the AMAZING SPIDER-MAN

THE GOBLIN LIVES

VOLUME 4

1967-1968

AMAZING SPIDER-MAN #53-67, SPECTACULAR SPIDER-MAN #1-2,
MARVEL SUPER-HEROES #14 AND NOT BRAND ECHH #6, #11

AMAZING SPIDER-MAN

WRITERS:
STAN LEE
WITH **GARY FRIEDRICH** & **ARNOLD DRAKE**

PENCILERS:
JOHN ROMITA
WITH **DON HECK, JIM MOONEY, ROSS ANDRU, LARRY LIEBER**
& **MARIE SEVERIN**

INKERS:
MIKE ESPOSITO
& **JIM MOONEY**
WITH **BILL EVERETT,
MARIE SEVERIN**
& **JOHN TARTAGLIONE**

LETTERERS:
SAM ROSEN
& **ART SIMEK**
WITH **AL KURZROK**
& **JOE ROSEN**

EDITOR:
STAN LEE

COLLECTION FRONT COVER ART:
JOHN ROMITA WITH
COLORS BY **PAUL MOUNTS**

COLLECTION BACK COVER ART:
JOHN ROMITA

SPIDER-MAN CREATED BY STAN LEE & STEVE DITKO

COLLECTION EDITOR: CORY SEDLMEIER
BOOK DESIGNER: NICKEL DESIGNWORKS
ART & COLOR RESTORATION: MICHAEL KELLEHER & KELLUSTRATION

SVP PRINT, SALES & MARKETING: DAVID GABRIEL   DIRECTOR, LICENSED PUBLISHING: SVEN LARSEN
EDITOR IN CHIEF: C.B. CEBULSKI   CHIEF CREATIVE OFFICER: JOE QUESADA
PRESIDENT: DAN BUCKLEY   EXECUTIVE PRODUCER: ALAN FINE

SPECIAL THANKS: GLEN BRUNSWICK, MIKE BURKEY, SCOTT DUNBIER, RALPH MACCHIO AND JEFF SHARPE

AMAZING SPIDER-MAN EPIC COLLECTION: THE GOBLIN LIVES. Contains material originally published in magazine form as AMAZING SPIDER-MAN #53-67, SPECTACULAR SPIDER-MAN #1-2, MARVEL SUPER-HEROES #14, and NOT BRAND ECHH #6 and #11. First printing 2019. ISBN 978-1-302-91780-7. Published by MARVEL WORLDWIDE, INC., a subsidiary of MARVEL ENTERTAINMENT, LLC. OFFICE OF PUBLICATION: 135 West 50th Street, New York, NY 10020. Copyright © 2019 MARVEL No similarity between any of the names, characters, persons, and/or institutions in this magazine with those of any living or dead person or institution is intended, and any such similarity which may exist is purely coincidental. Printed in the U.S.A. DAN BUCKLEY, President, Marvel Entertainment; JOHN NEE, Publisher; JOE QUESADA, Chief Creative Officer; TOM BREVOORT, SVP of Publishing; DAVID BOGART, SVP of Business Affairs & Operations, Publishing & Partnership; DAVID GABRIEL, SVP of Sales & Marketing, Publishing; JEFF YOUNGQUIST, VP of Production & Special Projects; DAN CARR, Executive Director of Publishing Technology; ALEX MORALES, Director of Publishing Operations; DAN EDINGTON, Managing Editor; SUSAN CRESPI, Production Manager; STAN LEE, Chairman Emeritus. For information regarding advertising in Marvel Comics or on Marvel.com, please contact Vit DeBellis, Custom Solutions & Integrated Advertising Manager, at vdebellis@marvel.com. For Marvel subscription inquiries, please call 888-511-5480. Manufactured between 4/26/2019 and 5/28/2019 by LSC COMMUNICATIONS INC., KENDALLVILLE, IN, USA.

10 9 8 7 6 5 4 3 2 1

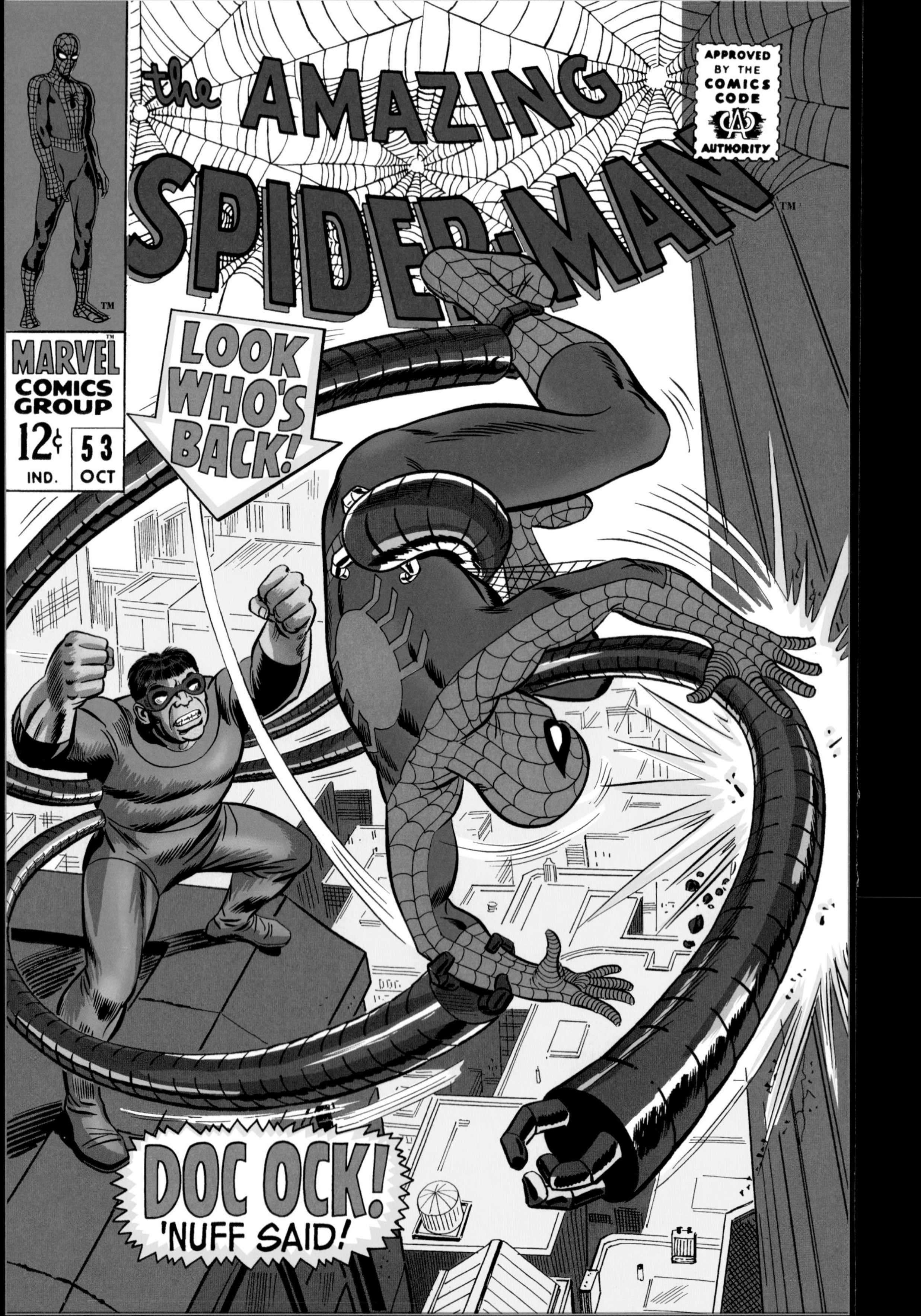
the AMAZING SPIDER-MAN™
APPROVED BY THE COMICS CODE AUTHORITY
MARVEL™ COMICS GROUP
12¢ IND.
53 OCT
LOOK WHO'S BACK!
DOC OCK!
'NUFF SAID!

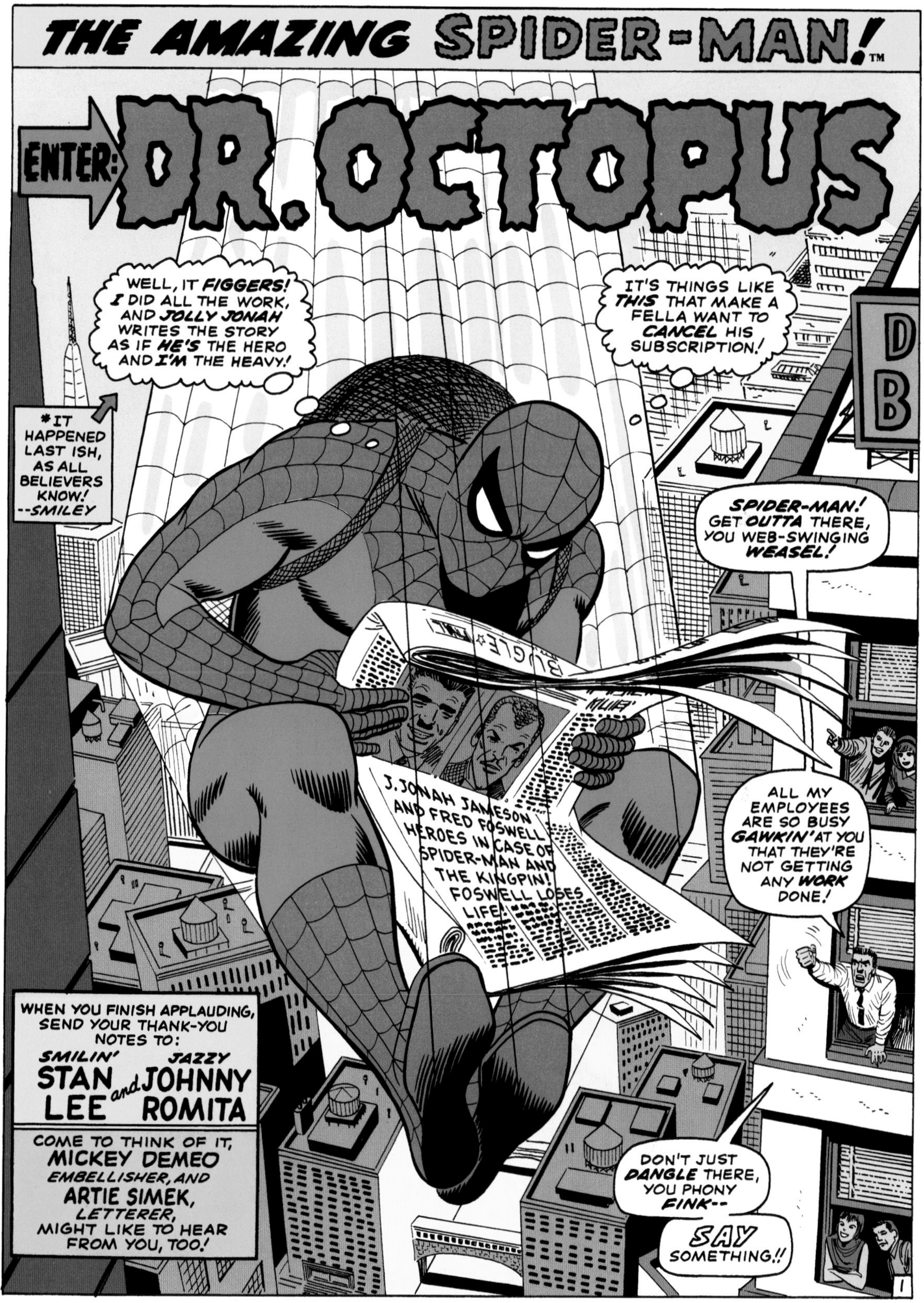
THE AMAZING SPIDER-MAN!™
ENTER: DR. OCTOPUS
WELL, IT FIGGERS! I DID ALL THE WORK, AND JOLLY JONAH WRITES THE STORY AS IF HE'S THE HERO AND I'M THE HEAVY!
*IT HAPPENED LAST ISH, AS ALL BELIEVERS KNOW! --SMILEY
IT'S THINGS LIKE THIS THAT MAKE A FELLA WANT TO CANCEL HIS SUBSCRIPTION!
D B
BUGLE
J. JONAH JAMESON AND FRED FOSWELL HEROES IN CASE OF SPIDER-MAN AND THE KINGPIN! FOSWELL LOSES LIFE!
SPIDER-MAN! GET OUTTA THERE, YOU WEB-SWINGING WEASEL!
ALL MY EMPLOYEES ARE SO BUSY GAWKIN' AT YOU THAT THEY'RE NOT GETTING ANY WORK DONE!
WHEN YOU FINISH APPLAUDING, SEND YOUR THANK-YOU NOTES TO: SMILIN' STAN LEE and JAZZY JOHNNY ROMITA
COME TO THINK OF IT, MICKEY DEMEO EMBELLISHER, AND ARTIE SIMEK, LETTERER, MIGHT LIKE TO HEAR FROM YOU, TOO!
DON'T JUST DANGLE THERE, YOU PHONY FINK--
SAY SOMETHING!!
1

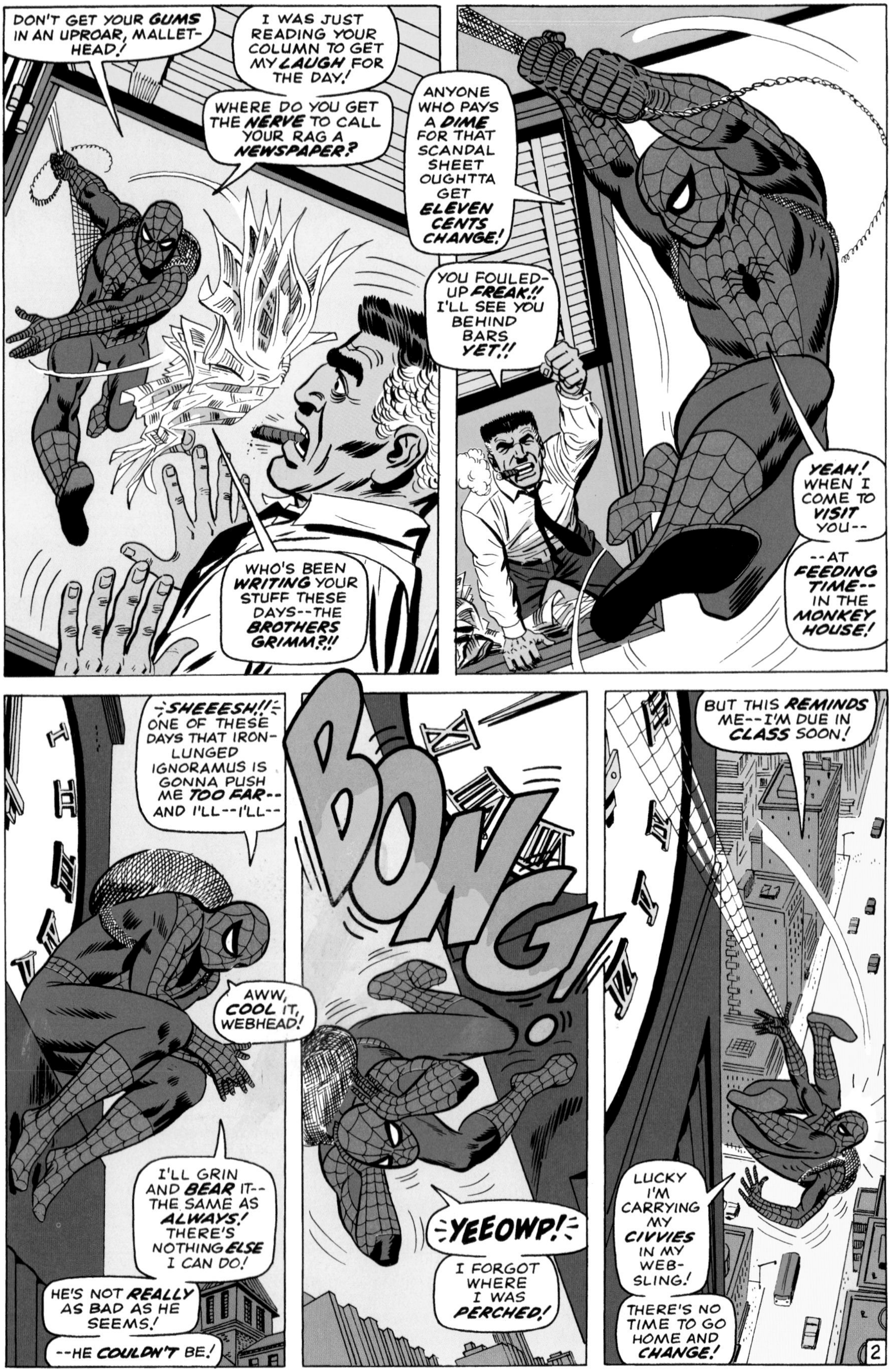
DON'T GET YOUR GUMS IN AN UPROAR, MALLET-HEAD!
I WAS JUST READING YOUR COLUMN TO GET MY LAUGH FOR THE DAY!
WHERE DO YOU GET THE NERVE TO CALL YOUR RAG A NEWSPAPER?
WHO'S BEEN WRITING YOUR STUFF THESE DAYS--THE BROTHERS GRIMM?!!
ANYONE WHO PAYS A DIME FOR THAT SCANDAL SHEET OUGHTTA GET ELEVEN CENTS CHANGE!
YOU FOULED-UP FREAK!! I'LL SEE YOU BEHIND BARS YET!!
YEAH! WHEN I COME TO VISIT YOU--
--AT FEEDING TIME--IN THE MONKEY HOUSE!
SHEEESH!! ONE OF THESE DAYS THAT IRON-LUNGED IGNORAMUS IS GONNA PUSH ME TOO FAR--AND I'LL--I'LL--
AWW, COOL IT, WEBHEAD!
I'LL GRIN AND BEAR IT--THE SAME AS ALWAYS! THERE'S NOTHING ELSE I CAN DO!
HE'S NOT REALLY AS BAD AS HE SEEMS!
--HE COULDN'T BE!
BONG!
YEEOWP!
I FORGOT WHERE I WAS PERCHED!
BUT THIS REMINDS ME--I'M DUE IN CLASS SOON!
LUCKY I'M CARRYING MY CIVVIES IN MY WEB-SLING!
THERE'S NO TIME TO GO HOME AND CHANGE!
2

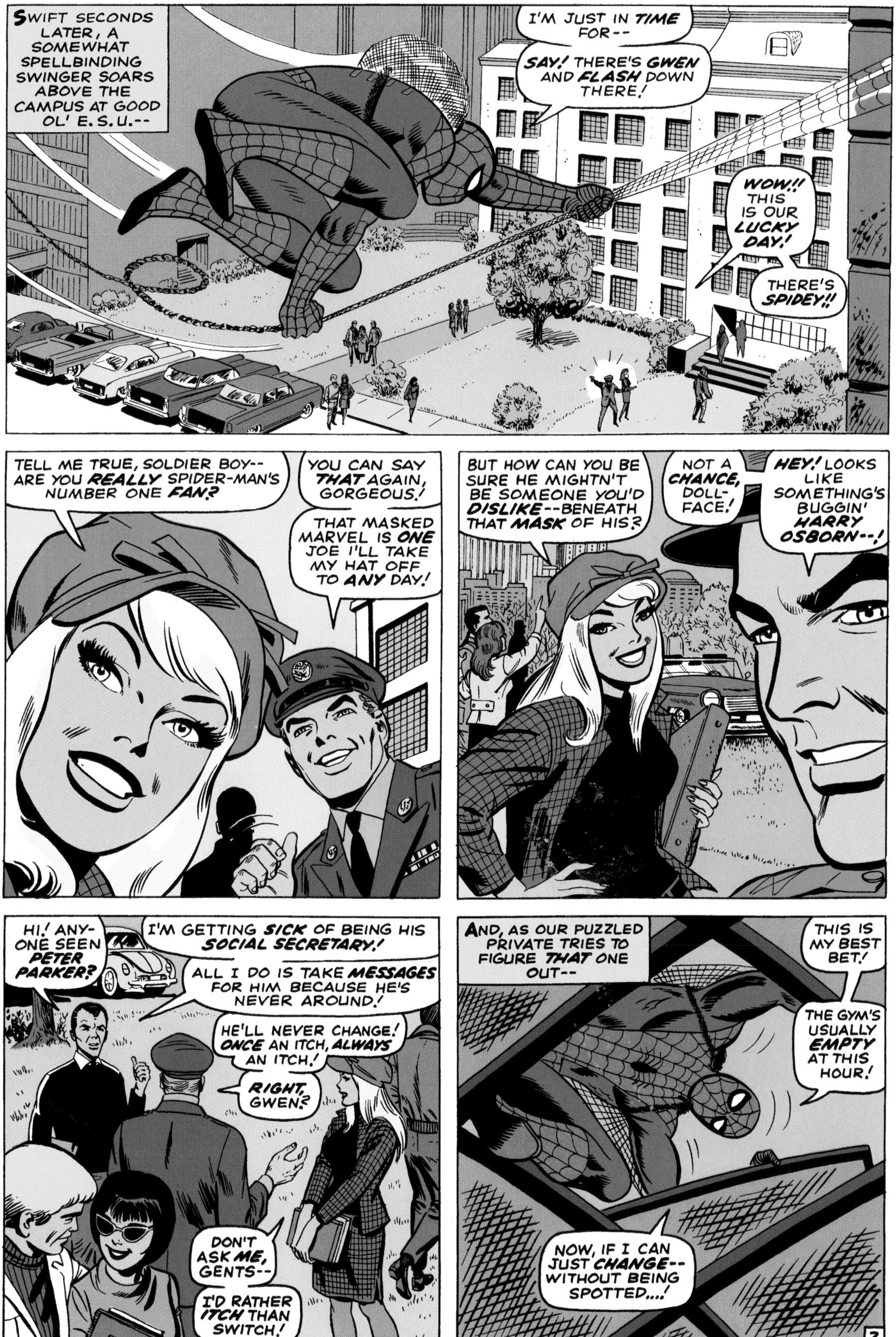
SWIFT SECONDS LATER, A SOMEWHAT SPELLBINDING SWINGER SOARS ABOVE THE CAMPUS AT GOOD OL' E.S.U.--
I'M JUST IN TIME FOR--
SAY! THERE'S GWEN AND FLASH DOWN THERE!
WOW!! THIS IS OUR LUCKY DAY!
THERE'S SPIDEY!!
TELL ME TRUE, SOLDIER BOY-- ARE YOU REALLY SPIDER-MAN'S NUMBER ONE FAN?
YOU CAN SAY THAT AGAIN, GORGEOUS!
THAT MASKED MARVEL IS ONE JOE I'LL TAKE MY HAT OFF TO ANY DAY!
BUT HOW CAN YOU BE SURE HE MIGHTN'T BE SOMEONE YOU'D DISLIKE--BENEATH THAT MASK OF HIS?
NOT A CHANCE, DOLL-FACE!
HEY! LOOKS LIKE SOMETHING'S BUGGIN' HARRY OSBORN--!
HI! ANYONE SEEN PETER PARKER?
I'M GETTING SICK OF BEING HIS SOCIAL SECRETARY!
ALL I DO IS TAKE MESSAGES FOR HIM BECAUSE HE'S NEVER AROUND!
HE'LL NEVER CHANGE! ONCE AN ITCH, ALWAYS AN ITCH!
RIGHT, GWEN?
DON'T ASK ME, GENTS--
I'D RATHER ITCH THAN SWITCH!
AND, AS OUR PUZZLED PRIVATE TRIES TO FIGURE THAT ONE OUT--
THIS IS MY BEST BET!
THE GYM'S USUALLY EMPTY AT THIS HOUR!
NOW, IF I CAN JUST CHANGE-- WITHOUT BEING SPOTTED...!
3

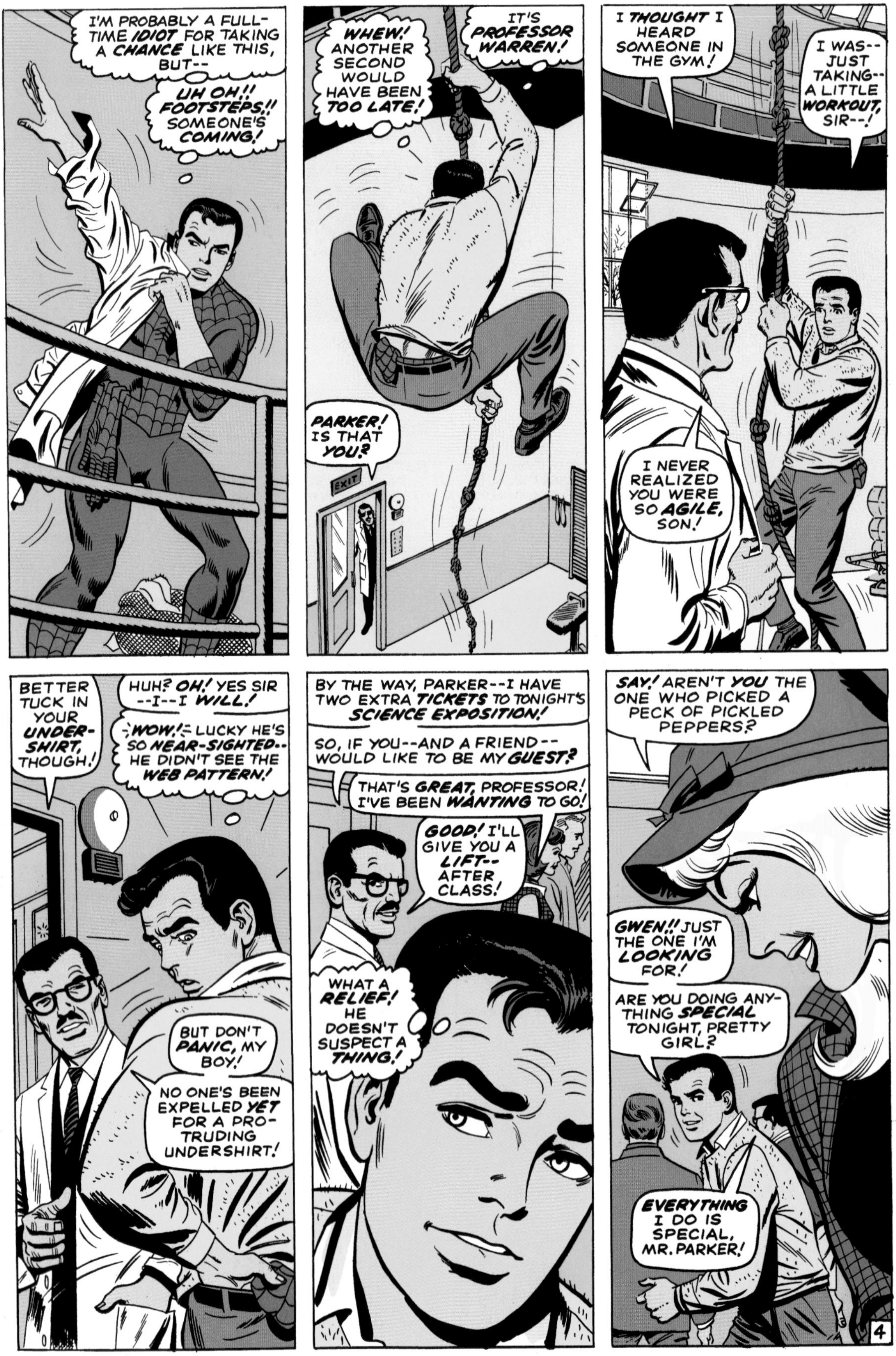
I'M PROBABLY A FULL-TIME IDIOT FOR TAKING A CHANCE LIKE THIS, BUT--
UH OH!! FOOTSTEPS!! SOMEONE'S COMING!
IT'S PROFESSOR WARREN!
WHEW! ANOTHER SECOND WOULD HAVE BEEN TOO LATE!
PARKER! IS THAT YOU?
EXIT
I THOUGHT I HEARD SOMEONE IN THE GYM!
I WAS--JUST TAKING--A LITTLE WORKOUT, SIR--!
I NEVER REALIZED YOU WERE SO AGILE, SON!
BETTER TUCK IN YOUR UNDER-SHIRT, THOUGH!
HUH? OH! YES SIR--I--I WILL!
WOW! LUCKY HE'S SO NEAR-SIGHTED--HE DIDN'T SEE THE WEB PATTERN!
BUT DON'T PANIC, MY BOY!
NO ONE'S BEEN EXPELLED YET FOR A PRO-TRUDING UNDERSHIRT!
BY THE WAY, PARKER--I HAVE TWO EXTRA TICKETS TO TONIGHT'S SCIENCE EXPOSITION!
SO, IF YOU--AND A FRIEND--WOULD LIKE TO BE MY GUEST?
THAT'S GREAT, PROFESSOR! I'VE BEEN WANTING TO GO!
GOOD! I'LL GIVE YOU A LIFT--AFTER CLASS!
WHAT A RELIEF! HE DOESN'T SUSPECT A THING!
SAY! AREN'T YOU THE ONE WHO PICKED A PECK OF PICKLED PEPPERS?
GWEN!! JUST THE ONE I'M LOOKING FOR!
ARE YOU DOING ANY-THING SPECIAL TONIGHT, PRETTY GIRL?
EVERYTHING I DO IS SPECIAL, MR. PARKER!
4

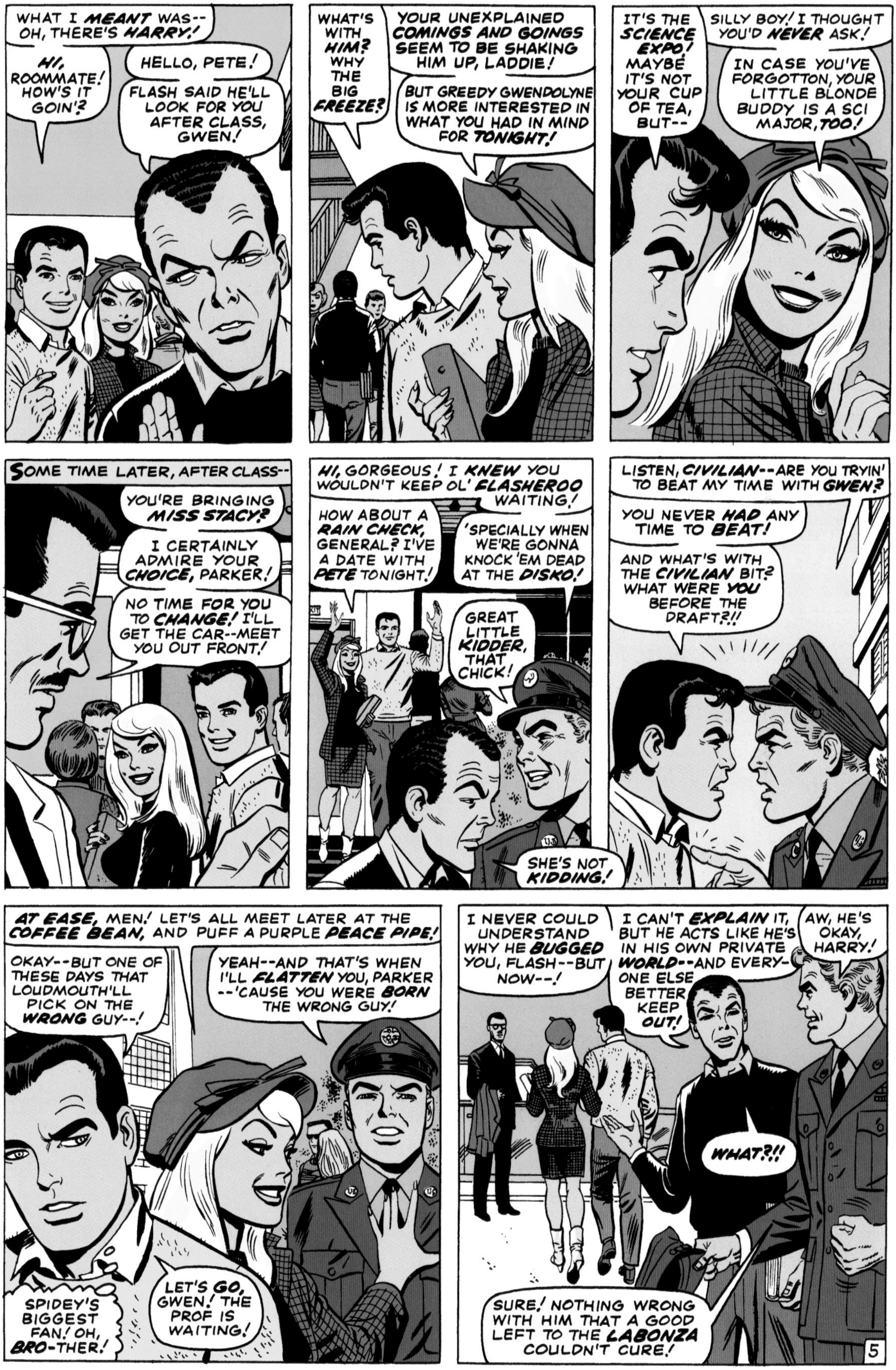
WHAT I MEANT WAS-- OH, THERE'S HARRY!
HI, ROOMMATE! HOW'S IT GOIN'?
HELLO, PETE!
FLASH SAID HE'LL LOOK FOR YOU AFTER CLASS, GWEN!
WHAT'S WITH HIM? WHY THE BIG FREEZE?
YOUR UNEXPLAINED COMINGS AND GOINGS SEEM TO BE SHAKING HIM UP, LADDIE!
BUT GREEDY GWENDOLYNE IS MORE INTERESTED IN WHAT YOU HAD IN MIND FOR TONIGHT!
IT'S THE SCIENCE EXPO! MAYBE IT'S NOT YOUR CUP OF TEA, BUT--
SILLY BOY! I THOUGHT YOU'D NEVER ASK!
IN CASE YOU'VE FORGOTTON, YOUR LITTLE BLONDE BUDDY IS A SCI MAJOR, TOO!
SOME TIME LATER, AFTER CLASS--
YOU'RE BRINGING MISS STACY?
I CERTAINLY ADMIRE YOUR CHOICE, PARKER!
NO TIME FOR YOU TO CHANGE! I'LL GET THE CAR--MEET YOU OUT FRONT!
HI, GORGEOUS! I KNEW YOU WOULDN'T KEEP OL' FLASHEROO WAITING!
HOW ABOUT A RAIN CHECK, GENERAL? I'VE A DATE WITH PETE TONIGHT!
'SPECIALLY WHEN WE'RE GONNA KNOCK 'EM DEAD AT THE DISKO!
GREAT LITTLE KIDDER, THAT CHICK!
SHE'S NOT KIDDING!
LISTEN, CIVILIAN--ARE YOU TRYIN' TO BEAT MY TIME WITH GWEN?
YOU NEVER HAD ANY TIME TO BEAT!
AND WHAT'S WITH THE CIVILIAN BIT? WHAT WERE YOU BEFORE THE DRAFT?!!
AT EASE, MEN! LET'S ALL MEET LATER AT THE COFFEE BEAN, AND PUFF A PURPLE PEACE PIPE!
OKAY--BUT ONE OF THESE DAYS THAT LOUDMOUTH'LL PICK ON THE WRONG GUY--!
YEAH--AND THAT'S WHEN I'LL FLATTEN YOU, PARKER --'CAUSE YOU WERE BORN THE WRONG GUY!
SPIDEY'S BIGGEST FAN! OH, BRO-THER!
LET'S GO, GWEN! THE PROF IS WAITING!
I NEVER COULD UNDERSTAND WHY HE BUGGED YOU, FLASH--BUT NOW--!
I CAN'T EXPLAIN IT, BUT HE ACTS LIKE HE'S IN HIS OWN PRIVATE WORLD--AND EVERY-ONE ELSE BETTER KEEP OUT!
AW, HE'S OKAY, HARRY!
WHAT?!!
SURE! NOTHING WRONG WITH HIM THAT A GOOD LEFT TO THE LABONZA COULDN'T CURE!
5

MINUTES LATER, IN PROFESSOR WARREN'S CAR--

I WONDER WHAT THEY'RE *FEATURING* AT THE SCIENCE EXHIBIT TODAY?

ACCORDING TO THE *PAPER*, IT'S A NEW TYPE OF *MISSILE DEFENSE*-- CALLED A *NULLIFIER!*

EXACTLY! AND, DO YOU KNOW HOW IT *WORKS?*

I IMAGINE IT NULLIFIES THE *HOMING DEVICES* OF ENEMY MISSILES!

YOU IMAGINE *RIGHT,* YOUNG LADY!

TODAY, THERE'LL BE A DEMONSTRATION OF THE NULLIFIER'S *STABILIZER CONTROL!*

SOMEHOW, IT ALL SEEMS LIKE THE START OF A *JAMES BOND* MOVIE--!

FOR MAXIMUM *SECURITY,* THE TWO *PARTS* OF THE STABILIZER WILL BE DELIVERED *SEPARATELY!*

IT SURE *DOES!*

BUT, THE *MOST* EXCITING PART IS JUST BEING WITH *GWEN!*

HOW CAN ANY-ONE SO *BEAUTIFUL* ALSO BE SO--*UH OH!!*

SOMETHING'S *WRONG!* MY *SPIDER SENSE* IS STARTING TO *TINGLE!*

PETE! YOU LOOK SO *STRANGE!* DO YOU--*FEEL* ALL RIGHT? PETE--?

WE'D BETTER SEE ABOUT FINDING OUR *SEATS!*

IT LOOKS AS THOUGH THE *DEMONSTRATION* IS ABOUT TO *BEGIN!*

I'M SURE YOU'LL SEE A *PRACTICAL* APPLICATION OF THE MANY SEEMINGLY UNRELATED *THEORIES* WE'VE BEEN DISCUSSING IN CLASS!

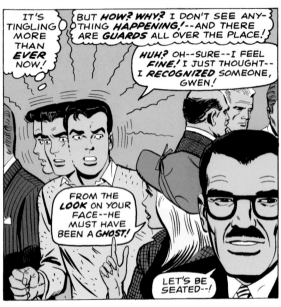

IT'S TINGLING MORE THAN *EVER* NOW!

BUT *HOW? WHY?* I DON'T SEE ANY-THING *HAPPENING,*--AND THERE ARE *GUARDS* ALL OVER THE PLACE!

HUH? OH--SURE--I FEEL *FINE!* I JUST THOUGHT-- I *RECOGNIZED* SOMEONE, GWEN!

FROM THE *LOOK* ON YOUR FACE--HE MUST HAVE BEEN A *GHOST!*

LET'S BE SEATED--!

THERE *MUST* BE SOME DANGER TO THE *NULLIFIER!* BUT-- I JUST *CAN'T* SLIP AWAY AND BECOME *SPIDER-MAN!*

NOT WITHOUT AROUS-ING TOO MANY *SUSPICIONS!!*

LADIES AND GENTLE-MEN--WITH *BOTH* PARTS OF THE STABILIZER SAFELY ON THIS PLATFORM, I SHALL *JOIN* THEM TOGETHER SO THAT OUR *DEMON-STRATION* CAN BEGIN--!

OBVIOUSLY, WE HAVE TAKEN EVERY PRECAUTION FOR *MAXIMUM SECURITY* WITH THIS VITAL DEVICE!

6

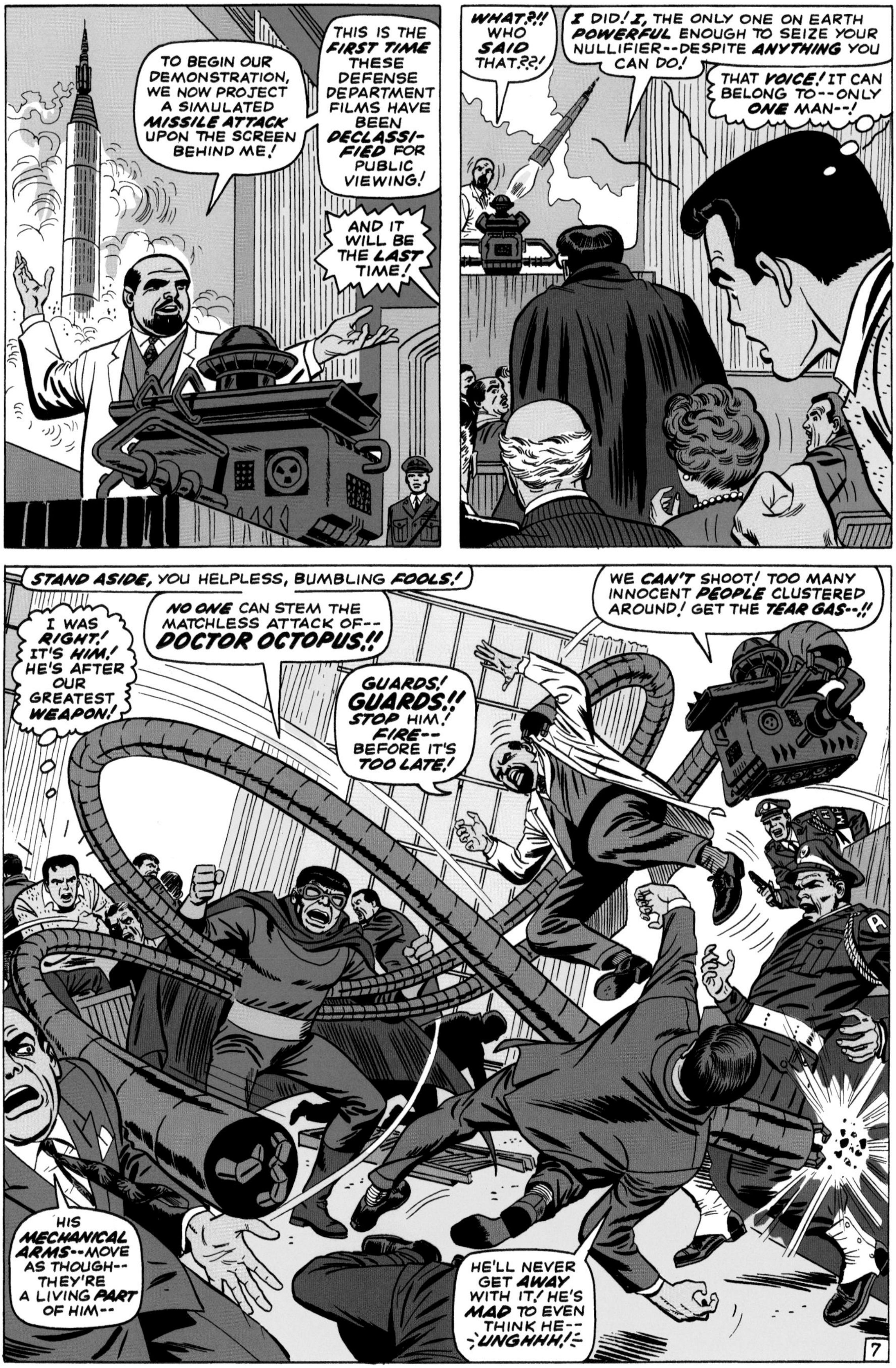
TO BEGIN OUR DEMONSTRATION, WE NOW PROJECT A SIMULATED MISSILE ATTACK UPON THE SCREEN BEHIND ME!
THIS IS THE FIRST TIME THESE DEFENSE DEPARTMENT FILMS HAVE BEEN DECLASSIFIED FOR PUBLIC VIEWING!
AND IT WILL BE THE LAST TIME!
WHAT?!! WHO SAID THAT?!?!
I DID! I, THE ONLY ONE ON EARTH POWERFUL ENOUGH TO SEIZE YOUR NULLIFIER--DESPITE ANYTHING YOU CAN DO!
THAT VOICE! IT CAN BELONG TO--ONLY ONE MAN--!
STAND ASIDE, YOU HELPLESS, BUMBLING FOOLS!
NO ONE CAN STEM THE MATCHLESS ATTACK OF-- DOCTOR OCTOPUS!!
I WAS RIGHT! IT'S HIM! HE'S AFTER OUR GREATEST WEAPON!
GUARDS! GUARDS!! STOP HIM! FIRE-- BEFORE IT'S TOO LATE!
WE CAN'T SHOOT! TOO MANY INNOCENT PEOPLE CLUSTERED AROUND! GET THE TEAR GAS--!!
HIS MECHANICAL ARMS--MOVE AS THOUGH--THEY'RE A LIVING PART OF HIM--
HE'LL NEVER GET AWAY WITH IT! HE'S MAD TO EVEN THINK HE-- UNGHHH!
7

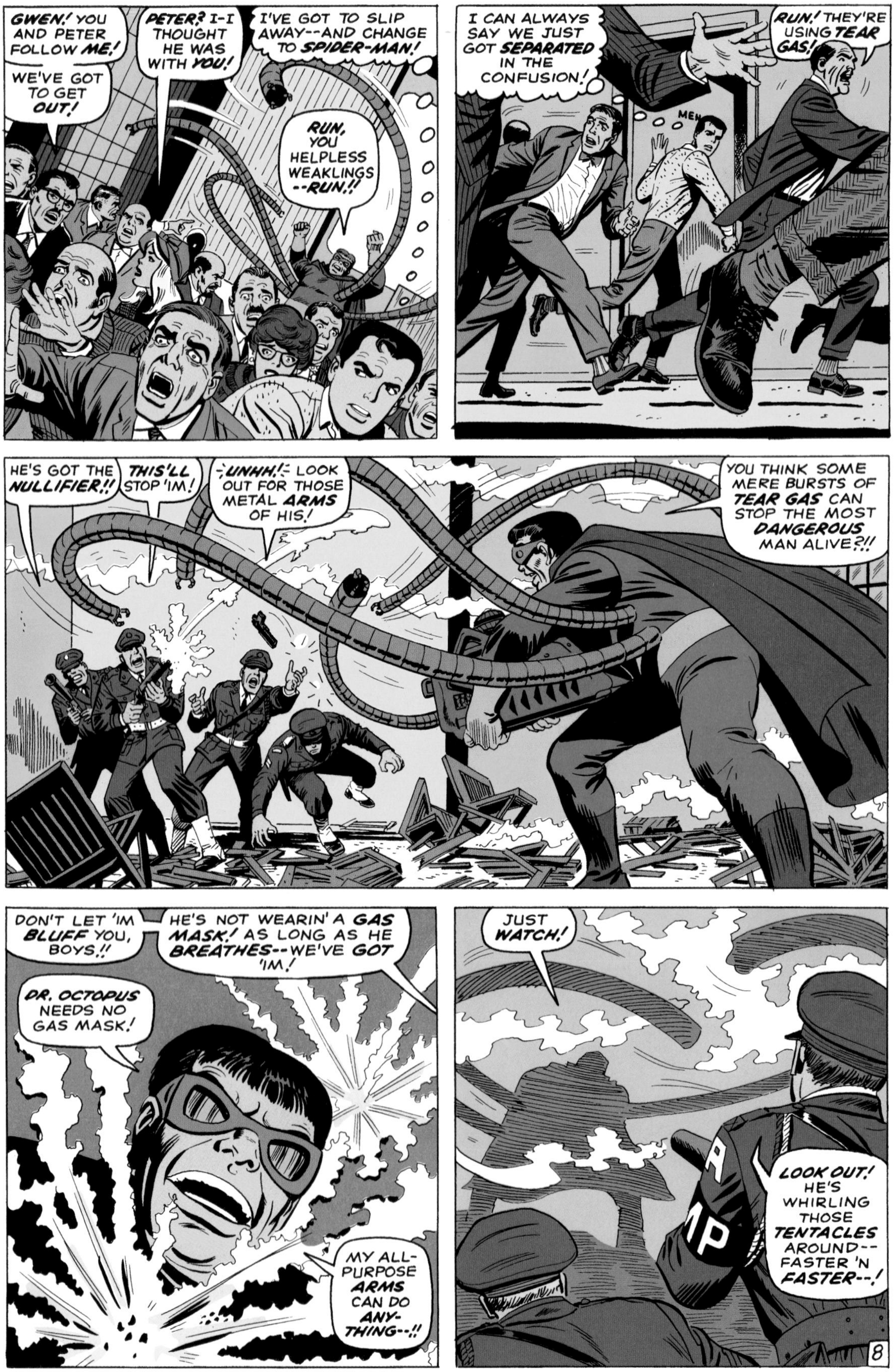
GWEN! YOU AND PETER FOLLOW ME!
WE'VE GOT TO GET OUT!
PETER? I-I THOUGHT HE WAS WITH YOU!
I'VE GOT TO SLIP AWAY--AND CHANGE TO SPIDER-MAN!
RUN, YOU HELPLESS WEAKLINGS --RUN!!
I CAN ALWAYS SAY WE JUST GOT SEPARATED IN THE CONFUSION!
RUN! THEY'RE USING TEAR GAS!
HE'S GOT THE NULLIFIER!!
THIS'LL STOP 'IM!
-UNHH!- LOOK OUT FOR THOSE METAL ARMS OF HIS!
YOU THINK SOME MERE BURSTS OF TEAR GAS CAN STOP THE MOST DANGEROUS MAN ALIVE?!!
DON'T LET 'IM BLUFF YOU, BOYS!!
HE'S NOT WEARIN' A GAS MASK! AS LONG AS HE BREATHES--WE'VE GOT 'IM!
DR. OCTOPUS NEEDS NO GAS MASK!
MY ALL-PURPOSE ARMS CAN DO ANY-THING--!!
JUST WATCH!
MP
LOOK OUT! HE'S WHIRLING THOSE TENTACLES AROUND--FASTER 'N FASTER--!
8

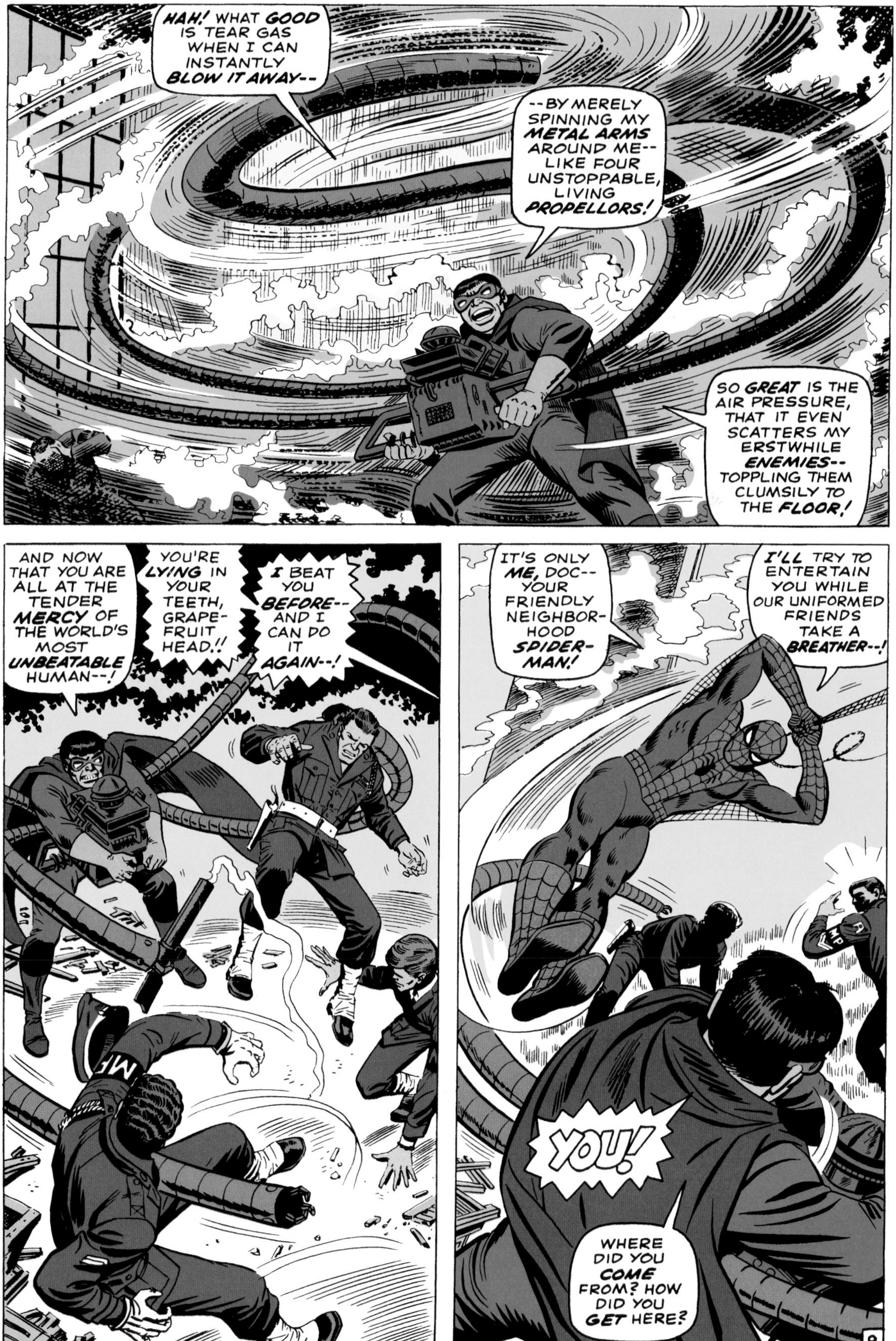
HAH! WHAT GOOD IS TEAR GAS WHEN I CAN INSTANTLY BLOW IT AWAY--
--BY MERELY SPINNING MY METAL ARMS AROUND ME-- LIKE FOUR UNSTOPPABLE, LIVING PROPELLORS!
SO GREAT IS THE AIR PRESSURE, THAT IT EVEN SCATTERS MY ERSTWHILE ENEMIES-- TOPPLING THEM CLUMSILY TO THE FLOOR!
AND NOW THAT YOU ARE ALL AT THE TENDER MERCY OF THE WORLD'S MOST UNBEATABLE HUMAN--!
YOU'RE LYING IN YOUR TEETH, GRAPE-FRUIT HEAD!!
I BEAT YOU BEFORE-- AND I CAN DO IT AGAIN--!
MP
IT'S ONLY ME, DOC-- YOUR FRIENDLY NEIGHBOR-HOOD SPIDER-MAN!
I'LL TRY TO ENTERTAIN YOU WHILE OUR UNIFORMED FRIENDS TAKE A BREATHER--!
MP
YOU!
WHERE DID YOU COME FROM? HOW DID YOU GET HERE?
9

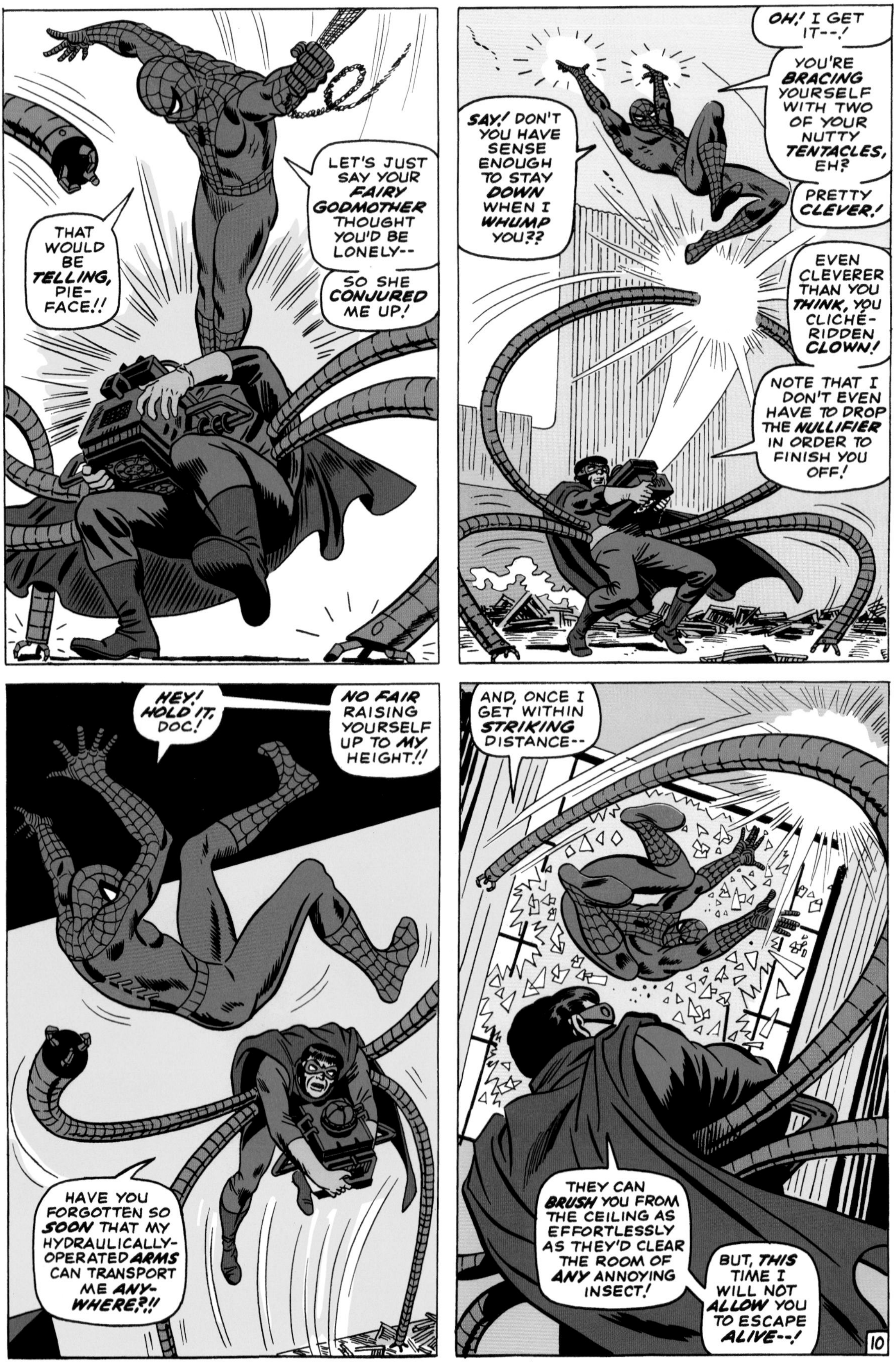
LET'S JUST SAY YOUR FAIRY GODMOTHER THOUGHT YOU'D BE LONELY--
SO SHE CONJURED ME UP!
THAT WOULD BE TELLING, PIE-FACE!!
OH! I GET IT--!
YOU'RE BRACING YOURSELF WITH TWO OF YOUR NUTTY TENTACLES, EH?
PRETTY CLEVER!
SAY! DON'T YOU HAVE SENSE ENOUGH TO STAY DOWN WHEN I WHUMP YOU??
EVEN CLEVERER THAN YOU THINK, YOU CLICHÉ-RIDDEN CLOWN!
NOTE THAT I DON'T EVEN HAVE TO DROP THE NULLIFIER IN ORDER TO FINISH YOU OFF!
HEY! HOLD IT, DOC!
NO FAIR RAISING YOURSELF UP TO MY HEIGHT!!
HAVE YOU FORGOTTEN SO SOON THAT MY HYDRAULICALLY-OPERATED ARMS CAN TRANSPORT ME ANY-WHERE?!!
AND, ONCE I GET WITHIN STRIKING DISTANCE--
THEY CAN BRUSH YOU FROM THE CEILING AS EFFORTLESSLY AS THEY'D CLEAR THE ROOM OF ANY ANNOYING INSECT!
BUT, THIS TIME I WILL NOT ALLOW YOU TO ESCAPE ALIVE--!
10

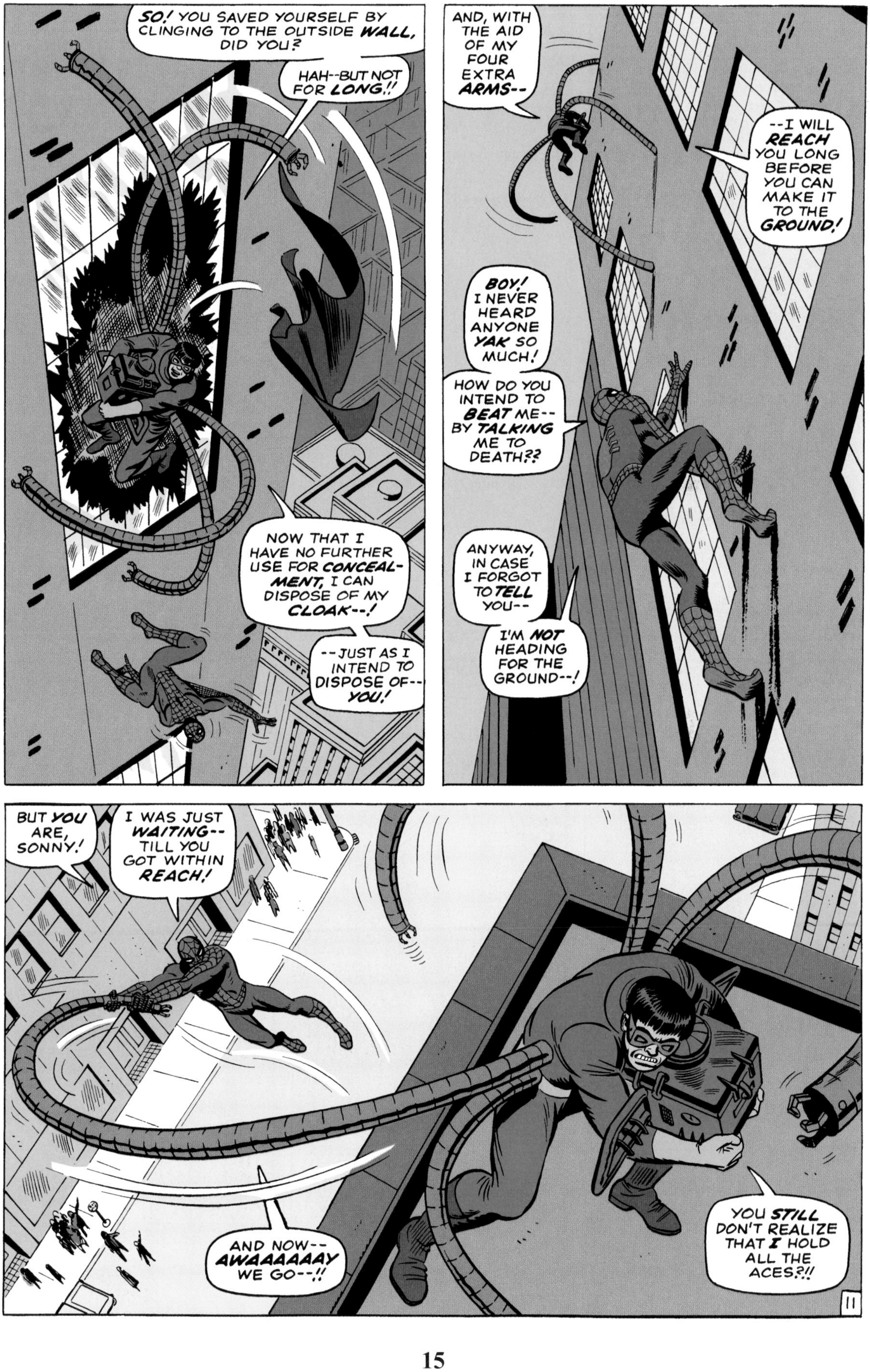
SO! YOU SAVED YOURSELF BY CLINGING TO THE OUTSIDE WALL, DID YOU?
HAH--BUT NOT FOR LONG!!
NOW THAT I HAVE NO FURTHER USE FOR CONCEAL-MENT, I CAN DISPOSE OF MY CLOAK--!
--JUST AS I INTEND TO DISPOSE OF--YOU!
AND, WITH THE AID OF MY FOUR EXTRA ARMS--
--I WILL REACH YOU LONG BEFORE YOU CAN MAKE IT TO THE GROUND!
BOY! I NEVER HEARD ANYONE YAK SO MUCH!
HOW DO YOU INTEND TO BEAT ME--BY TALKING ME TO DEATH??
ANYWAY, IN CASE I FORGOT TO TELL YOU--
I'M NOT HEADING FOR THE GROUND--!
BUT YOU ARE, SONNY!
I WAS JUST WAITING--TILL YOU GOT WITHIN REACH!
AND NOW--AWAAAAAAY WE GO--!!
YOU STILL DON'T REALIZE THAT I HOLD ALL THE ACES?!!
11

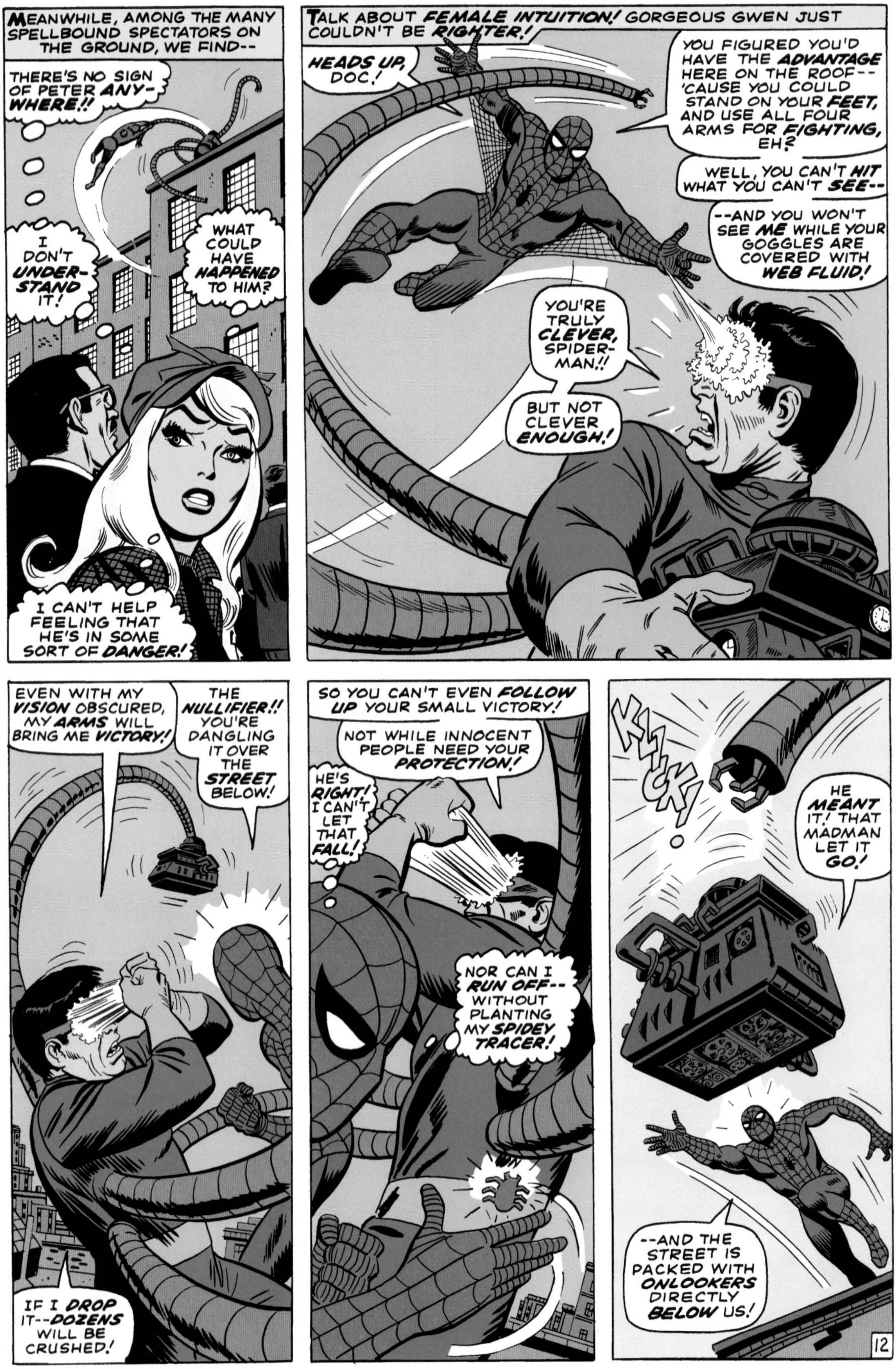
MEANWHILE, AMONG THE MANY SPELLBOUND SPECTATORS ON THE GROUND, WE FIND--
THERE'S NO SIGN OF PETER ANYWHERE!!
I DON'T UNDERSTAND IT!
WHAT COULD HAVE HAPPENED TO HIM?
I CAN'T HELP FEELING THAT HE'S IN SOME SORT OF DANGER!
TALK ABOUT FEMALE INTUITION! GORGEOUS GWEN JUST COULDN'T BE RIGHTER!
HEADS UP, DOC.!
YOU FIGURED YOU'D HAVE THE ADVANTAGE HERE ON THE ROOF-- 'CAUSE YOU COULD STAND ON YOUR FEET, AND USE ALL FOUR ARMS FOR FIGHTING, EH?
WELL, YOU CAN'T HIT WHAT YOU CAN'T SEE--
--AND YOU WON'T SEE ME WHILE YOUR GOGGLES ARE COVERED WITH WEB FLUID!
YOU'RE TRULY CLEVER, SPIDER-MAN!!
BUT NOT CLEVER ENOUGH!
EVEN WITH MY VISION OBSCURED, MY ARMS WILL BRING ME VICTORY!
THE NULLIFIER!! YOU'RE DANGLING IT OVER THE STREET BELOW!
IF I DROP IT--DOZENS WILL BE CRUSHED!
SO YOU CAN'T EVEN FOLLOW UP YOUR SMALL VICTORY!
NOT WHILE INNOCENT PEOPLE NEED YOUR PROTECTION!
HE'S RIGHT! I CAN'T LET THAT FALL!
NOR CAN I RUN OFF-- WITHOUT PLANTING MY SPIDEY TRACER!
KLIK!
HE MEANT IT! THAT MADMAN LET IT GO!
--AND THE STREET IS PACKED WITH ONLOOKERS DIRECTLY BELOW US!
12

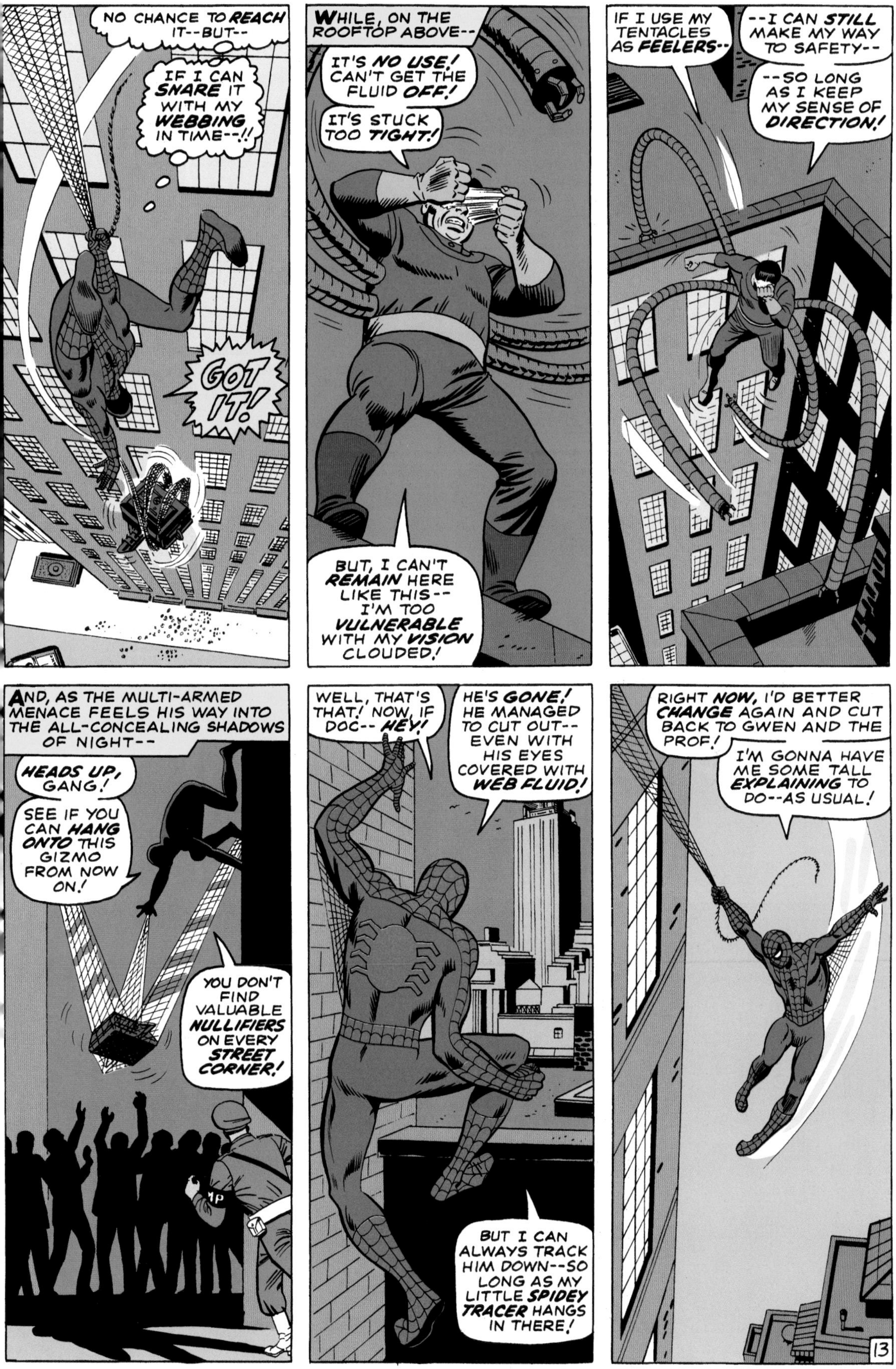
NO CHANCE TO REACH IT--BUT--
IF I CAN SNARE IT WITH MY WEBBING IN TIME--!!
GOT IT!
WHILE, ON THE ROOFTOP ABOVE--
IT'S NO USE! CAN'T GET THE FLUID OFF!
IT'S STUCK TOO TIGHT!
BUT, I CAN'T REMAIN HERE LIKE THIS--I'M TOO VULNERABLE WITH MY VISION CLOUDED!
IF I USE MY TENTACLES AS FEELERS--
--I CAN STILL MAKE MY WAY TO SAFETY--
--SO LONG AS I KEEP MY SENSE OF DIRECTION!
AND, AS THE MULTI-ARMED MENACE FEELS HIS WAY INTO THE ALL-CONCEALING SHADOWS OF NIGHT--
HEADS UP, GANG!
SEE IF YOU CAN HANG ONTO THIS GIZMO FROM NOW ON!
YOU DON'T FIND VALUABLE NULLIFIERS ON EVERY STREET CORNER!
MP
WELL, THAT'S THAT! NOW, IF DOC-- HEY!
HE'S GONE! HE MANAGED TO CUT OUT--EVEN WITH HIS EYES COVERED WITH WEB FLUID!
BUT I CAN ALWAYS TRACK HIM DOWN--SO LONG AS MY LITTLE SPIDEY TRACER HANGS IN THERE!
RIGHT NOW, I'D BETTER CHANGE AGAIN AND CUT BACK TO GWEN AND THE PROF!
I'M GONNA HAVE ME SOME TALL EXPLAINING TO DO--AS USUAL!
13

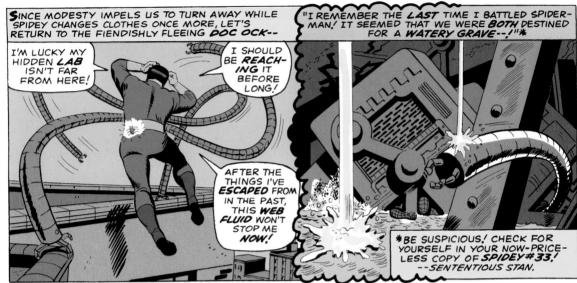

SINCE MODESTY IMPELS US TO TURN AWAY WHILE SPIDEY CHANGES CLOTHES ONCE MORE, LET'S RETURN TO THE FIENDISHLY FLEEING *DOC OCK*--

I'M LUCKY MY HIDDEN *LAB* ISN'T FAR FROM HERE!

I SHOULD BE *REACHING* IT BEFORE LONG!

AFTER THE THINGS I'VE *ESCAPED* FROM IN THE PAST, THIS *WEB FLUID* WON'T STOP ME *NOW!*

"I REMEMBER THE *LAST* TIME I BATTLED SPIDER-MAN! IT SEEMED THAT WE WERE *BOTH* DESTINED FOR A *WATERY GRAVE*--!"*

*BE SUSPICIOUS! CHECK FOR YOURSELF IN YOUR NOW-PRICE-LESS COPY OF *SPIDEY #33!* --SENTENTIOUS STAN.

"BUT, I HAD UNDER-ESTIMATED HIS *STRENGTH*-- THE STRENGTH WHICH *SAVED* HIM--!"

"JUST AS MY OWN HYDRAULIC-POWERED *ARMS* SAVED *ME*-- BY RAISING ME UP TO AN *AIR POCKET*--"

"--ALLOWING ME PRECIOUS TIME TO GRAPPLE FOR AN *OXYGEN TANK*, WHICH HAD BEEN PART OF MY BASIC EQUIPMENT--"

"--AND, ENABLING ME TO MAKE MY WAY INTO THE SAME *TUNNEL* AS THE ONE WHICH *SPIDER-MAN* HAD ESCAPED THRU, JUST SECONDS EARLIER!"

14.

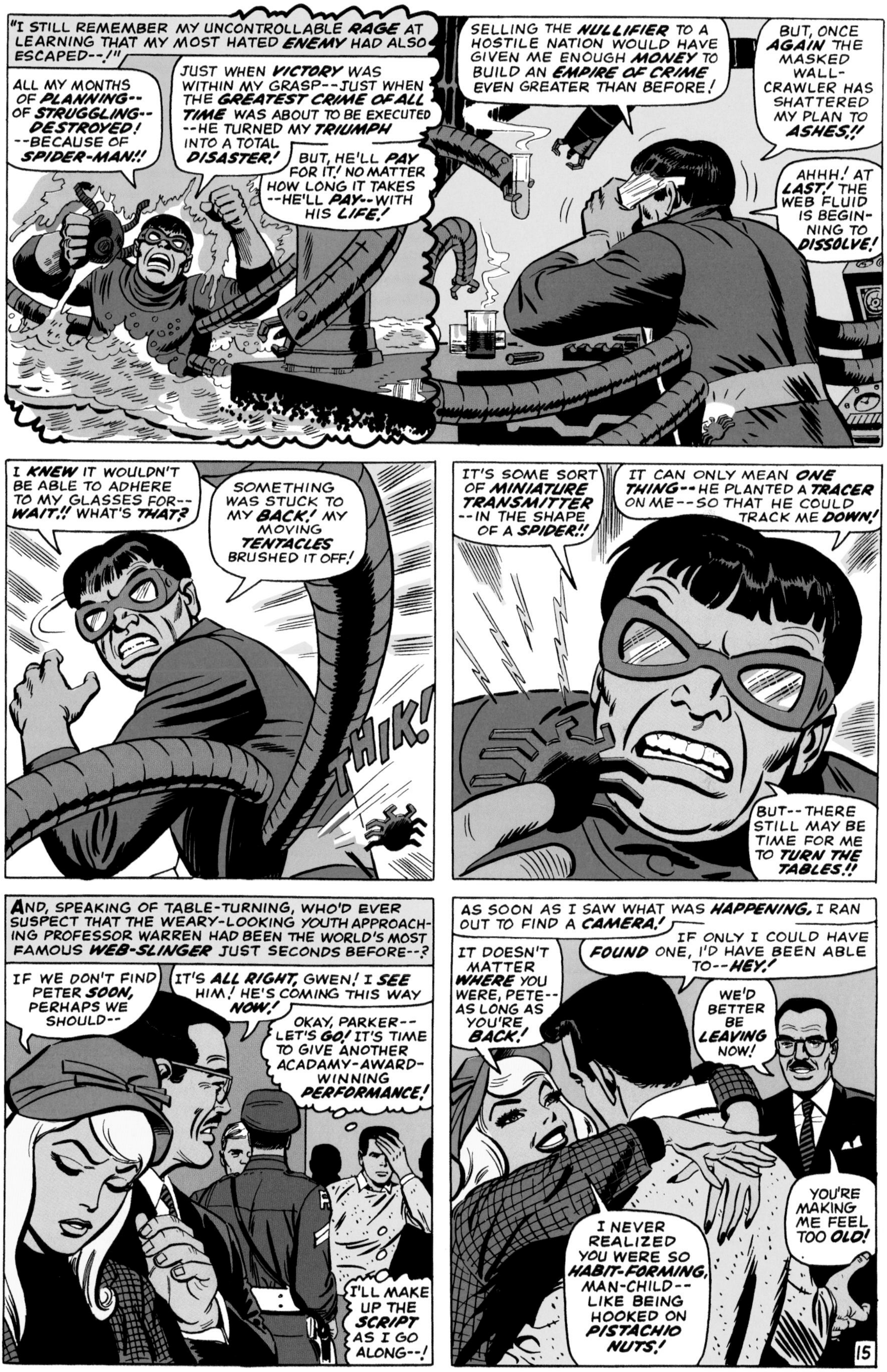
"I STILL REMEMBER MY UNCONTROLLABLE RAGE AT LEARNING THAT MY MOST HATED ENEMY HAD ALSO ESCAPED--!"
ALL MY MONTHS OF PLANNING-- OF STRUGGLING-- DESTROYED! --BECAUSE OF SPIDER-MAN!!
JUST WHEN VICTORY WAS WITHIN MY GRASP--JUST WHEN THE GREATEST CRIME OF ALL TIME WAS ABOUT TO BE EXECUTED --HE TURNED MY TRIUMPH INTO A TOTAL DISASTER!
BUT, HE'LL PAY FOR IT! NO MATTER HOW LONG IT TAKES --HE'LL PAY--WITH HIS LIFE!
SELLING THE NULLIFIER TO A HOSTILE NATION WOULD HAVE GIVEN ME ENOUGH MONEY TO BUILD AN EMPIRE OF CRIME EVEN GREATER THAN BEFORE!
BUT, ONCE AGAIN THE MASKED WALL-CRAWLER HAS SHATTERED MY PLAN TO ASHES!!
AHHH! AT LAST! THE WEB FLUID IS BEGINNING TO DISSOLVE!
I KNEW IT WOULDN'T BE ABLE TO ADHERE TO MY GLASSES FOR-- WAIT!! WHAT'S THAT?
SOMETHING WAS STUCK TO MY BACK! MY MOVING TENTACLES BRUSHED IT OFF!
THIK!
IT'S SOME SORT OF MINIATURE TRANSMITTER --IN THE SHAPE OF A SPIDER!!
IT CAN ONLY MEAN ONE THING-- HE PLANTED A TRACER ON ME--SO THAT HE COULD TRACK ME DOWN!
BUT--THERE STILL MAY BE TIME FOR ME TO TURN THE TABLES!!
AND, SPEAKING OF TABLE-TURNING, WHO'D EVER SUSPECT THAT THE WEARY-LOOKING YOUTH APPROACHING PROFESSOR WARREN HAD BEEN THE WORLD'S MOST FAMOUS WEB-SLINGER JUST SECONDS BEFORE--?
IF WE DON'T FIND PETER SOON, PERHAPS WE SHOULD--
IT'S ALL RIGHT, GWEN! I SEE HIM! HE'S COMING THIS WAY NOW!
OKAY, PARKER-- LET'S GO! IT'S TIME TO GIVE ANOTHER ACADAMY-AWARD-WINNING PERFORMANCE!
I'LL MAKE UP THE SCRIPT AS I GO ALONG--!
AS SOON AS I SAW WHAT WAS HAPPENING, I RAN OUT TO FIND A CAMERA!
IF ONLY I COULD HAVE FOUND ONE, I'D HAVE BEEN ABLE TO--HEY!
IT DOESN'T MATTER WHERE YOU WERE, PETE-- AS LONG AS YOU'RE BACK!
WE'D BETTER BE LEAVING NOW!
I NEVER REALIZED YOU WERE SO HABIT-FORMING, MAN-CHILD-- LIKE BEING HOOKED ON PISTACHIO NUTS!
YOU'RE MAKING ME FEEL TOO OLD!
15

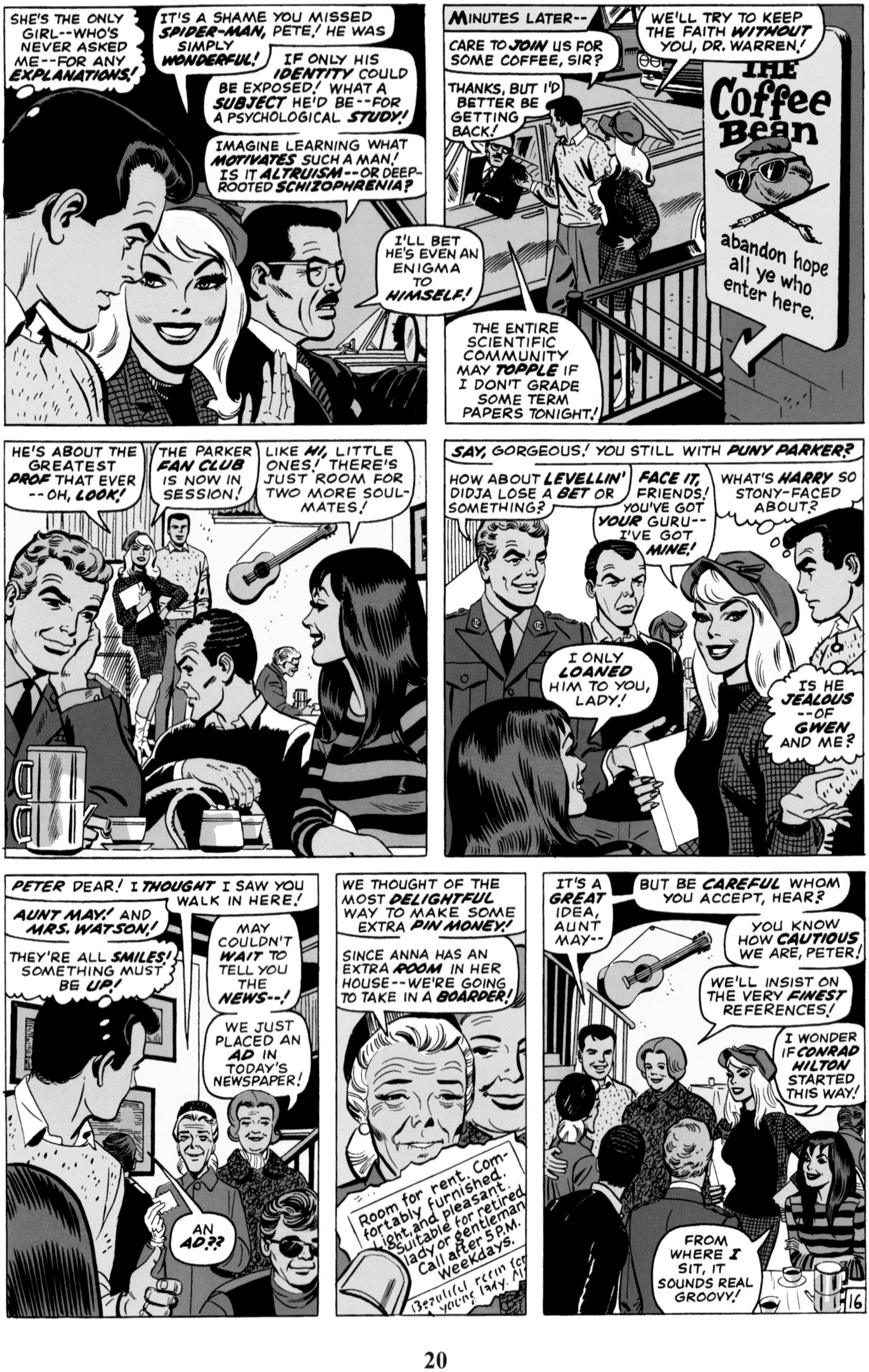
SHE'S THE ONLY GIRL--WHO'S NEVER ASKED ME--FOR ANY EXPLANATIONS!
IT'S A SHAME YOU MISSED SPIDER-MAN, PETE! HE WAS SIMPLY WONDERFUL!
IF ONLY HIS IDENTITY COULD BE EXPOSED! WHAT A SUBJECT HE'D BE--FOR A PSYCHOLOGICAL STUDY!
IMAGINE LEARNING WHAT MOTIVATES SUCH A MAN! IS IT ALTRUISM--OR DEEP-ROOTED SCHIZOPHRENIA?
I'LL BET HE'S EVEN AN ENIGMA TO HIMSELF!
MINUTES LATER--
CARE TO JOIN US FOR SOME COFFEE, SIR?
THANKS, BUT I'D BETTER BE GETTING BACK!
WE'LL TRY TO KEEP THE FAITH WITHOUT YOU, DR. WARREN!
THE Coffee Bean
abandon hope all ye who enter here.
THE ENTIRE SCIENTIFIC COMMUNITY MAY TOPPLE IF I DON'T GRADE SOME TERM PAPERS TONIGHT!
HE'S ABOUT THE GREATEST PROF THAT EVER --OH, LOOK!
THE PARKER FAN CLUB IS NOW IN SESSION!
LIKE HI, LITTLE ONES! THERE'S JUST ROOM FOR TWO MORE SOUL-MATES!
SAY, GORGEOUS! YOU STILL WITH PUNY PARKER?
HOW ABOUT LEVELLIN' DIDJA LOSE A BET OR SOMETHING?
FACE IT, FRIENDS! YOU'VE GOT YOUR GURU-- I'VE GOT MINE!
WHAT'S HARRY SO STONY-FACED ABOUT?
I ONLY LOANED HIM TO YOU, LADY!
IS HE JEALOUS --OF GWEN AND ME?
PETER DEAR! I THOUGHT I SAW YOU WALK IN HERE!
AUNT MAY! AND MRS. WATSON!
THEY'RE ALL SMILES! SOMETHING MUST BE UP!
MAY COULDN'T WAIT TO TELL YOU THE NEWS--!
WE JUST PLACED AN AD IN TODAY'S NEWSPAPER!
AN AD??
WE THOUGHT OF THE MOST DELIGHTFUL WAY TO MAKE SOME EXTRA PIN MONEY!
SINCE ANNA HAS AN EXTRA ROOM IN HER HOUSE--WE'RE GOING TO TAKE IN A BOARDER!
Room for rent. Comfortably furnished. Light, and pleasant. Suitable for retired lady or gentleman. Call after 5 P.M. Weekdays.
IT'S A GREAT IDEA, AUNT MAY--
BUT BE CAREFUL WHOM YOU ACCEPT, HEAR?
YOU KNOW HOW CAUTIOUS WE ARE, PETER!
WE'LL INSIST ON THE VERY FINEST REFERENCES!
I WONDER IF CONRAD HILTON STARTED THIS WAY!
FROM WHERE I SIT, IT SOUNDS REAL GROOVY!
16

THIS IS MY CHANCE TO *CUT OUT* NOW, AND GET BACK TO THE TRAIL OF *DOC OCK!*

SEE YOU *LATER*, GROUP! I'LL MAKE SURE NO ONE *FLIRTS* WITH THESE TWO PUSSYWILLOWS ON THEIR WAY HOME!

NO SKIN OFF *MY* NOSE! NOW WE DON'T HAVE ONE FELLA TOO *MANY!*

AW, *ONE* TIGER'S AS GOOD AS *ANOTHER*, SO LONG AS HE'S A REAL LIVE *MALE!*

EVEN WHEN NO ONE'S *AROUND*, HE'S ONE FELLA TOO *MANY!*

METHINKS THE LADY DOTH *PROTEST* TOO MUCH!

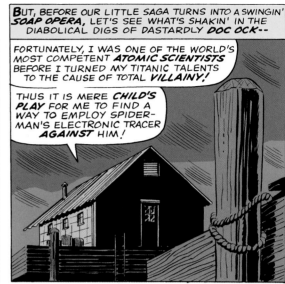

BUT, BEFORE OUR LITTLE SAGA TURNS INTO A SWINGIN' *SOAP OPERA*, LET'S SEE WHAT'S SHAKIN' IN THE DIABOLICAL DIGS OF DASTARDLY *DOC OCK*--

FORTUNATELY, I WAS ONE OF THE WORLD'S MOST COMPETENT *ATOMIC SCIENTISTS* BEFORE I TURNED MY TITANIC TALENTS TO THE CAUSE OF TOTAL *VILLAINY!*

THUS IT IS MERE *CHILD'S PLAY* FOR ME TO FIND A WAY TO EMPLOY SPIDER-MAN'S ELECTRONIC TRACER *AGAINST* HIM!

ALL I NEED DO IS CONSTRUCT A MAKESHIFT *REPLICA* OF MYSELF--SETTING IT IN FRONT OF A DUMMY *CONTROL PANEL*--!

THE SHEER *SIMPLICITY* OF THIS TRAP WILL MAKE IT VIRTUALLY *ESCAPE-PROOF!!*

THERE! EVERYTHING IS READY--AND WAITING--FOR THE ARRIVAL OF MY *DOOMED* ARCH-FOE!

THERE CAN BE NO DOUBT THAT HE *WILL* ARRIVE!!

SINCE I HAVE TAKEN THE PRECAUTION OF PLACING HIS OWN *SPIDER TRACER* EXACTLY WHERE I *WANT* IT!

AND, BEFORE THE NIGHT GETS VERY MUCH OLDER--

AUNT MAY AND MRS. WATSON ARE SAFELY BACK AT HOME--AND THEY GAVE ME THE PERFECT *EXCUSE* TO DUCK OUT OF THE *COFFEE BEAN*--

SO NOW I'M FREE AS A *BIRD* TO TAKE OFF AFTER THAT MULTI-ARMED *MISFIT!!*

I'VE JUST GOTTA PICK UP MY *TRACER SIGNAL*, AND THEN-- *ZOWEEE!*

[17]

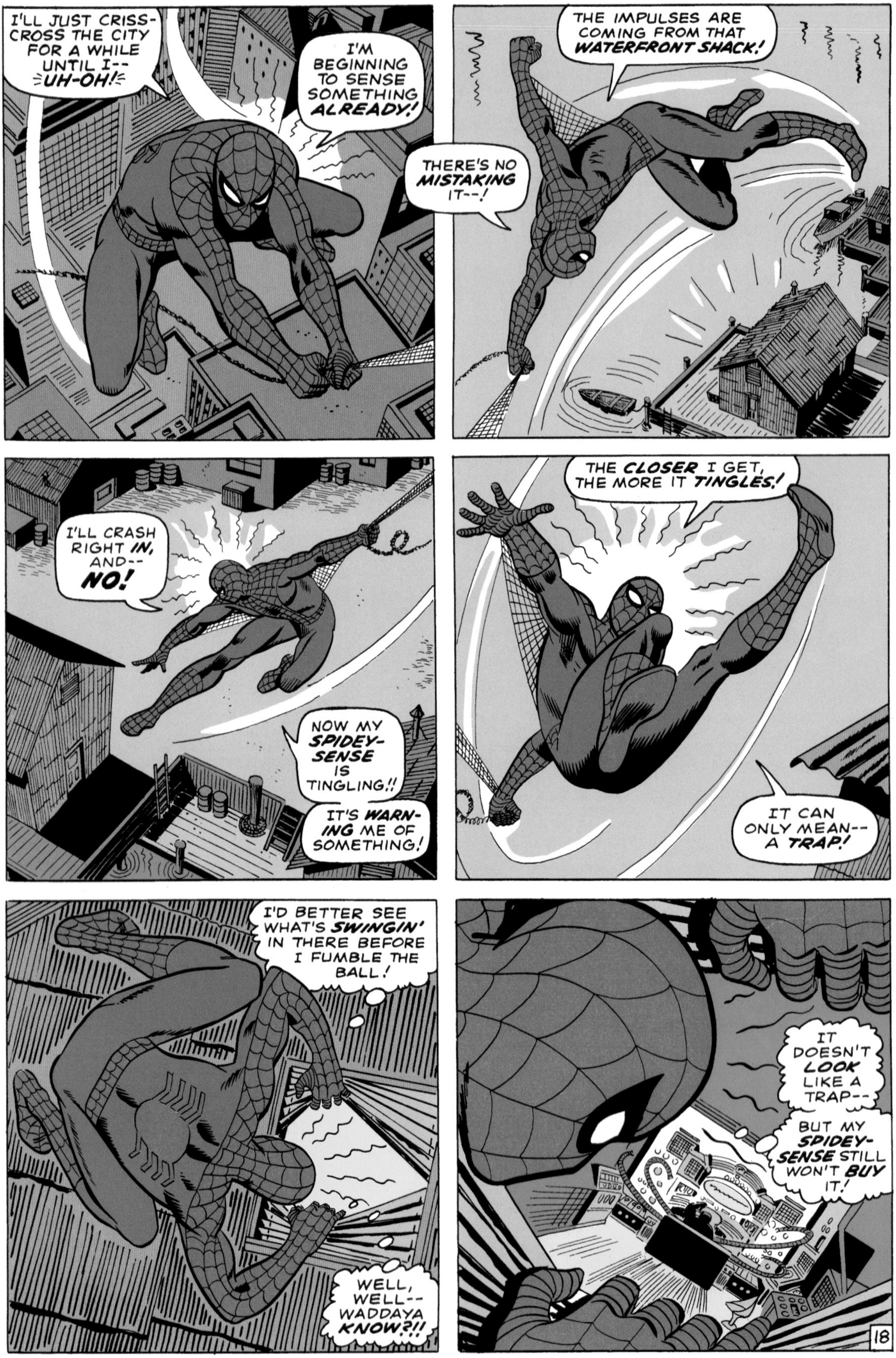
I'LL JUST CRISS-CROSS THE CITY FOR A WHILE UNTIL I-- UH-OH!
I'M BEGINNING TO SENSE SOMETHING ALREADY!
THERE'S NO MISTAKING IT--!
THE IMPULSES ARE COMING FROM THAT WATERFRONT SHACK!
I'LL CRASH RIGHT IN, AND-- NO!
NOW MY SPIDEY-SENSE IS TINGLING!!
IT'S WARNING ME OF SOMETHING!
THE CLOSER I GET, THE MORE IT TINGLES!
IT CAN ONLY MEAN-- A TRAP!
I'D BETTER SEE WHAT'S SWINGIN' IN THERE BEFORE I FUMBLE THE BALL!
WELL, WELL-- WADDAYA KNOW?!!
IT DOESN'T LOOK LIKE A TRAP--
BUT MY SPIDEY-SENSE STILL WON'T BUY IT!
18

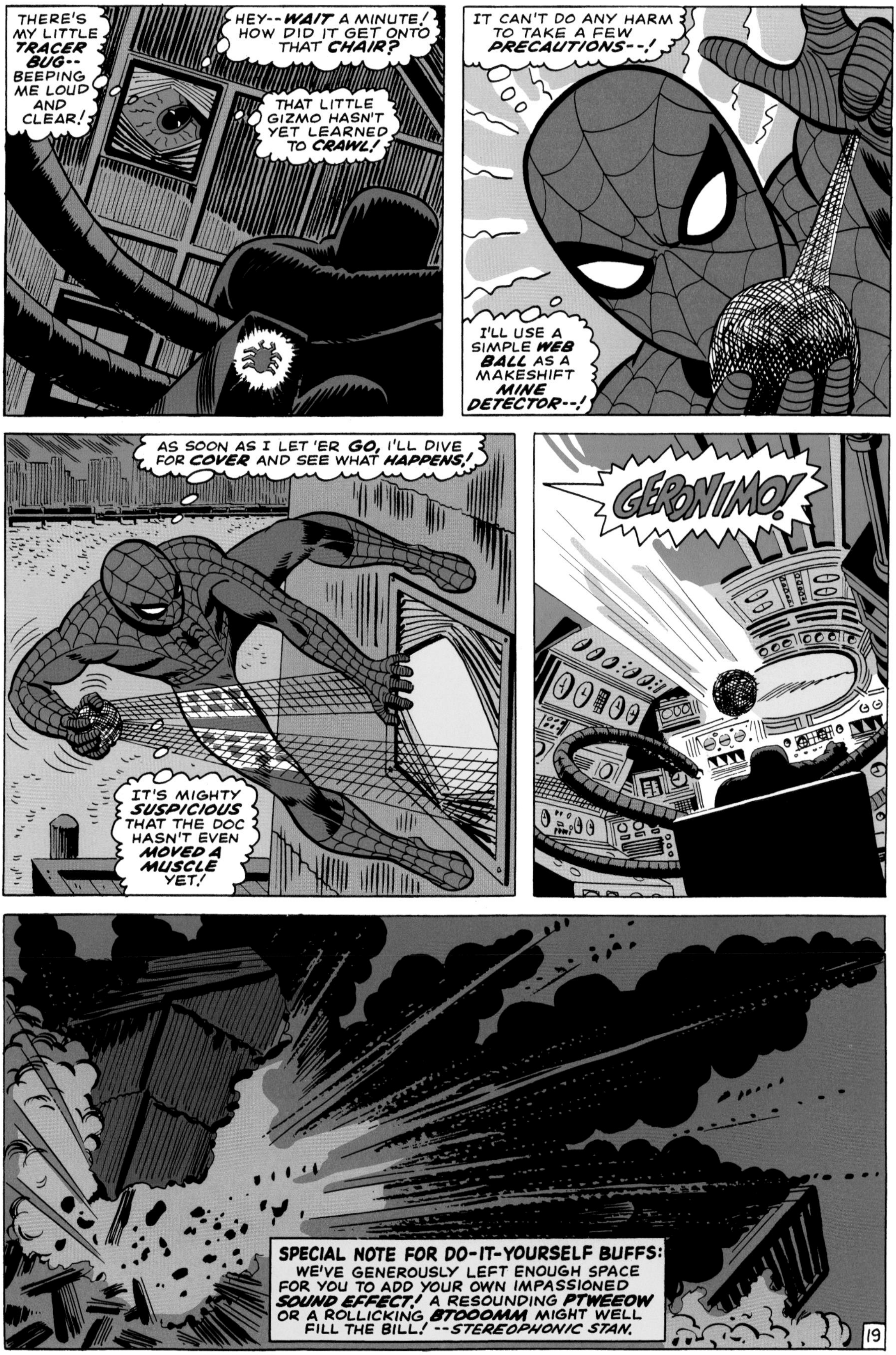
THERE'S MY LITTLE TRACER BUG-- BEEPING ME LOUD AND CLEAR!
HEY--WAIT A MINUTE! HOW DID IT GET ONTO THAT CHAIR?
THAT LITTLE GIZMO HASN'T YET LEARNED TO CRAWL!
IT CAN'T DO ANY HARM TO TAKE A FEW PRECAUTIONS--!
I'LL USE A SIMPLE WEB BALL AS A MAKESHIFT MINE DETECTOR--!
AS SOON AS I LET 'ER GO, I'LL DIVE FOR COVER AND SEE WHAT HAPPENS!
IT'S MIGHTY SUSPICIOUS THAT THE DOC HASN'T EVEN MOVED A MUSCLE YET!
GERONIMO!
SPECIAL NOTE FOR DO-IT-YOURSELF BUFFS:
WE'VE GENEROUSLY LEFT ENOUGH SPACE FOR YOU TO ADD YOUR OWN IMPASSIONED SOUND EFFECT! A RESOUNDING PTWEEOW OR A ROLLICKING BTOOOMM MIGHT WELL FILL THE BILL! --STEREOPHONIC STAN.
19

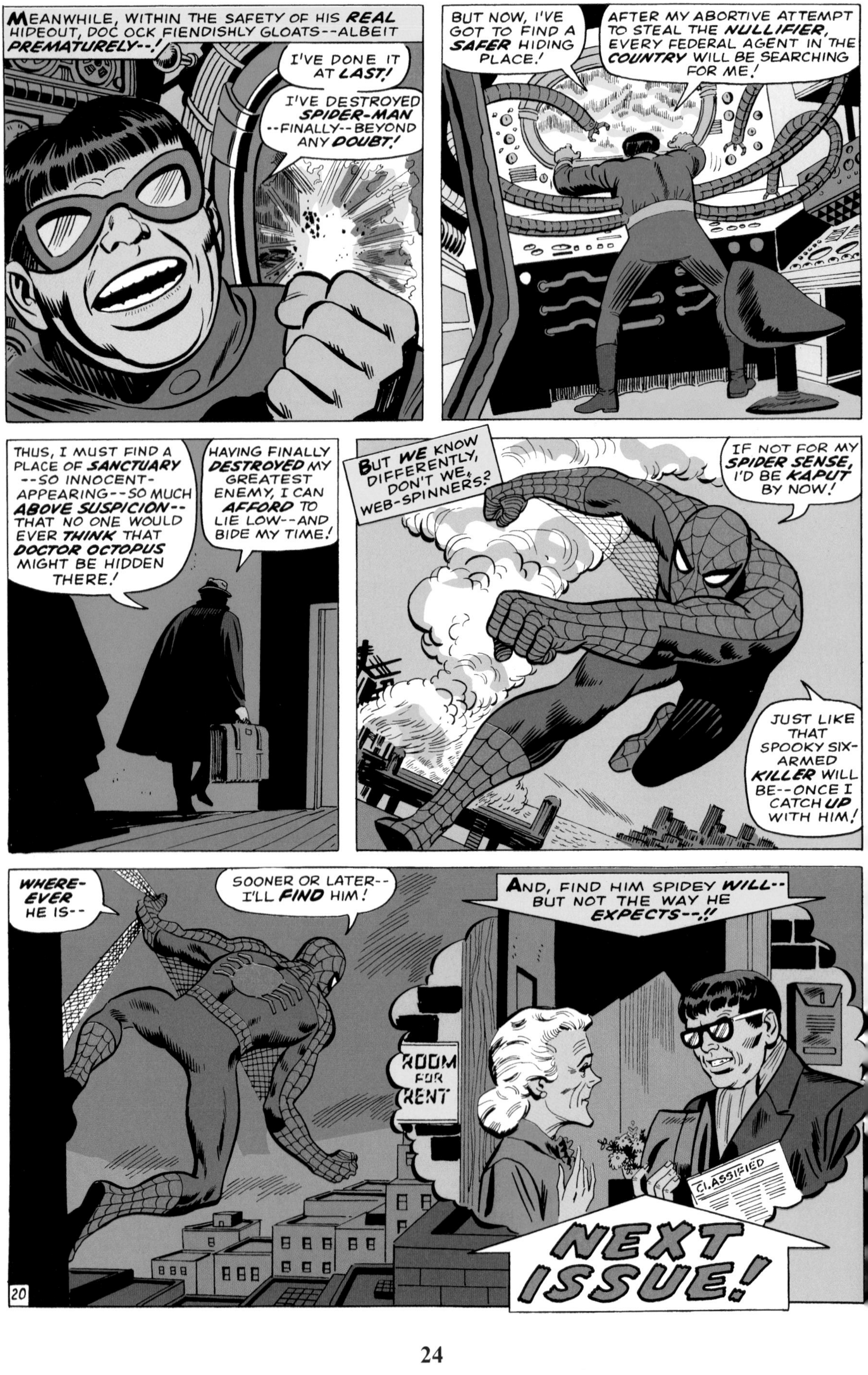
MEANWHILE, WITHIN THE SAFETY OF HIS REAL HIDEOUT, DOC OCK FIENDISHLY GLOATS--ALBEIT PREMATURELY--!
I'VE DONE IT AT LAST!
I'VE DESTROYED SPIDER-MAN --FINALLY--BEYOND ANY DOUBT!
BUT NOW, I'VE GOT TO FIND A SAFER HIDING PLACE!
AFTER MY ABORTIVE ATTEMPT TO STEAL THE NULLIFIER, EVERY FEDERAL AGENT IN THE COUNTRY WILL BE SEARCHING FOR ME!
THUS, I MUST FIND A PLACE OF SANCTUARY --SO INNOCENT-APPEARING--SO MUCH ABOVE SUSPICION--THAT NO ONE WOULD EVER THINK THAT DOCTOR OCTOPUS MIGHT BE HIDDEN THERE!
HAVING FINALLY DESTROYED MY GREATEST ENEMY, I CAN AFFORD TO LIE LOW--AND BIDE MY TIME!
BUT WE KNOW DIFFERENTLY, DON'T WE, WEB-SPINNERS?
IF NOT FOR MY SPIDER SENSE, I'D BE KAPUT BY NOW!
JUST LIKE THAT SPOOKY SIX-ARMED KILLER WILL BE--ONCE I CATCH UP WITH HIM!
WHERE-EVER HE IS--
SOONER OR LATER--I'LL FIND HIM!
AND, FIND HIM SPIDEY WILL--BUT NOT THE WAY HE EXPECTS--!!
ROOM FOR RENT
CLASSIFIED
NEXT ISSUE!
20

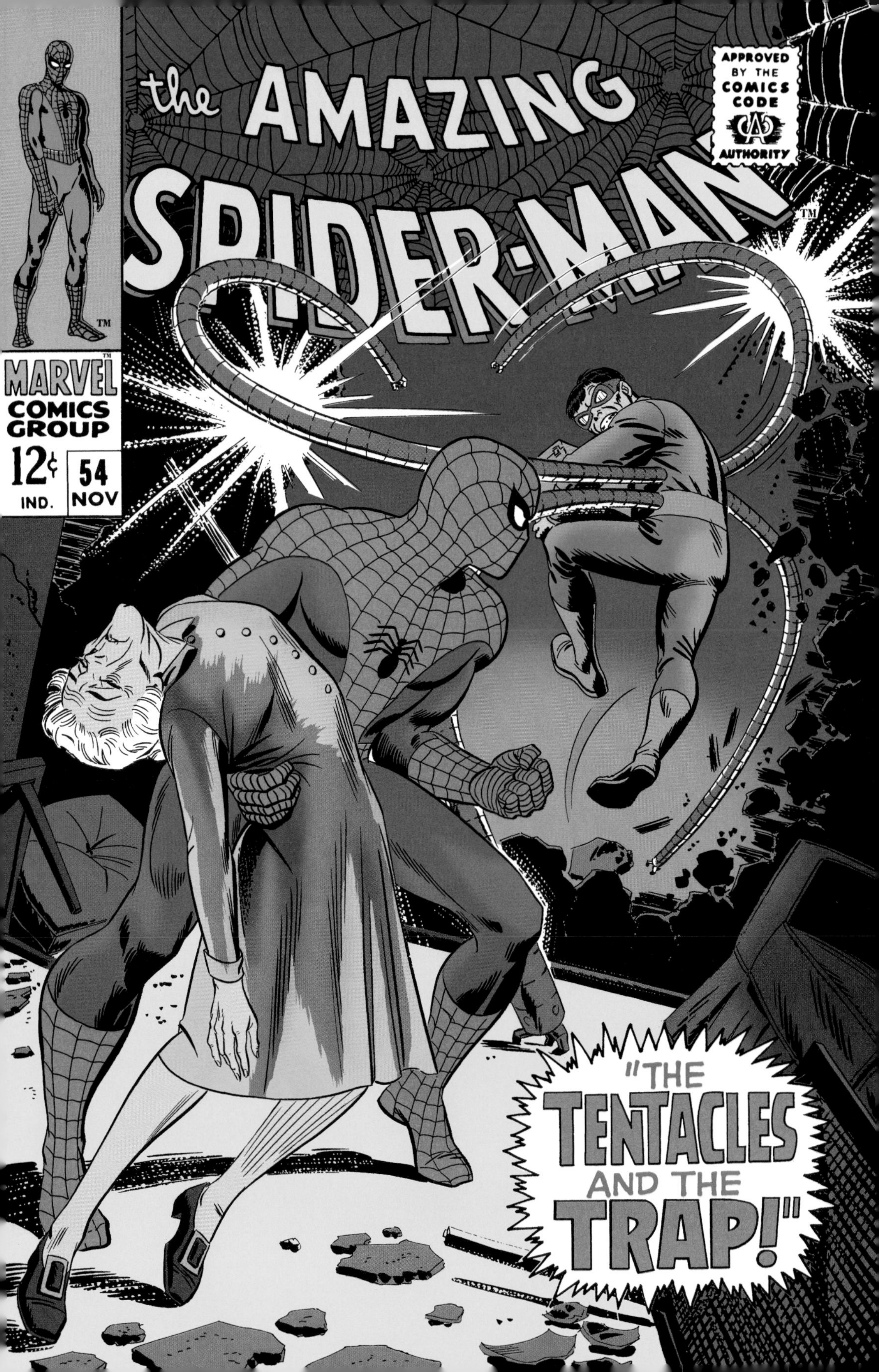
the AMAZING SPIDER-MAN
APPROVED BY THE COMICS CODE AUTHORITY
MARVEL COMICS GROUP
12¢ IND.
54 NOV
"THE TENTACLES AND THE TRAP!"

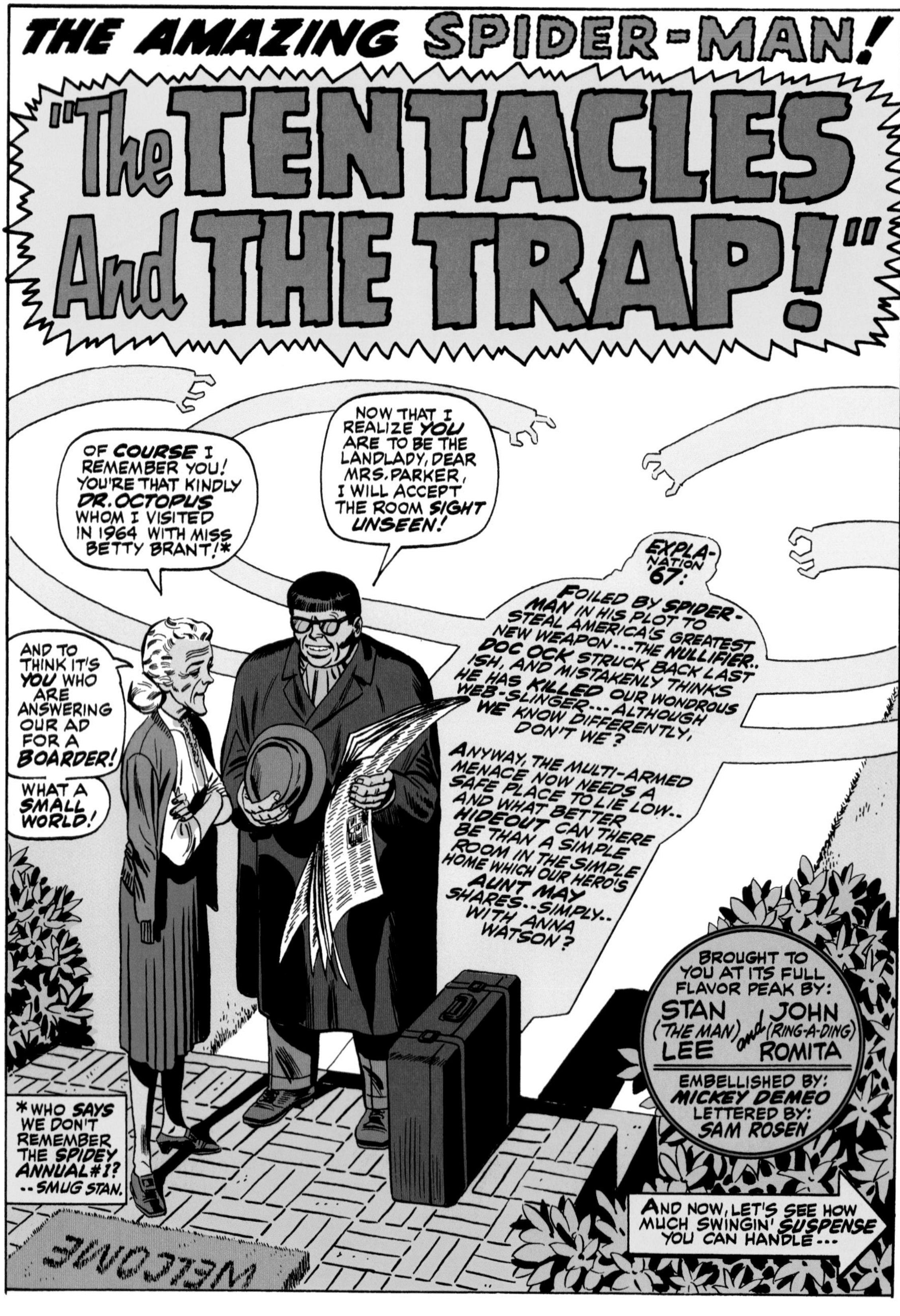

THE AMAZING SPIDER-MAN!
"The TENTACLES And THE TRAP!"
OF COURSE I REMEMBER YOU! YOU'RE THAT KINDLY DR. OCTOPUS WHOM I VISITED IN 1964 WITH MISS BETTY BRANT!*
NOW THAT I REALIZE YOU ARE TO BE THE LANDLADY, DEAR MRS. PARKER, I WILL ACCEPT THE ROOM SIGHT UNSEEN!
EXPLA-NATION '67:
FOILED BY SPIDER-MAN IN HIS PLOT TO STEAL AMERICA'S GREATEST NEW WEAPON... THE NULLIFIER.. DOC OCK STRUCK BACK LAST ISH, AND MISTAKENLY THINKS HE HAS KILLED OUR WONDROUS WEB-SLINGER... ALTHOUGH WE KNOW DIFFERENTLY, DON'T WE?
ANYWAY, THE MULTI-ARMED MENACE NOW NEEDS A SAFE PLACE TO LIE LOW.. AND WHAT BETTER HIDEOUT CAN THERE BE THAN A SIMPLE ROOM IN THE SIMPLE HOME WHICH OUR HERO'S AUNT MAY SHARES..SIMPLY.. WITH ANNA WATSON?
AND TO THINK IT'S YOU WHO ARE ANSWERING OUR AD FOR A BOARDER!
WHAT A SMALL WORLD!
BROUGHT TO YOU AT ITS FULL FLAVOR PEAK BY: STAN (THE MAN) LEE and JOHN (RING-A-DING) ROMITA
EMBELLISHED BY: MICKEY DEMEO
LETTERED BY: SAM ROSEN
*WHO SAYS WE DON'T REMEMBER THE SPIDEY ANNUAL #1? --SMUG STAN.
AND NOW, LET'S SEE HOW MUCH SWINGIN' SUSPENSE YOU CAN HANDLE...
WELCOME

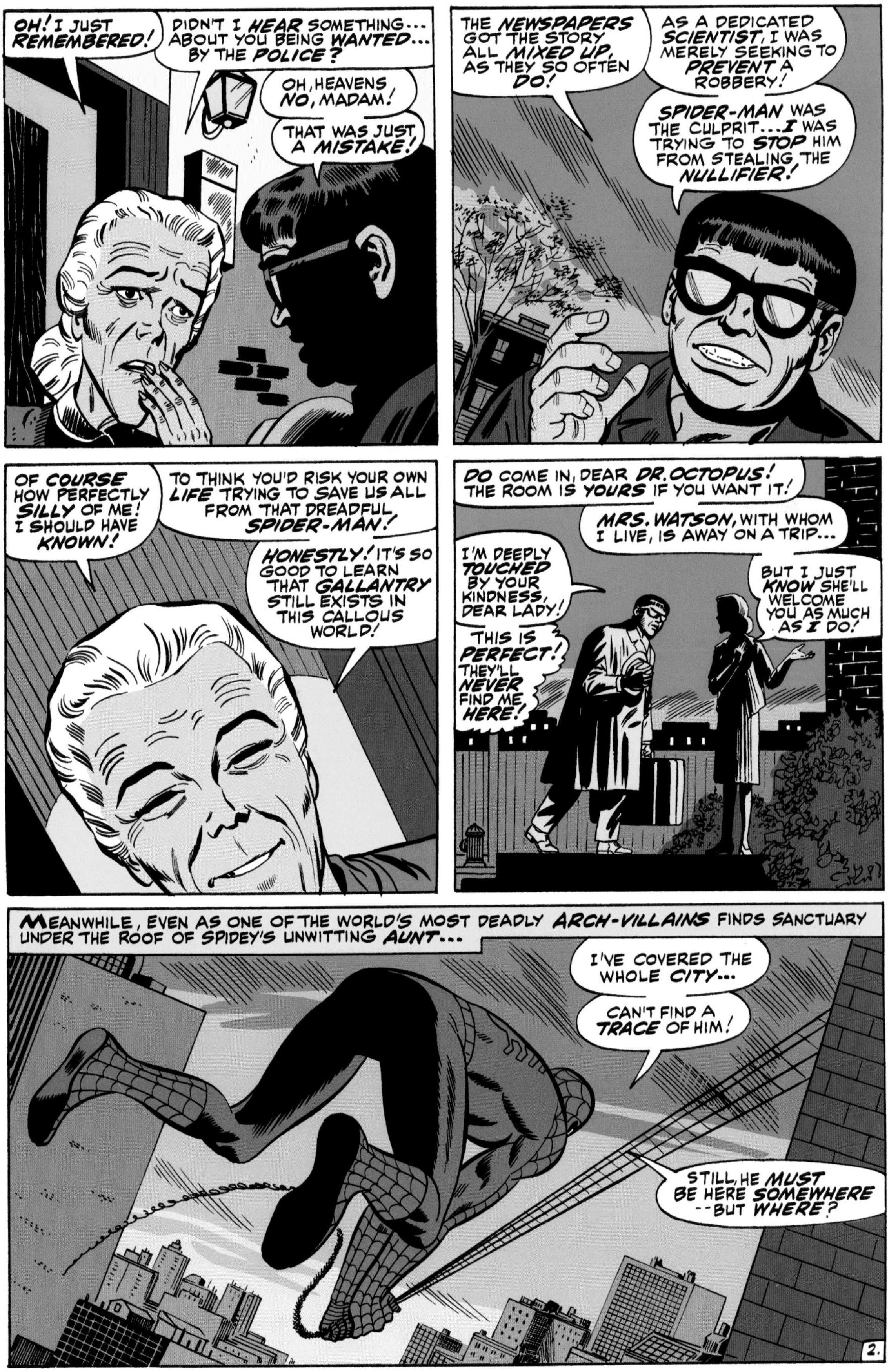
OH! I JUST REMEMBERED!
DIDN'T I HEAR SOMETHING... ABOUT YOU BEING WANTED... BY THE POLICE?
OH, HEAVENS NO, MADAM!
THAT WAS JUST A MISTAKE!
THE NEWSPAPERS GOT THE STORY ALL MIXED UP, AS THEY SO OFTEN DO!
AS A DEDICATED SCIENTIST, I WAS MERELY SEEKING TO PREVENT A ROBBERY!
SPIDER-MAN WAS THE CULPRIT... I WAS TRYING TO STOP HIM FROM STEALING THE NULLIFIER!
OF COURSE HOW PERFECTLY SILLY OF ME! I SHOULD HAVE KNOWN!
TO THINK YOU'D RISK YOUR OWN LIFE TRYING TO SAVE US ALL FROM THAT DREADFUL SPIDER-MAN!
HONESTLY! IT'S SO GOOD TO LEARN THAT GALLANTRY STILL EXISTS IN THIS CALLOUS WORLD!
DO COME IN, DEAR DR. OCTOPUS! THE ROOM IS YOURS IF YOU WANT IT!
MRS. WATSON, WITH WHOM I LIVE, IS AWAY ON A TRIP...
BUT I JUST KNOW SHE'LL WELCOME YOU AS MUCH AS I DO!
I'M DEEPLY TOUCHED BY YOUR KINDNESS, DEAR LADY!
THIS IS PERFECT! THEY'LL NEVER FIND ME HERE!
MEANWHILE, EVEN AS ONE OF THE WORLD'S MOST DEADLY ARCH-VILLAINS FINDS SANCTUARY UNDER THE ROOF OF SPIDEY'S UNWITTING AUNT...
I'VE COVERED THE WHOLE CITY...
CAN'T FIND A TRACE OF HIM!
STILL, HE MUST BE HERE SOMEWHERE --BUT WHERE?
2.

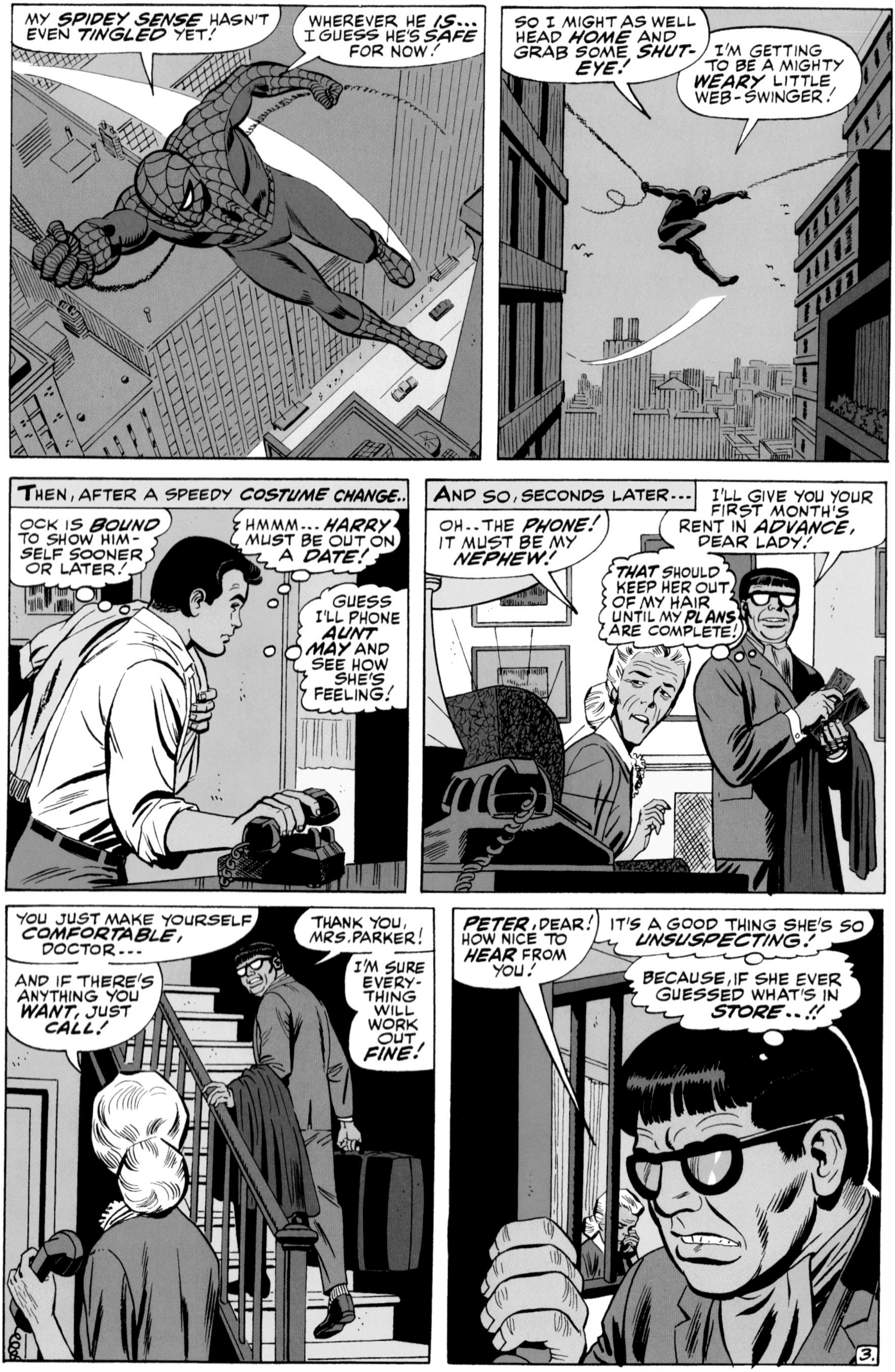
MY SPIDEY SENSE HASN'T EVEN TINGLED YET!
WHEREVER HE IS... I GUESS HE'S SAFE FOR NOW!
SO I MIGHT AS WELL HEAD HOME AND GRAB SOME SHUT-EYE!
I'M GETTING TO BE A MIGHTY WEARY LITTLE WEB-SWINGER!
THEN, AFTER A SPEEDY COSTUME CHANGE..
OCK IS BOUND TO SHOW HIMSELF SOONER OR LATER!
HMMM... HARRY MUST BE OUT ON A DATE!
GUESS I'LL PHONE AUNT MAY AND SEE HOW SHE'S FEELING!
AND SO, SECONDS LATER...
OH.. THE PHONE! IT MUST BE MY NEPHEW!
I'LL GIVE YOU YOUR FIRST MONTH'S RENT IN ADVANCE, DEAR LADY!
THAT SHOULD KEEP HER OUT OF MY HAIR UNTIL MY PLANS ARE COMPLETE!
YOU JUST MAKE YOURSELF COMFORTABLE, DOCTOR---
AND IF THERE'S ANYTHING YOU WANT, JUST CALL!
THANK YOU, MRS. PARKER!
I'M SURE EVERYTHING WILL WORK OUT FINE!
PETER, DEAR! HOW NICE TO HEAR FROM YOU!
IT'S A GOOD THING SHE'S SO UNSUSPECTING!
BECAUSE, IF SHE EVER GUESSED WHAT'S IN STORE..!!
3.

1709-4987

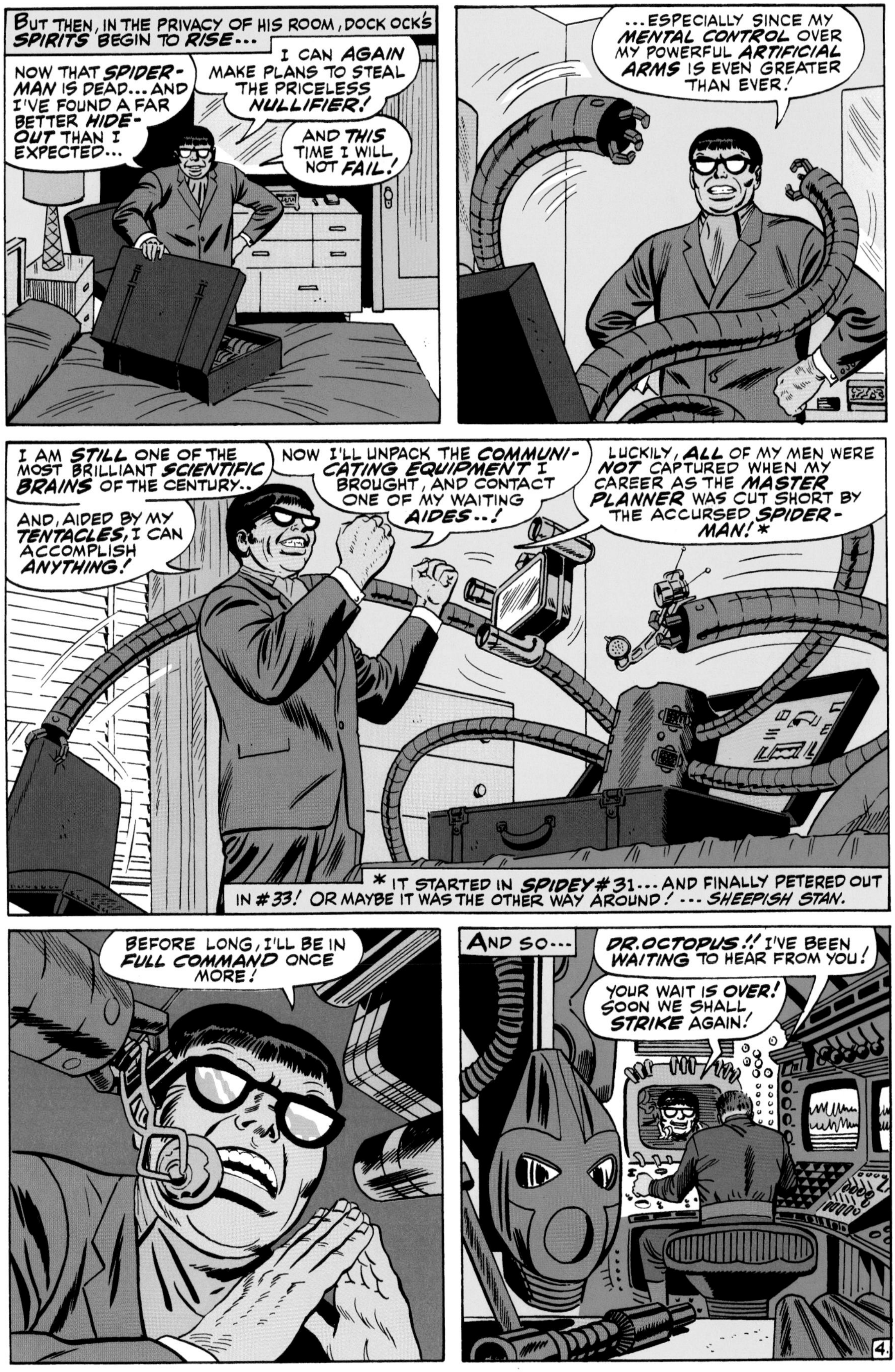

BUT THEN, IN THE PRIVACY OF HIS ROOM, DOCK OCK'S SPIRITS BEGIN TO RISE...
NOW THAT SPIDER-MAN IS DEAD... AND I'VE FOUND A FAR BETTER HIDE-OUT THAN I EXPECTED...
I CAN AGAIN MAKE PLANS TO STEAL THE PRICELESS NULLIFIER!
AND THIS TIME I WILL NOT FAIL!
...ESPECIALLY SINCE MY MENTAL CONTROL OVER MY POWERFUL ARTIFICIAL ARMS IS EVEN GREATER THAN EVER!
I AM STILL ONE OF THE MOST BRILLIANT SCIENTIFIC BRAINS OF THE CENTURY..
AND, AIDED BY MY TENTACLES, I CAN ACCOMPLISH ANYTHING!
NOW I'LL UNPACK THE COMMUNICATING EQUIPMENT I BROUGHT, AND CONTACT ONE OF MY WAITING AIDES..!
LUCKILY, ALL OF MY MEN WERE NOT CAPTURED WHEN MY CAREER AS THE MASTER PLANNER WAS CUT SHORT BY THE ACCURSED SPIDER-MAN! *
* IT STARTED IN SPIDEY #31... AND FINALLY PETERED OUT IN #33! OR MAYBE IT WAS THE OTHER WAY AROUND! --- SHEEPISH STAN.
BEFORE LONG, I'LL BE IN FULL COMMAND ONCE MORE!
AND SO...
DR. OCTOPUS!! I'VE BEEN WAITING TO HEAR FROM YOU!
YOUR WAIT IS OVER! SOON WE SHALL STRIKE AGAIN!
4.

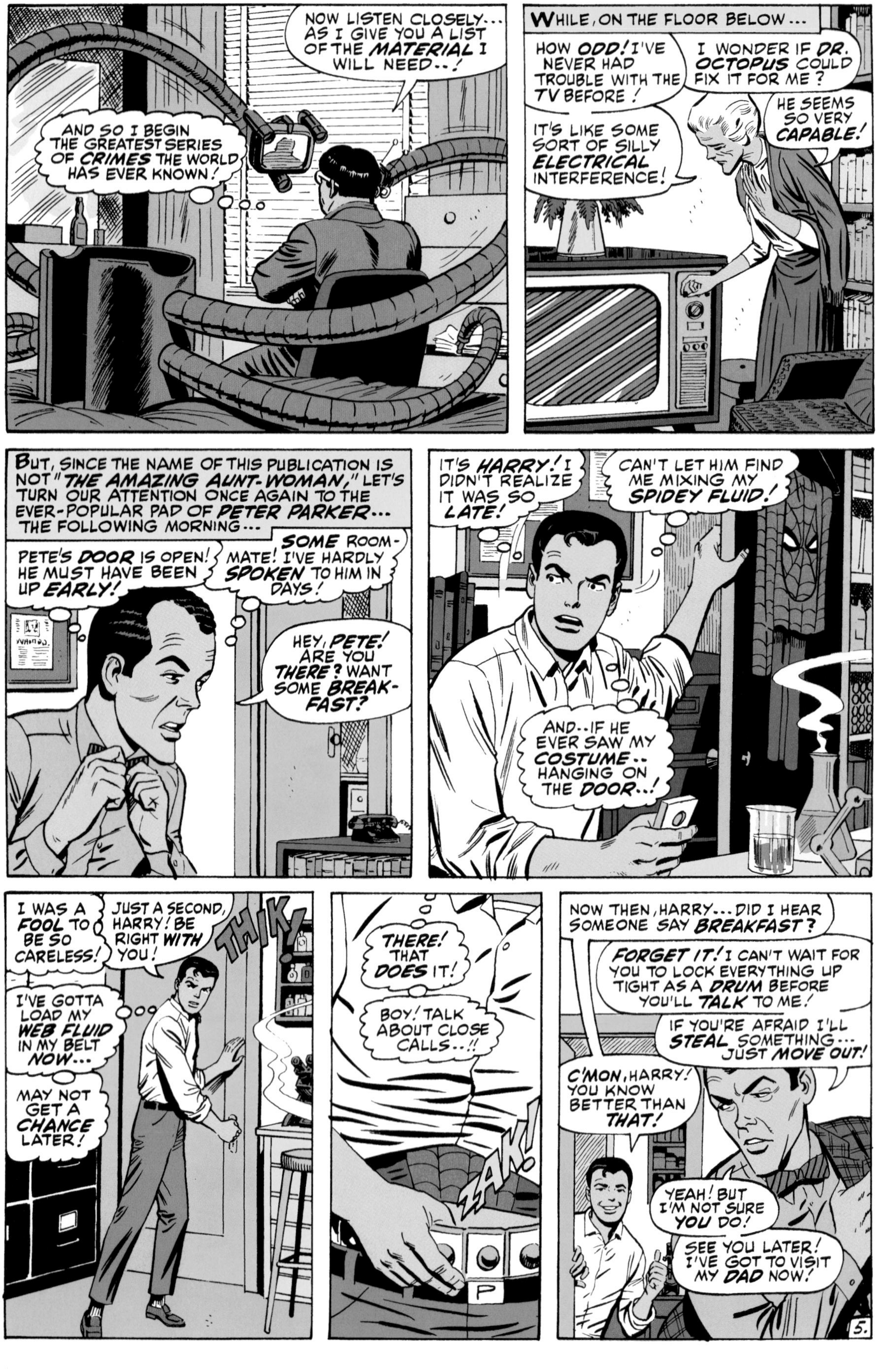
NOW LISTEN CLOSELY... AS I GIVE YOU A LIST OF THE MATERIAL I WILL NEED..!
AND SO I BEGIN THE GREATEST SERIES OF CRIMES THE WORLD HAS EVER KNOWN!
WHILE, ON THE FLOOR BELOW...
HOW ODD! I'VE NEVER HAD TROUBLE WITH THE TV BEFORE!
I WONDER IF DR. OCTOPUS COULD FIX IT FOR ME?
HE SEEMS SO VERY CAPABLE!
IT'S LIKE SOME SORT OF SILLY ELECTRICAL INTERFERENCE!
BUT, SINCE THE NAME OF THIS PUBLICATION IS NOT "THE AMAZING AUNT-WOMAN," LET'S TURN OUR ATTENTION ONCE AGAIN TO THE EVER-POPULAR PAD OF PETER PARKER... THE FOLLOWING MORNING...
PETE'S DOOR IS OPEN! HE MUST HAVE BEEN UP EARLY!
SOME ROOM-MATE! I'VE HARDLY SPOKEN TO HIM IN DAYS!
HEY, PETE! ARE YOU THERE? WANT SOME BREAK-FAST?
IT'S HARRY! I DIDN'T REALIZE IT WAS SO LATE!
CAN'T LET HIM FIND ME MIXING MY SPIDEY FLUID!
AND..IF HE EVER SAW MY COSTUME.. HANGING ON THE DOOR..!
I WAS A FOOL TO BE SO CARELESS!
JUST A SECOND, HARRY! BE RIGHT WITH YOU!
THIK!
I'VE GOTTA LOAD MY WEB FLUID IN MY BELT NOW...
MAY NOT GET A CHANCE LATER!
THERE! THAT DOES IT!
BOY! TALK ABOUT CLOSE CALLS..!!
ZAK!
P
NOW THEN, HARRY... DID I HEAR SOMEONE SAY BREAKFAST?
FORGET IT! I CAN'T WAIT FOR YOU TO LOCK EVERYTHING UP TIGHT AS A DRUM BEFORE YOU'LL TALK TO ME!
IF YOU'RE AFRAID I'LL STEAL SOMETHING... JUST MOVE OUT!
C'MON, HARRY! YOU KNOW BETTER THAN THAT!
YEAH! BUT I'M NOT SURE YOU DO!
SEE YOU LATER! I'VE GOT TO VISIT MY DAD NOW!
5.

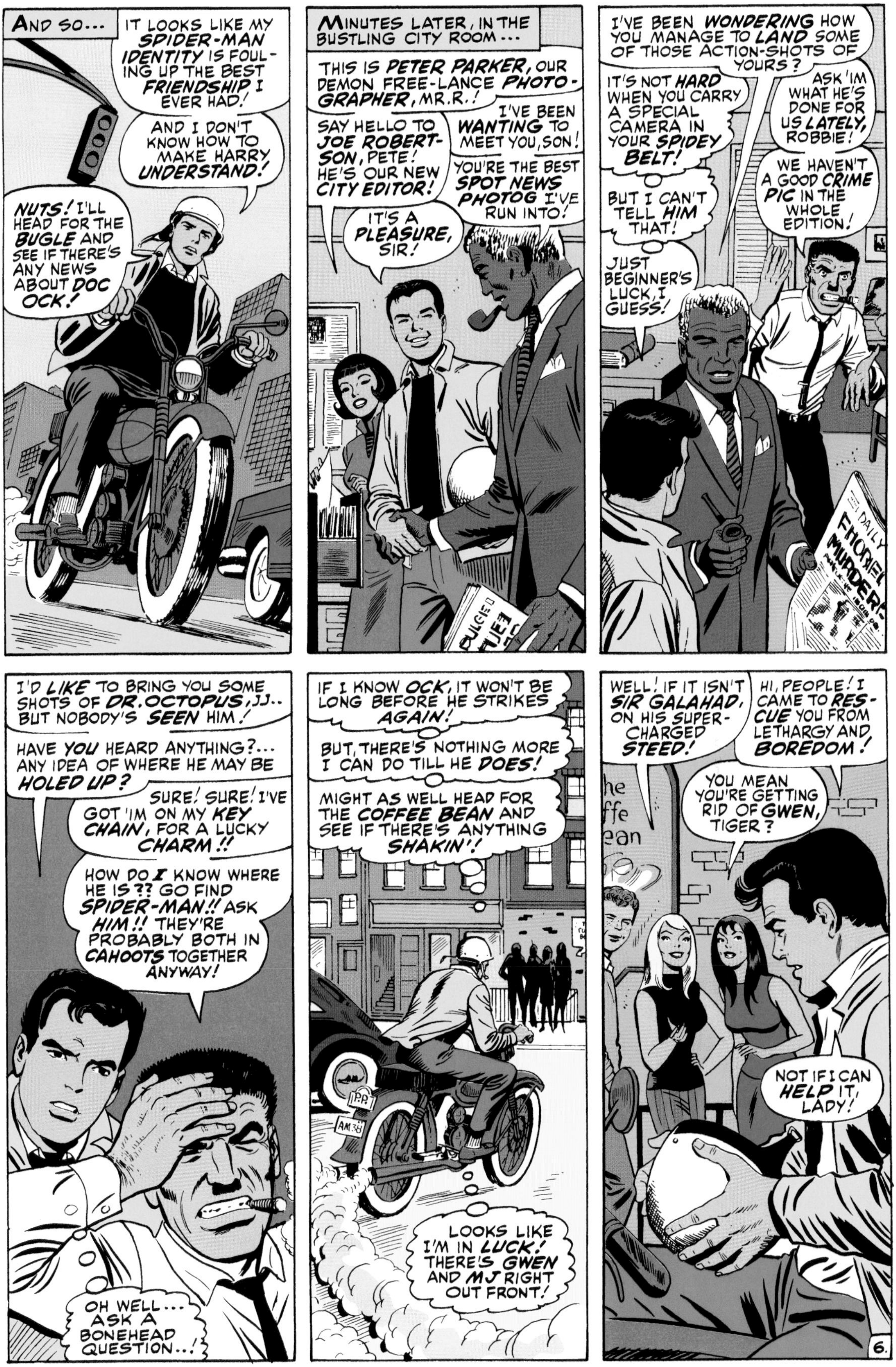
AND SO...
IT LOOKS LIKE MY SPIDER-MAN IDENTITY IS FOULING UP THE BEST FRIENDSHIP I EVER HAD!
AND I DON'T KNOW HOW TO MAKE HARRY UNDERSTAND!
NUTS! I'LL HEAD FOR THE BUGLE AND SEE IF THERE'S ANY NEWS ABOUT DOC OCK!
MINUTES LATER, IN THE BUSTLING CITY ROOM...
THIS IS PETER PARKER, OUR DEMON FREE-LANCE PHOTOGRAPHER, MR. R.!
SAY HELLO TO JOE ROBERTSON, PETE! HE'S OUR NEW CITY EDITOR!
I'VE BEEN WANTING TO MEET YOU, SON!
YOU'RE THE BEST SPOT NEWS PHOTOG I'VE RUN INTO!
IT'S A PLEASURE, SIR!
I'VE BEEN WONDERING HOW YOU MANAGE TO LAND SOME OF THOSE ACTION-SHOTS OF YOURS?
IT'S NOT HARD WHEN YOU CARRY A SPECIAL CAMERA IN YOUR SPIDEY BELT!
BUT I CAN'T TELL HIM THAT!
JUST BEGINNER'S LUCK, I GUESS!
ASK 'IM WHAT HE'S DONE FOR US LATELY, ROBBIE!
WE HAVEN'T A GOOD CRIME PIC IN THE WHOLE EDITION!
I'D LIKE TO BRING YOU SOME SHOTS OF DR. OCTOPUS, JJ.. BUT NOBODY'S SEEN HIM!
HAVE YOU HEARD ANYTHING?... ANY IDEA OF WHERE HE MAY BE HOLED UP?
SURE! SURE! I'VE GOT 'IM ON MY KEY CHAIN, FOR A LUCKY CHARM!!
HOW DO I KNOW WHERE HE IS?? GO FIND SPIDER-MAN!! ASK HIM!! THEY'RE PROBABLY BOTH IN CAHOOTS TOGETHER ANYWAY!
OH WELL... ASK A BONEHEAD QUESTION...!
IF I KNOW OCK, IT WON'T BE LONG BEFORE HE STRIKES AGAIN!
BUT, THERE'S NOTHING MORE I CAN DO TILL HE DOES!
MIGHT AS WELL HEAD FOR THE COFFEE BEAN AND SEE IF THERE'S ANYTHING SHAKIN'!
LOOKS LIKE I'M IN LUCK! THERE'S GWEN AND MJ RIGHT OUT FRONT!
WELL! IF IT ISN'T SIR GALAHAD, ON HIS SUPER-CHARGED STEED!
HI, PEOPLE! I CAME TO RESCUE YOU FROM LETHARGY AND BOREDOM!
YOU MEAN YOU'RE GETTING RID OF GWEN, TIGER?
NOT IF I CAN HELP IT, LADY!
6.

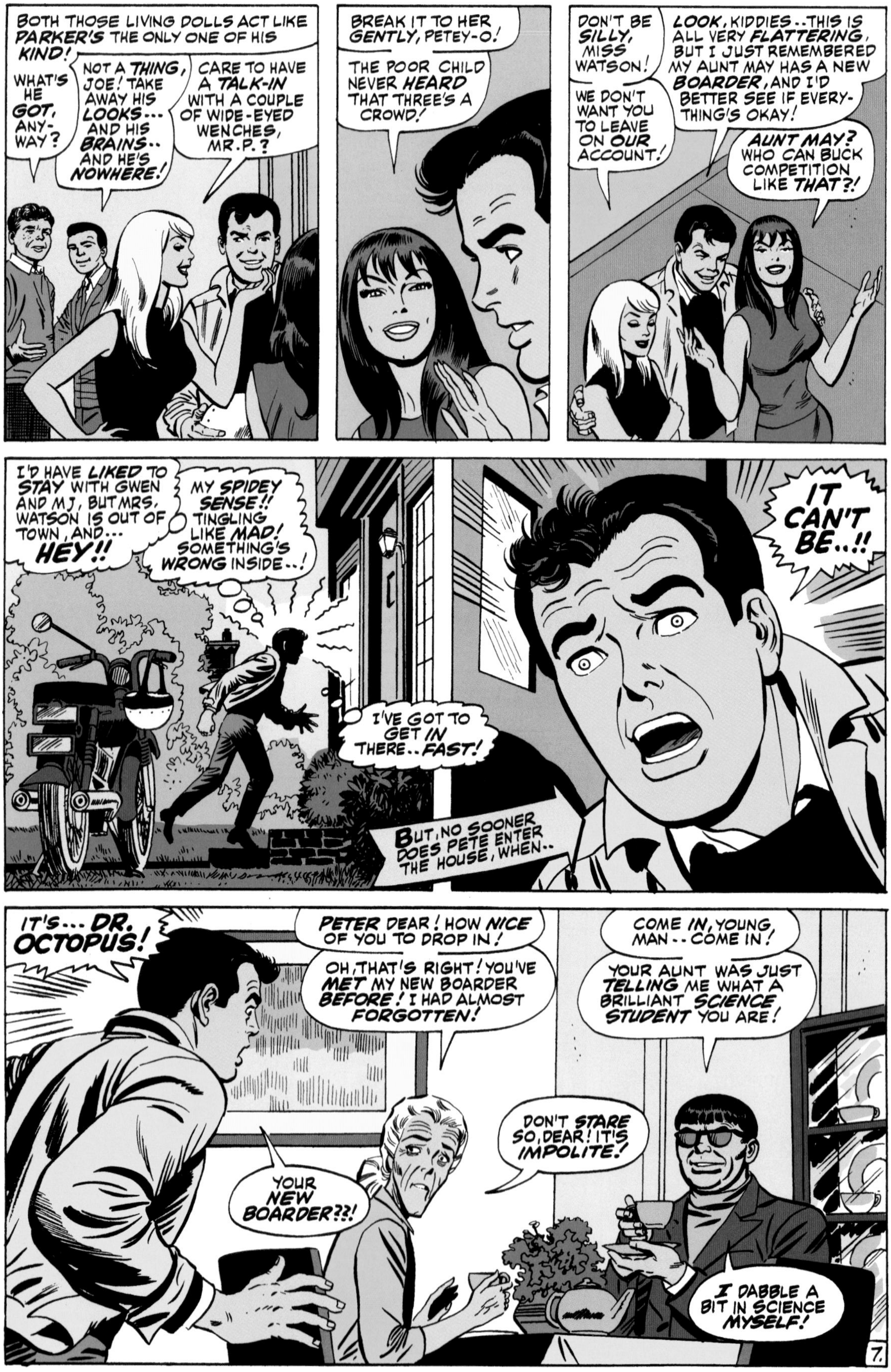

BOTH THOSE LIVING DOLLS ACT LIKE PARKER'S THE ONLY ONE OF HIS KIND!
WHAT'S HE GOT, ANYWAY?
NOT A THING, JOE! TAKE AWAY HIS LOOKS... AND HIS BRAINS.. AND HE'S NOWHERE!
CARE TO HAVE A TALK-IN WITH A COUPLE OF WIDE-EYED WENCHES, MR.P.?
BREAK IT TO HER GENTLY, PETEY-O!
THE POOR CHILD NEVER HEARD THAT THREE'S A CROWD!
DON'T BE SILLY, MISS WATSON!
WE DON'T WANT YOU TO LEAVE ON OUR ACCOUNT!
LOOK, KIDDIES.. THIS IS ALL VERY FLATTERING, BUT I JUST REMEMBERED MY AUNT MAY HAS A NEW BOARDER, AND I'D BETTER SEE IF EVERYTHING'S OKAY!
AUNT MAY? WHO CAN BUCK COMPETITION LIKE THAT?!
I'D HAVE LIKED TO STAY WITH GWEN AND MJ, BUT MRS. WATSON IS OUT OF TOWN, AND... HEY!!
MY SPIDEY SENSE!! TINGLING LIKE MAD! SOMETHING'S WRONG INSIDE..!
I'VE GOT TO GET IN THERE.. FAST!
BUT, NO SOONER DOES PETE ENTER THE HOUSE, WHEN..
IT CAN'T BE..!!
IT'S... DR. OCTOPUS!
PETER DEAR! HOW NICE OF YOU TO DROP IN!
OH, THAT'S RIGHT! YOU'VE MET MY NEW BOARDER BEFORE! I HAD ALMOST FORGOTTEN!
YOUR NEW BOARDER??!
DON'T STARE SO, DEAR! IT'S IMPOLITE!
COME IN, YOUNG MAN -- COME IN!
YOUR AUNT WAS JUST TELLING ME WHAT A BRILLIANT SCIENCE STUDENT YOU ARE!
I DABBLE A BIT IN SCIENCE MYSELF!
7.

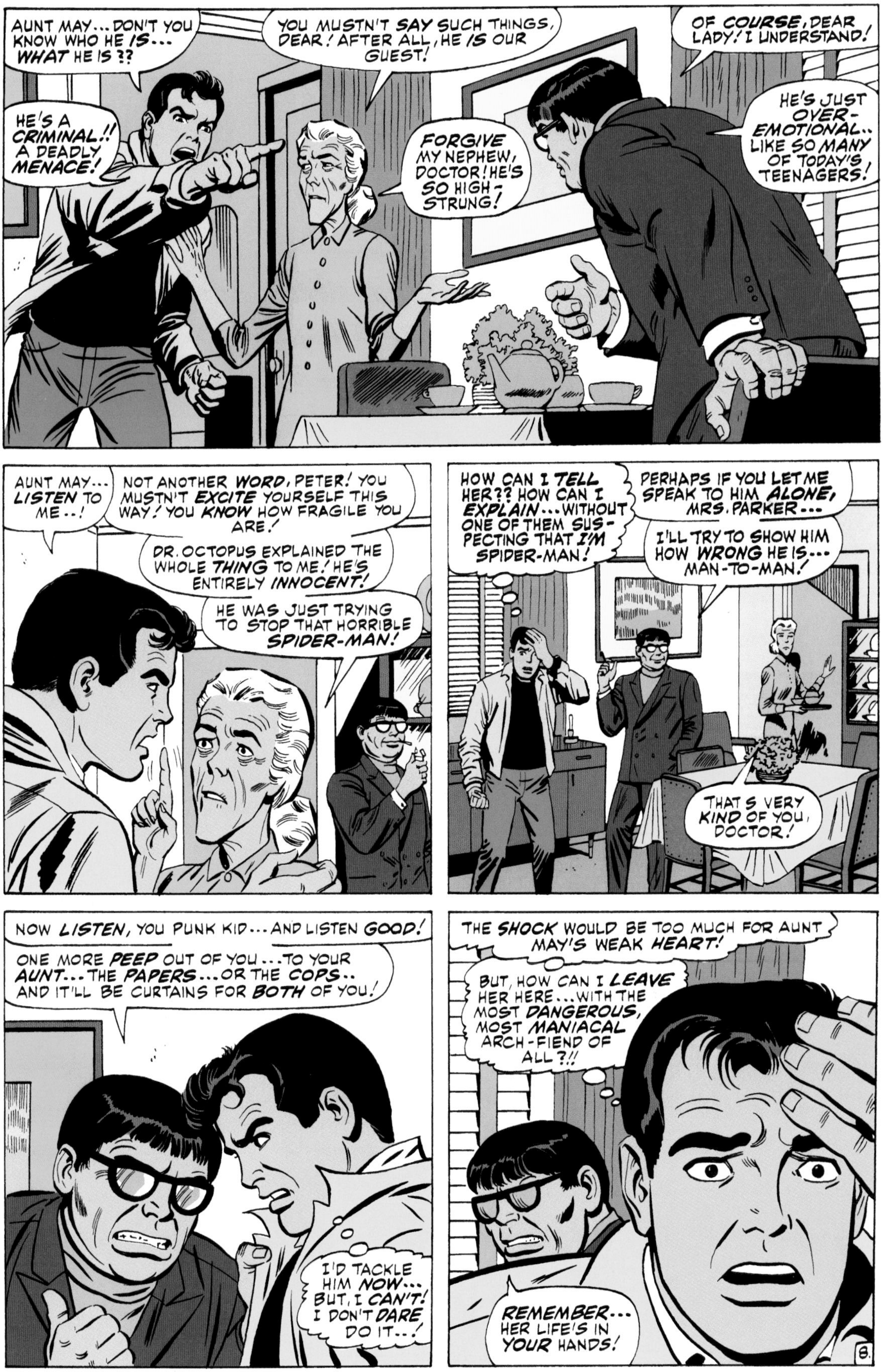
AUNT MAY... DON'T YOU KNOW WHO HE IS... WHAT HE IS ??
HE'S A CRIMINAL!! A DEADLY MENACE!
YOU MUSTN'T SAY SUCH THINGS, DEAR! AFTER ALL, HE IS OUR GUEST!
FORGIVE MY NEPHEW, DOCTOR! HE'S SO HIGH-STRUNG!
OF COURSE, DEAR LADY! I UNDERSTAND!
HE'S JUST OVER-EMOTIONAL.. LIKE SO MANY OF TODAY'S TEENAGERS!
AUNT MAY... LISTEN TO ME..!
NOT ANOTHER WORD, PETER! YOU MUSTN'T EXCITE YOURSELF THIS WAY! YOU KNOW HOW FRAGILE YOU ARE!
DR. OCTOPUS EXPLAINED THE WHOLE THING TO ME! HE'S ENTIRELY INNOCENT!
HE WAS JUST TRYING TO STOP THAT HORRIBLE SPIDER-MAN!
HOW CAN I TELL HER?? HOW CAN I EXPLAIN... WITHOUT ONE OF THEM SUSPECTING THAT I'M SPIDER-MAN!
PERHAPS IF YOU LET ME SPEAK TO HIM ALONE, MRS. PARKER...
I'LL TRY TO SHOW HIM HOW WRONG HE IS... MAN-TO-MAN!
THAT'S VERY KIND OF YOU, DOCTOR!
NOW LISTEN, YOU PUNK KID... AND LISTEN GOOD!
ONE MORE PEEP OUT OF YOU... TO YOUR AUNT... THE PAPERS... OR THE COPS.. AND IT'LL BE CURTAINS FOR BOTH OF YOU!
I'D TACKLE HIM NOW... BUT, I CAN'T! I DON'T DARE DO IT..!
THE SHOCK WOULD BE TOO MUCH FOR AUNT MAY'S WEAK HEART!
BUT, HOW CAN I LEAVE HER HERE... WITH THE MOST DANGEROUS, MOST MANIACAL ARCH-FIEND OF ALL?!!
REMEMBER... HER LIFE'S IN YOUR HANDS!
8.

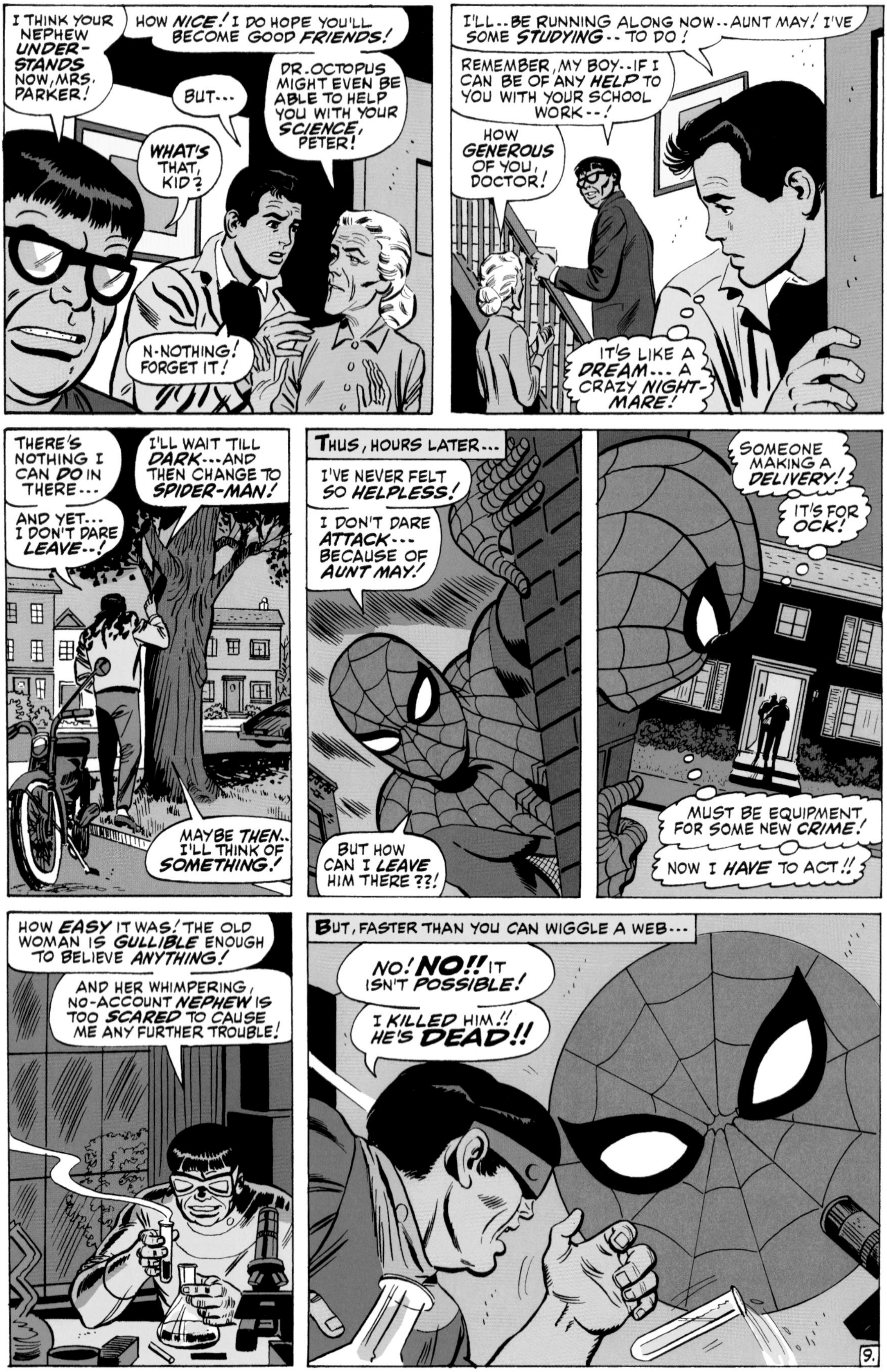
I THINK YOUR NEPHEW UNDERSTANDS NOW, MRS. PARKER!
HOW NICE! I DO HOPE YOU'LL BECOME GOOD FRIENDS!
BUT...
DR. OCTOPUS MIGHT EVEN BE ABLE TO HELP YOU WITH YOUR SCIENCE, PETER!
WHAT'S THAT, KID?
N-NOTHING! FORGET IT!
I'LL.. BE RUNNING ALONG NOW.. AUNT MAY! I'VE SOME STUDYING.. TO DO!
REMEMBER, MY BOY..IF I CAN BE OF ANY HELP TO YOU WITH YOUR SCHOOL WORK..!
HOW GENEROUS OF YOU, DOCTOR!
IT'S LIKE A DREAM... A CRAZY NIGHTMARE!
THERE'S NOTHING I CAN DO IN THERE...
AND YET... I DON'T DARE LEAVE..!
I'LL WAIT TILL DARK...AND THEN CHANGE TO SPIDER-MAN!
MAYBE THEN.. I'LL THINK OF SOMETHING!
THUS, HOURS LATER...
I'VE NEVER FELT SO HELPLESS!
I DON'T DARE ATTACK... BECAUSE OF AUNT MAY!
BUT HOW CAN I LEAVE HIM THERE??!
SOMEONE MAKING A DELIVERY!
IT'S FOR OCK!
MUST BE EQUIPMENT FOR SOME NEW CRIME!
NOW I HAVE TO ACT!!
HOW EASY IT WAS! THE OLD WOMAN IS GULLIBLE ENOUGH TO BELIEVE ANYTHING!
AND HER WHIMPERING, NO-ACCOUNT NEPHEW IS TOO SCARED TO CAUSE ME ANY FURTHER TROUBLE!
BUT, FASTER THAN YOU CAN WIGGLE A WEB...
NO! NO!! IT ISN'T POSSIBLE!
I KILLED HIM!! HE'S DEAD!!
9.

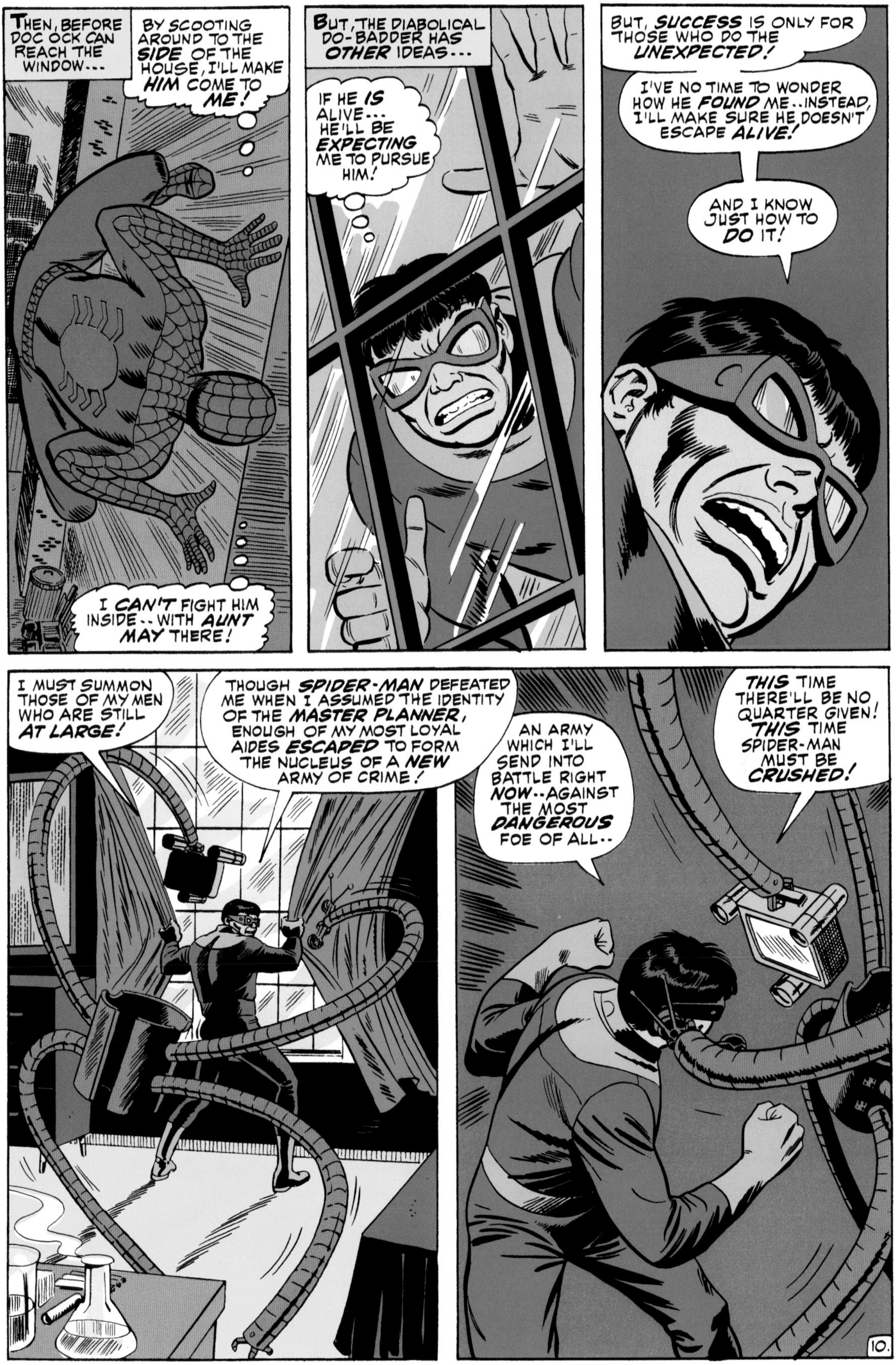

THEN, BEFORE DOC OCK CAN REACH THE WINDOW...
BY SCOOTING AROUND TO THE SIDE OF THE HOUSE, I'LL MAKE HIM COME TO ME!
I CAN'T FIGHT HIM INSIDE.. WITH AUNT MAY THERE!
BUT, THE DIABOLICAL DO-BADDER HAS OTHER IDEAS...
IF HE IS ALIVE... HE'LL BE EXPECTING ME TO PURSUE HIM!
BUT, SUCCESS IS ONLY FOR THOSE WHO DO THE UNEXPECTED!
I'VE NO TIME TO WONDER HOW HE FOUND ME..INSTEAD, I'LL MAKE SURE HE DOESN'T ESCAPE ALIVE!
AND I KNOW JUST HOW TO DO IT!
I MUST SUMMON THOSE OF MY MEN WHO ARE STILL AT LARGE!
THOUGH SPIDER-MAN DEFEATED ME WHEN I ASSUMED THE IDENTITY OF THE MASTER PLANNER, ENOUGH OF MY MOST LOYAL AIDES ESCAPED TO FORM THE NUCLEUS OF A NEW ARMY OF CRIME!
AN ARMY WHICH I'LL SEND INTO BATTLE RIGHT NOW..AGAINST THE MOST DANGEROUS FOE OF ALL..
THIS TIME THERE'LL BE NO QUARTER GIVEN! THIS TIME SPIDER-MAN MUST BE CRUSHED!
10.

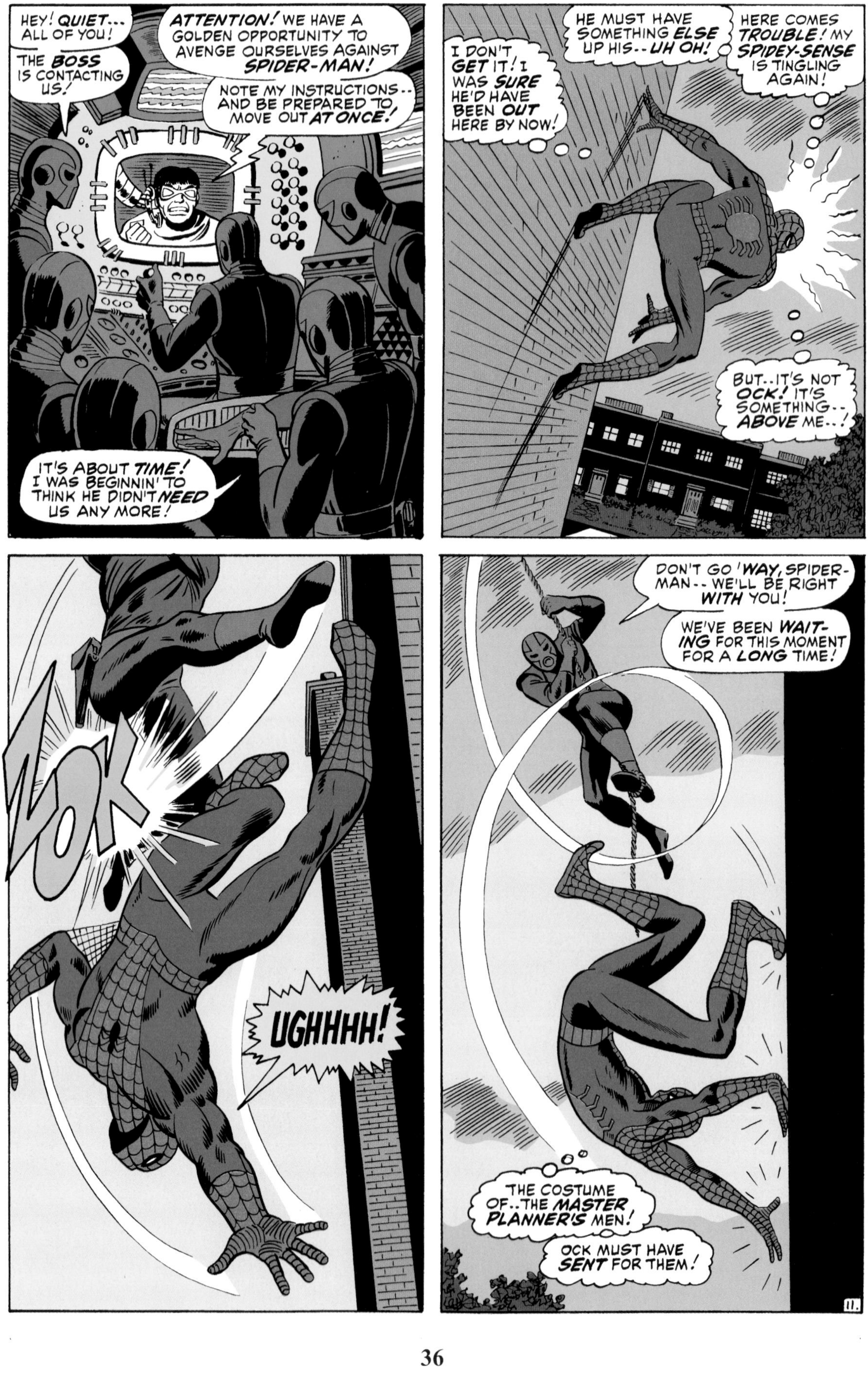

HEY! QUIET... ALL OF YOU!
THE BOSS IS CONTACTING US!
ATTENTION! WE HAVE A GOLDEN OPPORTUNITY TO AVENGE OURSELVES AGAINST SPIDER-MAN!
NOTE MY INSTRUCTIONS-- AND BE PREPARED TO MOVE OUT AT ONCE!
IT'S ABOUT TIME! I WAS BEGINNIN' TO THINK HE DIDN'T NEED US ANY MORE!
I DON'T GET IT! I WAS SURE HE'D HAVE BEEN OUT HERE BY NOW!
HE MUST HAVE SOMETHING ELSE UP HIS-- UH OH!
HERE COMES TROUBLE! MY SPIDEY-SENSE IS TINGLING AGAIN!
BUT--IT'S NOT OCK! IT'S SOMETHING-- ABOVE ME--!
WOK
UGHHHH!
DON'T GO 'WAY, SPIDER-MAN-- WE'LL BE RIGHT WITH YOU!
WE'VE BEEN WAITING FOR THIS MOMENT FOR A LONG TIME!
THE COSTUME OF--THE MASTER PLANNER'S MEN!
OCK MUST HAVE SENT FOR THEM!
11.

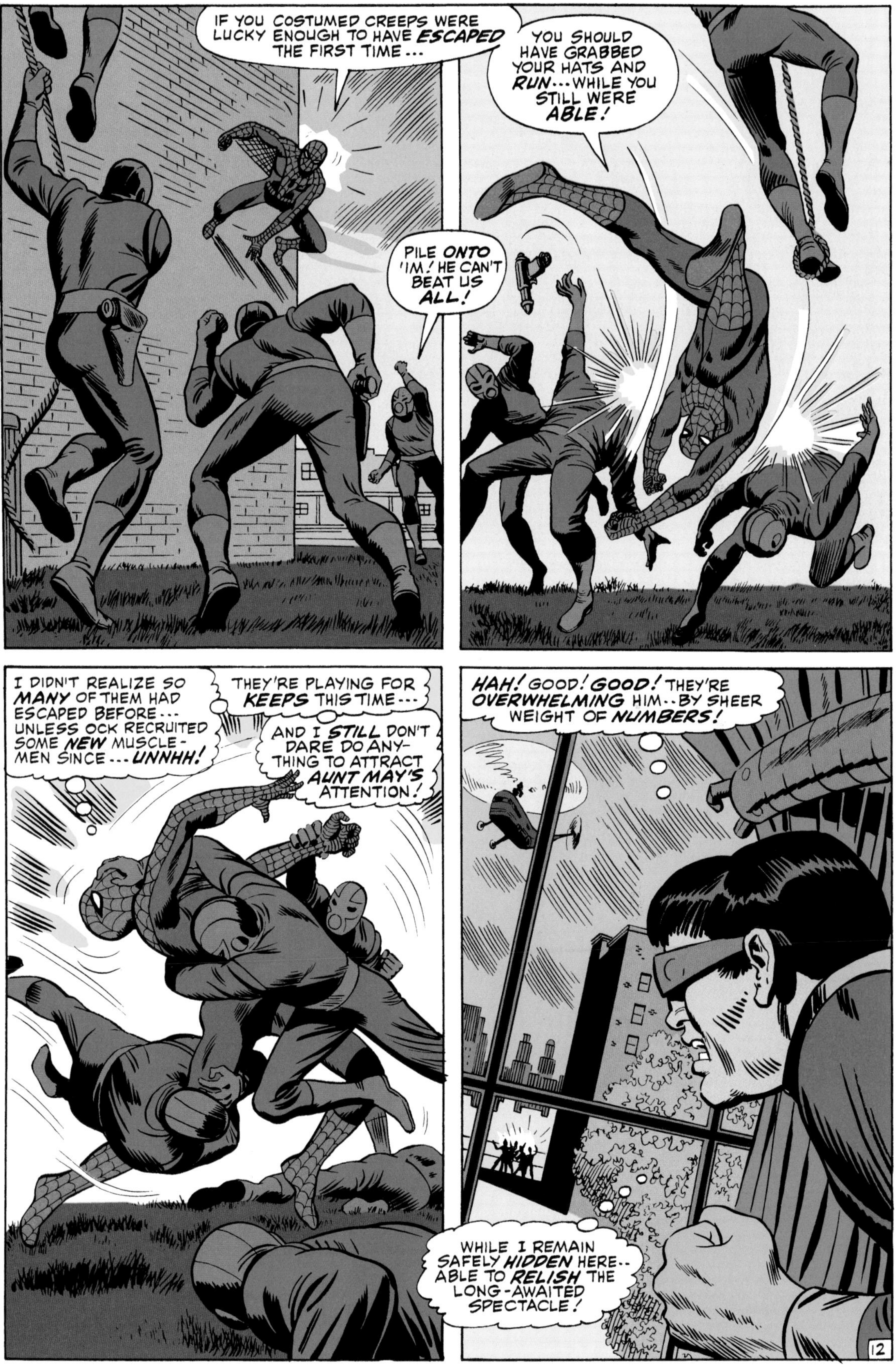
IF YOU COSTUMED CREEPS WERE LUCKY ENOUGH TO HAVE ESCAPED THE FIRST TIME...
YOU SHOULD HAVE GRABBED YOUR HATS AND RUN...WHILE YOU STILL WERE ABLE!
PILE ONTO 'IM! HE CAN'T BEAT US ALL!
I DIDN'T REALIZE SO MANY OF THEM HAD ESCAPED BEFORE... UNLESS OCK RECRUITED SOME NEW MUSCLE-MEN SINCE...UNNHH!
THEY'RE PLAYING FOR KEEPS THIS TIME...
AND I STILL DON'T DARE DO ANY-THING TO ATTRACT AUNT MAY'S ATTENTION!
HAH! GOOD! GOOD! THEY'RE OVERWHELMING HIM..BY SHEER WEIGHT OF NUMBERS!
WHILE I REMAIN SAFELY HIDDEN HERE.. ABLE TO RELISH THE LONG-AWAITED SPECTACLE!
12

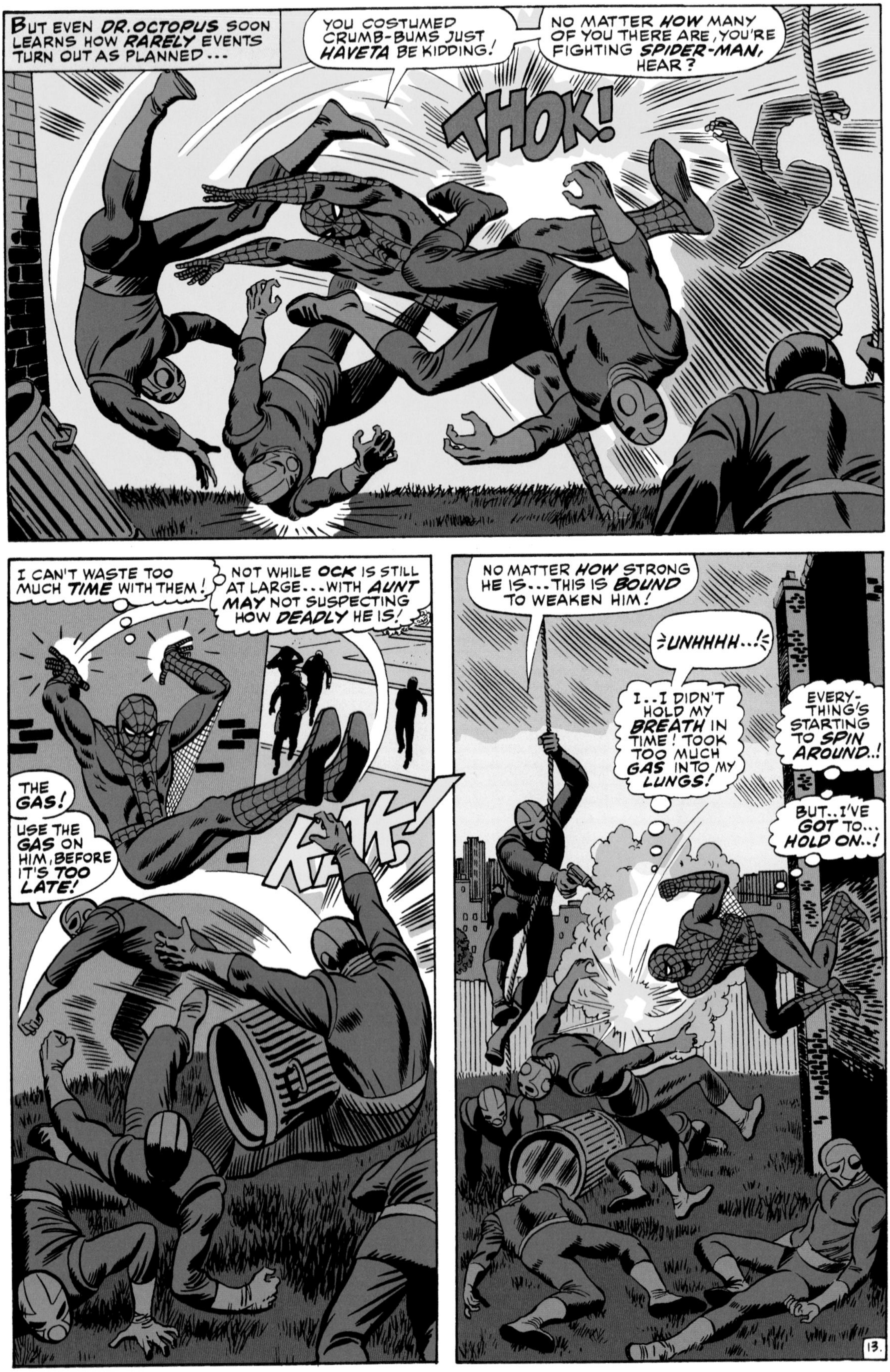

BUT EVEN DR. OCTOPUS SOON LEARNS HOW RARELY EVENTS TURN OUT AS PLANNED...
YOU COSTUMED CRUMB-BUMS JUST HAVETA BE KIDDING!
NO MATTER HOW MANY OF YOU THERE ARE, YOU'RE FIGHTING SPIDER-MAN, HEAR?
THOK!
I CAN'T WASTE TOO MUCH TIME WITH THEM!
NOT WHILE OCK IS STILL AT LARGE... WITH AUNT MAY NOT SUSPECTING HOW DEADLY HE IS!
THE GAS!
USE THE GAS ON HIM, BEFORE IT'S TOO LATE!
KRAK!
NO MATTER HOW STRONG HE IS... THIS IS BOUND TO WEAKEN HIM!
UNHHHH..!
I..I DIDN'T HOLD MY BREATH IN TIME! TOOK TOO MUCH GAS INTO MY LUNGS!
EVERY-THING'S STARTING TO SPIN AROUND..!
BUT.. I'VE GOT TO... HOLD ON..!
13.

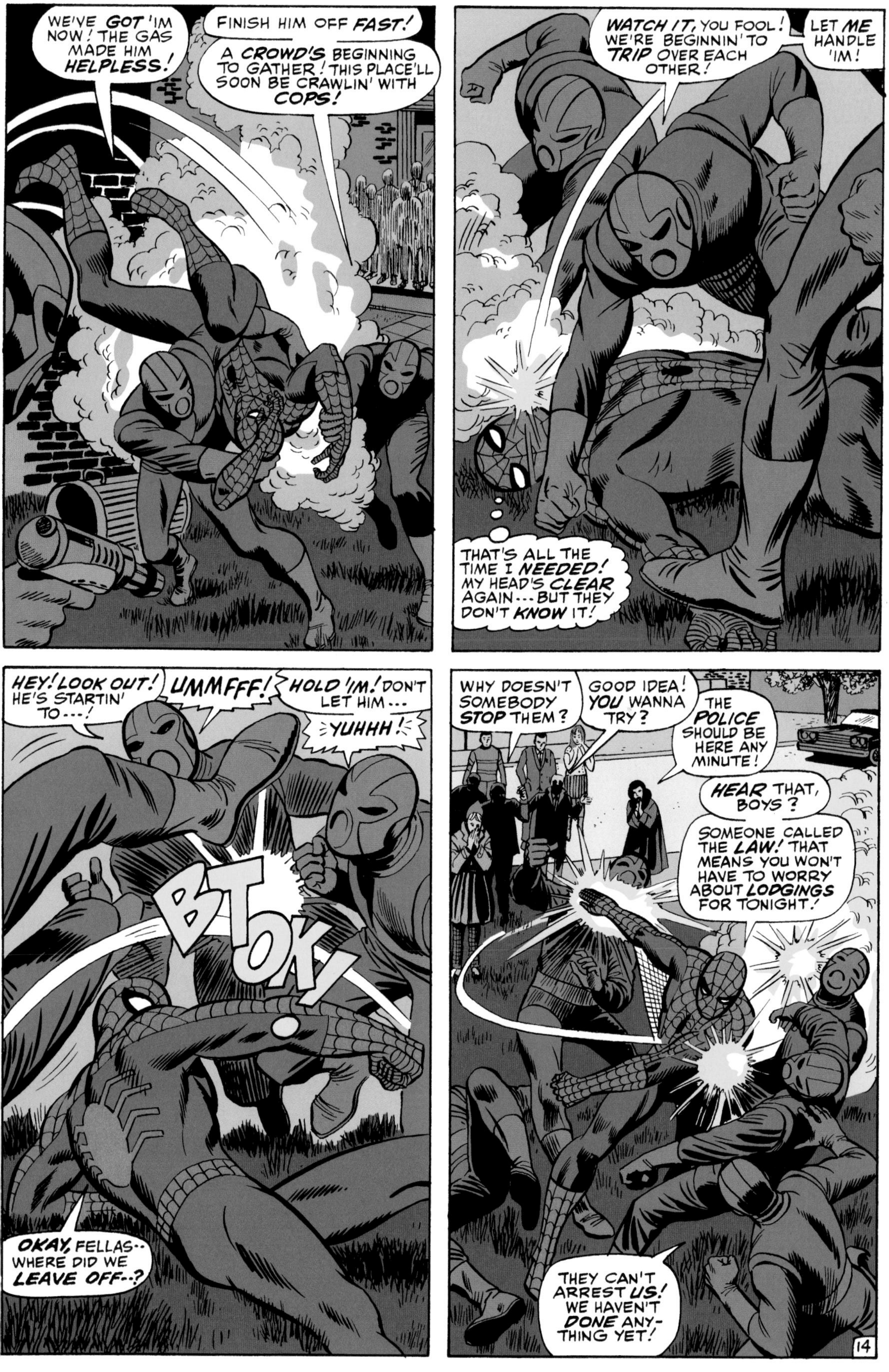

WE'VE GOT 'IM NOW! THE GAS MADE HIM HELPLESS!
FINISH HIM OFF FAST!
A CROWD'S BEGINNING TO GATHER! THIS PLACE'LL SOON BE CRAWLIN' WITH COPS!
WATCH IT, YOU FOOL! WE'RE BEGINNIN' TO TRIP OVER EACH OTHER!
LET ME HANDLE 'IM!
THAT'S ALL THE TIME I NEEDED! MY HEAD'S CLEAR AGAIN--- BUT THEY DON'T KNOW IT!
HEY! LOOK OUT! HE'S STARTIN' TO---!
UMMFFF!
HOLD 'IM! DON'T LET HIM---
YUHHH!
BTOK!
OKAY, FELLAS-- WHERE DID WE LEAVE OFF--?
WHY DOESN'T SOMEBODY STOP THEM?
GOOD IDEA! YOU WANNA TRY?
THE POLICE SHOULD BE HERE ANY MINUTE!
HEAR THAT, BOYS?
SOMEONE CALLED THE LAW! THAT MEANS YOU WON'T HAVE TO WORRY ABOUT LODGINGS FOR TONIGHT!
THEY CAN'T ARREST US! WE HAVEN'T DONE ANY-THING YET!
14

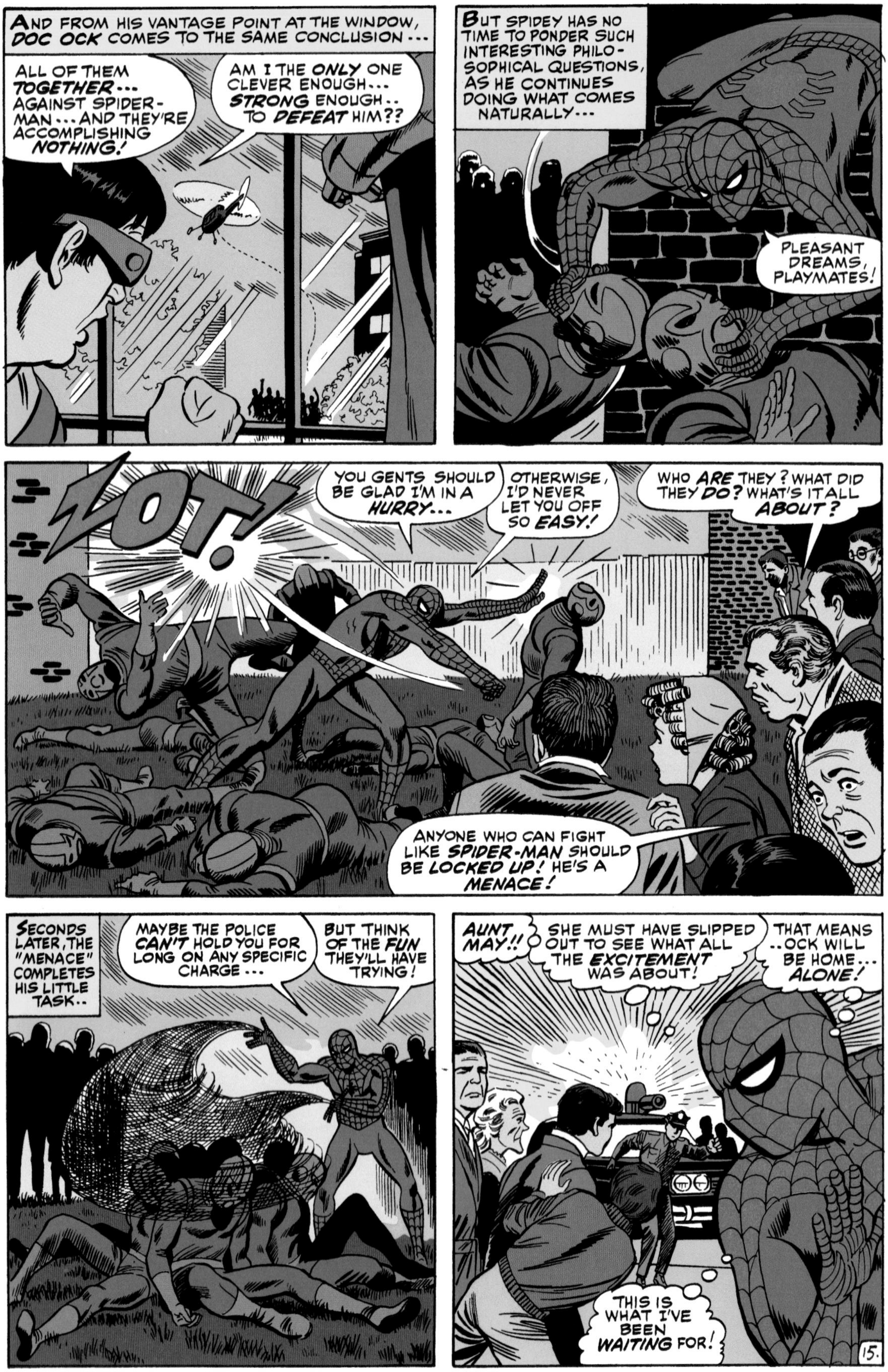
AND FROM HIS VANTAGE POINT AT THE WINDOW, DOC OCK COMES TO THE SAME CONCLUSION ...
ALL OF THEM TOGETHER ... AGAINST SPIDER-MAN ... AND THEY'RE ACCOMPLISHING NOTHING!
AM I THE ONLY ONE CLEVER ENOUGH ... STRONG ENOUGH .. TO DEFEAT HIM??
BUT SPIDEY HAS NO TIME TO PONDER SUCH INTERESTING PHILO-SOPHICAL QUESTIONS, AS HE CONTINUES DOING WHAT COMES NATURALLY ...
PLEASANT DREAMS, PLAYMATES!
ZOT!
YOU GENTS SHOULD BE GLAD I'M IN A HURRY...
OTHERWISE, I'D NEVER LET YOU OFF SO EASY!
WHO ARE THEY? WHAT DID THEY DO? WHAT'S IT ALL ABOUT?
ANYONE WHO CAN FIGHT LIKE SPIDER-MAN SHOULD BE LOCKED UP! HE'S A MENACE!
SECONDS LATER, THE "MENACE" COMPLETES HIS LITTLE TASK..
MAYBE THE POLICE CAN'T HOLD YOU FOR LONG ON ANY SPECIFIC CHARGE ...
BUT THINK OF THE FUN THEY'LL HAVE TRYING!
AUNT MAY!!
SHE MUST HAVE SLIPPED OUT TO SEE WHAT ALL THE EXCITEMENT WAS ABOUT!
THAT MEANS ..OCK WILL BE HOME... ALONE!
THIS IS WHAT I'VE BEEN WAITING FOR!
15.

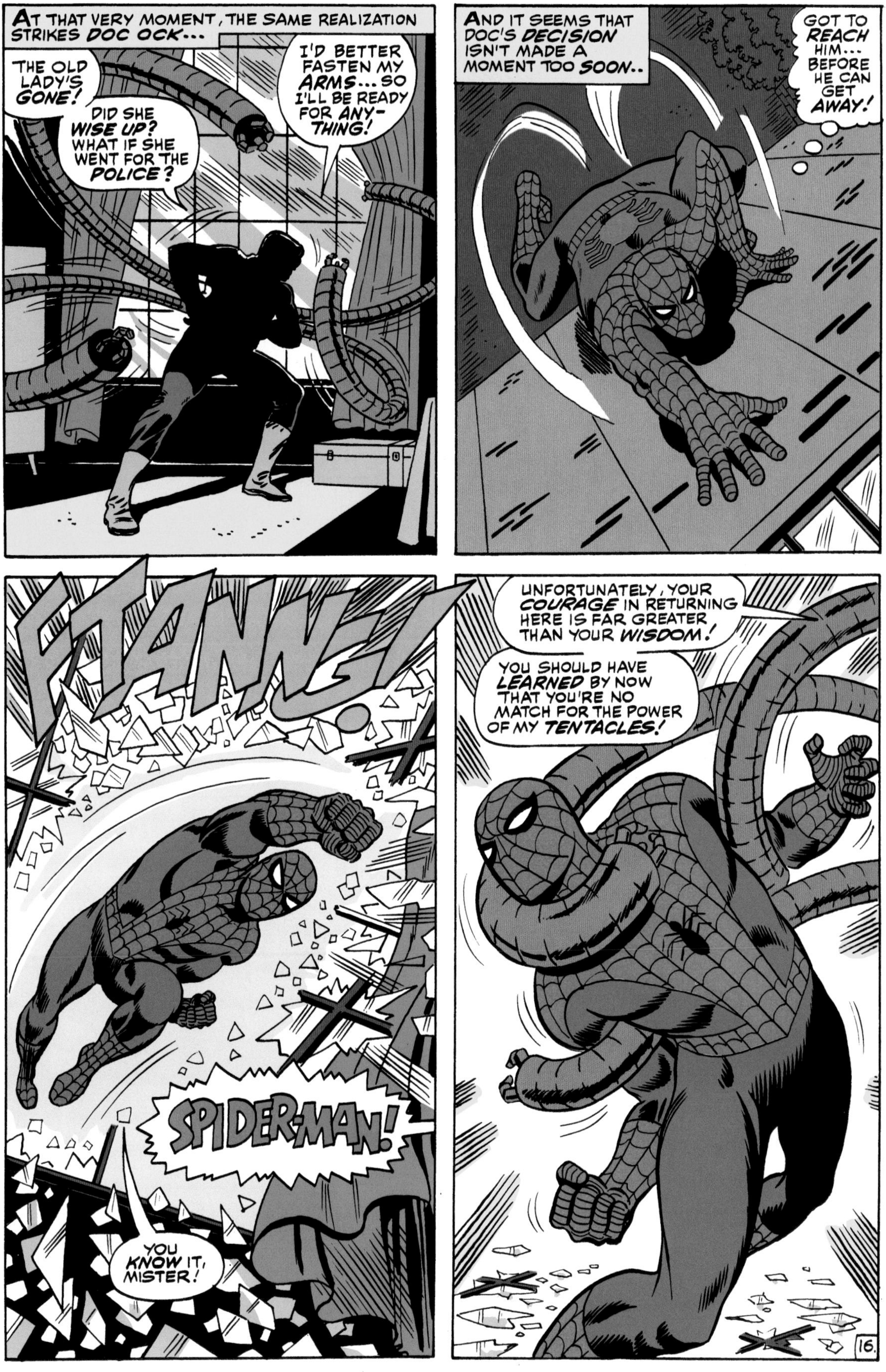
AT THAT VERY MOMENT, THE SAME REALIZATION STRIKES DOC OCK...
THE OLD LADY'S GONE!
DID SHE WISE UP? WHAT IF SHE WENT FOR THE POLICE?
I'D BETTER FASTEN MY ARMS... SO I'LL BE READY FOR ANY-THING!
AND IT SEEMS THAT DOC'S DECISION ISN'T MADE A MOMENT TOO SOON..
GOT TO REACH HIM... BEFORE HE CAN GET AWAY!
KRANNG!
SPIDER-MAN!
YOU KNOW IT, MISTER!
UNFORTUNATELY, YOUR COURAGE IN RETURNING HERE IS FAR GREATER THAN YOUR WISDOM!
YOU SHOULD HAVE LEARNED BY NOW THAT YOU'RE NO MATCH FOR THE POWER OF MY TENTACLES!
16.

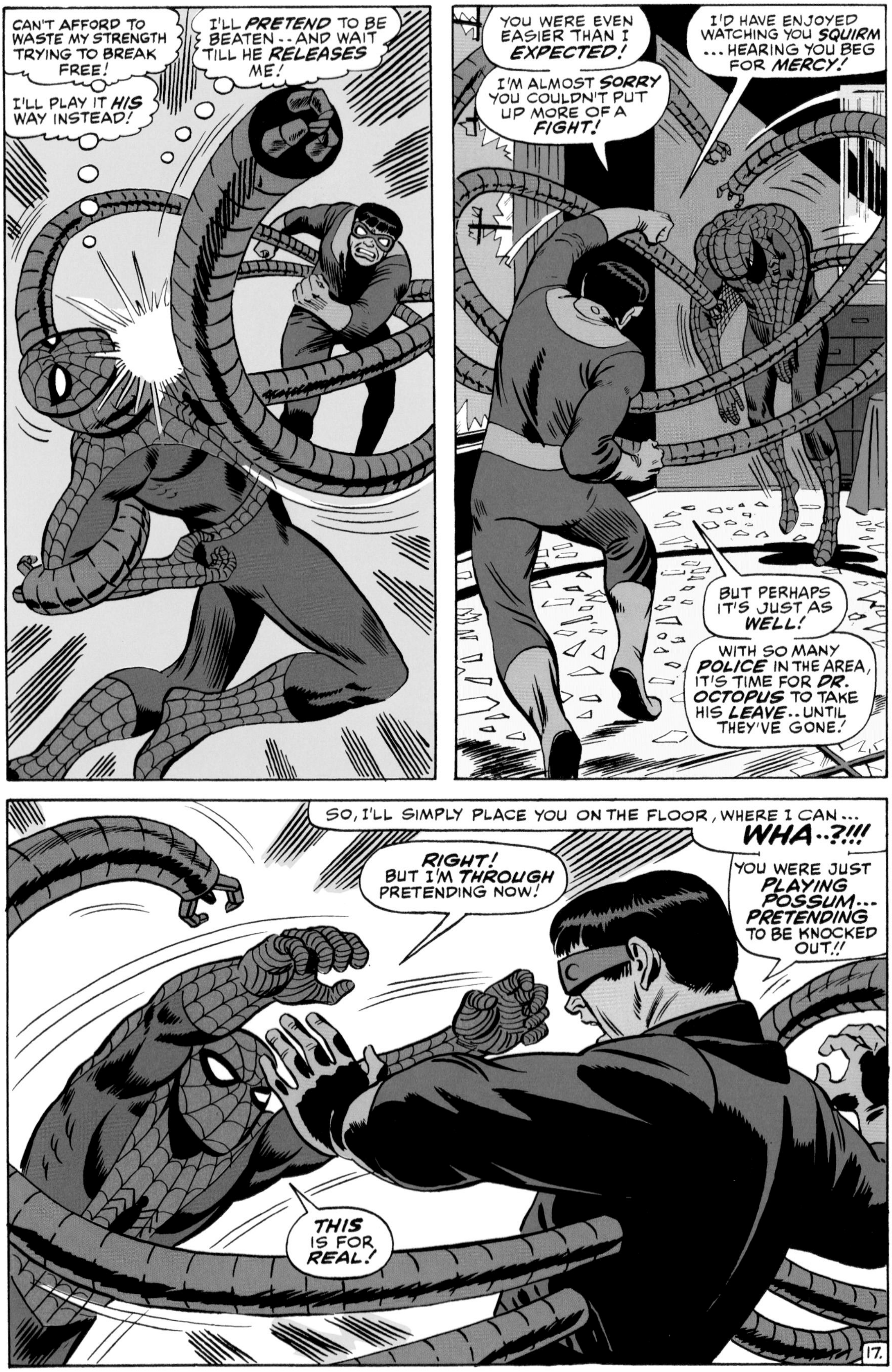
CAN'T AFFORD TO WASTE MY STRENGTH TRYING TO BREAK FREE!
I'LL PLAY IT HIS WAY INSTEAD!
I'LL PRETEND TO BE BEATEN -- AND WAIT TILL HE RELEASES ME!
YOU WERE EVEN EASIER THAN I EXPECTED!
I'M ALMOST SORRY YOU COULDN'T PUT UP MORE OF A FIGHT!
I'D HAVE ENJOYED WATCHING YOU SQUIRM ... HEARING YOU BEG FOR MERCY!
BUT PERHAPS IT'S JUST AS WELL!
WITH SO MANY POLICE IN THE AREA, IT'S TIME FOR DR. OCTOPUS TO TAKE HIS LEAVE.. UNTIL THEY'VE GONE!
SO, I'LL SIMPLY PLACE YOU ON THE FLOOR, WHERE I CAN ... WHA..?!!!
RIGHT! BUT I'M THROUGH PRETENDING NOW!
YOU WERE JUST PLAYING POSSUM... PRETENDING TO BE KNOCKED OUT!!
THIS IS FOR REAL!
17.

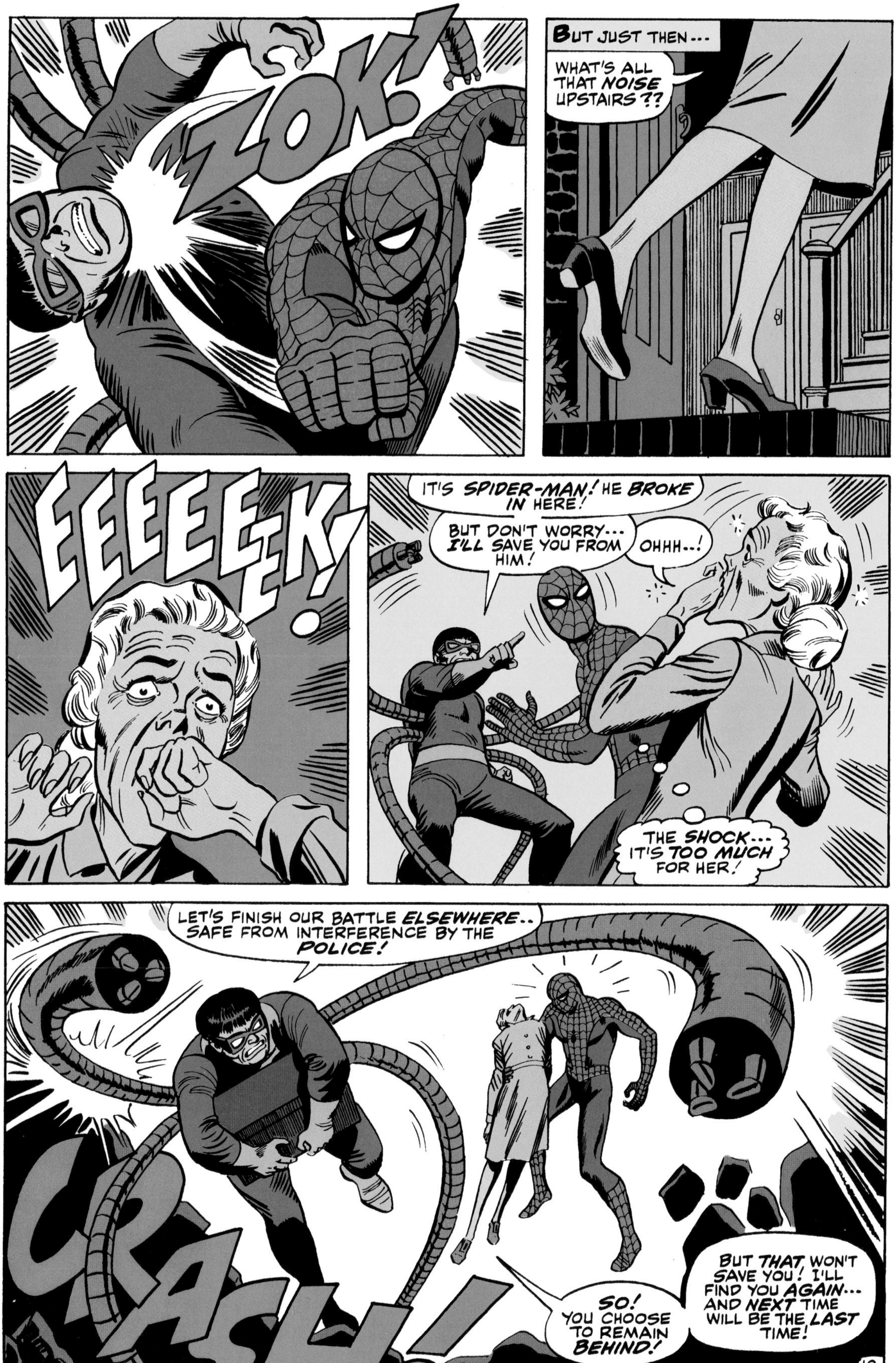
ZOK!
BUT JUST THEN...
WHAT'S ALL THAT NOISE UPSTAIRS??
EEEEEEEK!
IT'S SPIDER-MAN! HE BROKE IN HERE!
BUT DON'T WORRY... I'LL SAVE YOU FROM HIM!
OHHH...!
THE SHOCK... IT'S TOO MUCH FOR HER!
LET'S FINISH OUR BATTLE ELSEWHERE.. SAFE FROM INTERFERENCE BY THE POLICE!
CRASH!
SO! YOU CHOOSE TO REMAIN BEHIND!
BUT THAT WON'T SAVE YOU! I'LL FIND YOU AGAIN... AND NEXT TIME WILL BE THE LAST TIME!
18.

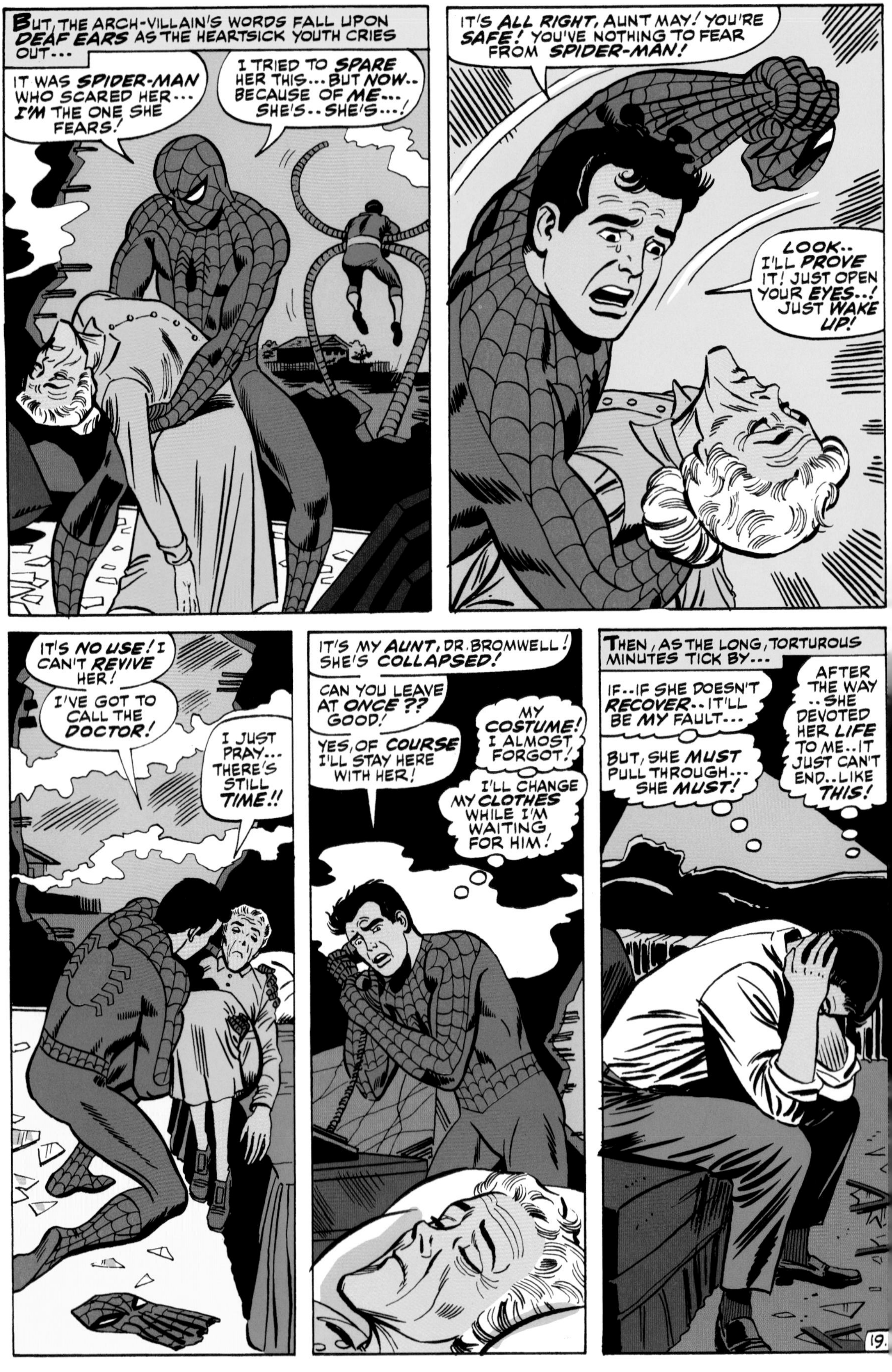

BUT, THE ARCH-VILLAIN'S WORDS FALL UPON DEAF EARS AS THE HEARTSICK YOUTH CRIES OUT...
IT WAS SPIDER-MAN WHO SCARED HER... I'M THE ONE SHE FEARS!
I TRIED TO SPARE HER THIS... BUT NOW.. BECAUSE OF ME... SHE'S.. SHE'S...!
IT'S ALL RIGHT, AUNT MAY! YOU'RE SAFE! YOU'VE NOTHING TO FEAR FROM SPIDER-MAN!
LOOK.. I'LL PROVE IT! JUST OPEN YOUR EYES..! JUST WAKE UP!
IT'S NO USE! I CAN'T REVIVE HER!
I'VE GOT TO CALL THE DOCTOR!
I JUST PRAY... THERE'S STILL TIME!!
IT'S MY AUNT, DR. BROMWELL! SHE'S COLLAPSED!
CAN YOU LEAVE AT ONCE?? GOOD!
YES, OF COURSE I'LL STAY HERE WITH HER!
MY COSTUME! I ALMOST FORGOT!
I'LL CHANGE MY CLOTHES WHILE I'M WAITING FOR HIM!
THEN, AS THE LONG, TORTUROUS MINUTES TICK BY...
IF--IF SHE DOESN'T RECOVER.. IT'LL BE MY FAULT...
BUT, SHE MUST PULL THROUGH... SHE MUST!
AFTER THE WAY ..SHE DEVOTED HER LIFE TO ME..IT JUST CAN'T END..LIKE THIS!
19.

THEN, TWENTY MINUTES *LATER*, TO THE HEARTSICK YOUTH'S INDESCRIBABLE *RELIEF*---

LUCK WAS *WITH* US THIS TIME, PETER!

YOUR AUNT WILL PULL THROUGH!

DO YOU KNOW WHAT *CAUSED* THE SHOCK?

I, EH.. I'M NOT QUITE *SURE*..!

WELL, SEE TO IT SHE GETS PLENTY OF *REST*, SON!

AT HER AGE, THE *NEXT* SUCH ATTACK COULD BE *FATAL*!

I'LL DROP BY AGAIN.. IN THE MORNING!

I COULDN'T EVEN TELL HIM THE *TRUTH*... ABOUT *SPIDER-MAN*!

IT WAS *FOOLISH* OF ME---TO HAVE TAKEN OFF MY *MASK* BEFORE!

IF SHE *HAD* LEARNED WHO I REALLY *AM*.. IT MIGHT HAVE MADE THINGS *WORSE* THAN EVER!

BUT WHAT HAPPENS *NEXT*?

WHERE DO WE GO FROM *HERE*?

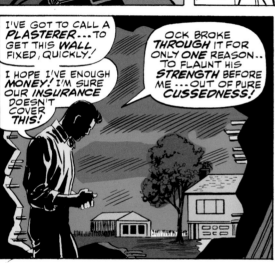

I'VE GOT TO CALL A *PLASTERER*---TO GET THIS *WALL* FIXED, QUICKLY!

I HOPE I'VE ENOUGH *MONEY*! I'M SURE OUR *INSURANCE* DOESN'T COVER *THIS*!

OCK BROKE *THROUGH* IT FOR ONLY *ONE* REASON.. TO FLAUNT HIS *STRENGTH* BEFORE ME ---OUT OF PURE *CUSSEDNESS*!

BUT NOW HE'LL LEARN HOW CUSSED *SPIDER-MAN* CAN BE!

I'LL SHOW HIM WHAT STRENGTH REALLY *IS*!

HE WON'T GET *ANOTHER* CHANCE TO RETURN AND JEOPARDIZE THE LIFE OF *AUNT MAY*!

NO MATTER *WHERE* HE IS, I'LL *FIND* HIM!

AND *THIS* TIME, NOTHING WILL *STOP* ME FROM RIDDING THE WORLD *FOREVER* OF THE MENACE OF *DR. OCTOPUS*!

BE HERE WHEN: DISASTER STRIKES SPIDER-MAN!

BUT EVEN *SPIDEY* CANNOT SUSPECT THE STARTLING *FATE* THAT AWAITS HIM WHEN THEY MEET *AGAIN* NEXT ISH!

20.

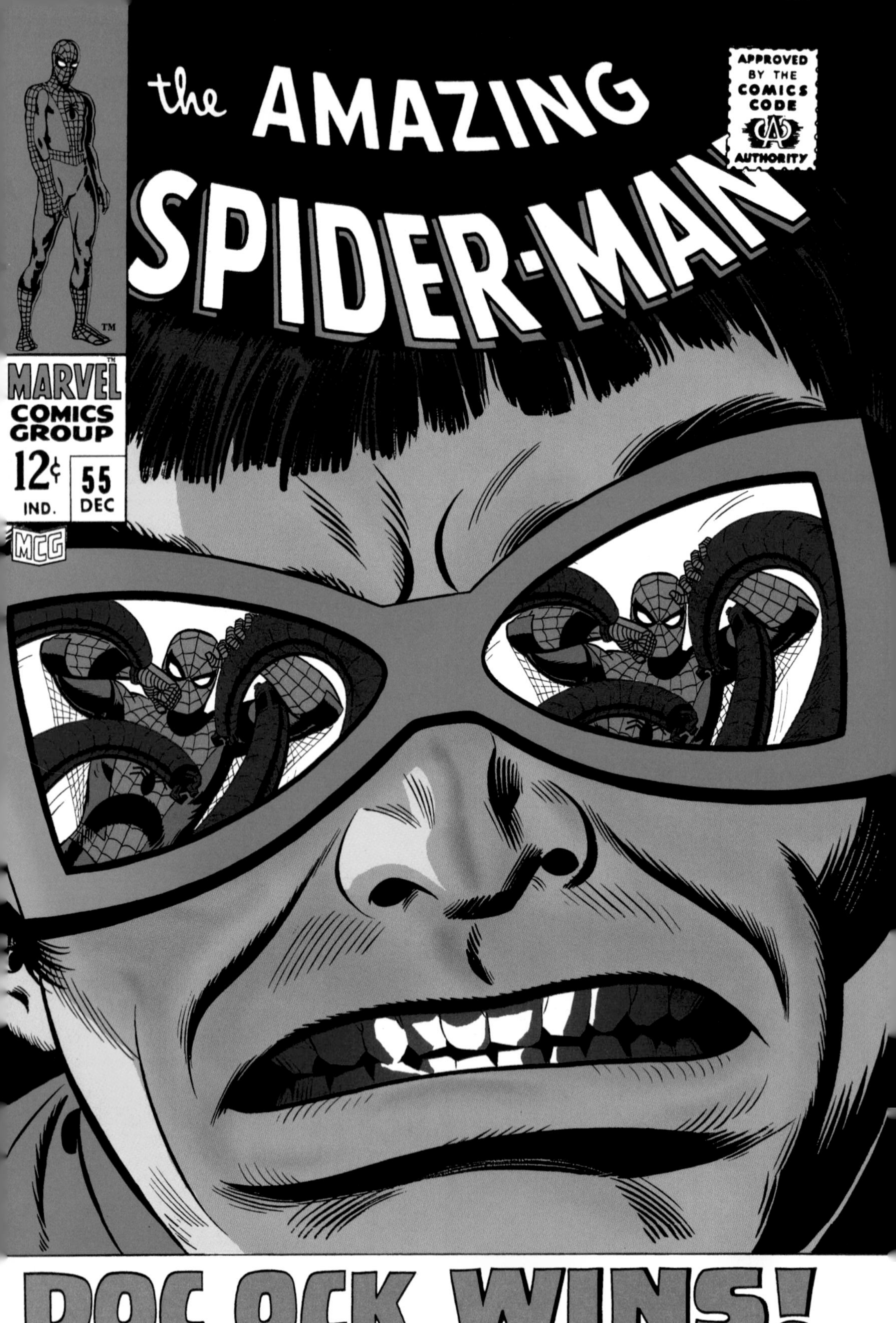

the AMAZING SPIDER-MAN
APPROVED BY THE COMICS CODE AUTHORITY
MARVEL COMICS GROUP
12¢
IND.
55
DEC
MCG
DOC OCK WINS!

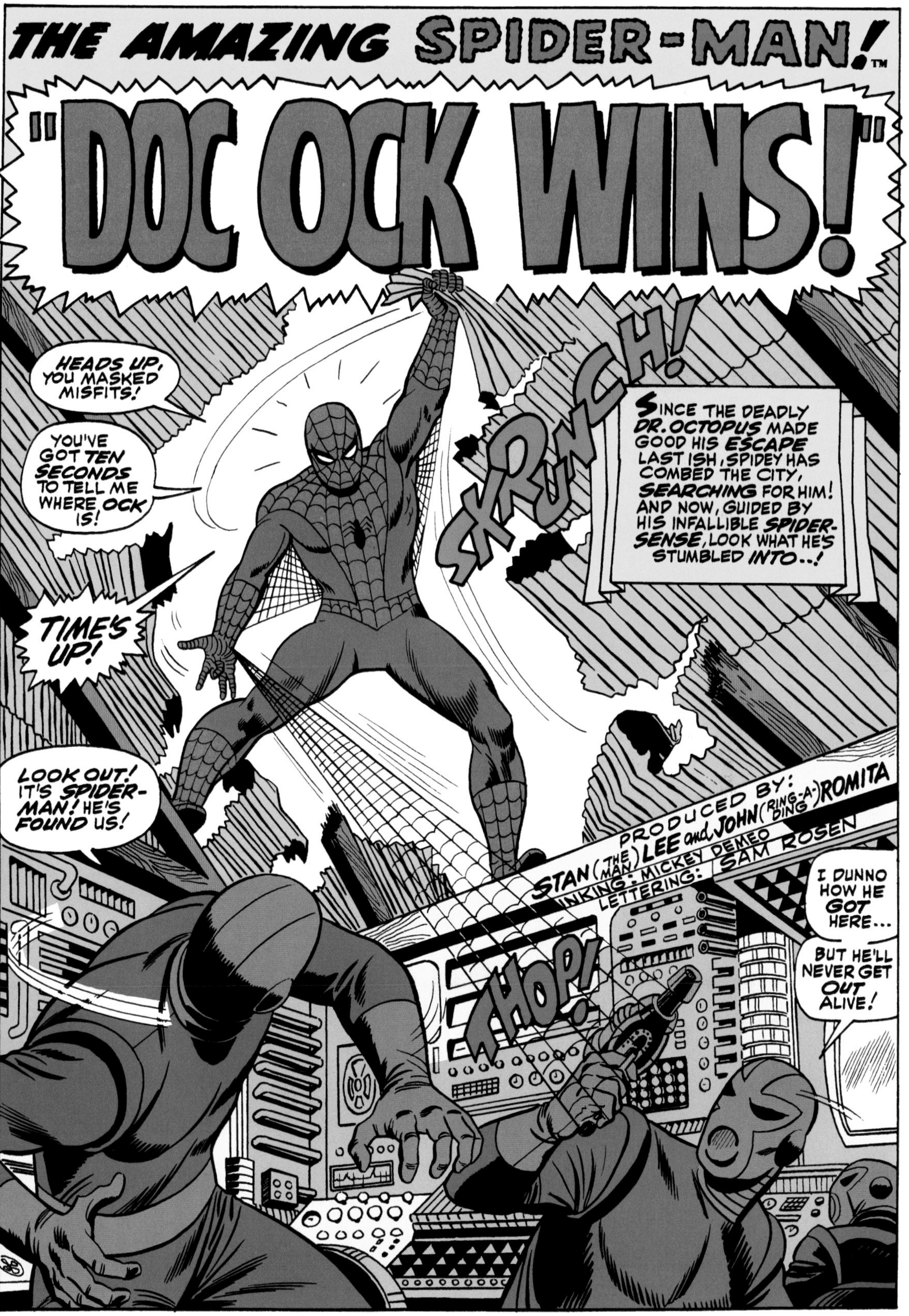
THE AMAZING SPIDER-MAN!™
"DOC OCK WINS!"
HEADS UP, YOU MASKED MISFITS!
YOU'VE GOT TEN SECONDS TO TELL ME WHERE OCK IS!
TIME'S UP!
SKRUNCH!
SINCE THE DEADLY DR. OCTOPUS MADE GOOD HIS ESCAPE LAST ISH, SPIDEY HAS COMBED THE CITY, SEARCHING FOR HIM! AND NOW, GUIDED BY HIS INFALLIBLE SPIDER-SENSE, LOOK WHAT HE'S STUMBLED INTO..!
LOOK OUT! IT'S SPIDER-MAN! HE'S FOUND US!
PRODUCED BY: STAN (THE MAN) LEE and JOHN (RING-A-DING) ROMITA
INKING: MICKEY DEMEO
LETTERING: SAM ROSEN
I DUNNO HOW HE GOT HERE...
BUT HE'LL NEVER GET OUT ALIVE!
THOP!

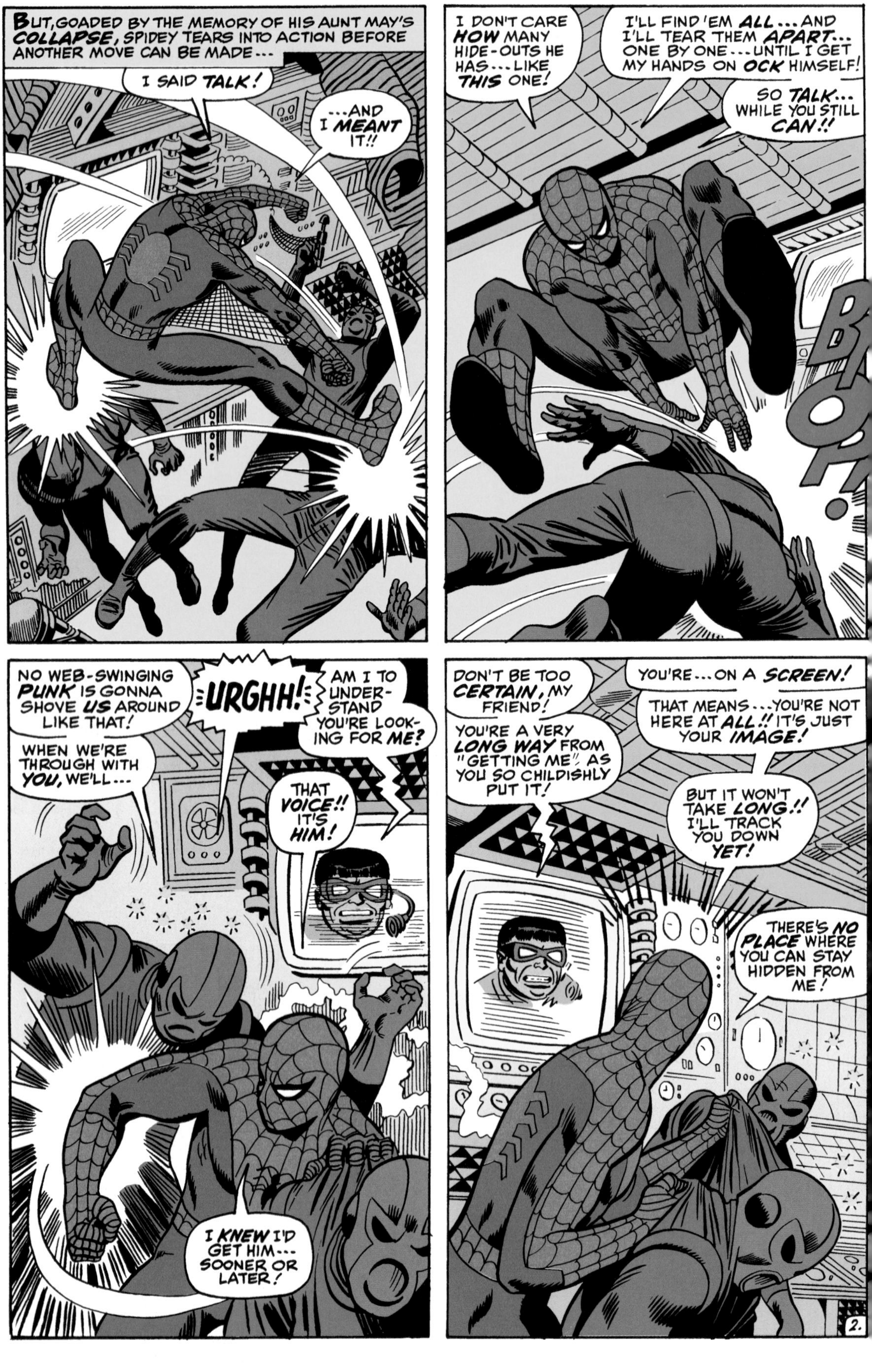

BUT, GOADED BY THE MEMORY OF HIS AUNT MAY'S COLLAPSE, SPIDEY TEARS INTO ACTION BEFORE ANOTHER MOVE CAN BE MADE...
I SAID TALK!
...AND I MEANT IT!!
I DON'T CARE HOW MANY HIDE-OUTS HE HAS...LIKE THIS ONE!
I'LL FIND 'EM ALL...AND I'LL TEAR THEM APART... ONE BY ONE...UNTIL I GET MY HANDS ON OCK HIMSELF!
SO TALK... WHILE YOU STILL CAN!!
NO WEB-SWINGING PUNK IS GONNA SHOVE US AROUND LIKE THAT!
WHEN WE'RE THROUGH WITH YOU, WE'LL...
URGHH!
AM I TO UNDERSTAND YOU'RE LOOKING FOR ME?
THAT VOICE!! IT'S HIM!
I KNEW I'D GET HIM... SOONER OR LATER!
DON'T BE TOO CERTAIN, MY FRIEND!
YOU'RE A VERY LONG WAY FROM "GETTING ME", AS YOU SO CHILDISHLY PUT IT!
YOU'RE...ON A SCREEN!
THAT MEANS...YOU'RE NOT HERE AT ALL!! IT'S JUST YOUR IMAGE!
BUT IT WON'T TAKE LONG!! I'LL TRACK YOU DOWN YET!
THERE'S NO PLACE WHERE YOU CAN STAY HIDDEN FROM ME!
2.

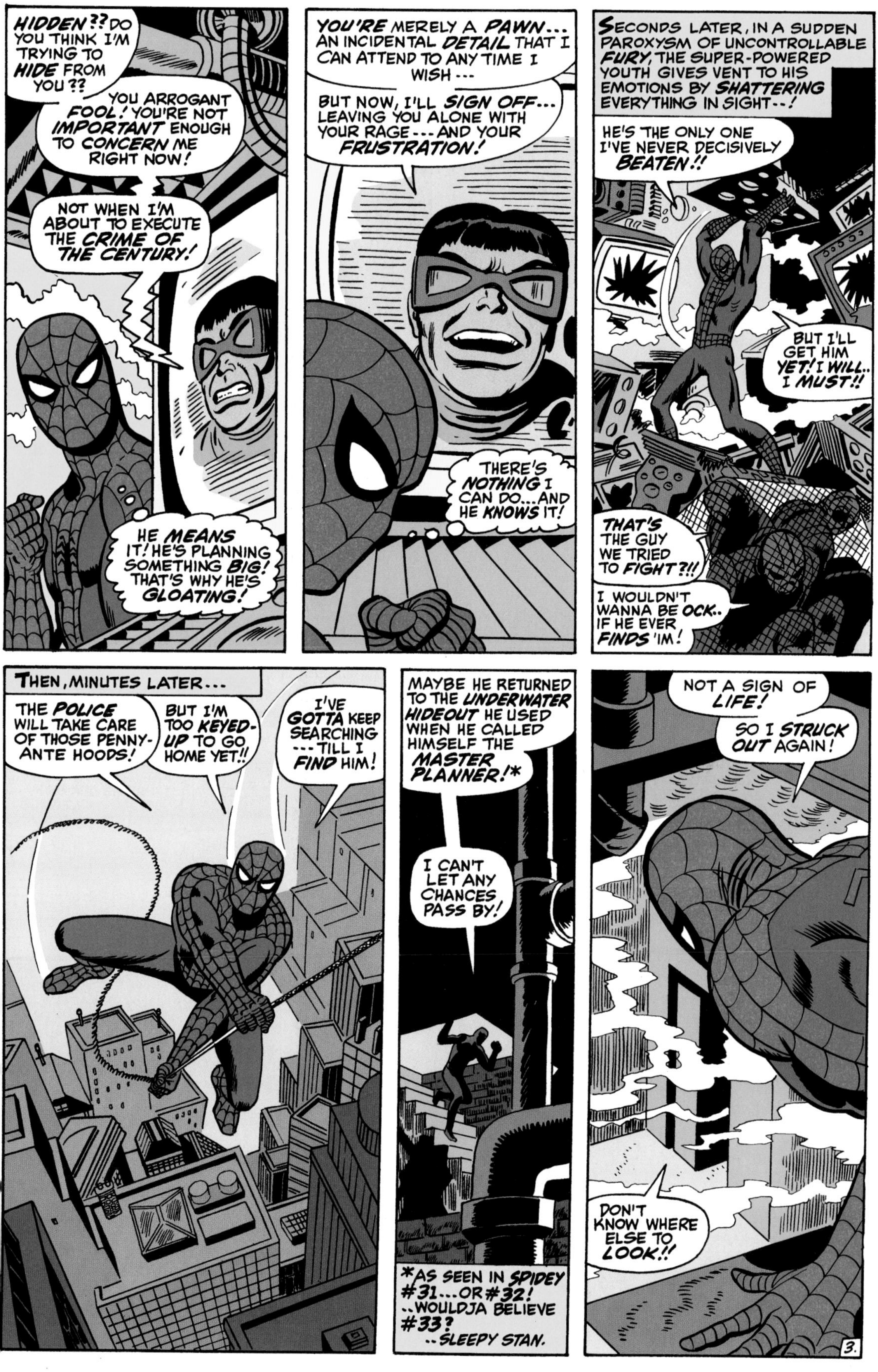
HIDDEN?? DO YOU THINK I'M TRYING TO HIDE FROM YOU??
YOU ARROGANT FOOL! YOU'RE NOT IMPORTANT ENOUGH TO CONCERN ME RIGHT NOW!
NOT WHEN I'M ABOUT TO EXECUTE THE CRIME OF THE CENTURY!
HE MEANS IT! HE'S PLANNING SOMETHING BIG! THAT'S WHY HE'S GLOATING!
YOU'RE MERELY A PAWN... AN INCIDENTAL DETAIL THAT I CAN ATTEND TO ANY TIME I WISH---
BUT NOW, I'LL SIGN OFF... LEAVING YOU ALONE WITH YOUR RAGE---AND YOUR FRUSTRATION!
THERE'S NOTHING I CAN DO...AND HE KNOWS IT!
SECONDS LATER, IN A SUDDEN PAROXYSM OF UNCONTROLLABLE FURY, THE SUPER-POWERED YOUTH GIVES VENT TO HIS EMOTIONS BY SHATTERING EVERYTHING IN SIGHT--!
HE'S THE ONLY ONE I'VE NEVER DECISIVELY BEATEN!!
BUT I'LL GET HIM YET! I WILL.. I MUST!!
THAT'S THE GUY WE TRIED TO FIGHT?!!
I WOULDN'T WANNA BE OCK.. IF HE EVER FINDS 'IM!
THEN, MINUTES LATER...
THE POLICE WILL TAKE CARE OF THOSE PENNY-ANTE HOODS!
BUT I'M TOO KEYED-UP TO GO HOME YET!!
I'VE GOTTA KEEP SEARCHING ---TILL I FIND HIM!
MAYBE HE RETURNED TO THE UNDERWATER HIDEOUT HE USED WHEN HE CALLED HIMSELF THE MASTER PLANNER!*
I CAN'T LET ANY CHANCES PASS BY!
*AS SEEN IN SPIDEY #31...OR #32! ..WOULDJA BELIEVE #33? --SLEEPY STAN.
NOT A SIGN OF LIFE!
SO I STRUCK OUT AGAIN!
DON'T KNOW WHERE ELSE TO LOOK!!
3.

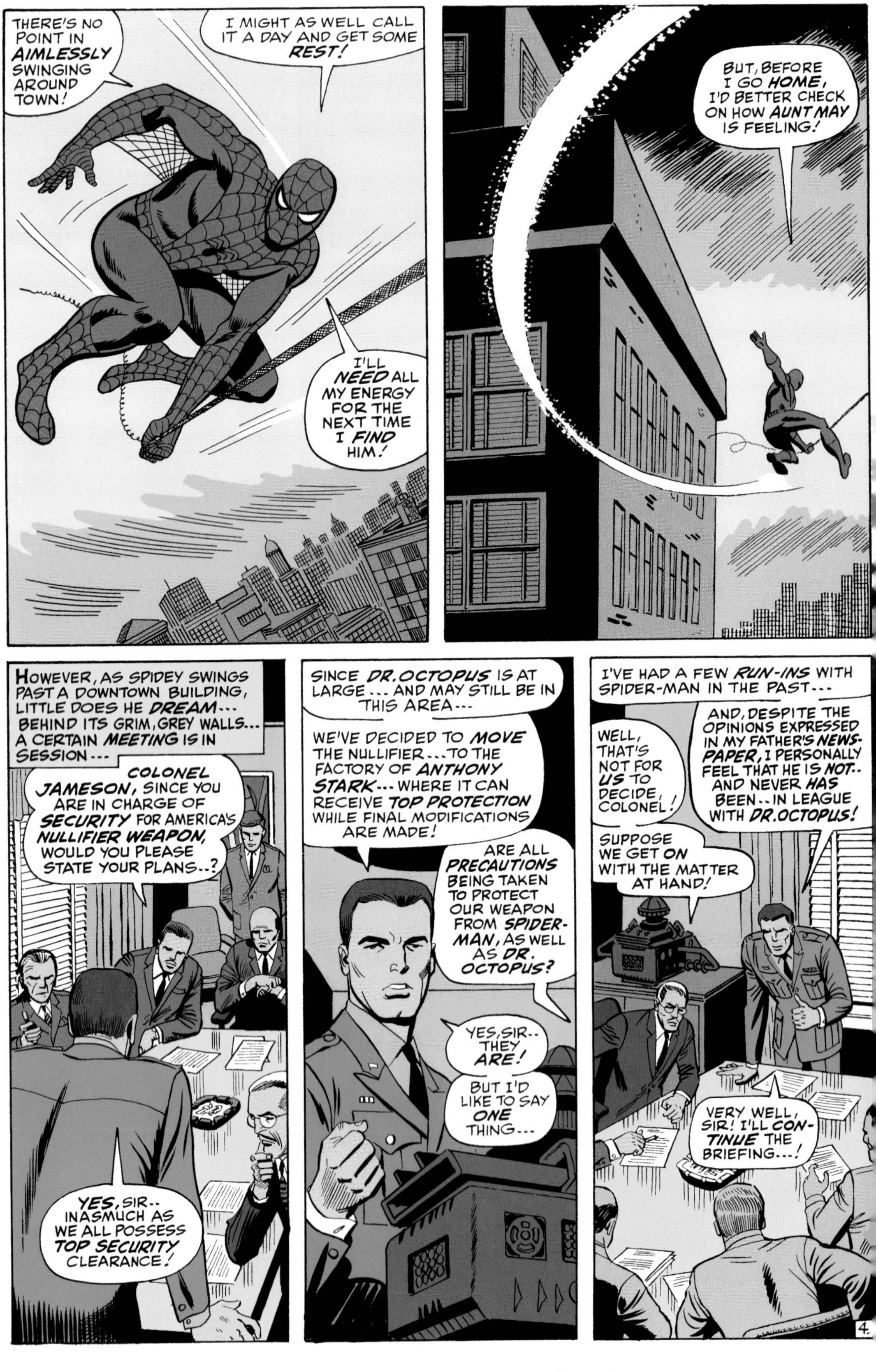
THERE'S NO POINT IN AIMLESSLY SWINGING AROUND TOWN!
I MIGHT AS WELL CALL IT A DAY AND GET SOME REST!
I'LL NEED ALL MY ENERGY FOR THE NEXT TIME I FIND HIM!
BUT, BEFORE I GO HOME, I'D BETTER CHECK ON HOW AUNT MAY IS FEELING!
HOWEVER, AS SPIDEY SWINGS PAST A DOWNTOWN BUILDING, LITTLE DOES HE DREAM... BEHIND ITS GRIM, GREY WALLS... A CERTAIN MEETING IS IN SESSION...
COLONEL JAMESON, SINCE YOU ARE IN CHARGE OF SECURITY FOR AMERICA'S NULLIFIER WEAPON, WOULD YOU PLEASE STATE YOUR PLANS..?
YES, SIR.. INASMUCH AS WE ALL POSSESS TOP SECURITY CLEARANCE!
SINCE DR. OCTOPUS IS AT LARGE... AND MAY STILL BE IN THIS AREA...
WE'VE DECIDED TO MOVE THE NULLIFIER... TO THE FACTORY OF ANTHONY STARK... WHERE IT CAN RECEIVE TOP PROTECTION WHILE FINAL MODIFICATIONS ARE MADE!
ARE ALL PRECAUTIONS BEING TAKEN TO PROTECT OUR WEAPON FROM SPIDER-MAN, AS WELL AS DR. OCTOPUS?
YES, SIR.. THEY ARE!
BUT I'D LIKE TO SAY ONE THING...
I'VE HAD A FEW RUN-INS WITH SPIDER-MAN IN THE PAST...
AND, DESPITE THE OPINIONS EXPRESSED IN MY FATHER'S NEWSPAPER, I PERSONALLY FEEL THAT HE IS NOT.. AND NEVER HAS BEEN.. IN LEAGUE WITH DR. OCTOPUS!
WELL, THAT'S NOT FOR US TO DECIDE, COLONEL!
SUPPOSE WE GET ON WITH THE MATTER AT HAND!
VERY WELL, SIR! I'LL CONTINUE THE BRIEFING...!
4.

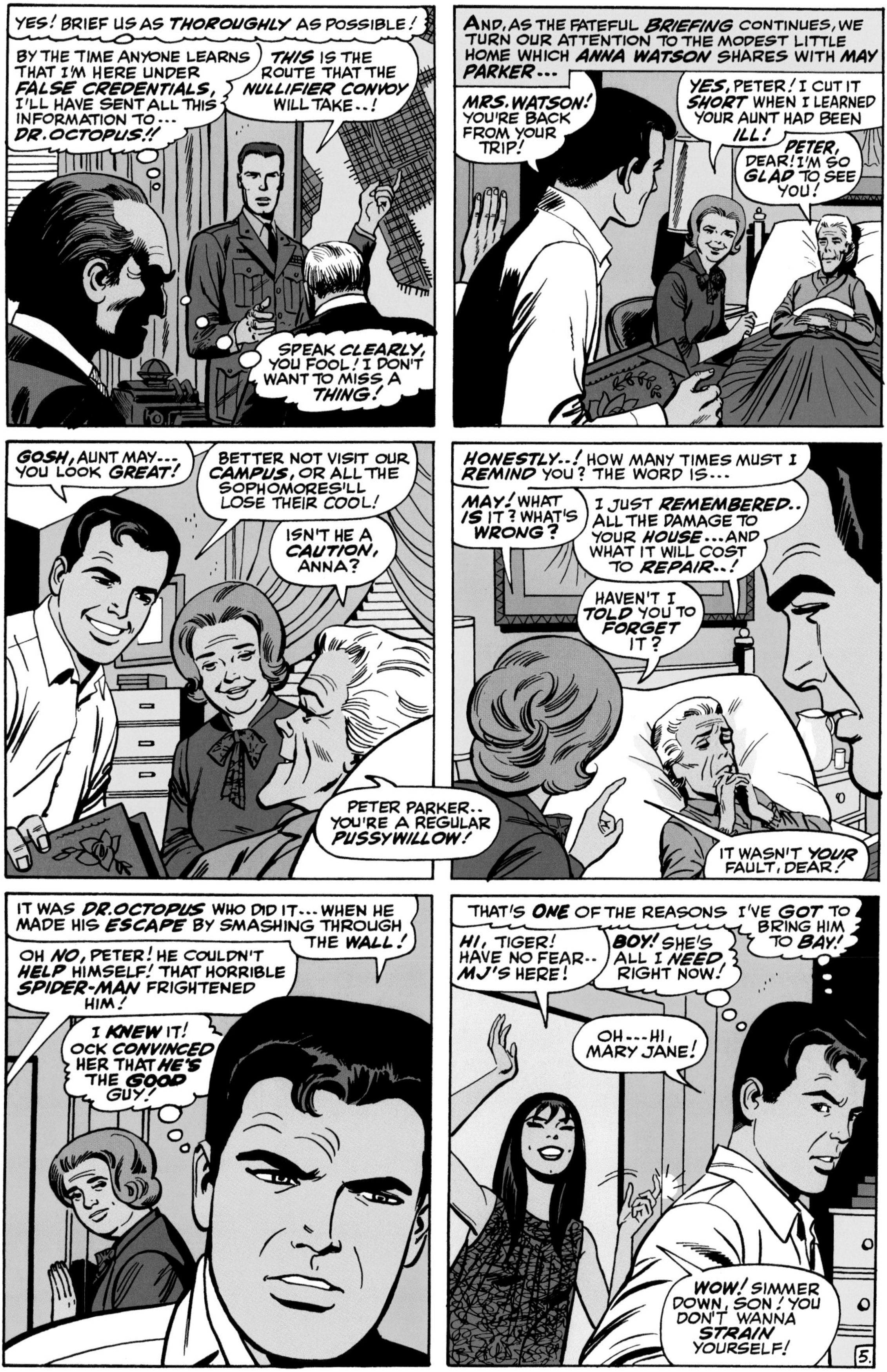
YES! BRIEF US AS THOROUGHLY AS POSSIBLE!
BY THE TIME ANYONE LEARNS THAT I'M HERE UNDER FALSE CREDENTIALS, I'LL HAVE SENT ALL THIS INFORMATION TO... DR. OCTOPUS!!
THIS IS THE ROUTE THAT THE NULLIFIER CONVOY WILL TAKE..!
SPEAK CLEARLY, YOU FOOL! I DON'T WANT TO MISS A THING!
AND, AS THE FATEFUL BRIEFING CONTINUES, WE TURN OUR ATTENTION TO THE MODEST LITTLE HOME WHICH ANNA WATSON SHARES WITH MAY PARKER...
MRS. WATSON! YOU'RE BACK FROM YOUR TRIP!
YES, PETER! I CUT IT SHORT WHEN I LEARNED YOUR AUNT HAD BEEN ILL!
PETER, DEAR! I'M SO GLAD TO SEE YOU!
GOSH, AUNT MAY... YOU LOOK GREAT!
BETTER NOT VISIT OUR CAMPUS, OR ALL THE SOPHOMORES'LL LOSE THEIR COOL!
ISN'T HE A CAUTION, ANNA?
PETER PARKER.. YOU'RE A REGULAR PUSSYWILLOW!
HONESTLY..! HOW MANY TIMES MUST I REMIND YOU? THE WORD IS...
MAY! WHAT IS IT? WHAT'S WRONG?
I JUST REMEMBERED.. ALL THE DAMAGE TO YOUR HOUSE...AND WHAT IT WILL COST TO REPAIR..!
HAVEN'T I TOLD YOU TO FORGET IT?
IT WASN'T YOUR FAULT, DEAR!
IT WAS DR. OCTOPUS WHO DID IT... WHEN HE MADE HIS ESCAPE BY SMASHING THROUGH THE WALL!
OH NO, PETER! HE COULDN'T HELP HIMSELF! THAT HORRIBLE SPIDER-MAN FRIGHTENED HIM!
I KNEW IT! OCK CONVINCED HER THAT HE'S THE GOOD GUY!
THAT'S ONE OF THE REASONS I'VE GOT TO BRING HIM TO BAY!
HI, TIGER! HAVE NO FEAR.. MJ'S HERE!
BOY! SHE'S ALL I NEED RIGHT NOW!
OH---HI, MARY JANE!
WOW! SIMMER DOWN, SON! YOU DON'T WANNA STRAIN YOURSELF!
5.

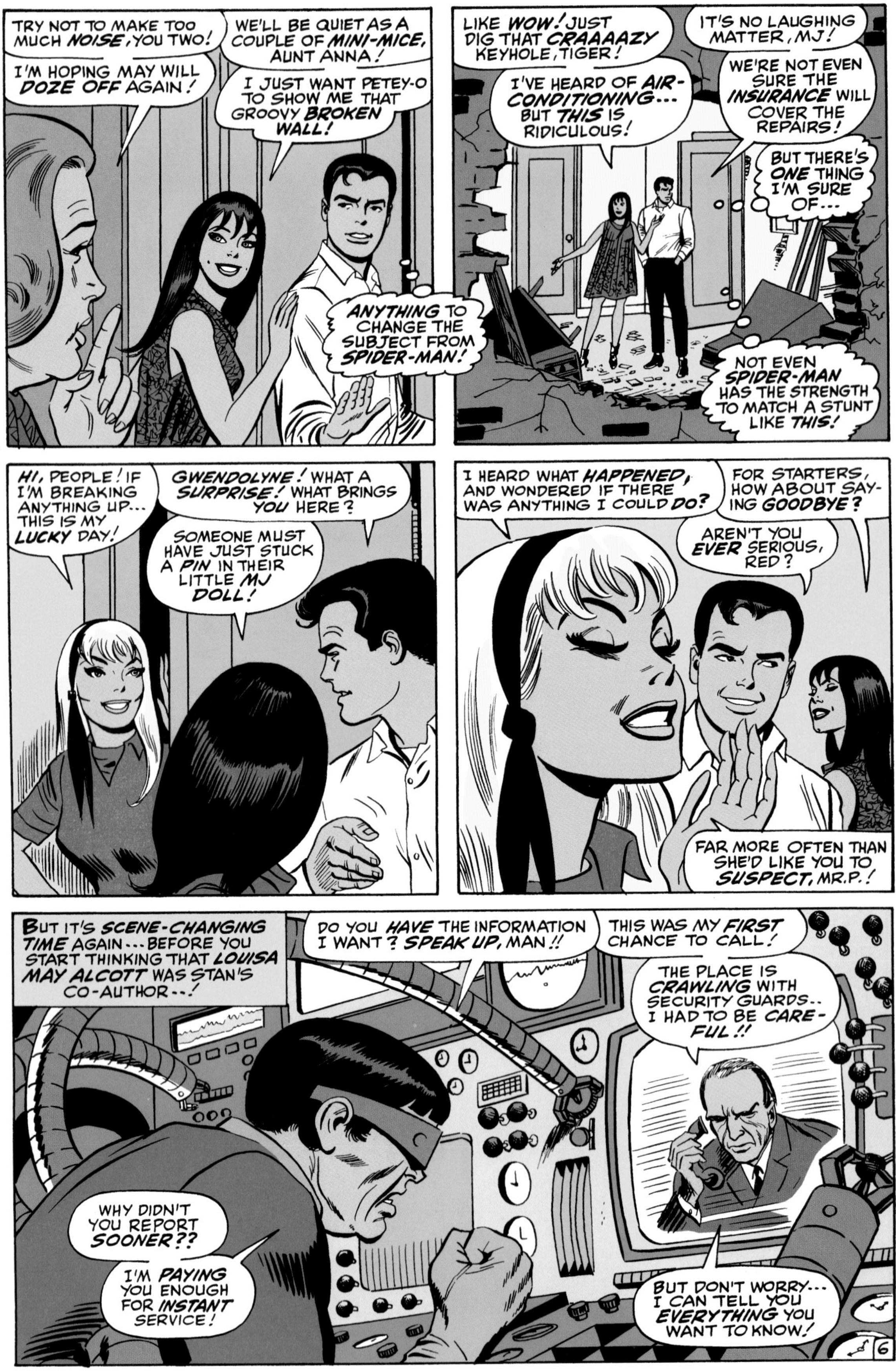
TRY NOT TO MAKE TOO MUCH NOISE, YOU TWO!
I'M HOPING MAY WILL DOZE OFF AGAIN!
WE'LL BE QUIET AS A COUPLE OF MINI-MICE, AUNT ANNA!
I JUST WANT PETEY-O TO SHOW ME THAT GROOVY BROKEN WALL!
ANYTHING TO CHANGE THE SUBJECT FROM SPIDER-MAN!
LIKE WOW! JUST DIG THAT CRAAAAZY KEYHOLE, TIGER!
I'VE HEARD OF AIR-CONDITIONING... BUT THIS IS RIDICULOUS!
IT'S NO LAUGHING MATTER, MJ!
WE'RE NOT EVEN SURE THE INSURANCE WILL COVER THE REPAIRS!
BUT THERE'S ONE THING I'M SURE OF...
NOT EVEN SPIDER-MAN HAS THE STRENGTH TO MATCH A STUNT LIKE THIS!
HI, PEOPLE! IF I'M BREAKING ANYTHING UP... THIS IS MY LUCKY DAY!
GWENDOLYNE! WHAT A SURPRISE! WHAT BRINGS YOU HERE?
SOMEONE MUST HAVE JUST STUCK A PIN IN THEIR LITTLE MJ DOLL!
I HEARD WHAT HAPPENED, AND WONDERED IF THERE WAS ANYTHING I COULD DO?
FOR STARTERS, HOW ABOUT SAYING GOODBYE?
AREN'T YOU EVER SERIOUS, RED?
FAR MORE OFTEN THAN SHE'D LIKE YOU TO SUSPECT, MR.P.!
BUT IT'S SCENE-CHANGING TIME AGAIN... BEFORE YOU START THINKING THAT LOUISA MAY ALCOTT WAS STAN'S CO-AUTHOR--!
DO YOU HAVE THE INFORMATION I WANT? SPEAK UP, MAN!!
THIS WAS MY FIRST CHANCE TO CALL!
THE PLACE IS CRAWLING WITH SECURITY GUARDS.. I HAD TO BE CAREFUL!!
WHY DIDN'T YOU REPORT SOONER??
I'M PAYING YOU ENOUGH FOR INSTANT SERVICE!
BUT DON'T WORRY... I CAN TELL YOU EVERYTHING YOU WANT TO KNOW!
6

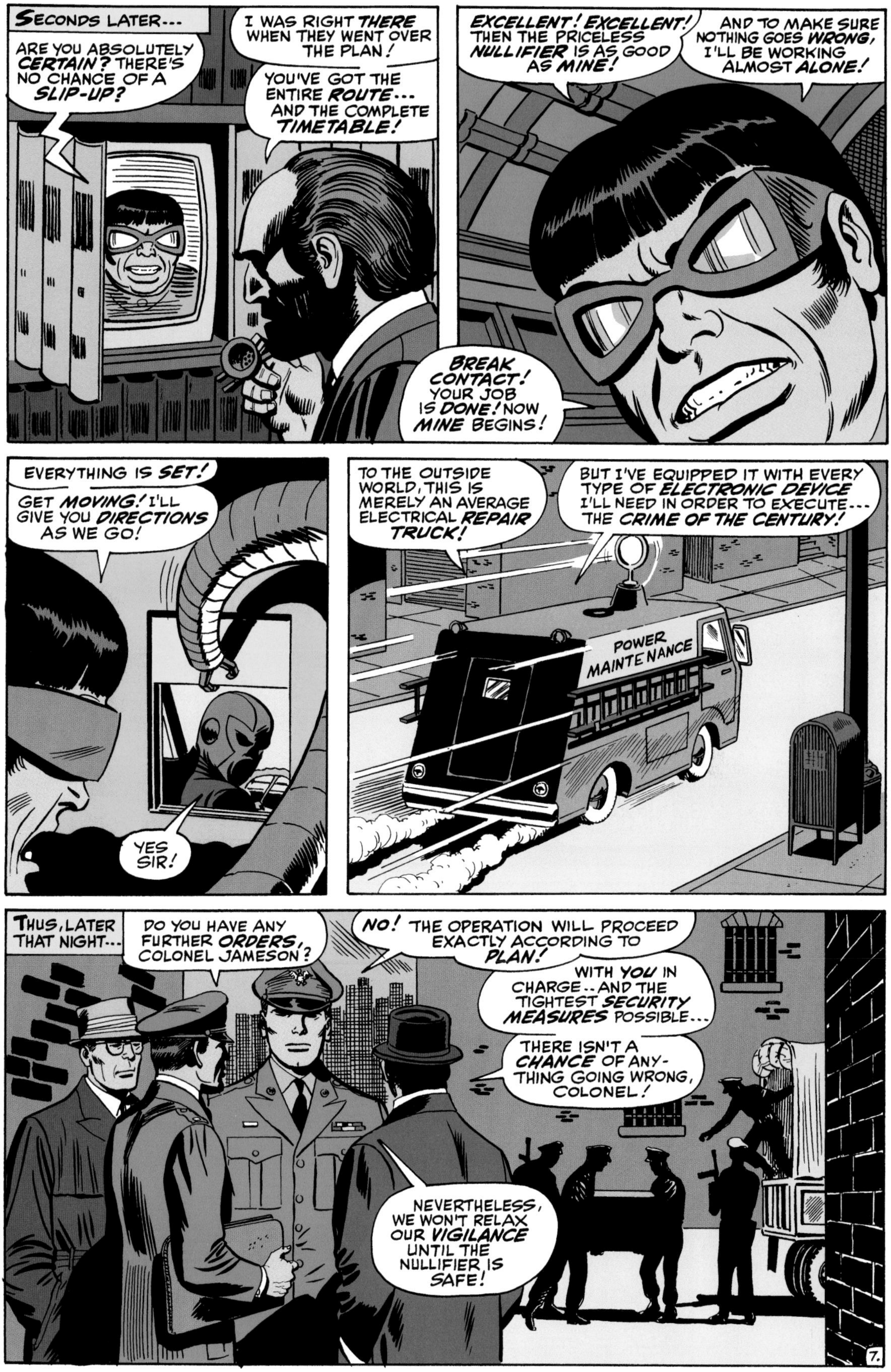

SECONDS LATER...
ARE YOU ABSOLUTELY CERTAIN? THERE'S NO CHANCE OF A SLIP-UP?
I WAS RIGHT THERE WHEN THEY WENT OVER THE PLAN!
YOU'VE GOT THE ENTIRE ROUTE... AND THE COMPLETE TIMETABLE!
EXCELLENT! EXCELLENT! THEN THE PRICELESS NULLIFIER IS AS GOOD AS MINE!
AND TO MAKE SURE NOTHING GOES WRONG, I'LL BE WORKING ALMOST ALONE!
BREAK CONTACT! YOUR JOB IS DONE! NOW MINE BEGINS!
EVERYTHING IS SET!
GET MOVING! I'LL GIVE YOU DIRECTIONS AS WE GO!
YES SIR!
TO THE OUTSIDE WORLD, THIS IS MERELY AN AVERAGE ELECTRICAL REPAIR TRUCK!
BUT I'VE EQUIPPED IT WITH EVERY TYPE OF ELECTRONIC DEVICE I'LL NEED IN ORDER TO EXECUTE... THE CRIME OF THE CENTURY!
POWER MAINTENANCE
THUS, LATER THAT NIGHT...
DO YOU HAVE ANY FURTHER ORDERS, COLONEL JAMESON?
NO! THE OPERATION WILL PROCEED EXACTLY ACCORDING TO PLAN!
WITH YOU IN CHARGE.. AND THE TIGHTEST SECURITY MEASURES POSSIBLE...
THERE ISN'T A CHANCE OF ANYTHING GOING WRONG, COLONEL!
NEVERTHELESS, WE WON'T RELAX OUR VIGILANCE UNTIL THE NULLIFIER IS SAFE!
7.

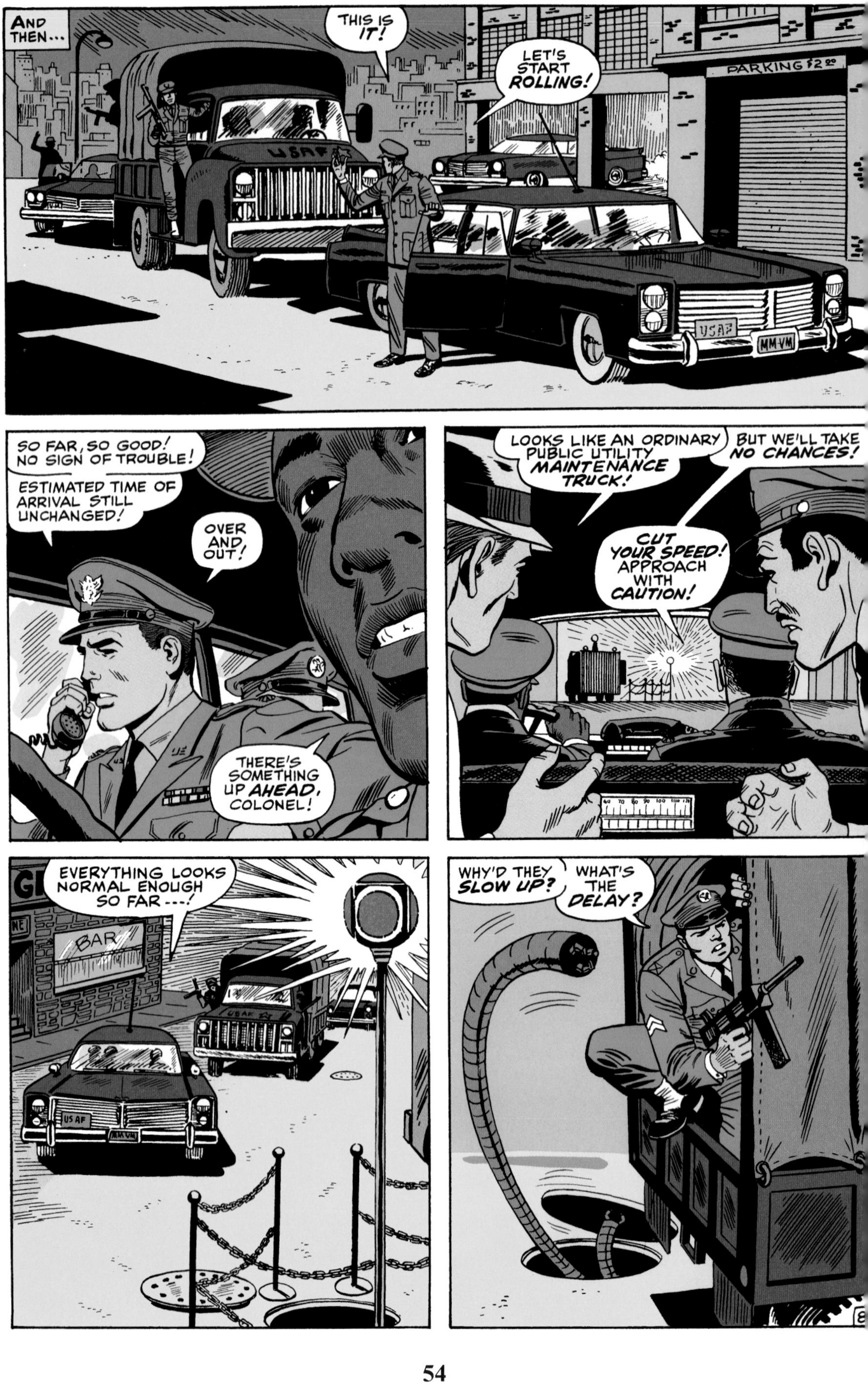
AND THEN...
THIS IS IT!
LET'S START ROLLING!
PARKING $2.00
USAF
SO FAR, SO GOOD! NO SIGN OF TROUBLE!
ESTIMATED TIME OF ARRIVAL STILL UNCHANGED!
OVER AND OUT!
THERE'S SOMETHING UP AHEAD, COLONEL!
LOOKS LIKE AN ORDINARY PUBLIC UTILITY MAINTENANCE TRUCK!
BUT WE'LL TAKE NO CHANCES!
CUT YOUR SPEED! APPROACH WITH CAUTION!
EVERYTHING LOOKS NORMAL ENOUGH SO FAR---!
BAR
WHY'D THEY SLOW UP?
WHAT'S THE DELAY?

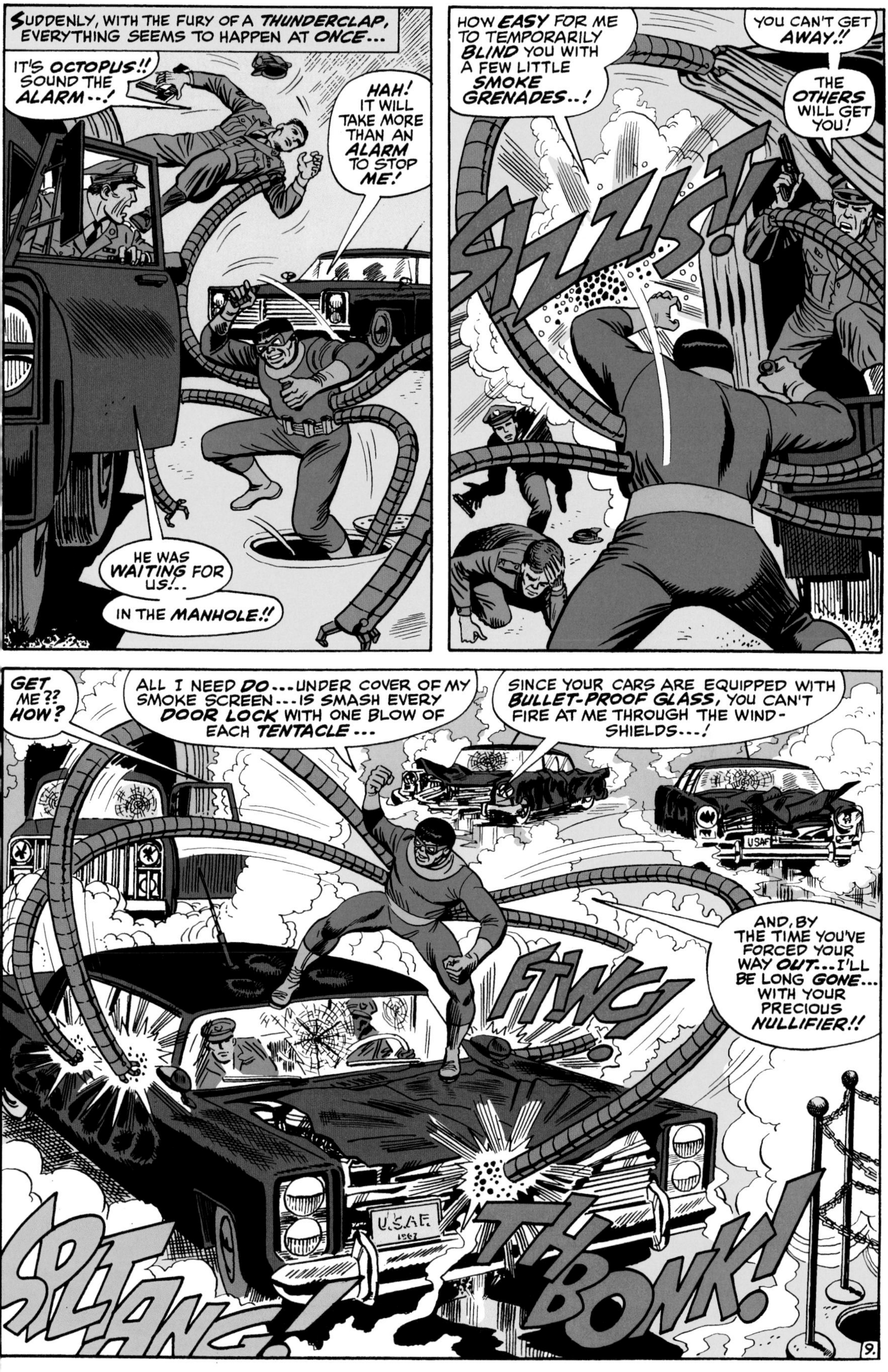
SUDDENLY, WITH THE FURY OF A THUNDERCLAP, EVERYTHING SEEMS TO HAPPEN AT ONCE...
IT'S OCTOPUS!! SOUND THE ALARM..!
HAH! IT WILL TAKE MORE THAN AN ALARM TO STOP ME!
HE WAS WAITING FOR US!..
IN THE MANHOLE!!
HOW EASY FOR ME TO TEMPORARILY BLIND YOU WITH A FEW LITTLE SMOKE GRENADES..!
YOU CAN'T GET AWAY!!
THE OTHERS WILL GET YOU!
SSZZIST!!
GET ME?? HOW?
ALL I NEED DO...UNDER COVER OF MY SMOKE SCREEN...IS SMASH EVERY DOOR LOCK WITH ONE BLOW OF EACH TENTACLE...
SINCE YOUR CARS ARE EQUIPPED WITH BULLET-PROOF GLASS, YOU CAN'T FIRE AT ME THROUGH THE WIND-SHIELDS...!
AND, BY THE TIME YOU'VE FORCED YOUR WAY OUT...I'LL BE LONG GONE... WITH YOUR PRECIOUS NULLIFIER!!
FTWG!
U.S.A.F.
SPLTANG!
THBONK!
9.

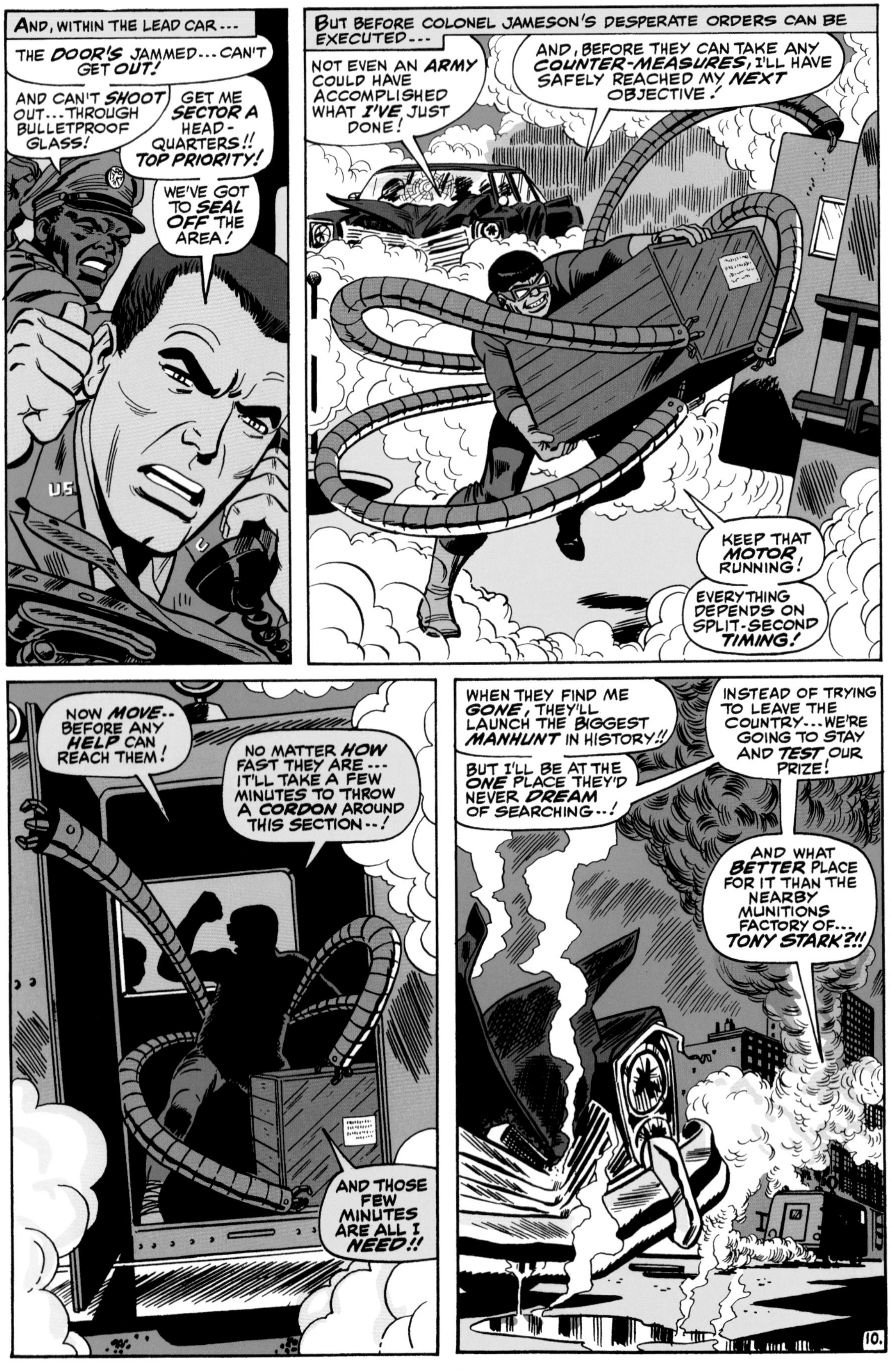
AND, WITHIN THE LEAD CAR ---
THE DOOR'S JAMMED... CAN'T GET OUT!
AND CAN'T SHOOT OUT... THROUGH BULLETPROOF GLASS!
GET ME SECTOR A HEAD-QUARTERS!! TOP PRIORITY!
WE'VE GOT TO SEAL OFF THE AREA!
BUT BEFORE COLONEL JAMESON'S DESPERATE ORDERS CAN BE EXECUTED ---
NOT EVEN AN ARMY COULD HAVE ACCOMPLISHED WHAT I'VE JUST DONE!
AND, BEFORE THEY CAN TAKE ANY COUNTER-MEASURES, I'LL HAVE SAFELY REACHED MY NEXT OBJECTIVE!
KEEP THAT MOTOR RUNNING!
EVERYTHING DEPENDS ON SPLIT-SECOND TIMING!
NOW MOVE-- BEFORE ANY HELP CAN REACH THEM!
NO MATTER HOW FAST THEY ARE --- IT'LL TAKE A FEW MINUTES TO THROW A CORDON AROUND THIS SECTION--!
AND THOSE FEW MINUTES ARE ALL I NEED!!
WHEN THEY FIND ME GONE, THEY'LL LAUNCH THE BIGGEST MANHUNT IN HISTORY!!
BUT I'LL BE AT THE ONE PLACE THEY'D NEVER DREAM OF SEARCHING--!
INSTEAD OF TRYING TO LEAVE THE COUNTRY--- WE'RE GOING TO STAY AND TEST OUR PRIZE!
AND WHAT BETTER PLACE FOR IT THAN THE NEARBY MUNITIONS FACTORY OF... TONY STARK?!!
10.

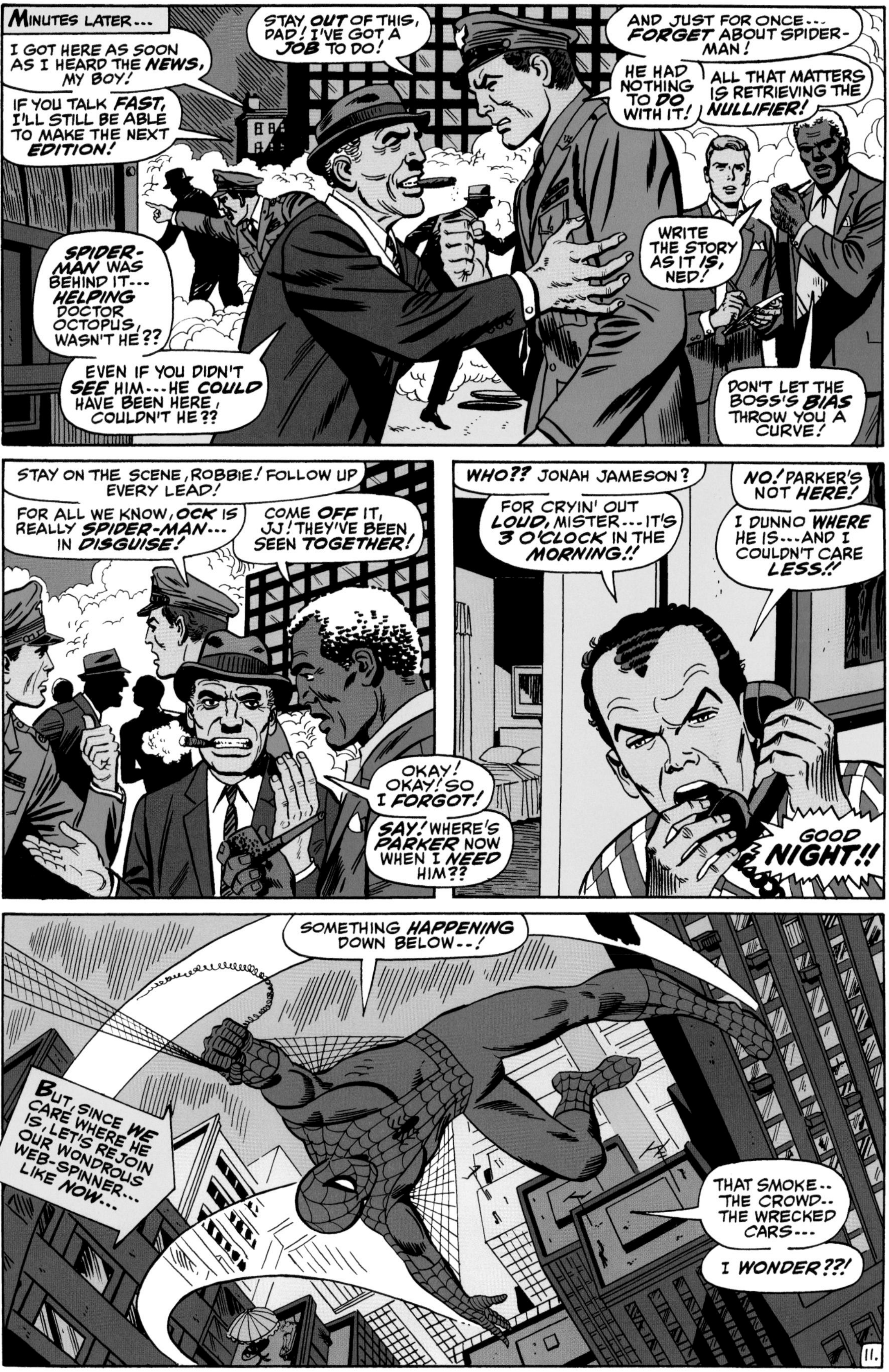
MINUTES LATER...
I GOT HERE AS SOON AS I HEARD THE NEWS, MY BOY!
IF YOU TALK FAST, I'LL STILL BE ABLE TO MAKE THE NEXT EDITION!
STAY OUT OF THIS, DAD! I'VE GOT A JOB TO DO!
AND JUST FOR ONCE... FORGET ABOUT SPIDER-MAN!
HE HAD NOTHING TO DO WITH IT!
ALL THAT MATTERS IS RETRIEVING THE NULLIFIER!
SPIDER-MAN WAS BEHIND IT--- HELPING DOCTOR OCTOPUS, WASN'T HE??
EVEN IF YOU DIDN'T SEE HIM--- HE COULD HAVE BEEN HERE, COULDN'T HE??
WRITE THE STORY AS IT IS, NED!
DON'T LET THE BOSS'S BIAS THROW YOU A CURVE!
STAY ON THE SCENE, ROBBIE! FOLLOW UP EVERY LEAD!
FOR ALL WE KNOW, OCK IS REALLY SPIDER-MAN... IN DISGUISE!
COME OFF IT, JJ! THEY'VE BEEN SEEN TOGETHER!
OKAY! OKAY! SO I FORGOT!
SAY! WHERE'S PARKER NOW WHEN I NEED HIM??
WHO?? JONAH JAMESON?
FOR CRYIN' OUT LOUD, MISTER---IT'S 3 O'CLOCK IN THE MORNING!!
NO! PARKER'S NOT HERE!
I DUNNO WHERE HE IS---AND I COULDN'T CARE LESS!!
GOOD NIGHT!!
BUT, SINCE WE CARE WHERE HE IS, LET'S REJOIN OUR WONDROUS WEB-SPINNER... LIKE NOW...
SOMETHING HAPPENING DOWN BELOW--!
THAT SMOKE.. THE CROWD.. THE WRECKED CARS---
I WONDER??!
11.

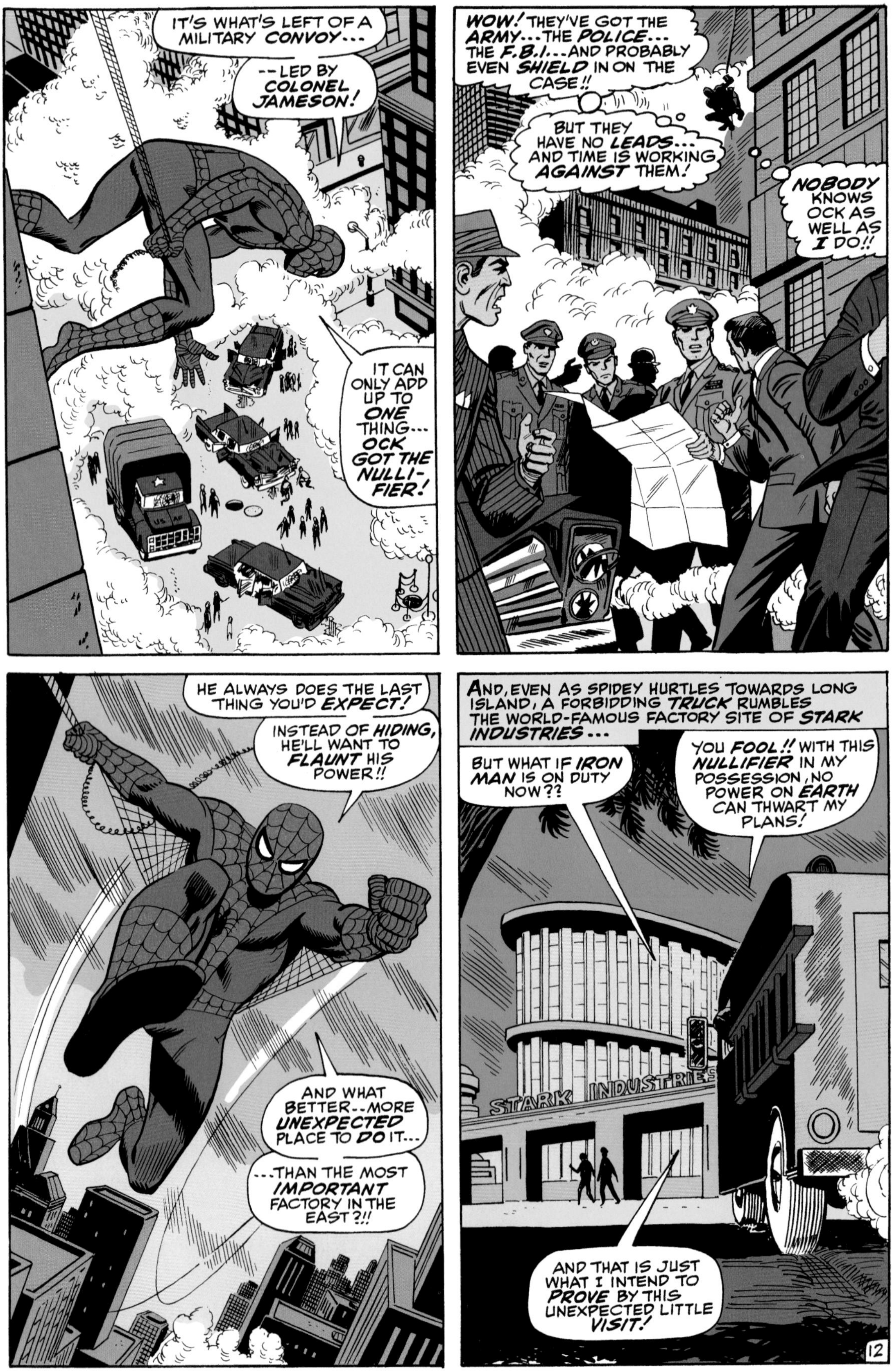
IT'S WHAT'S LEFT OF A MILITARY CONVOY...
--LED BY COLONEL JAMESON!
IT CAN ONLY ADD UP TO ONE THING... OCK GOT THE NULLIFIER!
WOW! THEY'VE GOT THE ARMY... THE POLICE... THE F.B.I... AND PROBABLY EVEN SHIELD IN ON THE CASE!!
BUT THEY HAVE NO LEADS... AND TIME IS WORKING AGAINST THEM!
NOBODY KNOWS OCK AS WELL AS I DO!!
HE ALWAYS DOES THE LAST THING YOU'D EXPECT!
INSTEAD OF HIDING, HE'LL WANT TO FLAUNT HIS POWER!!
AND WHAT BETTER--MORE UNEXPECTED PLACE TO DO IT...
...THAN THE MOST IMPORTANT FACTORY IN THE EAST?!!
AND, EVEN AS SPIDEY HURTLES TOWARDS LONG ISLAND, A FORBIDDING TRUCK RUMBLES THE WORLD-FAMOUS FACTORY SITE OF STARK INDUSTRIES...
BUT WHAT IF IRON MAN IS ON DUTY NOW??
YOU FOOL!! WITH THIS NULLIFIER IN MY POSSESSION, NO POWER ON EARTH CAN THWART MY PLANS!
STARK INDUSTRIES
AND THAT IS JUST WHAT I INTEND TO PROVE BY THIS UNEXPECTED LITTLE VISIT!
12

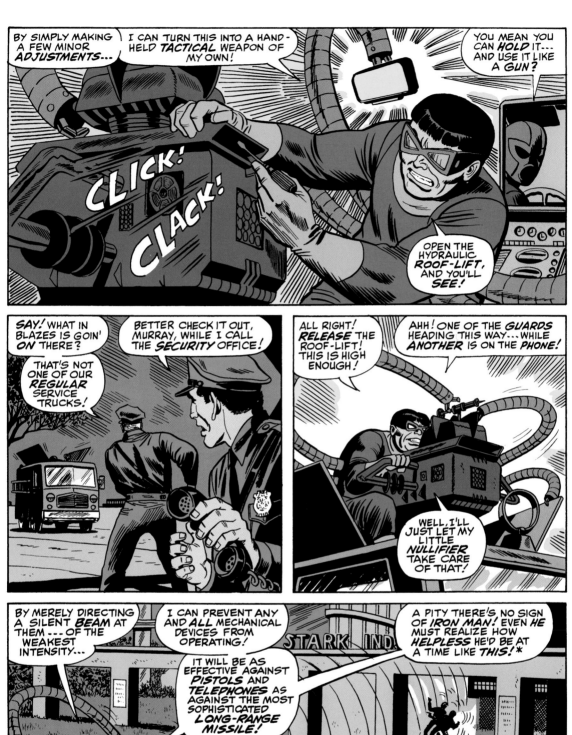

BY SIMPLY MAKING A FEW MINOR *ADJUSTMENTS*...

I CAN TURN THIS INTO A HAND-HELD *TACTICAL* WEAPON OF MY OWN!

YOU MEAN YOU CAN *HOLD* IT... AND USE IT LIKE A *GUN*?

CLICK! CLACK!

OPEN THE HYDRAULIC *ROOF-LIFT,* AND YOU'LL *SEE!*

SAY! WHAT IN BLAZES IS GOIN' *ON* THERE?

THAT'S NOT ONE OF OUR *REGULAR* SERVICE TRUCKS!

BETTER CHECK IT OUT, MURRAY, WHILE I CALL THE *SECURITY* OFFICE!

ALL RIGHT! *RELEASE* THE ROOF-LIFT! THIS IS HIGH ENOUGH!

AHH! ONE OF THE *GUARDS* HEADING THIS WAY... WHILE *ANOTHER* IS ON THE *PHONE!*

WELL, I'LL JUST LET MY LITTLE *NULLIFIER* TAKE CARE OF THAT!

BY MERELY DIRECTING A SILENT *BEAM* AT THEM --- OF THE WEAKEST INTENSITY...

I CAN PREVENT ANY AND *ALL* MECHANICAL DEVICES FROM OPERATING!

IT WILL BE AS EFFECTIVE AGAINST *PISTOLS* AND *TELEPHONES* AS AGAINST THE MOST SOPHISTICATED *LONG-RANGE MISSILE!*

A PITY THERE'S NO SIGN OF *IRON MAN!* EVEN *HE* MUST REALIZE HOW *HELPLESS* HE'D BE AT A TIME LIKE *THIS!**

STARK IND.

*IT'S AN EVEN *GREATER* PITY, AS ALL RABID READERS OF THE CURRENT *SUSPENSE #96* MUST KNOW, THAT THE GREAT GOLDEN GLADIATOR NOW LIES MORTALLY *WOUNDED,* IN ANOTHER SECTION OF THE SPRAWLING FACTORY... AFTER HIS TITANIC BATTLE WITH THE *GREY GARGOYLE!*

BUT NOW, BACK TO OUR OWN FRANTIC FUN AND GAMES...

13

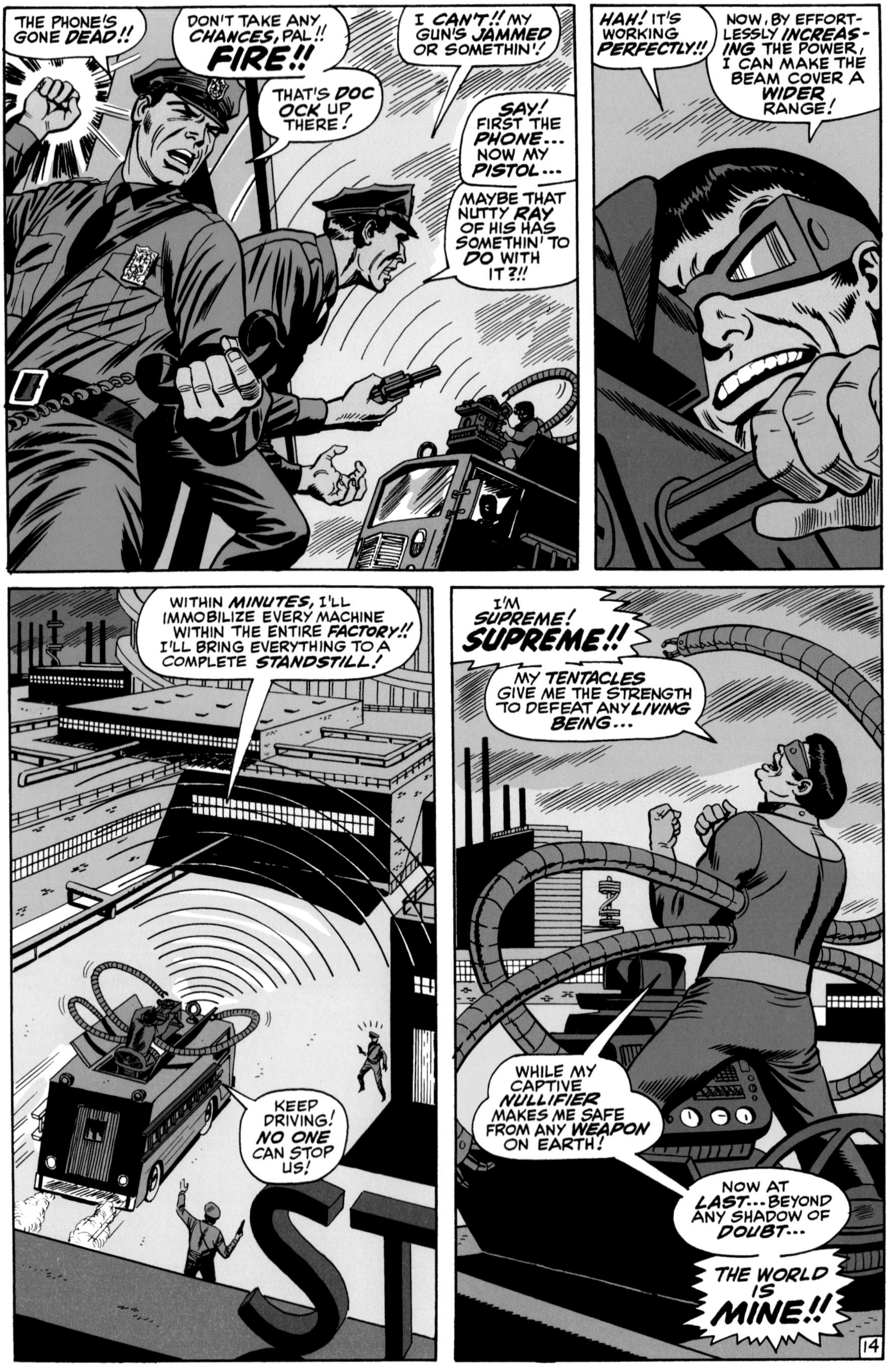
THE PHONE'S GONE DEAD!!
DON'T TAKE ANY CHANCES, PAL!! FIRE!!
THAT'S DOC OCK UP THERE!
I CAN'T!! MY GUN'S JAMMED OR SOMETHIN'!
SAY! FIRST THE PHONE... NOW MY PISTOL...
MAYBE THAT NUTTY RAY OF HIS HAS SOMETHIN' TO DO WITH IT?!!
HAH! IT'S WORKING PERFECTLY!!
NOW, BY EFFORTLESSLY INCREASING THE POWER, I CAN MAKE THE BEAM COVER A WIDER RANGE!
WITHIN MINUTES, I'LL IMMOBILIZE EVERY MACHINE WITHIN THE ENTIRE FACTORY!! I'LL BRING EVERYTHING TO A COMPLETE STANDSTILL!
KEEP DRIVING! NO ONE CAN STOP US!
I'M SUPREME! SUPREME!!
MY TENTACLES GIVE ME THE STRENGTH TO DEFEAT ANY LIVING BEING...
WHILE MY CAPTIVE NULLIFIER MAKES ME SAFE FROM ANY WEAPON ON EARTH!
NOW AT LAST... BEYOND ANY SHADOW OF DOUBT...
THE WORLD IS MINE!!
14

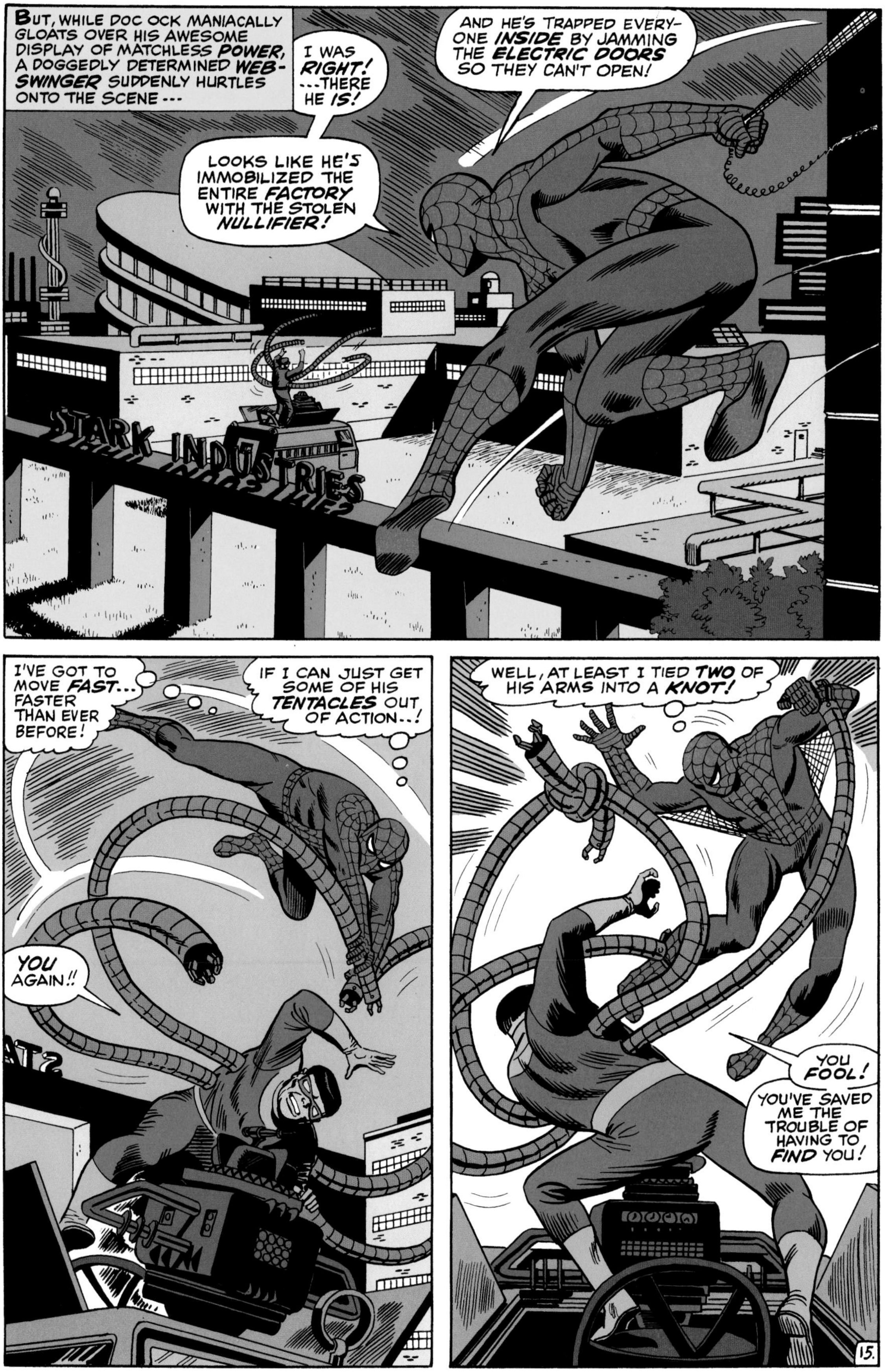
BUT, WHILE DOC OCK MANIACALLY GLOATS OVER HIS AWESOME DISPLAY OF MATCHLESS POWER, A DOGGEDLY DETERMINED WEB-SWINGER SUDDENLY HURTLES ONTO THE SCENE ---
I WAS RIGHT! ---THERE HE IS!
AND HE'S TRAPPED EVERY-ONE INSIDE BY JAMMING THE ELECTRIC DOORS SO THEY CAN'T OPEN!
LOOKS LIKE HE'S IMMOBILIZED THE ENTIRE FACTORY WITH THE STOLEN NULLIFIER!
STARK INDUSTRIES
I'VE GOT TO MOVE FAST... FASTER THAN EVER BEFORE!
IF I CAN JUST GET SOME OF HIS TENTACLES OUT OF ACTION..!
YOU AGAIN!!
WELL, AT LEAST I TIED TWO OF HIS ARMS INTO A KNOT!
YOU FOOL!
YOU'VE SAVED ME THE TROUBLE OF HAVING TO FIND YOU!
15.

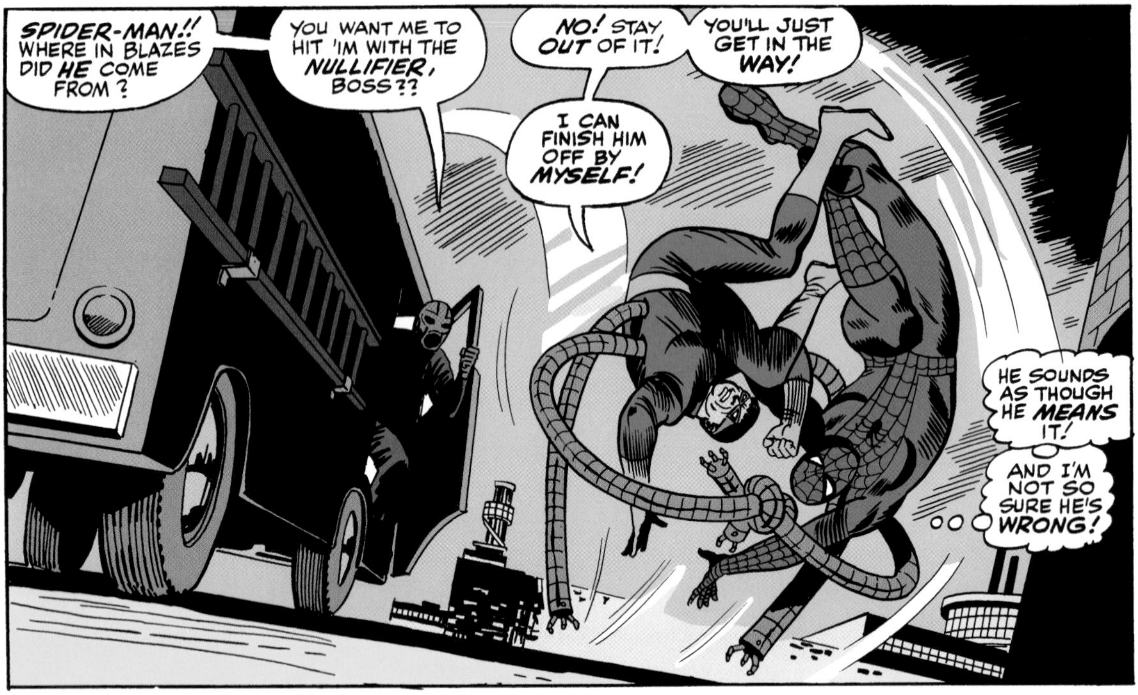
SPIDER-MAN!! WHERE IN BLAZES DID HE COME FROM?
YOU WANT ME TO HIT 'IM WITH THE NULLIFIER, BOSS??
NO! STAY OUT OF IT!
YOU'LL JUST GET IN THE WAY!
I CAN FINISH HIM OFF BY MYSELF!
HE SOUNDS AS THOUGH HE MEANS IT!
AND I'M NOT SO SURE HE'S WRONG!

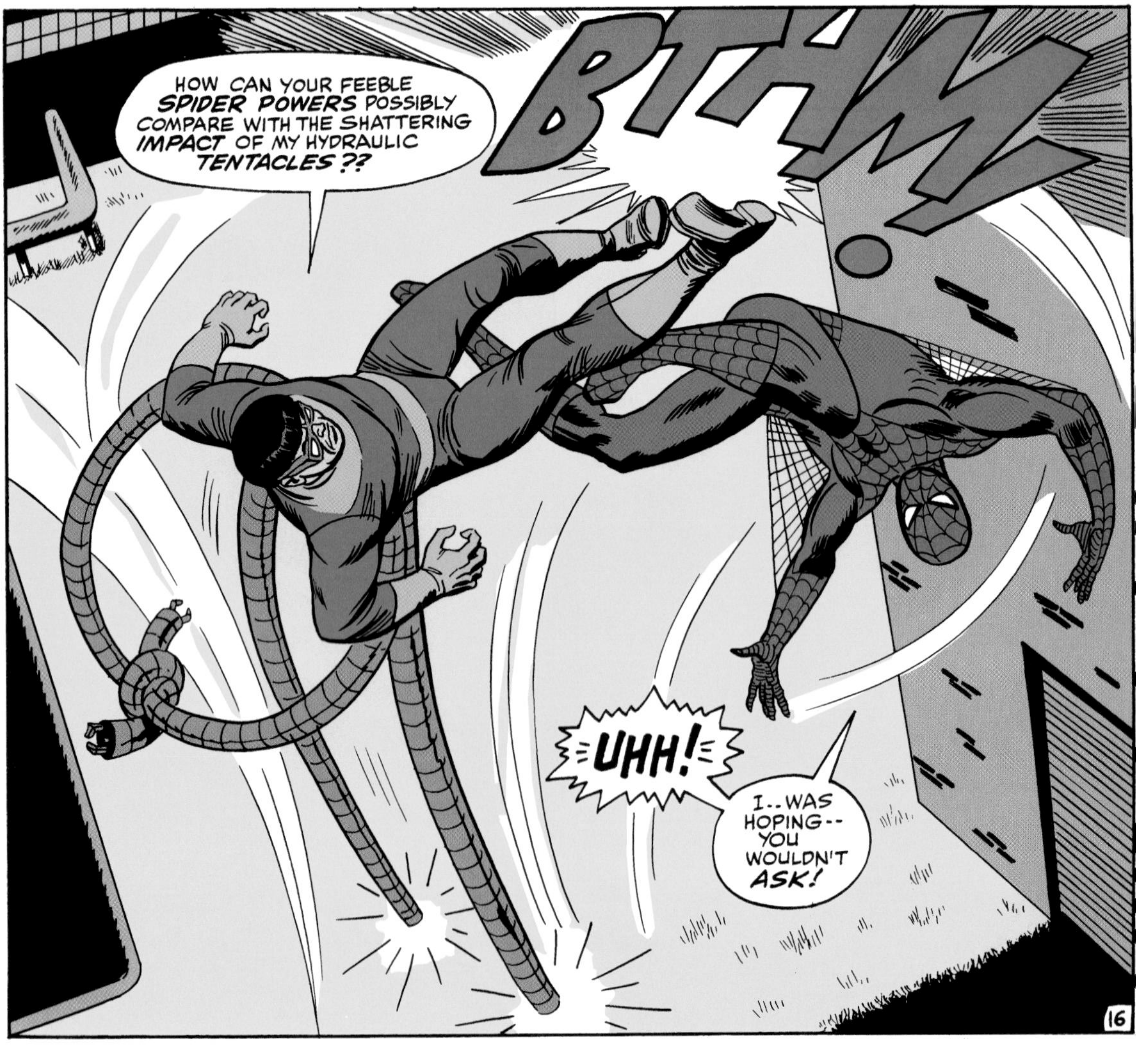
BTHM!
HOW CAN YOUR FEEBLE SPIDER POWERS POSSIBLY COMPARE WITH THE SHATTERING IMPACT OF MY HYDRAULIC TENTACLES??
UHH!
I--WAS HOPING--YOU WOULDN'T ASK!
16

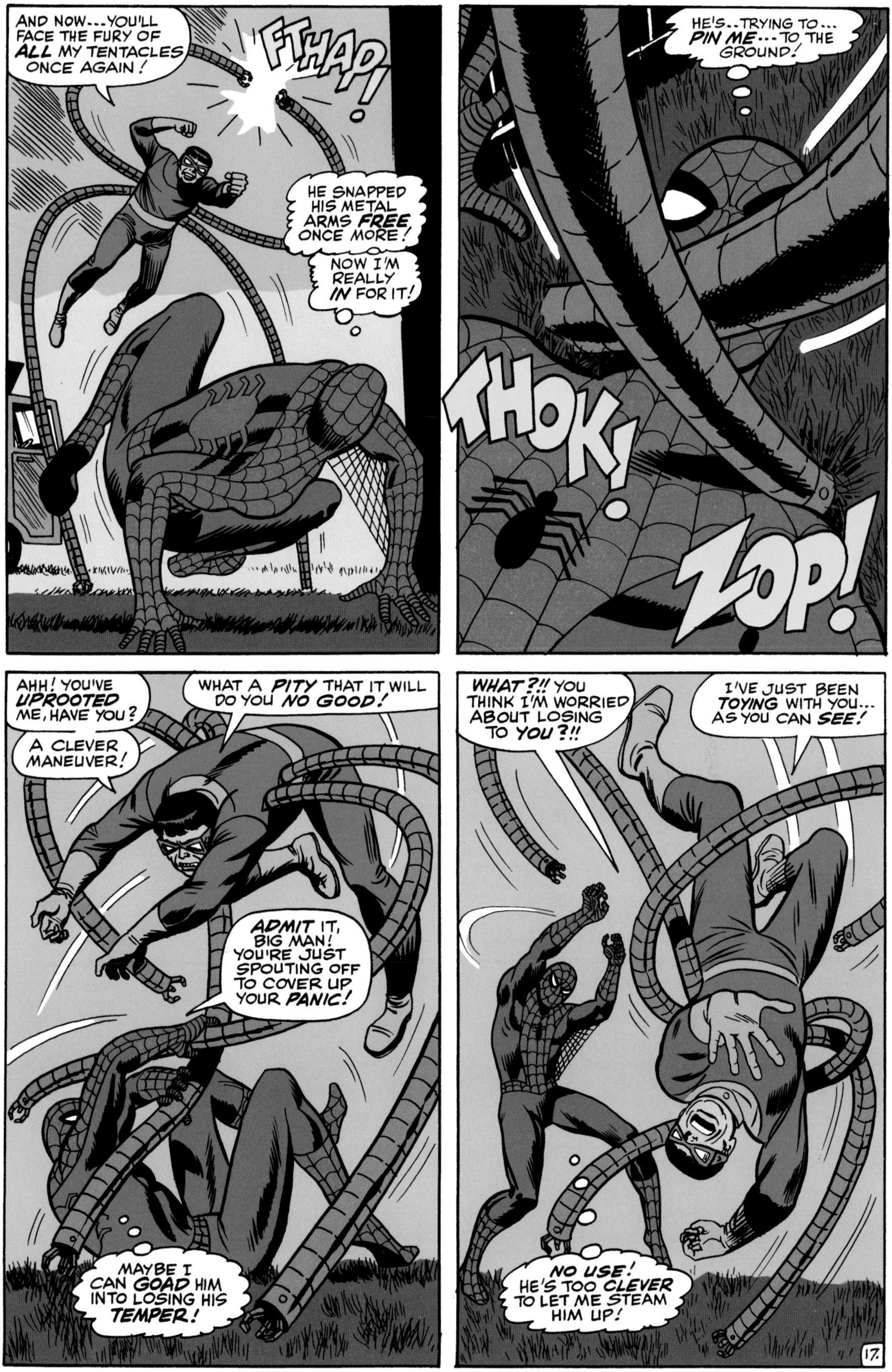
AND NOW...YOU'LL FACE THE FURY OF ALL MY TENTACLES ONCE AGAIN!
FTHAP!
HE SNAPPED HIS METAL ARMS FREE ONCE MORE!
NOW I'M REALLY IN FOR IT!
HE'S..TRYING TO... PIN ME...TO THE GROUND!
THOK!
ZOP!
AHH! YOU'VE UPROOTED ME, HAVE YOU?
A CLEVER MANEUVER!
WHAT A PITY THAT IT WILL DO YOU NO GOOD!
ADMIT IT, BIG MAN! YOU'RE JUST SPOUTING OFF TO COVER UP YOUR PANIC!
MAYBE I CAN GOAD HIM INTO LOSING HIS TEMPER!
WHAT?!! YOU THINK I'M WORRIED ABOUT LOSING TO YOU?!!
I'VE JUST BEEN TOYING WITH YOU... AS YOU CAN SEE!
NO USE! HE'S TOO CLEVER TO LET ME STEAM HIM UP!
17.

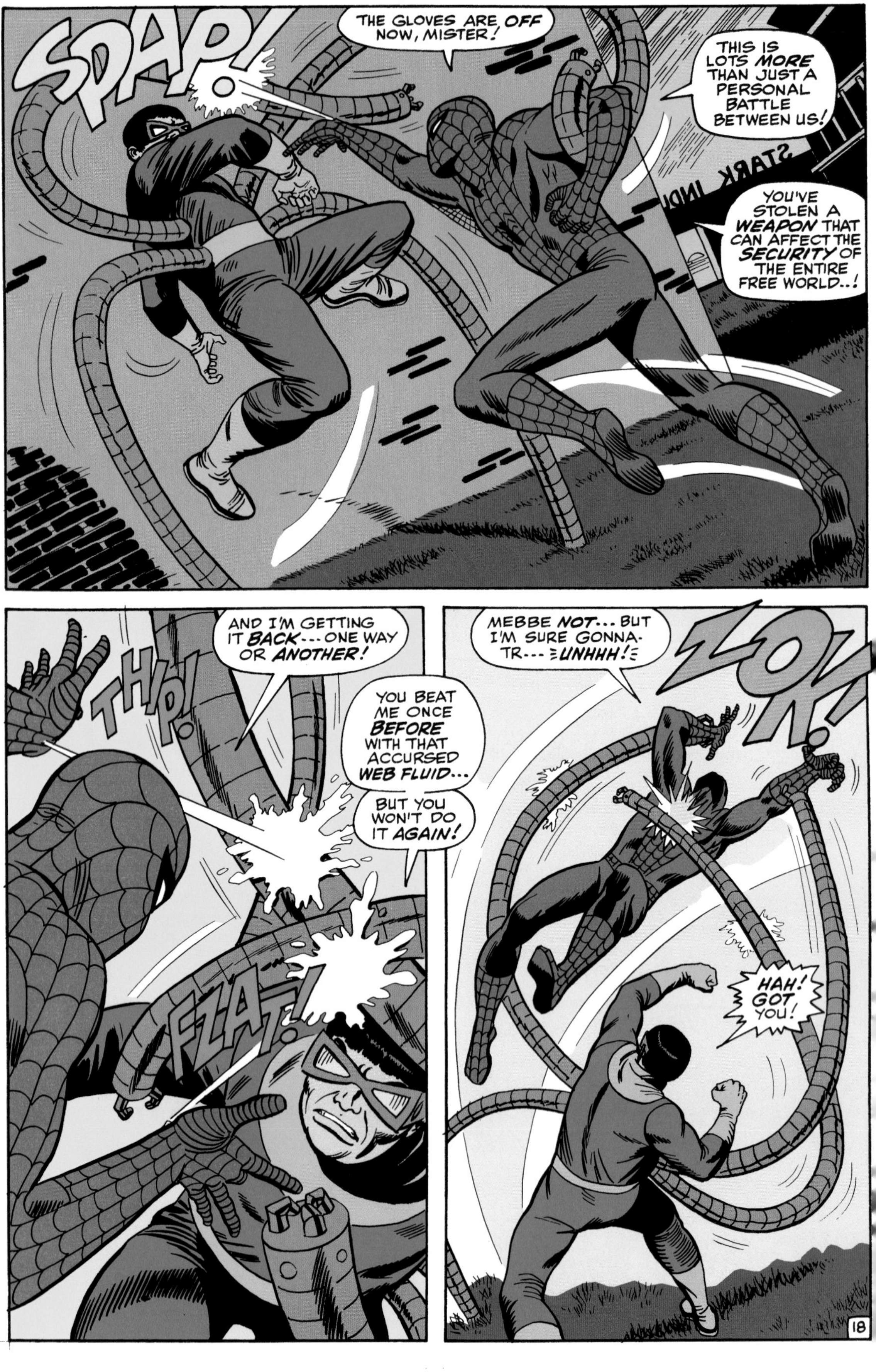
SPAP!
THE GLOVES ARE OFF NOW, MISTER!
THIS IS LOTS MORE THAN JUST A PERSONAL BATTLE BETWEEN US!
YOU'VE STOLEN A WEAPON THAT CAN AFFECT THE SECURITY OF THE ENTIRE FREE WORLD..!
STARK INDU
AND I'M GETTING IT BACK--- ONE WAY OR ANOTHER!
THIP!
YOU BEAT ME ONCE BEFORE WITH THAT ACCURSED WEB FLUID...
BUT YOU WON'T DO IT AGAIN!
FZAT!
MEBBE NOT... BUT I'M SURE GONNA-TR---UNHHH!
ZOK!
HAH! GOT YOU!
18

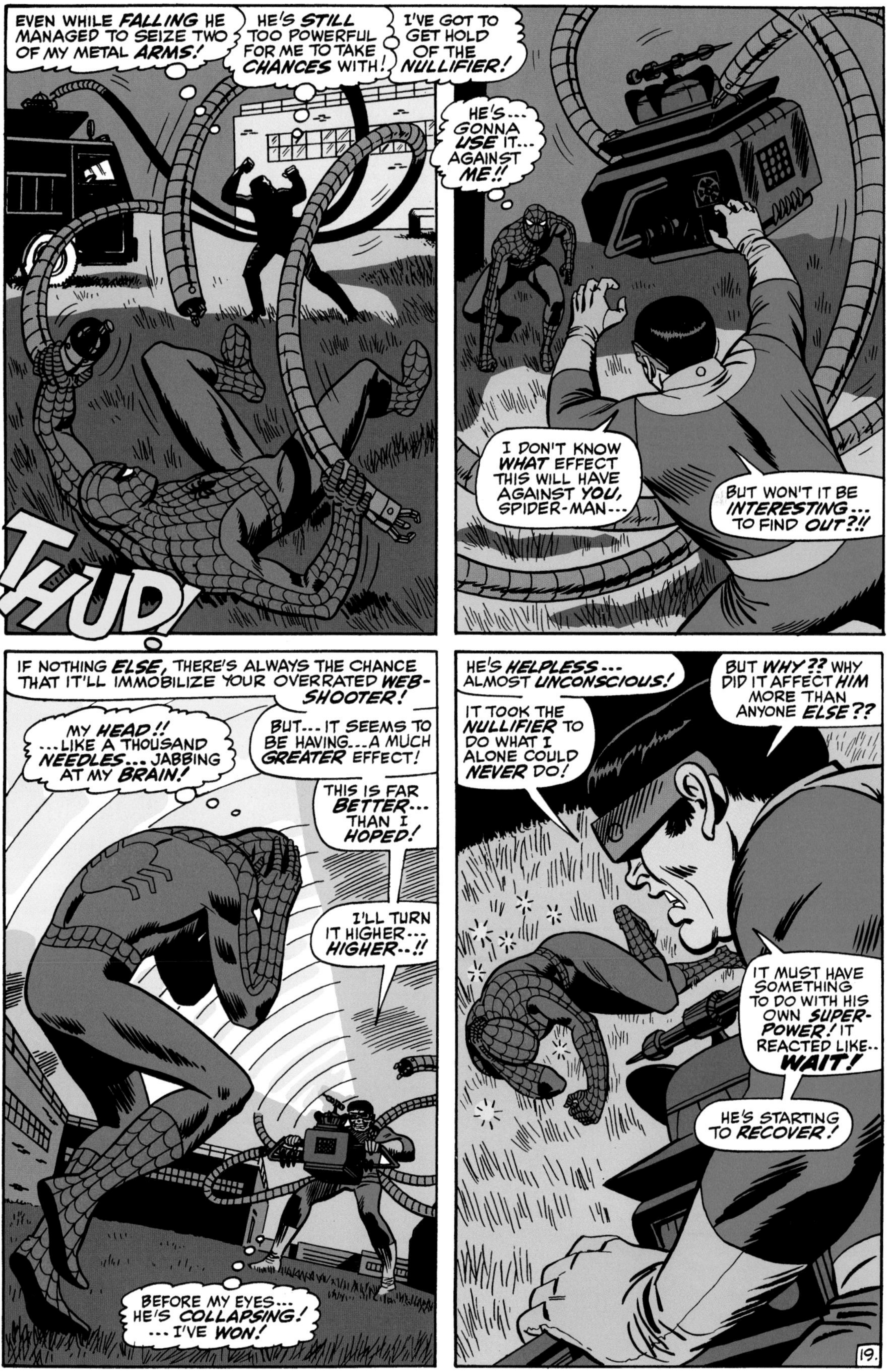
EVEN WHILE FALLING HE MANAGED TO SEIZE TWO OF MY METAL ARMS!
HE'S STILL TOO POWERFUL FOR ME TO TAKE CHANCES WITH!
I'VE GOT TO GET HOLD OF THE NULLIFIER!
THUD!
HE'S... GONNA USE IT... AGAINST ME!!
I DON'T KNOW WHAT EFFECT THIS WILL HAVE AGAINST YOU, SPIDER-MAN---
BUT WON'T IT BE INTERESTING... TO FIND OUT?!!
IF NOTHING ELSE, THERE'S ALWAYS THE CHANCE THAT IT'LL IMMOBILIZE YOUR OVERRATED WEB-SHOOTER!
MY HEAD!! ...LIKE A THOUSAND NEEDLES... JABBING AT MY BRAIN!
BUT--- IT SEEMS TO BE HAVING... A MUCH GREATER EFFECT!
THIS IS FAR BETTER... THAN I HOPED!
I'LL TURN IT HIGHER--- HIGHER--!!
BEFORE MY EYES... HE'S COLLAPSING! --- I'VE WON!
HE'S HELPLESS--- ALMOST UNCONSCIOUS!
IT TOOK THE NULLIFIER TO DO WHAT I ALONE COULD NEVER DO!
BUT WHY?? WHY DID IT AFFECT HIM MORE THAN ANYONE ELSE??
IT MUST HAVE SOMETHING TO DO WITH HIS OWN SUPER-POWER! IT REACTED LIKE.. WAIT!
HE'S STARTING TO RECOVER!
19.

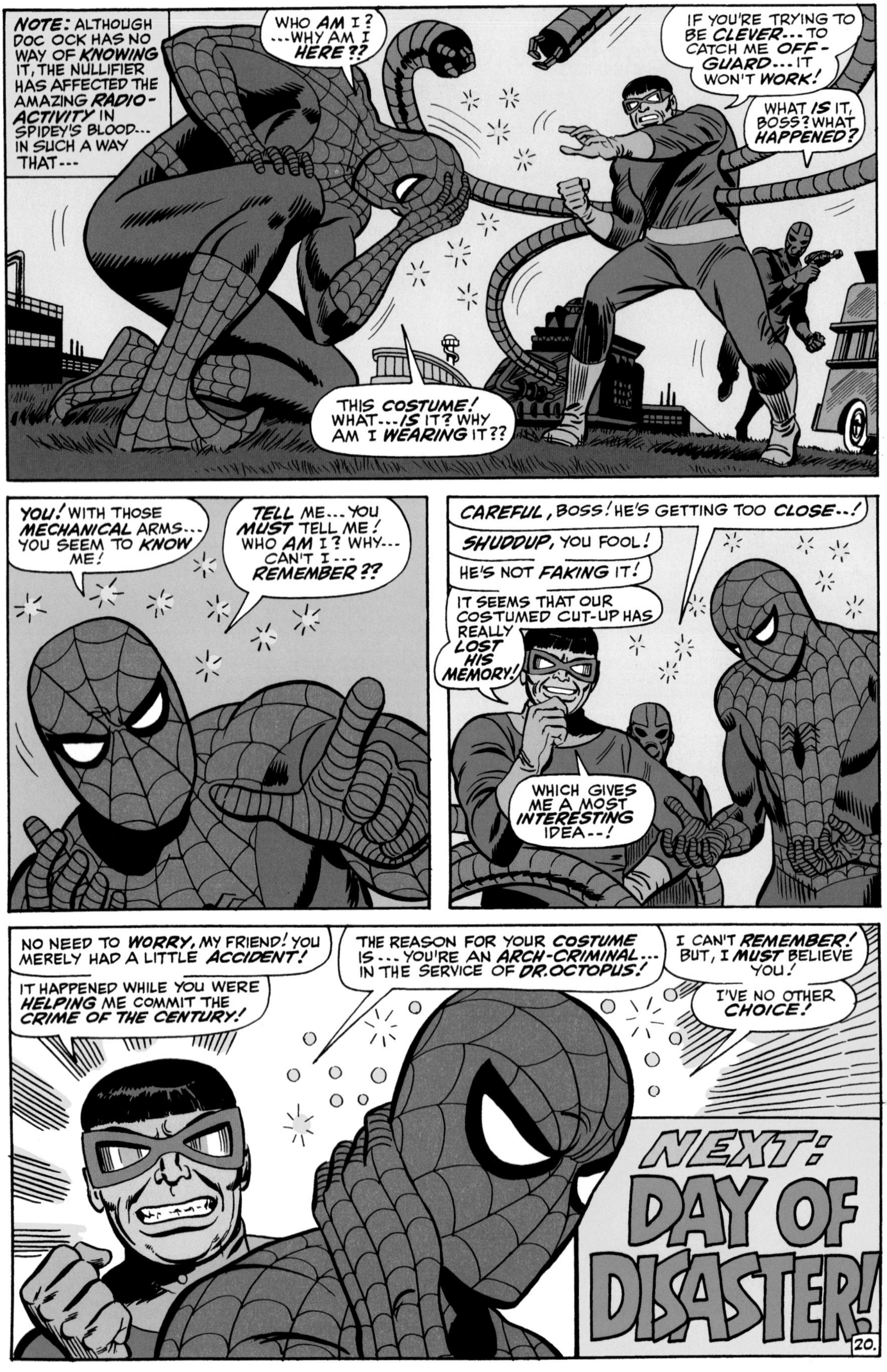

NOTE: ALTHOUGH DOC OCK HAS NO WAY OF KNOWING IT, THE NULLIFIER HAS AFFECTED THE AMAZING RADIO-ACTIVITY IN SPIDEY'S BLOOD... IN SUCH A WAY THAT---
WHO AM I? ---WHY AM I HERE??
IF YOU'RE TRYING TO BE CLEVER--- TO CATCH ME OFF-GUARD--- IT WON'T WORK!
WHAT IS IT, BOSS? WHAT HAPPENED?
THIS COSTUME! WHAT---IS IT? WHY AM I WEARING IT??
YOU! WITH THOSE MECHANICAL ARMS... YOU SEEM TO KNOW ME!
TELL ME... YOU MUST TELL ME! WHO AM I? WHY--- CAN'T I --- REMEMBER??
CAREFUL, BOSS! HE'S GETTING TOO CLOSE--!
SHUDDUP, YOU FOOL!
HE'S NOT FAKING IT!
IT SEEMS THAT OUR COSTUMED CUT-UP HAS REALLY LOST HIS MEMORY!
WHICH GIVES ME A MOST INTERESTING IDEA--!
NO NEED TO WORRY, MY FRIEND! YOU MERELY HAD A LITTLE ACCIDENT!
IT HAPPENED WHILE YOU WERE HELPING ME COMMIT THE CRIME OF THE CENTURY!
THE REASON FOR YOUR COSTUME IS... YOU'RE AN ARCH-CRIMINAL... IN THE SERVICE OF DR. OCTOPUS!
I CAN'T REMEMBER! BUT, I MUST BELIEVE YOU!
I'VE NO OTHER CHOICE!
NEXT: DAY OF DISASTER!
20.

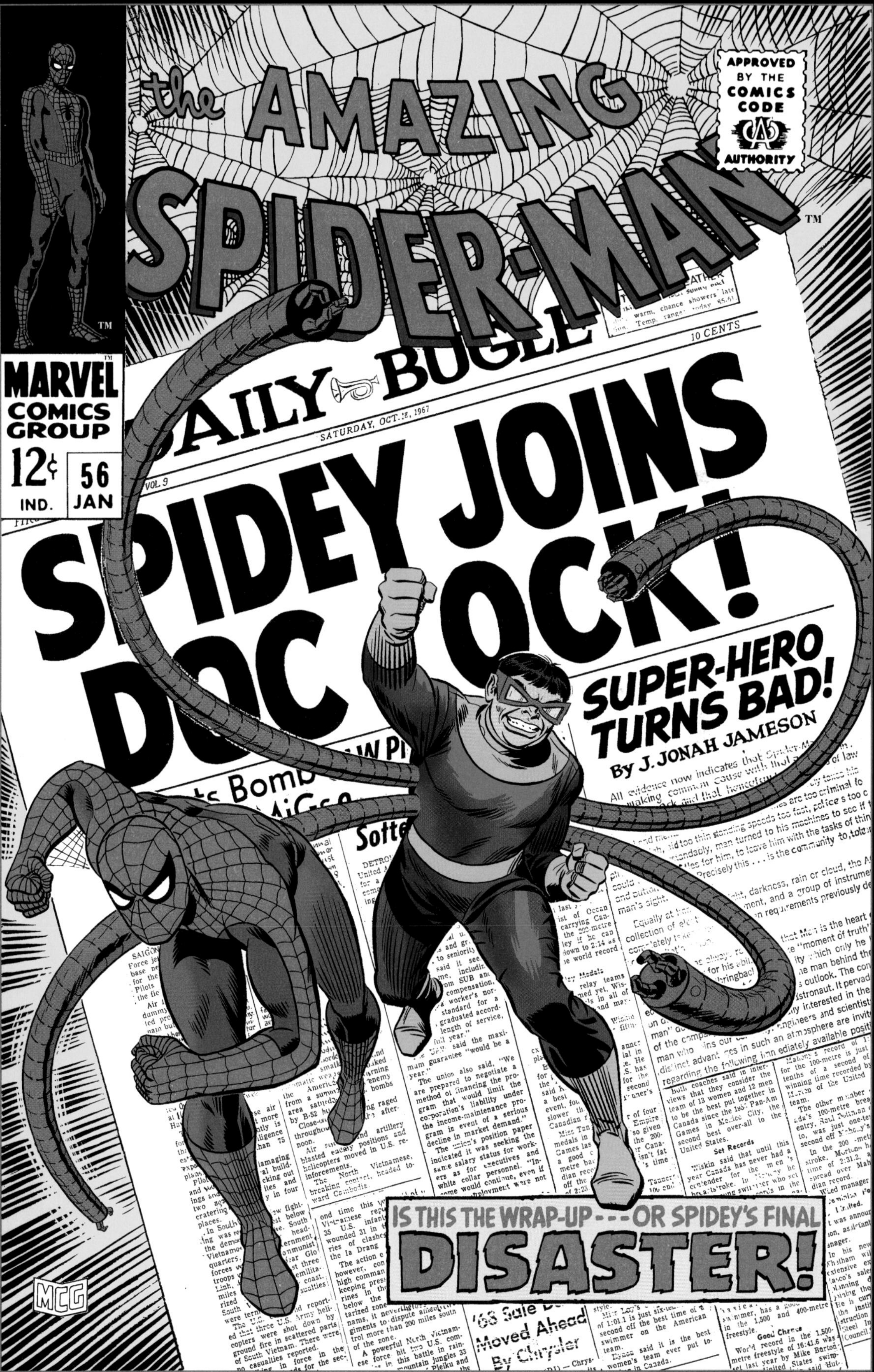
the AMAZING SPIDER-MAN
APPROVED BY THE COMICS CODE AUTHORITY
MARVEL COMICS GROUP
12¢
IND.
56
JAN
AILY BUGLE
10 CENTS
SPIDEY JOINS
DOC
OCK!
SUPER-HERO TURNS BAD!
By J. JONAH JAMESON
IS THIS THE WRAP-UP---OR SPIDEY'S FINAL
DISASTER!
Moved Ahead

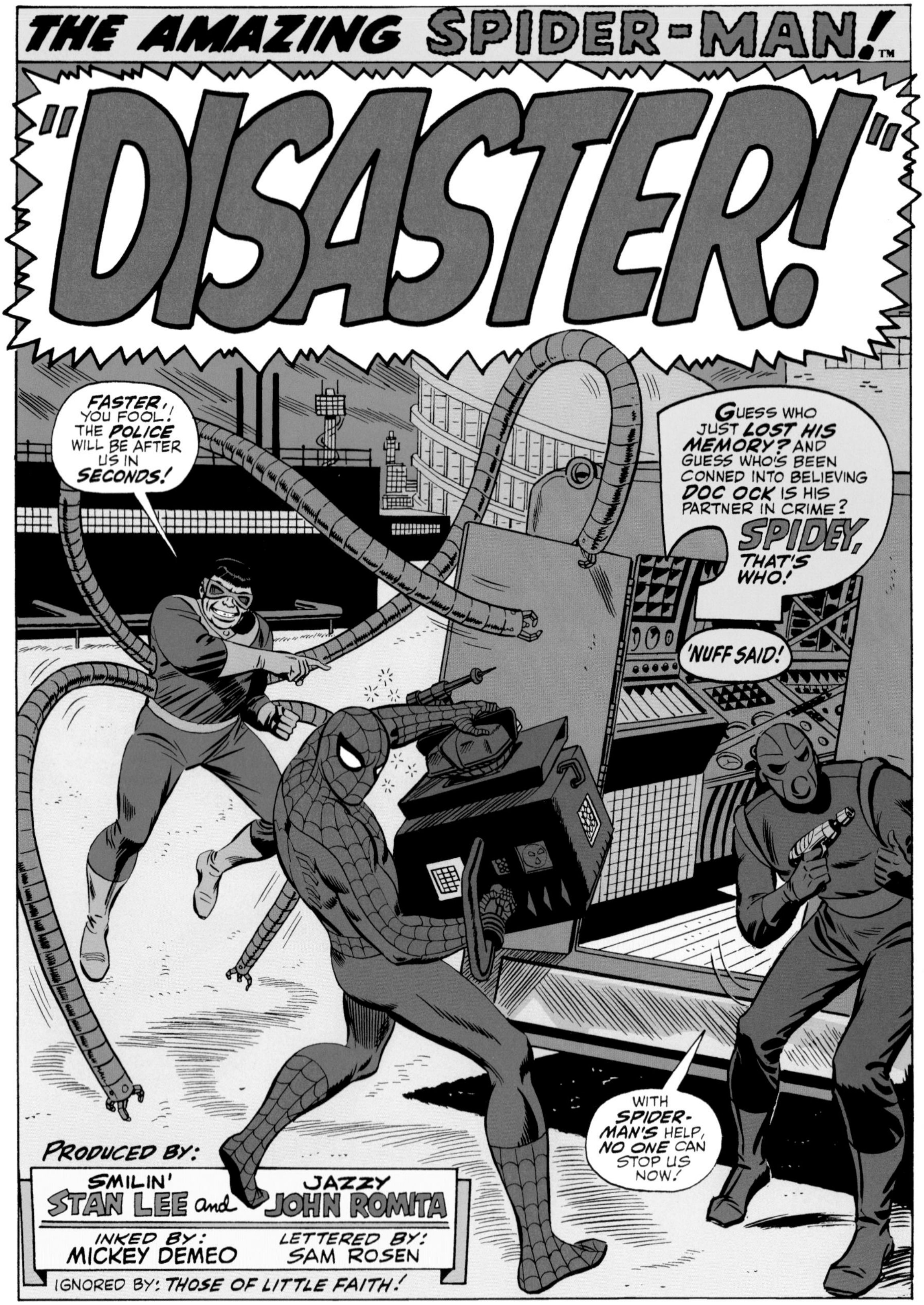
THE AMAZING SPIDER-MAN!™
"DISASTER!"
FASTER, YOU FOOL! THE POLICE WILL BE AFTER US IN SECONDS!
GUESS WHO JUST LOST HIS MEMORY? AND GUESS WHO'S BEEN CONNED INTO BELIEVING DOC OCK IS HIS PARTNER IN CRIME? SPIDEY, THAT'S WHO!
'NUFF SAID!
WITH SPIDER-MAN'S HELP, NO ONE CAN STOP US NOW!
PRODUCED BY:
SMILIN' STAN LEE and JAZZY JOHN ROMITA
INKED BY: MICKEY DEMEO
LETTERED BY: SAM ROSEN
IGNORED BY: THOSE OF LITTLE FAITH!

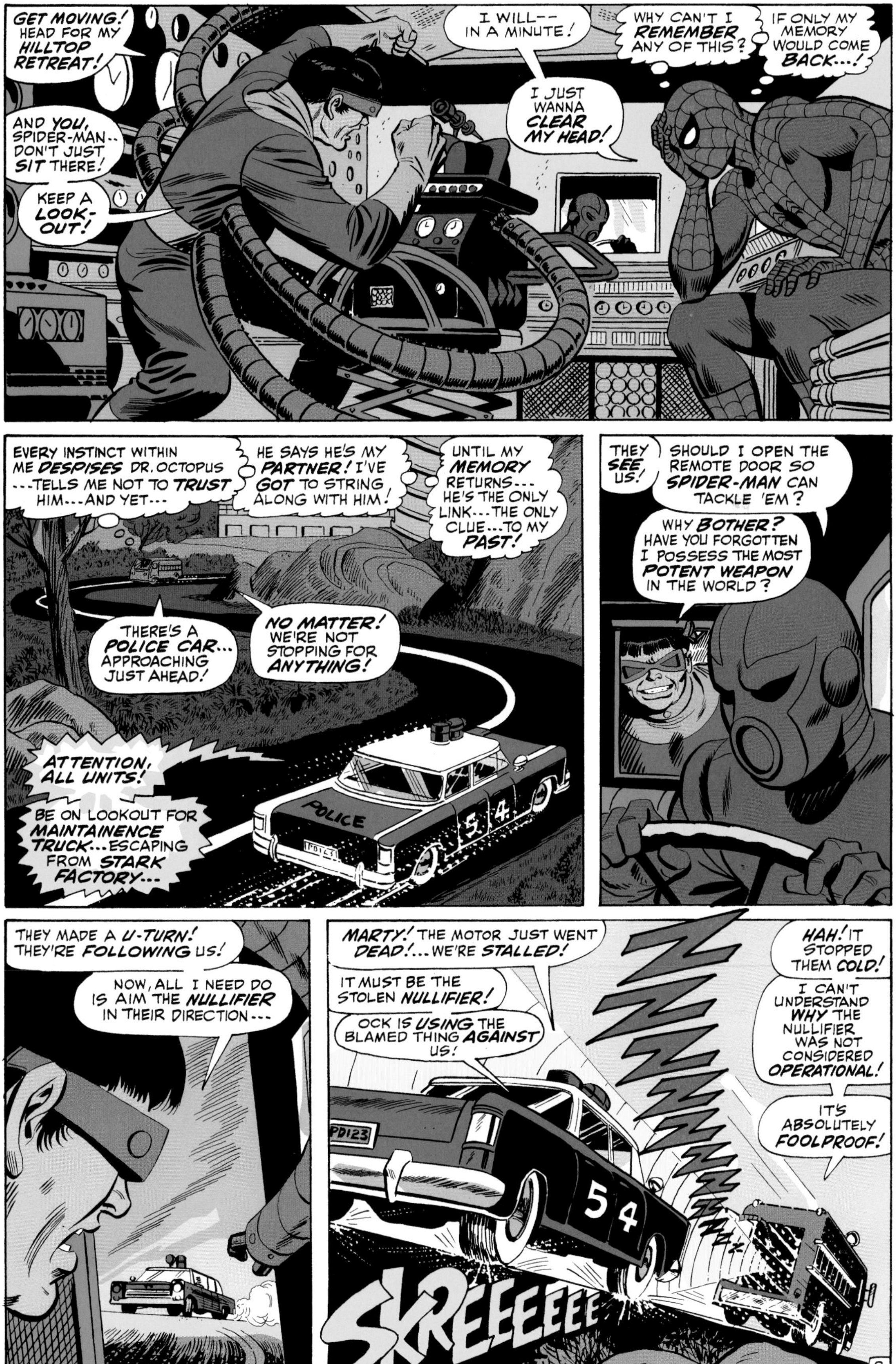
GET MOVING! HEAD FOR MY HILLTOP RETREAT!
AND YOU, SPIDER-MAN-- DON'T JUST SIT THERE!
KEEP A LOOK-OUT!
I WILL-- IN A MINUTE!
I JUST WANNA CLEAR MY HEAD!
WHY CAN'T I REMEMBER ANY OF THIS?
IF ONLY MY MEMORY WOULD COME BACK--!
EVERY INSTINCT WITHIN ME DESPISES DR. OCTOPUS --TELLS ME NOT TO TRUST HIM--AND YET--
HE SAYS HE'S MY PARTNER! I'VE GOT TO STRING ALONG WITH HIM!
UNTIL MY MEMORY RETURNS-- HE'S THE ONLY LINK--THE ONLY CLUE--TO MY PAST!
THERE'S A POLICE CAR-- APPROACHING JUST AHEAD!
NO MATTER! WE'RE NOT STOPPING FOR ANYTHING!
ATTENTION, ALL UNITS!
BE ON LOOKOUT FOR MAINTAINENCE TRUCK--ESCAPING FROM STARK FACTORY--
POLICE
54
THEY SEE US!
SHOULD I OPEN THE REMOTE DOOR SO SPIDER-MAN CAN TACKLE 'EM?
WHY BOTHER? HAVE YOU FORGOTTEN I POSSESS THE MOST POTENT WEAPON IN THE WORLD?
THEY MADE A U-TURN! THEY'RE FOLLOWING US!
NOW, ALL I NEED DO IS AIM THE NULLIFIER IN THEIR DIRECTION--
MARTY! THE MOTOR JUST WENT DEAD!--WE'RE STALLED!
IT MUST BE THE STOLEN NULLIFIER!
OCK IS USING THE BLAMED THING AGAINST US!
PD123
54
ZZZZZZZZZZZZ
SKREEEEEE
HAH! IT STOPPED THEM COLD!
I CAN'T UNDERSTAND WHY THE NULLIFIER WAS NOT CONSIDERED OPERATIONAL!
IT'S ABSOLUTELY FOOLPROOF!
2.

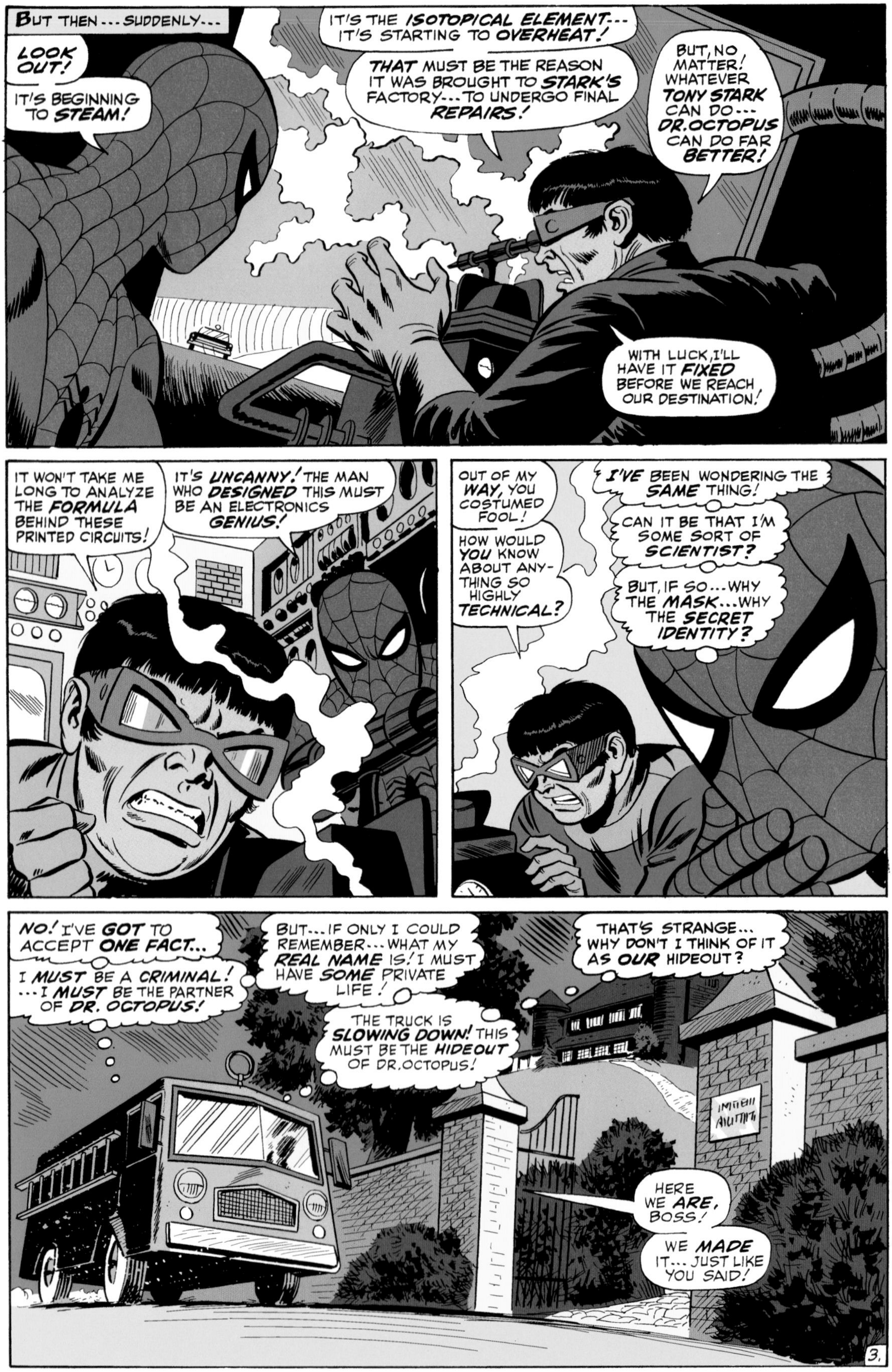
BUT THEN ... SUDDENLY...
LOOK OUT!
IT'S BEGINNING TO STEAM!
IT'S THE ISOTOPICAL ELEMENT--- IT'S STARTING TO OVERHEAT!
THAT MUST BE THE REASON IT WAS BROUGHT TO STARK'S FACTORY--- TO UNDERGO FINAL REPAIRS!
BUT, NO MATTER! WHATEVER TONY STARK CAN DO--- DR. OCTOPUS CAN DO FAR BETTER!
WITH LUCK, I'LL HAVE IT FIXED BEFORE WE REACH OUR DESTINATION!
IT WON'T TAKE ME LONG TO ANALYZE THE FORMULA BEHIND THESE PRINTED CIRCUITS!
IT'S UNCANNY! THE MAN WHO DESIGNED THIS MUST BE AN ELECTRONICS GENIUS!
OUT OF MY WAY, YOU COSTUMED FOOL!
HOW WOULD YOU KNOW ABOUT ANY-THING SO HIGHLY TECHNICAL?
I'VE BEEN WONDERING THE SAME THING!
CAN IT BE THAT I'M SOME SORT OF SCIENTIST?
BUT, IF SO... WHY THE MASK... WHY THE SECRET IDENTITY?
NO! I'VE GOT TO ACCEPT ONE FACT...
I MUST BE A CRIMINAL! ... I MUST BE THE PARTNER OF DR. OCTOPUS!
BUT... IF ONLY I COULD REMEMBER... WHAT MY REAL NAME IS! I MUST HAVE SOME PRIVATE LIFE!
THE TRUCK IS SLOWING DOWN! THIS MUST BE THE HIDEOUT OF DR. OCTOPUS!
THAT'S STRANGE... WHY DON'T I THINK OF IT AS OUR HIDEOUT?
HERE WE ARE, BOSS!
WE MADE IT... JUST LIKE YOU SAID!
3.

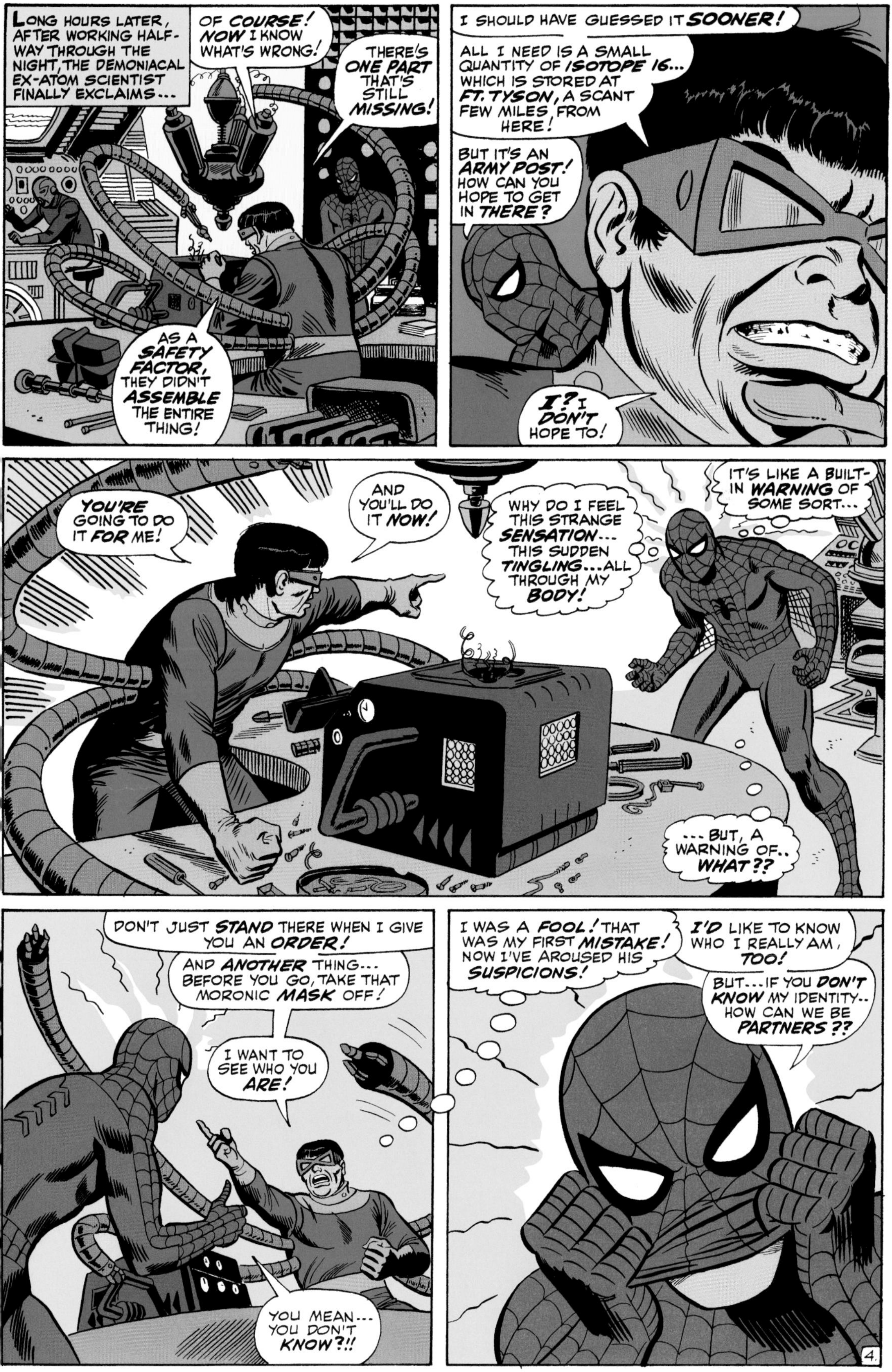
LONG HOURS LATER, AFTER WORKING HALF-WAY THROUGH THE NIGHT, THE DEMONIACAL EX-ATOM SCIENTIST FINALLY EXCLAIMS...
OF COURSE! NOW I KNOW WHAT'S WRONG!
THERE'S ONE PART THAT'S STILL MISSING!
AS A SAFETY FACTOR, THEY DIDN'T ASSEMBLE THE ENTIRE THING!
I SHOULD HAVE GUESSED IT SOONER!
ALL I NEED IS A SMALL QUANTITY OF ISOTOPE 16... WHICH IS STORED AT FT. TYSON, A SCANT FEW MILES FROM HERE!
BUT IT'S AN ARMY POST! HOW CAN YOU HOPE TO GET IN THERE?
I? I DON'T HOPE TO!
YOU'RE GOING TO DO IT FOR ME!
AND YOU'LL DO IT NOW!
WHY DO I FEEL THIS STRANGE SENSATION... THIS SUDDEN TINGLING... ALL THROUGH MY BODY!
IT'S LIKE A BUILT-IN WARNING OF SOME SORT...
... BUT, A WARNING OF.. WHAT??
DON'T JUST STAND THERE WHEN I GIVE YOU AN ORDER!
AND ANOTHER THING... BEFORE YOU GO, TAKE THAT MORONIC MASK OFF!
I WANT TO SEE WHO YOU ARE!
YOU MEAN... YOU DON'T KNOW?!!
I WAS A FOOL! THAT WAS MY FIRST MISTAKE! NOW I'VE AROUSED HIS SUSPICIONS!
I'D LIKE TO KNOW WHO I REALLY AM, TOO!
BUT... IF YOU DON'T KNOW MY IDENTITY.. HOW CAN WE BE PARTNERS??
4.

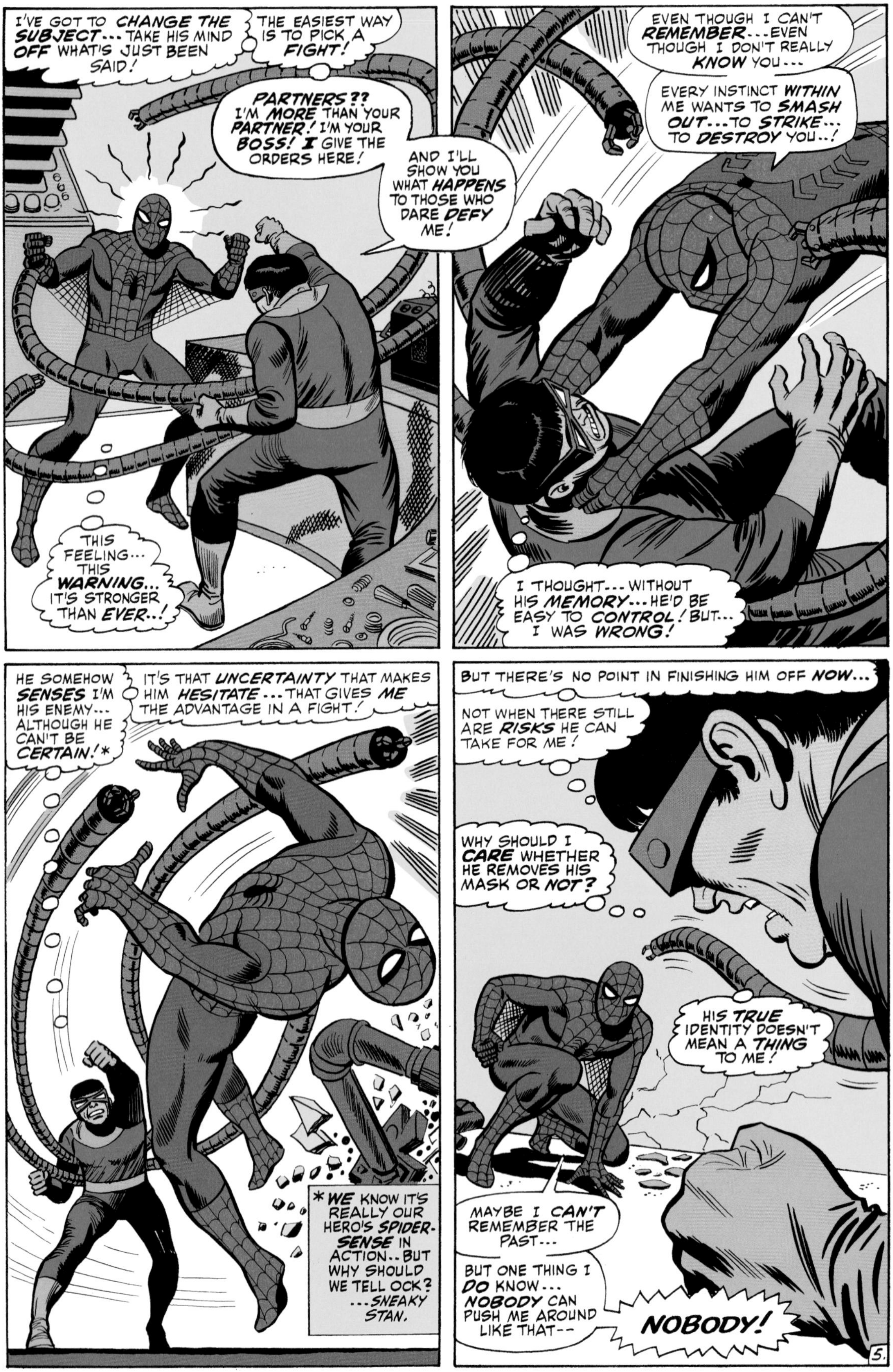
I'VE GOT TO CHANGE THE SUBJECT... TAKE HIS MIND OFF WHAT'S JUST BEEN SAID!
THE EASIEST WAY IS TO PICK A FIGHT!
PARTNERS?? I'M MORE THAN YOUR PARTNER! I'M YOUR BOSS! I GIVE THE ORDERS HERE!
AND I'LL SHOW YOU WHAT HAPPENS TO THOSE WHO DARE DEFY ME!
THIS FEELING... THIS WARNING... IT'S STRONGER THAN EVER..!
EVEN THOUGH I CAN'T REMEMBER... EVEN THOUGH I DON'T REALLY KNOW YOU...
EVERY INSTINCT WITHIN ME WANTS TO SMASH OUT... TO STRIKE... TO DESTROY YOU..!
I THOUGHT... WITHOUT HIS MEMORY... HE'D BE EASY TO CONTROL! BUT... I WAS WRONG!
HE SOMEHOW SENSES I'M HIS ENEMY... ALTHOUGH HE CAN'T BE CERTAIN!*
IT'S THAT UNCERTAINTY THAT MAKES HIM HESITATE... THAT GIVES ME THE ADVANTAGE IN A FIGHT!
*WE KNOW IT'S REALLY OUR HERO'S SPIDER-SENSE IN ACTION.. BUT WHY SHOULD WE TELL OCK? ...SNEAKY STAN.
BUT THERE'S NO POINT IN FINISHING HIM OFF NOW...
NOT WHEN THERE STILL ARE RISKS HE CAN TAKE FOR ME!
WHY SHOULD I CARE WHETHER HE REMOVES HIS MASK OR NOT?
HIS TRUE IDENTITY DOESN'T MEAN A THING TO ME!
MAYBE I CAN'T REMEMBER THE PAST...
BUT ONE THING I DO KNOW... NOBODY CAN PUSH ME AROUND LIKE THAT--
NOBODY!
5.

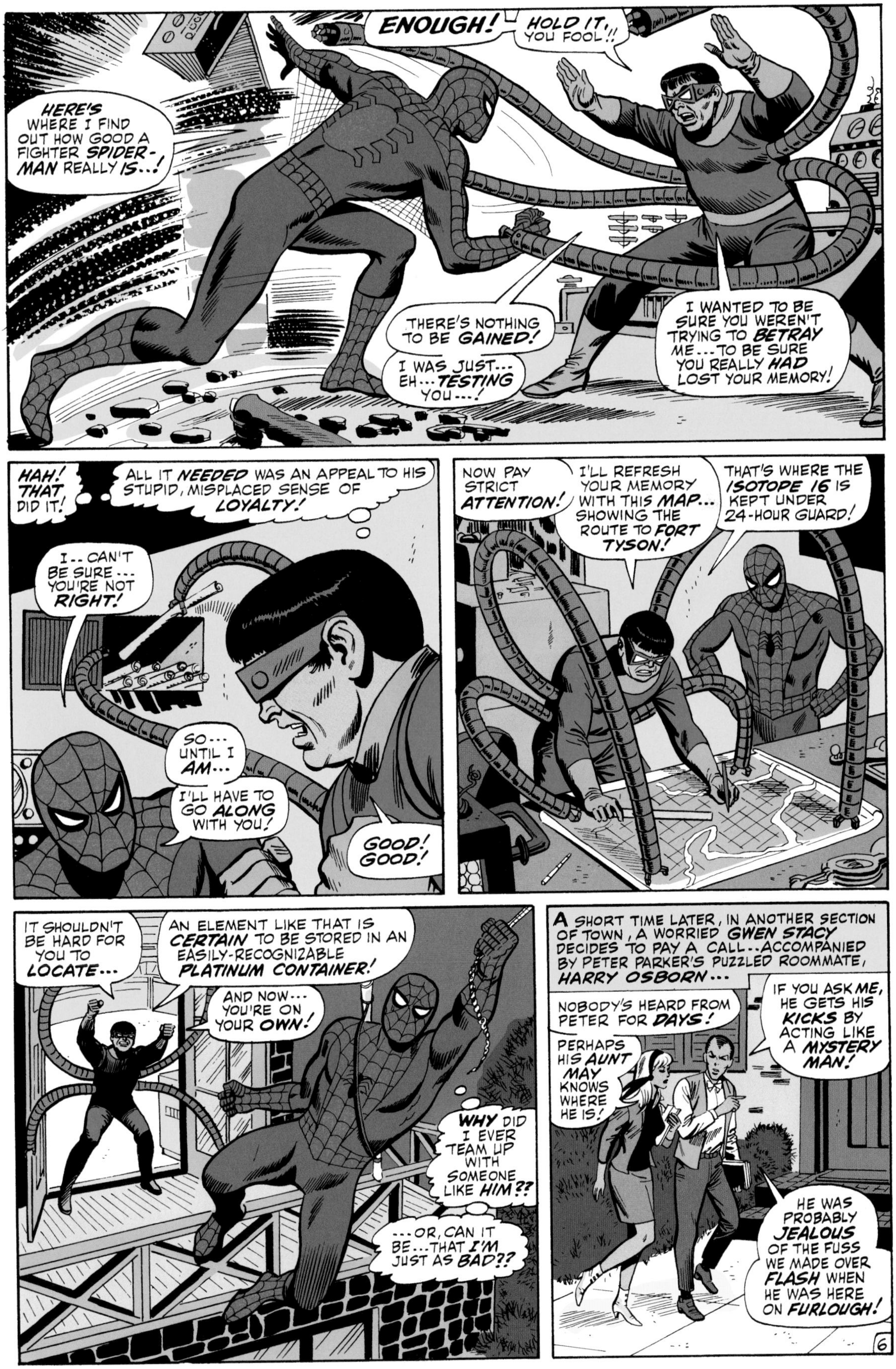
HERE'S WHERE I FIND OUT HOW GOOD A FIGHTER SPIDER-MAN REALLY IS..!
ENOUGH!
HOLD IT, YOU FOOL!!
THERE'S NOTHING TO BE GAINED!
I WAS JUST... EH...TESTING YOU...!
I WANTED TO BE SURE YOU WEREN'T TRYING TO BETRAY ME...TO BE SURE YOU REALLY HAD LOST YOUR MEMORY!
HAH! THAT DID IT!
ALL IT NEEDED WAS AN APPEAL TO HIS STUPID, MISPLACED SENSE OF LOYALTY!
I.. CAN'T BE SURE... YOU'RE NOT RIGHT!
SO... UNTIL I AM...
I'LL HAVE TO GO ALONG WITH YOU!
GOOD! GOOD!
NOW PAY STRICT ATTENTION!
I'LL REFRESH YOUR MEMORY WITH THIS MAP... SHOWING THE ROUTE TO FORT TYSON!
THAT'S WHERE THE ISOTOPE 16 IS KEPT UNDER 24-HOUR GUARD!
IT SHOULDN'T BE HARD FOR YOU TO LOCATE...
AN ELEMENT LIKE THAT IS CERTAIN TO BE STORED IN AN EASILY-RECOGNIZABLE PLATINUM CONTAINER!
AND NOW... YOU'RE ON YOUR OWN!
WHY DID I EVER TEAM UP WITH SOMEONE LIKE HIM??
...OR, CAN IT BE...THAT I'M JUST AS BAD??
A SHORT TIME LATER, IN ANOTHER SECTION OF TOWN, A WORRIED GWEN STACY DECIDES TO PAY A CALL..ACCOMPANIED BY PETER PARKER'S PUZZLED ROOMMATE, HARRY OSBORN...
NOBODY'S HEARD FROM PETER FOR DAYS!
PERHAPS HIS AUNT MAY KNOWS WHERE HE IS!
IF YOU ASK ME, HE GETS HIS KICKS BY ACTING LIKE A MYSTERY MAN!
HE WAS PROBABLY JEALOUS OF THE FUSS WE MADE OVER FLASH WHEN HE WAS HERE ON FURLOUGH!
6

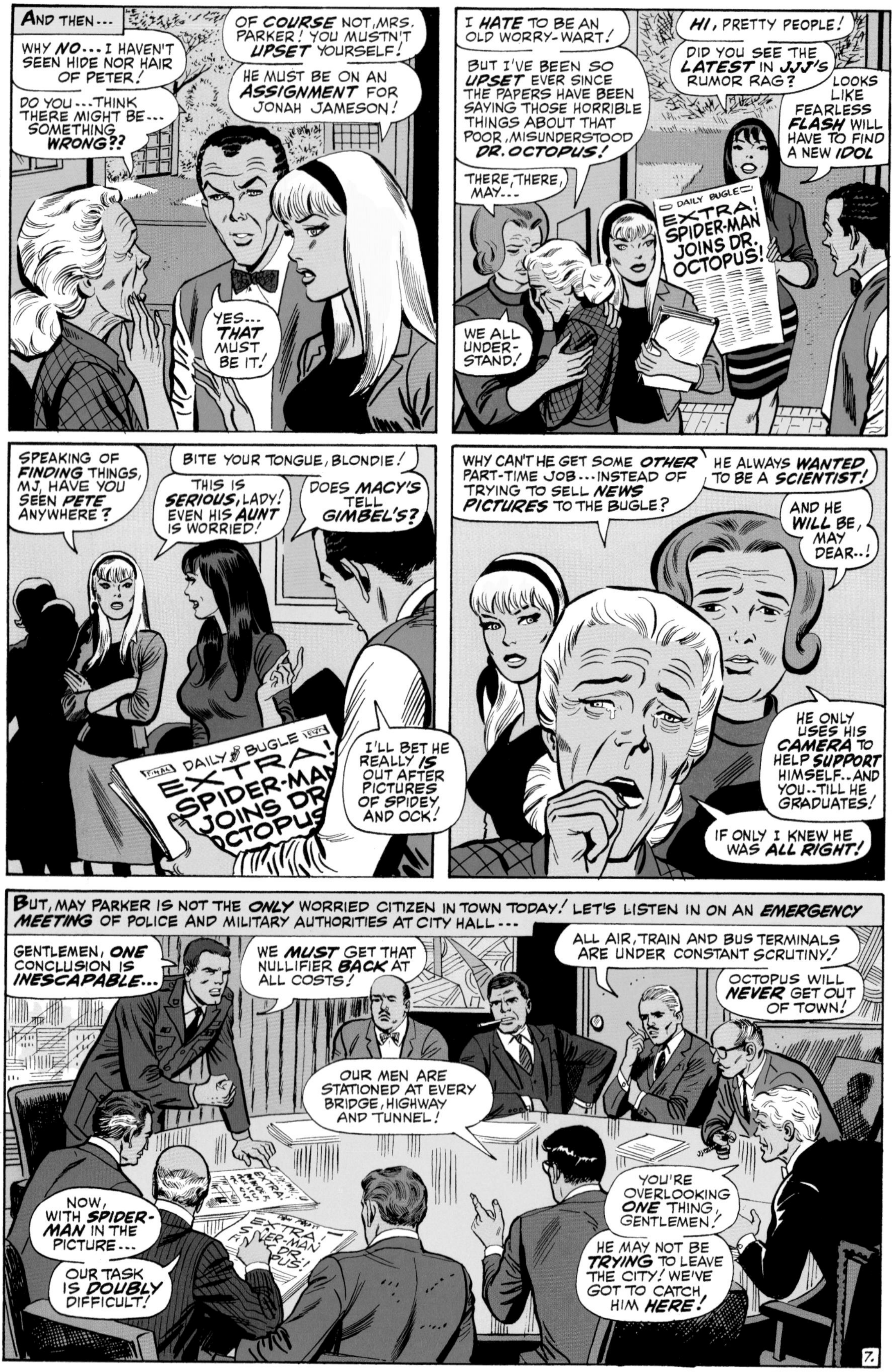
AND THEN...
WHY NO... I HAVEN'T SEEN HIDE NOR HAIR OF PETER!
DO YOU... THINK THERE MIGHT BE... SOMETHING WRONG??
OF COURSE NOT, MRS. PARKER! YOU MUSTN'T UPSET YOURSELF!
HE MUST BE ON AN ASSIGNMENT FOR JONAH JAMESON!
YES... THAT MUST BE IT!
I HATE TO BE AN OLD WORRY-WART!
BUT I'VE BEEN SO UPSET EVER SINCE THE PAPERS HAVE BEEN SAYING THOSE HORRIBLE THINGS ABOUT THAT POOR, MISUNDERSTOOD DR. OCTOPUS!
THERE, THERE, MAY...
WE ALL UNDERSTAND!
HI, PRETTY PEOPLE!
DID YOU SEE THE LATEST IN JJJ'S RUMOR RAG?
LOOKS LIKE FEARLESS FLASH WILL HAVE TO FIND A NEW IDOL
DAILY BUGLE EXTRA! SPIDER-MAN JOINS DR. OCTOPUS!
SPEAKING OF FINDING THINGS, MJ, HAVE YOU SEEN PETE ANYWHERE?
BITE YOUR TONGUE, BLONDIE!
THIS IS SERIOUS, LADY! EVEN HIS AUNT IS WORRIED!
DOES MACY'S TELL GIMBEL'S?
FINAL DAILY BUGLE EXTRA! SPIDER-MAN JOINS DR. OCTOPUS
I'LL BET HE REALLY IS OUT AFTER PICTURES OF SPIDEY AND OCK!
WHY CAN'T HE GET SOME OTHER PART-TIME JOB... INSTEAD OF TRYING TO SELL NEWS PICTURES TO THE BUGLE?
HE ALWAYS WANTED TO BE A SCIENTIST!
AND HE WILL BE, MAY DEAR..!
HE ONLY USES HIS CAMERA TO HELP SUPPORT HIMSELF.. AND YOU.. TILL HE GRADUATES!
IF ONLY I KNEW HE WAS ALL RIGHT!
BUT, MAY PARKER IS NOT THE ONLY WORRIED CITIZEN IN TOWN TODAY! LET'S LISTEN IN ON AN EMERGENCY MEETING OF POLICE AND MILITARY AUTHORITIES AT CITY HALL...
GENTLEMEN, ONE CONCLUSION IS INESCAPABLE...
WE MUST GET THAT NULLIFIER BACK AT ALL COSTS!
ALL AIR, TRAIN AND BUS TERMINALS ARE UNDER CONSTANT SCRUTINY!
OCTOPUS WILL NEVER GET OUT OF TOWN!
OUR MEN ARE STATIONED AT EVERY BRIDGE, HIGHWAY AND TUNNEL!
NOW, WITH SPIDER-MAN IN THE PICTURE...
OUR TASK IS DOUBLY DIFFICULT!
YOU'RE OVERLOOKING ONE THING, GENTLEMEN!
HE MAY NOT BE TRYING TO LEAVE THE CITY! WE'VE GOT TO CATCH HIM HERE!
7.

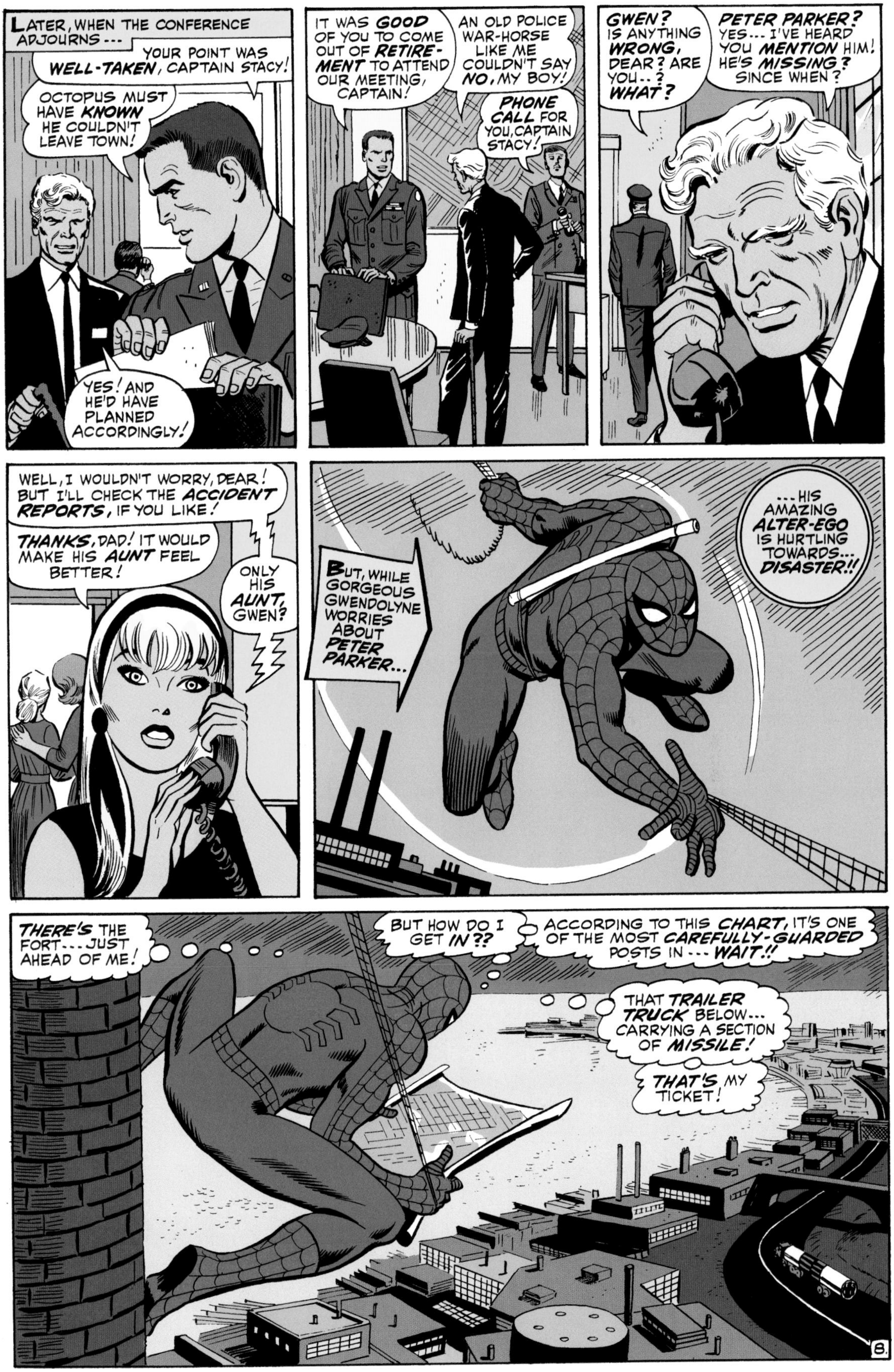
LATER, WHEN THE CONFERENCE ADJOURNS ---
YOUR POINT WAS WELL-TAKEN, CAPTAIN STACY!
OCTOPUS MUST HAVE KNOWN HE COULDN'T LEAVE TOWN!
YES! AND HE'D HAVE PLANNED ACCORDINGLY!
IT WAS GOOD OF YOU TO COME OUT OF RETIREMENT TO ATTEND OUR MEETING, CAPTAIN!
AN OLD POLICE WAR-HORSE LIKE ME COULDN'T SAY NO, MY BOY!
PHONE CALL FOR YOU, CAPTAIN STACY!
GWEN? IS ANYTHING WRONG, DEAR? ARE YOU--? WHAT?
PETER PARKER? YES--- I'VE HEARD YOU MENTION HIM! HE'S MISSING? SINCE WHEN?
WELL, I WOULDN'T WORRY, DEAR! BUT I'LL CHECK THE ACCIDENT REPORTS, IF YOU LIKE!
THANKS, DAD! IT WOULD MAKE HIS AUNT FEEL BETTER!
ONLY HIS AUNT, GWEN?
BUT, WHILE GORGEOUS GWENDOLYNE WORRIES ABOUT PETER PARKER...
...HIS AMAZING ALTER-EGO IS HURTLING TOWARDS... DISASTER!!
THERE'S THE FORT--- JUST AHEAD OF ME!
BUT HOW DO I GET IN??
ACCORDING TO THIS CHART, IT'S ONE OF THE MOST CAREFULLY-GUARDED POSTS IN --- WAIT!!
THAT TRAILER TRUCK BELOW... CARRYING A SECTION OF MISSILE!
THAT'S MY TICKET!
8

I *STILL* DON'T FEEL RIGHT ABOUT INVADING A MILITARY POST...!

BUT, UNTIL I GET MY *MEMORY* BACK...I'VE GOT TO SEE THIS THROUGH!

I DON'T EVEN DARE *THINK* OF WHAT WOULD HAPPEN ---

...IF MY MEMORY SOMEHOW *NEVER* RETURNS!

THE ONLY THING I CAN'T *UNDERSTAND* IS ---

IF I REALLY *AM* A CRIMINAL... WHY IS THIS SO *DISTASTEFUL* TO ME ??

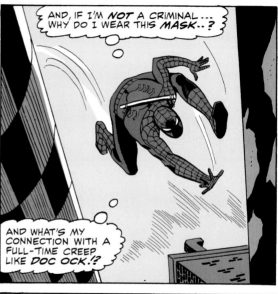

AND, IF I'M *NOT* A CRIMINAL... WHY DO I WEAR THIS *MASK*..?

AND WHAT'S MY CONNECTION WITH A FULL-TIME CREEP LIKE *DOC OCK*.!?

BUT I'D BETTER *FORGET* ABOUT THAT NOW!

AT LEAST-- UNTIL THE *JOB* IS DONE!

THAT *VENT* BELOW IS JUST WHAT I NEED!

WOW! I'M *LIFTING* IT LIKE IT'S *NOTHING!*

SURE WISH I COULD REMEMBER HOW I *GOT* MY POWERS!

9.

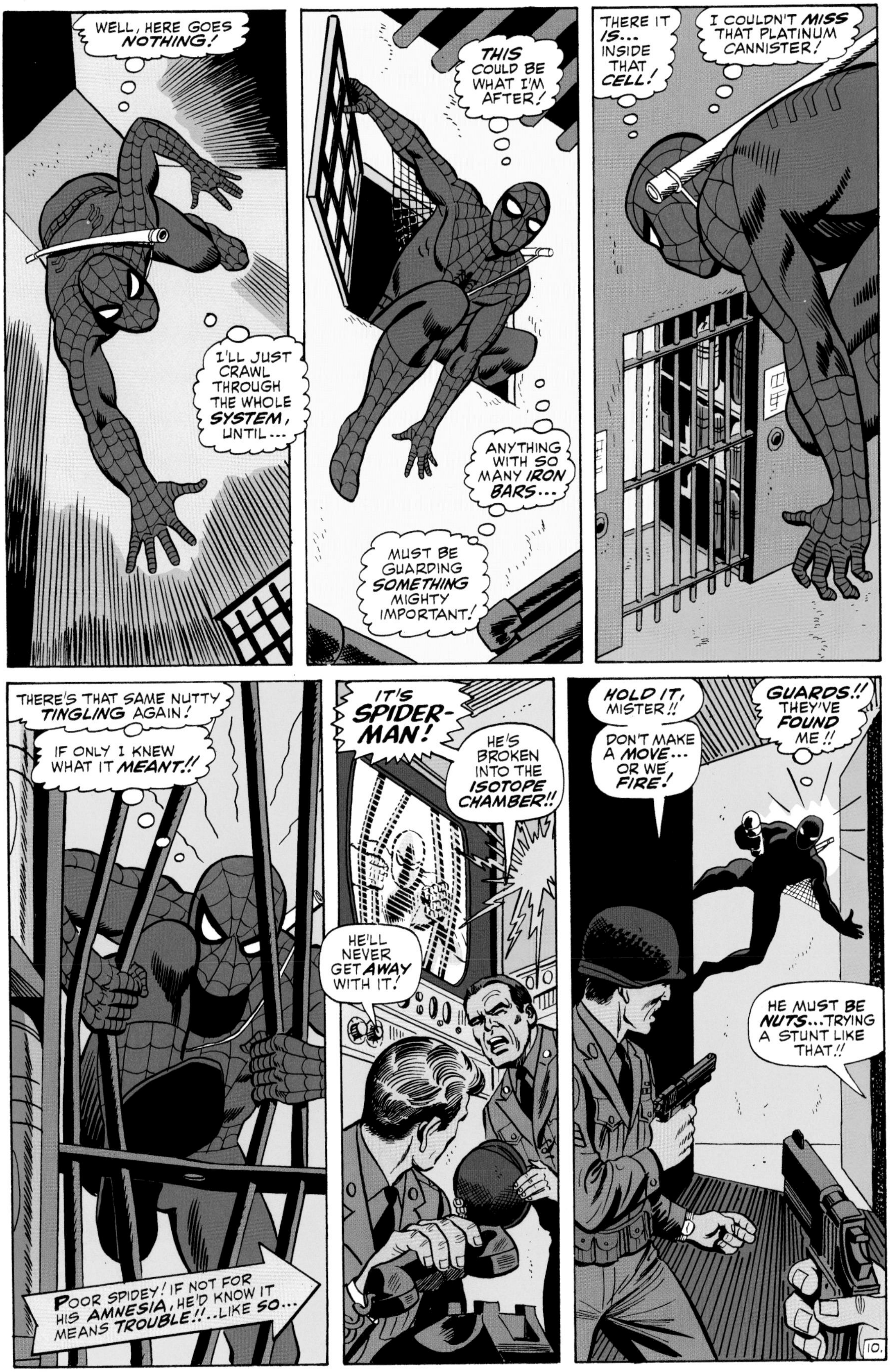
WELL, HERE GOES NOTHING!
I'LL JUST CRAWL THROUGH THE WHOLE SYSTEM, UNTIL...
THIS COULD BE WHAT I'M AFTER!
ANYTHING WITH SO MANY IRON BARS...
MUST BE GUARDING SOMETHING MIGHTY IMPORTANT!
THERE IT IS... INSIDE THAT CELL!
I COULDN'T MISS THAT PLATINUM CANNISTER!
THERE'S THAT SAME NUTTY TINGLING AGAIN!
IF ONLY I KNEW WHAT IT MEANT!!
POOR SPIDEY! IF NOT FOR HIS AMNESIA, HE'D KNOW IT MEANS TROUBLE!!..LIKE SO...
IT'S SPIDER-MAN!
HE'S BROKEN INTO THE ISOTOPE CHAMBER!!
HE'LL NEVER GET AWAY WITH IT!
HOLD IT, MISTER!!
DON'T MAKE A MOVE... OR WE FIRE!
GUARDS!! THEY'VE FOUND ME!!
HE MUST BE NUTS...TRYING A STUNT LIKE THAT!!
10.

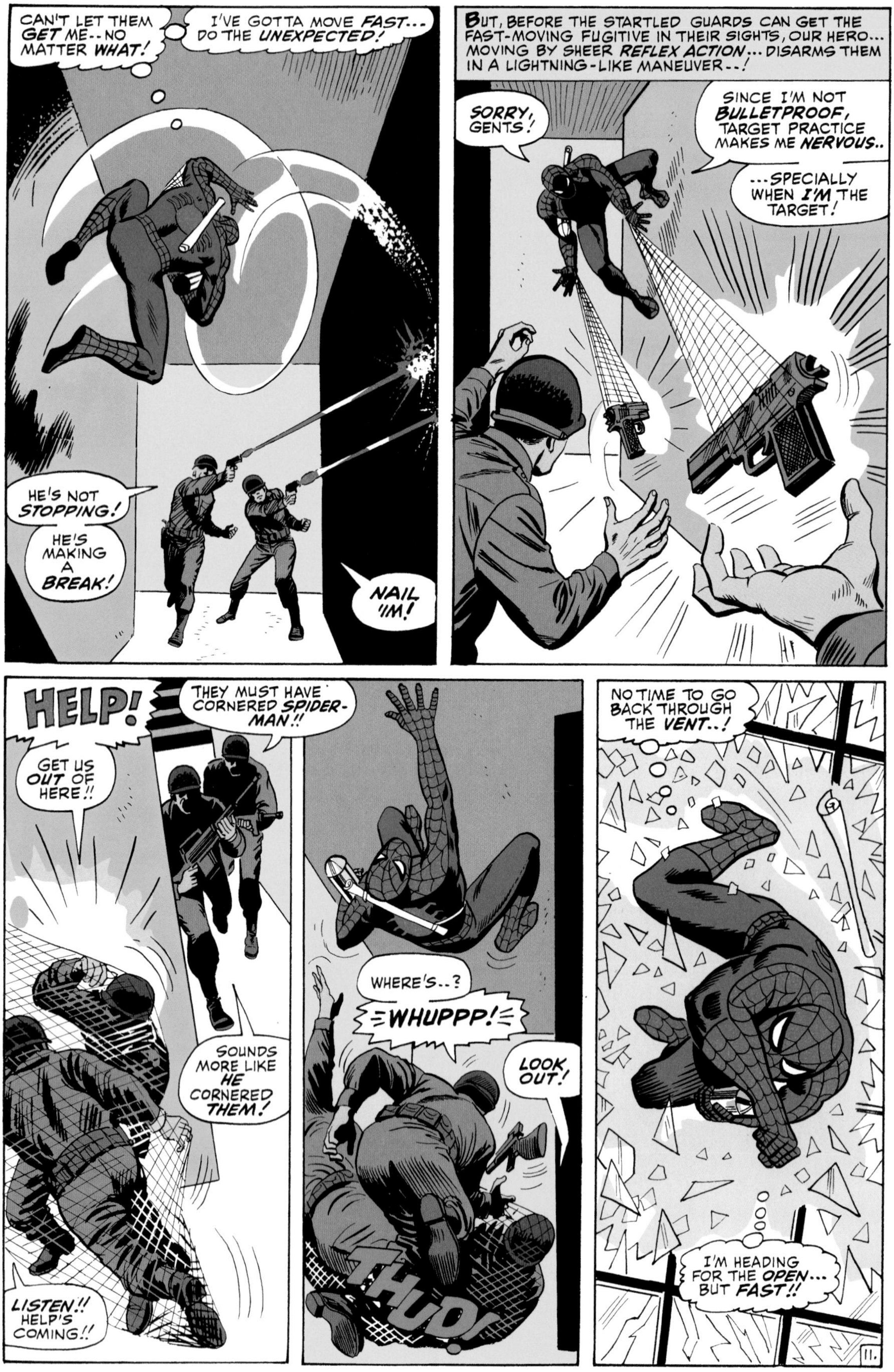
CAN'T LET THEM GET ME--NO MATTER WHAT!
I'VE GOTTA MOVE FAST... DO THE UNEXPECTED!
HE'S NOT STOPPING!
HE'S MAKING A BREAK!
NAIL 'IM!
BUT, BEFORE THE STARTLED GUARDS CAN GET THE FAST-MOVING FUGITIVE IN THEIR SIGHTS, OUR HERO... MOVING BY SHEER REFLEX ACTION... DISARMS THEM IN A LIGHTNING-LIKE MANEUVER--!
SORRY, GENTS!
SINCE I'M NOT BULLETPROOF, TARGET PRACTICE MAKES ME NERVOUS..
...SPECIALLY WHEN I'M THE TARGET!
HELP!
GET US OUT OF HERE!!
LISTEN!! HELP'S COMING!!
THEY MUST HAVE CORNERED SPIDER-MAN!!
SOUNDS MORE LIKE HE CORNERED THEM!
WHERE'S..?
WHUPPP!
LOOK OUT!
THUD!
NO TIME TO GO BACK THROUGH THE VENT..!
I'M HEADING FOR THE OPEN... BUT FAST!!
11.

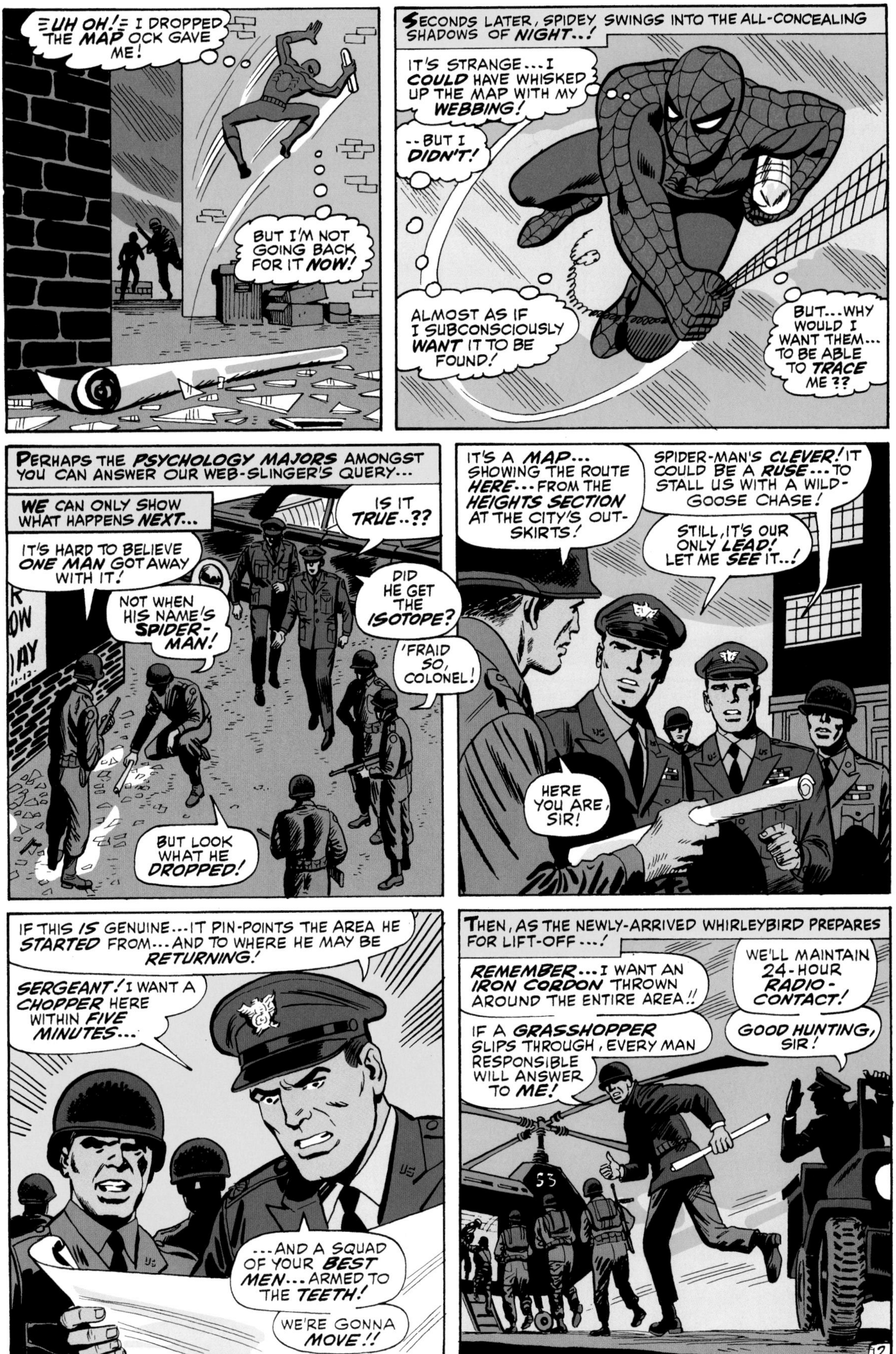
UH OH! I DROPPED THE MAP OCK GAVE ME!
BUT I'M NOT GOING BACK FOR IT NOW!
SECONDS LATER, SPIDEY SWINGS INTO THE ALL-CONCEALING SHADOWS OF NIGHT..!
IT'S STRANGE... I COULD HAVE WHISKED UP THE MAP WITH MY WEBBING!
--BUT I DIDN'T!
ALMOST AS IF I SUBCONSCIOUSLY WANT IT TO BE FOUND!
BUT...WHY WOULD I WANT THEM... TO BE ABLE TO TRACE ME??
PERHAPS THE PSYCHOLOGY MAJORS AMONGST YOU CAN ANSWER OUR WEB-SLINGER'S QUERY...
WE CAN ONLY SHOW WHAT HAPPENS NEXT...
IT'S HARD TO BELIEVE ONE MAN GOT AWAY WITH IT!
NOT WHEN HIS NAME'S SPIDER-MAN!
IS IT TRUE..??
DID HE GET THE ISOTOPE?
'FRAID SO, COLONEL!
BUT LOOK WHAT HE DROPPED!
IT'S A MAP... SHOWING THE ROUTE HERE... FROM THE HEIGHTS SECTION AT THE CITY'S OUT-SKIRTS!
SPIDER-MAN'S CLEVER! IT COULD BE A RUSE... TO STALL US WITH A WILD-GOOSE CHASE!
STILL, IT'S OUR ONLY LEAD! LET ME SEE IT...!
HERE YOU ARE, SIR!
IF THIS IS GENUINE... IT PIN-POINTS THE AREA HE STARTED FROM... AND TO WHERE HE MAY BE RETURNING!
SERGEANT! I WANT A CHOPPER HERE WITHIN FIVE MINUTES...
...AND A SQUAD OF YOUR BEST MEN... ARMED TO THE TEETH!
WE'RE GONNA MOVE!!
THEN, AS THE NEWLY-ARRIVED WHIRLEYBIRD PREPARES FOR LIFT-OFF...!
REMEMBER... I WANT AN IRON CORDON THROWN AROUND THE ENTIRE AREA!!
IF A GRASSHOPPER SLIPS THROUGH, EVERY MAN RESPONSIBLE WILL ANSWER TO ME!
WE'LL MAINTAIN 24-HOUR RADIO-CONTACT!
GOOD HUNTING, SIR!
53
12.

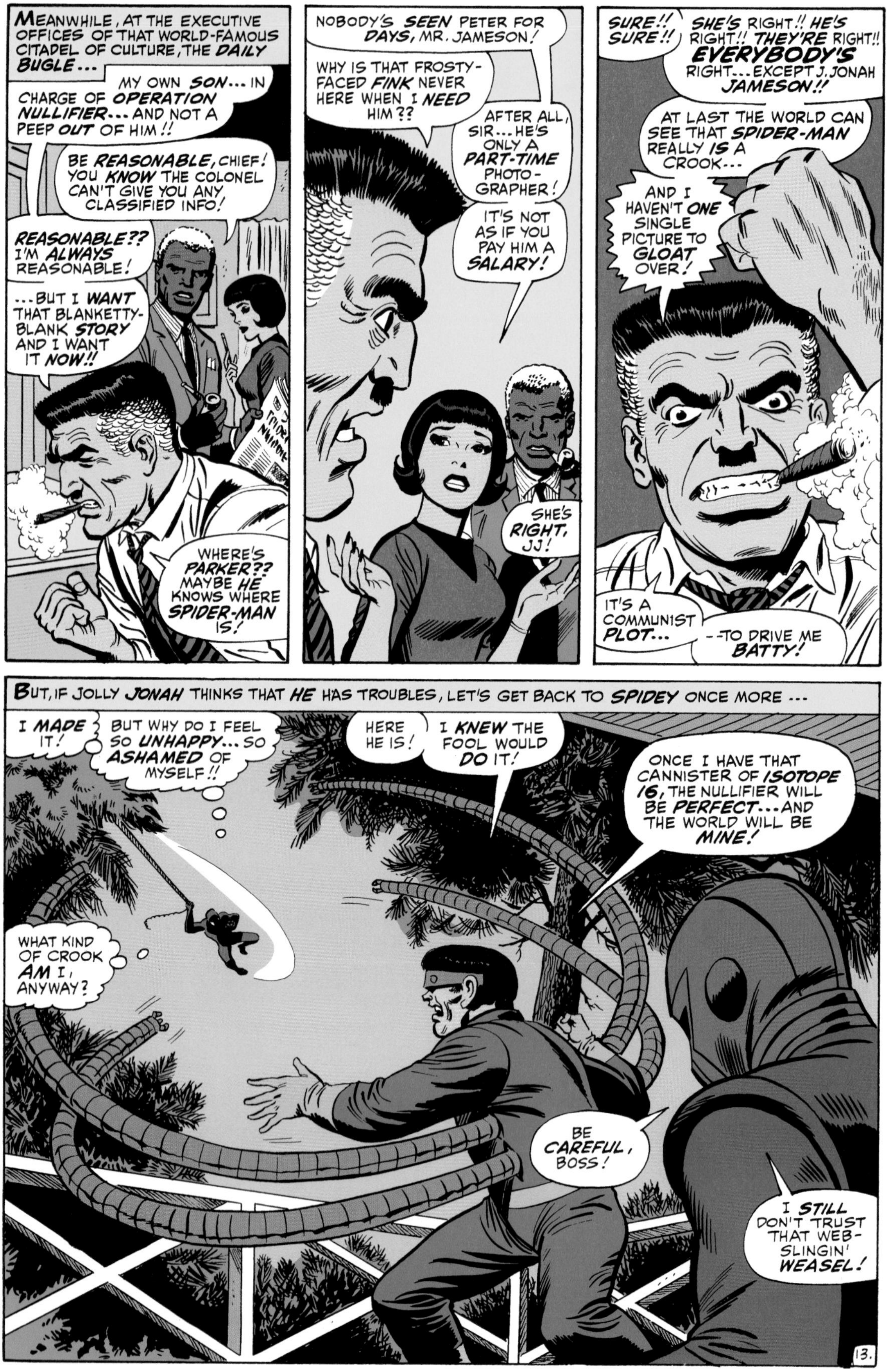

MEANWHILE, AT THE EXECUTIVE OFFICES OF THAT WORLD-FAMOUS CITADEL OF CULTURE, THE DAILY BUGLE...
MY OWN SON... IN CHARGE OF OPERATION NULLIFIER... AND NOT A PEEP OUT OF HIM!!
BE REASONABLE, CHIEF! YOU KNOW THE COLONEL CAN'T GIVE YOU ANY CLASSIFIED INFO!
REASONABLE?? I'M ALWAYS REASONABLE!
...BUT I WANT THAT BLANKETTY-BLANK STORY AND I WANT IT NOW!!
WHERE'S PARKER?? MAYBE HE KNOWS WHERE SPIDER-MAN IS!
NOBODY'S SEEN PETER FOR DAYS, MR. JAMESON!
WHY IS THAT FROSTY-FACED FINK NEVER HERE WHEN I NEED HIM??
AFTER ALL, SIR... HE'S ONLY A PART-TIME PHOTO-GRAPHER!
IT'S NOT AS IF YOU PAY HIM A SALARY!
SHE'S RIGHT, JJ!
SURE!! SURE!!
SHE'S RIGHT!! HE'S RIGHT!! THEY'RE RIGHT!! EVERYBODY'S RIGHT... EXCEPT J. JONAH JAMESON!!
AT LAST THE WORLD CAN SEE THAT SPIDER-MAN REALLY IS A CROOK...
AND I HAVEN'T ONE SINGLE PICTURE TO GLOAT OVER!
IT'S A COMMUNIST PLOT...
--TO DRIVE ME BATTY!
BUT, IF JOLLY JONAH THINKS THAT HE HAS TROUBLES, LET'S GET BACK TO SPIDEY ONCE MORE ---
I MADE IT!
BUT WHY DO I FEEL SO UNHAPPY... SO ASHAMED OF MYSELF!!
WHAT KIND OF CROOK AM I, ANYWAY?
HERE HE IS!
I KNEW THE FOOL WOULD DO IT!
ONCE I HAVE THAT CANNISTER OF ISOTOPE 16, THE NULLIFIER WILL BE PERFECT... AND THE WORLD WILL BE MINE!
BE CAREFUL, BOSS!
I STILL DON'T TRUST THAT WEB-SLINGIN' WEASEL!
13.

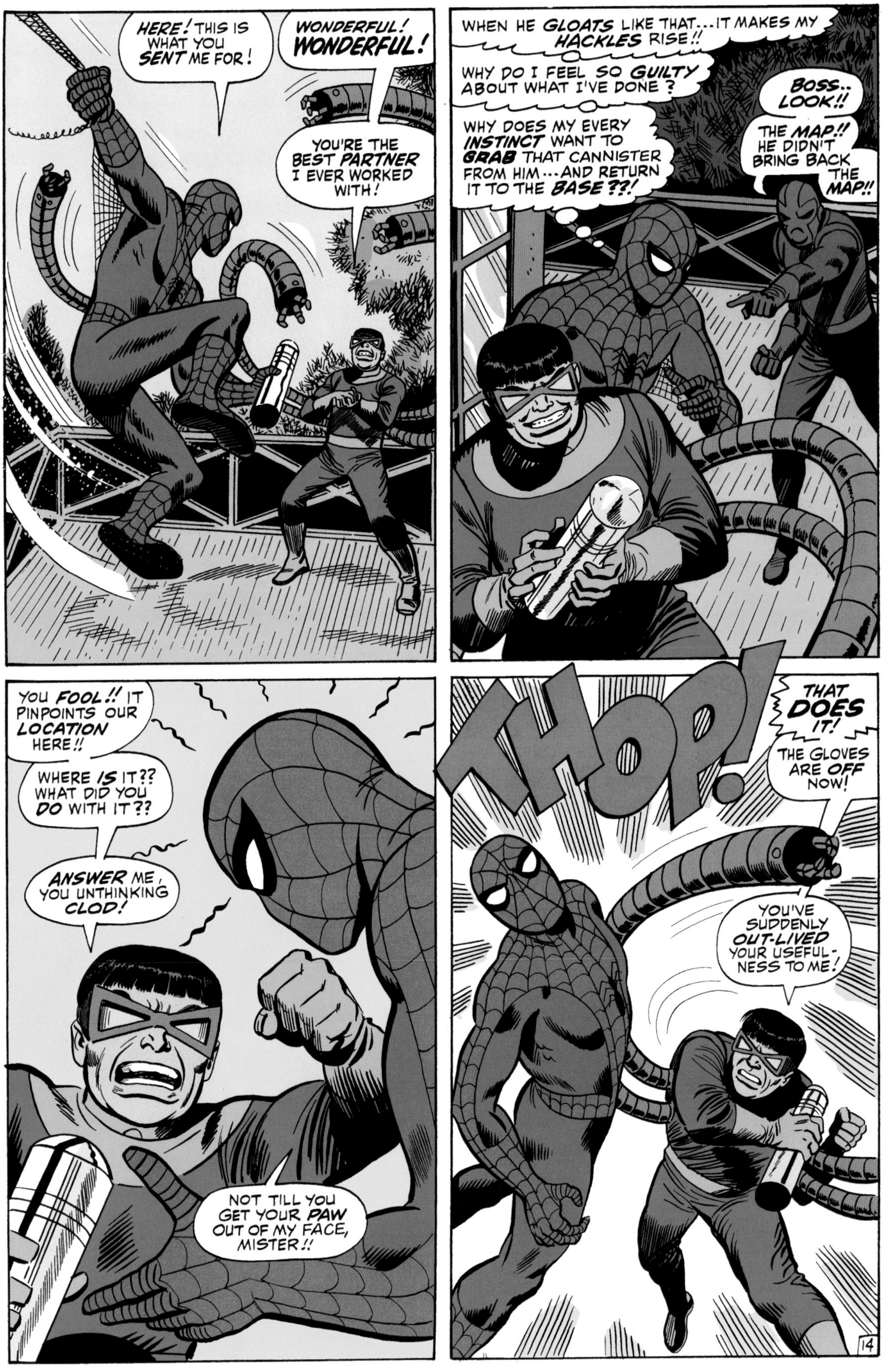
HERE! THIS IS WHAT YOU SENT ME FOR!
WONDERFUL! WONDERFUL!
YOU'RE THE BEST PARTNER I EVER WORKED WITH!
WHEN HE GLOATS LIKE THAT...IT MAKES MY HACKLES RISE!!
WHY DO I FEEL SO GUILTY ABOUT WHAT I'VE DONE?
WHY DOES MY EVERY INSTINCT WANT TO GRAB THAT CANNISTER FROM HIM...AND RETURN IT TO THE BASE??!
BOSS.. LOOK!!
THE MAP!! HE DIDN'T BRING BACK THE MAP!!
YOU FOOL!! IT PINPOINTS OUR LOCATION HERE!!
WHERE IS IT?? WHAT DID YOU DO WITH IT??
ANSWER ME, YOU UNTHINKING CLOD!
NOT TILL YOU GET YOUR PAW OUT OF MY FACE, MISTER!!
THOP!
THAT DOES IT!
THE GLOVES ARE OFF NOW!
YOU'VE SUDDENLY OUT-LIVED YOUR USEFUL-NESS TO ME!
14

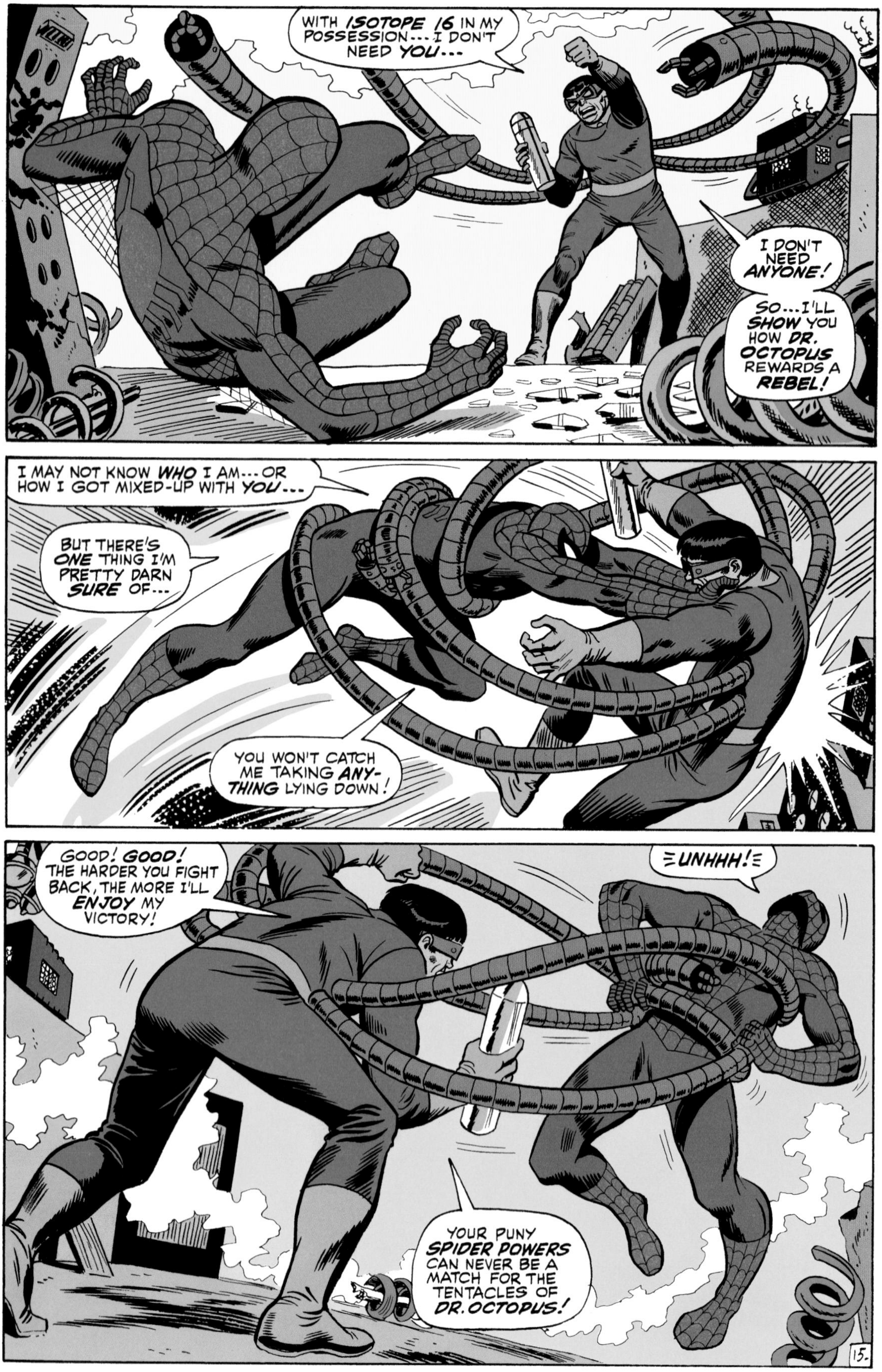

WITH ISOTOPE 16 IN MY POSSESSION... I DON'T NEED YOU...
I DON'T NEED ANYONE!
SO...I'LL SHOW YOU HOW DR. OCTOPUS REWARDS A REBEL!
I MAY NOT KNOW WHO I AM... OR HOW I GOT MIXED-UP WITH YOU...
BUT THERE'S ONE THING I'M PRETTY DARN SURE OF...
YOU WON'T CATCH ME TAKING ANY-THING LYING DOWN!
GOOD! GOOD! THE HARDER YOU FIGHT BACK, THE MORE I'LL ENJOY MY VICTORY!
UNHHH!
YOUR PUNY SPIDER POWERS CAN NEVER BE A MATCH FOR THE TENTACLES OF DR. OCTOPUS!
15.

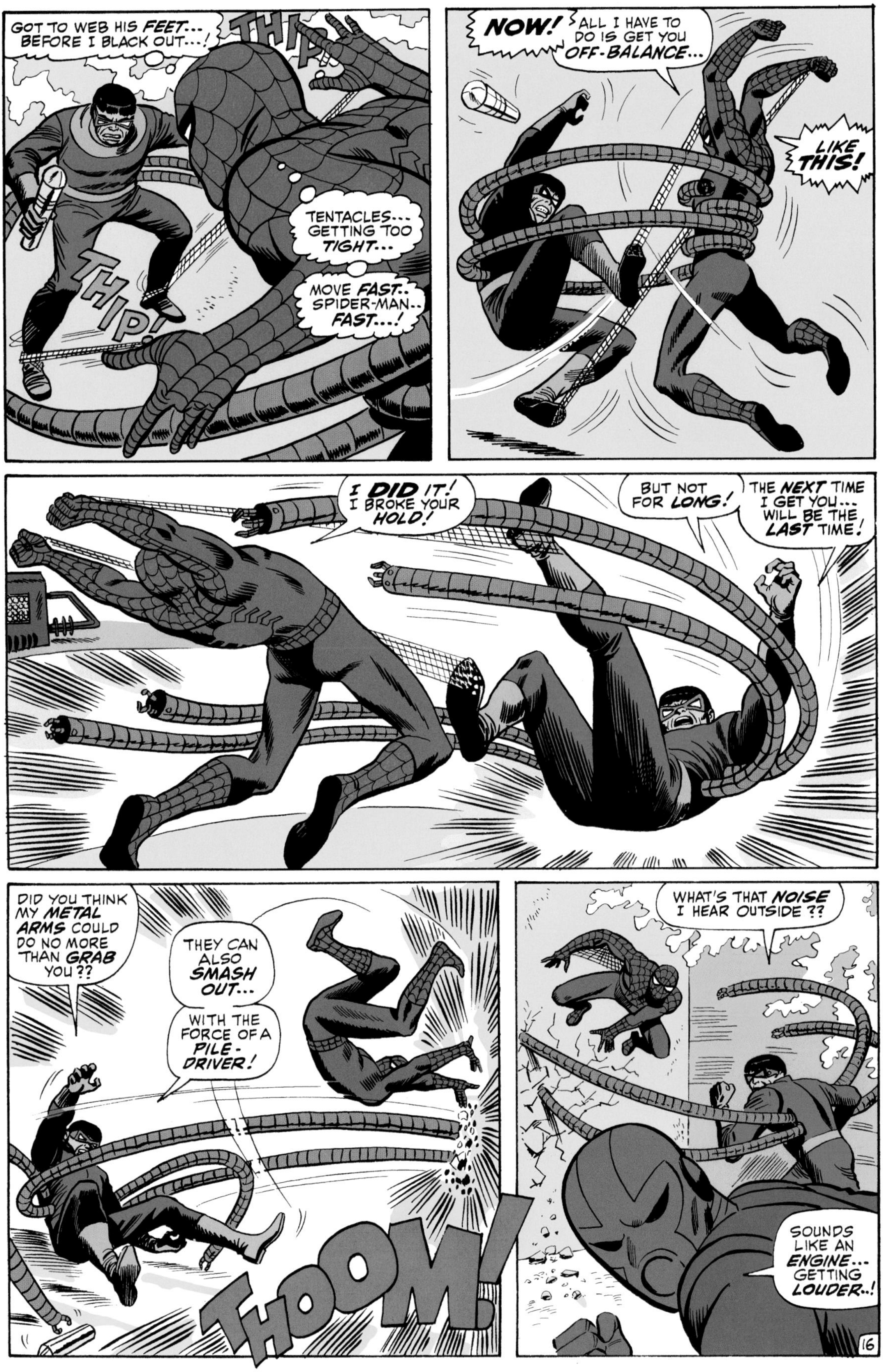
GOT TO WEB HIS FEET... BEFORE I BLACK OUT...!
THIP!
TENTACLES... GETTING TOO TIGHT...
MOVE FAST.. SPIDER-MAN.. FAST...!
THIP!
NOW!
ALL I HAVE TO DO IS GET YOU OFF-BALANCE...
LIKE THIS!
I DID IT! I BROKE YOUR HOLD!
BUT NOT FOR LONG!
THE NEXT TIME I GET YOU... WILL BE THE LAST TIME!
DID YOU THINK MY METAL ARMS COULD DO NO MORE THAN GRAB YOU??
THEY CAN ALSO SMASH OUT...
WITH THE FORCE OF A PILE-DRIVER!
THOOM!
WHAT'S THAT NOISE I HEAR OUTSIDE??
SOUNDS LIKE AN ENGINE... GETTING LOUDER..!
16

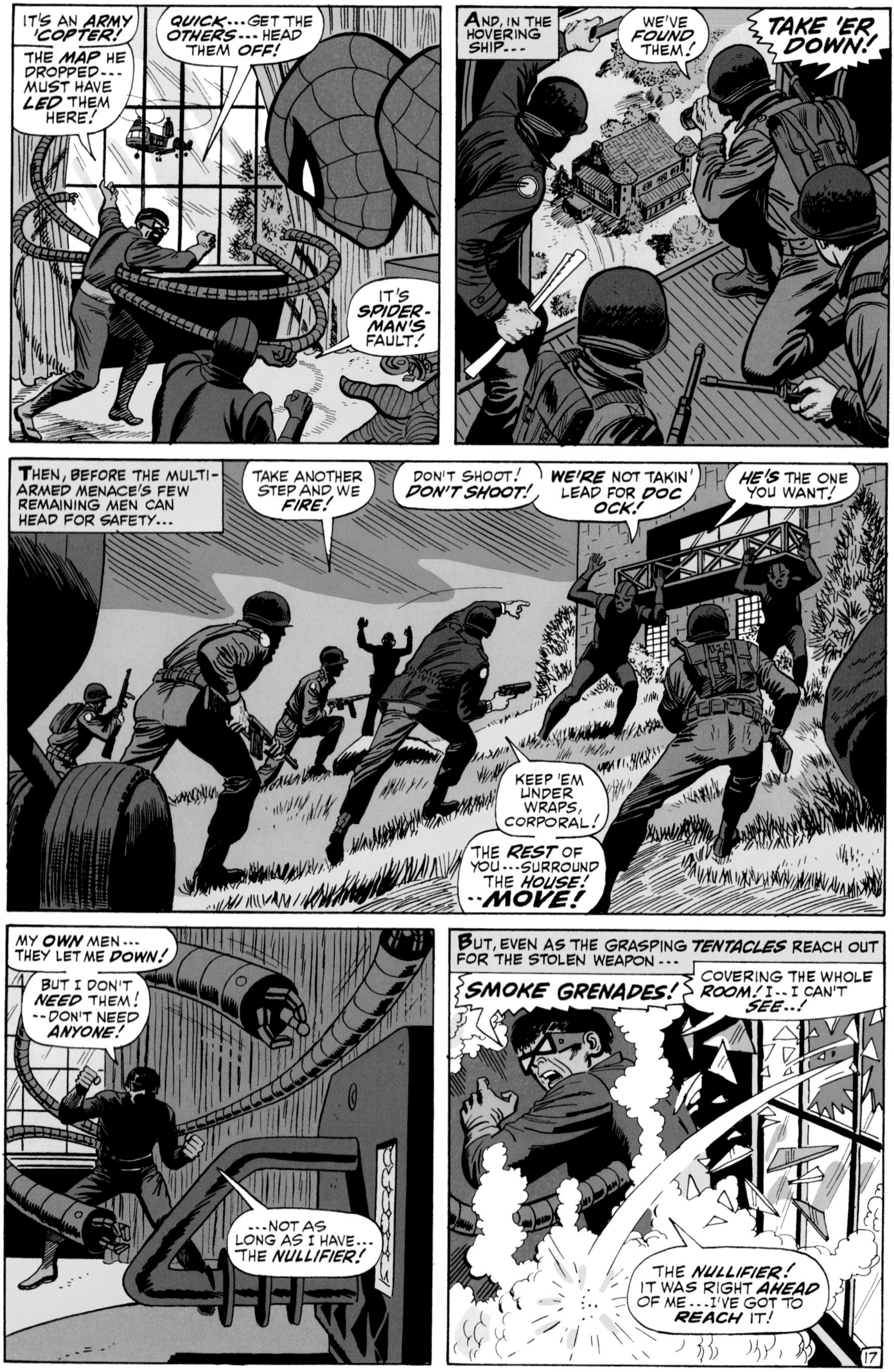
IT'S AN ARMY 'COPTER!
THE MAP HE DROPPED--- MUST HAVE LED THEM HERE!
QUICK---GET THE OTHERS--- HEAD THEM OFF!
IT'S SPIDER-MAN'S FAULT!
AND, IN THE HOVERING SHIP---
WE'VE FOUND THEM!
TAKE 'ER DOWN!
THEN, BEFORE THE MULTI-ARMED MENACE'S FEW REMAINING MEN CAN HEAD FOR SAFETY...
TAKE ANOTHER STEP AND WE FIRE!
DON'T SHOOT! DON'T SHOOT!
WE'RE NOT TAKIN' LEAD FOR DOC OCK!
HE'S THE ONE YOU WANT!
KEEP 'EM UNDER WRAPS, CORPORAL!
THE REST OF YOU---SURROUND THE HOUSE! --MOVE!
MY OWN MEN--- THEY LET ME DOWN!
BUT I DON'T NEED THEM! --DON'T NEED ANYONE!
---NOT AS LONG AS I HAVE--- THE NULLIFIER!
BUT, EVEN AS THE GRASPING TENTACLES REACH OUT FOR THE STOLEN WEAPON---
SMOKE GRENADES!
COVERING THE WHOLE ROOM! I--I CAN'T SEE--!
THE NULLIFIER! IT WAS RIGHT AHEAD OF ME---I'VE GOT TO REACH IT!
17

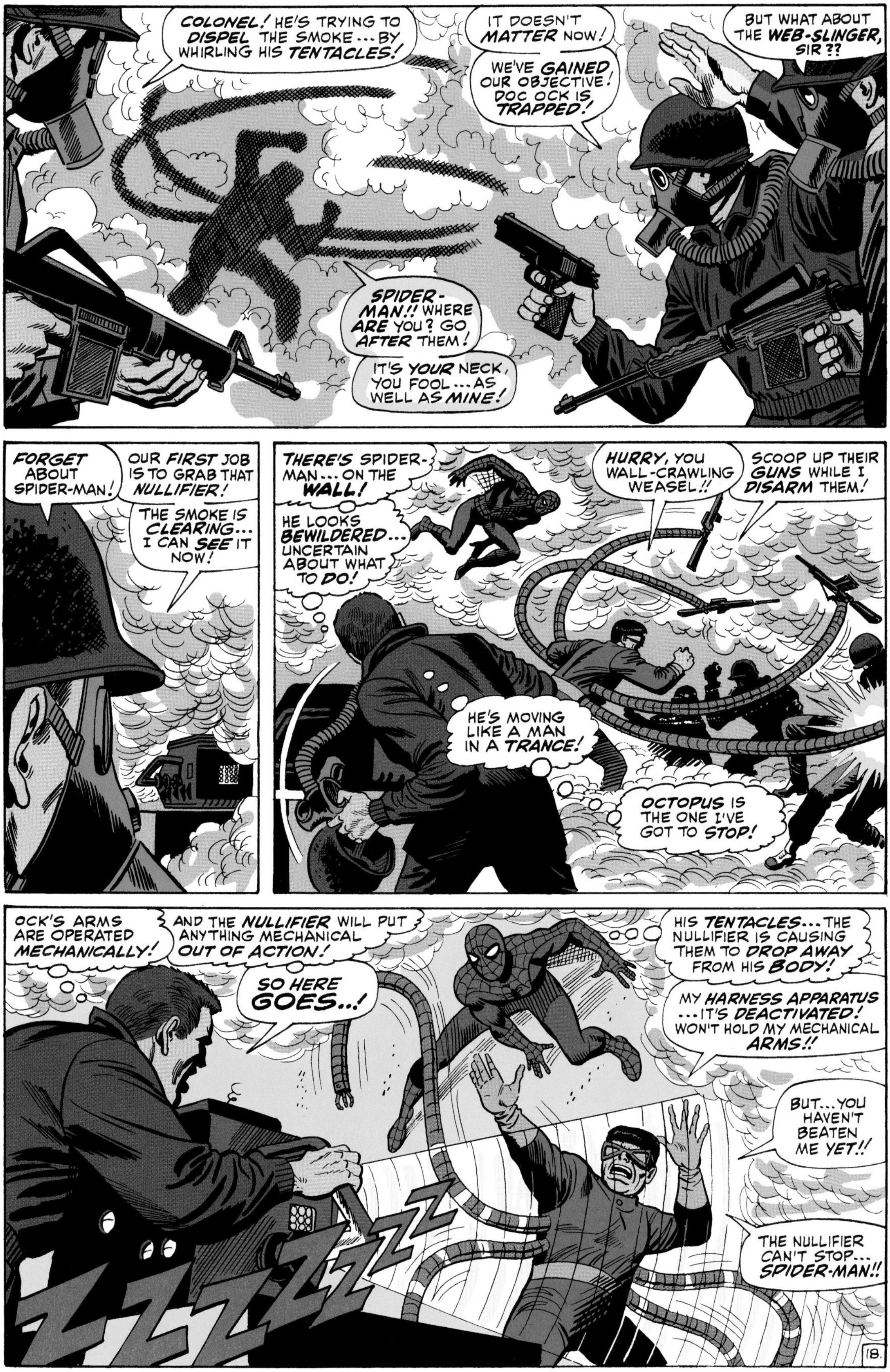
COLONEL! HE'S TRYING TO DISPEL THE SMOKE... BY WHIRLING HIS TENTACLES!
IT DOESN'T MATTER NOW!
WE'VE GAINED OUR OBJECTIVE! DOC OCK IS TRAPPED!
BUT WHAT ABOUT THE WEB-SLINGER, SIR??
SPIDER-MAN!! WHERE ARE YOU? GO AFTER THEM!
IT'S YOUR NECK, YOU FOOL... AS WELL AS MINE!
FORGET ABOUT SPIDER-MAN!
OUR FIRST JOB IS TO GRAB THAT NULLIFIER!
THE SMOKE IS CLEARING... I CAN SEE IT NOW!
THERE'S SPIDER-MAN... ON THE WALL!
HE LOOKS BEWILDERED... UNCERTAIN ABOUT WHAT TO DO!
HURRY, YOU WALL-CRAWLING WEASEL!!
SCOOP UP THEIR GUNS WHILE I DISARM THEM!
HE'S MOVING LIKE A MAN IN A TRANCE!
OCTOPUS IS THE ONE I'VE GOT TO STOP!
OCK'S ARMS ARE OPERATED MECHANICALLY!
AND THE NULLIFIER WILL PUT ANYTHING MECHANICAL OUT OF ACTION!
SO HERE GOES...!
HIS TENTACLES... THE NULLIFIER IS CAUSING THEM TO DROP AWAY FROM HIS BODY!
MY HARNESS APPARATUS... IT'S DEACTIVATED! WON'T HOLD MY MECHANICAL ARMS!!
BUT... YOU HAVEN'T BEATEN ME YET!!
THE NULLIFIER CAN'T STOP... SPIDER-MAN!!
ZZZZZZZZ
18.

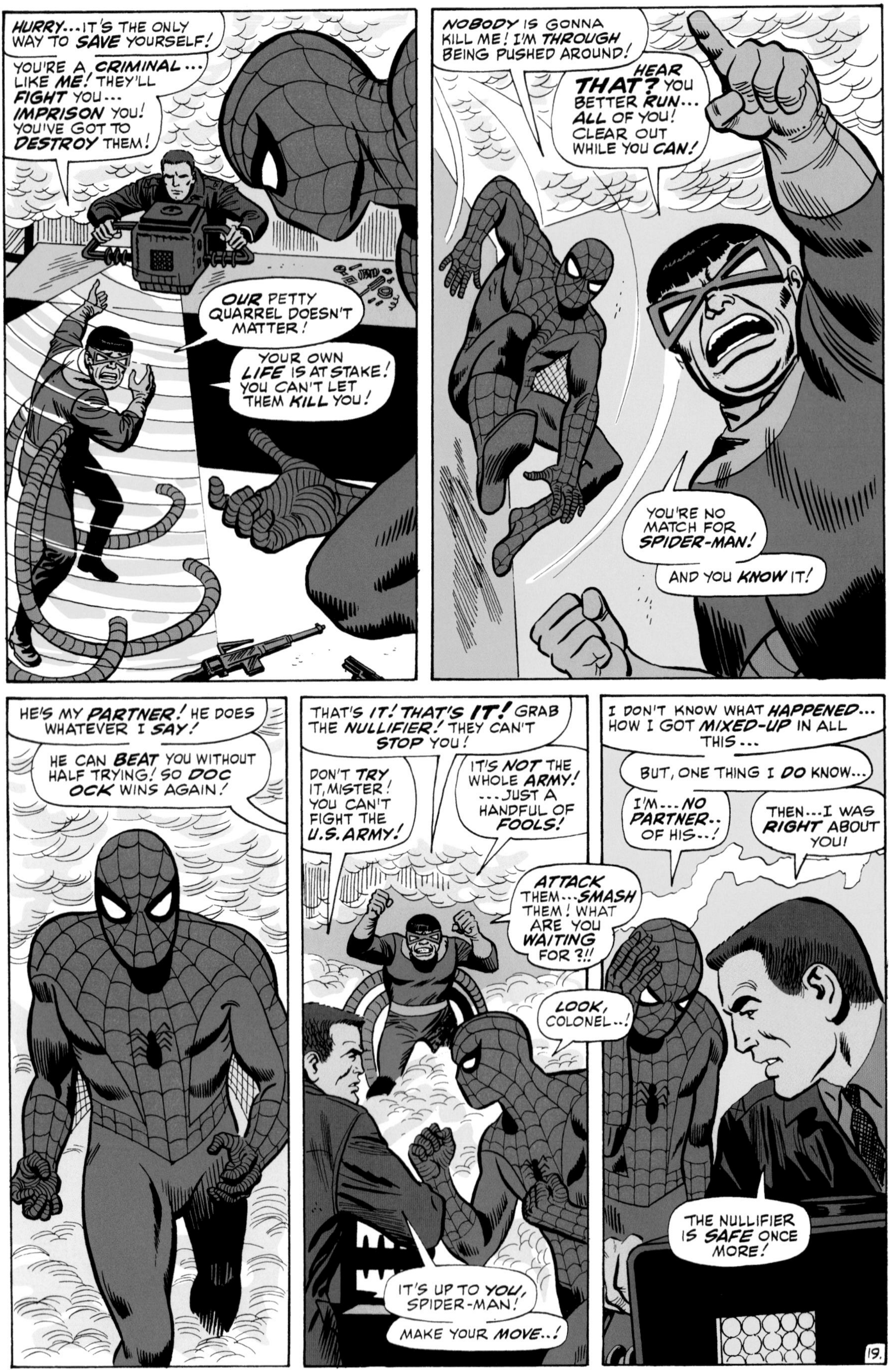

HURRY...IT'S THE ONLY WAY TO SAVE YOURSELF!
YOU'RE A CRIMINAL... LIKE ME! THEY'LL FIGHT YOU... IMPRISON YOU! YOU'VE GOT TO DESTROY THEM!
OUR PETTY QUARREL DOESN'T MATTER!
YOUR OWN LIFE IS AT STAKE! YOU CAN'T LET THEM KILL YOU!
NOBODY IS GONNA KILL ME! I'M THROUGH BEING PUSHED AROUND!
HEAR THAT? YOU BETTER RUN... ALL OF YOU! CLEAR OUT WHILE YOU CAN!
YOU'RE NO MATCH FOR SPIDER-MAN!
AND YOU KNOW IT!
HE'S MY PARTNER! HE DOES WHATEVER I SAY!
HE CAN BEAT YOU WITHOUT HALF TRYING! SO DOC OCK WINS AGAIN!
THAT'S IT! THAT'S IT! GRAB THE NULLIFIER! THEY CAN'T STOP YOU!
DON'T TRY IT, MISTER! YOU CAN'T FIGHT THE U.S. ARMY!
IT'S NOT THE WHOLE ARMY! ...JUST A HANDFUL OF FOOLS!
ATTACK THEM...SMASH THEM! WHAT ARE YOU WAITING FOR?!!
LOOK, COLONEL..!
IT'S UP TO YOU, SPIDER-MAN!
MAKE YOUR MOVE..!
I DON'T KNOW WHAT HAPPENED... HOW I GOT MIXED-UP IN ALL THIS...
BUT, ONE THING I DO KNOW...
I'M...NO PARTNER.. OF HIS..!
THEN...I WAS RIGHT ABOUT YOU!
THE NULLIFIER IS SAFE ONCE MORE!
19.

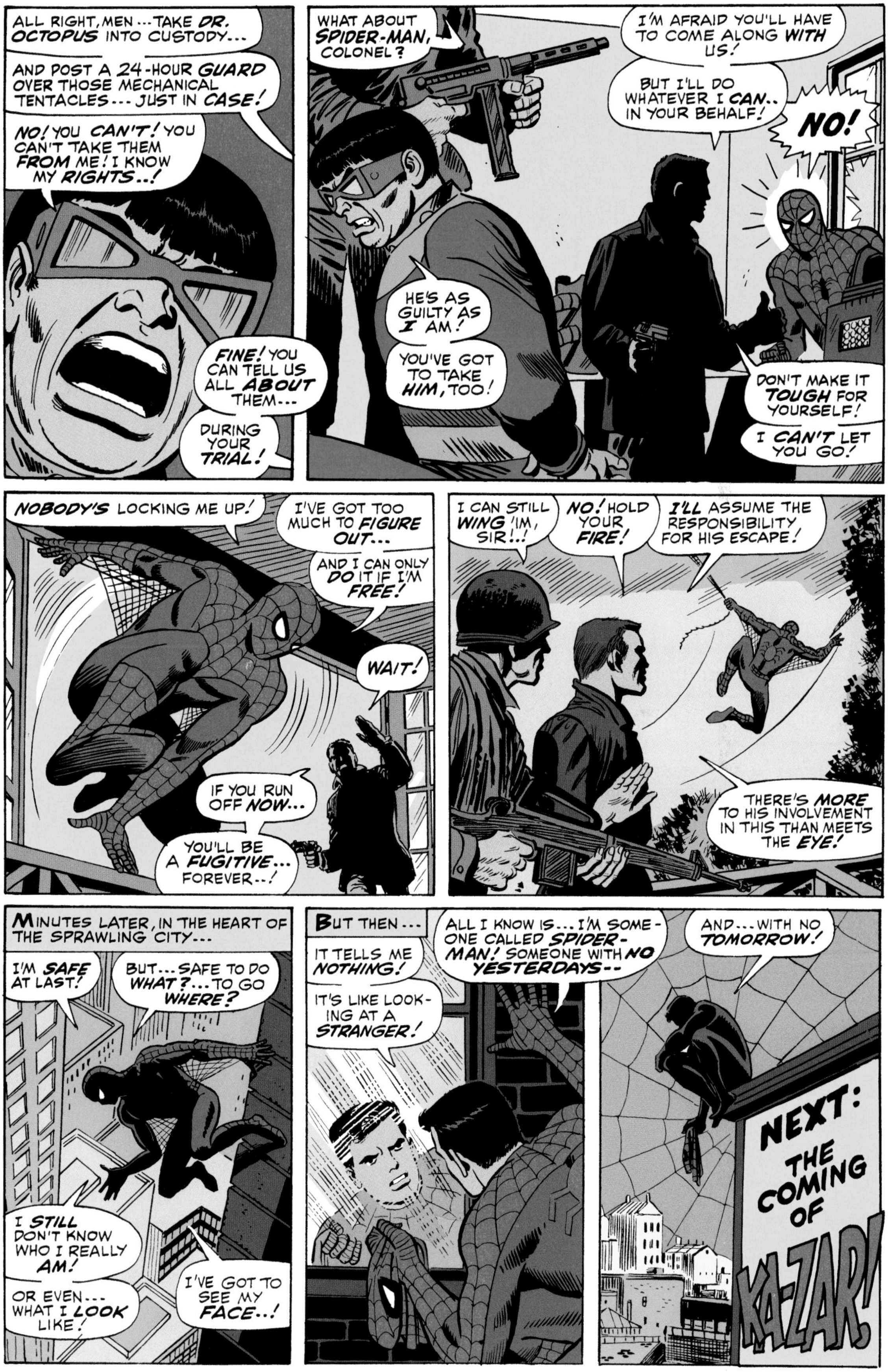
ALL RIGHT, MEN ... TAKE DR. OCTOPUS INTO CUSTODY...
AND POST A 24-HOUR GUARD OVER THOSE MECHANICAL TENTACLES... JUST IN CASE!
NO! YOU CAN'T! YOU CAN'T TAKE THEM FROM ME! I KNOW MY RIGHTS..!
FINE! YOU CAN TELL US ALL ABOUT THEM...
DURING YOUR TRIAL!
WHAT ABOUT SPIDER-MAN, COLONEL?
HE'S AS GUILTY AS I AM!
YOU'VE GOT TO TAKE HIM, TOO!
I'M AFRAID YOU'LL HAVE TO COME ALONG WITH US!
BUT I'LL DO WHATEVER I CAN.. IN YOUR BEHALF!
NO!
DON'T MAKE IT TOUGH FOR YOURSELF!
I CAN'T LET YOU GO!
NOBODY'S LOCKING ME UP!
I'VE GOT TOO MUCH TO FIGURE OUT...
AND I CAN ONLY DO IT IF I'M FREE!
WAIT!
IF YOU RUN OFF NOW...
YOU'LL BE A FUGITIVE... FOREVER..!
I CAN STILL WING 'IM, SIR..!
NO! HOLD YOUR FIRE!
I'LL ASSUME THE RESPONSIBILITY FOR HIS ESCAPE!
THERE'S MORE TO HIS INVOLVEMENT IN THIS THAN MEETS THE EYE!
MINUTES LATER, IN THE HEART OF THE SPRAWLING CITY...
I'M SAFE AT LAST!
BUT... SAFE TO DO WHAT?... TO GO WHERE?
I STILL DON'T KNOW WHO I REALLY AM!
OR EVEN... WHAT I LOOK LIKE!
I'VE GOT TO SEE MY FACE..!
BUT THEN...
IT TELLS ME NOTHING!
IT'S LIKE LOOKING AT A STRANGER!
ALL I KNOW IS... I'M SOMEONE CALLED SPIDER-MAN! SOMEONE WITH NO YESTERDAYS--
AND... WITH NO TOMORROW!
NEXT: THE COMING OF KA-ZAR!

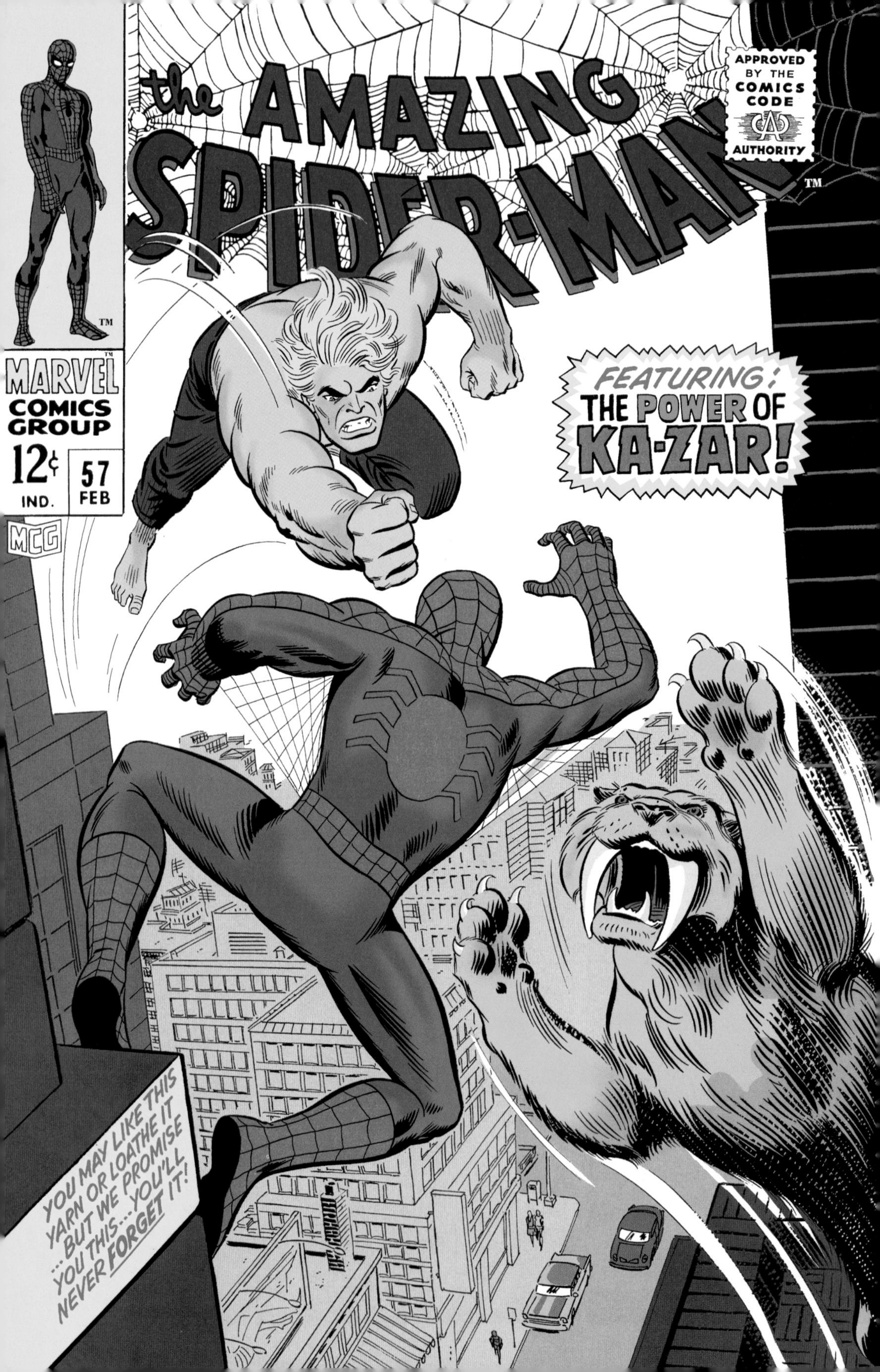
APPROVED BY THE COMICS CODE AUTHORITY
the AMAZING SPIDER-MAN
MARVEL COMICS GROUP
12¢ IND.
57 FEB
MCG
FEATURING: THE POWER OF KA-ZAR!
YOU MAY LIKE THIS YARN OR LOATHE IT ...BUT WE PROMISE YOU THIS...YOU'LL NEVER FORGET IT!

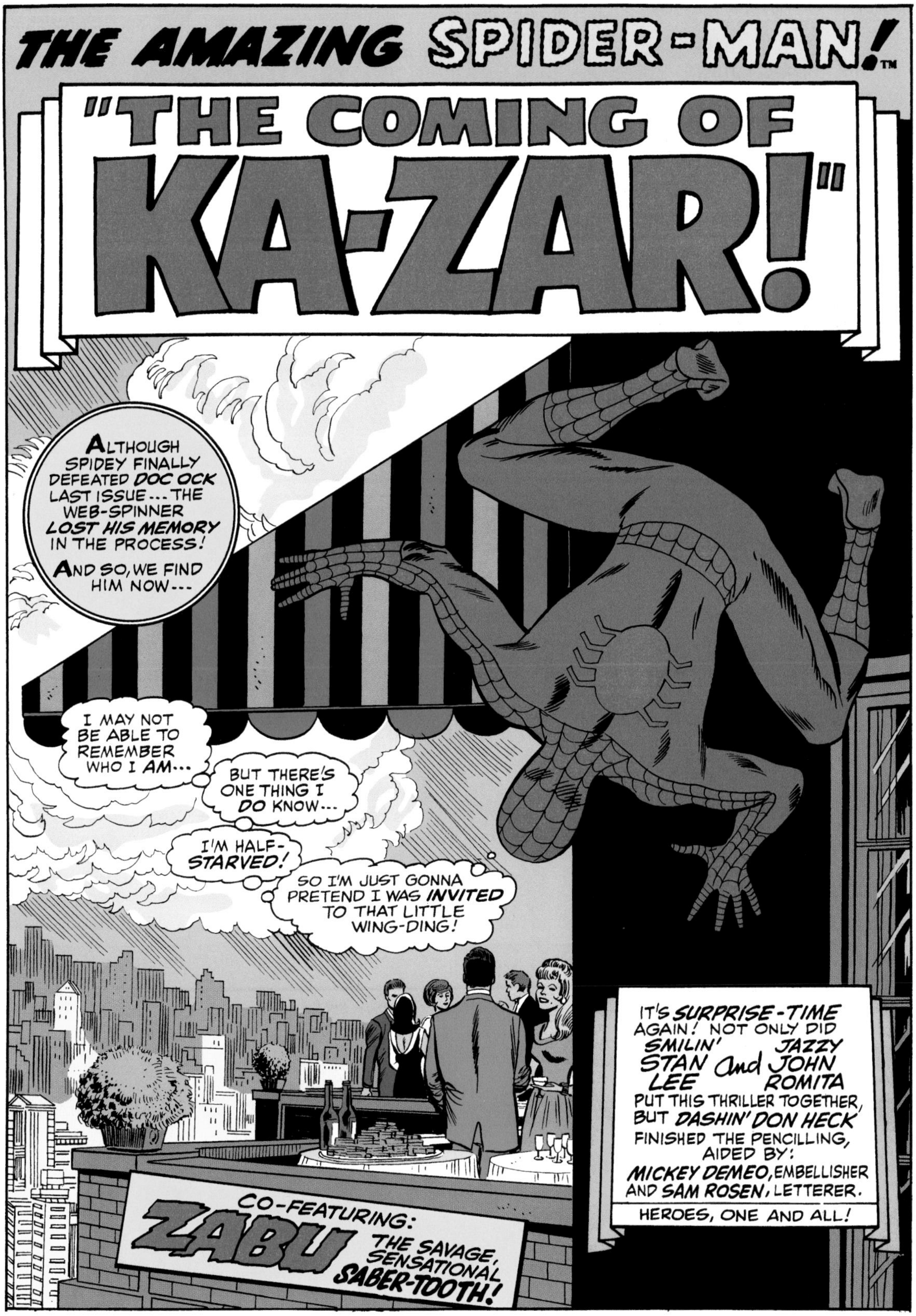
THE AMAZING SPIDER-MAN!
"THE COMING OF KA-ZAR!"
ALTHOUGH SPIDEY FINALLY DEFEATED DOC OCK LAST ISSUE... THE WEB-SPINNER LOST HIS MEMORY IN THE PROCESS! AND SO, WE FIND HIM NOW---
I MAY NOT BE ABLE TO REMEMBER WHO I AM...
BUT THERE'S ONE THING I DO KNOW...
I'M HALF-STARVED!
SO I'M JUST GONNA PRETEND I WAS INVITED TO THAT LITTLE WING-DING!
IT'S SURPRISE-TIME AGAIN! NOT ONLY DID SMILIN' STAN LEE And JAZZY JOHN ROMITA PUT THIS THRILLER TOGETHER, BUT DASHIN' DON HECK FINISHED THE PENCILLING, AIDED BY: MICKEY DEMEO, EMBELLISHER AND SAM ROSEN, LETTERER.
HEROES, ONE AND ALL!
CO-FEATURING: ZABU THE SAVAGE, SENSATIONAL SABER-TOOTH!

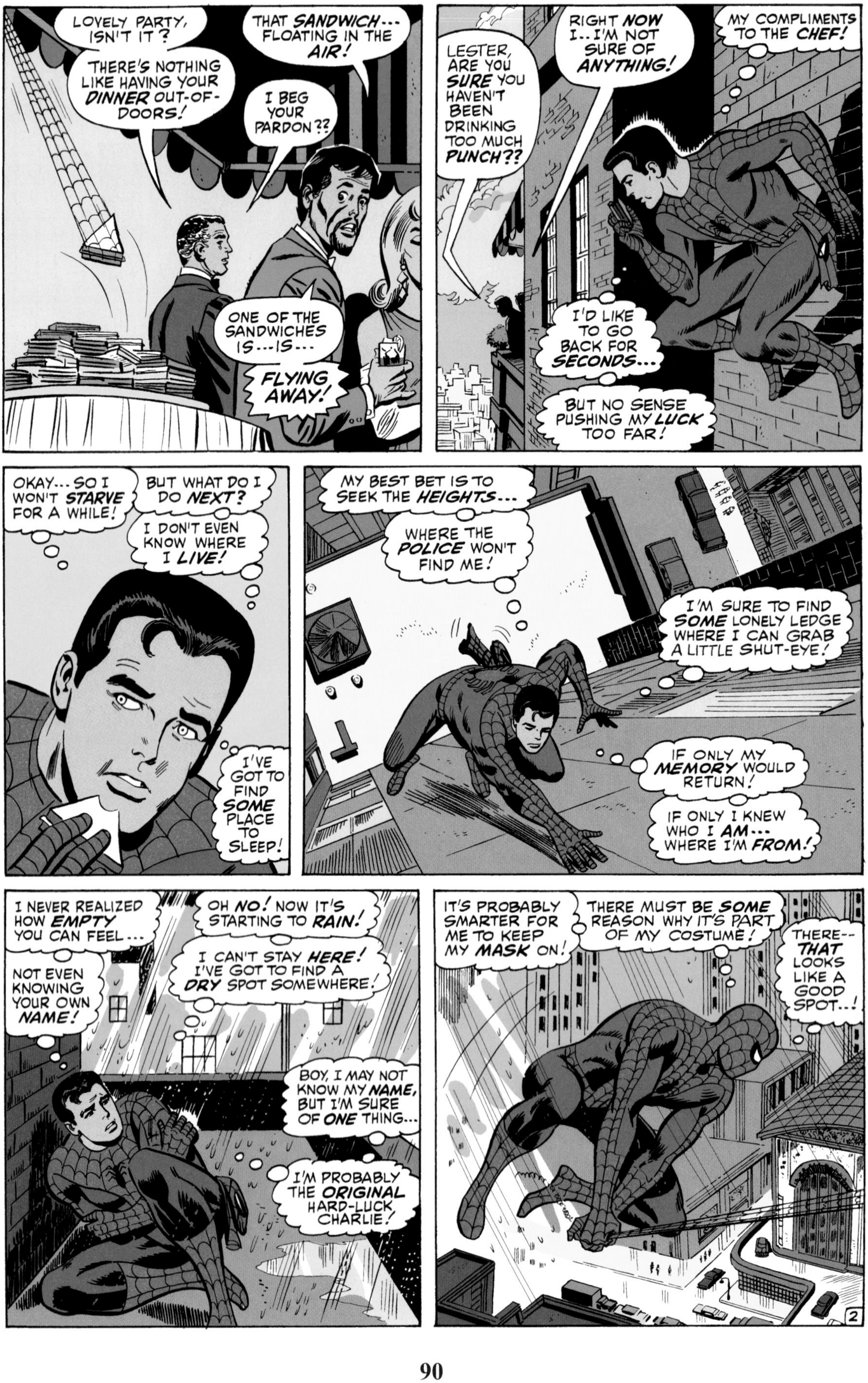
LOVELY PARTY, ISN'T IT?
THERE'S NOTHING LIKE HAVING YOUR DINNER OUT-OF-DOORS!
THAT SANDWICH... FLOATING IN THE AIR!
I BEG YOUR PARDON??
ONE OF THE SANDWICHES IS---IS---
FLYING AWAY!
LESTER, ARE YOU SURE YOU HAVEN'T BEEN DRINKING TOO MUCH PUNCH??
RIGHT NOW I.. I'M NOT SURE OF ANYTHING!
MY COMPLIMENTS TO THE CHEF!
I'D LIKE TO GO BACK FOR SECONDS...
BUT NO SENSE PUSHING MY LUCK TOO FAR!
OKAY... SO I WON'T STARVE FOR A WHILE!
BUT WHAT DO I DO NEXT?
I DON'T EVEN KNOW WHERE I LIVE!
I'VE GOT TO FIND SOME PLACE TO SLEEP!
MY BEST BET IS TO SEEK THE HEIGHTS...
WHERE THE POLICE WON'T FIND ME!
I'M SURE TO FIND SOME LONELY LEDGE WHERE I CAN GRAB A LITTLE SHUT-EYE!
IF ONLY MY MEMORY WOULD RETURN!
IF ONLY I KNEW WHO I AM... WHERE I'M FROM!
I NEVER REALIZED HOW EMPTY YOU CAN FEEL...
NOT EVEN KNOWING YOUR OWN NAME!
OH NO! NOW IT'S STARTING TO RAIN!
I CAN'T STAY HERE! I'VE GOT TO FIND A DRY SPOT SOMEWHERE!
BOY, I MAY NOT KNOW MY NAME, BUT I'M SURE OF ONE THING...
I'M PROBABLY THE ORIGINAL HARD-LUCK CHARLIE!
IT'S PROBABLY SMARTER FOR ME TO KEEP MY MASK ON!
THERE MUST BE SOME REASON WHY IT'S PART OF MY COSTUME!
THERE-- THAT LOOKS LIKE A GOOD SPOT...!
2

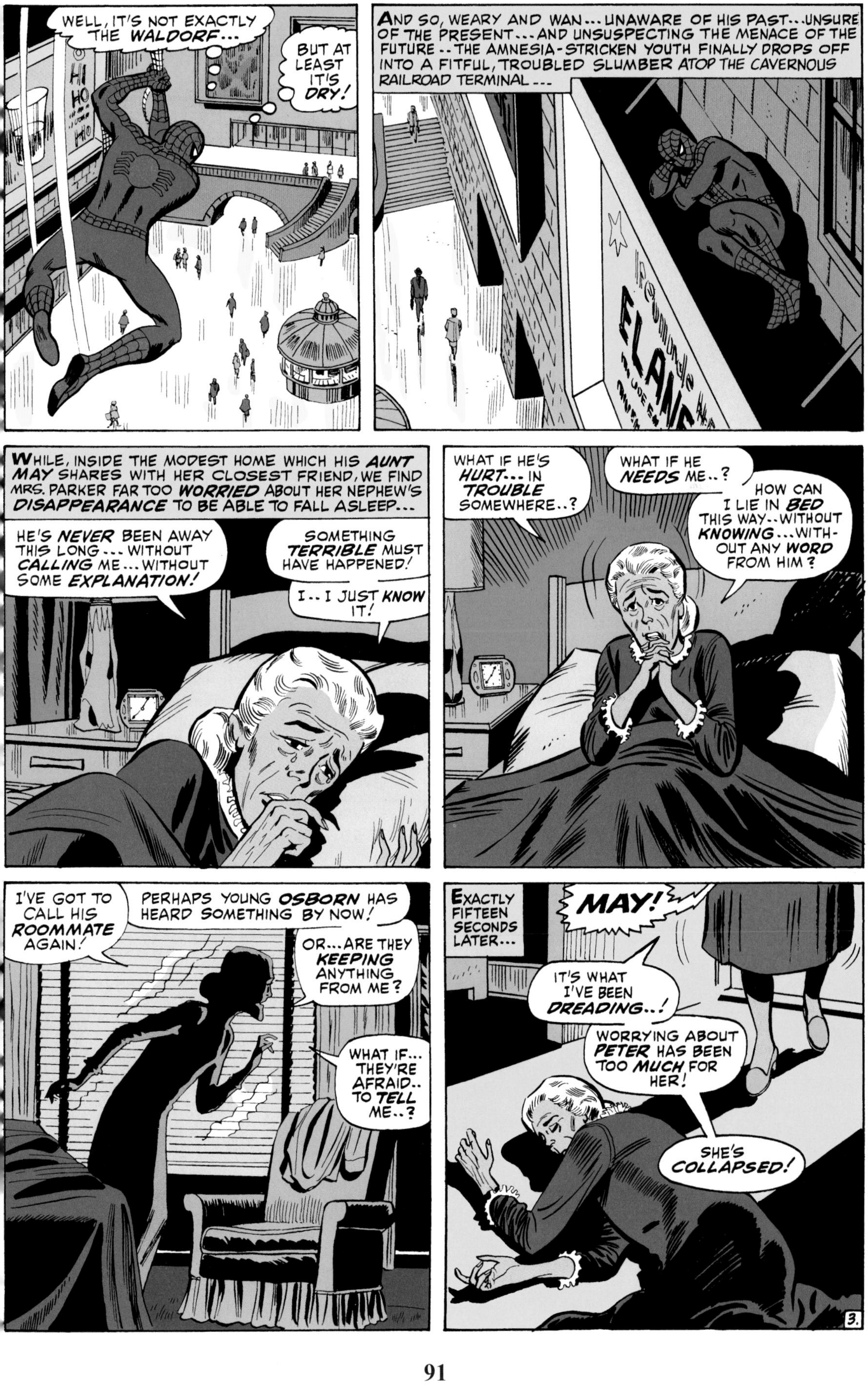
WELL, IT'S NOT EXACTLY THE WALDORF...
BUT AT LEAST IT'S DRY!
AND SO, WEARY AND WAN... UNAWARE OF HIS PAST... UNSURE OF THE PRESENT... AND UNSUSPECTING THE MENACE OF THE FUTURE -- THE AMNESIA-STRICKEN YOUTH FINALLY DROPS OFF INTO A FITFUL, TROUBLED SLUMBER ATOP THE CAVERNOUS RAILROAD TERMINAL---
WHILE, INSIDE THE MODEST HOME WHICH HIS AUNT MAY SHARES WITH HER CLOSEST FRIEND, WE FIND MRS. PARKER FAR TOO WORRIED ABOUT HER NEPHEW'S DISAPPEARANCE TO BE ABLE TO FALL ASLEEP...
HE'S NEVER BEEN AWAY THIS LONG... WITHOUT CALLING ME... WITHOUT SOME EXPLANATION!
SOMETHING TERRIBLE MUST HAVE HAPPENED!
I.. I JUST KNOW IT!
WHAT IF HE'S HURT... IN TROUBLE SOMEWHERE..?
WHAT IF HE NEEDS ME..?
HOW CAN I LIE IN BED THIS WAY--WITHOUT KNOWING...WITH-OUT ANY WORD FROM HIM?
I'VE GOT TO CALL HIS ROOMMATE AGAIN!
PERHAPS YOUNG OSBORN HAS HEARD SOMETHING BY NOW!
OR...ARE THEY KEEPING ANYTHING FROM ME?
WHAT IF... THEY'RE AFRAID.. TO TELL ME..?
EXACTLY FIFTEEN SECONDS LATER...
MAY!
IT'S WHAT I'VE BEEN DREADING..!
WORRYING ABOUT PETER HAS BEEN TOO MUCH FOR HER!
SHE'S COLLAPSED!
3.

DR. BROMWELL... YOU'VE GOT TO COME AT *ONCE!*

OR... PERHAPS IT WOULD BE BETTER... TO SEND AN *AMBULANCE!*

AND, AS THINGS SEEM TO GET FROM BAD TO WORSE...

IF I HAD *MY* WAY, YOU'D BE BUSTED TO *PRIVATE*, COLONEL JAMESON!

HE HAD NO *RIGHT*, TO LET *SPIDER-MAN* ESCAPE!

LET'S NOT FLY OFF THE HANDLE UNTIL WE'VE HEARD FROM THE *COLONEL*, GENTLEMEN!

THANK YOU, CAPTAIN STACY!

COLONEL JAMESON IS UNDER *MY* COMMAND!

HIS ORDERS WERE TO RETRIEVE THE STOLEN *NULLIFIER*...

--*NOT* TO APPREHEND COSTUMED CRIMINALS!

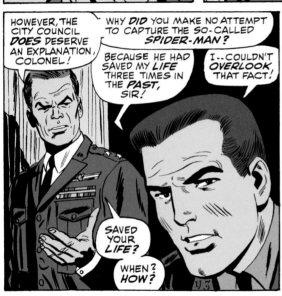

HOWEVER, THE CITY COUNCIL *DOES* DESERVE AN EXPLANATION, COLONEL!

WHY *DID* YOU MAKE NO ATTEMPT TO CAPTURE THE SO-CALLED *SPIDER-MAN?*

BECAUSE HE HAD SAVED MY *LIFE* THREE TIMES IN THE *PAST*, SIR!

I...COULDN'T *OVERLOOK*, THAT FACT!

SAVED YOUR *LIFE?*

WHEN? HOW?

I'VE MADE A *STUDY* OF SPIDER-MAN'S RECORD, GENERAL!

ONE OF HIS *EARLIEST* EXPLOITS WAS SAVING A *SPACE CRAFT* WHICH THE COLONEL WAS PILOTING...

WHILE HE LATER RESCUED HIM FROM THE *RHINO*... AND FINALLY FROM *DR. OCTOPUS* HIMSELF! *

IN FACT, HIS *RECORD* MAKES IT DIFFICULT TO BELIEVE SPIDER-MAN COULD REALLY HAVE TURNED *BAD!*

I CAN SEE YOUR *POINT*, CAPTAIN STACEY!

*SPI. # 1, 41 AND 56. --SUCCINCT STAN.

FINALLY, AT THE CONCLUSION OF THE STORMY MEETING...

I NEVER KNEW YOU WERE SO *FAMILIAR* WITH SPIDER-MAN'S BACKGROUND, CAPTAIN!

AS AN EX-POLICE OFFICER, I FIND HIS HISTORY *FASCINATING!*

JOHN! I THOUGHT YOU'D NEVER COME *OUT*, BLAST IT!

THE MORE I *LEARN*... THE MORE HE *MYSTIFIES* ME!

IS IT *TRUE?* DID YOU LET THAT WEBBED WEASEL *ESCAPE??*

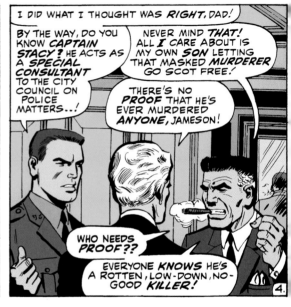

I DID WHAT I THOUGHT WAS *RIGHT*, DAD!

BY THE WAY, DO YOU KNOW *CAPTAIN STACY?* HE ACTS AS A *SPECIAL CONSULTANT* TO THE CITY COUNCIL ON POLICE MATTERS...!

NEVER MIND *THAT!* ALL *I* CARE ABOUT IS MY OWN *SON* LETTING THAT MASKED *MURDERER* GO SCOT FREE!

THERE'S NO *PROOF* THAT HE'S EVER MURDERED *ANYONE*, JAMESON!

WHO NEEDS *PROOF??*

EVERYONE *KNOWS* HE'S A ROTTEN, LOW-DOWN, NO-GOOD *KILLER!*

4.

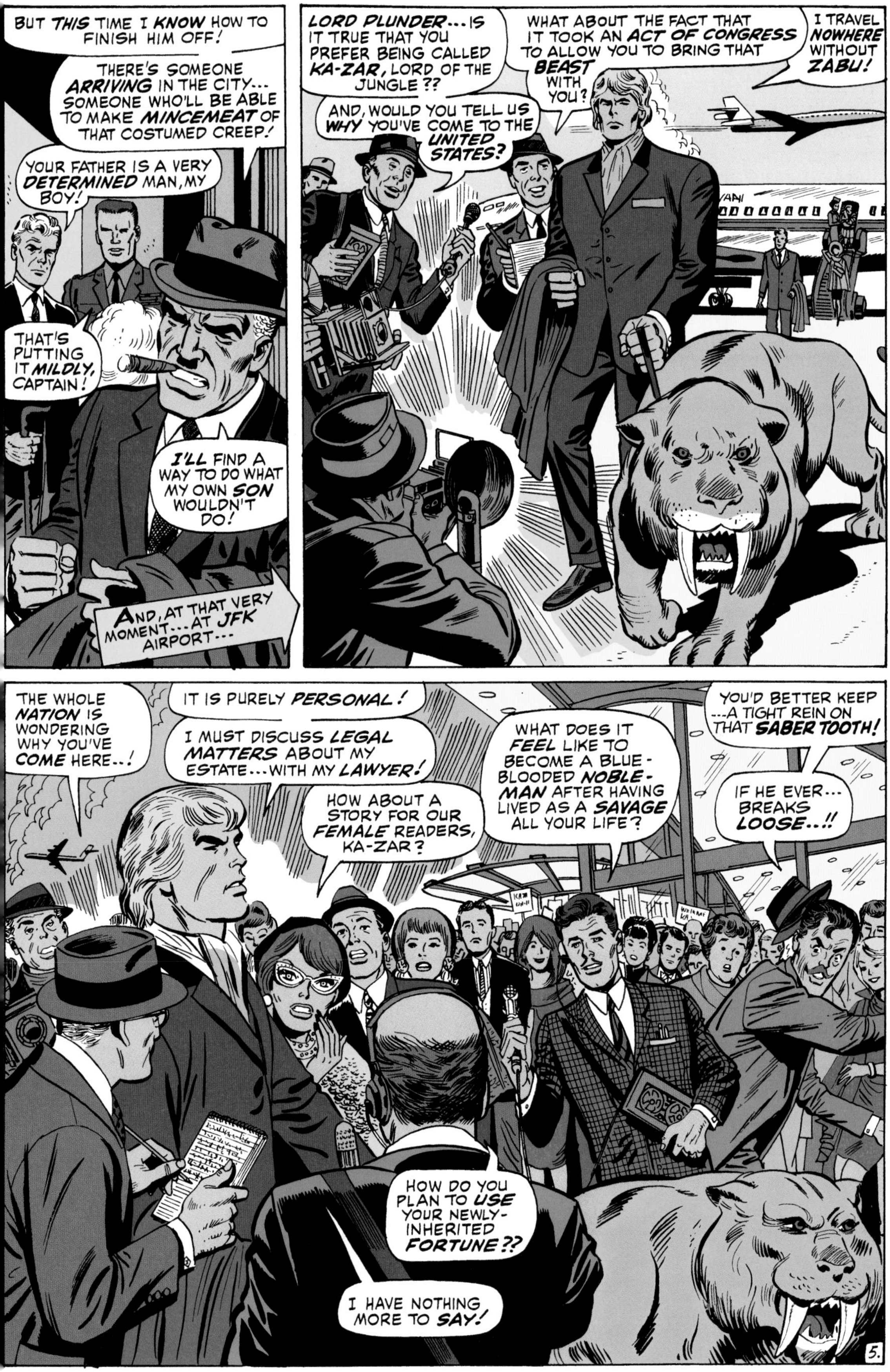

BUT THIS TIME I KNOW HOW TO FINISH HIM OFF!
THERE'S SOMEONE ARRIVING IN THE CITY... SOMEONE WHO'LL BE ABLE TO MAKE MINCEMEAT OF THAT COSTUMED CREEP!
YOUR FATHER IS A VERY DETERMINED MAN, MY BOY!
THAT'S PUTTING IT MILDLY, CAPTAIN!
I'LL FIND A WAY TO DO WHAT MY OWN SON WOULDN'T DO!
AND, AT THAT VERY MOMENT... AT JFK AIRPORT...
LORD PLUNDER... IS IT TRUE THAT YOU PREFER BEING CALLED KA-ZAR, LORD OF THE JUNGLE??
AND, WOULD YOU TELL US WHY YOU'VE COME TO THE UNITED STATES?
WHAT ABOUT THE FACT THAT IT TOOK AN ACT OF CONGRESS TO ALLOW YOU TO BRING THAT BEAST WITH YOU?
I TRAVEL NOWHERE WITHOUT ZABU!
THE WHOLE NATION IS WONDERING WHY YOU'VE COME HERE..!
IT IS PURELY PERSONAL!
I MUST DISCUSS LEGAL MATTERS ABOUT MY ESTATE... WITH MY LAWYER!
HOW ABOUT A STORY FOR OUR FEMALE READERS, KA-ZAR?
WHAT DOES IT FEEL LIKE TO BECOME A BLUE-BLOODED NOBLEMAN AFTER HAVING LIVED AS A SAVAGE ALL YOUR LIFE?
YOU'D BETTER KEEP ...A TIGHT REIN ON THAT SABER TOOTH!
IF HE EVER... BREAKS LOOSE...!!
HOW DO YOU PLAN TO USE YOUR NEWLY-INHERITED FORTUNE??
I HAVE NOTHING MORE TO SAY!
5.

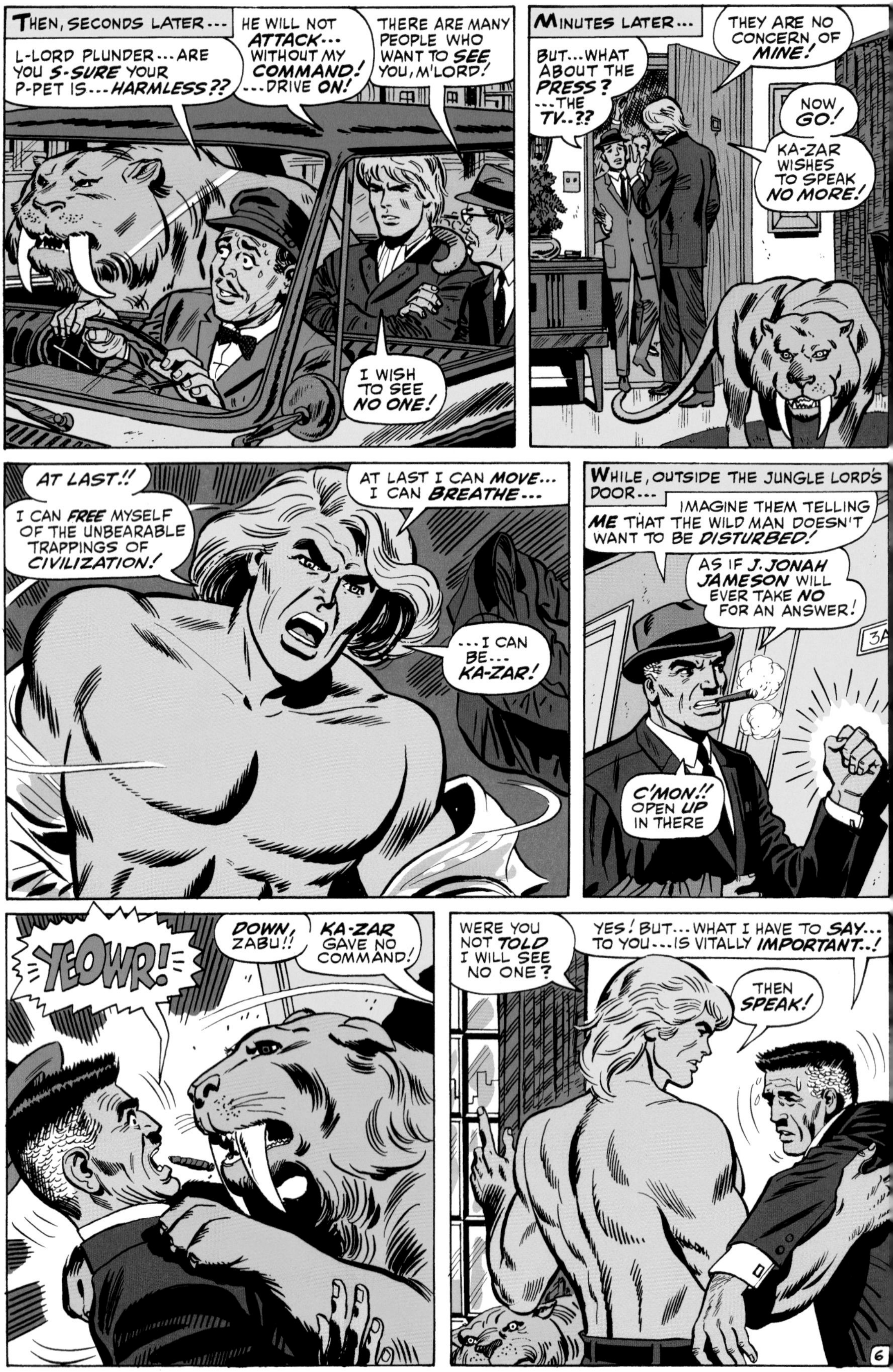

THEN, SECONDS LATER---
L-LORD PLUNDER---ARE YOU S-SURE YOUR P-PET IS---HARMLESS??
HE WILL NOT ATTACK--- WITHOUT MY COMMAND! ---DRIVE ON!
THERE ARE MANY PEOPLE WHO WANT TO SEE YOU, M'LORD!
I WISH TO SEE NO ONE!
MINUTES LATER---
BUT---WHAT ABOUT THE PRESS? ---THE TV..??
THEY ARE NO CONCERN OF MINE!
NOW GO!
KA-ZAR WISHES TO SPEAK NO MORE!
AT LAST!!
I CAN FREE MYSELF OF THE UNBEARABLE TRAPPINGS OF CIVILIZATION!
AT LAST I CAN MOVE--- I CAN BREATHE---
---I CAN BE--- KA-ZAR!
WHILE, OUTSIDE THE JUNGLE LORD'S DOOR---
IMAGINE THEM TELLING ME THAT THE WILD MAN DOESN'T WANT TO BE DISTURBED!
AS IF J. JONAH JAMESON WILL EVER TAKE NO FOR AN ANSWER!
C'MON!! OPEN UP IN THERE
YEOWR!
DOWN, ZABU!!
KA-ZAR GAVE NO COMMAND!
WERE YOU NOT TOLD I WILL SEE NO ONE?
YES! BUT---WHAT I HAVE TO SAY--- TO YOU---IS VITALLY IMPORTANT--!
THEN SPEAK!
6

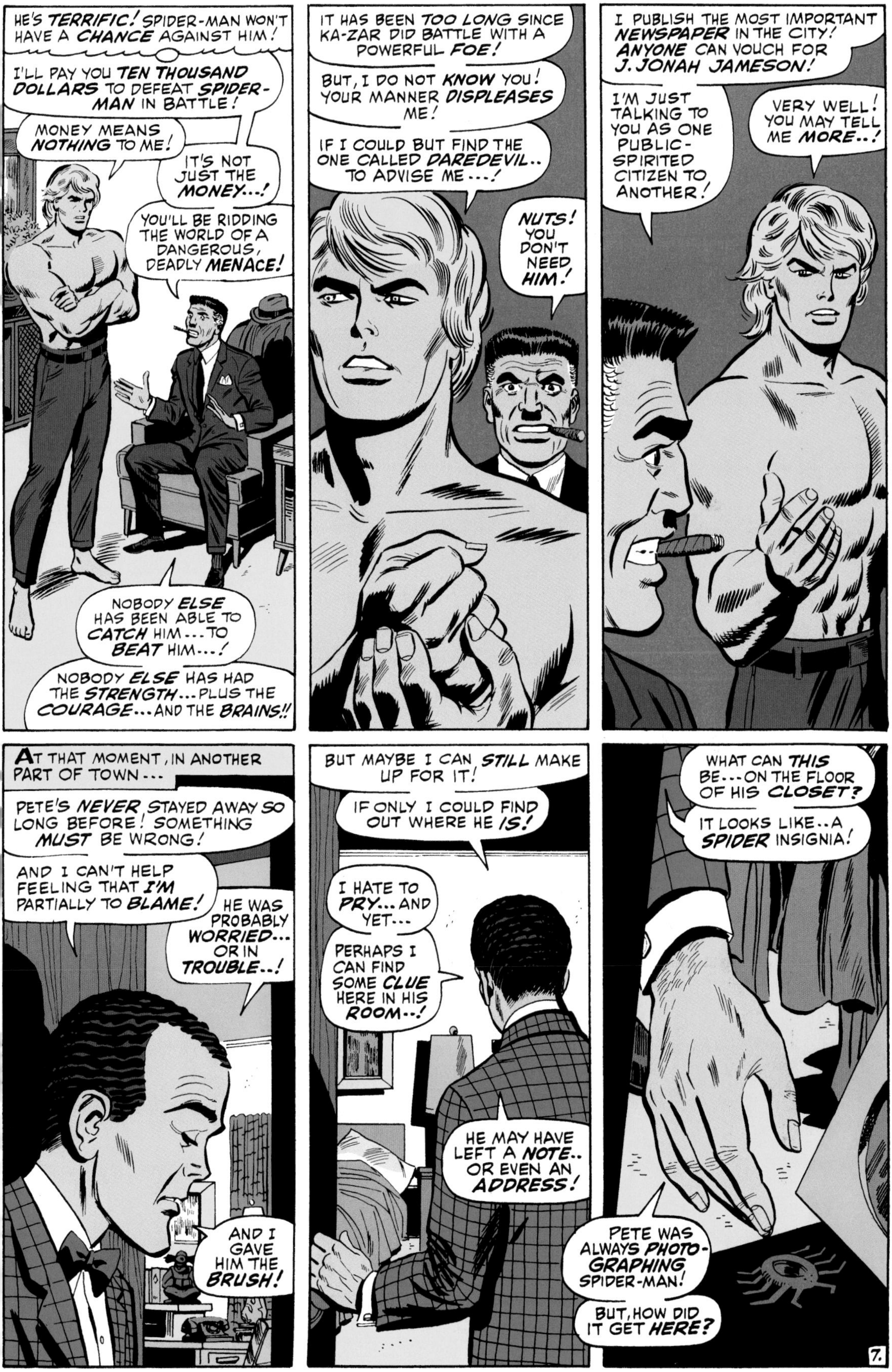

HE'S TERRIFIC! SPIDER-MAN WON'T HAVE A CHANCE AGAINST HIM!
I'LL PAY YOU TEN THOUSAND DOLLARS TO DEFEAT SPIDER-MAN IN BATTLE!
MONEY MEANS NOTHING TO ME!
IT'S NOT JUST THE MONEY...!
YOU'LL BE RIDDING THE WORLD OF A DANGEROUS, DEADLY MENACE!
NOBODY ELSE HAS BEEN ABLE TO CATCH HIM... TO BEAT HIM...!
NOBODY ELSE HAS HAD THE STRENGTH... PLUS THE COURAGE... AND THE BRAINS!!
IT HAS BEEN TOO LONG SINCE KA-ZAR DID BATTLE WITH A POWERFUL FOE!
BUT, I DO NOT KNOW YOU! YOUR MANNER DISPLEASES ME!
IF I COULD BUT FIND THE ONE CALLED DAREDEVIL.. TO ADVISE ME...!
NUTS! YOU DON'T NEED HIM!
I PUBLISH THE MOST IMPORTANT NEWSPAPER IN THE CITY! ANYONE CAN VOUCH FOR J. JONAH JAMESON!
I'M JUST TALKING TO YOU AS ONE PUBLIC-SPIRITED CITIZEN TO ANOTHER!
VERY WELL! YOU MAY TELL ME MORE..!
AT THAT MOMENT, IN ANOTHER PART OF TOWN...
PETE'S NEVER STAYED AWAY SO LONG BEFORE! SOMETHING MUST BE WRONG!
AND I CAN'T HELP FEELING THAT I'M PARTIALLY TO BLAME!
HE WAS PROBABLY WORRIED... OR IN TROUBLE..!
AND I GAVE HIM THE BRUSH!
BUT MAYBE I CAN STILL MAKE UP FOR IT!
IF ONLY I COULD FIND OUT WHERE HE IS!
I HATE TO PRY... AND YET...
PERHAPS I CAN FIND SOME CLUE HERE IN HIS ROOM..!
HE MAY HAVE LEFT A NOTE.. OR EVEN AN ADDRESS!
WHAT CAN THIS BE... ON THE FLOOR OF HIS CLOSET?
IT LOOKS LIKE.. A SPIDER INSIGNIA!
PETE WAS ALWAYS PHOTOGRAPHING SPIDER-MAN!
BUT, HOW DID IT GET HERE?
7.

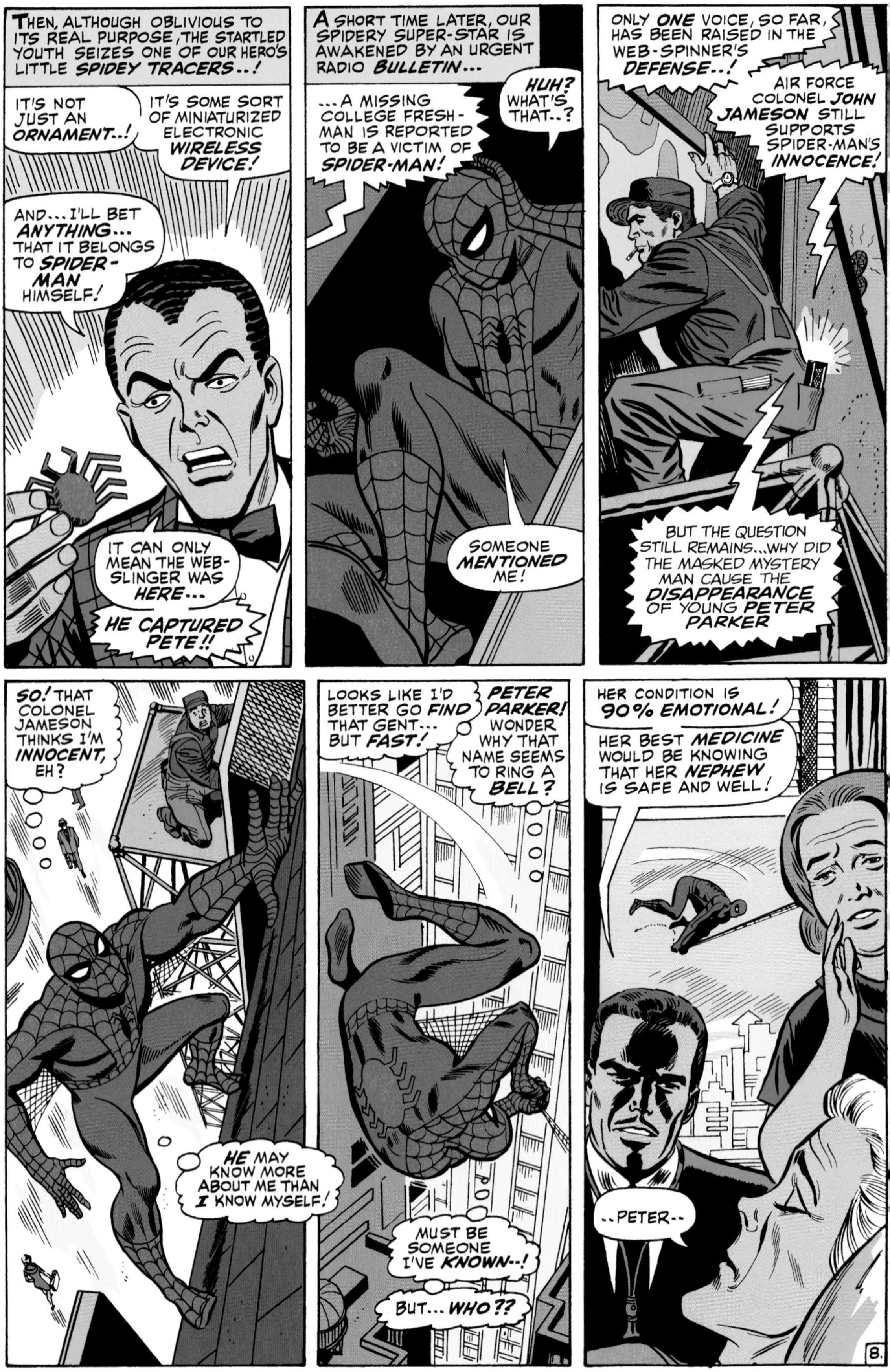

THEN, ALTHOUGH OBLIVIOUS TO ITS REAL PURPOSE, THE STARTLED YOUTH SEIZES ONE OF OUR HERO'S LITTLE SPIDEY TRACERS..!
IT'S NOT JUST AN ORNAMENT..!
IT'S SOME SORT OF MINIATURIZED ELECTRONIC WIRELESS DEVICE!
AND... I'LL BET ANYTHING... THAT IT BELONGS TO SPIDER-MAN HIMSELF!
IT CAN ONLY MEAN THE WEB-SLINGER WAS HERE...
HE CAPTURED PETE!!
A SHORT TIME LATER, OUR SPIDERY SUPER-STAR IS AWAKENED BY AN URGENT RADIO BULLETIN...
...A MISSING COLLEGE FRESHMAN IS REPORTED TO BE A VICTIM OF SPIDER-MAN!
HUH? WHAT'S THAT..?
SOMEONE MENTIONED ME!
ONLY ONE VOICE, SO FAR, HAS BEEN RAISED IN THE WEB-SPINNER'S DEFENSE..!
AIR FORCE COLONEL JOHN JAMESON STILL SUPPORTS SPIDER-MAN'S INNOCENCE!
BUT THE QUESTION STILL REMAINS...WHY DID THE MASKED MYSTERY MAN CAUSE THE DISAPPEARANCE OF YOUNG PETER PARKER
SO! THAT COLONEL JAMESON THINKS I'M INNOCENT, EH?
HE MAY KNOW MORE ABOUT ME THAN I KNOW MYSELF!
LOOKS LIKE I'D BETTER GO FIND THAT GENT... BUT FAST!
PETER PARKER! WONDER WHY THAT NAME SEEMS TO RING A BELL?
MUST BE SOMEONE I'VE KNOWN--!
BUT... WHO??
HER CONDITION IS 90% EMOTIONAL!
HER BEST MEDICINE WOULD BE KNOWING THAT HER NEPHEW IS SAFE AND WELL!
..PETER--
8.

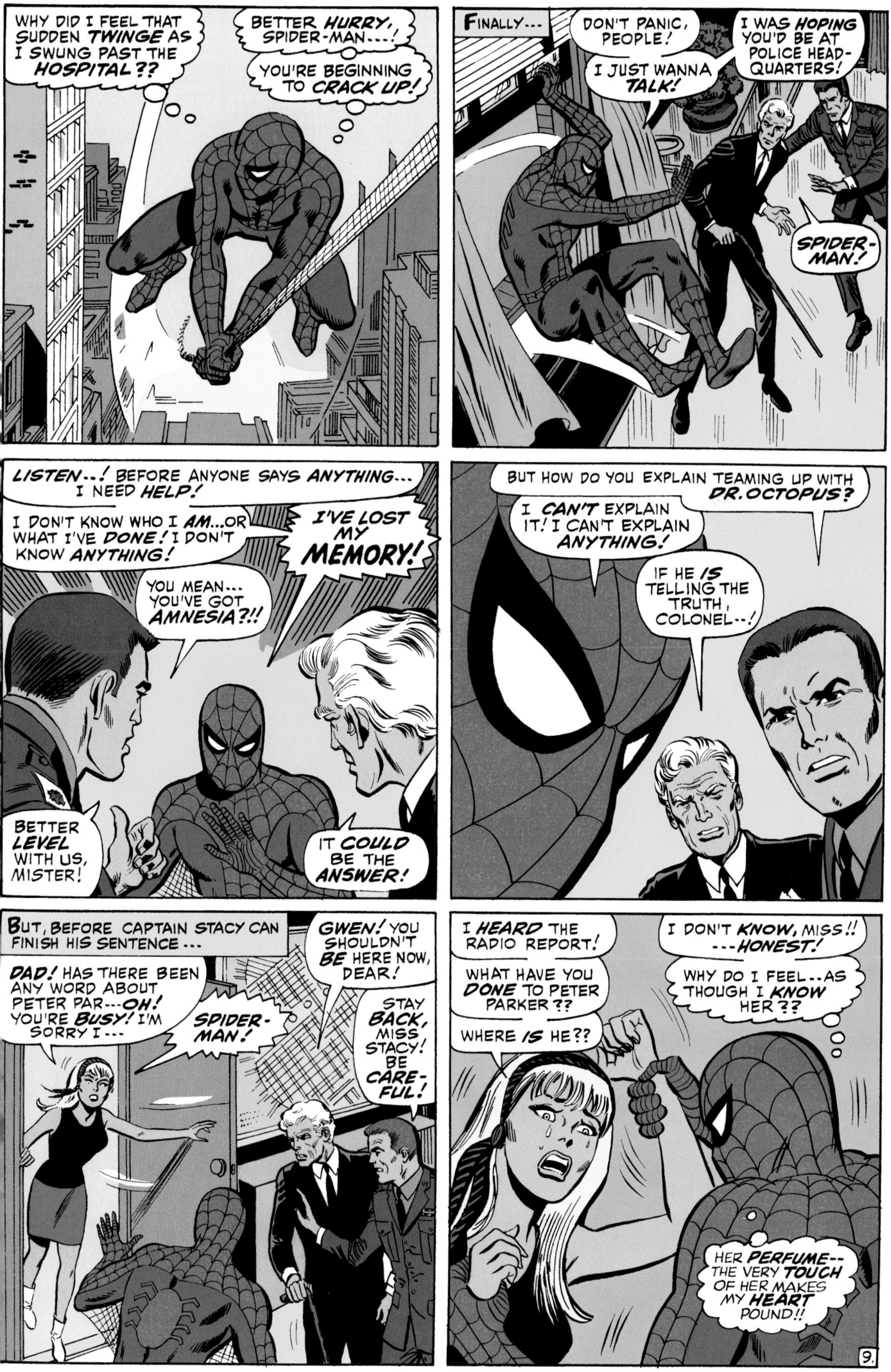
WHY DID I FEEL THAT SUDDEN TWINGE AS I SWUNG PAST THE HOSPITAL??
BETTER HURRY, SPIDER-MAN---!
YOU'RE BEGINNING TO CRACK UP!
FINALLY...
DON'T PANIC, PEOPLE!
I JUST WANNA TALK!
I WAS HOPING YOU'D BE AT POLICE HEAD-QUARTERS!
SPIDER-MAN!
LISTEN--! BEFORE ANYONE SAYS ANYTHING... I NEED HELP!
I DON'T KNOW WHO I AM...OR WHAT I'VE DONE! I DON'T KNOW ANYTHING!
I'VE LOST MY MEMORY!
YOU MEAN... YOU'VE GOT AMNESIA?!!
BETTER LEVEL WITH US, MISTER!
IT COULD BE THE ANSWER!
BUT HOW DO YOU EXPLAIN TEAMING UP WITH DR. OCTOPUS?
I CAN'T EXPLAIN IT! I CAN'T EXPLAIN ANYTHING!
IF HE IS TELLING THE TRUTH, COLONEL--!
BUT, BEFORE CAPTAIN STACY CAN FINISH HIS SENTENCE...
DAD! HAS THERE BEEN ANY WORD ABOUT PETER PAR---OH! YOU'RE BUSY! I'M SORRY I ---
SPIDER-MAN!
GWEN! YOU SHOULDN'T BE HERE NOW, DEAR!
STAY BACK, MISS STACY! BE CARE-FUL!
I HEARD THE RADIO REPORT!
WHAT HAVE YOU DONE TO PETER PARKER??
WHERE IS HE??
I DON'T KNOW, MISS!! ---HONEST!
WHY DO I FEEL--AS THOUGH I KNOW HER??
HER PERFUME-- THE VERY TOUCH OF HER MAKES MY HEART POUND!!
9

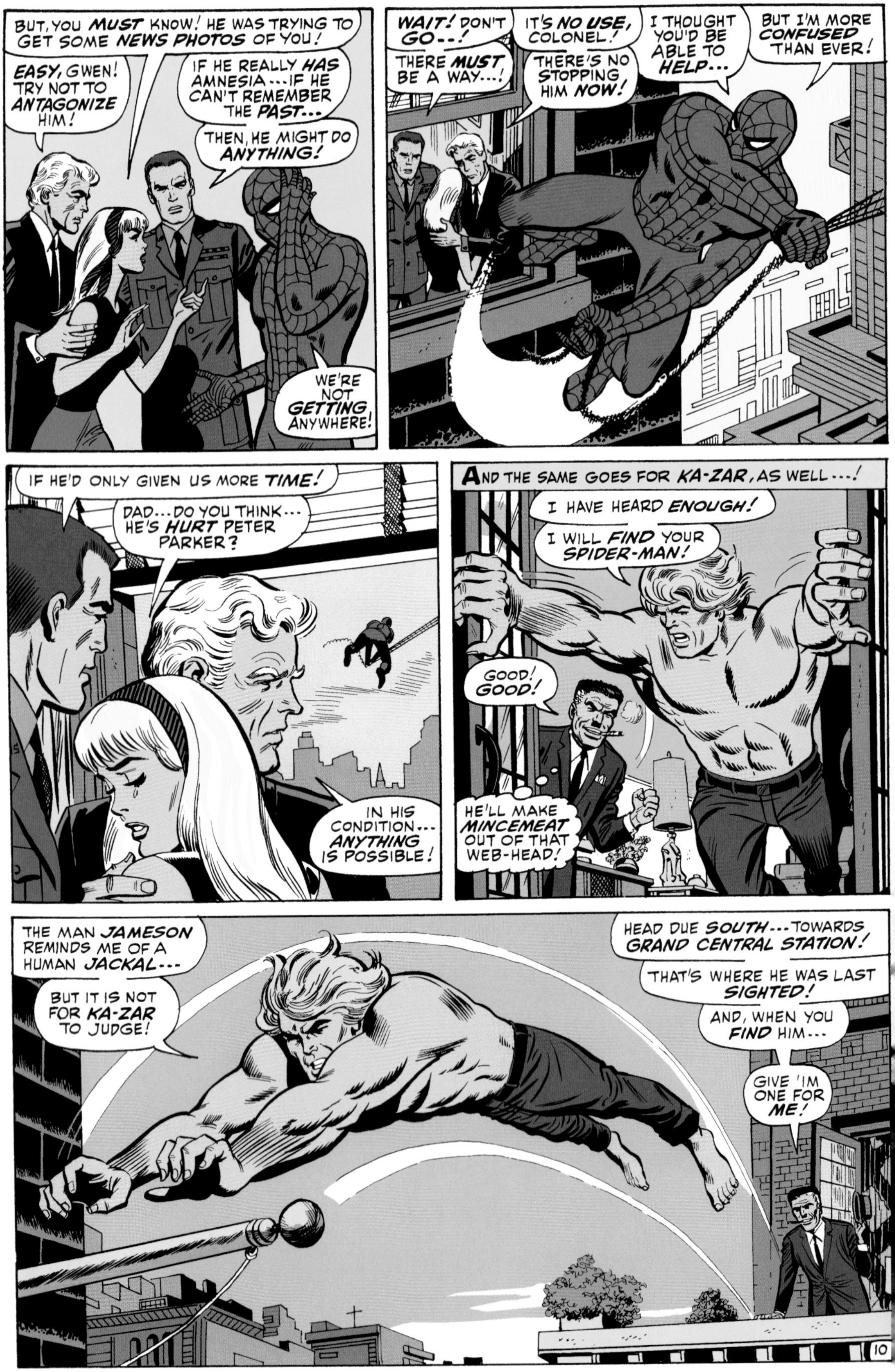
BUT, YOU MUST KNOW! HE WAS TRYING TO GET SOME NEWS PHOTOS OF YOU!
EASY, GWEN! TRY NOT TO ANTAGONIZE HIM!
IF HE REALLY HAS AMNESIA... IF HE CAN'T REMEMBER THE PAST...
THEN, HE MIGHT DO ANYTHING!
WE'RE NOT GETTING ANYWHERE!
WAIT! DON'T GO--!
THERE MUST BE A WAY...!
IT'S NO USE, COLONEL!
THERE'S NO STOPPING HIM NOW!
I THOUGHT YOU'D BE ABLE TO HELP...
BUT I'M MORE CONFUSED THAN EVER!
IF HE'D ONLY GIVEN US MORE TIME!
DAD... DO YOU THINK... HE'S HURT PETER PARKER?
IN HIS CONDITION... ANYTHING IS POSSIBLE!
AND THE SAME GOES FOR KA-ZAR, AS WELL...!
I HAVE HEARD ENOUGH!
I WILL FIND YOUR SPIDER-MAN!
GOOD! GOOD!
HE'LL MAKE MINCEMEAT OUT OF THAT WEB-HEAD!
THE MAN JAMESON REMINDS ME OF A HUMAN JACKAL...
BUT IT IS NOT FOR KA-ZAR TO JUDGE!
HEAD DUE SOUTH... TOWARDS GRAND CENTRAL STATION!
THAT'S WHERE HE WAS LAST SIGHTED!
AND, WHEN YOU FIND HIM...
GIVE 'IM ONE FOR ME!
10

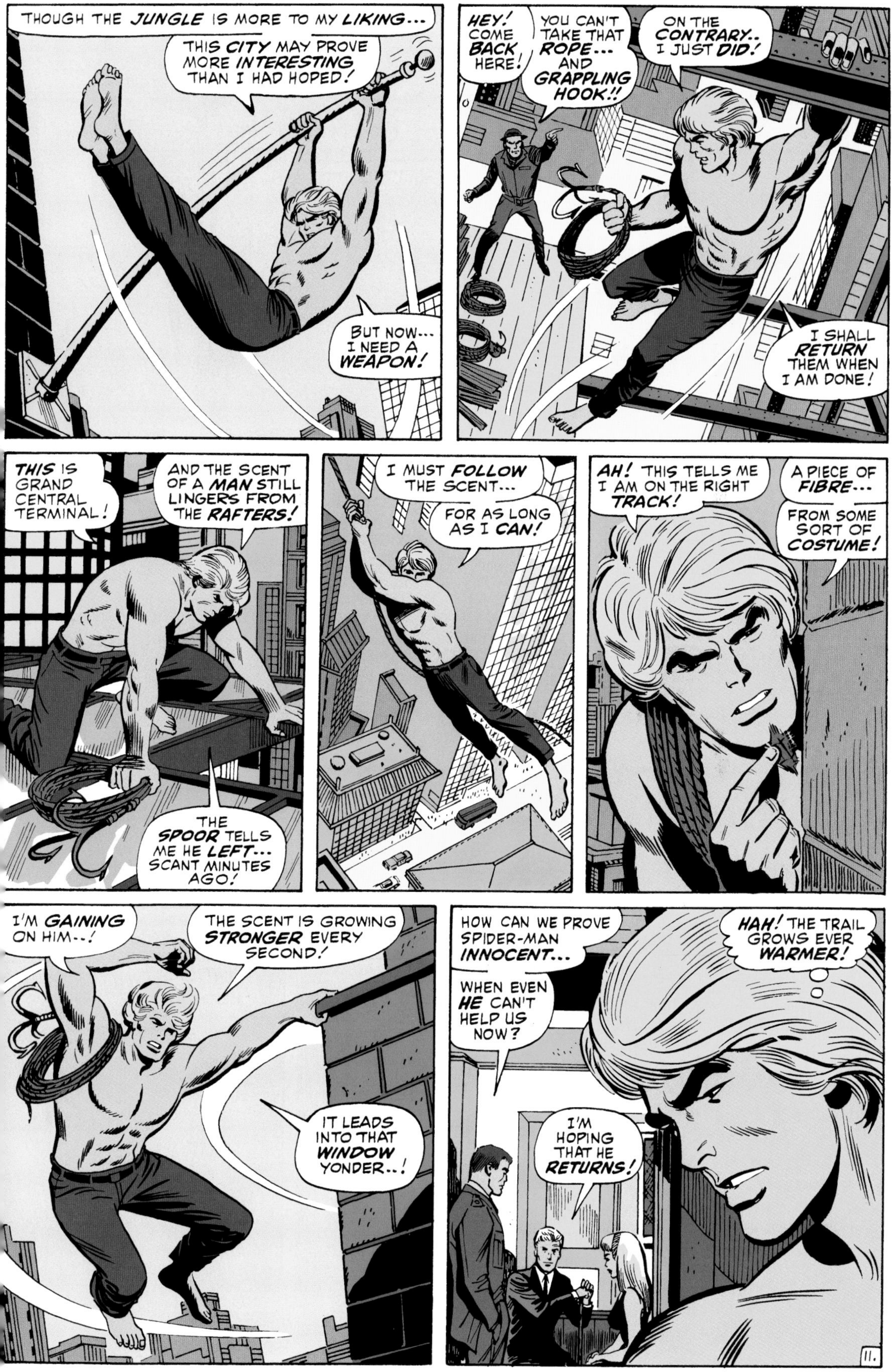

THOUGH THE JUNGLE IS MORE TO MY LIKING...
THIS CITY MAY PROVE MORE INTERESTING THAN I HAD HOPED!
BUT NOW... I NEED A WEAPON!
HEY! COME BACK HERE!
YOU CAN'T TAKE THAT ROPE... AND GRAPPLING HOOK!!
ON THE CONTRARY.. I JUST DID!
I SHALL RETURN THEM WHEN I AM DONE!
THIS IS GRAND CENTRAL TERMINAL!
AND THE SCENT OF A MAN STILL LINGERS FROM THE RAFTERS!
THE SPOOR TELLS ME HE LEFT... SCANT MINUTES AGO!
I MUST FOLLOW THE SCENT...
FOR AS LONG AS I CAN!
AH! THIS TELLS ME I AM ON THE RIGHT TRACK!
A PIECE OF FIBRE...
FROM SOME SORT OF COSTUME!
I'M GAINING ON HIM--!
THE SCENT IS GROWING STRONGER EVERY SECOND!
IT LEADS INTO THAT WINDOW YONDER..!
HOW CAN WE PROVE SPIDER-MAN INNOCENT...
WHEN EVEN HE CAN'T HELP US NOW?
I'M HOPING THAT HE RETURNS!
HAH! THE TRAIL GROWS EVER WARMER!
11.

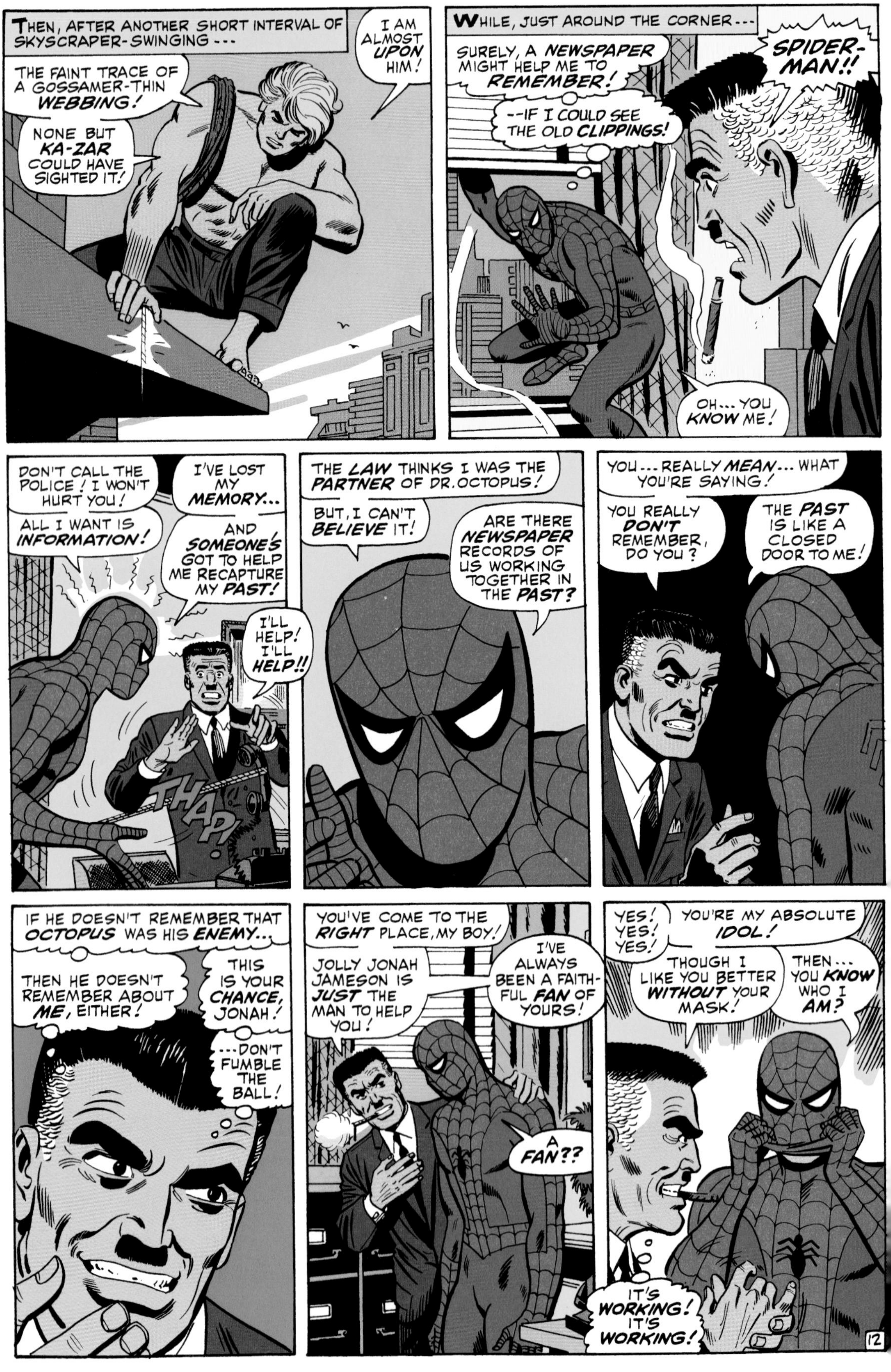

THEN, AFTER ANOTHER SHORT INTERVAL OF SKYSCRAPER-SWINGING ---
THE FAINT TRACE OF A GOSSAMER-THIN WEBBING!
NONE BUT KA-ZAR COULD HAVE SIGHTED IT!
I AM ALMOST UPON HIM!
WHILE, JUST AROUND THE CORNER ---
SURELY, A NEWSPAPER MIGHT HELP ME TO REMEMBER!
--IF I COULD SEE THE OLD CLIPPINGS!
SPIDER-MAN!!
OH... YOU KNOW ME!
DON'T CALL THE POLICE! I WON'T HURT YOU!
ALL I WANT IS INFORMATION!
I'VE LOST MY MEMORY...
AND SOMEONE'S GOT TO HELP ME RECAPTURE MY PAST!
I'LL HELP! I'LL HELP!!
THAP!
THE LAW THINKS I WAS THE PARTNER OF DR. OCTOPUS!
BUT, I CAN'T BELIEVE IT!
ARE THERE NEWSPAPER RECORDS OF US WORKING TOGETHER IN THE PAST?
YOU... REALLY MEAN... WHAT YOU'RE SAYING!
YOU REALLY DON'T REMEMBER, DO YOU?
THE PAST IS LIKE A CLOSED DOOR TO ME!
IF HE DOESN'T REMEMBER THAT OCTOPUS WAS HIS ENEMY...
THEN HE DOESN'T REMEMBER ABOUT ME, EITHER!
THIS IS YOUR CHANCE, JONAH!
...DON'T FUMBLE THE BALL!
YOU'VE COME TO THE RIGHT PLACE, MY BOY!
JOLLY JONAH JAMESON IS JUST THE MAN TO HELP YOU!
I'VE ALWAYS BEEN A FAITH-FUL FAN OF YOURS!
A FAN??
YES! YES! YES!
YOU'RE MY ABSOLUTE IDOL!
THOUGH I LIKE YOU BETTER WITHOUT YOUR MASK!
THEN... YOU KNOW WHO I AM?
IT'S WORKING! IT'S WORKING!
12

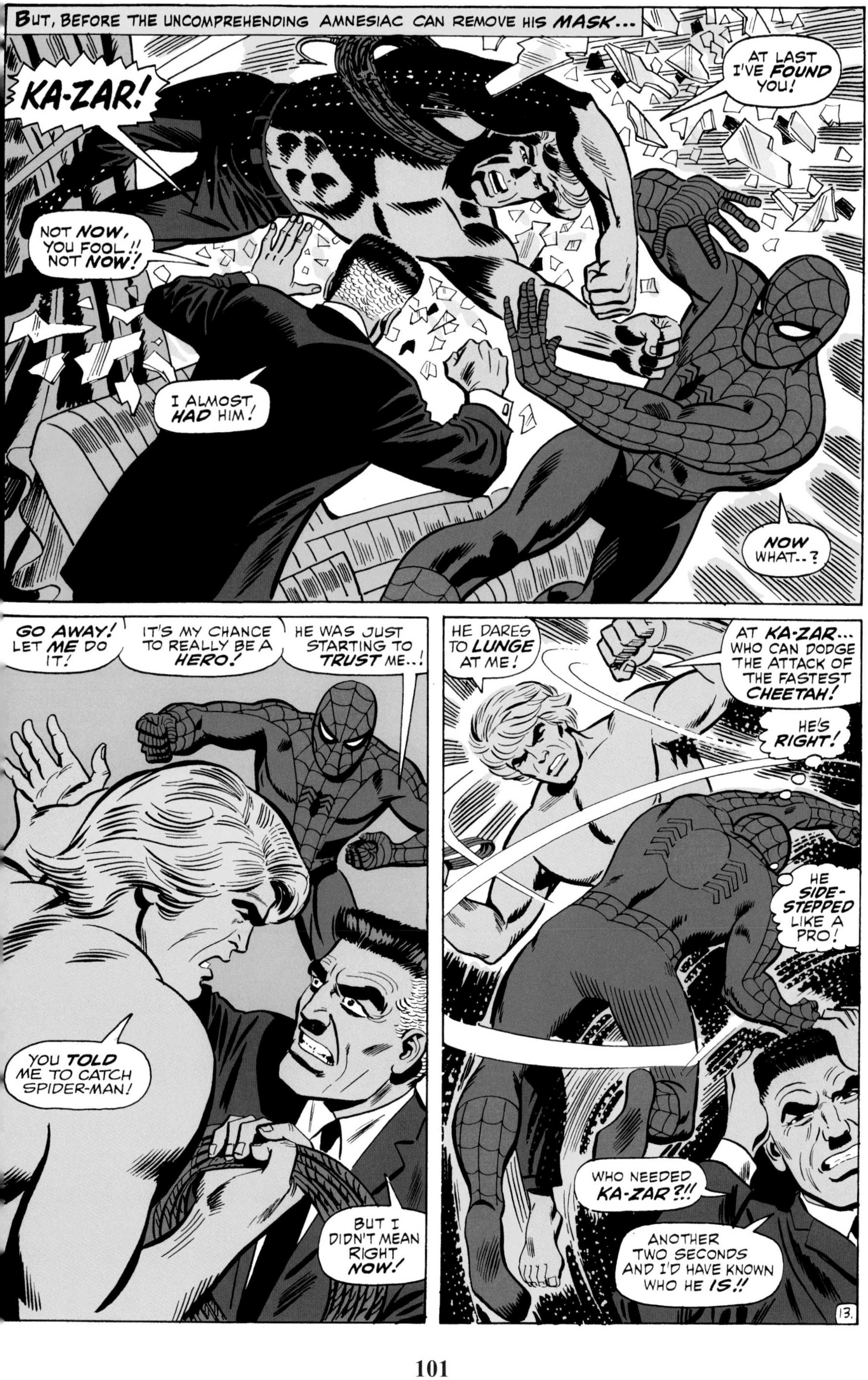
BUT, BEFORE THE UNCOMPREHENDING AMNESIAC CAN REMOVE HIS MASK...
KA-ZAR!
AT LAST I'VE FOUND YOU!
NOT NOW, YOU FOOL!! NOT NOW!
I ALMOST HAD HIM!
NOW WHAT..?
GO AWAY! LET ME DO IT!
IT'S MY CHANCE TO REALLY BE A HERO!
HE WAS JUST STARTING TO TRUST ME..!
YOU TOLD ME TO CATCH SPIDER-MAN!
BUT I DIDN'T MEAN RIGHT NOW!
HE DARES TO LUNGE AT ME!
AT KA-ZAR... WHO CAN DODGE THE ATTACK OF THE FASTEST CHEETAH!
HE'S RIGHT!
HE SIDE-STEPPED LIKE A PRO!
WHO NEEDED KA-ZAR?!!
ANOTHER TWO SECONDS AND I'D HAVE KNOWN WHO HE IS!!
13.

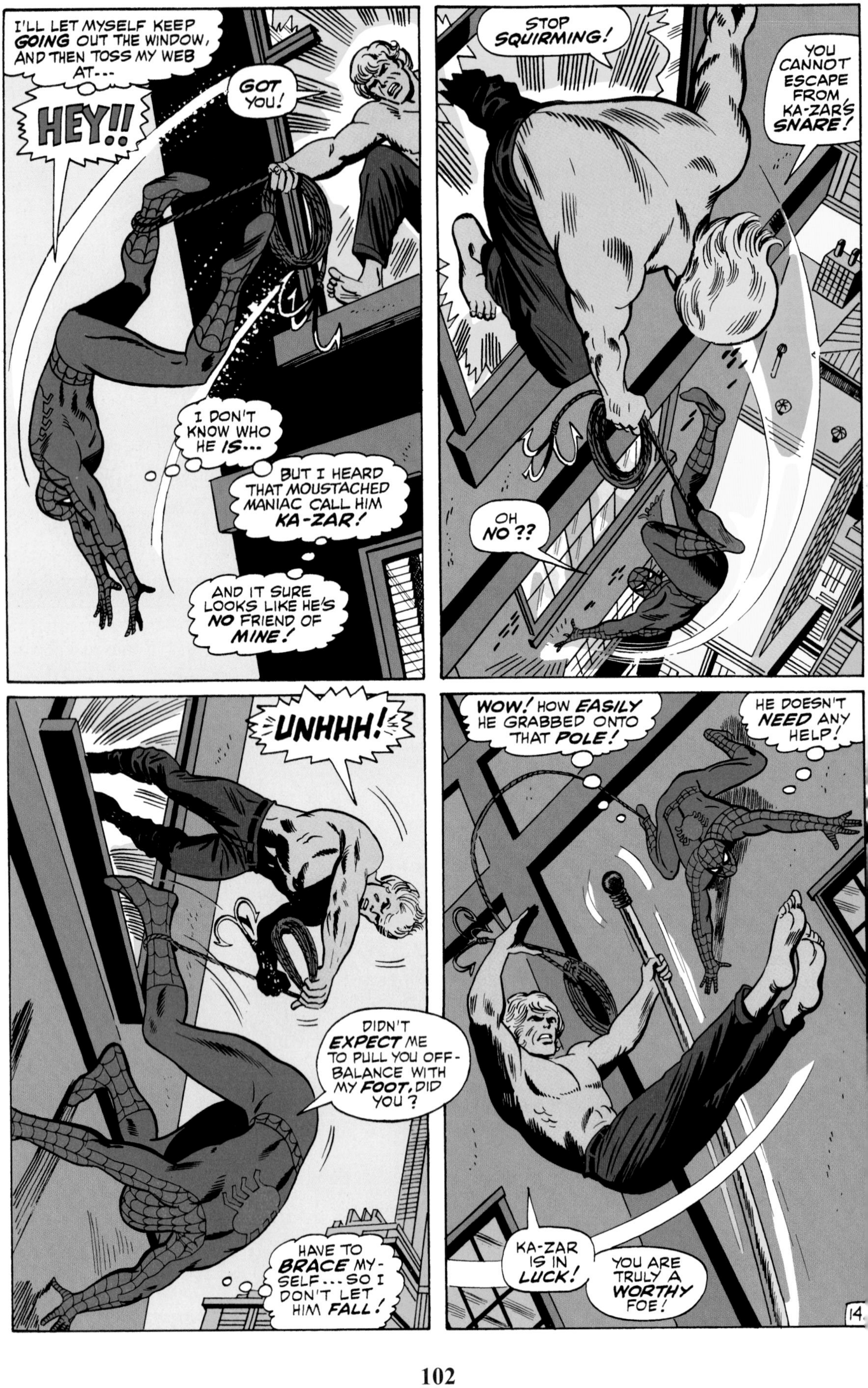
I'LL LET MYSELF KEEP GOING OUT THE WINDOW, AND THEN TOSS MY WEB AT---
HEY!!
GOT YOU!
I DON'T KNOW WHO HE IS---
BUT I HEARD THAT MOUSTACHED MANIAC CALL HIM KA-ZAR!
AND IT SURE LOOKS LIKE HE'S NO FRIEND OF MINE!
STOP SQUIRMING!
YOU CANNOT ESCAPE FROM KA-ZAR'S SNARE!
OH NO??
UNHHH!
DIDN'T EXPECT ME TO PULL YOU OFF-BALANCE WITH MY FOOT, DID YOU?
HAVE TO BRACE MY-SELF--- SO I DON'T LET HIM FALL!
WOW! HOW EASILY HE GRABBED ONTO THAT POLE!
HE DOESN'T NEED ANY HELP!
KA-ZAR IS IN LUCK!
YOU ARE TRULY A WORTHY FOE!
14

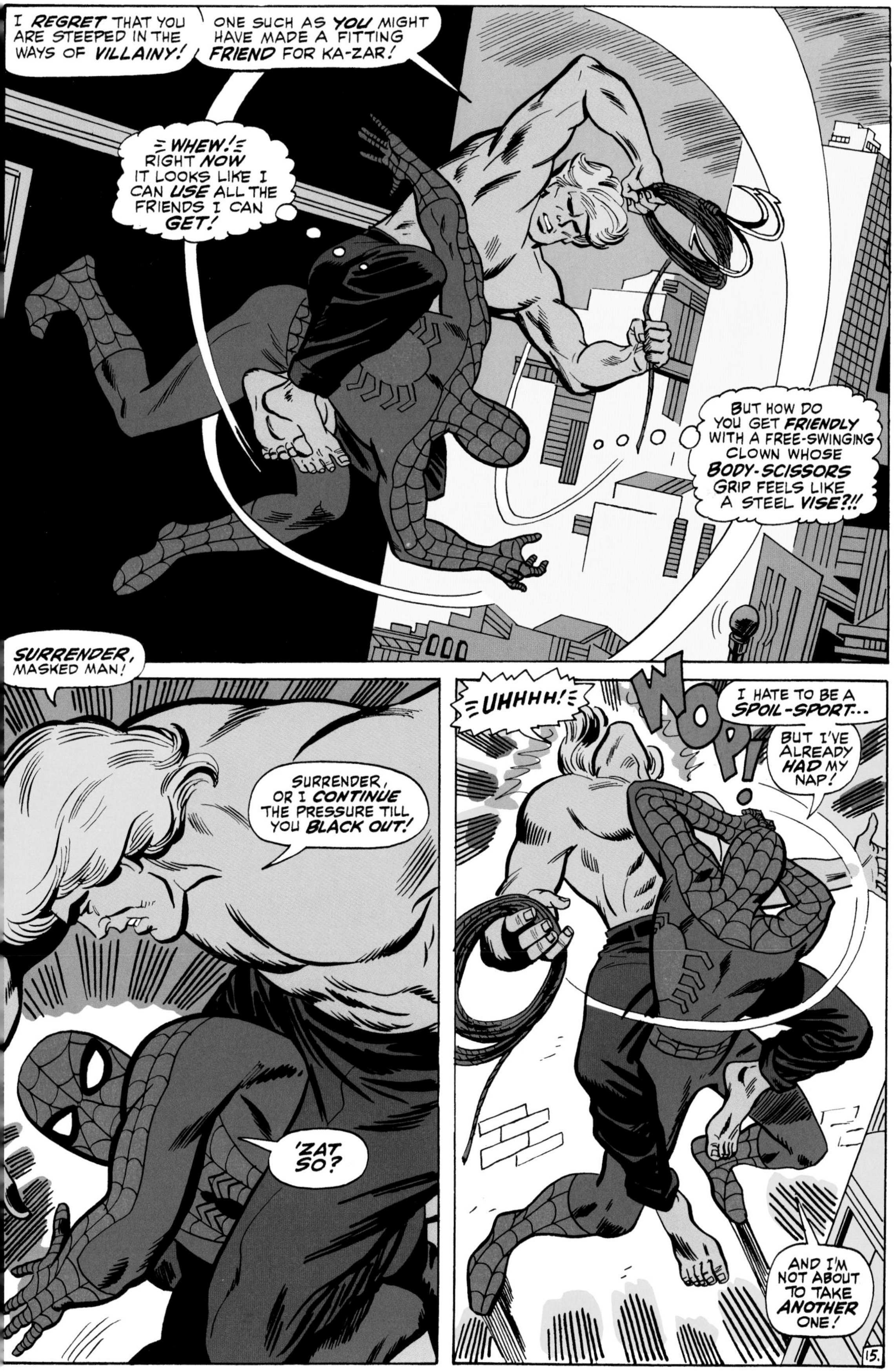
I REGRET THAT YOU ARE STEEPED IN THE WAYS OF VILLAINY!
ONE SUCH AS YOU MIGHT HAVE MADE A FITTING FRIEND FOR KA-ZAR!
WHEW! RIGHT NOW IT LOOKS LIKE I CAN USE ALL THE FRIENDS I CAN GET!
BUT HOW DO YOU GET FRIENDLY WITH A FREE-SWINGING CLOWN WHOSE BODY-SCISSORS GRIP FEELS LIKE A STEEL VISE?!!
SURRENDER, MASKED MAN!
SURRENDER, OR I CONTINUE THE PRESSURE TILL YOU BLACK OUT!
'ZAT SO?
UHHHH!
WOP!
I HATE TO BE A SPOIL-SPORT...
BUT I'VE ALREADY HAD MY NAP!
AND I'M NOT ABOUT TO TAKE ANOTHER ONE!
15.

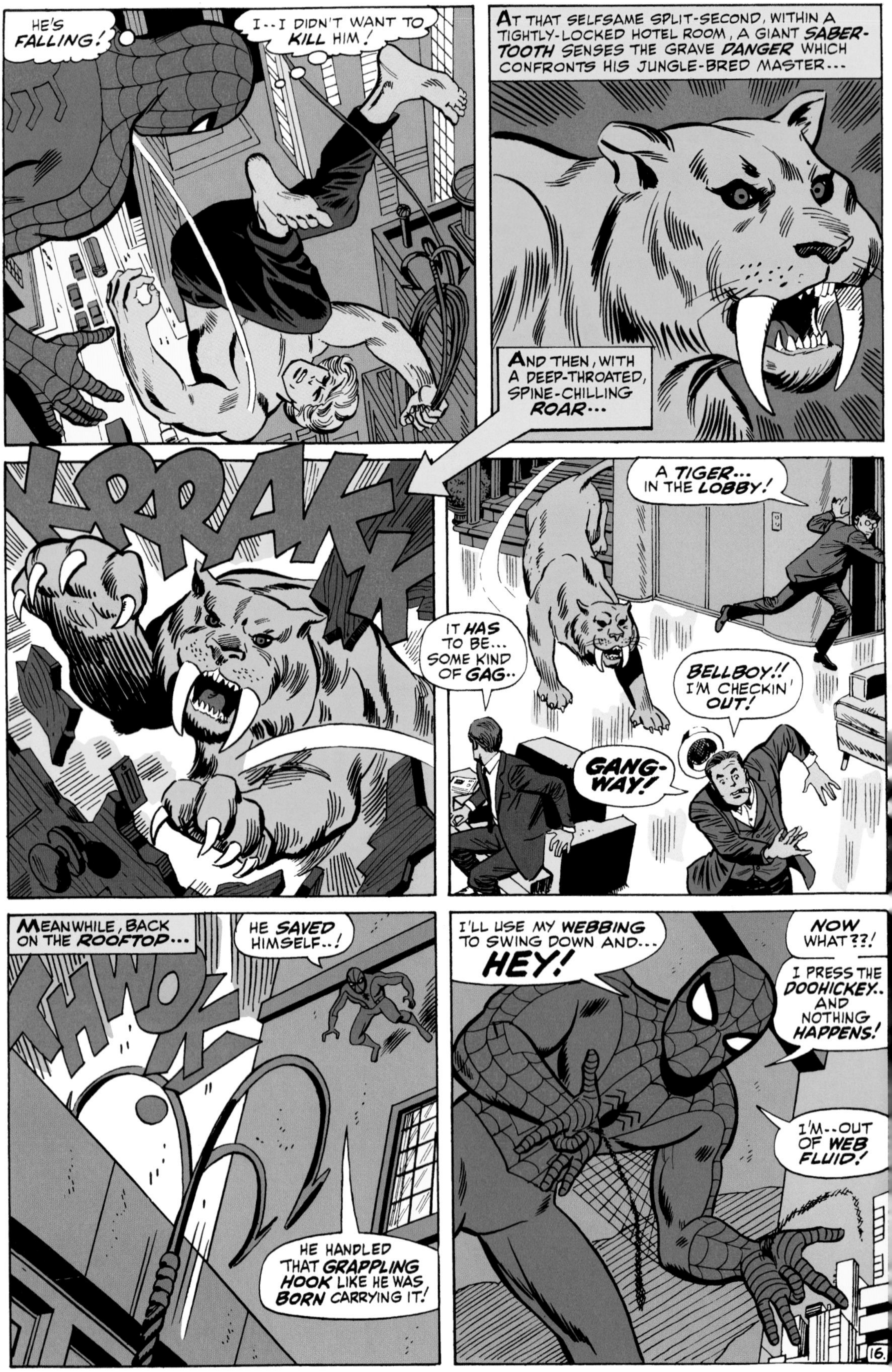
HE'S FALLING!
I--I DIDN'T WANT TO KILL HIM!
AT THAT SELFSAME SPLIT-SECOND, WITHIN A TIGHTLY-LOCKED HOTEL ROOM, A GIANT SABER-TOOTH SENSES THE GRAVE DANGER WHICH CONFRONTS HIS JUNGLE-BRED MASTER...
AND THEN, WITH A DEEP-THROATED, SPINE-CHILLING ROAR...
KRRAKK
A TIGER... IN THE LOBBY!
IT HAS TO BE... SOME KIND OF GAG..
BELLBOY!! I'M CHECKIN' OUT!
GANG-WAY!
MEANWHILE, BACK ON THE ROOFTOP...
HE SAVED HIMSELF..!
THWOK
HE HANDLED THAT GRAPPLING HOOK LIKE HE WAS BORN CARRYING IT!
I'LL USE MY WEBBING TO SWING DOWN AND... HEY!
NOW WHAT??!
I PRESS THE DOOHICKEY.. AND NOTHING HAPPENS!
I'M--OUT OF WEB FLUID!
16.

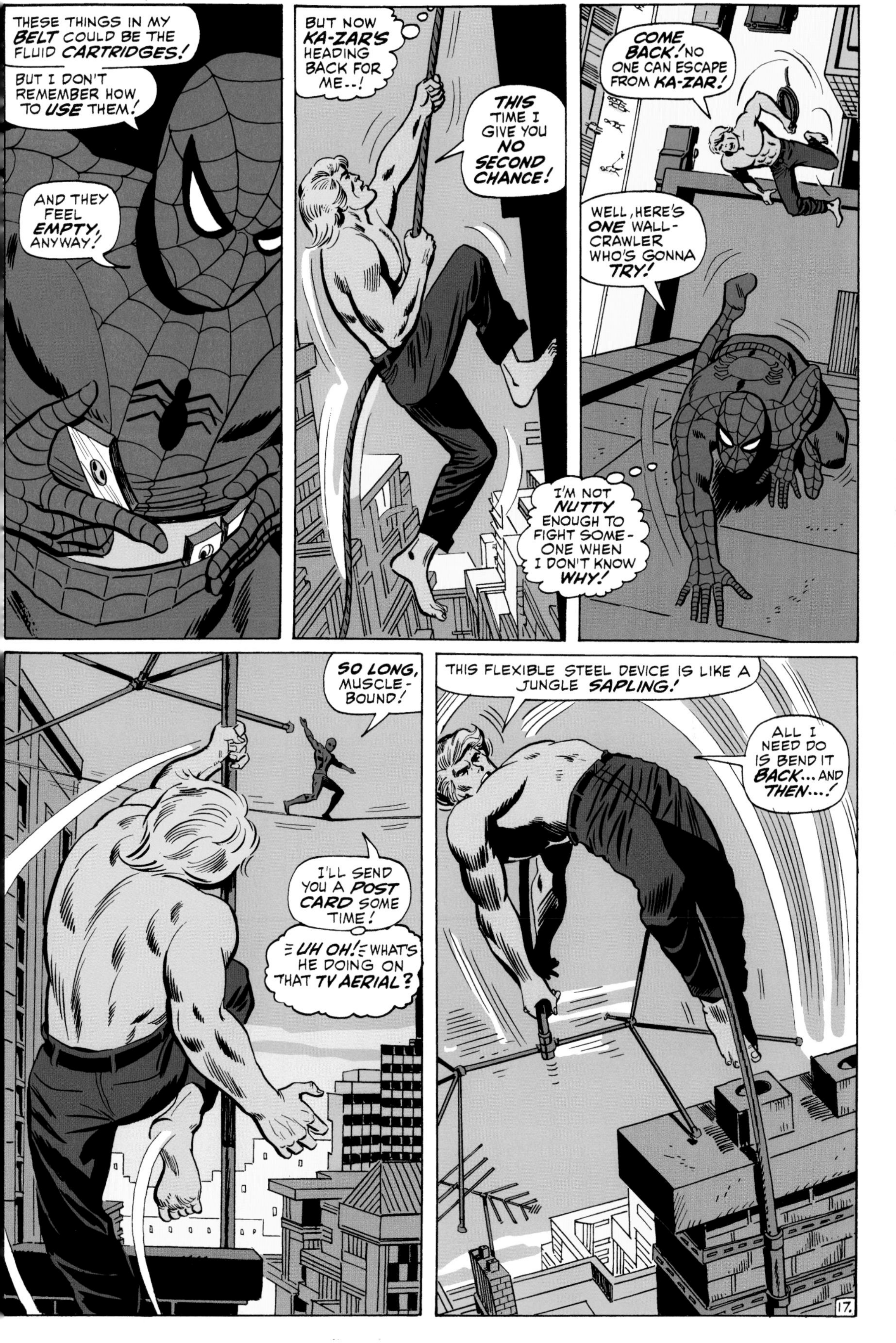
THESE THINGS IN MY BELT COULD BE THE FLUID CARTRIDGES!
BUT I DON'T REMEMBER HOW TO USE THEM!
AND THEY FEEL EMPTY, ANYWAY!
BUT NOW KA-ZAR'S HEADING BACK FOR ME..!
THIS TIME I GIVE YOU NO SECOND CHANCE!
COME BACK! NO ONE CAN ESCAPE FROM KA-ZAR!
WELL, HERE'S ONE WALL-CRAWLER WHO'S GONNA TRY!
I'M NOT NUTTY ENOUGH TO FIGHT SOME-ONE WHEN I DON'T KNOW WHY!
SO LONG, MUSCLE-BOUND!
I'LL SEND YOU A POST CARD SOME TIME!
UH OH! WHAT'S HE DOING ON THAT TV AERIAL?
THIS FLEXIBLE STEEL DEVICE IS LIKE A JUNGLE SAPLING!
ALL I NEED DO IS BEND IT BACK... AND THEN...!
17.

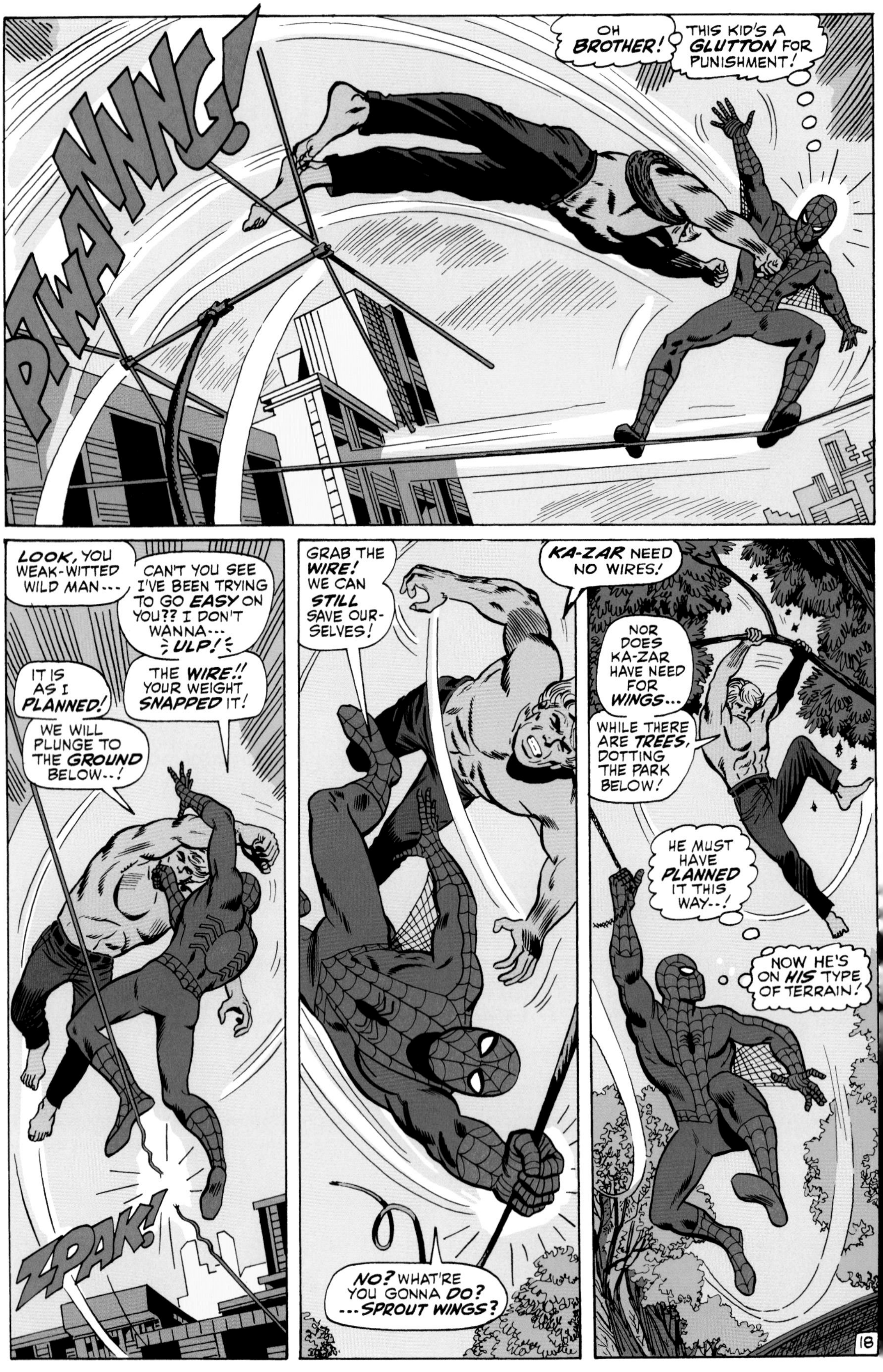
PTWANNG!
OH BROTHER!
THIS KID'S A GLUTTON FOR PUNISHMENT!
LOOK, YOU WEAK-WITTED WILD MAN---
CAN'T YOU SEE I'VE BEEN TRYING TO GO EASY ON YOU?? I DON'T WANNA---
ULP!
THE WIRE!! YOUR WEIGHT SNAPPED IT!
IT IS AS I PLANNED!
WE WILL PLUNGE TO THE GROUND BELOW--!
ZPAK!
GRAB THE WIRE! WE CAN STILL SAVE OUR-SELVES!
KA-ZAR NEED NO WIRES!
NO? WHAT'RE YOU GONNA DO? ---SPROUT WINGS?
NOR DOES KA-ZAR HAVE NEED FOR WINGS...
WHILE THERE ARE TREES, DOTTING THE PARK BELOW!
HE MUST HAVE PLANNED IT THIS WAY--!
NOW HE'S ON HIS TYPE OF TERRAIN!
18

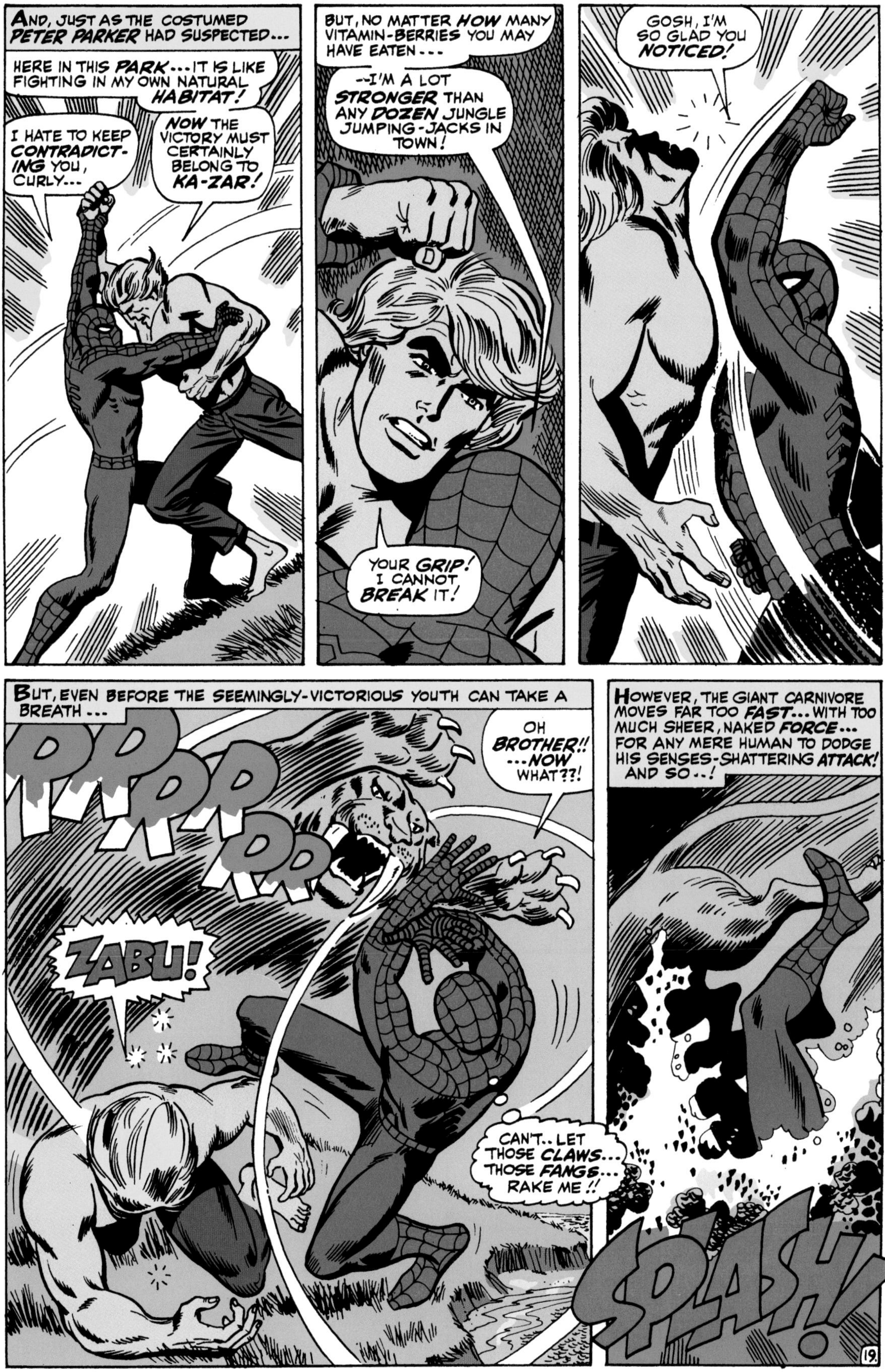
AND, JUST AS THE COSTUMED PETER PARKER HAD SUSPECTED...
HERE IN THIS PARK... IT IS LIKE FIGHTING IN MY OWN NATURAL HABITAT!
NOW THE VICTORY MUST CERTAINLY BELONG TO KA-ZAR!
I HATE TO KEEP CONTRADICTING YOU, CURLY...
BUT, NO MATTER HOW MANY VITAMIN-BERRIES YOU MAY HAVE EATEN---
--I'M A LOT STRONGER THAN ANY DOZEN JUNGLE JUMPING-JACKS IN TOWN!
YOUR GRIP! I CANNOT BREAK IT!
GOSH, I'M SO GLAD YOU NOTICED!
BUT, EVEN BEFORE THE SEEMINGLY-VICTORIOUS YOUTH CAN TAKE A BREATH...
OH BROTHER!! ...NOW WHAT??!
ZABU!
CAN'T.. LET THOSE CLAWS... THOSE FANGS... RAKE ME!!
HOWEVER, THE GIANT CARNIVORE MOVES FAR TOO FAST... WITH TOO MUCH SHEER, NAKED FORCE... FOR ANY MERE HUMAN TO DODGE HIS SENSES-SHATTERING ATTACK! AND SO..!
SPLASH!
19.

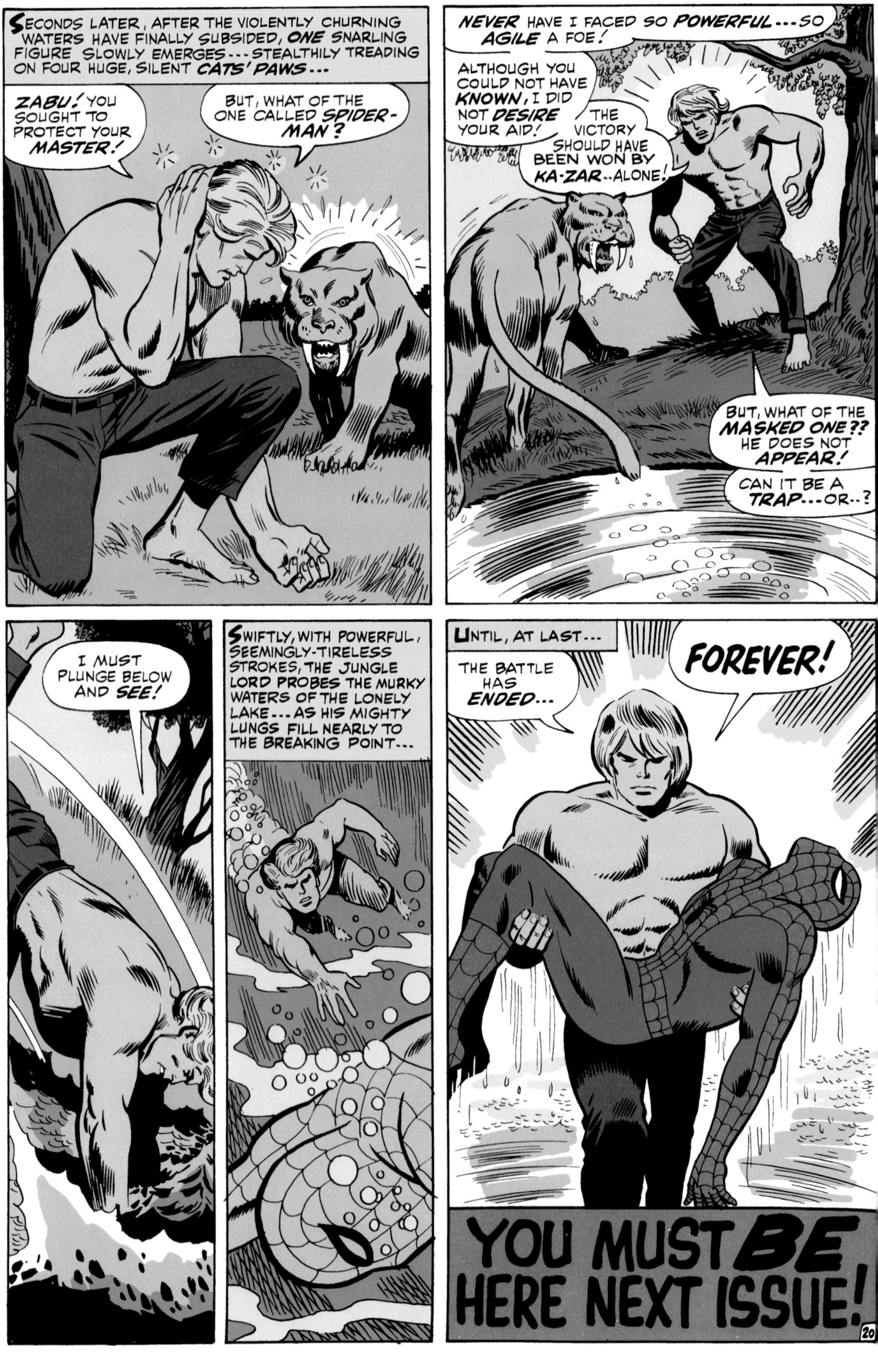
SECONDS LATER, AFTER THE VIOLENTLY CHURNING WATERS HAVE FINALLY SUBSIDED, ONE SNARLING FIGURE SLOWLY EMERGES--- STEALTHILY TREADING ON FOUR HUGE, SILENT CATS' PAWS---
ZABU! YOU SOUGHT TO PROTECT YOUR MASTER!
BUT, WHAT OF THE ONE CALLED SPIDER-MAN?
NEVER HAVE I FACED SO POWERFUL---SO AGILE A FOE!
ALTHOUGH YOU COULD NOT HAVE KNOWN, I DID NOT DESIRE YOUR AID!
THE VICTORY SHOULD HAVE BEEN WON BY KA-ZAR--ALONE!
BUT, WHAT OF THE MASKED ONE?? HE DOES NOT APPEAR!
CAN IT BE A TRAP---OR--?
I MUST PLUNGE BELOW AND SEE!
SWIFTLY, WITH POWERFUL, SEEMINGLY-TIRELESS STROKES, THE JUNGLE LORD PROBES THE MURKY WATERS OF THE LONELY LAKE---AS HIS MIGHTY LUNGS FILL NEARLY TO THE BREAKING POINT---
UNTIL, AT LAST---
THE BATTLE HAS ENDED---
FOREVER!
YOU MUST BE HERE NEXT ISSUE!
20

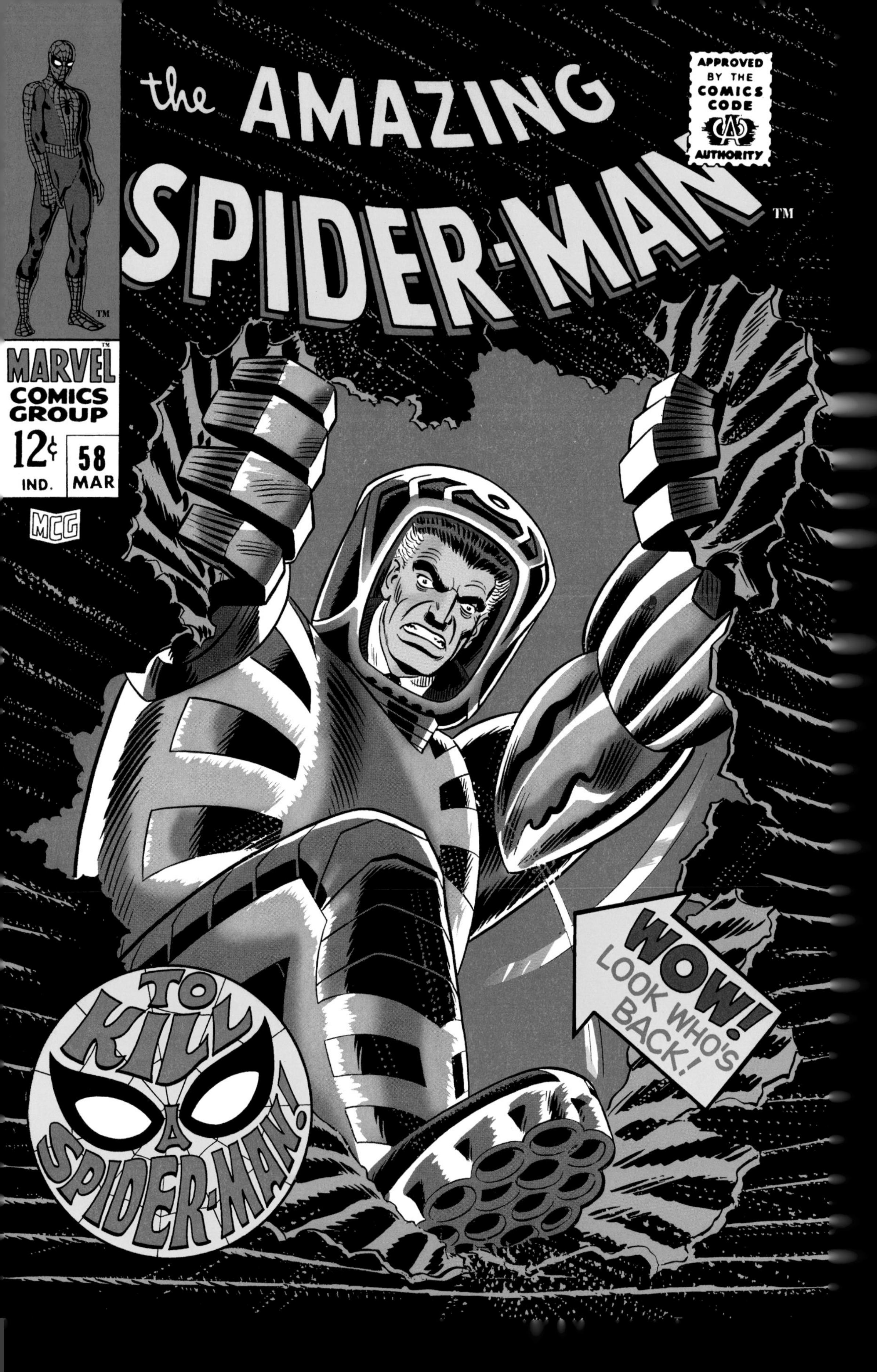

the AMAZING SPIDER-MAN™
APPROVED BY THE COMICS CODE AUTHORITY
MARVEL COMICS GROUP
12¢ IND.
58 MAR
MCG
WOW! LOOK WHO'S BACK!
TO KILL A SPIDER-MAN!

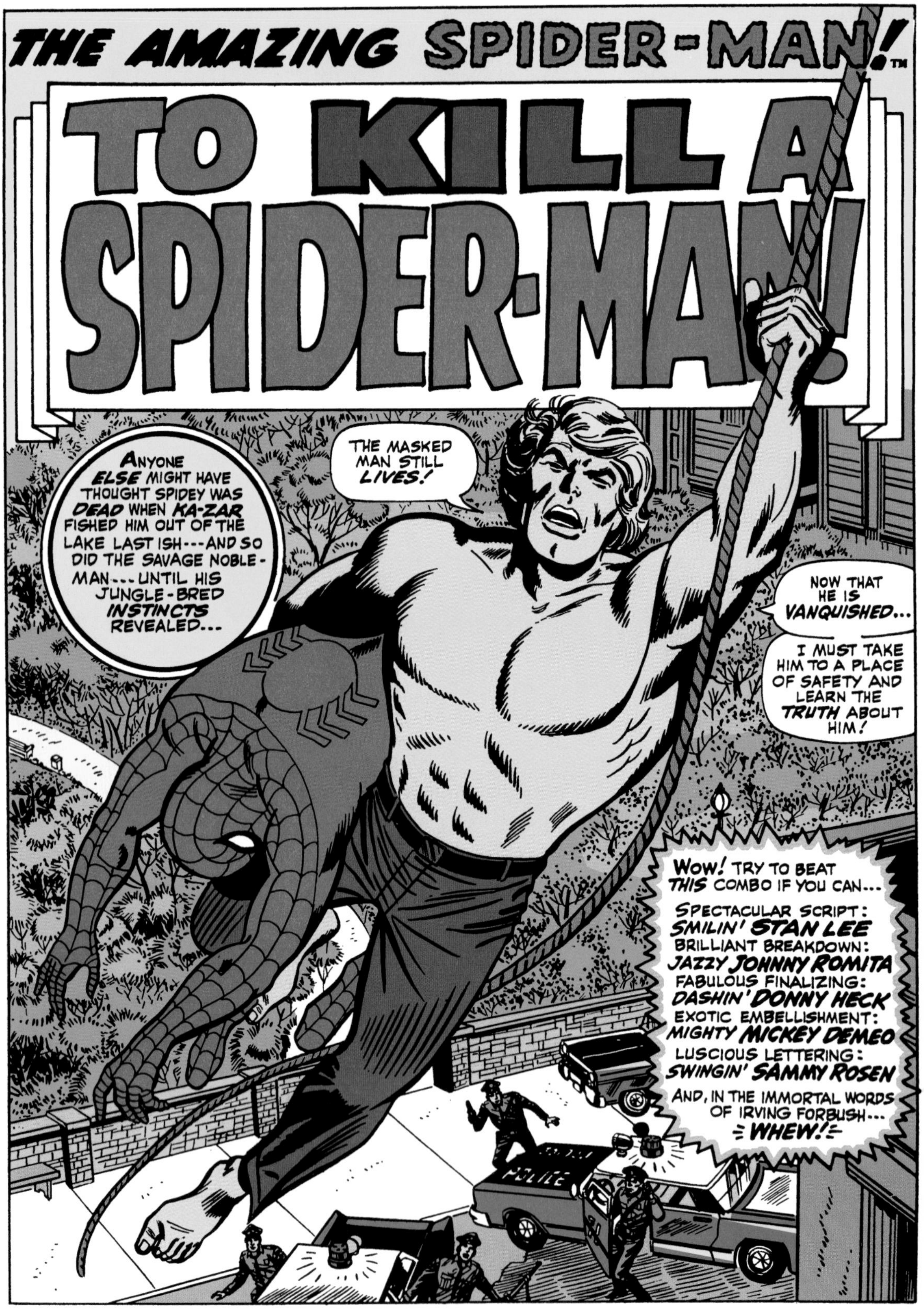
THE AMAZING SPIDER-MAN!™
TO KILL A SPIDER-MAN!
ANYONE ELSE MIGHT HAVE THOUGHT SPIDEY WAS DEAD WHEN KA-ZAR FISHED HIM OUT OF THE LAKE LAST ISH---AND SO DID THE SAVAGE NOBLE-MAN--- UNTIL HIS JUNGLE-BRED INSTINCTS REVEALED...
THE MASKED MAN STILL LIVES!
NOW THAT HE IS VANQUISHED...
I MUST TAKE HIM TO A PLACE OF SAFETY AND LEARN THE TRUTH ABOUT HIM!
WOW! TRY TO BEAT THIS COMBO IF YOU CAN...
SPECTACULAR SCRIPT: SMILIN' STAN LEE
BRILLIANT BREAKDOWN: JAZZY JOHNNY ROMITA
FABULOUS FINALIZING: DASHIN' DONNY HECK
EXOTIC EMBELLISHMENT: MIGHTY MICKEY DEMEO
LUSCIOUS LETTERING: SWINGIN' SAMMY ROSEN
AND, IN THE IMMORTAL WORDS OF IRVING FORBUSH... WHEW!
POLICE

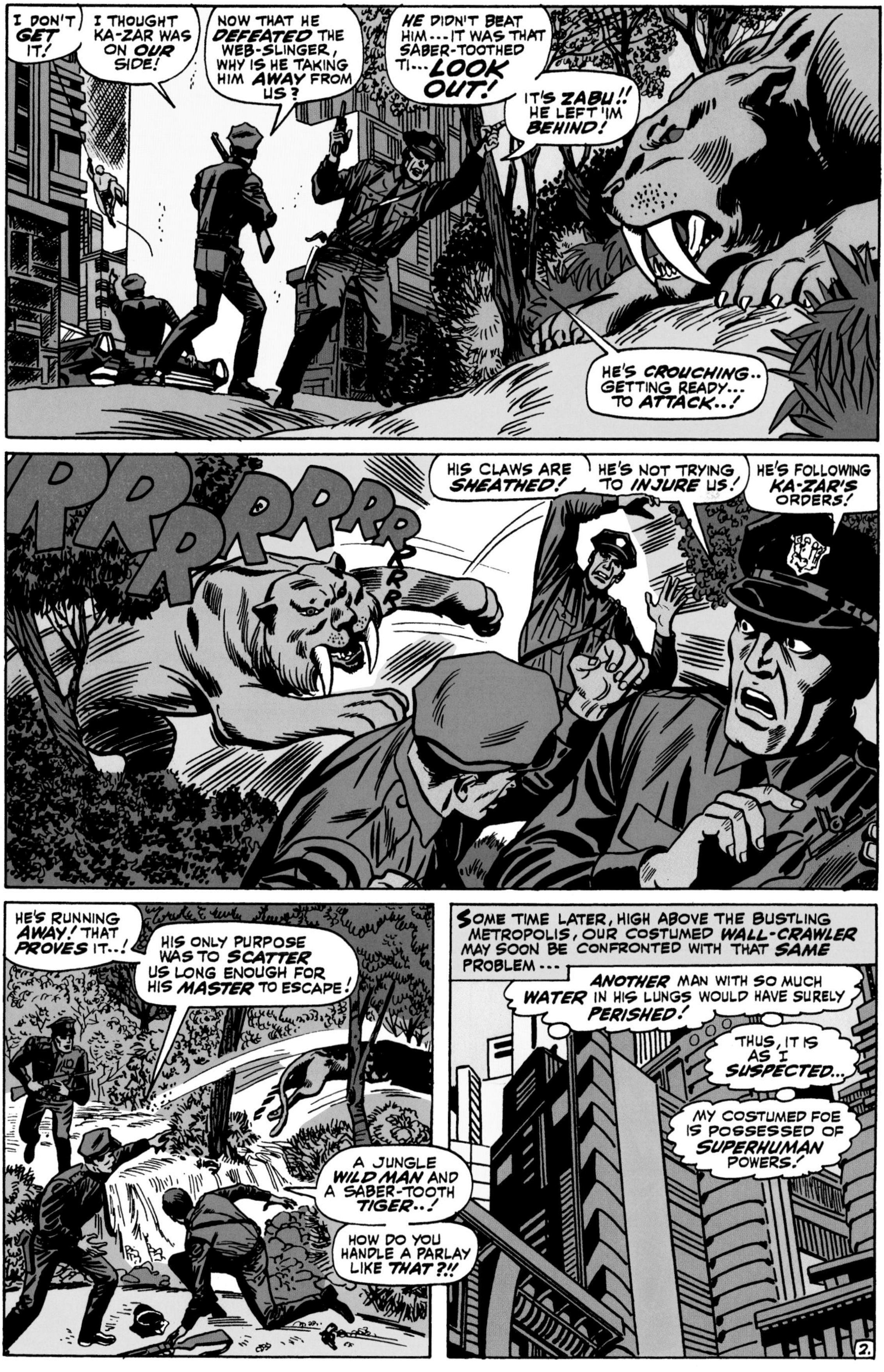
I DON'T GET IT!
I THOUGHT KA-ZAR WAS ON OUR SIDE!
NOW THAT HE DEFEATED THE WEB-SLINGER, WHY IS HE TAKING HIM AWAY FROM US?
HE DIDN'T BEAT HIM---IT WAS THAT SABER-TOOTHED TI... LOOK OUT!
IT'S ZABU!! HE LEFT 'IM BEHIND!
HE'S CROUCHING.. GETTING READY... TO ATTACK..!
RRRRRRRRRRRR
HIS CLAWS ARE SHEATHED!
HE'S NOT TRYING TO INJURE US!
HE'S FOLLOWING KA-ZAR'S ORDERS!
HE'S RUNNING AWAY! THAT PROVES IT..!
HIS ONLY PURPOSE WAS TO SCATTER US LONG ENOUGH FOR HIS MASTER TO ESCAPE!
A JUNGLE WILD MAN AND A SABER-TOOTH TIGER..!
HOW DO YOU HANDLE A PARLAY LIKE THAT?!!
SOME TIME LATER, HIGH ABOVE THE BUSTLING METROPOLIS, OUR COSTUMED WALL-CRAWLER MAY SOON BE CONFRONTED WITH THAT SAME PROBLEM---
ANOTHER MAN WITH SO MUCH WATER IN HIS LUNGS WOULD HAVE SURELY PERISHED!
THUS, IT IS AS I SUSPECTED...
MY COSTUMED FOE IS POSSESSED OF SUPERHUMAN POWERS!
2.

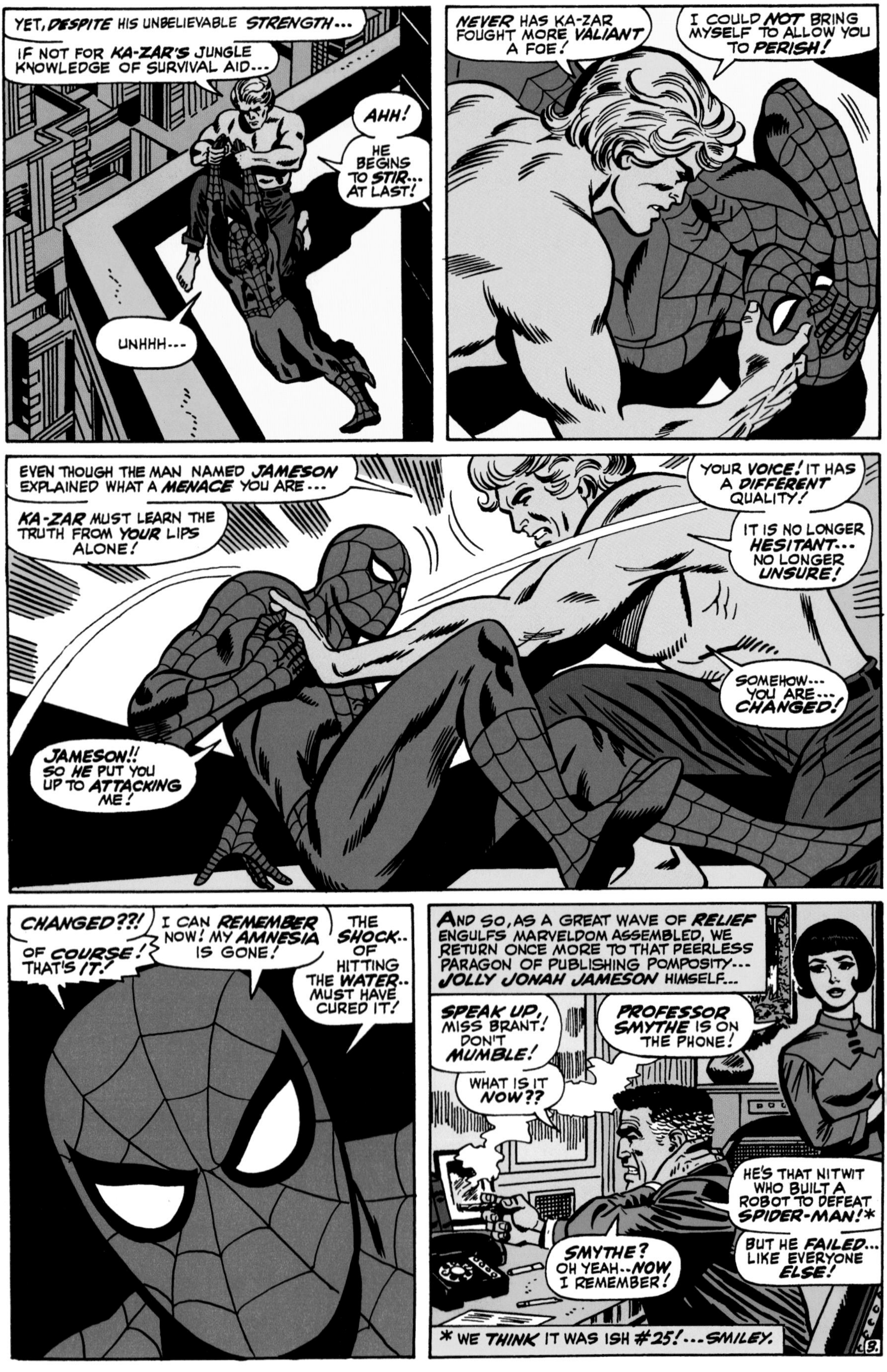
YET, DESPITE HIS UNBELIEVABLE STRENGTH...
IF NOT FOR KA-ZAR'S JUNGLE KNOWLEDGE OF SURVIVAL AID...
AHH!
HE BEGINS TO STIR... AT LAST!
UNHHH---
NEVER HAS KA-ZAR FOUGHT MORE VALIANT A FOE!
I COULD NOT BRING MYSELF TO ALLOW YOU TO PERISH!
EVEN THOUGH THE MAN NAMED JAMESON EXPLAINED WHAT A MENACE YOU ARE...
KA-ZAR MUST LEARN THE TRUTH FROM YOUR LIPS ALONE!
YOUR VOICE! IT HAS A DIFFERENT QUALITY!
IT IS NO LONGER HESITANT... NO LONGER UNSURE!
SOMEHOW--- YOU ARE--- CHANGED!
JAMESON!! SO HE PUT YOU UP TO ATTACKING ME!
CHANGED??!
OF COURSE! THAT'S IT!
I CAN REMEMBER NOW! MY AMNESIA IS GONE!
THE SHOCK.. OF HITTING THE WATER.. MUST HAVE CURED IT!
AND SO, AS A GREAT WAVE OF RELIEF ENGULFS MARVELDOM ASSEMBLED, WE RETURN ONCE MORE TO THAT PEERLESS PARAGON OF PUBLISHING POMPOSITY--- JOLLY JONAH JAMESON HIMSELF...
SPEAK UP, MISS BRANT! DON'T MUMBLE!
PROFESSOR SMYTHE IS ON THE PHONE!
WHAT IS IT NOW??
HE'S THAT NITWIT WHO BUILT A ROBOT TO DEFEAT SPIDER-MAN!*
SMYTHE? OH YEAH--NOW I REMEMBER!
BUT HE FAILED... LIKE EVERYONE ELSE!
* WE THINK IT WAS ISH #25!... SMILEY.
9.

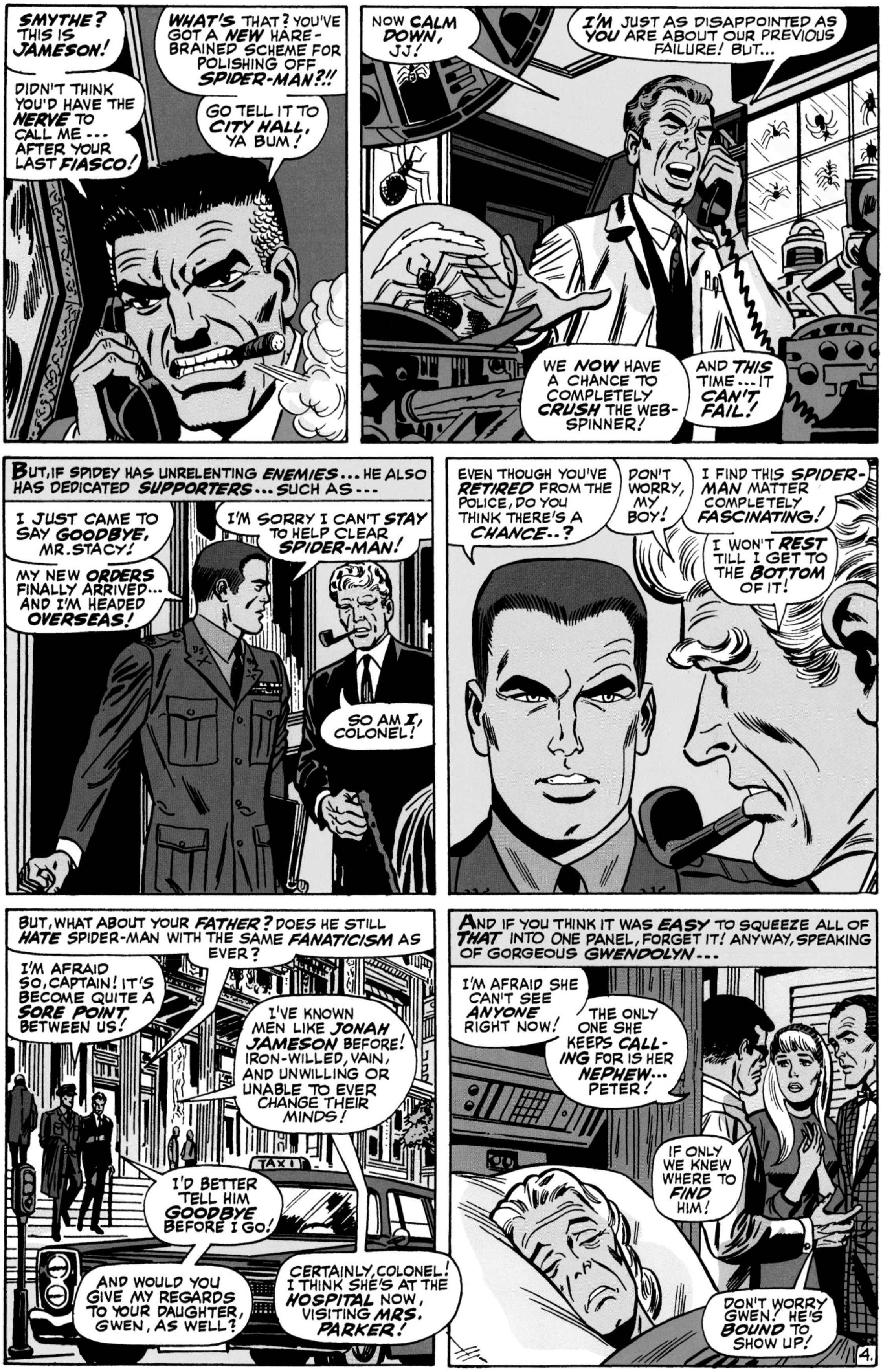
SMYTHE? THIS IS JAMESON!
DIDN'T THINK YOU'D HAVE THE NERVE TO CALL ME --- AFTER YOUR LAST FIASCO!
WHAT'S THAT? YOU'VE GOT A NEW HARE-BRAINED SCHEME FOR POLISHING OFF SPIDER-MAN?!!
GO TELL IT TO CITY HALL, YA BUM!
NOW CALM DOWN, JJ!
I'M JUST AS DISAPPOINTED AS YOU ARE ABOUT OUR PREVIOUS FAILURE! BUT...
WE NOW HAVE A CHANCE TO COMPLETELY CRUSH THE WEB-SPINNER!
AND THIS TIME... IT CAN'T FAIL!
BUT, IF SPIDEY HAS UNRELENTING ENEMIES... HE ALSO HAS DEDICATED SUPPORTERS... SUCH AS---
I JUST CAME TO SAY GOODBYE, MR. STACY!
MY NEW ORDERS FINALLY ARRIVED... AND I'M HEADED OVERSEAS!
I'M SORRY I CAN'T STAY TO HELP CLEAR SPIDER-MAN!
SO AM I, COLONEL!
EVEN THOUGH YOU'VE RETIRED FROM THE POLICE, DO YOU THINK THERE'S A CHANCE..?
DON'T WORRY, MY BOY!
I FIND THIS SPIDER-MAN MATTER COMPLETELY FASCINATING!
I WON'T REST TILL I GET TO THE BOTTOM OF IT!
BUT, WHAT ABOUT YOUR FATHER? DOES HE STILL HATE SPIDER-MAN WITH THE SAME FANATICISM AS EVER?
I'M AFRAID SO, CAPTAIN! IT'S BECOME QUITE A SORE POINT BETWEEN US!
I'VE KNOWN MEN LIKE JONAH JAMESON BEFORE! IRON-WILLED, VAIN, AND UNWILLING OR UNABLE TO EVER CHANGE THEIR MINDS!
TAXI
I'D BETTER TELL HIM GOODBYE BEFORE I GO!
AND WOULD YOU GIVE MY REGARDS TO YOUR DAUGHTER, GWEN, AS WELL?
CERTAINLY, COLONEL! I THINK SHE'S AT THE HOSPITAL NOW, VISITING MRS. PARKER!
AND IF YOU THINK IT WAS EASY TO SQUEEZE ALL OF THAT INTO ONE PANEL, FORGET IT! ANYWAY, SPEAKING OF GORGEOUS GWENDOLYN---
I'M AFRAID SHE CAN'T SEE ANYONE RIGHT NOW!
THE ONLY ONE SHE KEEPS CALLING FOR IS HER NEPHEW... PETER!
IF ONLY WE KNEW WHERE TO FIND HIM!
DON'T WORRY GWEN! HE'S BOUND TO SHOW UP!
4.

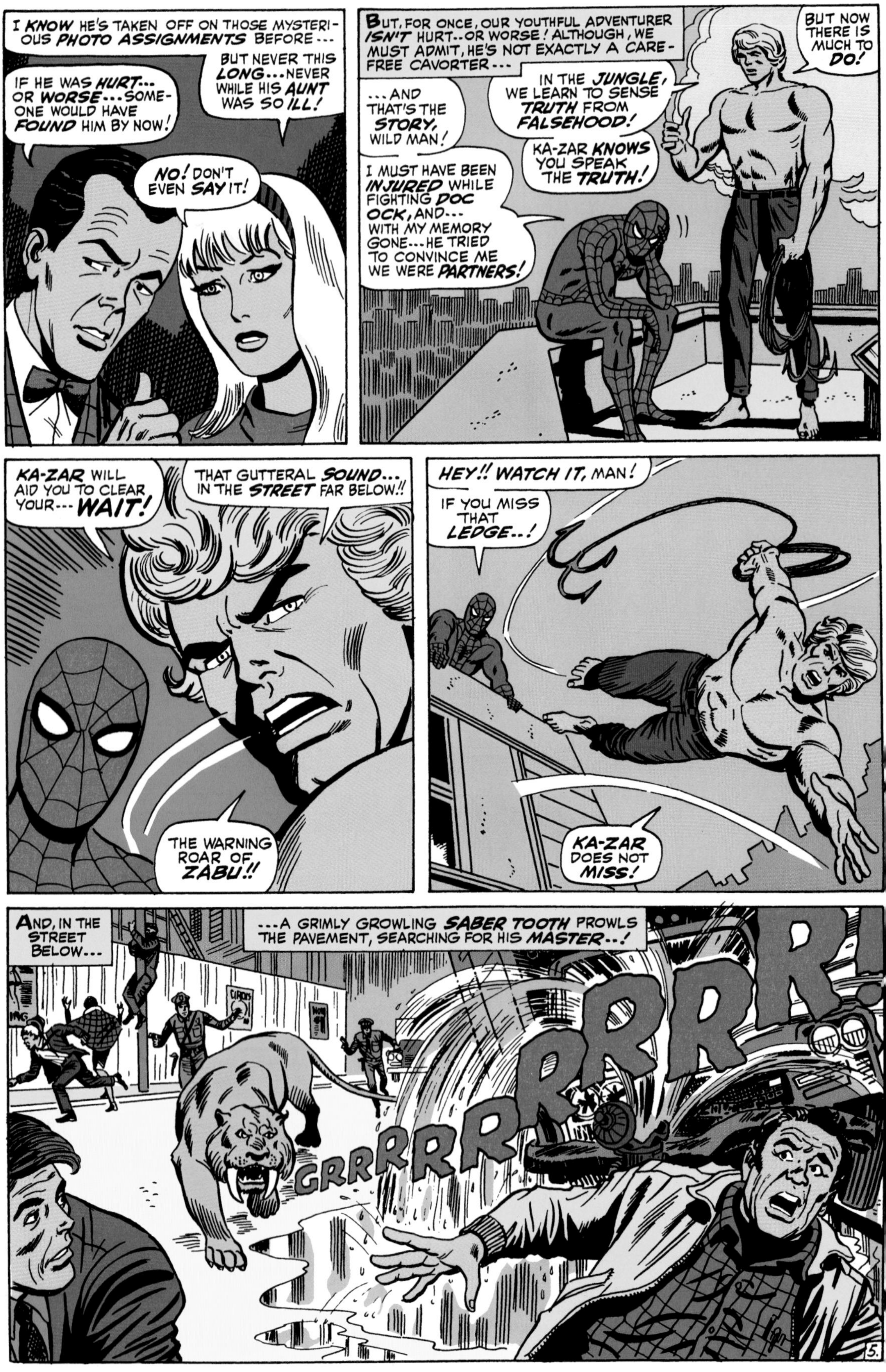
I KNOW HE'S TAKEN OFF ON THOSE MYSTERIOUS PHOTO ASSIGNMENTS BEFORE---
BUT NEVER THIS LONG...NEVER WHILE HIS AUNT WAS SO ILL!
IF HE WAS HURT...OR WORSE...SOMEONE WOULD HAVE FOUND HIM BY NOW!
NO! DON'T EVEN SAY IT!
BUT, FOR ONCE, OUR YOUTHFUL ADVENTURER ISN'T HURT--OR WORSE! ALTHOUGH, WE MUST ADMIT, HE'S NOT EXACTLY A CAREFREE CAVORTER---
BUT NOW THERE IS MUCH TO DO!
...AND THAT'S THE STORY, WILD MAN!
I MUST HAVE BEEN INJURED WHILE FIGHTING DOC OCK, AND--- WITH MY MEMORY GONE---HE TRIED TO CONVINCE ME WE WERE PARTNERS!
IN THE JUNGLE, WE LEARN TO SENSE TRUTH FROM FALSEHOOD!
KA-ZAR KNOWS YOU SPEAK THE TRUTH!
KA-ZAR WILL AID YOU TO CLEAR YOUR--- WAIT!
THAT GUTTERAL SOUND... IN THE STREET FAR BELOW!!
THE WARNING ROAR OF ZABU!!
HEY!! WATCH IT, MAN!
IF YOU MISS THAT LEDGE..!
KA-ZAR DOES NOT MISS!
AND, IN THE STREET BELOW---
...A GRIMLY GROWLING SABER TOOTH PROWLS THE PAVEMENT, SEARCHING FOR HIS MASTER..!
GRRRRRRRRRRRR!
5.

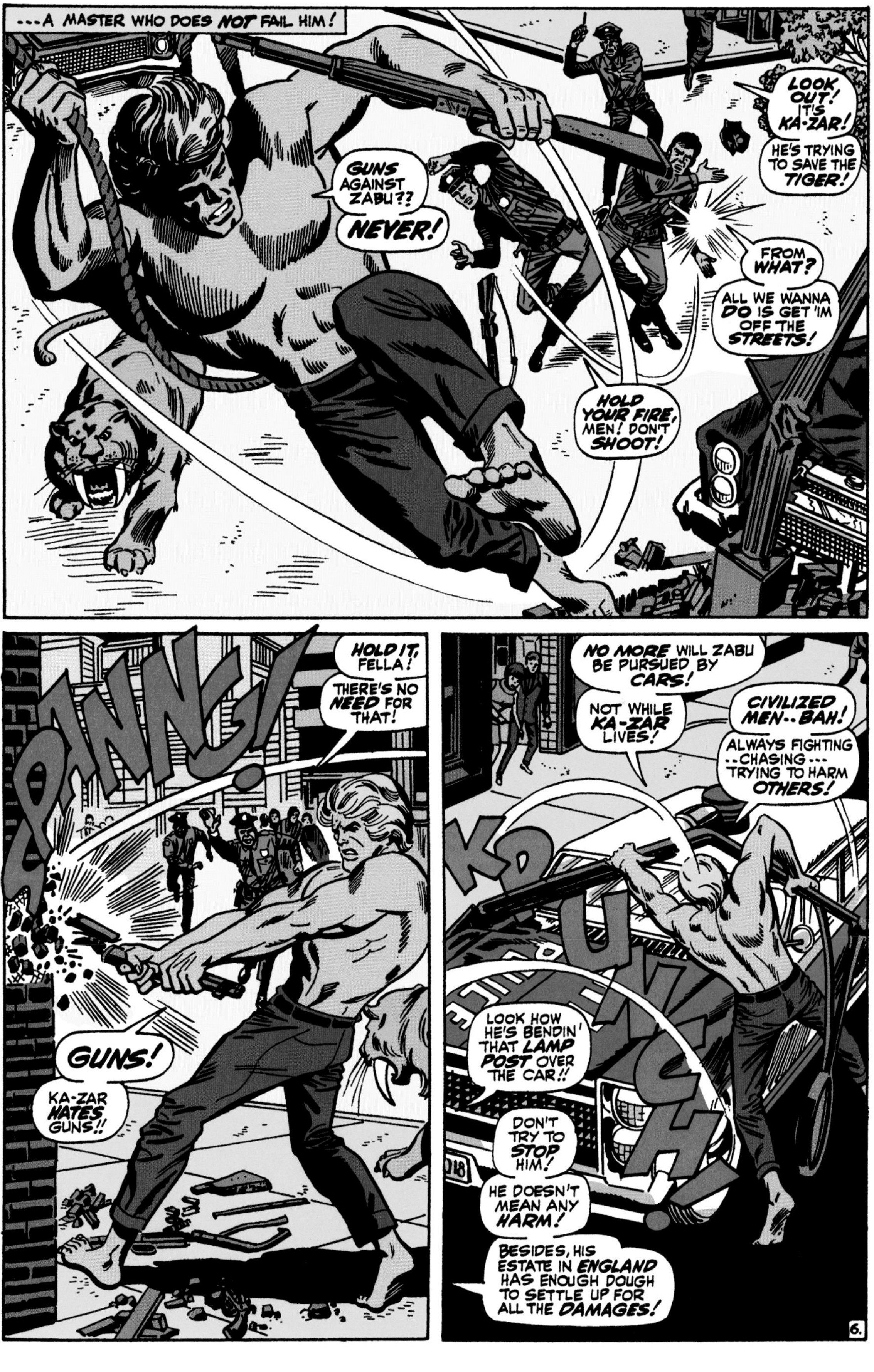

...A MASTER WHO DOES NOT FAIL HIM!
GUNS AGAINST ZABU?? NEVER!
LOOK OUT! IT'S KA-ZAR!
HE'S TRYING TO SAVE THE TIGER!
FROM WHAT?
ALL WE WANNA DO IS GET 'IM OFF THE STREETS!
HOLD YOUR FIRE, MEN! DON'T SHOOT!
HOLD IT, FELLA!
THERE'S NO NEED FOR THAT!
GUNS!
KA-ZAR HATES GUNS!!
NO MORE WILL ZABU BE PURSUED BY CARS!
NOT WHILE KA-ZAR LIVES!
CIVILIZED MEN..BAH!
ALWAYS FIGHTING ..CHASING... TRYING TO HARM OTHERS!
LOOK HOW HE'S BENDIN' THAT LAMP POST OVER THE CAR!!
DON'T TRY TO STOP HIM!
HE DOESN'T MEAN ANY HARM!
BESIDES, HIS ESTATE IN ENGLAND HAS ENOUGH DOUGH TO SETTLE UP FOR ALL THE DAMAGES!
6.

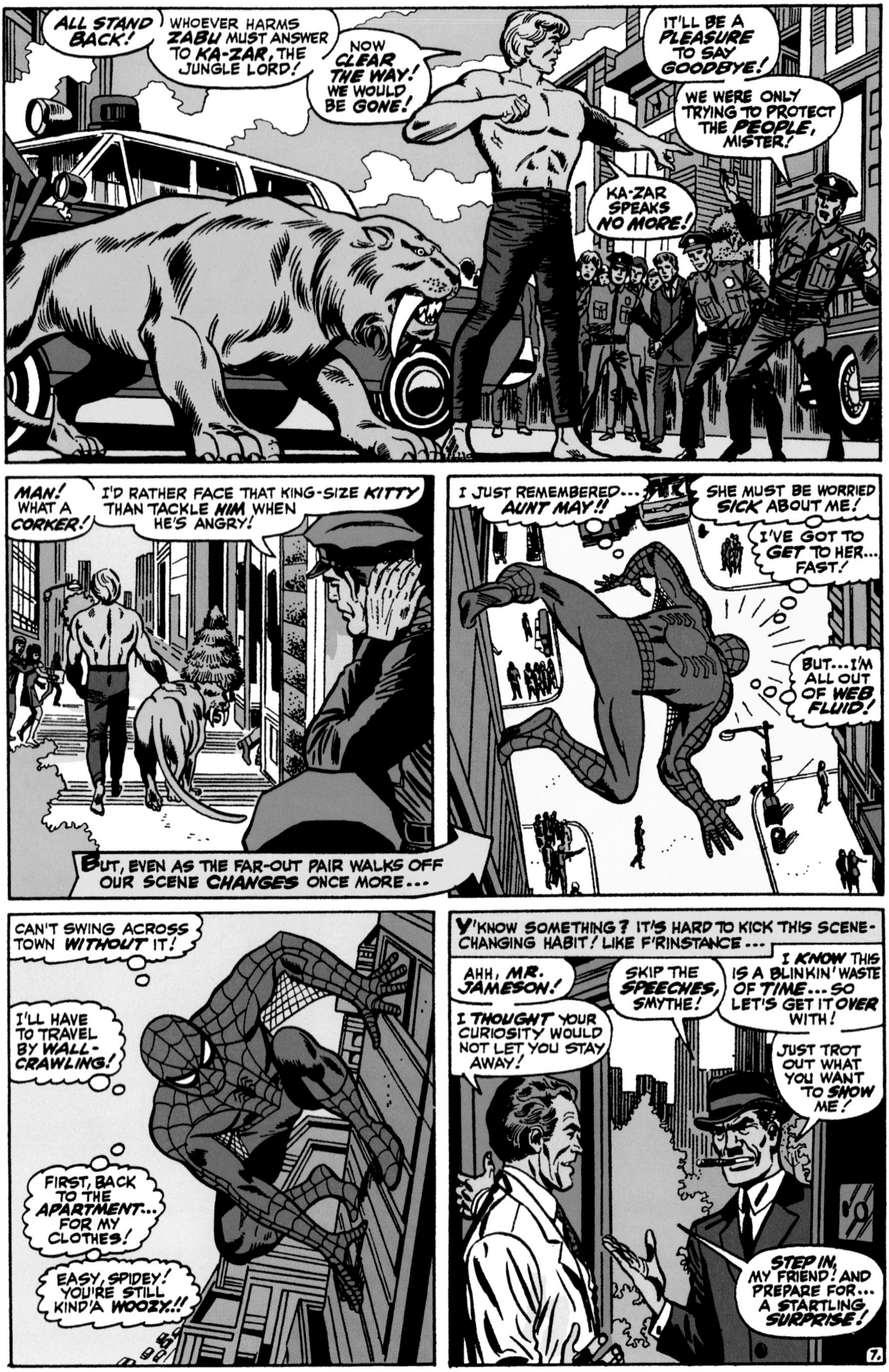
ALL STAND BACK!
WHOEVER HARMS ZABU MUST ANSWER TO KA-ZAR, THE JUNGLE LORD!
NOW CLEAR THE WAY! WE WOULD BE GONE!
IT'LL BE A PLEASURE TO SAY GOODBYE!
WE WERE ONLY TRYING TO PROTECT THE PEOPLE, MISTER!
KA-ZAR SPEAKS NO MORE!
MAN! WHAT A CORKER!
I'D RATHER FACE THAT KING-SIZE KITTY THAN TACKLE HIM WHEN HE'S ANGRY!
BUT, EVEN AS THE FAR-OUT PAIR WALKS OFF OUR SCENE CHANGES ONCE MORE...
I JUST REMEMBERED... AUNT MAY!!
SHE MUST BE WORRIED SICK ABOUT ME!
I'VE GOT TO GET TO HER... FAST!
BUT... I'M ALL OUT OF WEB FLUID!
CAN'T SWING ACROSS TOWN WITHOUT IT!
I'LL HAVE TO TRAVEL BY WALL-CRAWLING!
FIRST, BACK TO THE APARTMENT... FOR MY CLOTHES!
EASY, SPIDEY! YOU'RE STILL KIND'A WOOZY!!
Y'KNOW SOMETHING? IT'S HARD TO KICK THIS SCENE-CHANGING HABIT! LIKE F'RINSTANCE...
AHH, MR. JAMESON!
I THOUGHT YOUR CURIOSITY WOULD NOT LET YOU STAY AWAY!
SKIP THE SPEECHES, SMYTHE!
I KNOW THIS IS A BLINKIN' WASTE OF TIME... SO LET'S GET IT OVER WITH!
JUST TROT OUT WHAT YOU WANT TO SHOW ME!
STEP IN, MY FRIEND! AND PREPARE FOR... A STARTLING SURPRISE!
7.

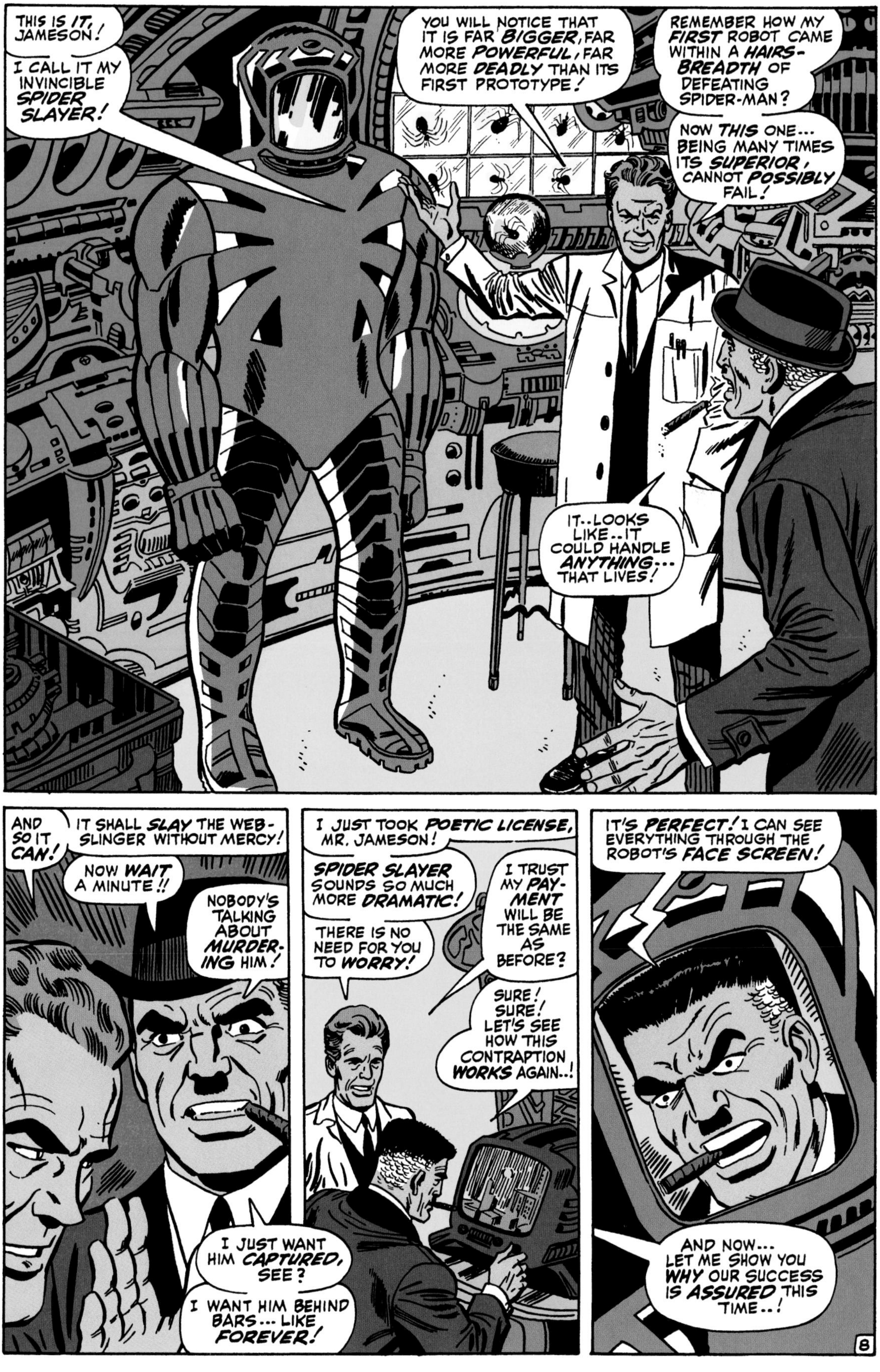
THIS IS IT, JAMESON!
I CALL IT MY INVINCIBLE SPIDER SLAYER!
YOU WILL NOTICE THAT IT IS FAR BIGGER, FAR MORE POWERFUL, FAR MORE DEADLY THAN ITS FIRST PROTOTYPE!
REMEMBER HOW MY FIRST ROBOT CAME WITHIN A HAIRS-BREADTH OF DEFEATING SPIDER-MAN?
NOW THIS ONE... BEING MANY TIMES ITS SUPERIOR, CANNOT POSSIBLY FAIL!
IT..LOOKS LIKE..IT COULD HANDLE ANYTHING... THAT LIVES!
AND SO IT CAN!
IT SHALL SLAY THE WEB-SLINGER WITHOUT MERCY!
NOW WAIT A MINUTE!!
NOBODY'S TALKING ABOUT MURDERING HIM!
I JUST WANT HIM CAPTURED, SEE?
I WANT HIM BEHIND BARS... LIKE FOREVER!
I JUST TOOK POETIC LICENSE, MR. JAMESON!
SPIDER SLAYER SOUNDS SO MUCH MORE DRAMATIC!
THERE IS NO NEED FOR YOU TO WORRY!
I TRUST MY PAYMENT WILL BE THE SAME AS BEFORE?
SURE! SURE! LET'S SEE HOW THIS CONTRAPTION WORKS AGAIN..!
IT'S PERFECT! I CAN SEE EVERYTHING THROUGH THE ROBOT'S FACE SCREEN!
AND NOW... LET ME SHOW YOU WHY OUR SUCCESS IS ASSURED THIS TIME..!
8

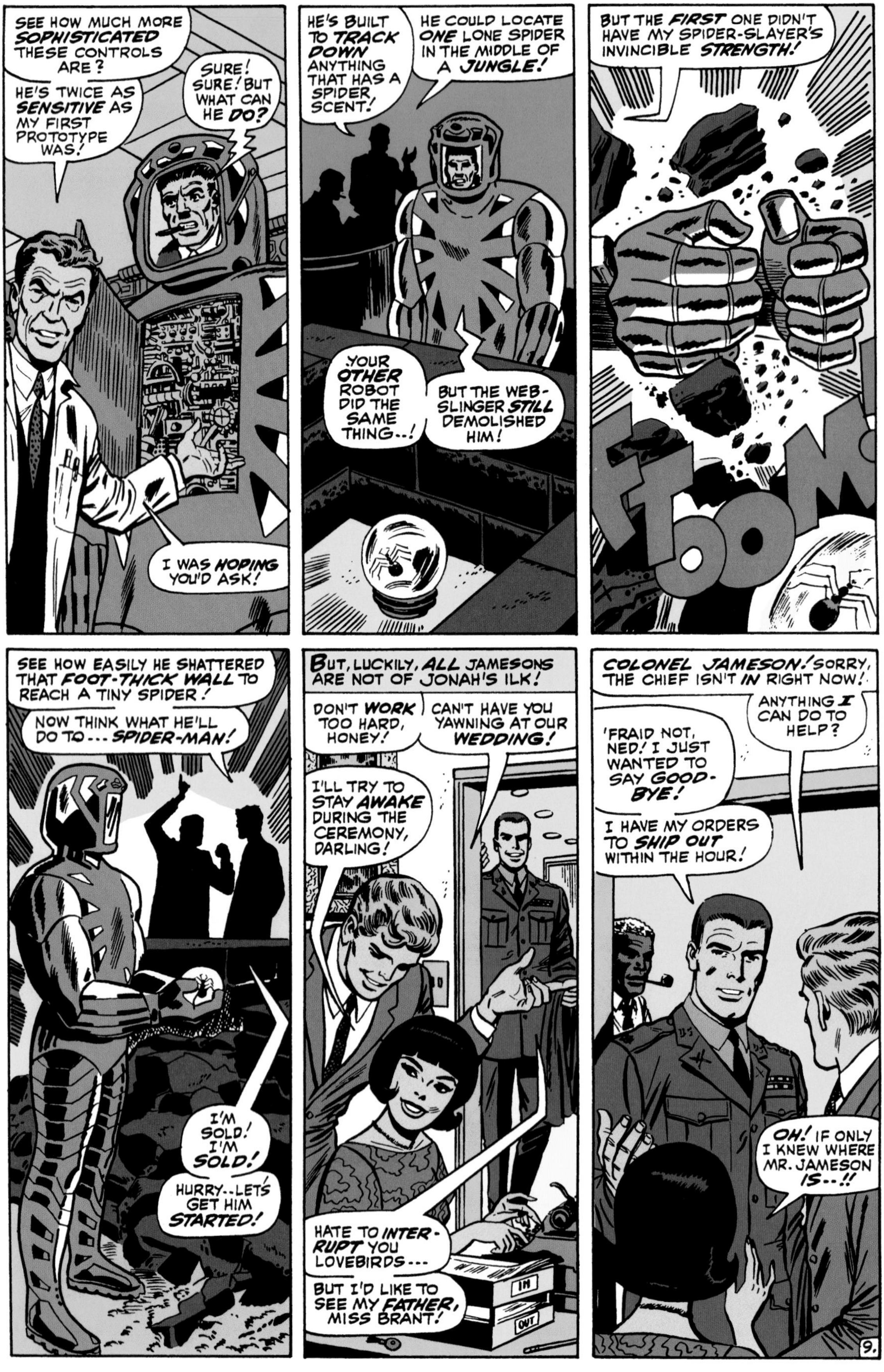

SEE HOW MUCH MORE SOPHISTICATED THESE CONTROLS ARE?
HE'S TWICE AS SENSITIVE AS MY FIRST PROTOTYPE WAS!
SURE! SURE! BUT WHAT CAN HE DO?
I WAS HOPING YOU'D ASK!
HE'S BUILT TO TRACK DOWN ANYTHING THAT HAS A SPIDER SCENT!
HE COULD LOCATE ONE LONE SPIDER IN THE MIDDLE OF A JUNGLE!
YOUR OTHER ROBOT DID THE SAME THING..!
BUT THE WEB-SLINGER STILL DEMOLISHED HIM!
BUT THE FIRST ONE DIDN'T HAVE MY SPIDER-SLAYER'S INVINCIBLE STRENGTH!
FTOOM!
SEE HOW EASILY HE SHATTERED THAT FOOT-THICK WALL TO REACH A TINY SPIDER!
NOW THINK WHAT HE'LL DO TO... SPIDER-MAN!
I'M SOLD! I'M SOLD!
HURRY..LET'S GET HIM STARTED!
BUT, LUCKILY, ALL JAMESONS ARE NOT OF JONAH'S ILK!
DON'T WORK TOO HARD, HONEY!
CAN'T HAVE YOU YAWNING AT OUR WEDDING!
I'LL TRY TO STAY AWAKE DURING THE CEREMONY, DARLING!
HATE TO INTER-RUPT YOU LOVEBIRDS---
BUT I'D LIKE TO SEE MY FATHER, MISS BRANT!
IN
OUT
COLONEL JAMESON! SORRY, THE CHIEF ISN'T IN RIGHT NOW!
ANYTHING I CAN DO TO HELP?
'FRAID NOT, NED! I JUST WANTED TO SAY GOOD-BYE!
I HAVE MY ORDERS TO SHIP OUT WITHIN THE HOUR!
OH! IF ONLY I KNEW WHERE MR. JAMESON IS..!!
9.

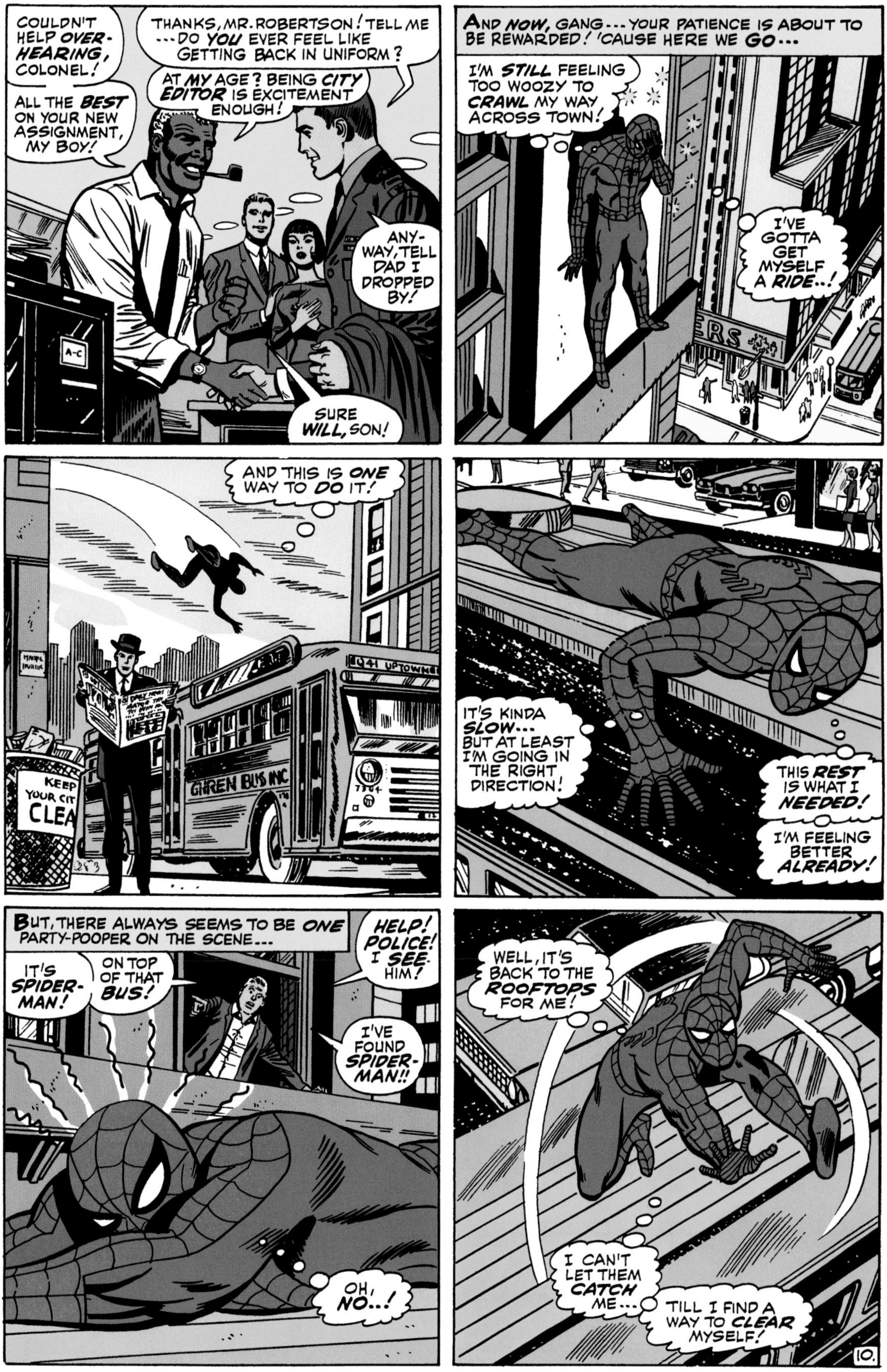
COULDN'T HELP OVER-HEARING, COLONEL!
THANKS, MR. ROBERTSON! TELL ME ...DO YOU EVER FEEL LIKE GETTING BACK IN UNIFORM?
AT MY AGE? BEING CITY EDITOR IS EXCITEMENT ENOUGH!
ALL THE BEST ON YOUR NEW ASSIGNMENT, MY BOY!
ANY-WAY, TELL DAD I DROPPED BY!
SURE WILL, SON!
AND NOW, GANG... YOUR PATIENCE IS ABOUT TO BE REWARDED! 'CAUSE HERE WE GO...
I'M STILL FEELING TOO WOOZY TO CRAWL MY WAY ACROSS TOWN!
I'VE GOTTA GET MYSELF A RIDE..!
AND THIS IS ONE WAY TO DO IT!
41 UPTOWN
GHREN BUS INC
KEEP YOUR CIT CLEA
IT'S KINDA SLOW... BUT AT LEAST I'M GOING IN THE RIGHT DIRECTION!
THIS REST IS WHAT I NEEDED!
I'M FEELING BETTER ALREADY!
BUT, THERE ALWAYS SEEMS TO BE ONE PARTY-POOPER ON THE SCENE...
IT'S SPIDER-MAN!
ON TOP OF THAT BUS!
HELP! POLICE! I SEE HIM!
I'VE FOUND SPIDER-MAN!!
OH, NO..!
WELL, IT'S BACK TO THE ROOFTOPS FOR ME!
I CAN'T LET THEM CATCH ME...
TILL I FIND A WAY TO CLEAR MYSELF!
10.

BUT, IF SPIDEY THINKS HE'LL HAVE TIME FOR MAKING LEISURE-LY *PLANS...* FORGET IT!!

HOP IN, *JAMESON!* WE'LL FOLLOW THE *SPIDER SLAYER* HERE IN MY CAR!

GOOD! I DON'T WANT TO BE TOO FAR *AWAY* WHEN HE CATCHES UP WITH THAT MASKED MISFIT!

HE WALKS LIKE HE KNOWS WHERE HE'S *GOING!*

MAYBE HE'S PICKED UP THE TRAIL *ALREADY!*

OF COURSE! IF SPIDER-MAN IS ANY-WHERE IN THE *CITY,* HE'S AS GOOD AS *TRAPPED!*

WHAT A *FUN* WAY TO PASS THE TIME!

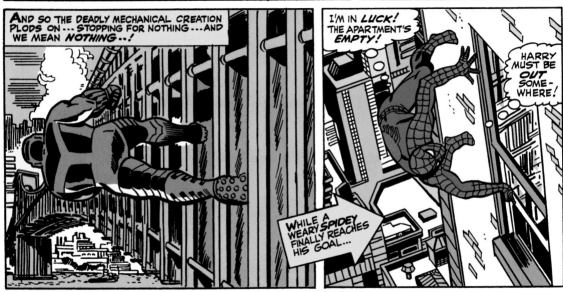

AND SO THE DEADLY MECHANICAL CREATION PLODS ON... STOPPING FOR NOTHING... AND WE MEAN *NOTHING*...!

I'M IN *LUCK!* THE APARTMENT'S *EMPTY!*

HARRY MUST BE *OUT* SOME-WHERE!

WHILE A WEARY *SPIDEY* FINALLY REACHES HIS GOAL...

FIRST THING TO DO IS GET OUT OF THESE DUDS AND CHECK WITH *AUNT MAY!*

≋ WHEW! ≋ I'VE NEVER FELT SO *TIRED* BEFORE!

NO ANSWER!

MAYBE IT'S JUST AS *WELL!* I'M NOT *SURE* WHAT I'D *TELL* HER, ANYWAY!

AFTER I GET SOME *SHUT-EYE,* I'LL... *SAY!* WHY'S MY SPIDEY-SENSE *TINGLING* LIKE THIS?!!

SOME-THING'S *WRONG!*

11.

120

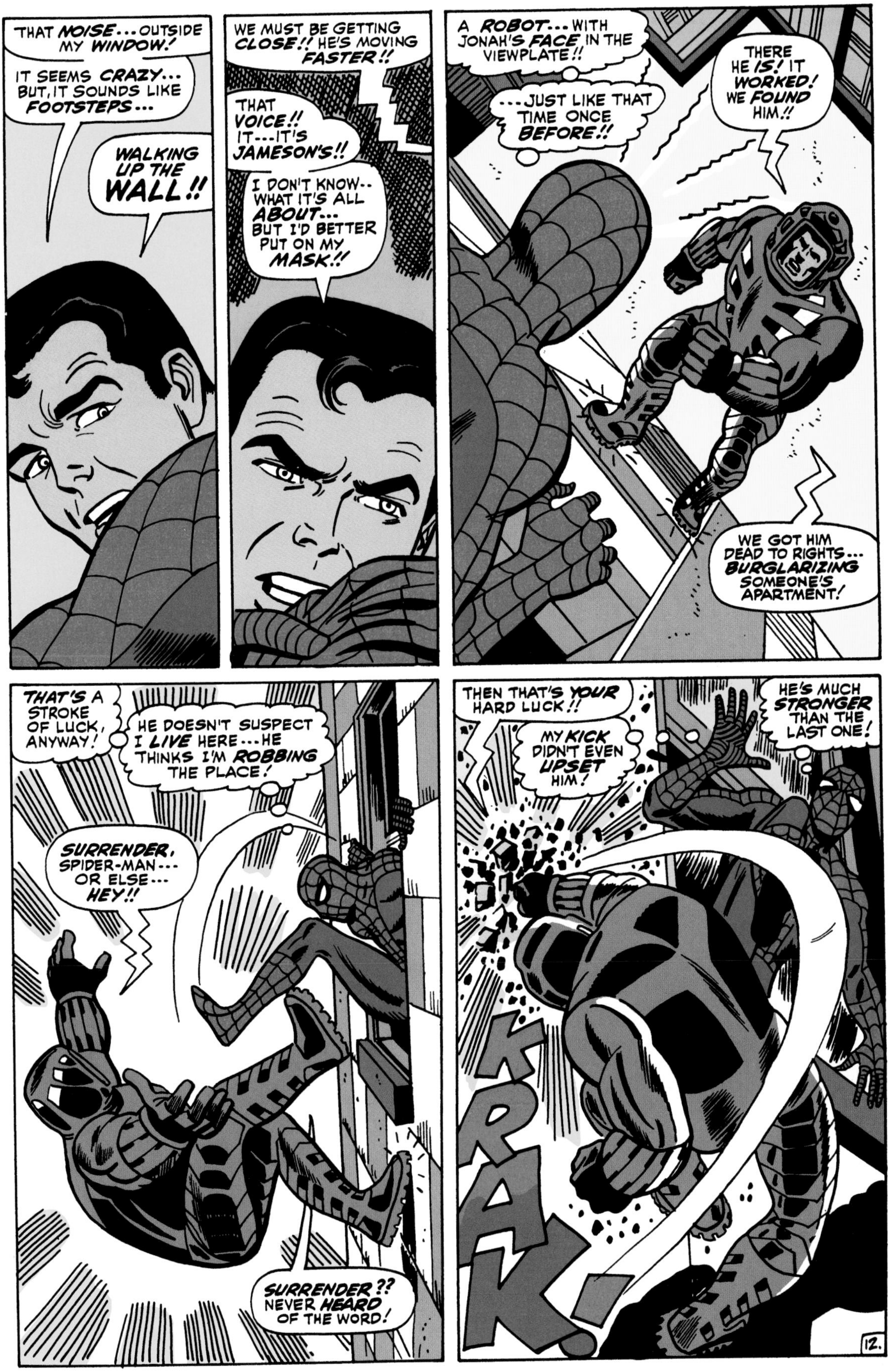
THAT NOISE... OUTSIDE MY WINDOW!
IT SEEMS CRAZY... BUT, IT SOUNDS LIKE FOOTSTEPS...
WALKING UP THE WALL!!
WE MUST BE GETTING CLOSE!! HE'S MOVING FASTER!!
THAT VOICE!! IT---IT'S JAMESON'S!!
I DON'T KNOW-- WHAT IT'S ALL ABOUT... BUT I'D BETTER PUT ON MY MASK!!
A ROBOT... WITH JONAH'S FACE IN THE VIEWPLATE!!
...JUST LIKE THAT TIME ONCE BEFORE!!
THERE HE IS! IT WORKED! WE FOUND HIM!!
WE GOT HIM DEAD TO RIGHTS... BURGLARIZING SOMEONE'S APARTMENT!
THAT'S A STROKE OF LUCK, ANYWAY!
HE DOESN'T SUSPECT I LIVE HERE...HE THINKS I'M ROBBING THE PLACE!
SURRENDER, SPIDER-MAN--- OR ELSE--- HEY!!
SURRENDER?? NEVER HEARD OF THE WORD!
THEN THAT'S YOUR HARD LUCK!!
MY KICK DIDN'T EVEN UPSET HIM!
HE'S MUCH STRONGER THAN THE LAST ONE!
KRAK!
12.

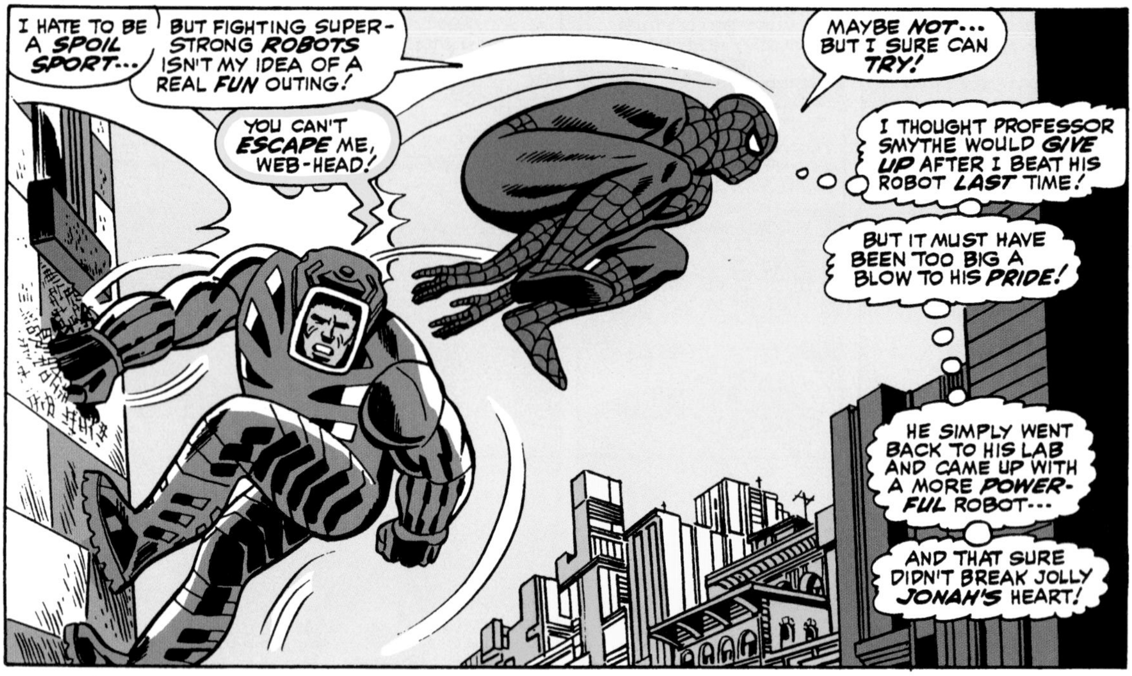
I HATE TO BE A SPOIL SPORT...
BUT FIGHTING SUPER-STRONG ROBOTS ISN'T MY IDEA OF A REAL FUN OUTING!
YOU CAN'T ESCAPE ME, WEB-HEAD!
MAYBE NOT... BUT I SURE CAN TRY!
I THOUGHT PROFESSOR SMYTHE WOULD GIVE UP AFTER I BEAT HIS ROBOT LAST TIME!
BUT IT MUST HAVE BEEN TOO BIG A BLOW TO HIS PRIDE!
HE SIMPLY WENT BACK TO HIS LAB AND CAME UP WITH A MORE POWER-FUL ROBOT---
AND THAT SURE DIDN'T BREAK JOLLY JONAH'S HEART!

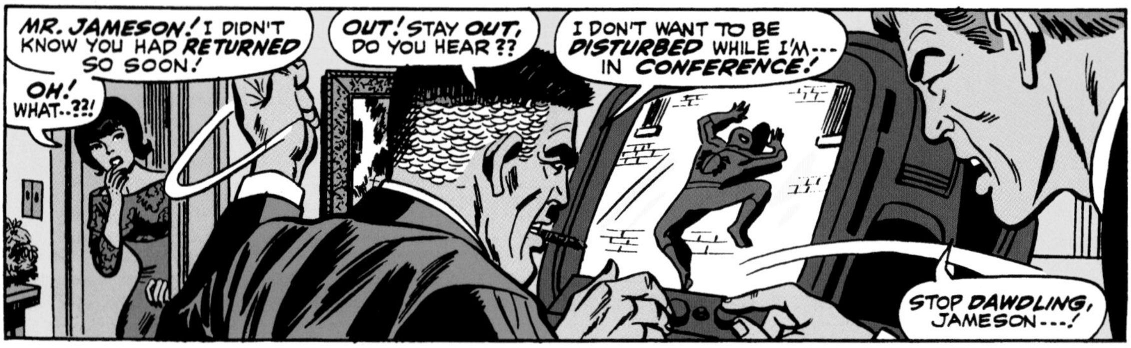
MR. JAMESON! I DIDN'T KNOW YOU HAD RETURNED SO SOON!
OH! WHAT-.??!
OUT! STAY OUT, DO YOU HEAR??
I DON'T WANT TO BE DISTURBED WHILE I'M--- IN CONFERENCE!
STOP DAWDLING, JAMESON---!

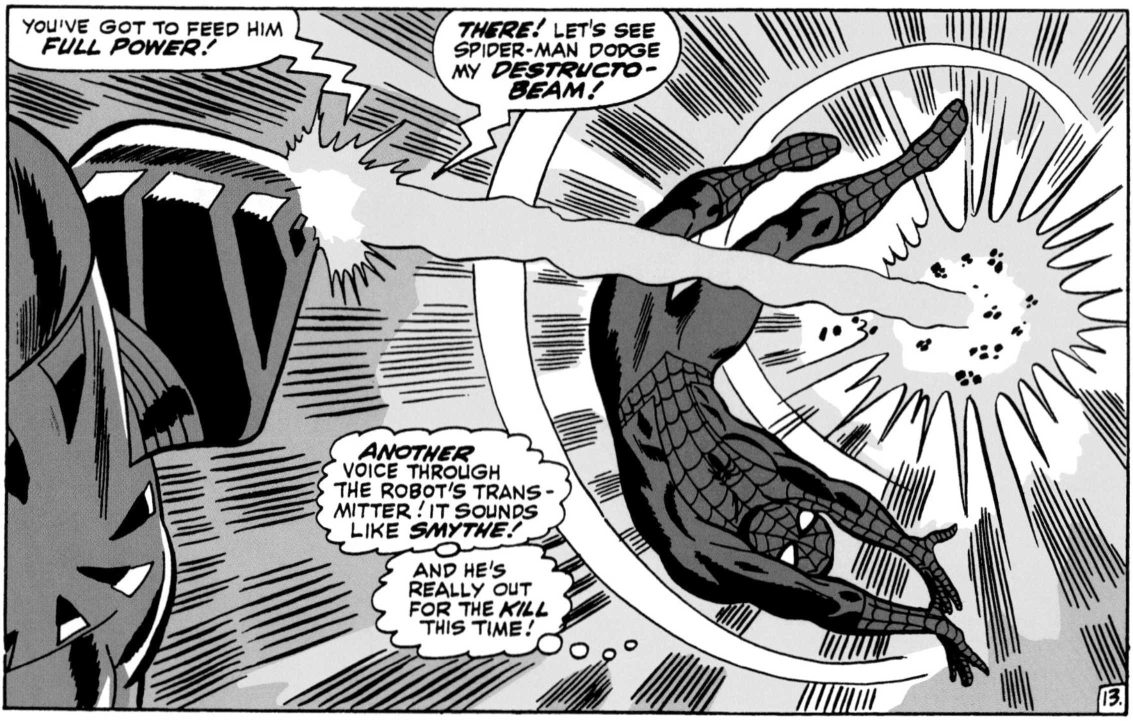
YOU'VE GOT TO FEED HIM FULL POWER!
THERE! LET'S SEE SPIDER-MAN DODGE MY DESTRUCTO-BEAM!
ANOTHER VOICE THROUGH THE ROBOT'S TRANS-MITTER! IT SOUNDS LIKE SMYTHE!
AND HE'S REALLY OUT FOR THE KILL THIS TIME!
13.

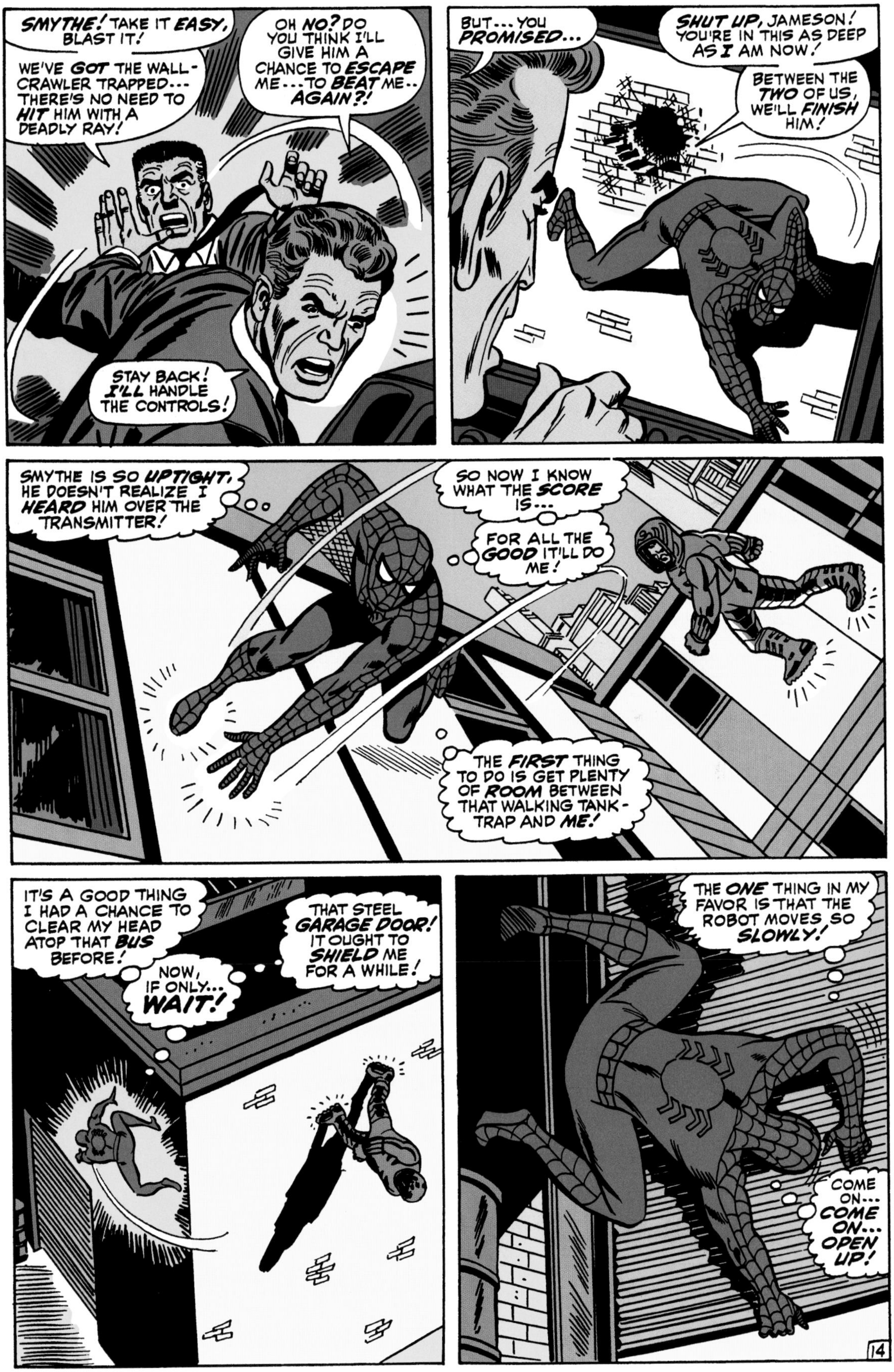
SMYTHE! TAKE IT EASY, BLAST IT!
WE'VE GOT THE WALL-CRAWLER TRAPPED--- THERE'S NO NEED TO HIT HIM WITH A DEADLY RAY!
OH NO? DO YOU THINK I'LL GIVE HIM A CHANCE TO ESCAPE ME---TO BEAT ME.. AGAIN?!
STAY BACK! I'LL HANDLE THE CONTROLS!
BUT... YOU PROMISED...
SHUT UP, JAMESON! YOU'RE IN THIS AS DEEP AS I AM NOW!
BETWEEN THE TWO OF US, WE'LL FINISH HIM!
SMYTHE IS SO UPTIGHT, HE DOESN'T REALIZE I HEARD HIM OVER THE TRANSMITTER!
SO NOW I KNOW WHAT THE SCORE IS...
FOR ALL THE GOOD IT'LL DO ME!
THE FIRST THING TO DO IS GET PLENTY OF ROOM BETWEEN THAT WALKING TANK-TRAP AND ME!
IT'S A GOOD THING I HAD A CHANCE TO CLEAR MY HEAD ATOP THAT BUS BEFORE!
THAT STEEL GARAGE DOOR! IT OUGHT TO SHIELD ME FOR A WHILE!
NOW, IF ONLY... WAIT!
THE ONE THING IN MY FAVOR IS THAT THE ROBOT MOVES SO SLOWLY!
COME ON... COME ON... OPEN UP!
14

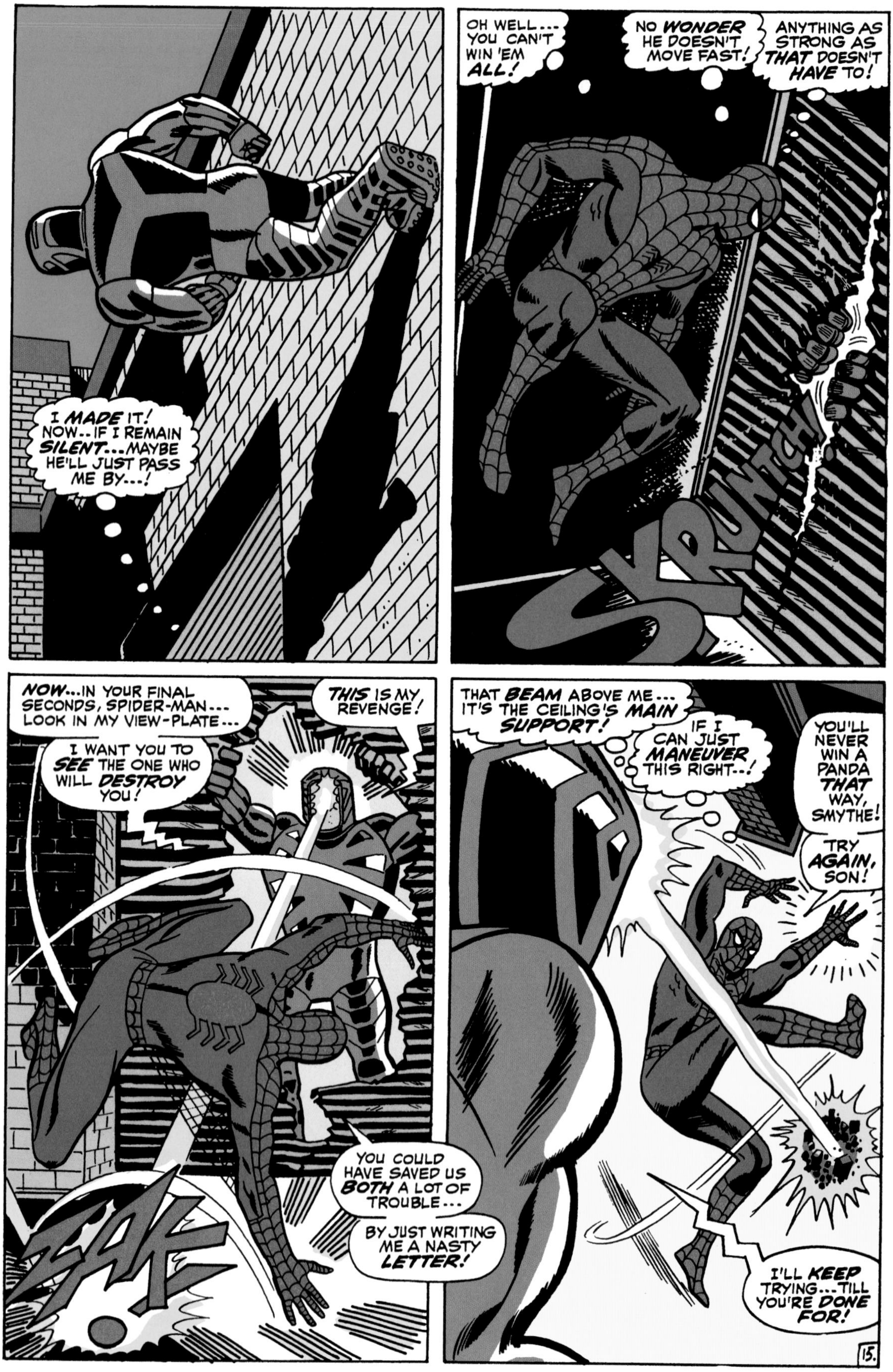
I MADE IT! NOW--IF I REMAIN SILENT...MAYBE HE'LL JUST PASS ME BY...!
OH WELL... YOU CAN'T WIN 'EM ALL!
NO WONDER HE DOESN'T MOVE FAST!
ANYTHING AS STRONG AS THAT DOESN'T HAVE TO!
SKRUNTCH!
NOW...IN YOUR FINAL SECONDS, SPIDER-MAN... LOOK IN MY VIEW-PLATE...
I WANT YOU TO SEE THE ONE WHO WILL DESTROY YOU!
THIS IS MY REVENGE!
ZAK
YOU COULD HAVE SAVED US BOTH A LOT OF TROUBLE...
BY JUST WRITING ME A NASTY LETTER!
THAT BEAM ABOVE ME... IT'S THE CEILING'S MAIN SUPPORT!
IF I CAN JUST MANEUVER THIS RIGHT--!
YOU'LL NEVER WIN A PANDA THAT WAY, SMYTHE!
TRY AGAIN, SON!
I'LL KEEP TRYING...TILL YOU'RE DONE FOR!
15.

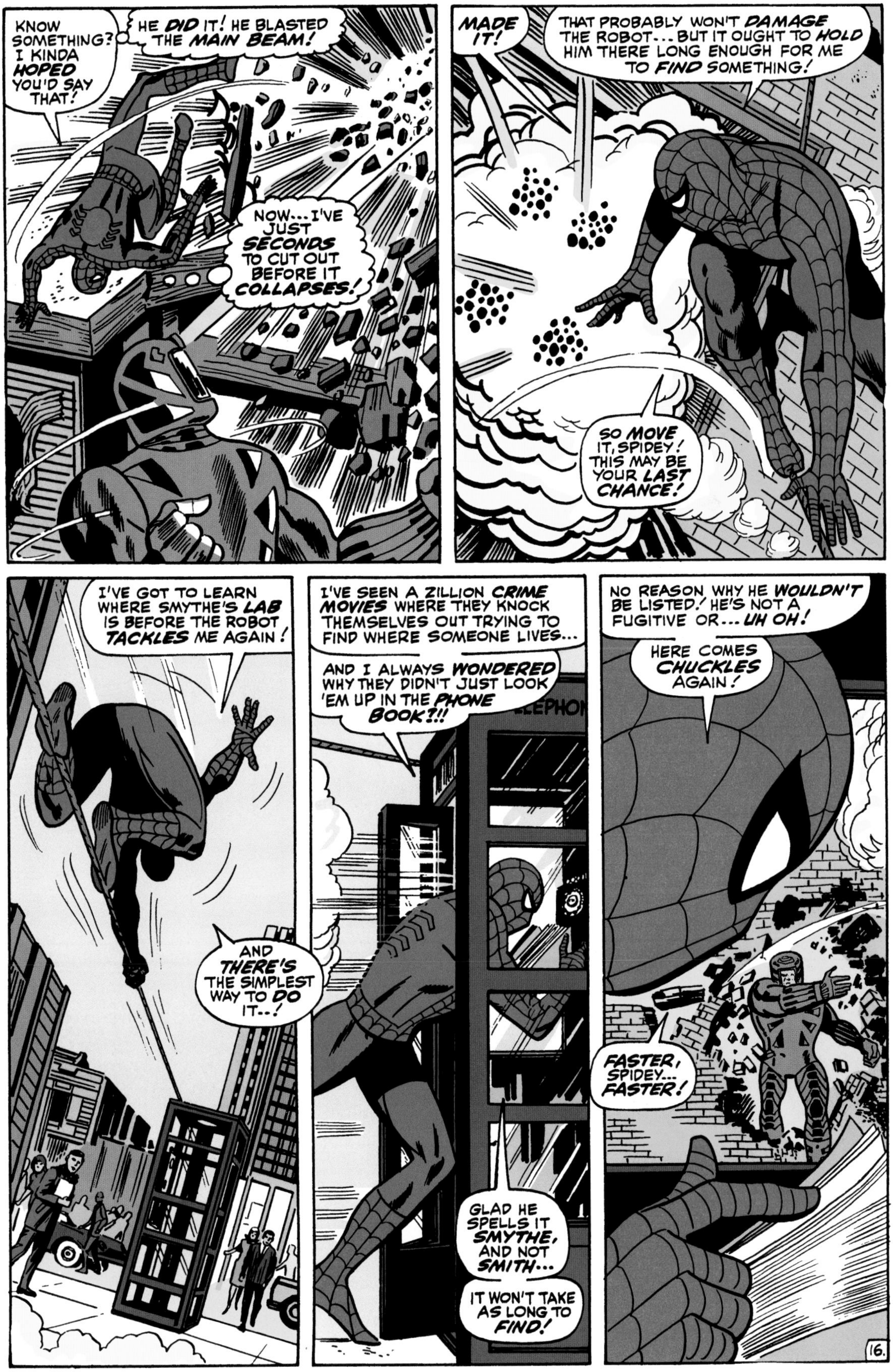

KNOW SOMETHING? I KINDA HOPED YOU'D SAY THAT!
HE DID IT! HE BLASTED THE MAIN BEAM!
NOW... I'VE JUST SECONDS TO CUT OUT BEFORE IT COLLAPSES!
MADE IT!
THAT PROBABLY WON'T DAMAGE THE ROBOT... BUT IT OUGHT TO HOLD HIM THERE LONG ENOUGH FOR ME TO FIND SOMETHING!
SO MOVE IT, SPIDEY! THIS MAY BE YOUR LAST CHANCE!
I'VE GOT TO LEARN WHERE SMYTHE'S LAB IS BEFORE THE ROBOT TACKLES ME AGAIN!
AND THERE'S THE SIMPLEST WAY TO DO IT..!
I'VE SEEN A ZILLION CRIME MOVIES WHERE THEY KNOCK THEMSELVES OUT TRYING TO FIND WHERE SOMEONE LIVES...
AND I ALWAYS WONDERED WHY THEY DIDN'T JUST LOOK 'EM UP IN THE PHONE BOOK?!!
GLAD HE SPELLS IT SMYTHE, AND NOT SMITH...
IT WON'T TAKE AS LONG TO FIND!
NO REASON WHY HE WOULDN'T BE LISTED! HE'S NOT A FUGITIVE OR... UH OH!
HERE COMES CHUCKLES AGAIN!
FASTER, SPIDEY... FASTER!
16.

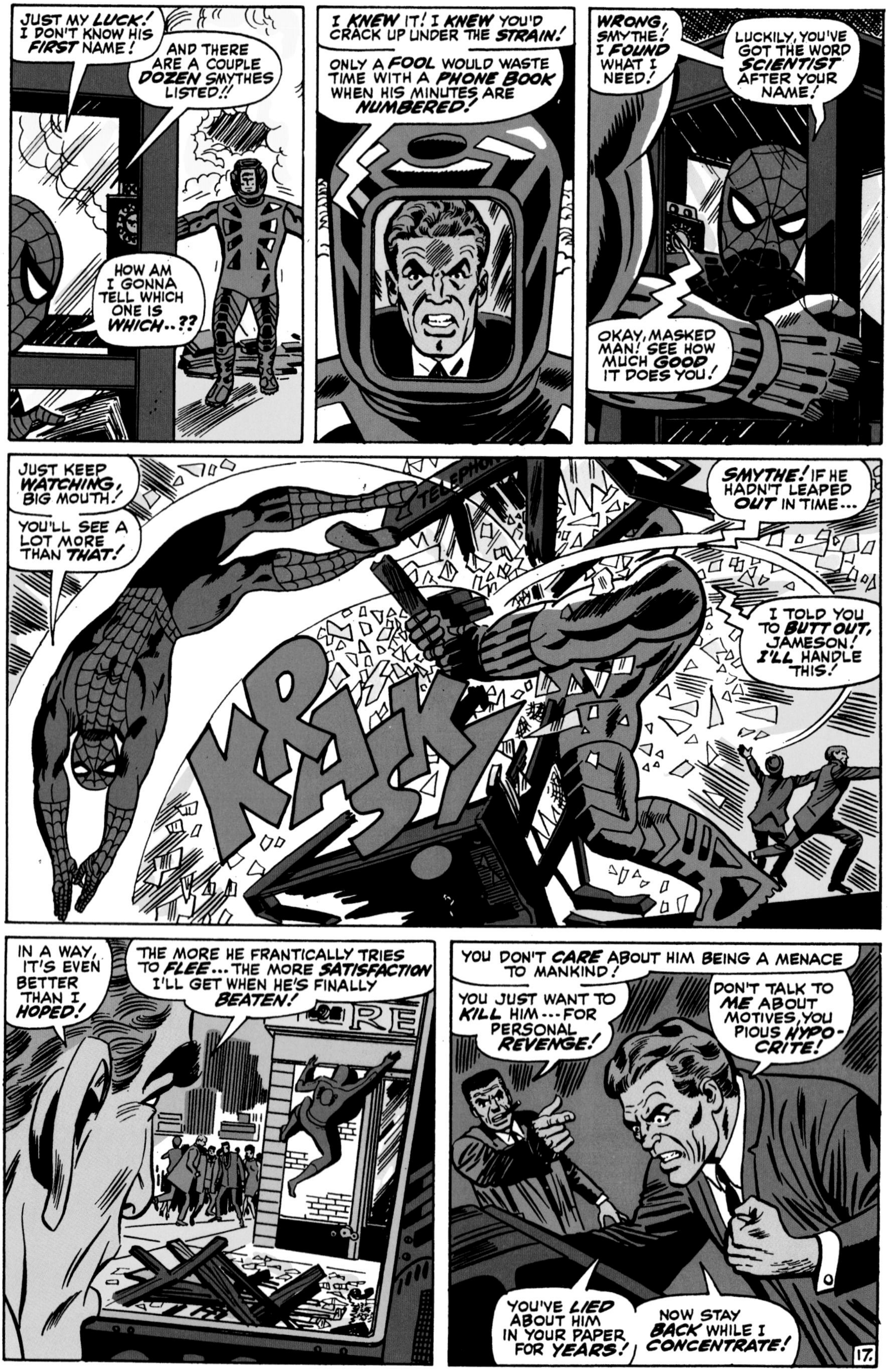

JUST MY LUCK! I DON'T KNOW HIS FIRST NAME!
AND THERE ARE A COUPLE DOZEN SMYTHES LISTED!!
HOW AM I GONNA TELL WHICH ONE IS WHICH..??
I KNEW IT! I KNEW YOU'D CRACK UP UNDER THE STRAIN!
ONLY A FOOL WOULD WASTE TIME WITH A PHONE BOOK WHEN HIS MINUTES ARE NUMBERED!
WRONG, SMYTHE! I FOUND WHAT I NEED!
LUCKILY, YOU'VE GOT THE WORD SCIENTIST AFTER YOUR NAME!
OKAY, MASKED MAN! SEE HOW MUCH GOOD IT DOES YOU!
JUST KEEP WATCHING, BIG MOUTH!
YOU'LL SEE A LOT MORE THAN THAT!
SMYTHE! IF HE HADN'T LEAPED OUT IN TIME...
I TOLD YOU TO BUTT OUT, JAMESON! I'LL HANDLE THIS!
KRAKK
IN A WAY, IT'S EVEN BETTER THAN I HOPED!
THE MORE HE FRANTICALLY TRIES TO FLEE... THE MORE SATISFACTION I'LL GET WHEN HE'S FINALLY BEATEN!
YOU DON'T CARE ABOUT HIM BEING A MENACE TO MANKIND!
YOU JUST WANT TO KILL HIM --- FOR PERSONAL REVENGE!
DON'T TALK TO ME ABOUT MOTIVES, YOU PIOUS HYPO-CRITE!
YOU'VE LIED ABOUT HIM IN YOUR PAPER FOR YEARS!
NOW STAY BACK WHILE I CONCENTRATE!
17.

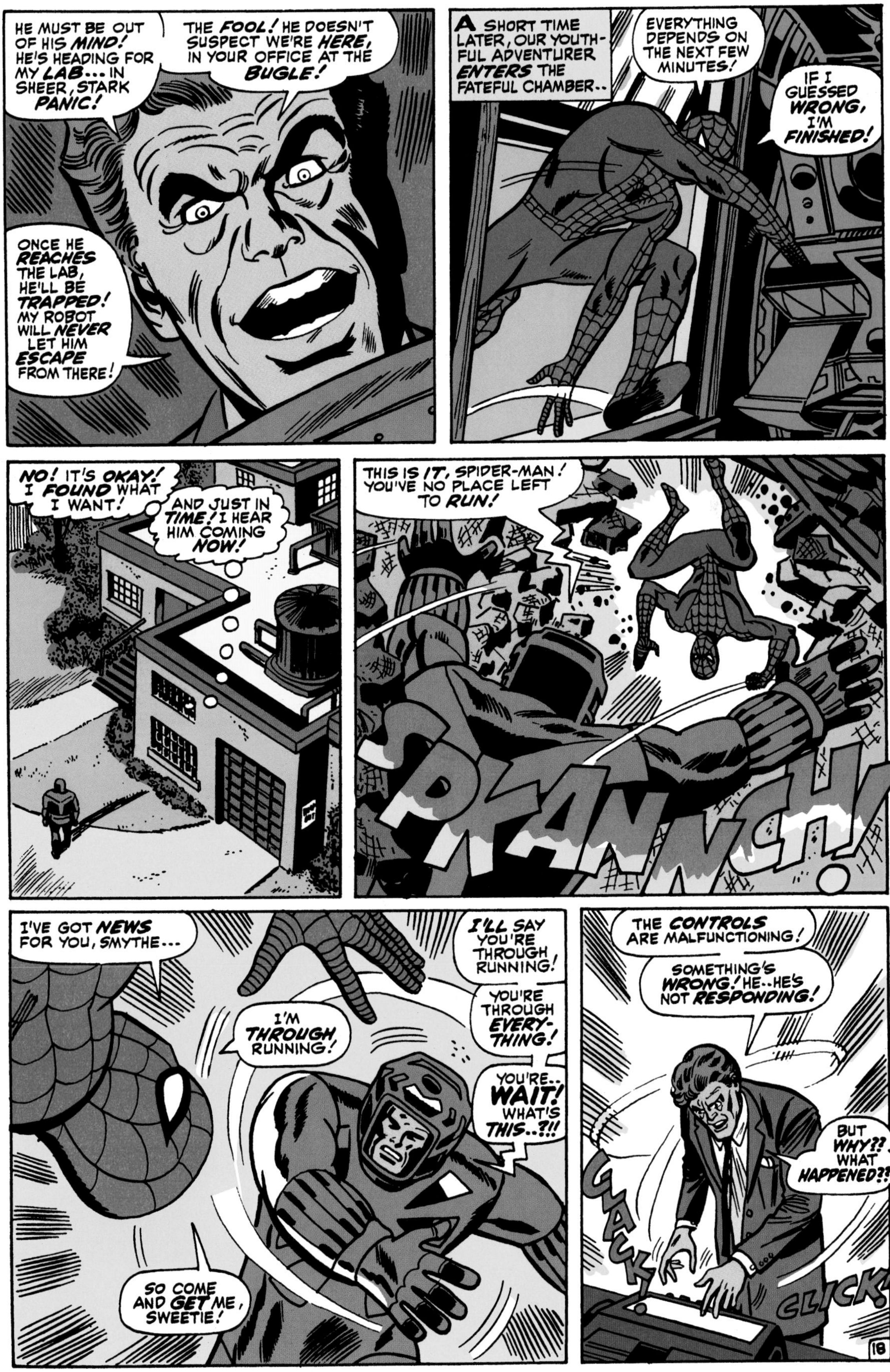
HE MUST BE OUT OF HIS MIND! HE'S HEADING FOR MY LAB... IN SHEER, STARK PANIC!
THE FOOL! HE DOESN'T SUSPECT WE'RE HERE, IN YOUR OFFICE AT THE BUGLE!
ONCE HE REACHES THE LAB, HE'LL BE TRAPPED! MY ROBOT WILL NEVER LET HIM ESCAPE FROM THERE!
A SHORT TIME LATER, OUR YOUTHFUL ADVENTURER ENTERS THE FATEFUL CHAMBER..
EVERYTHING DEPENDS ON THE NEXT FEW MINUTES!
IF I GUESSED WRONG, I'M FINISHED!
NO! IT'S OKAY! I FOUND WHAT I WANT!
AND JUST IN TIME! I HEAR HIM COMING NOW!
THIS IS IT, SPIDER-MAN! YOU'VE NO PLACE LEFT TO RUN!
SPLANNCH!
I'VE GOT NEWS FOR YOU, SMYTHE...
I'M THROUGH RUNNING!
SO COME AND GET ME, SWEETIE!
I'LL SAY YOU'RE THROUGH RUNNING!
YOU'RE THROUGH EVERYTHING!
YOU'RE.. WAIT! WHAT'S THIS..?!!
THE CONTROLS ARE MALFUNCTIONING!
SOMETHING'S WRONG! HE..HE'S NOT RESPONDING!
BUT WHY?? WHAT HAPPENED??
UUAUK!
CLICK!
18

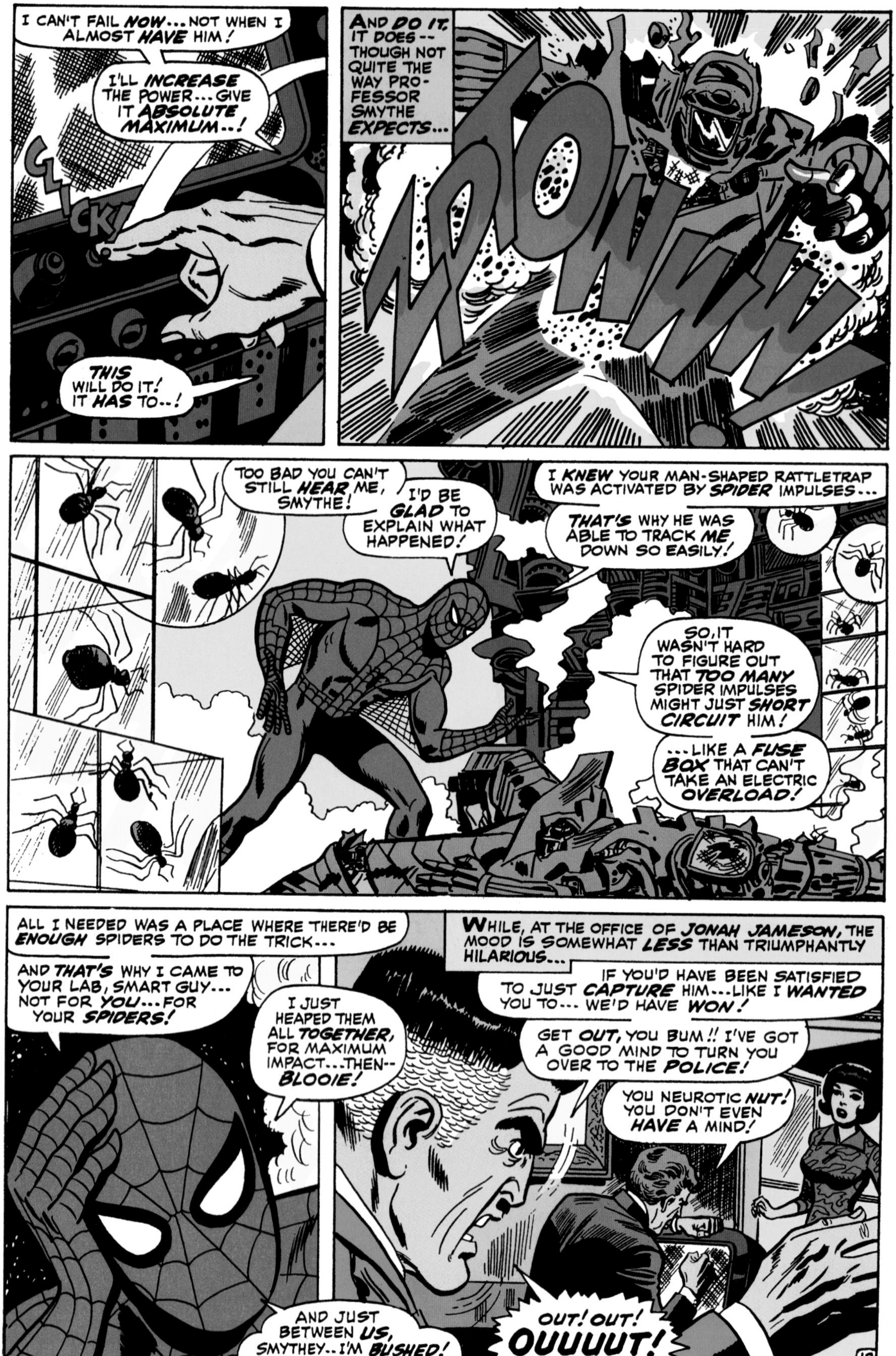
I CAN'T FAIL NOW... NOT WHEN I ALMOST HAVE HIM!
I'LL INCREASE THE POWER... GIVE IT ABSOLUTE MAXIMUM..!
CLICK!
THIS WILL DO IT! IT HAS TO..!
AND DO IT, IT DOES-- THOUGH NOT QUITE THE WAY PROFESSOR SMYTHE EXPECTS...
ZZOWWW!
TOO BAD YOU CAN'T STILL HEAR ME, SMYTHE!
I'D BE GLAD TO EXPLAIN WHAT HAPPENED!
I KNEW YOUR MAN-SHAPED RATTLETRAP WAS ACTIVATED BY SPIDER IMPULSES...
THAT'S WHY HE WAS ABLE TO TRACK ME DOWN SO EASILY!
SO, IT WASN'T HARD TO FIGURE OUT THAT TOO MANY SPIDER IMPULSES MIGHT JUST SHORT CIRCUIT HIM!
...LIKE A FUSE BOX THAT CAN'T TAKE AN ELECTRIC OVERLOAD!
ALL I NEEDED WAS A PLACE WHERE THERE'D BE ENOUGH SPIDERS TO DO THE TRICK...
AND THAT'S WHY I CAME TO YOUR LAB, SMART GUY... NOT FOR YOU... FOR YOUR SPIDERS!
I JUST HEAPED THEM ALL TOGETHER, FOR MAXIMUM IMPACT... THEN-- BLOOIE!
AND JUST BETWEEN US, SMYTHEY.. I'M BUSHED!
WHILE, AT THE OFFICE OF JONAH JAMESON, THE MOOD IS SOMEWHAT LESS THAN TRIUMPHANTLY HILARIOUS...
IF YOU'D HAVE BEEN SATISFIED TO JUST CAPTURE HIM... LIKE I WANTED YOU TO... WE'D HAVE WON!
GET OUT, YOU BUM!! I'VE GOT A GOOD MIND TO TURN YOU OVER TO THE POLICE!
YOU NEUROTIC NUT! YOU DON'T EVEN HAVE A MIND!
OUT! OUT! OUUUUT!
19

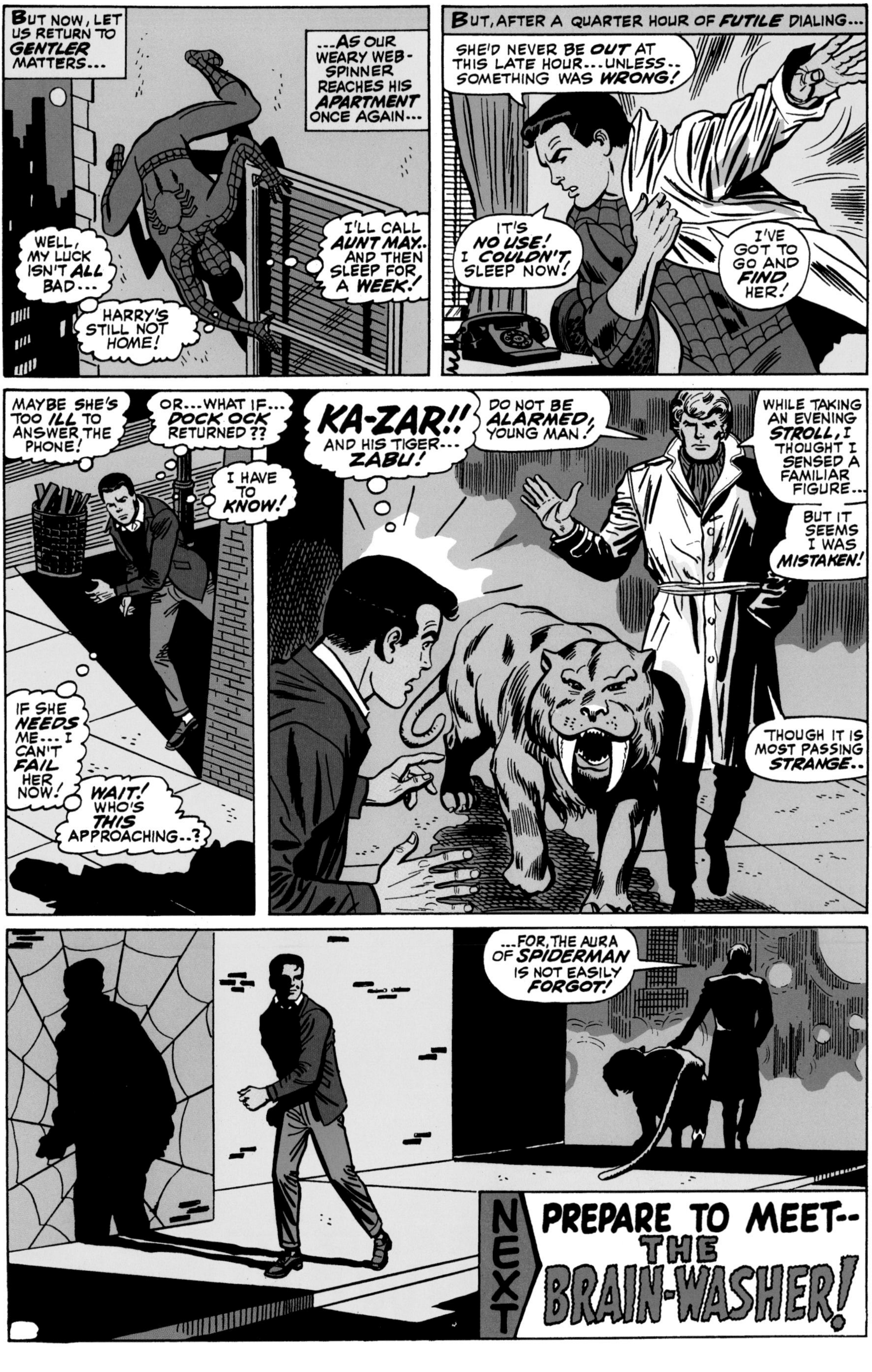

BUT NOW, LET US RETURN TO GENTLER MATTERS...
...AS OUR WEARY WEB-SPINNER REACHES HIS APARTMENT ONCE AGAIN...
WELL, MY LUCK ISN'T ALL BAD...
HARRY'S STILL NOT HOME!
I'LL CALL AUNT MAY.. AND THEN SLEEP FOR A WEEK!
BUT, AFTER A QUARTER HOUR OF FUTILE DIALING...
SHE'D NEVER BE OUT AT THIS LATE HOUR...UNLESS.. SOMETHING WAS WRONG!
IT'S NO USE! I COULDN'T SLEEP NOW!
I'VE GOT TO GO AND FIND HER!
MAYBE SHE'S TOO ILL TO ANSWER THE PHONE!
OR...WHAT IF... DOCK OCK RETURNED??
I HAVE TO KNOW!
IF SHE NEEDS ME... I CAN'T FAIL HER NOW!
WAIT! WHO'S THIS APPROACHING..?
KA-ZAR!! AND HIS TIGER--- ZABU!
DO NOT BE ALARMED, YOUNG MAN.
WHILE TAKING AN EVENING STROLL, I THOUGHT I SENSED A FAMILIAR FIGURE...
BUT IT SEEMS I WAS MISTAKEN!
THOUGH IT IS MOST PASSING STRANGE..
...FOR, THE AURA OF SPIDERMAN IS NOT EASILY FORGOT!
NEXT
PREPARE TO MEET-- THE BRAIN-WASHER!

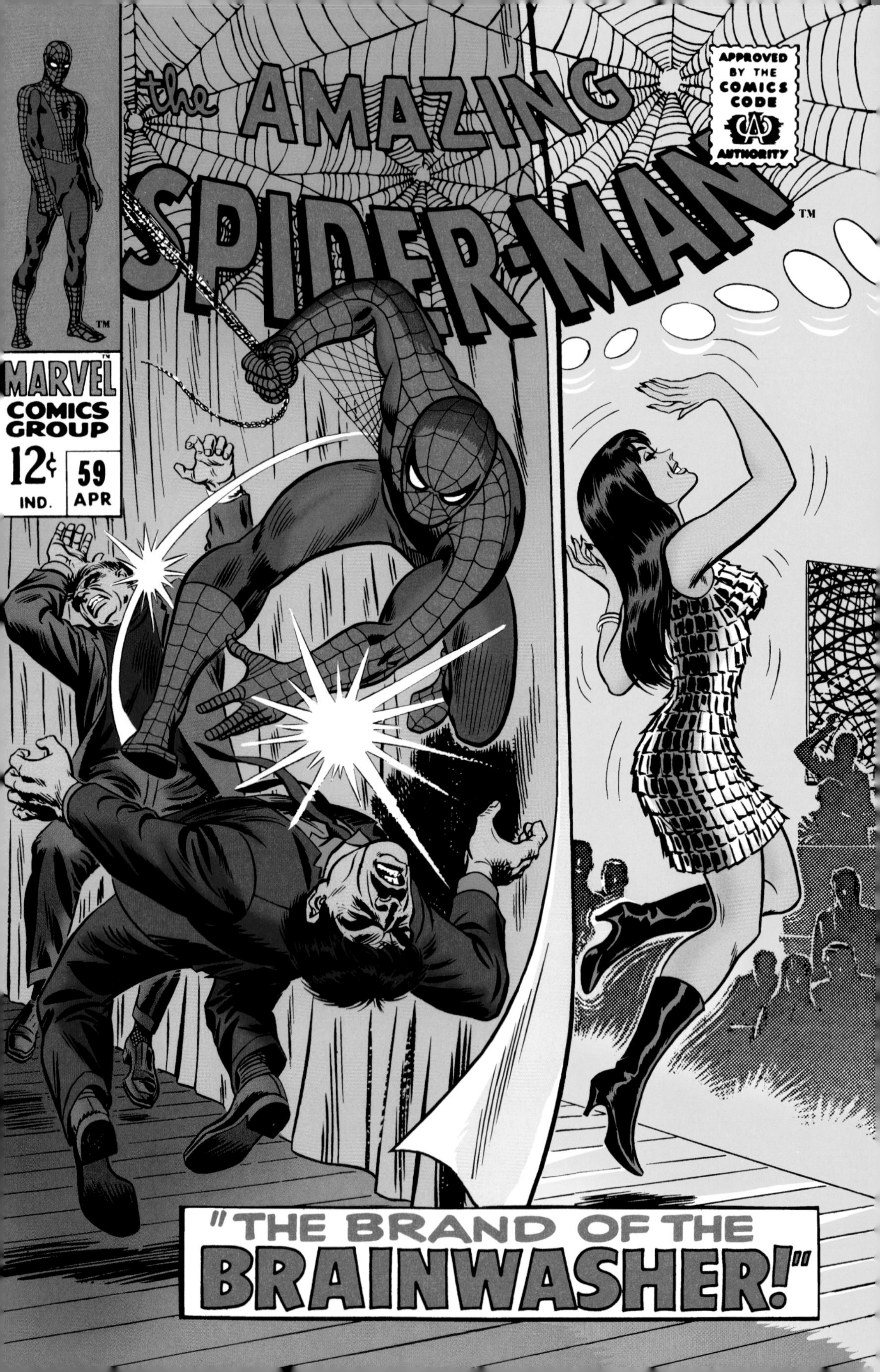

the AMAZING SPIDER-MAN™
APPROVED BY THE COMICS CODE AUTHORITY
MARVEL™ COMICS GROUP
12¢ IND.
59 APR
"THE BRAND OF THE BRAINWASHER!"

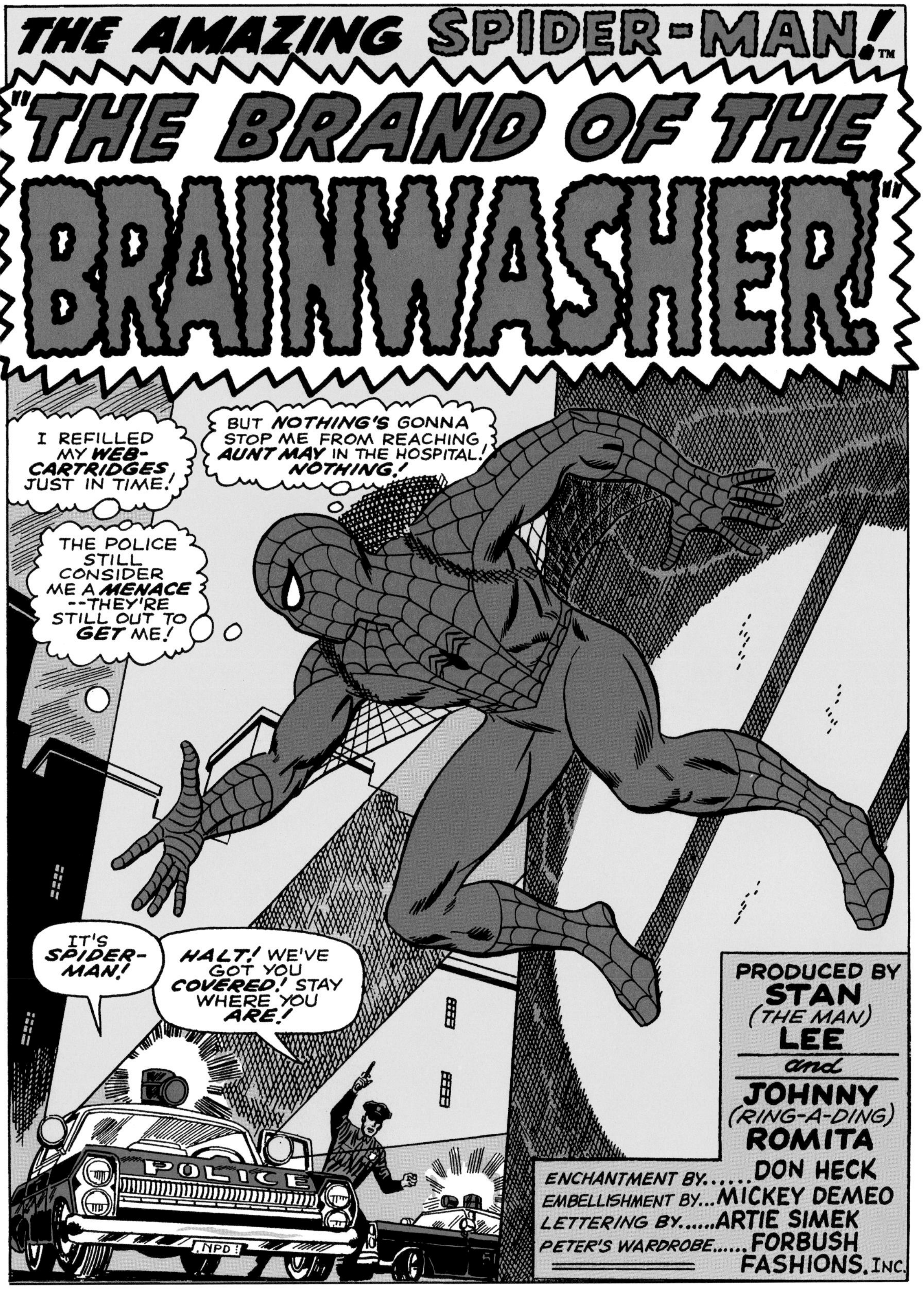
THE AMAZING SPIDER-MAN!
"THE BRAND OF THE BRAINWASHER!"
I REFILLED MY WEB-CARTRIDGES JUST IN TIME!
BUT NOTHING'S GONNA STOP ME FROM REACHING AUNT MAY IN THE HOSPITAL! NOTHING!
THE POLICE STILL CONSIDER ME A MENACE --THEY'RE STILL OUT TO GET ME!
IT'S SPIDER-MAN!
HALT! WE'VE GOT YOU COVERED! STAY WHERE YOU ARE!
POLICE
NPD
PRODUCED BY STAN (THE MAN) LEE and JOHNNY (RING-A-DING) ROMITA
ENCHANTMENT BY......DON HECK
EMBELLISHMENT BY...MICKEY DEMEO
LETTERING BY......ARTIE SIMEK
PETER'S WARDROBE......FORBUSH FASHIONS. INC.

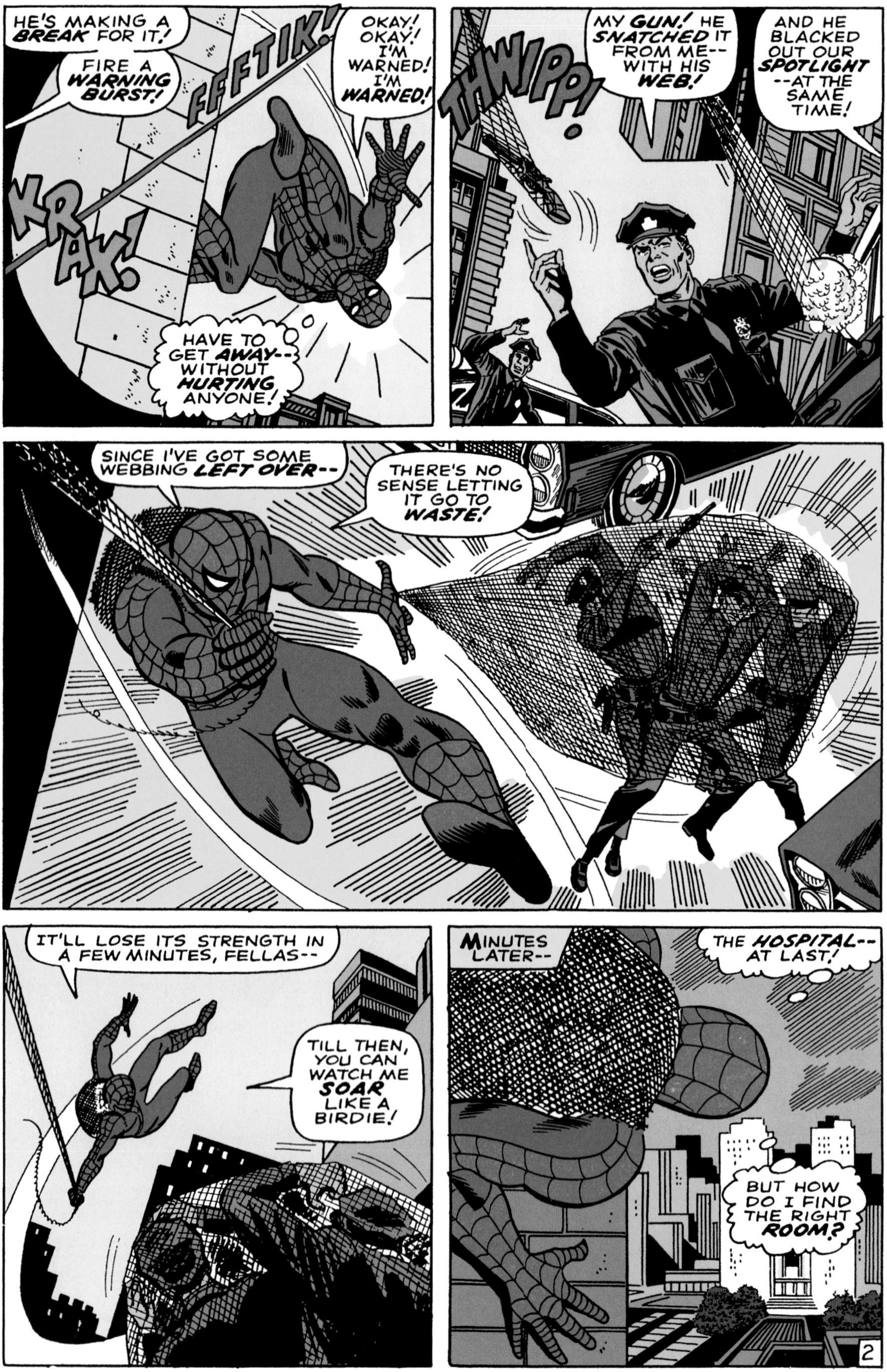
HE'S MAKING A BREAK FOR IT!
FIRE A WARNING BURST!
FFFTIK!
KRAK!
OKAY! OKAY! I'M WARNED! I'M WARNED!
HAVE TO GET AWAY-- WITHOUT HURTING ANYONE!
THWIPP!
MY GUN! HE SNATCHED IT FROM ME-- WITH HIS WEB!
AND HE BLACKED OUT OUR SPOTLIGHT --AT THE SAME TIME!
SINCE I'VE GOT SOME WEBBING LEFT OVER--
THERE'S NO SENSE LETTING IT GO TO WASTE!
IT'LL LOSE ITS STRENGTH IN A FEW MINUTES, FELLAS--
TILL THEN, YOU CAN WATCH ME SOAR LIKE A BIRDIE!
MINUTES LATER--
THE HOSPITAL-- AT LAST!
BUT HOW DO I FIND THE RIGHT ROOM?
2

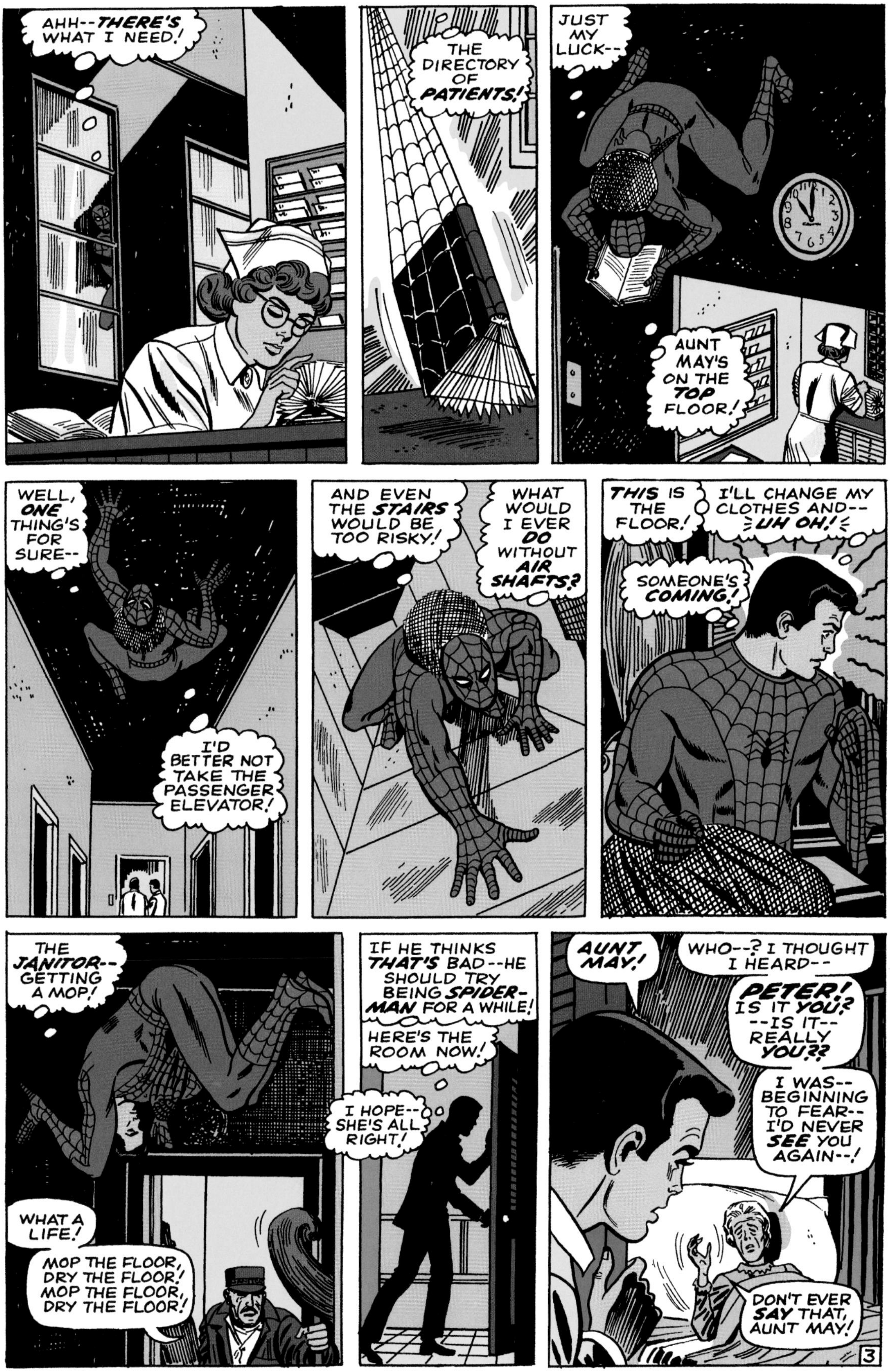
AHH--THERE'S WHAT I NEED!
THE DIRECTORY OF PATIENTS!
JUST MY LUCK--
AUNT MAY'S ON THE TOP FLOOR!
WELL, ONE THING'S FOR SURE--
I'D BETTER NOT TAKE THE PASSENGER ELEVATOR!
AND EVEN THE STAIRS WOULD BE TOO RISKY!
WHAT WOULD I EVER DO WITHOUT AIR SHAFTS?
THIS IS THE FLOOR!
I'LL CHANGE MY CLOTHES AND-- UH OH!
SOMEONE'S COMING!
THE JANITOR--GETTING A MOP!
WHAT A LIFE!
MOP THE FLOOR, DRY THE FLOOR! MOP THE FLOOR, DRY THE FLOOR!
IF HE THINKS THAT'S BAD--HE SHOULD TRY BEING SPIDER-MAN FOR A WHILE!
HERE'S THE ROOM NOW!
I HOPE--SHE'S ALL RIGHT!
AUNT MAY!
WHO--? I THOUGHT I HEARD--
PETER! IS IT YOU? --IS IT--REALLY YOU??
I WAS--BEGINNING TO FEAR--I'D NEVER SEE YOU AGAIN--!
DON'T EVER SAY THAT, AUNT MAY!
3

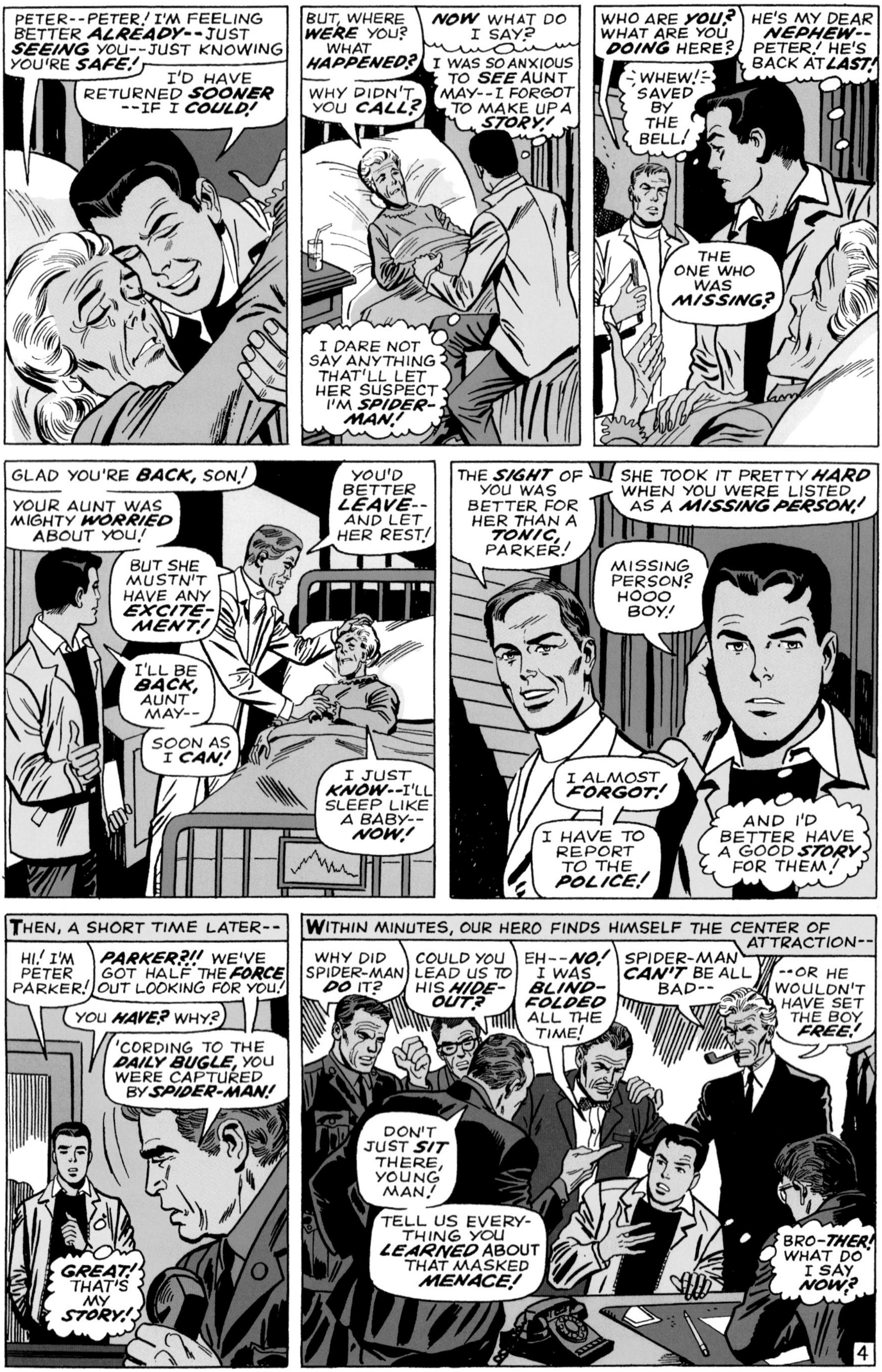
PETER--PETER! I'M FEELING BETTER ALREADY--JUST SEEING YOU--JUST KNOWING YOU'RE SAFE!
I'D HAVE RETURNED SOONER --IF I COULD!
BUT, WHERE WERE YOU? WHAT HAPPENED?
WHY DIDN'T YOU CALL?
NOW WHAT DO I SAY?
I WAS SO ANXIOUS TO SEE AUNT MAY--I FORGOT TO MAKE UP A STORY!
I DARE NOT SAY ANYTHING THAT'LL LET HER SUSPECT I'M SPIDER-MAN!
WHO ARE YOU? WHAT ARE YOU DOING HERE?
HE'S MY DEAR NEPHEW--PETER! HE'S BACK AT LAST!
WHEW! SAVED BY THE BELL!
THE ONE WHO WAS MISSING?
GLAD YOU'RE BACK, SON!
YOUR AUNT WAS MIGHTY WORRIED ABOUT YOU!
YOU'D BETTER LEAVE--AND LET HER REST!
BUT SHE MUSTN'T HAVE ANY EXCITEMENT!
I'LL BE BACK, AUNT MAY--
SOON AS I CAN!
I JUST KNOW--I'LL SLEEP LIKE A BABY--NOW!
THE SIGHT OF YOU WAS BETTER FOR HER THAN A TONIC, PARKER!
SHE TOOK IT PRETTY HARD WHEN YOU WERE LISTED AS A MISSING PERSON!
MISSING PERSON? HOOO BOY!
I ALMOST FORGOT!
I HAVE TO REPORT TO THE POLICE!
AND I'D BETTER HAVE A GOOD STORY FOR THEM!
THEN, A SHORT TIME LATER--
HI! I'M PETER PARKER!
PARKER?!! WE'VE GOT HALF THE FORCE OUT LOOKING FOR YOU!
YOU HAVE? WHY?
'CORDING TO THE DAILY BUGLE, YOU WERE CAPTURED BY SPIDER-MAN!
GREAT! THAT'S MY STORY!
WITHIN MINUTES, OUR HERO FINDS HIMSELF THE CENTER OF ATTRACTION--
WHY DID SPIDER-MAN DO IT?
COULD YOU LEAD US TO HIS HIDE-OUT?
EH--NO! I WAS BLIND-FOLDED ALL THE TIME!
SPIDER-MAN CAN'T BE ALL BAD--
--OR HE WOULDN'T HAVE SET THE BOY FREE!
DON'T JUST SIT THERE, YOUNG MAN!
TELL US EVERY-THING YOU LEARNED ABOUT THAT MASKED MENACE!
BRO-THER! WHAT DO I SAY NOW?
4

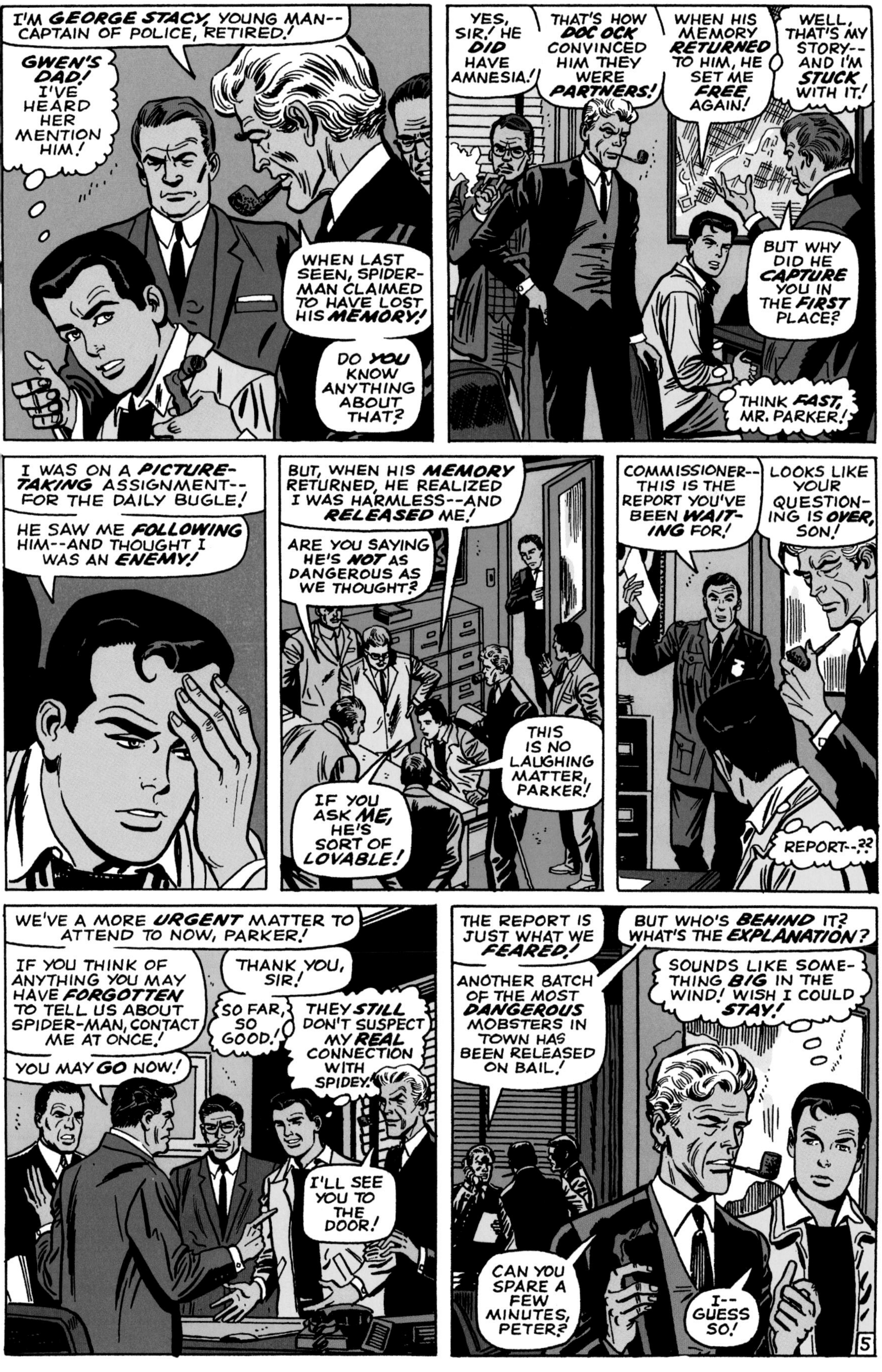
I'M GEORGE STACY, YOUNG MAN-- CAPTAIN OF POLICE, RETIRED!
GWEN'S DAD! I'VE HEARD HER MENTION HIM!
WHEN LAST SEEN, SPIDER-MAN CLAIMED TO HAVE LOST HIS MEMORY!
DO YOU KNOW ANYTHING ABOUT THAT?
YES, SIR! HE DID HAVE AMNESIA!
THAT'S HOW DOC OCK CONVINCED HIM THEY WERE PARTNERS!
WHEN HIS MEMORY RETURNED TO HIM, HE SET ME FREE AGAIN!
WELL, THAT'S MY STORY-- AND I'M STUCK WITH IT!
BUT WHY DID HE CAPTURE YOU IN THE FIRST PLACE?
THINK FAST, MR. PARKER!
I WAS ON A PICTURE-TAKING ASSIGNMENT-- FOR THE DAILY BUGLE!
HE SAW ME FOLLOWING HIM--AND THOUGHT I WAS AN ENEMY!
BUT, WHEN HIS MEMORY RETURNED, HE REALIZED I WAS HARMLESS--AND RELEASED ME!
ARE YOU SAYING HE'S NOT AS DANGEROUS AS WE THOUGHT?
THIS IS NO LAUGHING MATTER, PARKER!
IF YOU ASK ME, HE'S SORT OF LOVABLE!
COMMISSIONER-- THIS IS THE REPORT YOU'VE BEEN WAITING FOR!
LOOKS LIKE YOUR QUESTIONING IS OVER, SON!
REPORT--??
WE'VE A MORE URGENT MATTER TO ATTEND TO NOW, PARKER!
IF YOU THINK OF ANYTHING YOU MAY HAVE FORGOTTEN TO TELL US ABOUT SPIDER-MAN, CONTACT ME AT ONCE!
YOU MAY GO NOW!
THANK YOU, SIR!
SO FAR, SO GOOD!
THEY STILL DON'T SUSPECT MY REAL CONNECTION WITH SPIDEY!
I'LL SEE YOU TO THE DOOR!
THE REPORT IS JUST WHAT WE FEARED!
ANOTHER BATCH OF THE MOST DANGEROUS MOBSTERS IN TOWN HAS BEEN RELEASED ON BAIL!
BUT WHO'S BEHIND IT? WHAT'S THE EXPLANATION?
SOUNDS LIKE SOMETHING BIG IN THE WIND! WISH I COULD STAY!
CAN YOU SPARE A FEW MINUTES, PETER?
I-- GUESS SO!
5

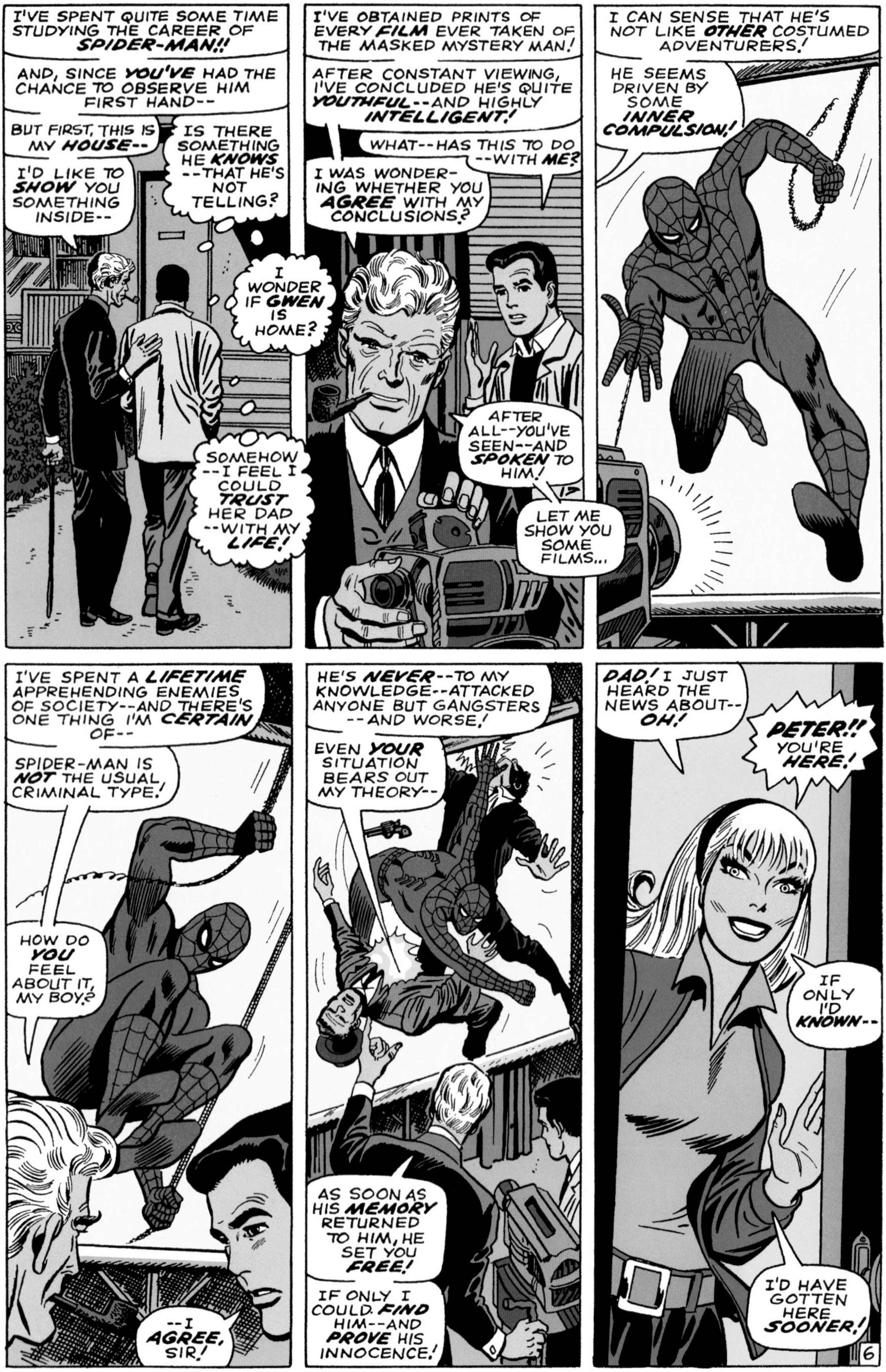
I'VE SPENT QUITE SOME TIME STUDYING THE CAREER OF SPIDER-MAN!!
AND, SINCE YOU'VE HAD THE CHANCE TO OBSERVE HIM FIRST HAND--
BUT FIRST, THIS IS MY HOUSE--
I'D LIKE TO SHOW YOU SOMETHING INSIDE--
IS THERE SOMETHING HE KNOWS--THAT HE'S NOT TELLING?
I WONDER IF GWEN IS HOME?
SOMEHOW--I FEEL I COULD TRUST HER DAD--WITH MY LIFE!
I'VE OBTAINED PRINTS OF EVERY FILM EVER TAKEN OF THE MASKED MYSTERY MAN!
AFTER CONSTANT VIEWING, I'VE CONCLUDED HE'S QUITE YOUTHFUL--AND HIGHLY INTELLIGENT!
WHAT--HAS THIS TO DO--WITH ME?
I WAS WONDERING WHETHER YOU AGREE WITH MY CONCLUSIONS?
AFTER ALL--YOU'VE SEEN--AND SPOKEN TO HIM!
LET ME SHOW YOU SOME FILMS...
I CAN SENSE THAT HE'S NOT LIKE OTHER COSTUMED ADVENTURERS!
HE SEEMS DRIVEN BY SOME INNER COMPULSION!
I'VE SPENT A LIFETIME APPREHENDING ENEMIES OF SOCIETY--AND THERE'S ONE THING I'M CERTAIN OF--
SPIDER-MAN IS NOT THE USUAL CRIMINAL TYPE!
HOW DO YOU FEEL ABOUT IT, MY BOY?
--I AGREE, SIR!
HE'S NEVER--TO MY KNOWLEDGE--ATTACKED ANYONE BUT GANGSTERS--AND WORSE!
EVEN YOUR SITUATION BEARS OUT MY THEORY--
AS SOON AS HIS MEMORY RETURNED TO HIM, HE SET YOU FREE!
IF ONLY I COULD FIND HIM--AND PROVE HIS INNOCENCE!
DAD! I JUST HEARD THE NEWS ABOUT--OH!
PETER!! YOU'RE HERE!
IF ONLY I'D KNOWN--
I'D HAVE GOTTEN HERE SOONER!
6

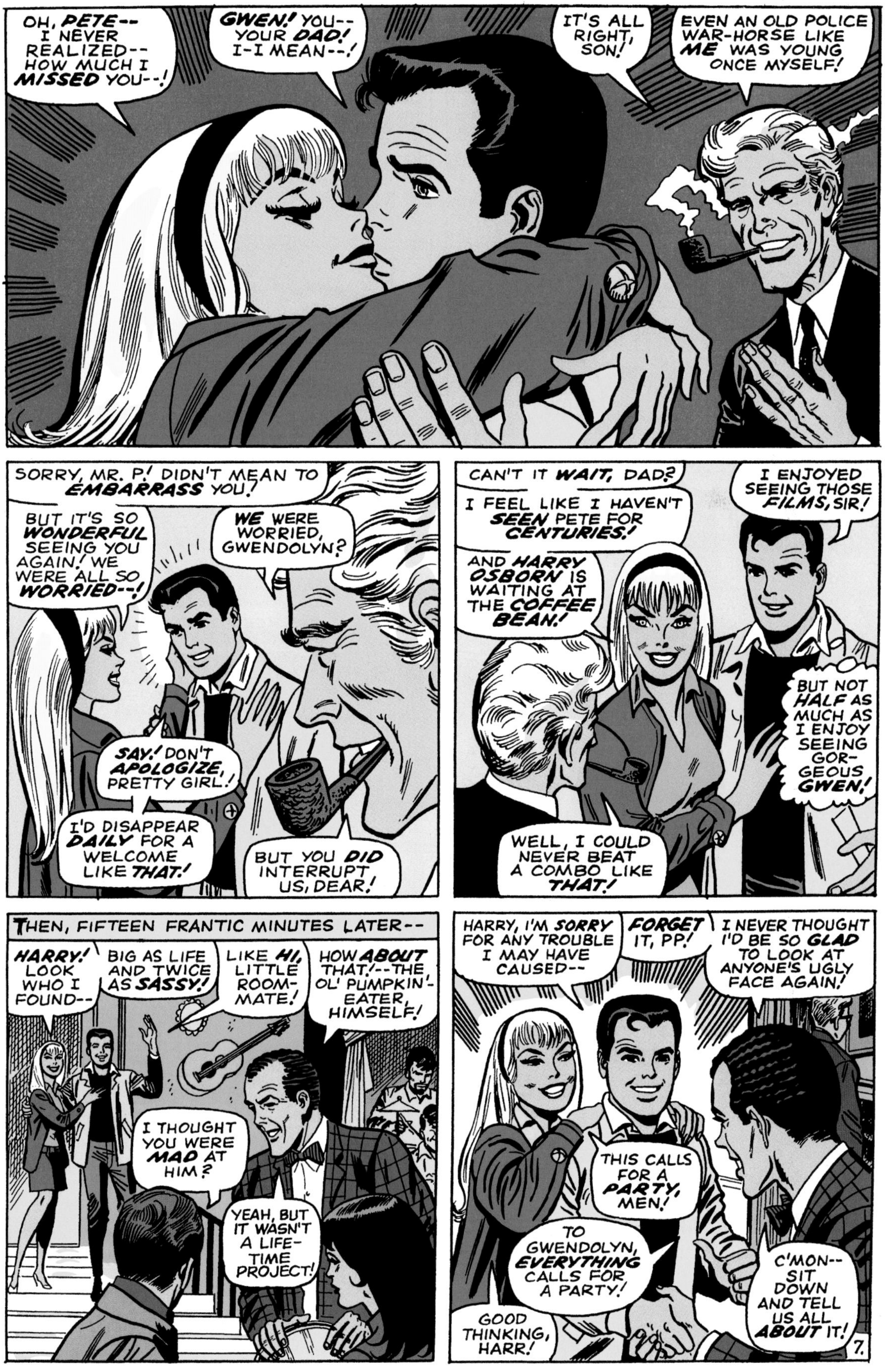

OH, PETE-- I NEVER REALIZED-- HOW MUCH I MISSED YOU--!
GWEN! YOU-- YOUR DAD! I-I MEAN--!
IT'S ALL RIGHT, SON!
EVEN AN OLD POLICE WAR-HORSE LIKE ME WAS YOUNG ONCE MYSELF!
SORRY, MR. P! DIDN'T MEAN TO EMBARRASS YOU!
BUT IT'S SO WONDERFUL SEEING YOU AGAIN! WE WERE ALL SO WORRIED--!
WE WERE WORRIED, GWENDOLYN?
SAY! DON'T APOLOGIZE, PRETTY GIRL!
I'D DISAPPEAR DAILY FOR A WELCOME LIKE THAT!
BUT YOU DID INTERRUPT US, DEAR!
CAN'T IT WAIT, DAD?
I FEEL LIKE I HAVEN'T SEEN PETE FOR CENTURIES!
AND HARRY OSBORN IS WAITING AT THE COFFEE BEAN!
I ENJOYED SEEING THOSE FILMS, SIR!
BUT NOT HALF AS MUCH AS I ENJOY SEEING GOR-GEOUS GWEN!
WELL, I COULD NEVER BEAT A COMBO LIKE THAT!
THEN, FIFTEEN FRANTIC MINUTES LATER--
HARRY! LOOK WHO I FOUND--
BIG AS LIFE AND TWICE AS SASSY!
LIKE HI, LITTLE ROOM-MATE!
HOW ABOUT THAT!--THE OL' PUMPKIN-EATER, HIMSELF!
I THOUGHT YOU WERE MAD AT HIM?
YEAH, BUT IT WASN'T A LIFE-TIME PROJECT!
HARRY, I'M SORRY FOR ANY TROUBLE I MAY HAVE CAUSED--
FORGET IT, PP!
I NEVER THOUGHT I'D BE SO GLAD TO LOOK AT ANYONE'S UGLY FACE AGAIN!
THIS CALLS FOR A PARTY, MEN!
TO GWENDOLYN, EVERYTHING CALLS FOR A PARTY!
GOOD THINKING, HARR!
C'MON-- SIT DOWN AND TELL US ALL ABOUT IT!
7.

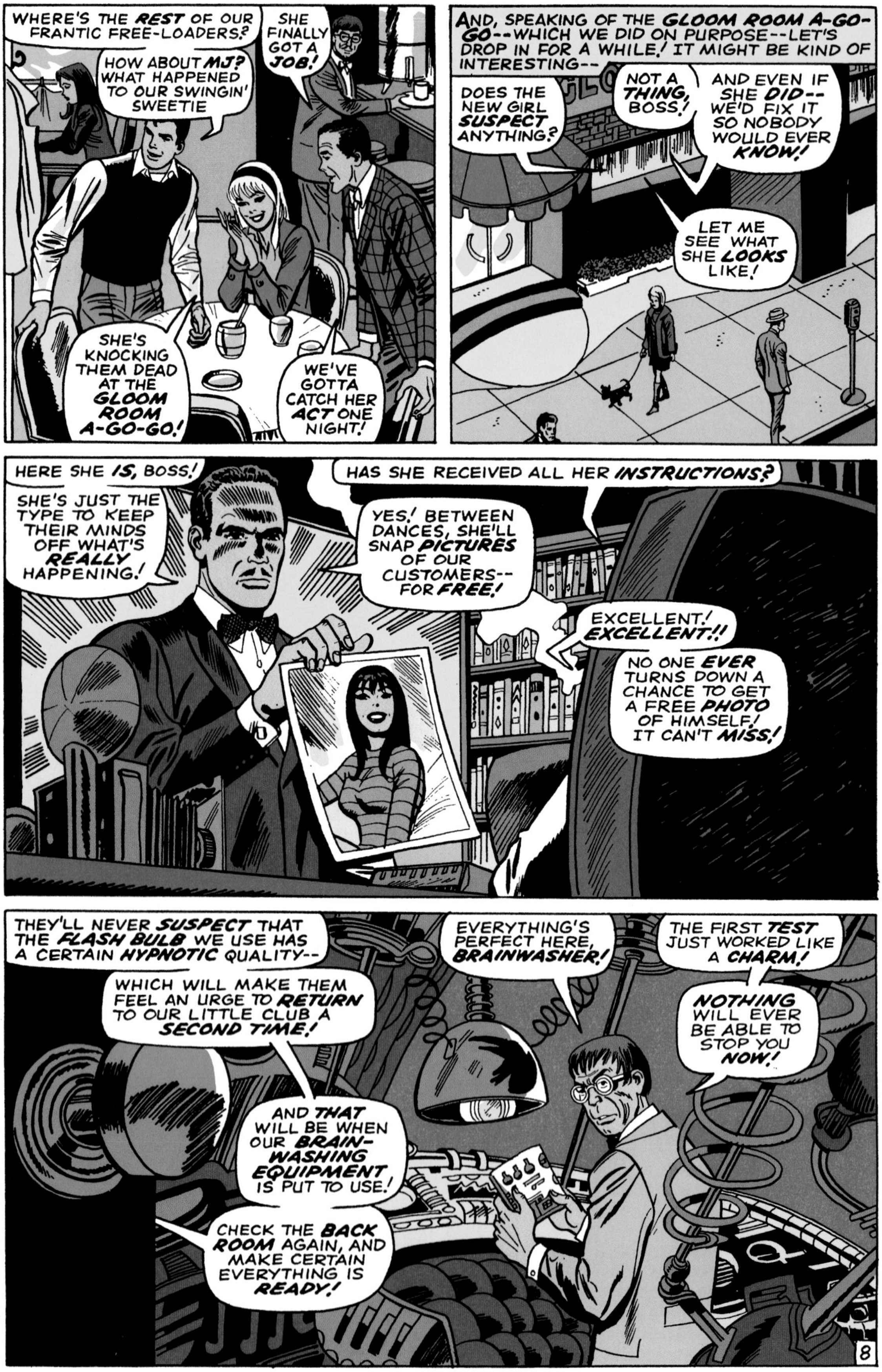

WHERE'S THE REST OF OUR FRANTIC FREE-LOADERS?
SHE FINALLY GOT A JOB!
HOW ABOUT MJ? WHAT HAPPENED TO OUR SWINGIN' SWEETIE
SHE'S KNOCKING THEM DEAD AT THE GLOOM ROOM A-GO-GO!
WE'VE GOTTA CATCH HER ACT ONE NIGHT!
AND, SPEAKING OF THE GLOOM ROOM A-GO-GO--WHICH WE DID ON PURPOSE--LET'S DROP IN FOR A WHILE! IT MIGHT BE KIND OF INTERESTING--
DOES THE NEW GIRL SUSPECT ANYTHING?
NOT A THING, BOSS!
AND EVEN IF SHE DID--WE'D FIX IT SO NOBODY WOULD EVER KNOW!
LET ME SEE WHAT SHE LOOKS LIKE!
HERE SHE IS, BOSS!
SHE'S JUST THE TYPE TO KEEP THEIR MINDS OFF WHAT'S REALLY HAPPENING!
HAS SHE RECEIVED ALL HER INSTRUCTIONS?
YES! BETWEEN DANCES, SHE'LL SNAP PICTURES OF OUR CUSTOMERS--FOR FREE!
EXCELLENT! EXCELLENT!!
NO ONE EVER TURNS DOWN A CHANCE TO GET A FREE PHOTO OF HIMSELF! IT CAN'T MISS!
THEY'LL NEVER SUSPECT THAT THE FLASH BULB WE USE HAS A CERTAIN HYPNOTIC QUALITY--
WHICH WILL MAKE THEM FEEL AN URGE TO RETURN TO OUR LITTLE CLUB A SECOND TIME!
AND THAT WILL BE WHEN OUR BRAIN-WASHING EQUIPMENT IS PUT TO USE!
CHECK THE BACK ROOM AGAIN, AND MAKE CERTAIN EVERYTHING IS READY!
EVERYTHING'S PERFECT HERE, BRAINWASHER!
THE FIRST TEST JUST WORKED LIKE A CHARM!
NOTHING WILL EVER BE ABLE TO STOP YOU NOW!
8

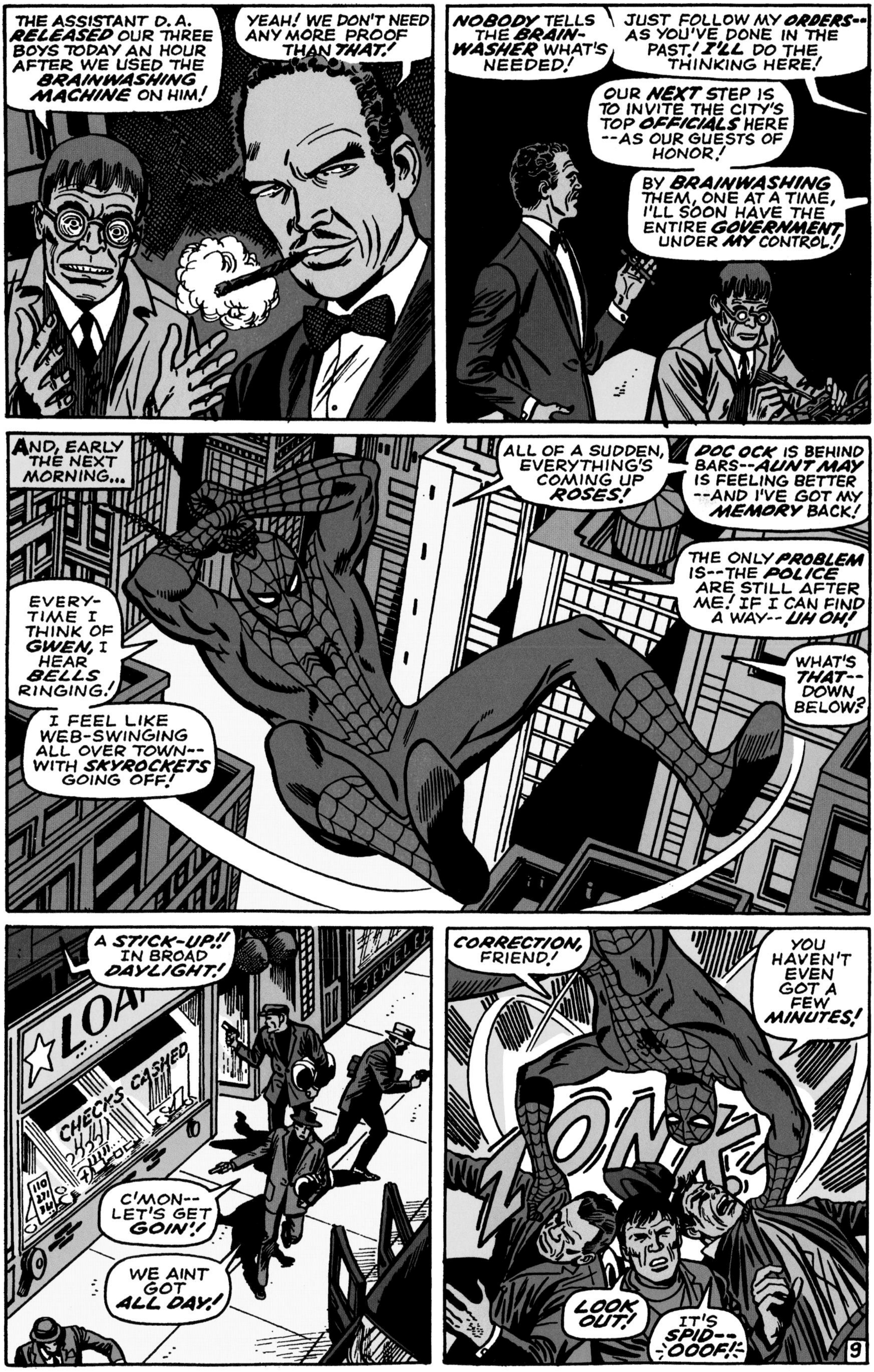
THE ASSISTANT D.A. RELEASED OUR THREE BOYS TODAY AN HOUR AFTER WE USED THE BRAINWASHING MACHINE ON HIM!
YEAH! WE DON'T NEED ANY MORE PROOF THAN THAT!
NOBODY TELLS THE BRAIN-WASHER WHAT'S NEEDED!
JUST FOLLOW MY ORDERS--AS YOU'VE DONE IN THE PAST! I'LL DO THE THINKING HERE!
OUR NEXT STEP IS TO INVITE THE CITY'S TOP OFFICIALS HERE --AS OUR GUESTS OF HONOR!
BY BRAINWASHING THEM, ONE AT A TIME, I'LL SOON HAVE THE ENTIRE GOVERNMENT UNDER MY CONTROL!
AND, EARLY THE NEXT MORNING...
ALL OF A SUDDEN, EVERYTHING'S COMING UP ROSES!
DOC OCK IS BEHIND BARS--AUNT MAY IS FEELING BETTER --AND I'VE GOT MY MEMORY BACK!
EVERY-TIME I THINK OF GWEN, I HEAR BELLS RINGING!
I FEEL LIKE WEB-SWINGING ALL OVER TOWN--WITH SKYROCKETS GOING OFF!
THE ONLY PROBLEM IS--THE POLICE ARE STILL AFTER ME! IF I CAN FIND A WAY-- UH OH!
WHAT'S THAT-- DOWN BELOW?
A STICK-UP!! IN BROAD DAYLIGHT!
LOA
CHECKS CASHED
C'MON-- LET'S GET GOIN'!
WE AINT GOT ALL DAY!
CORRECTION, FRIEND!
YOU HAVEN'T EVEN GOT A FEW MINUTES!
LOOK OUT!
IT'S SPID-- OOOF!
9

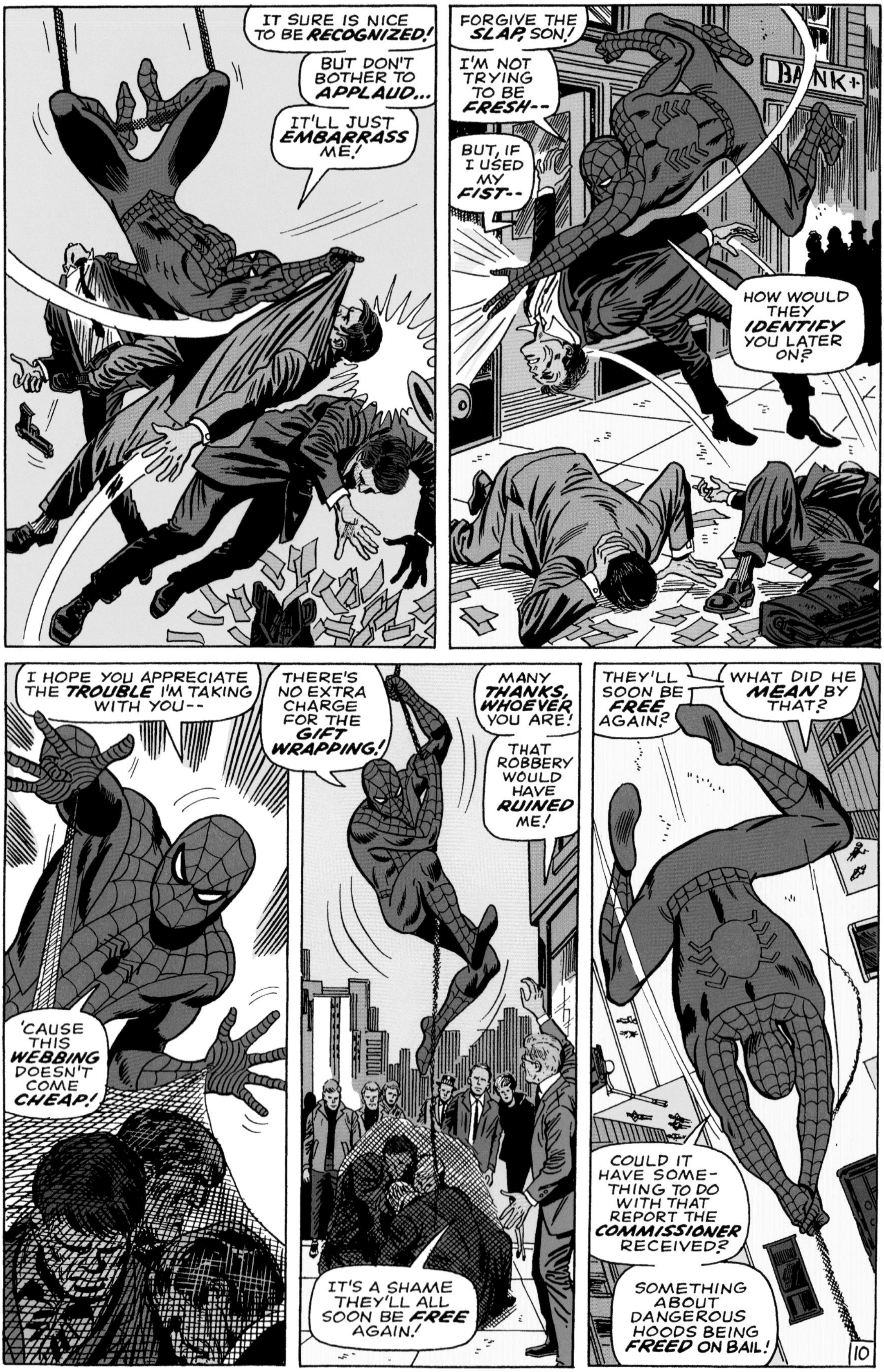

IT SURE IS NICE TO BE RECOGNIZED!
BUT DON'T BOTHER TO APPLAUD...
IT'LL JUST EMBARRASS ME!
FORGIVE THE SLAP, SON!
I'M NOT TRYING TO BE FRESH--
BUT, IF I USED MY FIST--
HOW WOULD THEY IDENTIFY YOU LATER ON?
BANK
I HOPE YOU APPRECIATE THE TROUBLE I'M TAKING WITH YOU--
'CAUSE THIS WEBBING DOESN'T COME CHEAP!
THERE'S NO EXTRA CHARGE FOR THE GIFT WRAPPING!
MANY THANKS, WHOEVER YOU ARE!
THAT ROBBERY WOULD HAVE RUINED ME!
IT'S A SHAME THEY'LL ALL SOON BE FREE AGAIN!
THEY'LL SOON BE FREE AGAIN?
WHAT DID HE MEAN BY THAT?
COULD IT HAVE SOME-THING TO DO WITH THAT REPORT THE COMMISSIONER RECEIVED?
SOMETHING ABOUT DANGEROUS HOODS BEING FREED ON BAIL!
10

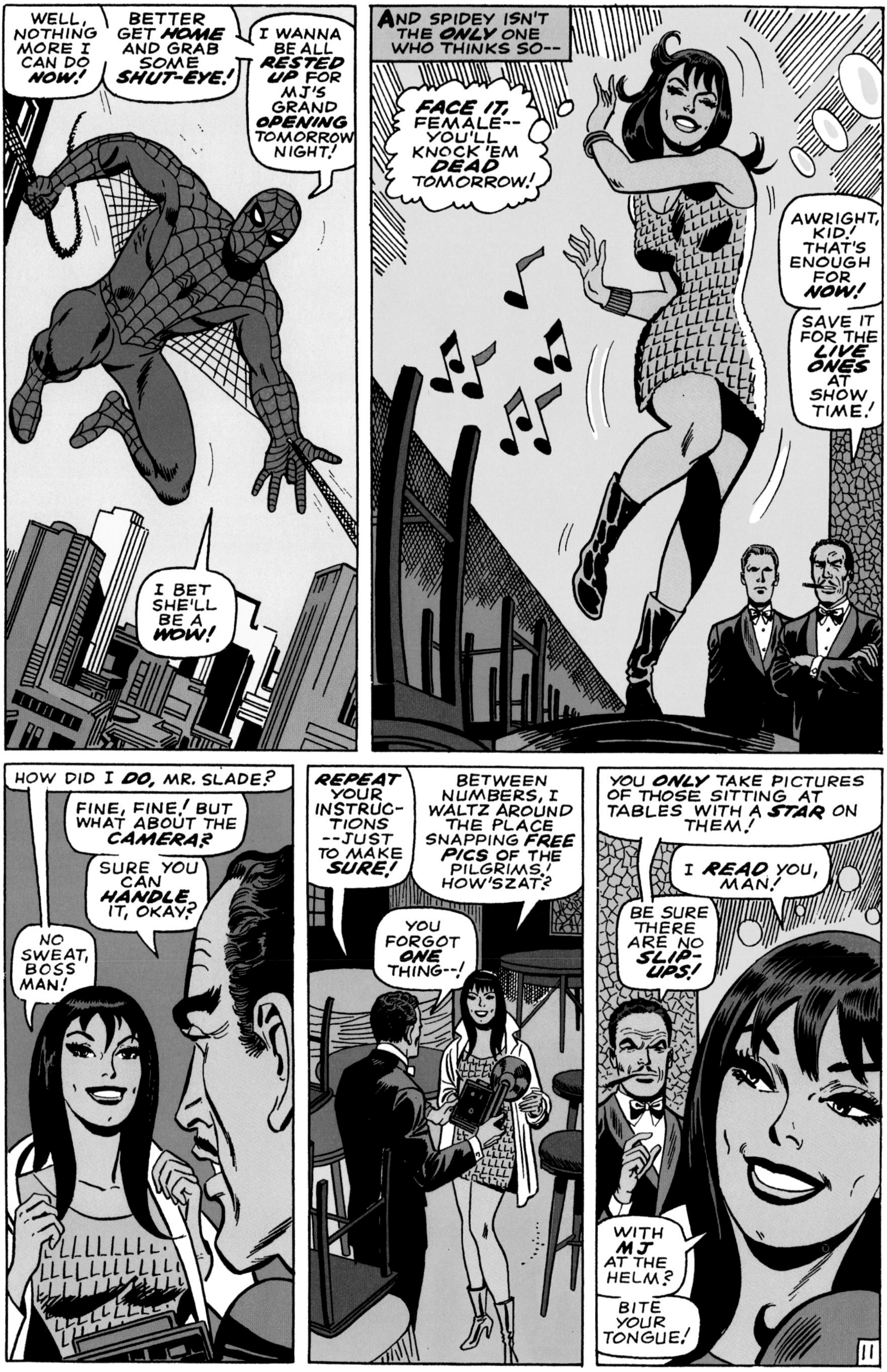
WELL, NOTHING MORE I CAN DO NOW!
BETTER GET HOME AND GRAB SOME SHUT-EYE!
I WANNA BE ALL RESTED UP FOR MJ'S GRAND OPENING TOMORROW NIGHT!
I BET SHE'LL BE A WOW!
AND SPIDEY ISN'T THE ONLY ONE WHO THINKS SO--
FACE IT, FEMALE-- YOU'LL KNOCK 'EM DEAD TOMORROW!
AWRIGHT, KID! THAT'S ENOUGH FOR NOW!
SAVE IT FOR THE LIVE ONES AT SHOW TIME!
HOW DID I DO, MR. SLADE?
FINE, FINE! BUT WHAT ABOUT THE CAMERA?
SURE YOU CAN HANDLE IT, OKAY?
NO SWEAT, BOSS MAN!
REPEAT YOUR INSTRUC- TIONS --JUST TO MAKE SURE!
BETWEEN NUMBERS, I WALTZ AROUND THE PLACE SNAPPING FREE PICS OF THE PILGRIMS! HOW'SZAT?
YOU FORGOT ONE THING--!
YOU ONLY TAKE PICTURES OF THOSE SITTING AT TABLES WITH A STAR ON THEM!
I READ YOU, MAN!
BE SURE THERE ARE NO SLIP-UPS!
WITH MJ AT THE HELM?
BITE YOUR TONGUE!
11

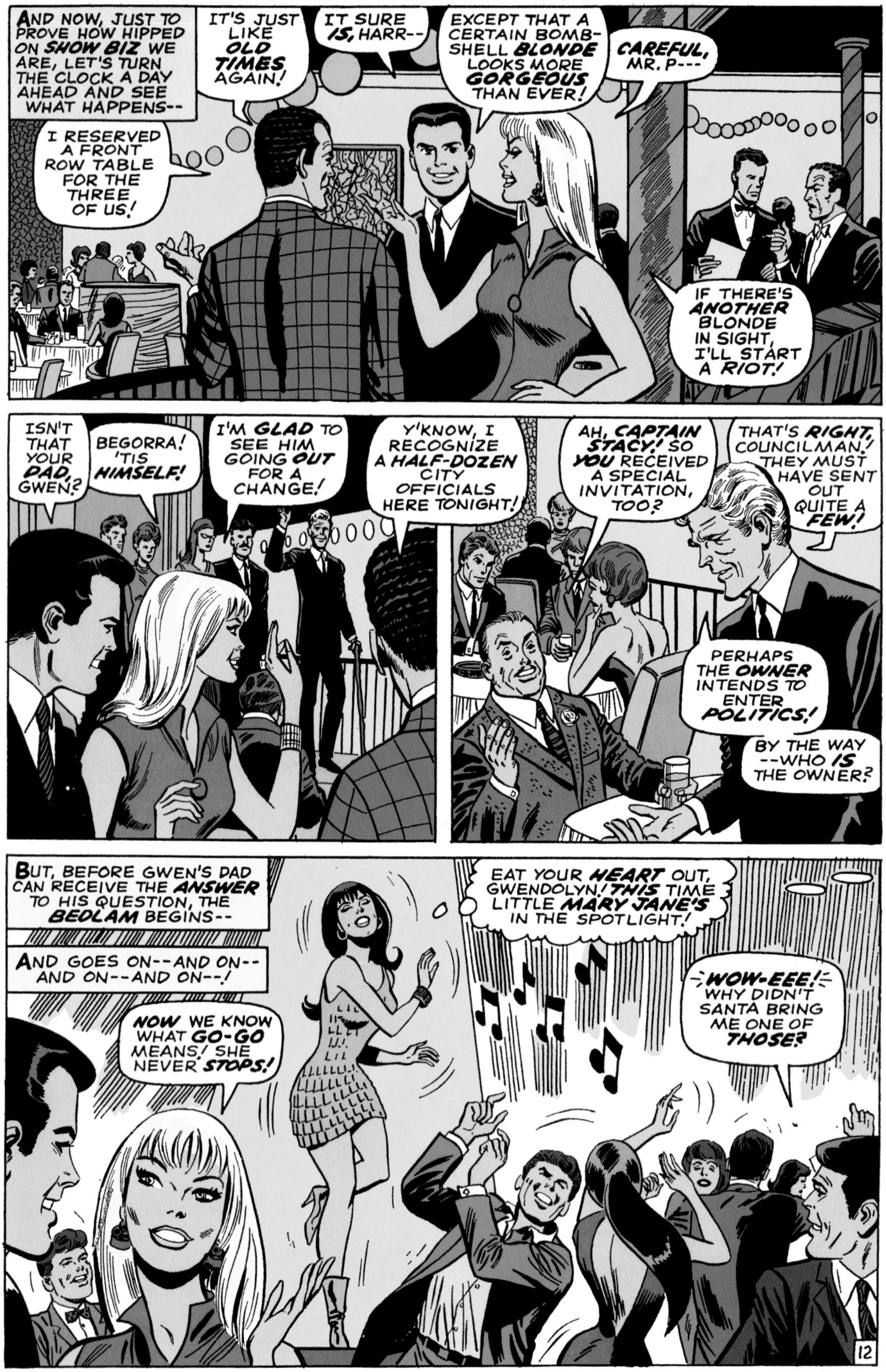
AND NOW, JUST TO PROVE HOW HIPPED ON SHOW BIZ WE ARE, LET'S TURN THE CLOCK A DAY AHEAD AND SEE WHAT HAPPENS--
IT'S JUST LIKE OLD TIMES AGAIN!
IT SURE IS, HARR--
EXCEPT THAT A CERTAIN BOMB-SHELL BLONDE LOOKS MORE GORGEOUS THAN EVER!
CAREFUL, MR. P---
I RESERVED A FRONT ROW TABLE FOR THE THREE OF US!
IF THERE'S ANOTHER BLONDE IN SIGHT, I'LL START A RIOT!
ISN'T THAT YOUR DAD, GWEN?
BEGORRA! 'TIS HIMSELF!
I'M GLAD TO SEE HIM GOING OUT FOR A CHANGE!
Y'KNOW, I RECOGNIZE A HALF-DOZEN CITY OFFICIALS HERE TONIGHT!
AH, CAPTAIN STACY! SO YOU RECEIVED A SPECIAL INVITATION, TOO?
THAT'S RIGHT, COUNCILMAN! THEY MUST HAVE SENT OUT QUITE A FEW!
PERHAPS THE OWNER INTENDS TO ENTER POLITICS!
BY THE WAY --WHO IS THE OWNER?
BUT, BEFORE GWEN'S DAD CAN RECEIVE THE ANSWER TO HIS QUESTION, THE BEDLAM BEGINS--
AND GOES ON--AND ON--AND ON--AND ON--!
EAT YOUR HEART OUT, GWENDOLYN! THIS TIME LITTLE MARY JANE'S IN THE SPOTLIGHT!
NOW WE KNOW WHAT GO-GO MEANS! SHE NEVER STOPS!
WOW-EEE! WHY DIDN'T SANTA BRING ME ONE OF THOSE?
12

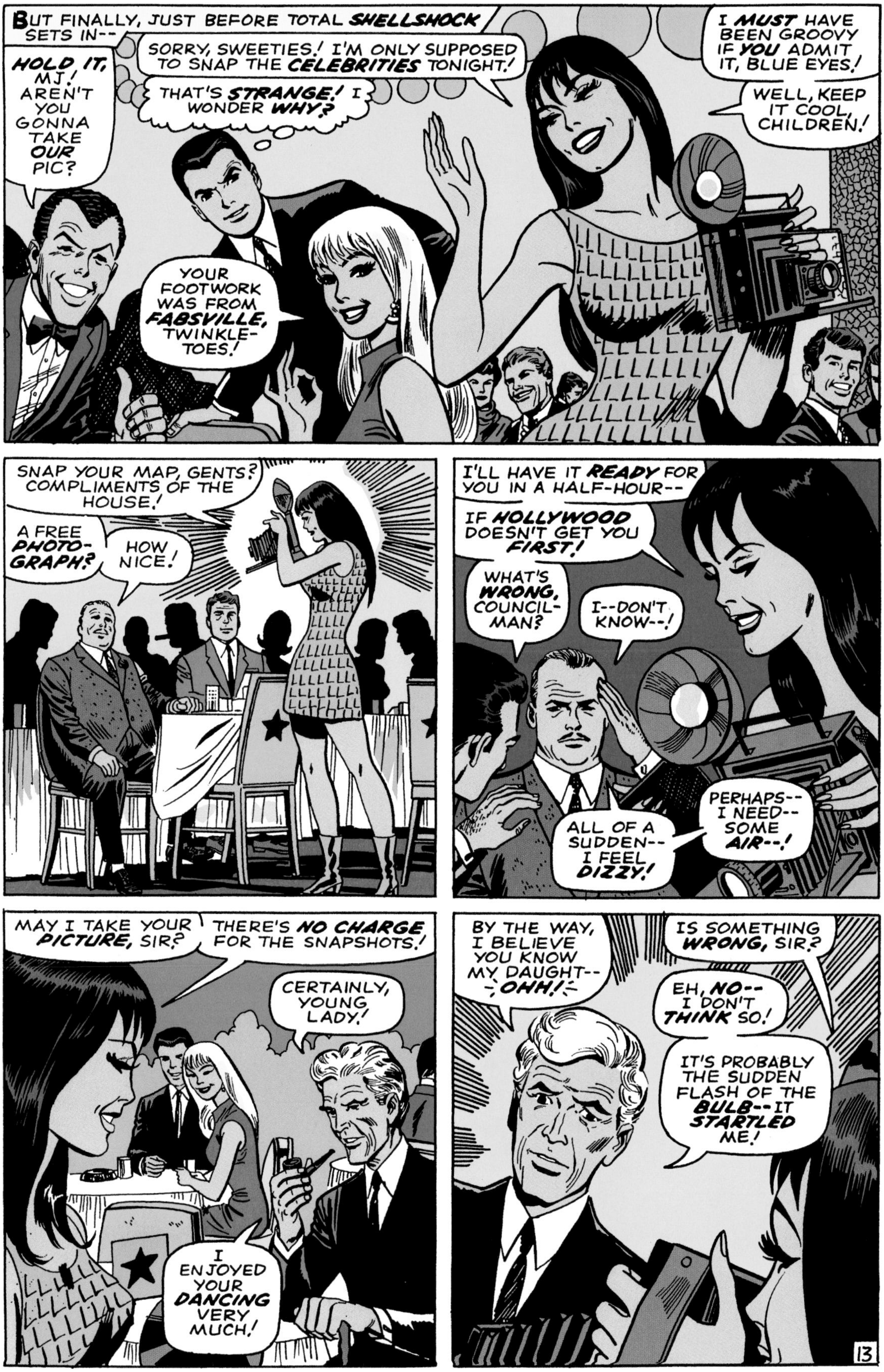
BUT FINALLY, JUST BEFORE TOTAL SHELLSHOCK SETS IN--
HOLD IT, MJ! AREN'T YOU GONNA TAKE OUR PIC?
SORRY, SWEETIES! I'M ONLY SUPPOSED TO SNAP THE CELEBRITIES TONIGHT!
THAT'S STRANGE! I WONDER WHY?
I MUST HAVE BEEN GROOVY IF YOU ADMIT IT, BLUE EYES!
WELL, KEEP IT COOL, CHILDREN!
YOUR FOOTWORK WAS FROM FABSVILLE, TWINKLE-TOES!
SNAP YOUR MAP, GENTS? COMPLIMENTS OF THE HOUSE!
A FREE PHOTO-GRAPH?
HOW NICE!
I'LL HAVE IT READY FOR YOU IN A HALF-HOUR--
IF HOLLYWOOD DOESN'T GET YOU FIRST!
WHAT'S WRONG, COUNCIL-MAN?
I--DON'T KNOW--!
ALL OF A SUDDEN-- I FEEL DIZZY!
PERHAPS-- I NEED-- SOME AIR--!
MAY I TAKE YOUR PICTURE, SIR?
THERE'S NO CHARGE FOR THE SNAPSHOTS!
CERTAINLY, YOUNG LADY!
I ENJOYED YOUR DANCING VERY MUCH!
BY THE WAY, I BELIEVE YOU KNOW MY DAUGHT-- OHH!
IS SOMETHING WRONG, SIR?
EH, NO-- I DON'T THINK SO!
IT'S PROBABLY THE SUDDEN FLASH OF THE BULB--IT STARTLED ME!
13

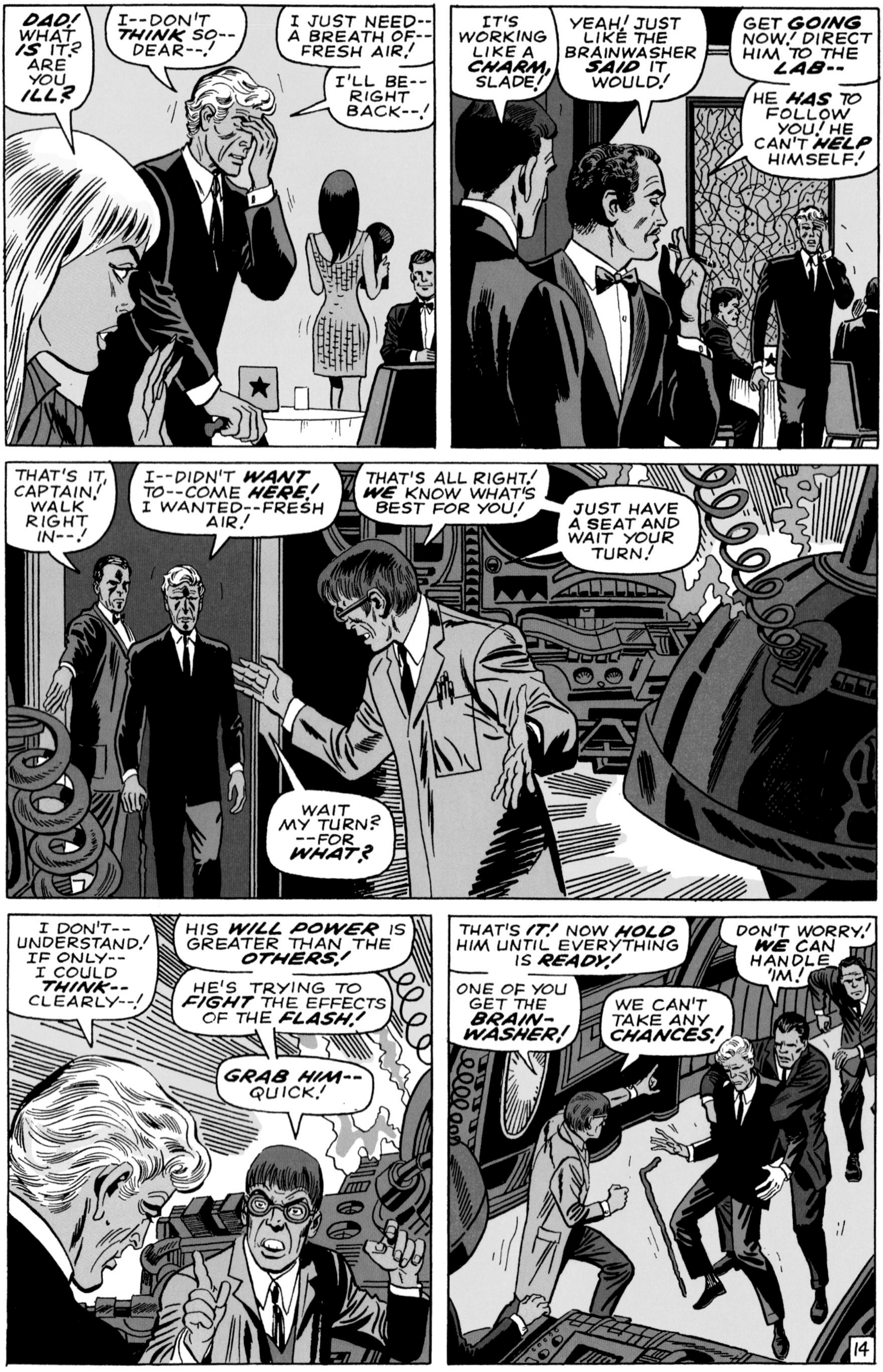
DAD! WHAT IS IT? ARE YOU ILL?
I--DON'T THINK SO-- DEAR--!
I JUST NEED-- A BREATH OF-- FRESH AIR!
I'LL BE-- RIGHT BACK--!
IT'S WORKING LIKE A CHARM, SLADE!
YEAH! JUST LIKE THE BRAINWASHER SAID IT WOULD!
GET GOING NOW! DIRECT HIM TO THE LAB--
HE HAS TO FOLLOW YOU! HE CAN'T HELP HIMSELF!
THAT'S IT, CAPTAIN! WALK RIGHT IN--!
I--DIDN'T WANT TO--COME HERE! I WANTED--FRESH AIR!
THAT'S ALL RIGHT! WE KNOW WHAT'S BEST FOR YOU!
JUST HAVE A SEAT AND WAIT YOUR TURN!
WAIT MY TURN? --FOR WHAT?
I DON'T-- UNDERSTAND! IF ONLY-- I COULD THINK-- CLEARLY--!
HIS WILL POWER IS GREATER THAN THE OTHERS!
HE'S TRYING TO FIGHT THE EFFECTS OF THE FLASH!
GRAB HIM-- QUICK!
THAT'S IT! NOW HOLD HIM UNTIL EVERYTHING IS READY!
ONE OF YOU GET THE BRAIN-WASHER!
WE CAN'T TAKE ANY CHANCES!
DON'T WORRY! WE CAN HANDLE 'IM!
14

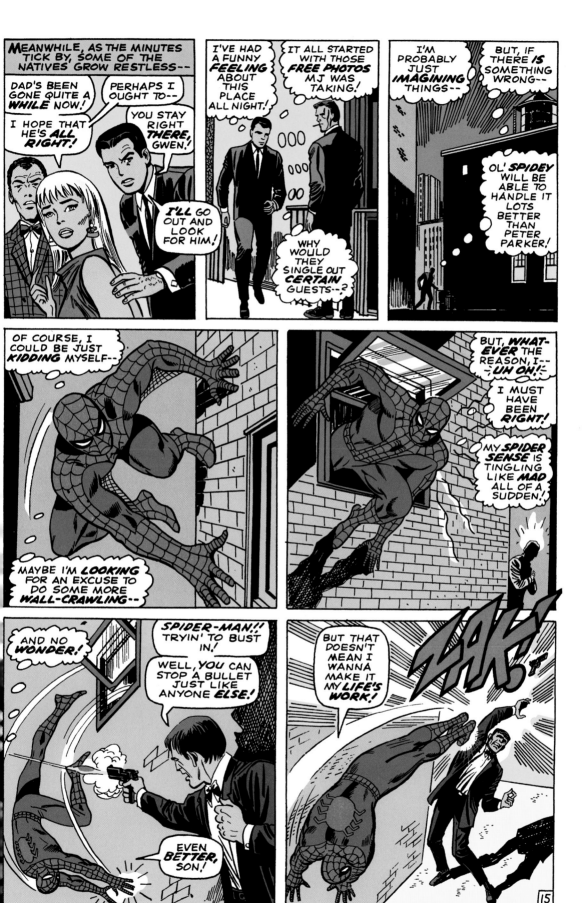

MEANWHILE, AS THE MINUTES TICK BY, SOME OF THE NATIVES' GROW RESTLESS--

DAD'S BEEN GONE QUITE A *WHILE* NOW!

PERHAPS I OUGHT TO--

I HOPE THAT HE'S *ALL RIGHT!*

YOU STAY RIGHT *THERE,* GWEN!

I'LL GO OUT AND LOOK FOR HIM!

I'VE HAD A FUNNY *FEELING* ABOUT THIS PLACE ALL NIGHT!

IT ALL STARTED WITH THOSE *FREE PHOTOS* MJ WAS TAKING!

WHY WOULD THEY SINGLE OUT *CERTAIN* GUESTS--?

I'M PROBABLY JUST *IMAGINING* THINGS--

BUT, IF THERE *IS* SOMETHING WRONG--

OL' *SPIDEY* WILL BE ABLE TO HANDLE IT LOTS BETTER THAN PETER PARKER!

OF COURSE, I COULD BE JUST *KIDDING* MYSELF--

MAYBE I'M *LOOKING* FOR AN EXCUSE TO DO SOME MORE *WALL-CRAWLING*--

BUT, *WHATEVER* THE REASON, I---UH OH!--

I MUST HAVE BEEN *RIGHT!*

MY *SPIDER SENSE* IS TINGLING LIKE *MAD* ALL OF A SUDDEN!

AND NO *WONDER!*

SPIDER-MAN!! TRYIN' TO BUST IN!

WELL, YOU CAN STOP A BULLET JUST LIKE ANYONE *ELSE!*

EVEN *BETTER,* SON!

BUT THAT DOESN'T MEAN I WANNA MAKE IT MY *LIFE'S WORK!*

ZAK!

15

145

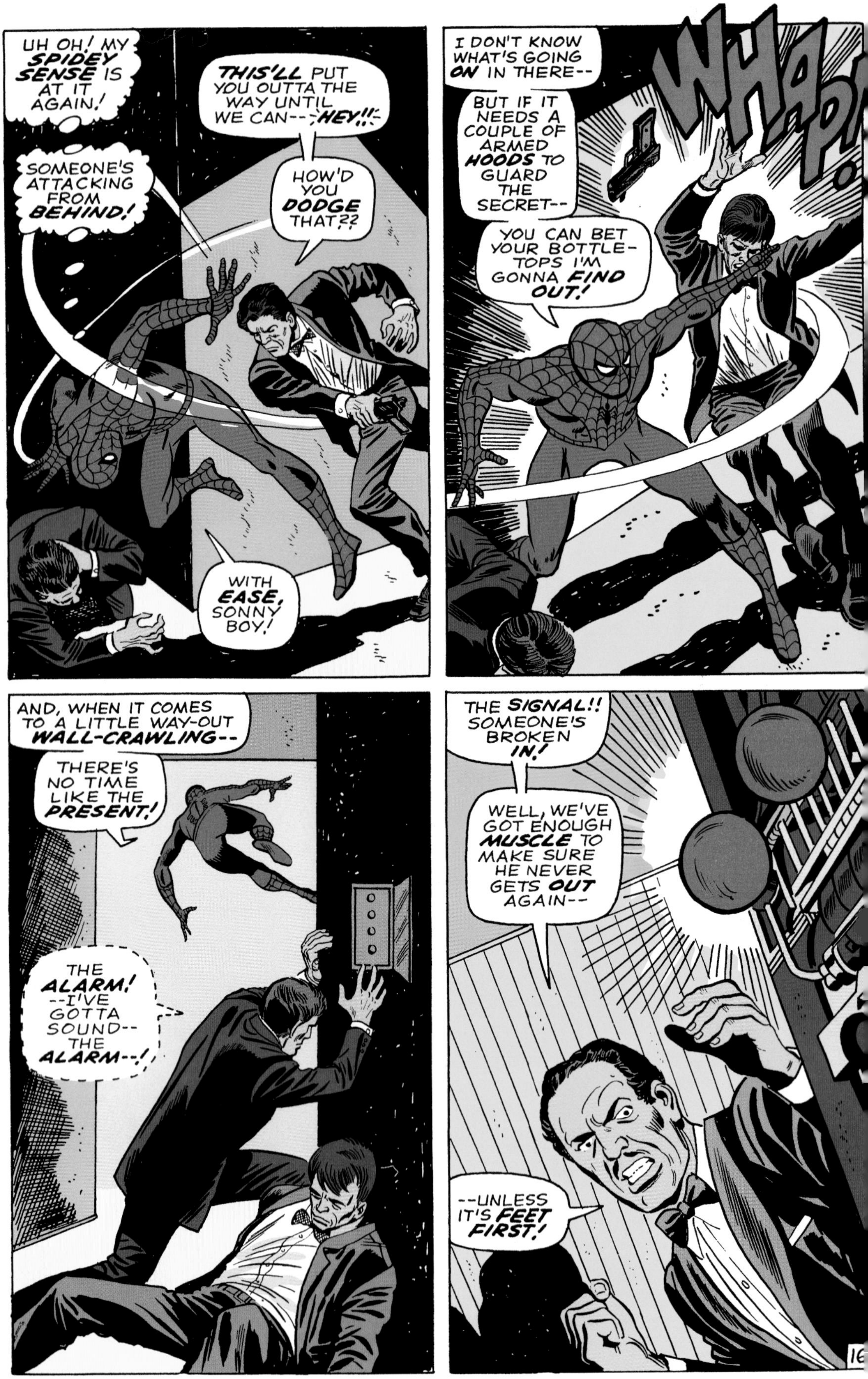

UH OH! MY SPIDEY SENSE IS AT IT AGAIN!
SOMEONE'S ATTACKING FROM BEHIND!
THIS'LL PUT YOU OUTTA THE WAY UNTIL WE CAN-- HEY!!
HOW'D YOU DODGE THAT??
WITH EASE, SONNY BOY!
I DON'T KNOW WHAT'S GOING ON IN THERE--
BUT IF IT NEEDS A COUPLE OF ARMED HOODS TO GUARD THE SECRET--
YOU CAN BET YOUR BOTTLE-TOPS I'M GONNA FIND OUT!
AND, WHEN IT COMES TO A LITTLE WAY-OUT WALL-CRAWLING--
THERE'S NO TIME LIKE THE PRESENT!
THE ALARM! --I'VE GOTTA SOUND-- THE ALARM--!
THE SIGNAL!! SOMEONE'S BROKEN IN!
WELL, WE'VE GOT ENOUGH MUSCLE TO MAKE SURE HE NEVER GETS OUT AGAIN--
--UNLESS IT'S FEET FIRST!

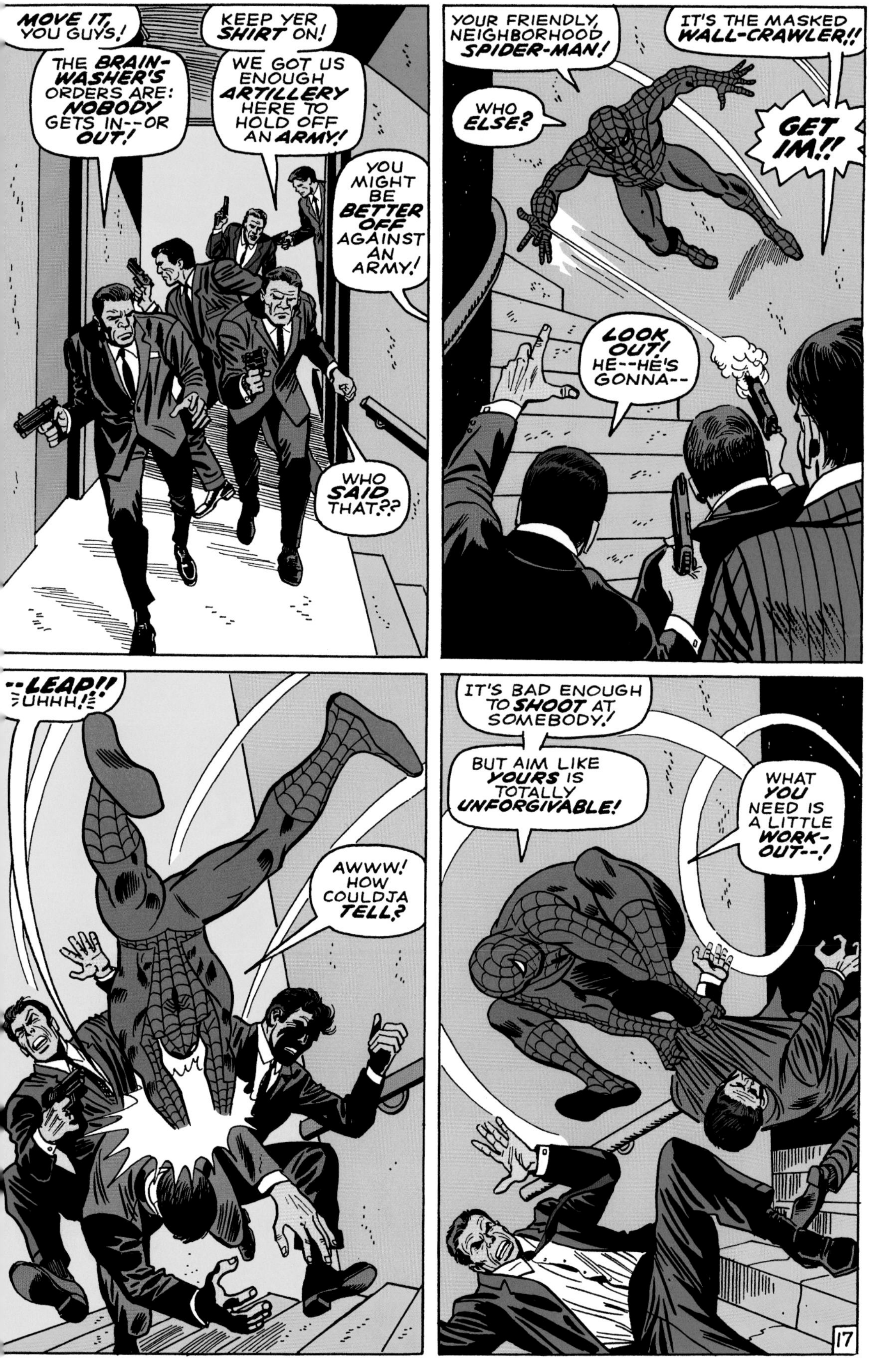
MOVE IT, YOU GUYS! THE BRAIN-WASHER'S ORDERS ARE: NOBODY GETS IN--OR OUT!
KEEP YER SHIRT ON! WE GOT US ENOUGH ARTILLERY HERE TO HOLD OFF AN ARMY!
YOU MIGHT BE BETTER OFF AGAINST AN ARMY!
WHO SAID THAT??
YOUR FRIENDLY, NEIGHBORHOOD SPIDER-MAN!
WHO ELSE?
IT'S THE MASKED WALL-CRAWLER!!
GET 'IM!!
LOOK OUT! HE--HE'S GONNA--
--LEAP!!
UHHH!
AWWW! HOW COULDJA TELL?
IT'S BAD ENOUGH TO SHOOT AT SOMEBODY!
BUT AIM LIKE YOURS IS TOTALLY UNFORGIVABLE!
WHAT YOU NEED IS A LITTLE WORK-OUT--!
17

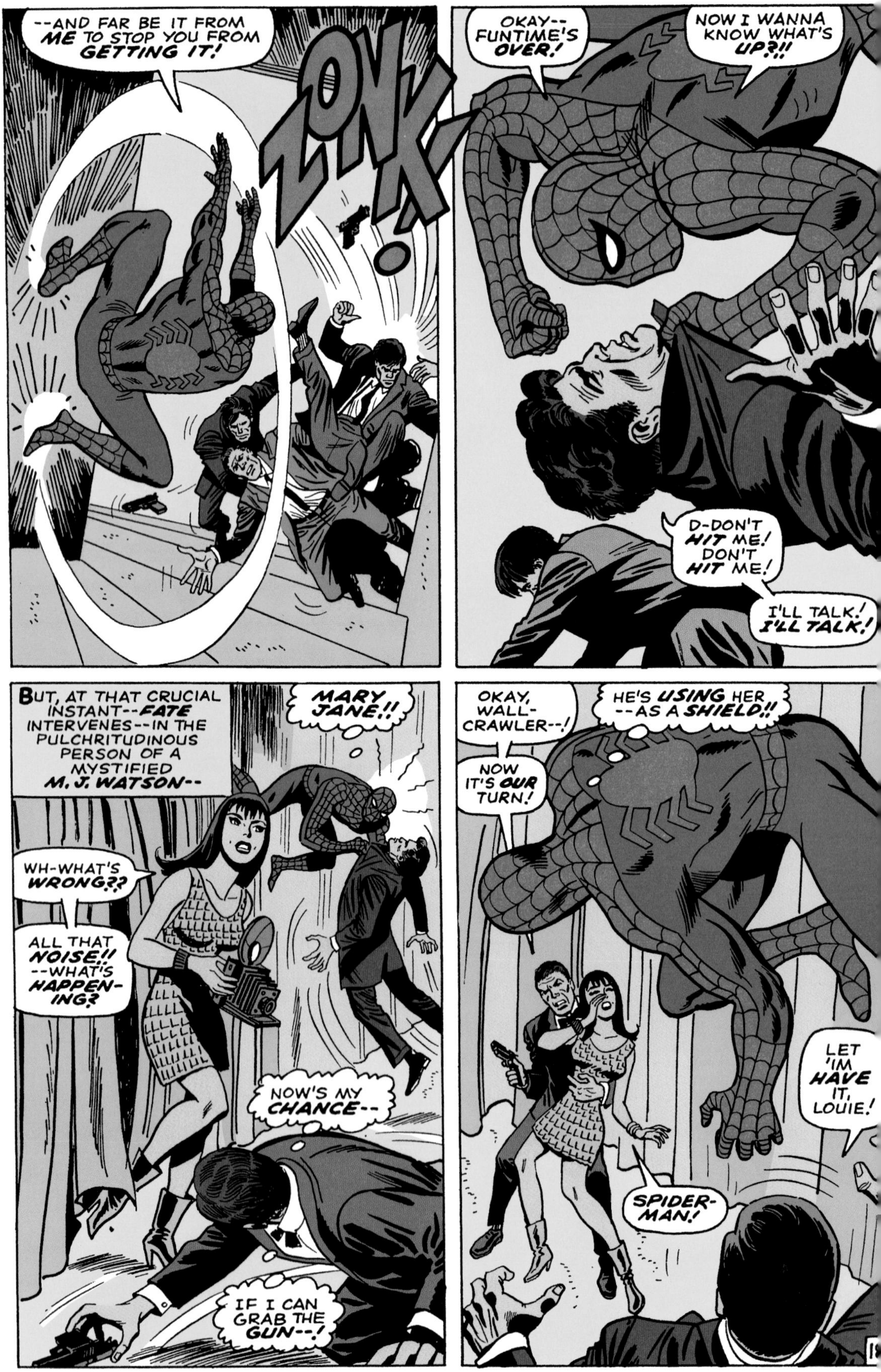
--AND FAR BE IT FROM ME TO STOP YOU FROM GETTING IT!
ZONK!
OKAY--FUNTIME'S OVER!
NOW I WANNA KNOW WHAT'S UP?!!
D-DON'T HIT ME! DON'T HIT ME!
I'LL TALK! I'LL TALK!
BUT, AT THAT CRUCIAL INSTANT--FATE INTERVENES--IN THE PULCHRITUDINOUS PERSON OF A MYSTIFIED M. J. WATSON--
MARY JANE!!
WH-WHAT'S WRONG??
ALL THAT NOISE!! --WHAT'S HAPPENING?
NOW'S MY CHANCE--
IF I CAN GRAB THE GUN--!
OKAY, WALL-CRAWLER--!
NOW IT'S OUR TURN!
HE'S USING HER --AS A SHIELD!!
LET 'IM HAVE IT, LOUIE!
SPIDER-MAN!

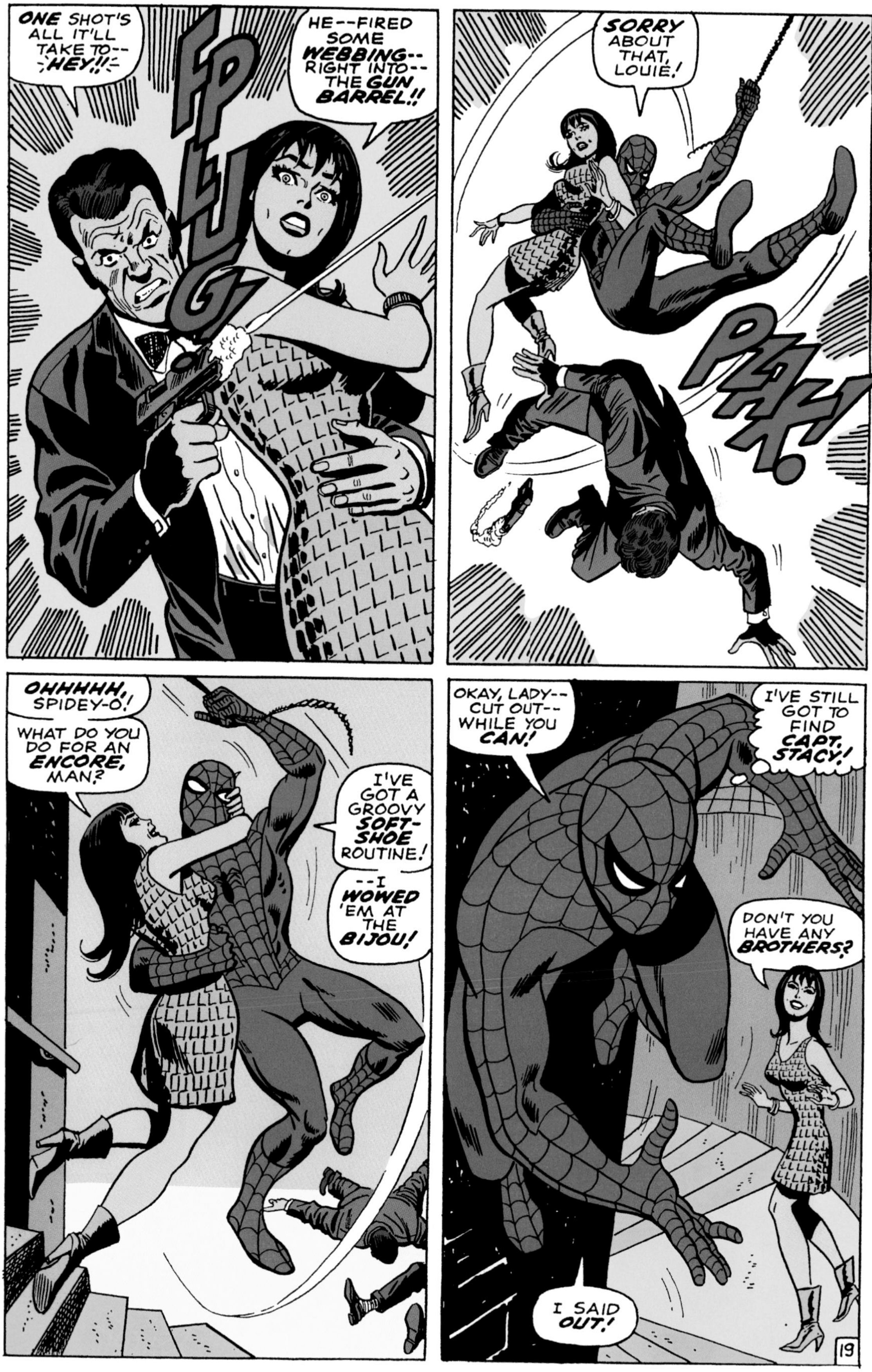
ONE SHOT'S ALL IT'LL TAKE TO-- HEY!!
FPLUG
HE--FIRED SOME WEBBING-- RIGHT INTO-- THE GUN BARREL!!
SORRY ABOUT THAT, LOUIE!
PLAK!
OHHHHH, SPIDEY-O!
WHAT DO YOU DO FOR AN ENCORE, MAN?
I'VE GOT A GROOVY SOFT-SHOE ROUTINE!
--I WOWED 'EM AT THE BIJOU!
OKAY, LADY-- CUT OUT-- WHILE YOU CAN!
I'VE STILL GOT TO FIND CAPT. STACY!
DON'T YOU HAVE ANY BROTHERS?
I SAID OUT!
19

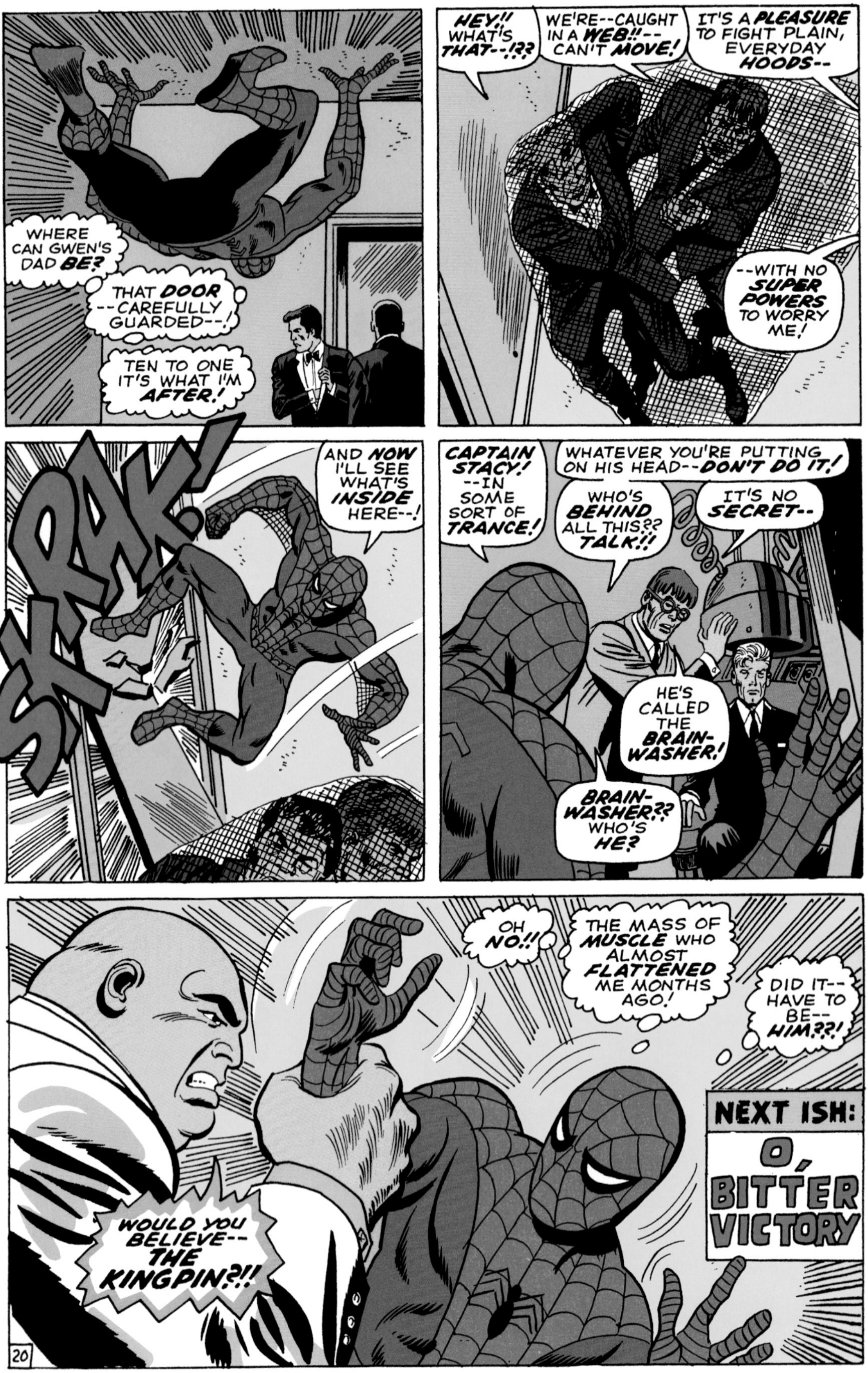
WHERE CAN GWEN'S DAD BE?
THAT DOOR --CAREFULLY GUARDED--!
TEN TO ONE IT'S WHAT I'M AFTER!
HEY!! WHAT'S THAT--!??
WE'RE--CAUGHT IN A WEB!!-- CAN'T MOVE!
IT'S A PLEASURE TO FIGHT PLAIN, EVERYDAY HOODS--
--WITH NO SUPER POWERS TO WORRY ME!
STRAK!
AND NOW I'LL SEE WHAT'S INSIDE HERE--!
CAPTAIN STACY! --IN SOME SORT OF TRANCE!
WHATEVER YOU'RE PUTTING ON HIS HEAD--DON'T DO IT!
WHO'S BEHIND ALL THIS?? TALK!!
IT'S NO SECRET--
HE'S CALLED THE BRAIN-WASHER!
BRAIN-WASHER?? WHO'S HE?
OH NO!!
THE MASS OF MUSCLE WHO ALMOST FLATTENED ME MONTHS AGO!
DID IT--HAVE TO BE--HIM??!
WOULD YOU BELIEVE--THE KINGPIN?!!
NEXT ISH:
O, BITTER VICTORY
20

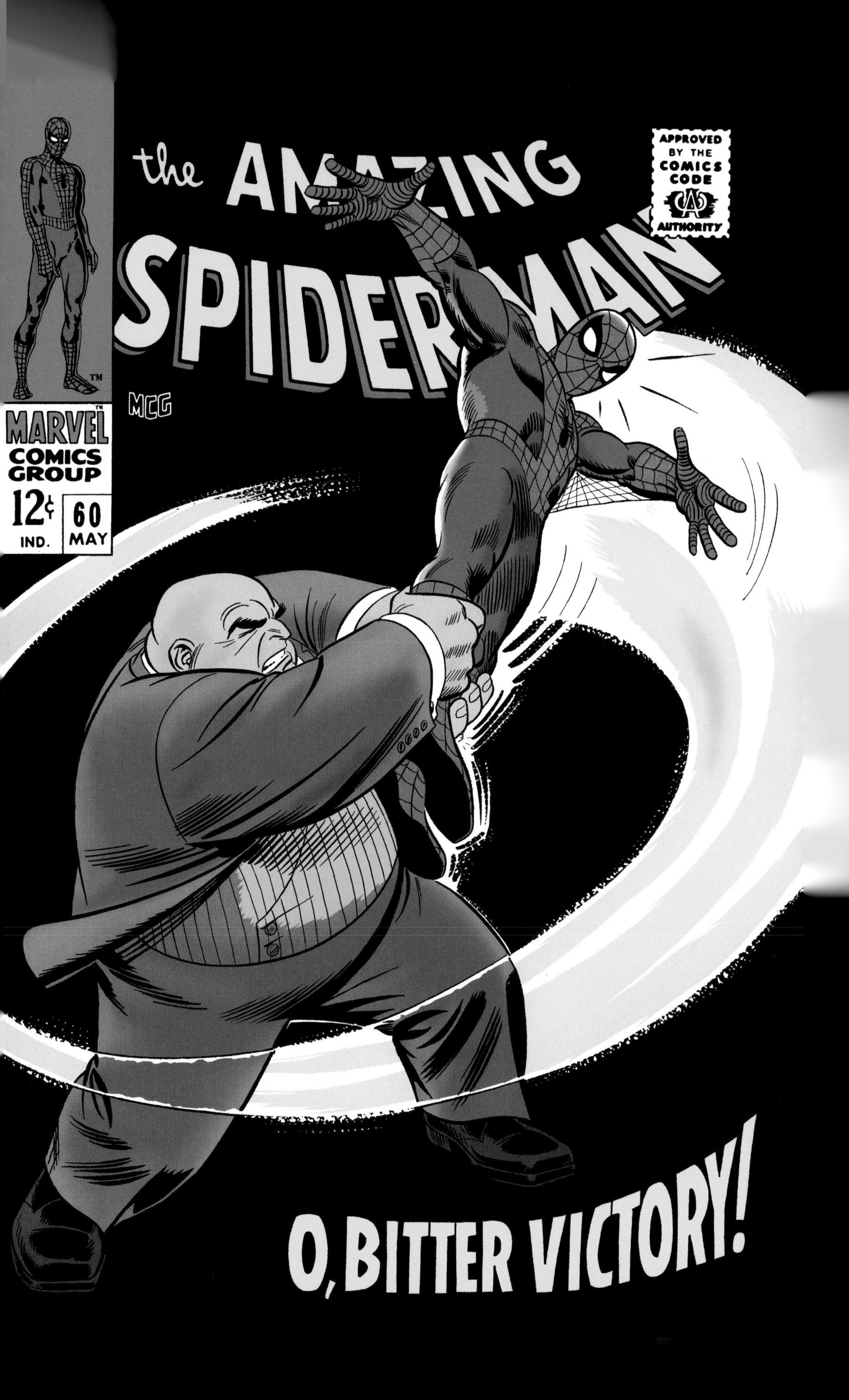
the AMAZING SPIDER-MAN
APPROVED BY THE COMICS CODE AUTHORITY
MARVEL COMICS GROUP
12¢ IND.
60 MAY
MCG
O, BITTER VICTORY!

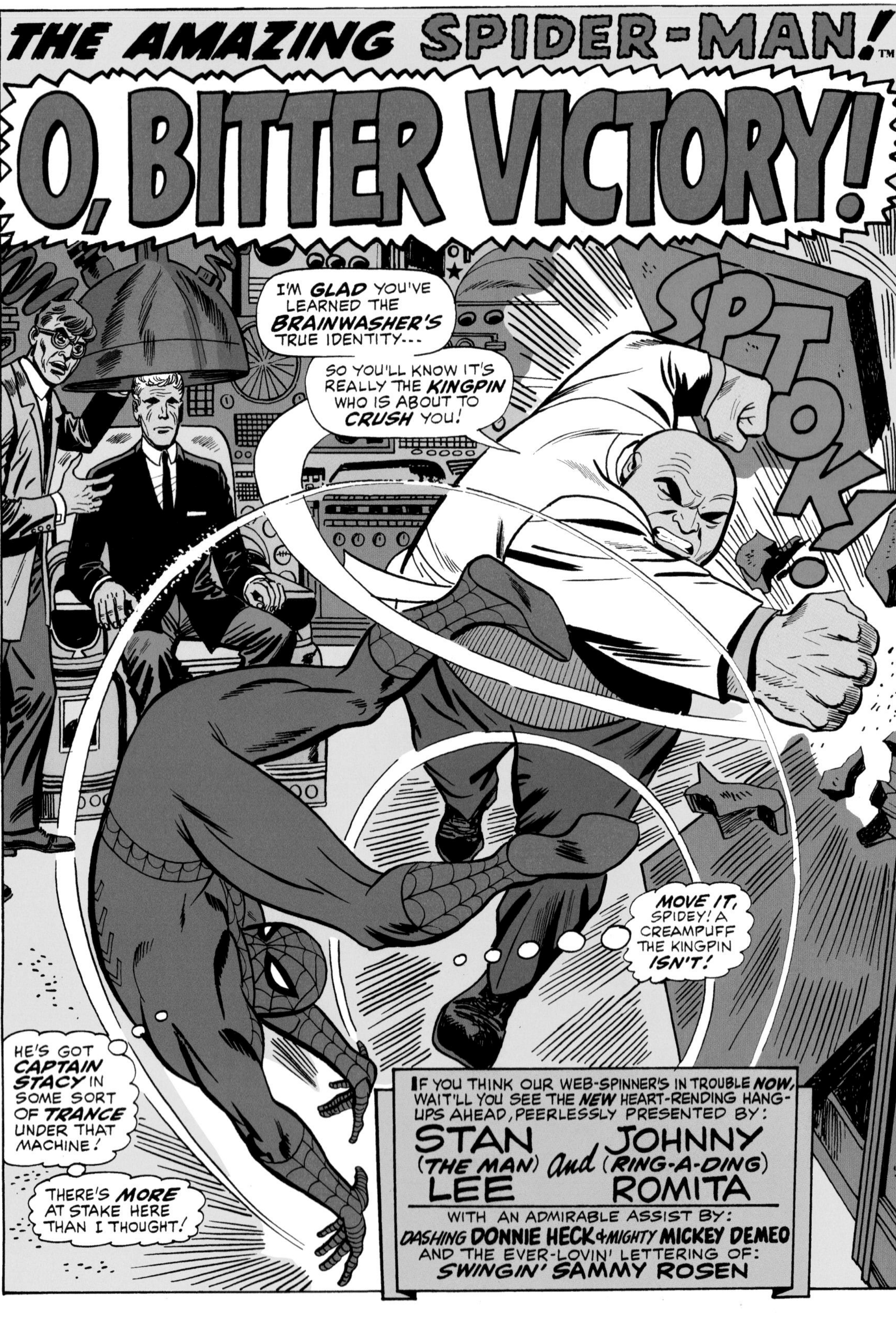
THE AMAZING SPIDER-MAN!
O, BITTER VICTORY!
I'M GLAD YOU'VE LEARNED THE BRAINWASHER'S TRUE IDENTITY---
SO YOU'LL KNOW IT'S REALLY THE KINGPIN WHO IS ABOUT TO CRUSH YOU!
SPTOK!
MOVE IT, SPIDEY! A CREAMPUFF THE KINGPIN ISN'T!
HE'S GOT CAPTAIN STACY IN SOME SORT OF TRANCE UNDER THAT MACHINE!
THERE'S MORE AT STAKE HERE THAN I THOUGHT!
IF YOU THINK OUR WEB-SPINNER'S IN TROUBLE NOW, WAIT'LL YOU SEE THE NEW HEART-RENDING HANG-UPS AHEAD, PEERLESSLY PRESENTED BY:
STAN (THE MAN) LEE and JOHNNY (RING-A-DING) ROMITA
WITH AN ADMIRABLE ASSIST BY:
DASHING DONNIE HECK & MIGHTY MICKEY DEMEO
AND THE EVER-LOVIN' LETTERING OF:
SWINGIN' SAMMY ROSEN

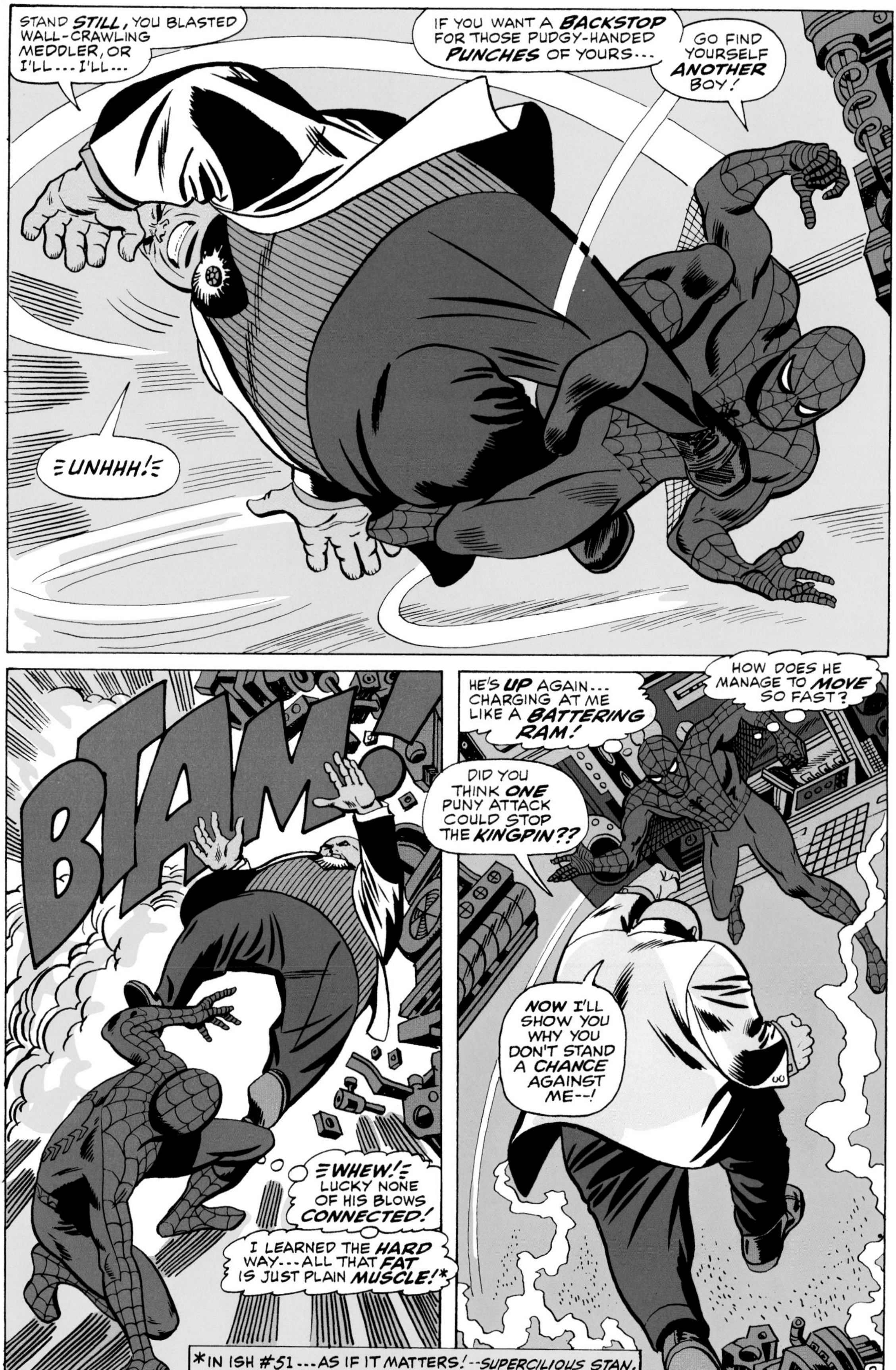
STAND STILL, YOU BLASTED WALL-CRAWLING MEDDLER, OR I'LL---I'LL---
IF YOU WANT A BACKSTOP FOR THOSE PUDGY-HANDED PUNCHES OF YOURS---
GO FIND YOURSELF ANOTHER BOY!
UNHHH!
BLAM!
WHEW! LUCKY NONE OF HIS BLOWS CONNECTED!
I LEARNED THE HARD WAY---ALL THAT FAT IS JUST PLAIN MUSCLE!*
HE'S UP AGAIN--- CHARGING AT ME LIKE A BATTERING RAM!
HOW DOES HE MANAGE TO MOVE SO FAST?
DID YOU THINK ONE PUNY ATTACK COULD STOP THE KINGPIN??
NOW I'LL SHOW YOU WHY YOU DON'T STAND A CHANCE AGAINST ME--!
*IN ISH #51---AS IF IT MATTERS!--SUPERCILIOUS STAN.
2.

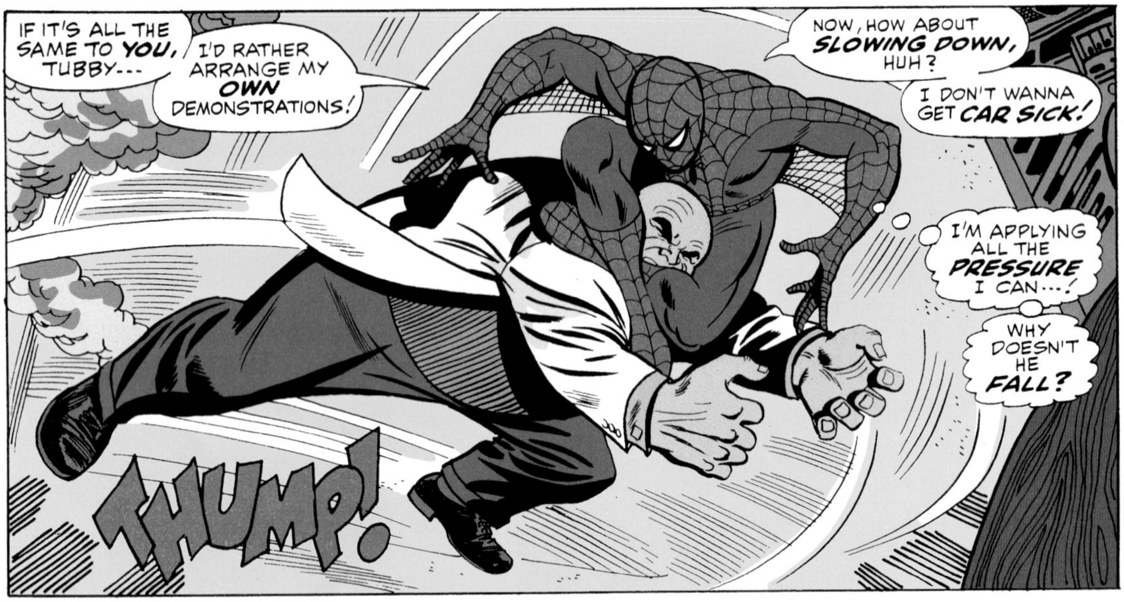
IF IT'S ALL THE SAME TO YOU, TUBBY---
I'D RATHER ARRANGE MY OWN DEMONSTRATIONS!
NOW, HOW ABOUT SLOWING DOWN, HUH?
I DON'T WANNA GET CAR SICK!
I'M APPLYING ALL THE PRESSURE I CAN---!
WHY DOESN'T HE FALL?
THUMP!

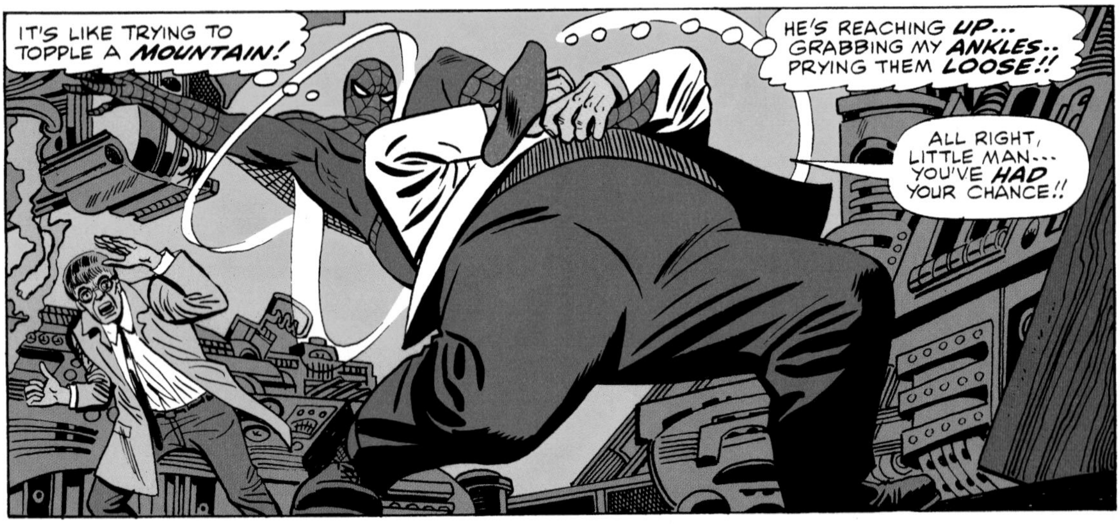
IT'S LIKE TRYING TO TOPPLE A MOUNTAIN!
HE'S REACHING UP... GRABBING MY ANKLES.. PRYING THEM LOOSE!!
ALL RIGHT, LITTLE MAN--- YOU'VE HAD YOUR CHANCE!!

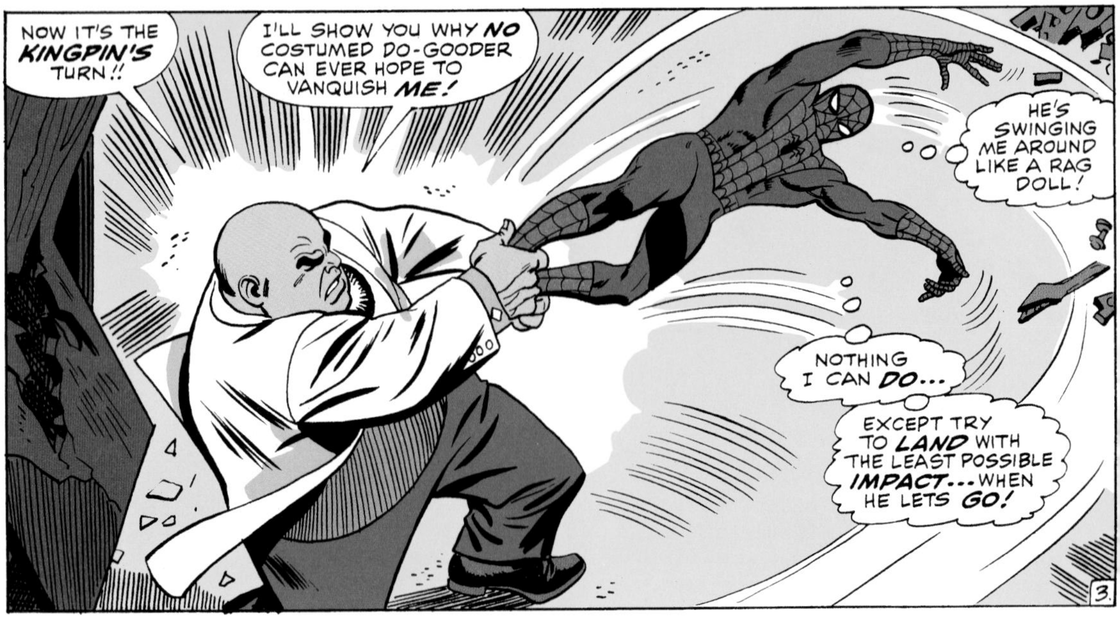
NOW IT'S THE KINGPIN'S TURN!!
I'LL SHOW YOU WHY NO COSTUMED DO-GOODER CAN EVER HOPE TO VANQUISH ME!
HE'S SWINGING ME AROUND LIKE A RAG DOLL!
NOTHING I CAN DO...
EXCEPT TRY TO LAND WITH THE LEAST POSSIBLE IMPACT---WHEN HE LETS GO!
3.

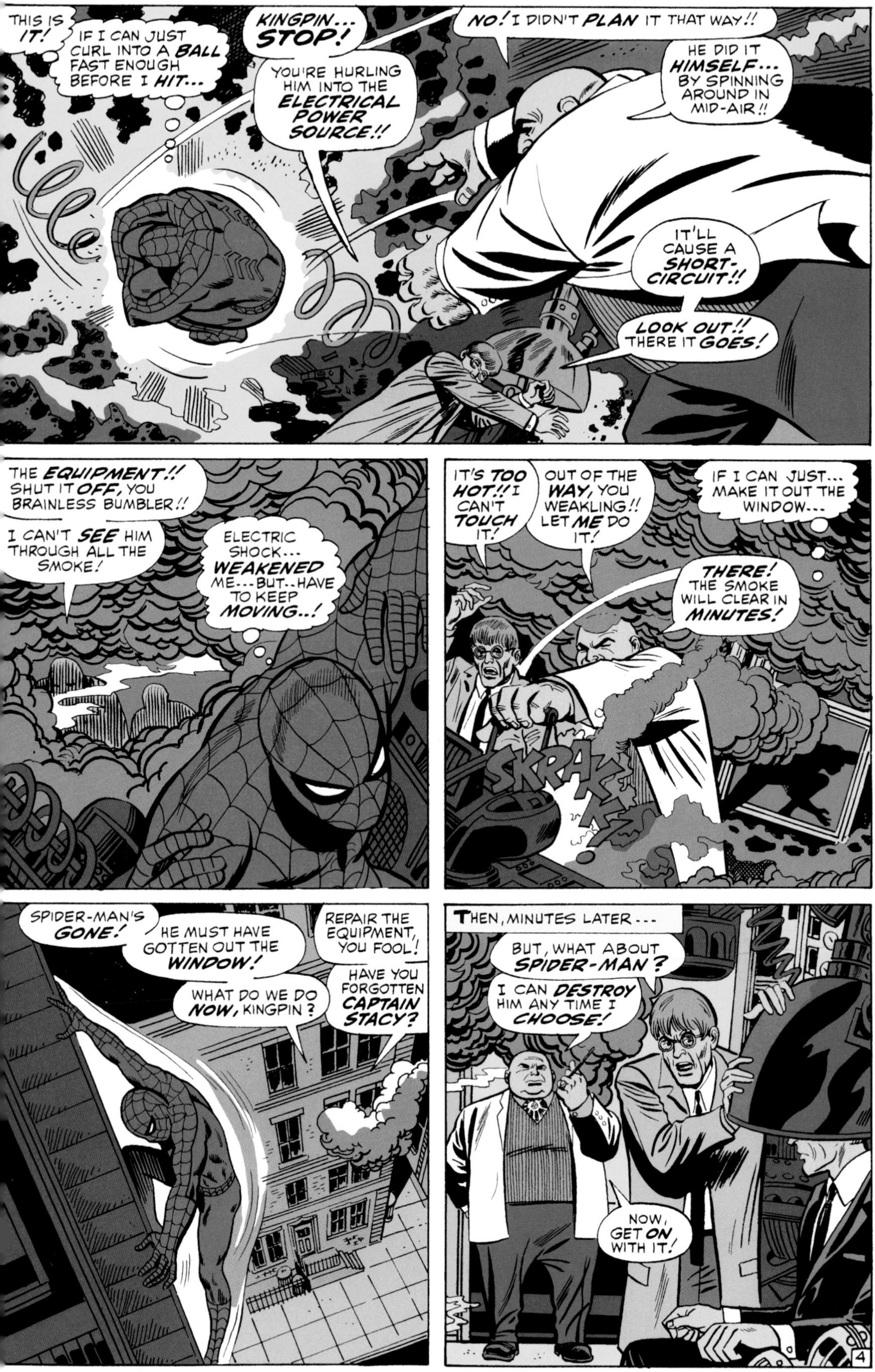

THIS IS IT!
IF I CAN JUST CURL INTO A BALL FAST ENOUGH BEFORE I HIT...
KINGPIN... STOP!
YOU'RE HURLING HIM INTO THE ELECTRICAL POWER SOURCE!!
NO! I DIDN'T PLAN IT THAT WAY!!
HE DID IT HIMSELF... BY SPINNING AROUND IN MID-AIR!!
IT'LL CAUSE A SHORT-CIRCUIT!!
LOOK OUT!! THERE IT GOES!
THE EQUIPMENT!! SHUT IT OFF, YOU BRAINLESS BUMBLER!!
I CAN'T SEE HIM THROUGH ALL THE SMOKE!
ELECTRIC SHOCK... WEAKENED ME... BUT.. HAVE TO KEEP MOVING..!
IT'S TOO HOT!! I CAN'T TOUCH IT!
OUT OF THE WAY, YOU WEAKLING!! LET ME DO IT!
IF I CAN JUST... MAKE IT OUT THE WINDOW...
THERE! THE SMOKE WILL CLEAR IN MINUTES!
SKRAKK
SPIDER-MAN'S GONE!
HE MUST HAVE GOTTEN OUT THE WINDOW!
REPAIR THE EQUIPMENT, YOU FOOL!
WHAT DO WE DO NOW, KINGPIN?
HAVE YOU FORGOTTEN CAPTAIN STACY?
THEN, MINUTES LATER ---
BUT, WHAT ABOUT SPIDER-MAN?
I CAN DESTROY HIM ANY TIME I CHOOSE!
NOW, GET ON WITH IT!
4

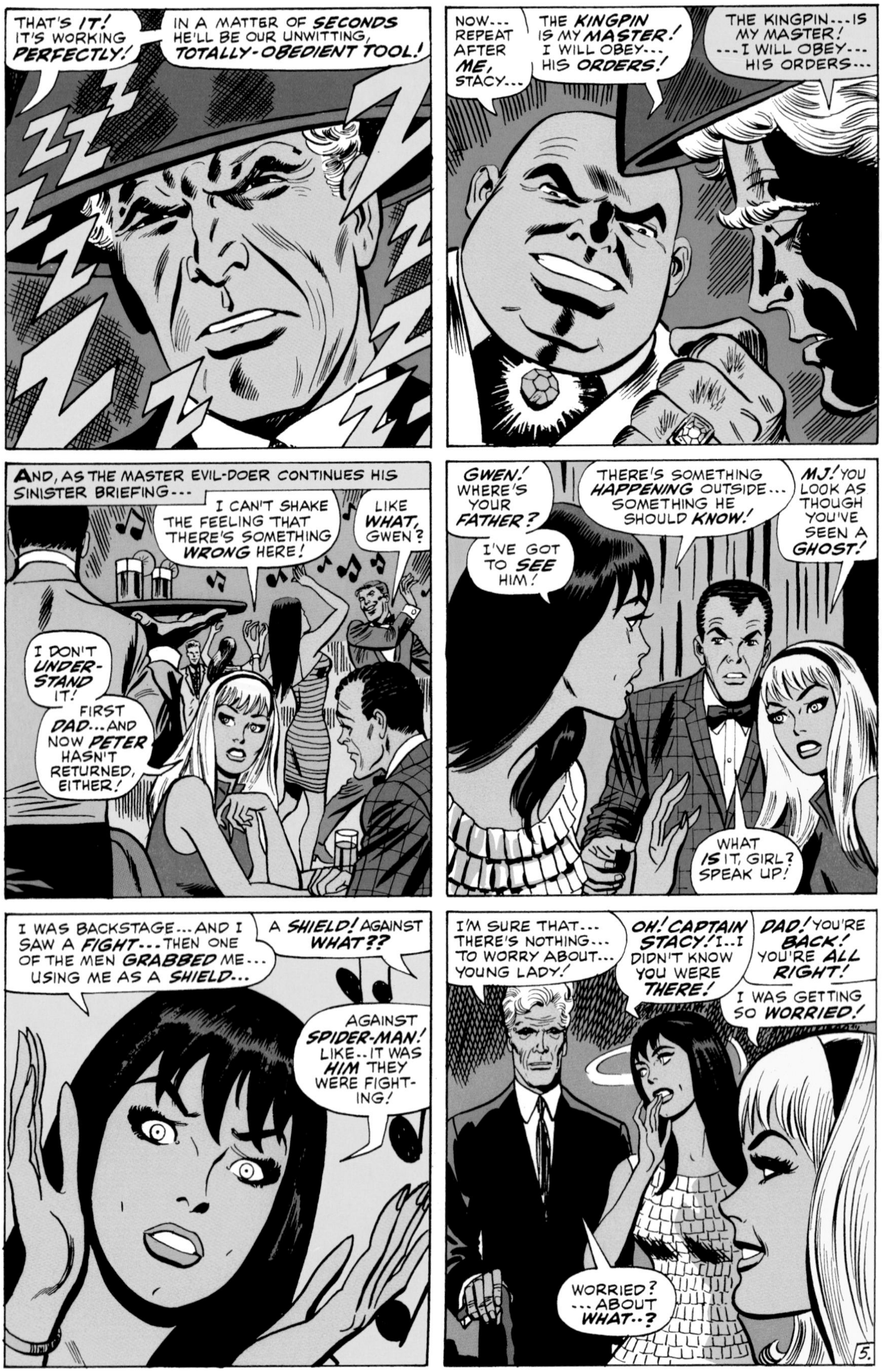
THAT'S IT! IT'S WORKING PERFECTLY!
IN A MATTER OF SECONDS HE'LL BE OUR UNWITTING, TOTALLY-OBEDIENT TOOL!
NOW--- REPEAT AFTER ME, STACY---
THE KINGPIN IS MY MASTER! I WILL OBEY--- HIS ORDERS!
THE KINGPIN---IS MY MASTER! ---I WILL OBEY--- HIS ORDERS---
AND, AS THE MASTER EVIL-DOER CONTINUES HIS SINISTER BRIEFING---
I CAN'T SHAKE THE FEELING THAT THERE'S SOMETHING WRONG HERE!
LIKE WHAT, GWEN?
I DON'T UNDERSTAND IT! FIRST DAD...AND NOW PETER HASN'T RETURNED, EITHER!
GWEN! WHERE'S YOUR FATHER?
I'VE GOT TO SEE HIM!
THERE'S SOMETHING HAPPENING OUTSIDE... SOMETHING HE SHOULD KNOW!
MJ! YOU LOOK AS THOUGH YOU'VE SEEN A GHOST!
WHAT IS IT, GIRL? SPEAK UP!
I WAS BACKSTAGE...AND I SAW A FIGHT---THEN ONE OF THE MEN GRABBED ME... USING ME AS A SHIELD...
A SHIELD! AGAINST WHAT??
AGAINST SPIDER-MAN! LIKE--IT WAS HIM THEY WERE FIGHTING!
I'M SURE THAT--- THERE'S NOTHING--- TO WORRY ABOUT--- YOUNG LADY!
OH! CAPTAIN STACY! I..I DIDN'T KNOW YOU WERE THERE!
DAD! YOU'RE BACK! YOU'RE ALL RIGHT!
I WAS GETTING SO WORRIED!
WORRIED? ...ABOUT WHAT..?
5.

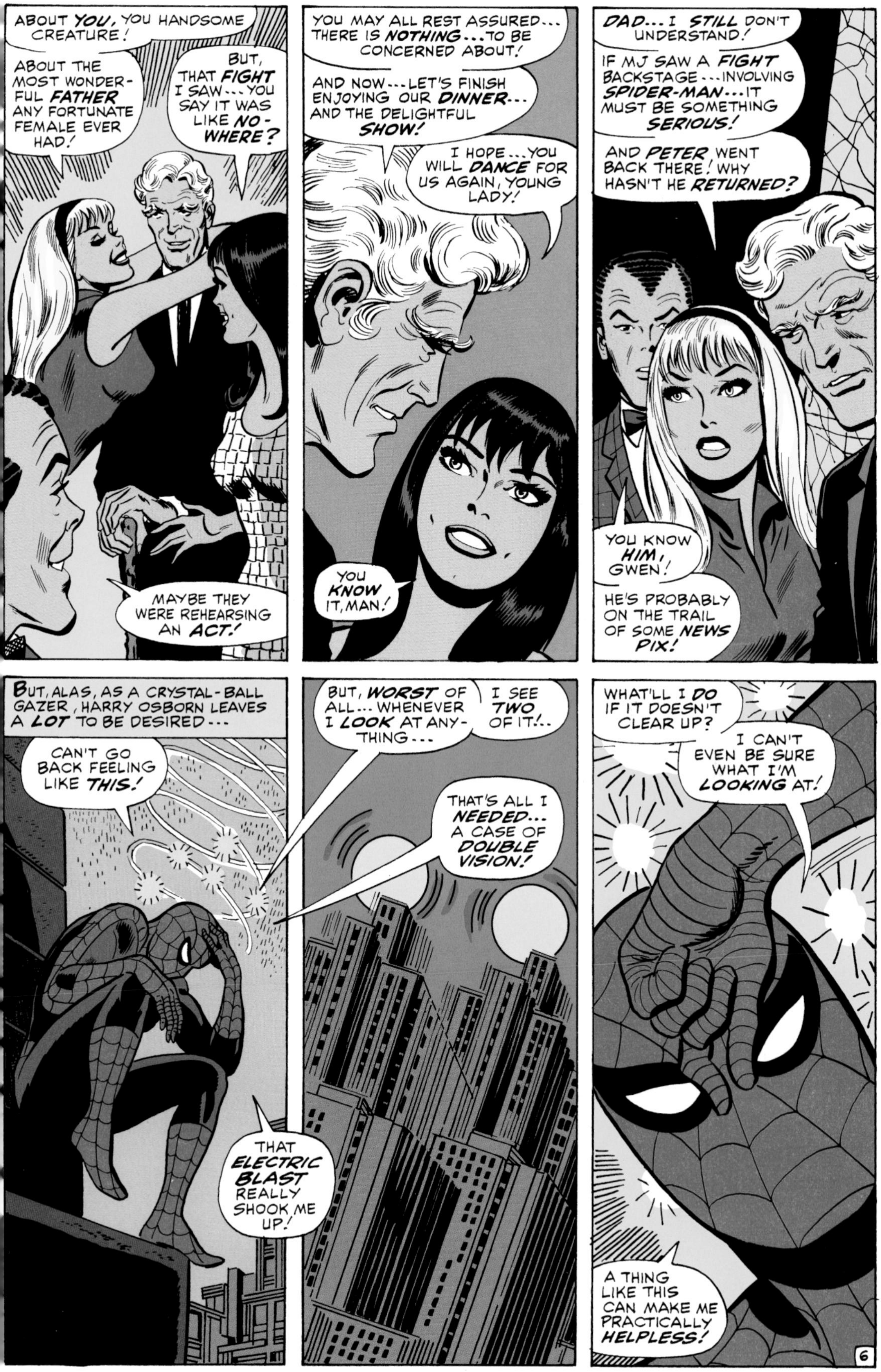
ABOUT YOU, YOU HANDSOME CREATURE!
ABOUT THE MOST WONDERFUL FATHER ANY FORTUNATE FEMALE EVER HAD!
BUT, THAT FIGHT I SAW... YOU SAY IT WAS LIKE NO-WHERE?
MAYBE THEY WERE REHEARSING AN ACT!
YOU MAY ALL REST ASSURED... THERE IS NOTHING... TO BE CONCERNED ABOUT!
AND NOW... LET'S FINISH ENJOYING OUR DINNER... AND THE DELIGHTFUL SHOW!
I HOPE... YOU WILL DANCE FOR US AGAIN, YOUNG LADY!
YOU KNOW IT, MAN!
DAD... I STILL DON'T UNDERSTAND!
IF MJ SAW A FIGHT BACKSTAGE... INVOLVING SPIDER-MAN... IT MUST BE SOMETHING SERIOUS!
AND PETER WENT BACK THERE! WHY HASN'T HE RETURNED?
YOU KNOW HIM, GWEN!
HE'S PROBABLY ON THE TRAIL OF SOME NEWS PIX!
BUT, ALAS, AS A CRYSTAL-BALL GAZER, HARRY OSBORN LEAVES A LOT TO BE DESIRED...
CAN'T GO BACK FEELING LIKE THIS!
THAT ELECTRIC BLAST REALLY SHOOK ME UP!
BUT, WORST OF ALL... WHENEVER I LOOK AT ANY-THING...
I SEE TWO OF IT!..
THAT'S ALL I NEEDED... A CASE OF DOUBLE VISION!
WHAT'LL I DO IF IT DOESN'T CLEAR UP?
I CAN'T EVEN BE SURE WHAT I'M LOOKING AT!
A THING LIKE THIS CAN MAKE ME PRACTICALLY HELPLESS!
6

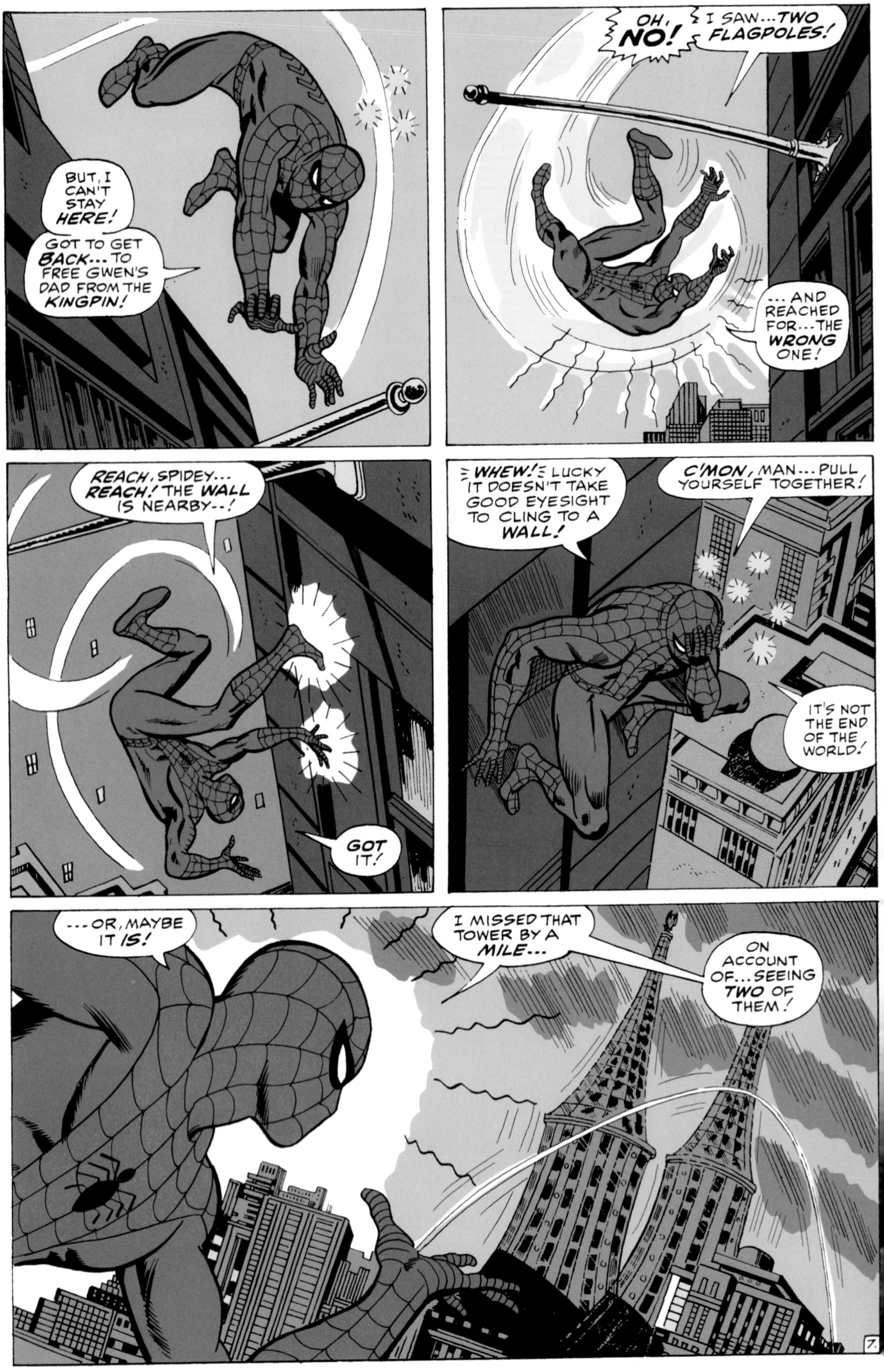
BUT, I CAN'T STAY HERE!
GOT TO GET BACK... TO FREE GWEN'S DAD FROM THE KINGPIN!
OH, NO!
I SAW...TWO FLAGPOLES!
...AND REACHED FOR...THE WRONG ONE!
REACH, SPIDEY... REACH! THE WALL IS NEARBY--!
GOT IT!
WHEW! LUCKY IT DOESN'T TAKE GOOD EYESIGHT TO CLING TO A WALL!
C'MON, MAN...PULL YOURSELF TOGETHER!
IT'S NOT THE END OF THE WORLD!
...OR, MAYBE IT IS!
I MISSED THAT TOWER BY A MILE...
ON ACCOUNT OF...SEEING TWO OF THEM!
7.

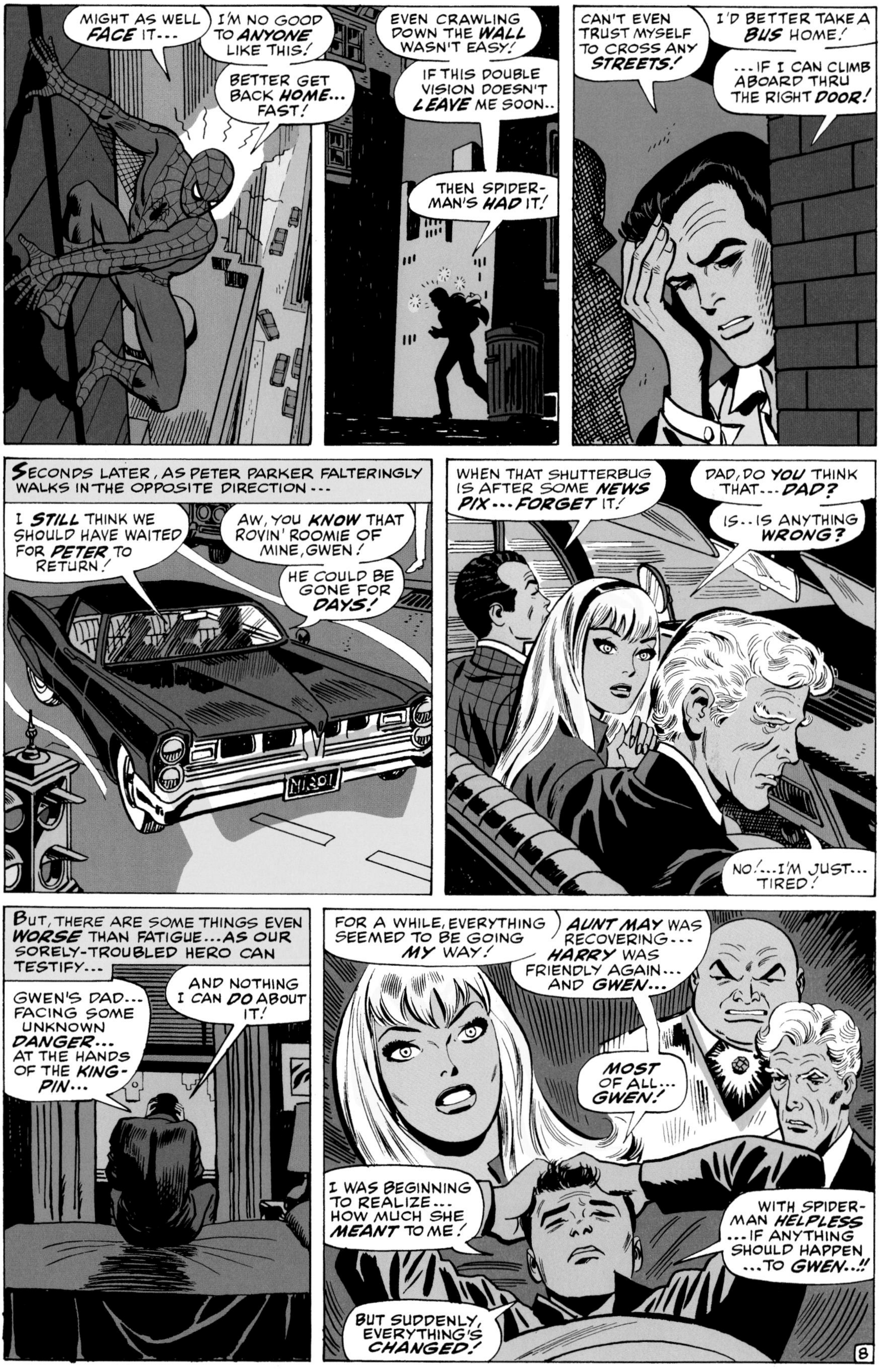
MIGHT AS WELL FACE IT---
I'M NO GOOD TO ANYONE LIKE THIS!
BETTER GET BACK HOME... FAST!
EVEN CRAWLING DOWN THE WALL WASN'T EASY!
IF THIS DOUBLE VISION DOESN'T LEAVE ME SOON..
THEN SPIDER-MAN'S HAD IT!
CAN'T EVEN TRUST MYSELF TO CROSS ANY STREETS!
I'D BETTER TAKE A BUS HOME!
...IF I CAN CLIMB ABOARD THRU THE RIGHT DOOR!
SECONDS LATER, AS PETER PARKER FALTERINGLY WALKS IN THE OPPOSITE DIRECTION---
I STILL THINK WE SHOULD HAVE WAITED FOR PETER TO RETURN!
AW, YOU KNOW THAT ROVIN' ROOMIE OF MINE, GWEN!
HE COULD BE GONE FOR DAYS!
WHEN THAT SHUTTERBUG IS AFTER SOME NEWS PIX---FORGET IT!
DAD, DO YOU THINK THAT---DAD?
IS--IS ANYTHING WRONG?
NO!...I'M JUST... TIRED!
BUT, THERE ARE SOME THINGS EVEN WORSE THAN FATIGUE...AS OUR SORELY-TROUBLED HERO CAN TESTIFY---
GWEN'S DAD... FACING SOME UNKNOWN DANGER... AT THE HANDS OF THE KING-PIN...
AND NOTHING I CAN DO ABOUT IT!
FOR A WHILE, EVERYTHING SEEMED TO BE GOING MY WAY!
AUNT MAY WAS RECOVERING--- HARRY WAS FRIENDLY AGAIN--- AND GWEN---
MOST OF ALL... GWEN!
I WAS BEGINNING TO REALIZE--- HOW MUCH SHE MEANT TO ME!
WITH SPIDER-MAN HELPLESS ...IF ANYTHING SHOULD HAPPEN ...TO GWEN..!!
BUT SUDDENLY, EVERYTHING'S CHANGED!
8

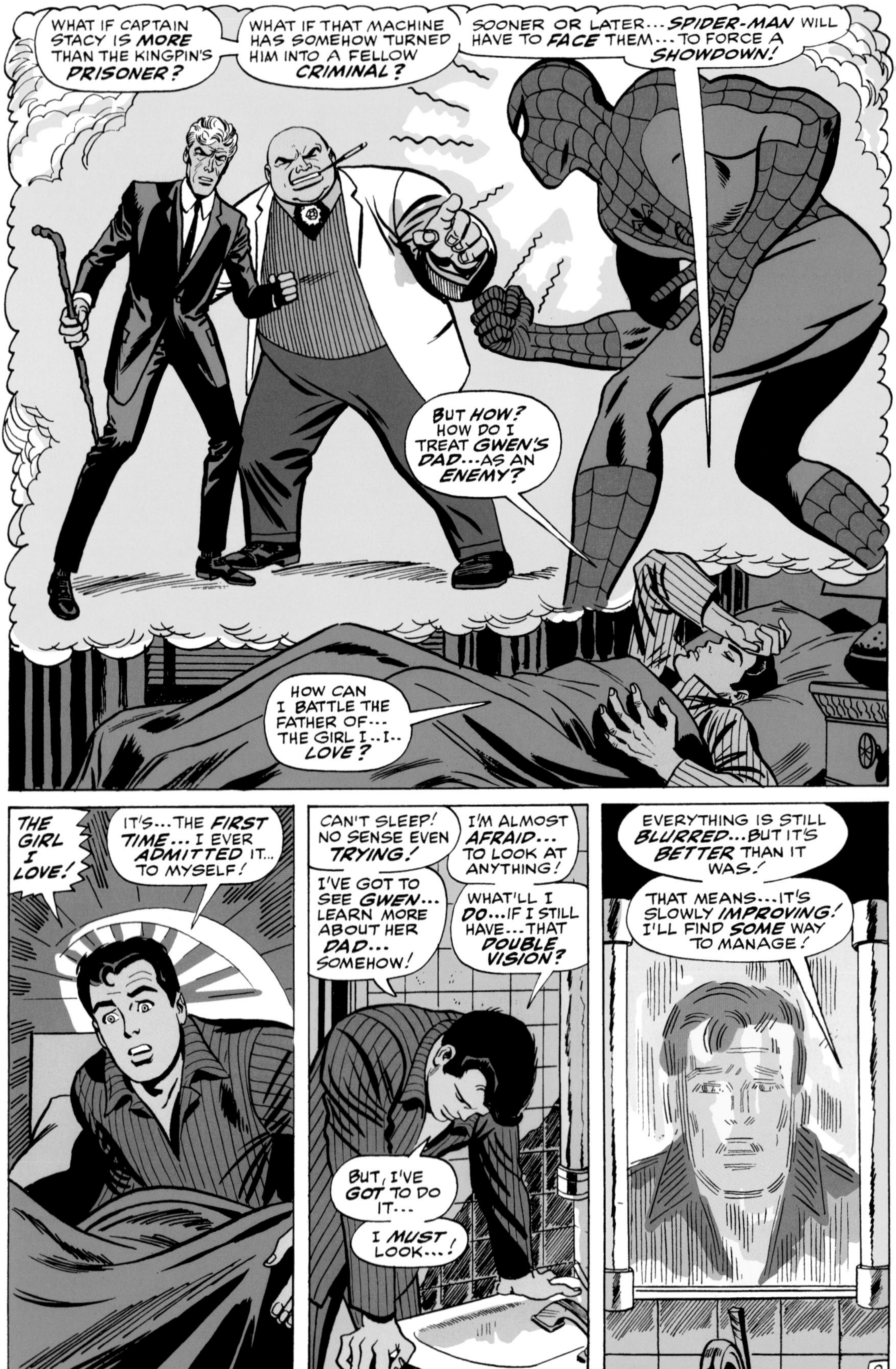
WHAT IF CAPTAIN STACY IS MORE THAN THE KINGPIN'S PRISONER?
WHAT IF THAT MACHINE HAS SOMEHOW TURNED HIM INTO A FELLOW CRIMINAL?
SOONER OR LATER... SPIDER-MAN WILL HAVE TO FACE THEM... TO FORCE A SHOWDOWN!
BUT HOW? HOW DO I TREAT GWEN'S DAD...AS AN ENEMY?
HOW CAN I BATTLE THE FATHER OF--- THE GIRL I..I.. LOVE?
THE GIRL I LOVE!
IT'S... THE FIRST TIME... I EVER ADMITTED IT... TO MYSELF!
CAN'T SLEEP! NO SENSE EVEN TRYING!
I'M ALMOST AFRAID... TO LOOK AT ANYTHING!
I'VE GOT TO SEE GWEN... LEARN MORE ABOUT HER DAD... SOMEHOW!
WHAT'LL I DO...IF I STILL HAVE... THAT DOUBLE VISION?
BUT, I'VE GOT TO DO IT...
I MUST LOOK...!
EVERYTHING IS STILL BLURRED...BUT IT'S BETTER THAN IT WAS!
THAT MEANS... IT'S SLOWLY IMPROVING! I'LL FIND SOME WAY TO MANAGE!
9

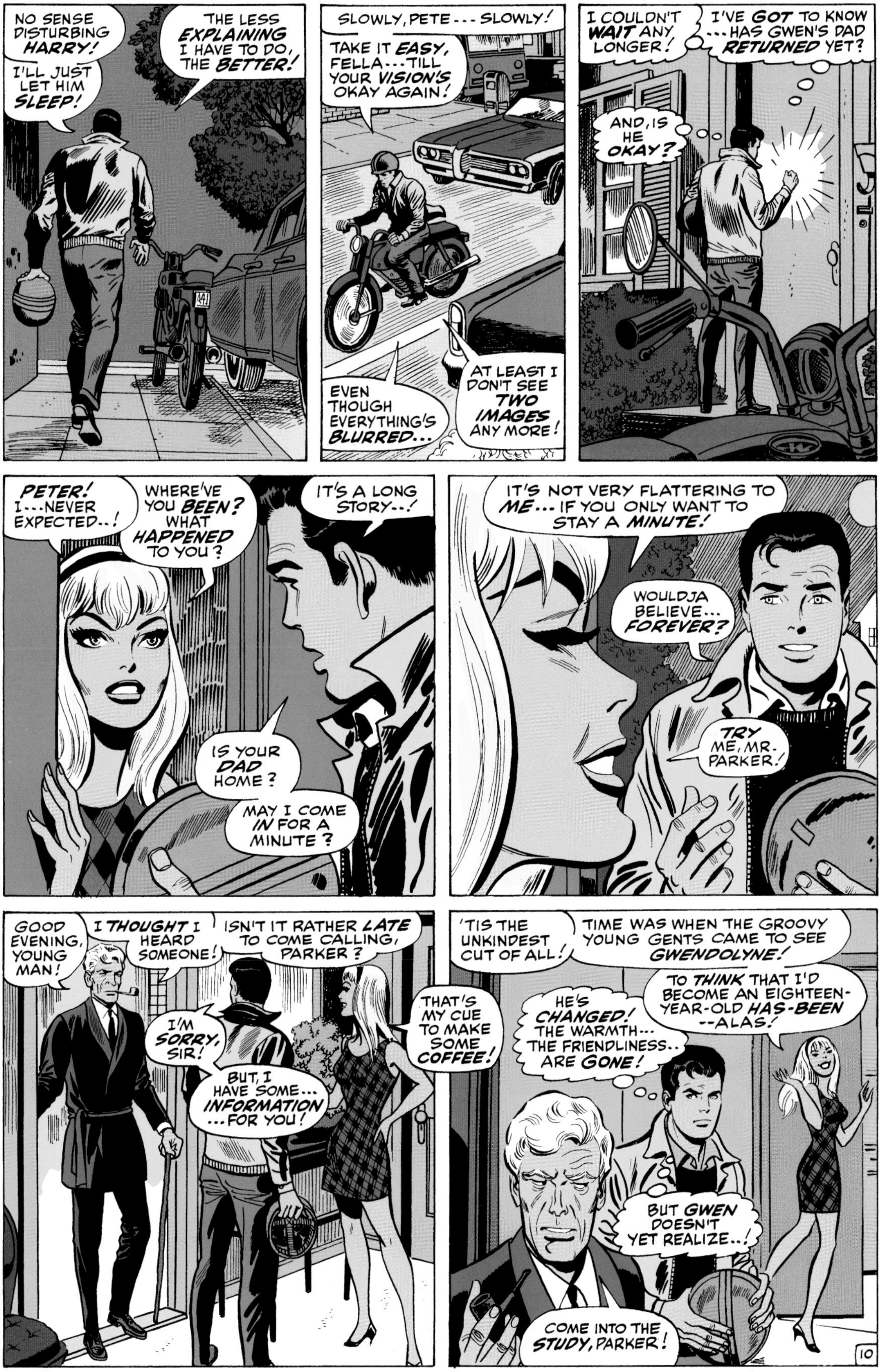
NO SENSE DISTURBING HARRY!
I'LL JUST LET HIM SLEEP!
THE LESS EXPLAINING I HAVE TO DO, THE BETTER!
SLOWLY, PETE --- SLOWLY!
TAKE IT EASY, FELLA--- TILL YOUR VISION'S OKAY AGAIN!
EVEN THOUGH EVERYTHING'S BLURRED...
AT LEAST I DON'T SEE TWO IMAGES ANY MORE!
I COULDN'T WAIT ANY LONGER!
I'VE GOT TO KNOW ---HAS GWEN'S DAD RETURNED YET?
AND, IS HE OKAY?
PETER! I---NEVER EXPECTED--!
WHERE'VE YOU BEEN? WHAT HAPPENED TO YOU?
IT'S A LONG STORY--!
IS YOUR DAD HOME?
MAY I COME IN FOR A MINUTE?
IT'S NOT VERY FLATTERING TO ME... IF YOU ONLY WANT TO STAY A MINUTE!
WOULDJA BELIEVE... FOREVER?
TRY ME, MR. PARKER!
GOOD EVENING, YOUNG MAN!
I THOUGHT I HEARD SOMEONE!
ISN'T IT RATHER LATE TO COME CALLING, PARKER?
I'M SORRY, SIR!
BUT, I HAVE SOME... INFORMATION ...FOR YOU!
THAT'S MY CUE TO MAKE SOME COFFEE!
'TIS THE UNKINDEST CUT OF ALL!
TIME WAS WHEN THE GROOVY YOUNG GENTS CAME TO SEE GWENDOLYNE!
TO THINK THAT I'D BECOME AN EIGHTEEN-YEAR-OLD HAS-BEEN --ALAS!
HE'S CHANGED! THE WARMTH--- THE FRIENDLINESS.. ARE GONE!
BUT GWEN DOESN'T YET REALIZE..!
COME INTO THE STUDY, PARKER!
10

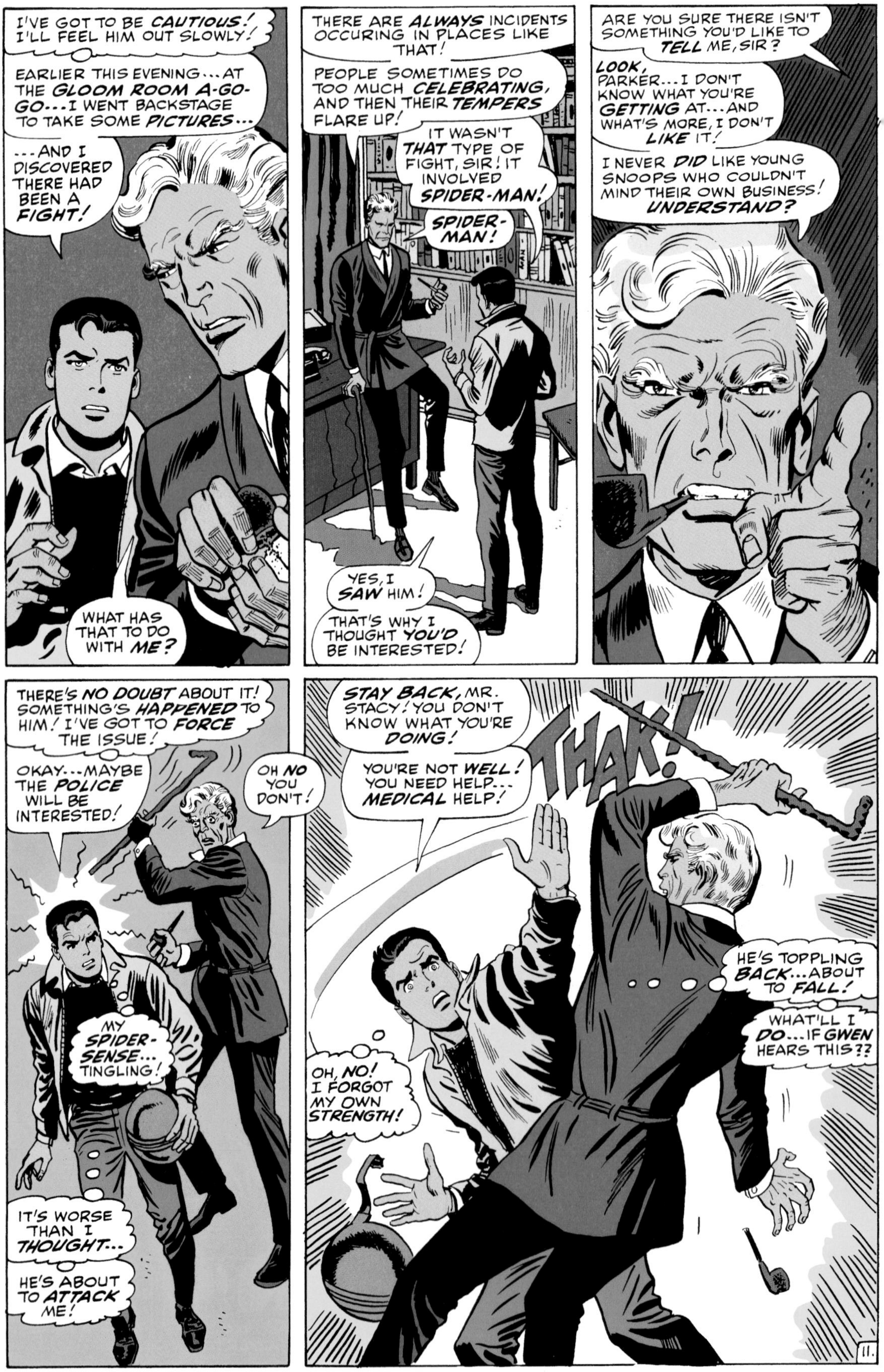

I'VE GOT TO BE CAUTIOUS! I'LL FEEL HIM OUT SLOWLY!
EARLIER THIS EVENING... AT THE GLOOM ROOM A-GO-GO... I WENT BACKSTAGE TO TAKE SOME PICTURES...
...AND I DISCOVERED THERE HAD BEEN A FIGHT!
WHAT HAS THAT TO DO WITH ME?
THERE ARE ALWAYS INCIDENTS OCCURING IN PLACES LIKE THAT!
PEOPLE SOMETIMES DO TOO MUCH CELEBRATING, AND THEN THEIR TEMPERS FLARE UP!
IT WASN'T THAT TYPE OF FIGHT, SIR! IT INVOLVED SPIDER-MAN!
SPIDER-MAN!
YES, I SAW HIM!
THAT'S WHY I THOUGHT YOU'D BE INTERESTED!
ARE YOU SURE THERE ISN'T SOMETHING YOU'D LIKE TO TELL ME, SIR?
LOOK, PARKER... I DON'T KNOW WHAT YOU'RE GETTING AT... AND WHAT'S MORE, I DON'T LIKE IT!
I NEVER DID LIKE YOUNG SNOOPS WHO COULDN'T MIND THEIR OWN BUSINESS! UNDERSTAND?
THERE'S NO DOUBT ABOUT IT! SOMETHING'S HAPPENED TO HIM! I'VE GOT TO FORCE THE ISSUE!
OKAY... MAYBE THE POLICE WILL BE INTERESTED!
OH NO YOU DON'T!
MY SPIDER-SENSE... TINGLING!
IT'S WORSE THAN I THOUGHT...
HE'S ABOUT TO ATTACK ME!
STAY BACK, MR. STACY! YOU DON'T KNOW WHAT YOU'RE DOING!
YOU'RE NOT WELL! YOU NEED HELP... MEDICAL HELP!
THAK!
HE'S TOPPLING BACK... ABOUT TO FALL!
WHAT'LL I DO... IF GWEN HEARS THIS??
OH, NO! I FORGOT MY OWN STRENGTH!
11.

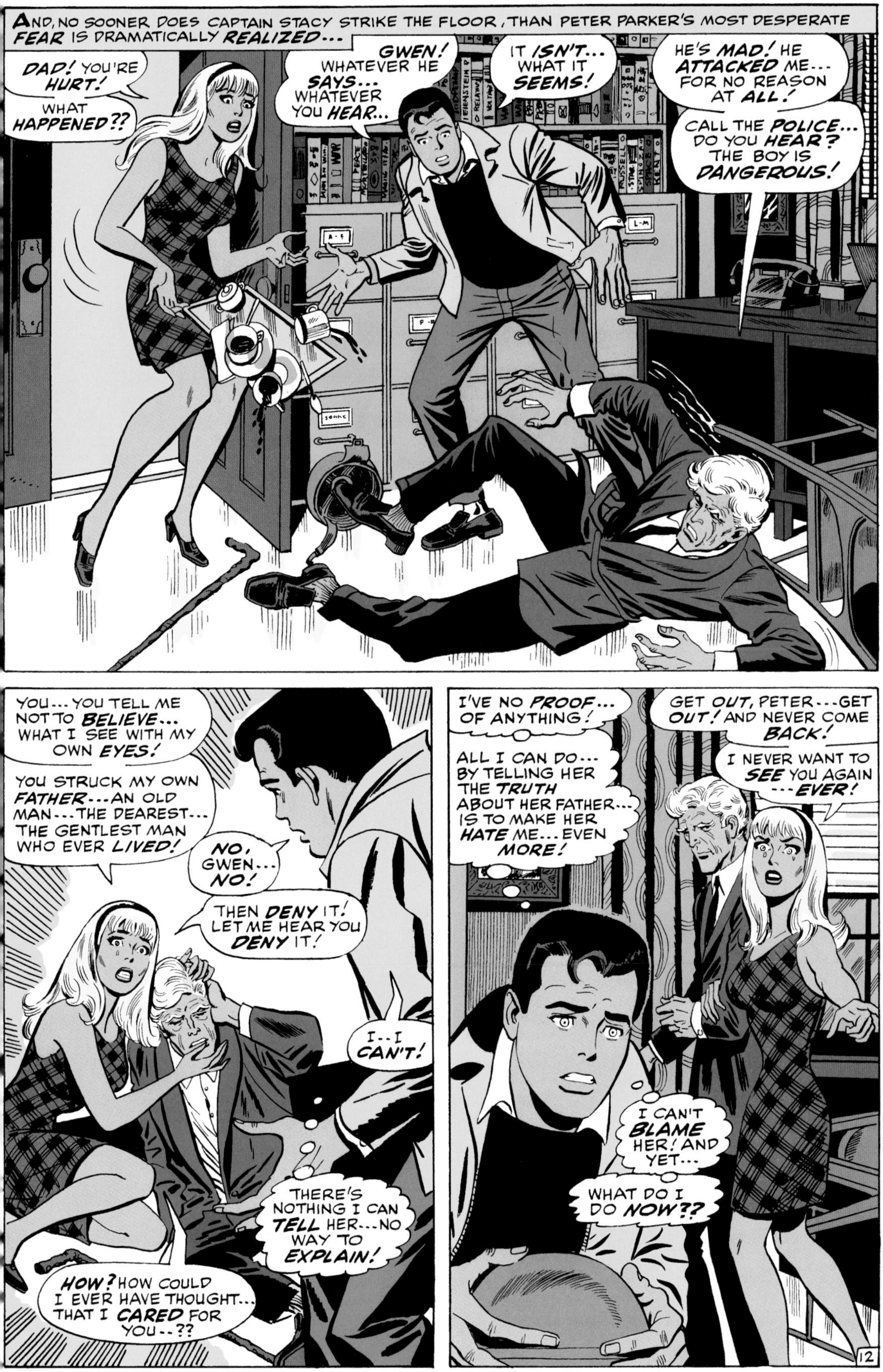
AND, NO SOONER DOES CAPTAIN STACY STRIKE THE FLOOR, THAN PETER PARKER'S MOST DESPERATE FEAR IS DRAMATICALLY REALIZED...
DAD! YOU'RE HURT! WHAT HAPPENED??
GWEN! WHATEVER HE SAYS... WHATEVER YOU HEAR...
IT ISN'T... WHAT IT SEEMS!
HE'S MAD! HE ATTACKED ME... FOR NO REASON AT ALL!
CALL THE POLICE... DO YOU HEAR? THE BOY IS DANGEROUS!
YOU... YOU TELL ME NOT TO BELIEVE... WHAT I SEE WITH MY OWN EYES!
YOU STRUCK MY OWN FATHER... AN OLD MAN... THE DEAREST... THE GENTLEST MAN WHO EVER LIVED!
NO, GWEN... NO!
THEN DENY IT! LET ME HEAR YOU DENY IT!
I.. I CAN'T!
THERE'S NOTHING I CAN TELL HER... NO WAY TO EXPLAIN!
HOW? HOW COULD I EVER HAVE THOUGHT... THAT I CARED FOR YOU..??
I'VE NO PROOF... OF ANYTHING!
ALL I CAN DO... BY TELLING HER THE TRUTH ABOUT HER FATHER... IS TO MAKE HER HATE ME... EVEN MORE!
GET OUT, PETER... GET OUT! AND NEVER COME BACK!
I NEVER WANT TO SEE YOU AGAIN ...EVER!
I CAN'T BLAME HER! AND YET...
WHAT DO I DO NOW??
12

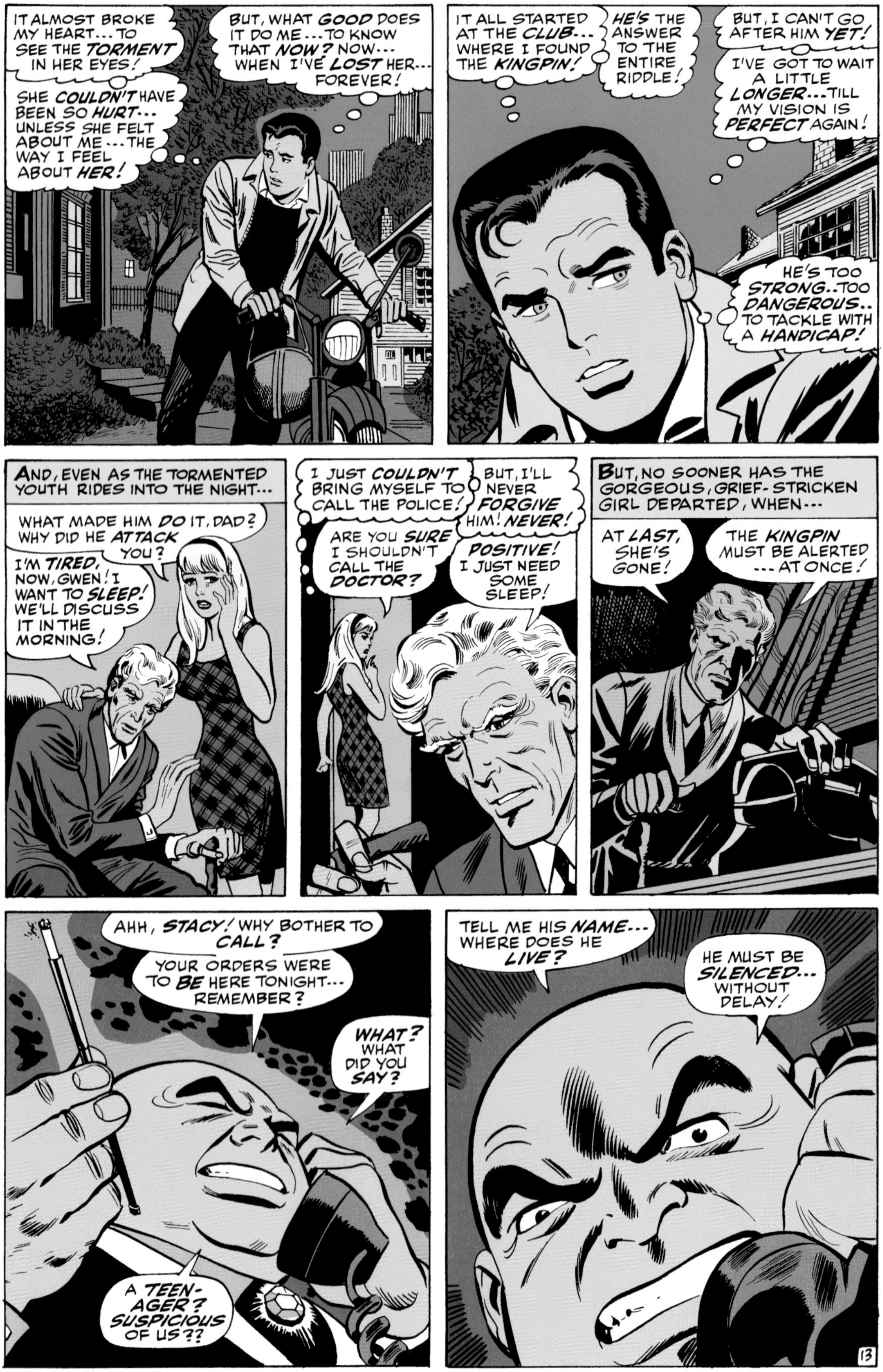

IT ALMOST BROKE MY HEART... TO SEE THE TORMENT IN HER EYES!
SHE COULDN'T HAVE BEEN SO HURT... UNLESS SHE FELT ABOUT ME... THE WAY I FEEL ABOUT HER!
BUT, WHAT GOOD DOES IT DO ME... TO KNOW THAT NOW? NOW... WHEN I'VE LOST HER... FOREVER!
IT ALL STARTED AT THE CLUB... WHERE I FOUND THE KINGPIN!
HE'S THE ANSWER TO THE ENTIRE RIDDLE!
BUT, I CAN'T GO AFTER HIM YET!
I'VE GOT TO WAIT A LITTLE LONGER... TILL MY VISION IS PERFECT AGAIN!
HE'S TOO STRONG.. TOO DANGEROUS.. TO TACKLE WITH A HANDICAP!
AND, EVEN AS THE TORMENTED YOUTH RIDES INTO THE NIGHT...
WHAT MADE HIM DO IT, DAD? WHY DID HE ATTACK YOU?
I'M TIRED, NOW, GWEN! I WANT TO SLEEP! WE'LL DISCUSS IT IN THE MORNING!
I JUST COULDN'T BRING MYSELF TO CALL THE POLICE!
BUT, I'LL NEVER FORGIVE HIM! NEVER!
ARE YOU SURE I SHOULDN'T CALL THE DOCTOR?
POSITIVE! I JUST NEED SOME SLEEP!
BUT, NO SOONER HAS THE GORGEOUS, GRIEF-STRICKEN GIRL DEPARTED, WHEN...
AT LAST, SHE'S GONE!
THE KINGPIN MUST BE ALERTED ...AT ONCE!
AHH, STACY! WHY BOTHER TO CALL?
YOUR ORDERS WERE TO BE HERE TONIGHT... REMEMBER?
WHAT? WHAT DID YOU SAY?
A TEEN-AGER? SUSPICIOUS OF US??
TELL ME HIS NAME... WHERE DOES HE LIVE?
HE MUST BE SILENCED... WITHOUT DELAY!
13

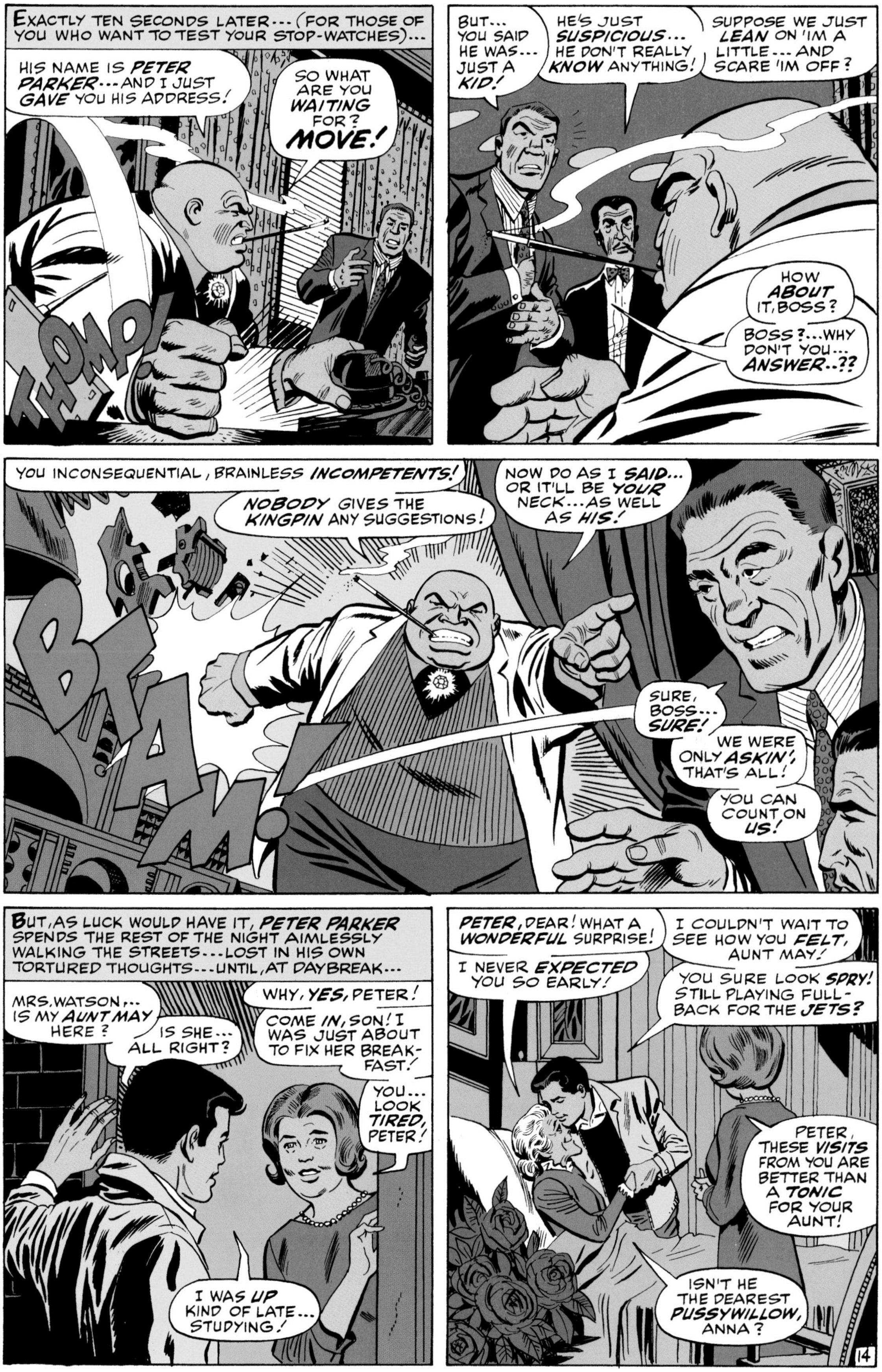
EXACTLY TEN SECONDS LATER... (FOR THOSE OF YOU WHO WANT TO TEST YOUR STOP-WATCHES)...
HIS NAME IS PETER PARKER... AND I JUST GAVE YOU HIS ADDRESS!
SO WHAT ARE YOU WAITING FOR? MOVE!
THOMP!
BUT... YOU SAID HE WAS... JUST A KID!
HE'S JUST SUSPICIOUS... HE DON'T REALLY KNOW ANYTHING!
SUPPOSE WE JUST LEAN ON 'IM A LITTLE... AND SCARE 'IM OFF?
HOW ABOUT IT, BOSS?
BOSS?...WHY DON'T YOU... ANSWER..??
YOU INCONSEQUENTIAL, BRAINLESS INCOMPETENTS!
NOBODY GIVES THE KINGPIN ANY SUGGESTIONS!
NOW DO AS I SAID... OR IT'LL BE YOUR NECK... AS WELL AS HIS!
BLAM!
SURE, BOSS... SURE!
WE WERE ONLY ASKIN', THAT'S ALL!
YOU CAN COUNT ON US!
BUT, AS LUCK WOULD HAVE IT, PETER PARKER SPENDS THE REST OF THE NIGHT AIMLESSLY WALKING THE STREETS... LOST IN HIS OWN TORTURED THOUGHTS... UNTIL, AT DAYBREAK...
MRS. WATSON,... IS MY AUNT MAY HERE?
IS SHE... ALL RIGHT?
WHY, YES, PETER!
COME IN, SON! I WAS JUST ABOUT TO FIX HER BREAK-FAST!
YOU... LOOK TIRED, PETER!
I WAS UP KIND OF LATE... STUDYING!
PETER, DEAR! WHAT A WONDERFUL SURPRISE!
I NEVER EXPECTED YOU SO EARLY!
I COULDN'T WAIT TO SEE HOW YOU FELT, AUNT MAY!
YOU SURE LOOK SPRY! STILL PLAYING FULL-BACK FOR THE JETS?
PETER, THESE VISITS FROM YOU ARE BETTER THAN A TONIC FOR YOUR AUNT!
ISN'T HE THE DEAREST PUSSYWILLOW, ANNA?
14

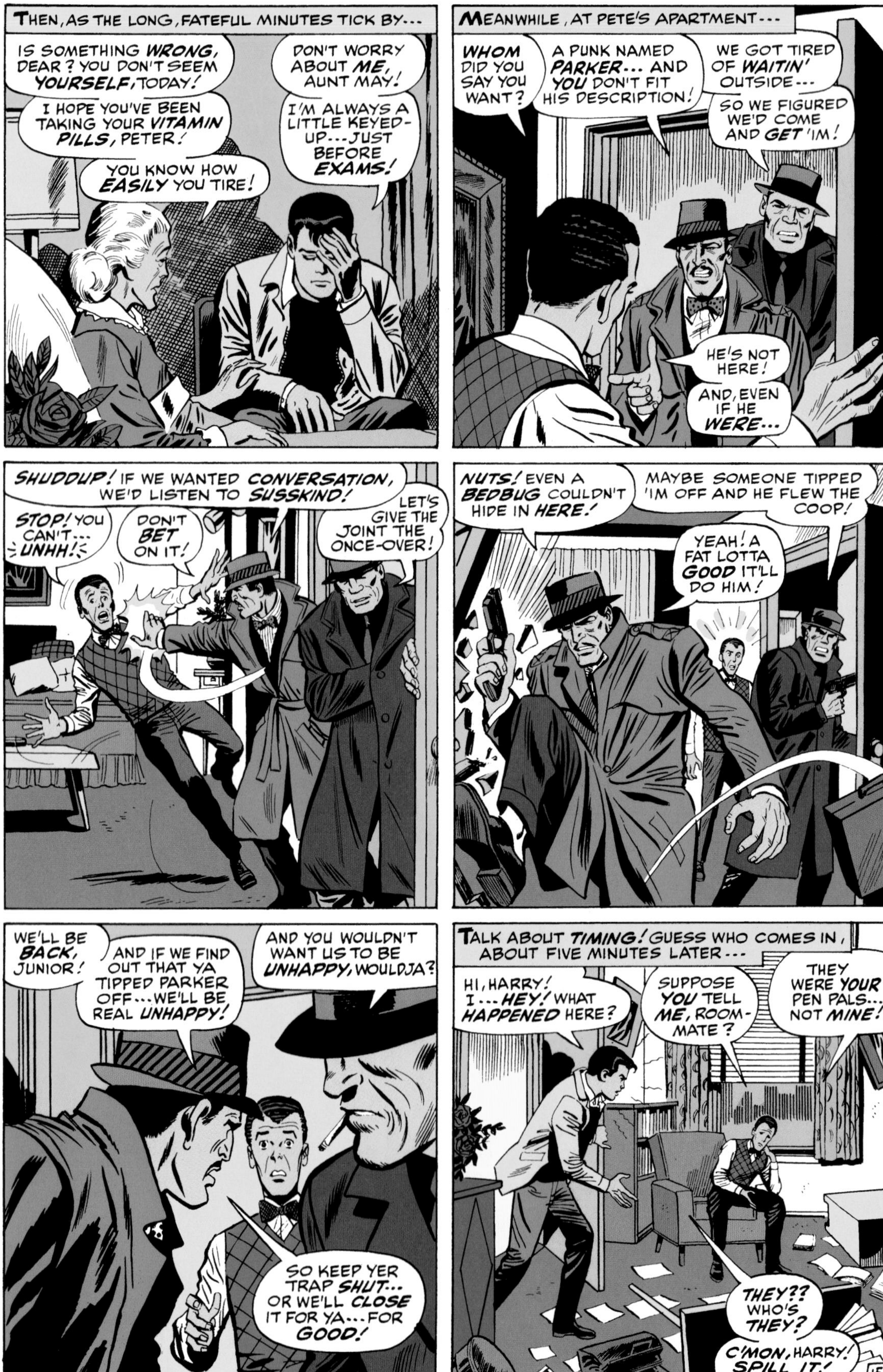

THEN, AS THE LONG, FATEFUL MINUTES TICK BY...
IS SOMETHING WRONG, DEAR? YOU DON'T SEEM YOURSELF, TODAY!
I HOPE YOU'VE BEEN TAKING YOUR VITAMIN PILLS, PETER!
YOU KNOW HOW EASILY YOU TIRE!
DON'T WORRY ABOUT ME, AUNT MAY!
I'M ALWAYS A LITTLE KEYED-UP...JUST BEFORE EXAMS!
MEANWHILE, AT PETE'S APARTMENT...
WHOM DID YOU SAY YOU WANT?
A PUNK NAMED PARKER... AND YOU DON'T FIT HIS DESCRIPTION!
WE GOT TIRED OF WAITIN' OUTSIDE...
SO WE FIGURED WE'D COME AND GET 'IM!
HE'S NOT HERE!
AND, EVEN IF HE WERE...
SHUDDUP! IF WE WANTED CONVERSATION, WE'D LISTEN TO SUSSKIND!
STOP! YOU CAN'T... UNHH!
DON'T BET ON IT!
LET'S GIVE THE JOINT THE ONCE-OVER!
NUTS! EVEN A BEDBUG COULDN'T HIDE IN HERE!
MAYBE SOMEONE TIPPED 'IM OFF AND HE FLEW THE COOP!
YEAH! A FAT LOTTA GOOD IT'LL DO HIM!
WE'LL BE BACK, JUNIOR!
AND IF WE FIND OUT THAT YA TIPPED PARKER OFF...WE'LL BE REAL UNHAPPY!
AND YOU WOULDN'T WANT US TO BE UNHAPPY, WOULDJA?
SO KEEP YER TRAP SHUT... OR WE'LL CLOSE IT FOR YA...FOR GOOD!
TALK ABOUT TIMING! GUESS WHO COMES IN, ABOUT FIVE MINUTES LATER...
HI, HARRY! I...HEY! WHAT HAPPENED HERE?
SUPPOSE YOU TELL ME, ROOM-MATE?
THEY WERE YOUR PEN PALS... NOT MINE!
THEY?? WHO'S THEY?
C'MON, HARRY! SPILL IT!
15

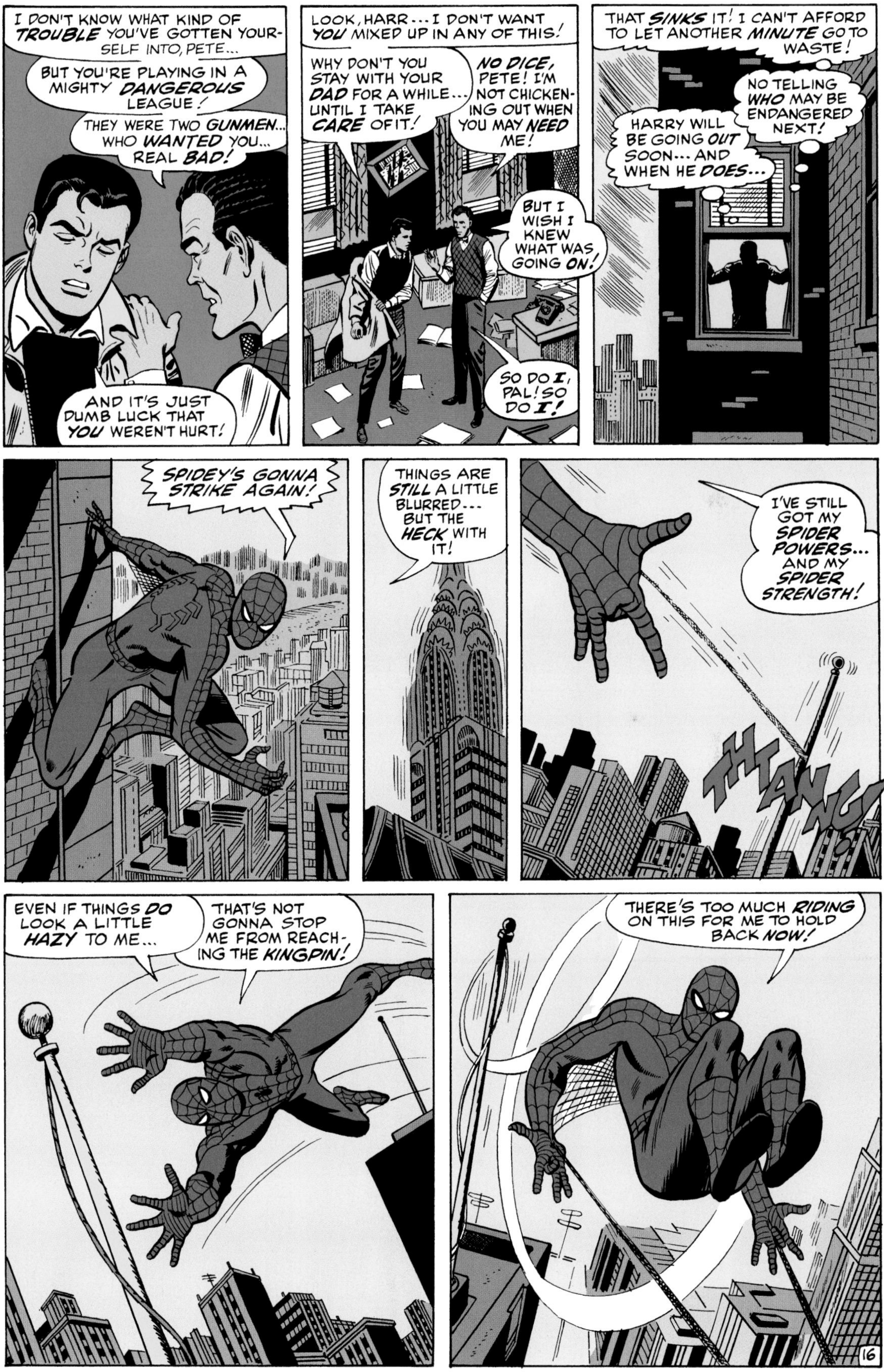
I DON'T KNOW WHAT KIND OF TROUBLE YOU'VE GOTTEN YOURSELF INTO, PETE...
BUT YOU'RE PLAYING IN A MIGHTY DANGEROUS LEAGUE!
THEY WERE TWO GUNMEN... WHO WANTED YOU... REAL BAD!
AND IT'S JUST DUMB LUCK THAT YOU WEREN'T HURT!
LOOK, HARR... I DON'T WANT YOU MIXED UP IN ANY OF THIS!
WHY DON'T YOU STAY WITH YOUR DAD FOR A WHILE... UNTIL I TAKE CARE OF IT!
NO DICE, PETE! I'M NOT CHICKENING OUT WHEN YOU MAY NEED ME!
BUT I WISH I KNEW WHAT WAS GOING ON!
SO DO I, PAL! SO DO I!
THAT SINKS IT! I CAN'T AFFORD TO LET ANOTHER MINUTE GO TO WASTE!
HARRY WILL BE GOING OUT SOON... AND WHEN HE DOES...
NO TELLING WHO MAY BE ENDANGERED NEXT!
SPIDEY'S GONNA STRIKE AGAIN!
THINGS ARE STILL A LITTLE BLURRED... BUT THE HECK WITH IT!
I'VE STILL GOT MY SPIDER POWERS... AND MY SPIDER STRENGTH!
THTANNG!
EVEN IF THINGS DO LOOK A LITTLE HAZY TO ME...
THAT'S NOT GONNA STOP ME FROM REACHING THE KINGPIN!
THERE'S TOO MUCH RIDING ON THIS FOR ME TO HOLD BACK NOW!
16

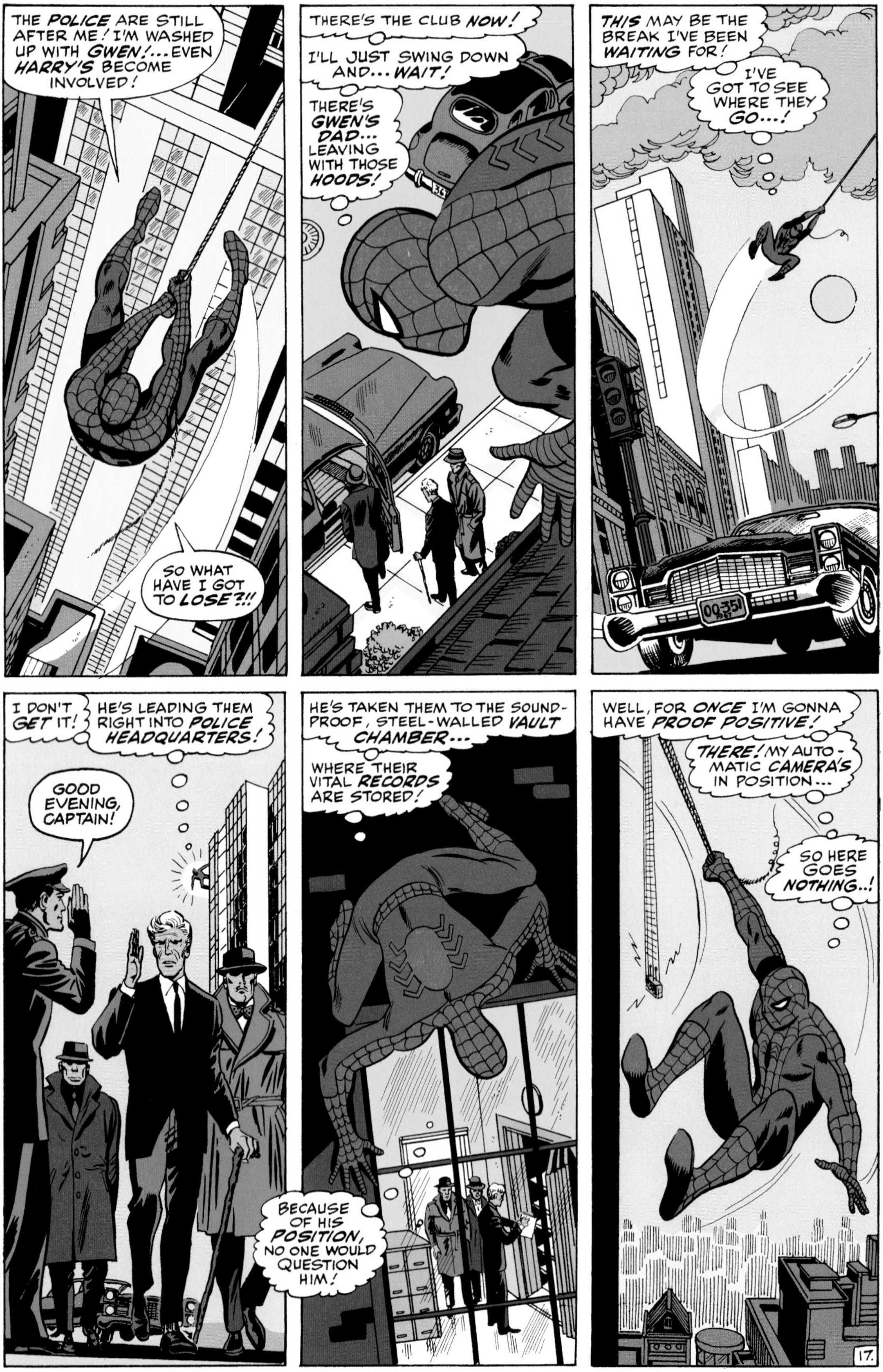
THE POLICE ARE STILL AFTER ME! I'M WASHED UP WITH GWEN!... EVEN HARRY'S BECOME INVOLVED!
SO WHAT HAVE I GOT TO LOSE?!!
THERE'S THE CLUB NOW!
I'LL JUST SWING DOWN AND... WAIT!
THERE'S GWEN'S DAD... LEAVING WITH THOSE HOODS!
THIS MAY BE THE BREAK I'VE BEEN WAITING FOR!
I'VE GOT TO SEE WHERE THEY GO...!
OO-351
I DON'T GET IT!
HE'S LEADING THEM RIGHT INTO POLICE HEADQUARTERS!
GOOD EVENING, CAPTAIN!
HE'S TAKEN THEM TO THE SOUND-PROOF, STEEL-WALLED VAULT CHAMBER...
WHERE THEIR VITAL RECORDS ARE STORED!
BECAUSE OF HIS POSITION, NO ONE WOULD QUESTION HIM!
WELL, FOR ONCE I'M GONNA HAVE PROOF POSITIVE!
THERE! MY AUTO-MATIC CAMERA'S IN POSITION...
SO HERE GOES NOTHING..!
17.

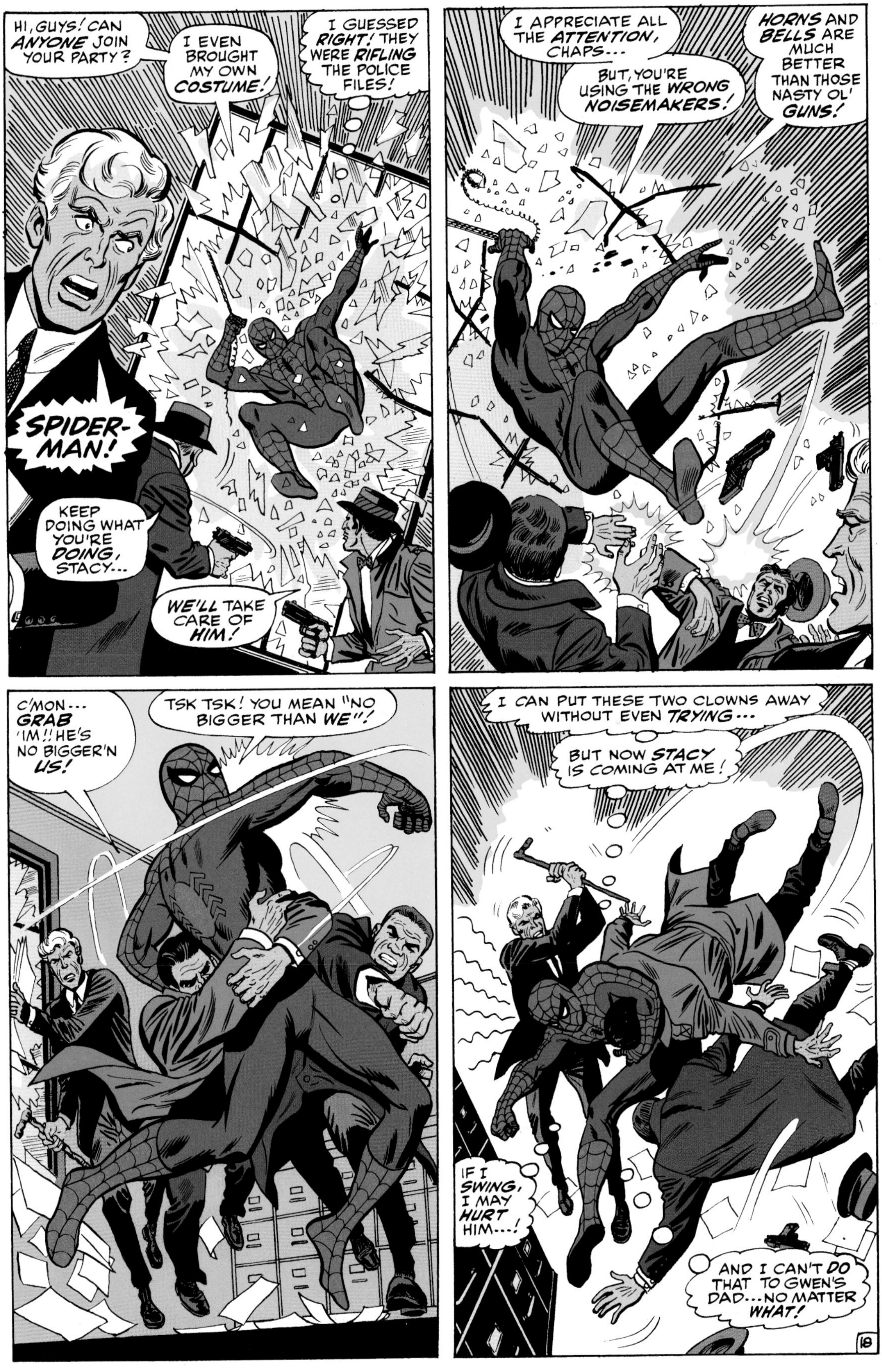
HI, GUYS! CAN ANYONE JOIN YOUR PARTY?
I EVEN BROUGHT MY OWN COSTUME!
I GUESSED RIGHT! THEY WERE RIFLING THE POLICE FILES!
SPIDER-MAN!
KEEP DOING WHAT YOU'RE DOING, STACY...
WE'LL TAKE CARE OF HIM!
I APPRECIATE ALL THE ATTENTION, CHAPS...
BUT, YOU'RE USING THE WRONG NOISEMAKERS!
HORNS AND BELLS ARE MUCH BETTER THAN THOSE NASTY OL' GUNS!
C'MON... GRAB 'IM!! HE'S NO BIGGER'N US!
TSK TSK! YOU MEAN "NO BIGGER THAN WE"!
I CAN PUT THESE TWO CLOWNS AWAY WITHOUT EVEN TRYING...
BUT NOW STACY IS COMING AT ME!
IF I SWING, I MAY HURT HIM...!
AND I CAN'T DO THAT TO GWEN'S DAD... NO MATTER WHAT!
18

THEN, AS THE DOUBT-RIDDEN WEB-SLINGER *HESITATES*...

THIS WILL GET HIM OFF OUR BACKS!

FTOK!

UNHHH!

THINK FAST, STACY! WHAT DO WE DO *NOW*?

DON'T *PANIC*, YOU FOOL! WE CAN GET THESE RECORDS SOME *OTHER* TIME...

BUT FIRST, WE NEED AN *ALIBI* FOR WHAT JUST HAPPENED!

WE'LL SAY WE SAW *SPIDER-MAN* BREAKING INTO THE FILE ROOM---AND TRIED TO *STOP* HIM!

NO ONE WILL HAVE REASON TO *DOUBT* US!

THEY *WILL*... IF MY *CAMERA* WAS WORKING!

RECORD. DEPT.

OH, MY *HEAD*!

IF NOT FOR MY SUPER-STRENGTH, I'D HAVE BEEN OUT FOR THE COUNT!

SECONDS LATER---

LUCKY I GOT *OUT* OF THERE IN TIME!

CAN'T WAIT TO SEE IF THE *PICTURES* ARE CLEAR!

THEN, AFTER A SPEEDY SESSION IN HIS APARTMENT-LAB DARKROOM---

I *DID* IT! THESE PIX SHOW STACY GOING THRU THE FILES *BEFORE* I BROKE IN...

THEY COMPLETELY *RIP* HIS ALIBI TO SHREDS!

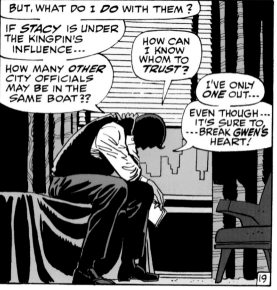

BUT, WHAT DO *I* DO WITH THEM?

IF *STACY* IS UNDER THE KINGPIN'S INFLUENCE...

HOW MANY *OTHER* CITY OFFICIALS MAY BE IN THE SAME BOAT??

HOW CAN I KNOW WHOM TO *TRUST*?

I'VE ONLY *ONE* OUT...

EVEN THOUGH--- IT'S SURE TO- ---BREAK *GWEN'S* HEART!

19

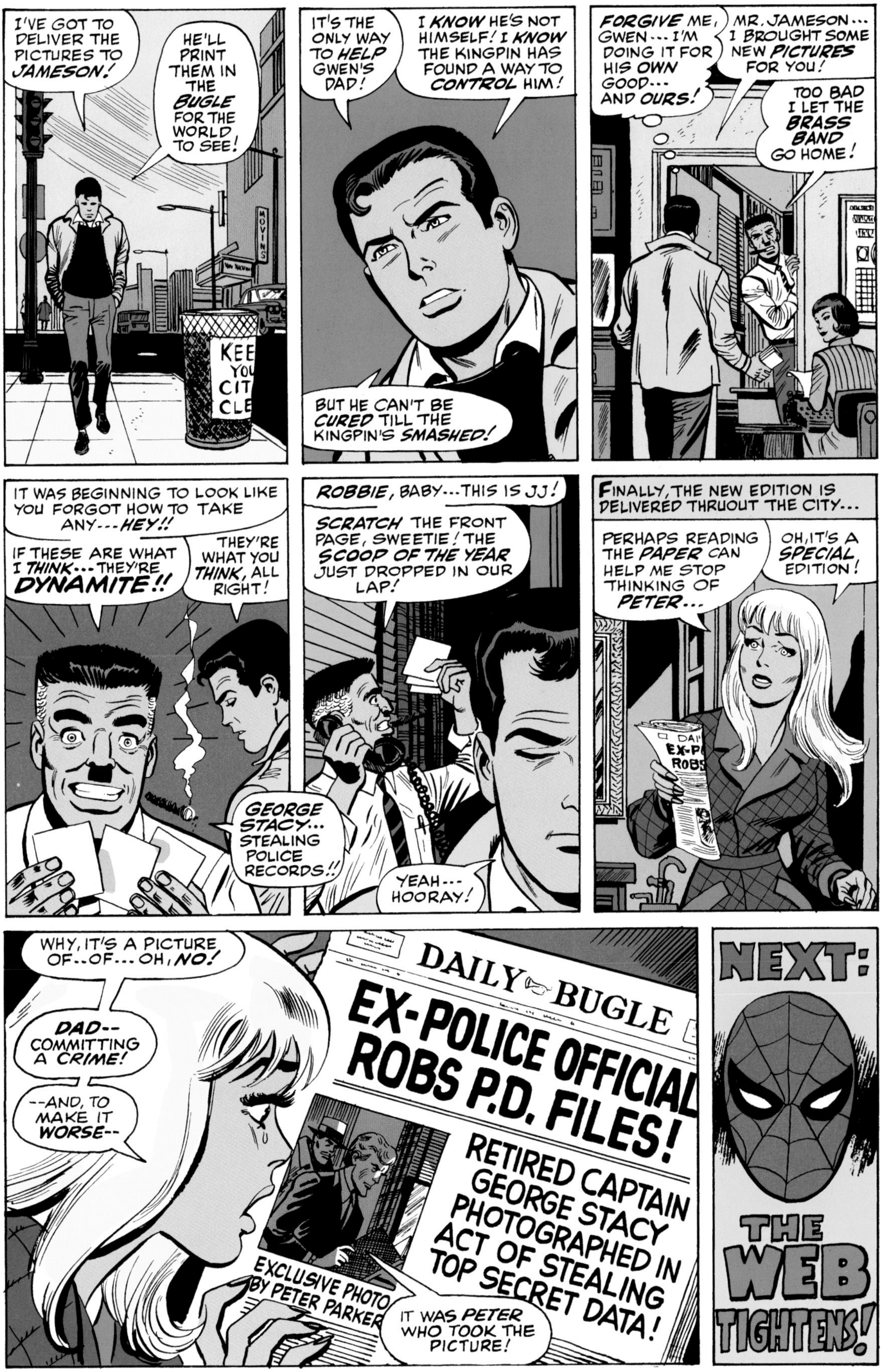
I'VE GOT TO DELIVER THE PICTURES TO JAMESON!
HE'LL PRINT THEM IN THE BUGLE FOR THE WORLD TO SEE!
KEE YOU CIT CLE
IT'S THE ONLY WAY TO HELP GWEN'S DAD!
I KNOW HE'S NOT HIMSELF! I KNOW THE KINGPIN HAS FOUND A WAY TO CONTROL HIM!
BUT HE CAN'T BE CURED TILL THE KINGPIN'S SMASHED!
FORGIVE ME, GWEN--- I'M DOING IT FOR HIS OWN GOOD--- AND OURS!
MR. JAMESON... I BROUGHT SOME NEW PICTURES FOR YOU!
TOO BAD I LET THE BRASS BAND GO HOME!
IT WAS BEGINNING TO LOOK LIKE YOU FORGOT HOW TO TAKE ANY---HEY!!
IF THESE ARE WHAT I THINK--- THEY'RE DYNAMITE!!
THEY'RE WHAT YOU THINK, ALL RIGHT!
GEORGE STACY... STEALING POLICE RECORDS!!
ROBBIE, BABY---THIS IS JJ!
SCRATCH THE FRONT PAGE, SWEETIE! THE SCOOP OF THE YEAR JUST DROPPED IN OUR LAP!
YEAH--- HOORAY!
FINALLY, THE NEW EDITION IS DELIVERED THRUOUT THE CITY...
PERHAPS READING THE PAPER CAN HELP ME STOP THINKING OF PETER...
OH, IT'S A SPECIAL EDITION!
WHY, IT'S A PICTURE OF--OF--- OH, NO!
DAD-- COMMITTING A CRIME!
--AND, TO MAKE IT WORSE--
DAILY BUGLE
EX-POLICE OFFICIAL ROBS P.D. FILES!
RETIRED CAPTAIN GEORGE STACY PHOTOGRAPHED IN ACT OF STEALING TOP SECRET DATA!
EXCLUSIVE PHOTO BY PETER PARKER
IT WAS PETER WHO TOOK THE PICTURE!
NEXT:
THE WEB TIGHTENS!

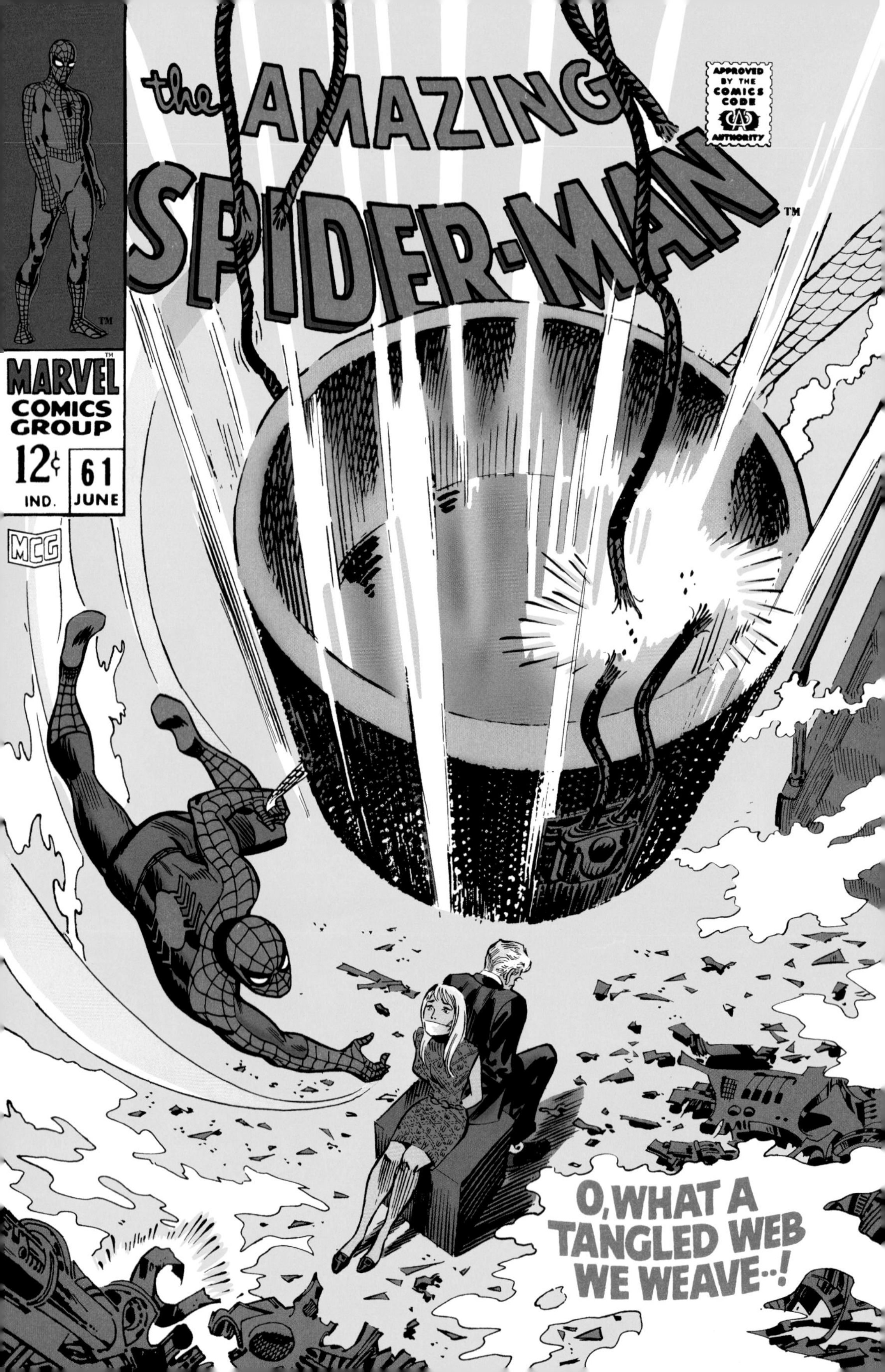

the AMAZING SPIDER-MAN
APPROVED BY THE COMICS CODE AUTHORITY
MARVEL COMICS GROUP
12¢
IND.
61
JUNE
MCG
O, WHAT A TANGLED WEB WE WEAVE..!

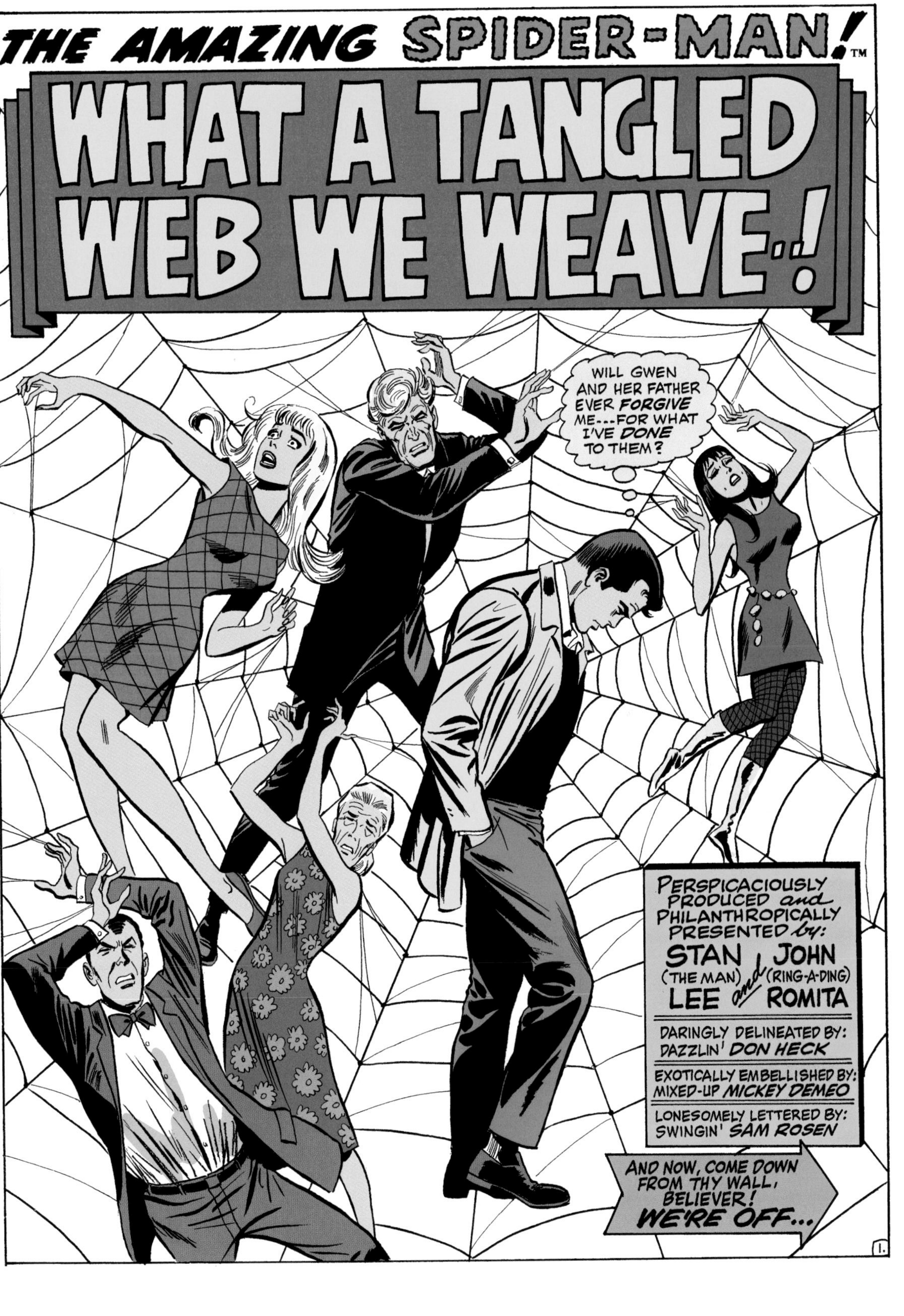
THE AMAZING SPIDER-MAN! ™
WHAT A TANGLED WEB WE WEAVE..!
WILL GWEN AND HER FATHER EVER FORGIVE ME---FOR WHAT I'VE DONE TO THEM?
PERSPICACIOUSLY PRODUCED and PHILANTHROPICALLY PRESENTED by: STAN (THE MAN) LEE and JOHN (RING-A-DING) ROMITA
DARINGLY DELINEATED BY: DAZZLIN' DON HECK
EXOTICALLY EMBELLISHED BY: MIXED-UP MICKEY DEMEO
LONESOMELY LETTERED BY: SWINGIN' SAM ROSEN
AND NOW, COME DOWN FROM THY WALL, BELIEVER! WE'RE OFF...
1.

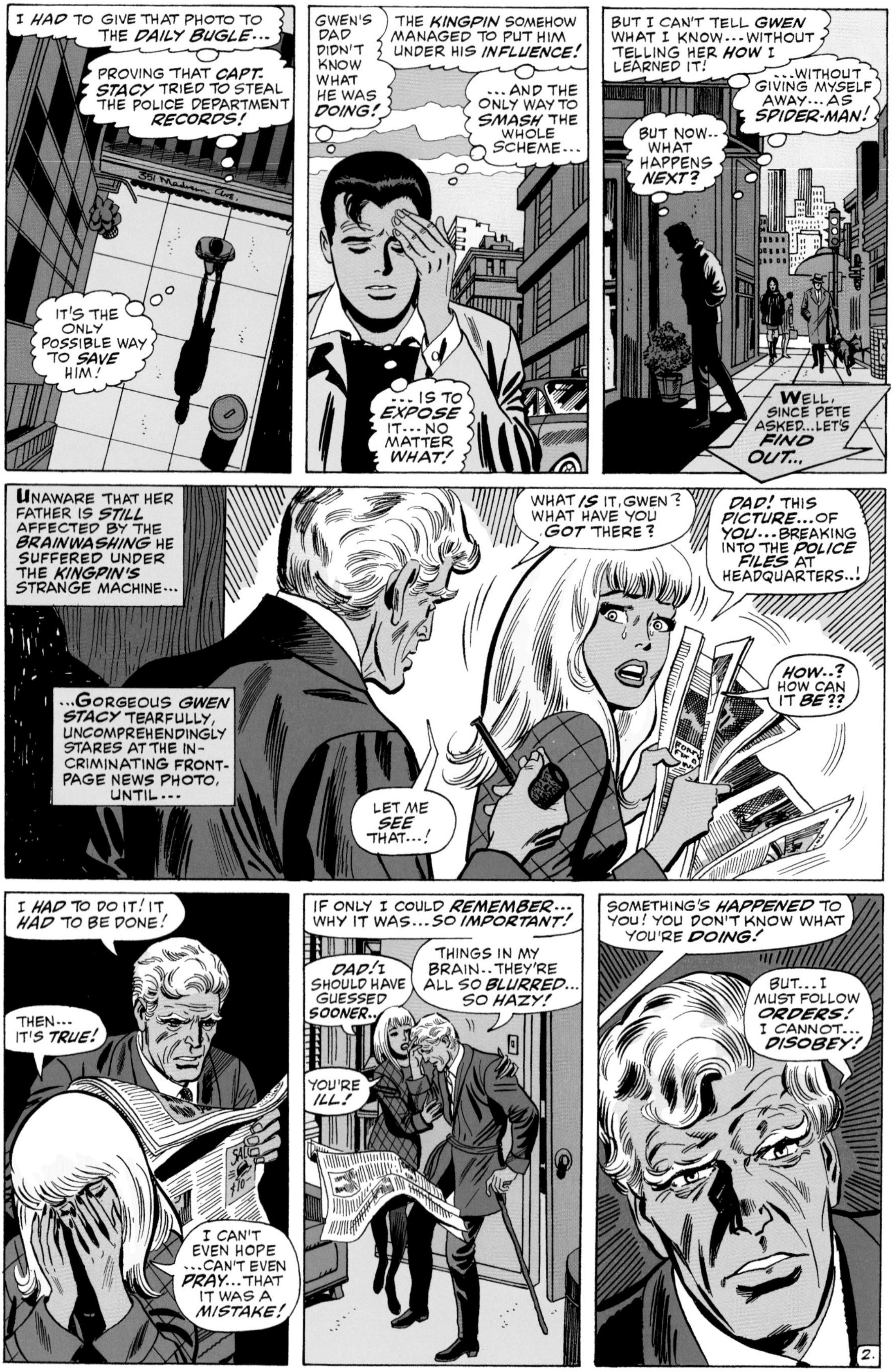
I HAD TO GIVE THAT PHOTO TO THE DAILY BUGLE...
PROVING THAT CAPT. STACY TRIED TO STEAL THE POLICE DEPARTMENT RECORDS!
IT'S THE ONLY POSSIBLE WAY TO SAVE HIM!
GWEN'S DAD DIDN'T KNOW WHAT HE WAS DOING!
THE KINGPIN SOMEHOW MANAGED TO PUT HIM UNDER HIS INFLUENCE!
...AND THE ONLY WAY TO SMASH THE WHOLE SCHEME...
...IS TO EXPOSE IT---NO MATTER WHAT!
BUT I CAN'T TELL GWEN WHAT I KNOW---WITHOUT TELLING HER HOW I LEARNED IT!
...WITHOUT GIVING MYSELF AWAY...AS SPIDER-MAN!
BUT NOW.. WHAT HAPPENS NEXT?
WELL, SINCE PETE ASKED...LET'S FIND OUT...
UNAWARE THAT HER FATHER IS STILL AFFECTED BY THE BRAINWASHING HE SUFFERED UNDER THE KINGPIN'S STRANGE MACHINE...
...GORGEOUS GWEN STACY TEARFULLY, UNCOMPREHENDINGLY STARES AT THE INCRIMINATING FRONT-PAGE NEWS PHOTO, UNTIL...
WHAT IS IT, GWEN? WHAT HAVE YOU GOT THERE?
DAD! THIS PICTURE...OF YOU...BREAKING INTO THE POLICE FILES AT HEADQUARTERS..!
HOW..? HOW CAN IT BE??
LET ME SEE THAT...!
I HAD TO DO IT! IT HAD TO BE DONE!
THEN... IT'S TRUE!
I CAN'T EVEN HOPE ...CAN'T EVEN PRAY...THAT IT WAS A MISTAKE!
IF ONLY I COULD REMEMBER... WHY IT WAS...SO IMPORTANT!
DAD! I SHOULD HAVE GUESSED SOONER..
THINGS IN MY BRAIN..THEY'RE ALL SO BLURRED... SO HAZY!
YOU'RE ILL!
SOMETHING'S HAPPENED TO YOU! YOU DON'T KNOW WHAT YOU'RE DOING!
BUT...I MUST FOLLOW ORDERS! I CANNOT... DISOBEY!
2.

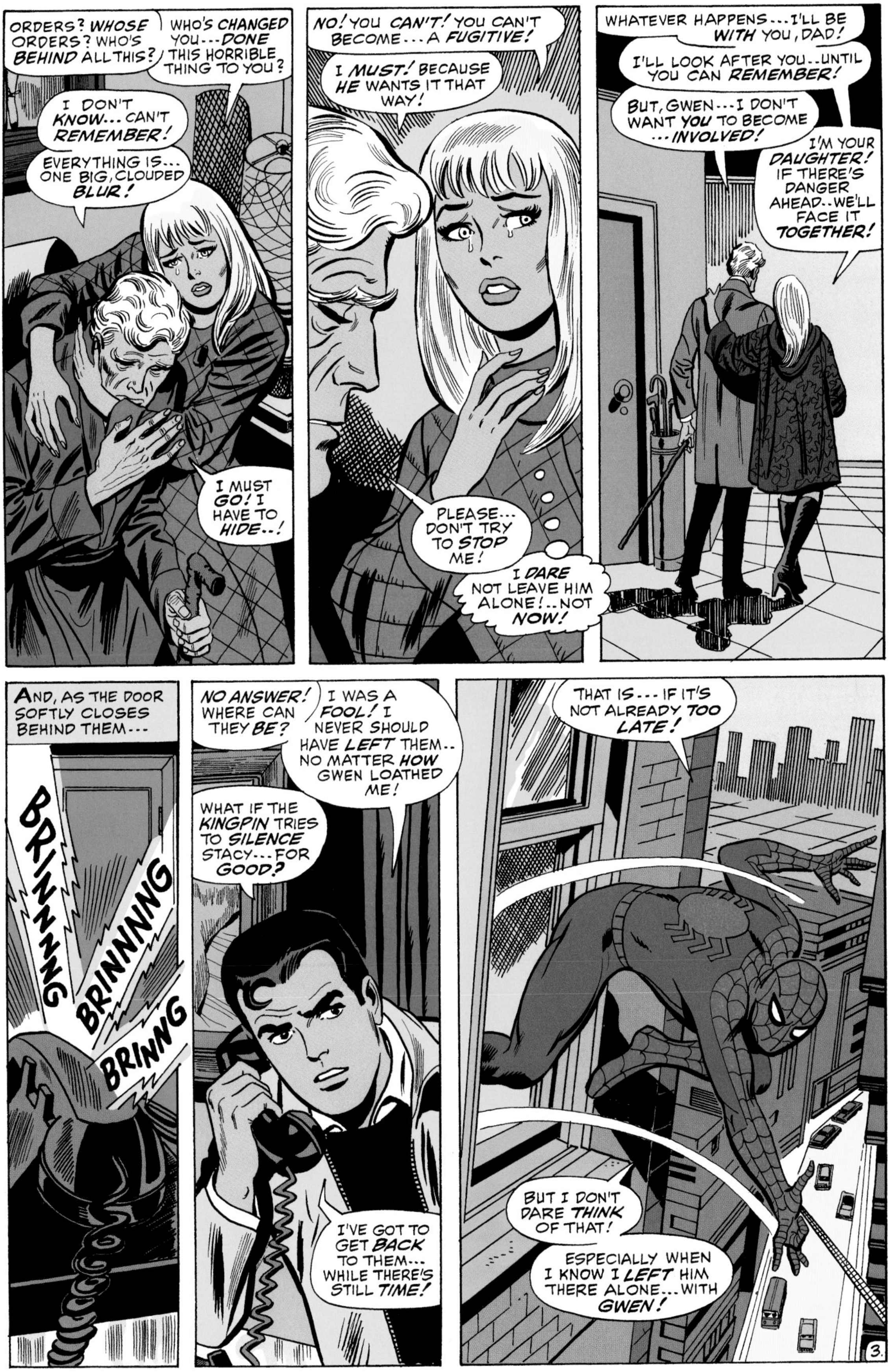
ORDERS? WHOSE ORDERS? WHO'S BEHIND ALL THIS?
WHO'S CHANGED YOU--- DONE THIS HORRIBLE THING TO YOU?
I DON'T KNOW... CAN'T REMEMBER!
EVERYTHING IS... ONE BIG, CLOUDED BLUR!
I MUST GO! I HAVE TO HIDE..!
NO! YOU CAN'T! YOU CAN'T BECOME... A FUGITIVE!
I MUST! BECAUSE HE WANTS IT THAT WAY!
PLEASE... DON'T TRY TO STOP ME!
I DARE NOT LEAVE HIM ALONE!.. NOT NOW!
WHATEVER HAPPENS... I'LL BE WITH YOU, DAD!
I'LL LOOK AFTER YOU.. UNTIL YOU CAN REMEMBER!
BUT, GWEN--- I DON'T WANT YOU TO BECOME ...INVOLVED!
I'M YOUR DAUGHTER! IF THERE'S DANGER AHEAD.. WE'LL FACE IT TOGETHER!
AND, AS THE DOOR SOFTLY CLOSES BEHIND THEM---
BRINNNNG
BRINNNNG
BRINNG
NO ANSWER! WHERE CAN THEY BE?
I WAS A FOOL! I NEVER SHOULD HAVE LEFT THEM.. NO MATTER HOW GWEN LOATHED ME!
WHAT IF THE KINGPIN TRIES TO SILENCE STACY... FOR GOOD?
I'VE GOT TO GET BACK TO THEM... WHILE THERE'S STILL TIME!
THAT IS... IF IT'S NOT ALREADY TOO LATE!
BUT I DON'T DARE THINK OF THAT!
ESPECIALLY WHEN I KNOW I LEFT HIM THERE ALONE... WITH GWEN!
3.

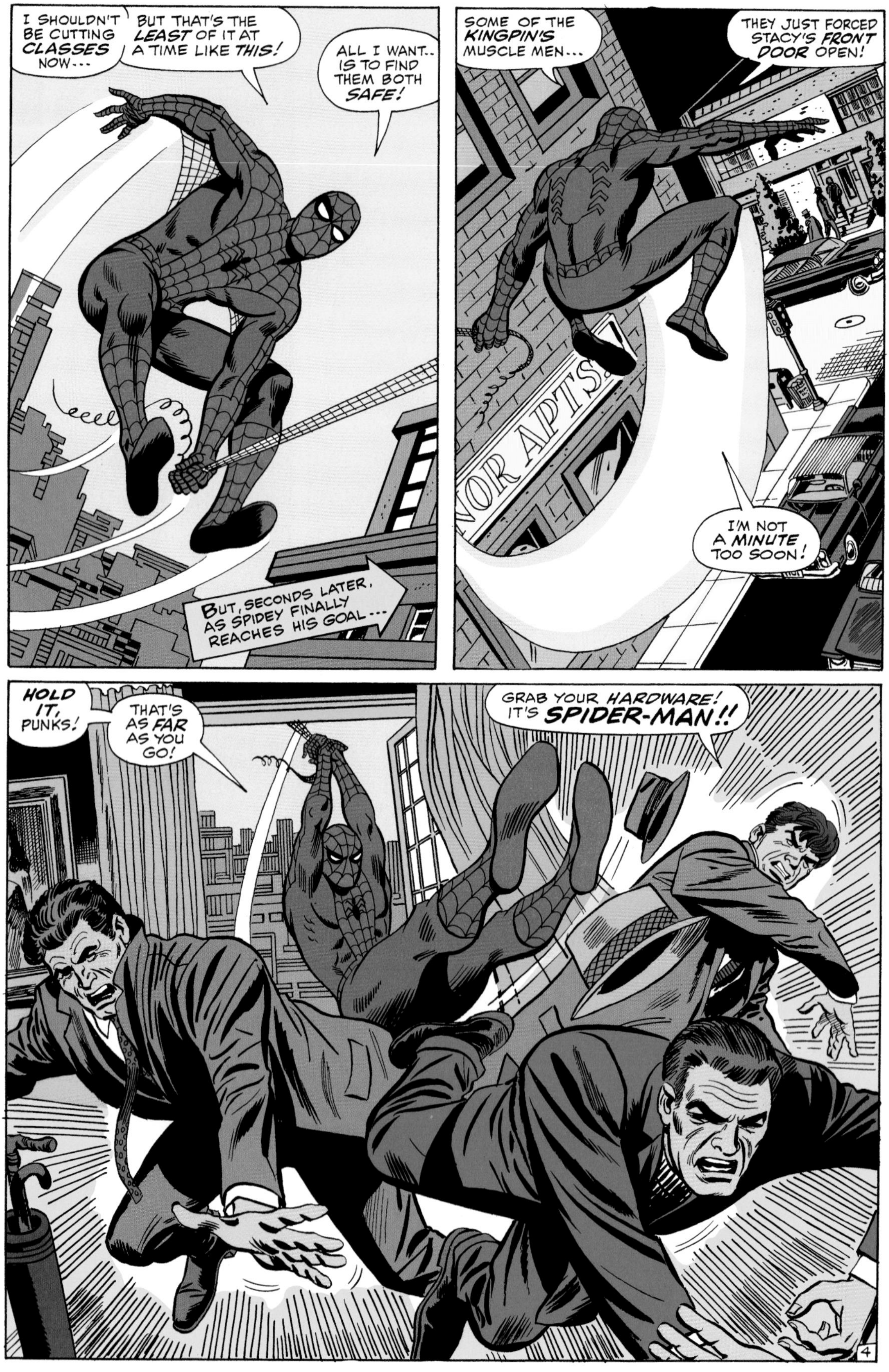
I SHOULDN'T BE CUTTING CLASSES NOW...
BUT THAT'S THE LEAST OF IT AT A TIME LIKE THIS!
ALL I WANT.. IS TO FIND THEM BOTH SAFE!
BUT, SECONDS LATER, AS SPIDEY FINALLY REACHES HIS GOAL...
SOME OF THE KINGPIN'S MUSCLE MEN...
THEY JUST FORCED STACY'S FRONT DOOR OPEN!
NOR APTS.
I'M NOT A MINUTE TOO SOON!
HOLD IT, PUNKS!
THAT'S AS FAR AS YOU GO!
GRAB YOUR HARDWARE! IT'S SPIDER-MAN!!
4

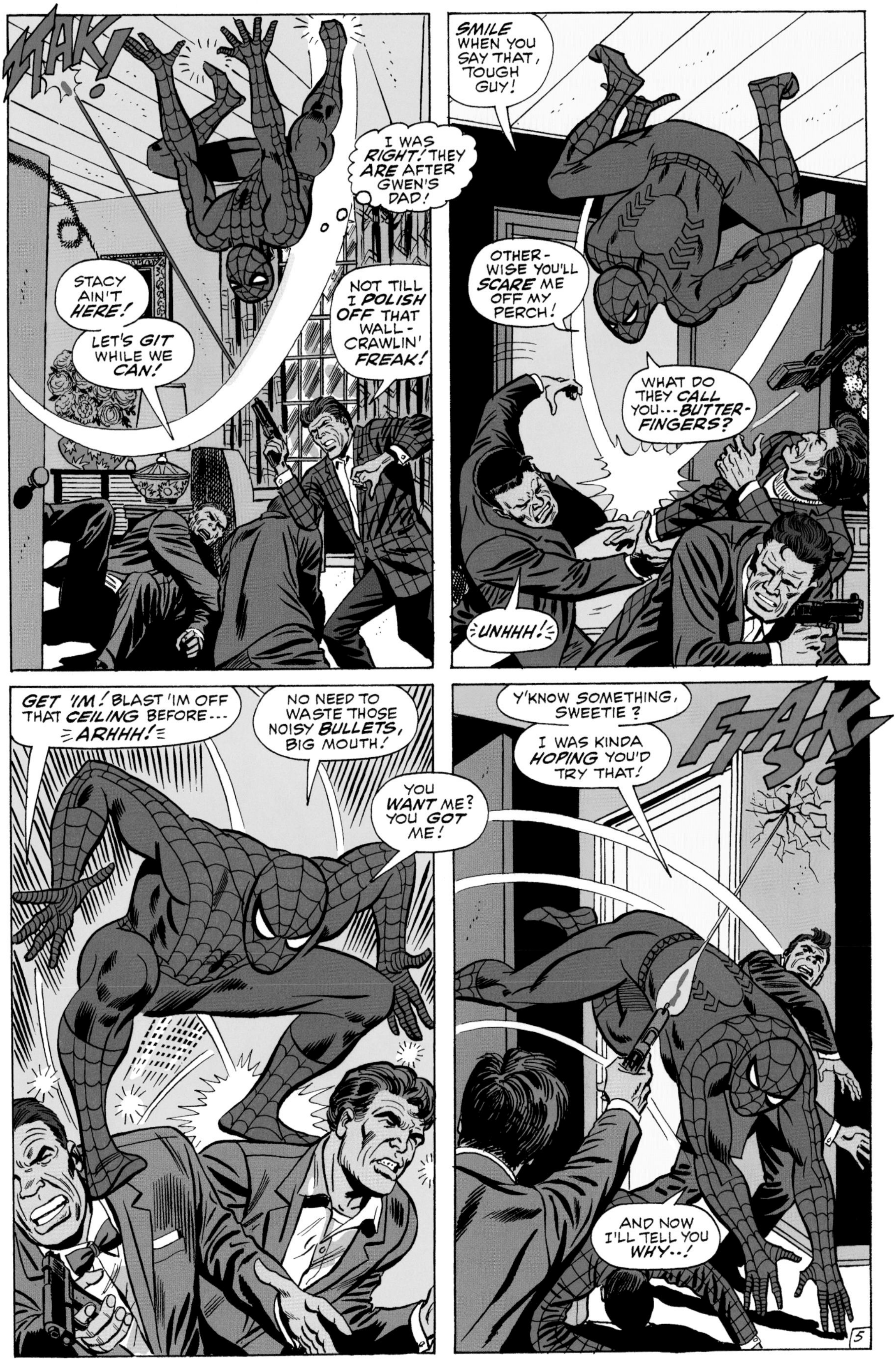
SKAK!
I WAS RIGHT! THEY ARE AFTER GWEN'S DAD!
STACY AIN'T HERE!
LET'S GIT WHILE WE CAN!
NOT TILL I POLISH OFF THAT WALL-CRAWLIN' FREAK!
SMILE WHEN YOU SAY THAT, TOUGH GUY!
OTHER-WISE YOU'LL SCARE ME OFF MY PERCH!
WHAT DO THEY CALL YOU--- BUTTER-FINGERS?
UNHHH!
GET 'IM! BLAST 'IM OFF THAT CEILING BEFORE--- ARHHH!
NO NEED TO WASTE THOSE NOISY BULLETS, BIG MOUTH!
YOU WANT ME? YOU GOT ME!
Y'KNOW SOMETHING, SWEETIE?
I WAS KINDA HOPING YOU'D TRY THAT!
FTAK!
AND NOW I'LL TELL YOU WHY--!
5

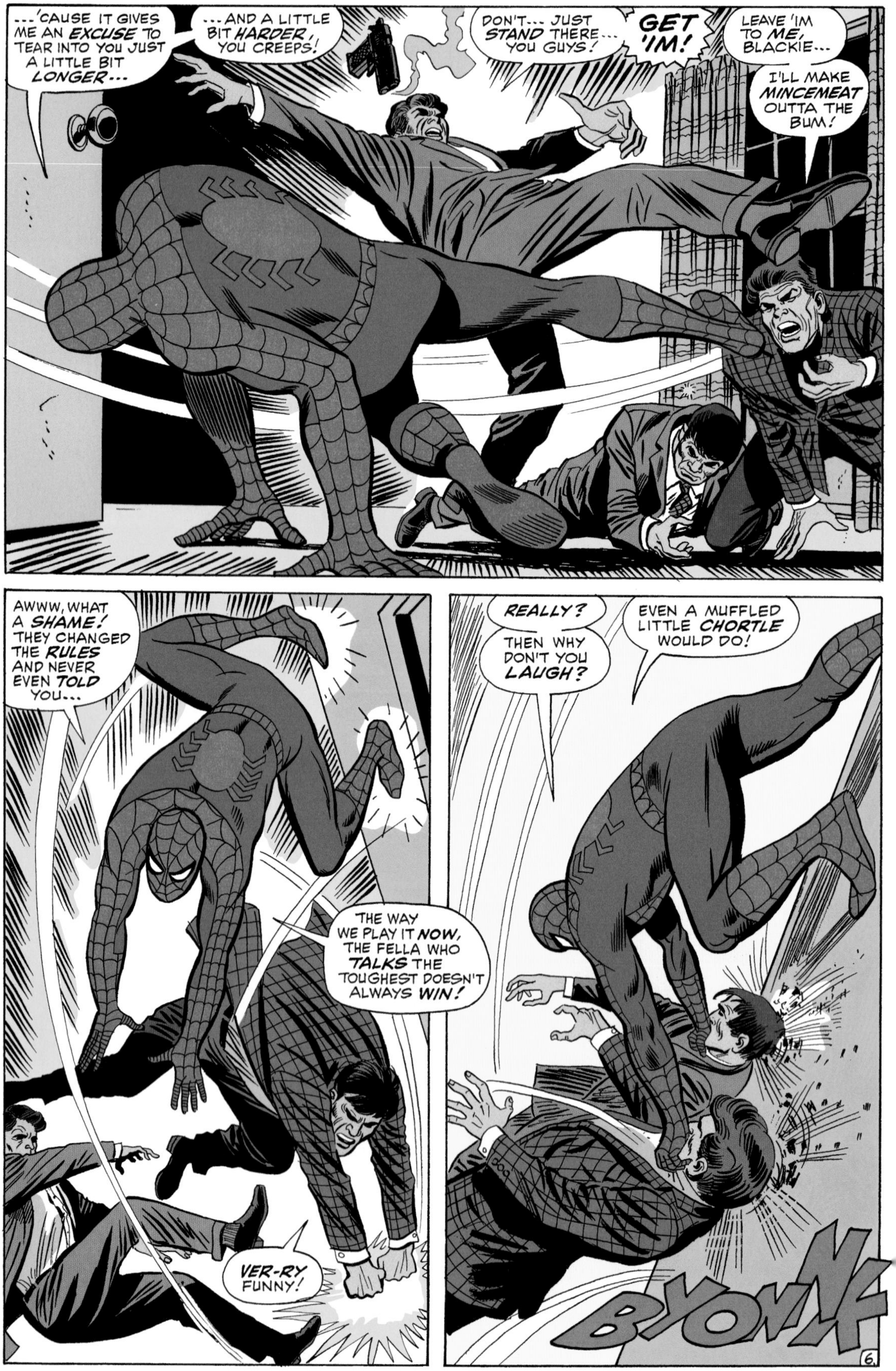
...'CAUSE IT GIVES ME AN EXCUSE TO TEAR INTO YOU JUST A LITTLE BIT LONGER...
...AND A LITTLE BIT HARDER, YOU CREEPS!
DON'T... JUST STAND THERE... YOU GUYS!
GET 'IM!
LEAVE 'IM TO ME, BLACKIE...
I'LL MAKE MINCEMEAT OUTTA THE BUM!
AWWW, WHAT A SHAME! THEY CHANGED THE RULES AND NEVER EVEN TOLD YOU...
THE WAY WE PLAY IT NOW, THE FELLA WHO TALKS THE TOUGHEST DOESN'T ALWAYS WIN!
VER-RY FUNNY!
REALLY?
THEN WHY DON'T YOU LAUGH?
EVEN A MUFFLED LITTLE CHORTLE WOULD DO!
BYONK
6

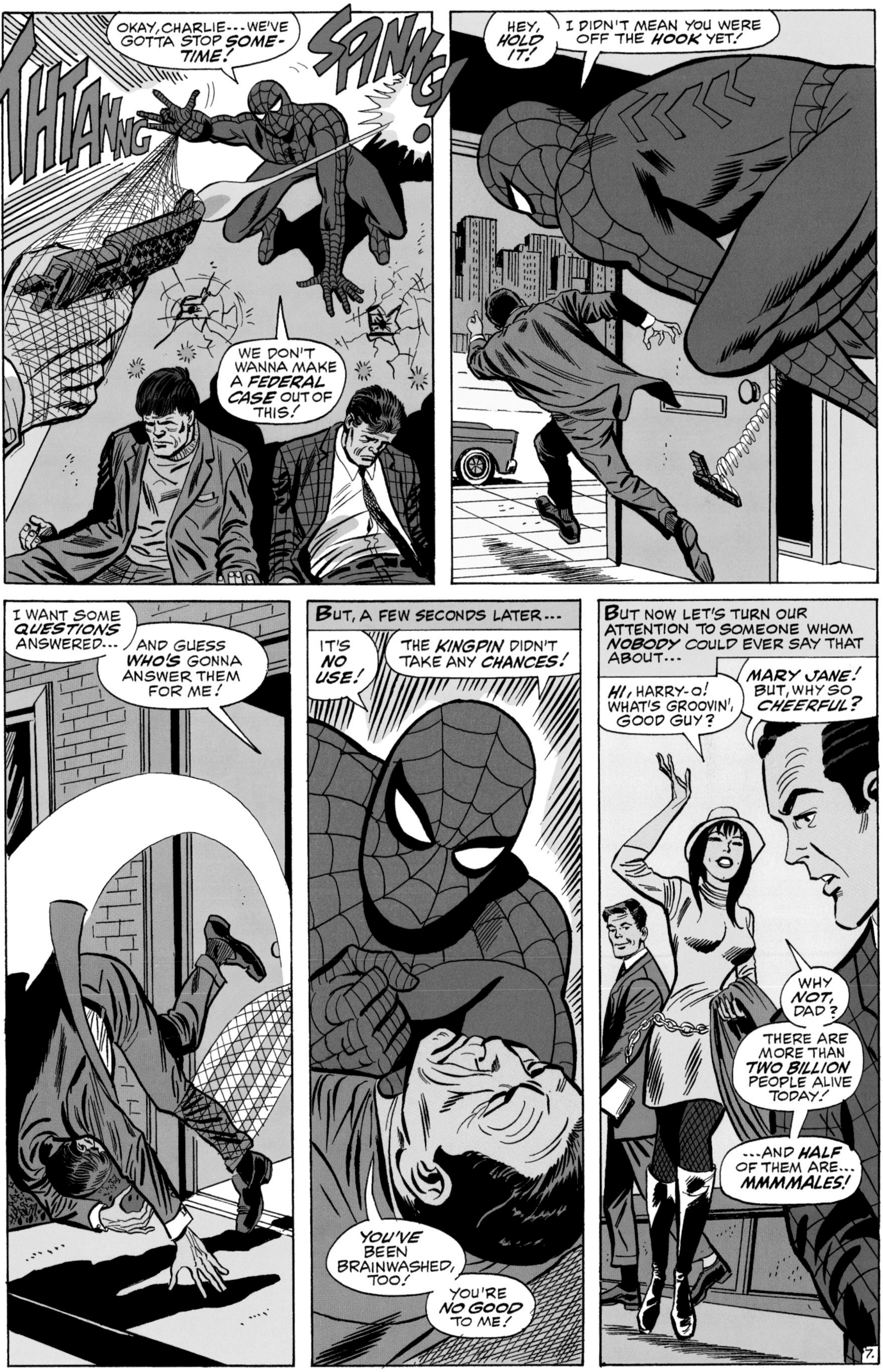
THTANNG
OKAY, CHARLIE--- WE'VE GOTTA STOP SOME-TIME!
SPANNG!
WE DON'T WANNA MAKE A FEDERAL CASE OUT OF THIS!
HEY, HOLD IT!
I DIDN'T MEAN YOU WERE OFF THE HOOK YET!
I WANT SOME QUESTIONS ANSWERED...
AND GUESS WHO'S GONNA ANSWER THEM FOR ME!
BUT, A FEW SECONDS LATER...
IT'S NO USE!
THE KINGPIN DIDN'T TAKE ANY CHANCES!
YOU'VE BEEN BRAINWASHED, TOO!
YOU'RE NO GOOD TO ME!
BUT NOW LET'S TURN OUR ATTENTION TO SOMEONE WHOM NOBODY COULD EVER SAY THAT ABOUT...
HI, HARRY-O! WHAT'S GROOVIN', GOOD GUY?
MARY JANE! BUT, WHY SO CHEERFUL?
WHY NOT, DAD?
THERE ARE MORE THAN TWO BILLION PEOPLE ALIVE TODAY!
...AND HALF OF THEM ARE... MMMMALES!
7.

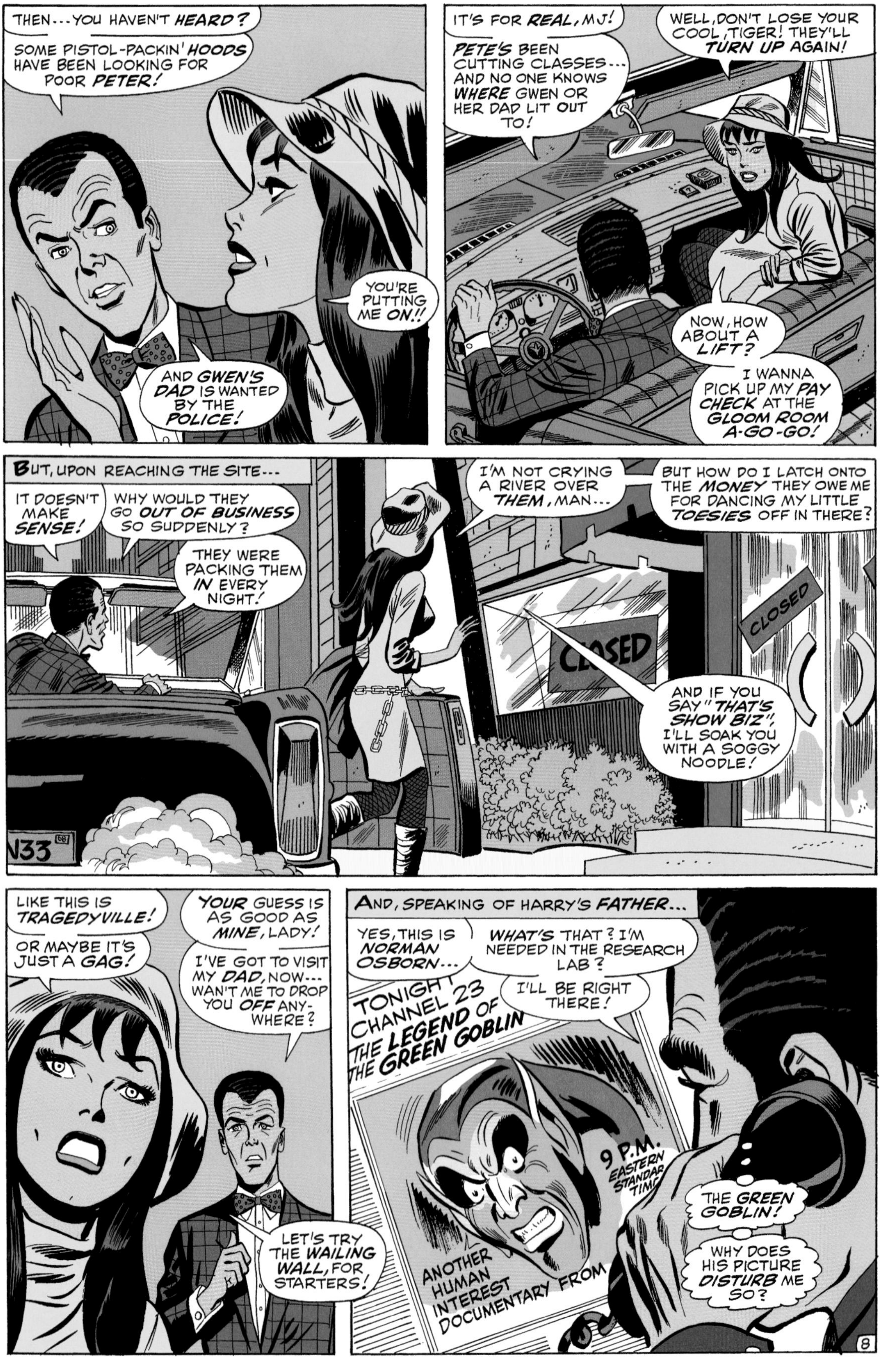
THEN... YOU HAVEN'T HEARD?
SOME PISTOL-PACKIN' HOODS HAVE BEEN LOOKING FOR POOR PETER!
YOU'RE PUTTING ME ON!!
AND GWEN'S DAD IS WANTED BY THE POLICE!
IT'S FOR REAL, MJ!
PETE'S BEEN CUTTING CLASSES... AND NO ONE KNOWS WHERE GWEN OR HER DAD LIT OUT TO!
WELL, DON'T LOSE YOUR COOL, TIGER! THEY'LL TURN UP AGAIN!
NOW, HOW ABOUT A LIFT?
I WANNA PICK UP MY PAY CHECK AT THE GLOOM ROOM A-GO-GO!
BUT, UPON REACHING THE SITE...
IT DOESN'T MAKE SENSE!
WHY WOULD THEY GO OUT OF BUSINESS SO SUDDENLY?
THEY WERE PACKING THEM IN EVERY NIGHT!
I'M NOT CRYING A RIVER OVER THEM, MAN...
BUT HOW DO I LATCH ONTO THE MONEY THEY OWE ME FOR DANCING MY LITTLE TOESIES OFF IN THERE?
CLOSED
CLOSED
AND IF YOU SAY "THAT'S SHOW BIZ", I'LL SOAK YOU WITH A SOGGY NOODLE!
N33 68
LIKE THIS IS TRAGEDYVILLE!
OR MAYBE IT'S JUST A GAG!
YOUR GUESS IS AS GOOD AS MINE, LADY!
I'VE GOT TO VISIT MY DAD, NOW--- WAN'T ME TO DROP YOU OFF ANY-WHERE?
LET'S TRY THE WAILING WALL, FOR STARTERS!
AND, SPEAKING OF HARRY'S FATHER...
YES, THIS IS NORMAN OSBORN...
WHAT'S THAT? I'M NEEDED IN THE RESEARCH LAB?
I'LL BE RIGHT THERE!
TONIGHT CHANNEL 23 THE LEGEND OF THE GREEN GOBLIN
9 P.M. EASTERN STANDAR TIM
ANOTHER HUMAN INTEREST DOCUMENTARY FROM
THE GREEN GOBLIN!
WHY DOES HIS PICTURE DISTURB ME SO?
8

EVERY TIME I HEAR THAT *NAME*, IT SENDS SHIVERS UP MY SPINE!

YOU SAY SOME NEW *EQUIPMENT* ARRIVED IN THE LAB...WITHOUT MY *AUTHORIZATION?*

ALL RIGHT! ALL RIGHT! JUST SIT TIGHT UNTIL I *GET* THERE!

NOW WHAT IN BLAZES CAN BE GOING ON?!!

WINKLER! IS THAT *YOU?* THE *SHIPPING DEPARTMENT* TELLS ME YOU ORDERED EXPENSIVE NEW *ELECTRONIC EQUIPMENT* WITHOUT MY SAY-SO!

EH, *YES*... I'M AFRAID I *DID*, MR. OSBORN!

CONFOUND IT, MAN!

YOU WORKED HERE LONG ENOUGH TO KNOW THE *RULES!*

THERE'S TO BE *NO EQUIPMENT* DELIVERED UNLESS THE ORDER HAS *MY SIGNATURE!*

BUT, YOU WERE *OUT OF TOWN*, MR. OSBORN --- AND WE *NEEDED* THE MATERIAL!

I *PERSONALLY* DOUBLE-CHECKED THE ENTIRE SHIPMENT!

ALL RIGHT, WINKLER... I'LL LET IT GO *THIS* TIME!

BUT, IN THE FUTURE, I WANT MY RULES *OBEYED* ---AND THAT MEANS BY *EVERYONE!*

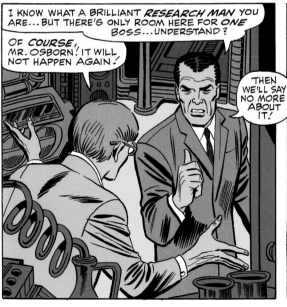

I KNOW WHAT A BRILLIANT *RESEARCH MAN* YOU ARE... BUT THERE'S ONLY ROOM HERE FOR *ONE* BOSS...UNDERSTAND?

OF *COURSE*, MR. OSBORN! IT WILL NOT HAPPEN AGAIN!

THEN WE'LL SAY NO MORE ABOUT IT!

HE'S *GONE!* I *TOLD* YOU WE COULD GET AWAY WITH IT!

IT WAS LUCKY FOR *HIM* THAT HE CHOSE TO *BELIEVE* YOU!

AND *NOW*, GENTLEMEN--- IT SEEMS WE HAVE FOUND A NEW *HIDING PLACE* FOR OUR *BRAIN-WASHING* MACHINE!

SINCE IT WAS *DESIGNED* FOR US BY *DR. WINKLER*, IT IS QUITE FITTING THAT IT SHOULD BE HOUSED IN WINKLER'S OWN *LABORATORY!*

BUT OSBORN *OWNS* THE JOINT! WHAT IF HE COMES SNOOPIN' *IN* HERE AN' SEES WHAT'S GOIN' *ON?*

DON'T BE A *FOOL!* OSBORN HAS *BIGGER* THINGS TO CONCERN HIMSELF WITH!

THIS SPOT IS *PERFECT* FOR US! NO ONE WOULD THINK TO SEARCH A RESPECTABLE *CHEMICAL PLANT* FOR THE *KINGPIN* AND HIS MEN!

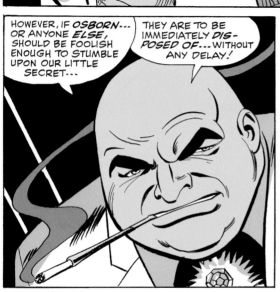

HOWEVER, IF *OSBORN*... OR ANYONE *ELSE*, SHOULD BE FOOLISH ENOUGH TO STUMBLE UPON OUR LITTLE SECRET...

THEY ARE TO BE IMMEDIATELY *DIS-POSED OF*...WITHOUT ANY DELAY!

...JUST AS YOU WILL *NOW* FIND, AND DISPOSE OF... *EX-CAPT. STACY!*

SINCE THE *POLICE* ARE AFTER HIM, HE CAN NO LONGER BE CONSIDERED A GOOD *SECURITY RISK!*

AND, AS A REWARD FOR TAKING THE PHOTOGRAPH WHICH *STARTED* IT ALL---

PETER PARKER IS TO BE *ELIMINATED* ALSO!

BUT YOUR *MAIN* TARGET... YOUR MOST *IMPORTANT* TARGET---IS TO BE *SPIDER-MAN!*

HE'S BEEN A *THORN* IN MY SIDE SINCE OUR FIRST MEETING!

I WANT HIM *CRUSHED*... JUST AS I'M CRUSHING THIS *STEEL CHAIR!*

IT WILL BE *HIS* LIFE...OR *YOURS!*

10

182

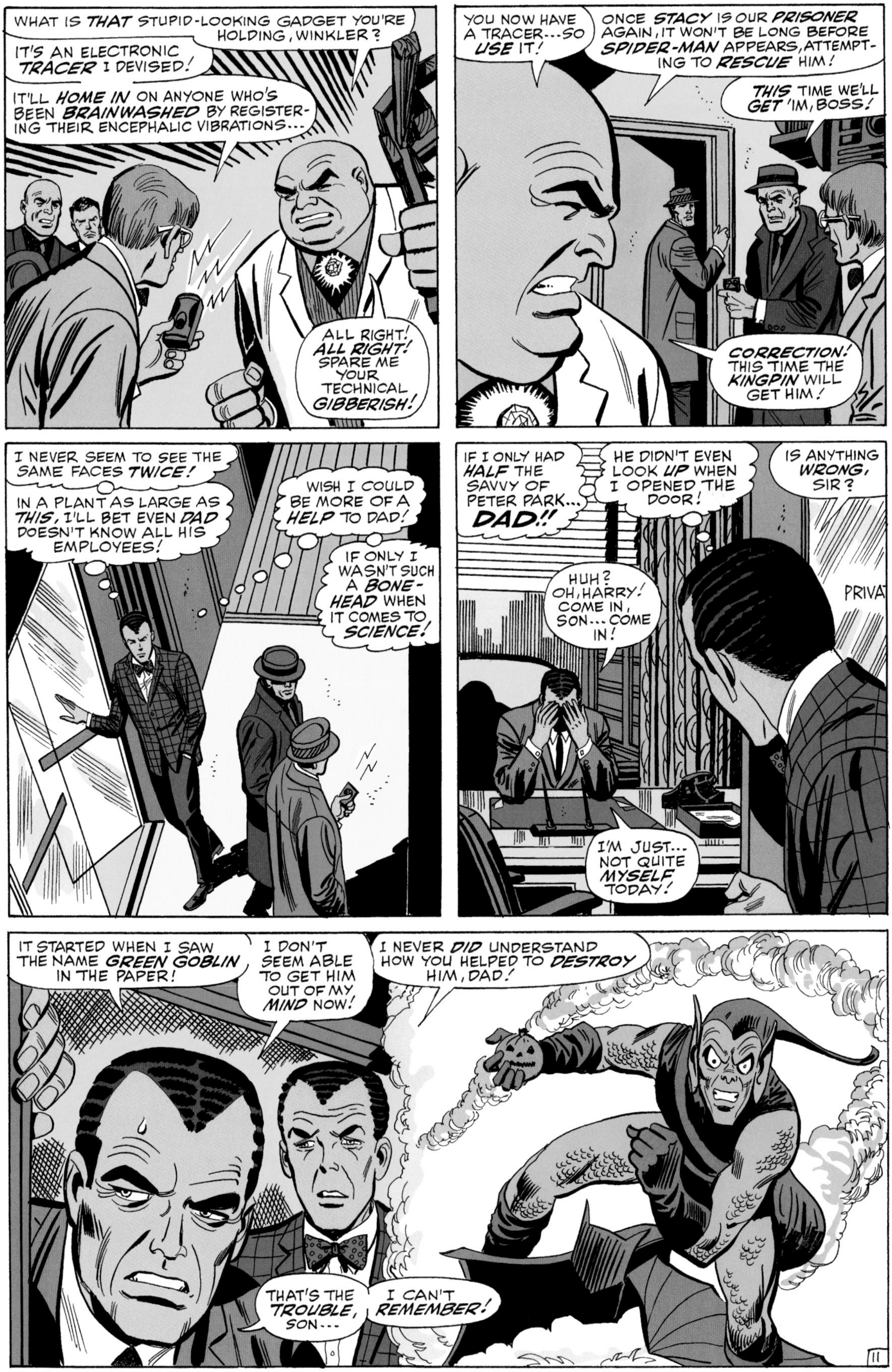

WHAT IS THAT STUPID-LOOKING GADGET YOU'RE HOLDING, WINKLER?
IT'S AN ELECTRONIC TRACER I DEVISED!
IT'LL HOME IN ON ANYONE WHO'S BEEN BRAINWASHED BY REGISTERING THEIR ENCEPHALIC VIBRATIONS...
ALL RIGHT! ALL RIGHT! SPARE ME YOUR TECHNICAL GIBBERISH!
YOU NOW HAVE A TRACER---SO USE IT!
ONCE STACY IS OUR PRISONER AGAIN, IT WON'T BE LONG BEFORE SPIDER-MAN APPEARS, ATTEMPTING TO RESCUE HIM!
THIS TIME WE'LL GET 'IM, BOSS!
CORRECTION! THIS TIME THE KINGPIN WILL GET HIM!
I NEVER SEEM TO SEE THE SAME FACES TWICE!
IN A PLANT AS LARGE AS THIS, I'LL BET EVEN DAD DOESN'T KNOW ALL HIS EMPLOYEES!
WISH I COULD BE MORE OF A HELP TO DAD!
IF ONLY I WASN'T SUCH A BONE-HEAD WHEN IT COMES TO SCIENCE!
IF I ONLY HAD HALF THE SAVVY OF PETER PARK... DAD!!
HE DIDN'T EVEN LOOK UP WHEN I OPENED THE DOOR!
IS ANYTHING WRONG, SIR?
PRIVAT
HUH? OH, HARRY! COME IN, SON... COME IN!
I'M JUST... NOT QUITE MYSELF TODAY!
IT STARTED WHEN I SAW THE NAME GREEN GOBLIN IN THE PAPER!
I DON'T SEEM ABLE TO GET HIM OUT OF MY MIND NOW!
I NEVER DID UNDERSTAND HOW YOU HELPED TO DESTROY HIM, DAD!
THAT'S THE TROUBLE, SON---
I CAN'T REMEMBER!
11

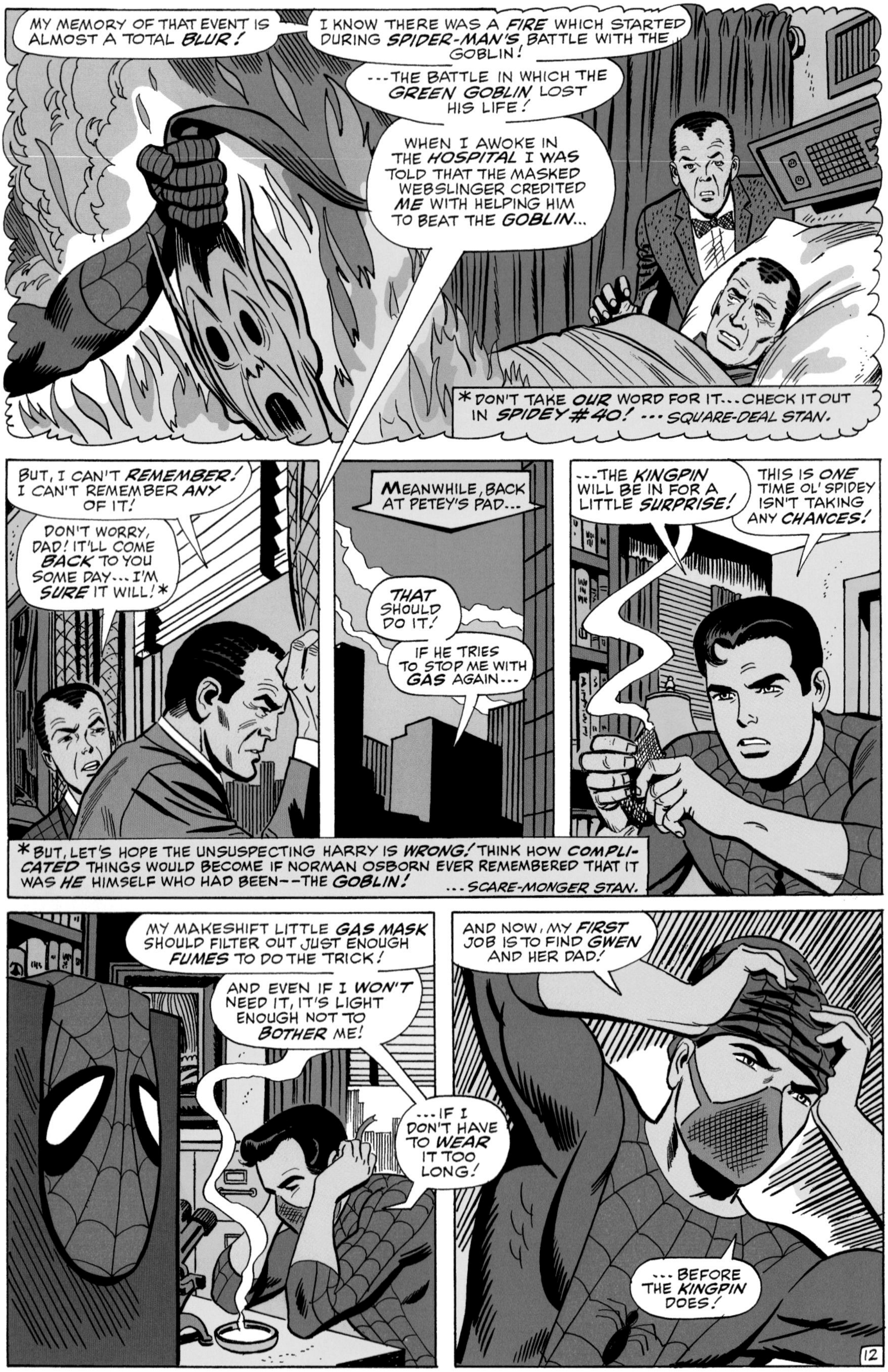
MY MEMORY OF THAT EVENT IS ALMOST A TOTAL BLUR!
I KNOW THERE WAS A FIRE WHICH STARTED DURING SPIDER-MAN'S BATTLE WITH THE GOBLIN!
---THE BATTLE IN WHICH THE GREEN GOBLIN LOST HIS LIFE!
WHEN I AWOKE IN THE HOSPITAL I WAS TOLD THAT THE MASKED WEBSLINGER CREDITED ME WITH HELPING HIM TO BEAT THE GOBLIN...
* DON'T TAKE OUR WORD FOR IT... CHECK IT OUT IN SPIDEY #40! ---SQUARE-DEAL STAN.
BUT, I CAN'T REMEMBER! I CAN'T REMEMBER ANY OF IT!
DON'T WORRY, DAD! IT'LL COME BACK TO YOU SOME DAY... I'M SURE IT WILL! *
MEANWHILE, BACK AT PETEY'S PAD...
THAT SHOULD DO IT!
IF HE TRIES TO STOP ME WITH GAS AGAIN...
---THE KINGPIN WILL BE IN FOR A LITTLE SURPRISE!
THIS IS ONE TIME OL' SPIDEY ISN'T TAKING ANY CHANCES!
* BUT, LET'S HOPE THE UNSUSPECTING HARRY IS WRONG! THINK HOW COMPLICATED THINGS WOULD BECOME IF NORMAN OSBORN EVER REMEMBERED THAT IT WAS HE HIMSELF WHO HAD BEEN--THE GOBLIN! ...SCARE-MONGER STAN.
MY MAKESHIFT LITTLE GAS MASK SHOULD FILTER OUT JUST ENOUGH FUMES TO DO THE TRICK!
AND EVEN IF I WON'T NEED IT, IT'S LIGHT ENOUGH NOT TO BOTHER ME!
...IF I DON'T HAVE TO WEAR IT TOO LONG!
AND NOW, MY FIRST JOB IS TO FIND GWEN AND HER DAD!
...BEFORE THE KINGPIN DOES!
12

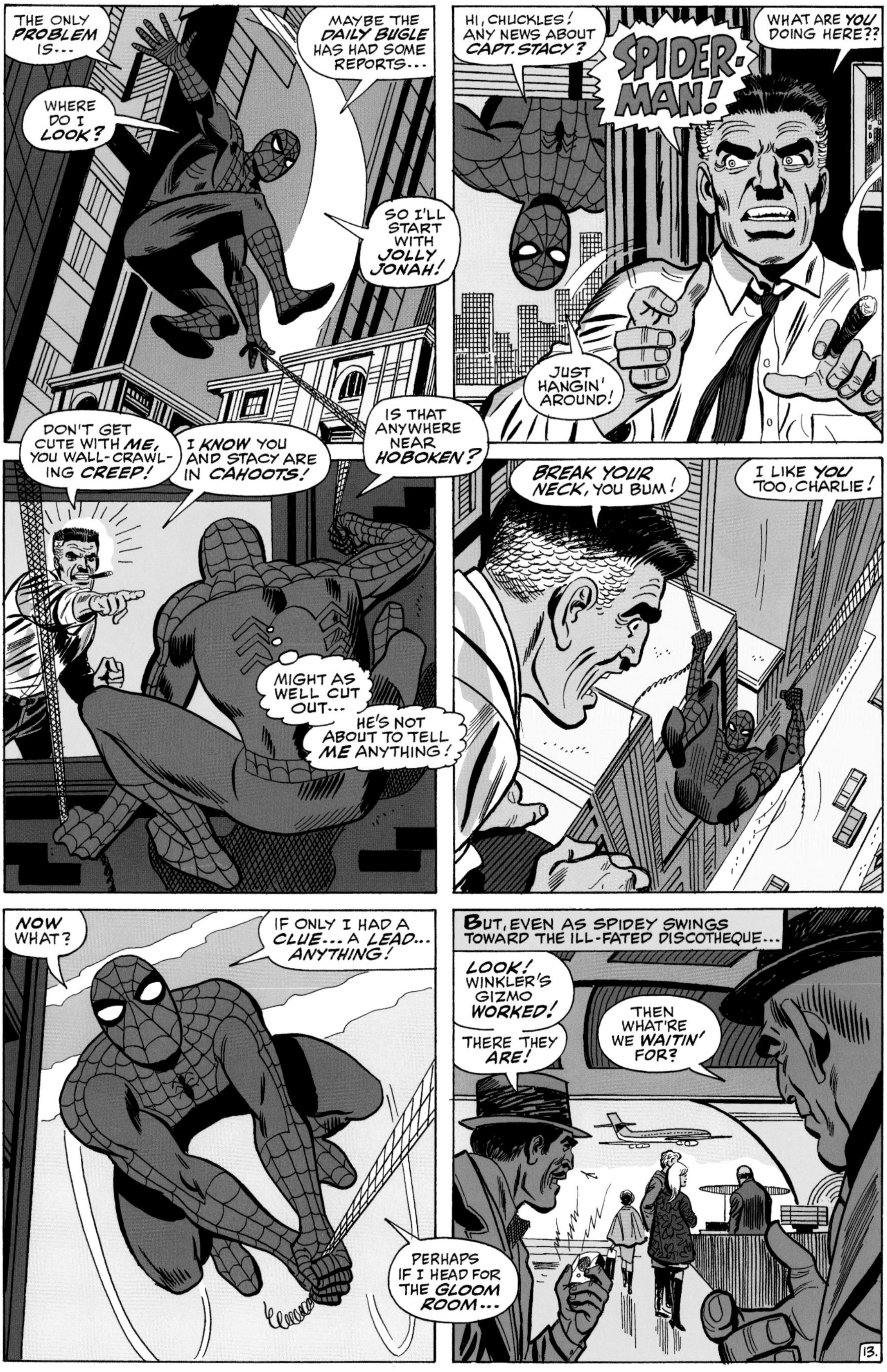
THE ONLY PROBLEM IS...
WHERE DO I LOOK?
MAYBE THE DAILY BUGLE HAS HAD SOME REPORTS...
SO I'LL START WITH JOLLY JONAH!
HI, CHUCKLES! ANY NEWS ABOUT CAPT. STACY?
SPIDER-MAN!
WHAT ARE YOU DOING HERE??
JUST HANGIN' AROUND!
DON'T GET CUTE WITH ME, YOU WALL-CRAWLING CREEP!
I KNOW YOU AND STACY ARE IN CAHOOTS!
IS THAT ANYWHERE NEAR HOBOKEN?
MIGHT AS WELL CUT OUT...
HE'S NOT ABOUT TO TELL ME ANYTHING!
BREAK YOUR NECK, YOU BUM!
I LIKE YOU TOO, CHARLIE!
NOW WHAT?
IF ONLY I HAD A CLUE... A LEAD... ANYTHING!
PERHAPS IF I HEAD FOR THE GLOOM ROOM...
BUT, EVEN AS SPIDEY SWINGS TOWARD THE ILL-FATED DISCOTHEQUE...
LOOK! WINKLER'S GIZMO WORKED!
THERE THEY ARE!
THEN WHAT'RE WE WAITIN' FOR?
13.

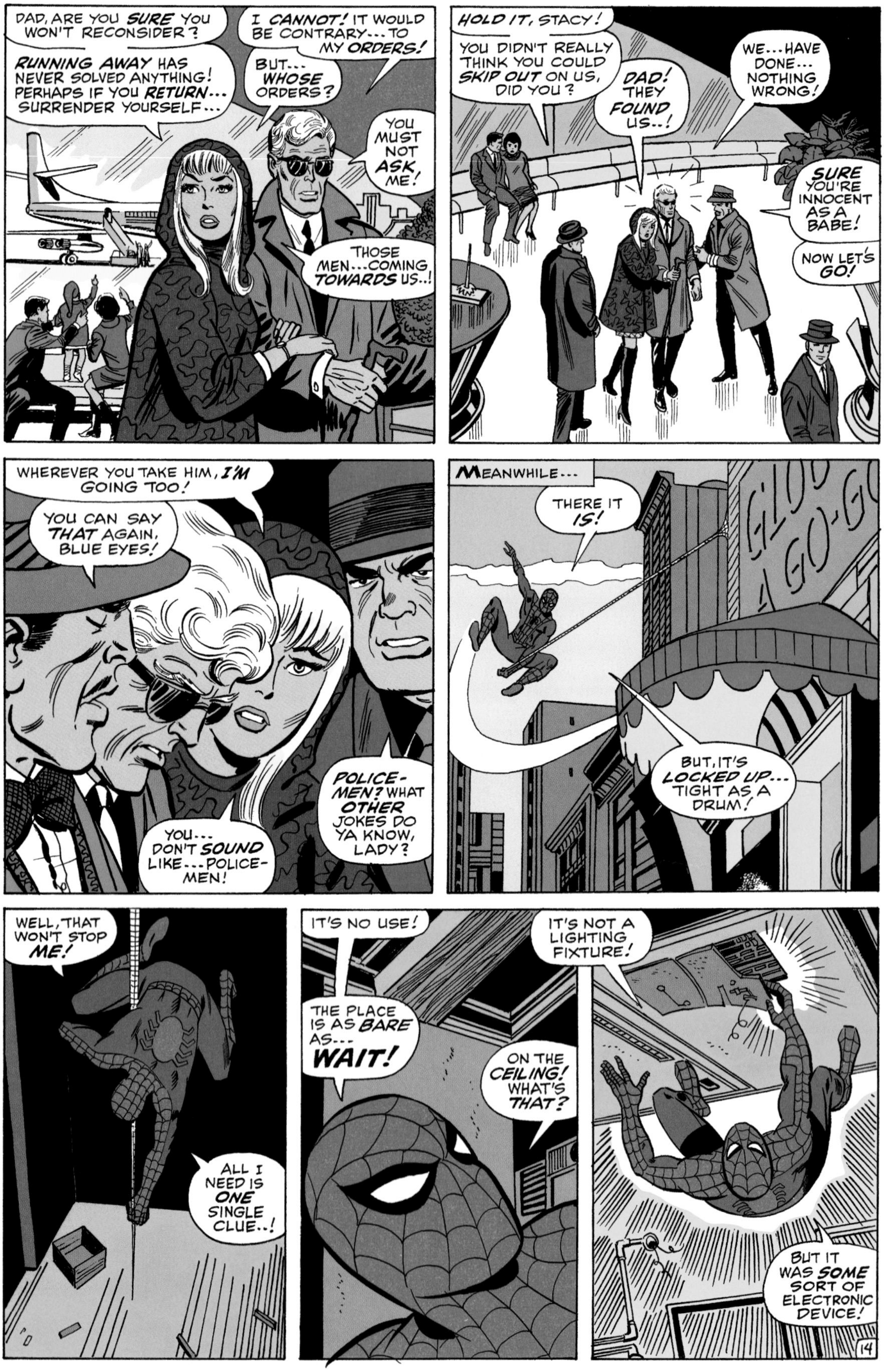
DAD, ARE YOU SURE YOU WON'T RECONSIDER?
RUNNING AWAY HAS NEVER SOLVED ANYTHING! PERHAPS IF YOU RETURN... SURRENDER YOURSELF...
I CANNOT! IT WOULD BE CONTRARY... TO MY ORDERS!
BUT... WHOSE ORDERS?
YOU MUST NOT ASK, ME!
THOSE MEN... COMING TOWARDS US..!
HOLD IT, STACY!
YOU DIDN'T REALLY THINK YOU COULD SKIP OUT ON US, DID YOU?
DAD! THEY FOUND US..!
WE... HAVE DONE... NOTHING WRONG!
SURE YOU'RE INNOCENT AS A BABE!
NOW LET'S GO!
WHEREVER YOU TAKE HIM, I'M GOING TOO!
YOU CAN SAY THAT AGAIN, BLUE EYES!
YOU... DON'T SOUND LIKE... POLICEMEN!
POLICE-MEN? WHAT OTHER JOKES DO YA KNOW, LADY?
MEANWHILE...
THERE IT IS!
BUT, IT'S LOCKED UP... TIGHT AS A DRUM!
WELL, THAT WON'T STOP ME!
ALL I NEED IS ONE SINGLE CLUE..!
IT'S NO USE!
THE PLACE IS AS BARE AS... WAIT!
ON THE CEILING! WHAT'S THAT?
IT'S NOT A LIGHTING FIXTURE!
BUT IT WAS SOME SORT OF ELECTRONIC DEVICE!
14

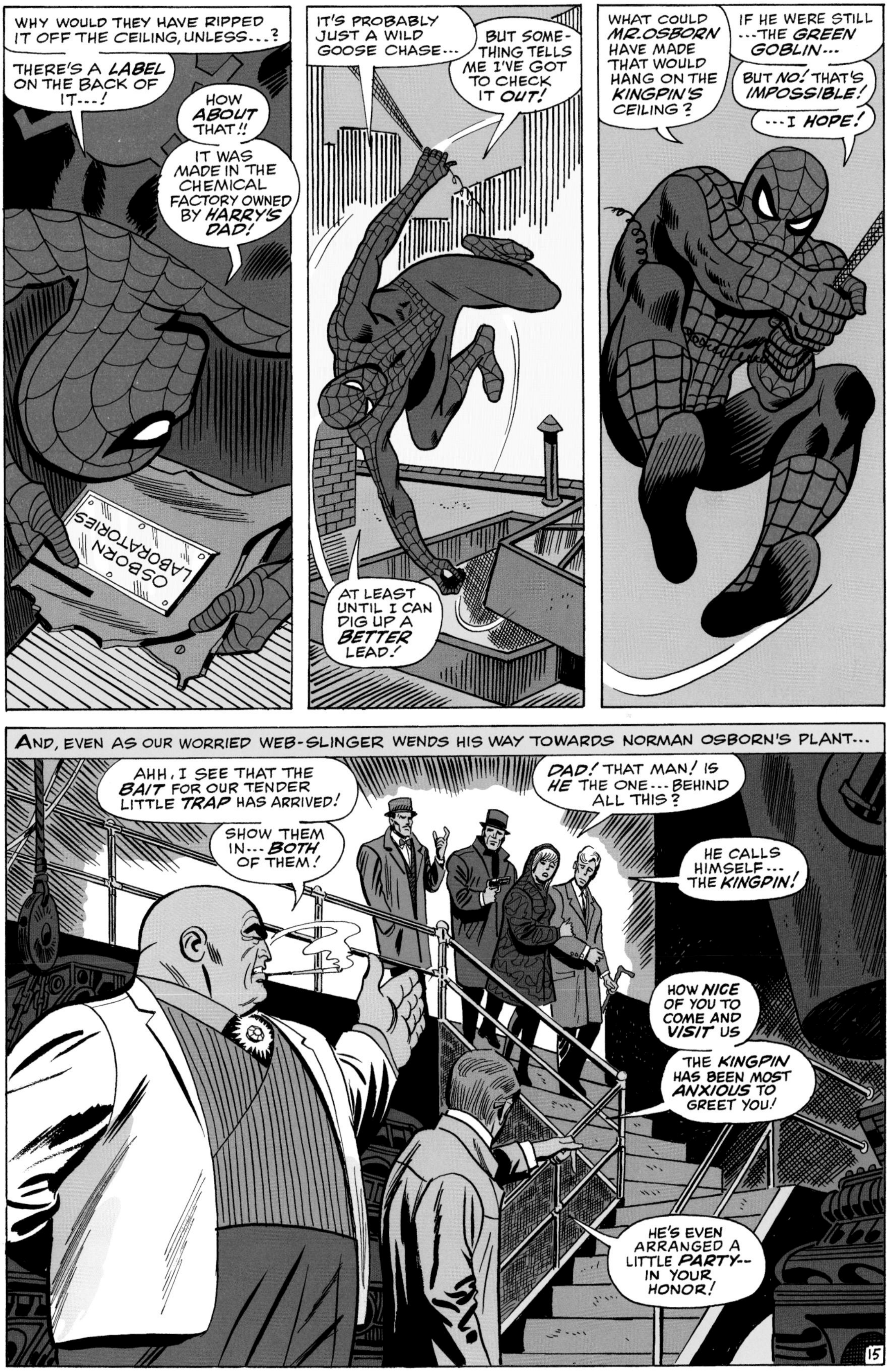
WHY WOULD THEY HAVE RIPPED IT OFF THE CEILING, UNLESS...?
THERE'S A LABEL ON THE BACK OF IT...!
HOW ABOUT THAT!!
IT WAS MADE IN THE CHEMICAL FACTORY OWNED BY HARRY'S DAD!
OSBORN LABORATORIES
IT'S PROBABLY JUST A WILD GOOSE CHASE...
BUT SOMETHING TELLS ME I'VE GOT TO CHECK IT OUT!
AT LEAST UNTIL I CAN DIG UP A BETTER LEAD!
WHAT COULD MR. OSBORN HAVE MADE THAT WOULD HANG ON THE KINGPIN'S CEILING?
IF HE WERE STILL ...THE GREEN GOBLIN...
BUT NO! THAT'S IMPOSSIBLE!
...I HOPE!
AND, EVEN AS OUR WORRIED WEB-SLINGER WENDS HIS WAY TOWARDS NORMAN OSBORN'S PLANT...
AHH, I SEE THAT THE BAIT FOR OUR TENDER LITTLE TRAP HAS ARRIVED!
SHOW THEM IN... BOTH OF THEM!
DAD! THAT MAN! IS HE THE ONE... BEHIND ALL THIS?
HE CALLS HIMSELF... THE KINGPIN!
HOW NICE OF YOU TO COME AND VISIT US
THE KINGPIN HAS BEEN MOST ANXIOUS TO GREET YOU!
HE'S EVEN ARRANGED A LITTLE PARTY-- IN YOUR HONOR!
15

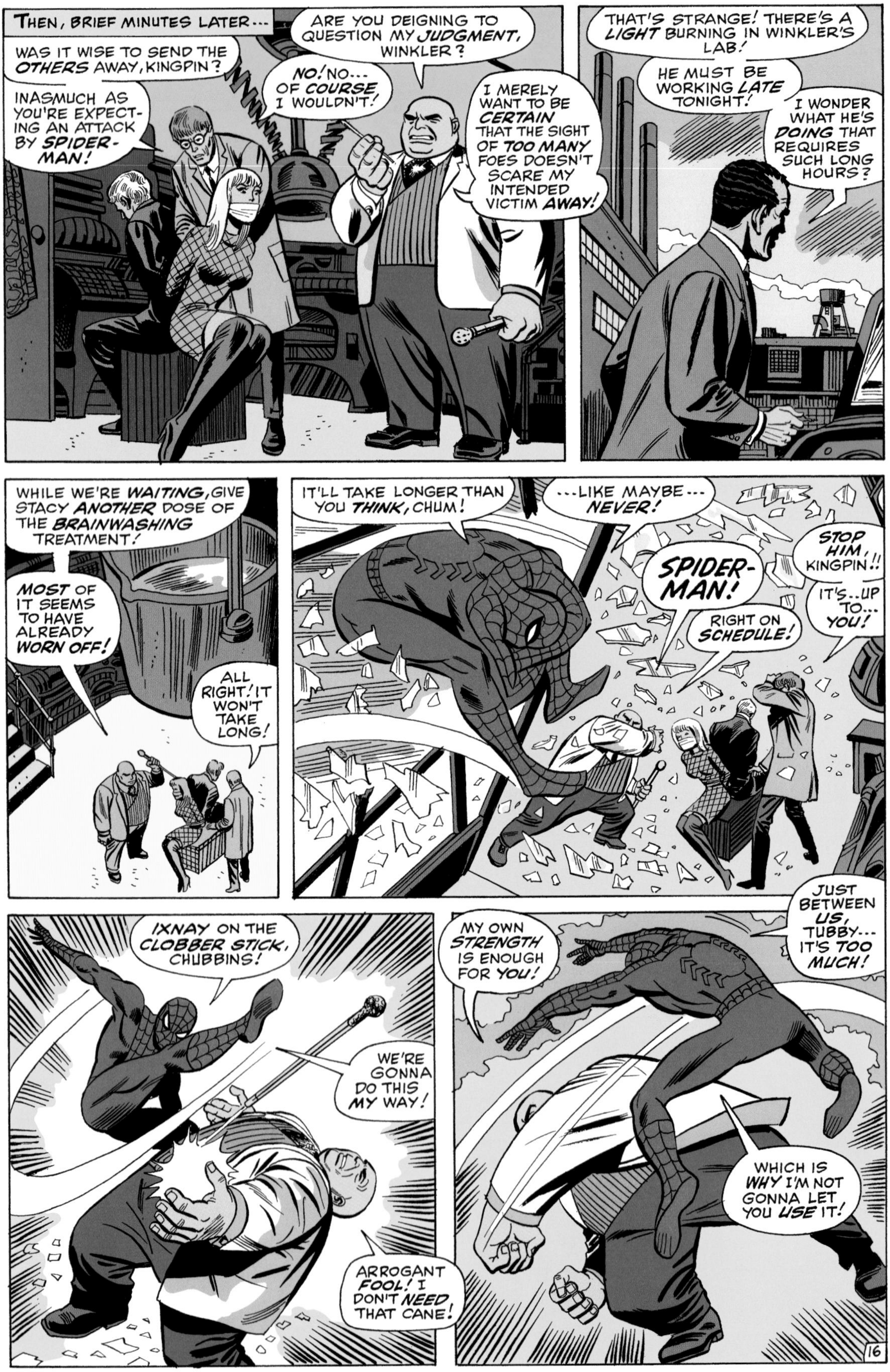
THEN, BRIEF MINUTES LATER...
WAS IT WISE TO SEND THE OTHERS AWAY, KINGPIN?
INASMUCH AS YOU'RE EXPECTING AN ATTACK BY SPIDER-MAN!
ARE YOU DEIGNING TO QUESTION MY JUDGMENT, WINKLER?
NO! NO--- OF COURSE I WOULDN'T!
I MERELY WANT TO BE CERTAIN THAT THE SIGHT OF TOO MANY FOES DOESN'T SCARE MY INTENDED VICTIM AWAY!
THAT'S STRANGE! THERE'S A LIGHT BURNING IN WINKLER'S LAB!
HE MUST BE WORKING LATE TONIGHT!
I WONDER WHAT HE'S DOING THAT REQUIRES SUCH LONG HOURS?
WHILE WE'RE WAITING, GIVE STACY ANOTHER DOSE OF THE BRAINWASHING TREATMENT!
MOST OF IT SEEMS TO HAVE ALREADY WORN OFF!
ALL RIGHT! IT WON'T TAKE LONG!
IT'LL TAKE LONGER THAN YOU THINK, CHUM!
---LIKE MAYBE--- NEVER!
SPIDER-MAN!
RIGHT ON SCHEDULE!
STOP HIM, KINGPIN!!
IT'S..UP TO... YOU!
IXNAY ON THE CLOBBER STICK, CHUBBINS!
WE'RE GONNA DO THIS MY WAY!
ARROGANT FOOL! I DON'T NEED THAT CANE!
MY OWN STRENGTH IS ENOUGH FOR YOU!
JUST BETWEEN US, TUBBY--- IT'S TOO MUCH!
WHICH IS WHY I'M NOT GONNA LET YOU USE IT!
16

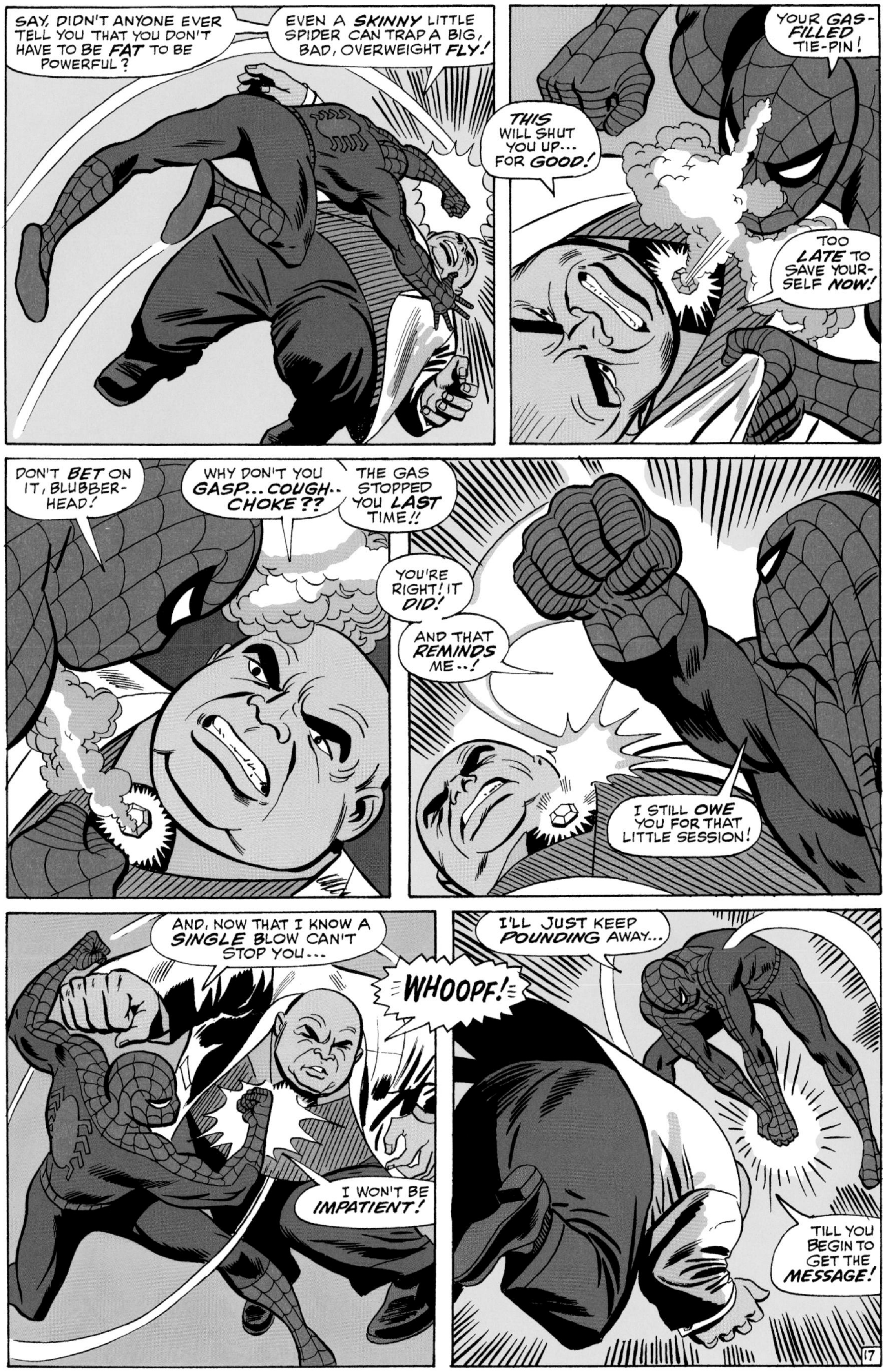

SAY, DIDN'T ANYONE EVER TELL YOU THAT YOU DON'T HAVE TO BE FAT TO BE POWERFUL?
EVEN A SKINNY LITTLE SPIDER CAN TRAP A BIG, BAD, OVERWEIGHT FLY!
YOUR GAS-FILLED TIE-PIN!
THIS WILL SHUT YOU UP... FOR GOOD!
TOO LATE TO SAVE YOURSELF NOW!
DON'T BET ON IT, BLUBBER-HEAD!
WHY DON'T YOU GASP... COUGH.. CHOKE??
THE GAS STOPPED YOU LAST TIME!!
YOU'RE RIGHT! IT DID!
AND THAT REMINDS ME..!
I STILL OWE YOU FOR THAT LITTLE SESSION!
AND, NOW THAT I KNOW A SINGLE BLOW CAN'T STOP YOU...
WHOOPF!
I WON'T BE IMPATIENT!
I'LL JUST KEEP POUNDING AWAY...
TILL YOU BEGIN TO GET THE MESSAGE!
17

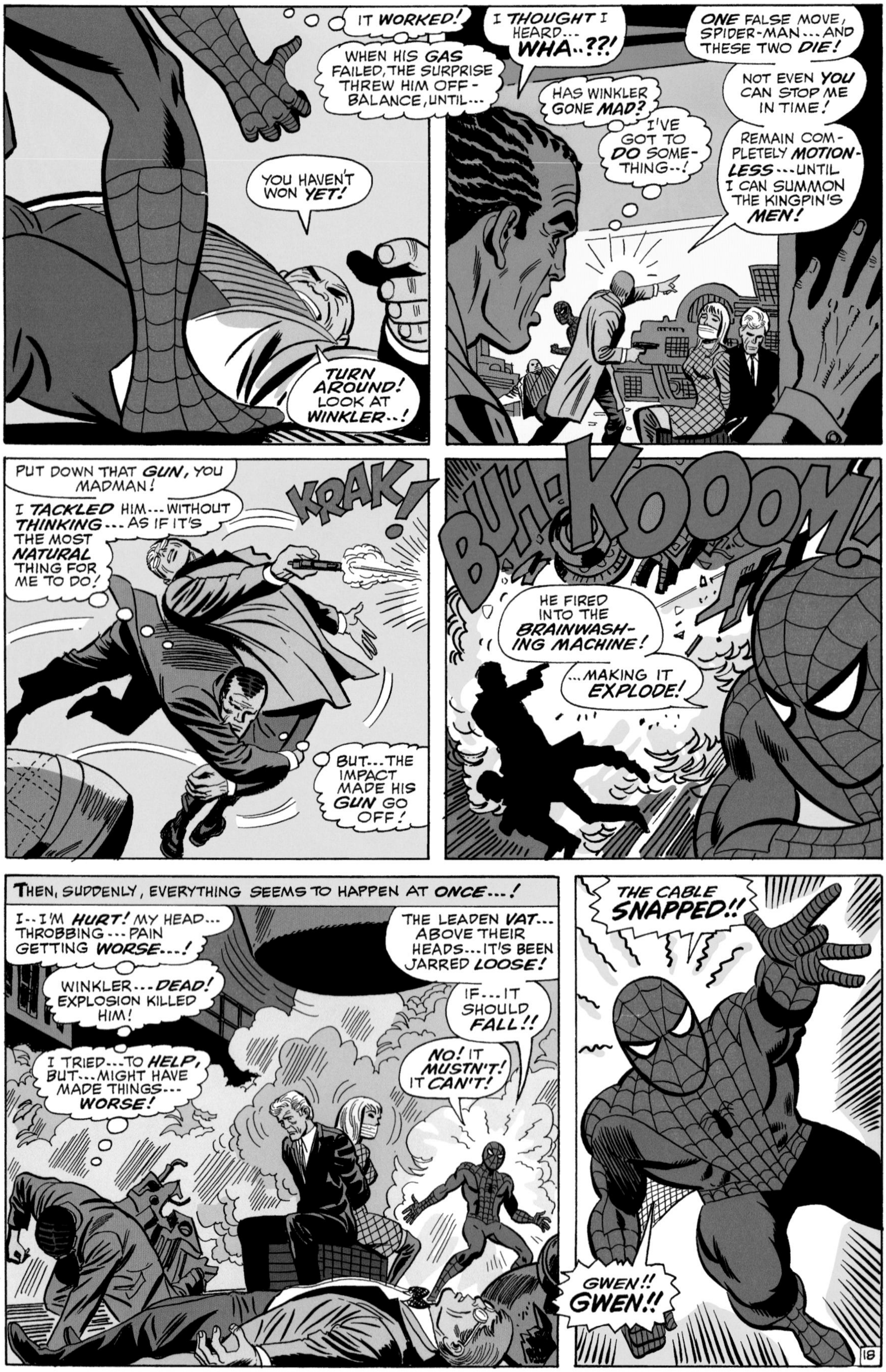
IT WORKED!
WHEN HIS GAS FAILED, THE SURPRISE THREW HIM OFF-BALANCE, UNTIL...
YOU HAVEN'T WON YET!
TURN AROUND! LOOK AT WINKLER..!
I THOUGHT I HEARD... WHA..??!
HAS WINKLER GONE MAD?
I'VE GOT TO DO SOMETHING..!
ONE FALSE MOVE, SPIDER-MAN... AND THESE TWO DIE!
NOT EVEN YOU CAN STOP ME IN TIME!
REMAIN COMPLETELY MOTIONLESS... UNTIL I CAN SUMMON THE KINGPIN'S MEN!
PUT DOWN THAT GUN, YOU MADMAN!
I TACKLED HIM... WITHOUT THINKING... AS IF IT'S THE MOST NATURAL THING FOR ME TO DO!
KRAK!
BUT... THE IMPACT MADE HIS GUN GO OFF!
BUH-KOOOM!
HE FIRED INTO THE BRAINWASHING MACHINE!
...MAKING IT EXPLODE!
THEN, SUDDENLY, EVERYTHING SEEMS TO HAPPEN AT ONCE...!
I.. I'M HURT! MY HEAD... THROBBING... PAIN GETTING WORSE...!
WINKLER... DEAD! EXPLOSION KILLED HIM!
I TRIED... TO HELP, BUT... MIGHT HAVE MADE THINGS... WORSE!
THE LEADEN VAT... ABOVE THEIR HEADS... IT'S BEEN JARRED LOOSE!
IF... IT SHOULD FALL!!
NO! IT MUSTN'T! IT CAN'T!
THE CABLE SNAPPED!!
GWEN!! GWEN!!
18

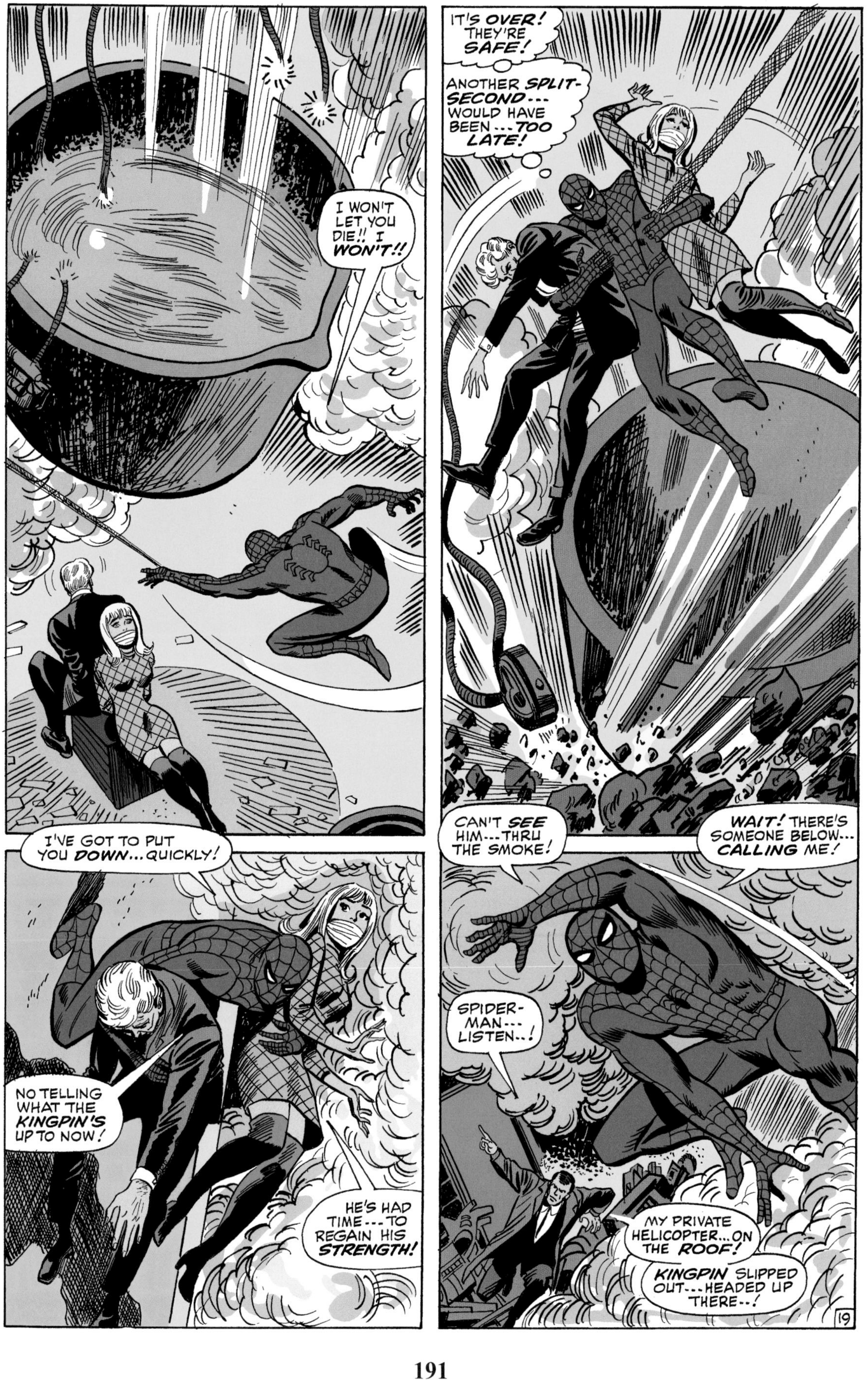
I WON'T LET YOU DIE!! I WON'T!!
IT'S OVER! THEY'RE SAFE!
ANOTHER SPLIT-SECOND--- WOULD HAVE BEEN...TOO LATE!
I'VE GOT TO PUT YOU DOWN...QUICKLY!
NO TELLING WHAT THE KINGPIN'S UP TO NOW!
HE'S HAD TIME---TO REGAIN HIS STRENGTH!
CAN'T SEE HIM---THRU THE SMOKE!
WAIT! THERE'S SOMEONE BELOW... CALLING ME!
SPIDER-MAN--- LISTEN--!
MY PRIVATE HELICOPTER...ON THE ROOF!
KINGPIN SLIPPED OUT---HEADED UP THERE--!
19

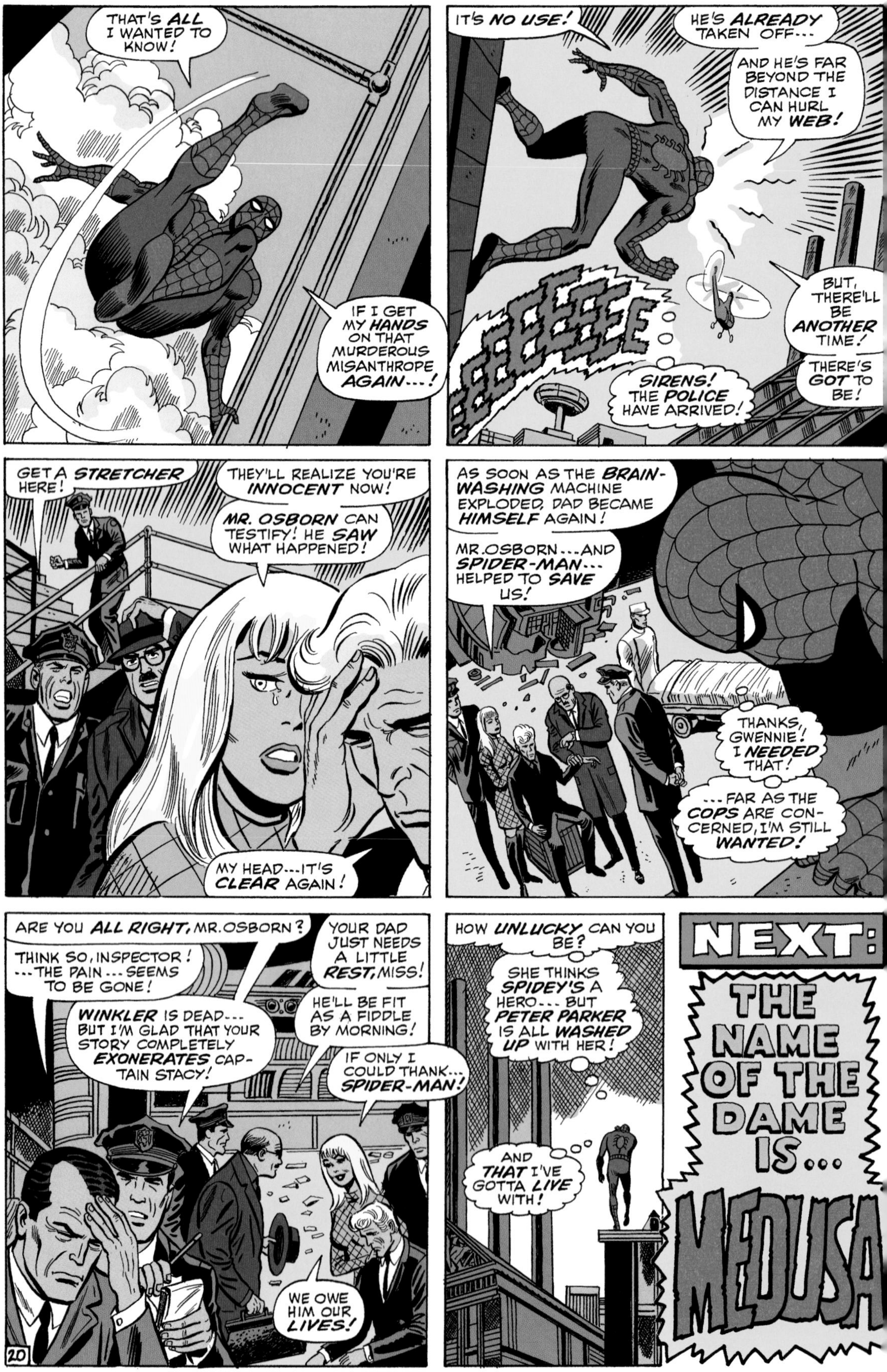
THAT'S ALL I WANTED TO KNOW!
IF I GET MY HANDS ON THAT MURDEROUS MISANTHROPE AGAIN...!
IT'S NO USE!
HE'S ALREADY TAKEN OFF---
AND HE'S FAR BEYOND THE DISTANCE I CAN HURL MY WEB!
EEEEEEEE
SIRENS! THE POLICE HAVE ARRIVED!
BUT, THERE'LL BE ANOTHER TIME!
THERE'S GOT TO BE!
GET A STRETCHER HERE!
THEY'LL REALIZE YOU'RE INNOCENT NOW!
MR. OSBORN CAN TESTIFY! HE SAW WHAT HAPPENED!
MY HEAD---IT'S CLEAR AGAIN!
AS SOON AS THE BRAIN-WASHING MACHINE EXPLODED, DAD BECAME HIMSELF AGAIN!
MR.OSBORN---AND SPIDER-MAN--- HELPED TO SAVE US!
THANKS, GWENNIE! I NEEDED THAT!
---FAR AS THE COPS ARE CON-CERNED, I'M STILL WANTED!
ARE YOU ALL RIGHT, MR.OSBORN?
THINK SO, INSPECTOR! ---THE PAIN --- SEEMS TO BE GONE!
WINKLER IS DEAD--- BUT I'M GLAD THAT YOUR STORY COMPLETELY EXONERATES CAP-TAIN STACY!
YOUR DAD JUST NEEDS A LITTLE REST, MISS!
HE'LL BE FIT AS A FIDDLE BY MORNING!
IF ONLY I COULD THANK... SPIDER-MAN!
WE OWE HIM OUR LIVES!
20
HOW UNLUCKY CAN YOU BE?
SHE THINKS SPIDEY'S A HERO--- BUT PETER PARKER IS ALL WASHED UP WITH HER!
AND THAT I'VE GOTTA LIVE WITH!
NEXT:
THE NAME OF THE DAME IS...
MEDUSA

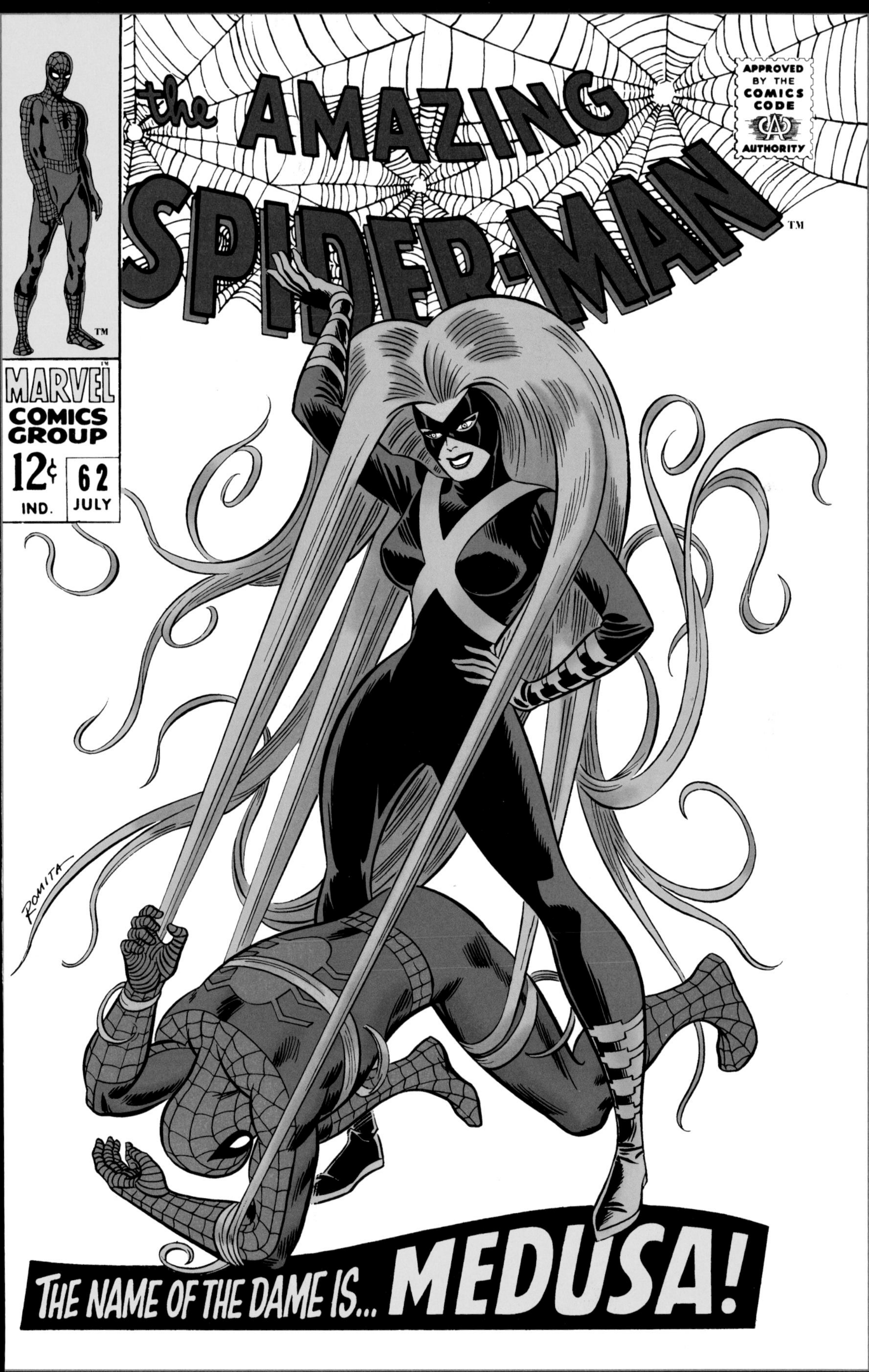
the AMAZING SPIDER-MAN™
APPROVED BY THE COMICS CODE AUTHORITY
MARVEL COMICS GROUP
12¢ IND.
62 JULY
ROMITA
THE NAME OF THE DAME IS... MEDUSA!

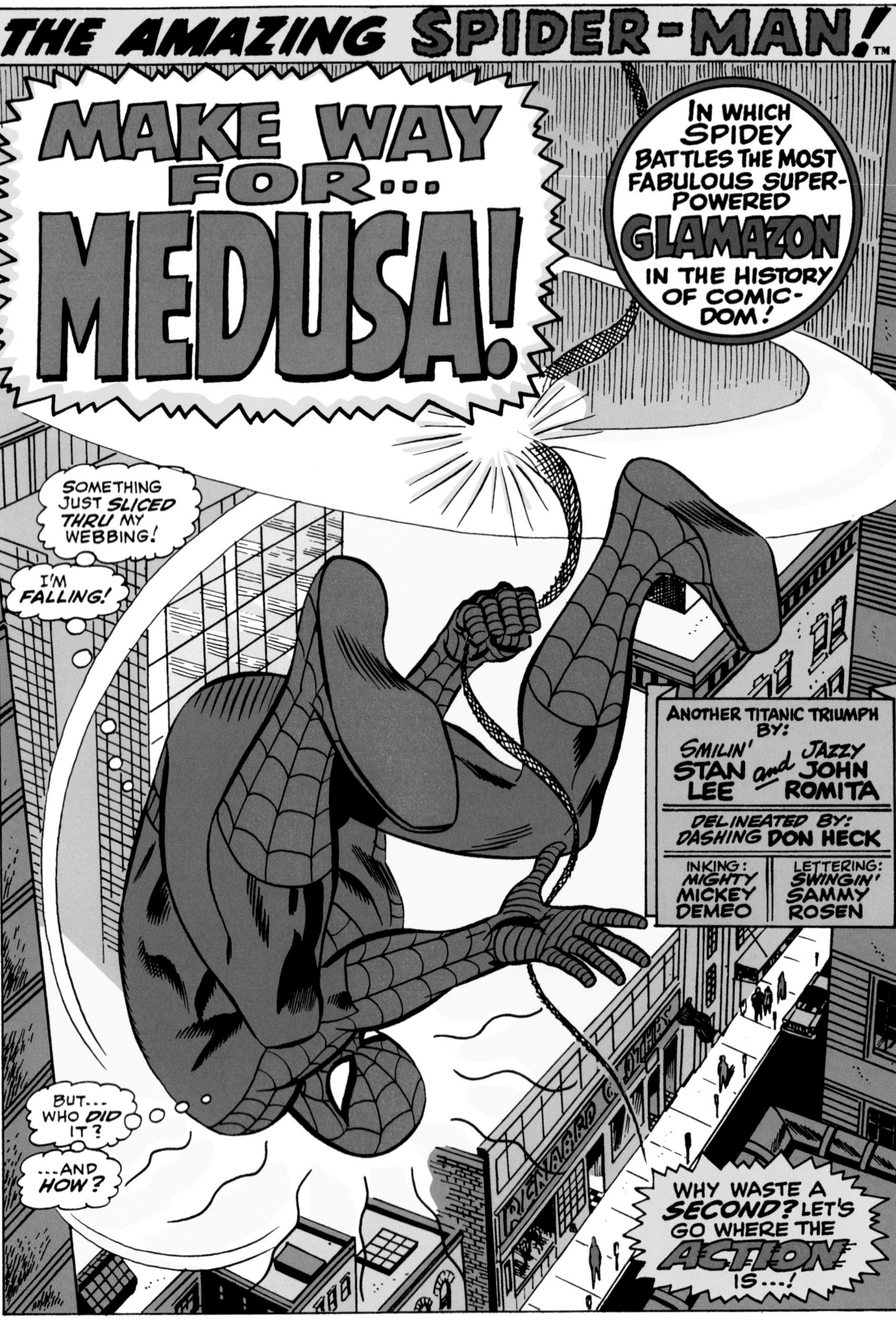
THE AMAZING SPIDER-MAN!™
MAKE WAY FOR... MEDUSA!
IN WHICH SPIDEY BATTLES THE MOST FABULOUS SUPER-POWERED GLAMAZON IN THE HISTORY OF COMIC-DOM!
SOMETHING JUST SLICED THRU MY WEBBING!
I'M FALLING!
BUT... WHO DID IT?
...AND HOW?
ANOTHER TITANIC TRIUMPH BY: SMILIN' STAN LEE and JAZZY JOHN ROMITA
DELINEATED BY: DASHING DON HECK
INKING: MIGHTY MICKEY DEMEO
LETTERING: SWINGIN' SAMMY ROSEN
WHY WASTE A SECOND? LET'S GO WHERE THE ACTION IS...!

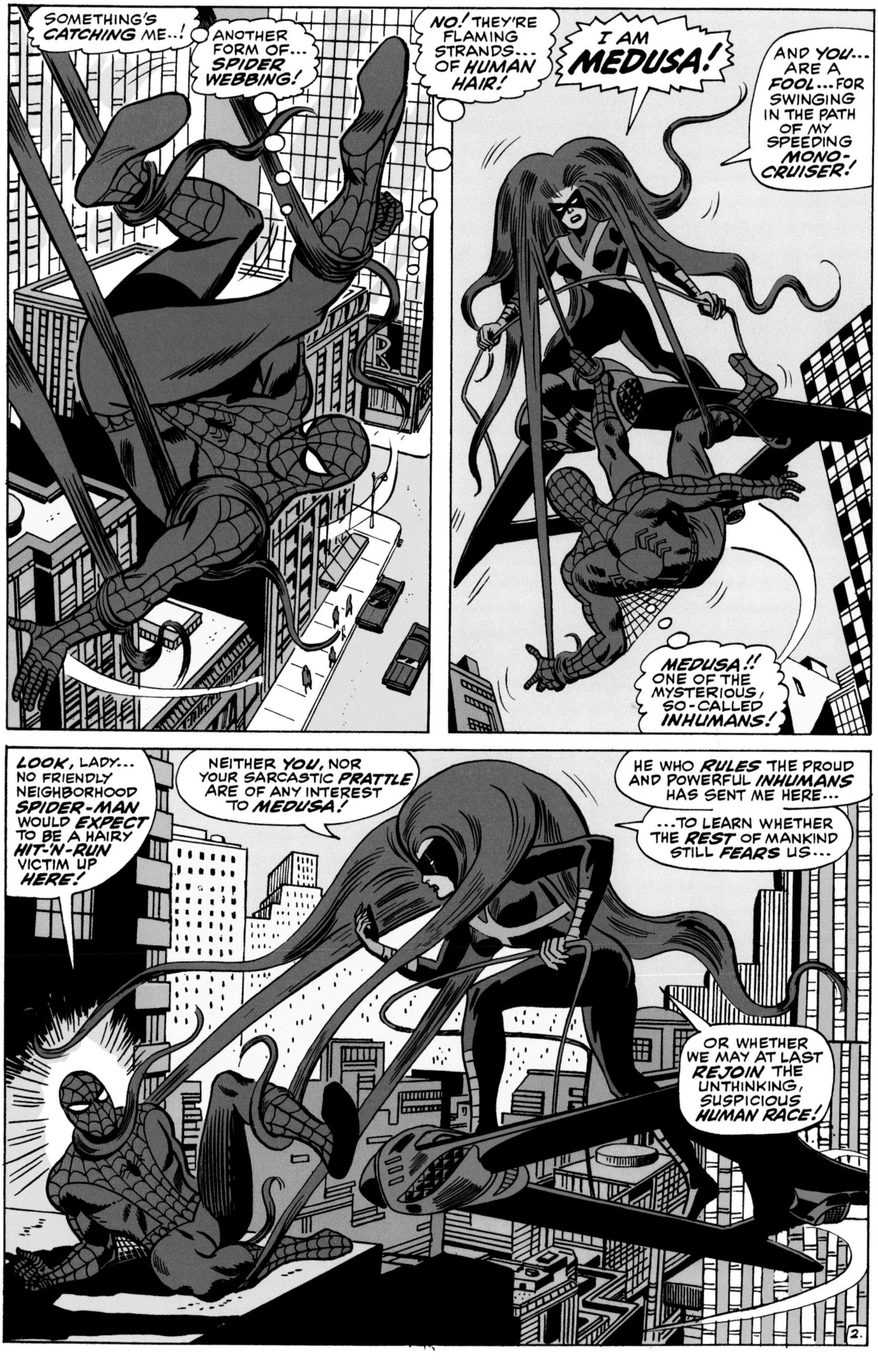
SOMETHING'S CATCHING ME..!
ANOTHER FORM OF... SPIDER WEBBING!
NO! THEY'RE FLAMING STRANDS... OF HUMAN HAIR!
I AM MEDUSA!
AND YOU... ARE A FOOL... FOR SWINGING IN THE PATH OF MY SPEEDING MONO-CRUISER!
MEDUSA!! ONE OF THE MYSTERIOUS, SO-CALLED INHUMANS!
LOOK, LADY... NO FRIENDLY NEIGHBORHOOD SPIDER-MAN WOULD EXPECT TO BE A HAIRY HIT-'N-RUN VICTIM UP HERE!
NEITHER YOU, NOR YOUR SARCASTIC PRATTLE ARE OF ANY INTEREST TO MEDUSA!
HE WHO RULES THE PROUD AND POWERFUL INHUMANS HAS SENT ME HERE...
...TO LEARN WHETHER THE REST OF MANKIND STILL FEARS US...
OR WHETHER WE MAY AT LAST REJOIN THE UNTHINKING, SUSPICIOUS HUMAN RACE!
2.

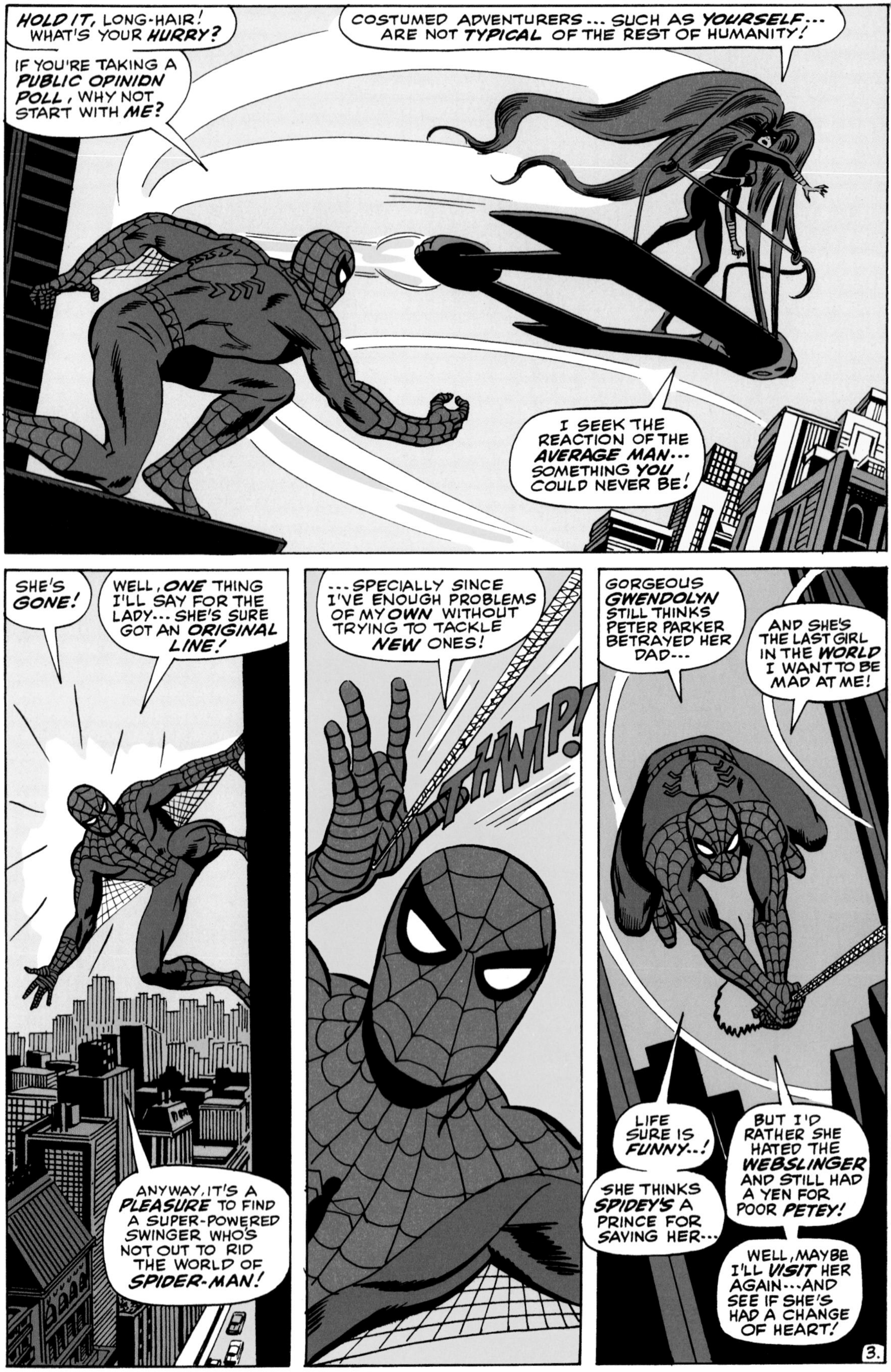
HOLD IT, LONG-HAIR! WHAT'S YOUR HURRY?
IF YOU'RE TAKING A PUBLIC OPINION POLL, WHY NOT START WITH ME?
COSTUMED ADVENTURERS... SUCH AS YOURSELF... ARE NOT TYPICAL OF THE REST OF HUMANITY!
I SEEK THE REACTION OF THE AVERAGE MAN... SOMETHING YOU COULD NEVER BE!
SHE'S GONE!
WELL, ONE THING I'LL SAY FOR THE LADY... SHE'S SURE GOT AN ORIGINAL LINE!
ANYWAY, IT'S A PLEASURE TO FIND A SUPER-POWERED SWINGER WHO'S NOT OUT TO RID THE WORLD OF SPIDER-MAN!
...SPECIALLY SINCE I'VE ENOUGH PROBLEMS OF MY OWN WITHOUT TRYING TO TACKLE NEW ONES!
THWIP!
GORGEOUS GWENDOLYN STILL THINKS PETER PARKER BETRAYED HER DAD...
AND SHE'S THE LAST GIRL IN THE WORLD I WANT TO BE MAD AT ME!
LIFE SURE IS FUNNY..!
SHE THINKS SPIDEY'S A PRINCE FOR SAVING HER...
BUT I'D RATHER SHE HATED THE WEBSLINGER AND STILL HAD A YEN FOR POOR PETEY!
WELL, MAYBE I'LL VISIT HER AGAIN... AND SEE IF SHE'S HAD A CHANGE OF HEART!
3.

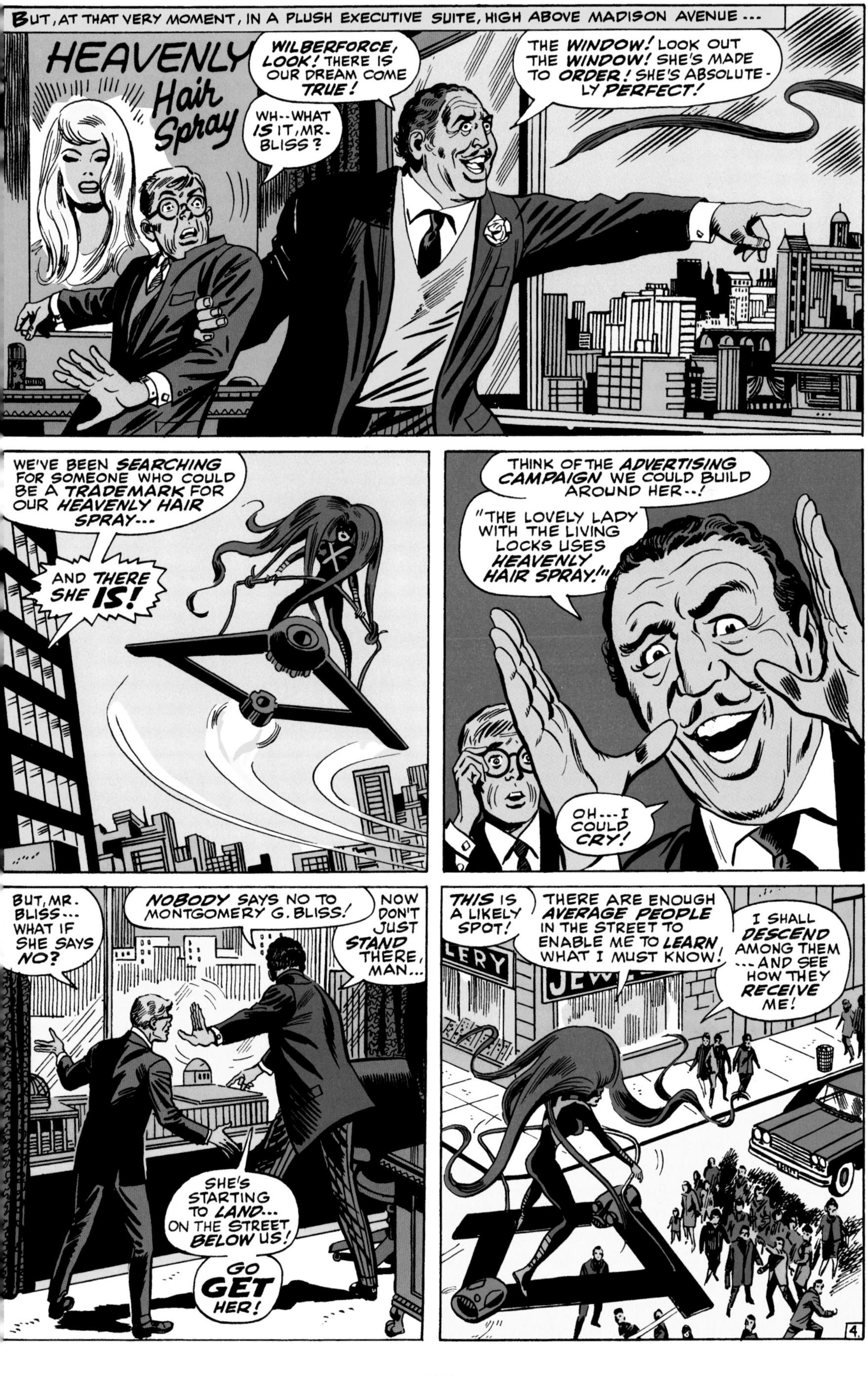
BUT, AT THAT VERY MOMENT, IN A PLUSH EXECUTIVE SUITE, HIGH ABOVE MADISON AVENUE...
HEAVENLY Hair Spray
WILBERFORCE, LOOK! THERE IS OUR DREAM COME TRUE!
WH--WHAT IS IT, MR. BLISS?
THE WINDOW! LOOK OUT THE WINDOW! SHE'S MADE TO ORDER! SHE'S ABSOLUTELY PERFECT!
WE'VE BEEN SEARCHING FOR SOMEONE WHO COULD BE A TRADEMARK FOR OUR HEAVENLY HAIR SPRAY...
AND THERE SHE IS!
THINK OF THE ADVERTISING CAMPAIGN WE COULD BUILD AROUND HER--!
"THE LOVELY LADY WITH THE LIVING LOCKS USES HEAVENLY HAIR SPRAY!"
OH...I COULD CRY!
BUT, MR. BLISS... WHAT IF SHE SAYS NO?
NOBODY SAYS NO TO MONTGOMERY G. BLISS!
NOW DON'T JUST STAND THERE, MAN...
SHE'S STARTING TO LAND... ON THE STREET BELOW US!
GO GET HER!
THIS IS A LIKELY SPOT!
THERE ARE ENOUGH AVERAGE PEOPLE IN THE STREET TO ENABLE ME TO LEARN WHAT I MUST KNOW!
I SHALL DESCEND AMONG THEM ...AND SEE HOW THEY RECEIVE ME!
4.

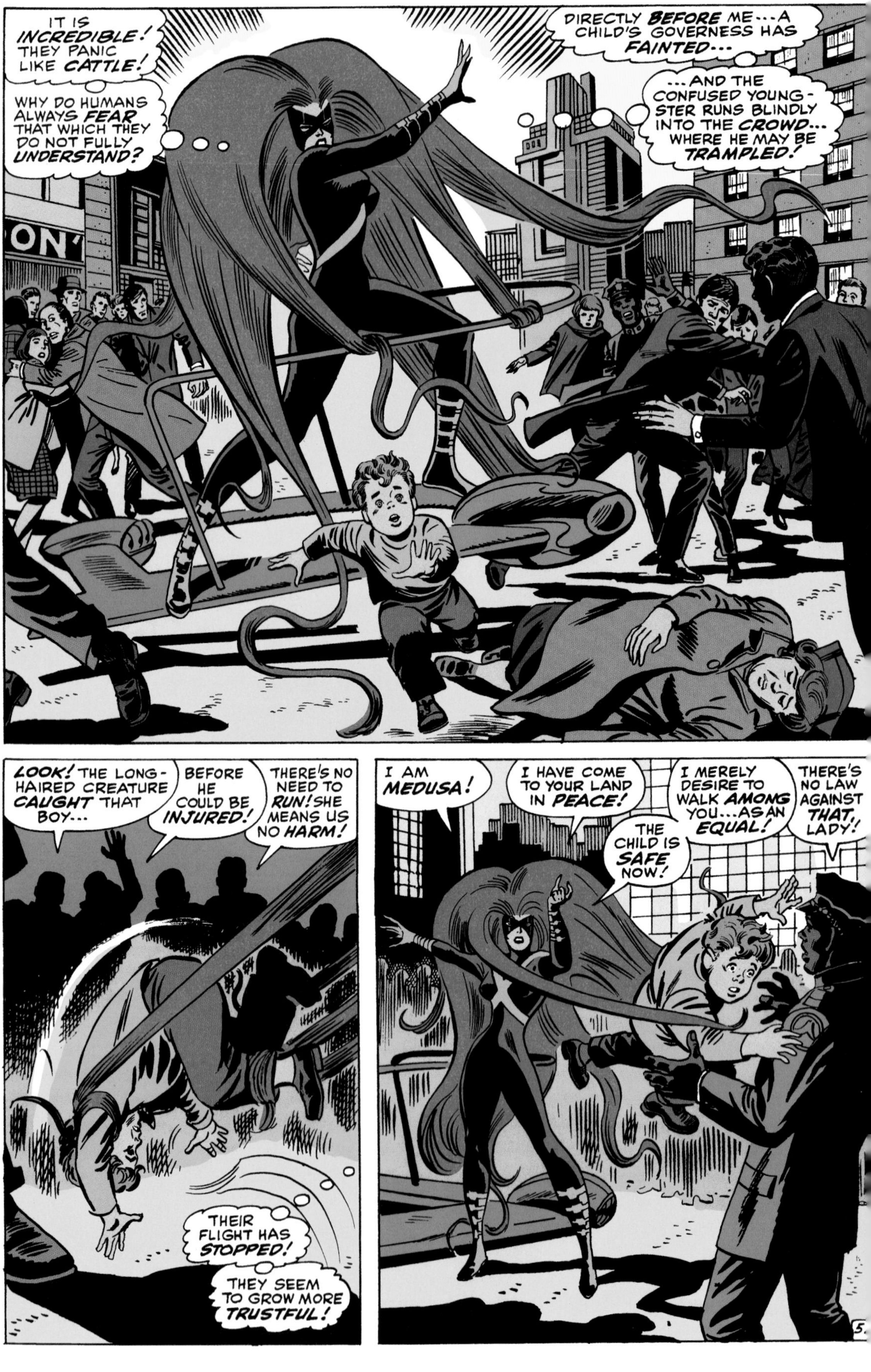
IT IS INCREDIBLE! THEY PANIC LIKE CATTLE!
WHY DO HUMANS ALWAYS FEAR THAT WHICH THEY DO NOT FULLY UNDERSTAND?
DIRECTLY BEFORE ME... A CHILD'S GOVERNESS HAS FAINTED...
...AND THE CONFUSED YOUNGSTER RUNS BLINDLY INTO THE CROWD... WHERE HE MAY BE TRAMPLED!
LOOK! THE LONG-HAIRED CREATURE CAUGHT THAT BOY...
BEFORE HE COULD BE INJURED!
THERE'S NO NEED TO RUN! SHE MEANS US NO HARM!
THEIR FLIGHT HAS STOPPED!
THEY SEEM TO GROW MORE TRUSTFUL!
I AM MEDUSA!
I HAVE COME TO YOUR LAND IN PEACE!
I MERELY DESIRE TO WALK AMONG YOU...AS AN EQUAL!
THE CHILD IS SAFE NOW!
THERE'S NO LAW AGAINST THAT, LADY!
5.

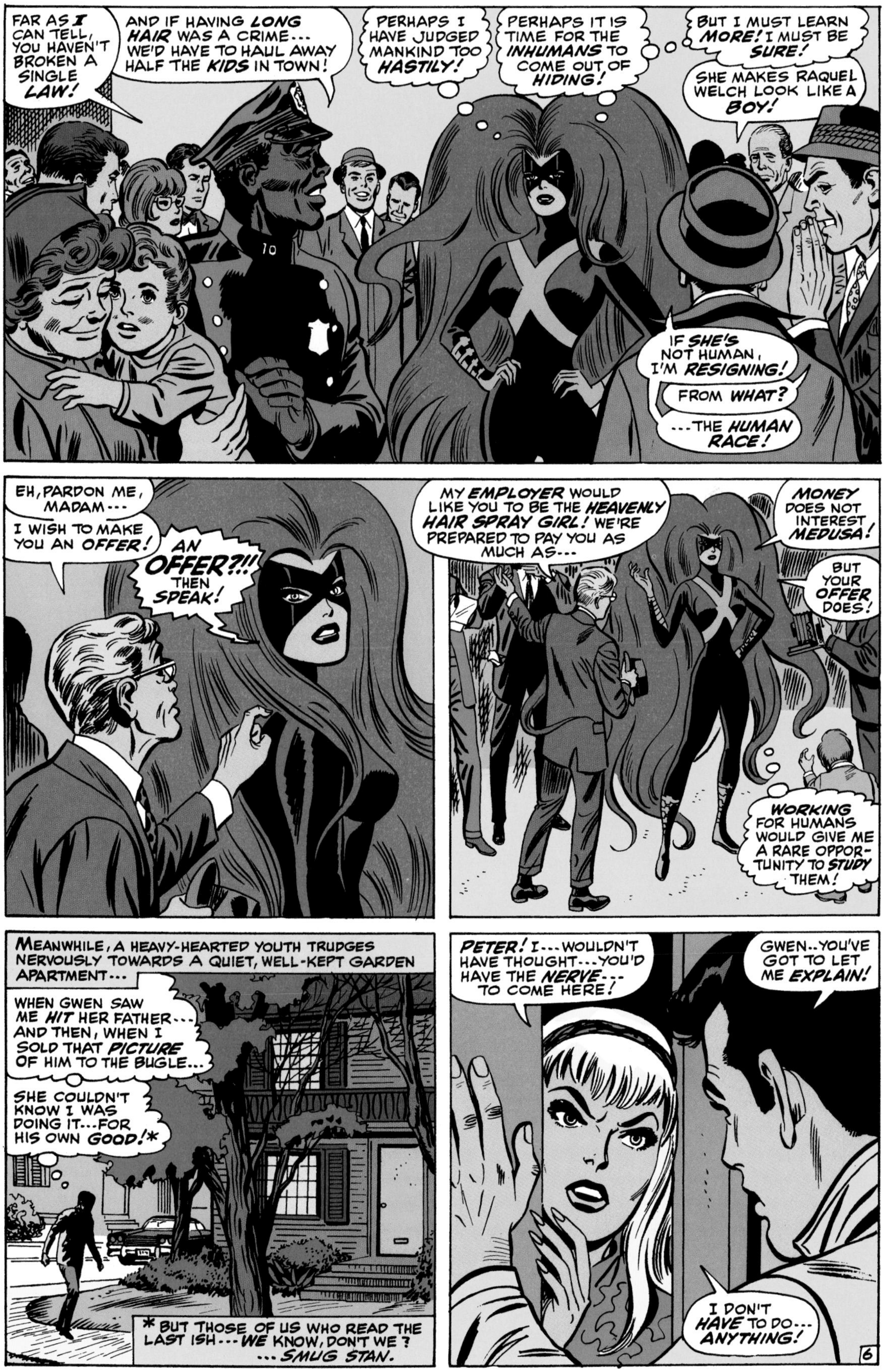
FAR AS I CAN TELL, YOU HAVEN'T BROKEN A SINGLE LAW!
AND IF HAVING LONG HAIR WAS A CRIME... WE'D HAVE TO HAUL AWAY HALF THE KIDS IN TOWN!
PERHAPS I HAVE JUDGED MANKIND TOO HASTILY!
PERHAPS IT IS TIME FOR THE INHUMANS TO COME OUT OF HIDING!
BUT I MUST LEARN MORE! I MUST BE SURE!
SHE MAKES RAQUEL WELCH LOOK LIKE A BOY!
IF SHE'S NOT HUMAN, I'M RESIGNING!
FROM WHAT?
...THE HUMAN RACE!
EH, PARDON ME, MADAM...
I WISH TO MAKE YOU AN OFFER!
AN OFFER?!! THEN SPEAK!
MY EMPLOYER WOULD LIKE YOU TO BE THE HEAVENLY HAIR SPRAY GIRL! WE'RE PREPARED TO PAY YOU AS MUCH AS...
MONEY DOES NOT INTEREST MEDUSA!
BUT YOUR OFFER DOES!
WORKING FOR HUMANS WOULD GIVE ME A RARE OPPORTUNITY TO STUDY THEM!
MEANWHILE, A HEAVY-HEARTED YOUTH TRUDGES NERVOUSLY TOWARDS A QUIET, WELL-KEPT GARDEN APARTMENT...
WHEN GWEN SAW ME HIT HER FATHER... AND THEN, WHEN I SOLD THAT PICTURE OF HIM TO THE BUGLE...
SHE COULDN'T KNOW I WAS DOING IT... FOR HIS OWN GOOD!*
* BUT THOSE OF US WHO READ THE LAST ISH... WE KNOW, DON'T WE? ...SMUG STAN.
PETER! I... WOULDN'T HAVE THOUGHT... YOU'D HAVE THE NERVE... TO COME HERE!
GWEN.. YOU'VE GOT TO LET ME EXPLAIN!
I DON'T HAVE TO DO... ANYTHING!
6

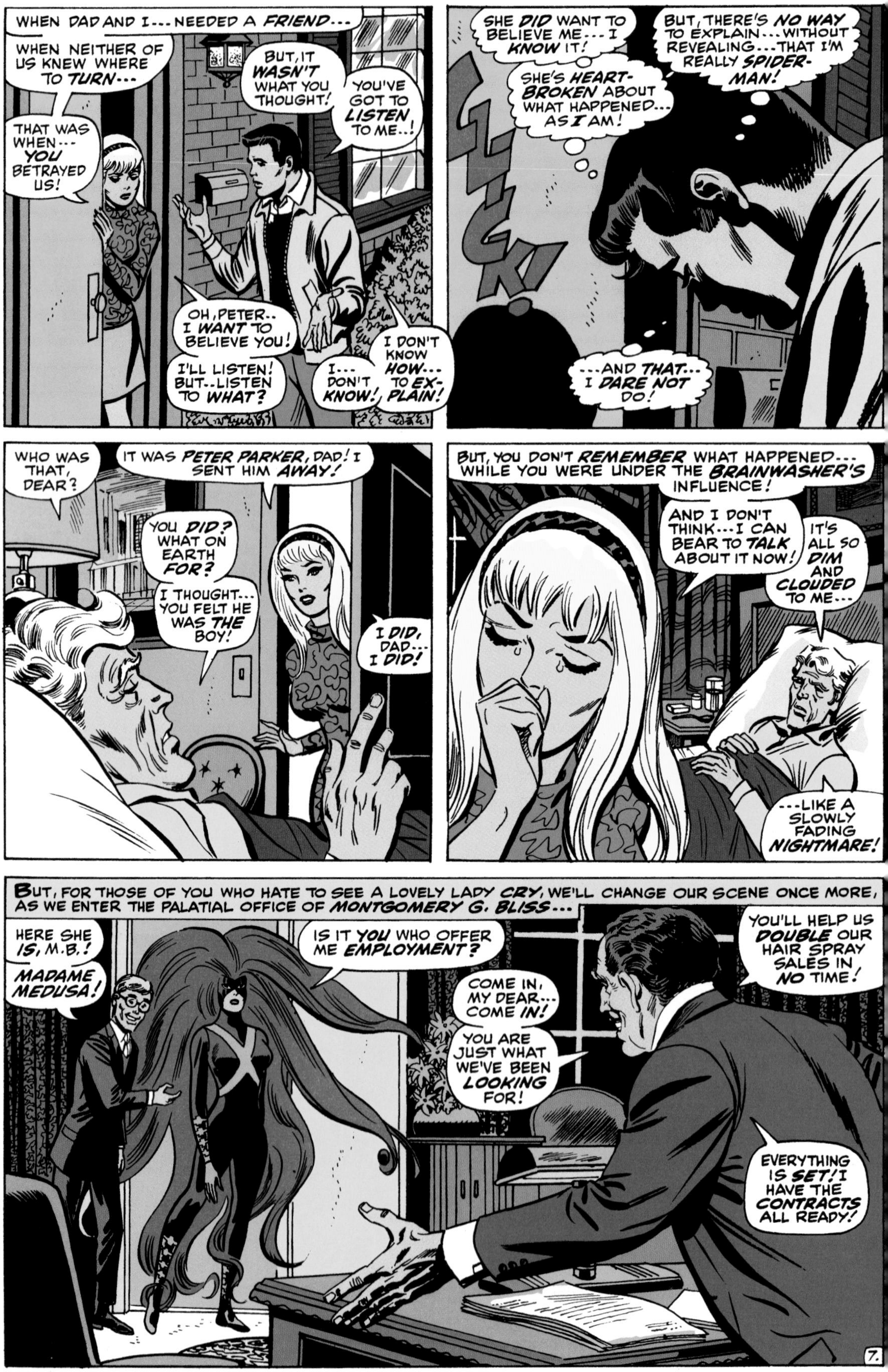
WHEN DAD AND I--- NEEDED A FRIEND---
WHEN NEITHER OF US KNEW WHERE TO TURN---
THAT WAS WHEN--- YOU BETRAYED US!
BUT, IT WASN'T WHAT YOU THOUGHT!
YOU'VE GOT TO LISTEN TO ME--!
OH, PETER-- I WANT TO BELIEVE YOU!
I'LL LISTEN! BUT--LISTEN TO WHAT?
I--- DON'T KNOW!
I DON'T KNOW HOW--- TO EX-PLAIN!
SHE DID WANT TO BELIEVE ME--- I KNOW IT!
SHE'S HEART-BROKEN ABOUT WHAT HAPPENED--- AS I AM!
BUT, THERE'S NO WAY TO EXPLAIN--- WITHOUT REVEALING--- THAT I'M REALLY SPIDER-MAN!
SLICK!
---AND THAT--- I DARE NOT DO!
WHO WAS THAT, DEAR?
IT WAS PETER PARKER, DAD! I SENT HIM AWAY!
YOU DID? WHAT ON EARTH FOR?
I THOUGHT--- YOU FELT HE WAS THE BOY!
I DID, DAD--- I DID!
BUT, YOU DON'T REMEMBER WHAT HAPPENED--- WHILE YOU WERE UNDER THE BRAINWASHER'S INFLUENCE!
AND I DON'T THINK--- I CAN BEAR TO TALK ABOUT IT NOW!
IT'S ALL SO DIM AND CLOUDED TO ME---
---LIKE A SLOWLY FADING NIGHTMARE!
BUT, FOR THOSE OF YOU WHO HATE TO SEE A LOVELY LADY CRY, WE'LL CHANGE OUR SCENE ONCE MORE, AS WE ENTER THE PALATIAL OFFICE OF MONTGOMERY G. BLISS---
HERE SHE IS, M.B.! MADAME MEDUSA!
IS IT YOU WHO OFFER ME EMPLOYMENT?
COME IN, MY DEAR--- COME IN!
YOU ARE JUST WHAT WE'VE BEEN LOOKING FOR!
YOU'LL HELP US DOUBLE OUR HAIR SPRAY SALES IN NO TIME!
EVERYTHING IS SET! I HAVE THE CONTRACTS ALL READY!
7.

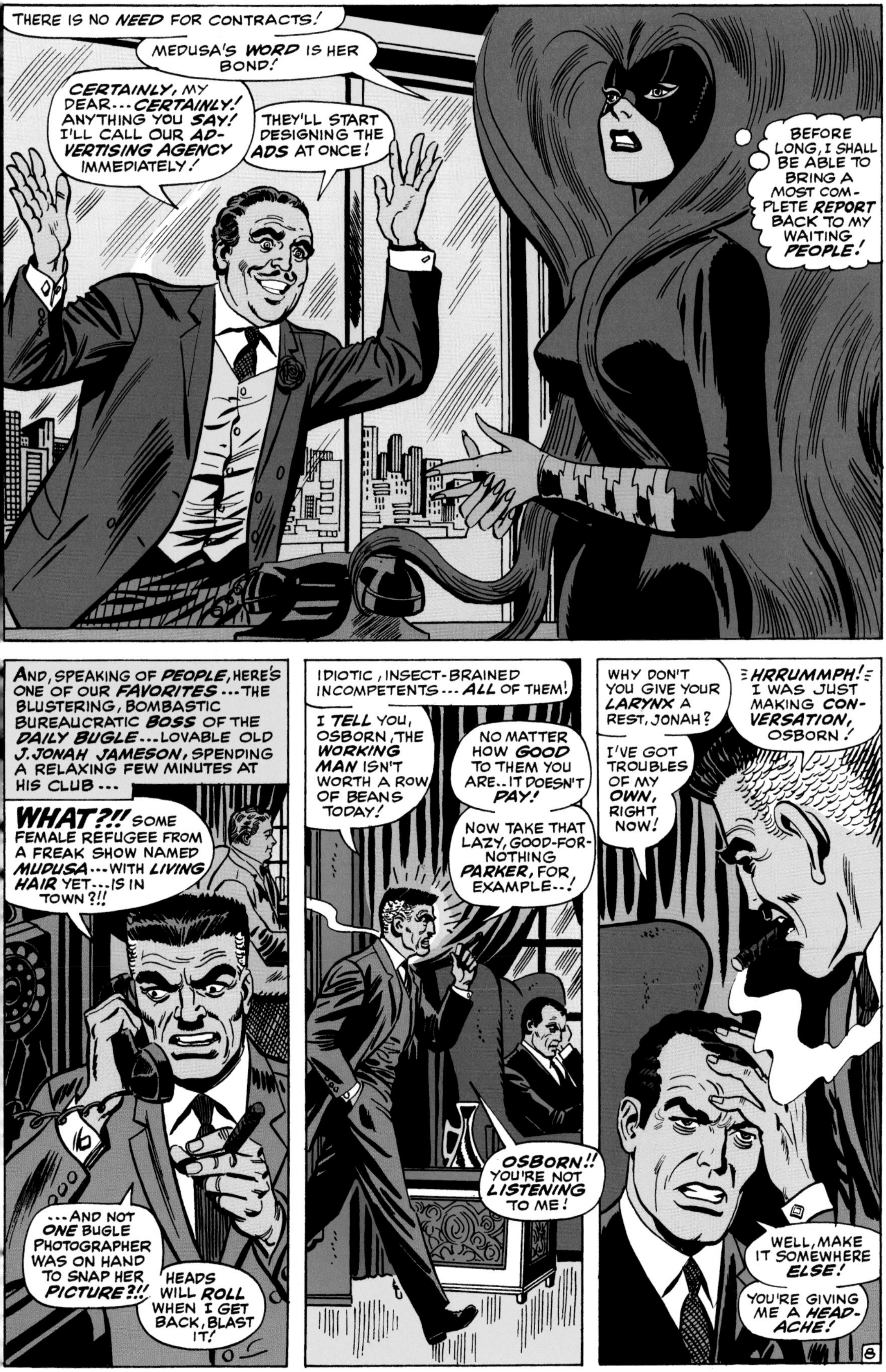

THERE IS NO NEED FOR CONTRACTS!
MEDUSA'S WORD IS HER BOND!
CERTAINLY, MY DEAR... CERTAINLY! ANYTHING YOU SAY! I'LL CALL OUR ADVERTISING AGENCY IMMEDIATELY!
THEY'LL START DESIGNING THE ADS AT ONCE!
BEFORE LONG, I SHALL BE ABLE TO BRING A MOST COMPLETE REPORT BACK TO MY WAITING PEOPLE!
AND, SPEAKING OF PEOPLE, HERE'S ONE OF OUR FAVORITES... THE BLUSTERING, BOMBASTIC BUREAUCRATIC BOSS OF THE DAILY BUGLE... LOVABLE OLD J. JONAH JAMESON, SPENDING A RELAXING FEW MINUTES AT HIS CLUB...
WHAT?!! SOME FEMALE REFUGEE FROM A FREAK SHOW NAMED MUDUSA... WITH LIVING HAIR YET... IS IN TOWN?!!
...AND NOT ONE BUGLE PHOTOGRAPHER WAS ON HAND TO SNAP HER PICTURE?!!
HEADS WILL ROLL WHEN I GET BACK, BLAST IT!
IDIOTIC, INSECT-BRAINED INCOMPETENTS... ALL OF THEM!
I TELL YOU, OSBORN, THE WORKING MAN ISN'T WORTH A ROW OF BEANS TODAY!
NO MATTER HOW GOOD TO THEM YOU ARE.. IT DOESN'T PAY!
NOW TAKE THAT LAZY, GOOD-FOR-NOTHING PARKER, FOR EXAMPLE--!
OSBORN!! YOU'RE NOT LISTENING TO ME!
WHY DON'T YOU GIVE YOUR LARYNX A REST, JONAH?
I'VE GOT TROUBLES OF MY OWN, RIGHT NOW!
HRRUMMPH! I WAS JUST MAKING CONVERSATION, OSBORN!
WELL, MAKE IT SOMEWHERE ELSE!
YOU'RE GIVING ME A HEADACHE!
8

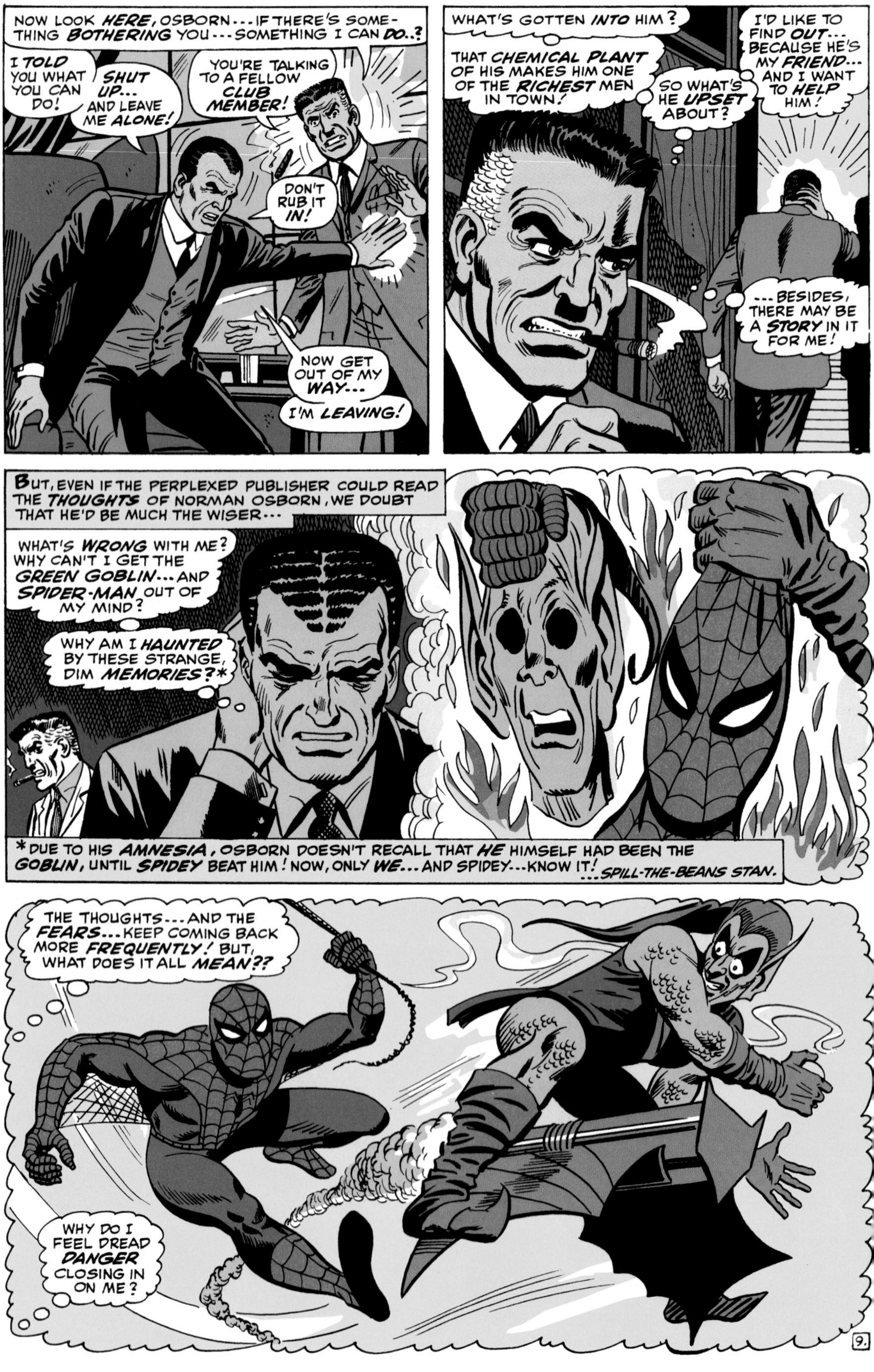
NOW LOOK HERE, OSBORN--- IF THERE'S SOME-THING BOTHERING YOU--- SOMETHING I CAN DO..?
I TOLD YOU WHAT YOU CAN DO!
SHUT UP... AND LEAVE ME ALONE!
YOU'RE TALKING TO A FELLOW CLUB MEMBER!
DON'T RUB IT IN!
NOW GET OUT OF MY WAY...
I'M LEAVING!
WHAT'S GOTTEN INTO HIM?
THAT CHEMICAL PLANT OF HIS MAKES HIM ONE OF THE RICHEST MEN IN TOWN!
SO WHAT'S HE UPSET ABOUT?
I'D LIKE TO FIND OUT... BECAUSE HE'S MY FRIEND... AND I WANT TO HELP HIM!
...BESIDES, THERE MAY BE A STORY IN IT FOR ME!
BUT, EVEN IF THE PERPLEXED PUBLISHER COULD READ THE THOUGHTS OF NORMAN OSBORN, WE DOUBT THAT HE'D BE MUCH THE WISER---
WHAT'S WRONG WITH ME? WHY CAN'T I GET THE GREEN GOBLIN... AND SPIDER-MAN OUT OF MY MIND?
WHY AM I HAUNTED BY THESE STRANGE, DIM MEMORIES?*
*DUE TO HIS AMNESIA, OSBORN DOESN'T RECALL THAT HE HIMSELF HAD BEEN THE GOBLIN, UNTIL SPIDEY BEAT HIM! NOW, ONLY WE... AND SPIDEY... KNOW IT! ...SPILL-THE-BEANS STAN.
THE THOUGHTS... AND THE FEARS... KEEP COMING BACK MORE FREQUENTLY! BUT, WHAT DOES IT ALL MEAN??
WHY DO I FEEL DREAD DANGER CLOSING IN ON ME?
9.

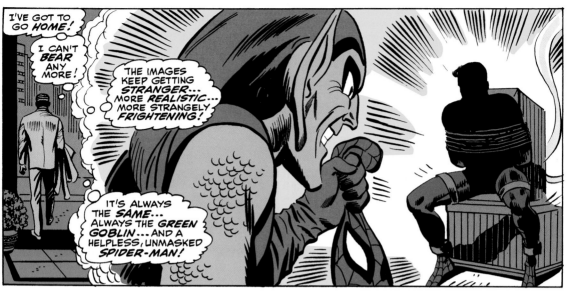

I'VE GOT TO GO *HOME!*

I CAN'T *BEAR* ANY *MORE!*

THE IMAGES KEEP GETTING *STRANGER...* MORE *REALISTIC...* MORE *STRANGELY FRIGHTENING!*

IT'S ALWAYS THE *SAME...* ALWAYS THE *GREEN GOBLIN...* AND A *HELPLESS, UNMASKED SPIDER-MAN!*

BUT I CAN NEVER REALLY SEE HIS *FACE...*

ALTHOUGH IT SEEMS TO GET *CLEARER* EVERY TIME!

I *MUST BE...* GOING *MAD!*

BUT, IF I *AM...* WHAT ABOUT MY *SON...* HARRY?

THERE'S NO ONE *ELSE...* TO LOOK *AFTER* HIM!

AND, IN CASE *YOU'RE* WORRIED ABOUT PETER'S ROOMMATE, TOO... LET'S LOOK IN ON HAPLESS *HARRY OSBORN...*

IT ISN'T *FAIR!* I STUDY AND STUDY... AND JUST GET *BY!*

WHILE EVERYTHING SEEMS TO COME SO *EASY* TO PETE!

HE WAS JUST BORN *LUCKY!*

HI, HARR...

I *DIDN'T THINK* YOU'D STILL BE *UP!*

HAVING TROUBLE WITH YOUR *COURSES?*

NO... I'M JUST TRYING TO LEARN TO LIVE WITHOUT *SLEEP!*

SORRY, PETE... DIDN'T MEAN TO *SNAP* AT YOU LIKE THAT!

HOW'S IT *GOING?* HAVE A GOOD TIME WITH *GWEN* TONIGHT?

GWEN? THAT LITTLE LADY CAN'T SEE ME FOR *DUST!*

ARE YOU *KIDDING?* SHE WAS *BATTY* ABOUT YOU! WHAT *HAPPENED?*

AW, IT'S A *LONG* STORY..!

NO SENSE BORING THE *TWO* OF US WITH MY *HANG-UPS!*

ANYWAY, THERE'S *NOTHING ELSE* LEFT TO HAPPEN!

BUT ALAS, PETEY DOESN'T SUSPECT HOW WOEFULLY *WRONG* HE IS! FOR, AT A MIDTOWN *PHOTO STUDIO...*

LOOK OUT! SHE'S A *TIGRESS!*

NO! SHE'S *PERFECT!*

THAT SAVAGE *EXCITEMENT* IS JUST WHAT WE *WANT!*

SHE'LL BE A *SENSATION!*

10.

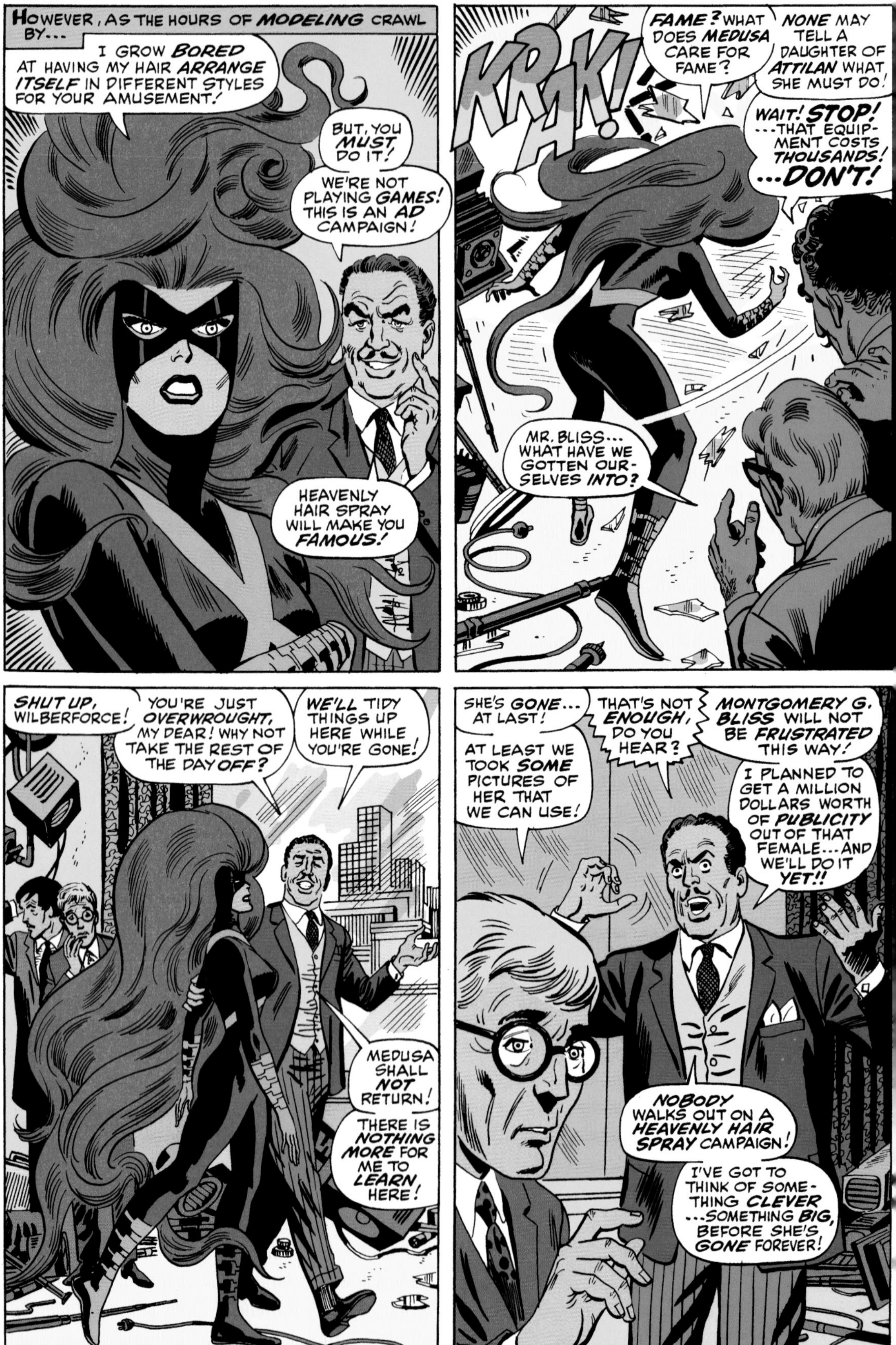
HOWEVER, AS THE HOURS OF MODELING CRAWL BY...
I GROW BORED AT HAVING MY HAIR ARRANGE ITSELF IN DIFFERENT STYLES FOR YOUR AMUSEMENT!
BUT, YOU MUST DO IT!
WE'RE NOT PLAYING GAMES! THIS IS AN AD CAMPAIGN!
HEAVENLY HAIR SPRAY WILL MAKE YOU FAMOUS!
KRAKK!
FAME? WHAT DOES MEDUSA CARE FOR FAME?
NONE MAY TELL A DAUGHTER OF ATTILAN WHAT SHE MUST DO!
WAIT! STOP! ---THAT EQUIPMENT COSTS THOUSANDS! ...DON'T!
MR. BLISS... WHAT HAVE WE GOTTEN OURSELVES INTO?
SHUT UP, WILBERFORCE!
YOU'RE JUST OVERWROUGHT, MY DEAR! WHY NOT TAKE THE REST OF THE DAY OFF?
WE'LL TIDY THINGS UP HERE WHILE YOU'RE GONE!
MEDUSA SHALL NOT RETURN!
THERE IS NOTHING MORE FOR ME TO LEARN, HERE!
SHE'S GONE... AT LAST!
AT LEAST WE TOOK SOME PICTURES OF HER THAT WE CAN USE!
THAT'S NOT ENOUGH, DO YOU HEAR?
MONTGOMERY G. BLISS WILL NOT BE FRUSTRATED THIS WAY!
I PLANNED TO GET A MILLION DOLLARS WORTH OF PUBLICITY OUT OF THAT FEMALE... AND WE'LL DO IT YET!!
NOBODY WALKS OUT ON A HEAVENLY HAIR SPRAY CAMPAIGN!
I'VE GOT TO THINK OF SOMETHING CLEVER ...SOMETHING BIG, BEFORE SHE'S GONE FOREVER!
11.

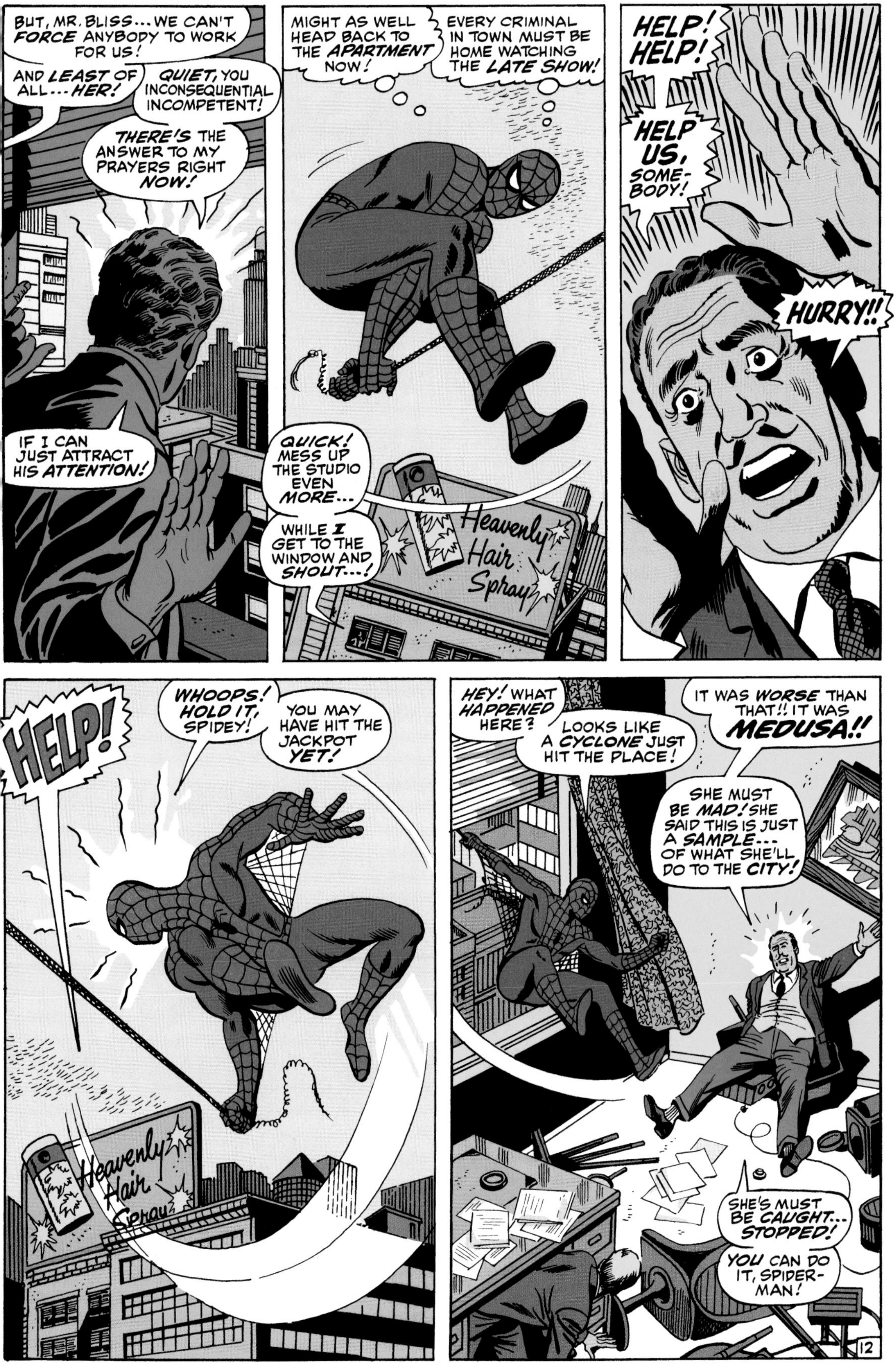

BUT, MR. BLISS... WE CAN'T FORCE ANYBODY TO WORK FOR US!
AND LEAST OF ALL... HER!
QUIET, YOU INCONSEQUENTIAL INCOMPETENT!
THERE'S THE ANSWER TO MY PRAYERS RIGHT NOW!
IF I CAN JUST ATTRACT HIS ATTENTION!
MIGHT AS WELL HEAD BACK TO THE APARTMENT NOW!
EVERY CRIMINAL IN TOWN MUST BE HOME WATCHING THE LATE SHOW!
QUICK! MESS UP THE STUDIO EVEN MORE...
WHILE I GET TO THE WINDOW AND SHOUT...!
Heavenly Hair Spray
HELP! HELP!
HELP US, SOMEBODY!
HURRY!!
HELP!
WHOOPS! HOLD IT, SPIDEY!
YOU MAY HAVE HIT THE JACKPOT YET!
Heavenly Hair Spray
HEY! WHAT HAPPENED HERE?
LOOKS LIKE A CYCLONE JUST HIT THE PLACE!
IT WAS WORSE THAN THAT!! IT WAS MEDUSA!!
SHE MUST BE MAD! SHE SAID THIS IS JUST A SAMPLE... OF WHAT SHE'LL DO TO THE CITY!
SHE'S MUST BE CAUGHT... STOPPED!
YOU CAN DO IT, SPIDER-MAN!
12

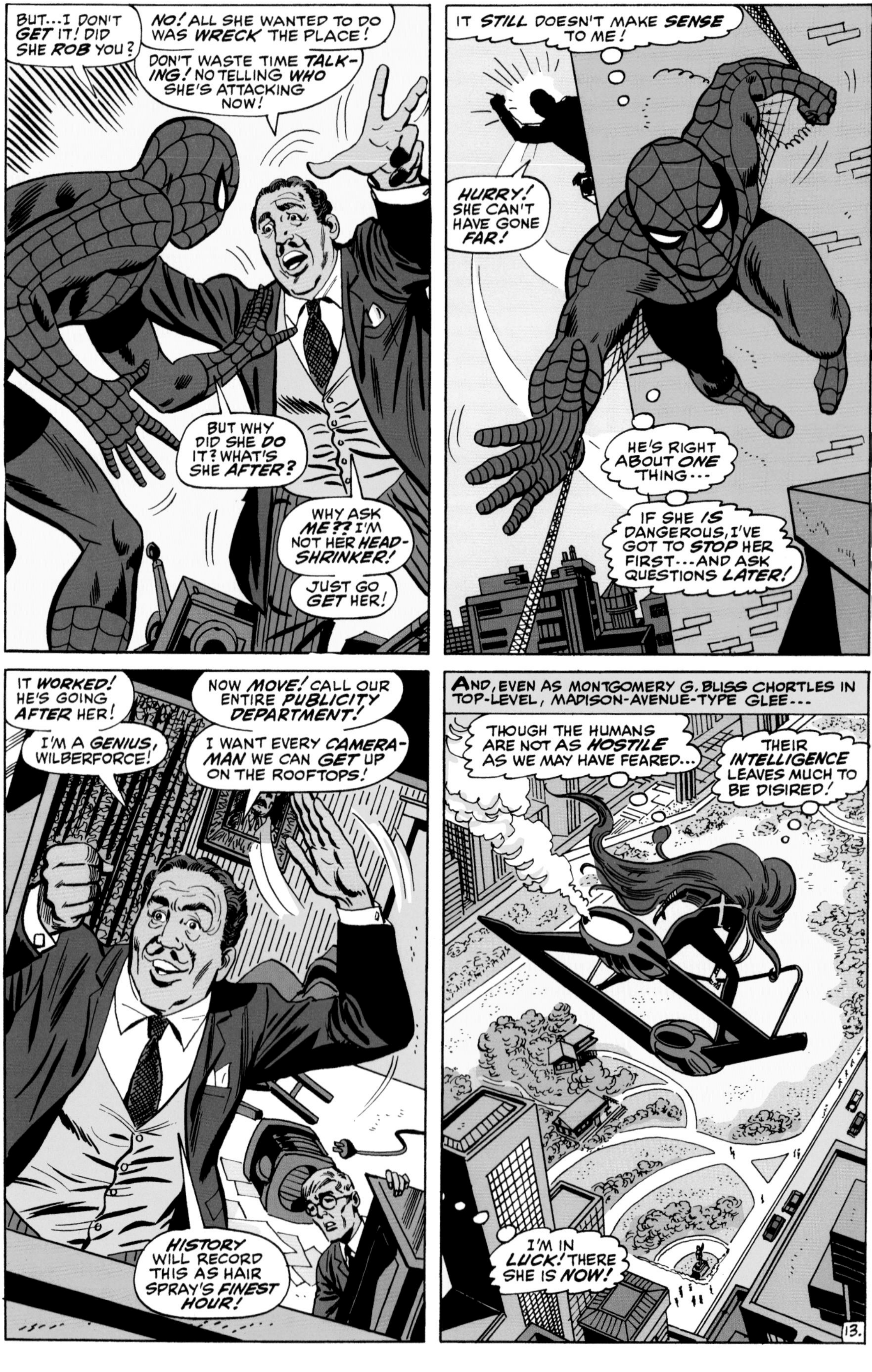
BUT...I DON'T GET IT! DID SHE ROB YOU?
NO! ALL SHE WANTED TO DO WAS WRECK THE PLACE!
DON'T WASTE TIME TALKING! NO TELLING WHO SHE'S ATTACKING NOW!
BUT WHY DID SHE DO IT? WHAT'S SHE AFTER?
WHY ASK ME?? I'M NOT HER HEAD-SHRINKER!
JUST GO GET HER!
IT STILL DOESN'T MAKE SENSE TO ME!
HURRY! SHE CAN'T HAVE GONE FAR!
HE'S RIGHT ABOUT ONE THING---
IF SHE IS DANGEROUS, I'VE GOT TO STOP HER FIRST---AND ASK QUESTIONS LATER!
IT WORKED! HE'S GOING AFTER HER!
I'M A GENIUS, WILBERFORCE!
NOW MOVE! CALL OUR ENTIRE PUBLICITY DEPARTMENT!
I WANT EVERY CAMERA-MAN WE CAN GET UP ON THE ROOFTOPS!
HISTORY WILL RECORD THIS AS HAIR SPRAY'S FINEST HOUR!
AND, EVEN AS MONTGOMERY G. BLISS CHORTLES IN TOP-LEVEL, MADISON-AVENUE-TYPE GLEE---
THOUGH THE HUMANS ARE NOT AS HOSTILE AS WE MAY HAVE FEARED...
THEIR INTELLIGENCE LEAVES MUCH TO BE DISIRED!
I'M IN LUCK! THERE SHE IS NOW!
13.

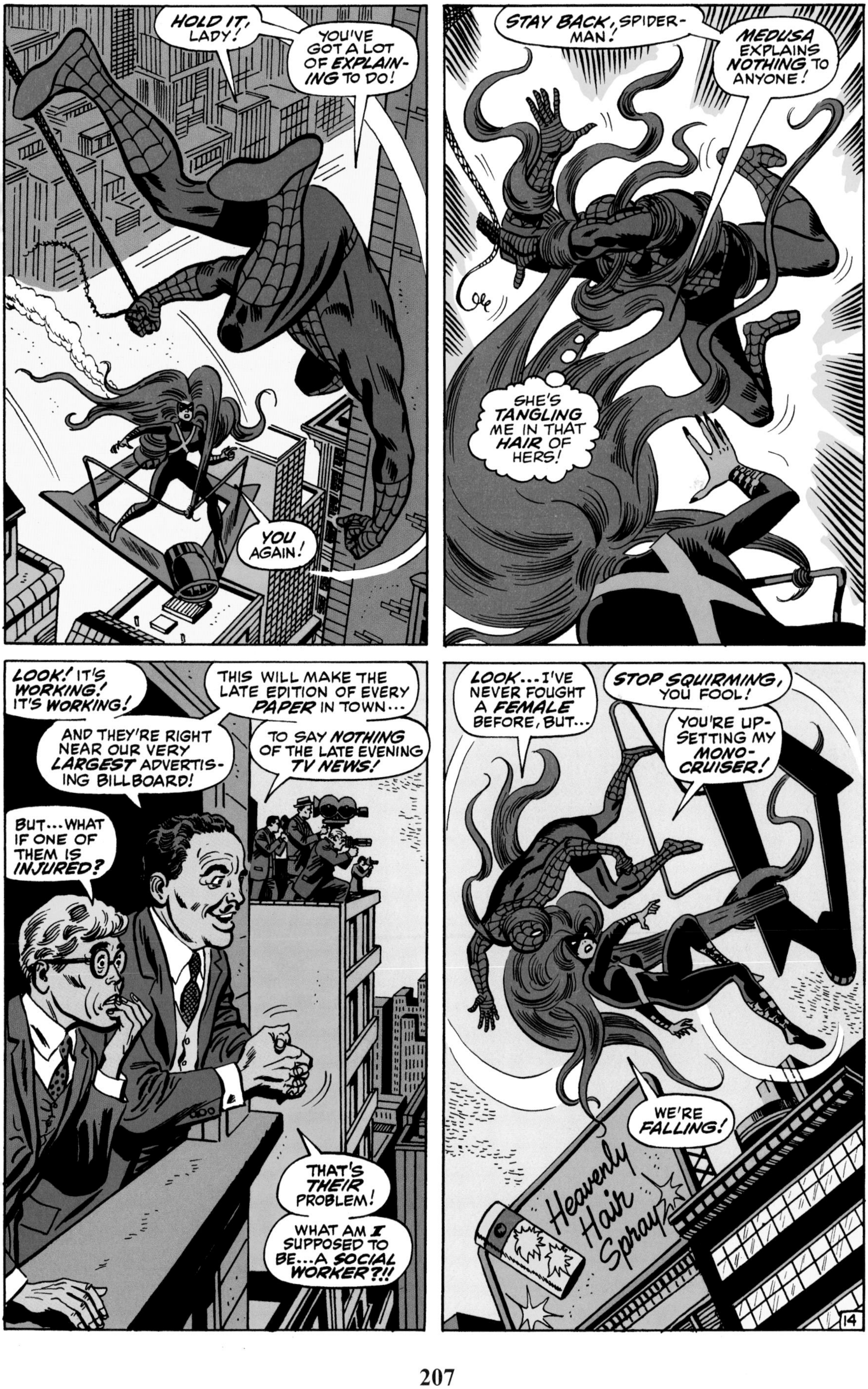
HOLD IT, LADY!
YOU'VE GOT A LOT OF EXPLAINING TO DO!
YOU AGAIN!
STAY BACK, SPIDER-MAN!
MEDUSA EXPLAINS NOTHING TO ANYONE!
SHE'S TANGLING ME IN THAT HAIR OF HERS!
LOOK! IT'S WORKING! IT'S WORKING!
THIS WILL MAKE THE LATE EDITION OF EVERY PAPER IN TOWN...
AND THEY'RE RIGHT NEAR OUR VERY LARGEST ADVERTISING BILLBOARD!
TO SAY NOTHING OF THE LATE EVENING TV NEWS!
BUT... WHAT IF ONE OF THEM IS INJURED?
THAT'S THEIR PROBLEM!
WHAT AM I SUPPOSED TO BE... A SOCIAL WORKER?!!
LOOK... I'VE NEVER FOUGHT A FEMALE BEFORE, BUT...
STOP SQUIRMING, YOU FOOL!
YOU'RE UPSETTING MY MONO-CRUISER!
WE'RE FALLING!
Heavenly Hair Spray
14

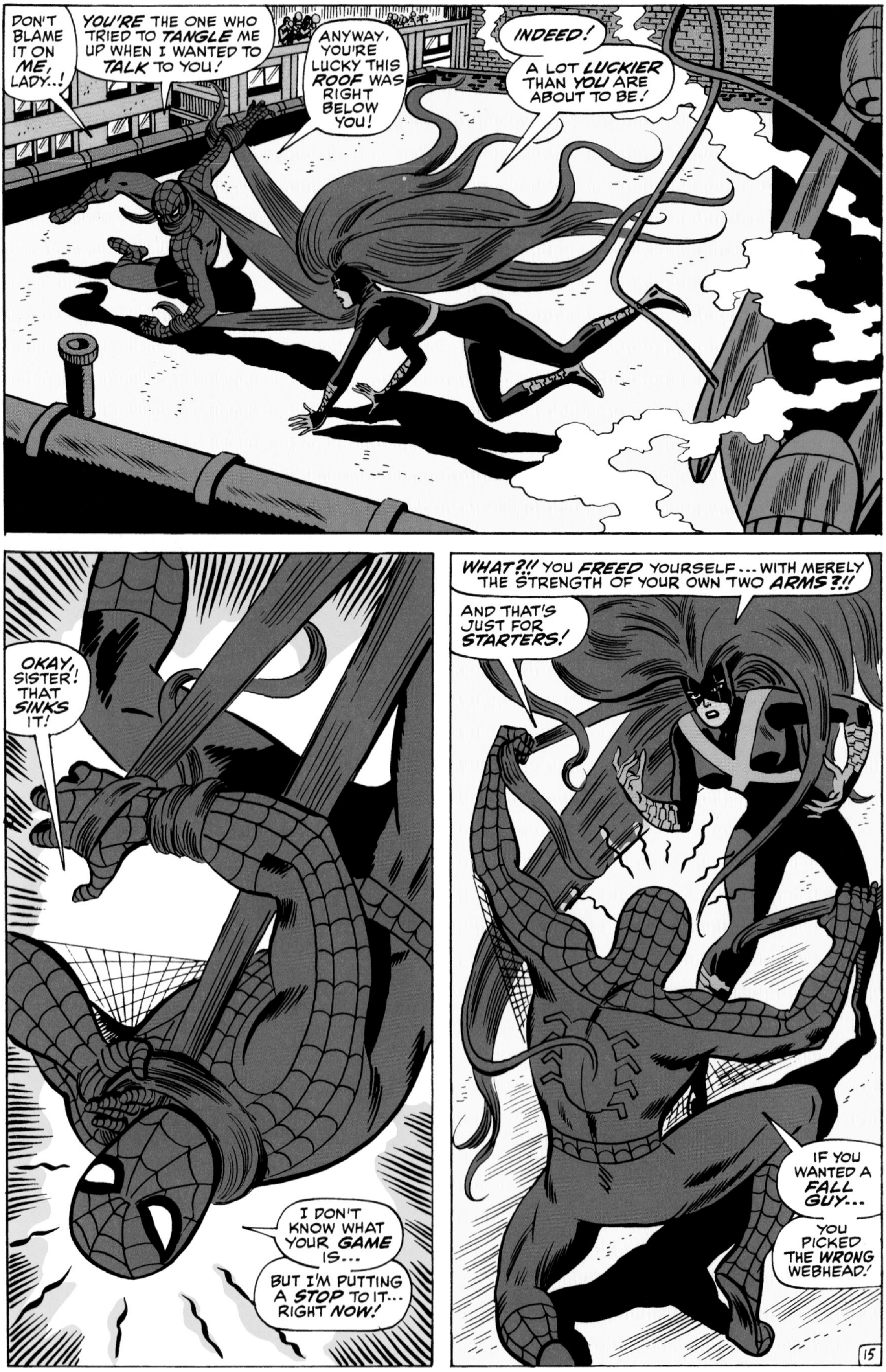
DON'T BLAME IT ON ME, LADY..!
YOU'RE THE ONE WHO TRIED TO TANGLE ME UP WHEN I WANTED TO TALK TO YOU!
ANYWAY, YOU'RE LUCKY THIS ROOF WAS RIGHT BELOW YOU!
INDEED!
A LOT LUCKIER THAN YOU ARE ABOUT TO BE!
OKAY, SISTER! THAT SINKS IT!
I DON'T KNOW WHAT YOUR GAME IS...
BUT I'M PUTTING A STOP TO IT... RIGHT NOW!
WHAT?!! YOU FREED YOURSELF... WITH MERELY THE STRENGTH OF YOUR OWN TWO ARMS?!!
AND THAT'S JUST FOR STARTERS!
IF YOU WANTED A FALL GUY...
YOU PICKED THE WRONG WEBHEAD!
15

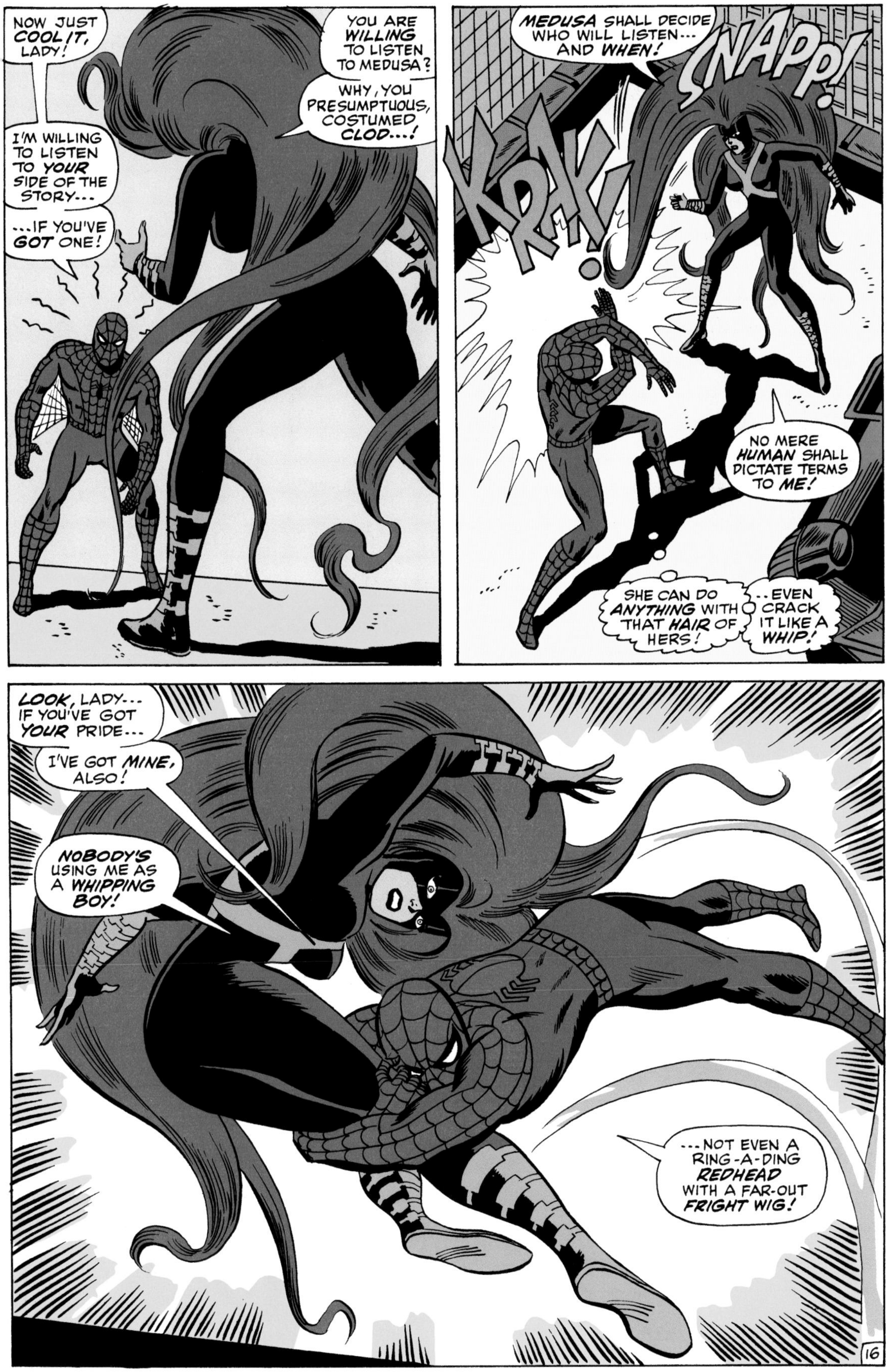
NOW JUST COOL IT, LADY!
I'M WILLING TO LISTEN TO YOUR SIDE OF THE STORY...
...IF YOU'VE GOT ONE!
YOU ARE WILLING TO LISTEN TO MEDUSA?
WHY, YOU PRESUMPTUOUS, COSTUMED CLOD...!
MEDUSA SHALL DECIDE WHO WILL LISTEN... AND WHEN!
SNAPP!
KRAK!
NO MERE HUMAN SHALL DICTATE TERMS TO ME!
SHE CAN DO ANYTHING WITH THAT HAIR OF HERS!
..EVEN CRACK IT LIKE A WHIP!
LOOK, LADY... IF YOU'VE GOT YOUR PRIDE...
I'VE GOT MINE, ALSO!
NOBODY'S USING ME AS A WHIPPING BOY!
...NOT EVEN A RING-A-DING REDHEAD WITH A FAR-OUT FRIGHT WIG!
16

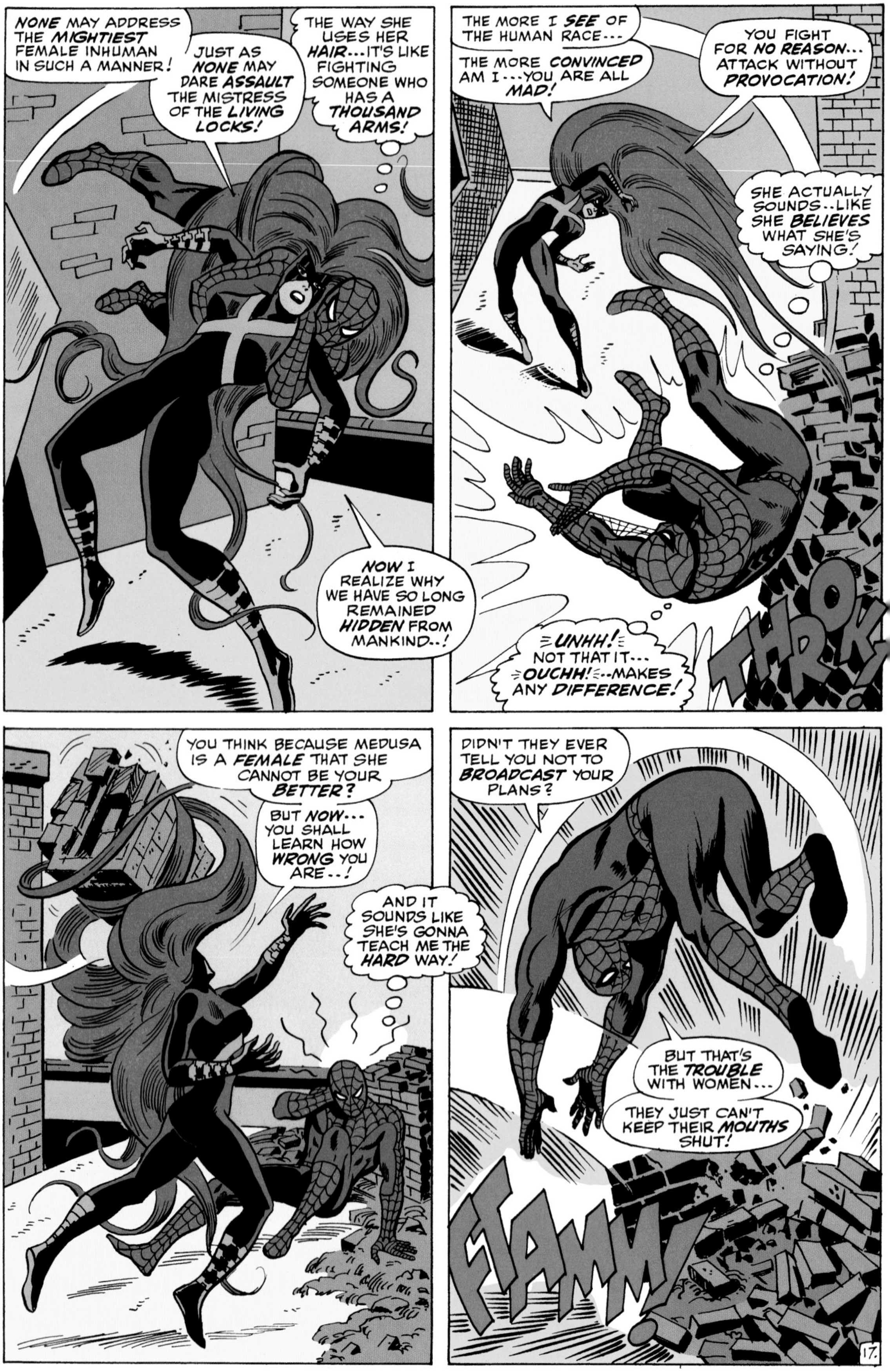
NONE MAY ADDRESS THE MIGHTIEST FEMALE INHUMAN IN SUCH A MANNER!
JUST AS NONE MAY DARE ASSAULT THE MISTRESS OF THE LIVING LOCKS!
THE WAY SHE USES HER HAIR...IT'S LIKE FIGHTING SOMEONE WHO HAS A THOUSAND ARMS!
NOW I REALIZE WHY WE HAVE SO LONG REMAINED HIDDEN FROM MANKIND..!
THE MORE I SEE OF THE HUMAN RACE---
THE MORE CONVINCED AM I---YOU ARE ALL MAD!
YOU FIGHT FOR NO REASON... ATTACK WITHOUT PROVOCATION!
SHE ACTUALLY SOUNDS..LIKE SHE BELIEVES WHAT SHE'S SAYING!
UNHH! NOT THAT IT--- OUCHH! --MAKES ANY DIFFERENCE!
THROK!
YOU THINK BECAUSE MEDUSA IS A FEMALE THAT SHE CANNOT BE YOUR BETTER?
BUT NOW--- YOU SHALL LEARN HOW WRONG YOU ARE--!
AND IT SOUNDS LIKE SHE'S GONNA TEACH ME THE HARD WAY!
DIDN'T THEY EVER TELL YOU NOT TO BROADCAST YOUR PLANS?
BUT THAT'S THE TROUBLE WITH WOMEN...
THEY JUST CAN'T KEEP THEIR MOUTHS SHUT!
CLAMM!
17.

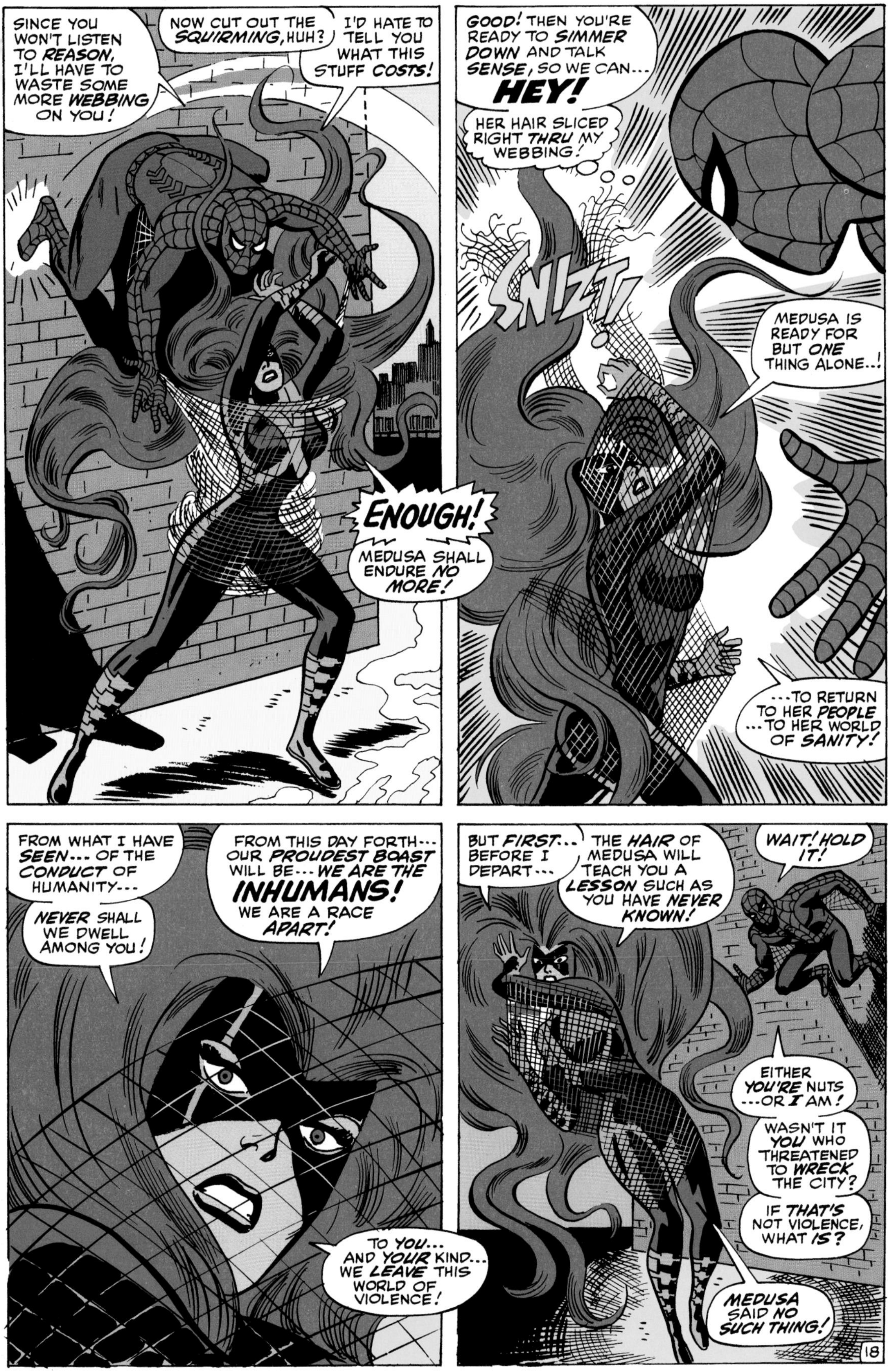
SINCE YOU WON'T LISTEN TO REASON, I'LL HAVE TO WASTE SOME MORE WEBBING ON YOU!
NOW CUT OUT THE SQUIRMING, HUH?
I'D HATE TO TELL YOU WHAT THIS STUFF COSTS!
ENOUGH!
MEDUSA SHALL ENDURE NO MORE!
GOOD! THEN YOU'RE READY TO SIMMER DOWN AND TALK SENSE, SO WE CAN... HEY!
HER HAIR SLICED RIGHT THRU MY WEBBING!
SNIZT!
MEDUSA IS READY FOR BUT ONE THING ALONE..!
...TO RETURN TO HER PEOPLE ...TO HER WORLD OF SANITY!
FROM WHAT I HAVE SEEN... OF THE CONDUCT OF HUMANITY...
NEVER SHALL WE DWELL AMONG YOU!
FROM THIS DAY FORTH... OUR PROUDEST BOAST WILL BE... WE ARE THE INHUMANS! WE ARE A RACE APART!
TO YOU... AND YOUR KIND... WE LEAVE THIS WORLD OF VIOLENCE!
BUT FIRST... BEFORE I DEPART...
THE HAIR OF MEDUSA WILL TEACH YOU A LESSON SUCH AS YOU HAVE NEVER KNOWN!
WAIT! HOLD IT!
EITHER YOU'RE NUTS ...OR I AM!
WASN'T IT YOU WHO THREATENED TO WRECK THE CITY?
IF THAT'S NOT VIOLENCE, WHAT IS?
MEDUSA SAID NO SUCH THING!
18

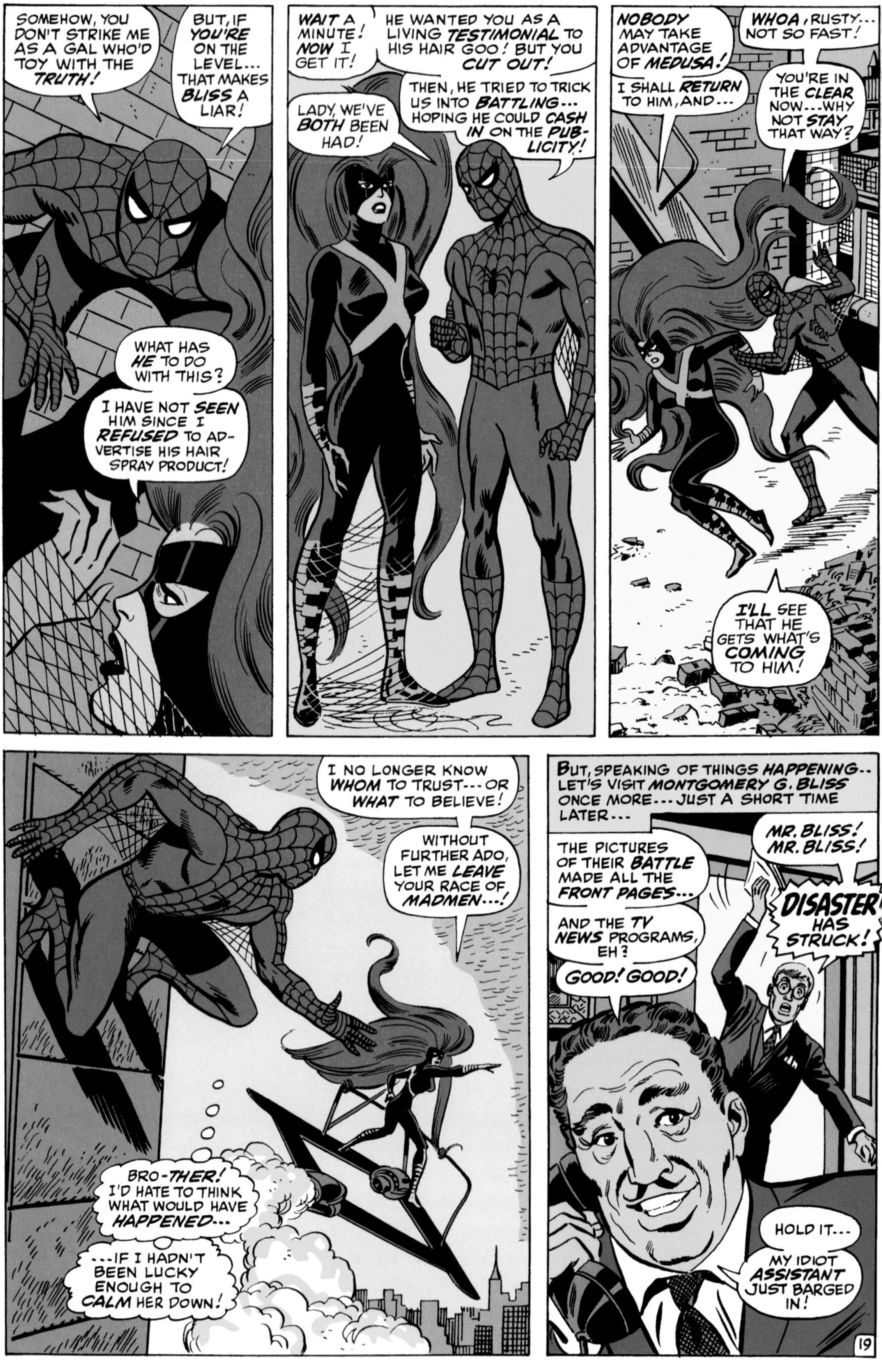
SOMEHOW, YOU DON'T STRIKE ME AS A GAL WHO'D TOY WITH THE TRUTH!
BUT, IF YOU'RE ON THE LEVEL... THAT MAKES BLISS A LIAR!
WHAT HAS HE TO DO WITH THIS?
I HAVE NOT SEEN HIM SINCE I REFUSED TO ADVERTISE HIS HAIR SPRAY PRODUCT!
WAIT A MINUTE! NOW I GET IT!
HE WANTED YOU AS A LIVING TESTIMONIAL TO HIS HAIR GOO! BUT YOU CUT OUT!
THEN, HE TRIED TO TRICK US INTO BATTLING... HOPING HE COULD CASH IN ON THE PUBLICITY!
LADY, WE'VE BOTH BEEN HAD!
NOBODY MAY TAKE ADVANTAGE OF MEDUSA!
I SHALL RETURN TO HIM, AND...
WHOA, RUSTY... NOT SO FAST!
YOU'RE IN THE CLEAR NOW---WHY NOT STAY THAT WAY?
I'LL SEE THAT HE GETS WHAT'S COMING TO HIM!
I NO LONGER KNOW WHOM TO TRUST--- OR WHAT TO BELIEVE!
WITHOUT FURTHER ADO, LET ME LEAVE YOUR RACE OF MADMEN...!
BRO-THER! I'D HATE TO THINK WHAT WOULD HAVE HAPPENED...
...IF I HADN'T BEEN LUCKY ENOUGH TO CALM HER DOWN!
BUT, SPEAKING OF THINGS HAPPENING.. LET'S VISIT MONTGOMERY G. BLISS ONCE MORE... JUST A SHORT TIME LATER...
THE PICTURES OF THEIR BATTLE MADE ALL THE FRONT PAGES...
AND THE TV NEWS PROGRAMS, EH?
GOOD! GOOD!
MR. BLISS! MR. BLISS!
DISASTER HAS STRUCK!
HOLD IT...
MY IDIOT ASSISTANT JUST BARGED IN!
19

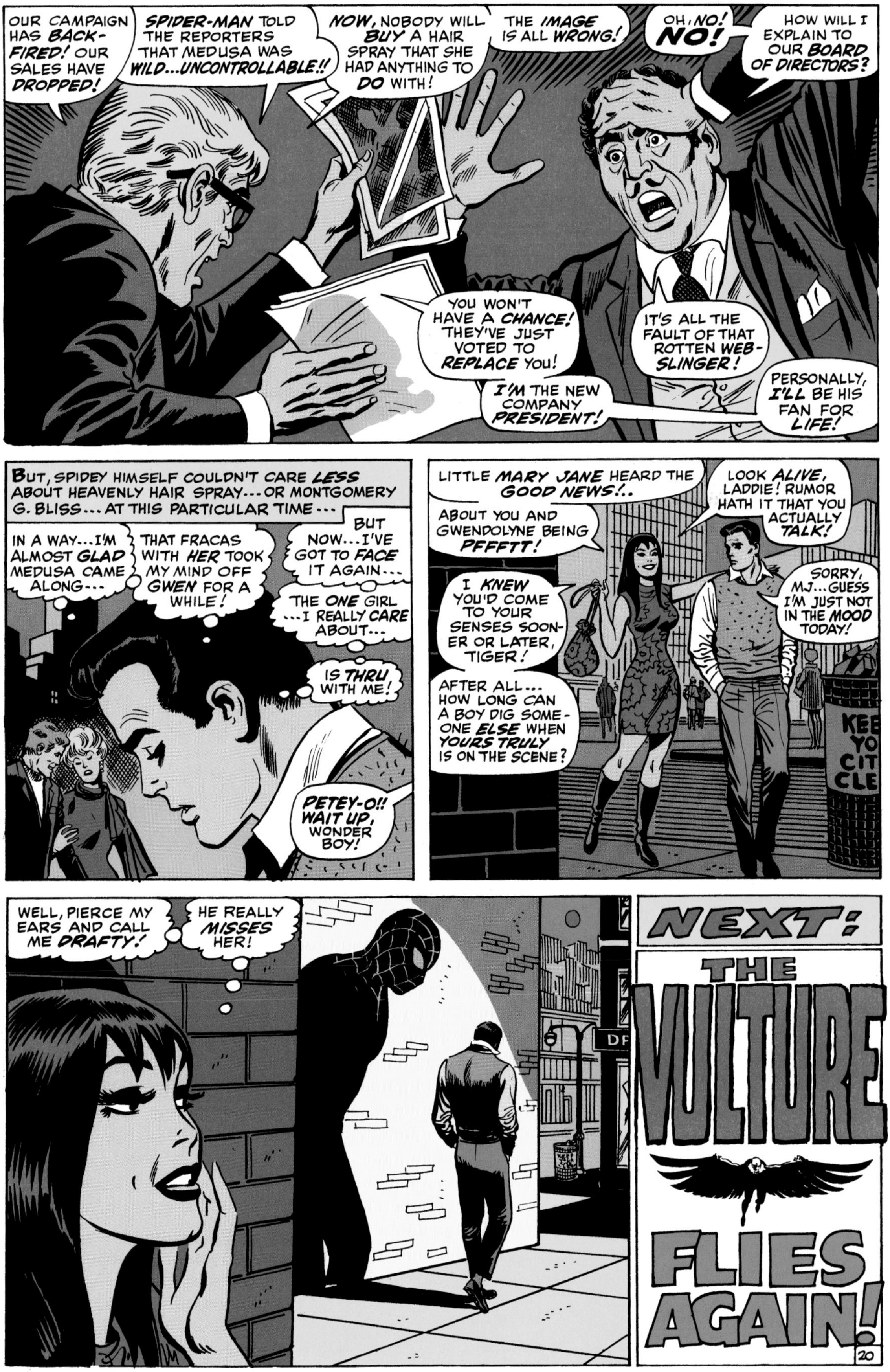

OUR CAMPAIGN HAS BACK-FIRED! OUR SALES HAVE DROPPED!
SPIDER-MAN TOLD THE REPORTERS THAT MEDUSA WAS WILD...UNCONTROLLABLE!!
NOW, NOBODY WILL BUY A HAIR SPRAY THAT SHE HAD ANYTHING TO DO WITH!
THE IMAGE IS ALL WRONG!
OH, NO! NO!
HOW WILL I EXPLAIN TO OUR BOARD OF DIRECTORS?
YOU WON'T HAVE A CHANCE! THEY'VE JUST VOTED TO REPLACE YOU!
IT'S ALL THE FAULT OF THAT ROTTEN WEB-SLINGER!
I'M THE NEW COMPANY PRESIDENT!
PERSONALLY, I'LL BE HIS FAN FOR LIFE!
BUT, SPIDEY HIMSELF COULDN'T CARE LESS ABOUT HEAVENLY HAIR SPRAY... OR MONTGOMERY G. BLISS... AT THIS PARTICULAR TIME...
IN A WAY...I'M ALMOST GLAD MEDUSA CAME ALONG...
THAT FRACAS WITH HER TOOK MY MIND OFF GWEN FOR A WHILE!
BUT NOW...I'VE GOT TO FACE IT AGAIN...
THE ONE GIRL ...I REALLY CARE ABOUT...
IS THRU WITH ME!
PETEY-O!! WAIT UP, WONDER BOY!
LITTLE MARY JANE HEARD THE GOOD NEWS!..
ABOUT YOU AND GWENDOLYNE BEING PFFFTT!
LOOK ALIVE, LADDIE! RUMOR HATH IT THAT YOU ACTUALLY TALK!
I KNEW YOU'D COME TO YOUR SENSES SOONER OR LATER, TIGER!
SORRY, MJ...GUESS I'M JUST NOT IN THE MOOD TODAY!
AFTER ALL... HOW LONG CAN A BOY DIG SOMEONE ELSE WHEN YOURS TRULY IS ON THE SCENE?
WELL, PIERCE MY EARS AND CALL ME DRAFTY!
HE REALLY MISSES HER!
NEXT: THE VULTURE FLIES AGAIN!
20

THE SPECTACULAR SPIDER-MAN™
35c
40¢ IN CAN.
JULY
"LO, THIS MONSTER!"
A BOOK-LENGTH SUPER-SPIDEY SPECTACULAR!

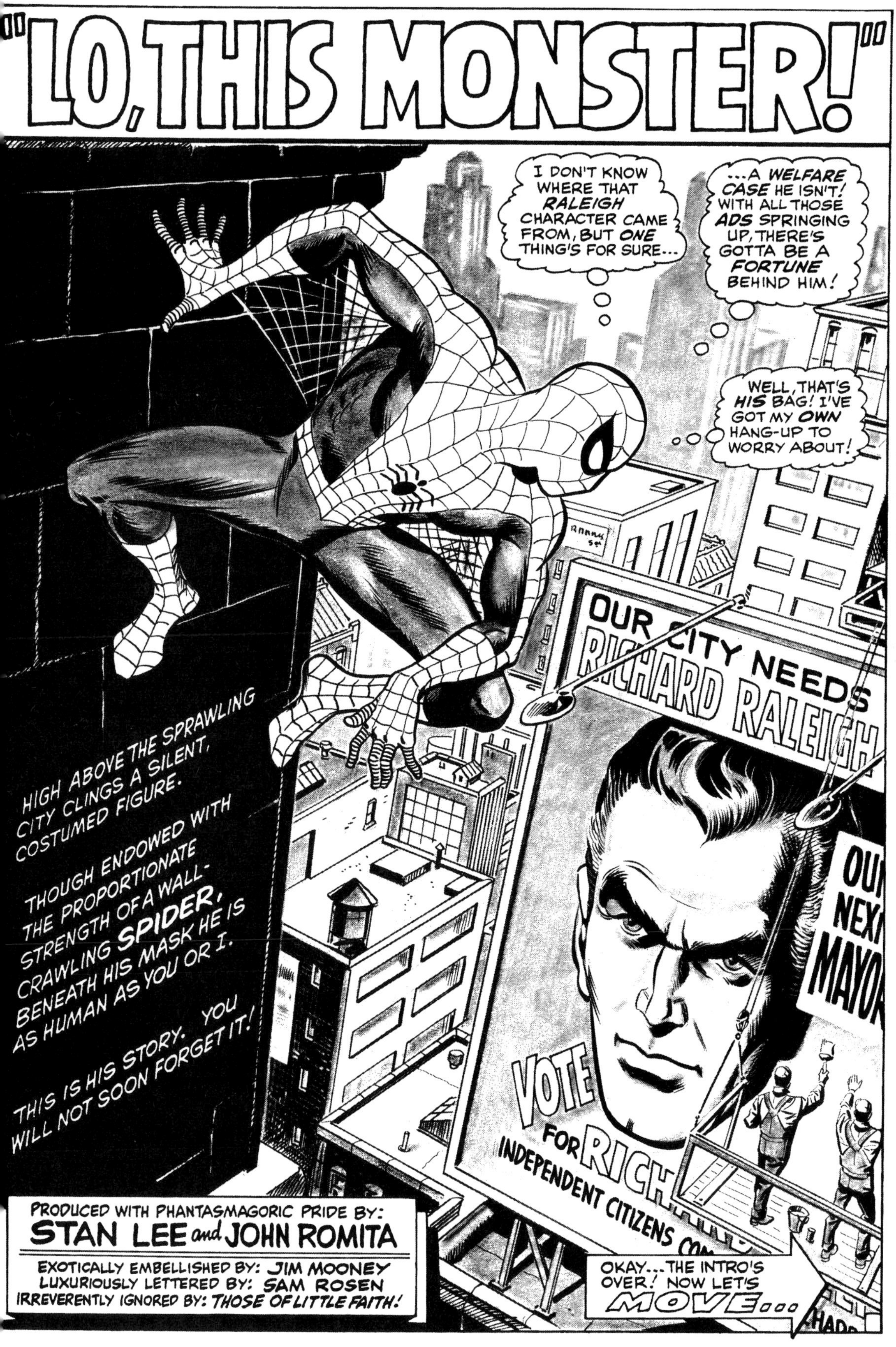

"LO, THIS MONSTER!"
HIGH ABOVE THE SPRAWLING CITY CLINGS A SILENT, COSTUMED FIGURE.
THOUGH ENDOWED WITH THE PROPORTIONATE STRENGTH OF A WALL-CRAWLING SPIDER, BENEATH HIS MASK HE IS AS HUMAN AS YOU OR I.
THIS IS HIS STORY. YOU WILL NOT SOON FORGET IT!
I DON'T KNOW WHERE THAT RALEIGH CHARACTER CAME FROM, BUT ONE THING'S FOR SURE...
...A WELFARE CASE HE ISN'T! WITH ALL THOSE ADS SPRINGING UP, THERE'S GOTTA BE A FORTUNE BEHIND HIM!
WELL, THAT'S HIS BAG! I'VE GOT MY OWN HANG-UP TO WORRY ABOUT!
OUR CITY NEEDS
RICHARD RALEIGH
VOTE
FOR
INDEPENDENT CITIZENS
PRODUCED WITH PHANTASMAGORIC PRIDE BY: STAN LEE and JOHN ROMITA
EXOTICALLY EMBELLISHED BY: JIM MOONEY
LUXURIOUSLY LETTERED BY: SAM ROSEN
IRREVERENTLY IGNORED BY: THOSE OF LITTLE FAITH!
OKAY... THE INTRO'S OVER! NOW LET'S MOVE...

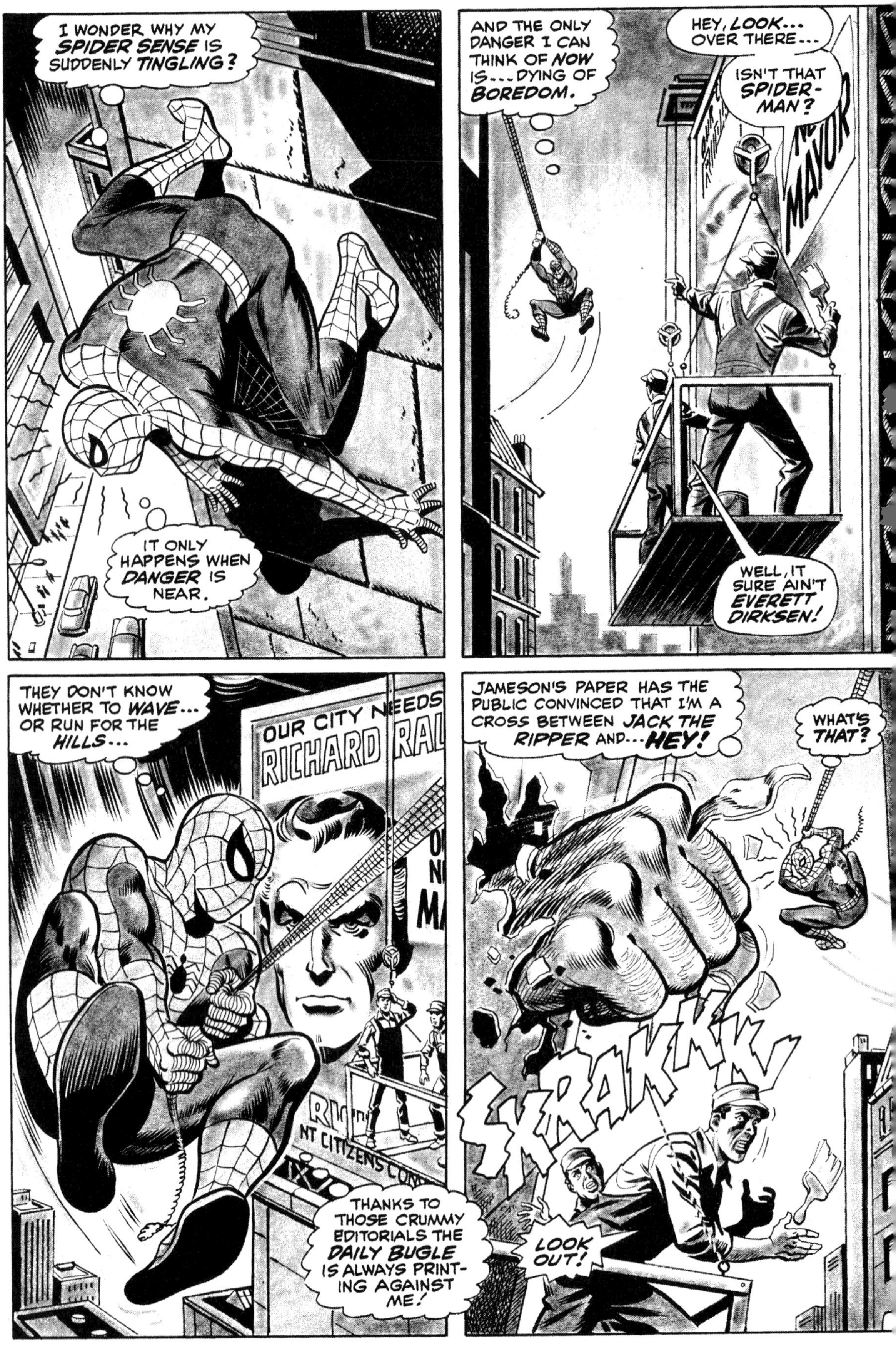
I WONDER WHY MY SPIDER SENSE IS SUDDENLY TINGLING?
IT ONLY HAPPENS WHEN DANGER IS NEAR.
AND THE ONLY DANGER I CAN THINK OF NOW IS...DYING OF BOREDOM.
HEY, LOOK... OVER THERE...
ISN'T THAT SPIDER-MAN?
MAYOR
WELL, IT SURE AIN'T EVERETT DIRKSEN!
THEY DON'T KNOW WHETHER TO WAVE... OR RUN FOR THE HILLS...
OUR CITY NEEDS
RICHARD RAL
NT CITIZENS COM
THANKS TO THOSE CRUMMY EDITORIALS THE DAILY BUGLE IS ALWAYS PRINTING AGAINST ME!
JAMESON'S PAPER HAS THE PUBLIC CONVINCED THAT I'M A CROSS BETWEEN JACK THE RIPPER AND...HEY!
WHAT'S THAT?
SKRAKKK
LOOK OUT!

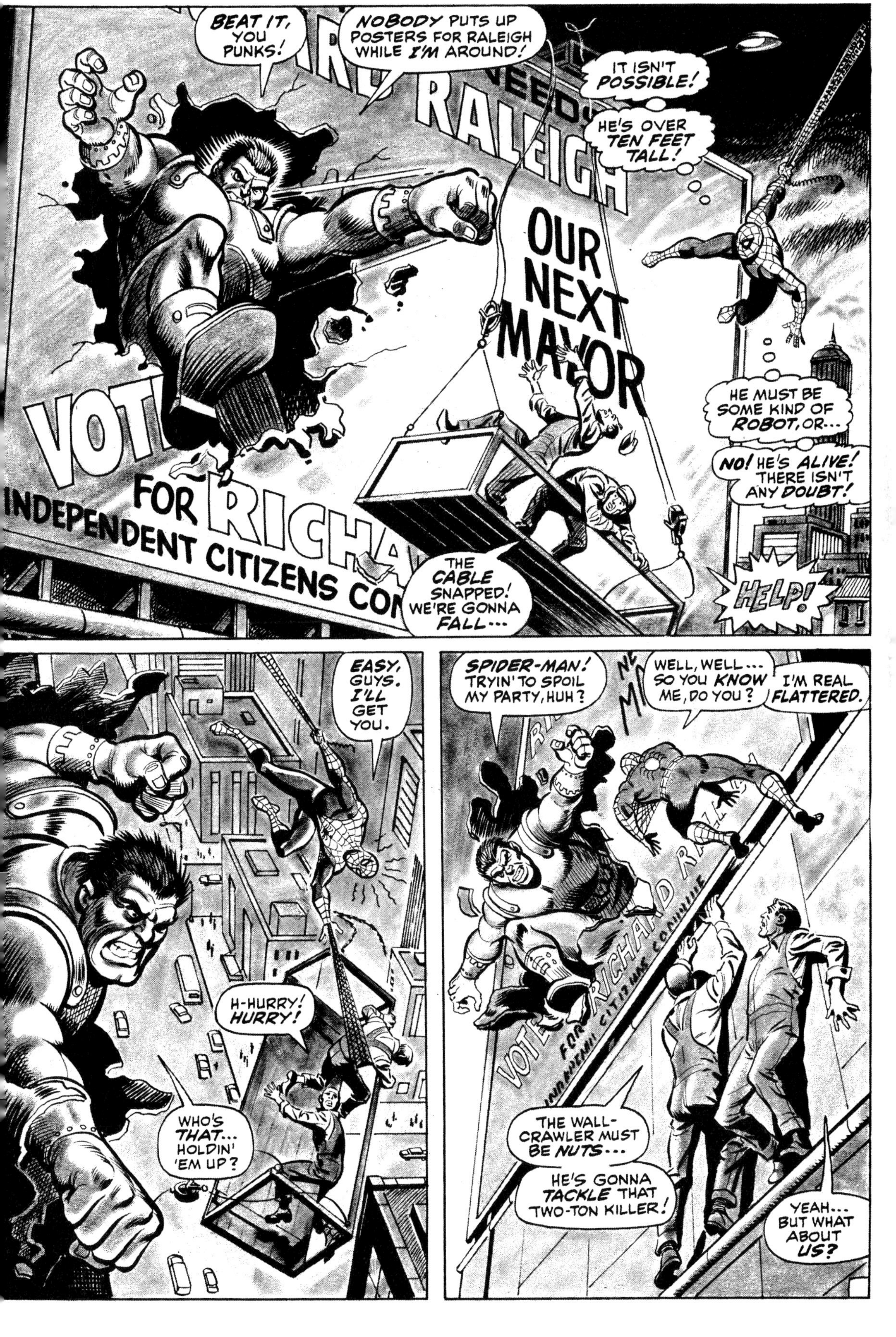
BEAT IT, YOU PUNKS!
NOBODY PUTS UP POSTERS FOR RALEIGH WHILE I'M AROUND!
RALEIGH
OUR NEXT MAYOR
FOR
INDEPENDENT CITIZENS
IT ISN'T POSSIBLE!
HE'S OVER TEN FEET TALL!
HE MUST BE SOME KIND OF ROBOT, OR...
NO! HE'S ALIVE! THERE ISN'T ANY DOUBT!
THE CABLE SNAPPED! WE'RE GONNA FALL...
HELP!
EASY, GUYS. I'LL GET YOU.
H-HURRY! HURRY!
WHO'S THAT... HOLDIN' 'EM UP?
SPIDER-MAN! TRYIN' TO SPOIL MY PARTY, HUH?
WELL, WELL... SO YOU KNOW ME, DO YOU?
I'M REAL FLATTERED.
THE WALL-CRAWLER MUST BE NUTS...
HE'S GONNA TACKLE THAT TWO-TON KILLER!
YEAH... BUT WHAT ABOUT US?

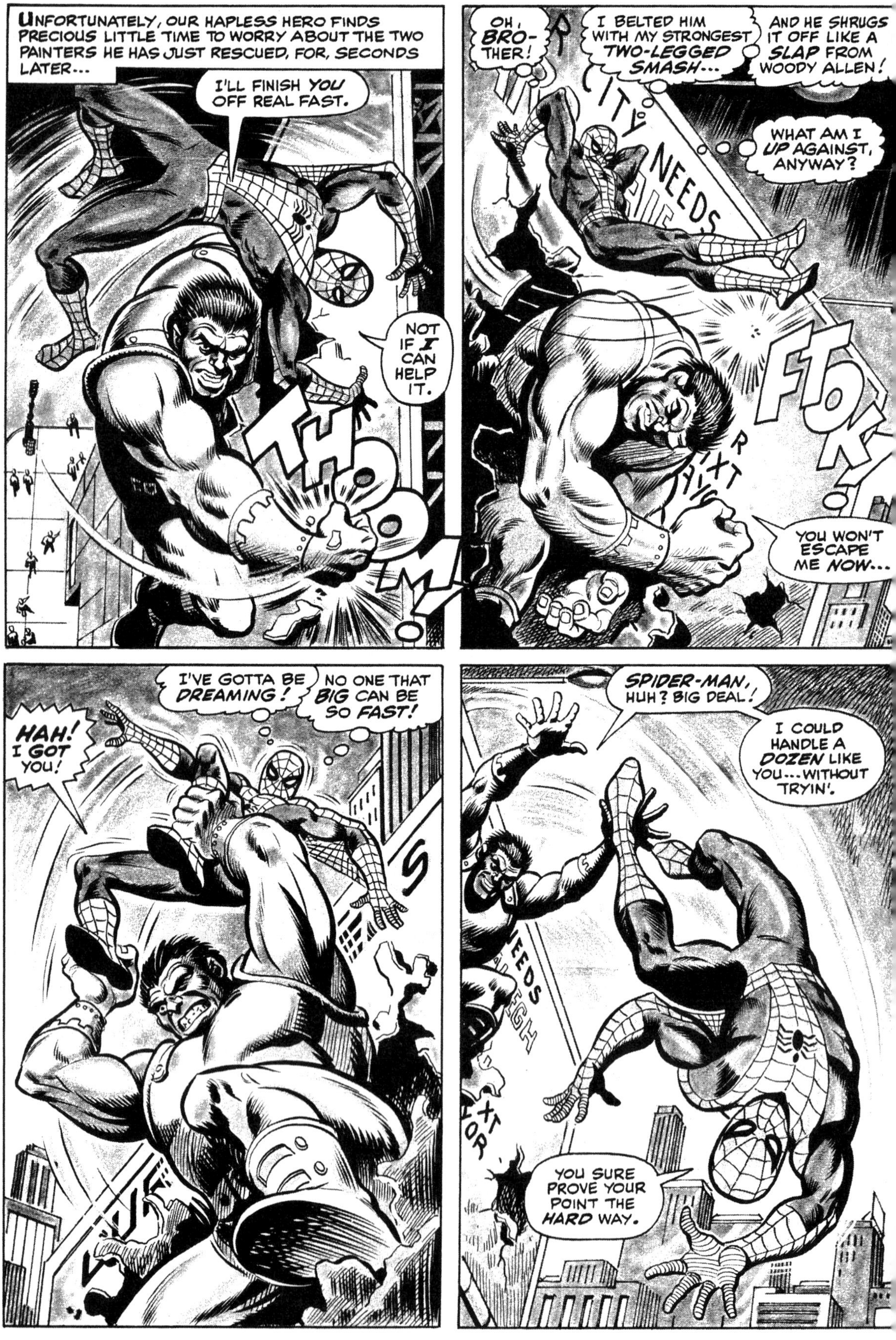

UNFORTUNATELY, OUR HAPLESS HERO FINDS PRECIOUS LITTLE TIME TO WORRY ABOUT THE TWO PAINTERS HE HAS JUST RESCUED, FOR, SECONDS LATER...
I'LL FINISH YOU OFF REAL FAST.
NOT IF I CAN HELP IT.
THOOOM!
OH, BROTHER!
I BELTED HIM WITH MY STRONGEST TWO-LEGGED SMASH...
AND HE SHRUGS IT OFF LIKE A SLAP FROM WOODY ALLEN!
WHAT AM I UP AGAINST, ANYWAY?
FTOK!
YOU WON'T ESCAPE ME NOW...
HAH! I GOT YOU!
I'VE GOTTA BE DREAMING!
NO ONE THAT BIG CAN BE SO FAST!
SPIDER-MAN, HUH? BIG DEAL!
I COULD HANDLE A DOZEN LIKE YOU... WITHOUT TRYIN'.
YOU SURE PROVE YOUR POINT THE HARD WAY.

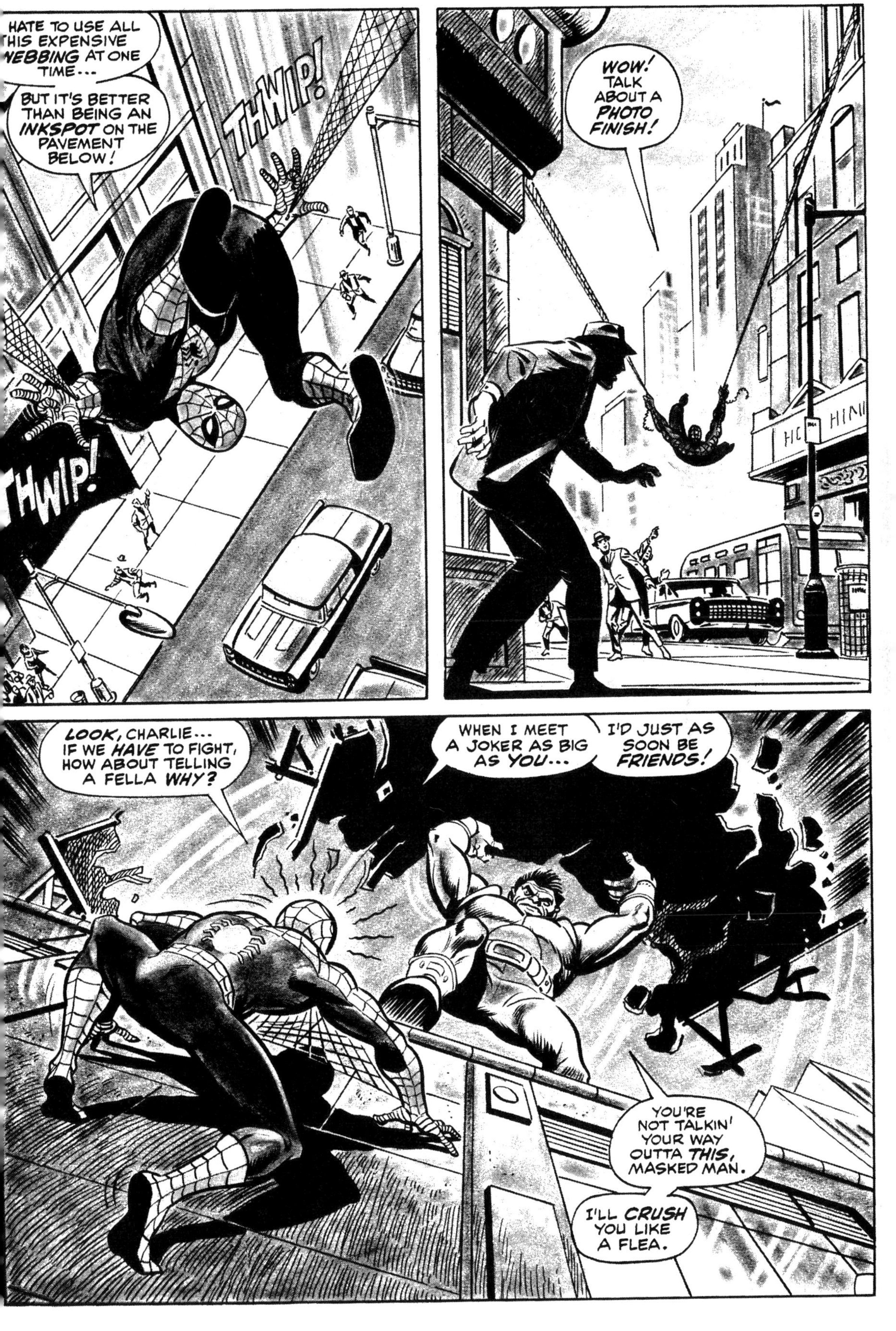
HATE TO USE ALL THIS EXPENSIVE WEBBING AT ONE TIME...
BUT IT'S BETTER THAN BEING AN INKSPOT ON THE PAVEMENT BELOW!
THWIP!
THWIP!
WOW! TALK ABOUT A PHOTO FINISH!
LOOK, CHARLIE... IF WE HAVE TO FIGHT, HOW ABOUT TELLING A FELLA WHY?
WHEN I MEET A JOKER AS BIG AS YOU...
I'D JUST AS SOON BE FRIENDS!
YOU'RE NOT TALKIN' YOUR WAY OUTTA THIS, MASKED MAN.
I'LL CRUSH YOU LIKE A FLEA.

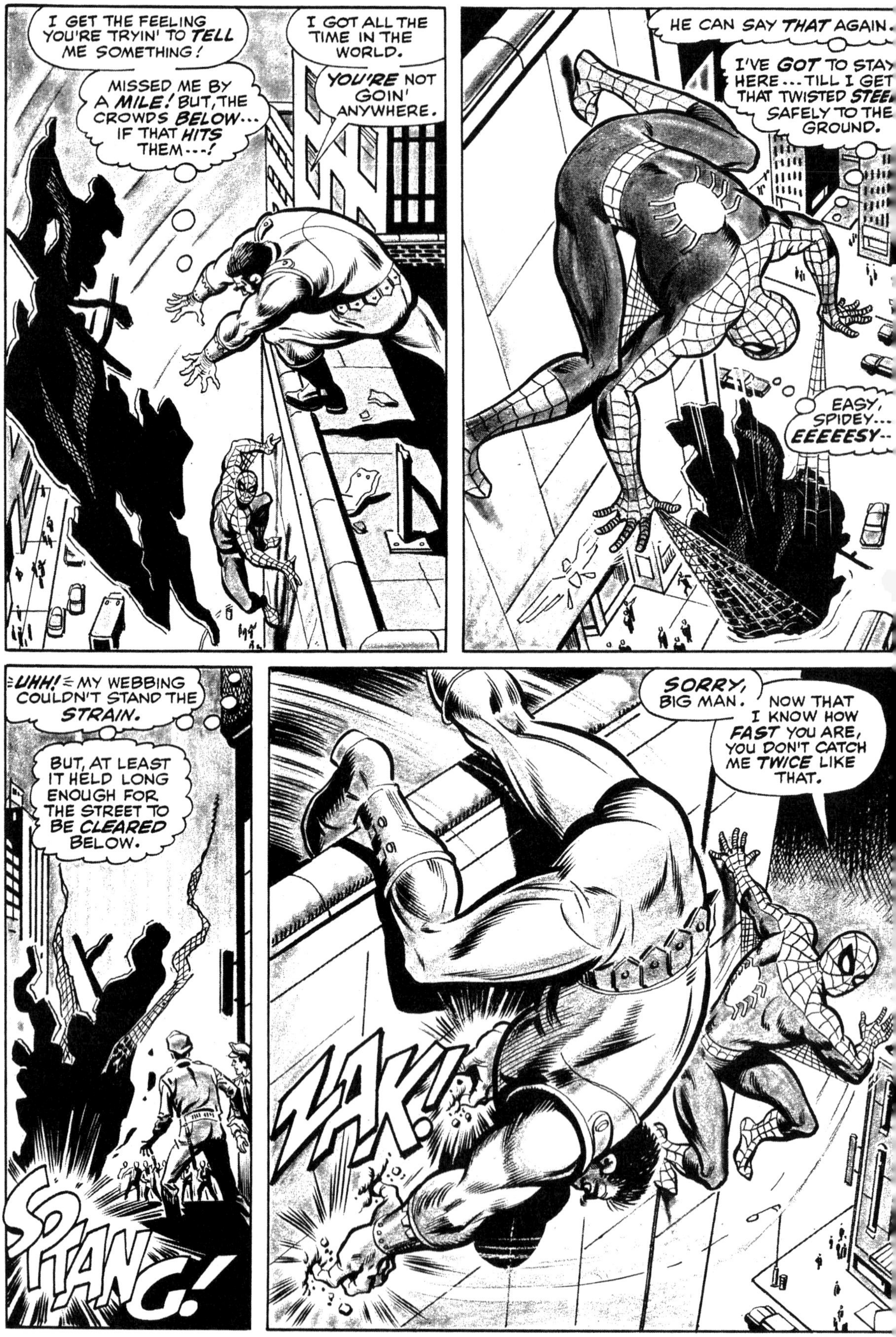
I GET THE FEELING YOU'RE TRYIN' TO TELL ME SOMETHING!
I GOT ALL THE TIME IN THE WORLD.
MISSED ME BY A MILE! BUT, THE CROWDS BELOW... IF THAT HITS THEM---!
YOU'RE NOT GOIN' ANYWHERE.
HE CAN SAY THAT AGAIN.
I'VE GOT TO STAY HERE...TILL I GET THAT TWISTED STEEL SAFELY TO THE GROUND.
EASY, SPIDEY... EEEEESY--
UHH! MY WEBBING COULDN'T STAND THE STRAIN.
BUT, AT LEAST IT HELD LONG ENOUGH FOR THE STREET TO BE CLEARED BELOW.
SPTANG!
SORRY, BIG MAN.
NOW THAT I KNOW HOW FAST YOU ARE, YOU DON'T CATCH ME TWICE LIKE THAT.
ZAK!

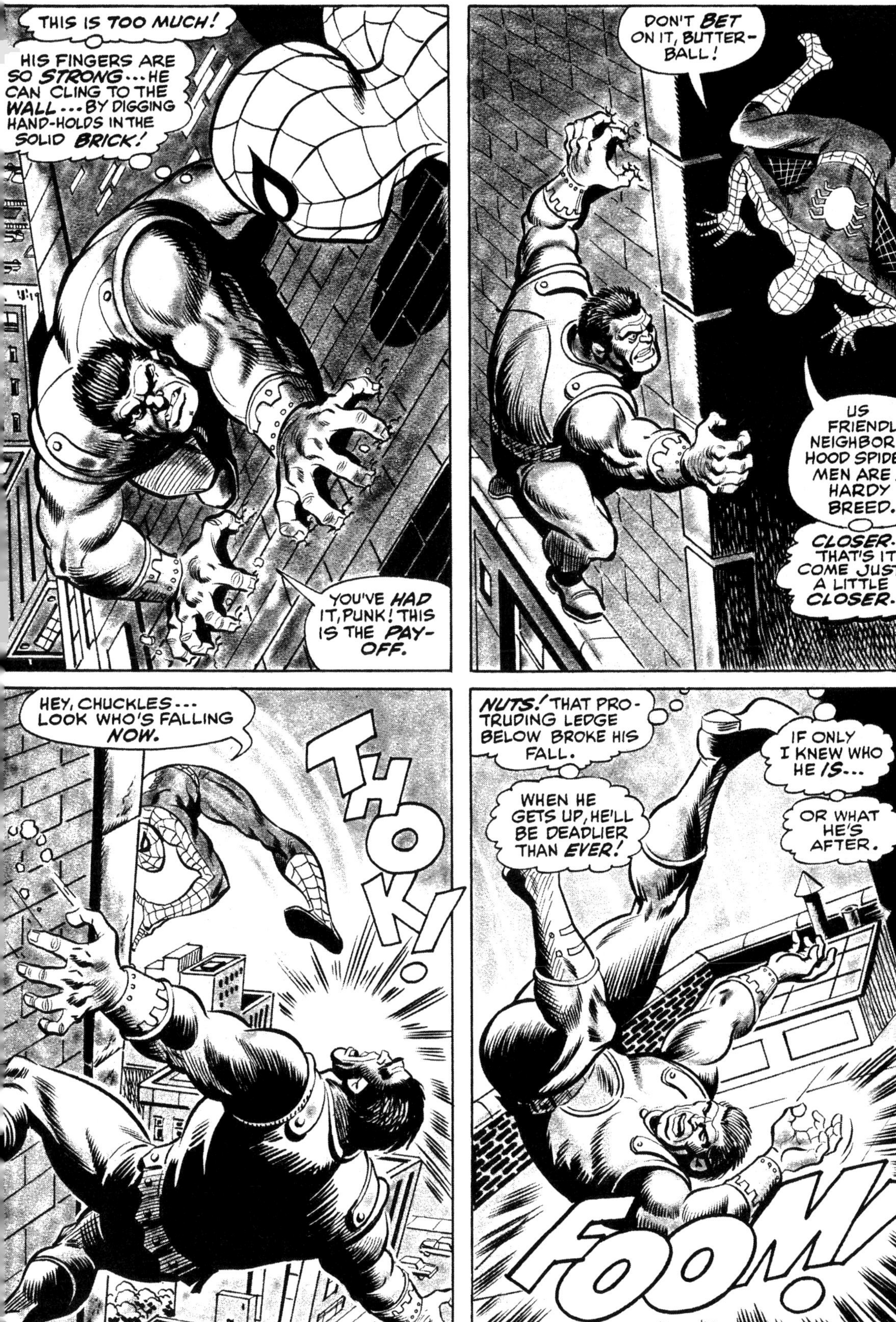
THIS IS TOO MUCH!
HIS FINGERS ARE SO STRONG... HE CAN CLING TO THE WALL... BY DIGGING HAND-HOLDS IN THE SOLID BRICK!
YOU'VE HAD IT, PUNK! THIS IS THE PAY-OFF.
DON'T BET ON IT, BUTTER-BALL!
US FRIENDLY NEIGHBOR-HOOD SPIDER-MEN ARE A HARDY BREED.
CLOSER... THAT'S IT. COME JUST A LITTLE CLOSER...
HEY, CHUCKLES... LOOK WHO'S FALLING NOW.
THOK!
NUTS! THAT PRO-TRUDING LEDGE BELOW BROKE HIS FALL.
WHEN HE GETS UP, HE'LL BE DEADLIER THAN EVER!
IF ONLY I KNEW WHO HE IS...
OR WHAT HE'S AFTER.
FOOM!

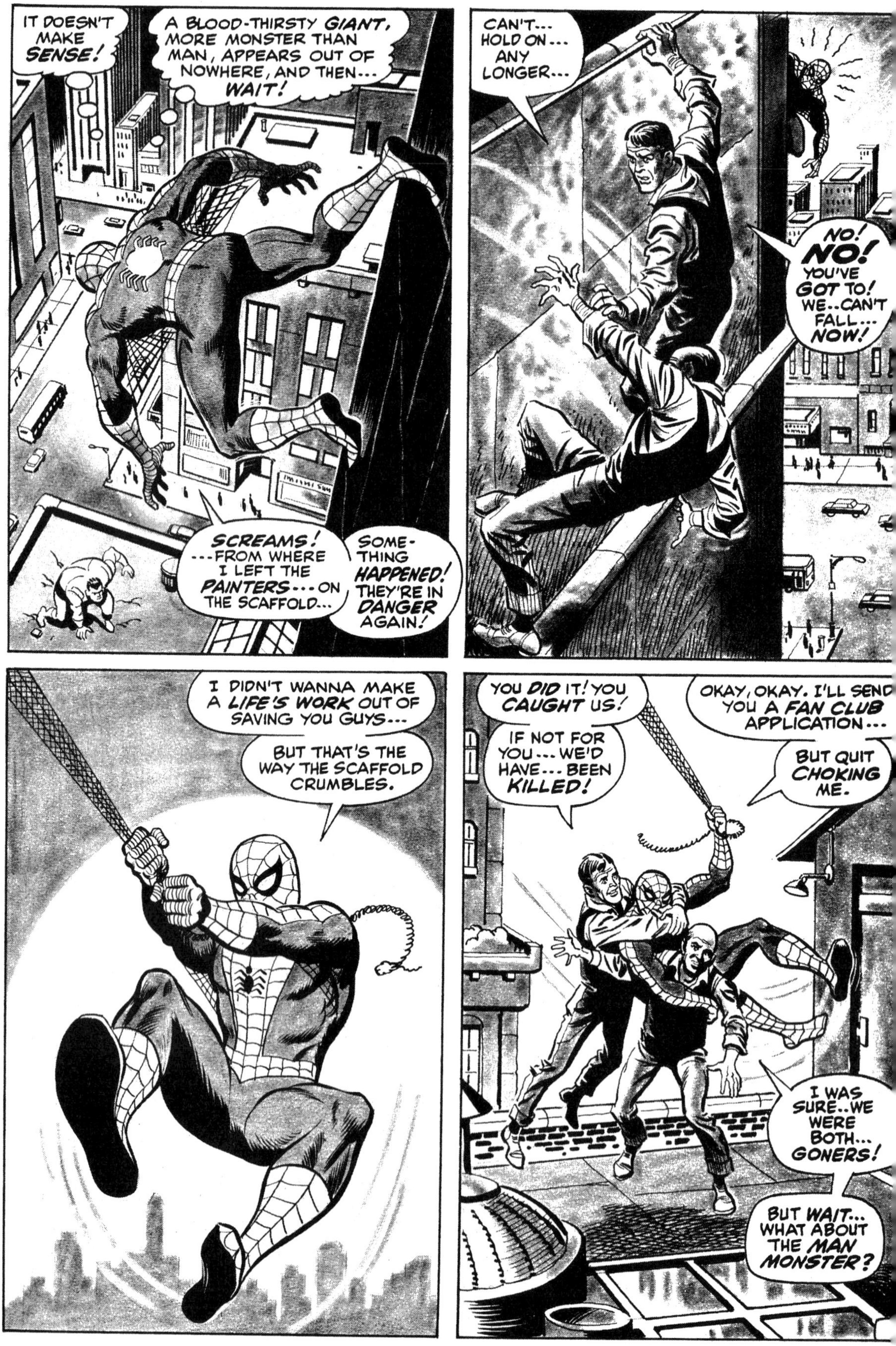
IT DOESN'T MAKE SENSE!
A BLOOD-THIRSTY GIANT, MORE MONSTER THAN MAN, APPEARS OUT OF NOWHERE, AND THEN... WAIT!
SCREAMS! ---FROM WHERE I LEFT THE PAINTERS---ON THE SCAFFOLD...
SOME-THING HAPPENED! THEY'RE IN DANGER AGAIN!
CAN'T... HOLD ON... ANY LONGER...
NO! NO! YOU'VE GOT TO! WE..CAN'T FALL... NOW!
I DIDN'T WANNA MAKE A LIFE'S WORK OUT OF SAVING YOU GUYS---
BUT THAT'S THE WAY THE SCAFFOLD CRUMBLES.
YOU DID IT! YOU CAUGHT US!
IF NOT FOR YOU... WE'D HAVE... BEEN KILLED!
OKAY, OKAY. I'LL SEND YOU A FAN CLUB APPLICATION...
BUT QUIT CHOKING ME.
I WAS SURE..WE WERE BOTH... GONERS!
BUT WAIT... WHAT ABOUT THE MAN MONSTER?

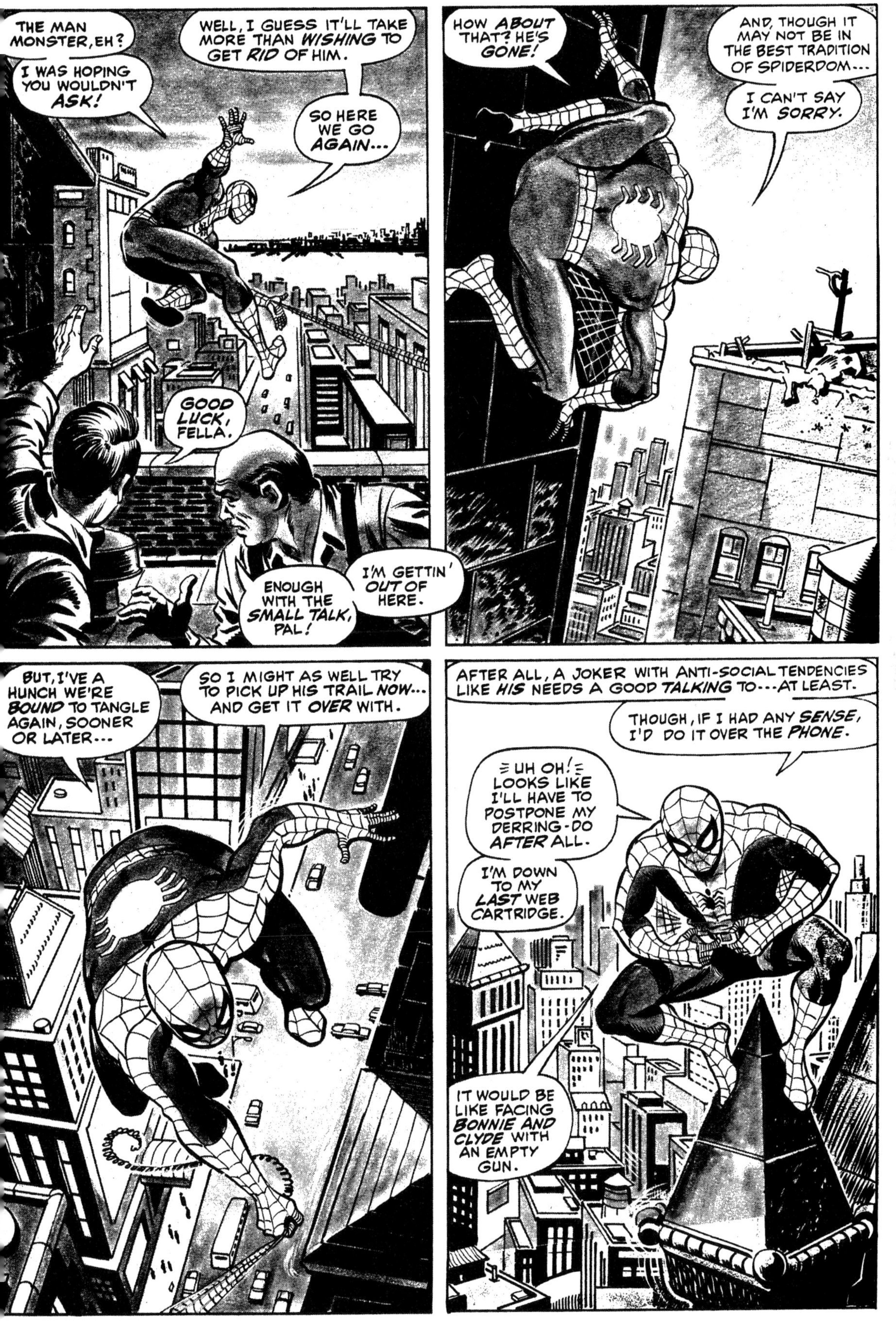
THE MAN MONSTER, EH?
I WAS HOPING YOU WOULDN'T ASK!
WELL, I GUESS IT'LL TAKE MORE THAN WISHING TO GET RID OF HIM.
SO HERE WE GO AGAIN...
GOOD LUCK, FELLA.
ENOUGH WITH THE SMALL TALK, PAL!
I'M GETTIN' OUT OF HERE.
HOW ABOUT THAT? HE'S GONE!
AND, THOUGH IT MAY NOT BE IN THE BEST TRADITION OF SPIDERDOM...
I CAN'T SAY I'M SORRY.
BUT, I'VE A HUNCH WE'RE BOUND TO TANGLE AGAIN, SOONER OR LATER...
SO I MIGHT AS WELL TRY TO PICK UP HIS TRAIL NOW... AND GET IT OVER WITH.
AFTER ALL, A JOKER WITH ANTI-SOCIAL TENDENCIES LIKE HIS NEEDS A GOOD TALKING TO... AT LEAST.
THOUGH, IF I HAD ANY SENSE, I'D DO IT OVER THE PHONE.
UH OH! LOOKS LIKE I'LL HAVE TO POSTPONE MY DERRING-DO AFTER ALL.
I'M DOWN TO MY LAST WEB CARTRIDGE.
IT WOULD BE LIKE FACING BONNIE AND CLYDE WITH AN EMPTY GUN.

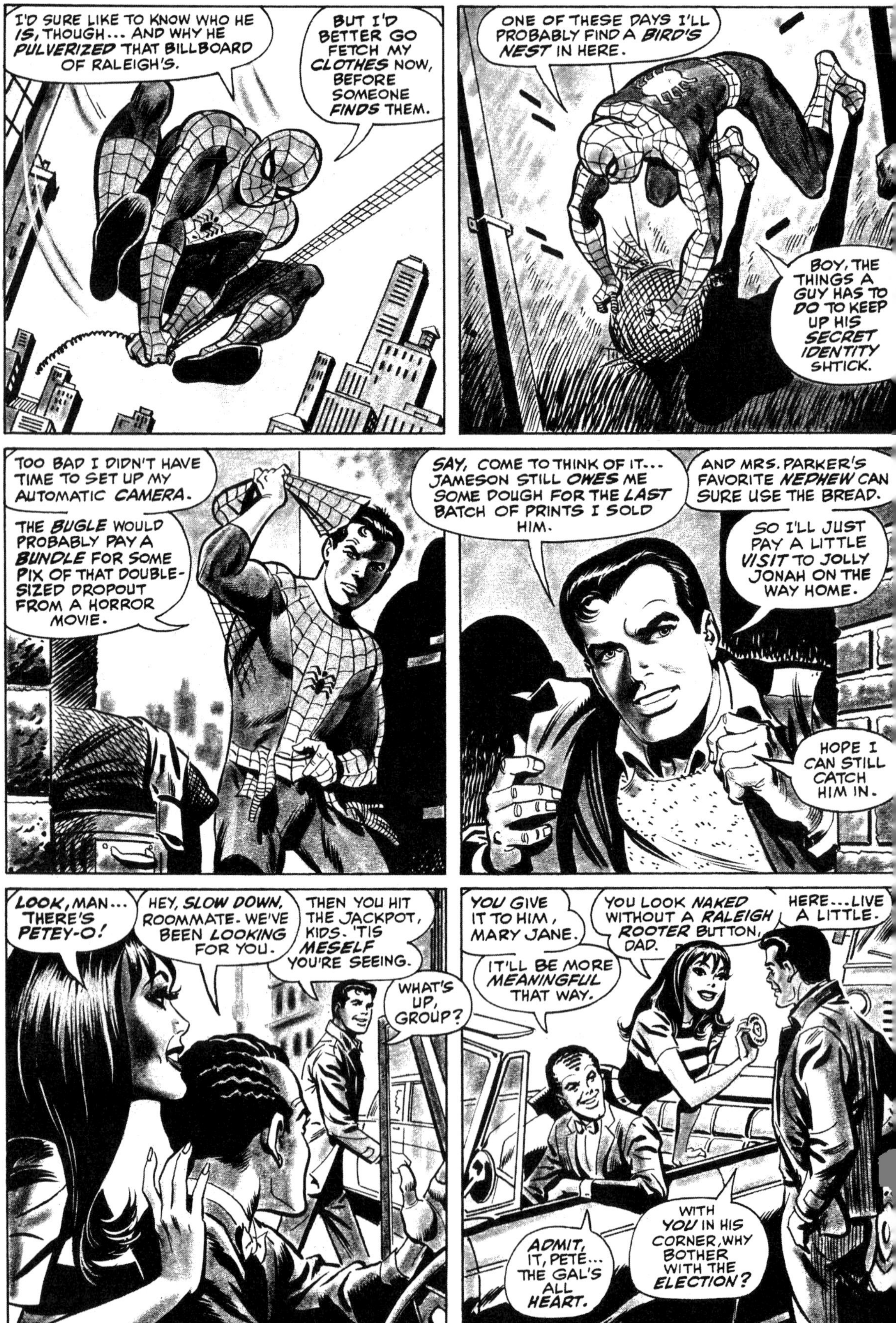

I'D SURE LIKE TO KNOW WHO HE *IS*, THOUGH... AND WHY HE *PULVERIZED* THAT BILLBOARD OF RALEIGH'S.
BUT I'D BETTER GO FETCH MY *CLOTHES* NOW, BEFORE SOMEONE *FINDS* THEM.
ONE OF THESE DAYS I'LL PROBABLY FIND A *BIRD'S NEST* IN HERE.
BOY, THE THINGS A GUY HAS TO *DO* TO KEEP UP HIS *SECRET IDENTITY* SHTICK.
TOO BAD I DIDN'T HAVE TIME TO SET UP MY AUTOMATIC *CAMERA*.
THE *BUGLE* WOULD PROBABLY PAY A *BUNDLE* FOR SOME PIX OF THAT DOUBLE-SIZED DROPOUT FROM A HORROR MOVIE.
SAY, COME TO THINK OF IT... JAMESON STILL *OWES* ME SOME DOUGH FOR THE *LAST* BATCH OF PRINTS I SOLD HIM.
AND MRS. PARKER'S FAVORITE *NEPHEW* CAN SURE USE THE BREAD.
SO I'LL JUST PAY A LITTLE *VISIT* TO JOLLY JONAH ON THE WAY HOME.
HOPE I CAN STILL CATCH HIM IN.
LOOK, MAN... THERE'S *PETEY-O!*
HEY, *SLOW DOWN*, ROOMMATE. WE'VE BEEN *LOOKING* FOR YOU.
THEN YOU HIT THE JACKPOT, KIDS. 'TIS *MESELF* YOU'RE SEEING.
WHAT'S UP, GROUP?
YOU GIVE IT TO HIM, MARY JANE.
IT'LL BE MORE *MEANINGFUL* THAT WAY.
YOU LOOK *NAKED* WITHOUT A *RALEIGH ROOTER* BUTTON, DAD.
HERE... LIVE A LITTLE.
ADMIT, IT, PETE... THE GAL'S ALL *HEART*.
WITH *YOU* IN HIS CORNER, WHY BOTHER WITH THE *ELECTION*?

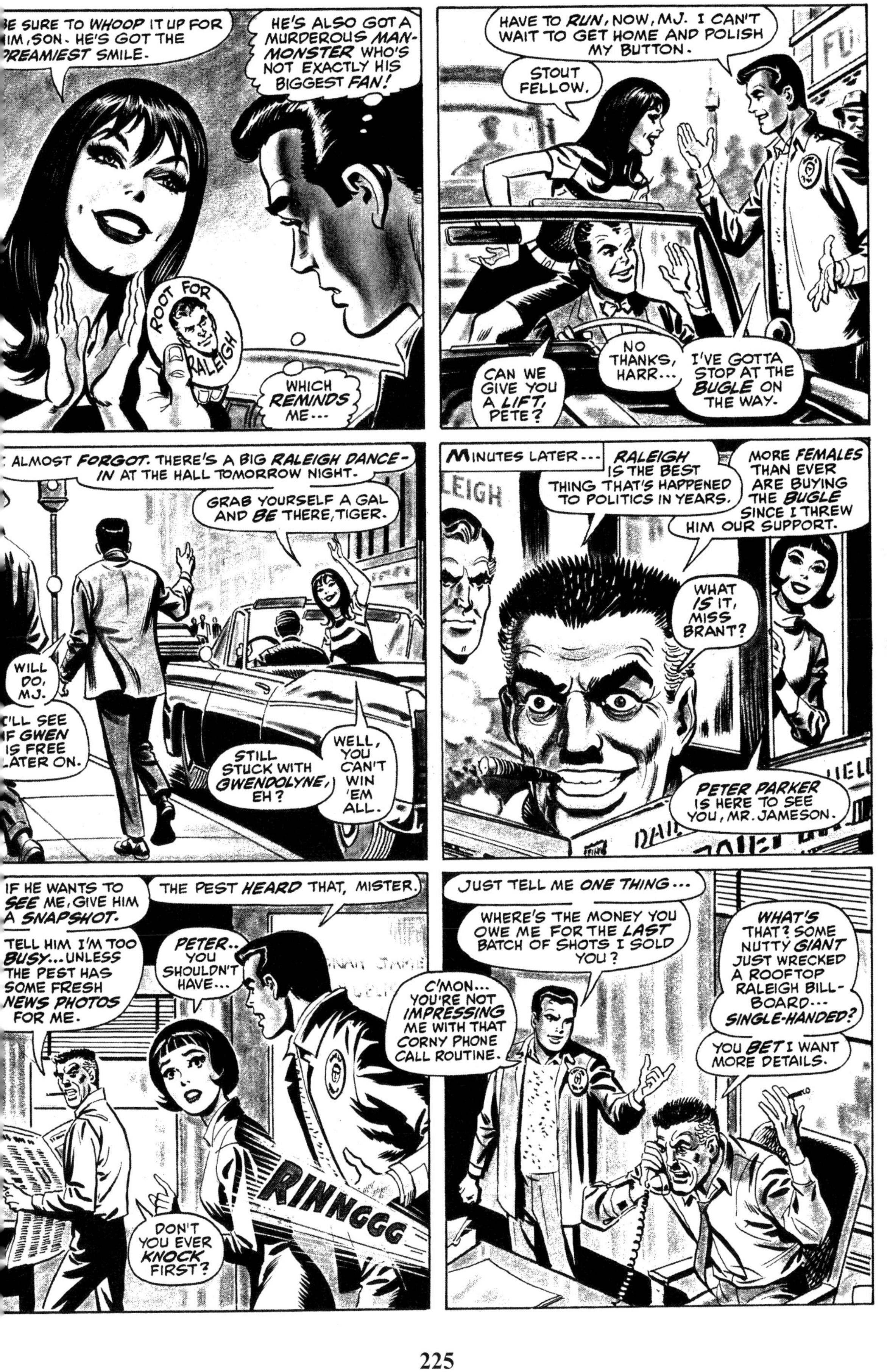

BE SURE TO WHOOP IT UP FOR HIM, SON. HE'S GOT THE DREAMIEST SMILE.
HE'S ALSO GOT A MURDEROUS MAN-MONSTER WHO'S NOT EXACTLY HIS BIGGEST FAN!
ROOT FOR RALEIGH
WHICH REMINDS ME---
HAVE TO RUN, NOW, MJ. I CAN'T WAIT TO GET HOME AND POLISH MY BUTTON.
STOUT FELLOW.
CAN WE GIVE YOU A LIFT, PETE?
NO THANKS, HARR...
I'VE GOTTA STOP AT THE BUGLE ON THE WAY.
I ALMOST FORGOT. THERE'S A BIG RALEIGH DANCE-IN AT THE HALL TOMORROW NIGHT.
GRAB YOURSELF A GAL AND BE THERE, TIGER.
WILL DO, MJ.
I'LL SEE IF GWEN IS FREE LATER ON.
STILL STUCK WITH GWENDOLYNE, EH?
WELL, YOU CAN'T WIN 'EM ALL.
MINUTES LATER---
RALEIGH IS THE BEST THING THAT'S HAPPENED TO POLITICS IN YEARS.
MORE FEMALES THAN EVER ARE BUYING THE BUGLE SINCE I THREW HIM OUR SUPPORT.
WHAT IS IT, MISS BRANT?
PETER PARKER IS HERE TO SEE YOU, MR. JAMESON.
IF HE WANTS TO SEE ME, GIVE HIM A SNAPSHOT.
THE PEST HEARD THAT, MISTER.
TELL HIM I'M TOO BUSY... UNLESS THE PEST HAS SOME FRESH NEWS PHOTOS FOR ME.
PETER.. YOU SHOULDN'T HAVE...
RINNGGG
DON'T YOU EVER KNOCK FIRST?
JUST TELL ME ONE THING...
WHERE'S THE MONEY YOU OWE ME FOR THE LAST BATCH OF SHOTS I SOLD YOU?
C'MON... YOU'RE NOT IMPRESSING ME WITH THAT CORNY PHONE CALL ROUTINE.
WHAT'S THAT? SOME NUTTY GIANT JUST WRECKED A ROOFTOP RALEIGH BILL-BOARD... SINGLE-HANDED?
YOU BET I WANT MORE DETAILS.

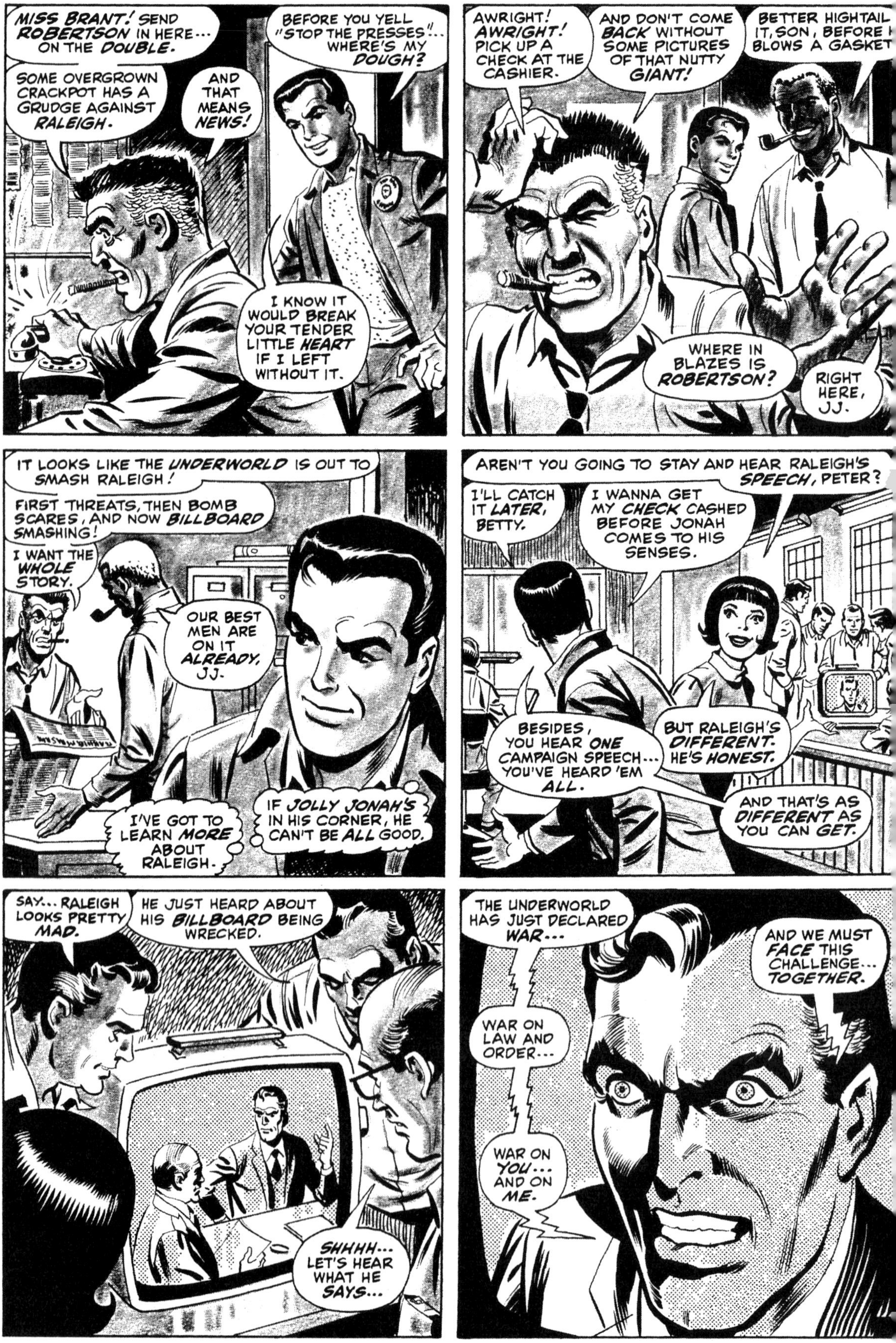
MISS BRANT! SEND ROBERTSON IN HERE... ON THE DOUBLE.
SOME OVERGROWN CRACKPOT HAS A GRUDGE AGAINST RALEIGH.
AND THAT MEANS NEWS!
BEFORE YOU YELL "STOP THE PRESSES"... WHERE'S MY DOUGH?
I KNOW IT WOULD BREAK YOUR TENDER LITTLE HEART IF I LEFT WITHOUT IT.
AWRIGHT! AWRIGHT! PICK UP A CHECK AT THE CASHIER.
AND DON'T COME BACK WITHOUT SOME PICTURES OF THAT NUTTY GIANT!
BETTER HIGHTAIL IT, SON, BEFORE H BLOWS A GASKET
WHERE IN BLAZES IS ROBERTSON?
RIGHT HERE, JJ.
IT LOOKS LIKE THE UNDERWORLD IS OUT TO SMASH RALEIGH!
FIRST THREATS, THEN BOMB SCARES, AND NOW BILLBOARD SMASHING!
I WANT THE WHOLE STORY.
OUR BEST MEN ARE ON IT ALREADY, JJ.
I'VE GOT TO LEARN MORE ABOUT RALEIGH.
IF JOLLY JONAH'S IN HIS CORNER, HE CAN'T BE ALL GOOD.
AREN'T YOU GOING TO STAY AND HEAR RALEIGH'S SPEECH, PETER?
I'LL CATCH IT LATER, BETTY.
I WANNA GET MY CHECK CASHED BEFORE JONAH COMES TO HIS SENSES.
BESIDES, YOU HEAR ONE CAMPAIGN SPEECH... YOU'VE HEARD 'EM ALL.
BUT RALEIGH'S DIFFERENT. HE'S HONEST.
AND THAT'S AS DIFFERENT AS YOU CAN GET.
SAY... RALEIGH LOOKS PRETTY MAD.
HE JUST HEARD ABOUT HIS BILLBOARD BEING WRECKED.
SHHHH... LET'S HEAR WHAT HE SAYS...
THE UNDERWORLD HAS JUST DECLARED WAR...
WAR ON LAW AND ORDER...
WAR ON YOU... AND ON ME.
AND WE MUST FACE THIS CHALLENGE... TOGETHER.

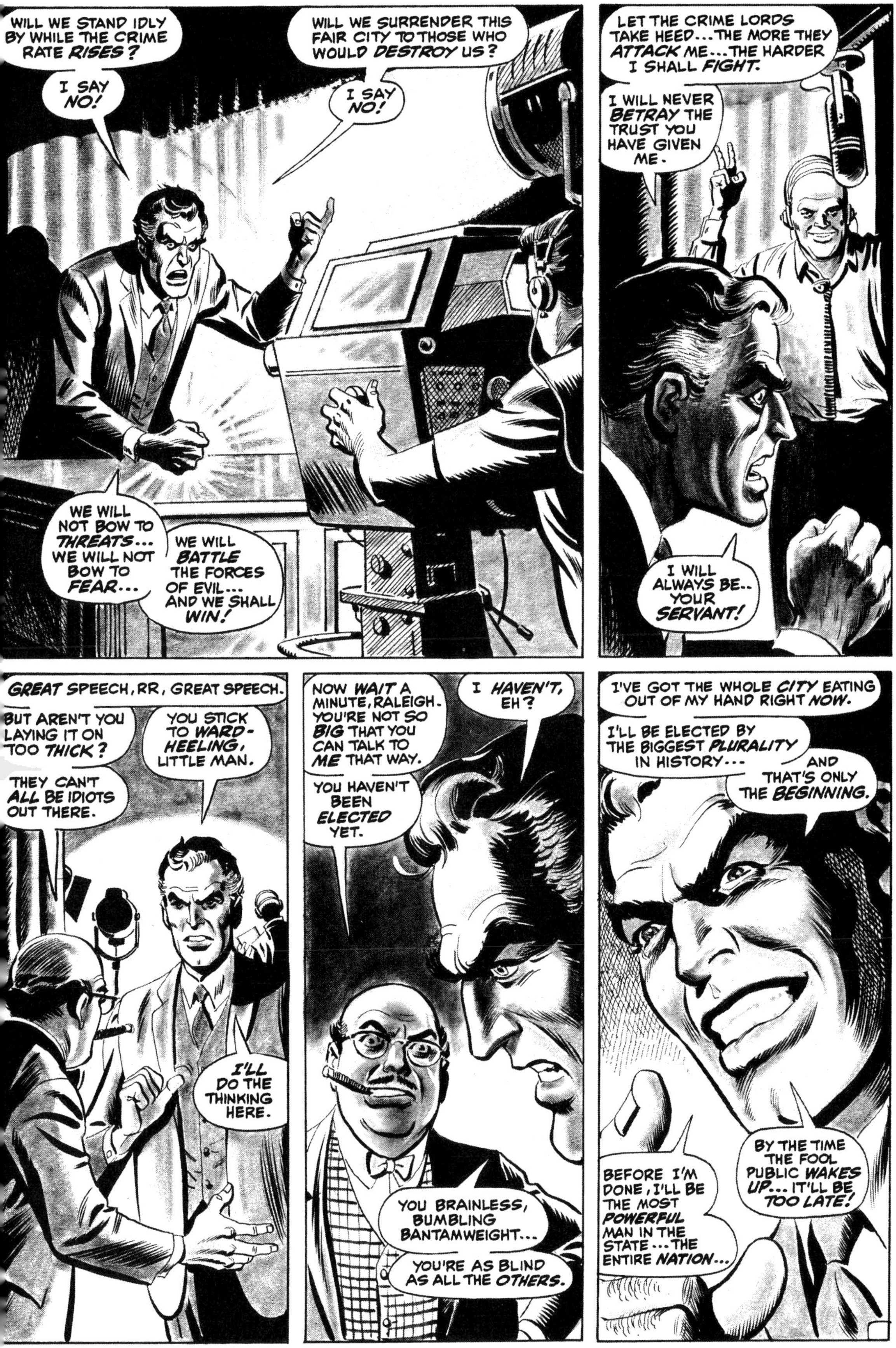

WILL WE STAND IDLY BY WHILE THE CRIME RATE RISES?
I SAY NO!
WILL WE SURRENDER THIS FAIR CITY TO THOSE WHO WOULD DESTROY US?
I SAY NO!
WE WILL NOT BOW TO THREATS... WE WILL NOT BOW TO FEAR...
WE WILL BATTLE THE FORCES OF EVIL... AND WE SHALL WIN!
LET THE CRIME LORDS TAKE HEED... THE MORE THEY ATTACK ME... THE HARDER I SHALL FIGHT.
I WILL NEVER BETRAY THE TRUST YOU HAVE GIVEN ME.
I WILL ALWAYS BE.. YOUR SERVANT!
GREAT SPEECH, RR, GREAT SPEECH.
BUT AREN'T YOU LAYING IT ON TOO THICK?
THEY CAN'T ALL BE IDIOTS OUT THERE.
YOU STICK TO WARD-HEELING, LITTLE MAN.
I'LL DO THE THINKING HERE.
NOW WAIT A MINUTE, RALEIGH. YOU'RE NOT SO BIG THAT YOU CAN TALK TO ME THAT WAY.
YOU HAVEN'T BEEN ELECTED YET.
I HAVEN'T, EH?
YOU BRAINLESS, BUMBLING BANTAMWEIGHT...
YOU'RE AS BLIND AS ALL THE OTHERS.
I'VE GOT THE WHOLE CITY EATING OUT OF MY HAND RIGHT NOW.
I'LL BE ELECTED BY THE BIGGEST PLURALITY IN HISTORY...
AND THAT'S ONLY THE BEGINNING.
BEFORE I'M DONE, I'LL BE THE MOST POWERFUL MAN IN THE STATE... THE ENTIRE NATION...
BY THE TIME THE FOOL PUBLIC WAKES UP... IT'LL BE TOO LATE!

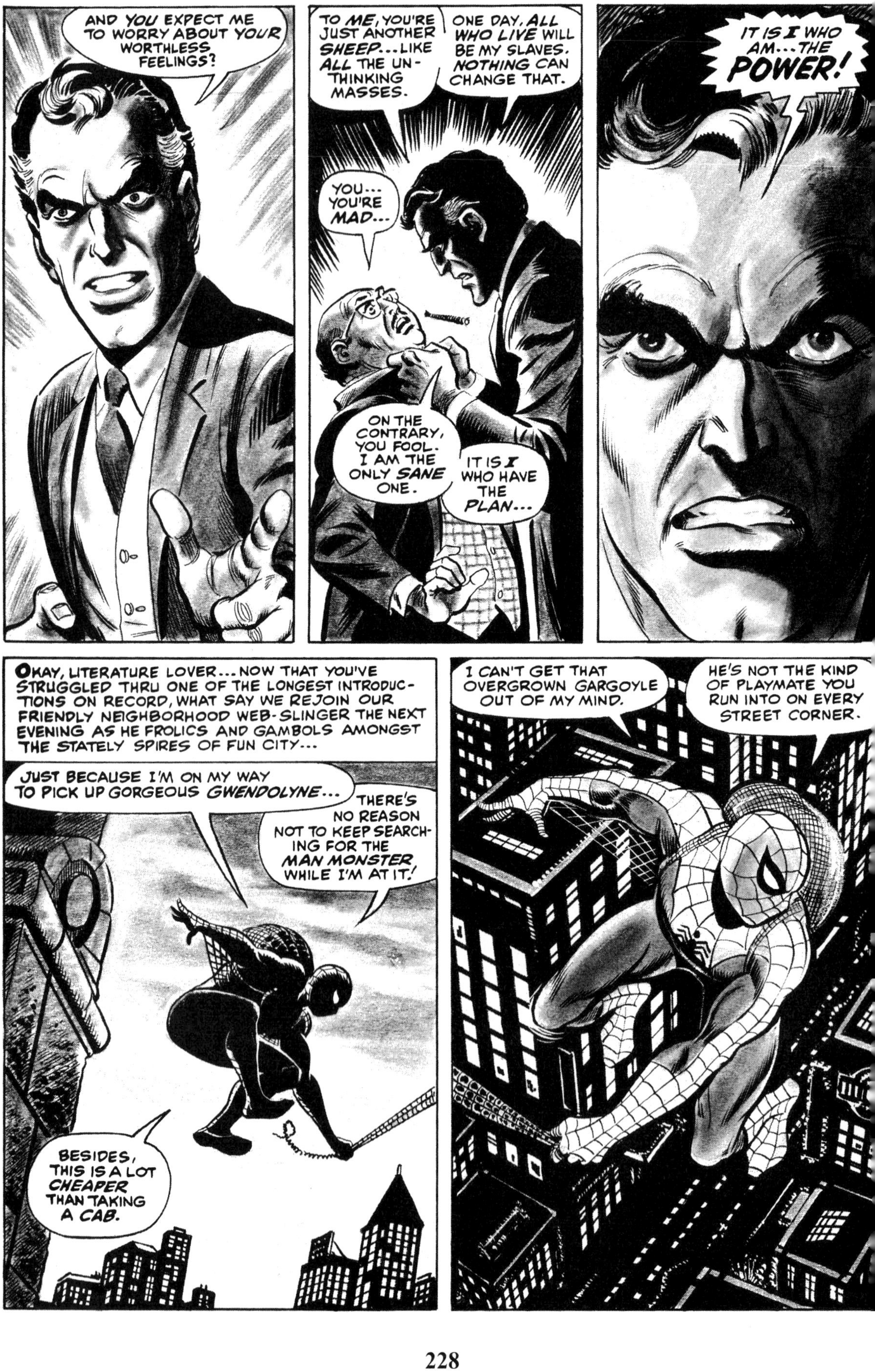
AND YOU EXPECT ME TO WORRY ABOUT YOUR WORTHLESS FEELINGS?
TO ME, YOU'RE JUST ANOTHER SHEEP... LIKE ALL THE UN-THINKING MASSES.
ONE DAY, ALL WHO LIVE WILL BE MY SLAVES. NOTHING CAN CHANGE THAT.
YOU... YOU'RE MAD...
ON THE CONTRARY, YOU FOOL. I AM THE ONLY SANE ONE.
IT IS I WHO HAVE THE PLAN...
IT IS I WHO AM... THE POWER!
OKAY, LITERATURE LOVER... NOW THAT YOU'VE STRUGGLED THRU ONE OF THE LONGEST INTRODUC-TIONS ON RECORD, WHAT SAY WE REJOIN OUR FRIENDLY NEIGHBORHOOD WEB-SLINGER THE NEXT EVENING AS HE FROLICS AND GAMBOLS AMONGST THE STATELY SPIRES OF FUN CITY...
JUST BECAUSE I'M ON MY WAY TO PICK UP GORGEOUS GWENDOLYNE...
THERE'S NO REASON NOT TO KEEP SEARCH-ING FOR THE MAN MONSTER WHILE I'M AT IT!
BESIDES, THIS IS A LOT CHEAPER THAN TAKING A CAB.
I CAN'T GET THAT OVERGROWN GARGOYLE OUT OF MY MIND.
HE'S NOT THE KIND OF PLAYMATE YOU RUN INTO ON EVERY STREET CORNER.

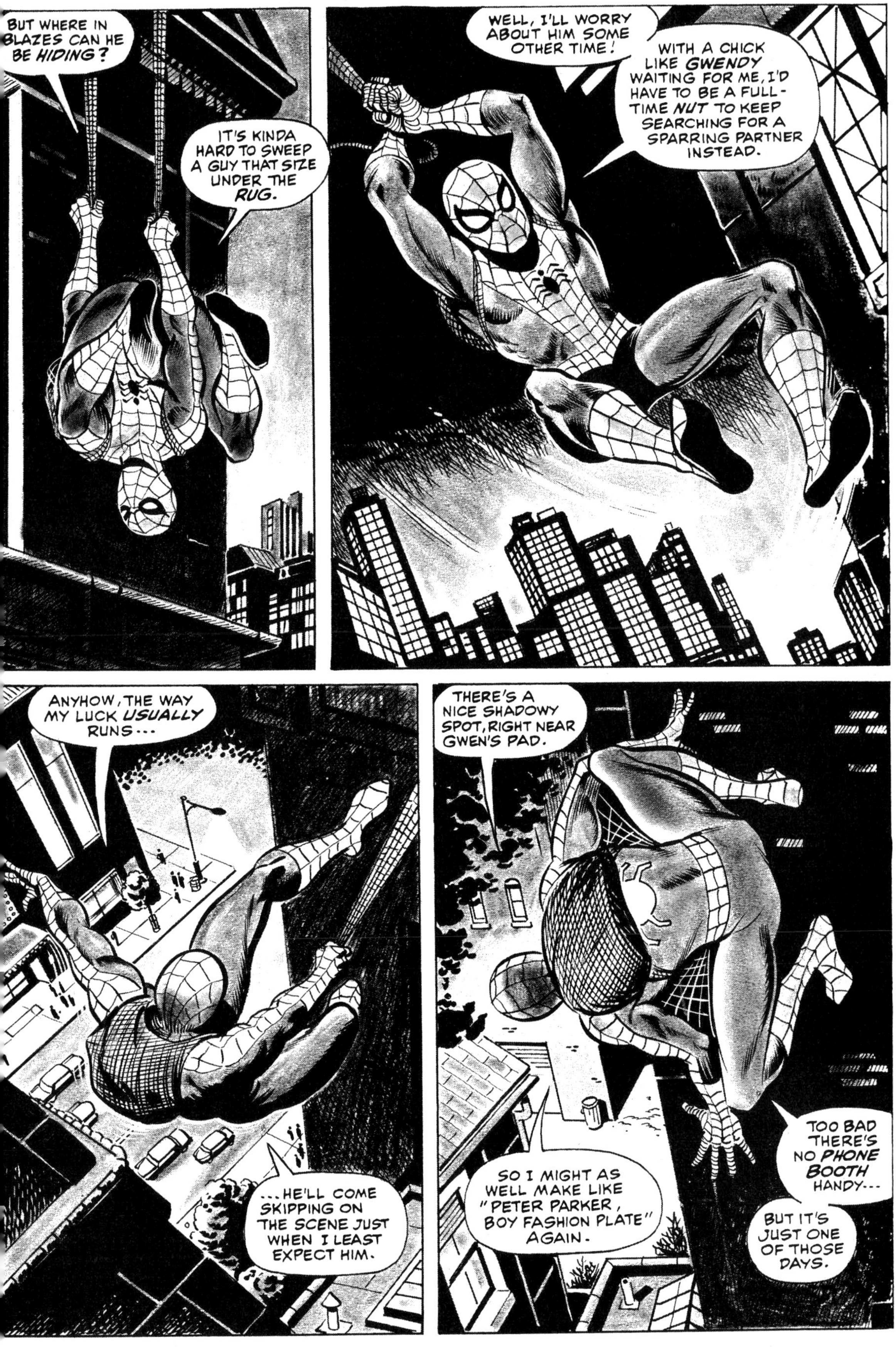

BUT WHERE IN BLAZES CAN HE BE HIDING?
IT'S KINDA HARD TO SWEEP A GUY THAT SIZE UNDER THE RUG.
WELL, I'LL WORRY ABOUT HIM SOME OTHER TIME!
WITH A CHICK LIKE GWENDY WAITING FOR ME, I'D HAVE TO BE A FULL-TIME NUT TO KEEP SEARCHING FOR A SPARRING PARTNER INSTEAD.
ANYHOW, THE WAY MY LUCK USUALLY RUNS...
...HE'LL COME SKIPPING ON THE SCENE JUST WHEN I LEAST EXPECT HIM.
THERE'S A NICE SHADOWY SPOT, RIGHT NEAR GWEN'S PAD.
SO I MIGHT AS WELL MAKE LIKE "PETER PARKER, BOY FASHION PLATE" AGAIN.
TOO BAD THERE'S NO PHONE BOOTH HANDY...
BUT IT'S JUST ONE OF THOSE DAYS.

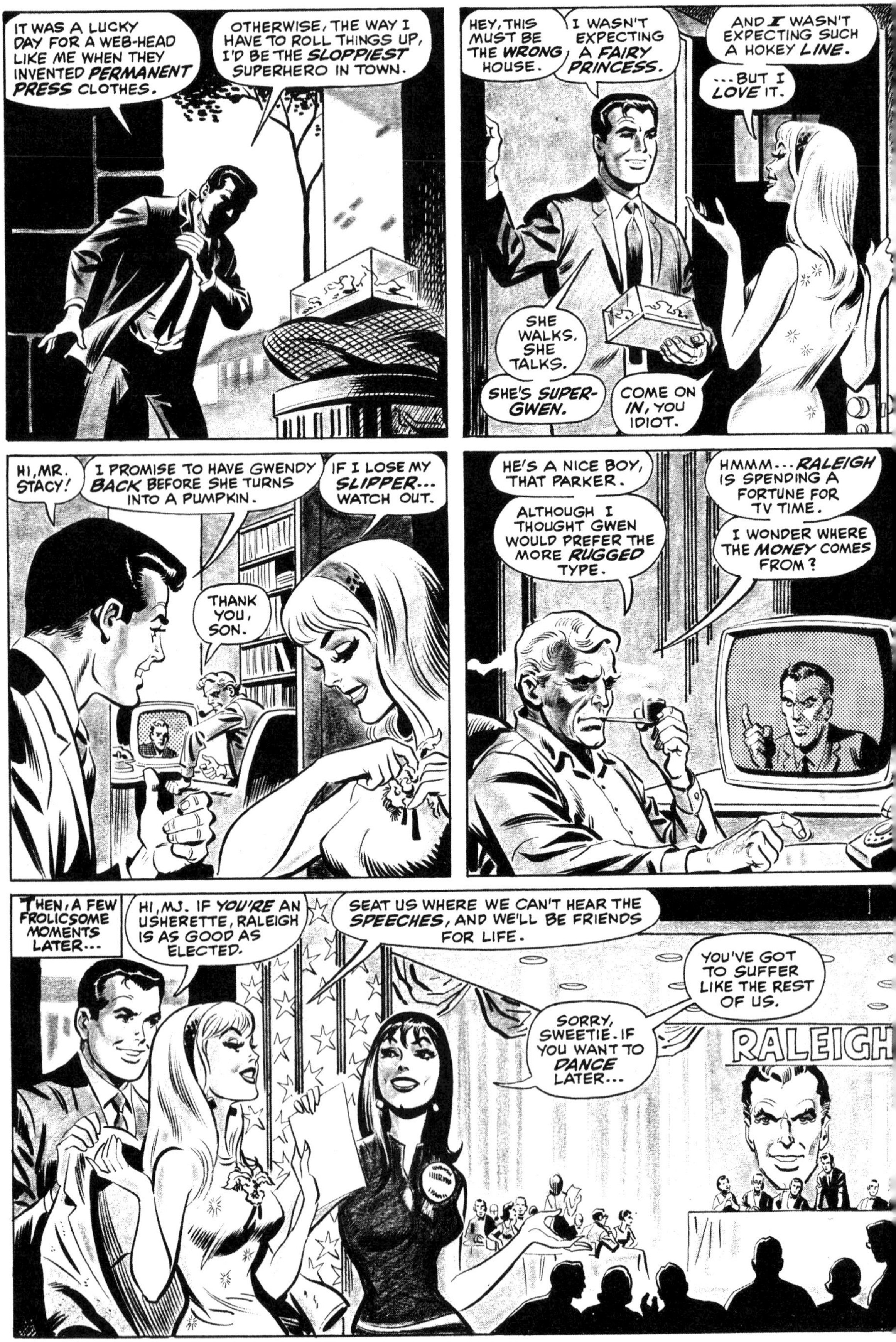
IT WAS A LUCKY DAY FOR A WEB-HEAD LIKE ME WHEN THEY INVENTED PERMANENT PRESS CLOTHES.
OTHERWISE, THE WAY I HAVE TO ROLL THINGS UP, I'D BE THE SLOPPIEST SUPERHERO IN TOWN.
HEY, THIS MUST BE THE WRONG HOUSE.
I WASN'T EXPECTING A FAIRY PRINCESS.
AND I WASN'T EXPECTING SUCH A HOKEY LINE.
...BUT I LOVE IT.
SHE WALKS. SHE TALKS.
SHE'S SUPER-GWEN.
COME ON IN, YOU IDIOT.
HI, MR. STACY!
I PROMISE TO HAVE GWENDY BACK BEFORE SHE TURNS INTO A PUMPKIN.
IF I LOSE MY SLIPPER... WATCH OUT.
THANK YOU, SON.
HE'S A NICE BOY, THAT PARKER.
ALTHOUGH I THOUGHT GWEN WOULD PREFER THE MORE RUGGED TYPE.
HMMM... RALEIGH IS SPENDING A FORTUNE FOR TV TIME.
I WONDER WHERE THE MONEY COMES FROM?
THEN, A FEW FROLICSOME MOMENTS LATER...
HI, MJ. IF YOU'RE AN USHERETTE, RALEIGH IS AS GOOD AS ELECTED.
SEAT US WHERE WE CAN'T HEAR THE SPEECHES, AND WE'LL BE FRIENDS FOR LIFE.
YOU'VE GOT TO SUFFER LIKE THE REST OF US.
SORRY, SWEETIE. IF YOU WANT TO DANCE LATER...
RALEIGH

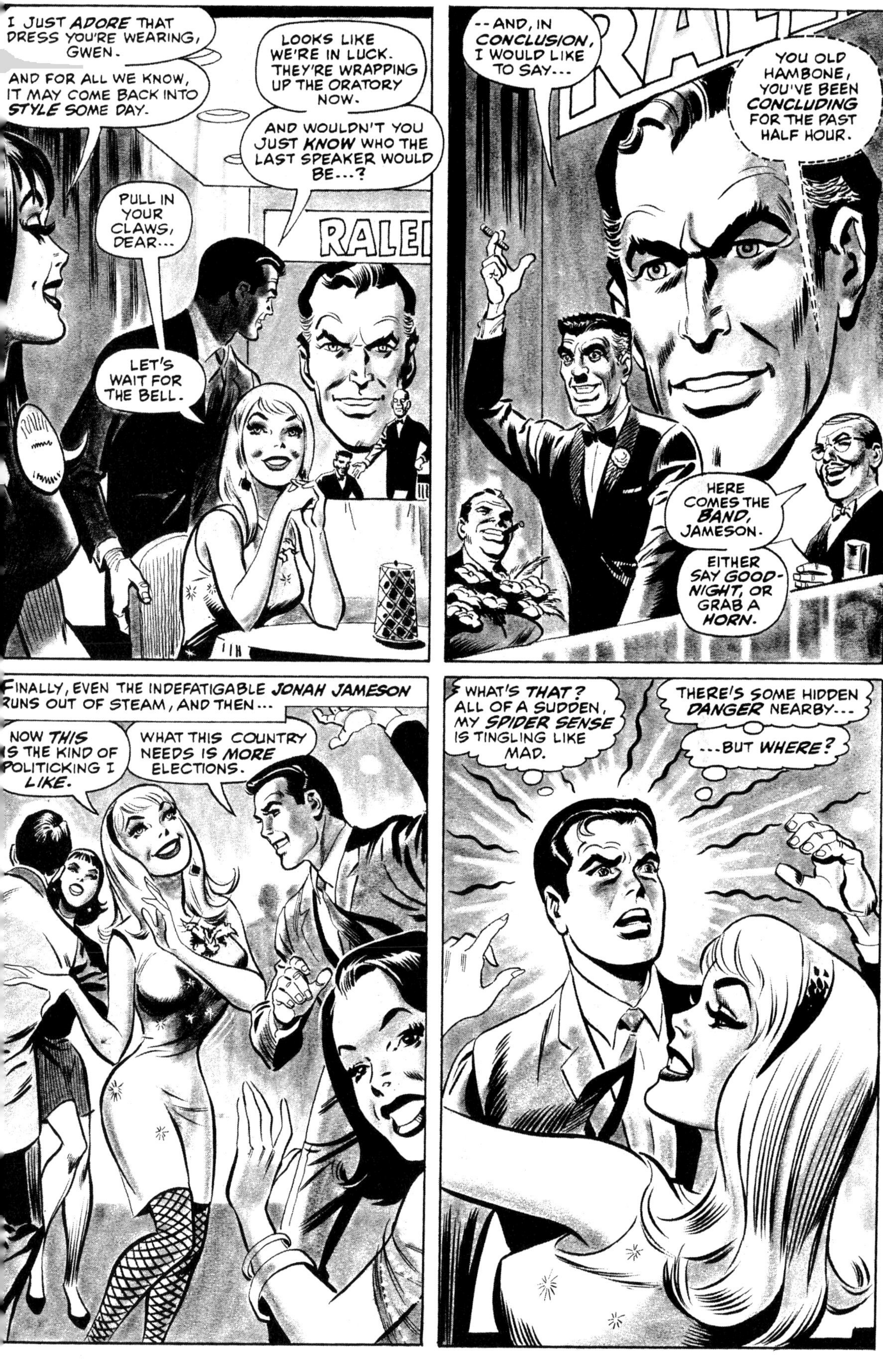
I JUST ADORE THAT DRESS YOU'RE WEARING, GWEN.
AND FOR ALL WE KNOW, IT MAY COME BACK INTO STYLE SOME DAY.
LOOKS LIKE WE'RE IN LUCK. THEY'RE WRAPPING UP THE ORATORY NOW.
AND WOULDN'T YOU JUST KNOW WHO THE LAST SPEAKER WOULD BE...?
PULL IN YOUR CLAWS, DEAR...
LET'S WAIT FOR THE BELL.
RALEI
--AND, IN CONCLUSION, I WOULD LIKE TO SAY...
YOU OLD HAMBONE, YOU'VE BEEN CONCLUDING FOR THE PAST HALF HOUR.
HERE COMES THE BAND, JAMESON.
EITHER SAY GOOD-NIGHT, OR GRAB A HORN.
FINALLY, EVEN THE INDEFATIGABLE JONAH JAMESON RUNS OUT OF STEAM, AND THEN...
NOW THIS IS THE KIND OF POLITICKING I LIKE.
WHAT THIS COUNTRY NEEDS IS MORE ELECTIONS.
WHAT'S THAT? ALL OF A SUDDEN, MY SPIDER SENSE IS TINGLING LIKE MAD.
THERE'S SOME HIDDEN DANGER NEARBY...
...BUT WHERE?

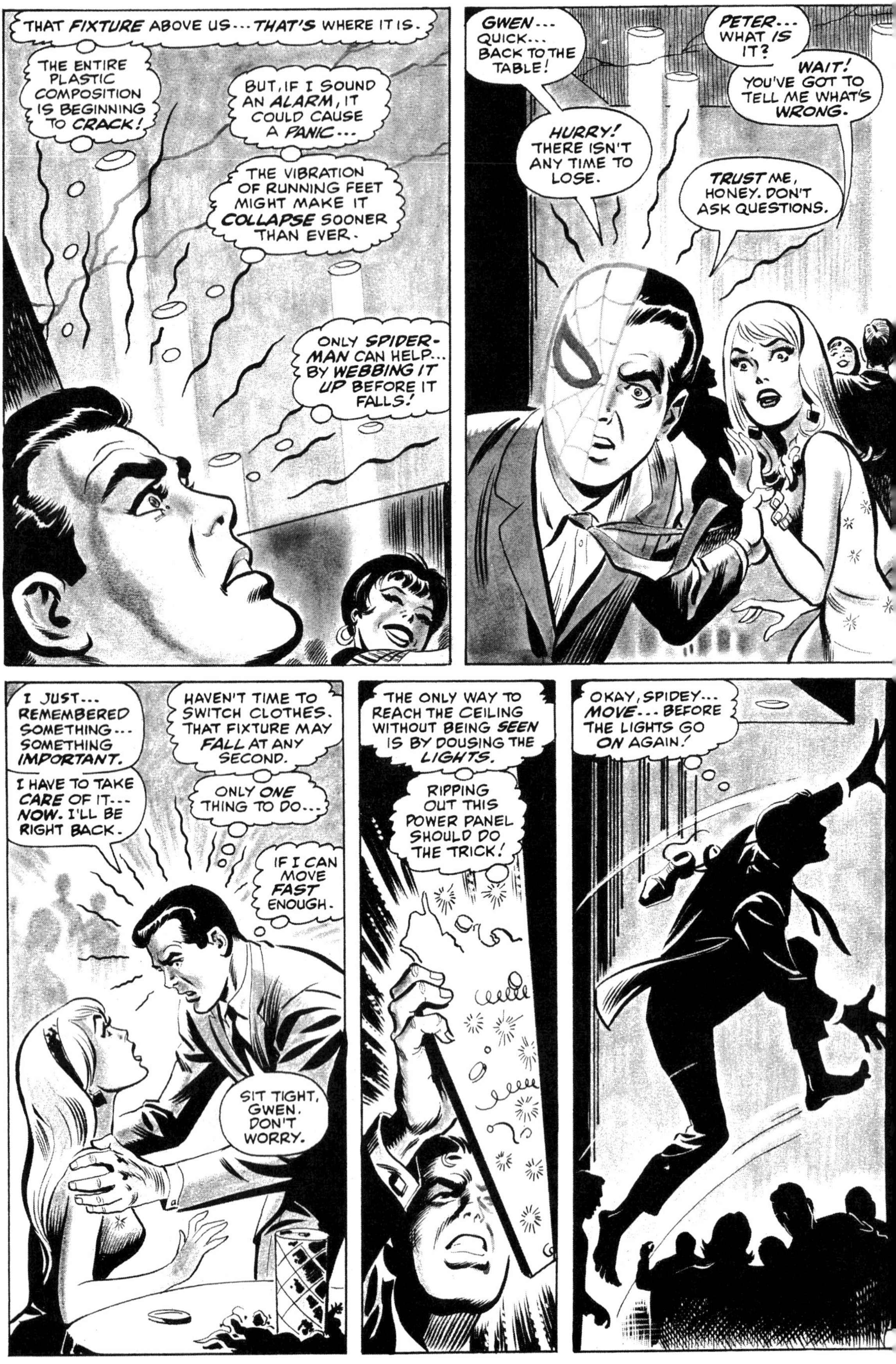

THAT FIXTURE ABOVE US... THAT'S WHERE IT IS.
THE ENTIRE PLASTIC COMPOSITION IS BEGINNING TO CRACK!
BUT, IF I SOUND AN ALARM, IT COULD CAUSE A PANIC...
THE VIBRATION OF RUNNING FEET MIGHT MAKE IT COLLAPSE SOONER THAN EVER.
ONLY SPIDER-MAN CAN HELP... BY WEBBING IT UP BEFORE IT FALLS!
GWEN... QUICK... BACK TO THE TABLE!
HURRY! THERE ISN'T ANY TIME TO LOSE.
PETER... WHAT IS IT?
WAIT! YOU'VE GOT TO TELL ME WHAT'S WRONG.
TRUST ME, HONEY. DON'T ASK QUESTIONS.
I JUST... REMEMBERED SOMETHING... SOMETHING IMPORTANT.
I HAVE TO TAKE CARE OF IT... NOW. I'LL BE RIGHT BACK.
HAVEN'T TIME TO SWITCH CLOTHES. THAT FIXTURE MAY FALL AT ANY SECOND.
ONLY ONE THING TO DO...
IF I CAN MOVE FAST ENOUGH.
SIT TIGHT, GWEN. DON'T WORRY.
THE ONLY WAY TO REACH THE CEILING WITHOUT BEING SEEN IS BY DOUSING THE LIGHTS.
RIPPING OUT THIS POWER PANEL SHOULD DO THE TRICK!
OKAY, SPIDEY... MOVE... BEFORE THE LIGHTS GO ON AGAIN!

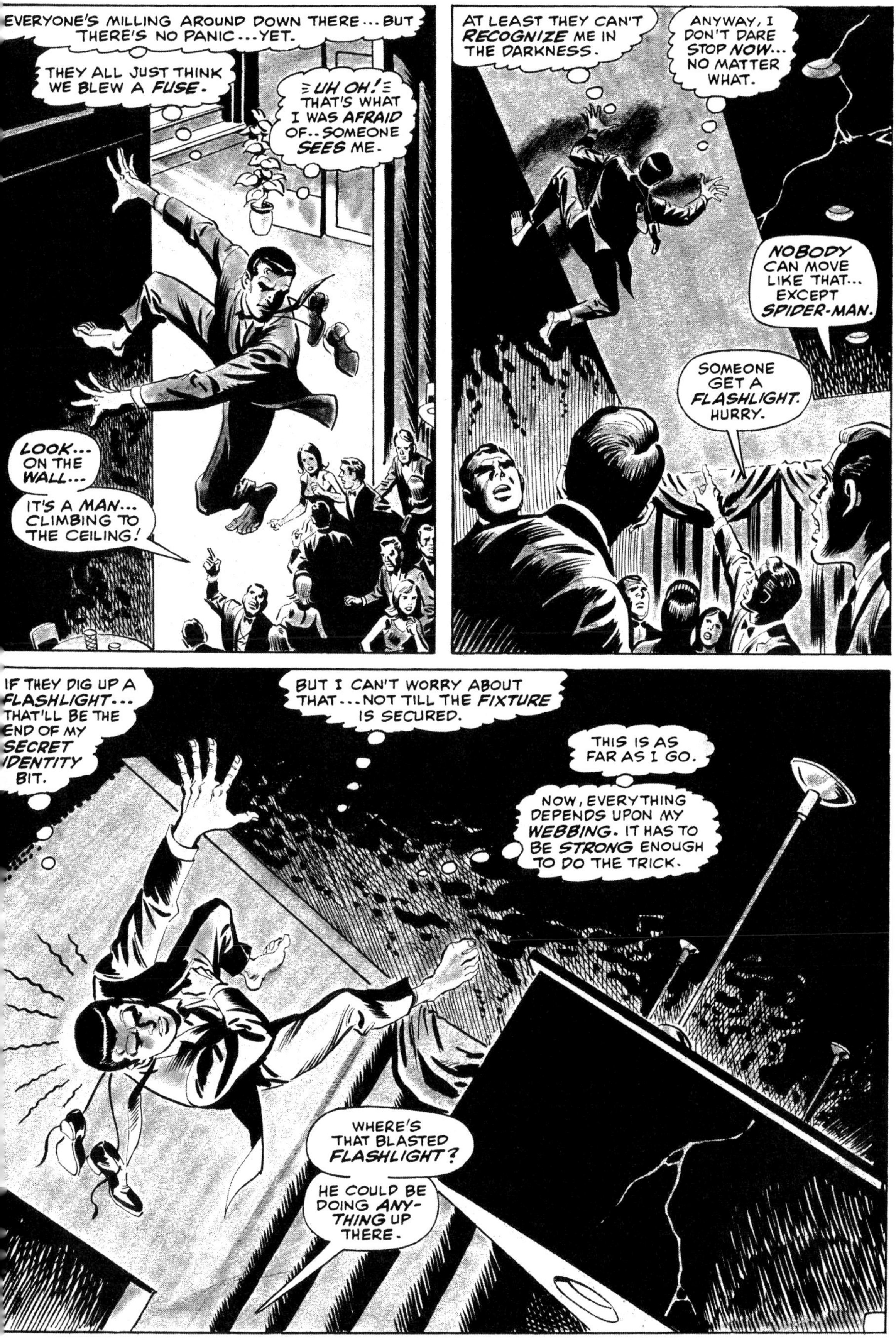
EVERYONE'S MILLING AROUND DOWN THERE... BUT THERE'S NO PANIC... YET.
THEY ALL JUST THINK WE BLEW A FUSE.
UH OH! THAT'S WHAT I WAS AFRAID OF.. SOMEONE SEES ME.
LOOK... ON THE WALL...
IT'S A MAN... CLIMBING TO THE CEILING!
AT LEAST THEY CAN'T RECOGNIZE ME IN THE DARKNESS.
ANYWAY, I DON'T DARE STOP NOW... NO MATTER WHAT.
NOBODY CAN MOVE LIKE THAT... EXCEPT SPIDER-MAN.
SOMEONE GET A FLASHLIGHT. HURRY.
IF THEY DIG UP A FLASHLIGHT--- THAT'LL BE THE END OF MY SECRET IDENTITY BIT.
BUT I CAN'T WORRY ABOUT THAT... NOT TILL THE FIXTURE IS SECURED.
THIS IS AS FAR AS I GO.
NOW, EVERYTHING DEPENDS UPON MY WEBBING. IT HAS TO BE STRONG ENOUGH TO DO THE TRICK.
WHERE'S THAT BLASTED FLASHLIGHT?
HE COULD BE DOING ANYTHING UP THERE.

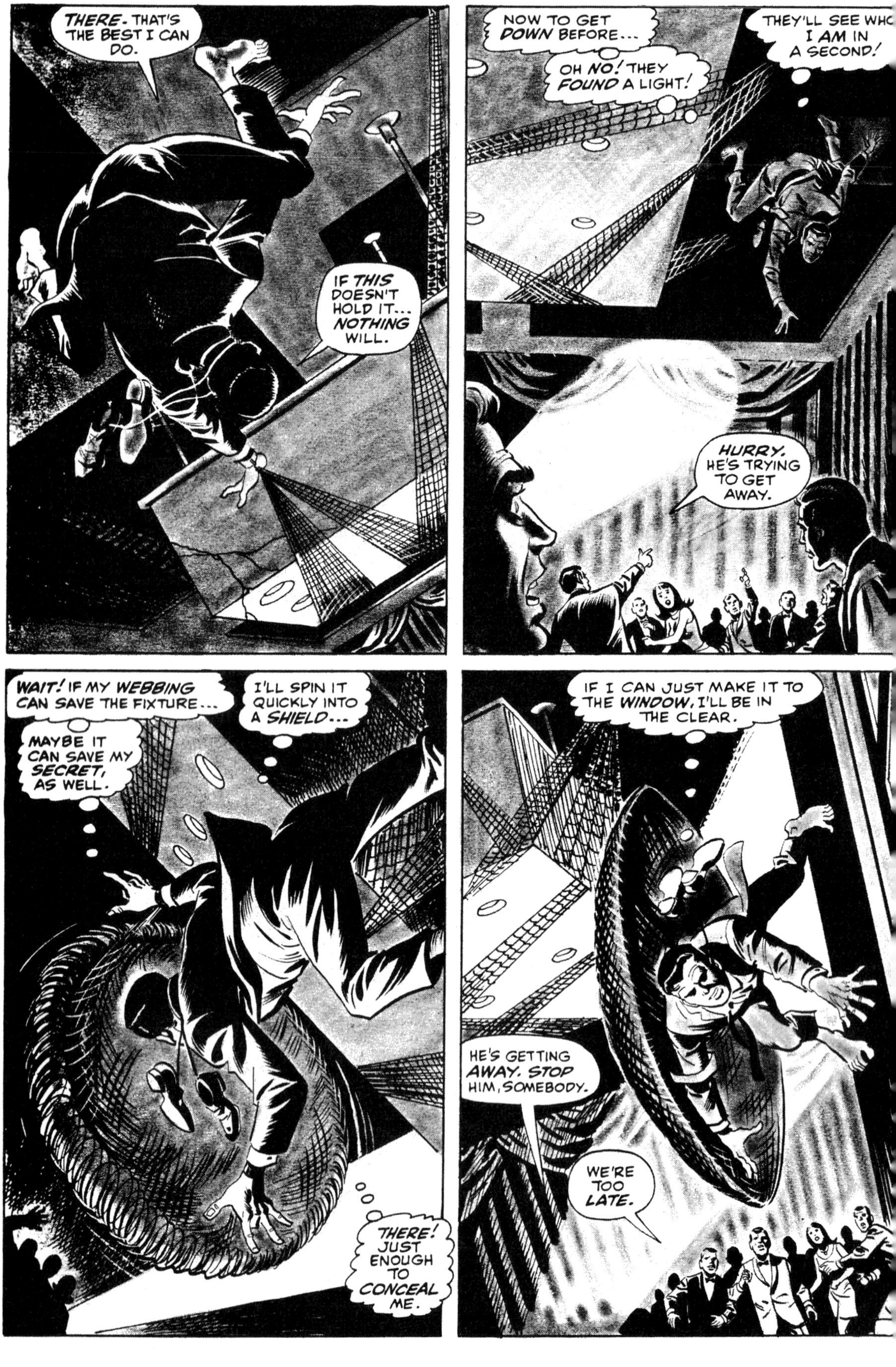
THERE- THAT'S THE BEST I CAN DO.
IF THIS DOESN'T HOLD IT... NOTHING WILL.
NOW TO GET DOWN BEFORE...
OH NO! THEY FOUND A LIGHT!
THEY'LL SEE WHO I AM IN A SECOND!
HURRY. HE'S TRYING TO GET AWAY.
WAIT! IF MY WEBBING CAN SAVE THE FIXTURE...
MAYBE IT CAN SAVE MY SECRET, AS WELL.
I'LL SPIN IT QUICKLY INTO A SHIELD...
THERE! JUST ENOUGH TO CONCEAL ME.
IF I CAN JUST MAKE IT TO THE WINDOW, I'LL BE IN THE CLEAR.
HE'S GETTING AWAY. STOP HIM, SOMEBODY.
WE'RE TOO LATE.

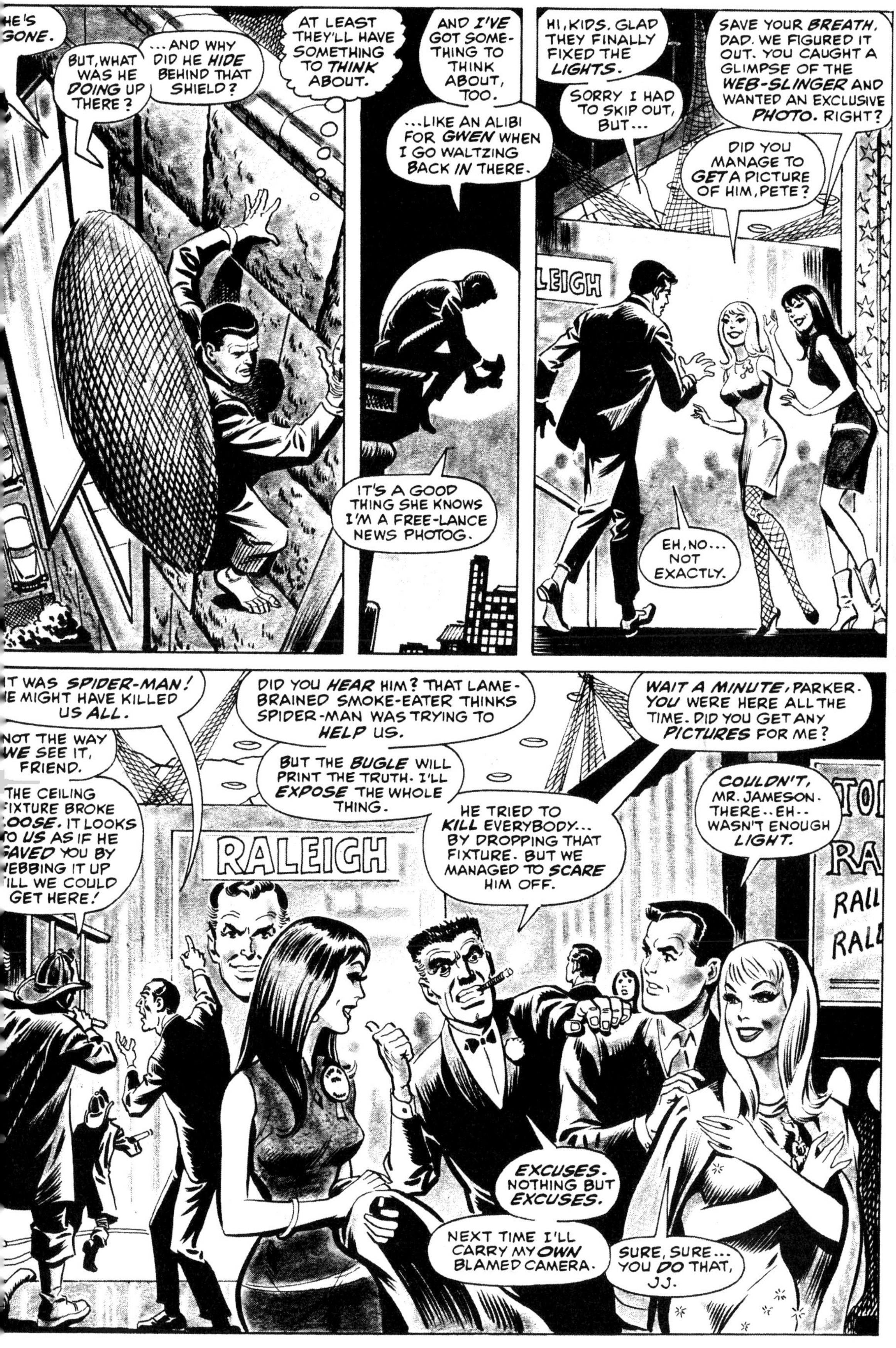

HE'S GONE.
BUT, WHAT WAS HE DOING UP THERE?
...AND WHY DID HE HIDE BEHIND THAT SHIELD?
AT LEAST THEY'LL HAVE SOMETHING TO THINK ABOUT.
AND I'VE GOT SOMETHING TO THINK ABOUT, TOO.
...LIKE AN ALIBI FOR GWEN WHEN I GO WALTZING BACK IN THERE.
IT'S A GOOD THING SHE KNOWS I'M A FREE-LANCE NEWS PHOTOG.
HI, KIDS. GLAD THEY FINALLY FIXED THE LIGHTS.
SORRY I HAD TO SKIP OUT, BUT...
SAVE YOUR BREATH, DAD. WE FIGURED IT OUT. YOU CAUGHT A GLIMPSE OF THE WEB-SLINGER AND WANTED AN EXCLUSIVE PHOTO. RIGHT?
DID YOU MANAGE TO GET A PICTURE OF HIM, PETE?
EH, NO... NOT EXACTLY.
RALEIGH
IT WAS SPIDER-MAN! HE MIGHT HAVE KILLED US ALL.
NOT THE WAY WE SEE IT, FRIEND.
THE CEILING FIXTURE BROKE LOOSE. IT LOOKS TO US AS IF HE SAVED YOU BY WEBBING IT UP TILL WE COULD GET HERE!
DID YOU HEAR HIM? THAT LAME-BRAINED SMOKE-EATER THINKS SPIDER-MAN WAS TRYING TO HELP US.
BUT THE BUGLE WILL PRINT THE TRUTH. I'LL EXPOSE THE WHOLE THING.
HE TRIED TO KILL EVERYBODY... BY DROPPING THAT FIXTURE. BUT WE MANAGED TO SCARE HIM OFF.
WAIT A MINUTE, PARKER. YOU WERE HERE ALL THE TIME. DID YOU GET ANY PICTURES FOR ME?
COULDN'T, MR. JAMESON. THERE.. EH.. WASN'T ENOUGH LIGHT.
RALEIGH
EXCUSES. NOTHING BUT EXCUSES.
NEXT TIME I'LL CARRY MY OWN BLAMED CAMERA.
SURE, SURE... YOU DO THAT, J.J.

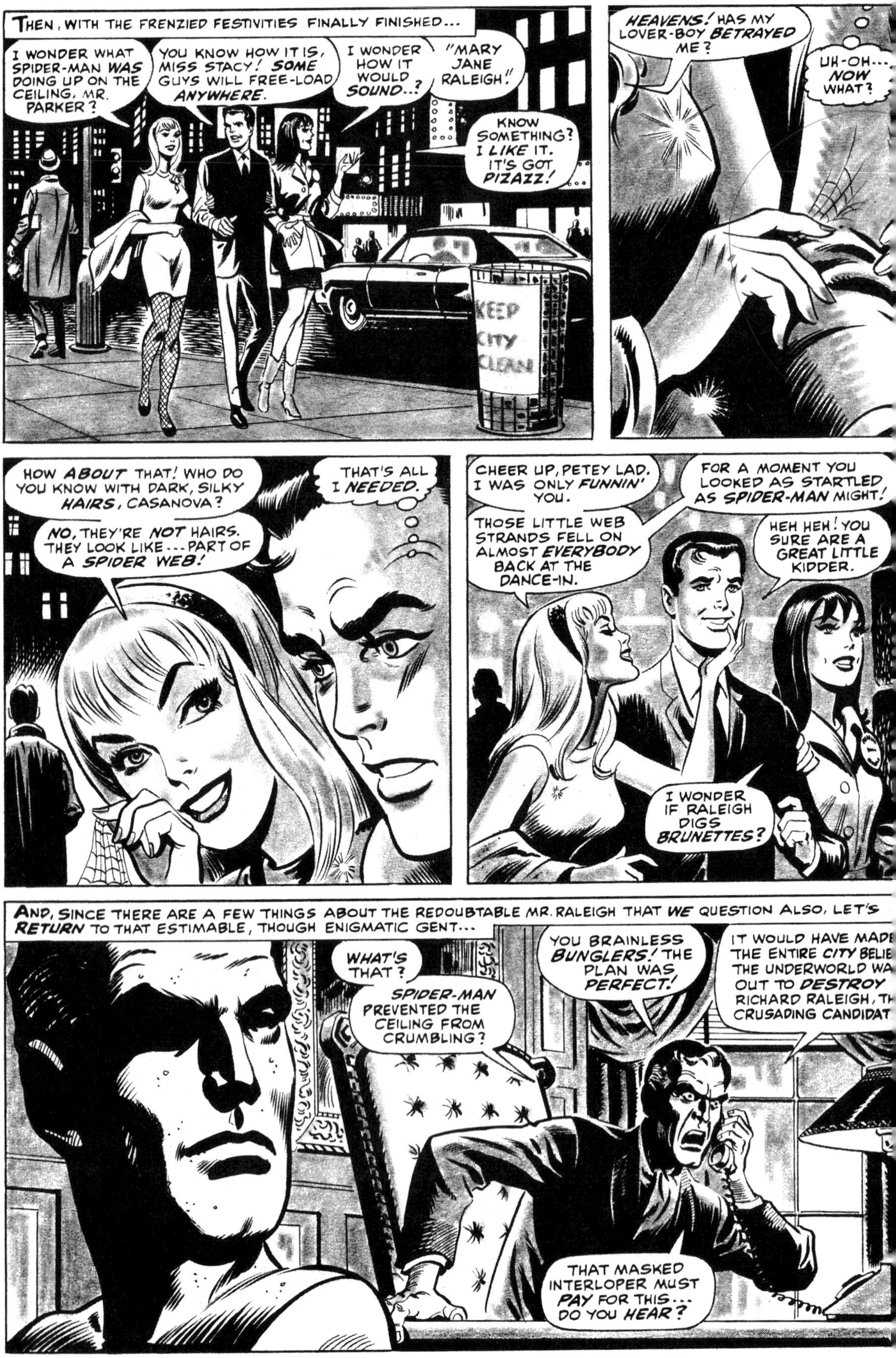
THEN, WITH THE FRENZIED FESTIVITIES FINALLY FINISHED...
I WONDER WHAT SPIDER-MAN WAS DOING UP ON THE CEILING, MR. PARKER?
YOU KNOW HOW IT IS, MISS STACY! SOME GUYS WILL FREE-LOAD ANYWHERE.
I WONDER HOW IT WOULD SOUND..?
"MARY JANE RALEIGH!"
KNOW SOMETHING? I LIKE IT. IT'S GOT PIZAZZ!
KEEP CITY CLEAN
HEAVENS! HAS MY LOVER-BOY BETRAYED ME?
UH-OH... NOW WHAT?
HOW ABOUT THAT! WHO DO YOU KNOW WITH DARK, SILKY HAIRS, CASANOVA?
THAT'S ALL I NEEDED.
NO, THEY'RE NOT HAIRS. THEY LOOK LIKE... PART OF A SPIDER WEB!
CHEER UP, PETEY LAD. I WAS ONLY FUNNIN' YOU.
FOR A MOMENT YOU LOOKED AS STARTLED AS SPIDER-MAN MIGHT!
THOSE LITTLE WEB STRANDS FELL ON ALMOST EVERYBODY BACK AT THE DANCE-IN.
HEH HEH! YOU SURE ARE A GREAT LITTLE KIDDER.
I WONDER IF RALEIGH DIGS BRUNETTES?
AND, SINCE THERE ARE A FEW THINGS ABOUT THE REDOUBTABLE MR. RALEIGH THAT WE QUESTION ALSO, LET'S RETURN TO THAT ESTIMABLE, THOUGH ENIGMATIC GENT...
WHAT'S THAT? SPIDER-MAN PREVENTED THE CEILING FROM CRUMBLING?
YOU BRAINLESS BUNGLERS! THE PLAN WAS PERFECT!
IT WOULD HAVE MADE THE ENTIRE CITY BELIE THE UNDERWORLD WA OUT TO DESTROY RICHARD RALEIGH, TH CRUSADING CANDIDAT
THAT MASKED INTERLOPER MUST PAY FOR THIS... DO YOU HEAR?

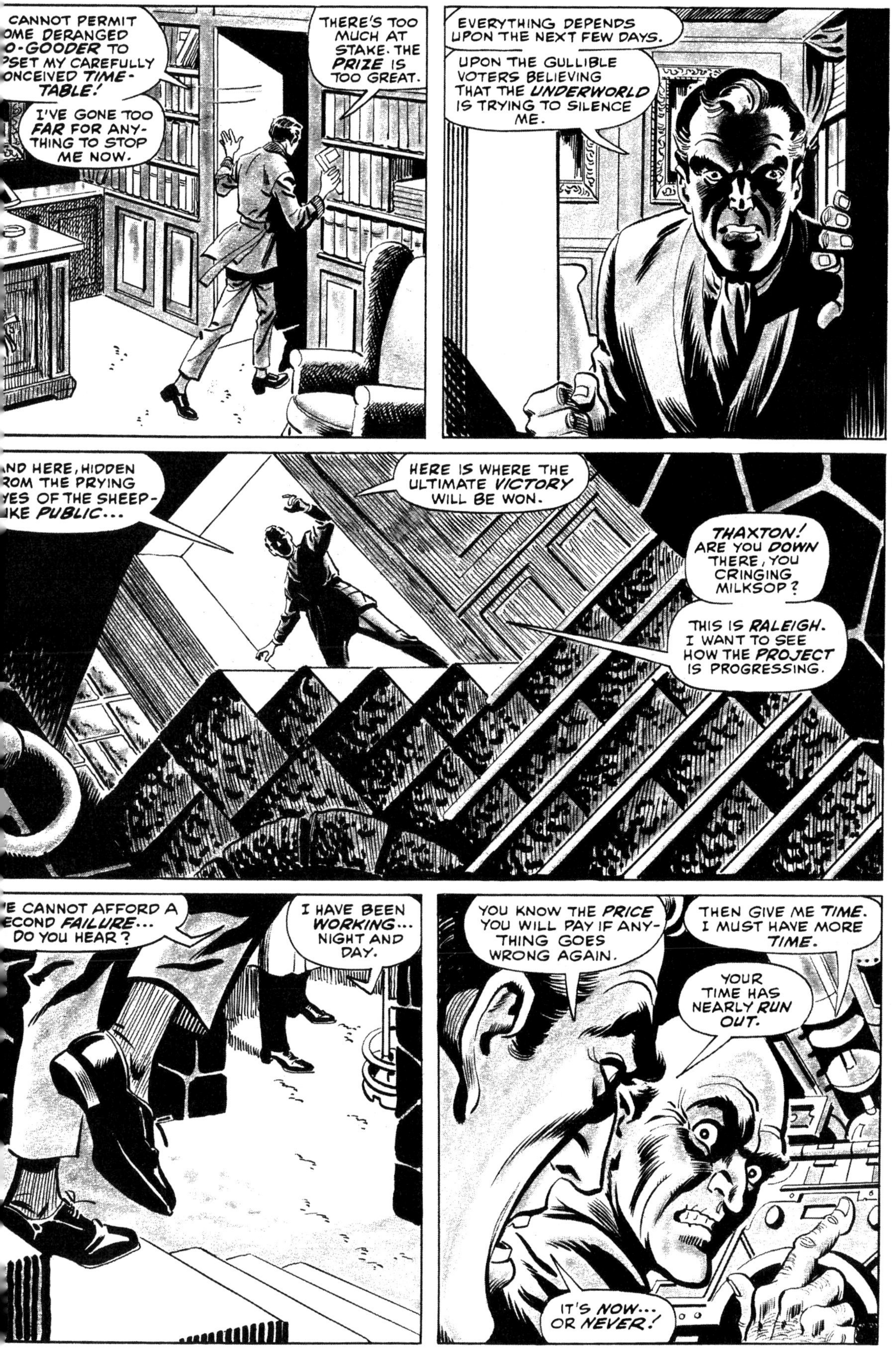
CANNOT PERMIT OME DERANGED O-GOODER TO PSET MY CAREFULLY ONCEIVED TIME-TABLE!
I'VE GONE TOO FAR FOR ANYTHING TO STOP ME NOW.
THERE'S TOO MUCH AT STAKE. THE PRIZE IS TOO GREAT.
EVERYTHING DEPENDS UPON THE NEXT FEW DAYS.
UPON THE GULLIBLE VOTERS BELIEVING THAT THE UNDERWORLD IS TRYING TO SILENCE ME.
ND HERE, HIDDEN ROM THE PRYING YES OF THE SHEEP-IKE PUBLIC...
HERE IS WHERE THE ULTIMATE VICTORY WILL BE WON.
THAXTON! ARE YOU DOWN THERE, YOU CRINGING MILKSOP?
THIS IS RALEIGH. I WANT TO SEE HOW THE PROJECT IS PROGRESSING.
E CANNOT AFFORD A ECOND FAILURE... DO YOU HEAR?
I HAVE BEEN WORKING... NIGHT AND DAY.
YOU KNOW THE PRICE YOU WILL PAY IF ANYTHING GOES WRONG AGAIN.
THEN GIVE ME TIME. I MUST HAVE MORE TIME.
YOUR TIME HAS NEARLY RUN OUT.
IT'S NOW... OR NEVER!

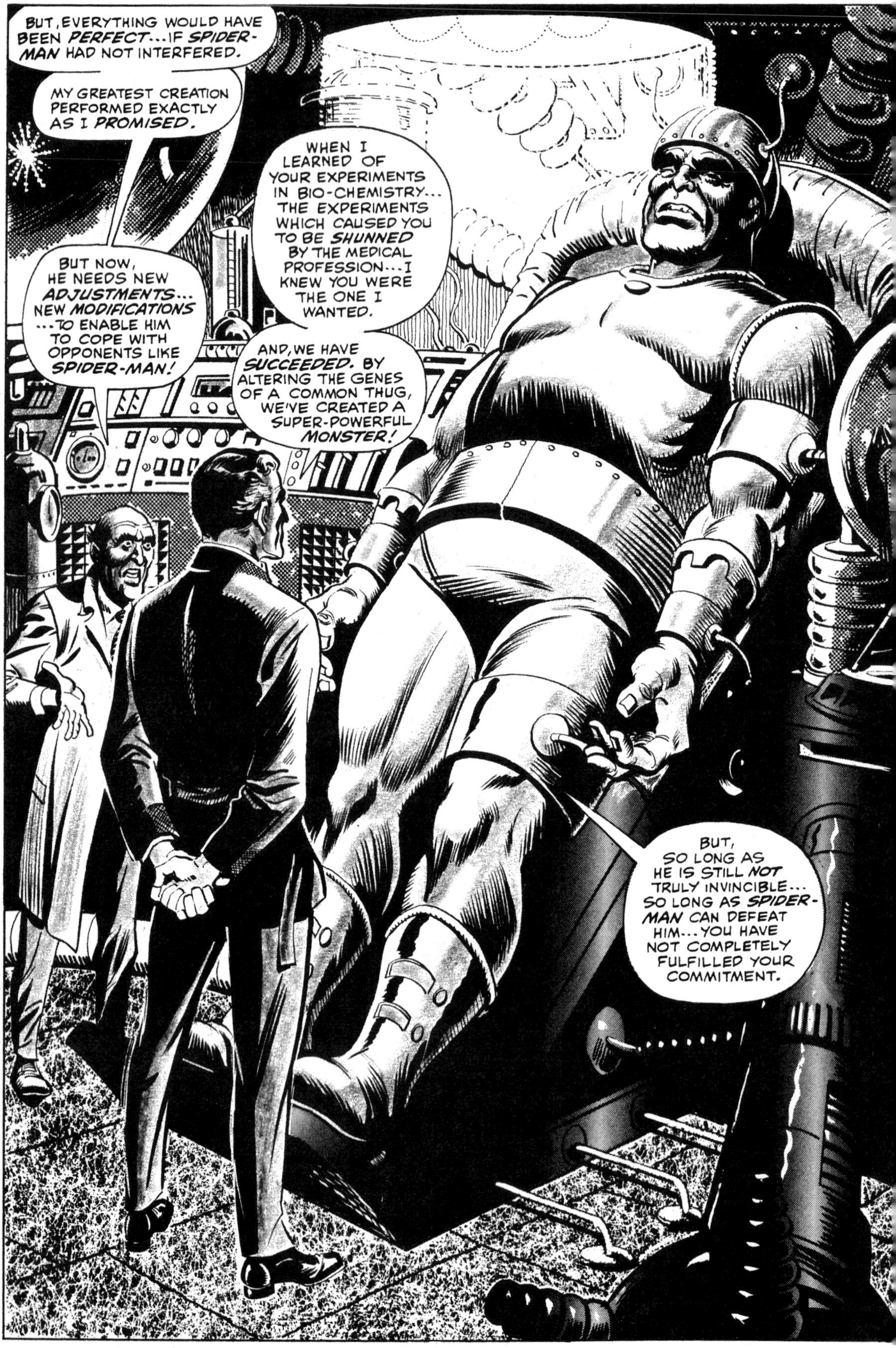
BUT, EVERYTHING WOULD HAVE BEEN PERFECT...IF SPIDER-MAN HAD NOT INTERFERED.
MY GREATEST CREATION PERFORMED EXACTLY AS I PROMISED.
BUT NOW, HE NEEDS NEW ADJUSTMENTS... NEW MODIFICATIONS ...TO ENABLE HIM TO COPE WITH OPPONENTS LIKE SPIDER-MAN!
WHEN I LEARNED OF YOUR EXPERIMENTS IN BIO-CHEMISTRY... THE EXPERIMENTS WHICH CAUSED YOU TO BE SHUNNED BY THE MEDICAL PROFESSION...I KNEW YOU WERE THE ONE I WANTED.
AND, WE HAVE SUCCEEDED. BY ALTERING THE GENES OF A COMMON THUG, WE'VE CREATED A SUPER-POWERFUL MONSTER!
BUT, SO LONG AS HE IS STILL NOT TRULY INVINCIBLE... SO LONG AS SPIDER-MAN CAN DEFEAT HIM...YOU HAVE NOT COMPLETELY FULFILLED YOUR COMMITMENT.

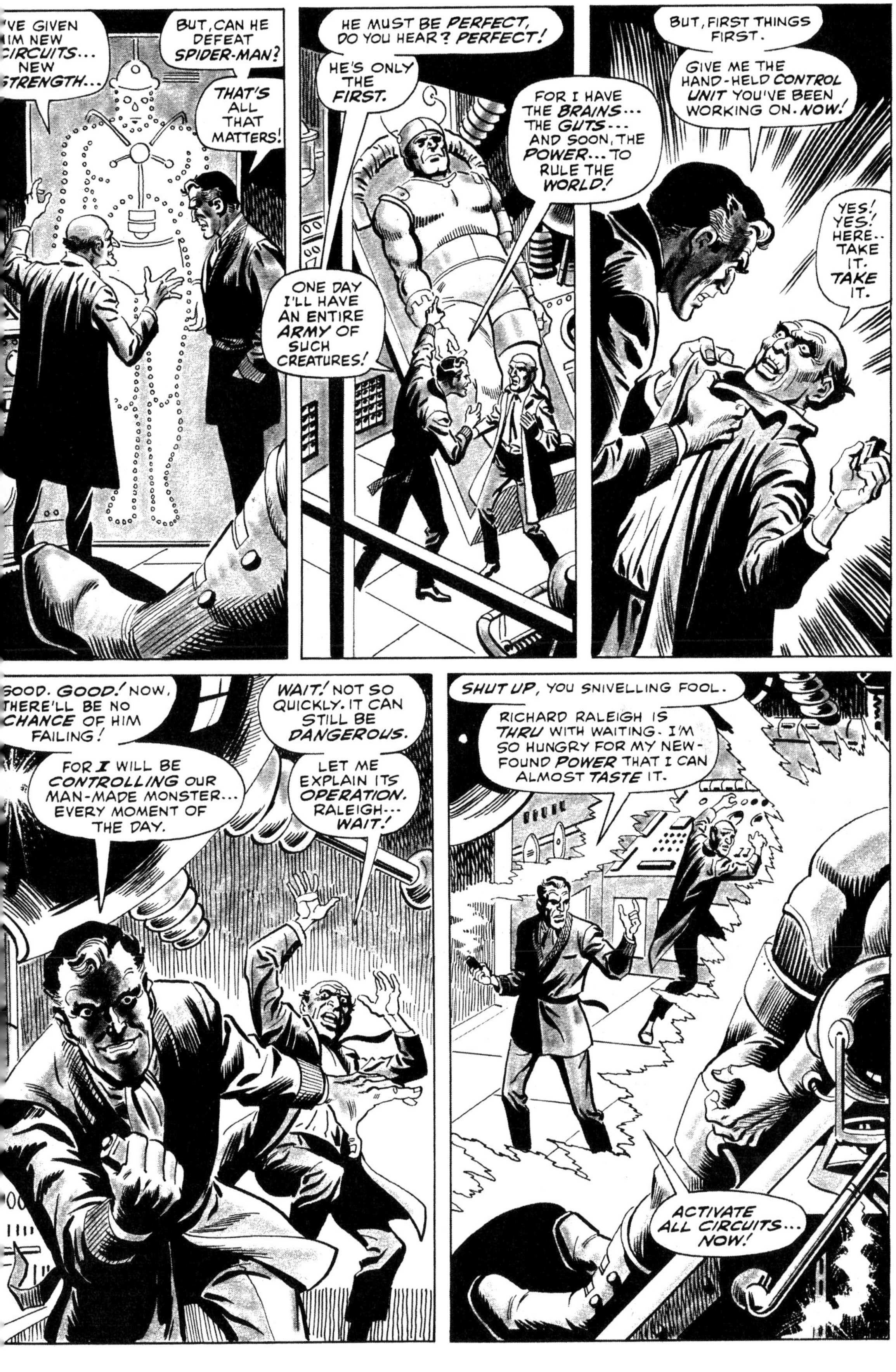
'VE GIVEN (H)IM NEW CIRCUITS... NEW STRENGTH...
BUT, CAN HE DEFEAT SPIDER-MAN?
THAT'S ALL THAT MATTERS!
HE MUST BE PERFECT, DO YOU HEAR? PERFECT!
HE'S ONLY THE FIRST.
FOR I HAVE THE BRAINS... THE GUTS... AND SOON, THE POWER... TO RULE THE WORLD!
ONE DAY I'LL HAVE AN ENTIRE ARMY OF SUCH CREATURES!
BUT, FIRST THINGS FIRST.
GIVE ME THE HAND-HELD CONTROL UNIT YOU'VE BEEN WORKING ON. NOW!
YES! YES! HERE.. TAKE IT. TAKE IT.
GOOD. GOOD! NOW, THERE'LL BE NO CHANCE OF HIM FAILING!
FOR I WILL BE CONTROLLING OUR MAN-MADE MONSTER... EVERY MOMENT OF THE DAY.
WAIT! NOT SO QUICKLY. IT CAN STILL BE DANGEROUS.
LET ME EXPLAIN ITS OPERATION. RALEIGH... WAIT!
SHUT UP, YOU SNIVELLING FOOL.
RICHARD RALEIGH IS THRU WITH WAITING. I'M SO HUNGRY FOR MY NEW-FOUND POWER THAT I CAN ALMOST TASTE IT.
ACTIVATE ALL CIRCUITS... NOW!

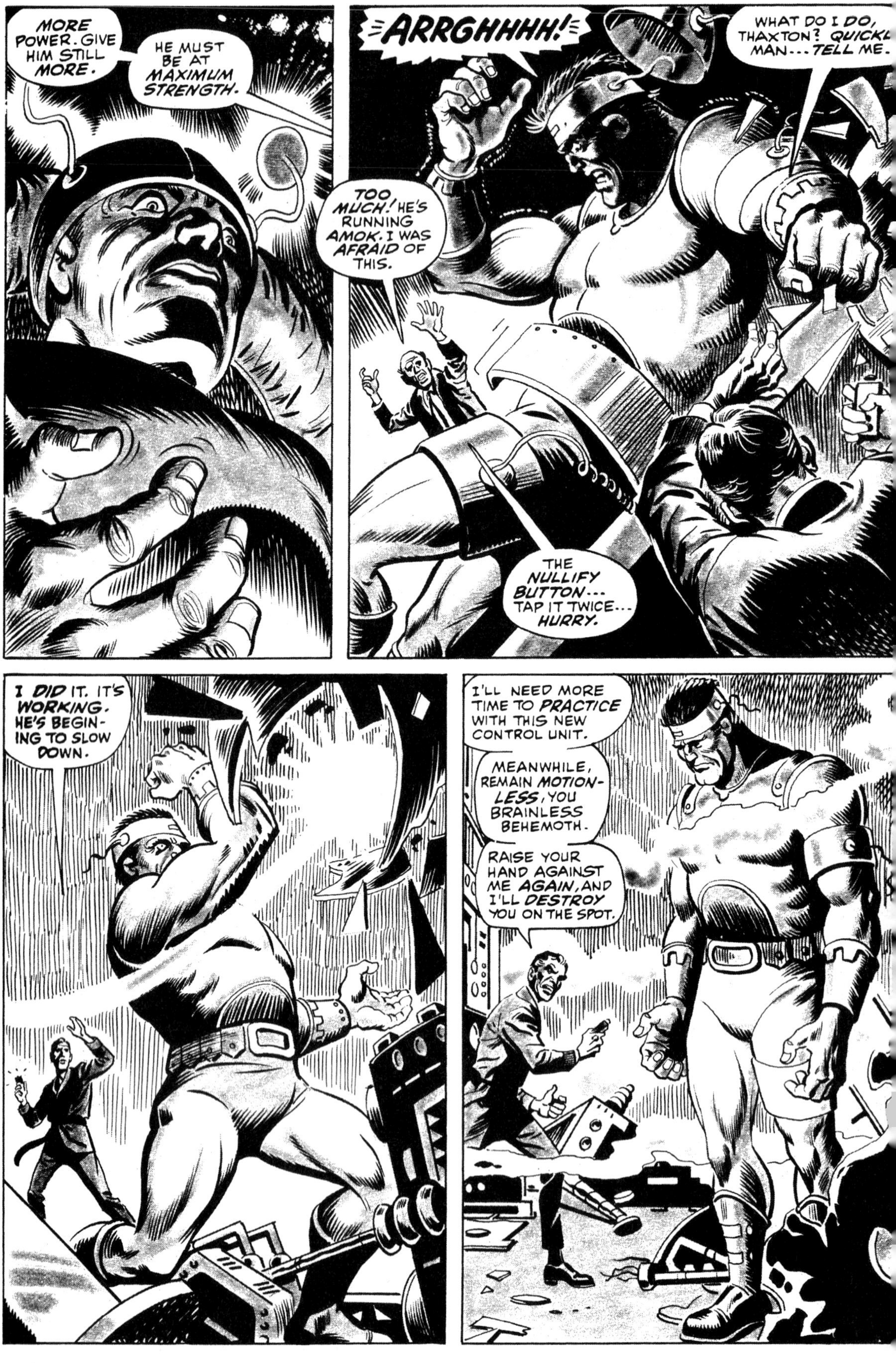
MORE POWER. GIVE HIM STILL MORE.
HE MUST BE AT MAXIMUM STRENGTH.
ARRGHHHH!
WHAT DO I DO, THAXTON? QUICKL MAN... TELL ME.
TOO MUCH! HE'S RUNNING AMOK. I WAS AFRAID OF THIS.
THE NULLIFY BUTTON... TAP IT TWICE... HURRY.
I DID IT. IT'S WORKING. HE'S BEGIN-ING TO SLOW DOWN.
I'LL NEED MORE TIME TO PRACTICE WITH THIS NEW CONTROL UNIT.
MEANWHILE, REMAIN MOTION-LESS, YOU BRAINLESS BEHEMOTH.
RAISE YOUR HAND AGAINST ME AGAIN, AND I'LL DESTROY YOU ON THE SPOT.

JUST A FEW MORE ADJUSTMENTS AND HE'LL BE *PERFECT*, MR. RALEIGH.

LET US *HOPE* SO, THAXTON... FOR *YOUR* SAKE.

AND NOW... I'LL ORDER OUR LITTLE CRIME WAVE TO *CONTINUE.*

MEANWHILE, *PETER PARKER* FINDS IT DIFFICULT TO CONCENTRATE UPON MATTERS SCHOLASTIC THE NEXT DAY---

THAT TEN-FOOT NIGHTMARE MAY STILL BE *AT LARGE*... ANYWHERE IN THE CITY.

PARKER...I HOPE WE'RE NOT *BORING* YOU.

HEY, PETE. BETTER GET *WITH* IT, SON!

HE DOESN'T EVEN *HEAR* YOU, HARRY!

WHAT'S WRONG, PAL O' MINE? YOU'VE BEEN IN A *DAZE* ALL DAY.

I DON'T KNOW, HARRY, PROBABLY JUST... SPRING FEVER.

IF YOU CAN USE A SOFT SHOULDER AND A SYMPATHETIC EAR...

I SURE *CAN*, LADY--- IF THE EYES AND LIPS GO ALONG *WITH* THEM.

WELL, YOU MAY BE UNDER THE WEATHER...BUT AT LEAST YOU'RE STILL *ALIVE.*

BUT, BEFORE WE SEGUE INTO *PEYTON PLACE*, LET'S SWITCH TO A PRIVATE MIDTOWN MEN'S CLUB, WHERE WE FIND...

HOW ABOUT JOINING OUR COMMITTEE TO RAISE FUNDS FOR RALEIGH'S CAMPAIGN, STACY?

I'LL THINK ABOUT IT, JAMESON.

THINK ABOUT IT? MY *NEWSPAPER* IS SQUARELY BEHIND THE MAN.

WHAT *MORE* DO YOU HAVE TO KNOW?

DIDN'T YOU *ALSO* PREDICT A *GOLD-WATER* LAND-SLIDE?

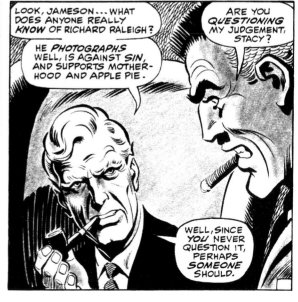

LOOK, JAMESON... WHAT DOES ANYONE REALLY *KNOW* OF RICHARD RALEIGH?

HE *PHOTOGRAPHS* WELL, IS AGAINST *SIN*, AND SUPPORTS MOTHER-HOOD AND APPLE PIE.

ARE YOU *QUESTIONING* MY JUDGEMENT, STACY?

WELL, SINCE *YOU* NEVER QUESTION IT, PERHAPS *SOMEONE* SHOULD.

241

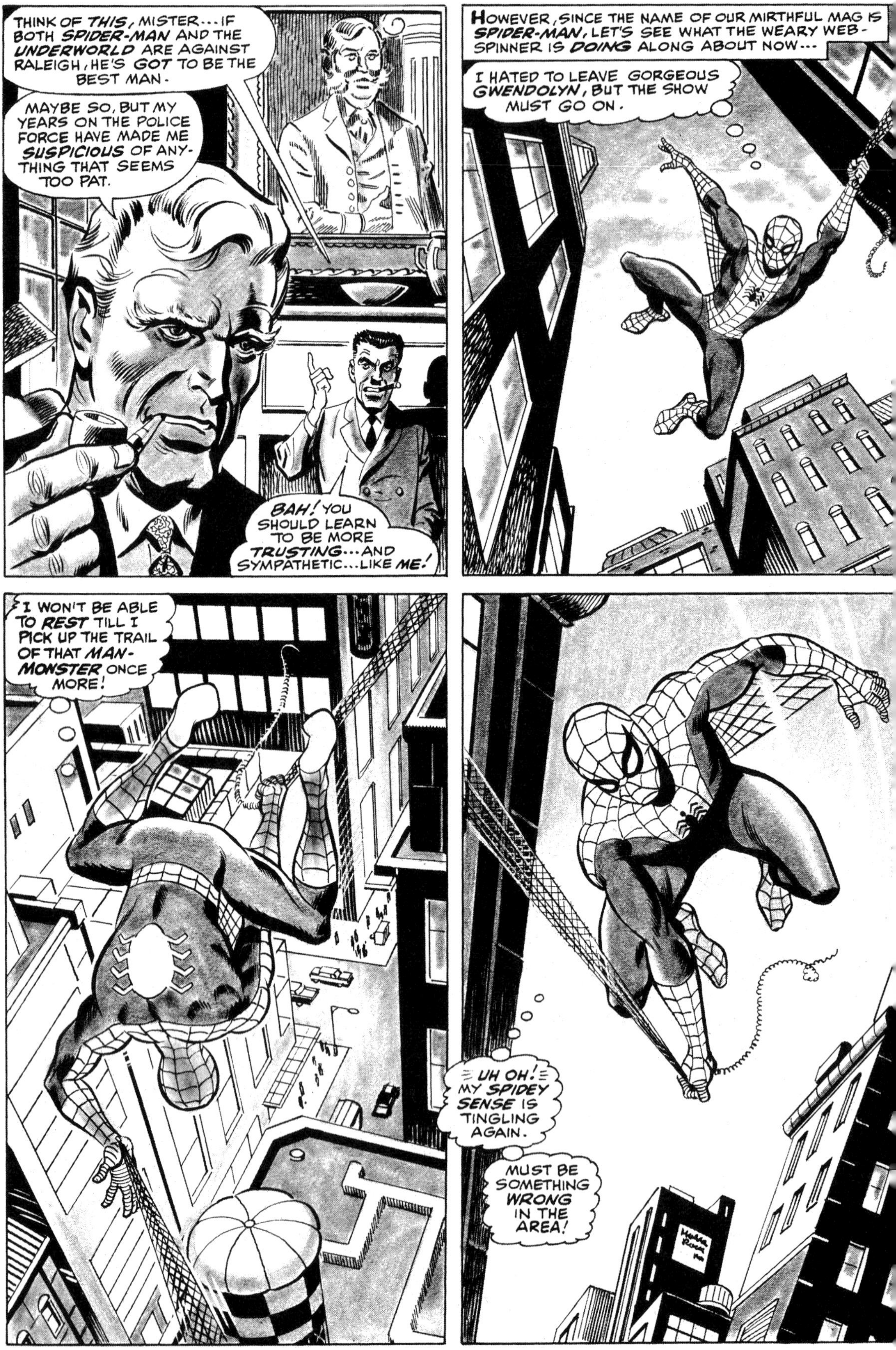
THINK OF THIS, MISTER... IF BOTH SPIDER-MAN AND THE UNDERWORLD ARE AGAINST RALEIGH, HE'S GOT TO BE THE BEST MAN.
MAYBE SO, BUT MY YEARS ON THE POLICE FORCE HAVE MADE ME SUSPICIOUS OF ANYTHING THAT SEEMS TOO PAT.
BAH! YOU SHOULD LEARN TO BE MORE TRUSTING... AND SYMPATHETIC... LIKE ME!
HOWEVER, SINCE THE NAME OF OUR MIRTHFUL MAG IS SPIDER-MAN, LET'S SEE WHAT THE WEARY WEB-SPINNER IS DOING ALONG ABOUT NOW...
I HATED TO LEAVE GORGEOUS GWENDOLYN, BUT THE SHOW MUST GO ON.
I WON'T BE ABLE TO REST TILL I PICK UP THE TRAIL OF THAT MAN-MONSTER ONCE MORE!
UH OH! MY SPIDEY SENSE IS TINGLING AGAIN.
MUST BE SOMETHING WRONG IN THE AREA!

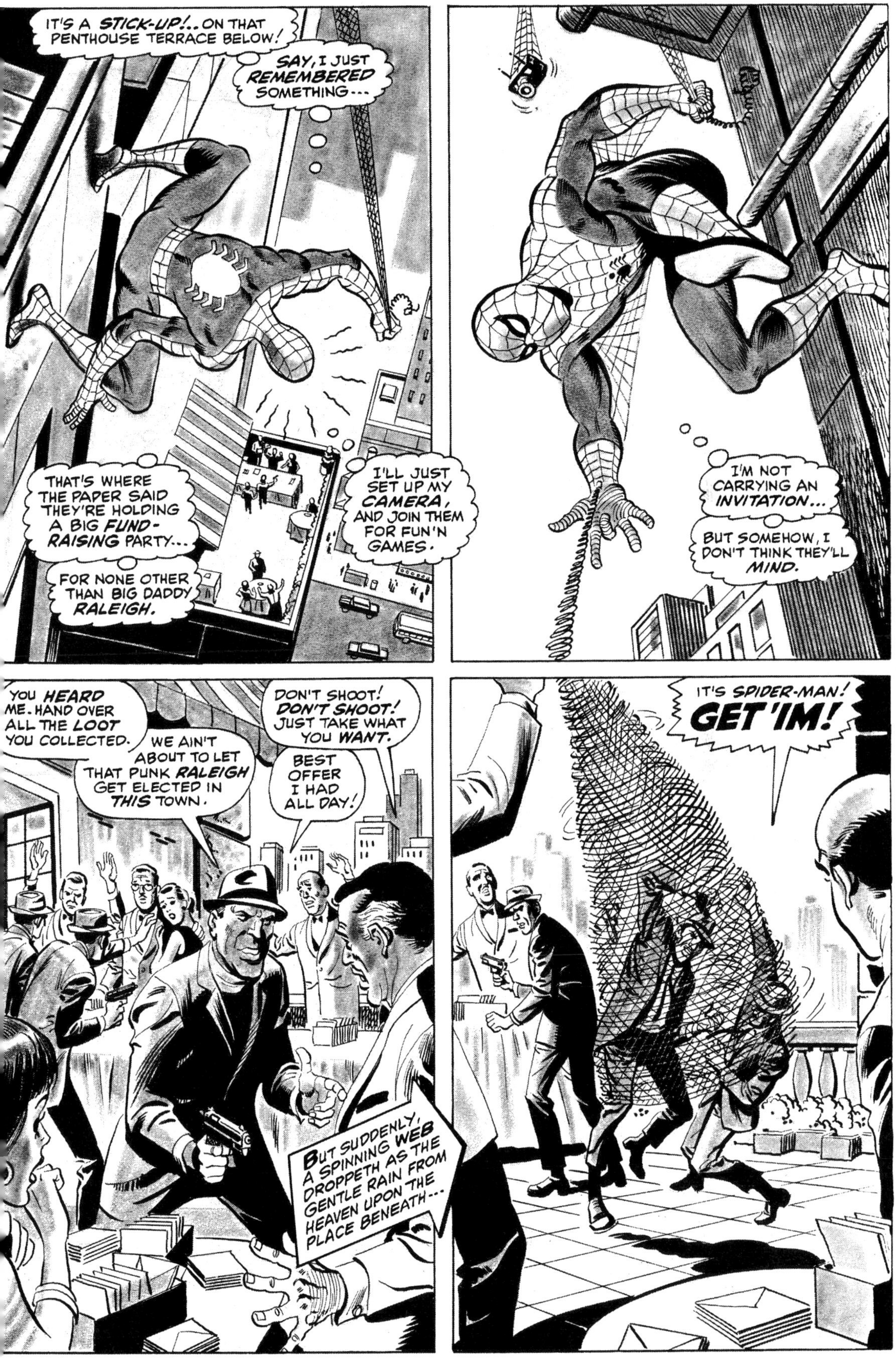
IT'S A STICK-UP!.. ON THAT PENTHOUSE TERRACE BELOW!
SAY, I JUST REMEMBERED SOMETHING...
THAT'S WHERE THE PAPER SAID THEY'RE HOLDING A BIG FUND-RAISING PARTY...
FOR NONE OTHER THAN BIG DADDY RALEIGH.
I'LL JUST SET UP MY CAMERA, AND JOIN THEM FOR FUN'N GAMES.
I'M NOT CARRYING AN INVITATION...
BUT SOMEHOW, I DON'T THINK THEY'LL MIND.
YOU HEARD ME. HAND OVER ALL THE LOOT YOU COLLECTED.
WE AIN'T ABOUT TO LET THAT PUNK RALEIGH GET ELECTED IN THIS TOWN.
DON'T SHOOT! DON'T SHOOT! JUST TAKE WHAT YOU WANT.
BEST OFFER I HAD ALL DAY!
BUT SUDDENLY, A SPINNING WEB DROPPETH AS THE GENTLE RAIN FROM HEAVEN UPON THE PLACE BENEATH...
IT'S SPIDER-MAN! GET 'IM!

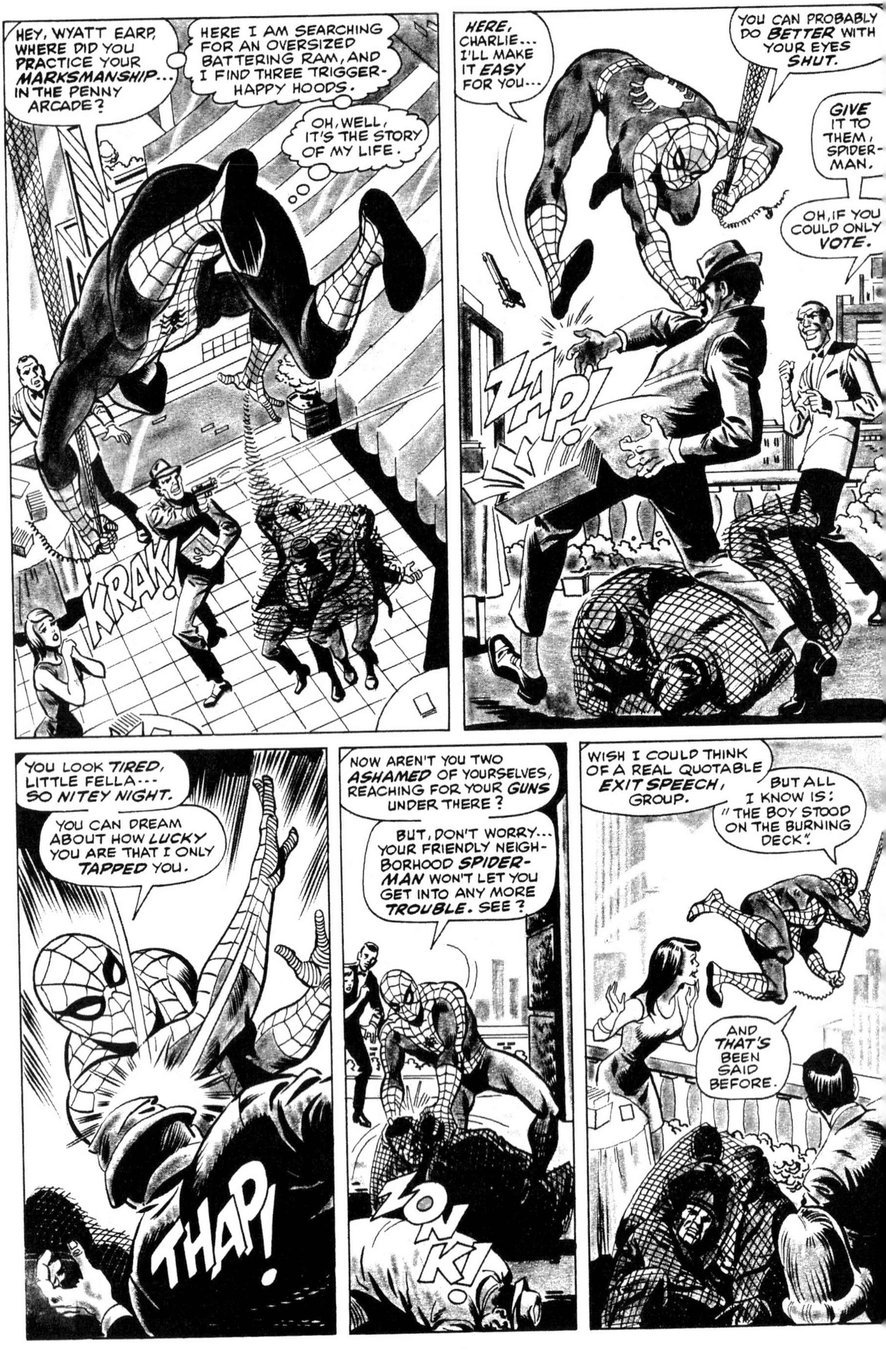
HEY, WYATT EARP, WHERE DID YOU PRACTICE YOUR MARKSMANSHIP... IN THE PENNY ARCADE?
HERE I AM SEARCHING FOR AN OVERSIZED BATTERING RAM, AND I FIND THREE TRIGGER-HAPPY HOODS.
OH, WELL, IT'S THE STORY OF MY LIFE.
KRAK!
HERE, CHARLIE... I'LL MAKE IT EASY FOR YOU...
YOU CAN PROBABLY DO BETTER WITH YOUR EYES SHUT.
GIVE IT TO THEM, SPIDER-MAN.
OH, IF YOU COULD ONLY VOTE.
ZAP!
YOU LOOK TIRED, LITTLE FELLA--- SO NITEY NIGHT.
YOU CAN DREAM ABOUT HOW LUCKY YOU ARE THAT I ONLY TAPPED YOU.
THAP!
NOW AREN'T YOU TWO ASHAMED OF YOURSELVES, REACHING FOR YOUR GUNS UNDER THERE?
BUT, DON'T WORRY... YOUR FRIENDLY NEIGHBORHOOD SPIDER-MAN WON'T LET YOU GET INTO ANY MORE TROUBLE. SEE?
ZONK!
WISH I COULD THINK OF A REAL QUOTABLE EXIT SPEECH, GROUP.
BUT ALL I KNOW IS: "THE BOY STOOD ON THE BURNING DECK".
AND THAT'S BEEN SAID BEFORE.

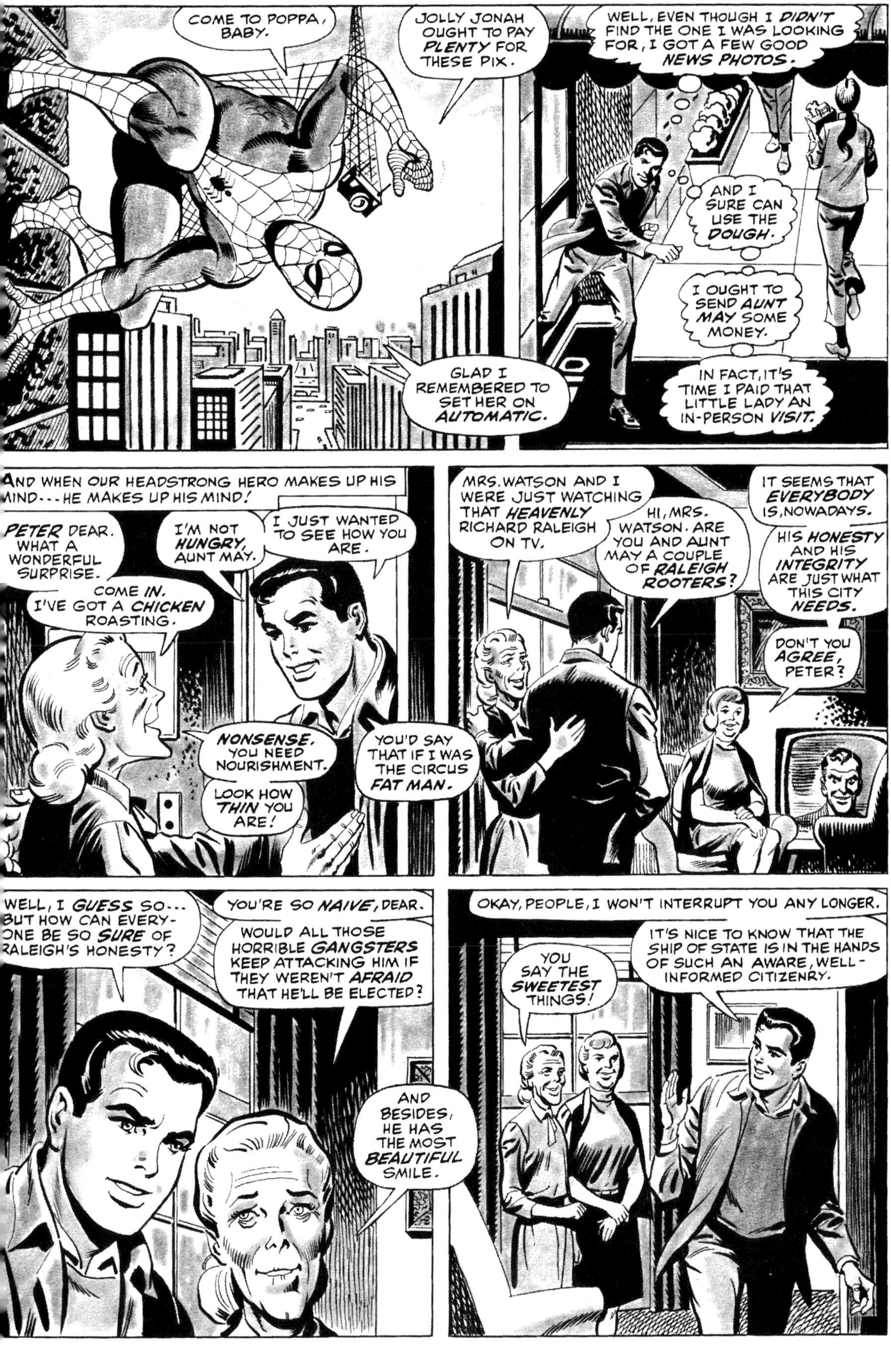

COME TO POPPA, BABY.
JOLLY JONAH OUGHT TO PAY PLENTY FOR THESE PIX.
GLAD I REMEMBERED TO SET HER ON AUTOMATIC.
WELL, EVEN THOUGH I DIDN'T FIND THE ONE I WAS LOOKING FOR, I GOT A FEW GOOD NEWS PHOTOS.
AND I SURE CAN USE THE DOUGH.
I OUGHT TO SEND AUNT MAY SOME MONEY.
IN FACT, IT'S TIME I PAID THAT LITTLE LADY AN IN-PERSON VISIT.
AND WHEN OUR HEADSTRONG HERO MAKES UP HIS MIND--- HE MAKES UP HIS MIND!
PETER DEAR. WHAT A WONDERFUL SURPRISE.
COME IN. I'VE GOT A CHICKEN ROASTING.
I'M NOT HUNGRY, AUNT MAY.
I JUST WANTED TO SEE HOW YOU ARE.
NONSENSE. YOU NEED NOURISHMENT.
LOOK HOW THIN YOU ARE!
YOU'D SAY THAT IF I WAS THE CIRCUS FAT MAN.
MRS. WATSON AND I WERE JUST WATCHING THAT HEAVENLY RICHARD RALEIGH ON TV.
HI, MRS. WATSON. ARE YOU AND AUNT MAY A COUPLE OF RALEIGH ROOTERS?
IT SEEMS THAT EVERYBODY IS, NOWADAYS.
HIS HONESTY AND HIS INTEGRITY ARE JUST WHAT THIS CITY NEEDS.
DON'T YOU AGREE, PETER?
WELL, I GUESS SO... BUT HOW CAN EVERYONE BE SO SURE OF RALEIGH'S HONESTY?
YOU'RE SO NAIVE, DEAR.
WOULD ALL THOSE HORRIBLE GANGSTERS KEEP ATTACKING HIM IF THEY WEREN'T AFRAID THAT HE'LL BE ELECTED?
AND BESIDES, HE HAS THE MOST BEAUTIFUL SMILE.
OKAY, PEOPLE, I WON'T INTERRUPT YOU ANY LONGER.
IT'S NICE TO KNOW THAT THE SHIP OF STATE IS IN THE HANDS OF SUCH AN AWARE, WELL-INFORMED CITIZENRY.
YOU SAY THE SWEETEST THINGS!

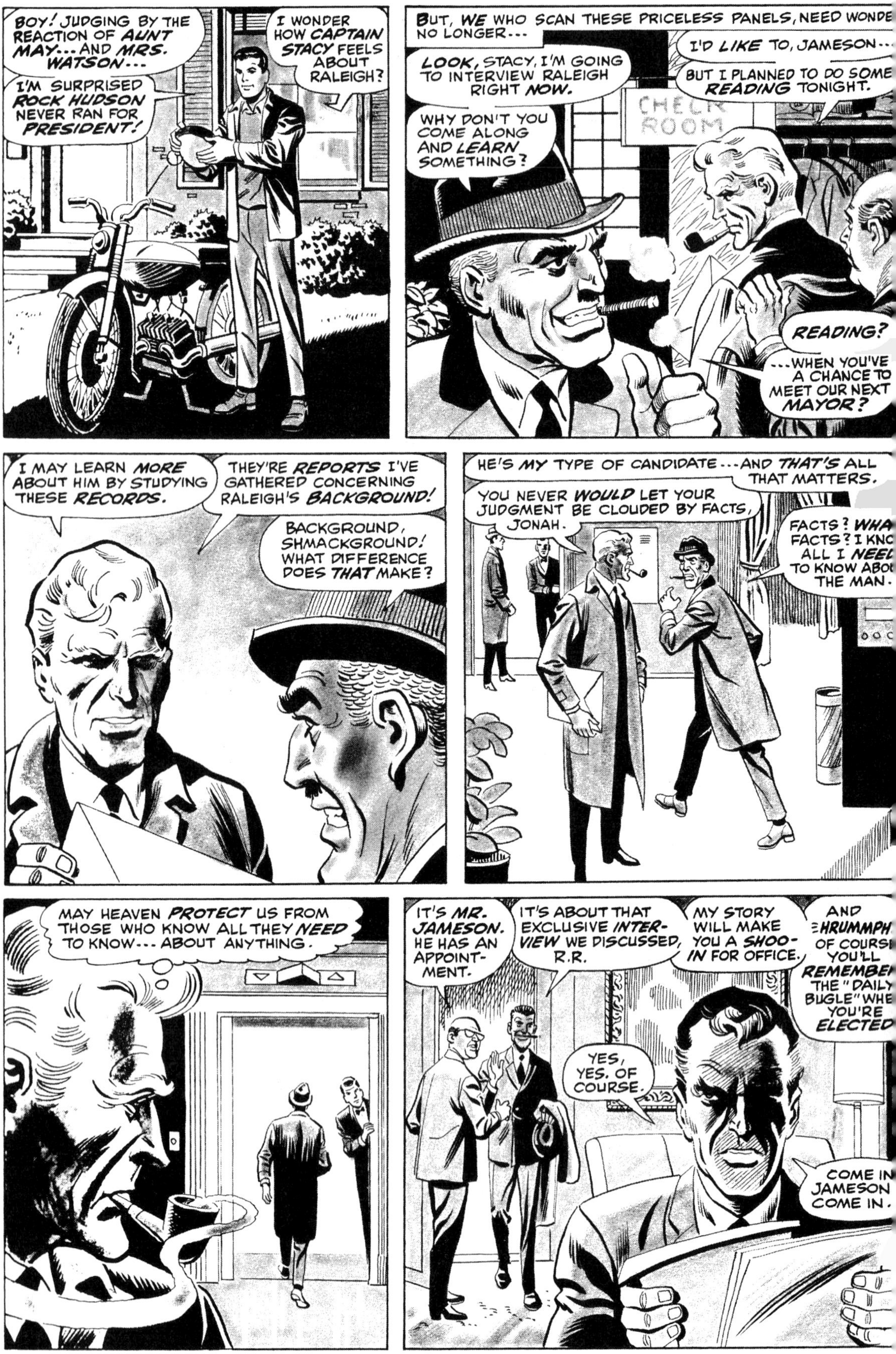
BOY! JUDGING BY THE REACTION OF AUNT MAY... AND MRS. WATSON...
I'M SURPRISED ROCK HUDSON NEVER RAN FOR PRESIDENT!
I WONDER HOW CAPTAIN STACY FEELS ABOUT RALEIGH?
BUT, WE WHO SCAN THESE PRICELESS PANELS, NEED WONDE NO LONGER---
LOOK, STACY, I'M GOING TO INTERVIEW RALEIGH RIGHT NOW.
WHY DON'T YOU COME ALONG AND LEARN SOMETHING?
CHECK ROOM
I'D LIKE TO, JAMESON...
BUT I PLANNED TO DO SOME READING TONIGHT.
READING?
...WHEN YOU'VE A CHANCE TO MEET OUR NEXT MAYOR?
I MAY LEARN MORE ABOUT HIM BY STUDYING THESE RECORDS.
THEY'RE REPORTS I'VE GATHERED CONCERNING RALEIGH'S BACKGROUND!
BACKGROUND, SHMACKGROUND! WHAT DIFFERENCE DOES THAT MAKE?
HE'S MY TYPE OF CANDIDATE---AND THAT'S ALL THAT MATTERS.
YOU NEVER WOULD LET YOUR JUDGMENT BE CLOUDED BY FACTS, JONAH.
FACTS? WHA FACTS? I KNO ALL I NEED TO KNOW ABO THE MAN.
MAY HEAVEN PROTECT US FROM THOSE WHO KNOW ALL THEY NEED TO KNOW--- ABOUT ANYTHING.
IT'S MR. JAMESON. HE HAS AN APPOINT-MENT.
IT'S ABOUT THAT EXCLUSIVE INTER-VIEW WE DISCUSSED, R.R.
MY STORY WILL MAKE YOU A SHOO-IN FOR OFFICE.
AND HRUMMPH OF COURS YOU'LL REMEMBE THE "DAILY BUGLE" WHE YOU'RE ELECTED
YES, YES. OF COURSE.
COME IN JAMESON COME IN.

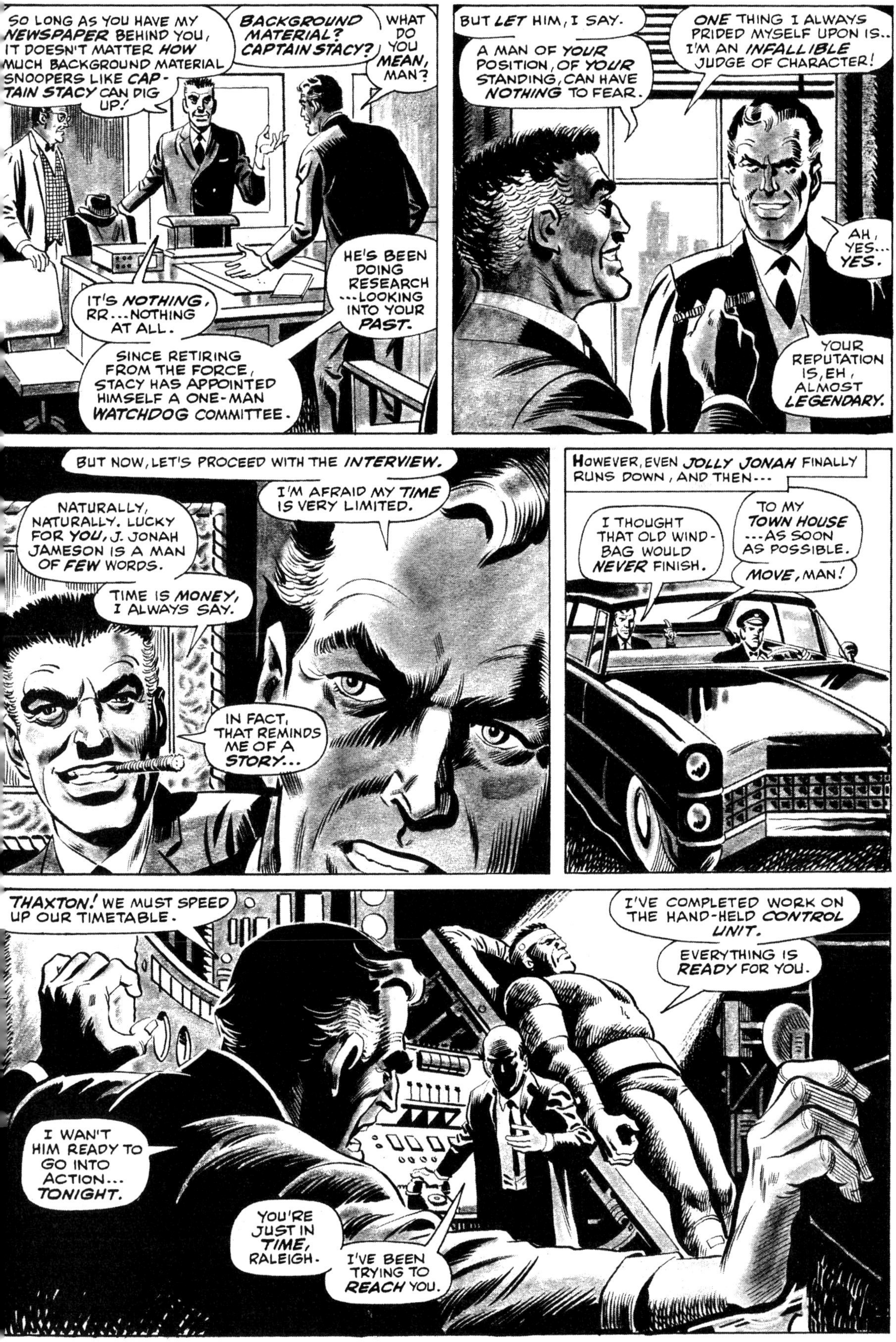
SO LONG AS YOU HAVE MY NEWSPAPER BEHIND YOU, IT DOESN'T MATTER HOW MUCH BACKGROUND MATERIAL SNOOPERS LIKE CAPTAIN STACY CAN DIG UP!
BACKGROUND MATERIAL? CAPTAIN STACY?
WHAT DO YOU MEAN, MAN?
HE'S BEEN DOING RESEARCH ...LOOKING INTO YOUR PAST.
IT'S NOTHING, RR...NOTHING AT ALL.
SINCE RETIRING FROM THE FORCE, STACY HAS APPOINTED HIMSELF A ONE-MAN WATCHDOG COMMITTEE.
BUT LET HIM, I SAY.
A MAN OF YOUR POSITION, OF YOUR STANDING, CAN HAVE NOTHING TO FEAR.
ONE THING I ALWAYS PRIDED MYSELF UPON IS.. I'M AN INFALLIBLE JUDGE OF CHARACTER!
AH, YES... YES.
YOUR REPUTATION IS, EH, ALMOST LEGENDARY.
BUT NOW, LET'S PROCEED WITH THE INTERVIEW.
I'M AFRAID MY TIME IS VERY LIMITED.
NATURALLY, NATURALLY. LUCKY FOR YOU, J. JONAH JAMESON IS A MAN OF FEW WORDS.
TIME IS MONEY, I ALWAYS SAY.
IN FACT, THAT REMINDS ME OF A STORY...
HOWEVER, EVEN JOLLY JONAH FINALLY RUNS DOWN, AND THEN---
I THOUGHT THAT OLD WIND-BAG WOULD NEVER FINISH.
TO MY TOWN HOUSE ---AS SOON AS POSSIBLE.
MOVE, MAN!
THAXTON! WE MUST SPEED UP OUR TIMETABLE.
I WAN'T HIM READY TO GO INTO ACTION... TONIGHT.
I'VE COMPLETED WORK ON THE HAND-HELD CONTROL UNIT.
EVERYTHING IS READY FOR YOU.
YOU'RE JUST IN TIME, RALEIGH.
I'VE BEEN TRYING TO REACH YOU.

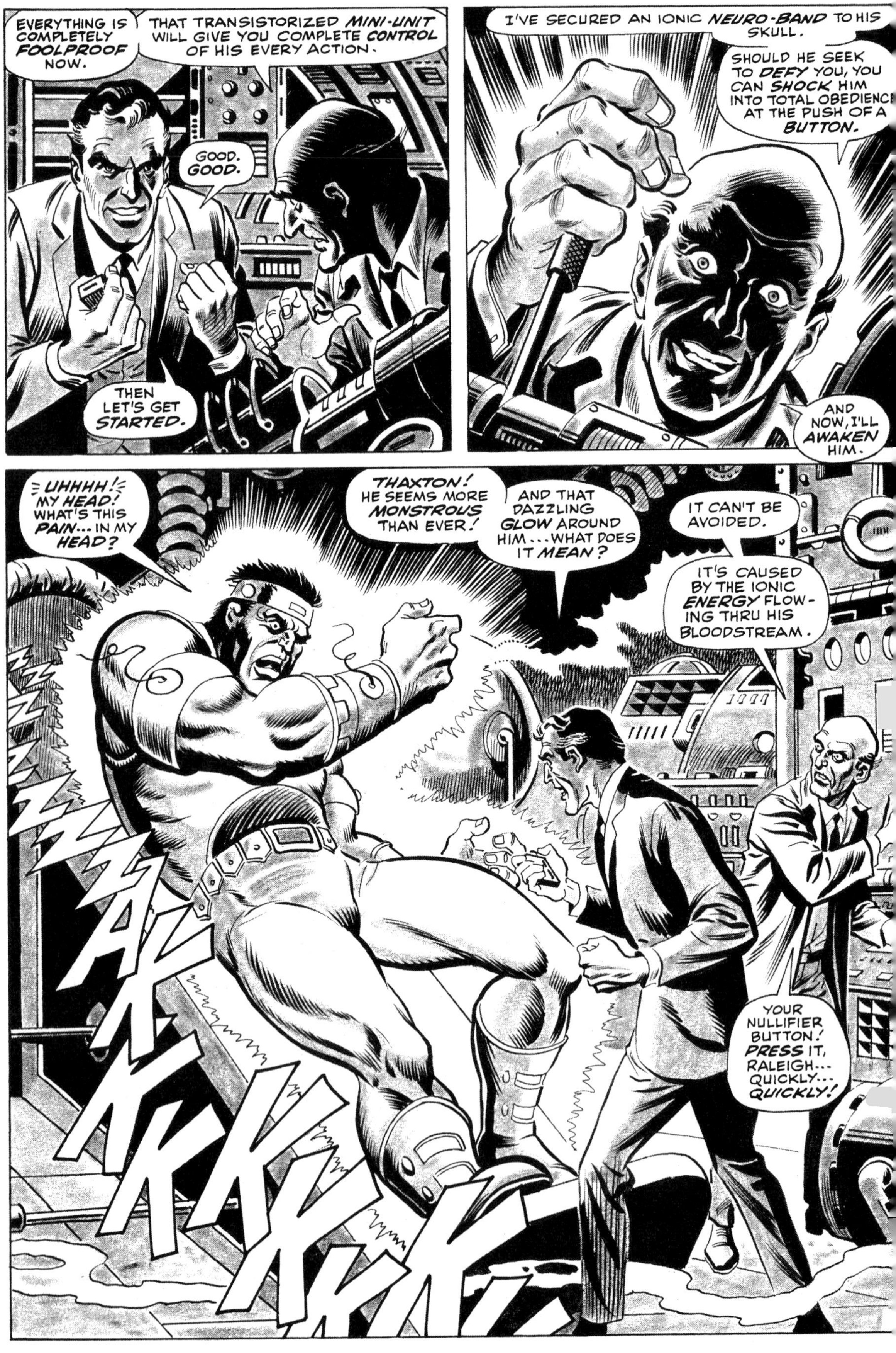
EVERYTHING IS COMPLETELY FOOLPROOF NOW.
THAT TRANSISTORIZED MINI-UNIT WILL GIVE YOU COMPLETE CONTROL OF HIS EVERY ACTION.
GOOD. GOOD.
THEN LET'S GET STARTED.
I'VE SECURED AN IONIC NEURO-BAND TO HIS SKULL.
SHOULD HE SEEK TO DEFY YOU, YOU CAN SHOCK HIM INTO TOTAL OBEDIENCE AT THE PUSH OF A BUTTON.
AND NOW, I'LL AWAKEN HIM.
UHHHH! MY HEAD! WHAT'S THIS PAIN... IN MY HEAD?
THAXTON! HE SEEMS MORE MONSTROUS THAN EVER!
AND THAT DAZZLING GLOW AROUND HIM... WHAT DOES IT MEAN?
IT CAN'T BE AVOIDED.
IT'S CAUSED BY THE IONIC ENERGY FLOWING THRU HIS BLOODSTREAM.
YOUR NULLIFIER BUTTON! PRESS IT, RALEIGH... QUICKLY... QUICKLY!
ZZZZAKKKKK!

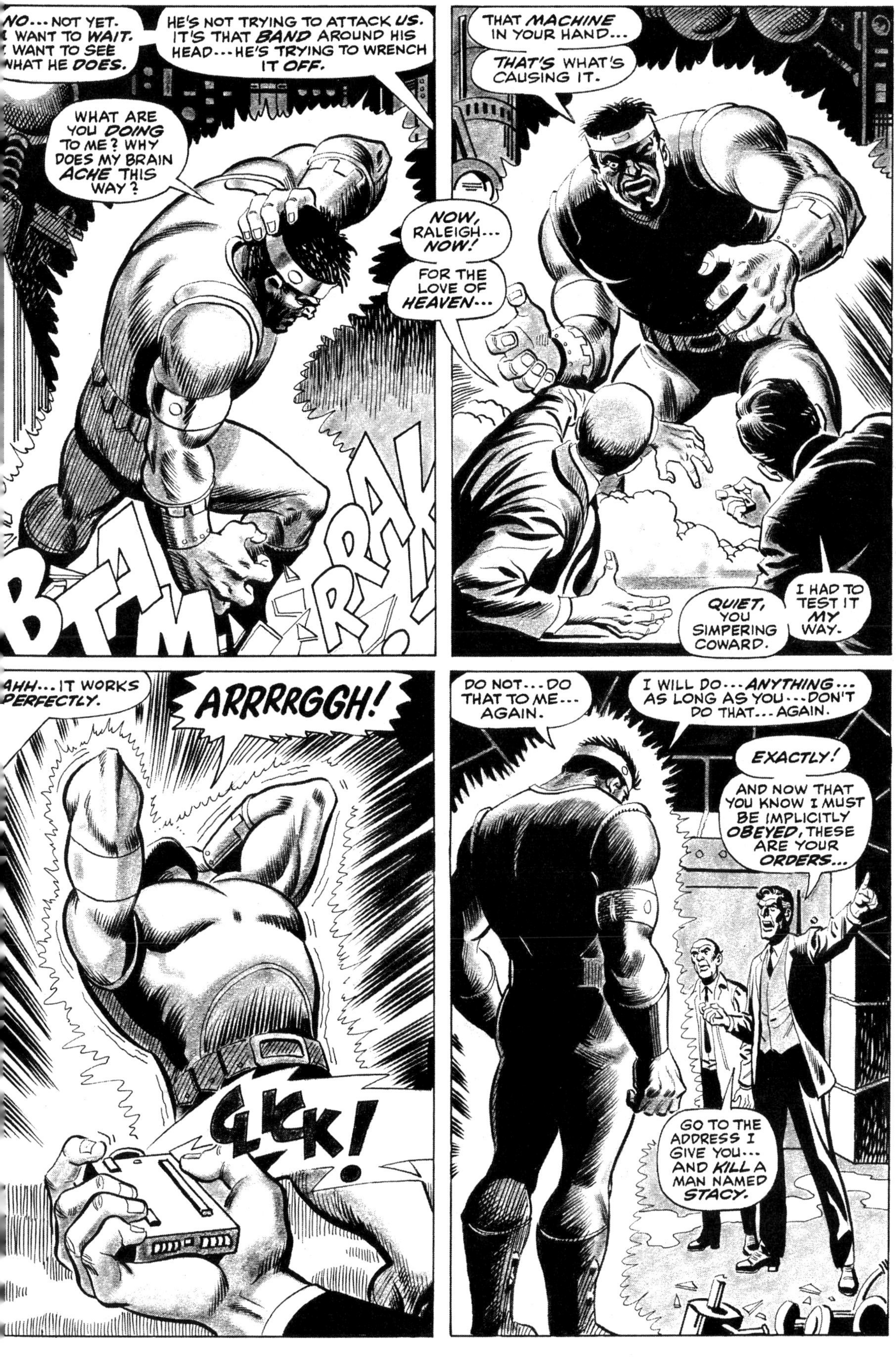

NO... NOT YET. I WANT TO WAIT. I WANT TO SEE WHAT HE DOES.
HE'S NOT TRYING TO ATTACK US. IT'S THAT BAND AROUND HIS HEAD... HE'S TRYING TO WRENCH IT OFF.
WHAT ARE YOU DOING TO ME? WHY DOES MY BRAIN ACHE THIS WAY?
BTAM!
KRRAK!
THAT MACHINE IN YOUR HAND...
THAT'S WHAT'S CAUSING IT.
NOW, RALEIGH... NOW!
FOR THE LOVE OF HEAVEN...
QUIET, YOU SIMPERING COWARD.
I HAD TO TEST IT MY WAY.
AHH... IT WORKS PERFECTLY.
ARRRRGGH!
CLICK!
DO NOT... DO THAT TO ME... AGAIN.
I WILL DO... ANYTHING... AS LONG AS YOU... DON'T DO THAT... AGAIN.
EXACTLY!
AND NOW THAT YOU KNOW I MUST BE IMPLICITLY OBEYED, THESE ARE YOUR ORDERS...
GO TO THE ADDRESS I GIVE YOU... AND KILL A MAN NAMED STACY.

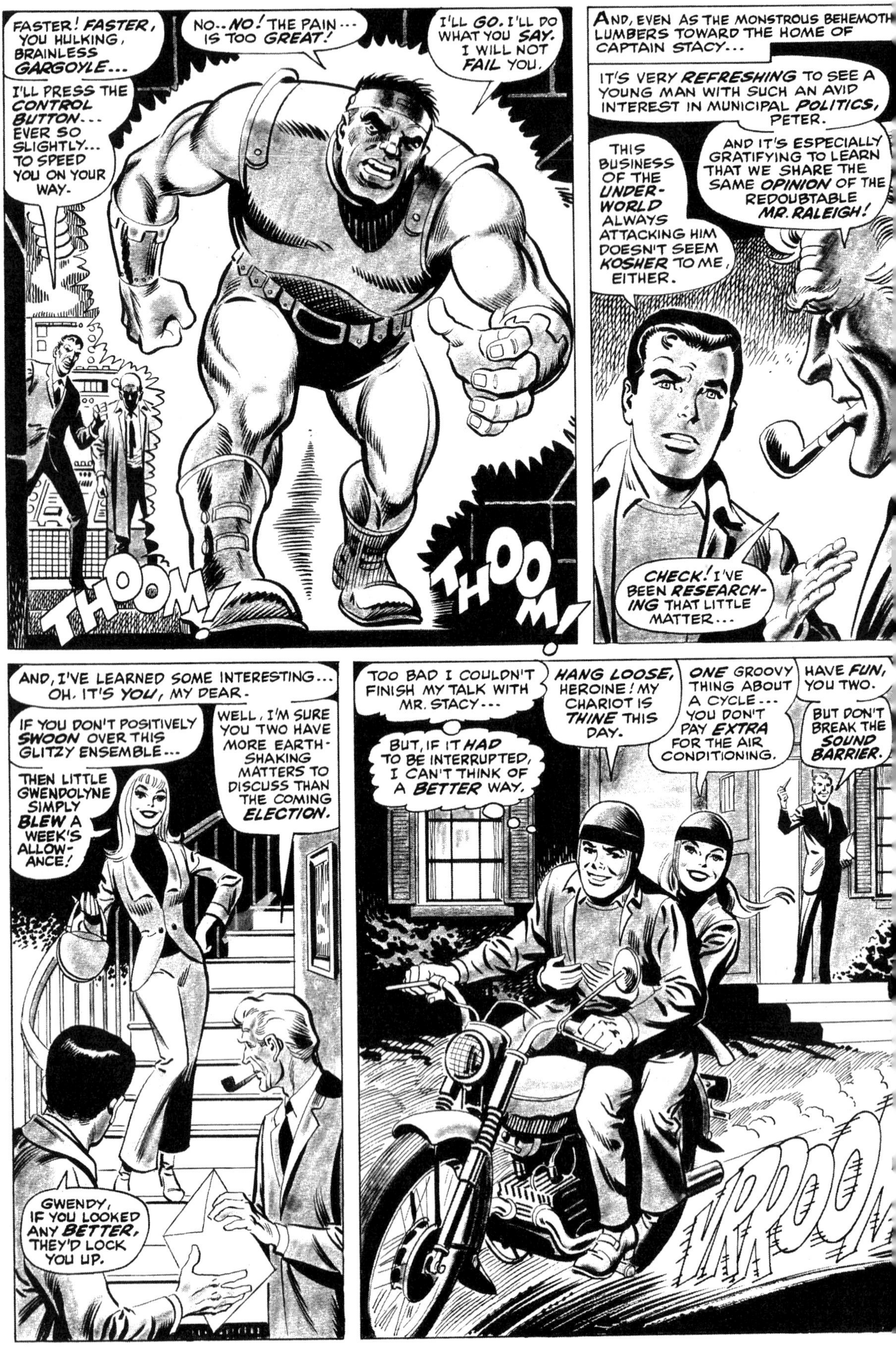
FASTER! FASTER, YOU HULKING, BRAINLESS GARGOYLE...
I'LL PRESS THE CONTROL BUTTON... EVER SO SLIGHTLY... TO SPEED YOU ON YOUR WAY.
NO.. NO! THE PAIN... IS TOO GREAT!
I'LL GO. I'LL DO WHAT YOU SAY. I WILL NOT FAIL YOU.
THOOM!
THOOM!
AND, EVEN AS THE MONSTROUS BEHEMOTH LUMBERS TOWARD THE HOME OF CAPTAIN STACY...
IT'S VERY REFRESHING TO SEE A YOUNG MAN WITH SUCH AN AVID INTEREST IN MUNICIPAL POLITICS, PETER.
AND IT'S ESPECIALLY GRATIFYING TO LEARN THAT WE SHARE THE SAME OPINION OF THE REDOUBTABLE MR. RALEIGH!
THIS BUSINESS OF THE UNDERWORLD ALWAYS ATTACKING HIM DOESN'T SEEM KOSHER TO ME, EITHER.
CHECK! I'VE BEEN RESEARCHING THAT LITTLE MATTER...
AND, I'VE LEARNED SOME INTERESTING... OH. IT'S YOU, MY DEAR.
IF YOU DON'T POSITIVELY SWOON OVER THIS GLITZY ENSEMBLE...
THEN LITTLE GWENDOLYNE SIMPLY BLEW A WEEK'S ALLOWANCE!
WELL, I'M SURE YOU TWO HAVE MORE EARTH-SHAKING MATTERS TO DISCUSS THAN THE COMING ELECTION.
GWENDY, IF YOU LOOKED ANY BETTER, THEY'D LOCK YOU UP.
TOO BAD I COULDN'T FINISH MY TALK WITH MR. STACY...
BUT, IF IT HAD TO BE INTERRUPTED, I CAN'T THINK OF A BETTER WAY.
HANG LOOSE, HEROINE! MY CHARIOT IS THINE THIS DAY.
ONE GROOVY THING ABOUT A CYCLE... YOU DON'T PAY EXTRA FOR THE AIR CONDITIONING.
HAVE FUN, YOU TWO.
BUT DON'T BREAK THE SOUND BARRIER.
VRROOM

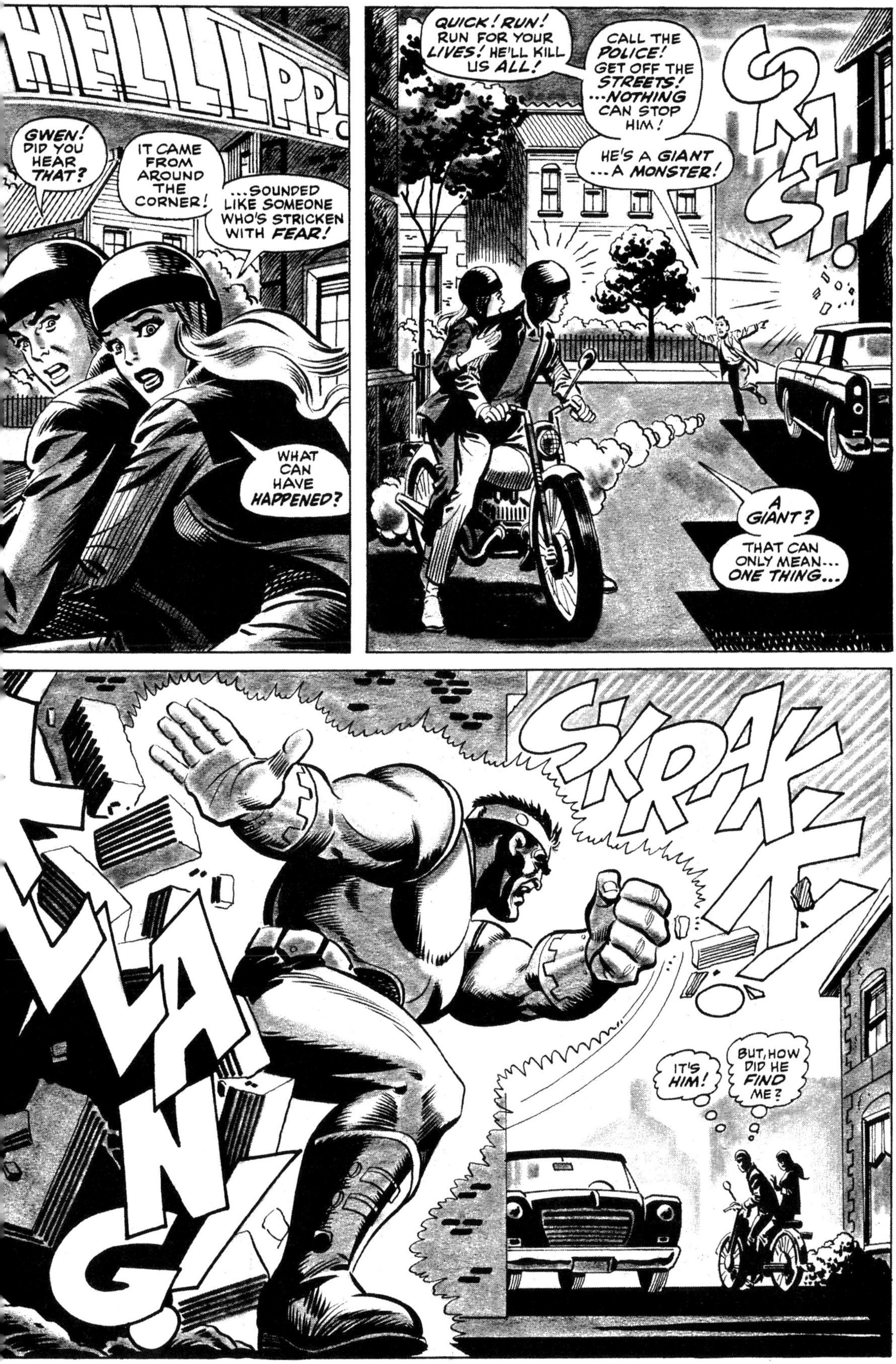
HELLLPP
GWEN! DID YOU HEAR THAT?
IT CAME FROM AROUND THE CORNER!
...SOUNDED LIKE SOMEONE WHO'S STRICKEN WITH FEAR!
WHAT CAN HAVE HAPPENED?
QUICK! RUN! RUN FOR YOUR LIVES! HE'LL KILL US ALL!
CALL THE POLICE! GET OFF THE STREETS! ...NOTHING CAN STOP HIM!
HE'S A GIANT ...A MONSTER!
A GIANT?
THAT CAN ONLY MEAN... ONE THING...
SKRAK!
IT'S HIM!
BUT, HOW DID HE FIND ME?

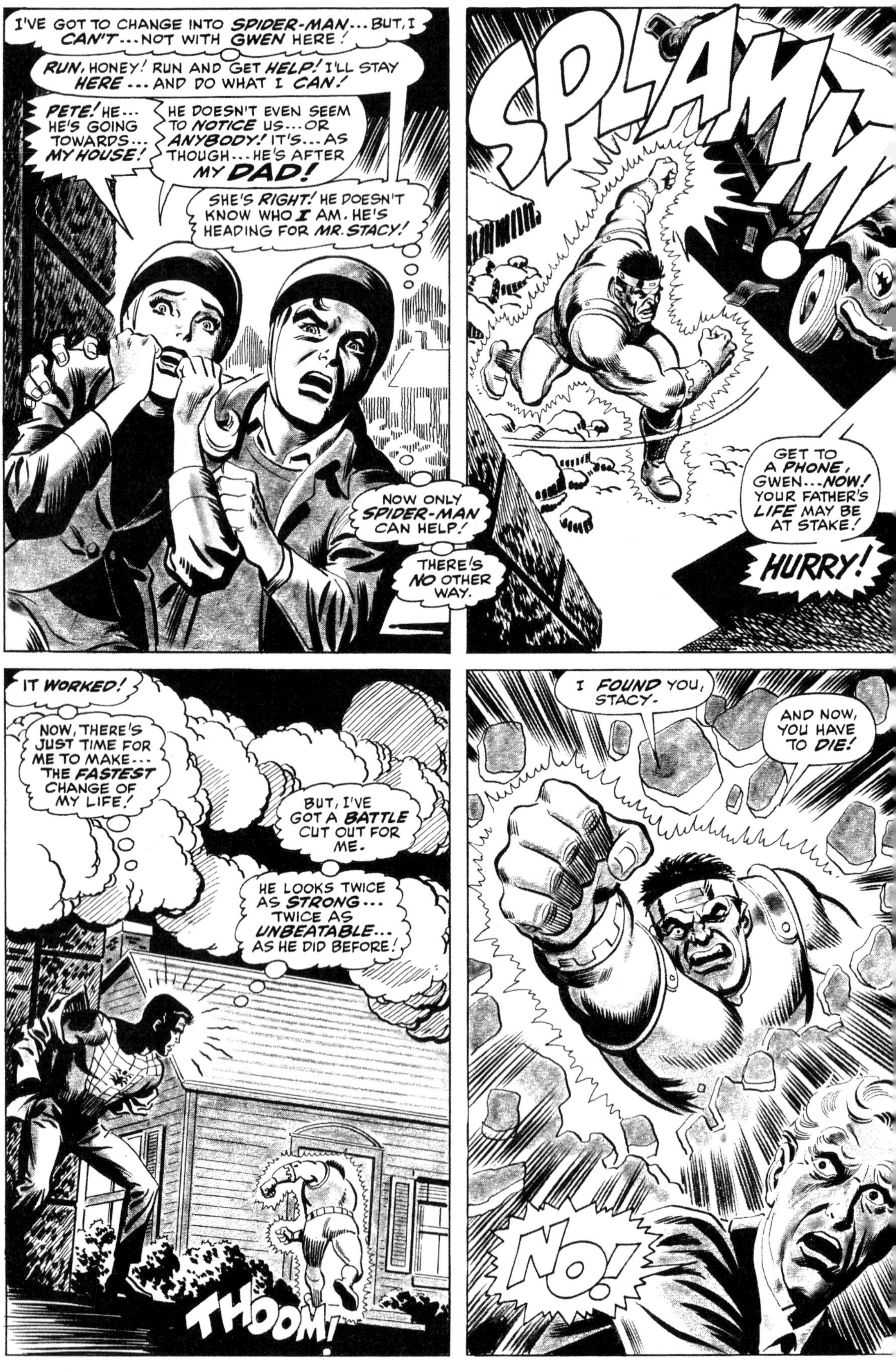
I'VE GOT TO CHANGE INTO SPIDER-MAN... BUT, I CAN'T... NOT WITH GWEN HERE!
RUN, HONEY! RUN AND GET HELP! I'LL STAY HERE... AND DO WHAT I CAN!
PETE! HE... HE'S GOING TOWARDS... MY HOUSE!
HE DOESN'T EVEN SEEM TO NOTICE US... OR ANYBODY! IT'S... AS THOUGH... HE'S AFTER MY DAD!
SHE'S RIGHT! HE DOESN'T KNOW WHO I AM. HE'S HEADING FOR MR. STACY!
NOW ONLY SPIDER-MAN CAN HELP!
THERE'S NO OTHER WAY.
SPLAM!
GET TO A PHONE, GWEN... NOW! YOUR FATHER'S LIFE MAY BE AT STAKE!
HURRY!
IT WORKED!
NOW, THERE'S JUST TIME FOR ME TO MAKE... THE FASTEST CHANGE OF MY LIFE!
BUT, I'VE GOT A BATTLE CUT OUT FOR ME.
HE LOOKS TWICE AS STRONG... TWICE AS UNBEATABLE... AS HE DID BEFORE!
THOOM!
I FOUND YOU, STACY.
AND NOW, YOU HAVE TO DIE!
NO!

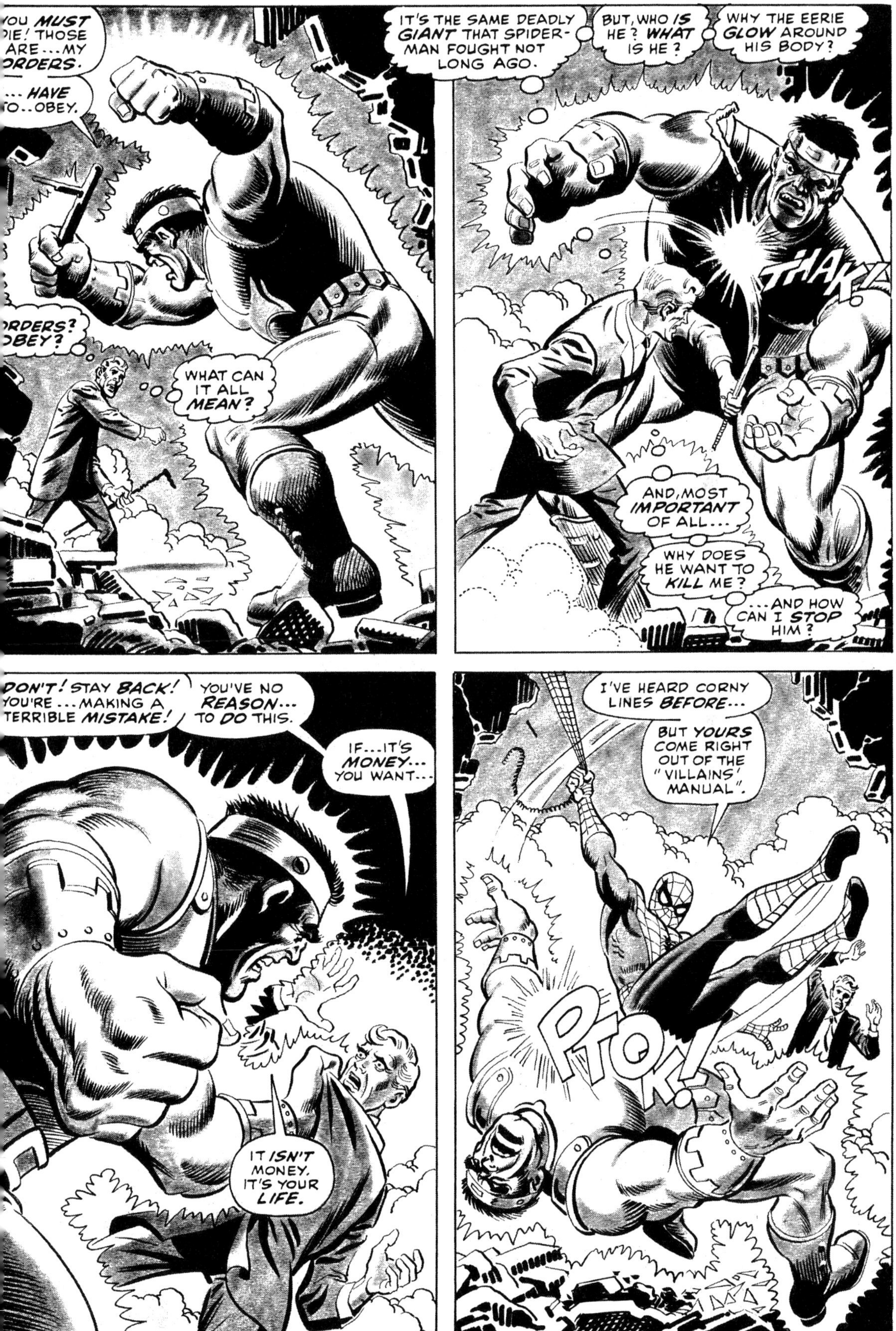

OU MUST IE! THOSE ARE...MY ORDERS.
...HAVE TO..OBEY.
ORDERS? OBEY?
WHAT CAN IT ALL MEAN?
IT'S THE SAME DEADLY GIANT THAT SPIDER-MAN FOUGHT NOT LONG AGO.
BUT, WHO IS HE? WHAT IS HE?
WHY THE EERIE GLOW AROUND HIS BODY?
THAK!
AND, MOST IMPORTANT OF ALL...
WHY DOES HE WANT TO KILL ME?
...AND HOW CAN I STOP HIM?
DON'T! STAY BACK! YOU'RE...MAKING A TERRIBLE MISTAKE!
YOU'VE NO REASON... TO DO THIS.
IF...IT'S MONEY... YOU WANT...
IT ISN'T MONEY. IT'S YOUR LIFE.
I'VE HEARD CORNY LINES BEFORE...
BUT YOURS COME RIGHT OUT OF THE "VILLAINS' MANUAL".
PTOK!

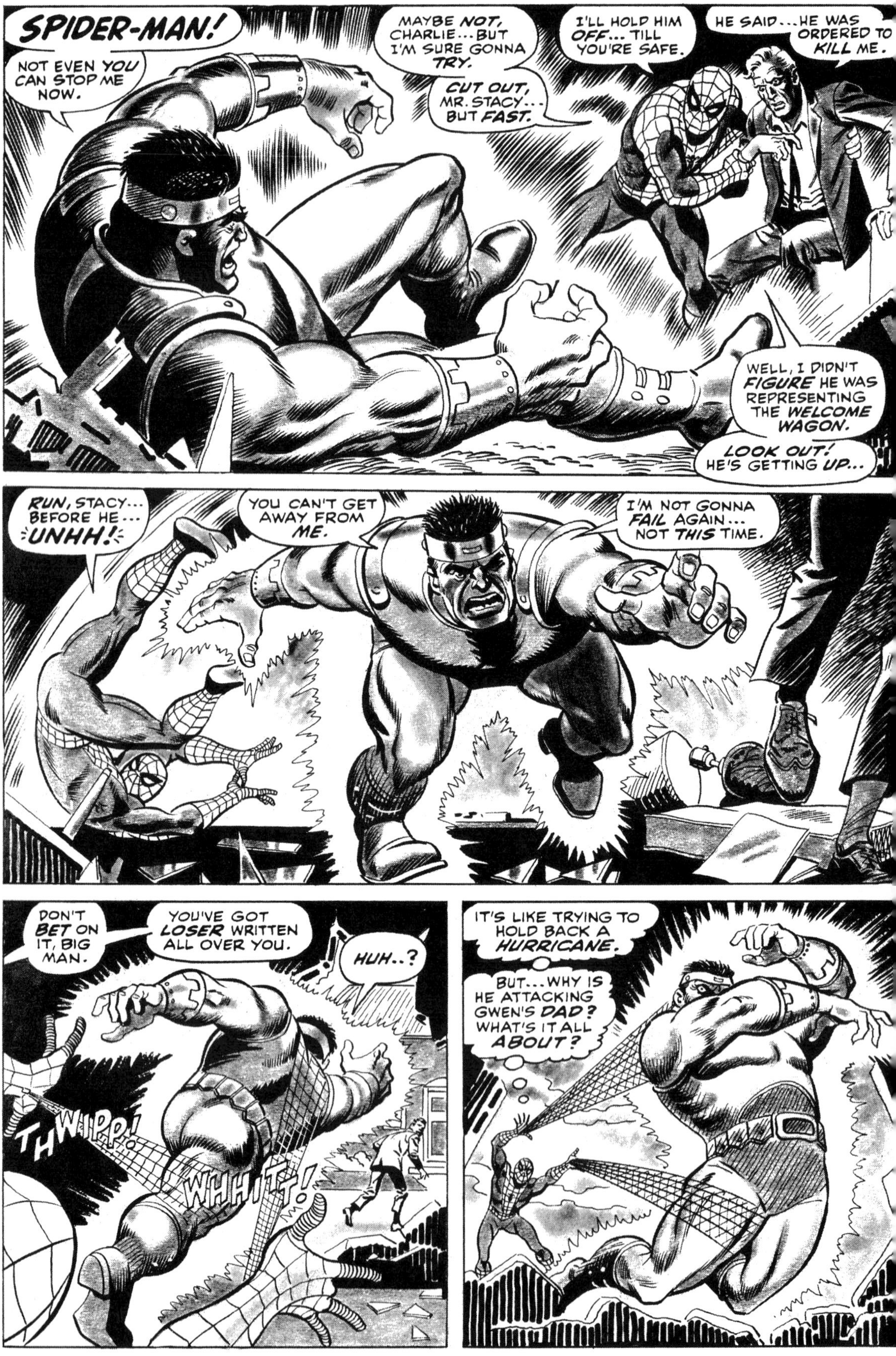
SPIDER-MAN!
NOT EVEN YOU CAN STOP ME NOW.
MAYBE NOT, CHARLIE... BUT I'M SURE GONNA TRY.
CUT OUT, MR. STACY... BUT FAST.
I'LL HOLD HIM OFF... TILL YOU'RE SAFE.
HE SAID... HE WAS ORDERED TO KILL ME.
WELL, I DIDN'T FIGURE HE WAS REPRESENTING THE WELCOME WAGON.
LOOK OUT! HE'S GETTING UP...
RUN, STACY... BEFORE HE... UNHH!
YOU CAN'T GET AWAY FROM ME.
I'M NOT GONNA FAIL AGAIN... NOT THIS TIME.
DON'T BET ON IT, BIG MAN.
YOU'VE GOT LOSER WRITTEN ALL OVER YOU.
HUH..?
THWIPP!
WHHITT!
IT'S LIKE TRYING TO HOLD BACK A HURRICANE.
BUT... WHY IS HE ATTACKING GWEN'S DAD? WHAT'S IT ALL ABOUT?

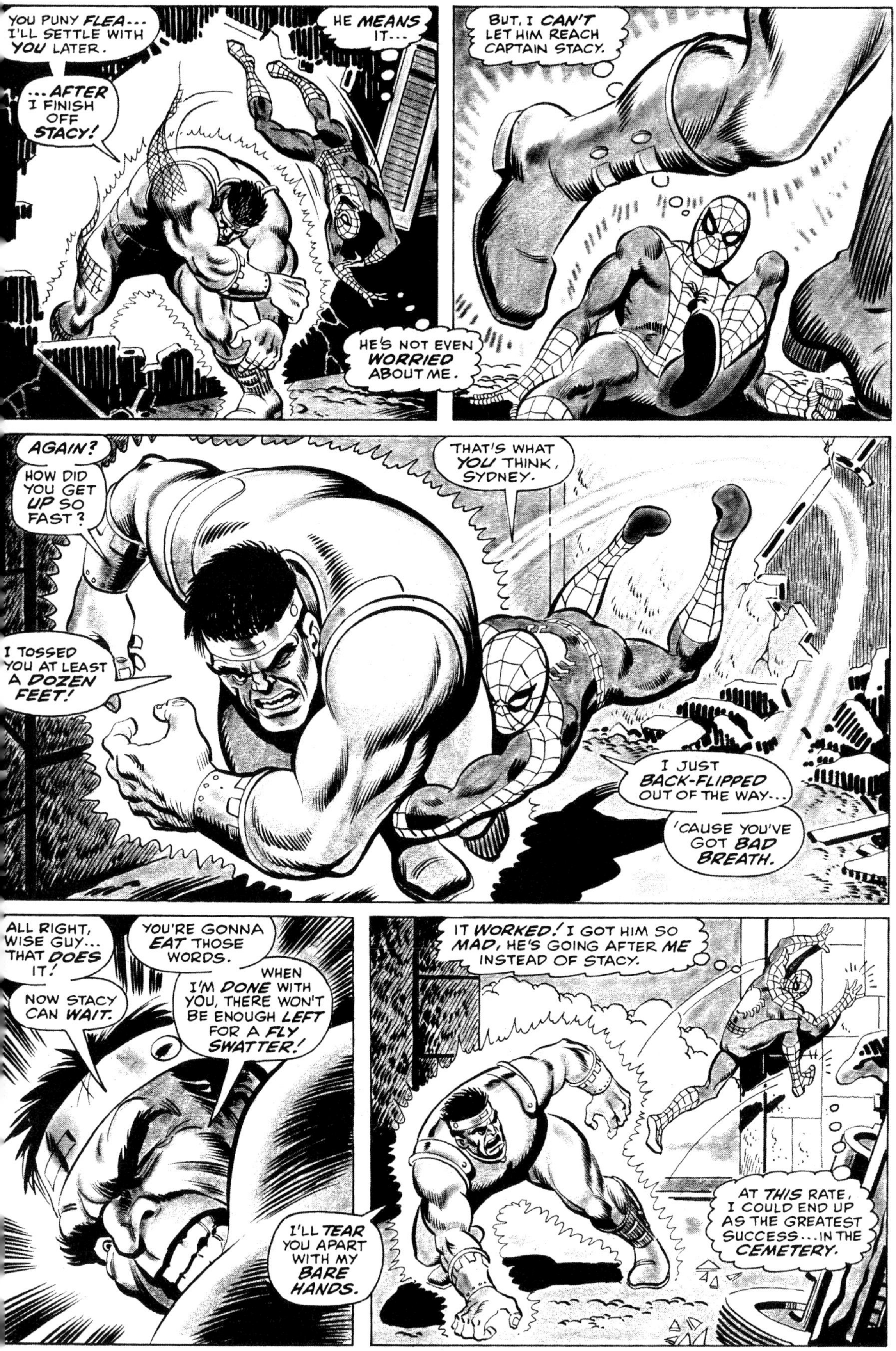

YOU PUNY FLEA... I'LL SETTLE WITH YOU LATER.
...AFTER I FINISH OFF STACY!
HE MEANS IT...
HE'S NOT EVEN WORRIED ABOUT ME.
BUT, I CAN'T LET HIM REACH CAPTAIN STACY.
AGAIN? HOW DID YOU GET UP SO FAST?
I TOSSED YOU AT LEAST A DOZEN FEET!
THAT'S WHAT YOU THINK, SYDNEY.
I JUST BACK-FLIPPED OUT OF THE WAY...
'CAUSE YOU'VE GOT BAD BREATH.
ALL RIGHT, WISE GUY... THAT DOES IT!
NOW STACY CAN WAIT.
YOU'RE GONNA EAT THOSE WORDS.
WHEN I'M DONE WITH YOU, THERE WON'T BE ENOUGH LEFT FOR A FLY SWATTER!
I'LL TEAR YOU APART WITH MY BARE HANDS.
IT WORKED! I GOT HIM SO MAD, HE'S GOING AFTER ME INSTEAD OF STACY.
AT THIS RATE, I COULD END UP AS THE GREATEST SUCCESS...IN THE CEMETERY.

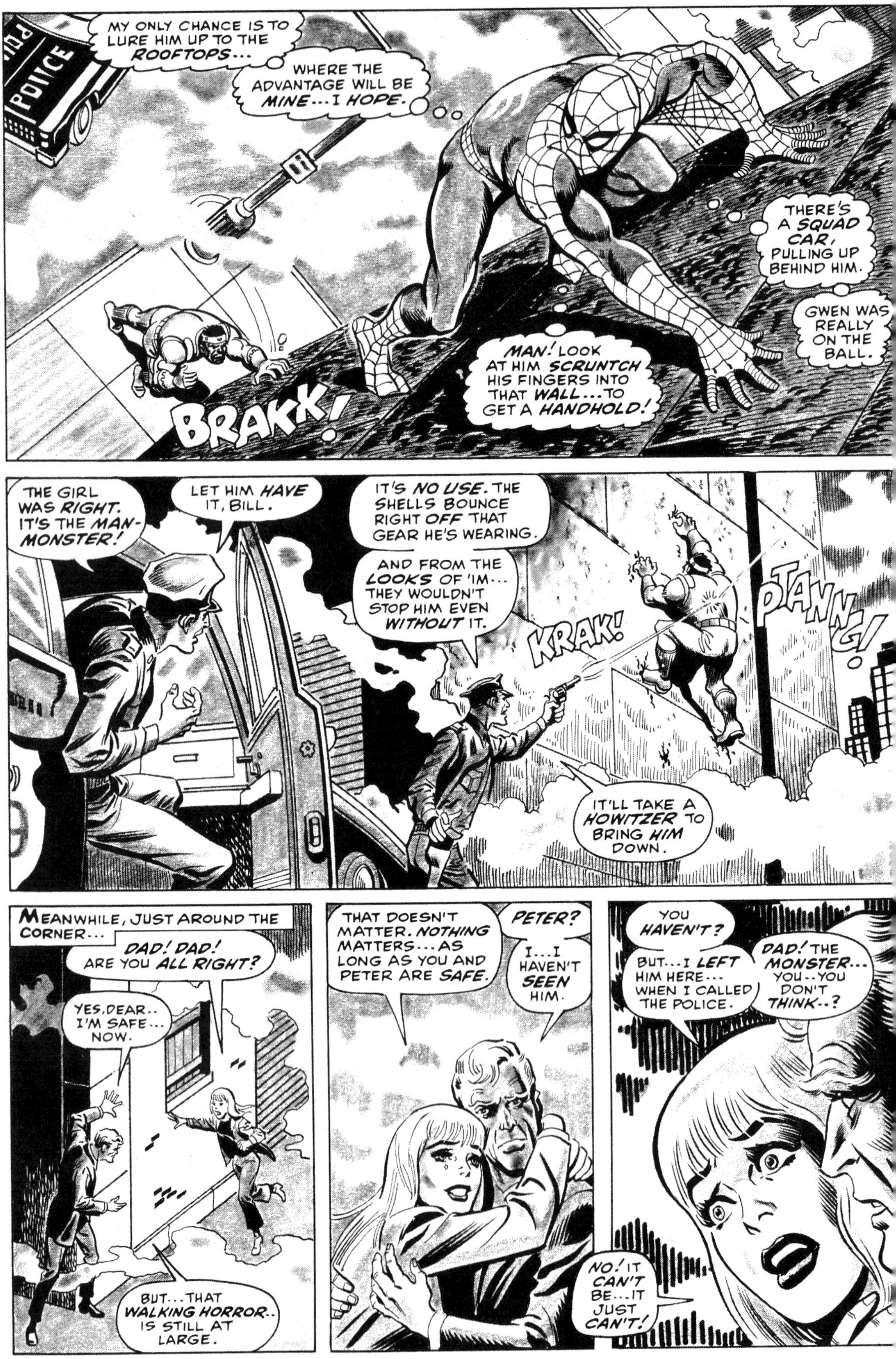
MY ONLY CHANCE IS TO LURE HIM UP TO THE ROOFTOPS...
WHERE THE ADVANTAGE WILL BE MINE...I HOPE.
THERE'S A SQUAD CAR, PULLING UP BEHIND HIM.
GWEN WAS REALLY ON THE BALL.
MAN! LOOK AT HIM SCRUNTCH HIS FINGERS INTO THAT WALL...TO GET A HANDHOLD!
BRAKK!
POLICE
THE GIRL WAS RIGHT. IT'S THE MAN-MONSTER!
LET HIM HAVE IT, BILL.
IT'S NO USE. THE SHELLS BOUNCE RIGHT OFF THAT GEAR HE'S WEARING.
AND FROM THE LOOKS OF 'IM... THEY WOULDN'T STOP HIM EVEN WITHOUT IT.
KRAK!
PTANNNG!
IT'LL TAKE A HOWITZER TO BRING HIM DOWN.
MEANWHILE, JUST AROUND THE CORNER...
DAD! DAD! ARE YOU ALL RIGHT?
YES, DEAR.. I'M SAFE... NOW.
BUT...THAT WALKING HORROR.. IS STILL AT LARGE.
THAT DOESN'T MATTER. NOTHING MATTERS...AS LONG AS YOU AND PETER ARE SAFE.
PETER?
I...I HAVEN'T SEEN HIM.
YOU HAVEN'T?
BUT...I LEFT HIM HERE... WHEN I CALLED THE POLICE.
DAD! THE MONSTER... YOU--YOU DON'T THINK--?
NO! IT CAN'T BE...IT JUST CAN'T!

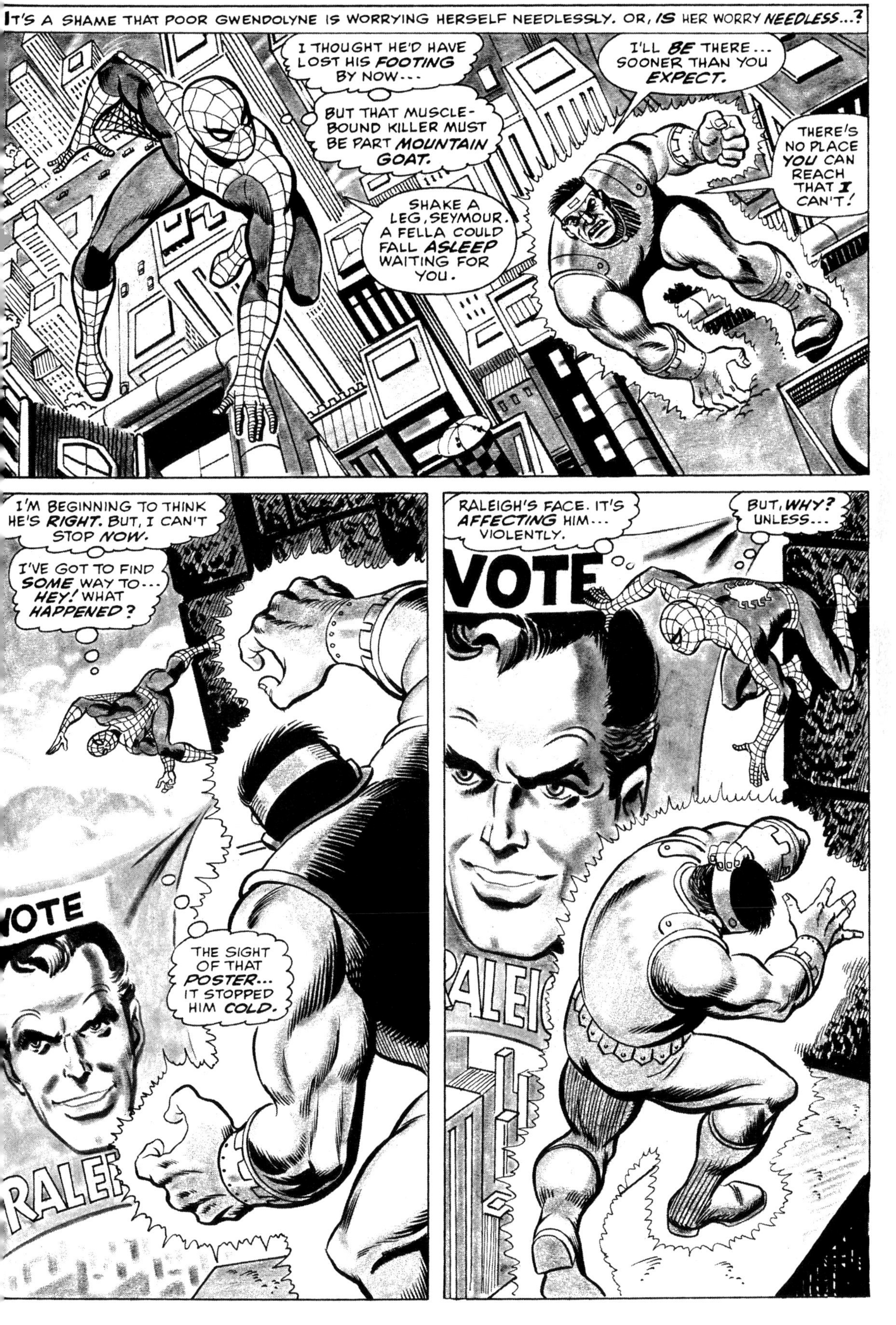

IT'S A SHAME THAT POOR GWENDOLYNE IS WORRYING HERSELF NEEDLESSLY. OR, IS HER WORRY NEEDLESS...?
I THOUGHT HE'D HAVE LOST HIS FOOTING BY NOW---
BUT THAT MUSCLE-BOUND KILLER MUST BE PART MOUNTAIN GOAT.
SHAKE A LEG, SEYMOUR. A FELLA COULD FALL ASLEEP WAITING FOR YOU.
I'LL BE THERE... SOONER THAN YOU EXPECT.
THERE'S NO PLACE YOU CAN REACH THAT I CAN'T!
I'M BEGINNING TO THINK HE'S RIGHT. BUT, I CAN'T STOP NOW.
I'VE GOT TO FIND SOME WAY TO--- HEY! WHAT HAPPENED?
THE SIGHT OF THAT POSTER... IT STOPPED HIM COLD.
VOTE
RALEI
RALEIGH'S FACE. IT'S AFFECTING HIM--- VIOLENTLY.
BUT, WHY? UNLESS---
VOTE
RALEI

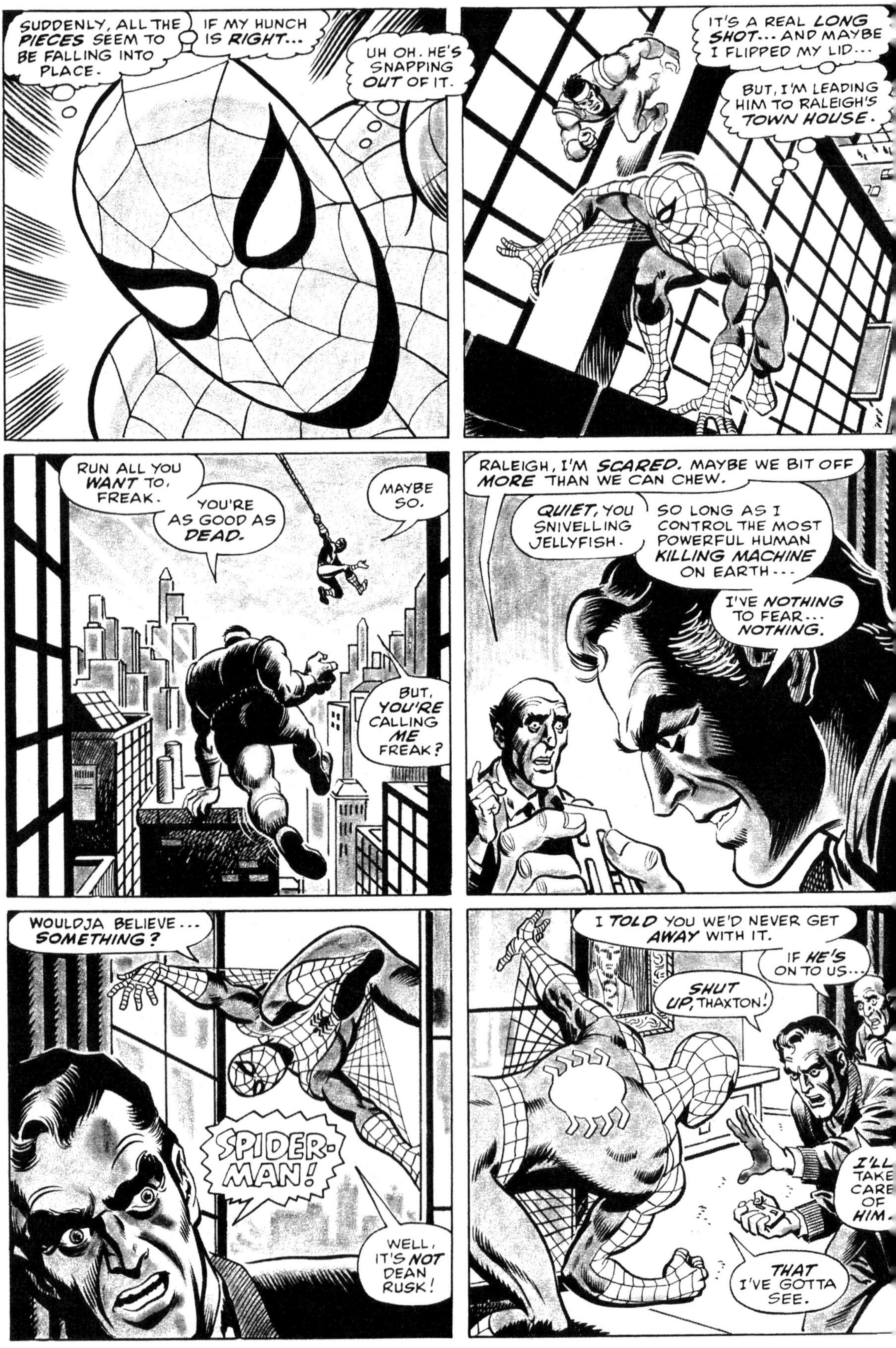
SUDDENLY, ALL THE PIECES SEEM TO BE FALLING INTO PLACE.
IF MY HUNCH IS RIGHT...
UH OH. HE'S SNAPPING OUT OF IT.
IT'S A REAL LONG SHOT... AND MAYBE I FLIPPED MY LID...
BUT, I'M LEADING HIM TO RALEIGH'S TOWN HOUSE.
RUN ALL YOU WANT TO, FREAK.
YOU'RE AS GOOD AS DEAD.
MAYBE SO.
BUT, YOU'RE CALLING ME FREAK?
RALEIGH, I'M SCARED. MAYBE WE BIT OFF MORE THAN WE CAN CHEW.
QUIET, YOU SNIVELLING JELLYFISH.
SO LONG AS I CONTROL THE MOST POWERFUL HUMAN KILLING MACHINE ON EARTH---
I'VE NOTHING TO FEAR... NOTHING.
WOULDJA BELIEVE... SOMETHING?
SPIDER-MAN!
WELL, IT'S NOT DEAN RUSK!
I TOLD YOU WE'D NEVER GET AWAY WITH IT.
IF HE'S ON TO US...
SHUT UP, THAXTON!
I'LL TAKE CARE OF HIM.
THAT I'VE GOTTA SEE.

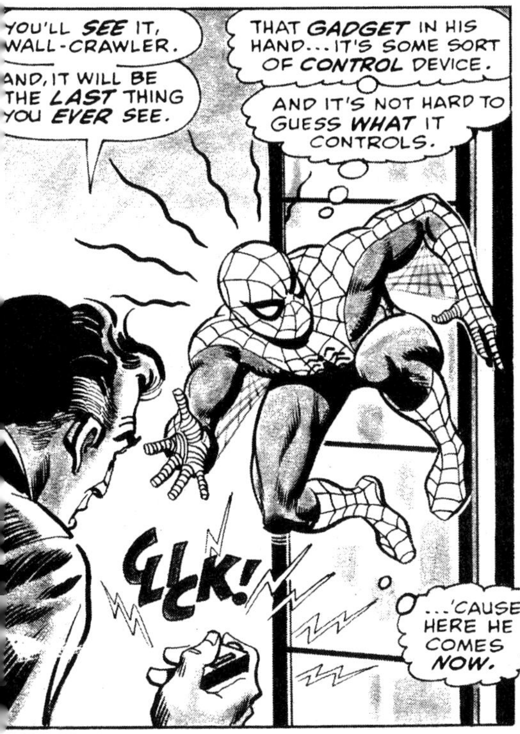
YOU'LL SEE IT, WALL-CRAWLER.
AND, IT WILL BE THE LAST THING YOU EVER SEE.
THAT GADGET IN HIS HAND... IT'S SOME SORT OF CONTROL DEVICE.
AND IT'S NOT HARD TO GUESS WHAT IT CONTROLS.
CLICK!
...'CAUSE HERE HE COMES NOW.

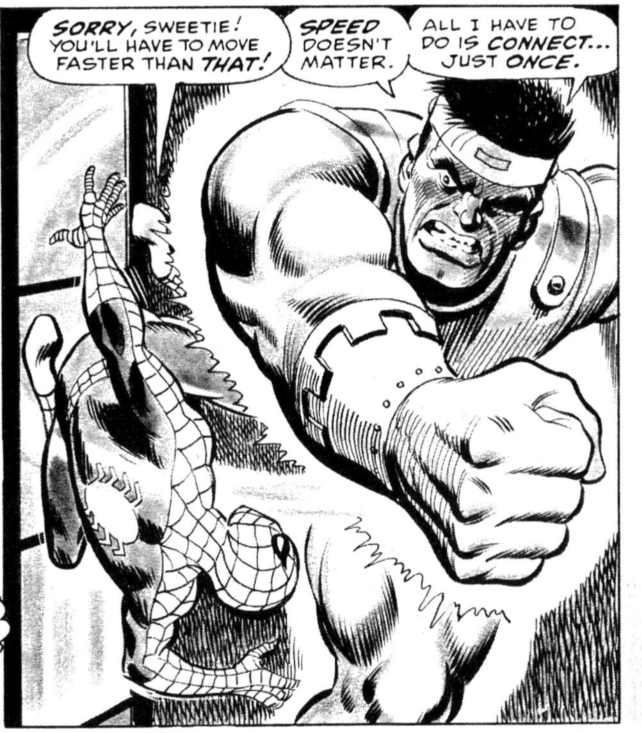
SORRY, SWEETIE! YOU'LL HAVE TO MOVE FASTER THAN THAT!
SPEED DOESN'T MATTER.
ALL I HAVE TO DO IS CONNECT... JUST ONCE.

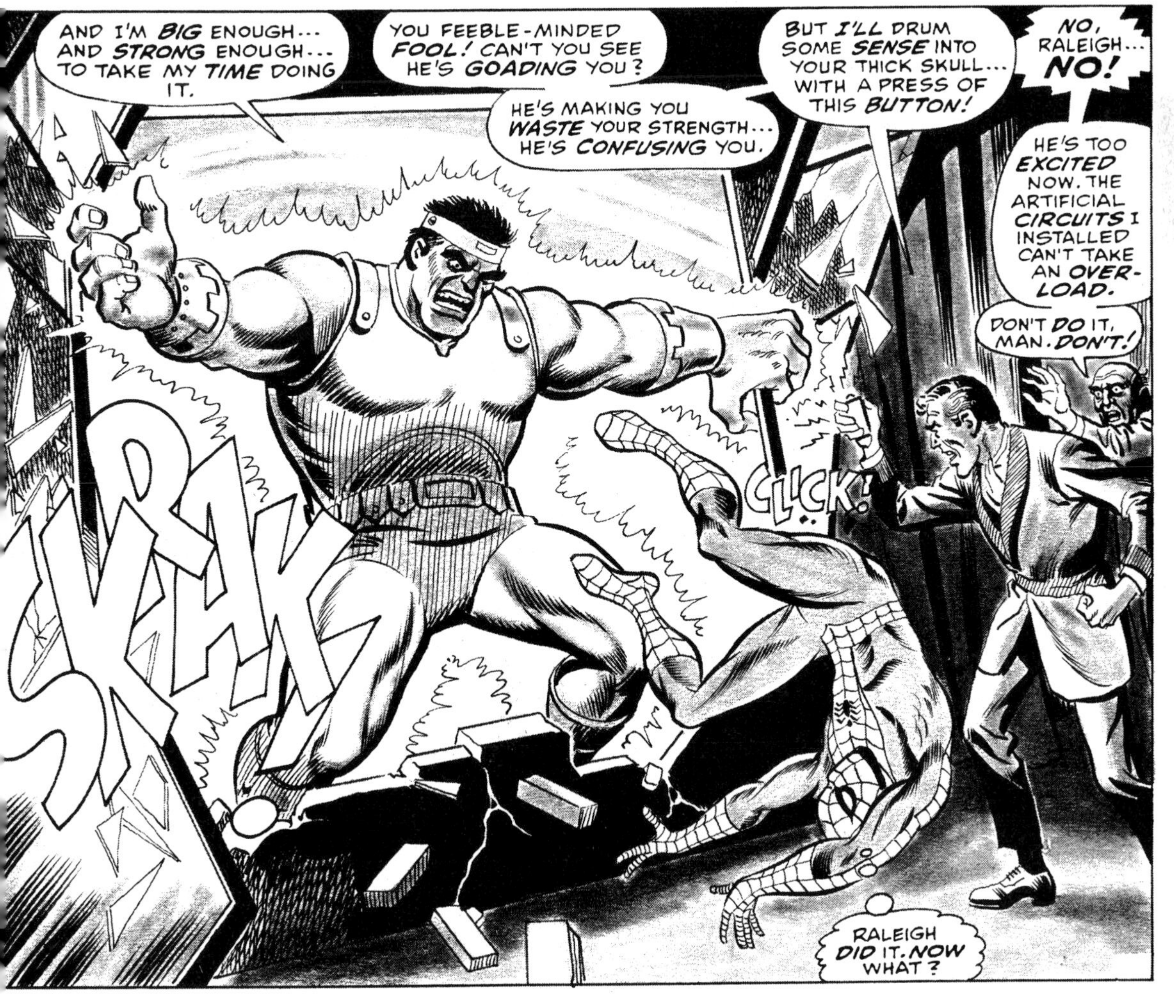
AND I'M BIG ENOUGH... AND STRONG ENOUGH... TO TAKE MY TIME DOING IT.
YOU FEEBLE-MINDED FOOL! CAN'T YOU SEE HE'S GOADING YOU?
HE'S MAKING YOU WASTE YOUR STRENGTH... HE'S CONFUSING YOU.
BUT I'LL DRUM SOME SENSE INTO YOUR THICK SKULL... WITH A PRESS OF THIS BUTTON!
NO, RALEIGH... NO!
HE'S TOO EXCITED NOW. THE ARTIFICIAL CIRCUITS I INSTALLED CAN'T TAKE AN OVER-LOAD.
DON'T DO IT, MAN. DON'T!
SKRAK
CLICK!
RALEIGH DID IT. NOW WHAT?

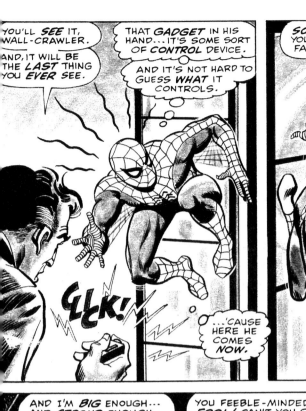

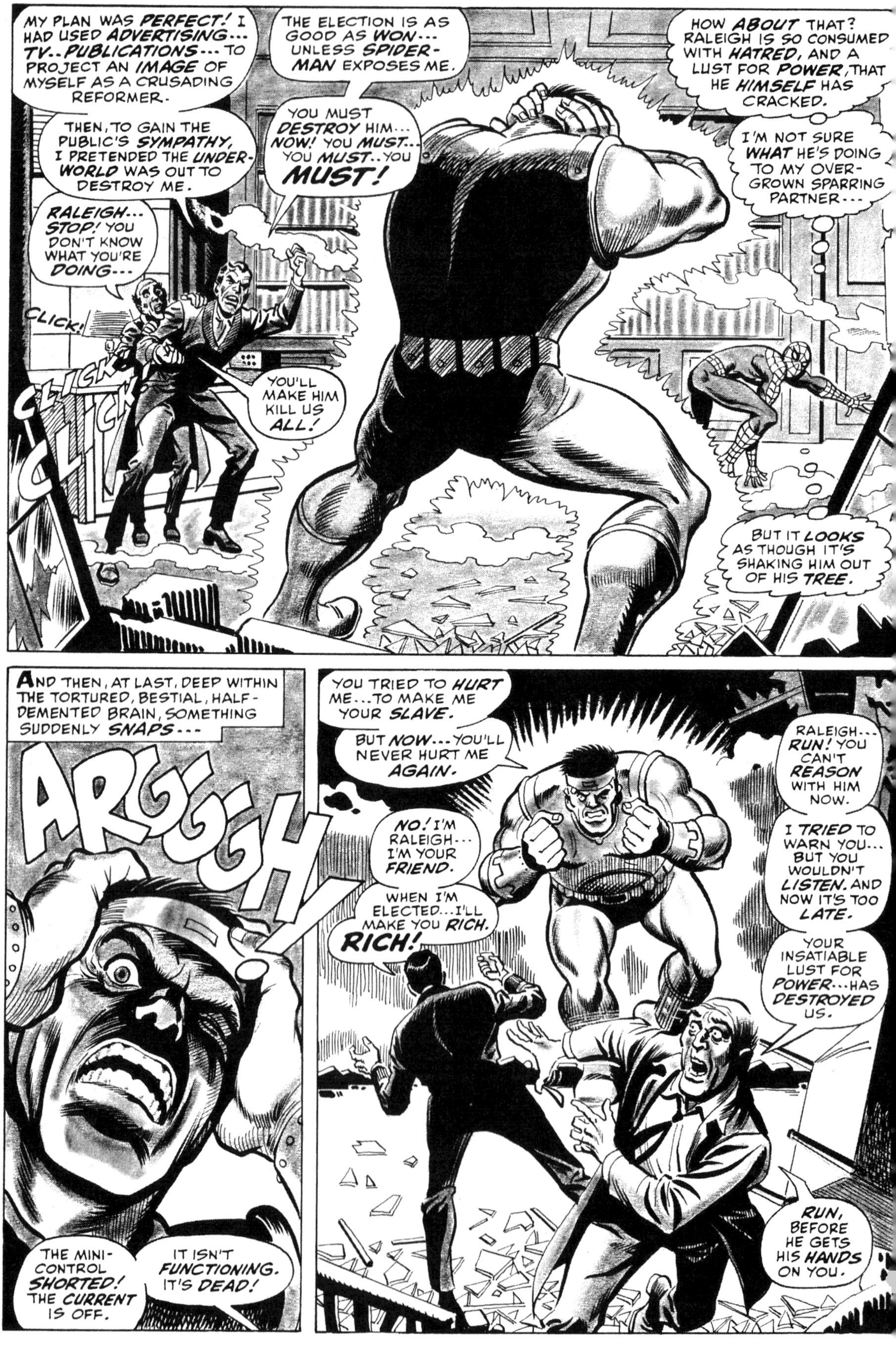
MY PLAN WAS PERFECT! I HAD USED ADVERTISING... TV..PUBLICATIONS... TO PROJECT AN IMAGE OF MYSELF AS A CRUSADING REFORMER.
THEN, TO GAIN THE PUBLIC'S SYMPATHY, I PRETENDED THE UNDER-WORLD WAS OUT TO DESTROY ME.
THE ELECTION IS AS GOOD AS WON... UNLESS SPIDER-MAN EXPOSES ME.
YOU MUST DESTROY HIM... NOW! YOU MUST... YOU MUST..YOU MUST!
RALEIGH... STOP! YOU DON'T KNOW WHAT YOU'RE DOING...
CLICK!
CLICK
CLICK
YOU'LL MAKE HIM KILL US ALL!
HOW ABOUT THAT? RALEIGH IS SO CONSUMED WITH HATRED, AND A LUST FOR POWER, THAT HE HIMSELF HAS CRACKED.
I'M NOT SURE WHAT HE'S DOING TO MY OVER-GROWN SPARRING PARTNER...
BUT IT LOOKS AS THOUGH IT'S SHAKING HIM OUT OF HIS TREE.
AND THEN, AT LAST, DEEP WITHIN THE TORTURED, BESTIAL, HALF-DEMENTED BRAIN, SOMETHING SUDDENLY SNAPS...
ARGGGH
THE MINI-CONTROL SHORTED! THE CURRENT IS OFF.
IT ISN'T FUNCTIONING. IT'S DEAD!
YOU TRIED TO HURT ME...TO MAKE ME YOUR SLAVE.
BUT NOW... YOU'LL NEVER HURT ME AGAIN.
NO! I'M RALEIGH... I'M YOUR FRIEND.
WHEN I'M ELECTED...I'LL MAKE YOU RICH. RICH!
RALEIGH... RUN! YOU CAN'T REASON WITH HIM NOW.
I TRIED TO WARN YOU... BUT YOU WOULDN'T LISTEN. AND NOW IT'S TOO LATE.
YOUR INSATIABLE LUST FOR POWER... HAS DESTROYED US.
RUN, BEFORE HE GETS HIS HANDS ON YOU.

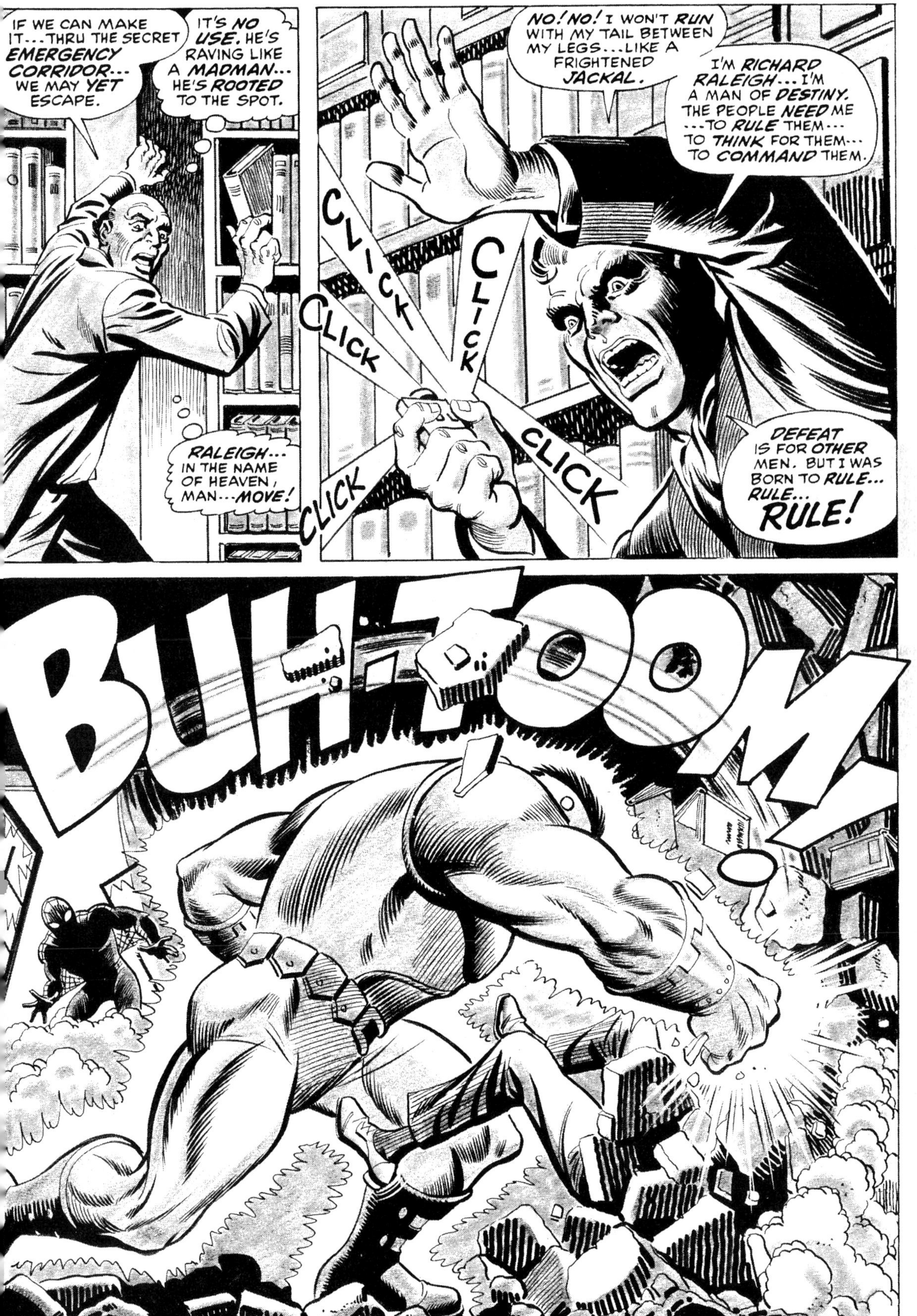

IF WE CAN MAKE IT... THRU THE SECRET EMERGENCY CORRIDOR... WE MAY YET ESCAPE.
IT'S NO USE. HE'S RAVING LIKE A MADMAN... HE'S ROOTED TO THE SPOT.
RALEIGH... IN THE NAME OF HEAVEN, MAN... MOVE!
NO! NO! I WON'T RUN WITH MY TAIL BETWEEN MY LEGS... LIKE A FRIGHTENED JACKAL.
I'M RICHARD RALEIGH... I'M A MAN OF DESTINY. THE PEOPLE NEED ME ...TO RULE THEM... TO THINK FOR THEM... TO COMMAND THEM.
CLICK
CLICK
CLICK
CLICK
CLICK
DEFEAT IS FOR OTHER MEN. BUT I WAS BORN TO RULE... RULE... RULE!
BUH-TOOM!

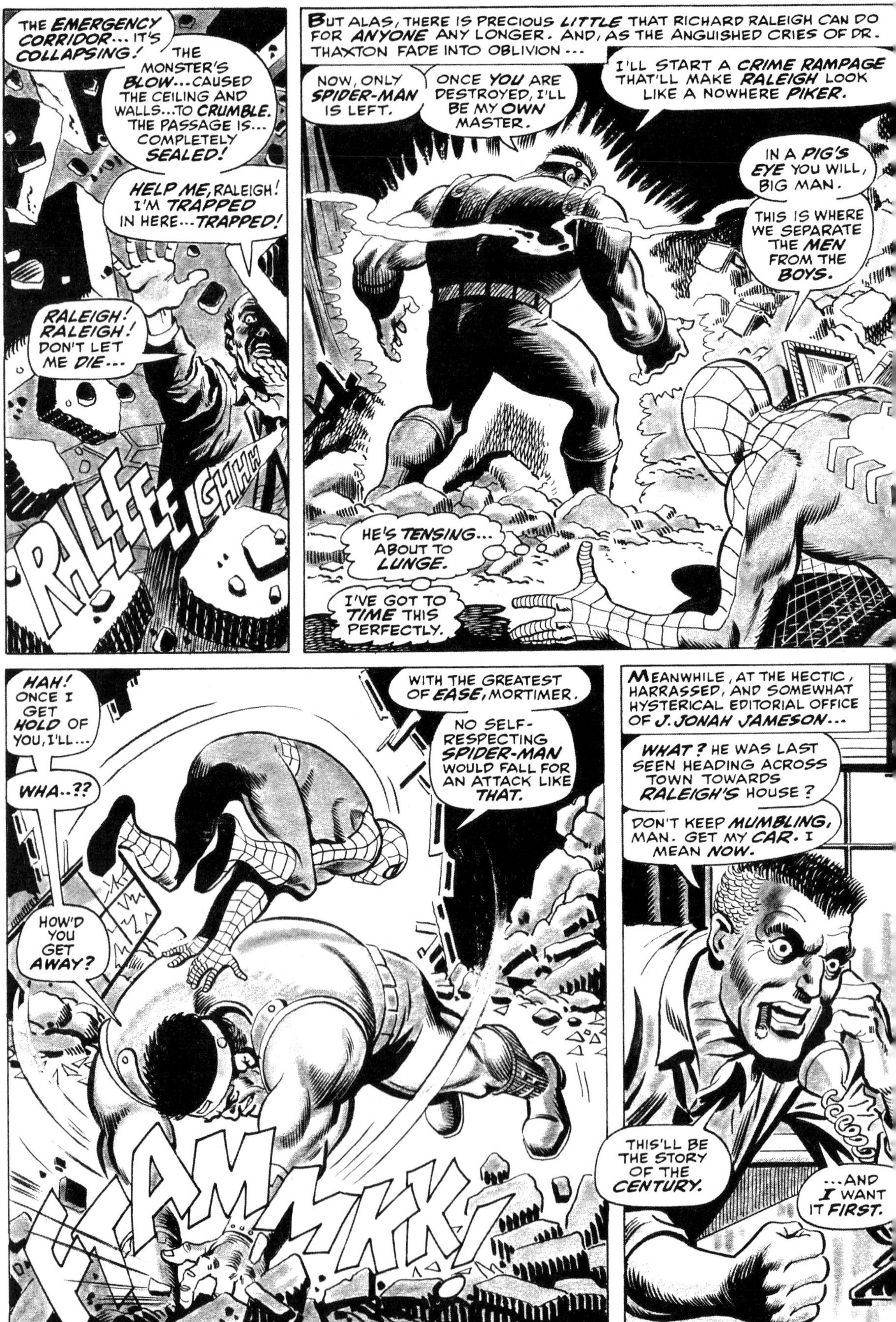
THE EMERGENCY CORRIDOR... IT'S COLLAPSING!
THE MONSTER'S BLOW...CAUSED THE CEILING AND WALLS...TO CRUMBLE. THE PASSAGE IS... COMPLETELY SEALED!
HELP ME, RALEIGH! I'M TRAPPED IN HERE...TRAPPED!
RALEIGH! RALEIGH! DON'T LET ME DIE...
RALEEEEIGHHH
BUT ALAS, THERE IS PRECIOUS LITTLE THAT RICHARD RALEIGH CAN DO FOR ANYONE ANY LONGER. AND, AS THE ANGUISHED CRIES OF DR. THAXTON FADE INTO OBLIVION...
NOW, ONLY SPIDER-MAN IS LEFT.
ONCE YOU ARE DESTROYED, I'LL BE MY OWN MASTER.
I'LL START A CRIME RAMPAGE THAT'LL MAKE RALEIGH LOOK LIKE A NOWHERE PIKER.
IN A PIG'S EYE YOU WILL, BIG MAN.
THIS IS WHERE WE SEPARATE THE MEN FROM THE BOYS.
HE'S TENSING... ABOUT TO LUNGE.
I'VE GOT TO TIME THIS PERFECTLY.
HAH! ONCE I GET HOLD OF YOU, I'LL...
WHA..??
WITH THE GREATEST OF EASE, MORTIMER.
NO SELF-RESPECTING SPIDER-MAN WOULD FALL FOR AN ATTACK LIKE THAT.
HOW'D YOU GET AWAY?
WHAMMKK!
MEANWHILE, AT THE HECTIC, HARRASSED, AND SOMEWHAT HYSTERICAL EDITORIAL OFFICE OF J. JONAH JAMESON...
WHAT? HE WAS LAST SEEN HEADING ACROSS TOWN TOWARDS RALEIGH'S HOUSE?
DON'T KEEP MUMBLING, MAN. GET MY CAR. I MEAN NOW.
THIS'LL BE THE STORY OF THE CENTURY.
...AND I WANT IT FIRST.

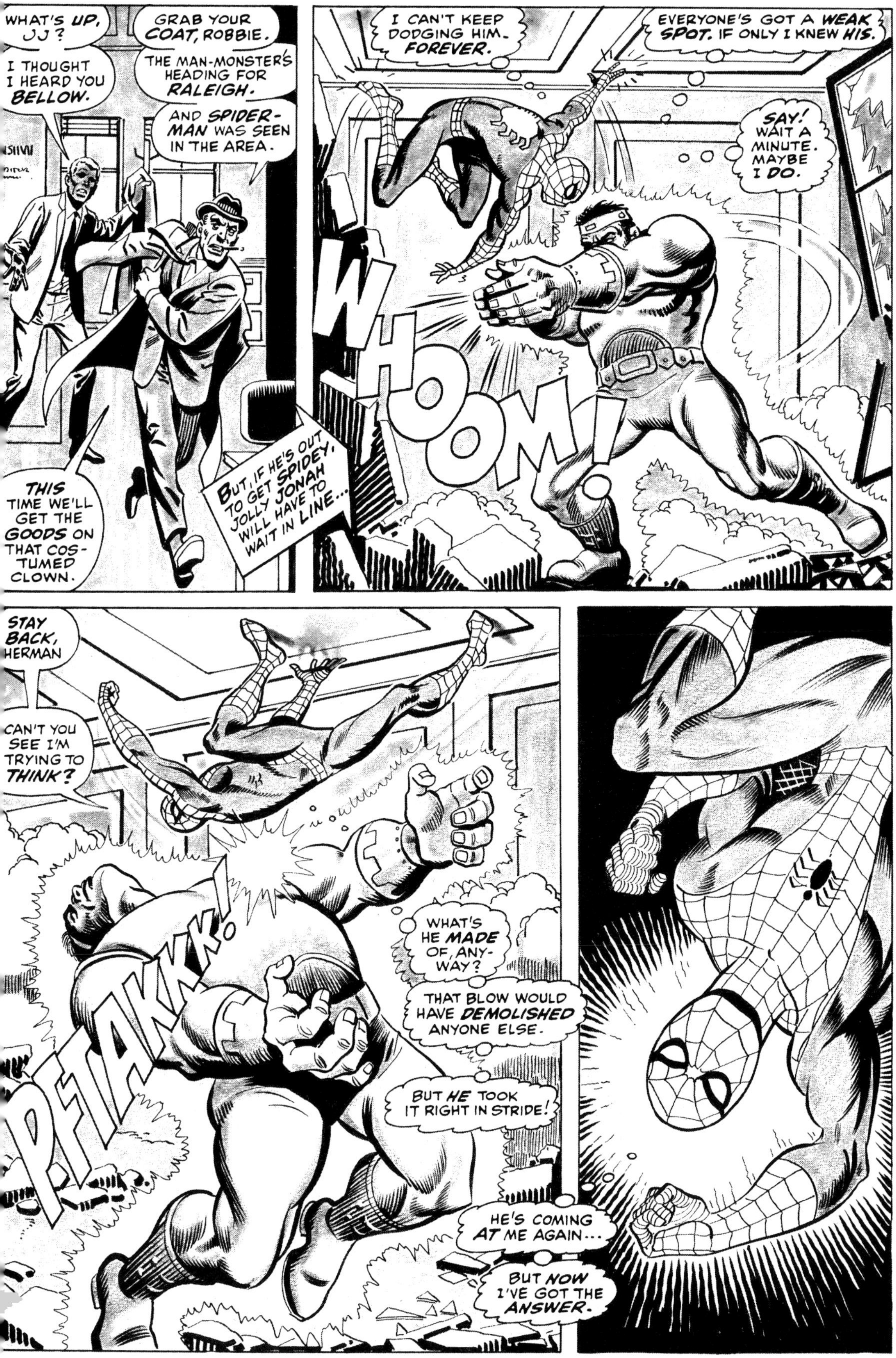
WHAT'S UP, JJ?
I THOUGHT I HEARD YOU BELLOW.
GRAB YOUR COAT, ROBBIE.
THE MAN-MONSTER'S HEADING FOR RALEIGH.
AND SPIDER-MAN WAS SEEN IN THE AREA.
THIS TIME WE'LL GET THE GOODS ON THAT COSTUMED CLOWN.
BUT, IF HE'S OUT TO GET SPIDEY, JOLLY JONAH WILL HAVE TO WAIT IN LINE...
I CAN'T KEEP DODGING HIM FOREVER.
EVERYONE'S GOT A WEAK SPOT. IF ONLY I KNEW HIS.
SAY! WAIT A MINUTE. MAYBE I DO.
WHOOOM!
STAY BACK, HERMAN
CAN'T YOU SEE I'M TRYING TO THINK?
PFTAKKK!
WHAT'S HE MADE OF, ANYWAY?
THAT BLOW WOULD HAVE DEMOLISHED ANYONE ELSE.
BUT HE TOOK IT RIGHT IN STRIDE!
HE'S COMING AT ME AGAIN...
BUT NOW I'VE GOT THE ANSWER.

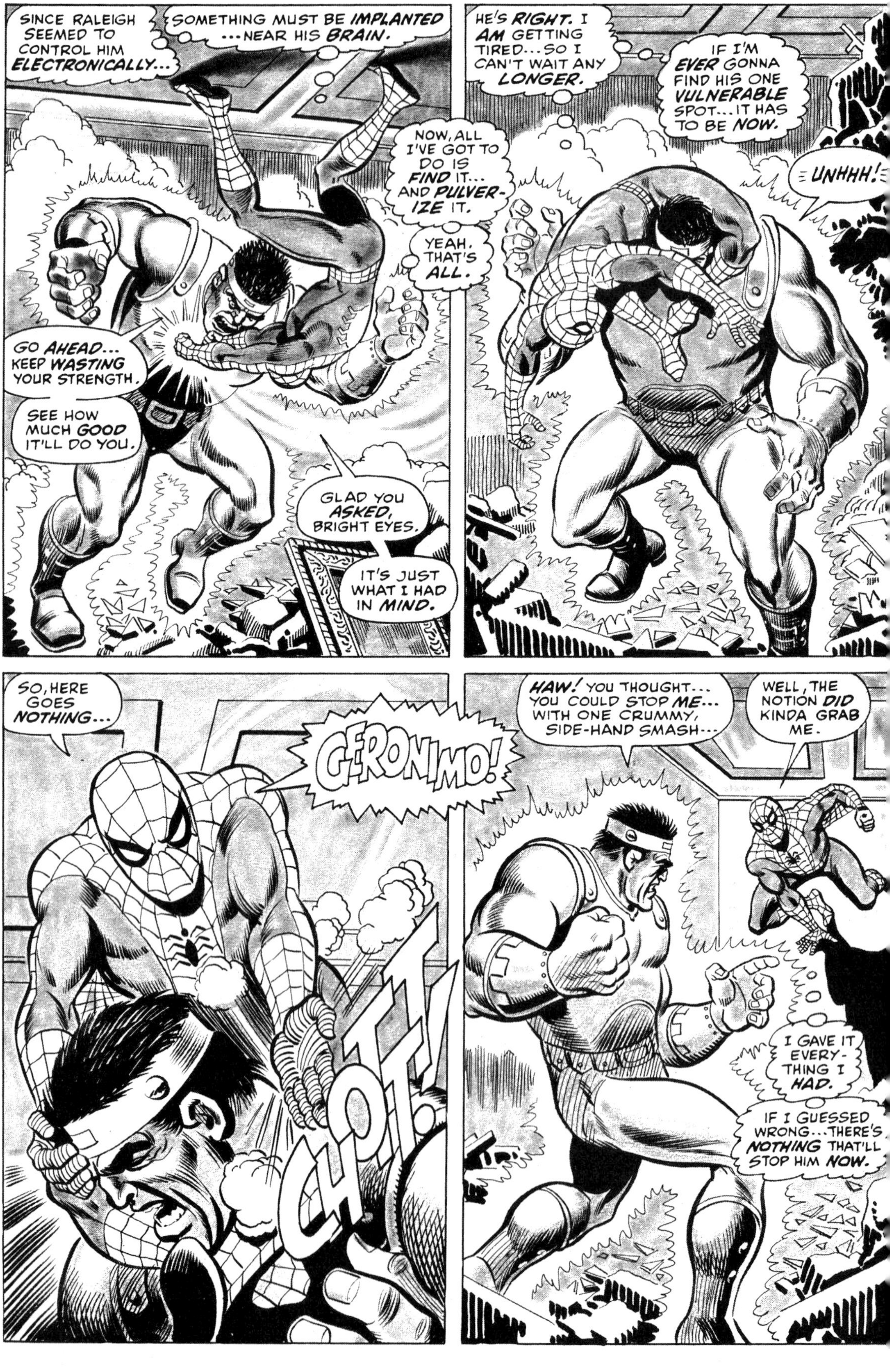
SINCE RALEIGH SEEMED TO CONTROL HIM ELECTRONICALLY...
SOMETHING MUST BE IMPLANTED ...NEAR HIS BRAIN.
NOW, ALL I'VE GOT TO DO IS FIND IT... AND PULVERIZE IT.
YEAH. THAT'S ALL.
GO AHEAD... KEEP WASTING YOUR STRENGTH.
SEE HOW MUCH GOOD IT'LL DO YOU.
GLAD YOU ASKED, BRIGHT EYES.
IT'S JUST WHAT I HAD IN MIND.
HE'S RIGHT. I AM GETTING TIRED... SO I CAN'T WAIT ANY LONGER.
IF I'M EVER GONNA FIND HIS ONE VULNERABLE SPOT... IT HAS TO BE NOW.
UNHHH!
SO, HERE GOES NOTHING...
GERONIMO!
CHOT!
HAW! YOU THOUGHT... YOU COULD STOP ME... WITH ONE CRUMMY, SIDE-HAND SMASH...
WELL, THE NOTION DID KINDA GRAB ME.
I GAVE IT EVERYTHING I HAD.
IF I GUESSED WRONG... THERE'S NOTHING THAT'LL STOP HIM NOW.

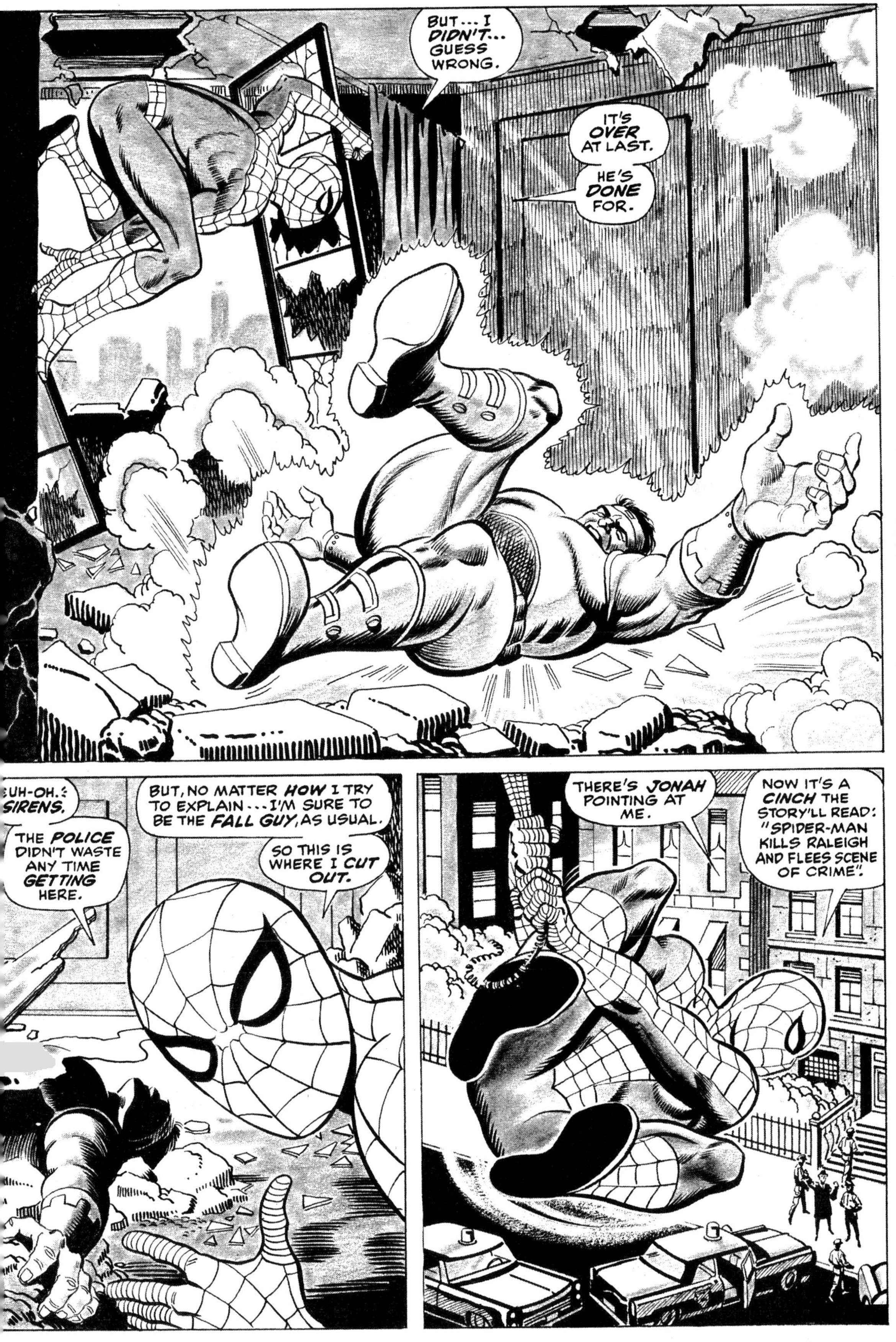

BUT... I DIDN'T... GUESS WRONG.
IT'S OVER AT LAST.
HE'S DONE FOR.
UH-OH. SIRENS.
THE POLICE DIDN'T WASTE ANY TIME GETTING HERE.
BUT, NO MATTER HOW I TRY TO EXPLAIN... I'M SURE TO BE THE FALL GUY, AS USUAL.
SO THIS IS WHERE I CUT OUT.
THERE'S JONAH POINTING AT ME.
NOW IT'S A CINCH THE STORY'LL READ: "SPIDER-MAN KILLS RALEIGH AND FLEES SCENE OF CRIME".

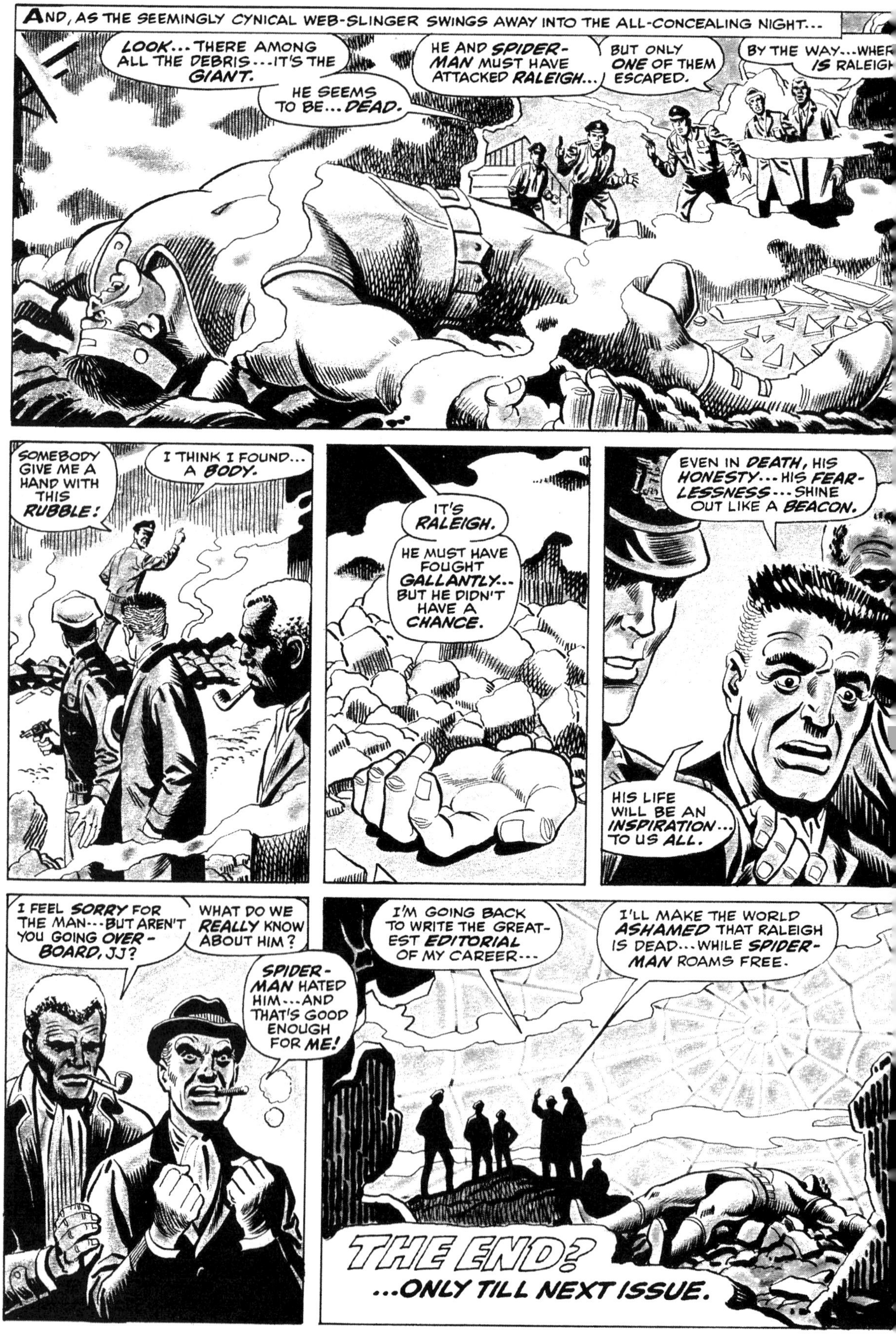
AND, AS THE SEEMINGLY CYNICAL WEB-SLINGER SWINGS AWAY INTO THE ALL-CONCEALING NIGHT...
LOOK... THERE AMONG ALL THE DEBRIS---IT'S THE GIANT.
HE SEEMS TO BE...DEAD.
HE AND SPIDER-MAN MUST HAVE ATTACKED RALEIGH...
BUT ONLY ONE OF THEM ESCAPED.
BY THE WAY...WHER IS RALEIGH
SOMEBODY GIVE ME A HAND WITH THIS RUBBLE!
I THINK I FOUND... A BODY.
IT'S RALEIGH.
HE MUST HAVE FOUGHT GALLANTLY... BUT HE DIDN'T HAVE A CHANCE.
EVEN IN DEATH, HIS HONESTY...HIS FEAR-LESSNESS...SHINE OUT LIKE A BEACON.
HIS LIFE WILL BE AN INSPIRATION... TO US ALL.
I FEEL SORRY FOR THE MAN---BUT AREN'T YOU GOING OVER-BOARD, JJ?
WHAT DO WE REALLY KNOW ABOUT HIM?
SPIDER-MAN HATED HIM...AND THAT'S GOOD ENOUGH FOR ME!
I'M GOING BACK TO WRITE THE GREAT-EST EDITORIAL OF MY CAREER---
I'LL MAKE THE WORLD ASHAMED THAT RALEIGH IS DEAD...WHILE SPIDER-MAN ROAMS FREE.
THE END?
...ONLY TILL NEXT ISSUE.

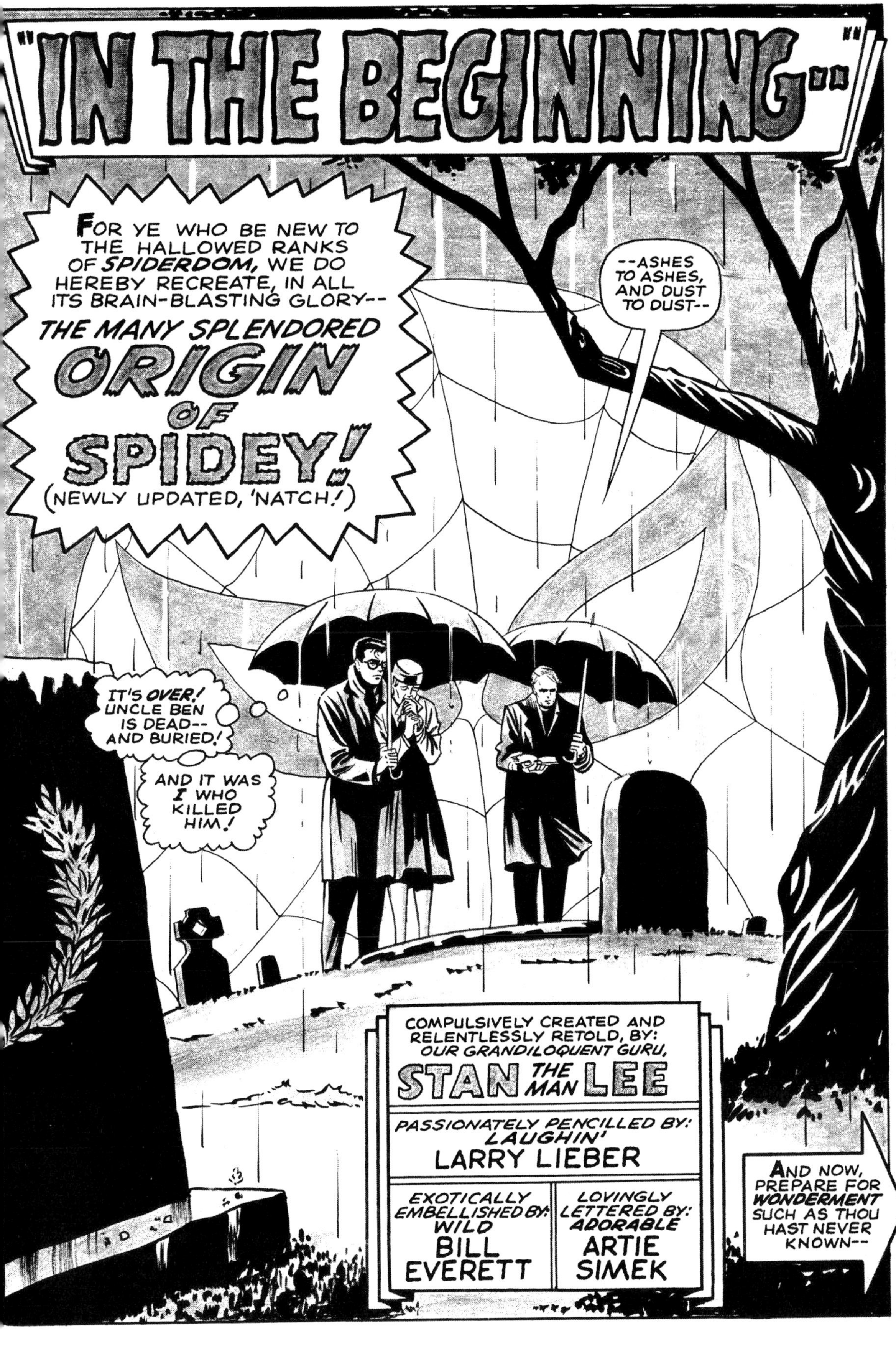
"IN THE BEGINNING--"
FOR YE WHO BE NEW TO THE HALLOWED RANKS OF SPIDERDOM, WE DO HEREBY RECREATE, IN ALL ITS BRAIN-BLASTING GLORY-- THE MANY SPLENDORED ORIGIN OF SPIDEY! (NEWLY UPDATED, 'NATCH!)
--ASHES TO ASHES, AND DUST TO DUST--
IT'S OVER! UNCLE BEN IS DEAD-- AND BURIED!
AND IT WAS I WHO KILLED HIM!
COMPULSIVELY CREATED AND RELENTLESSLY RETOLD, BY: OUR GRANDILOQUENT GURU, STAN THE MAN LEE
PASSIONATELY PENCILLED BY: LAUGHIN' LARRY LIEBER
EXOTICALLY EMBELLISHED BY: WILD BILL EVERETT
LOVINGLY LETTERED BY: ADORABLE ARTIE SIMEK
AND NOW, PREPARE FOR WONDERMENT SUCH AS THOU HAST NEVER KNOWN--

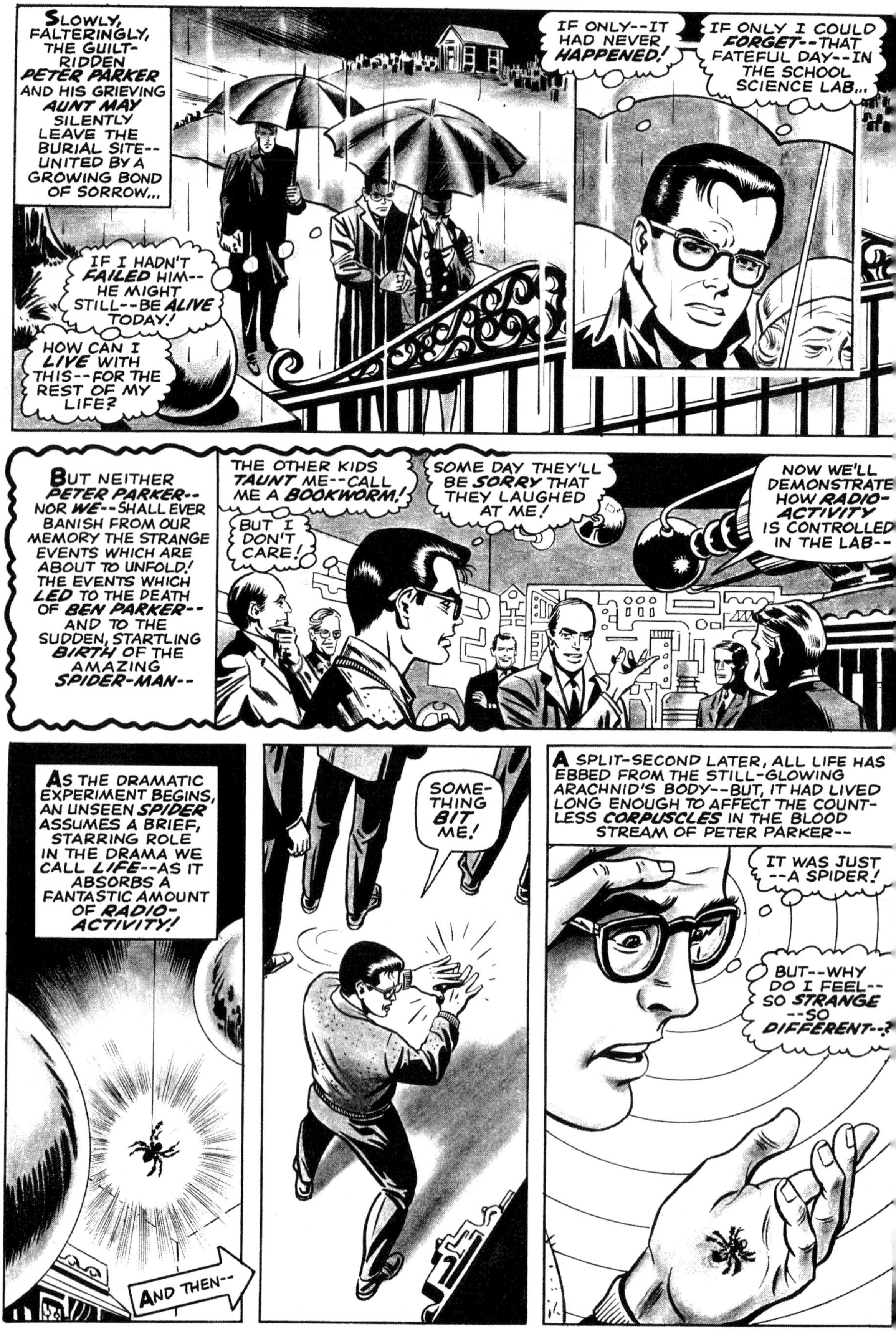
SLOWLY, FALTERINGLY, THE GUILT-RIDDEN PETER PARKER AND HIS GRIEVING AUNT MAY SILENTLY LEAVE THE BURIAL SITE--UNITED BY A GROWING BOND OF SORROW...
IF I HADN'T FAILED HIM--HE MIGHT STILL--BE ALIVE TODAY!
HOW CAN I LIVE WITH THIS--FOR THE REST OF MY LIFE?
IF ONLY--IT HAD NEVER HAPPENED!
IF ONLY I COULD FORGET--THAT FATEFUL DAY--IN THE SCHOOL SCIENCE LAB...
BUT NEITHER PETER PARKER--NOR WE--SHALL EVER BANISH FROM OUR MEMORY THE STRANGE EVENTS WHICH ARE ABOUT TO UNFOLD! THE EVENTS WHICH LED TO THE DEATH OF BEN PARKER--AND TO THE SUDDEN, STARTLING BIRTH OF THE AMAZING SPIDER-MAN--
THE OTHER KIDS TAUNT ME--CALL ME A BOOKWORM!
BUT I DON'T CARE!
SOME DAY THEY'LL BE SORRY THAT THEY LAUGHED AT ME!
NOW WE'LL DEMONSTRATE HOW RADIO-ACTIVITY IS CONTROLLED IN THE LAB--
AS THE DRAMATIC EXPERIMENT BEGINS, AN UNSEEN SPIDER ASSUMES A BRIEF, STARRING ROLE IN THE DRAMA WE CALL LIFE--AS IT ABSORBS A FANTASTIC AMOUNT OF RADIO-ACTIVITY!
AND THEN--
SOME-THING BIT ME!
A SPLIT-SECOND LATER, ALL LIFE HAS EBBED FROM THE STILL-GLOWING ARACHNID'S BODY--BUT, IT HAD LIVED LONG ENOUGH TO AFFECT THE COUNTLESS CORPUSCLES IN THE BLOOD STREAM OF PETER PARKER--
IT WAS JUST --A SPIDER!
BUT--WHY DO I FEEL--SO STRANGE --SO DIFFERENT--?

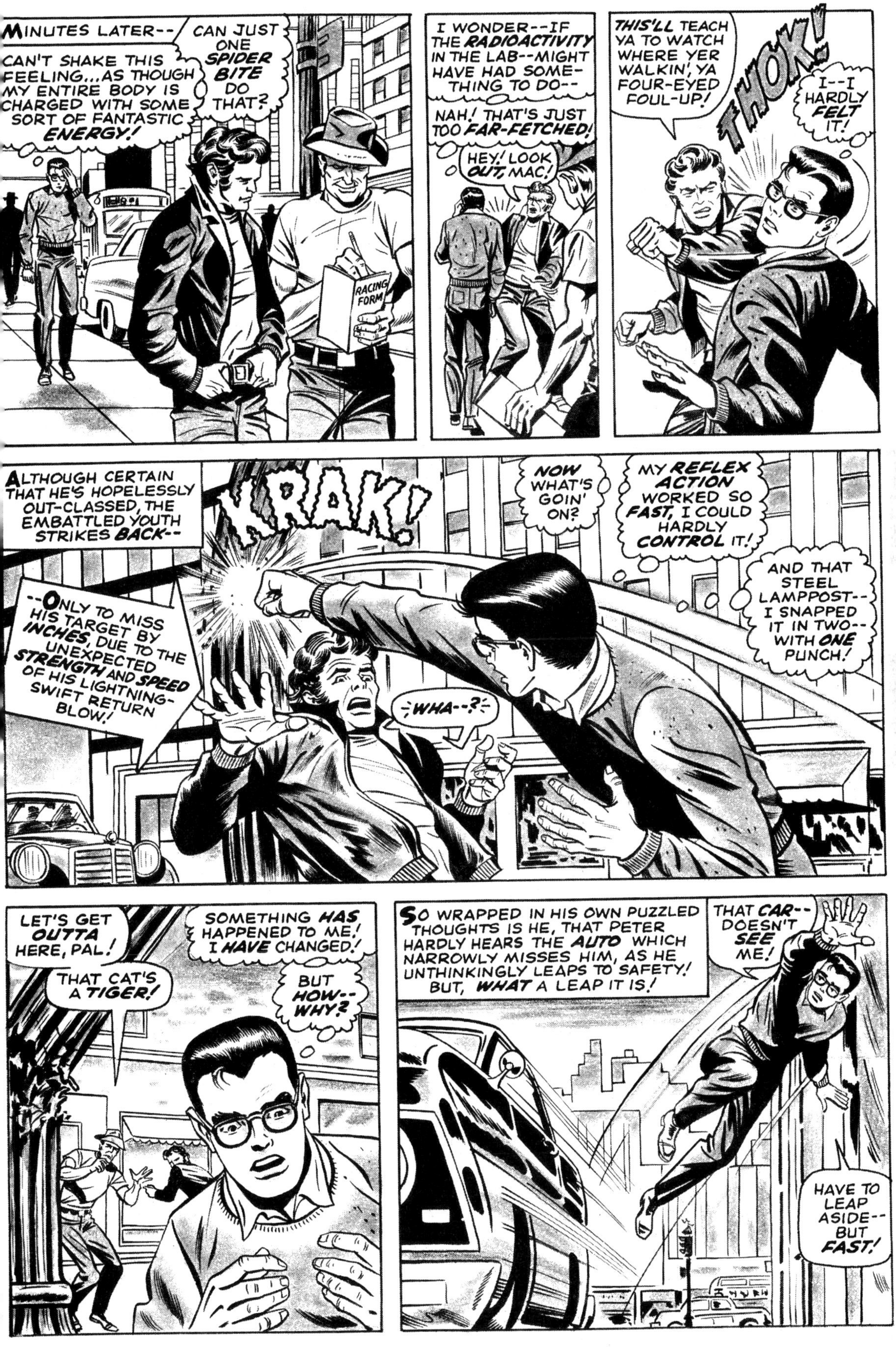
MINUTES LATER--
CAN'T SHAKE THIS FEELING...AS THOUGH MY ENTIRE BODY IS CHARGED WITH SOME SORT OF FANTASTIC ENERGY!
CAN JUST ONE SPIDER BITE DO THAT?
RACING FORM
I WONDER--IF THE RADIOACTIVITY IN THE LAB--MIGHT HAVE HAD SOMETHING TO DO--
NAH! THAT'S JUST TOO FAR-FETCHED!
HEY! LOOK OUT, MAC!
THIS'LL TEACH YA TO WATCH WHERE YER WALKIN', YA FOUR-EYED FOUL-UP!
THOK!
I--I HARDLY FELT IT!
ALTHOUGH CERTAIN THAT HE'S HOPELESSLY OUT-CLASSED, THE EMBATTLED YOUTH STRIKES BACK--
KRAK!
NOW WHAT'S GOIN' ON?
MY REFLEX ACTION WORKED SO FAST, I COULD HARDLY CONTROL IT!
AND THAT STEEL LAMPPOST--I SNAPPED IT IN TWO--WITH ONE PUNCH!
--ONLY TO MISS HIS TARGET BY INCHES, DUE TO THE UNEXPECTED STRENGTH AND SPEED OF HIS LIGHTNING-SWIFT RETURN BLOW!
WHA--?
LET'S GET OUTTA HERE, PAL!
THAT CAT'S A TIGER!
SOMETHING HAS HAPPENED TO ME! I HAVE CHANGED!
BUT HOW--WHY?
SO WRAPPED IN HIS OWN PUZZLED THOUGHTS IS HE, THAT PETER HARDLY HEARS THE AUTO WHICH NARROWLY MISSES HIM, AS HE UNTHINKINGLY LEAPS TO SAFETY! BUT, WHAT A LEAP IT IS!
THAT CAR--DOESN'T SEE ME!
HAVE TO LEAP ASIDE--BUT FAST!

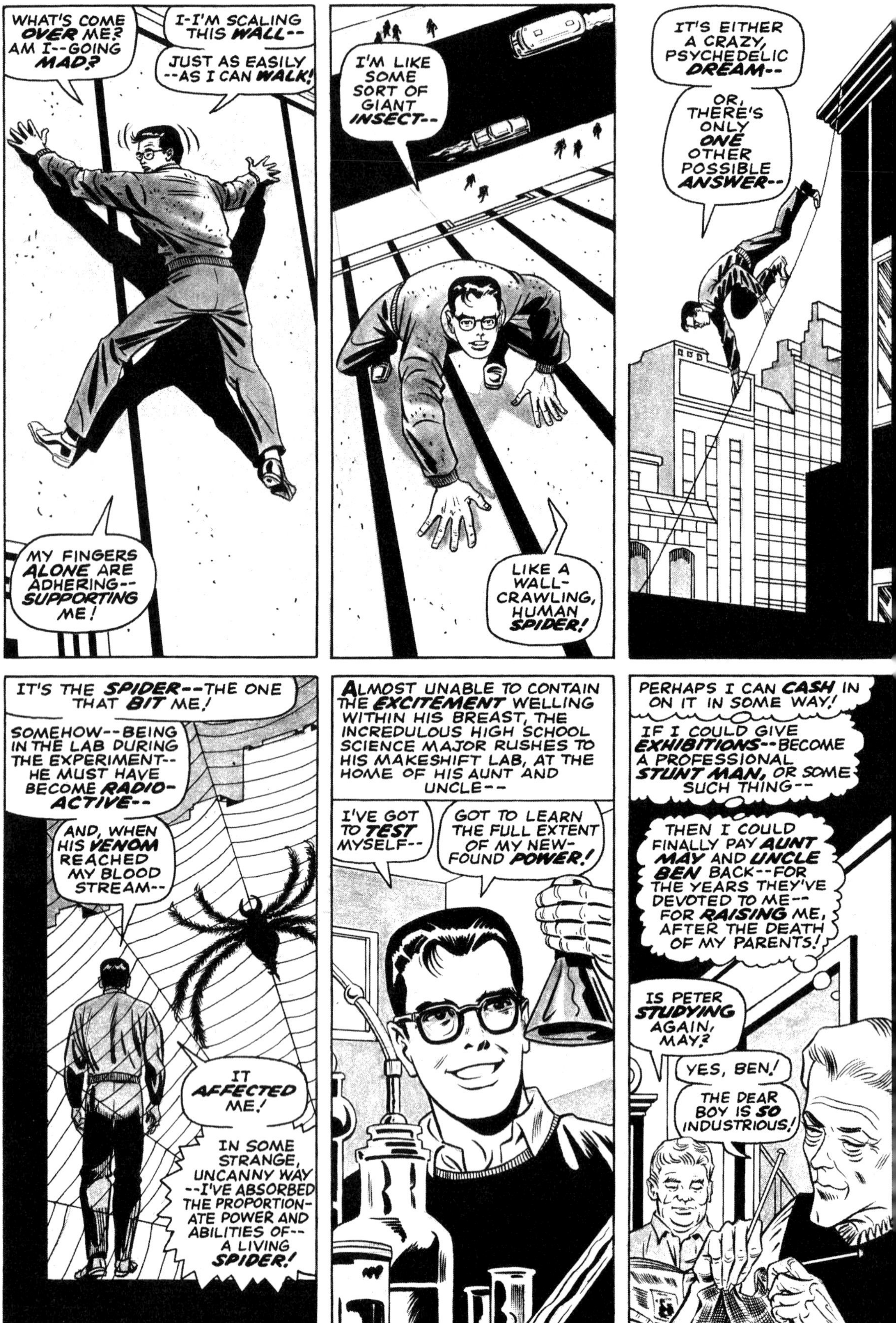
WHAT'S COME OVER ME? AM I--GOING MAD?
I-I'M SCALING THIS WALL--
JUST AS EASILY --AS I CAN WALK!
MY FINGERS ALONE ARE ADHERING-- SUPPORTING ME!
I'M LIKE SOME SORT OF GIANT INSECT--
LIKE A WALL-CRAWLING, HUMAN SPIDER!
IT'S EITHER A CRAZY, PSYCHEDELIC DREAM--
OR, THERE'S ONLY ONE OTHER POSSIBLE ANSWER--
IT'S THE SPIDER--THE ONE THAT BIT ME!
SOMEHOW--BEING IN THE LAB DURING THE EXPERIMENT-- HE MUST HAVE BECOME RADIO-ACTIVE--
AND, WHEN HIS VENOM REACHED MY BLOOD STREAM--
IT AFFECTED ME!
IN SOME STRANGE, UNCANNY WAY --I'VE ABSORBED THE PROPORTION-ATE POWER AND ABILITIES OF-- A LIVING SPIDER!
ALMOST UNABLE TO CONTAIN THE EXCITEMENT WELLING WITHIN HIS BREAST, THE INCREDULOUS HIGH SCHOOL SCIENCE MAJOR RUSHES TO HIS MAKESHIFT LAB, AT THE HOME OF HIS AUNT AND UNCLE--
I'VE GOT TO TEST MYSELF--
GOT TO LEARN THE FULL EXTENT OF MY NEW-FOUND POWER!
PERHAPS I CAN CASH IN ON IT IN SOME WAY!
IF I COULD GIVE EXHIBITIONS--BECOME A PROFESSIONAL STUNT MAN, OR SOME SUCH THING--
THEN I COULD FINALLY PAY AUNT MAY AND UNCLE BEN BACK--FOR THE YEARS THEY'VE DEVOTED TO ME-- FOR RAISING ME, AFTER THE DEATH OF MY PARENTS!
IS PETER STUDYING AGAIN, MAY?
YES, BEN!
THE DEAR BOY IS SO INDUSTRIOUS!

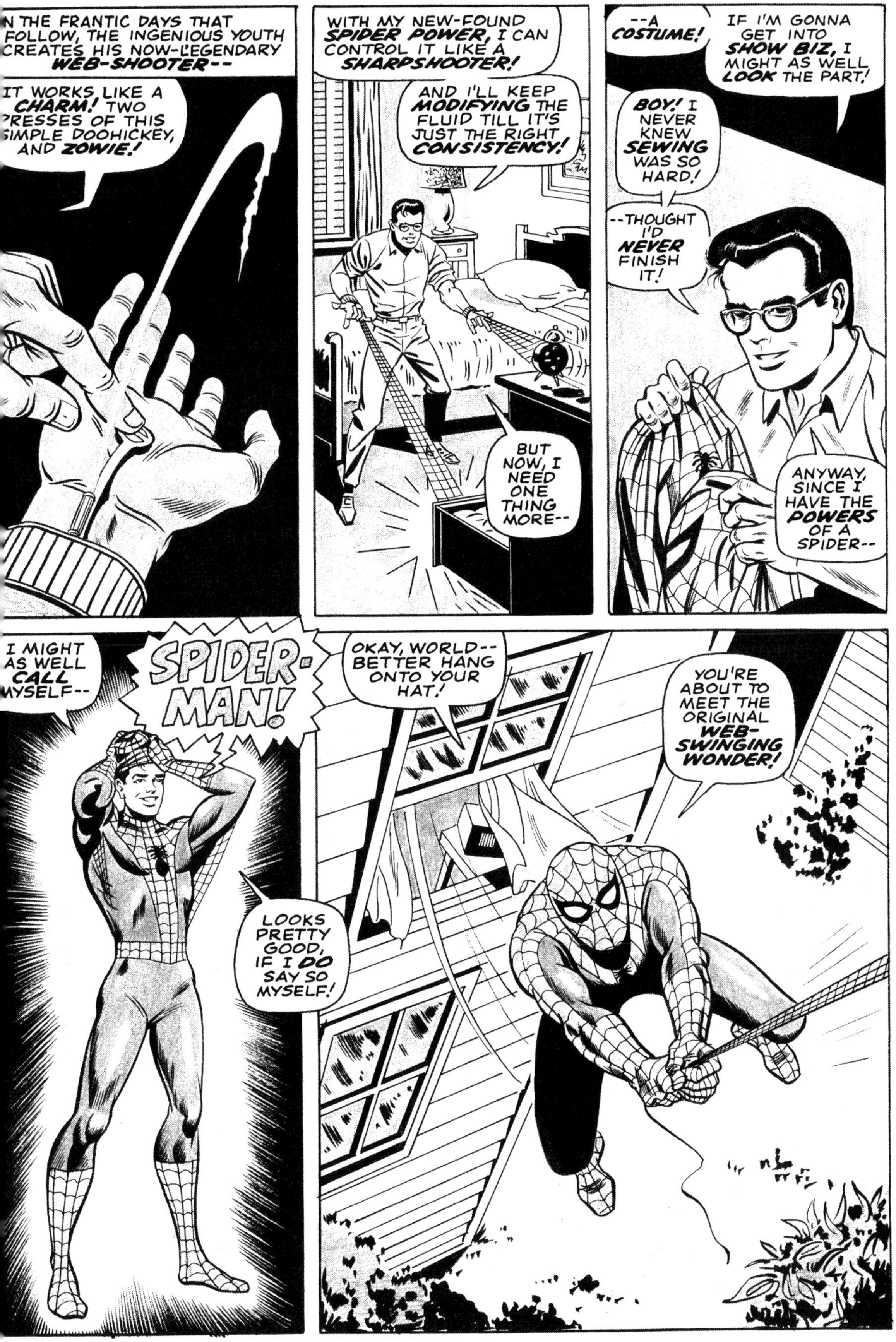
N THE FRANTIC DAYS THAT FOLLOW, THE INGENIOUS YOUTH CREATES HIS NOW-LEGENDARY WEB-SHOOTER--
IT WORKS LIKE A CHARM! TWO PRESSES OF THIS SIMPLE DOOHICKEY, AND ZOWIE!
WITH MY NEW-FOUND SPIDER POWER, I CAN CONTROL IT LIKE A SHARPSHOOTER!
AND I'LL KEEP MODIFYING THE FLUID TILL IT'S JUST THE RIGHT CONSISTENCY!
BUT NOW, I NEED ONE THING MORE--
--A COSTUME!
IF I'M GONNA GET INTO SHOW BIZ, I MIGHT AS WELL LOOK THE PART!
BOY! I NEVER KNEW SEWING WAS SO HARD!
--THOUGHT I'D NEVER FINISH IT!
ANYWAY, SINCE I HAVE THE POWERS OF A SPIDER--
I MIGHT AS WELL CALL MYSELF--
SPIDER-MAN!
LOOKS PRETTY GOOD, IF I DO SAY SO MYSELF!
OKAY, WORLD-- BETTER HANG ONTO YOUR HAT!
YOU'RE ABOUT TO MEET THE ORIGINAL WEB-SWINGING WONDER!

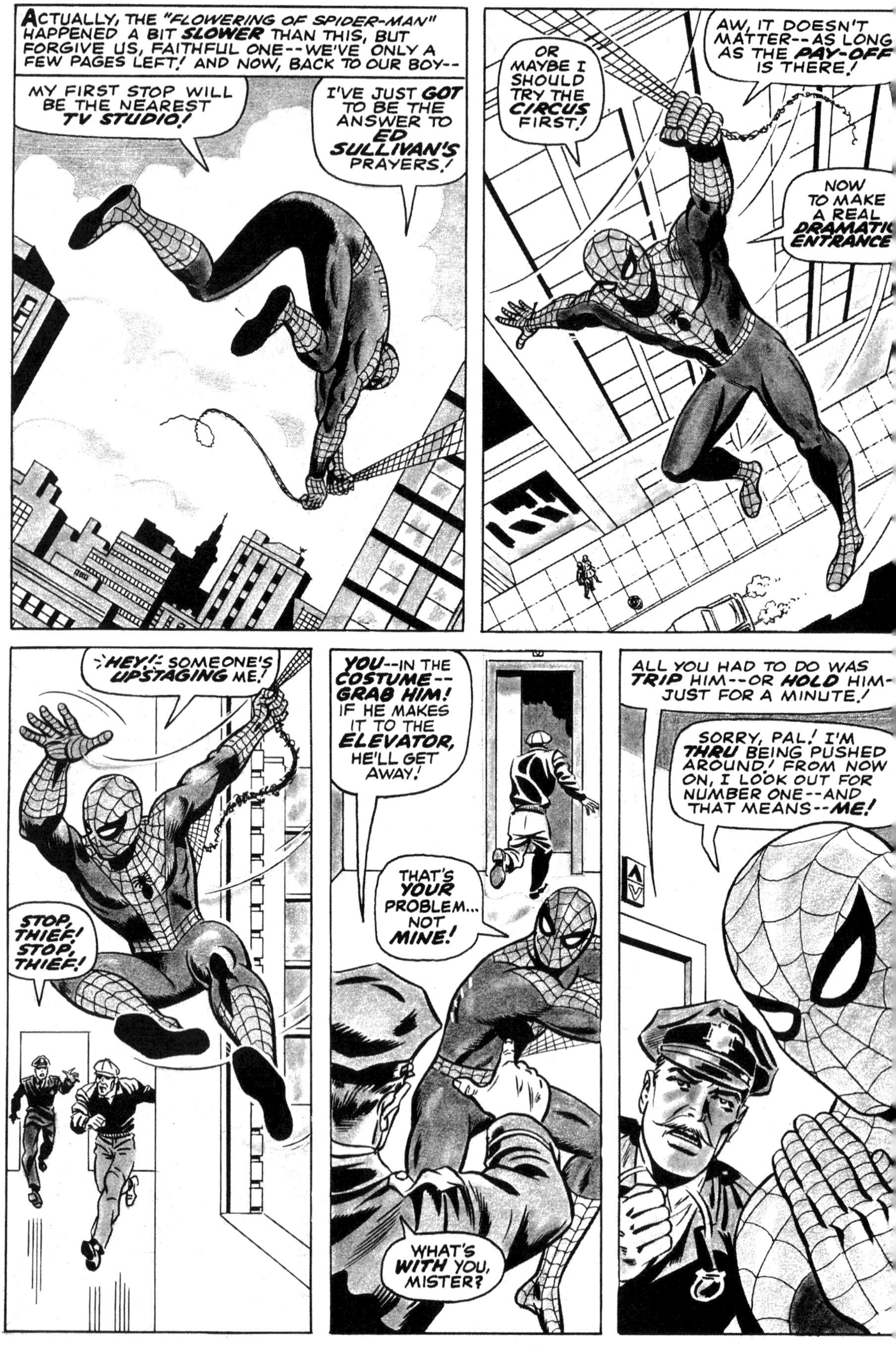
ACTUALLY, THE "FLOWERING OF SPIDER-MAN" HAPPENED A BIT SLOWER THAN THIS, BUT FORGIVE US, FAITHFUL ONE--WE'VE ONLY A FEW PAGES LEFT! AND NOW, BACK TO OUR BOY--
MY FIRST STOP WILL BE THE NEAREST TV STUDIO!
I'VE JUST GOT TO BE THE ANSWER TO ED SULLIVAN'S PRAYERS!
OR MAYBE I SHOULD TRY THE CIRCUS FIRST!
AW, IT DOESN'T MATTER--AS LONG AS THE PAY-OFF IS THERE!
NOW TO MAKE A REAL DRAMATIC ENTRANCE
HEY! SOMEONE'S UPSTAGING ME!
STOP, THIEF! STOP, THIEF!
YOU--IN THE COSTUME--GRAB HIM! IF HE MAKES IT TO THE ELEVATOR, HE'LL GET AWAY!
THAT'S YOUR PROBLEM... NOT MINE!
WHAT'S WITH YOU, MISTER?
ALL YOU HAD TO DO WAS TRIP HIM--OR HOLD HIM--JUST FOR A MINUTE!
SORRY, PAL! I'M THRU BEING PUSHED AROUND! FROM NOW ON, I LOOK OUT FOR NUMBER ONE--AND THAT MEANS--ME!

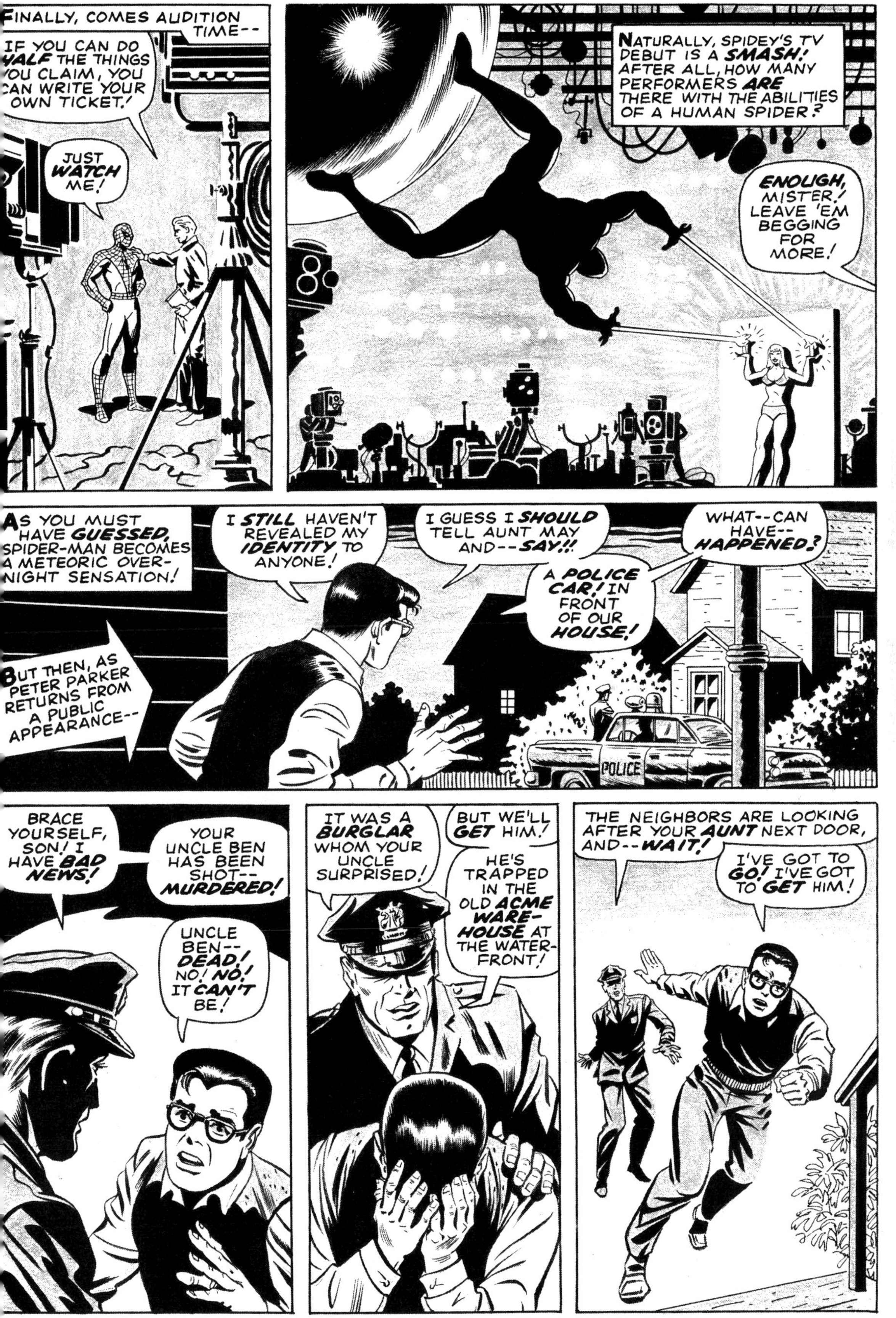
FINALLY, COMES AUDITION TIME--
IF YOU CAN DO HALF THE THINGS YOU CLAIM, YOU CAN WRITE YOUR OWN TICKET!
JUST WATCH ME!
NATURALLY, SPIDEY'S TV DEBUT IS A SMASH! AFTER ALL, HOW MANY PERFORMERS ARE THERE WITH THE ABILITIES OF A HUMAN SPIDER?
ENOUGH, MISTER! LEAVE 'EM BEGGING FOR MORE!
AS YOU MUST HAVE GUESSED, SPIDER-MAN BECOMES A METEORIC OVER-NIGHT SENSATION!
BUT THEN, AS PETER PARKER RETURNS FROM A PUBLIC APPEARANCE--
I STILL HAVEN'T REVEALED MY IDENTITY TO ANYONE!
I GUESS I SHOULD TELL AUNT MAY AND--SAY!!
A POLICE CAR! IN FRONT OF OUR HOUSE!
WHAT--CAN HAVE--HAPPENED?
POLICE
BRACE YOURSELF, SON! I HAVE BAD NEWS!
YOUR UNCLE BEN HAS BEEN SHOT--MURDERED!
UNCLE BEN--DEAD! NO! NO! IT CAN'T BE!
IT WAS A BURGLAR WHOM YOUR UNCLE SURPRISED!
BUT WE'LL GET HIM!
HE'S TRAPPED IN THE OLD ACME WARE-HOUSE AT THE WATER-FRONT!
THE NEIGHBORS ARE LOOKING AFTER YOUR AUNT NEXT DOOR, AND--WAIT!
I'VE GOT TO GO! I'VE GOT TO GET HIM!

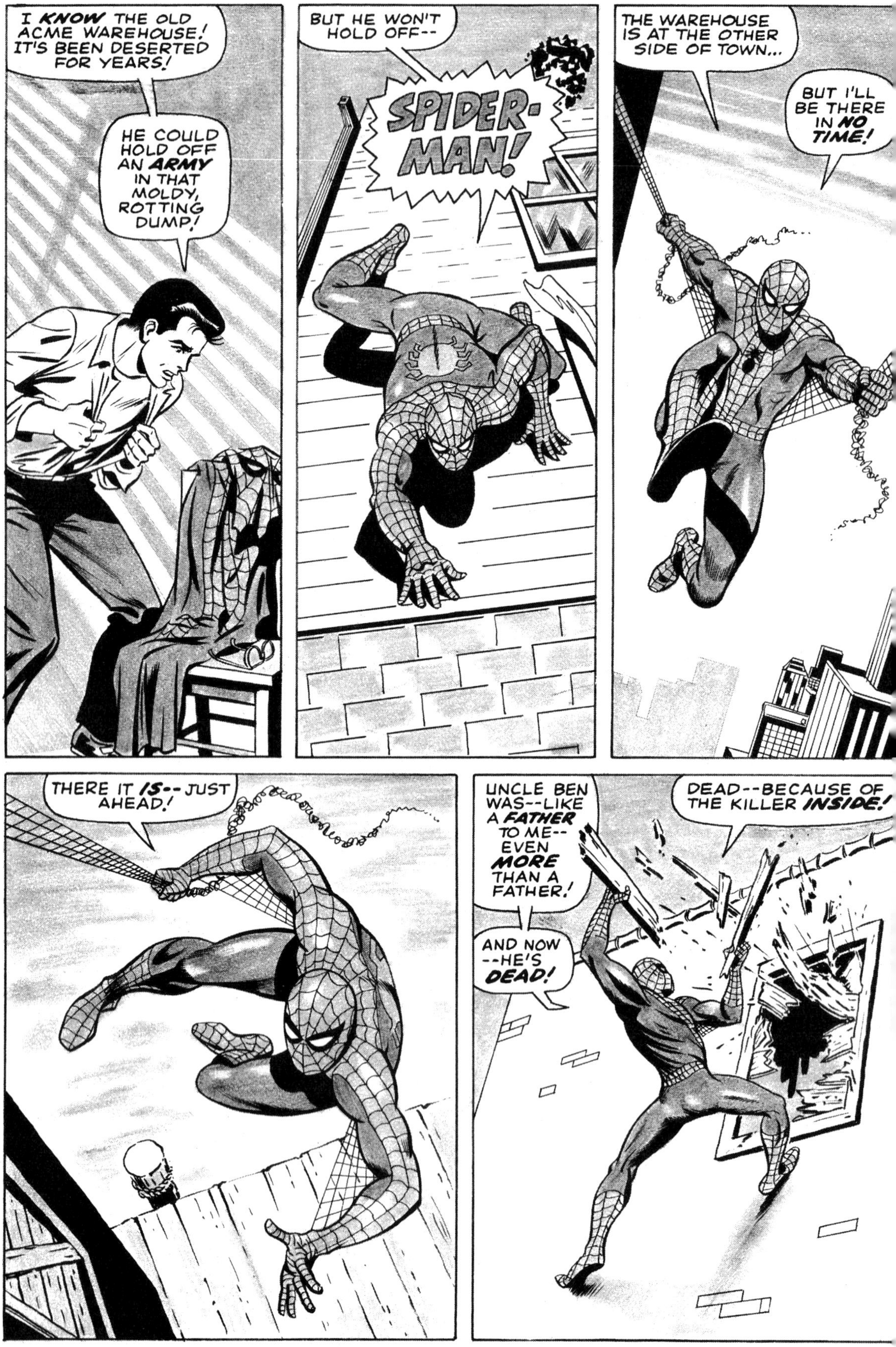
I KNOW THE OLD ACME WAREHOUSE! IT'S BEEN DESERTED FOR YEARS!
HE COULD HOLD OFF AN ARMY IN THAT MOLDY, ROTTING DUMP!
BUT HE WON'T HOLD OFF--
SPIDER-MAN!
THE WAREHOUSE IS AT THE OTHER SIDE OF TOWN...
BUT I'LL BE THERE IN NO TIME!
THERE IT IS-- JUST AHEAD!
UNCLE BEN WAS--LIKE A FATHER TO ME-- EVEN MORE THAN A FATHER!
AND NOW --HE'S DEAD!
DEAD--BECAUSE OF THE KILLER INSIDE!

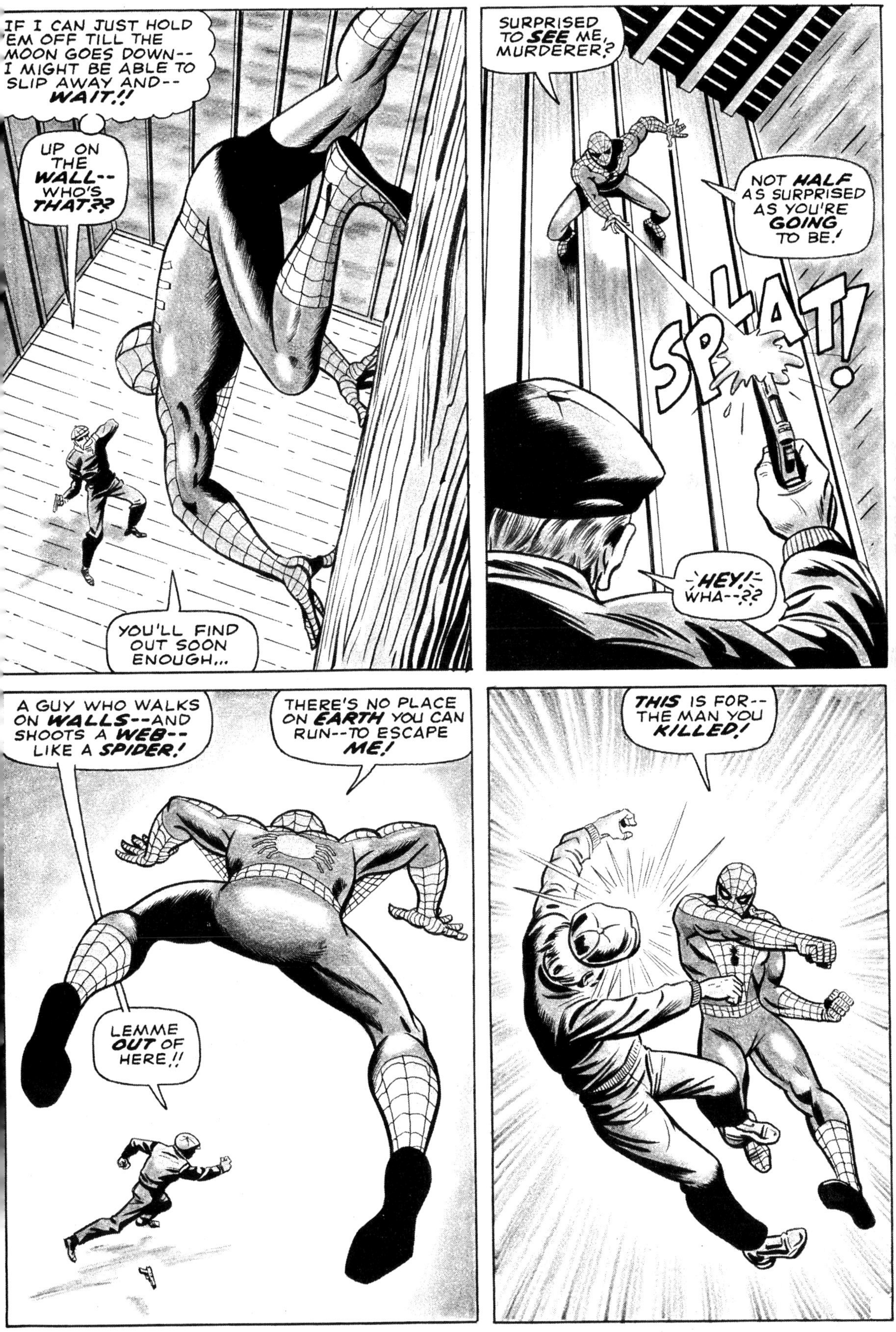
IF I CAN JUST HOLD 'EM OFF TILL THE MOON GOES DOWN-- I MIGHT BE ABLE TO SLIP AWAY AND-- WAIT.!!
UP ON THE WALL-- WHO'S THAT.??
YOU'LL FIND OUT SOON ENOUGH...
SURPRISED TO SEE ME, MURDERER?
NOT HALF AS SURPRISED AS YOU'RE GOING TO BE!
SPLAT!
HEY! WHA--??
A GUY WHO WALKS ON WALLS--AND SHOOTS A WEB-- LIKE A SPIDER!
THERE'S NO PLACE ON EARTH YOU CAN RUN--TO ESCAPE ME!
LEMME OUT OF HERE!!
THIS IS FOR-- THE MAN YOU KILLED!

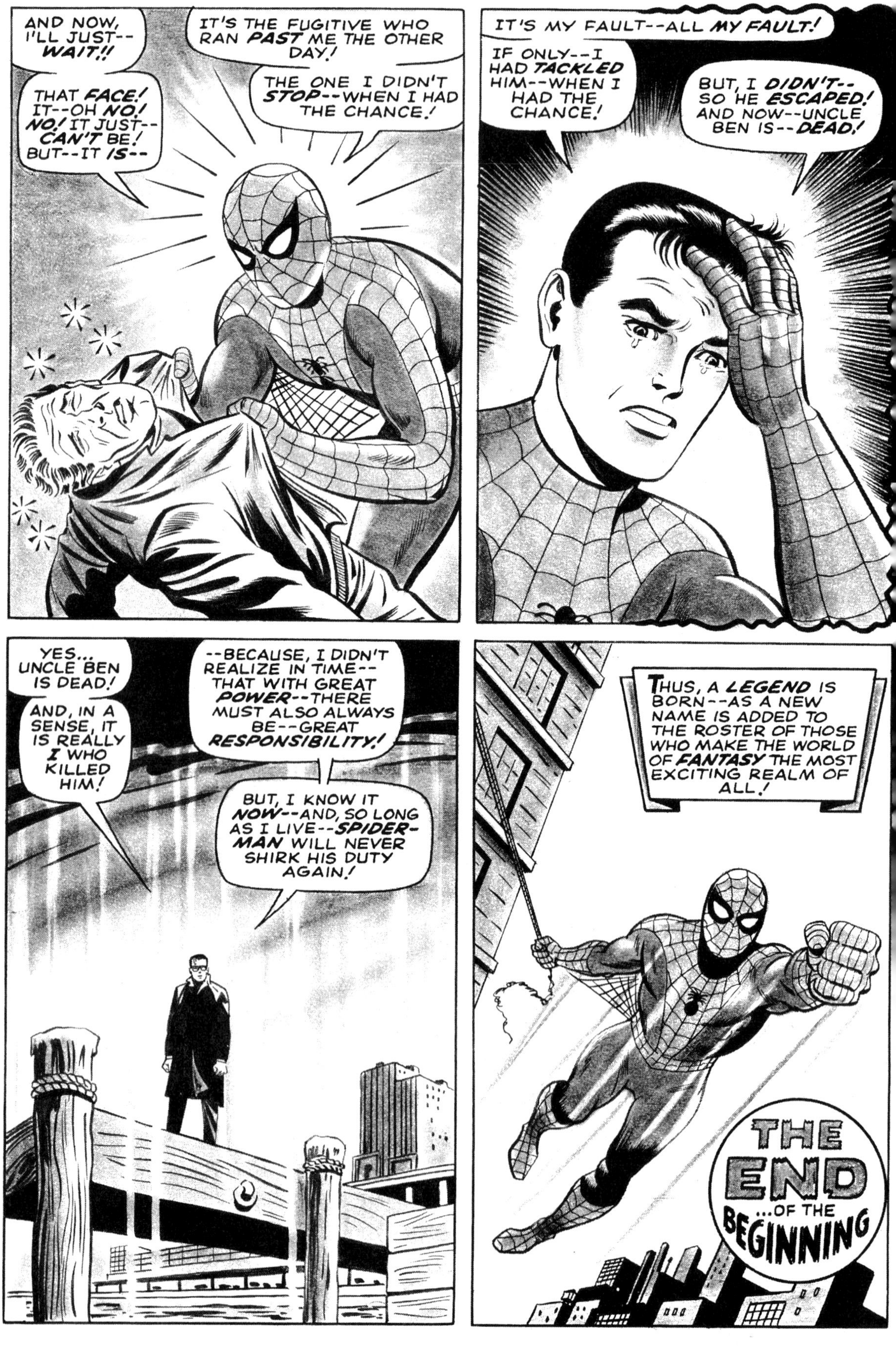
AND NOW, I'LL JUST-- WAIT!!
IT'S THE FUGITIVE WHO RAN PAST ME THE OTHER DAY!
THAT FACE! IT--OH NO! NO! IT JUST-- CAN'T BE! BUT--IT IS--
THE ONE I DIDN'T STOP--WHEN I HAD THE CHANCE!
IT'S MY FAULT--ALL MY FAULT!
IF ONLY--I HAD TACKLED HIM--WHEN I HAD THE CHANCE!
BUT, I DIDN'T-- SO HE ESCAPED! AND NOW--UNCLE BEN IS--DEAD!
YES... UNCLE BEN IS DEAD!
AND, IN A SENSE, IT IS REALLY I WHO KILLED HIM!
--BECAUSE, I DIDN'T REALIZE IN TIME-- THAT WITH GREAT POWER--THERE MUST ALSO ALWAYS BE--GREAT RESPONSIBILITY!
BUT, I KNOW IT NOW--AND, SO LONG AS I LIVE--SPIDER-MAN WILL NEVER SHIRK HIS DUTY AGAIN!
THUS, A LEGEND IS BORN--AS A NEW NAME IS ADDED TO THE ROSTER OF THOSE WHO MAKE THE WORLD OF FANTASY THE MOST EXCITING REALM OF ALL!
THE END ...OF THE BEGINNING

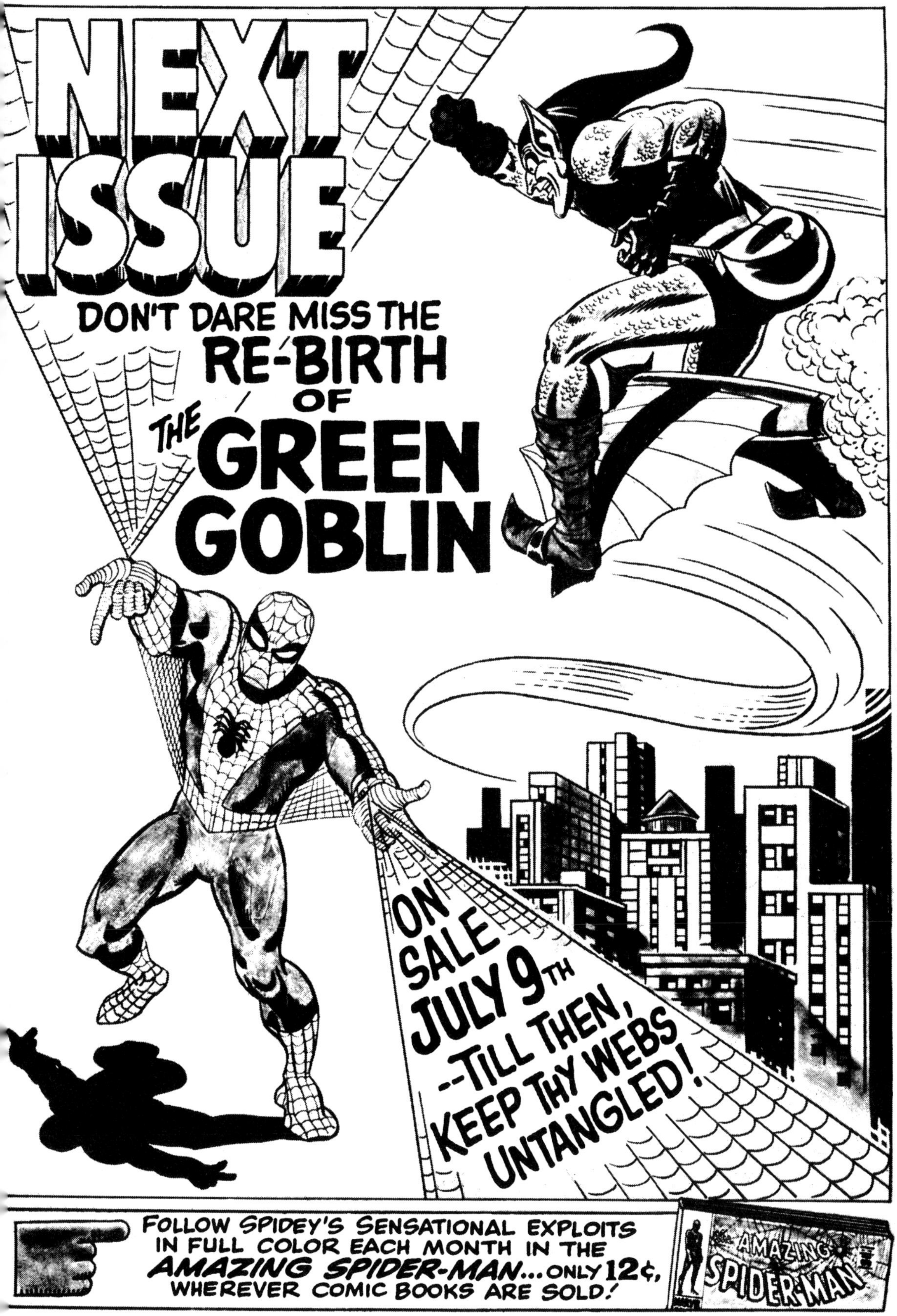

NEXT ISSUE
DON'T DARE MISS THE RE-BIRTH OF THE GREEN GOBLIN
ON SALE JULY 9TH --TILL THEN, KEEP THY WEBS UNTANGLED!
FOLLOW SPIDEY'S SENSATIONAL EXPLOITS IN FULL COLOR EACH MONTH IN THE AMAZING SPIDER-MAN... ONLY 12¢, WHEREVER COMIC BOOKS ARE SOLD!
AMAZING SPIDER-MAN

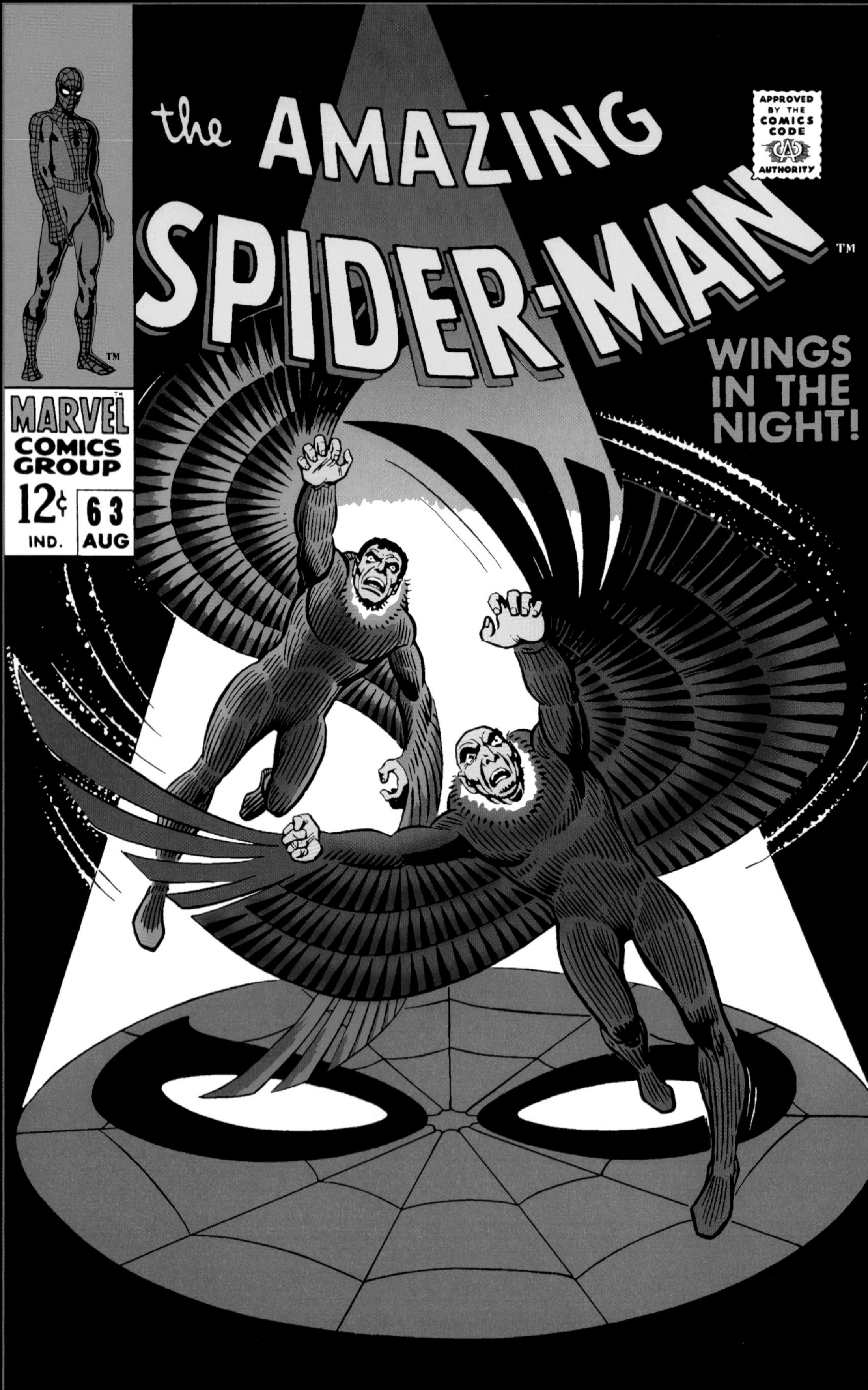

the AMAZING
SPIDER-MAN
TM
APPROVED BY THE COMICS CODE AUTHORITY
MARVEL COMICS GROUP
12¢
IND.
63
AUG
WINGS IN THE NIGHT!

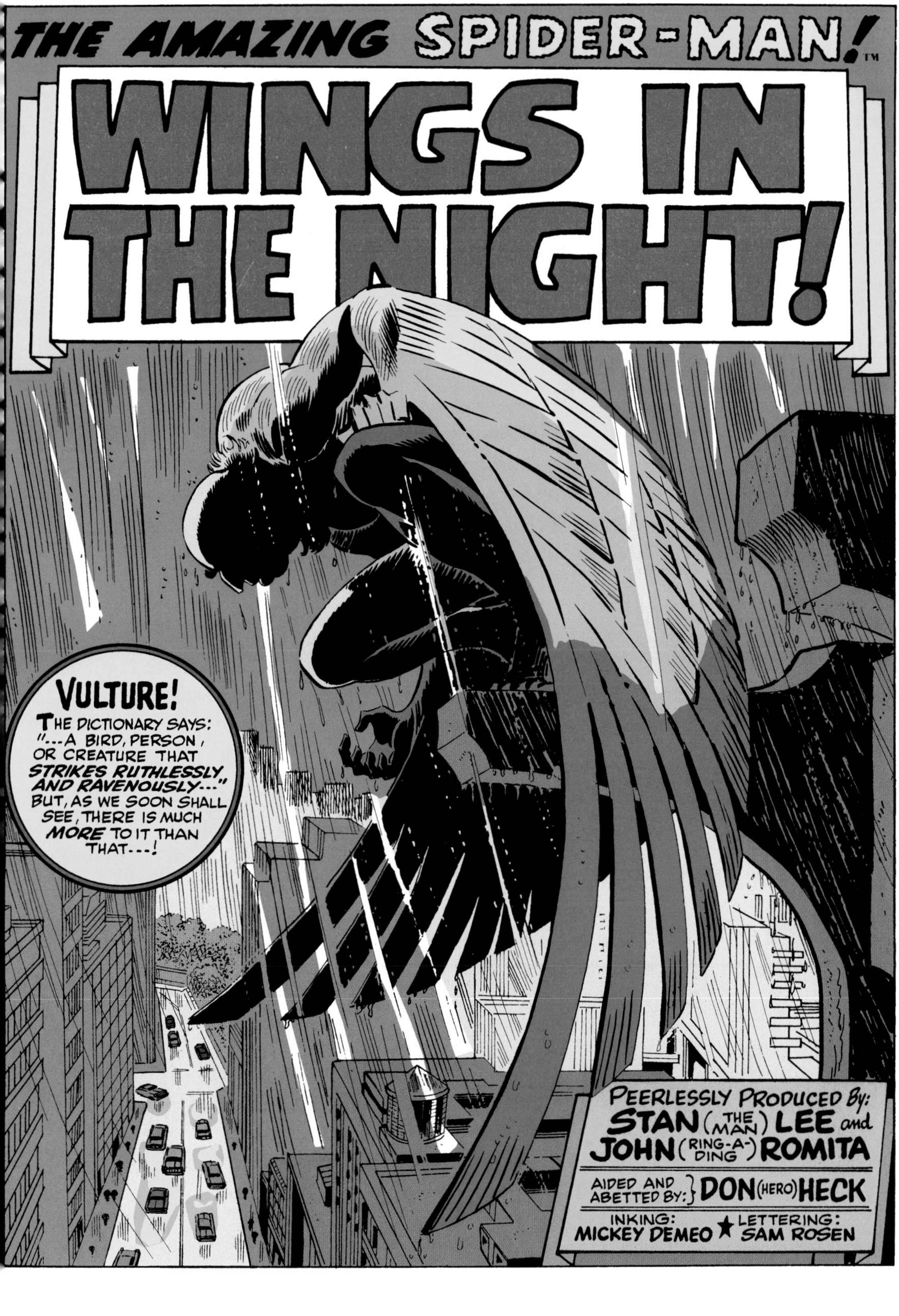
THE AMAZING SPIDER-MAN!
WINGS IN THE NIGHT!
VULTURE!
THE DICTIONARY SAYS: "...A BIRD, PERSON, OR CREATURE THAT STRIKES RUTHLESSLY AND RAVENOUSLY..." BUT, AS WE SOON SHALL SEE, THERE IS MUCH MORE TO IT THAN THAT---!
PEERLESSLY PRODUCED BY: STAN (THE MAN) LEE and JOHN (RING-A-DING) ROMITA
AIDED AND ABETTED BY: DON (HERO) HECK
INKING: MICKEY DEMEO ★ LETTERING: SAM ROSEN

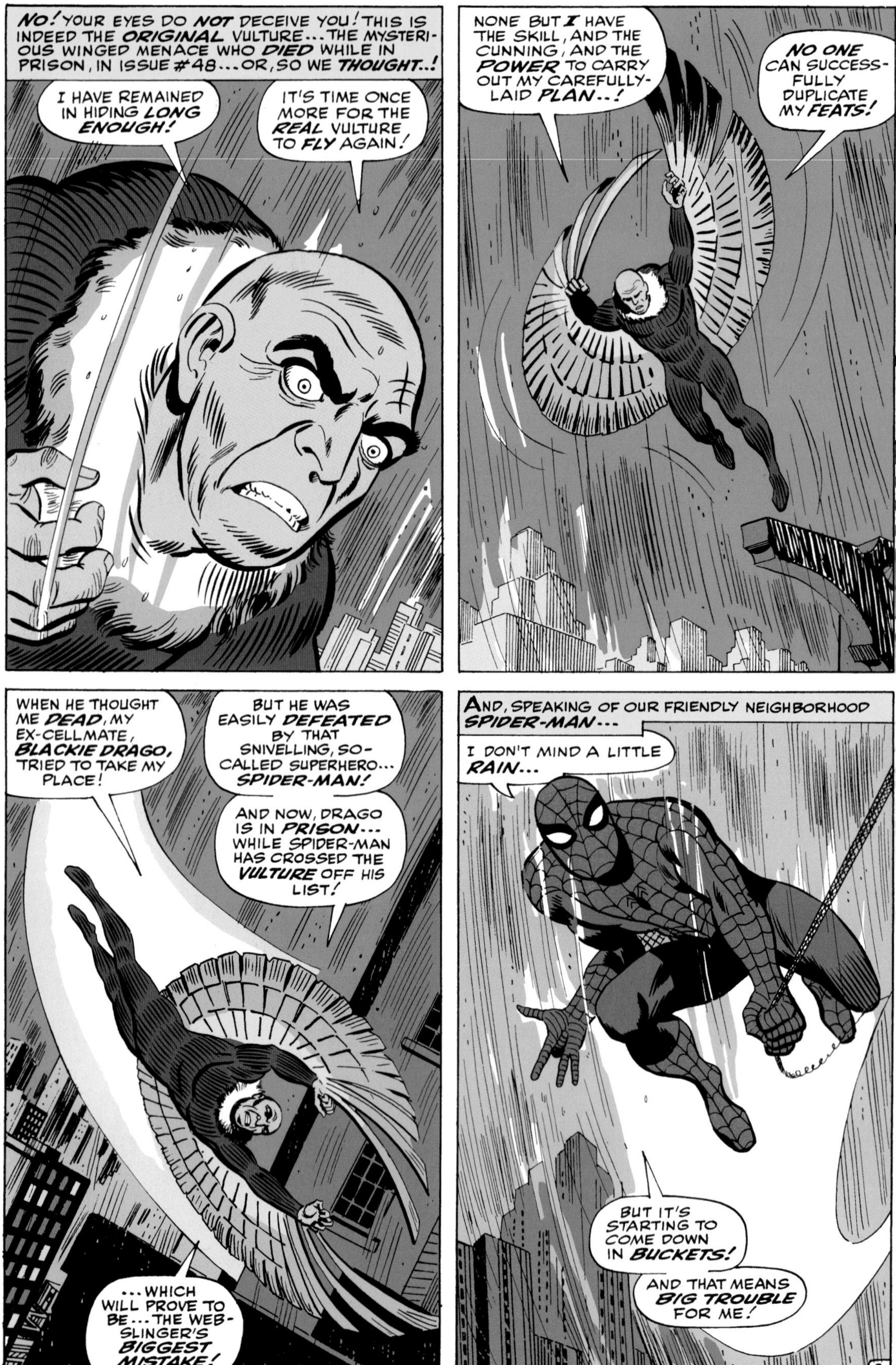
NO! YOUR EYES DO NOT DECEIVE YOU! THIS IS INDEED THE ORIGINAL VULTURE... THE MYSTERIOUS WINGED MENACE WHO DIED WHILE IN PRISON, IN ISSUE #48... OR, SO WE THOUGHT..!
I HAVE REMAINED IN HIDING LONG ENOUGH!
IT'S TIME ONCE MORE FOR THE REAL VULTURE TO FLY AGAIN!
NONE BUT I HAVE THE SKILL, AND THE CUNNING, AND THE POWER TO CARRY OUT MY CAREFULLY-LAID PLAN..!
NO ONE CAN SUCCESSFULLY DUPLICATE MY FEATS!
WHEN HE THOUGHT ME DEAD, MY EX-CELLMATE, BLACKIE DRAGO, TRIED TO TAKE MY PLACE!
BUT HE WAS EASILY DEFEATED BY THAT SNIVELLING, SO-CALLED SUPERHERO... SPIDER-MAN!
AND NOW, DRAGO IS IN PRISON... WHILE SPIDER-MAN HAS CROSSED THE VULTURE OFF HIS LIST!
...WHICH WILL PROVE TO BE... THE WEB-SLINGER'S BIGGEST MISTAKE!
AND, SPEAKING OF OUR FRIENDLY NEIGHBORHOOD SPIDER-MAN...
I DON'T MIND A LITTLE RAIN...
BUT IT'S STARTING TO COME DOWN IN BUCKETS!
AND THAT MEANS BIG TROUBLE FOR ME!
2.

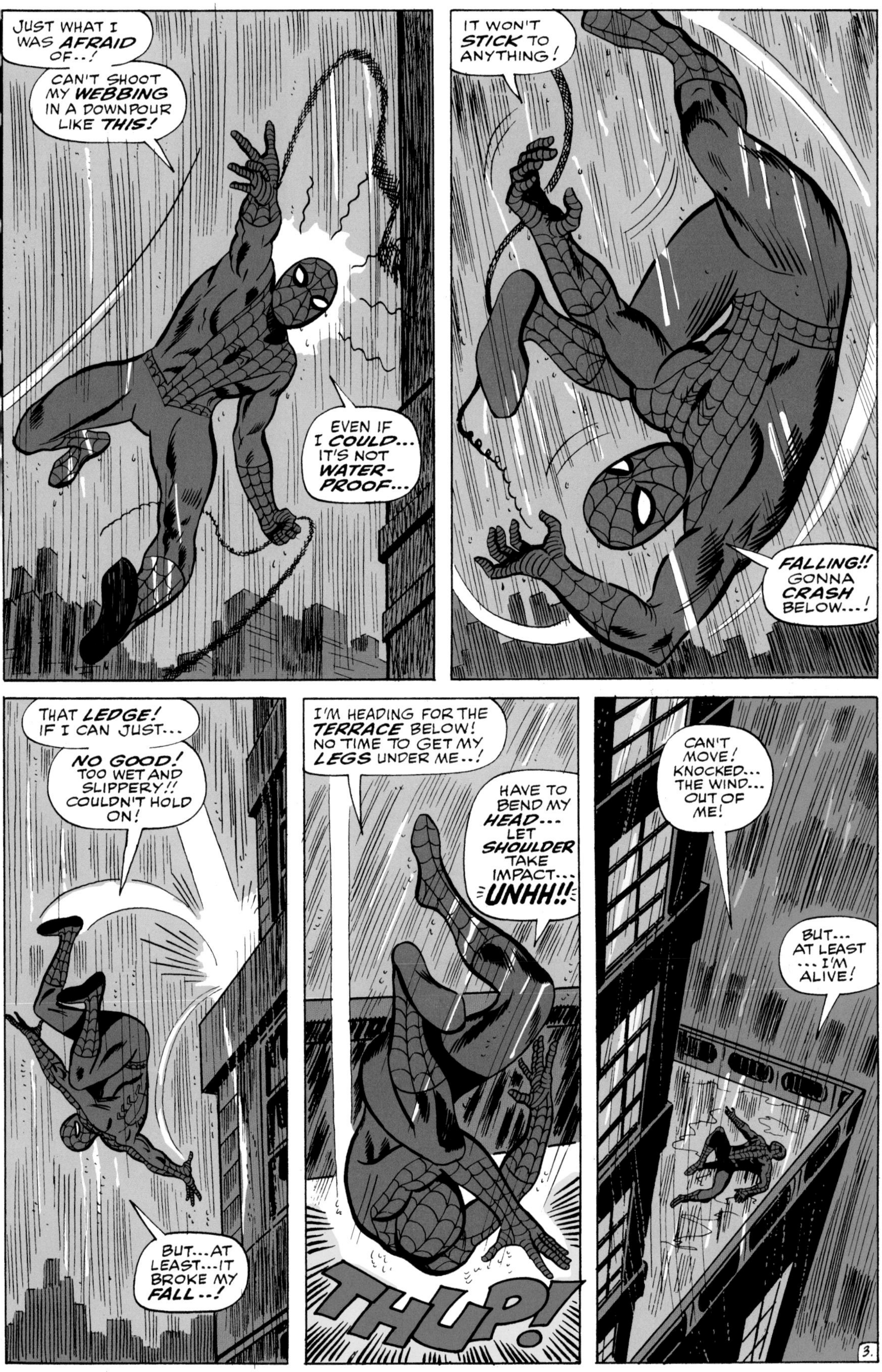
JUST WHAT I WAS AFRAID OF--!
CAN'T SHOOT MY WEBBING IN A DOWNPOUR LIKE THIS!
EVEN IF I COULD... IT'S NOT WATER-PROOF...
IT WON'T STICK TO ANYTHING!
FALLING!! GONNA CRASH BELOW...!
THAT LEDGE! IF I CAN JUST...
NO GOOD! TOO WET AND SLIPPERY!! COULDN'T HOLD ON!
BUT...AT LEAST...IT BROKE MY FALL--!
I'M HEADING FOR THE TERRACE BELOW! NO TIME TO GET MY LEGS UNDER ME--!
HAVE TO BEND MY HEAD... LET SHOULDER TAKE IMPACT... UNHH!!
THUP!
CAN'T MOVE! KNOCKED... THE WIND... OUT OF ME!
BUT... AT LEAST ... I'M ALIVE!
3.

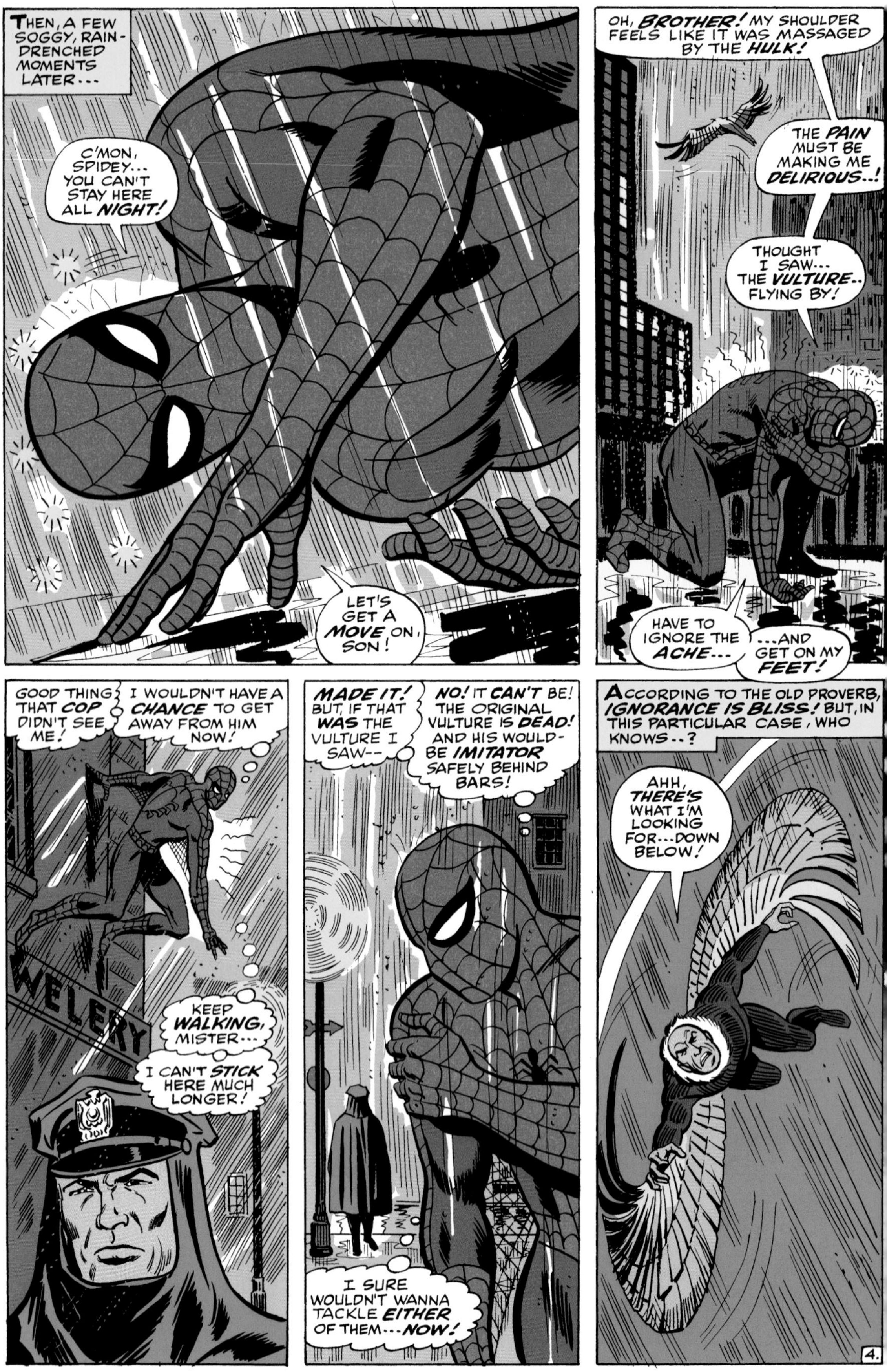
THEN, A FEW SOGGY, RAIN-DRENCHED MOMENTS LATER...
C'MON, SPIDEY... YOU CAN'T STAY HERE ALL NIGHT!
LET'S GET A MOVE ON, SON!
OH, BROTHER! MY SHOULDER FEELS LIKE IT WAS MASSAGED BY THE HULK!
THE PAIN MUST BE MAKING ME DELIRIOUS..!
THOUGHT I SAW... THE VULTURE.. FLYING BY!
HAVE TO IGNORE THE ACHE...
...AND GET ON MY FEET!
GOOD THING THAT COP DIDN'T SEE ME!
I WOULDN'T HAVE A CHANCE TO GET AWAY FROM HIM NOW!
KEEP WALKING, MISTER...
I CAN'T STICK HERE MUCH LONGER!
MADE IT! BUT, IF THAT WAS THE VULTURE I SAW--
NO! IT CAN'T BE! THE ORIGINAL VULTURE IS DEAD! AND HIS WOULD-BE IMITATOR SAFELY BEHIND BARS!
I SURE WOULDN'T WANNA TACKLE EITHER OF THEM---NOW!
ACCORDING TO THE OLD PROVERB, IGNORANCE IS BLISS! BUT, IN THIS PARTICULAR CASE, WHO KNOWS..?
AHH, THERE'S WHAT I'M LOOKING FOR...DOWN BELOW!
4.

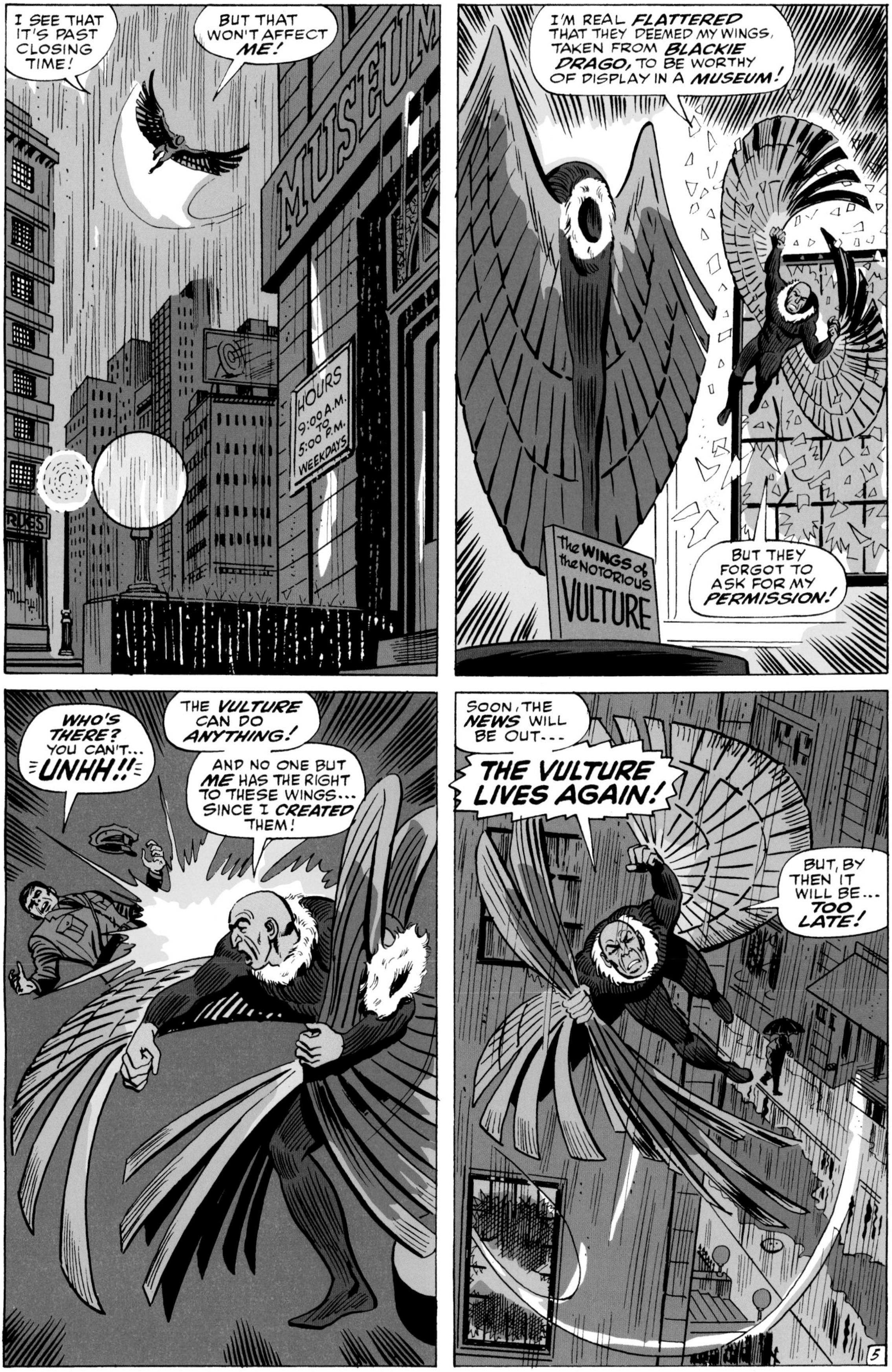
I SEE THAT IT'S PAST CLOSING TIME!
BUT THAT WON'T AFFECT ME!
MUSEUM
HOURS 9:00 A.M. TO 5:00 P.M. WEEKDAYS
I'M REAL FLATTERED THAT THEY DEEMED MY WINGS, TAKEN FROM BLACKIE DRAGO, TO BE WORTHY OF DISPLAY IN A MUSEUM!
The WINGS of the NOTORIOUS VULTURE
BUT THEY FORGOT TO ASK FOR MY PERMISSION!
WHO'S THERE? YOU CAN'T... UNHH!!
THE VULTURE CAN DO ANYTHING!
AND NO ONE BUT ME HAS THE RIGHT TO THESE WINGS... SINCE I CREATED THEM!
SOON, THE NEWS WILL BE OUT---
THE VULTURE LIVES AGAIN!
BUT, BY THEN IT WILL BE... TOO LATE!
5

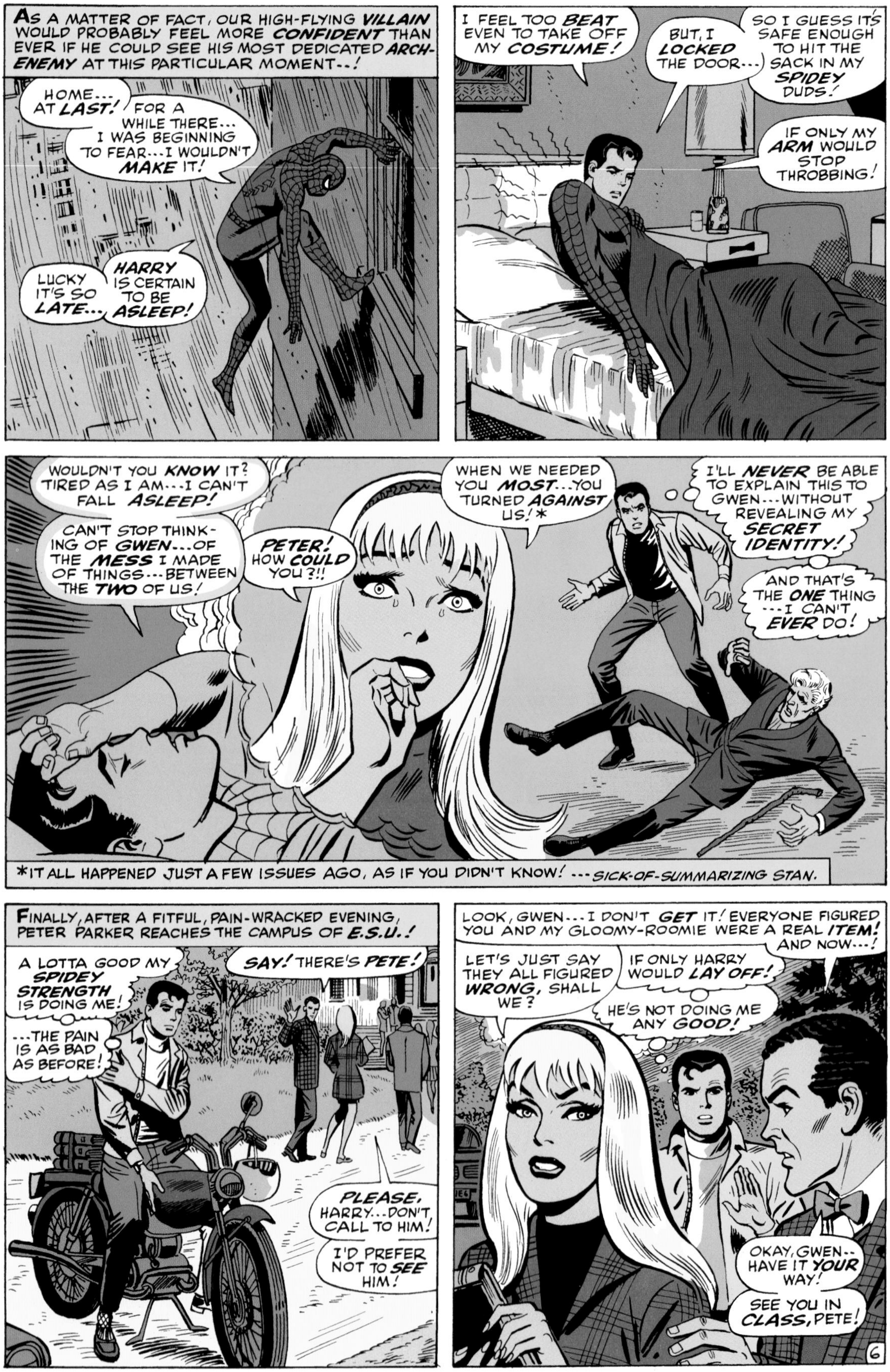

AS A MATTER OF FACT, OUR HIGH-FLYING VILLAIN WOULD PROBABLY FEEL MORE CONFIDENT THAN EVER IF HE COULD SEE HIS MOST DEDICATED ARCH-ENEMY AT THIS PARTICULAR MOMENT--!
HOME... AT LAST!
FOR A WHILE THERE... I WAS BEGINNING TO FEAR...I WOULDN'T MAKE IT!
LUCKY IT'S SO LATE...
HARRY IS CERTAIN TO BE ASLEEP!
I FEEL TOO BEAT EVEN TO TAKE OFF MY COSTUME!
BUT, I LOCKED THE DOOR...
SO I GUESS IT'S SAFE ENOUGH TO HIT THE SACK IN MY SPIDEY DUDS!
IF ONLY MY ARM WOULD STOP THROBBING!
WOULDN'T YOU KNOW IT? TIRED AS I AM---I CAN'T FALL ASLEEP!
CAN'T STOP THINKING OF GWEN...OF THE MESS I MADE OF THINGS---BETWEEN THE TWO OF US!
PETER! HOW COULD YOU?!!
WHEN WE NEEDED YOU MOST...YOU TURNED AGAINST US!*
I'LL NEVER BE ABLE TO EXPLAIN THIS TO GWEN---WITHOUT REVEALING MY SECRET IDENTITY!
AND THAT'S THE ONE THING ---I CAN'T EVER DO!
*IT ALL HAPPENED JUST A FEW ISSUES AGO, AS IF YOU DIDN'T KNOW! ---SICK-OF-SUMMARIZING STAN.
FINALLY, AFTER A FITFUL, PAIN-WRACKED EVENING, PETER PARKER REACHES THE CAMPUS OF E.S.U.!
A LOTTA GOOD MY SPIDEY STRENGTH IS DOING ME!
...THE PAIN IS AS BAD AS BEFORE!
SAY! THERE'S PETE!
PLEASE, HARRY...DON'T CALL TO HIM!
I'D PREFER NOT TO SEE HIM!
LOOK, GWEN...I DON'T GET IT! EVERYONE FIGURED YOU AND MY GLOOMY-ROOMIE WERE A REAL ITEM! AND NOW...!
LET'S JUST SAY THEY ALL FIGURED WRONG, SHALL WE?
IF ONLY HARRY WOULD LAY OFF!
HE'S NOT DOING ME ANY GOOD!
OKAY, GWEN-- HAVE IT YOUR WAY!
SEE YOU IN CLASS, PETE!
6

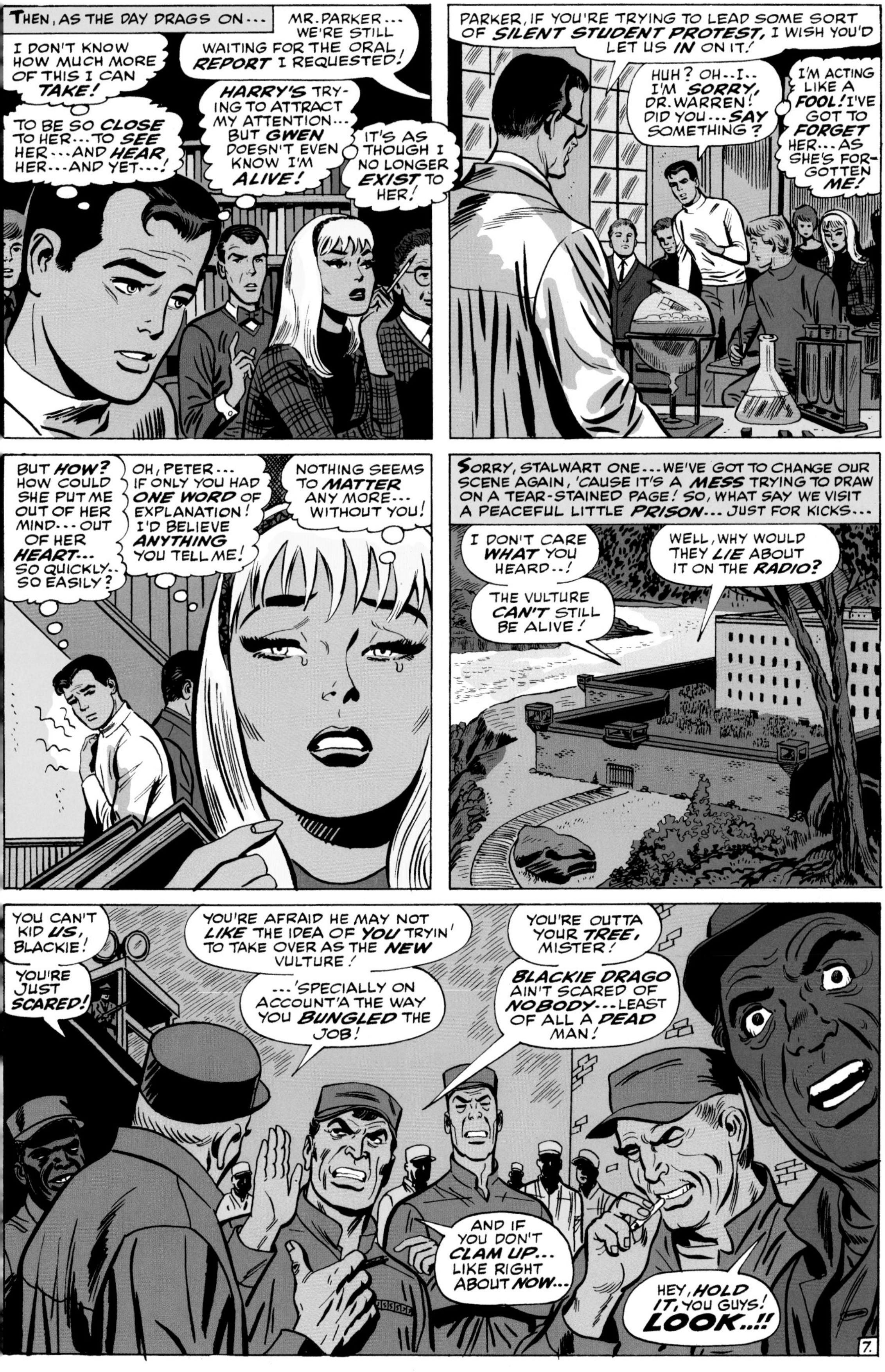
THEN, AS THE DAY DRAGS ON...
MR. PARKER... WE'RE STILL WAITING FOR THE ORAL REPORT I REQUESTED!
I DON'T KNOW HOW MUCH MORE OF THIS I CAN TAKE!
TO BE SO CLOSE TO HER... TO SEE HER... AND HEAR HER... AND YET...!
HARRY'S TRYING TO ATTRACT MY ATTENTION... BUT GWEN DOESN'T EVEN KNOW I'M ALIVE!
IT'S AS THOUGH I NO LONGER EXIST TO HER!
PARKER, IF YOU'RE TRYING TO LEAD SOME SORT OF SILENT STUDENT PROTEST, I WISH YOU'D LET US IN ON IT!
HUH? OH--I.. I'M SORRY, DR. WARREN! DID YOU... SAY SOMETHING?
I'M ACTING LIKE A FOOL! I'VE GOT TO FORGET HER... AS SHE'S FORGOTTEN ME!
BUT HOW? HOW COULD SHE PUT ME OUT OF HER MIND... OUT OF HER HEART... SO QUICKLY.. SO EASILY?
OH, PETER... IF ONLY YOU HAD ONE WORD OF EXPLANATION! I'D BELIEVE ANYTHING YOU TELL ME!
NOTHING SEEMS TO MATTER ANY MORE... WITHOUT YOU!
SORRY, STALWART ONE... WE'VE GOT TO CHANGE OUR SCENE AGAIN, 'CAUSE IT'S A MESS TRYING TO DRAW ON A TEAR-STAINED PAGE! SO, WHAT SAY WE VISIT A PEACEFUL LITTLE PRISON... JUST FOR KICKS...
I DON'T CARE WHAT YOU HEARD--!
THE VULTURE CAN'T STILL BE ALIVE!
WELL, WHY WOULD THEY LIE ABOUT IT ON THE RADIO?
YOU CAN'T KID US, BLACKIE!
YOU'RE JUST SCARED!
YOU'RE AFRAID HE MAY NOT LIKE THE IDEA OF YOU TRYIN' TO TAKE OVER AS THE NEW VULTURE!
...'SPECIALLY ON ACCOUNT'A THE WAY YOU BUNGLED THE JOB!
YOU'RE OUTTA YOUR TREE, MISTER!
BLACKIE DRAGO AIN'T SCARED OF NOBODY... LEAST OF ALL A DEAD MAN!
AND IF YOU DON'T CLAM UP... LIKE RIGHT ABOUT NOW...
HEY, HOLD IT, YOU GUYS! LOOK..!!
7.

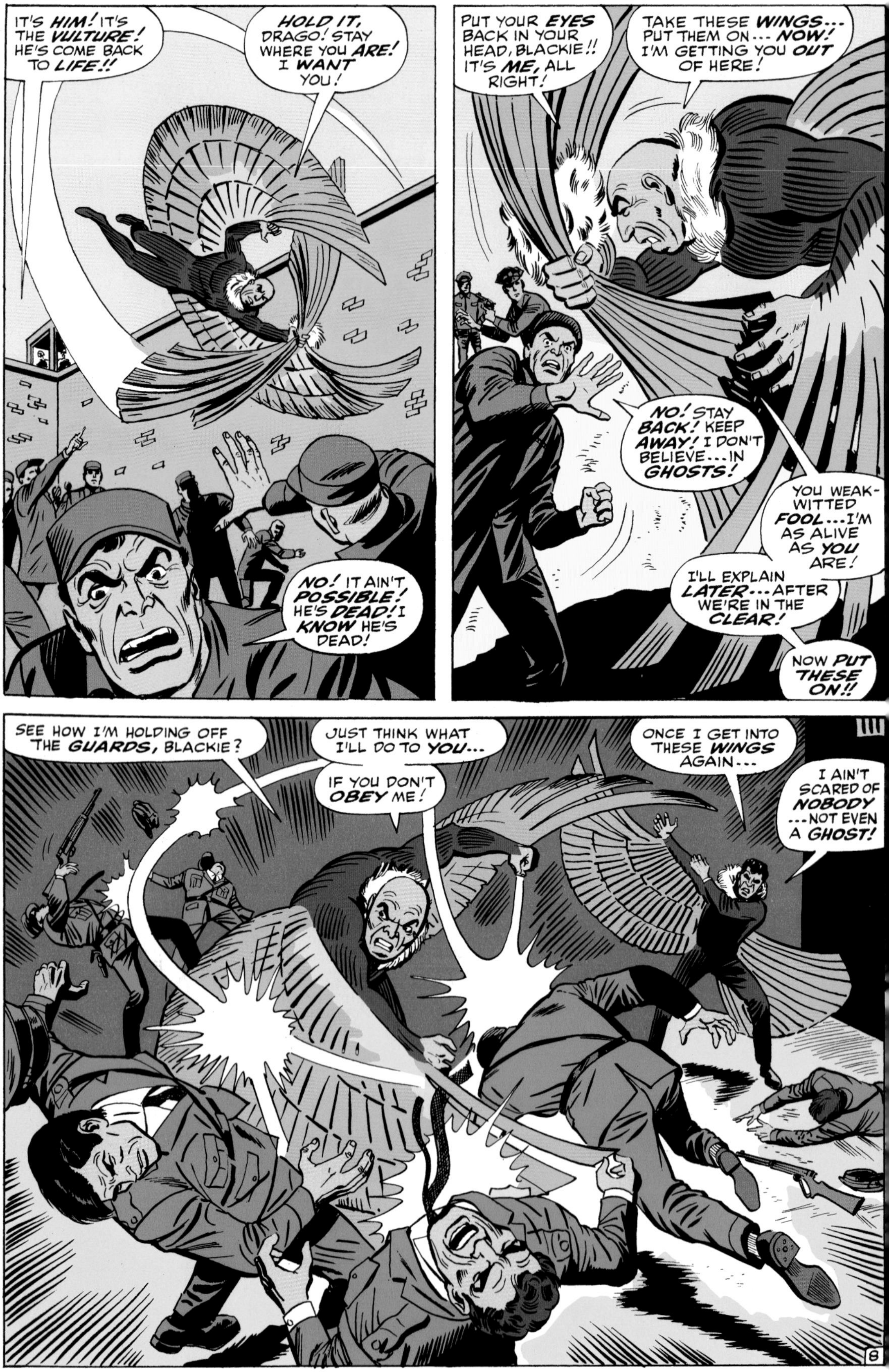
IT'S HIM! IT'S THE VULTURE! HE'S COME BACK TO LIFE!!
HOLD IT, DRAGO! STAY WHERE YOU ARE! I WANT YOU!
NO! IT AIN'T POSSIBLE! HE'S DEAD! I KNOW HE'S DEAD!
PUT YOUR EYES BACK IN YOUR HEAD, BLACKIE!! IT'S ME, ALL RIGHT!
TAKE THESE WINGS... PUT THEM ON... NOW! I'M GETTING YOU OUT OF HERE!
NO! STAY BACK! KEEP AWAY! I DON'T BELIEVE... IN GHOSTS!
YOU WEAK-WITTED FOOL... I'M AS ALIVE AS YOU ARE!
I'LL EXPLAIN LATER... AFTER WE'RE IN THE CLEAR!
NOW PUT THESE ON!!
SEE HOW I'M HOLDING OFF THE GUARDS, BLACKIE?
JUST THINK WHAT I'LL DO TO YOU...
IF YOU DON'T OBEY ME!
ONCE I GET INTO THESE WINGS AGAIN...
I AIN'T SCARED OF NOBODY ...NOT EVEN A GHOST!

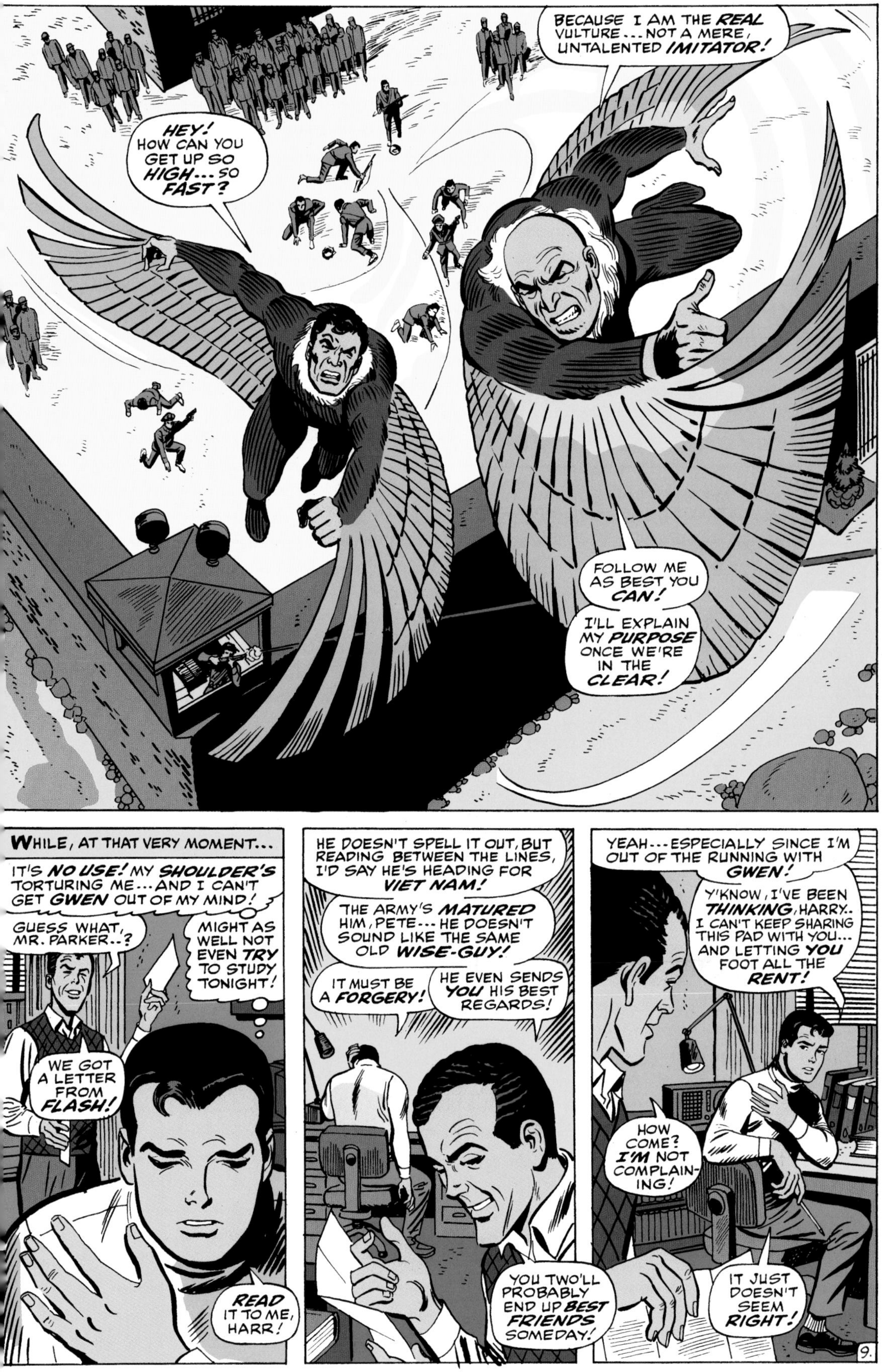
HEY! HOW CAN YOU GET UP SO HIGH... SO FAST?
BECAUSE I AM THE REAL VULTURE... NOT A MERE, UNTALENTED IMITATOR!
FOLLOW ME AS BEST YOU CAN!
I'LL EXPLAIN MY PURPOSE ONCE WE'RE IN THE CLEAR!
WHILE, AT THAT VERY MOMENT...
IT'S NO USE! MY SHOULDER'S TORTURING ME... AND I CAN'T GET GWEN OUT OF MY MIND!
GUESS WHAT, MR. PARKER..?
MIGHT AS WELL NOT EVEN TRY TO STUDY TONIGHT!
WE GOT A LETTER FROM FLASH!
READ IT TO ME, HARR!
HE DOESN'T SPELL IT OUT, BUT READING BETWEEN THE LINES, I'D SAY HE'S HEADING FOR VIET NAM!
THE ARMY'S MATURED HIM, PETE... HE DOESN'T SOUND LIKE THE SAME OLD WISE-GUY!
IT MUST BE A FORGERY!
HE EVEN SENDS YOU HIS BEST REGARDS!
YOU TWO'LL PROBABLY END UP BEST FRIENDS SOMEDAY!
YEAH... ESPECIALLY SINCE I'M OUT OF THE RUNNING WITH GWEN!
Y'KNOW, I'VE BEEN THINKING, HARRY.. I CAN'T KEEP SHARING THIS PAD WITH YOU... AND LETTING YOU FOOT ALL THE RENT!
HOW COME? I'M NOT COMPLAIN-ING!
IT JUST DOESN'T SEEM RIGHT!
9.

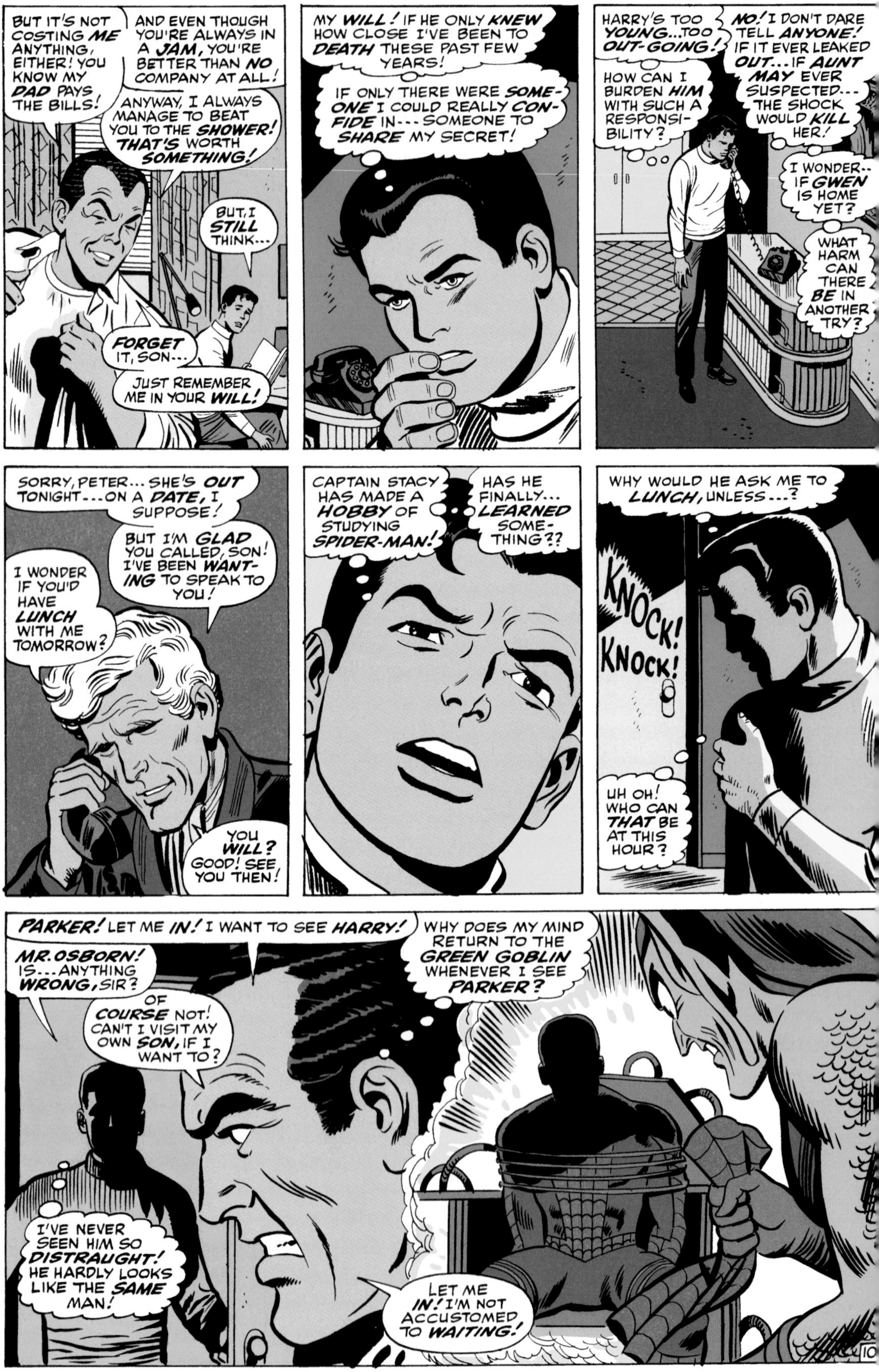

BUT IT'S NOT COSTING ME ANYTHING, EITHER! YOU KNOW MY DAD PAYS THE BILLS!
AND EVEN THOUGH YOU'RE ALWAYS IN A JAM, YOU'RE BETTER THAN NO COMPANY AT ALL!
ANYWAY, I ALWAYS MANAGE TO BEAT YOU TO THE SHOWER! THAT'S WORTH SOMETHING!
BUT, I STILL THINK...
FORGET IT, SON...
JUST REMEMBER ME IN YOUR WILL!
MY WILL! IF HE ONLY KNEW HOW CLOSE I'VE BEEN TO DEATH THESE PAST FEW YEARS!
IF ONLY THERE WERE SOME-ONE I COULD REALLY CON-FIDE IN--- SOMEONE TO SHARE MY SECRET!
HARRY'S TOO YOUNG...TOO OUT-GOING!
HOW CAN I BURDEN HIM WITH SUCH A RESPONSI-BILITY?
NO! I DON'T DARE TELL ANYONE! IF IT EVER LEAKED OUT...IF AUNT MAY EVER SUSPECTED--- THE SHOCK WOULD KILL HER!
I WONDER-- IF GWEN IS HOME YET?
WHAT HARM CAN THERE BE IN ANOTHER TRY?
SORRY, PETER... SHE'S OUT TONIGHT---ON A DATE, I SUPPOSE!
BUT I'M GLAD YOU CALLED, SON! I'VE BEEN WANTING TO SPEAK TO YOU!
I WONDER IF YOU'D HAVE LUNCH WITH ME TOMORROW?
YOU WILL? GOOD! SEE YOU THEN!
CAPTAIN STACY HAS MADE A HOBBY OF STUDYING SPIDER-MAN!
HAS HE FINALLY... LEARNED SOME-THING??
WHY WOULD HE ASK ME TO LUNCH, UNLESS ...?
KNOCK! KNOCK!
UH OH! WHO CAN THAT BE AT THIS HOUR?
PARKER! LET ME IN! I WANT TO SEE HARRY!
MR. OSBORN! IS... ANYTHING WRONG, SIR?
OF COURSE NOT! CAN'T I VISIT MY OWN SON, IF I WANT TO?
WHY DOES MY MIND RETURN TO THE GREEN GOBLIN WHENEVER I SEE PARKER?
I'VE NEVER SEEN HIM SO DISTRAUGHT! HE HARDLY LOOKS LIKE THE SAME MAN!
LET ME IN! I'M NOT ACCUSTOMED TO WAITING!
10

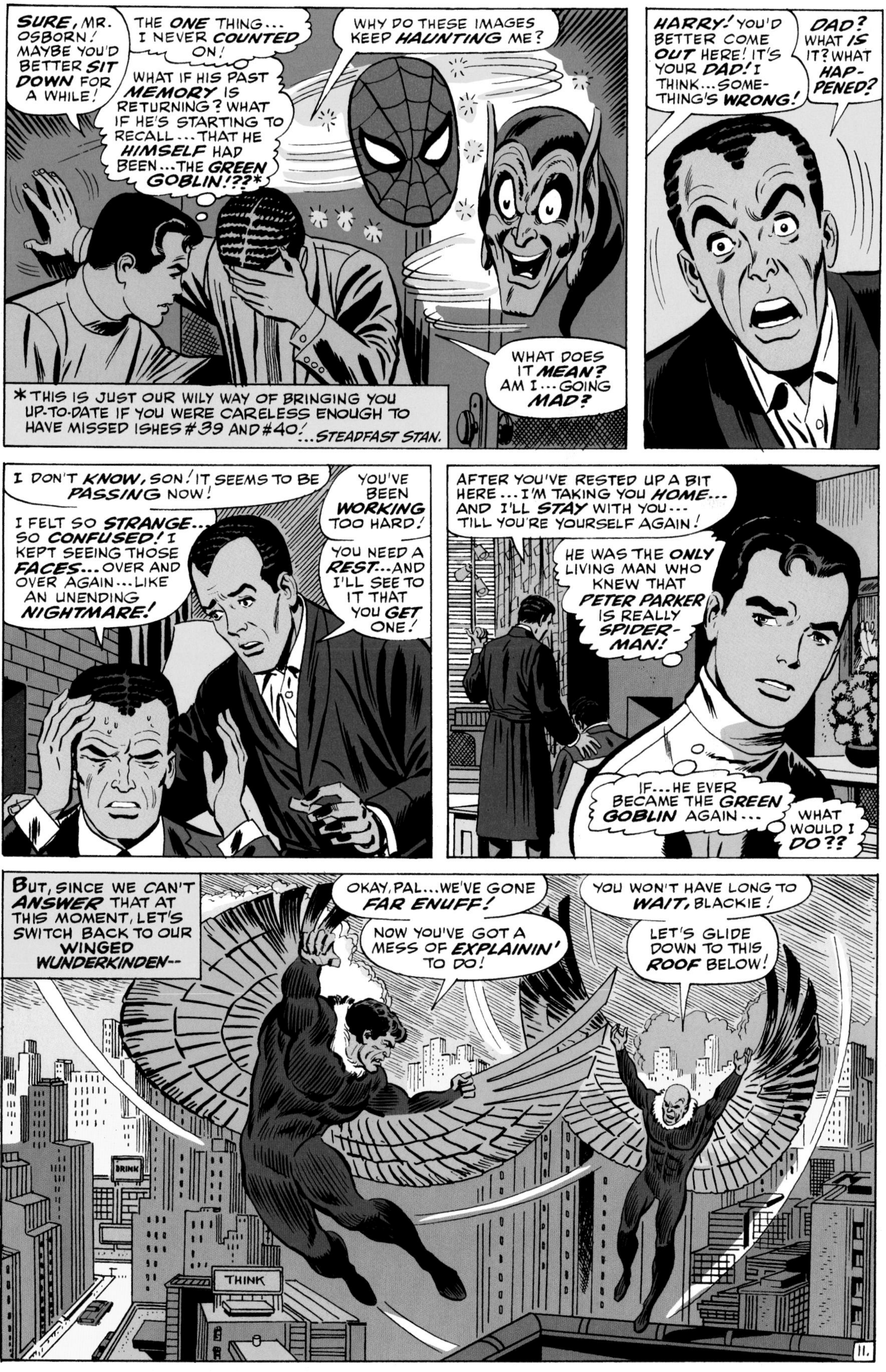
SURE, MR. OSBORN! MAYBE YOU'D BETTER SIT DOWN FOR A WHILE!
THE ONE THING... I NEVER COUNTED ON!
WHAT IF HIS PAST MEMORY IS RETURNING? WHAT IF HE'S STARTING TO RECALL... THAT HE HIMSELF HAD BEEN... THE GREEN GOBLIN!??*
WHY DO THESE IMAGES KEEP HAUNTING ME?
WHAT DOES IT MEAN? AM I... GOING MAD?
*THIS IS JUST OUR WILY WAY OF BRINGING YOU UP-TO-DATE IF YOU WERE CARELESS ENOUGH TO HAVE MISSED ISHES #39 AND #40! ...STEADFAST STAN.
HARRY! YOU'D BETTER COME OUT HERE! IT'S YOUR DAD! I THINK... SOME-THING'S WRONG!
DAD? WHAT IS IT? WHAT HAP-PENED?
I DON'T KNOW, SON! IT SEEMS TO BE PASSING NOW!
I FELT SO STRANGE... SO CONFUSED! I KEPT SEEING THOSE FACES... OVER AND OVER AGAIN... LIKE AN UNENDING NIGHTMARE!
YOU'VE BEEN WORKING TOO HARD!
YOU NEED A REST... AND I'LL SEE TO IT THAT YOU GET ONE!
AFTER YOU'VE RESTED UP A BIT HERE... I'M TAKING YOU HOME... AND I'LL STAY WITH YOU... TILL YOU'RE YOURSELF AGAIN!
HE WAS THE ONLY LIVING MAN WHO KNEW THAT PETER PARKER IS REALLY SPIDER-MAN!
IF... HE EVER BECAME THE GREEN GOBLIN AGAIN...
WHAT WOULD I DO??
BUT, SINCE WE CAN'T ANSWER THAT AT THIS MOMENT, LET'S SWITCH BACK TO OUR WINGED WUNDERKINDEN--
OKAY, PAL... WE'VE GONE FAR ENUFF!
NOW YOU'VE GOT A MESS OF EXPLAININ' TO DO!
YOU WON'T HAVE LONG TO WAIT, BLACKIE!
LET'S GLIDE DOWN TO THIS ROOF BELOW!
DRINK
THINK
11.

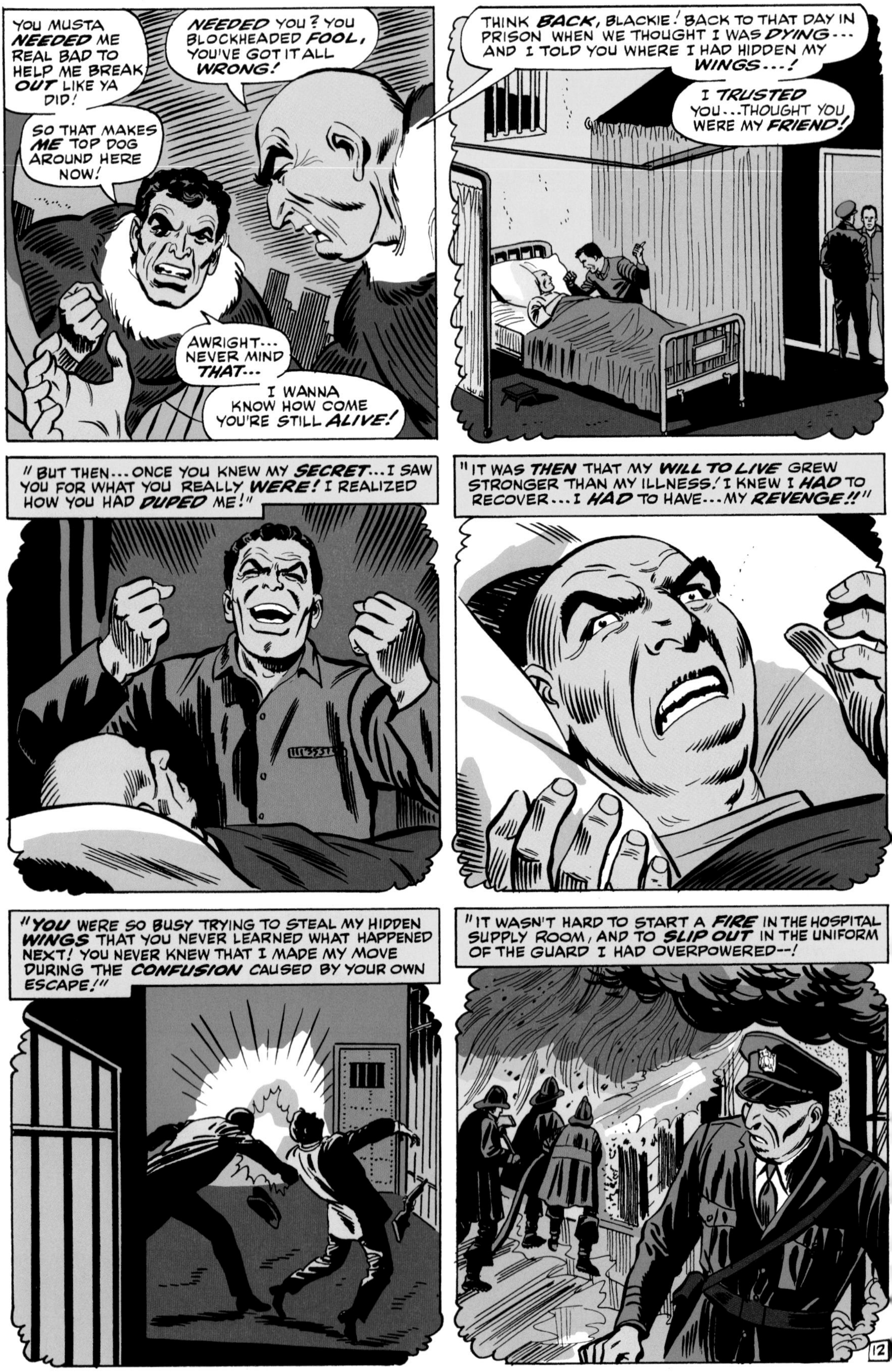

YOU MUSTA NEEDED ME REAL BAD TO HELP ME BREAK OUT LIKE YA DID!
NEEDED YOU? YOU BLOCKHEADED FOOL, YOU'VE GOT IT ALL WRONG!
SO THAT MAKES ME TOP DOG AROUND HERE NOW!
AWRIGHT--- NEVER MIND THAT---
I WANNA KNOW HOW COME YOU'RE STILL ALIVE!
THINK BACK, BLACKIE! BACK TO THAT DAY IN PRISON WHEN WE THOUGHT I WAS DYING--- AND I TOLD YOU WHERE I HAD HIDDEN MY WINGS---!
I TRUSTED YOU---THOUGHT YOU WERE MY FRIEND!
"BUT THEN---ONCE YOU KNEW MY SECRET---I SAW YOU FOR WHAT YOU REALLY WERE! I REALIZED HOW YOU HAD DUPED ME!"
"IT WAS THEN THAT MY WILL TO LIVE GREW STRONGER THAN MY ILLNESS! I KNEW I HAD TO RECOVER---I HAD TO HAVE---MY REVENGE!!"
"YOU WERE SO BUSY TRYING TO STEAL MY HIDDEN WINGS THAT YOU NEVER LEARNED WHAT HAPPENED NEXT! YOU NEVER KNEW THAT I MADE MY MOVE DURING THE CONFUSION CAUSED BY YOUR OWN ESCAPE!"
"IT WASN'T HARD TO START A FIRE IN THE HOSPITAL SUPPLY ROOM, AND TO SLIP OUT IN THE UNIFORM OF THE GUARD I HAD OVERPOWERED--!
12

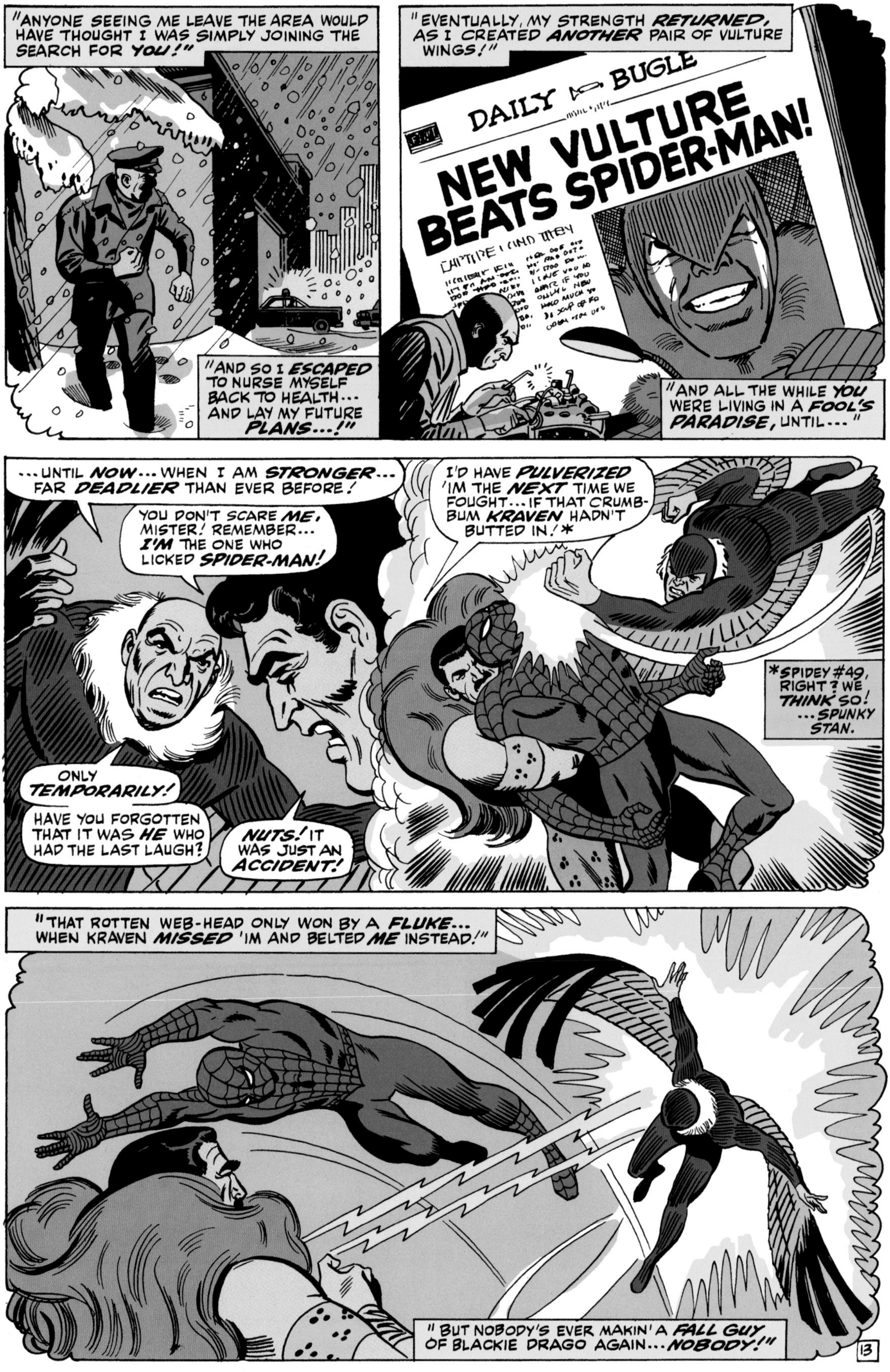

"ANYONE SEEING ME LEAVE THE AREA WOULD HAVE THOUGHT I WAS SIMPLY JOINING THE SEARCH FOR YOU!"
"AND SO I ESCAPED TO NURSE MYSELF BACK TO HEALTH... AND LAY MY FUTURE PLANS...!"
"EVENTUALLY, MY STRENGTH RETURNED, AS I CREATED ANOTHER PAIR OF VULTURE WINGS!"
DAILY BUGLE
NEW VULTURE BEATS SPIDER-MAN!
"AND ALL THE WHILE YOU WERE LIVING IN A FOOL'S PARADISE, UNTIL..."
...UNTIL NOW... WHEN I AM STRONGER... FAR DEADLIER THAN EVER BEFORE!
YOU DON'T SCARE ME, MISTER! REMEMBER... I'M THE ONE WHO LICKED SPIDER-MAN!
ONLY TEMPORARILY!
HAVE YOU FORGOTTEN THAT IT WAS HE WHO HAD THE LAST LAUGH?
NUTS! IT WAS JUST AN ACCIDENT!
I'D HAVE PULVERIZED 'IM THE NEXT TIME WE FOUGHT... IF THAT CRUMB-BUM KRAVEN HADN'T BUTTED IN!*
*SPIDEY #49, RIGHT? WE THINK SO! ...SPUNKY STAN.
"THAT ROTTEN WEB-HEAD ONLY WON BY A FLUKE... WHEN KRAVEN MISSED 'IM AND BELTED ME INSTEAD!"
"BUT NOBODY'S EVER MAKIN' A FALL GUY OF BLACKIE DRAGO AGAIN... NOBODY!"
13

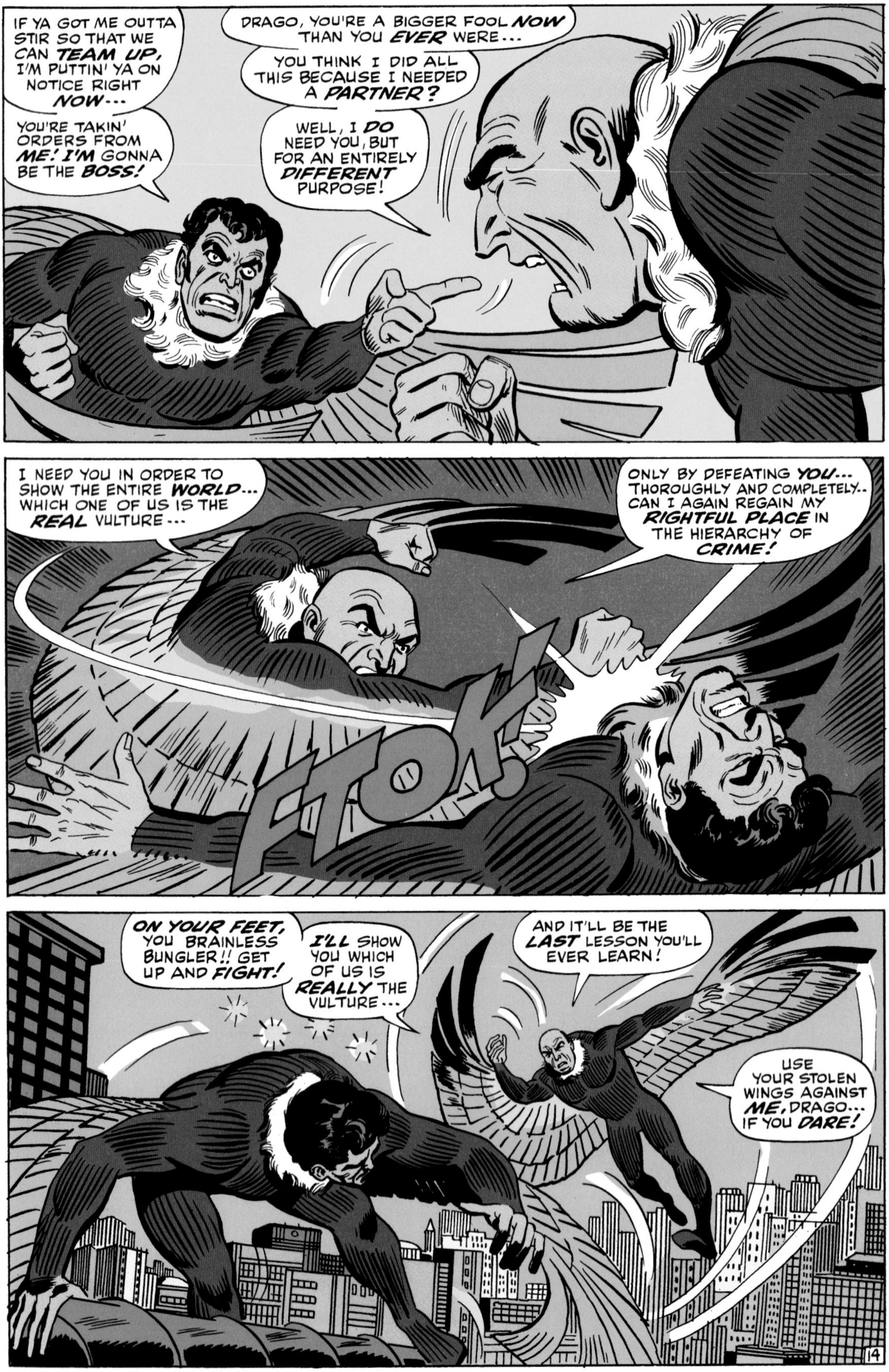
IF YA GOT ME OUTTA STIR SO THAT WE CAN TEAM UP, I'M PUTTIN' YA ON NOTICE RIGHT NOW...
YOU'RE TAKIN' ORDERS FROM ME! I'M GONNA BE THE BOSS!
DRAGO, YOU'RE A BIGGER FOOL NOW THAN YOU EVER WERE...
YOU THINK I DID ALL THIS BECAUSE I NEEDED A PARTNER?
WELL, I DO NEED YOU, BUT FOR AN ENTIRELY DIFFERENT PURPOSE!
I NEED YOU IN ORDER TO SHOW THE ENTIRE WORLD... WHICH ONE OF US IS THE REAL VULTURE...
ONLY BY DEFEATING YOU... THOROUGHLY AND COMPLETELY.. CAN I AGAIN REGAIN MY RIGHTFUL PLACE IN THE HIERARCHY OF CRIME!
FTOK!
ON YOUR FEET, YOU BRAINLESS BUNGLER!! GET UP AND FIGHT!
I'LL SHOW YOU WHICH OF US IS REALLY THE VULTURE...
AND IT'LL BE THE LAST LESSON YOU'LL EVER LEARN!
USE YOUR STOLEN WINGS AGAINST ME, DRAGO... IF YOU DARE!
14

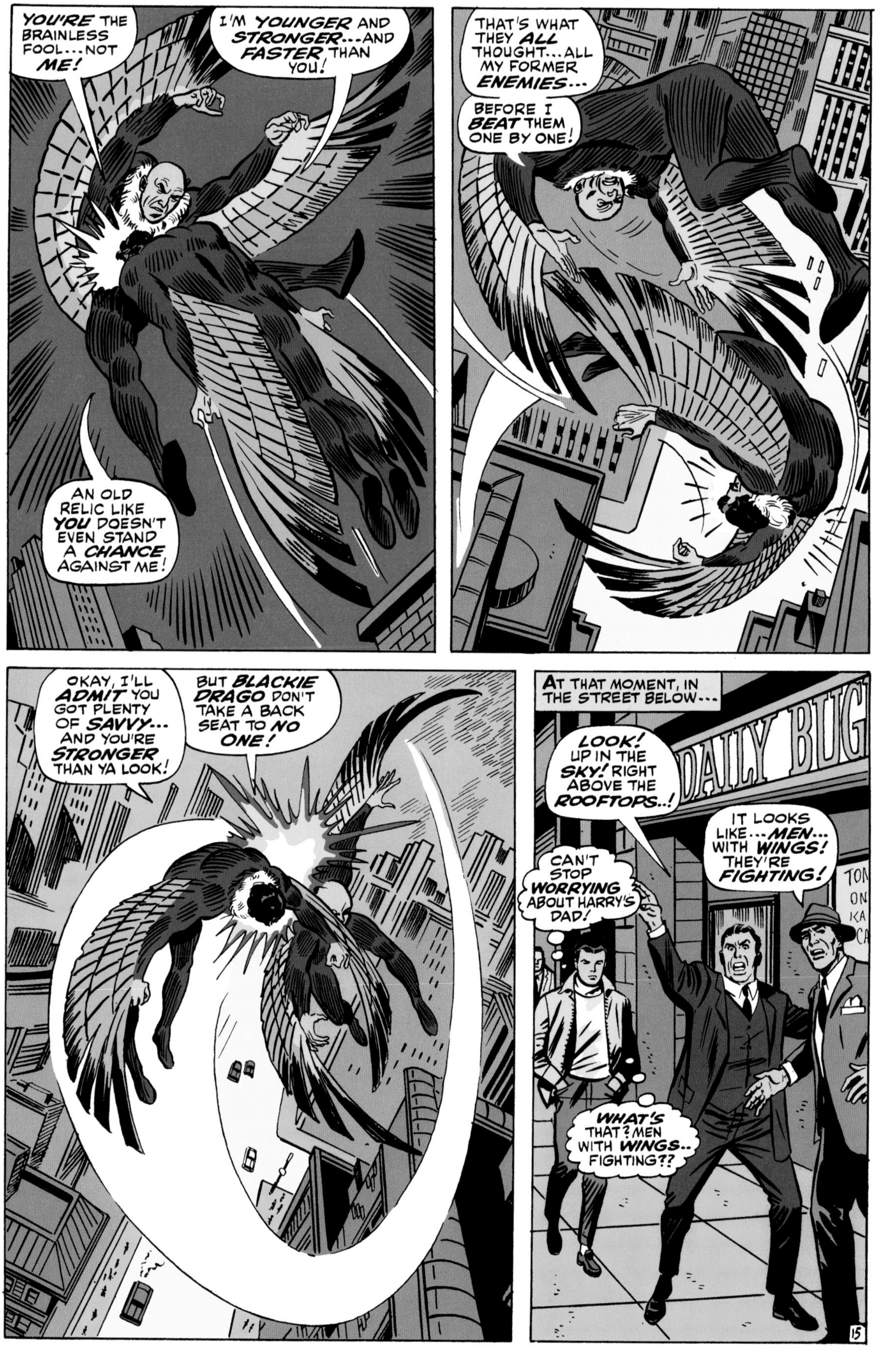
YOU'RE THE BRAINLESS FOOL... NOT ME!
I'M YOUNGER AND STRONGER... AND FASTER THAN YOU!
AN OLD RELIC LIKE YOU DOESN'T EVEN STAND A CHANCE AGAINST ME!
THAT'S WHAT THEY ALL THOUGHT... ALL MY FORMER ENEMIES...
BEFORE I BEAT THEM ONE BY ONE!
OKAY, I'LL ADMIT YOU GOT PLENTY OF SAVVY... AND YOU'RE STRONGER THAN YA LOOK!
BUT BLACKIE DRAGO DON'T TAKE A BACK SEAT TO NO ONE!
AT THAT MOMENT, IN THE STREET BELOW...
DAILY BUG
LOOK! UP IN THE SKY! RIGHT ABOVE THE ROOFTOPS..!
IT LOOKS LIKE... MEN... WITH WINGS! THEY'RE FIGHTING!
CAN'T STOP WORRYING ABOUT HARRY'S DAD!
WHAT'S THAT? MEN WITH WINGS.. FIGHTING??
15

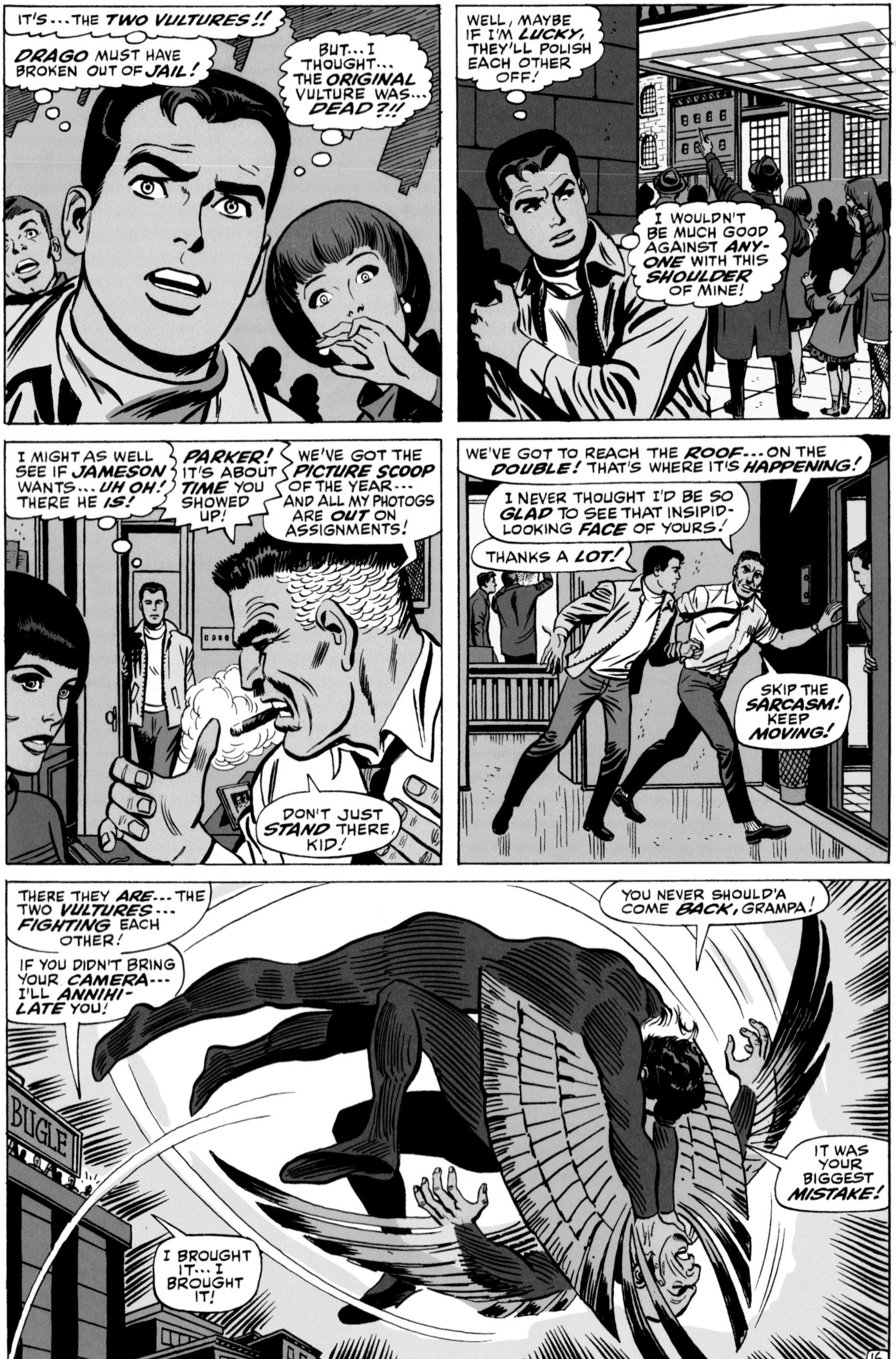
IT'S... THE TWO VULTURES!!
DRAGO MUST HAVE BROKEN OUT OF JAIL!
BUT... I THOUGHT... THE ORIGINAL VULTURE WAS... DEAD?!!
WELL, MAYBE IF I'M LUCKY, THEY'LL POLISH EACH OTHER OFF!
I WOULDN'T BE MUCH GOOD AGAINST ANY-ONE WITH THIS SHOULDER OF MINE!
I MIGHT AS WELL SEE IF JAMESON WANTS... UH OH! THERE HE IS!
PARKER! IT'S ABOUT TIME YOU SHOWED UP!
WE'VE GOT THE PICTURE SCOOP OF THE YEAR--- AND ALL MY PHOTOGS ARE OUT ON ASSIGNMENTS!
DON'T JUST STAND THERE, KID!
WE'VE GOT TO REACH THE ROOF... ON THE DOUBLE! THAT'S WHERE IT'S HAPPENING!
I NEVER THOUGHT I'D BE SO GLAD TO SEE THAT INSIPID-LOOKING FACE OF YOURS!
THANKS A LOT!
SKIP THE SARCASM! KEEP MOVING!
THERE THEY ARE--- THE TWO VULTURES--- FIGHTING EACH OTHER!
IF YOU DIDN'T BRING YOUR CAMERA--- I'LL ANNIHI-LATE YOU!
YOU NEVER SHOULD'A COME BACK, GRAMPA!
IT WAS YOUR BIGGEST MISTAKE!
I BROUGHT IT... I BROUGHT IT!
BUGLE
16

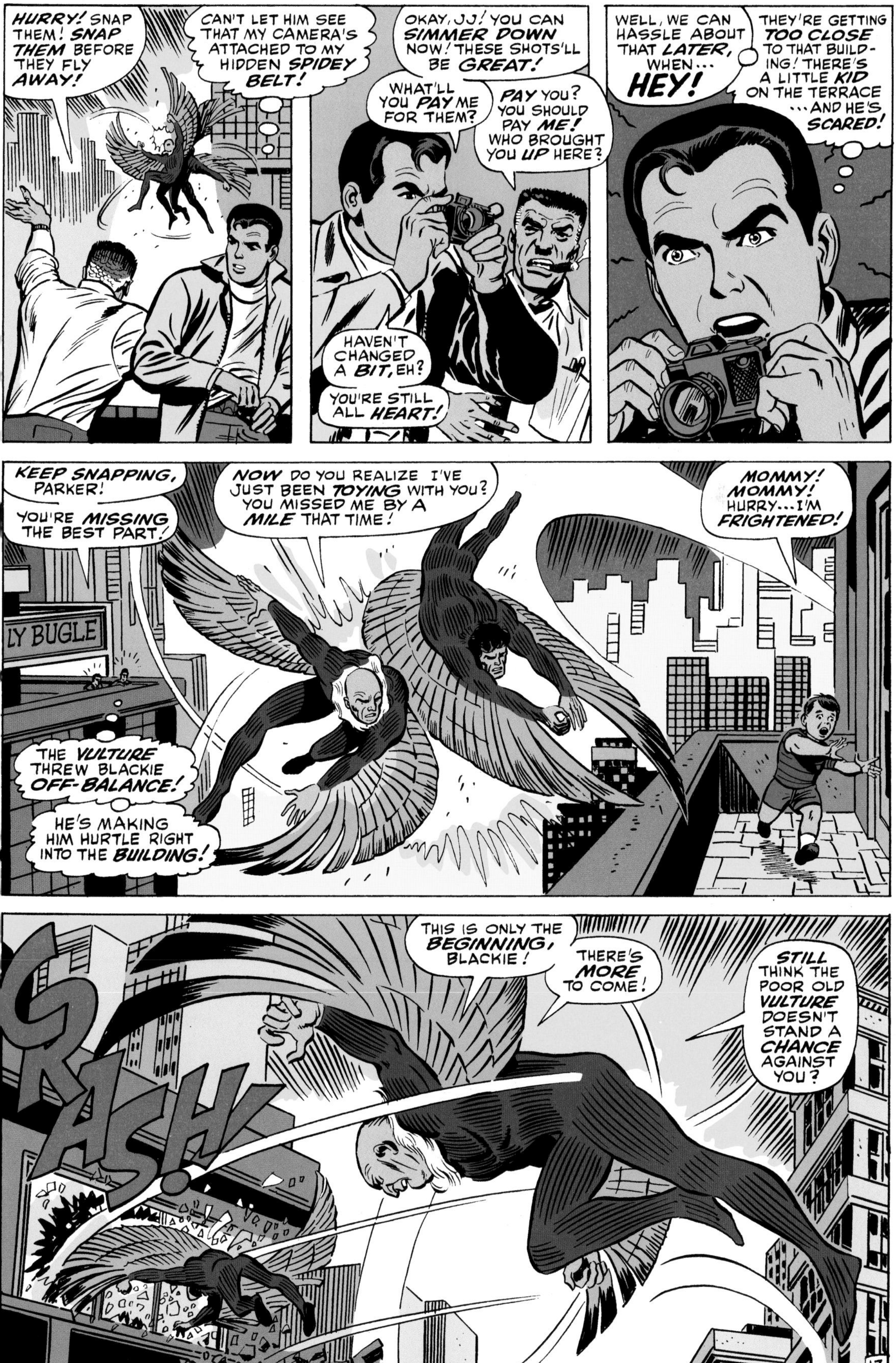
HURRY! SNAP THEM! SNAP THEM BEFORE THEY FLY AWAY!
CAN'T LET HIM SEE THAT MY CAMERA'S ATTACHED TO MY HIDDEN SPIDEY BELT!
OKAY, JJ! YOU CAN SIMMER DOWN NOW! THESE SHOTS'LL BE GREAT!
WHAT'LL YOU PAY ME FOR THEM?
PAY YOU? YOU SHOULD PAY ME! WHO BROUGHT YOU UP HERE?
HAVEN'T CHANGED A BIT, EH?
YOU'RE STILL ALL HEART!
WELL, WE CAN HASSLE ABOUT THAT LATER, WHEN... HEY!
THEY'RE GETTING TOO CLOSE TO THAT BUILDING! THERE'S A LITTLE KID ON THE TERRACE ...AND HE'S SCARED!
KEEP SNAPPING, PARKER!
YOU'RE MISSING THE BEST PART!
NOW DO YOU REALIZE I'VE JUST BEEN TOYING WITH YOU? YOU MISSED ME BY A MILE THAT TIME!
MOMMY! MOMMY! HURRY... I'M FRIGHTENED!
LY BUGLE
THE VULTURE THREW BLACKIE OFF-BALANCE!
HE'S MAKING HIM HURTLE RIGHT INTO THE BUILDING!
CRASH!
THIS IS ONLY THE BEGINNING, BLACKIE!
THERE'S MORE TO COME!
STILL THINK THE POOR OLD VULTURE DOESN'T STAND A CHANCE AGAINST YOU?
17.

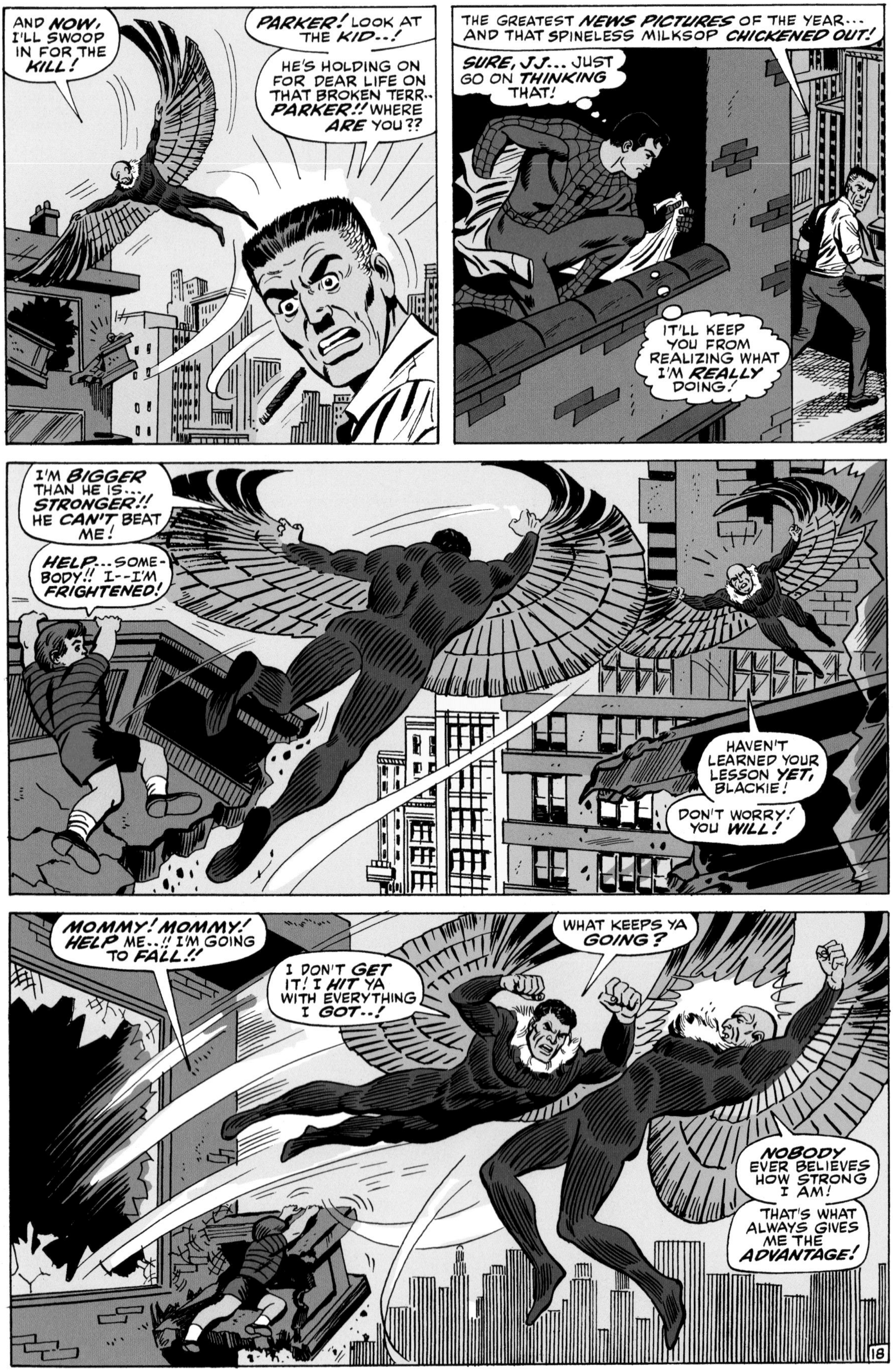
AND NOW, I'LL SWOOP IN FOR THE KILL!
PARKER! LOOK AT THE KID--!
HE'S HOLDING ON FOR DEAR LIFE ON THAT BROKEN TERR.. PARKER!! WHERE ARE YOU??
THE GREATEST NEWS PICTURES OF THE YEAR... AND THAT SPINELESS MILKSOP CHICKENED OUT!
SURE, JJ... JUST GO ON THINKING THAT!
IT'LL KEEP YOU FROM REALIZING WHAT I'M REALLY DOING!
I'M BIGGER THAN HE IS... STRONGER!! HE CAN'T BEAT ME!
HELP... SOME-BODY!! I--I'M FRIGHTENED!
HAVEN'T LEARNED YOUR LESSON YET, BLACKIE!
DON'T WORRY! YOU WILL!
MOMMY! MOMMY! HELP ME..!! I'M GOING TO FALL!!
I DON'T GET IT! I HIT YA WITH EVERYTHING I GOT--!
WHAT KEEPS YA GOING?
NOBODY EVER BELIEVES HOW STRONG I AM!
THAT'S WHAT ALWAYS GIVES ME THE ADVANTAGE!
18

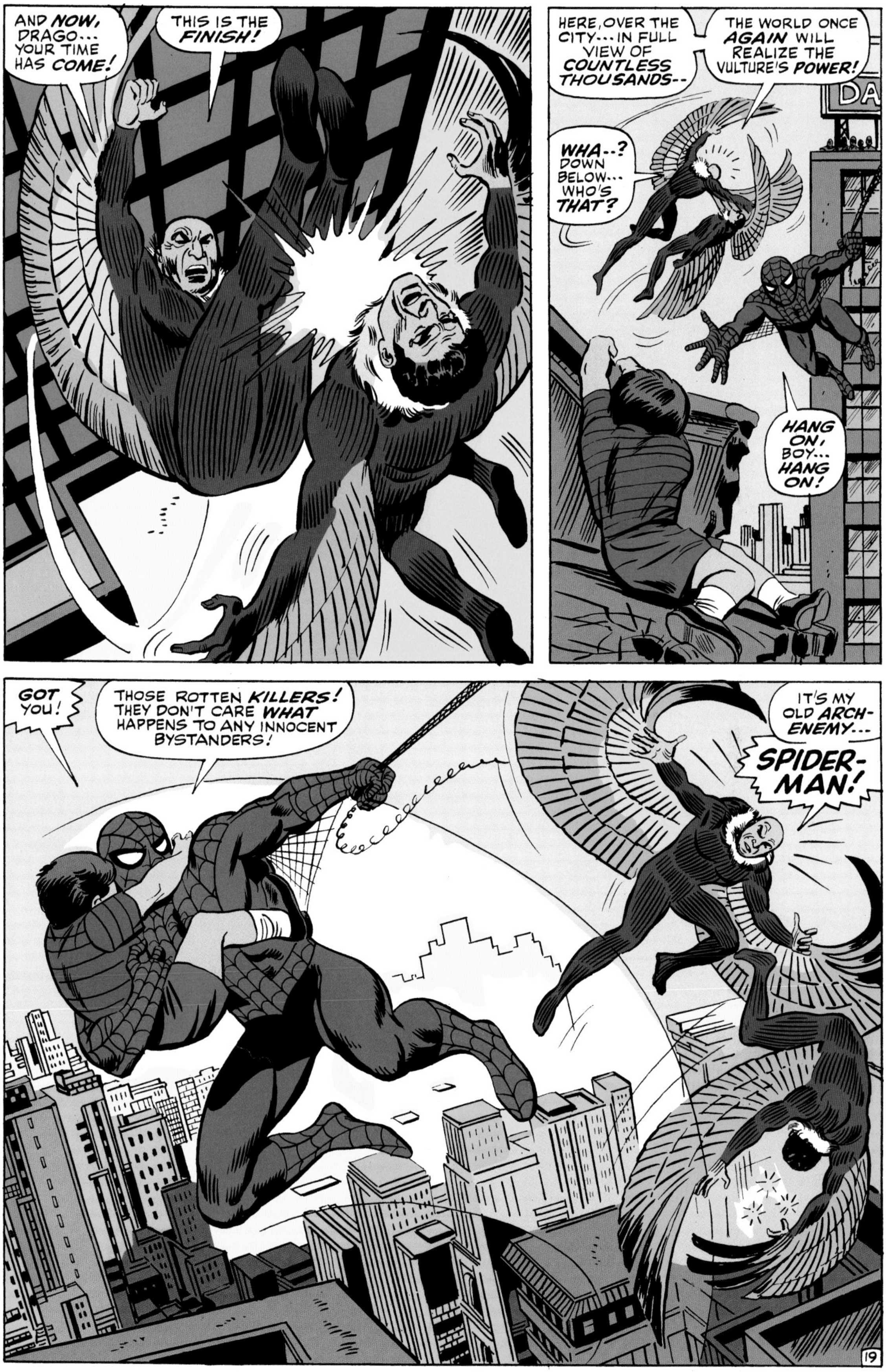
AND NOW, DRAGO... YOUR TIME HAS COME!
THIS IS THE FINISH!
HERE, OVER THE CITY... IN FULL VIEW OF COUNTLESS THOUSANDS--
THE WORLD ONCE AGAIN WILL REALIZE THE VULTURE'S POWER!
DA
WHA--? DOWN BELOW... WHO'S THAT?
HANG ON, BOY... HANG ON!
GOT YOU!
THOSE ROTTEN KILLERS! THEY DON'T CARE WHAT HAPPENS TO ANY INNOCENT BYSTANDERS!
IT'S MY OLD ARCH-ENEMY...
SPIDER-MAN!
19

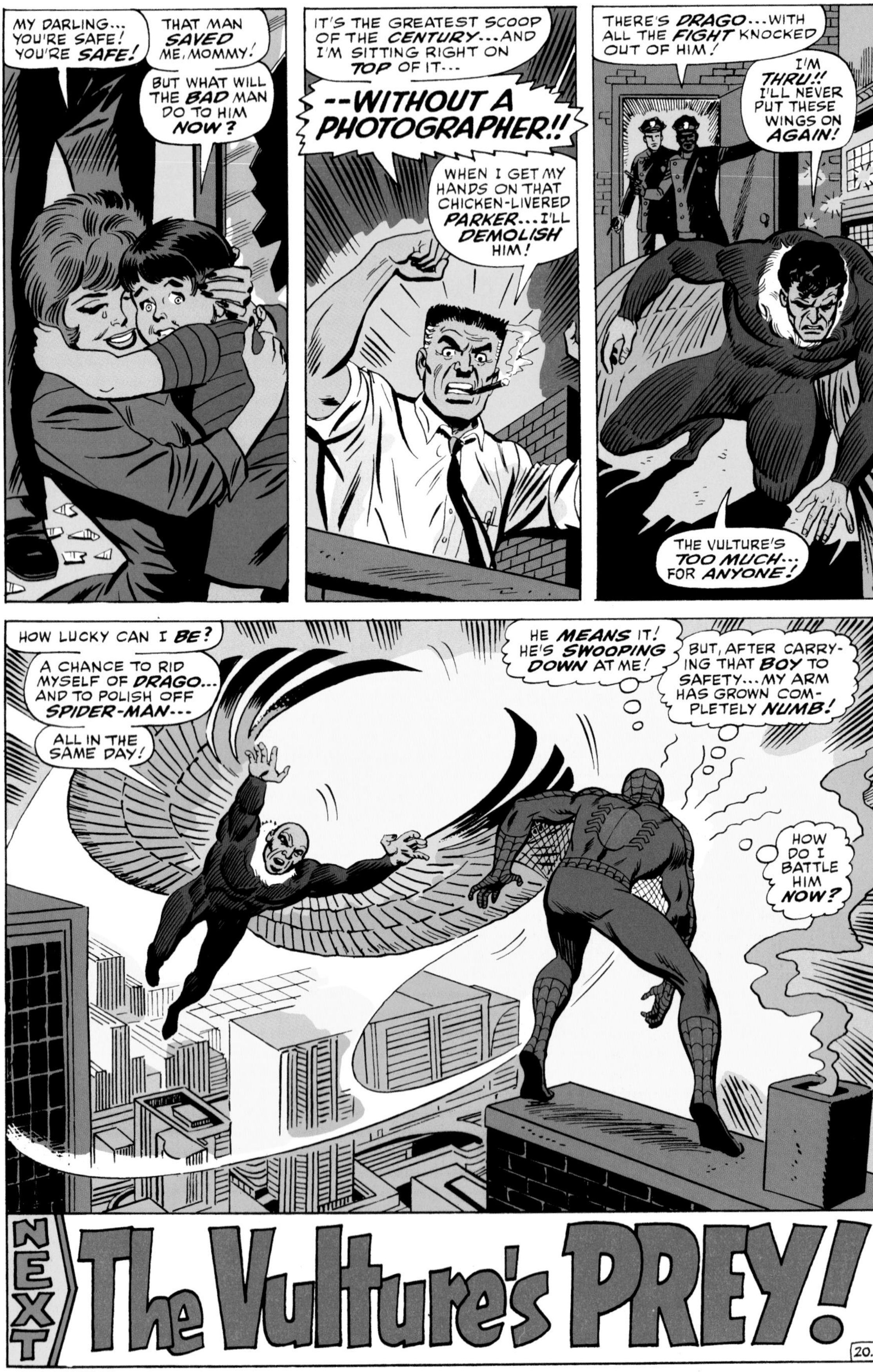
MY DARLING... YOU'RE SAFE! YOU'RE SAFE!
THAT MAN SAVED ME, MOMMY!
BUT WHAT WILL THE BAD MAN DO TO HIM NOW?
IT'S THE GREATEST SCOOP OF THE CENTURY...AND I'M SITTING RIGHT ON TOP OF IT---
--WITHOUT A PHOTOGRAPHER!!
WHEN I GET MY HANDS ON THAT CHICKEN-LIVERED PARKER...I'LL DEMOLISH HIM!
THERE'S DRAGO...WITH ALL THE FIGHT KNOCKED OUT OF HIM!
I'M THRU!! I'LL NEVER PUT THESE WINGS ON AGAIN!
THE VULTURE'S TOO MUCH... FOR ANYONE!
HOW LUCKY CAN I BE?
A CHANCE TO RID MYSELF OF DRAGO... AND TO POLISH OFF SPIDER-MAN---
ALL IN THE SAME DAY!
HE MEANS IT! HE'S SWOOPING DOWN AT ME!
BUT, AFTER CARRYING THAT BOY TO SAFETY...MY ARM HAS GROWN COMPLETELY NUMB!
HOW DO I BATTLE HIM NOW?
NEXT The Vulture's PREY!
20.

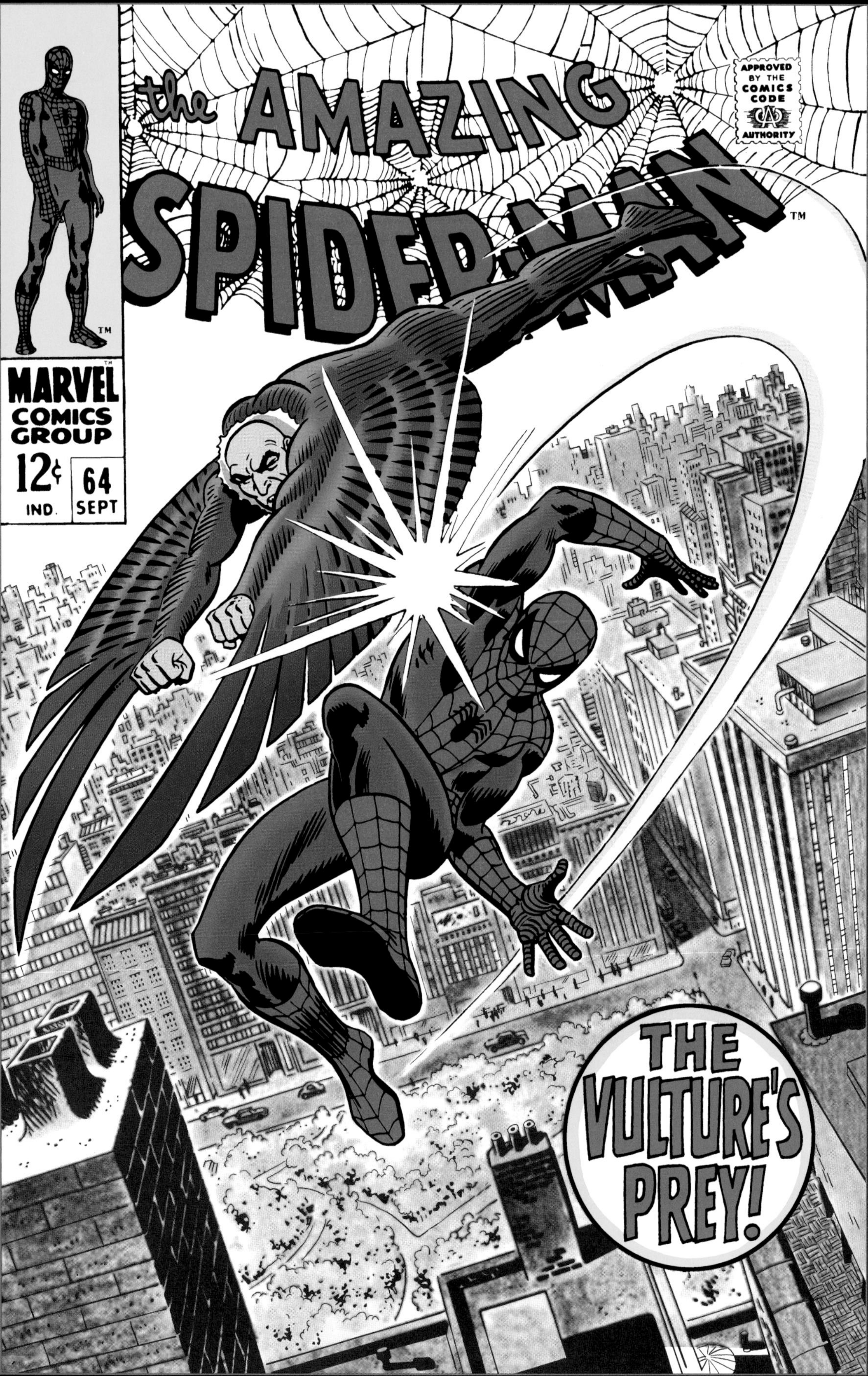

the AMAZING SPIDER-MAN ™
APPROVED BY THE COMICS CODE AUTHORITY
MARVEL COMICS GROUP
12¢ IND.
64 SEPT
THE VULTURE'S PREY!

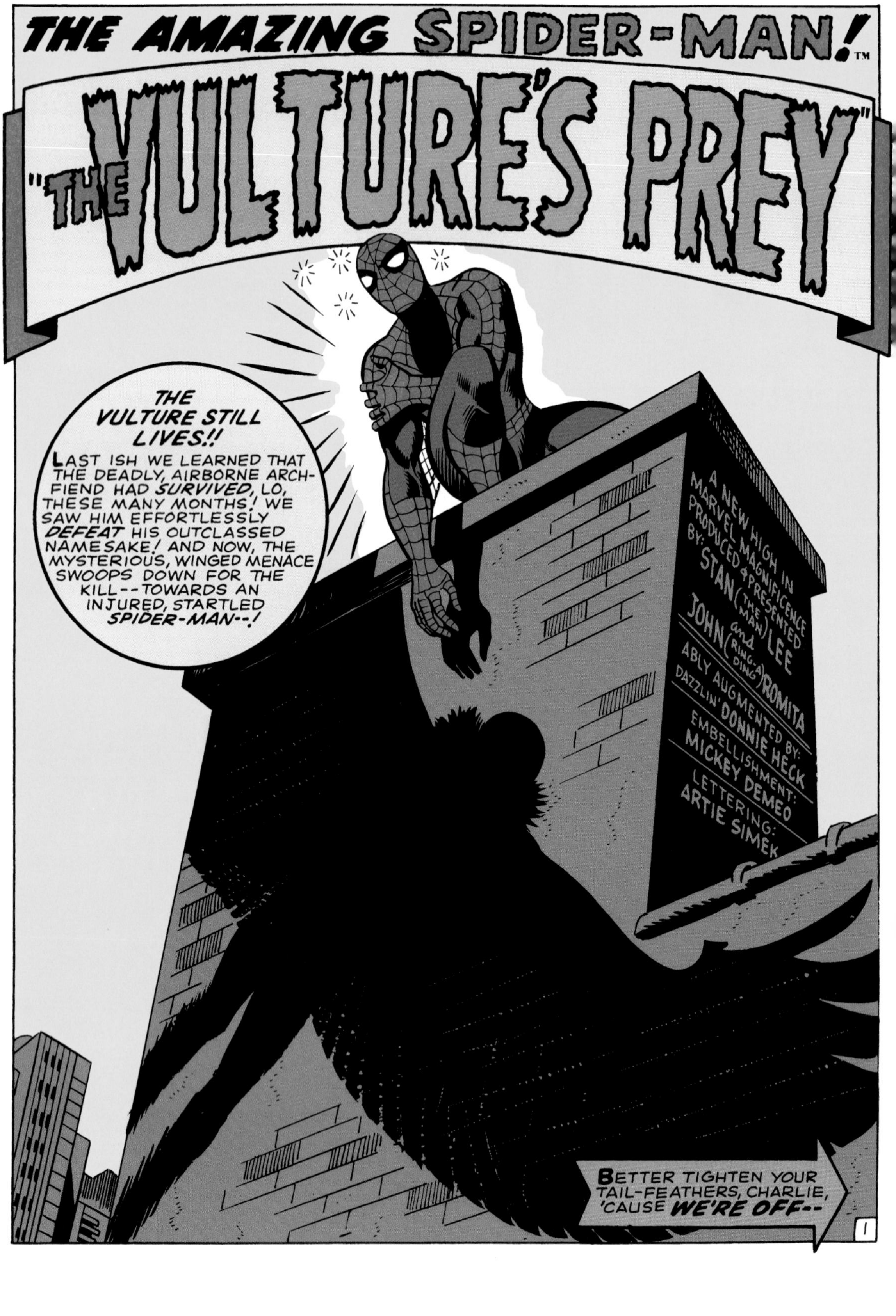
THE AMAZING SPIDER-MAN!™
"THE VULTURE'S PREY"
THE VULTURE STILL LIVES!! LAST ISH WE LEARNED THAT THE DEADLY, AIRBORNE ARCH-FIEND HAD SURVIVED, LO, THESE MANY MONTHS! WE SAW HIM EFFORTLESSLY DEFEAT HIS OUTCLASSED NAMESAKE! AND NOW, THE MYSTERIOUS, WINGED MENACE SWOOPS DOWN FOR THE KILL--TOWARDS AN INJURED, STARTLED SPIDER-MAN--!
A NEW HIGH IN MARVEL MAGNIFICENCE PRODUCED & PRESENTED BY: STAN (THE MAN) LEE and JOHN (RING-A DING) ROMITA
ABLY AUGMENTED BY: DAZZLIN' DONNIE HECK
EMBELLISHMENT: MICKEY DEMEO
LETTERING: ARTIE SIMEK
BETTER TIGHTEN YOUR TAIL-FEATHERS, CHARLIE, 'CAUSE WE'RE OFF--
1

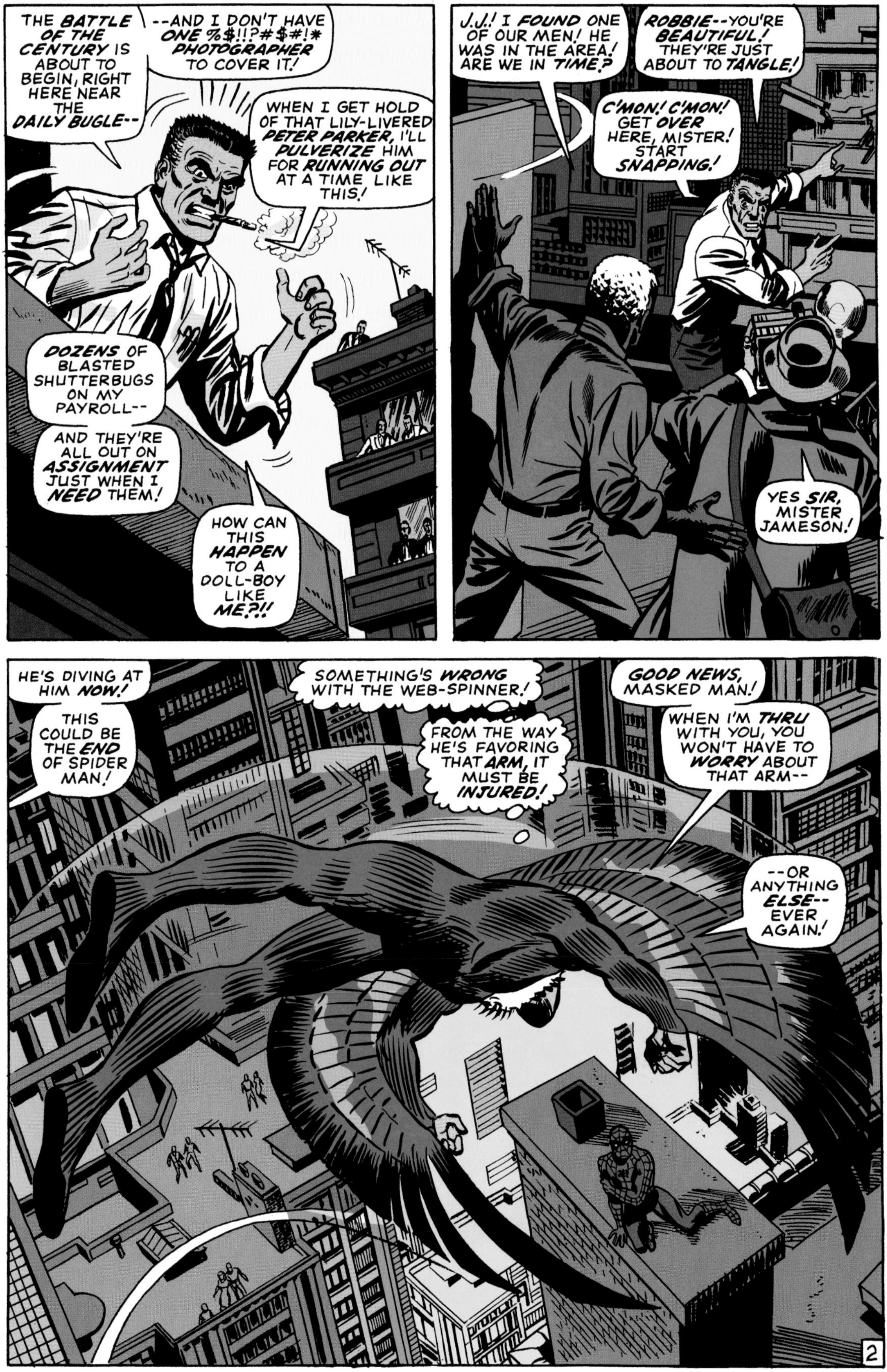
THE BATTLE OF THE CENTURY IS ABOUT TO BEGIN, RIGHT HERE NEAR THE DAILY BUGLE--
--AND I DON'T HAVE ONE %$!!?#$#!* PHOTOGRAPHER TO COVER IT!
WHEN I GET HOLD OF THAT LILY-LIVERED PETER PARKER, I'LL PULVERIZE HIM FOR RUNNING OUT AT A TIME LIKE THIS!
DOZENS OF BLASTED SHUTTERBUGS ON MY PAYROLL--
AND THEY'RE ALL OUT ON ASSIGNMENT JUST WHEN I NEED THEM!
HOW CAN THIS HAPPEN TO A DOLL-BOY LIKE ME?!!
J.J.! I FOUND ONE OF OUR MEN! HE WAS IN THE AREA! ARE WE IN TIME?
ROBBIE--YOU'RE BEAUTIFUL! THEY'RE JUST ABOUT TO TANGLE!
C'MON! C'MON! GET OVER HERE, MISTER! START SNAPPING!
YES SIR, MISTER JAMESON!
HE'S DIVING AT HIM NOW!
THIS COULD BE THE END OF SPIDER MAN!
SOMETHING'S WRONG WITH THE WEB-SPINNER!
FROM THE WAY HE'S FAVORING THAT ARM, IT MUST BE INJURED!
GOOD NEWS, MASKED MAN!
WHEN I'M THRU WITH YOU, YOU WON'T HAVE TO WORRY ABOUT THAT ARM--
--OR ANYTHING ELSE-- EVER AGAIN!
2

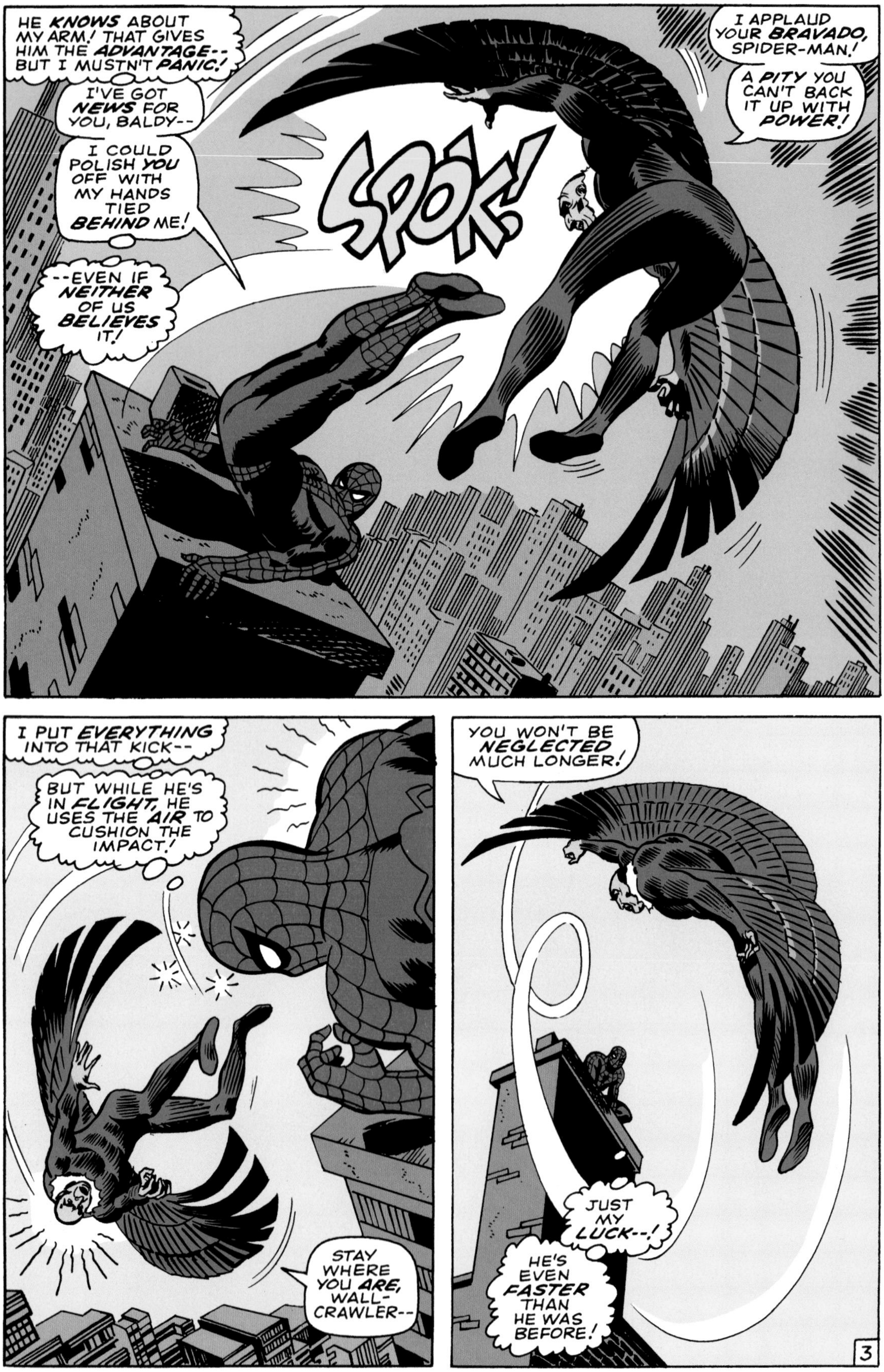
HE KNOWS ABOUT MY ARM! THAT GIVES HIM THE ADVANTAGE-- BUT I MUSTN'T PANIC!
I'VE GOT NEWS FOR YOU, BALDY--
I COULD POLISH YOU OFF WITH MY HANDS TIED BEHIND ME!
--EVEN IF NEITHER OF US BELIEVES IT!
SPOK!
I APPLAUD YOUR BRAVADO, SPIDER-MAN!
A PITY YOU CAN'T BACK IT UP WITH POWER!
I PUT EVERYTHING INTO THAT KICK--
BUT WHILE HE'S IN FLIGHT, HE USES THE AIR TO CUSHION THE IMPACT!
STAY WHERE YOU ARE, WALL-CRAWLER--
YOU WON'T BE NEGLECTED MUCH LONGER!
JUST MY LUCK--!
HE'S EVEN FASTER THAN HE WAS BEFORE!
3

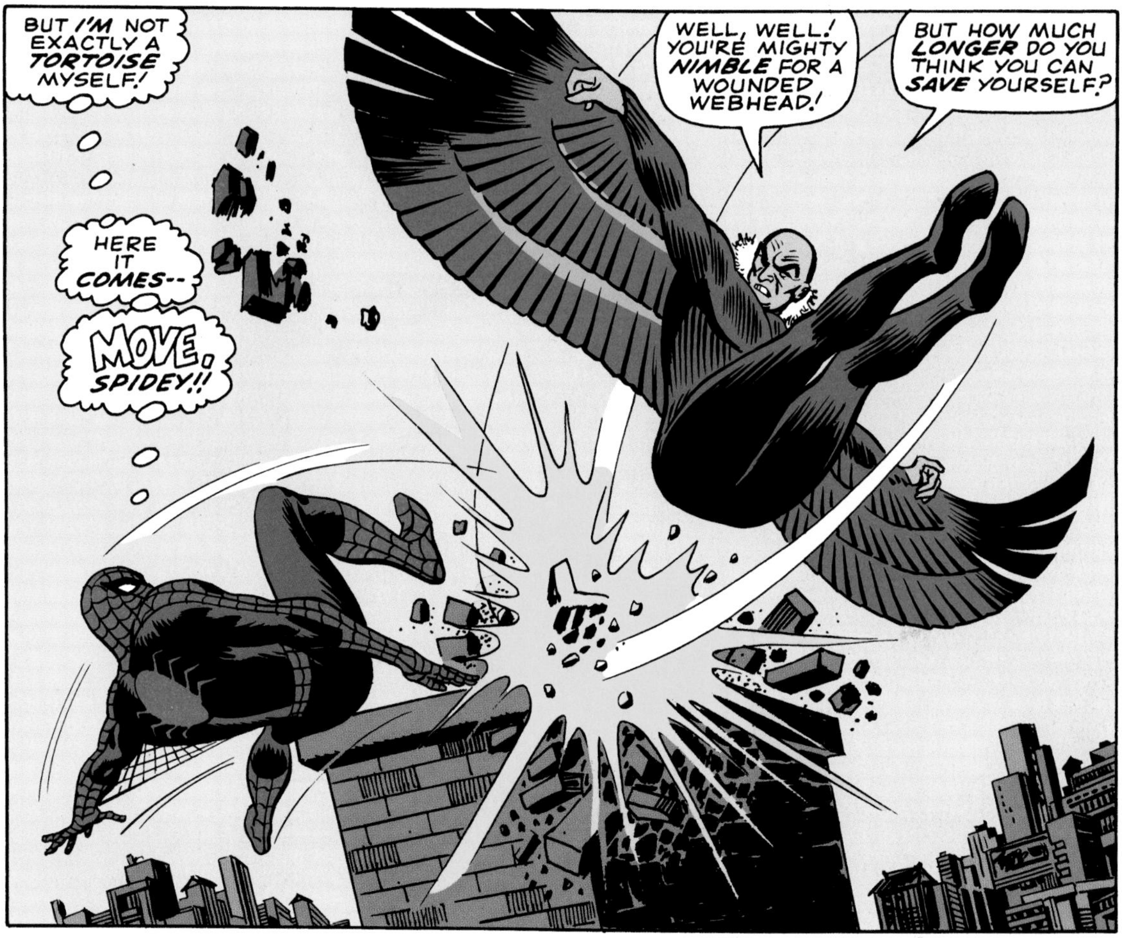
BUT I'M NOT EXACTLY A TORTOISE MYSELF!
WELL, WELL! YOU'RE MIGHTY NIMBLE FOR A WOUNDED WEBHEAD!
BUT HOW MUCH LONGER DO YOU THINK YOU CAN SAVE YOURSELF?
HERE IT COMES--
MOVE, SPIDEY!!

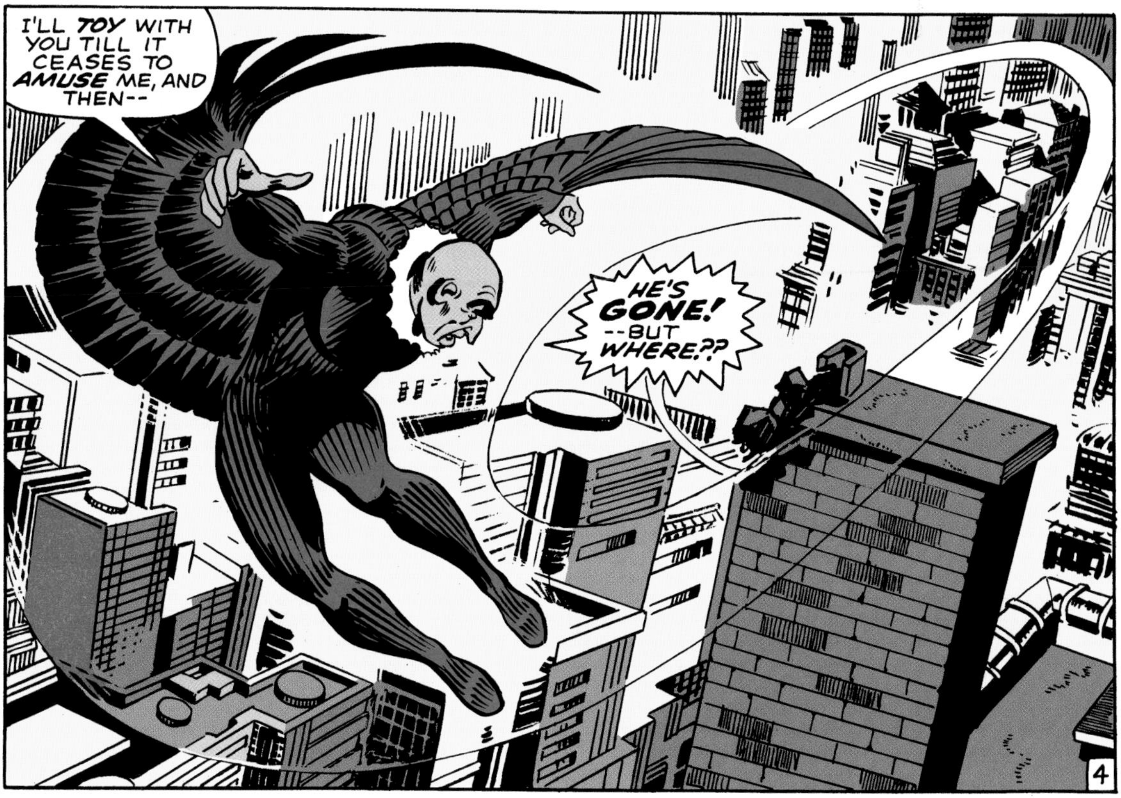
I'LL TOY WITH YOU TILL IT CEASES TO AMUSE ME, AND THEN--
HE'S GONE! --BUT WHERE??
4

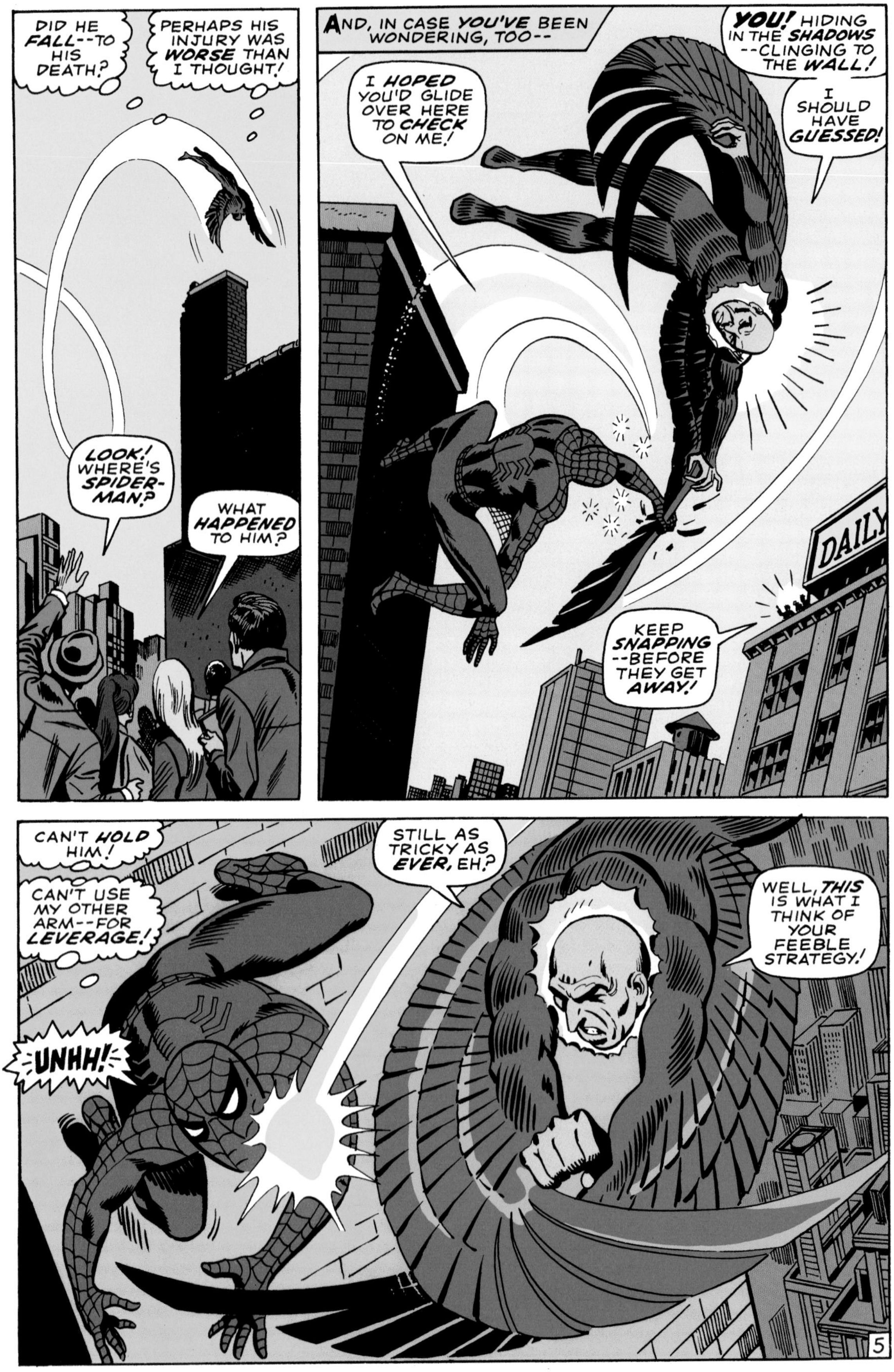
DID HE FALL--TO HIS DEATH?
PERHAPS HIS INJURY WAS WORSE THAN I THOUGHT!
LOOK! WHERE'S SPIDER-MAN?
WHAT HAPPENED TO HIM?
AND, IN CASE YOU'VE BEEN WONDERING, TOO--
YOU! HIDING IN THE SHADOWS --CLINGING TO THE WALL!
I SHOULD HAVE GUESSED!
I HOPED YOU'D GLIDE OVER HERE TO CHECK ON ME!
DAILY
KEEP SNAPPING --BEFORE THEY GET AWAY!
CAN'T HOLD HIM!
CAN'T USE MY OTHER ARM--FOR LEVERAGE!
STILL AS TRICKY AS EVER, EH?
WELL, THIS IS WHAT I THINK OF YOUR FEEBLE STRATEGY!
UNHH!
5

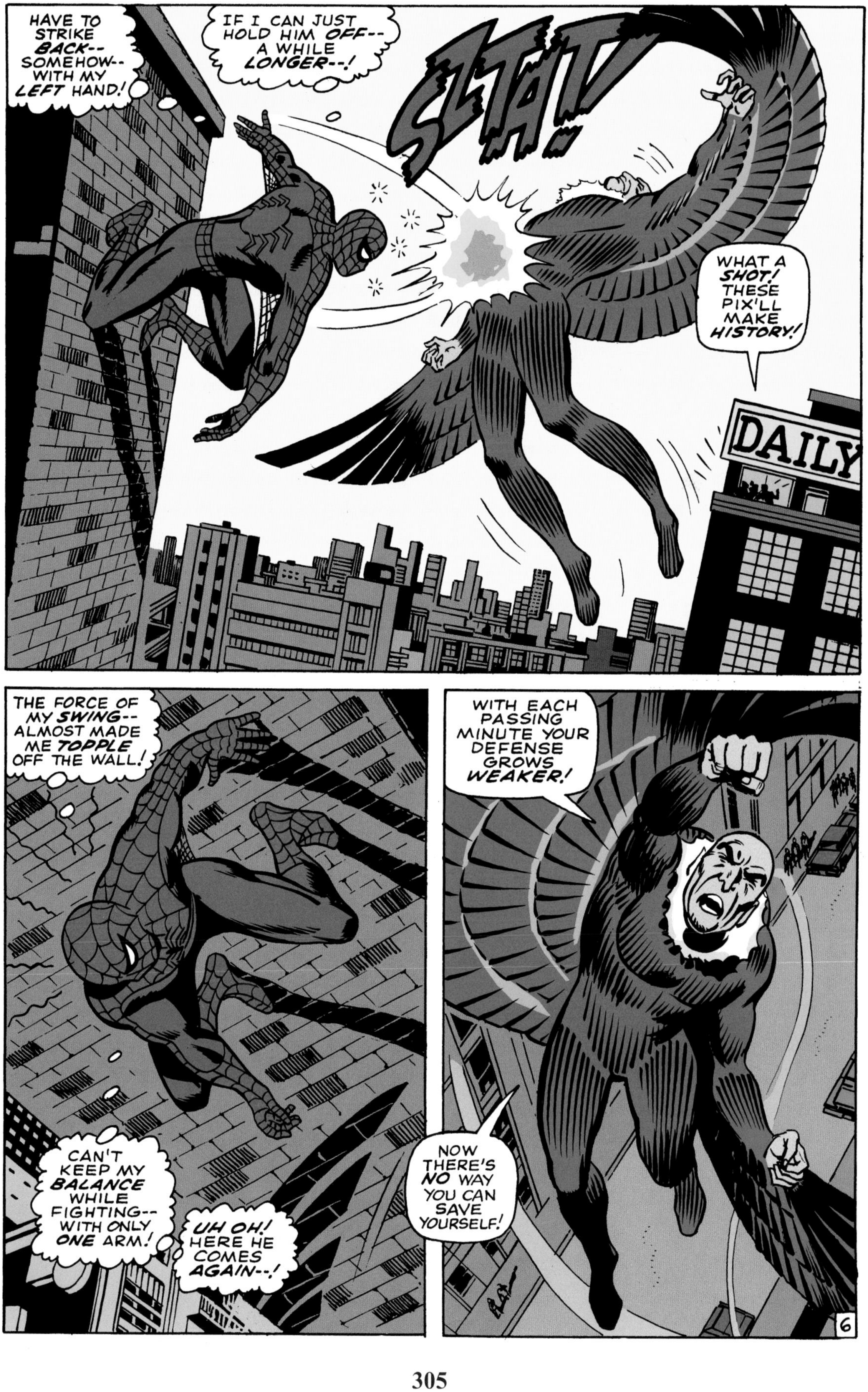
HAVE TO STRIKE BACK-- SOMEHOW-- WITH MY LEFT HAND!
IF I CAN JUST HOLD HIM OFF-- A WHILE LONGER--!
WHAT A SHOT! THESE PIX'LL MAKE HISTORY!
DAILY
THE FORCE OF MY SWING-- ALMOST MADE ME TOPPLE OFF THE WALL!
CAN'T KEEP MY BALANCE WHILE FIGHTING-- WITH ONLY ONE ARM!
UH OH! HERE HE COMES AGAIN--!
WITH EACH PASSING MINUTE YOUR DEFENSE GROWS WEAKER!
NOW THERE'S NO WAY YOU CAN SAVE YOURSELF!
6

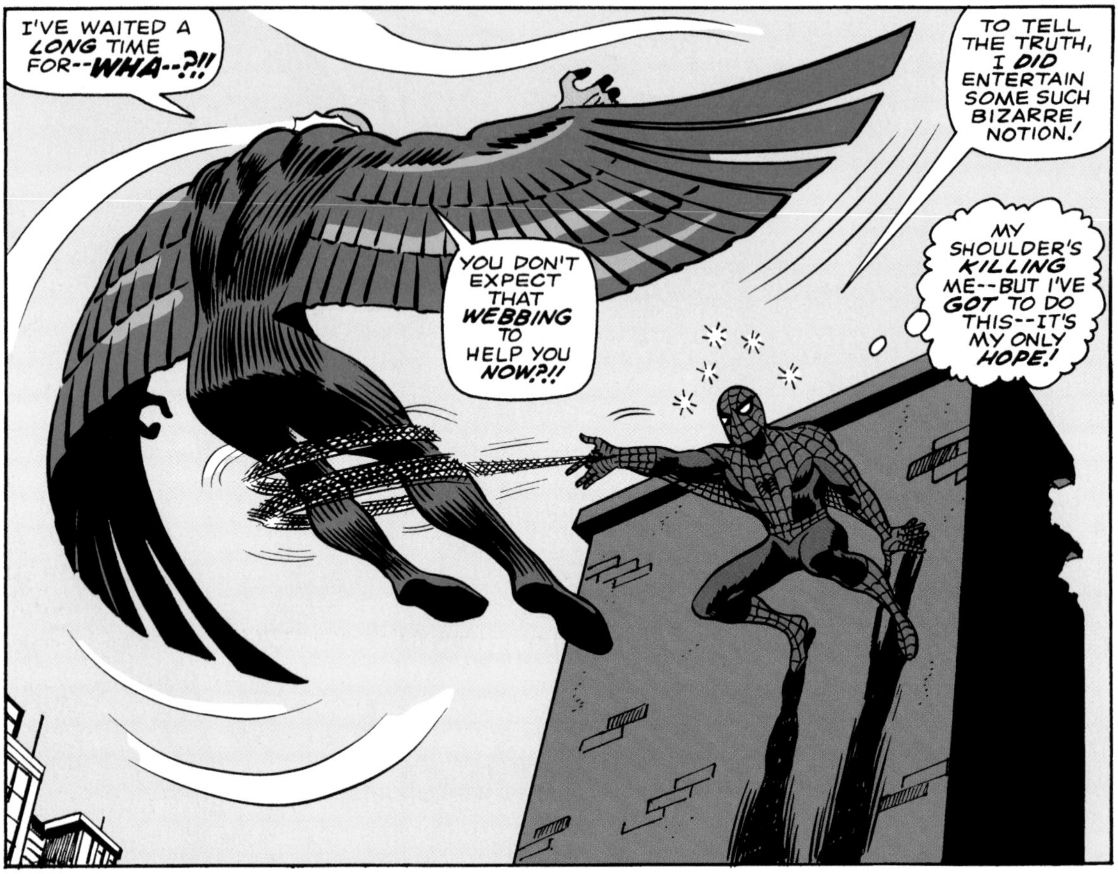
I'VE WAITED A LONG TIME FOR--WHA--?!!
TO TELL THE TRUTH, I DID ENTERTAIN SOME SUCH BIZARRE NOTION!
YOU DON'T EXPECT THAT WEBBING TO HELP YOU NOW?!!
MY SHOULDER'S KILLING ME--BUT I'VE GOT TO DO THIS--IT'S MY ONLY HOPE!

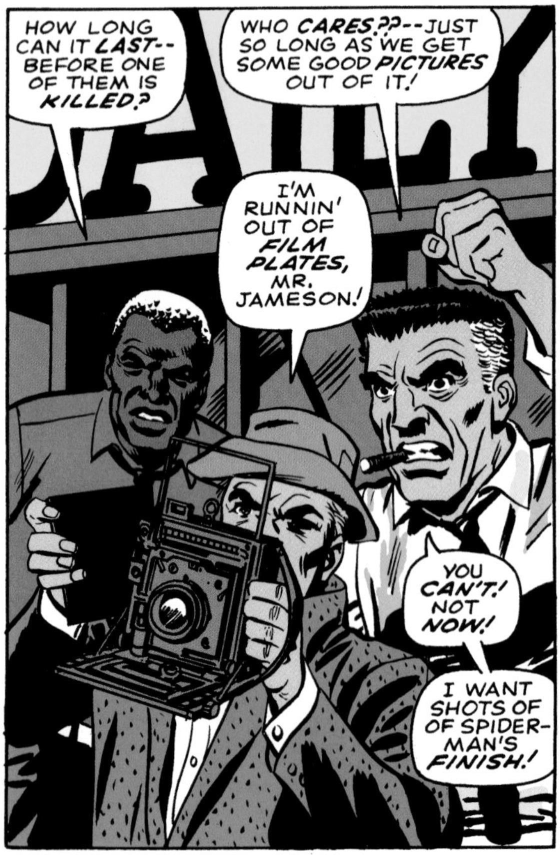
HOW LONG CAN IT LAST--BEFORE ONE OF THEM IS KILLED?
WHO CARES??--JUST SO LONG AS WE GET SOME GOOD PICTURES OUT OF IT!
I'M RUNNIN' OUT OF FILM PLATES, MR. JAMESON!
YOU CAN'T! NOT NOW!
I WANT SHOTS OF OF SPIDER-MAN'S FINISH!

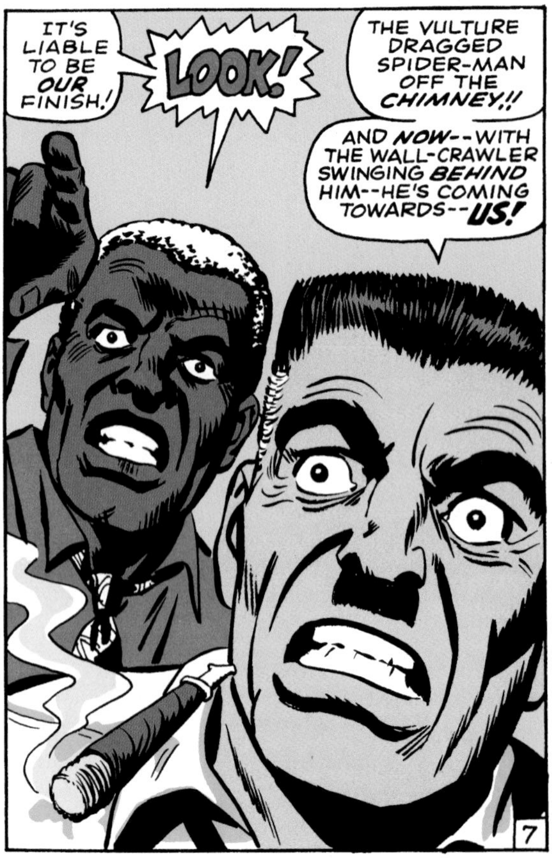
IT'S LIABLE TO BE OUR FINISH!
LOOK!
THE VULTURE DRAGGED SPIDER-MAN OFF THE CHIMNEY!!
AND NOW--WITH THE WALL-CRAWLER SWINGING BEHIND HIM--HE'S COMING TOWARDS--US!
7

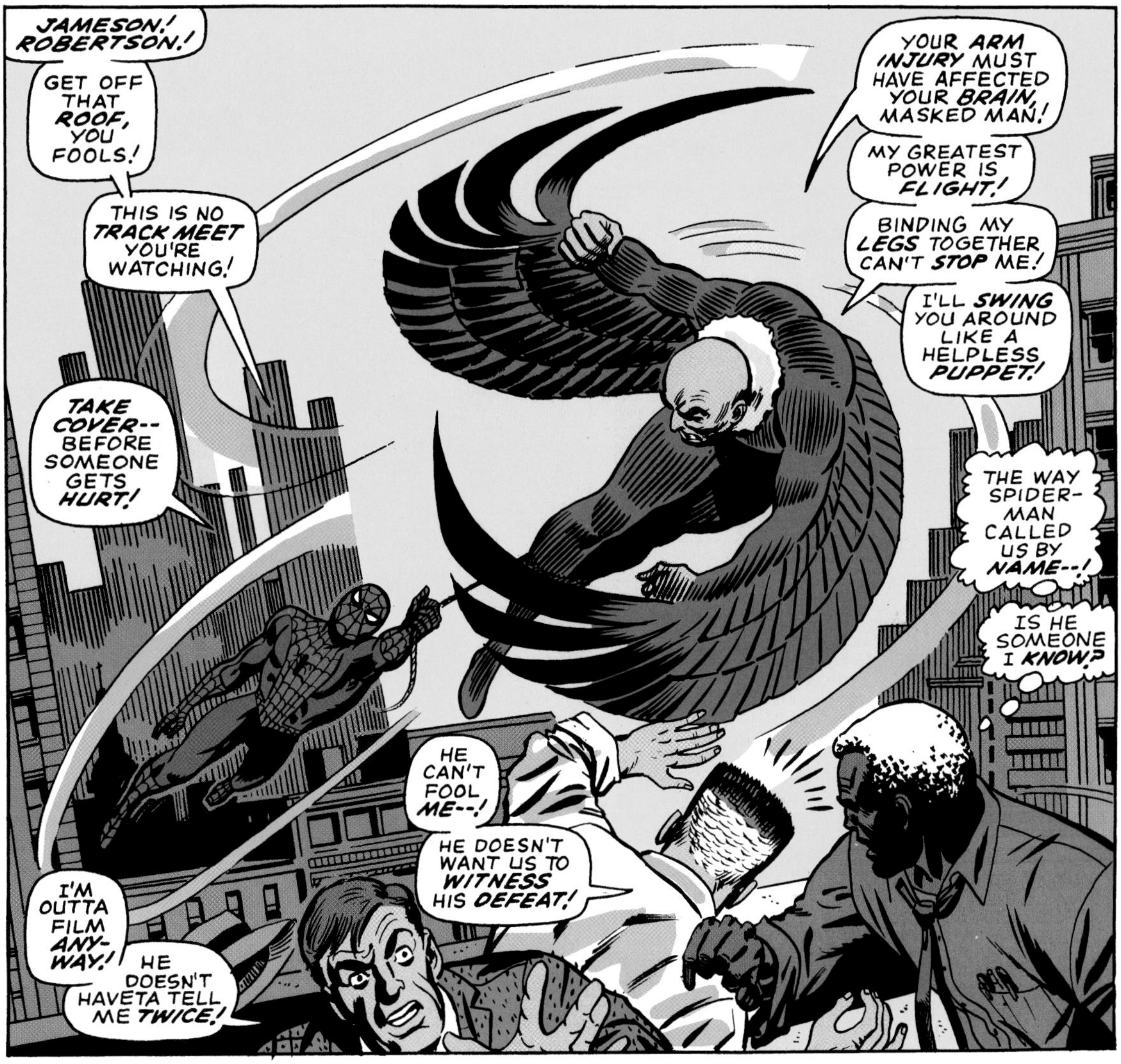
JAMESON! ROBERTSON!
GET OFF THAT ROOF, YOU FOOLS!
THIS IS NO TRACK MEET YOU'RE WATCHING!
TAKE COVER-- BEFORE SOMEONE GETS HURT!
YOUR ARM INJURY MUST HAVE AFFECTED YOUR BRAIN, MASKED MAN!
MY GREATEST POWER IS FLIGHT!
BINDING MY LEGS TOGETHER CAN'T STOP ME!
I'LL SWING YOU AROUND LIKE A HELPLESS PUPPET!
THE WAY SPIDER-MAN CALLED US BY NAME--!
IS HE SOMEONE I KNOW?
HE CAN'T FOOL ME--!
HE DOESN'T WANT US TO WITNESS HIS DEFEAT!
I'M OUTTA FILM ANY-WAY!
HE DOESN'T HAVETA TELL ME TWICE!

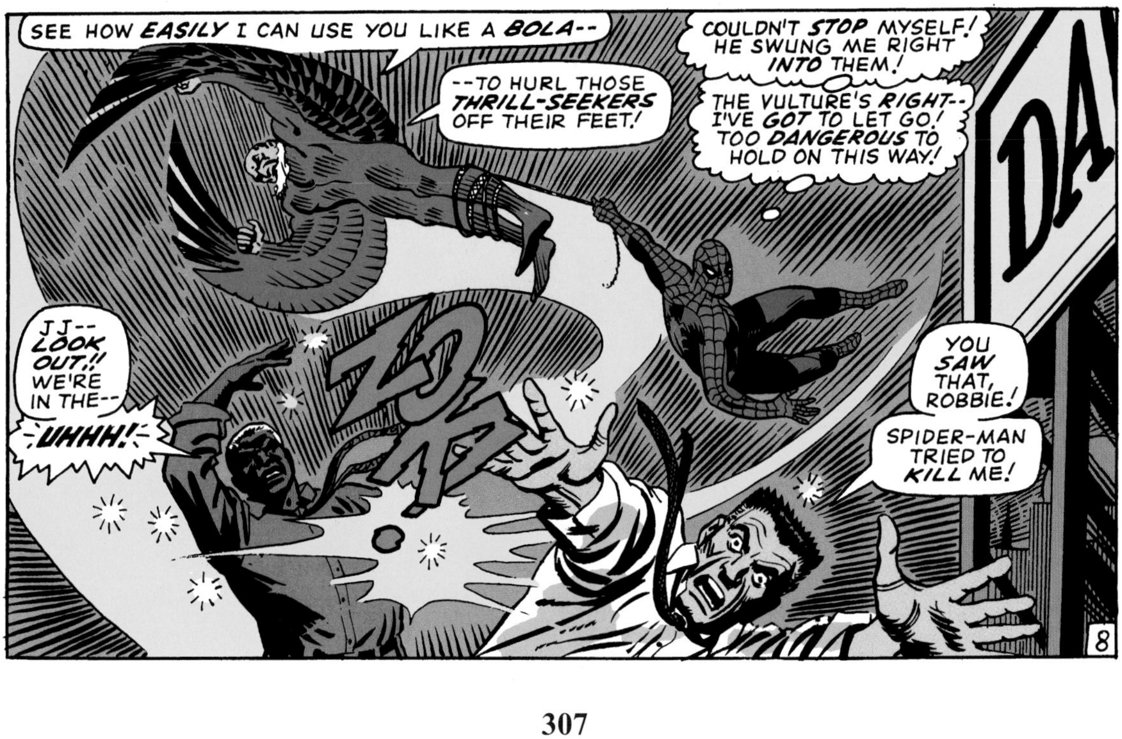
SEE HOW EASILY I CAN USE YOU LIKE A BOLA--
--TO HURL THOSE THRILL-SEEKERS OFF THEIR FEET!
COULDN'T STOP MYSELF! HE SWUNG ME RIGHT INTO THEM!
THE VULTURE'S RIGHT-- I'VE GOT TO LET GO! TOO DANGEROUS TO HOLD ON THIS WAY!
DA
JJ-- LOOK OUT!! WE'RE IN THE--
-UHHH!-
ZOK
YOU SAW THAT, ROBBIE!
SPIDER-MAN TRIED TO KILL ME!
8

THEY WERE *LUCKY*-- I ONLY *GRAZED* THEM!

THOP!!

T-HUP!

SPIDER-MAN-- WATCH IT! HE'S COMING AT YOU AGAIN!

WHAT ARE YOU WARNING *HIM* FOR?--

I'M ROOTING FOR THE *VULTURE!*

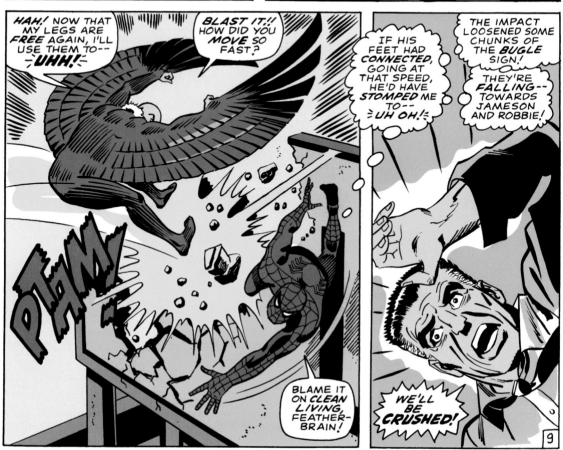

HAH! NOW THAT MY LEGS ARE *FREE* AGAIN, I'LL USE THEM TO--

--UHH!--

BLAST IT!! HOW DID YOU *MOVE* SO FAST?

IF HIS FEET HAD *CONNECTED*, GOING AT THAT SPEED, HE'D HAVE *STOMPED* ME TO-- UH OH!

THE IMPACT *LOOSENED* SOME CHUNKS OF THE *BUGLE* SIGN!

THEY'RE *FALLING*-- TOWARDS JAMESON AND ROBBIE!

PLAM!

BLAME IT ON *CLEAN LIVING*, FEATHER-BRAIN!

WE'LL BE *CRUSHED!*

9

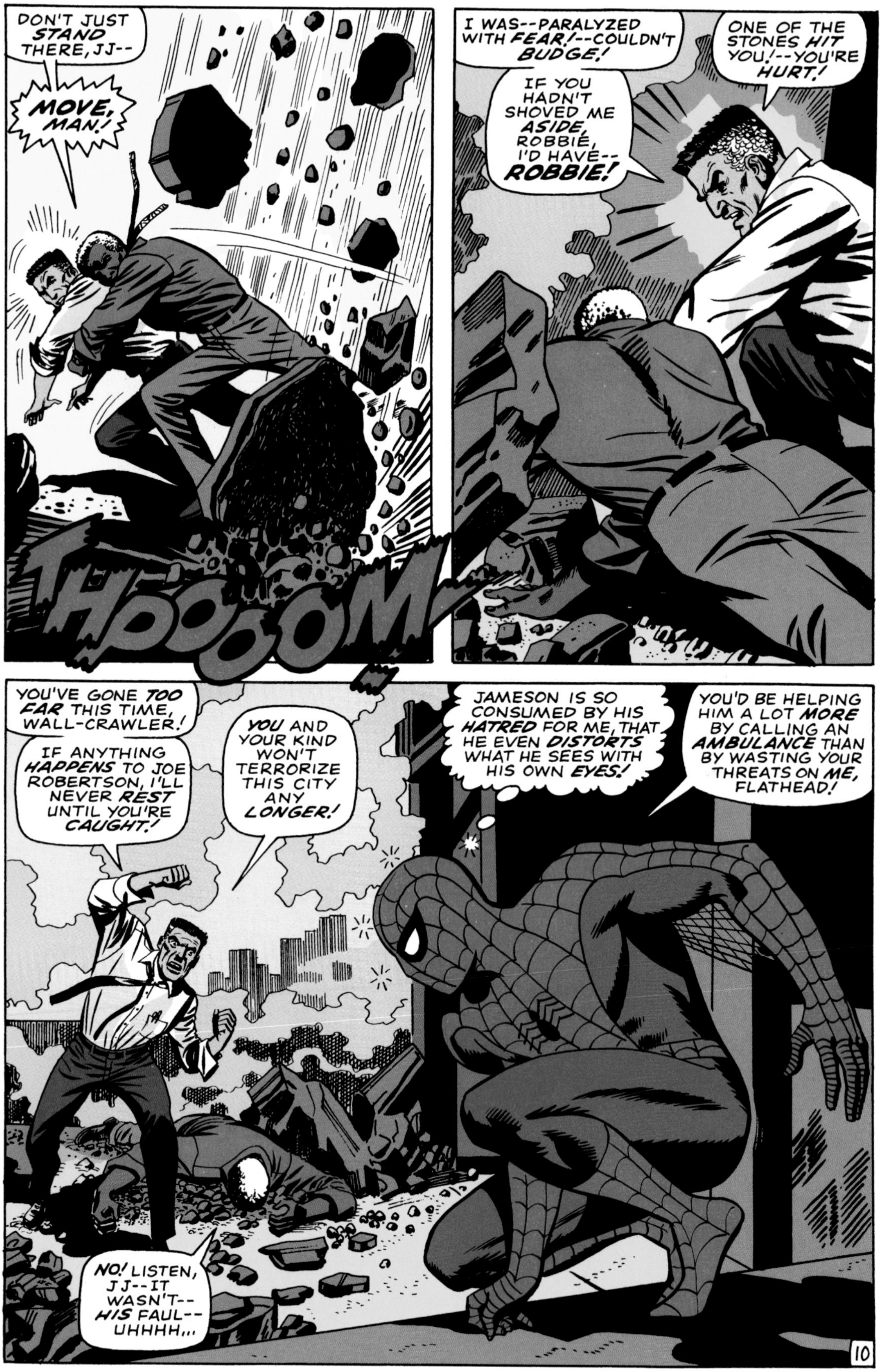
DON'T JUST STAND THERE, JJ--
MOVE, MAN!
THOOOOM
I WAS--PARALYZED WITH FEAR!--COULDN'T BUDGE!
IF YOU HADN'T SHOVED ME ASIDE, ROBBIE, I'D HAVE-- ROBBIE!
ONE OF THE STONES HIT YOU!--YOU'RE HURT!
YOU'VE GONE TOO FAR THIS TIME, WALL-CRAWLER!
IF ANYTHING HAPPENS TO JOE ROBERTSON, I'LL NEVER REST UNTIL YOU'RE CAUGHT!
YOU AND YOUR KIND WON'T TERRORIZE THIS CITY ANY LONGER!
JAMESON IS SO CONSUMED BY HIS HATRED FOR ME, THAT HE EVEN DISTORTS WHAT HE SEES WITH HIS OWN EYES!
YOU'D BE HELPING HIM A LOT MORE BY CALLING AN AMBULANCE THAN BY WASTING YOUR THREATS ON ME, FLATHEAD!
NO! LISTEN, JJ--IT WASN'T-- HIS FAUL-- UHHHH...
10

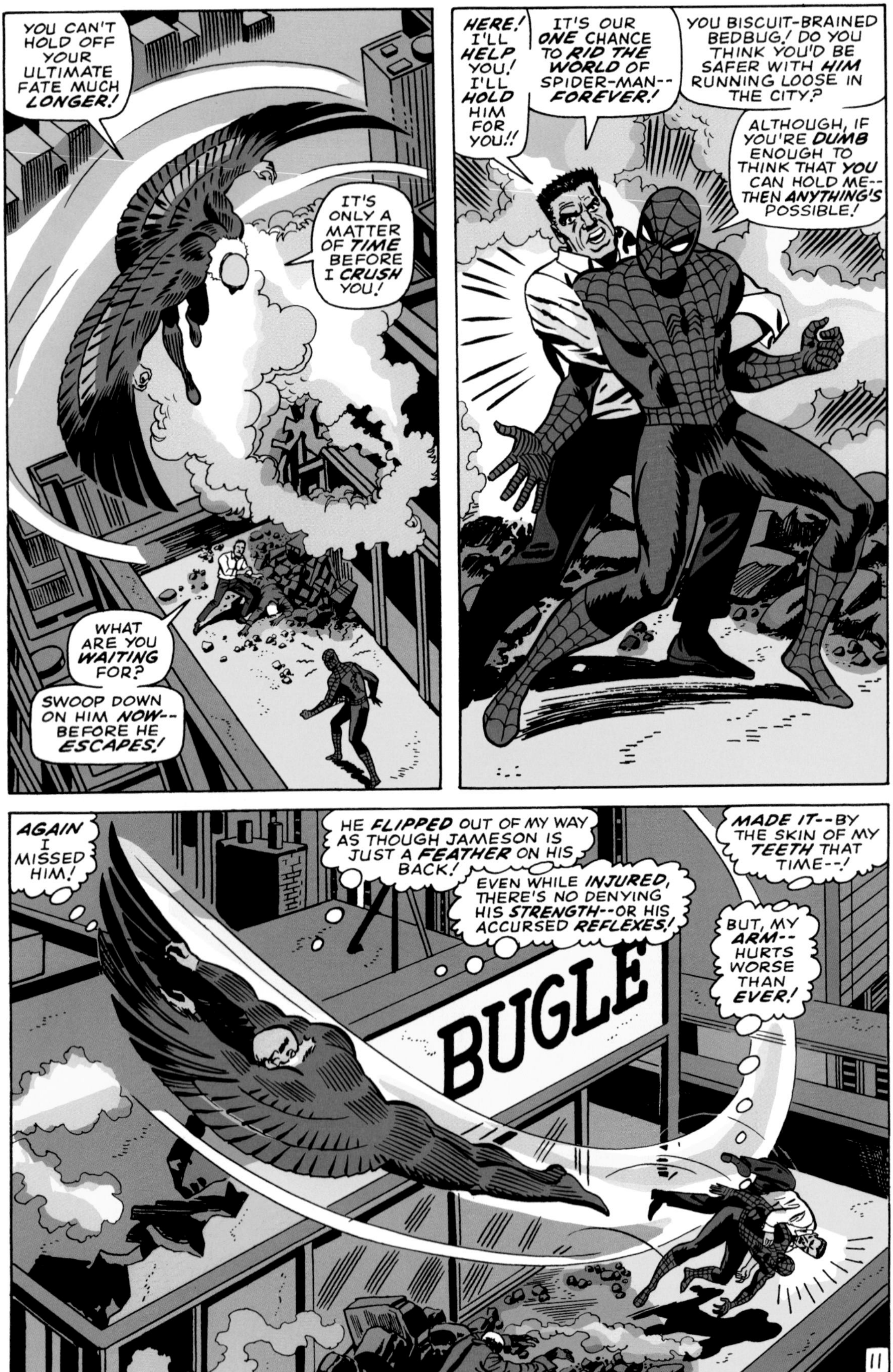
YOU CAN'T HOLD OFF YOUR ULTIMATE FATE MUCH LONGER!
IT'S ONLY A MATTER OF TIME BEFORE I CRUSH YOU!
WHAT ARE YOU WAITING FOR?
SWOOP DOWN ON HIM NOW-- BEFORE HE ESCAPES!
HERE! I'LL HELP YOU! I'LL HOLD HIM FOR YOU!!
IT'S OUR ONE CHANCE TO RID THE WORLD OF SPIDER-MAN-- FOREVER!
YOU BISCUIT-BRAINED BEDBUG! DO YOU THINK YOU'D BE SAFER WITH HIM RUNNING LOOSE IN THE CITY?
ALTHOUGH, IF YOU'RE DUMB ENOUGH TO THINK THAT YOU CAN HOLD ME-- THEN ANYTHING'S POSSIBLE!
AGAIN I MISSED HIM!
HE FLIPPED OUT OF MY WAY AS THOUGH JAMESON IS JUST A FEATHER ON HIS BACK!
EVEN WHILE INJURED, THERE'S NO DENYING HIS STRENGTH--OR HIS ACCURSED REFLEXES!
BUGLE
MADE IT--BY THE SKIN OF MY TEETH THAT TIME--!
BUT, MY ARM-- HURTS WORSE THAN EVER!
11

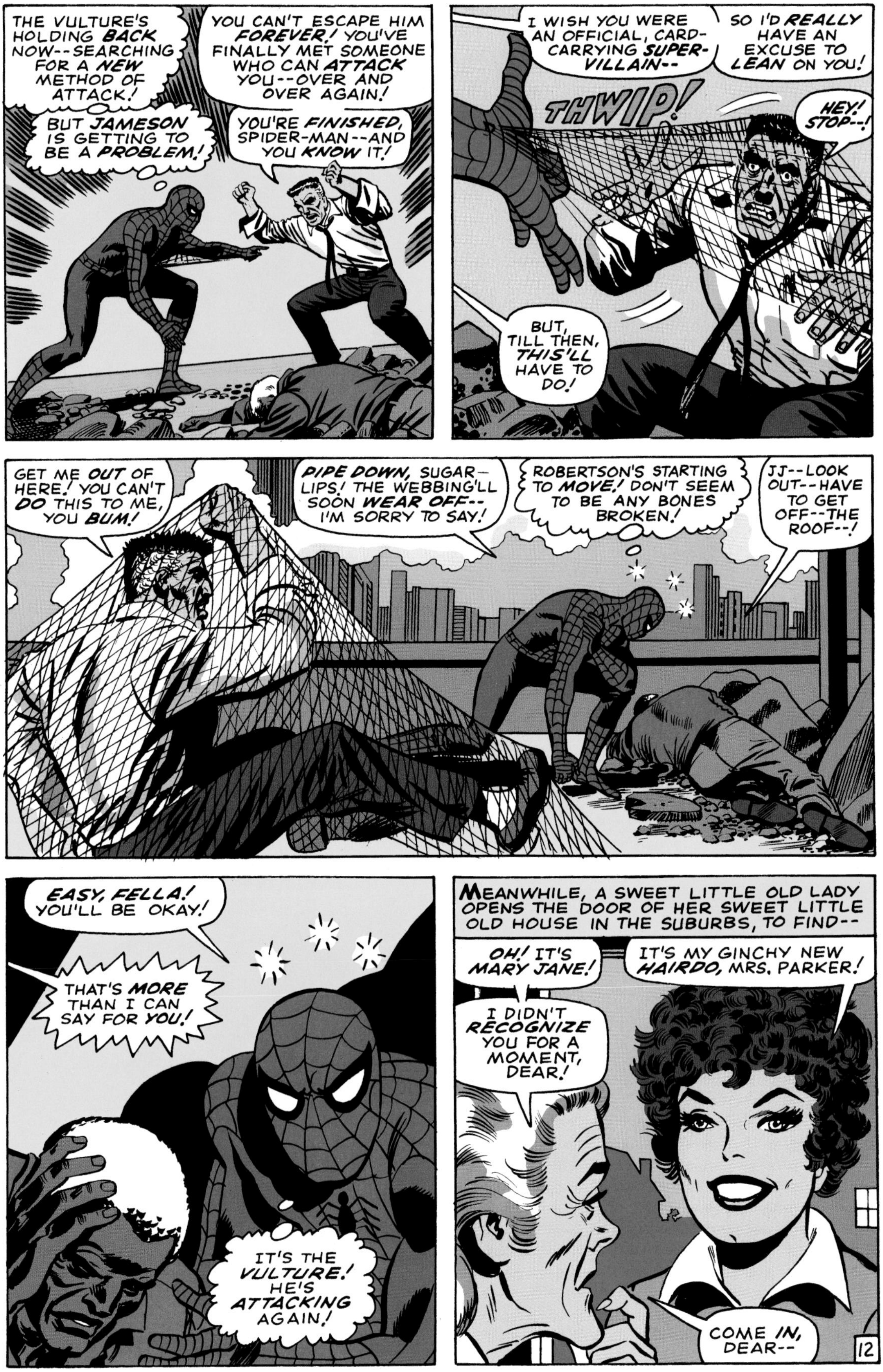
THE VULTURE'S HOLDING BACK NOW--SEARCHING FOR A NEW METHOD OF ATTACK!
BUT JAMESON IS GETTING TO BE A PROBLEM!
YOU CAN'T ESCAPE HIM FOREVER! YOU'VE FINALLY MET SOMEONE WHO CAN ATTACK YOU--OVER AND OVER AGAIN!
YOU'RE FINISHED, SPIDER-MAN--AND YOU KNOW IT!
I WISH YOU WERE AN OFFICIAL, CARD-CARRYING SUPER-VILLAIN--
SO I'D REALLY HAVE AN EXCUSE TO LEAN ON YOU!
THWIP!
HEY! STOP--!
BUT, TILL THEN, THIS'LL HAVE TO DO!
GET ME OUT OF HERE! YOU CAN'T DO THIS TO ME, YOU BUM!
PIPE DOWN, SUGAR-LIPS! THE WEBBING'LL SOON WEAR OFF--I'M SORRY TO SAY!
ROBERTSON'S STARTING TO MOVE! DON'T SEEM TO BE ANY BONES BROKEN!
JJ--LOOK OUT--HAVE TO GET OFF--THE ROOF--!
EASY, FELLA! YOU'LL BE OKAY!
THAT'S MORE THAN I CAN SAY FOR YOU!
IT'S THE VULTURE! HE'S ATTACKING AGAIN!
MEANWHILE, A SWEET LITTLE OLD LADY OPENS THE DOOR OF HER SWEET LITTLE OLD HOUSE IN THE SUBURBS, TO FIND--
OH! IT'S MARY JANE!
I DIDN'T RECOGNIZE YOU FOR A MOMENT, DEAR!
IT'S MY GINCHY NEW HAIRDO, MRS. PARKER!
COME IN, DEAR--
12

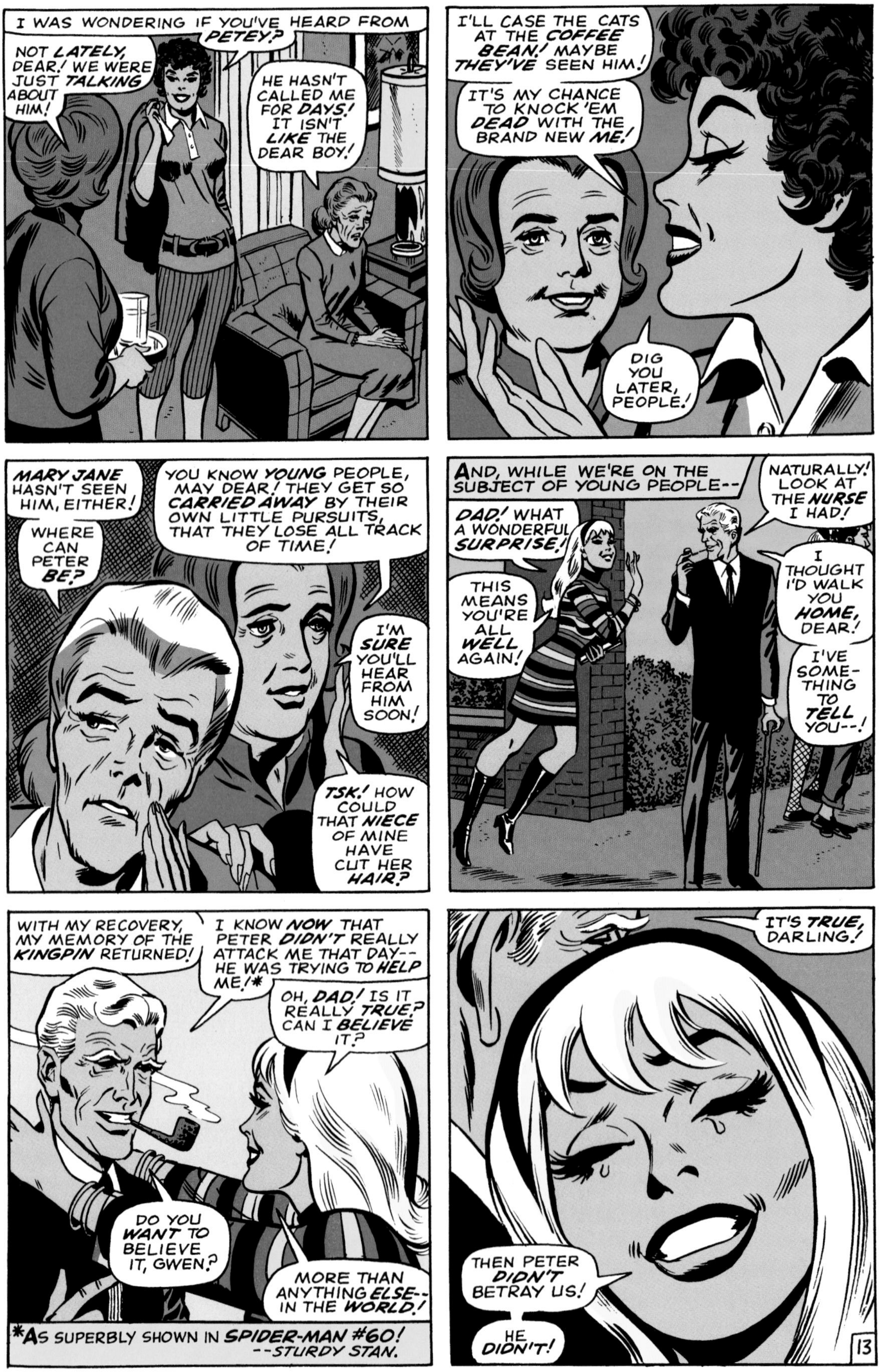
I WAS WONDERING IF YOU'VE HEARD FROM PETEY?
NOT LATELY, DEAR! WE WERE JUST TALKING ABOUT HIM!
HE HASN'T CALLED ME FOR DAYS! IT ISN'T LIKE THE DEAR BOY!
I'LL CASE THE CATS AT THE COFFEE BEAN! MAYBE THEY'VE SEEN HIM!
IT'S MY CHANCE TO KNOCK 'EM DEAD WITH THE BRAND NEW ME!
DIG YOU LATER, PEOPLE!
MARY JANE HASN'T SEEN HIM, EITHER!
WHERE CAN PETER BE?
YOU KNOW YOUNG PEOPLE, MAY DEAR! THEY GET SO CARRIED AWAY BY THEIR OWN LITTLE PURSUITS, THAT THEY LOSE ALL TRACK OF TIME!
I'M SURE YOU'LL HEAR FROM HIM SOON!
TSK! HOW COULD THAT NIECE OF MINE HAVE CUT HER HAIR?
AND, WHILE WE'RE ON THE SUBJECT OF YOUNG PEOPLE--
DAD! WHAT A WONDERFUL SURPRISE!
THIS MEANS YOU'RE ALL WELL AGAIN!
NATURALLY! LOOK AT THE NURSE I HAD!
I THOUGHT I'D WALK YOU HOME, DEAR!
I'VE SOMETHING TO TELL YOU--!
WITH MY RECOVERY, MY MEMORY OF THE KINGPIN RETURNED!
I KNOW NOW THAT PETER DIDN'T REALLY ATTACK ME THAT DAY-- HE WAS TRYING TO HELP ME!*
OH, DAD! IS IT REALLY TRUE? CAN I BELIEVE IT?
DO YOU WANT TO BELIEVE IT, GWEN?
MORE THAN ANYTHING ELSE-- IN THE WORLD!
*AS SUPERBLY SHOWN IN SPIDER-MAN #60! --STURDY STAN.
IT'S TRUE, DARLING!
THEN PETER DIDN'T BETRAY US!
HE DIDN'T!
13

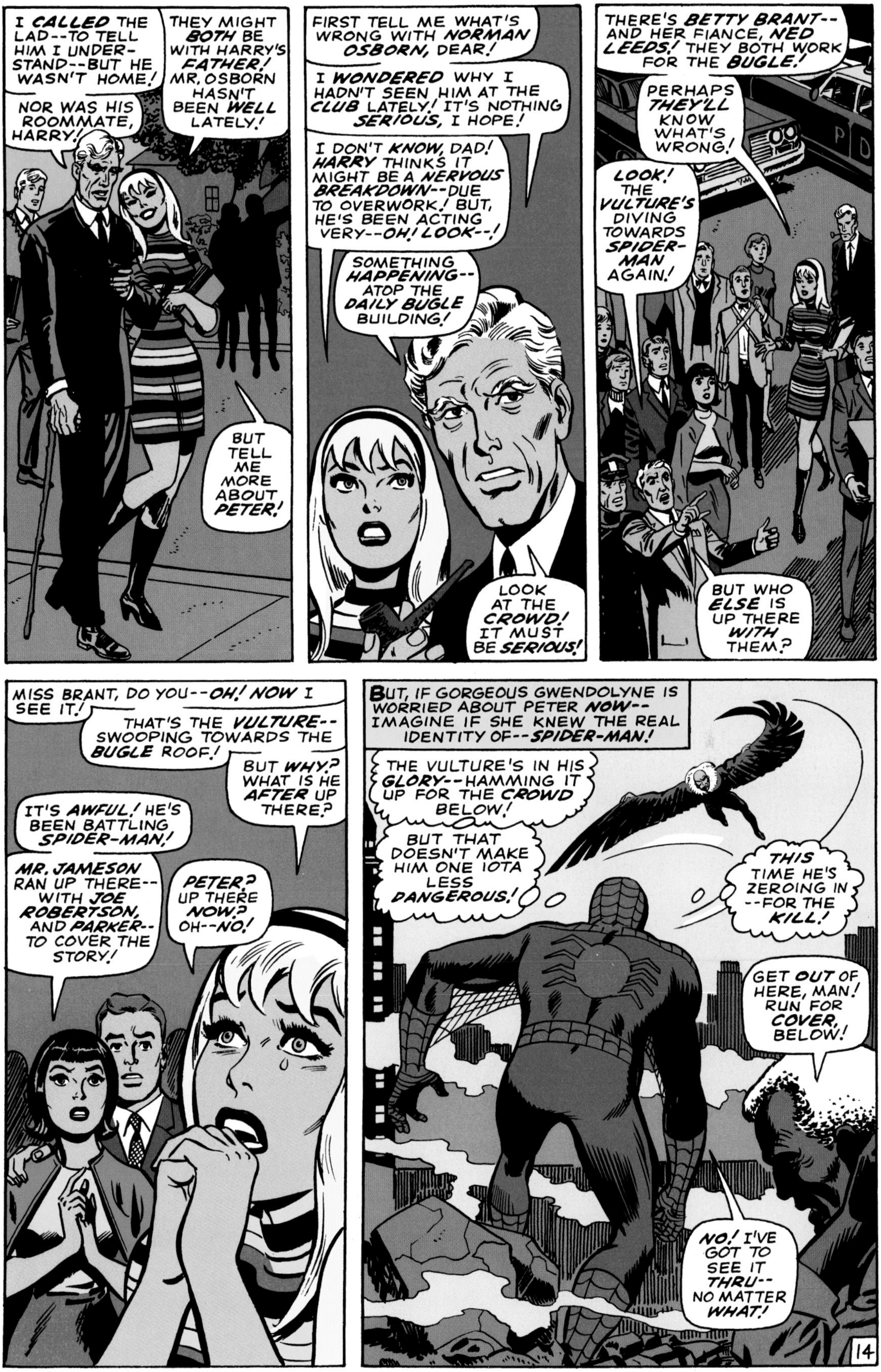
I CALLED THE LAD--TO TELL HIM I UNDERSTAND--BUT HE WASN'T HOME!
NOR WAS HIS ROOMMATE, HARRY!
THEY MIGHT BOTH BE WITH HARRY'S FATHER! MR. OSBORN HASN'T BEEN WELL LATELY!
BUT TELL ME MORE ABOUT PETER!
FIRST TELL ME WHAT'S WRONG WITH NORMAN OSBORN, DEAR!
I WONDERED WHY I HADN'T SEEN HIM AT THE CLUB LATELY! IT'S NOTHING SERIOUS, I HOPE!
I DON'T KNOW, DAD! HARRY THINKS IT MIGHT BE A NERVOUS BREAKDOWN--DUE TO OVERWORK! BUT, HE'S BEEN ACTING VERY--OH! LOOK--!
SOMETHING HAPPENING--ATOP THE DAILY BUGLE BUILDING!
LOOK AT THE CROWD! IT MUST BE SERIOUS!
THERE'S BETTY BRANT--AND HER FIANCE, NED LEEDS! THEY BOTH WORK FOR THE BUGLE!
PERHAPS THEY'LL KNOW WHAT'S WRONG!
LOOK! THE VULTURE'S DIVING TOWARDS SPIDER-MAN AGAIN!
BUT WHO ELSE IS UP THERE WITH THEM?
MISS BRANT, DO YOU--OH! NOW I SEE IT!
THAT'S THE VULTURE--SWOOPING TOWARDS THE BUGLE ROOF!
BUT WHY? WHAT IS HE AFTER UP THERE?
IT'S AWFUL! HE'S BEEN BATTLING SPIDER-MAN!
MR. JAMESON RAN UP THERE--WITH JOE ROBERTSON, AND PARKER--TO COVER THE STORY!
PETER? UP THERE NOW? OH--NO!
BUT, IF GORGEOUS GWENDOLYNE IS WORRIED ABOUT PETER NOW--IMAGINE IF SHE KNEW THE REAL IDENTITY OF--SPIDER-MAN!
THE VULTURE'S IN HIS GLORY--HAMMING IT UP FOR THE CROWD BELOW!
BUT THAT DOESN'T MAKE HIM ONE IOTA LESS DANGEROUS!
THIS TIME HE'S ZEROING IN--FOR THE KILL!
GET OUT OF HERE, MAN! RUN FOR COVER, BELOW!
NO! I'VE GOT TO SEE IT THRU--NO MATTER WHAT!
14

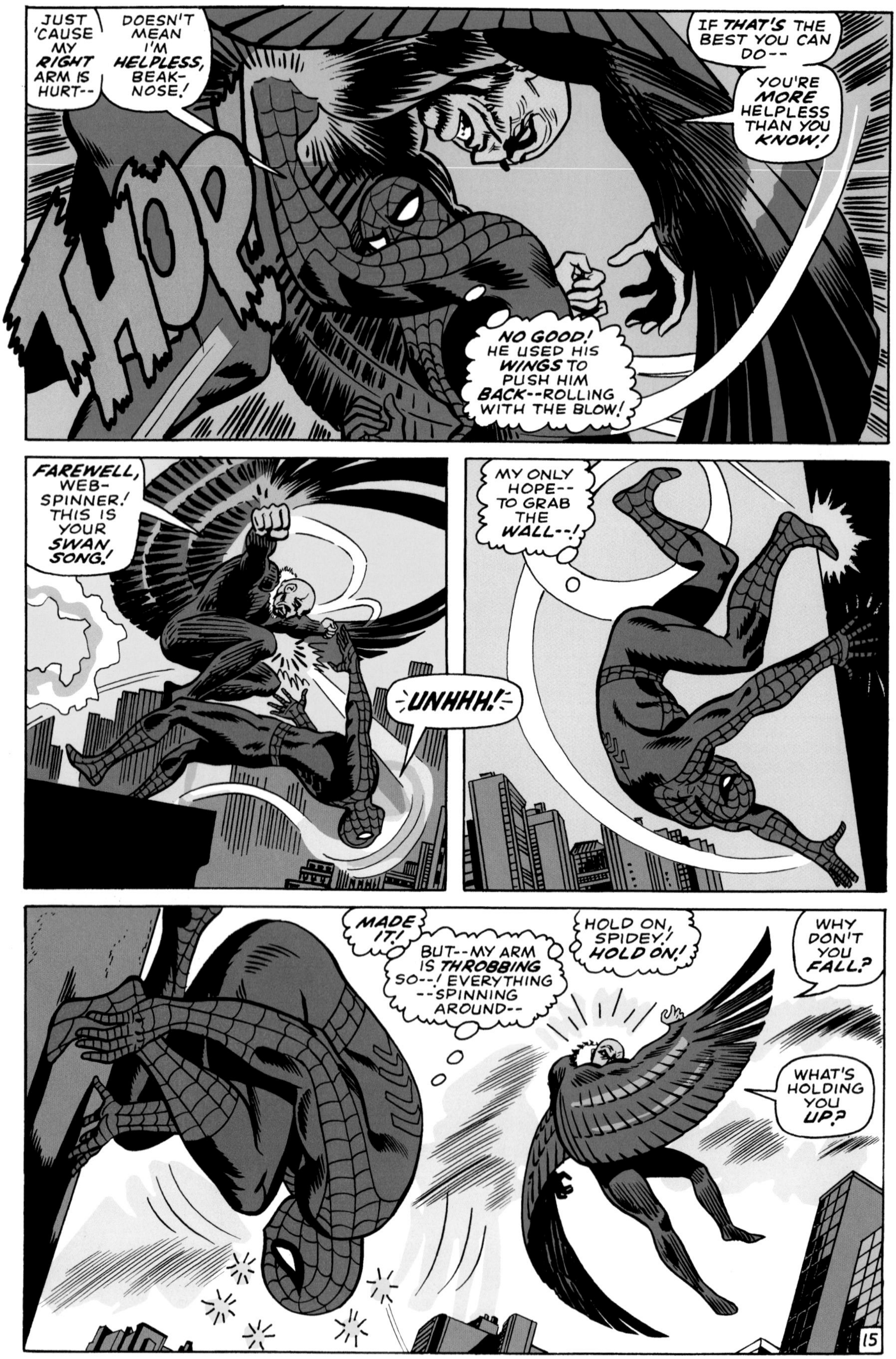
JUST 'CAUSE MY RIGHT ARM IS HURT--
DOESN'T MEAN I'M HELPLESS, BEAK-NOSE!
THOP
IF THAT'S THE BEST YOU CAN DO--
YOU'RE MORE HELPLESS THAN YOU KNOW!
NO GOOD! HE USED HIS WINGS TO PUSH HIM BACK--ROLLING WITH THE BLOW!
FAREWELL, WEB-SPINNER! THIS IS YOUR SWAN SONG!
UNHHH!
MY ONLY HOPE-- TO GRAB THE WALL--!
MADE IT!
BUT--MY ARM IS THROBBING SO--! EVERYTHING --SPINNING AROUND--
HOLD ON, SPIDEY! HOLD ON!
WHY DON'T YOU FALL?
WHAT'S HOLDING YOU UP?
15

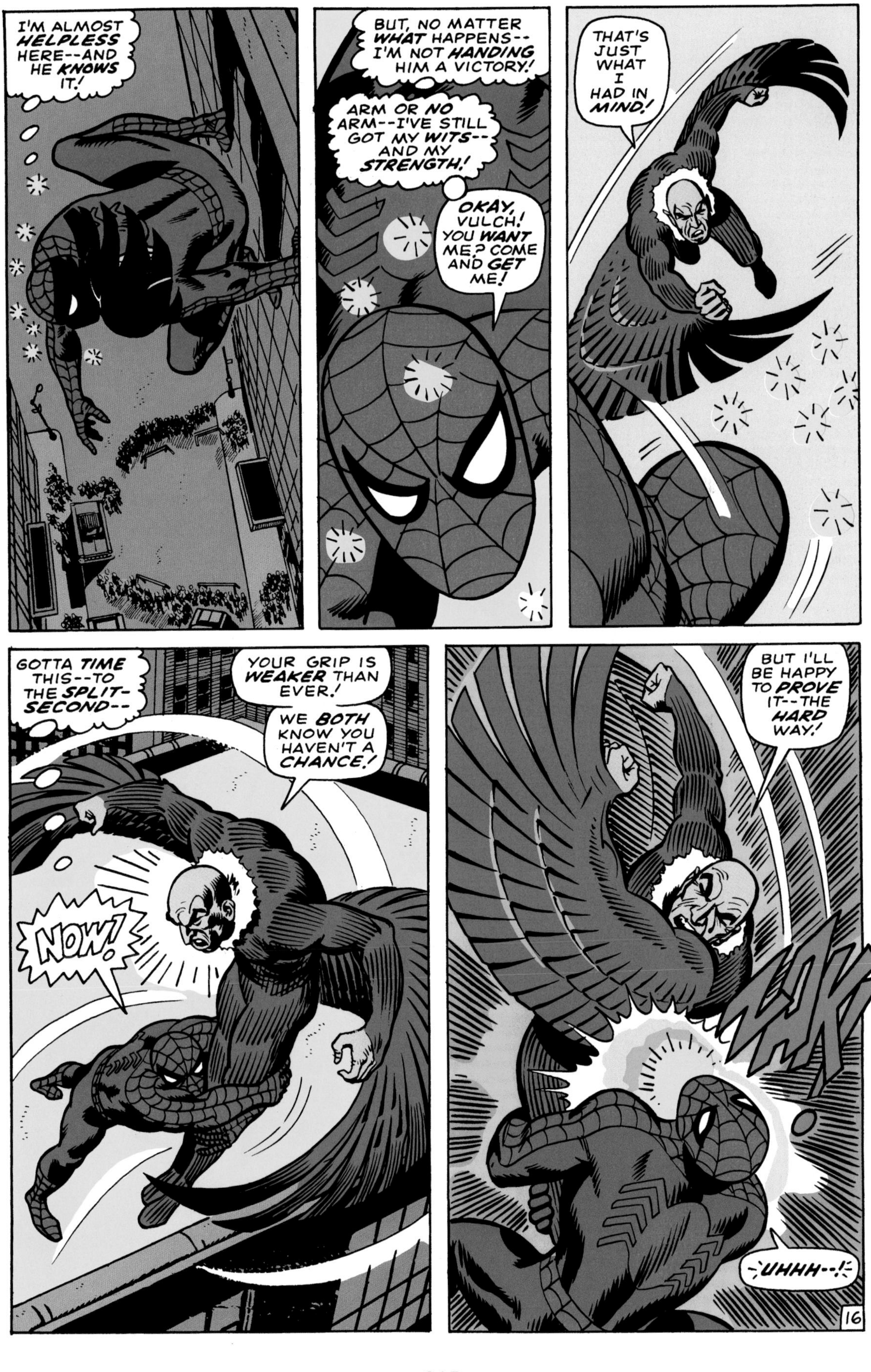
I'M ALMOST HELPLESS HERE--AND HE KNOWS IT!
BUT, NO MATTER WHAT HAPPENS--I'M NOT HANDING HIM A VICTORY!
ARM OR NO ARM--I'VE STILL GOT MY WITS--AND MY STRENGTH!
OKAY, VULCH! YOU WANT ME? COME AND GET ME!
THAT'S JUST WHAT I HAD IN MIND!
GOTTA TIME THIS--TO THE SPLIT-SECOND--
YOUR GRIP IS WEAKER THAN EVER!
WE BOTH KNOW YOU HAVEN'T A CHANCE!
NOW!
BUT I'LL BE HAPPY TO PROVE IT--THE HARD WAY!
-UHHH--!-
16

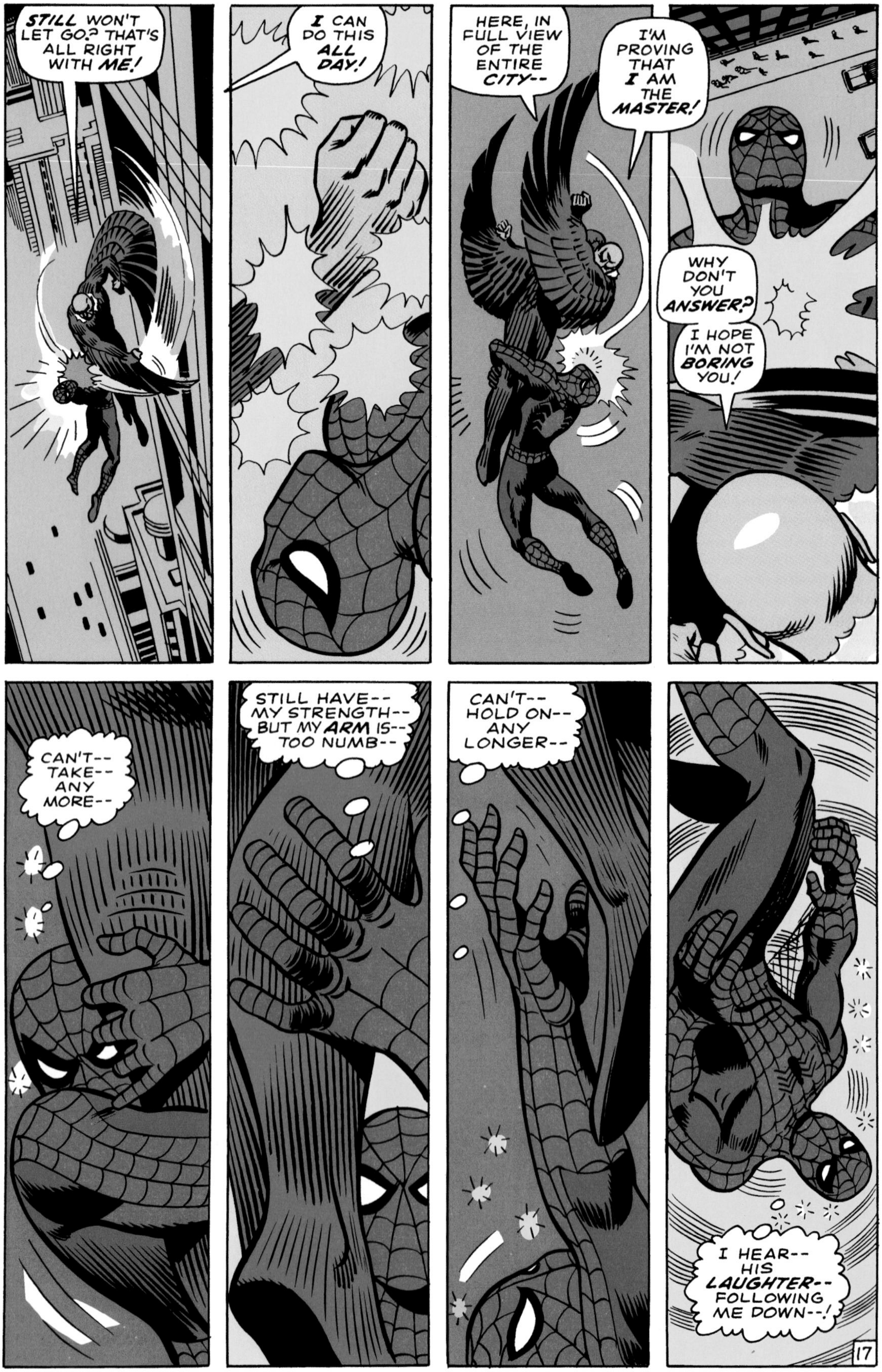
STILL WON'T LET GO? THAT'S ALL RIGHT WITH ME!
I CAN DO THIS ALL DAY!
HERE, IN FULL VIEW OF THE ENTIRE CITY--
I'M PROVING THAT I AM THE MASTER!
WHY DON'T YOU ANSWER?
I HOPE I'M NOT BORING YOU!
CAN'T-- TAKE-- ANY MORE--
STILL HAVE-- MY STRENGTH-- BUT MY ARM IS-- TOO NUMB--
CAN'T-- HOLD ON-- ANY LONGER--
I HEAR-- HIS LAUGHTER-- FOLLOWING ME DOWN--!
17

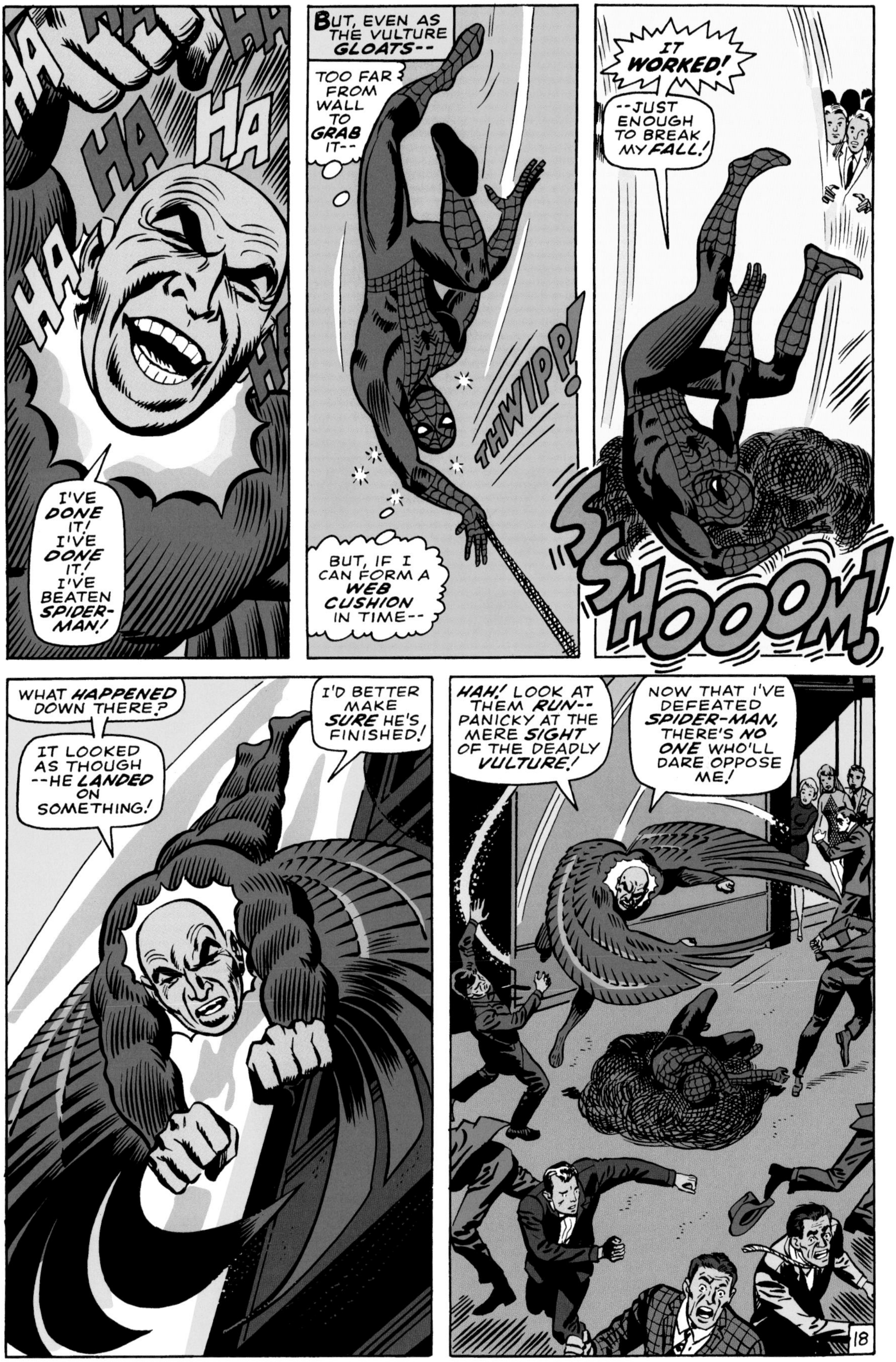
HA HA HA HA HA HA HA HA
I'VE DONE IT! I'VE DONE IT! I'VE BEATEN SPIDER-MAN!
BUT, EVEN AS THE VULTURE GLOATS--
TOO FAR FROM WALL TO GRAB IT--
BUT, IF I CAN FORM A WEB CUSHION IN TIME--
THWIPP!
IT WORKED!
--JUST ENOUGH TO BREAK MY FALL!
SSHOOOM!
WHAT HAPPENED DOWN THERE?
IT LOOKED AS THOUGH --HE LANDED ON SOMETHING!
I'D BETTER MAKE SURE HE'S FINISHED!
HAH! LOOK AT THEM RUN-- PANICKY AT THE MERE SIGHT OF THE DEADLY VULTURE!
NOW THAT I'VE DEFEATED SPIDER-MAN, THERE'S NO ONE WHO'LL DARE OPPOSE ME!
18

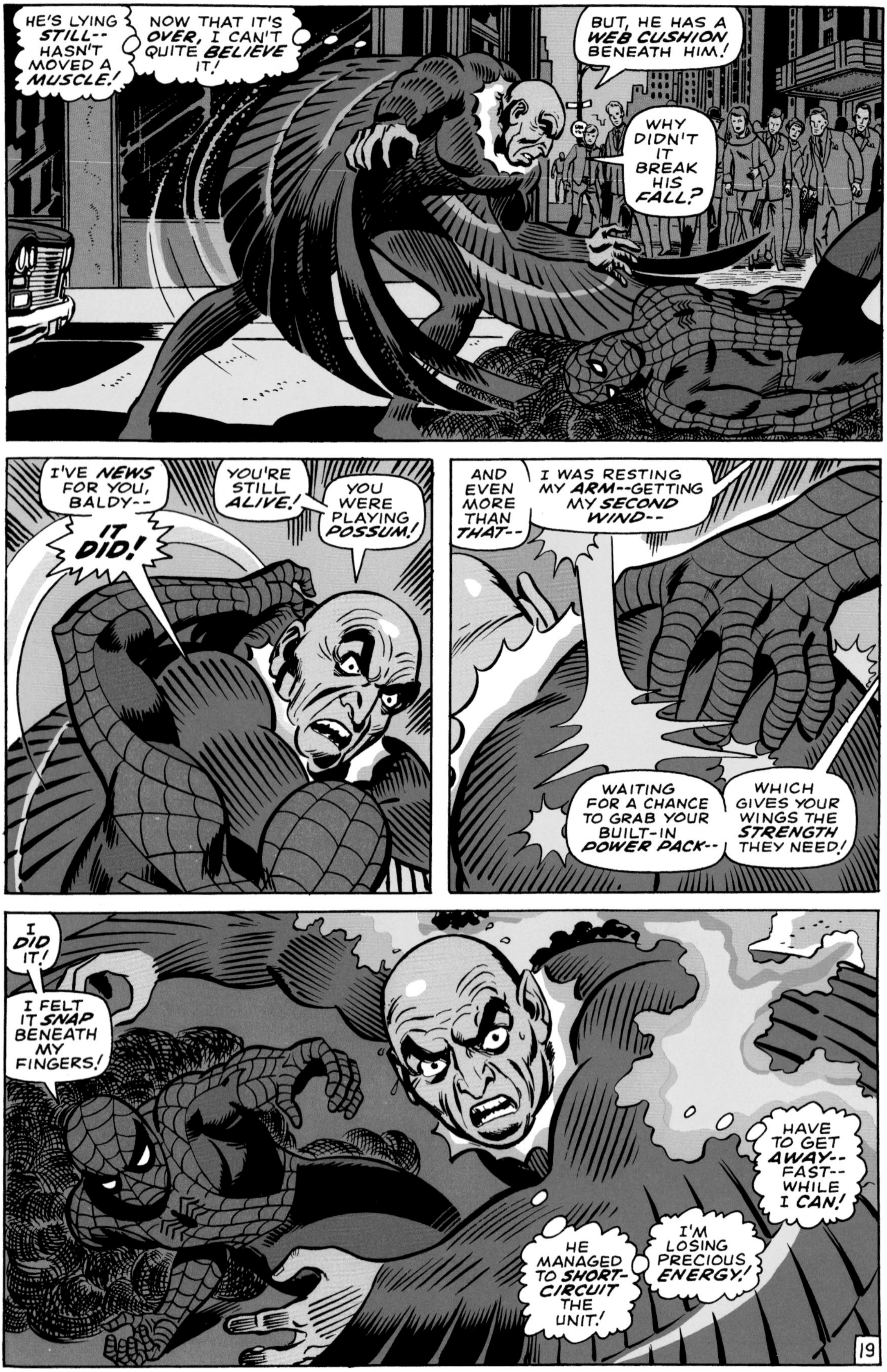
HE'S LYING STILL-- HASN'T MOVED A MUSCLE!
NOW THAT IT'S OVER, I CAN'T QUITE BELIEVE IT!
BUT, HE HAS A WEB CUSHION BENEATH HIM!
WHY DIDN'T IT BREAK HIS FALL?
I'VE NEWS FOR YOU, BALDY--
IT DID!
YOU'RE STILL ALIVE!
YOU WERE PLAYING POSSUM!
AND EVEN MORE THAN THAT--
I WAS RESTING MY ARM--GETTING MY SECOND WIND--
WAITING FOR A CHANCE TO GRAB YOUR BUILT-IN POWER PACK--
WHICH GIVES YOUR WINGS THE STRENGTH THEY NEED!
I DID IT!
I FELT IT SNAP BENEATH MY FINGERS!
HAVE TO GET AWAY-- FAST-- WHILE I CAN!
I'M LOSING PRECIOUS ENERGY!
HE MANAGED TO SHORT-CIRCUIT THE UNIT!
19

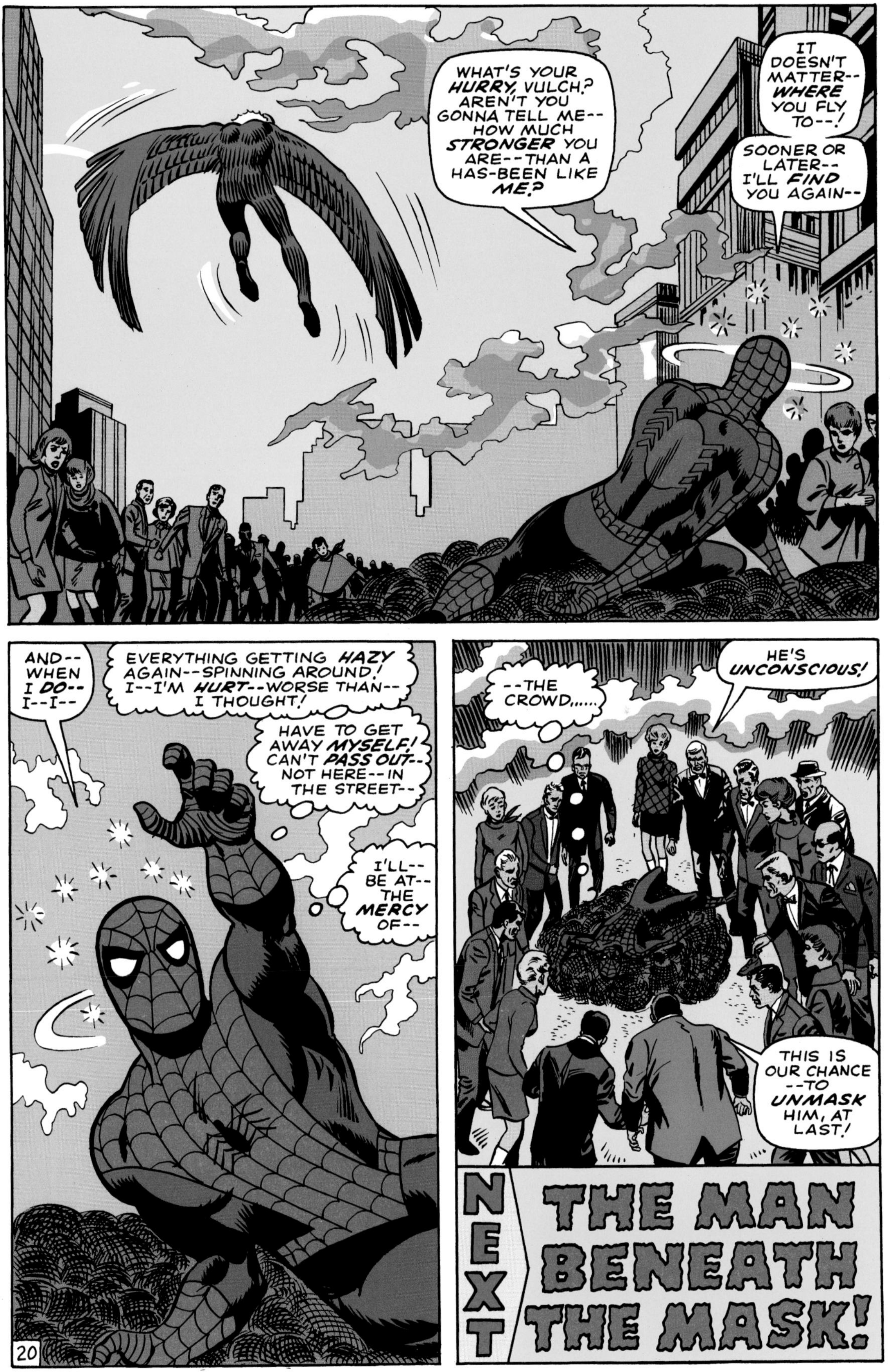

WHAT'S YOUR HURRY, VULCH? AREN'T YOU GONNA TELL ME-- HOW MUCH STRONGER YOU ARE--THAN A HAS-BEEN LIKE ME?
IT DOESN'T MATTER-- WHERE YOU FLY TO--!
SOONER OR LATER-- I'LL FIND YOU AGAIN--
AND-- WHEN I DO-- I--I--
EVERYTHING GETTING HAZY AGAIN--SPINNING AROUND! I--I'M HURT--WORSE THAN-- I THOUGHT!
HAVE TO GET AWAY MYSELF! CAN'T PASS OUT-- NOT HERE--IN THE STREET--
I'LL-- BE AT-- THE MERCY OF--
20
--THE CROWD,.....
HE'S UNCONSCIOUS!
THIS IS OUR CHANCE --TO UNMASK HIM, AT LAST!
NEXT
THE MAN BENEATH THE MASK!

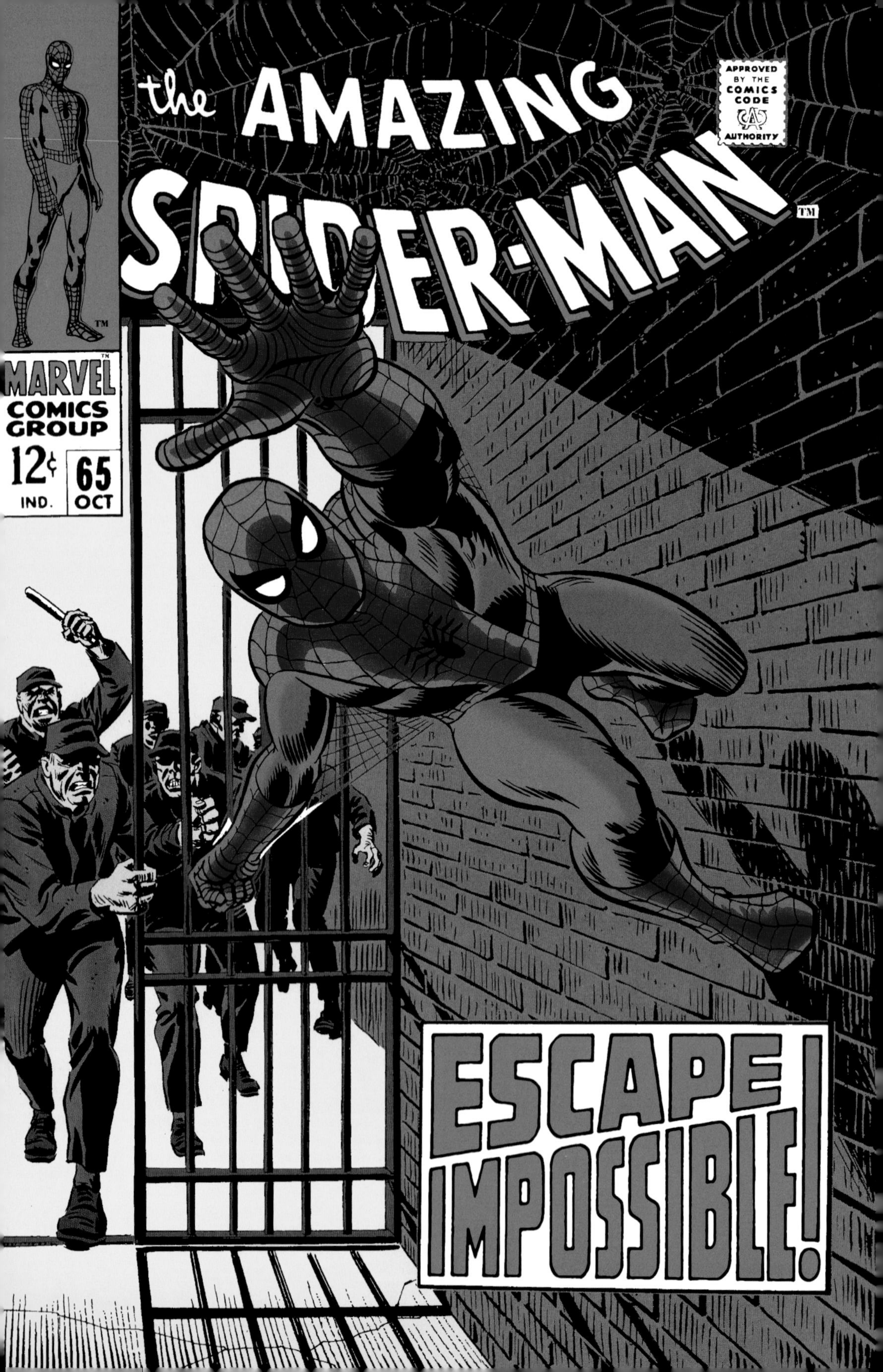
the AMAZING
SPIDER-MAN™
APPROVED BY THE COMICS CODE AUTHORITY
MARVEL™ COMICS GROUP
12¢ IND.
65 OCT
ESCAPE IMPOSSIBLE!

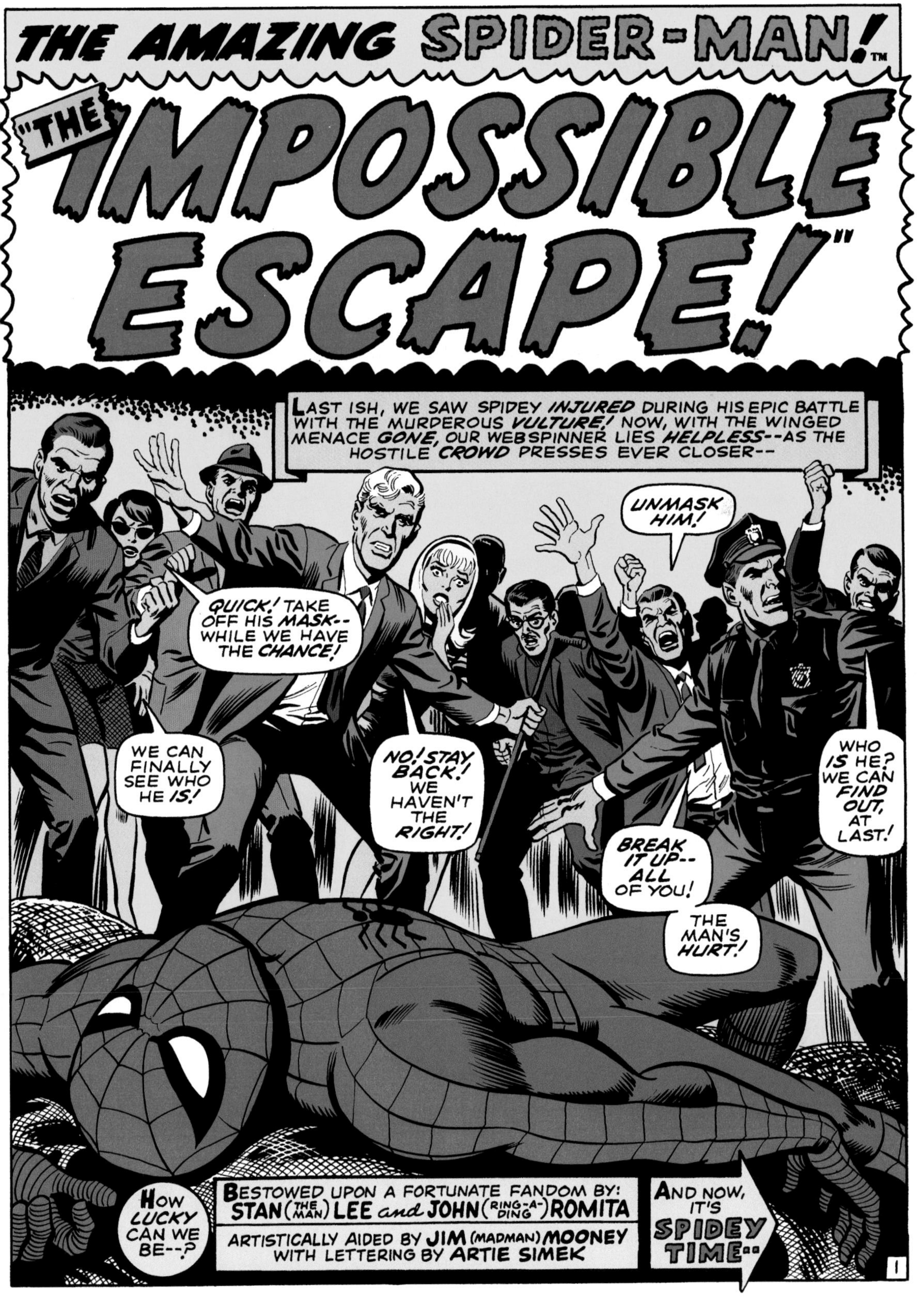
THE AMAZING SPIDER-MAN!
"THE IMPOSSIBLE ESCAPE!"
LAST ISH, WE SAW SPIDEY INJURED DURING HIS EPIC BATTLE WITH THE MURDEROUS VULTURE! NOW, WITH THE WINGED MENACE GONE, OUR WEBSPINNER LIES HELPLESS--AS THE HOSTILE CROWD PRESSES EVER CLOSER--
QUICK! TAKE OFF HIS MASK-- WHILE WE HAVE THE CHANCE!
UNMASK HIM!
WE CAN FINALLY SEE WHO HE IS!
NO! STAY BACK! WE HAVEN'T THE RIGHT!
WHO IS HE? WE CAN FIND OUT, AT LAST!
BREAK IT UP-- ALL OF YOU!
THE MAN'S HURT!
HOW LUCKY CAN WE BE--?
BESTOWED UPON A FORTUNATE FANDOM BY: STAN (THE MAN) LEE and JOHN (RING-A-DING) ROMITA
ARTISTICALLY AIDED BY JIM (MADMAN) MOONEY WITH LETTERING BY ARTIE SIMEK
AND NOW, IT'S SPIDEY TIME..
1

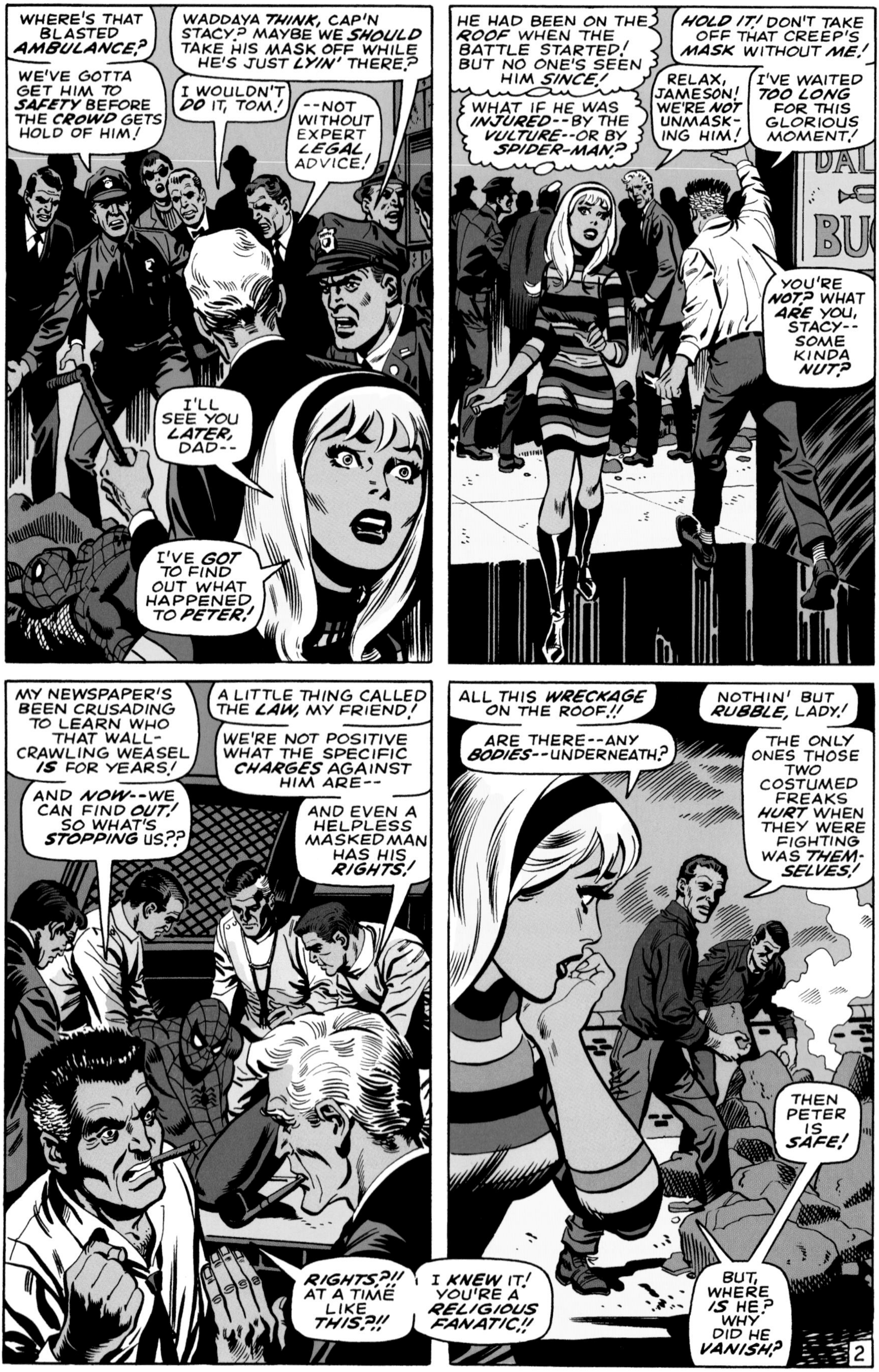
WHERE'S THAT BLASTED AMBULANCE?
WE'VE GOTTA GET HIM TO SAFETY BEFORE THE CROWD GETS HOLD OF HIM!
WADDAYA THINK, CAP'N STACY? MAYBE WE SHOULD TAKE HIS MASK OFF WHILE HE'S JUST LYIN' THERE?
I WOULDN'T DO IT, TOM!
--NOT WITHOUT EXPERT LEGAL ADVICE!
I'LL SEE YOU LATER, DAD--
I'VE GOT TO FIND OUT WHAT HAPPENED TO PETER!
HE HAD BEEN ON THE ROOF WHEN THE BATTLE STARTED! BUT NO ONE'S SEEN HIM SINCE!
WHAT IF HE WAS INJURED--BY THE VULTURE--OR BY SPIDER-MAN?
HOLD IT! DON'T TAKE OFF THAT CREEP'S MASK WITHOUT ME!
RELAX, JAMESON! WE'RE NOT UNMASKING HIM!
I'VE WAITED TOO LONG FOR THIS GLORIOUS MOMENT!
YOU'RE NOT? WHAT ARE YOU, STACY--SOME KINDA NUT?
MY NEWSPAPER'S BEEN CRUSADING TO LEARN WHO THAT WALL-CRAWLING WEASEL IS FOR YEARS!
AND NOW--WE CAN FIND OUT! SO WHAT'S STOPPING US??
A LITTLE THING CALLED THE LAW, MY FRIEND!
WE'RE NOT POSITIVE WHAT THE SPECIFIC CHARGES AGAINST HIM ARE--
AND EVEN A HELPLESS MASKED MAN HAS HIS RIGHTS!
RIGHTS?!! AT A TIME LIKE THIS?!!
I KNEW IT! YOU'RE A RELIGIOUS FANATIC!!
ALL THIS WRECKAGE ON THE ROOF!!
ARE THERE--ANY BODIES--UNDERNEATH?
NOTHIN' BUT RUBBLE, LADY!
THE ONLY ONES THOSE TWO COSTUMED FREAKS HURT WHEN THEY WERE FIGHTING WAS THEMSELVES!
THEN PETER IS SAFE!
BUT, WHERE IS HE? WHY DID HE VANISH?
2

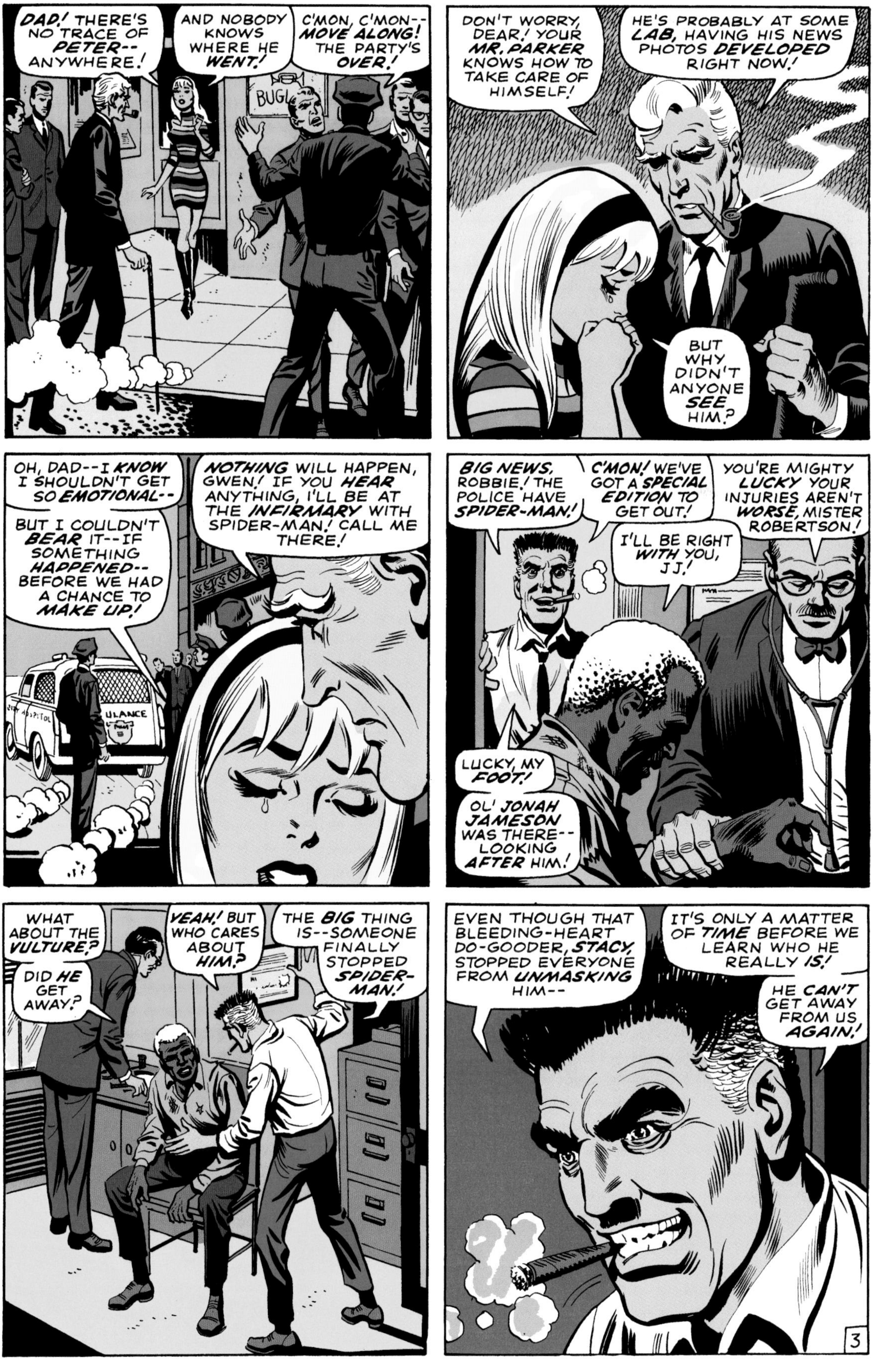
DAD! THERE'S NO TRACE OF PETER--ANYWHERE!
AND NOBODY KNOWS WHERE HE WENT!
C'MON, C'MON--MOVE ALONG! THE PARTY'S OVER!
BUGL
DON'T WORRY, DEAR! YOUR MR. PARKER KNOWS HOW TO TAKE CARE OF HIMSELF!
HE'S PROBABLY AT SOME LAB, HAVING HIS NEWS PHOTOS DEVELOPED RIGHT NOW!
BUT WHY DIDN'T ANYONE SEE HIM?
OH, DAD--I KNOW I SHOULDN'T GET SO EMOTIONAL--
BUT I COULDN'T BEAR IT--IF SOMETHING HAPPENED--BEFORE WE HAD A CHANCE TO MAKE UP!
NOTHING WILL HAPPEN, GWEN! IF YOU HEAR ANYTHING, I'LL BE AT THE INFIRMARY WITH SPIDER-MAN! CALL ME THERE!
ULANCE
BIG NEWS, ROBBIE! THE POLICE HAVE SPIDER-MAN!
C'MON! WE'VE GOT A SPECIAL EDITION TO GET OUT!
YOU'RE MIGHTY LUCKY YOUR INJURIES AREN'T WORSE, MISTER ROBERTSON!
I'LL BE RIGHT WITH YOU, JJ!
LUCKY, MY FOOT!
OL' JONAH JAMESON WAS THERE--LOOKING AFTER HIM!
WHAT ABOUT THE VULTURE?
DID HE GET AWAY?
YEAH! BUT WHO CARES ABOUT HIM?
THE BIG THING IS--SOMEONE FINALLY STOPPED SPIDER-MAN!
EVEN THOUGH THAT BLEEDING-HEART DO-GOODER, STACY, STOPPED EVERYONE FROM UNMASKING HIM--
IT'S ONLY A MATTER OF TIME BEFORE WE LEARN WHO HE REALLY IS!
HE CAN'T GET AWAY FROM US AGAIN!
3

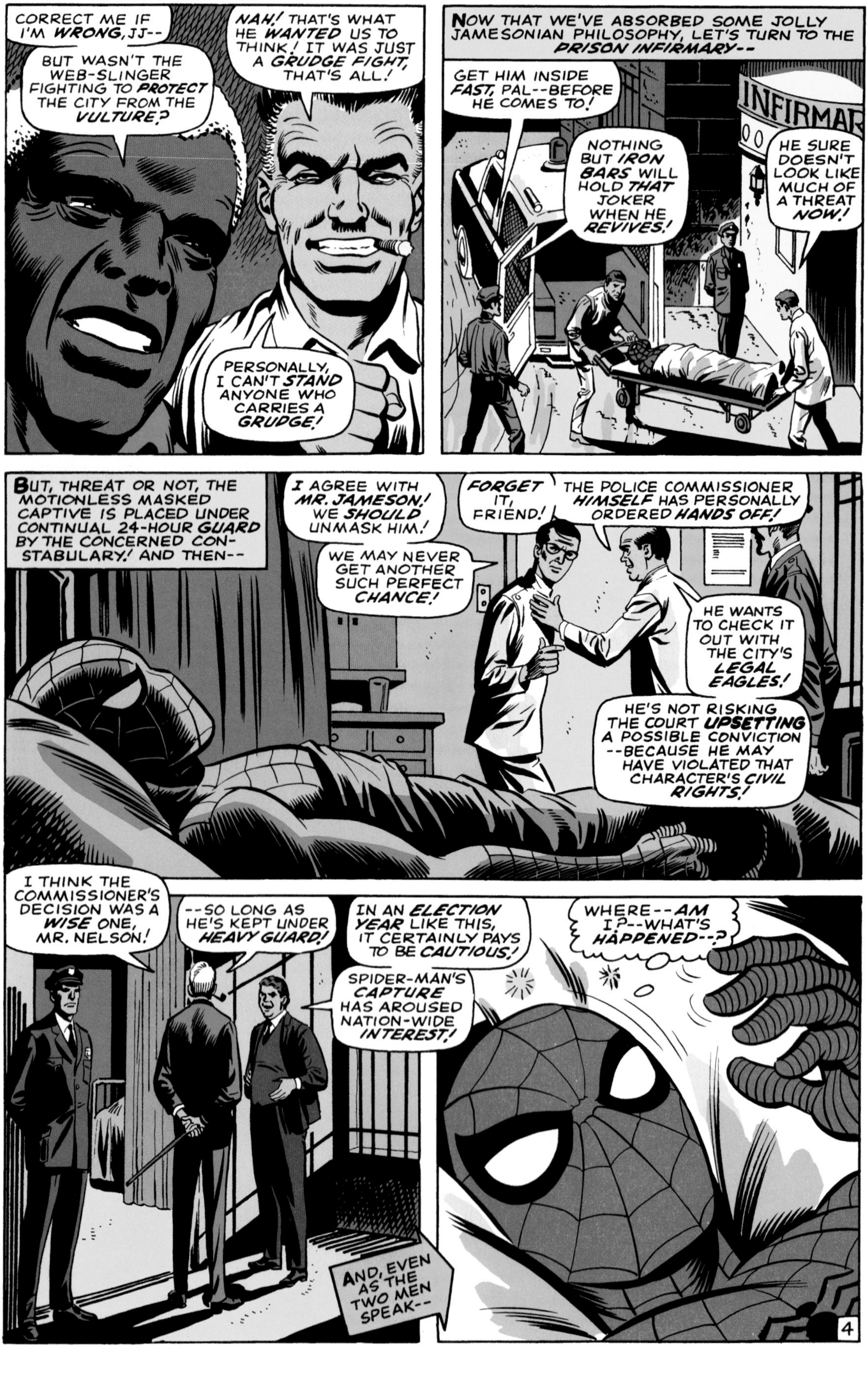
CORRECT ME IF I'M WRONG, JJ--
BUT WASN'T THE WEB-SLINGER FIGHTING TO PROTECT THE CITY FROM THE VULTURE?
NAH! THAT'S WHAT HE WANTED US TO THINK! IT WAS JUST A GRUDGE FIGHT, THAT'S ALL!
PERSONALLY, I CAN'T STAND ANYONE WHO CARRIES A GRUDGE!
NOW THAT WE'VE ABSORBED SOME JOLLY JAMESONIAN PHILOSOPHY, LET'S TURN TO THE PRISON INFIRMARY--
GET HIM INSIDE FAST, PAL--BEFORE HE COMES TO!
INFIRMAR
NOTHING BUT IRON BARS WILL HOLD THAT JOKER WHEN HE REVIVES!
HE SURE DOESN'T LOOK LIKE MUCH OF A THREAT NOW!
BUT, THREAT OR NOT, THE MOTIONLESS MASKED CAPTIVE IS PLACED UNDER CONTINUAL 24-HOUR GUARD BY THE CONCERNED CONSTABULARY! AND THEN--
I AGREE WITH MR. JAMESON! WE SHOULD UNMASK HIM!
WE MAY NEVER GET ANOTHER SUCH PERFECT CHANCE!
FORGET IT, FRIEND!
THE POLICE COMMISSIONER HIMSELF HAS PERSONALLY ORDERED HANDS OFF!
HE WANTS TO CHECK IT OUT WITH THE CITY'S LEGAL EAGLES!
HE'S NOT RISKING THE COURT UPSETTING A POSSIBLE CONVICTION --BECAUSE HE MAY HAVE VIOLATED THAT CHARACTER'S CIVIL RIGHTS!
I THINK THE COMMISSIONER'S DECISION WAS A WISE ONE, MR. NELSON!
--SO LONG AS HE'S KEPT UNDER HEAVY GUARD!
IN AN ELECTION YEAR LIKE THIS, IT CERTAINLY PAYS TO BE CAUTIOUS!
SPIDER-MAN'S CAPTURE HAS AROUSED NATION-WIDE INTEREST!
AND, EVEN AS THE TWO MEN SPEAK--
WHERE--AM I?--WHAT'S HAPPENED--?
4

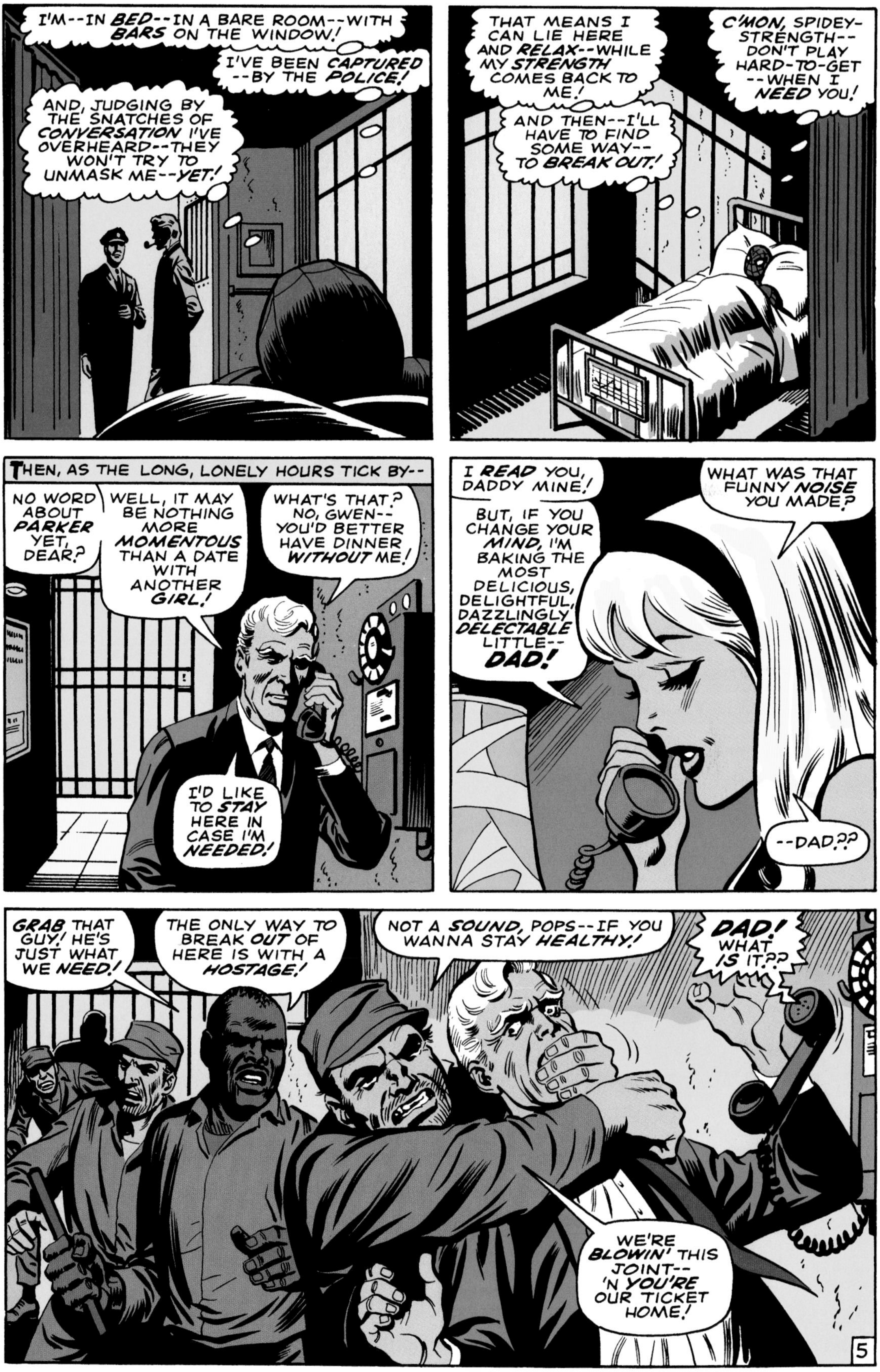
I'M--IN BED--IN A BARE ROOM--WITH BARS ON THE WINDOW!
I'VE BEEN CAPTURED--BY THE POLICE!
AND, JUDGING BY THE SNATCHES OF CONVERSATION I'VE OVERHEARD--THEY WON'T TRY TO UNMASK ME--YET!
THAT MEANS I CAN LIE HERE AND RELAX--WHILE MY STRENGTH COMES BACK TO ME!
AND THEN--I'LL HAVE TO FIND SOME WAY--TO BREAK OUT!
C'MON, SPIDEY-STRENGTH--DON'T PLAY HARD-TO-GET--WHEN I NEED YOU!
THEN, AS THE LONG, LONELY HOURS TICK BY--
NO WORD ABOUT PARKER YET, DEAR?
WELL, IT MAY BE NOTHING MORE MOMENTOUS THAN A DATE WITH ANOTHER GIRL!
WHAT'S THAT? NO, GWEN--YOU'D BETTER HAVE DINNER WITHOUT ME!
I'D LIKE TO STAY HERE IN CASE I'M NEEDED!
I READ YOU, DADDY MINE!
BUT, IF YOU CHANGE YOUR MIND, I'M BAKING THE MOST DELICIOUS, DELIGHTFUL, DAZZLINGLY DELECTABLE LITTLE--
DAD!
WHAT WAS THAT FUNNY NOISE YOU MADE?
--DAD??
GRAB THAT GUY! HE'S JUST WHAT WE NEED!
THE ONLY WAY TO BREAK OUT OF HERE IS WITH A HOSTAGE!
NOT A SOUND, POPS--IF YOU WANNA STAY HEALTHY!
DAD! WHAT IS IT??
WE'RE BLOWIN' THIS JOINT--'N YOU'RE OUR TICKET HOME!
5

IT SOUNDS LIKE--SOME SORT OF A *SCUFFLE!*

DAD! ARE YOU ALL RIGHT! WHY DON'T YOU ANSWER? *DAD!*

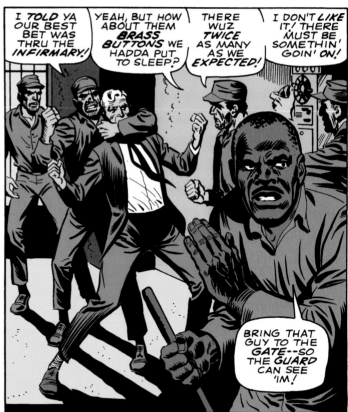

I *TOLD* YA OUR BEST BET WAS THRU THE *INFIRMARY!*

YEAH, BUT HOW ABOUT THEM *BRASS BUTTONS* WE HADDA PUT TO SLEEP?

THERE WUZ *TWICE* AS MANY AS WE *EXPECTED!*

I DON'T *LIKE* IT! THERE *MUST* BE SOMETHIN' GOIN' ON!

BRING THAT GUY TO THE *GATE*--SO THE *GUARD* CAN SEE 'IM!

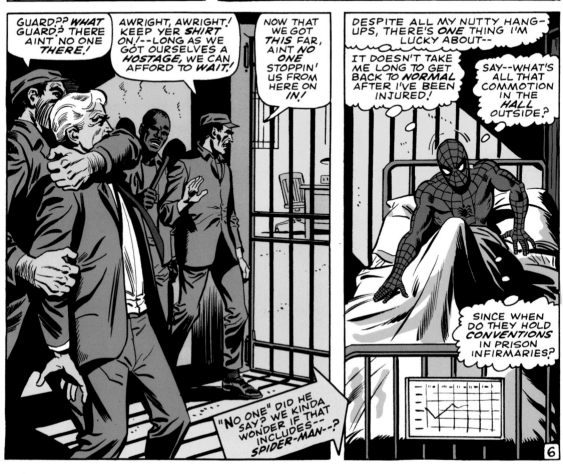

GUARD?? *WHAT* GUARD? THERE AINT NO ONE *THERE!*

AWRIGHT, AWRIGHT! KEEP YER *SHIRT* ON!--LONG AS WE GOT OURSELVES A *HOSTAGE,* WE CAN AFFORD TO *WAIT!*

NOW THAT WE GOT *THIS* FAR, AIN'T *NO ONE* STOPPIN' US FROM HERE ON *IN!*

"NO ONE" DID HE SAY? WE KINDA WONDER IF THAT INCLUDES--? *SPIDER-MAN--?*

DESPITE ALL MY NUTTY HANG-UPS, THERE'S *ONE* THING I'M LUCKY ABOUT--

IT DOESN'T TAKE ME LONG TO GET BACK TO *NORMAL* AFTER I'VE BEEN INJURED!

SAY--WHAT'S ALL THAT COMMOTION IN THE *HALL* OUTSIDE?

SINCE WHEN DO THEY HOLD *CONVENTIONS* IN PRISON INFIRMARIES?

6

326

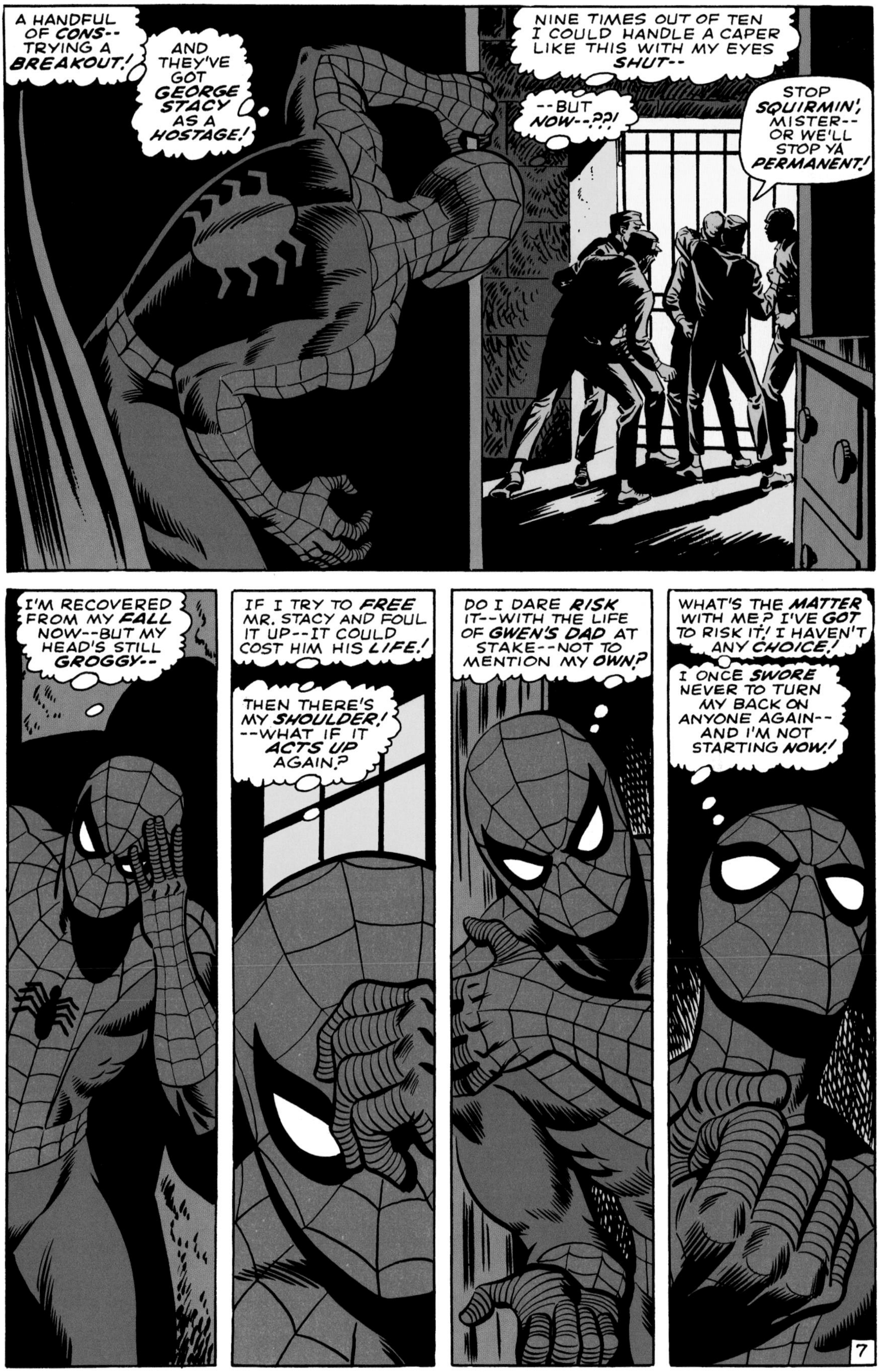
A HANDFUL OF CONS--TRYING A BREAKOUT!
AND THEY'VE GOT GEORGE STACY AS A HOSTAGE!
NINE TIMES OUT OF TEN I COULD HANDLE A CAPER LIKE THIS WITH MY EYES SHUT--
--BUT NOW--??!
STOP SQUIRMIN', MISTER--OR WE'LL STOP YA PERMANENT!
I'M RECOVERED FROM MY FALL NOW--BUT MY HEAD'S STILL GROGGY--
IF I TRY TO FREE MR. STACY AND FOUL IT UP--IT COULD COST HIM HIS LIFE!
THEN THERE'S MY SHOULDER! --WHAT IF IT ACTS UP AGAIN?
DO I DARE RISK IT--WITH THE LIFE OF GWEN'S DAD AT STAKE--NOT TO MENTION MY OWN?
WHAT'S THE MATTER WITH ME? I'VE GOT TO RISK IT! I HAVEN'T ANY CHOICE!
I ONCE SWORE NEVER TO TURN MY BACK ON ANYONE AGAIN--AND I'M NOT STARTING NOW!
7

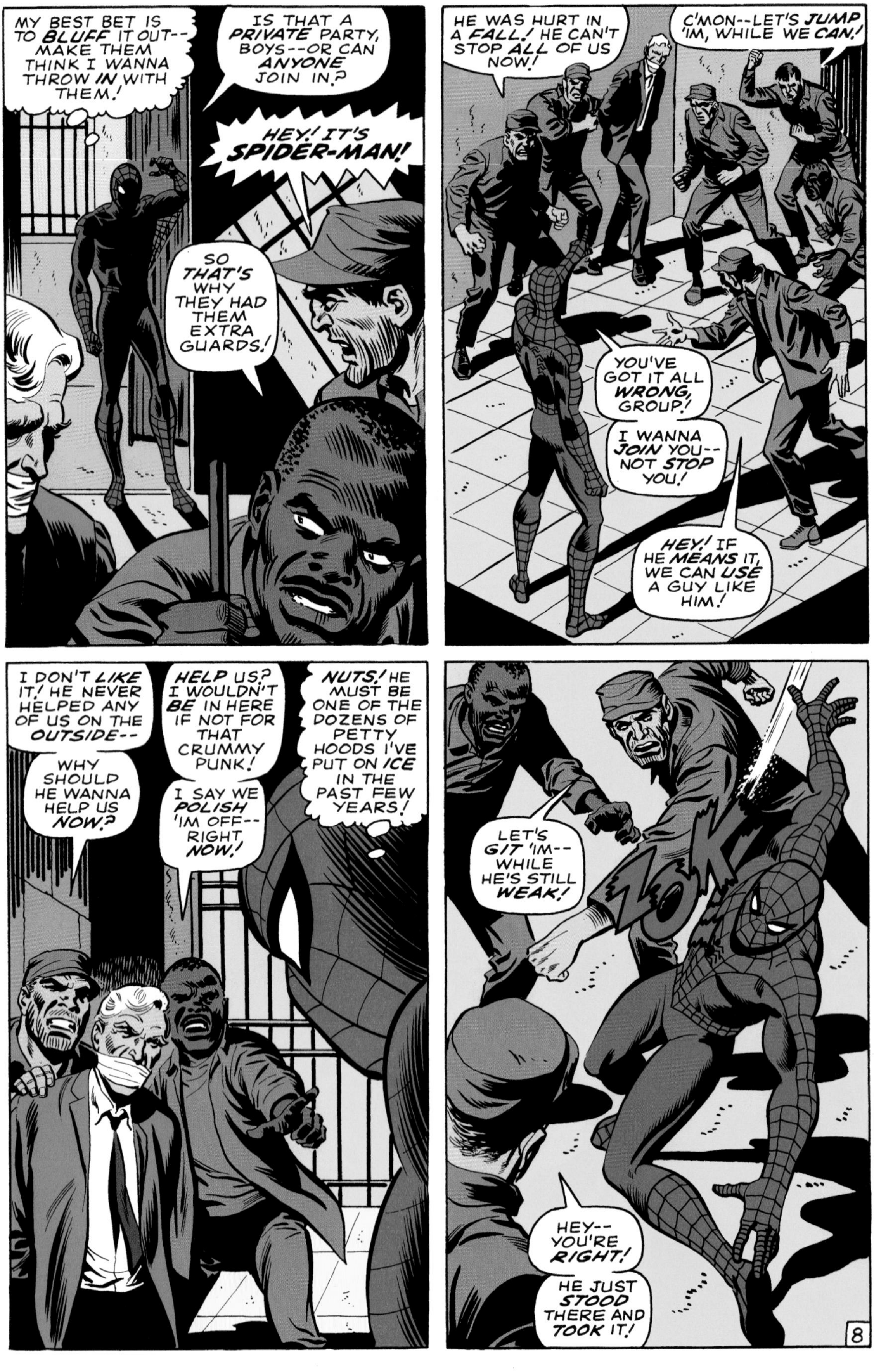

MY BEST BET IS TO BLUFF IT OUT--MAKE THEM THINK I WANNA THROW IN WITH THEM!
IS THAT A PRIVATE PARTY, BOYS--OR CAN ANYONE JOIN IN?
HEY! IT'S SPIDER-MAN!
SO THAT'S WHY THEY HAD THEM EXTRA GUARDS!
HE WAS HURT IN A FALL! HE CAN'T STOP ALL OF US NOW!
C'MON--LET'S JUMP 'IM, WHILE WE CAN!
YOU'VE GOT IT ALL WRONG, GROUP!
I WANNA JOIN YOU--NOT STOP YOU!
HEY! IF HE MEANS IT, WE CAN USE A GUY LIKE HIM!
I DON'T LIKE IT! HE NEVER HELPED ANY OF US ON THE OUTSIDE--
WHY SHOULD HE WANNA HELP US NOW?
HELP US? I WOULDN'T BE IN HERE IF NOT FOR THAT CRUMMY PUNK!
I SAY WE POLISH 'IM OFF--RIGHT NOW!
NUTS! HE MUST BE ONE OF THE DOZENS OF PETTY HOODS I'VE PUT ON ICE IN THE PAST FEW YEARS!
LET'S GIT 'IM--WHILE HE'S STILL WEAK!
ZOK!
HEY--YOU'RE RIGHT!
HE JUST STOOD THERE AND TOOK IT!
8

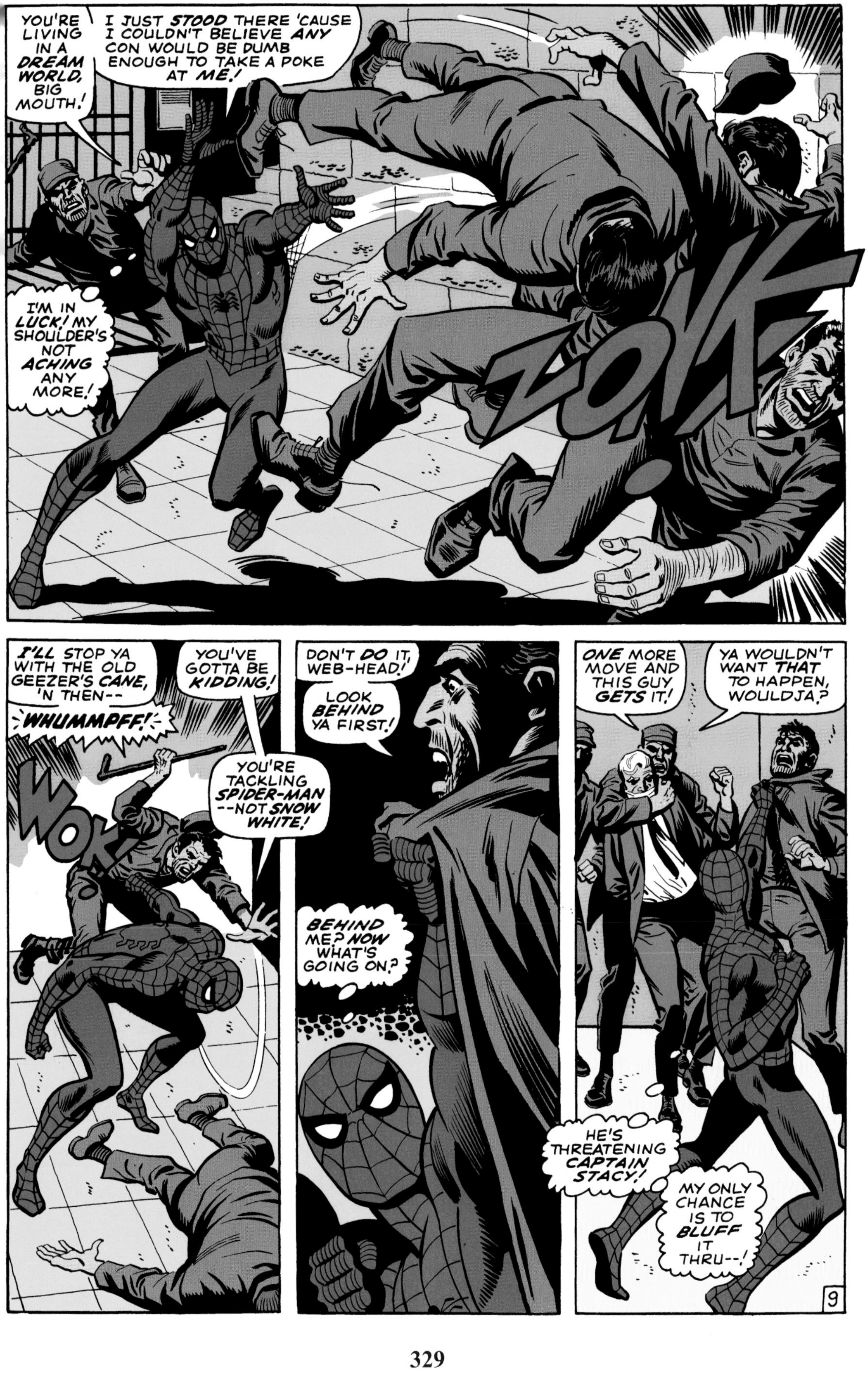
YOU'RE LIVING IN A DREAM WORLD, BIG MOUTH!
I JUST STOOD THERE 'CAUSE I COULDN'T BELIEVE ANY CON WOULD BE DUMB ENOUGH TO TAKE A POKE AT ME!
I'M IN LUCK! MY SHOULDER'S NOT ACHING ANY MORE!
ZOK!
I'LL STOP YA WITH THE OLD GEEZER'S CANE, 'N THEN--
WHUMMPFF!
WOK!
YOU'VE GOTTA BE KIDDING!
YOU'RE TACKLING SPIDER-MAN --NOT SNOW WHITE!
DON'T DO IT, WEB-HEAD!
LOOK BEHIND YA FIRST!
BEHIND ME? NOW WHAT'S GOING ON?
ONE MORE MOVE AND THIS GUY GETS IT!
YA WOULDN'T WANT THAT TO HAPPEN, WOULDJA?
HE'S THREATENING CAPTAIN STACY!
MY ONLY CHANCE IS TO BLUFF IT THRU--!
9

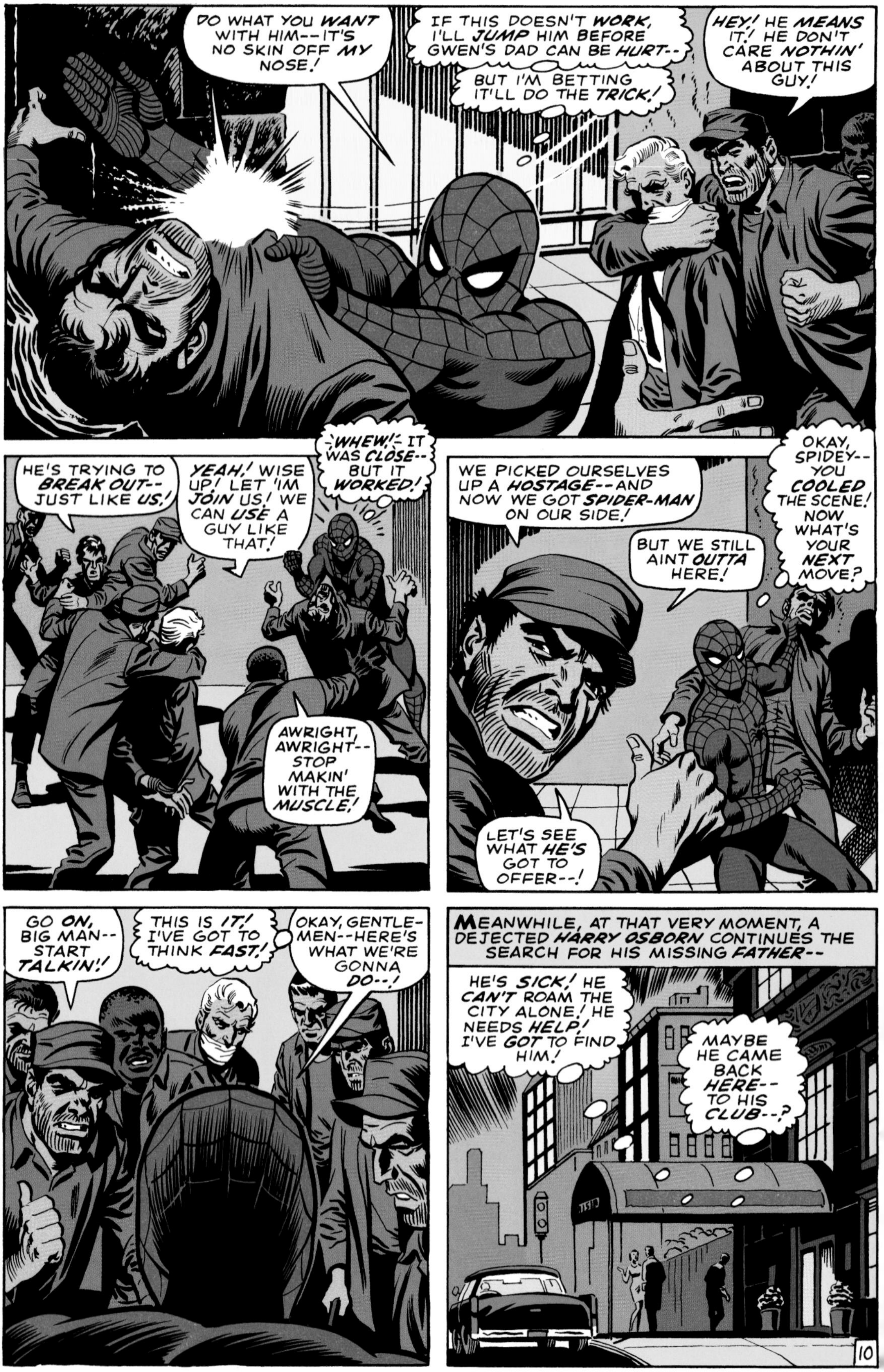
DO WHAT YOU WANT WITH HIM--IT'S NO SKIN OFF MY NOSE!
IF THIS DOESN'T WORK, I'LL JUMP HIM BEFORE GWEN'S DAD CAN BE HURT--
BUT I'M BETTING IT'LL DO THE TRICK!
HEY! HE MEANS IT! HE DON'T CARE NOTHIN' ABOUT THIS GUY!
HE'S TRYING TO BREAK OUT--JUST LIKE US!
YEAH! WISE UP! LET 'IM JOIN US! WE CAN USE A GUY LIKE THAT!
-WHEW!- IT WAS CLOSE--BUT IT WORKED!
AWRIGHT, AWRIGHT--STOP MAKIN' WITH THE MUSCLE!
WE PICKED OURSELVES UP A HOSTAGE--AND NOW WE GOT SPIDER-MAN ON OUR SIDE!
BUT WE STILL AINT OUTTA HERE!
OKAY, SPIDEY--YOU COOLED THE SCENE! NOW WHAT'S YOUR NEXT MOVE?
LET'S SEE WHAT HE'S GOT TO OFFER--!
GO ON, BIG MAN--START TALKIN'!
THIS IS IT! I'VE GOT TO THINK FAST!
OKAY, GENTLE-MEN--HERE'S WHAT WE'RE GONNA DO--!
MEANWHILE, AT THAT VERY MOMENT, A DEJECTED HARRY OSBORN CONTINUES THE SEARCH FOR HIS MISSING FATHER--
HE'S SICK! HE CAN'T ROAM THE CITY ALONE! HE NEEDS HELP! I'VE GOT TO FIND HIM!
MAYBE HE CAME BACK HERE--TO HIS CLUB--?
10

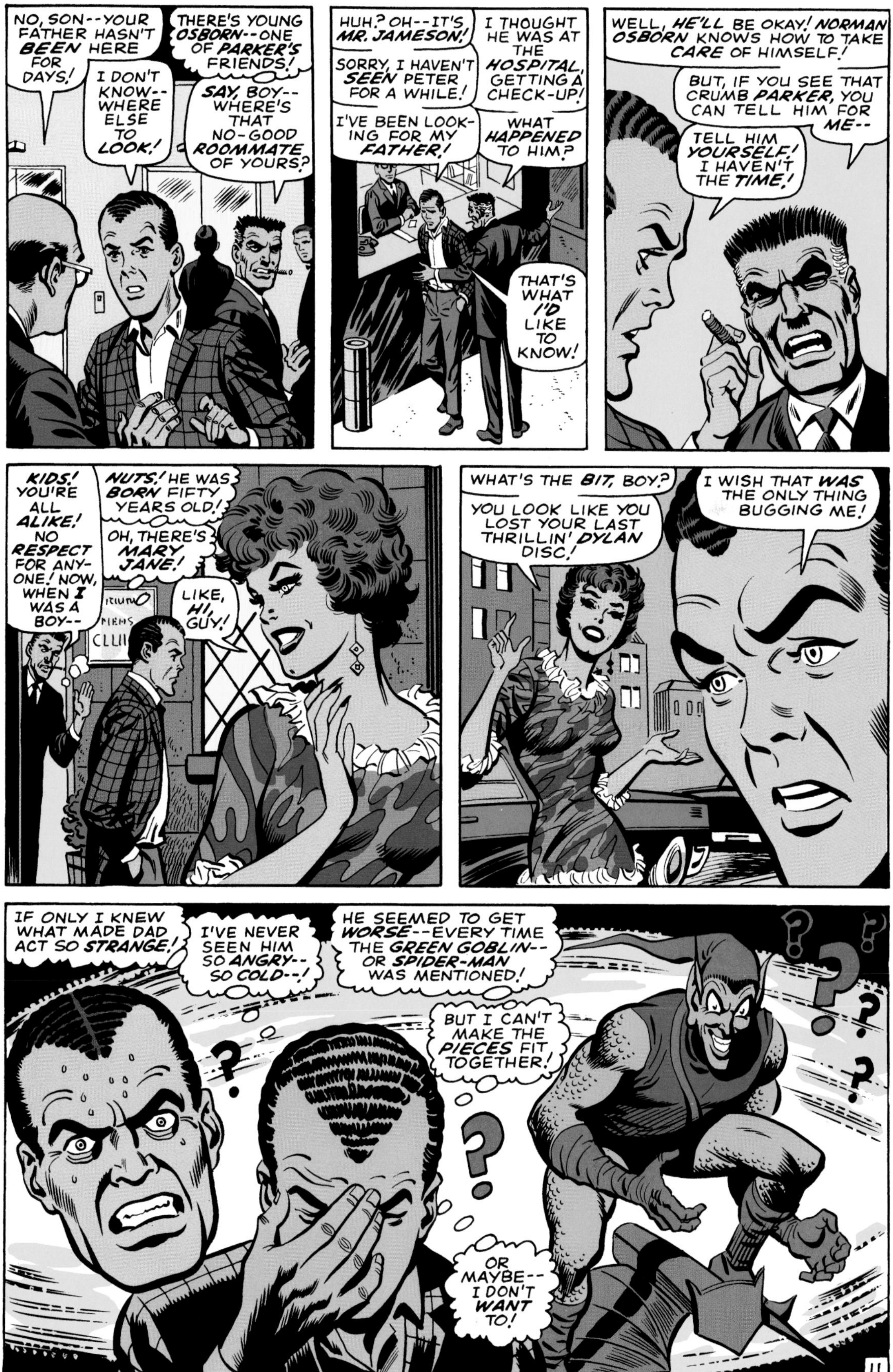
NO, SON--YOUR FATHER HASN'T BEEN HERE FOR DAYS!
I DON'T KNOW--WHERE ELSE TO LOOK!
THERE'S YOUNG OSBORN--ONE OF PARKER'S FRIENDS!
SAY, BOY--WHERE'S THAT NO-GOOD ROOMMATE OF YOURS?
HUH? OH--IT'S MR. JAMESON!
SORRY, I HAVEN'T SEEN PETER FOR A WHILE!
I'VE BEEN LOOKING FOR MY FATHER!
I THOUGHT HE WAS AT THE HOSPITAL, GETTING A CHECK-UP!
WHAT HAPPENED TO HIM?
THAT'S WHAT I'D LIKE TO KNOW!
WELL, HE'LL BE OKAY! NORMAN OSBORN KNOWS HOW TO TAKE CARE OF HIMSELF!
BUT, IF YOU SEE THAT CRUMB PARKER, YOU CAN TELL HIM FOR ME--
TELL HIM YOURSELF! I HAVEN'T THE TIME!
KIDS! YOU'RE ALL ALIKE! NO RESPECT FOR ANYONE! NOW, WHEN I WAS A BOY--
NUTS! HE WAS BORN FIFTY YEARS OLD!
OH, THERE'S MARY JANE!
LIKE, HI, GUY!
WHAT'S THE BIT, BOY?
YOU LOOK LIKE YOU LOST YOUR LAST THRILLIN' DYLAN DISC!
I WISH THAT WAS THE ONLY THING BUGGING ME!
IF ONLY I KNEW WHAT MADE DAD ACT SO STRANGE!
I'VE NEVER SEEN HIM SO ANGRY--SO COLD--!
HE SEEMED TO GET WORSE--EVERY TIME THE GREEN GOBLIN--OR SPIDER-MAN WAS MENTIONED!
BUT I CAN'T MAKE THE PIECES FIT TOGETHER!
OR MAYBE--I DON'T WANT TO!
11

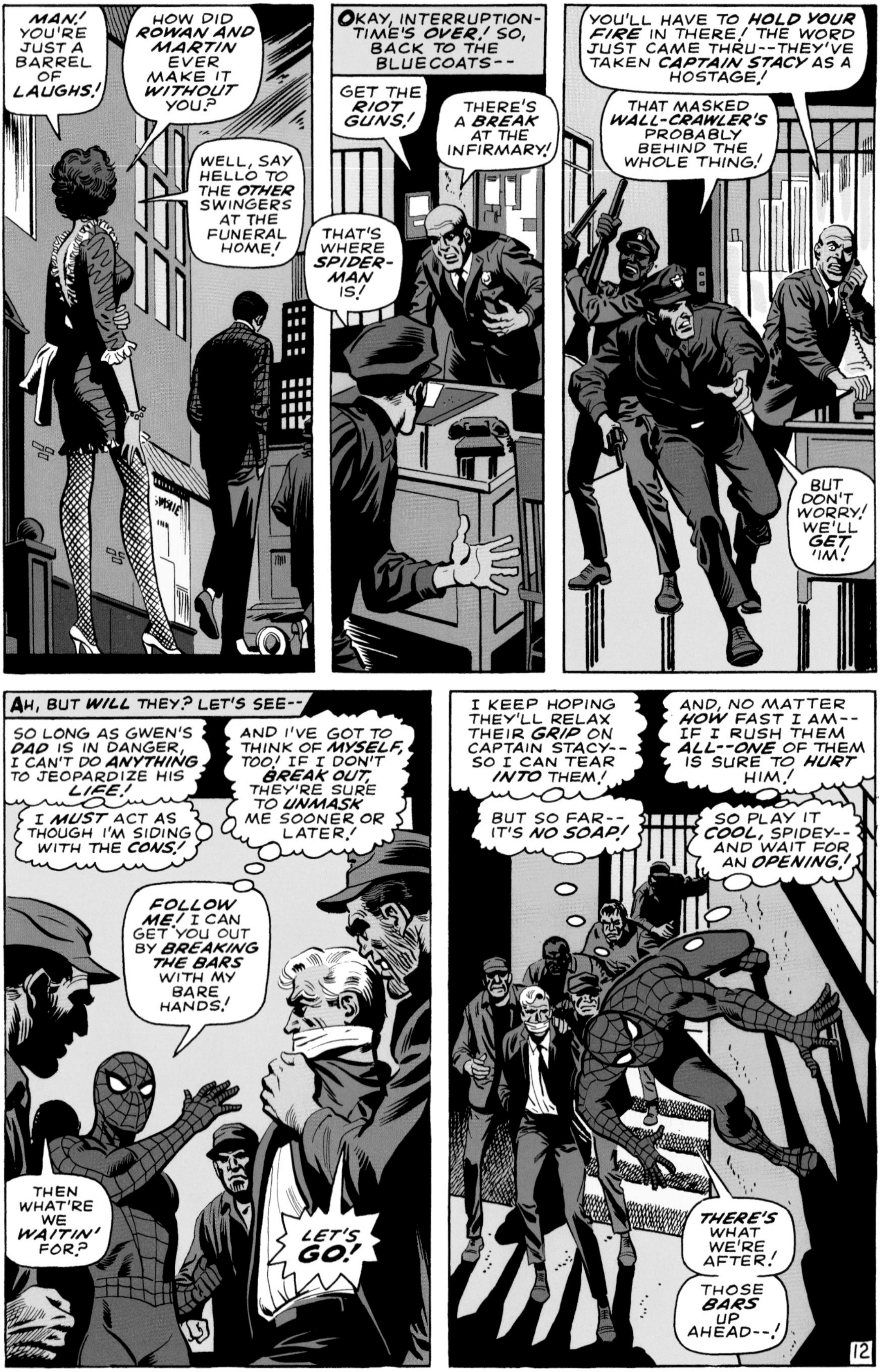
MAN! YOU'RE JUST A BARREL OF LAUGHS!
HOW DID ROWAN AND MARTIN EVER MAKE IT WITHOUT YOU?
WELL, SAY HELLO TO THE OTHER SWINGERS AT THE FUNERAL HOME!
OKAY, INTERRUPTION-TIME'S OVER! SO, BACK TO THE BLUECOATS--
GET THE RIOT GUNS!
THERE'S A BREAK AT THE INFIRMARY!
THAT'S WHERE SPIDER-MAN IS!
YOU'LL HAVE TO HOLD YOUR FIRE IN THERE! THE WORD JUST CAME THRU--THEY'VE TAKEN CAPTAIN STACY AS A HOSTAGE!
THAT MASKED WALL-CRAWLER'S PROBABLY BEHIND THE WHOLE THING!
BUT DON'T WORRY! WE'LL GET 'IM!
AH, BUT WILL THEY? LET'S SEE--
SO LONG AS GWEN'S DAD IS IN DANGER, I CAN'T DO ANYTHING TO JEOPARDIZE HIS LIFE!
I MUST ACT AS THOUGH I'M SIDING WITH THE CONS!
AND I'VE GOT TO THINK OF MYSELF, TOO! IF I DON'T BREAK OUT, THEY'RE SURE TO UNMASK ME SOONER OR LATER!
FOLLOW ME! I CAN GET YOU OUT BY BREAKING THE BARS WITH MY BARE HANDS!
THEN WHAT'RE WE WAITIN' FOR?
LET'S GO!
I KEEP HOPING THEY'LL RELAX THEIR GRIP ON CAPTAIN STACY--SO I CAN TEAR INTO THEM!
AND, NO MATTER HOW FAST I AM--IF I RUSH THEM ALL--ONE OF THEM IS SURE TO HURT HIM!
BUT SO FAR--IT'S NO SOAP!
SO PLAY IT COOL, SPIDEY--AND WAIT FOR AN OPENING!
THERE'S WHAT WE'RE AFTER!
THOSE BARS UP AHEAD--!
12

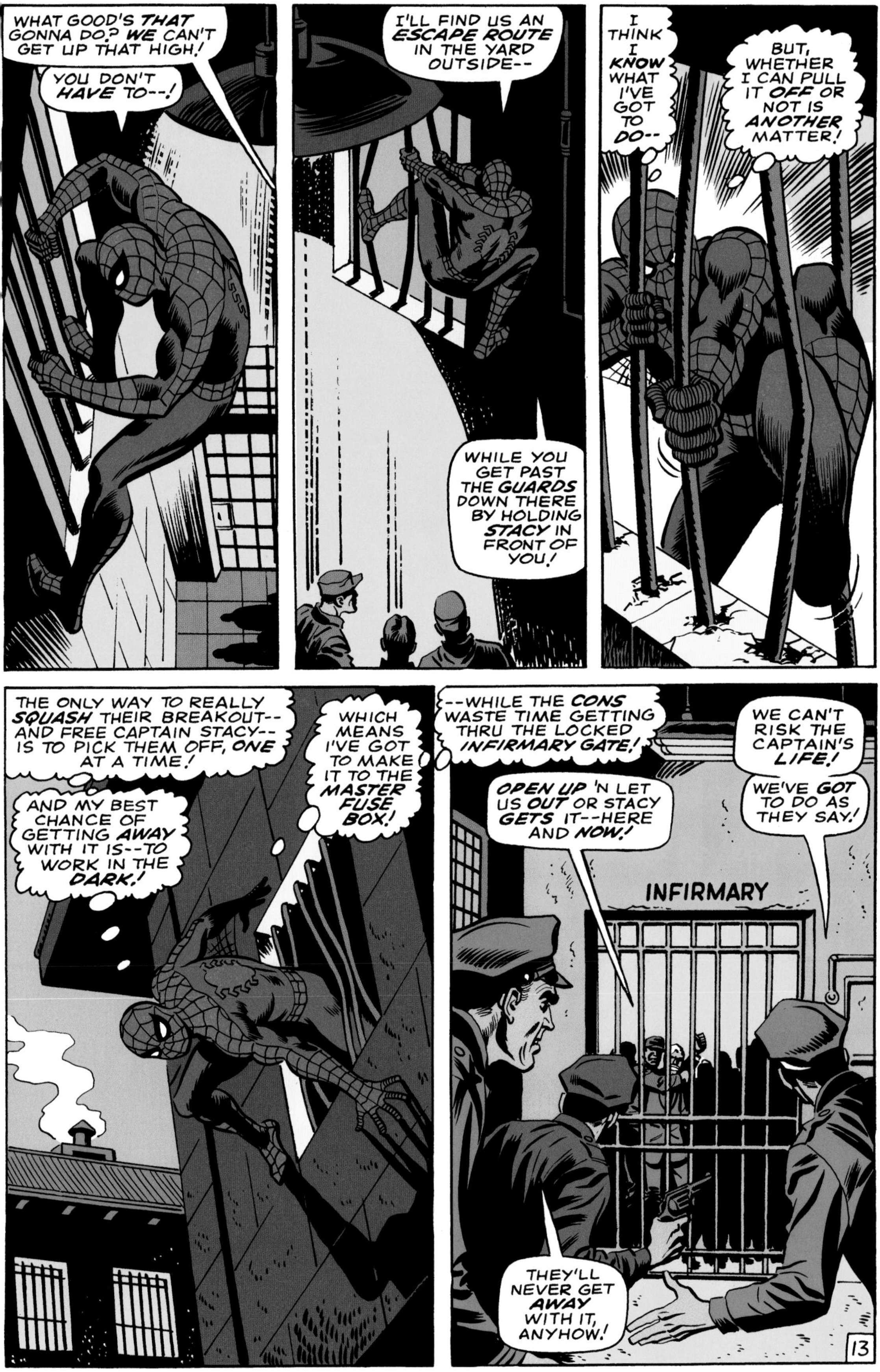
WHAT GOOD'S THAT GONNA DO? WE CAN'T GET UP THAT HIGH!
YOU DON'T HAVE TO--!
I'LL FIND US AN ESCAPE ROUTE IN THE YARD OUTSIDE--
WHILE YOU GET PAST THE GUARDS DOWN THERE BY HOLDING STACY IN FRONT OF YOU!
I THINK I KNOW WHAT I'VE GOT TO DO--
BUT, WHETHER I CAN PULL IT OFF OR NOT IS ANOTHER MATTER!
THE ONLY WAY TO REALLY SQUASH THEIR BREAKOUT--AND FREE CAPTAIN STACY--IS TO PICK THEM OFF, ONE AT A TIME!
AND MY BEST CHANCE OF GETTING AWAY WITH IT IS--TO WORK IN THE DARK!
WHICH MEANS I'VE GOT TO MAKE IT TO THE MASTER FUSE BOX!
--WHILE THE CONS WASTE TIME GETTING THRU THE LOCKED INFIRMARY GATE!
OPEN UP 'N LET US OUT OR STACY GETS IT--HERE AND NOW!
WE CAN'T RISK THE CAPTAIN'S LIFE!
WE'VE GOT TO DO AS THEY SAY!
INFIRMARY
THEY'LL NEVER GET AWAY WITH IT, ANYHOW!
13

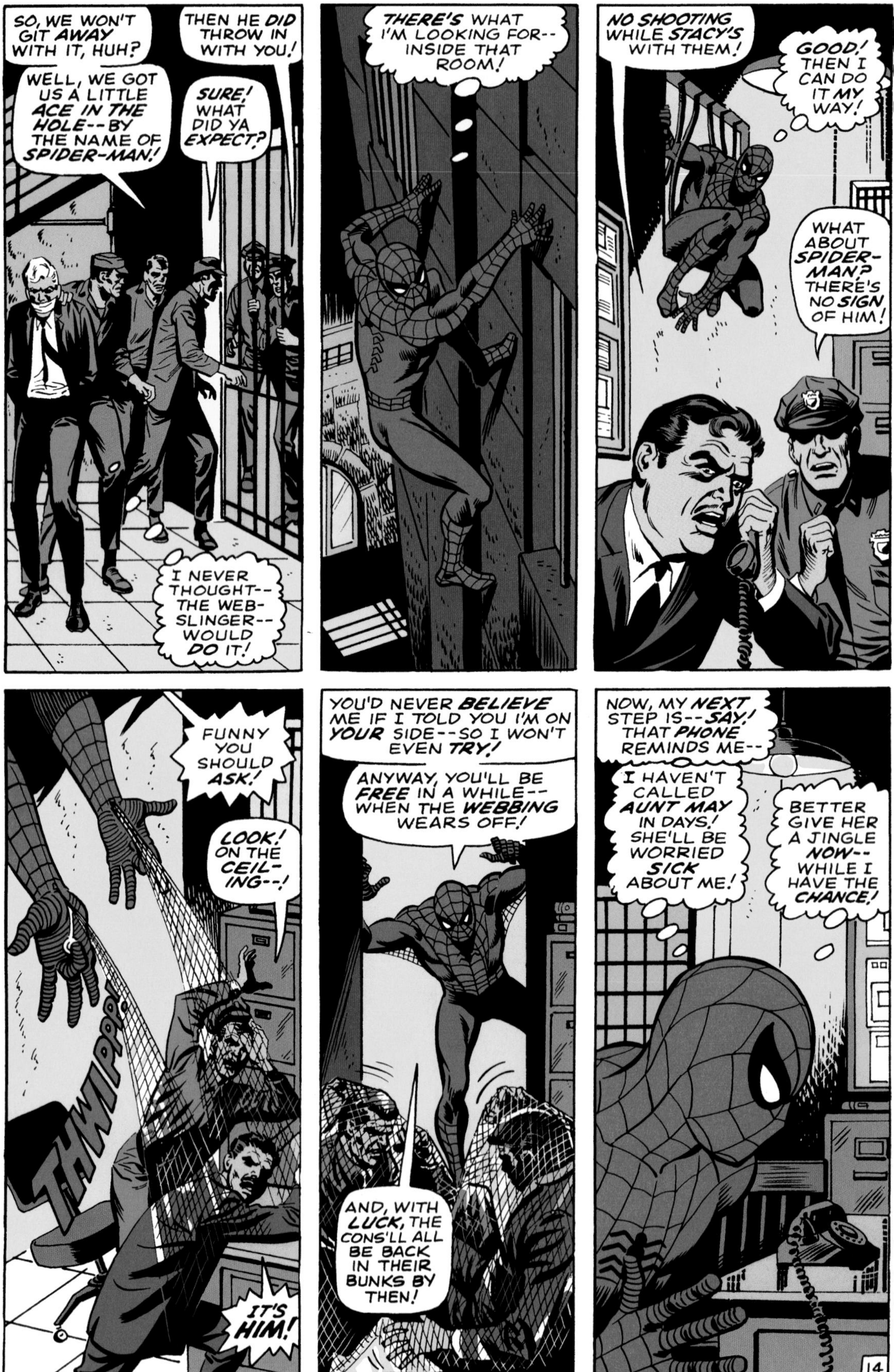

SO, WE WON'T GIT AWAY WITH IT, HUH?
THEN HE DID THROW IN WITH YOU!
WELL, WE GOT US A LITTLE ACE IN THE HOLE--BY THE NAME OF SPIDER-MAN!
SURE! WHAT DID YA EXPECT?
I NEVER THOUGHT-- THE WEB-SLINGER-- WOULD DO IT!
THERE'S WHAT I'M LOOKING FOR-- INSIDE THAT ROOM!
NO SHOOTING WHILE STACY'S WITH THEM!
GOOD! THEN I CAN DO IT MY WAY!
WHAT ABOUT SPIDER-MAN? THERE'S NO SIGN OF HIM!
FUNNY YOU SHOULD ASK!
LOOK! ON THE CEIL-ING--!
THWIPP!
IT'S HIM!
YOU'D NEVER BELIEVE ME IF I TOLD YOU I'M ON YOUR SIDE--SO I WON'T EVEN TRY!
ANYWAY, YOU'LL BE FREE IN A WHILE-- WHEN THE WEBBING WEARS OFF!
AND, WITH LUCK, THE CONS'LL ALL BE BACK IN THEIR BUNKS BY THEN!
NOW, MY NEXT STEP IS--SAY! THAT PHONE REMINDS ME--
I HAVEN'T CALLED AUNT MAY IN DAYS! SHE'LL BE WORRIED SICK ABOUT ME!
BETTER GIVE HER A JINGLE NOW-- WHILE I HAVE THE CHANCE!
14

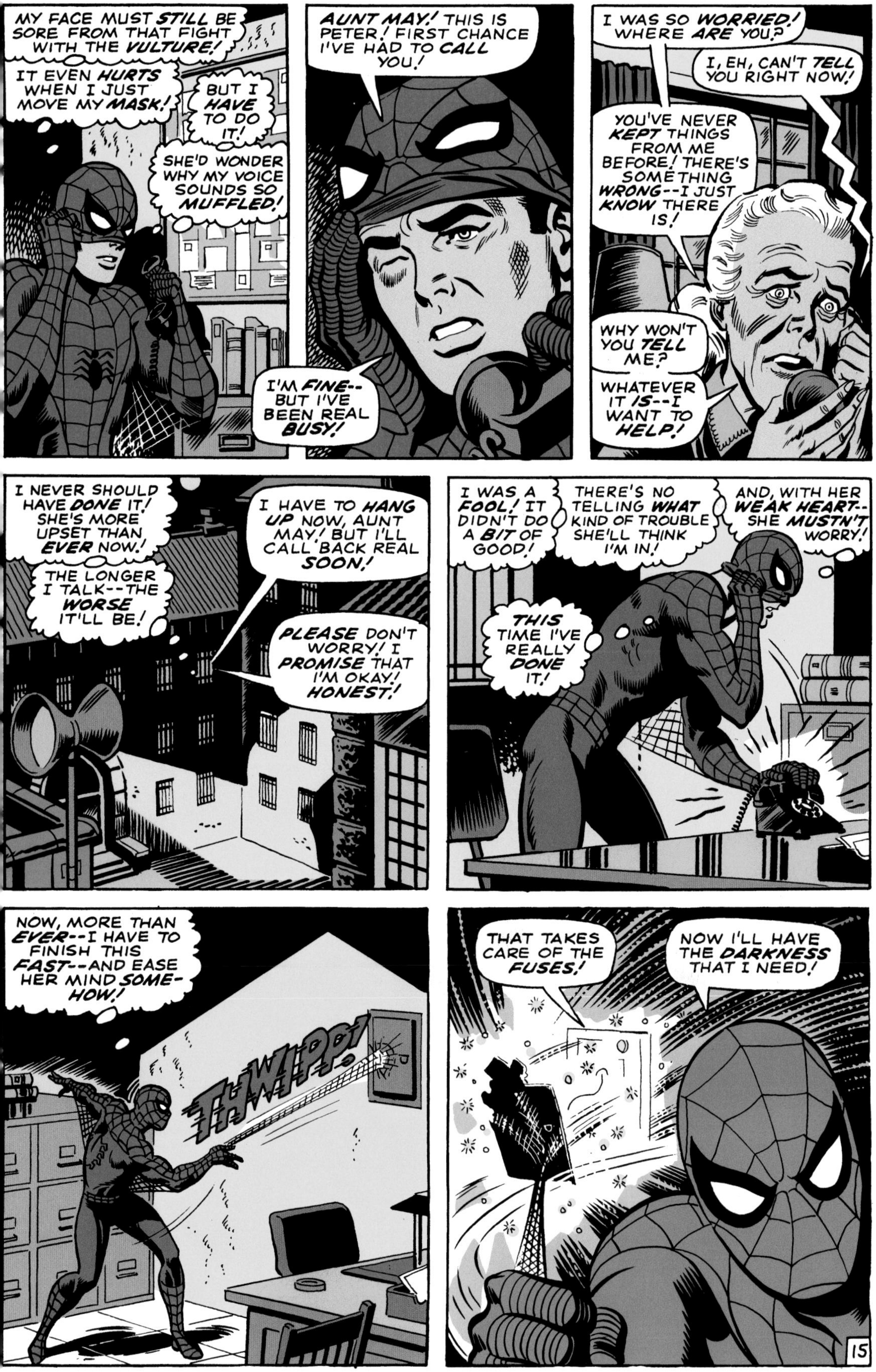
MY FACE MUST STILL BE SORE FROM THAT FIGHT WITH THE VULTURE!
IT EVEN HURTS WHEN I JUST MOVE MY MASK!
BUT I HAVE TO DO IT!
SHE'D WONDER WHY MY VOICE SOUNDS SO MUFFLED!
AUNT MAY! THIS IS PETER! FIRST CHANCE I'VE HAD TO CALL YOU!
I'M FINE-- BUT I'VE BEEN REAL BUSY!
I WAS SO WORRIED! WHERE ARE YOU?
I, EH, CAN'T TELL YOU RIGHT NOW!
YOU'VE NEVER KEPT THINGS FROM ME BEFORE! THERE'S SOMETHING WRONG--I JUST KNOW THERE IS!
WHY WON'T YOU TELL ME?
WHATEVER IT IS--I WANT TO HELP!
I NEVER SHOULD HAVE DONE IT! SHE'S MORE UPSET THAN EVER NOW!
THE LONGER I TALK--THE WORSE IT'LL BE!
I HAVE TO HANG UP NOW, AUNT MAY! BUT I'LL CALL BACK REAL SOON!
PLEASE DON'T WORRY! I PROMISE THAT I'M OKAY! HONEST!
I WAS A FOOL! IT DIDN'T DO A BIT OF GOOD!
THERE'S NO TELLING WHAT KIND OF TROUBLE SHE'LL THINK I'M IN!
AND, WITH HER WEAK HEART-- SHE MUSTN'T WORRY!
THIS TIME I'VE REALLY DONE IT!
NOW, MORE THAN EVER--I HAVE TO FINISH THIS FAST--AND EASE HER MIND SOME-HOW!
THWIPP!
THAT TAKES CARE OF THE FUSES!
NOW I'LL HAVE THE DARKNESS THAT I NEED!
15

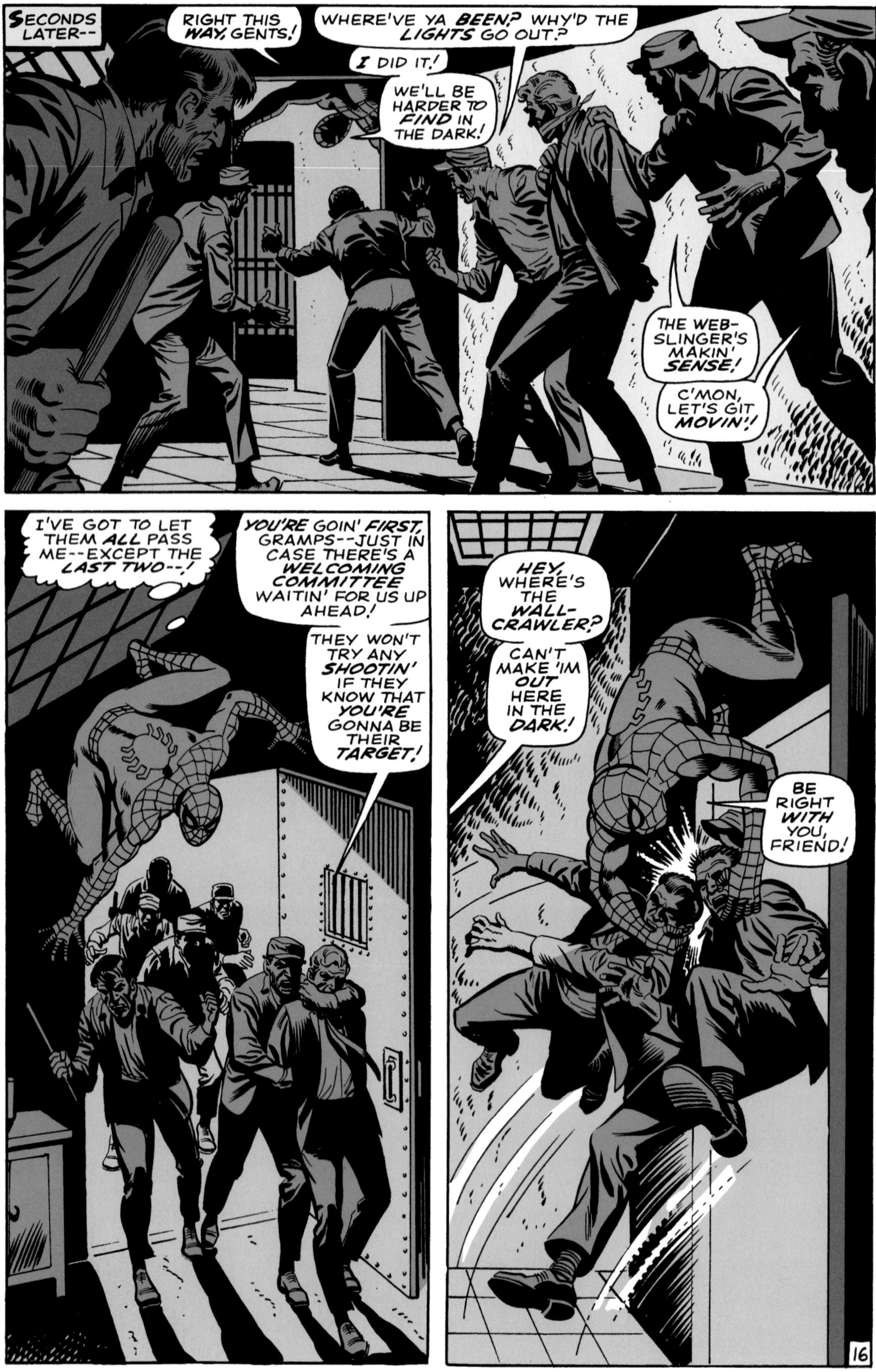
SECONDS LATER--
RIGHT THIS WAY, GENTS!
WHERE'VE YA BEEN? WHY'D THE LIGHTS GO OUT?
I DID IT!
WE'LL BE HARDER TO FIND IN THE DARK!
THE WEB-SLINGER'S MAKIN' SENSE!
C'MON, LET'S GIT MOVIN'!
I'VE GOT TO LET THEM ALL PASS ME--EXCEPT THE LAST TWO--!
YOU'RE GOIN' FIRST, GRAMPS--JUST IN CASE THERE'S A WELCOMING COMMITTEE WAITIN' FOR US UP AHEAD!
THEY WON'T TRY ANY SHOOTIN' IF THEY KNOW THAT YOU'RE GONNA BE THEIR TARGET!
HEY, WHERE'S THE WALL-CRAWLER?
CAN'T MAKE 'IM OUT HERE IN THE DARK!
BE RIGHT WITH YOU, FRIEND!
16

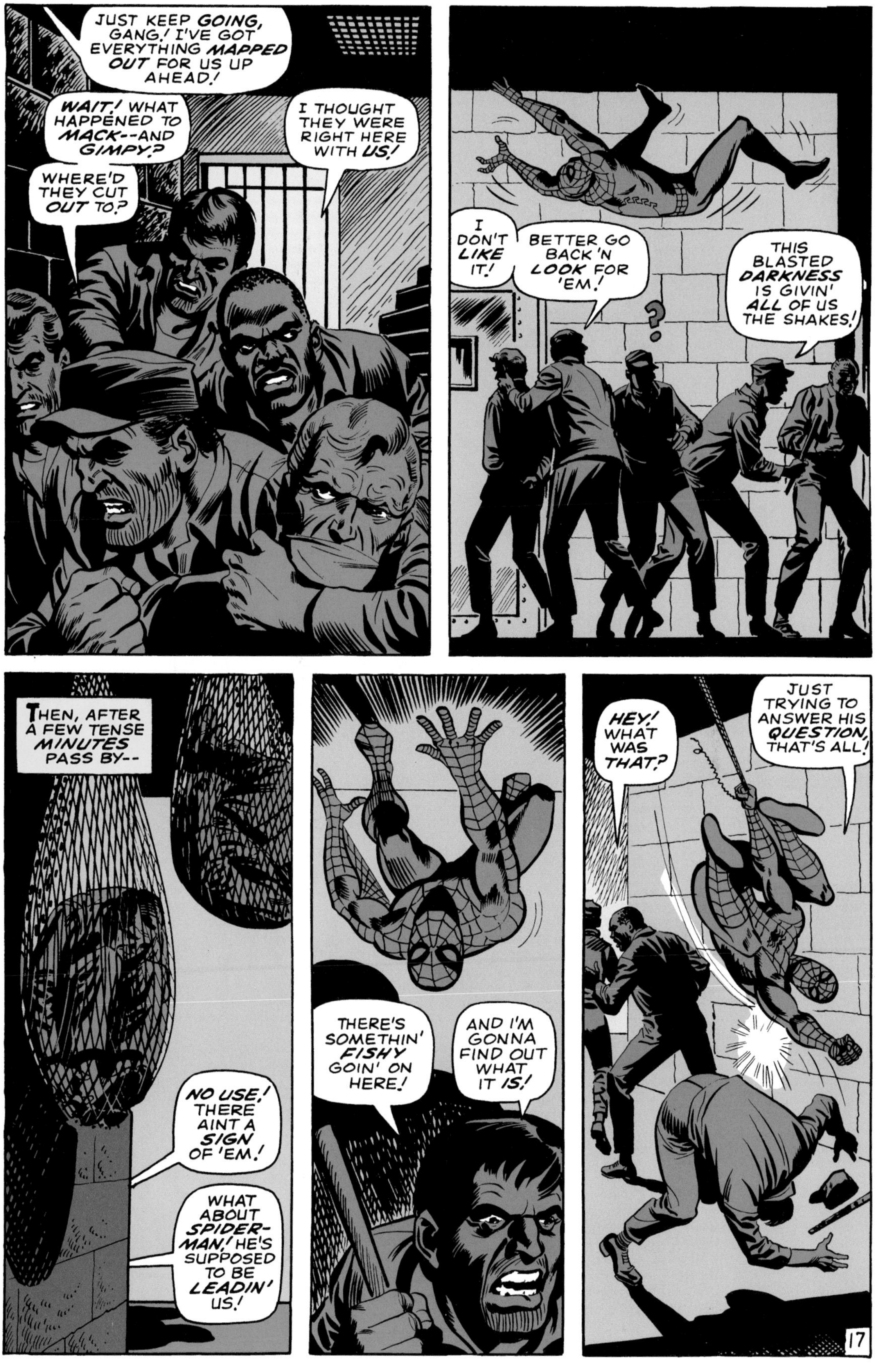

JUST KEEP GOING, GANG! I'VE GOT EVERYTHING MAPPED OUT FOR US UP AHEAD!
WAIT! WHAT HAPPENED TO MACK--AND GIMPY?
I THOUGHT THEY WERE RIGHT HERE WITH US!
WHERE'D THEY CUT OUT TO?
I DON'T LIKE IT!
BETTER GO BACK 'N LOOK FOR 'EM!
?
THIS BLASTED DARKNESS IS GIVIN' ALL OF US THE SHAKES!
THEN, AFTER A FEW TENSE MINUTES PASS BY--
NO USE! THERE AINT A SIGN OF 'EM!
WHAT ABOUT SPIDER-MAN! HE'S SUPPOSED TO BE LEADIN' US!
THERE'S SOMETHIN' FISHY GOIN' ON HERE!
AND I'M GONNA FIND OUT WHAT IT IS!
HEY! WHAT WAS THAT?
JUST TRYING TO ANSWER HIS QUESTION, THAT'S ALL!
17

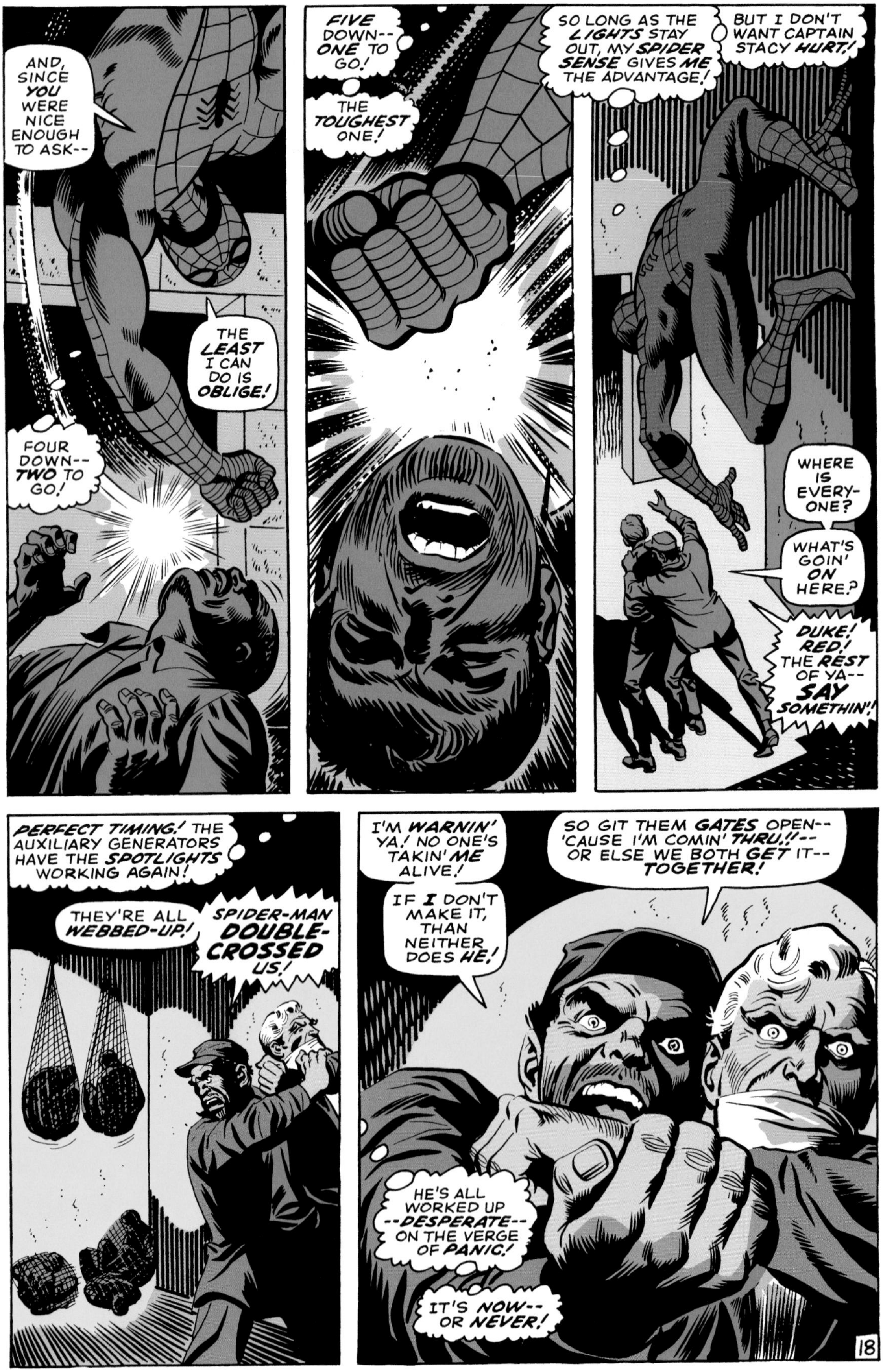

AND, SINCE YOU WERE NICE ENOUGH TO ASK--
THE LEAST I CAN DO IS OBLIGE!
FOUR DOWN--TWO TO GO!
FIVE DOWN--ONE TO GO!
THE TOUGHEST ONE!
SO LONG AS THE LIGHTS STAY OUT, MY SPIDER SENSE GIVES ME THE ADVANTAGE!
BUT I DON'T WANT CAPTAIN STACY HURT!
WHERE IS EVERYONE?
WHAT'S GOIN' ON HERE?
DUKE! RED! THE REST OF YA--SAY SOMETHIN'!
PERFECT TIMING! THE AUXILIARY GENERATORS HAVE THE SPOTLIGHTS WORKING AGAIN!
THEY'RE ALL WEBBED-UP!
SPIDER-MAN DOUBLE-CROSSED US!
I'M WARNIN' YA! NO ONE'S TAKIN' ME ALIVE!
IF I DON'T MAKE IT, THAN NEITHER DOES HE!
SO GIT THEM GATES OPEN--'CAUSE I'M COMIN' THRU!!--OR ELSE WE BOTH GET IT--TOGETHER!
HE'S ALL WORKED UP--DESPERATE--ON THE VERGE OF PANIC!
IT'S NOW--OR NEVER!
18

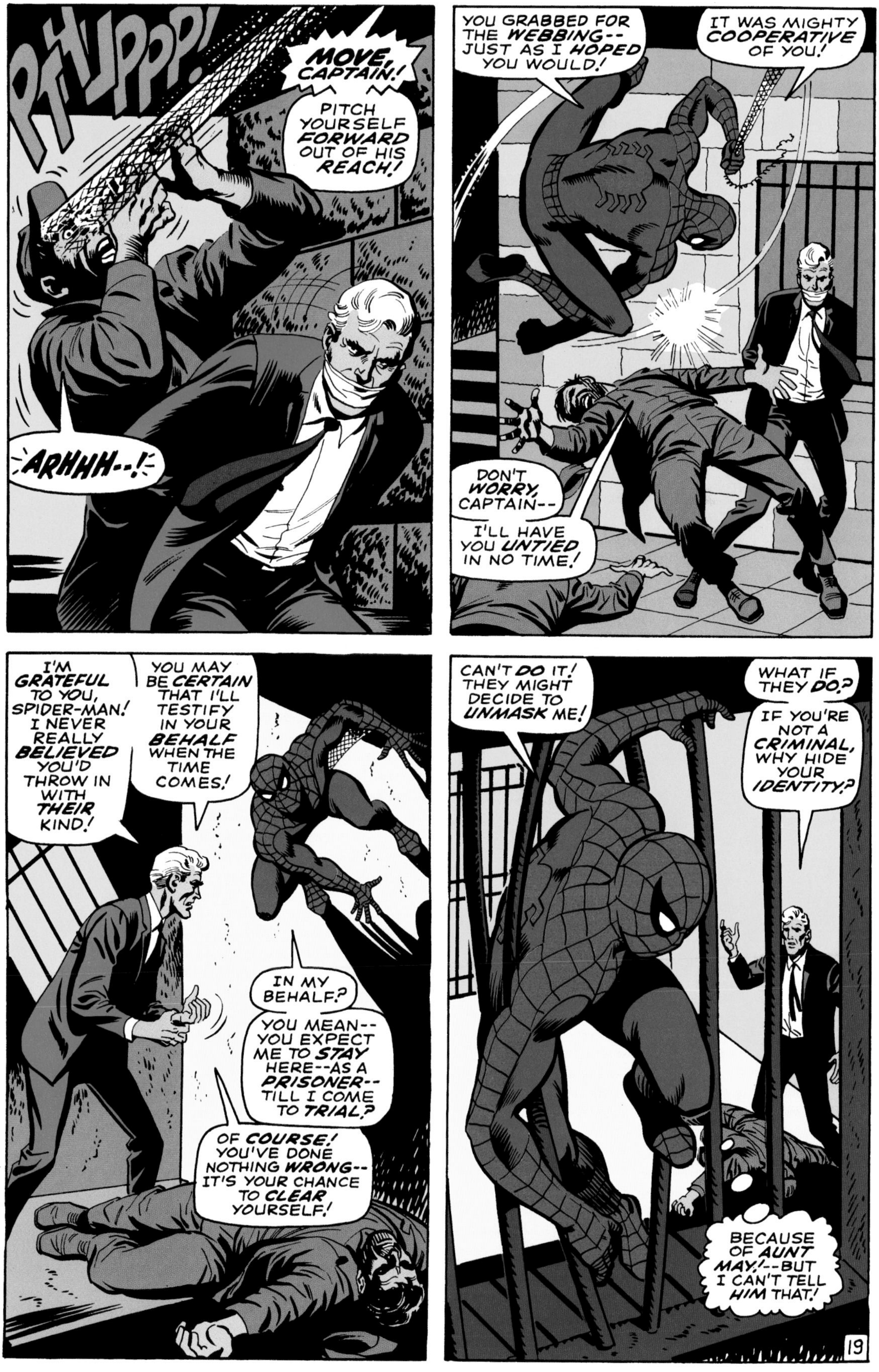
PTHUPPP!
MOVE, CAPTAIN!
PITCH YOURSELF FORWARD OUT OF HIS REACH!
ARHHH--!
YOU GRABBED FOR THE WEBBING-- JUST AS I HOPED YOU WOULD!
IT WAS MIGHTY COOPERATIVE OF YOU!
DON'T WORRY, CAPTAIN--
I'LL HAVE YOU UNTIED IN NO TIME!
I'M GRATEFUL TO YOU, SPIDER-MAN! I NEVER REALLY BELIEVED YOU'D THROW IN WITH THEIR KIND!
YOU MAY BE CERTAIN THAT I'LL TESTIFY IN YOUR BEHALF WHEN THE TIME COMES!
IN MY BEHALF?
YOU MEAN-- YOU EXPECT ME TO STAY HERE--AS A PRISONER-- TILL I COME TO TRIAL?
OF COURSE! YOU'VE DONE NOTHING WRONG-- IT'S YOUR CHANCE TO CLEAR YOURSELF!
CAN'T DO IT! THEY MIGHT DECIDE TO UNMASK ME!
WHAT IF THEY DO?
IF YOU'RE NOT A CRIMINAL, WHY HIDE YOUR IDENTITY?
BECAUSE OF AUNT MAY!--BUT I CAN'T TELL HIM THAT!
19

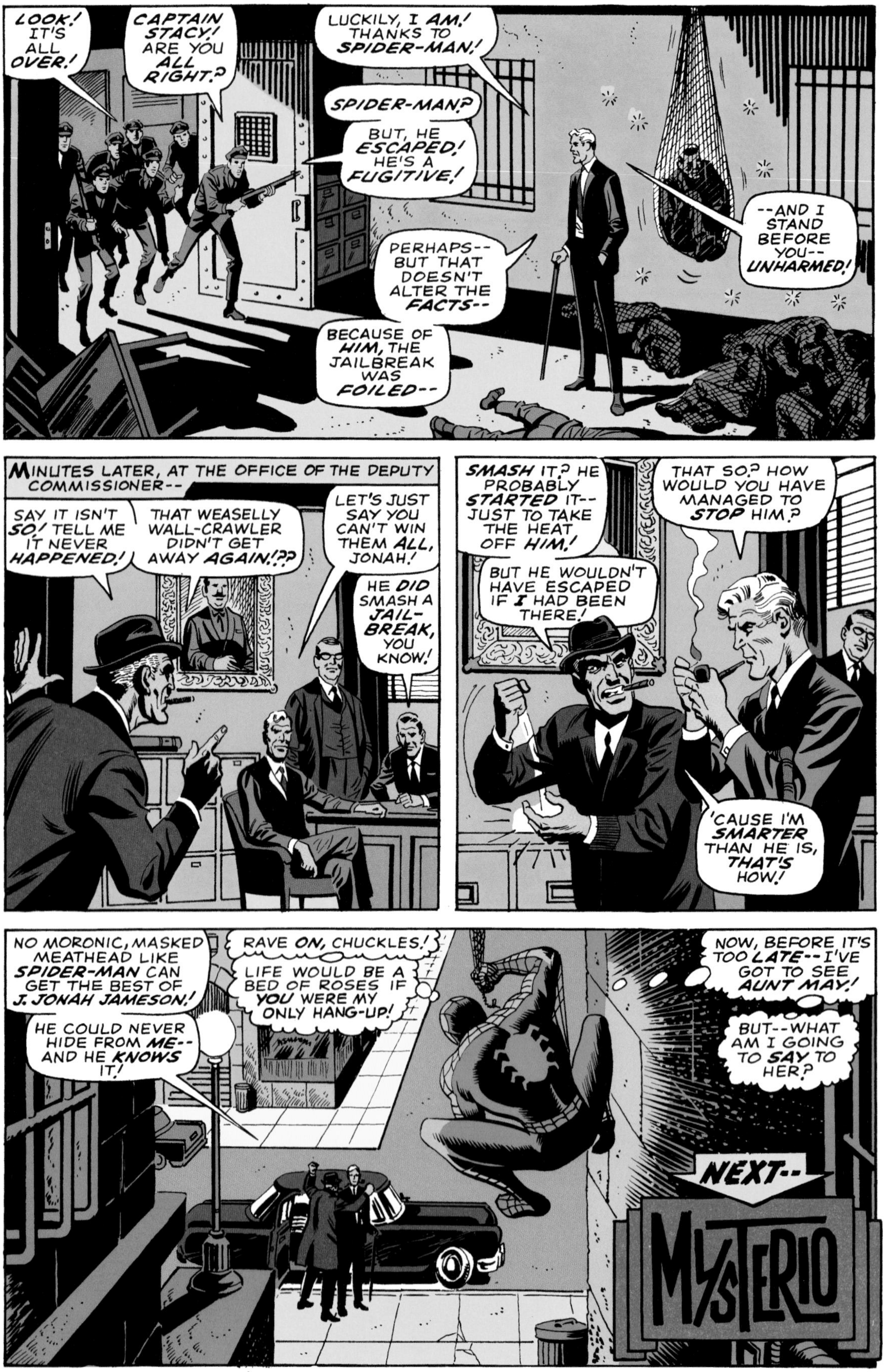
LOOK! IT'S ALL OVER!
CAPTAIN STACY! ARE YOU ALL RIGHT?
LUCKILY, I AM! THANKS TO SPIDER-MAN!
SPIDER-MAN?
BUT, HE ESCAPED! HE'S A FUGITIVE!
PERHAPS-- BUT THAT DOESN'T ALTER THE FACTS--
BECAUSE OF HIM, THE JAILBREAK WAS FOILED--
--AND I STAND BEFORE YOU-- UNHARMED!
MINUTES LATER, AT THE OFFICE OF THE DEPUTY COMMISSIONER--
SAY IT ISN'T SO! TELL ME IT NEVER HAPPENED!
THAT WEASELLY WALL-CRAWLER DIDN'T GET AWAY AGAIN!??
LET'S JUST SAY YOU CAN'T WIN THEM ALL, JONAH!
HE DID SMASH A JAIL-BREAK, YOU KNOW!
SMASH IT? HE PROBABLY STARTED IT-- JUST TO TAKE THE HEAT OFF HIM!
BUT HE WOULDN'T HAVE ESCAPED IF I HAD BEEN THERE!
THAT SO? HOW WOULD YOU HAVE MANAGED TO STOP HIM?
'CAUSE I'M SMARTER THAN HE IS, THAT'S HOW!
NO MORONIC, MASKED MEATHEAD LIKE SPIDER-MAN CAN GET THE BEST OF J. JONAH JAMESON!
HE COULD NEVER HIDE FROM ME-- AND HE KNOWS IT!
RAVE ON, CHUCKLES!
LIFE WOULD BE A BED OF ROSES IF YOU WERE MY ONLY HANG-UP!
NOW, BEFORE IT'S TOO LATE--I'VE GOT TO SEE AUNT MAY!
BUT--WHAT AM I GOING TO SAY TO HER?
NEXT--
MYSTERIO

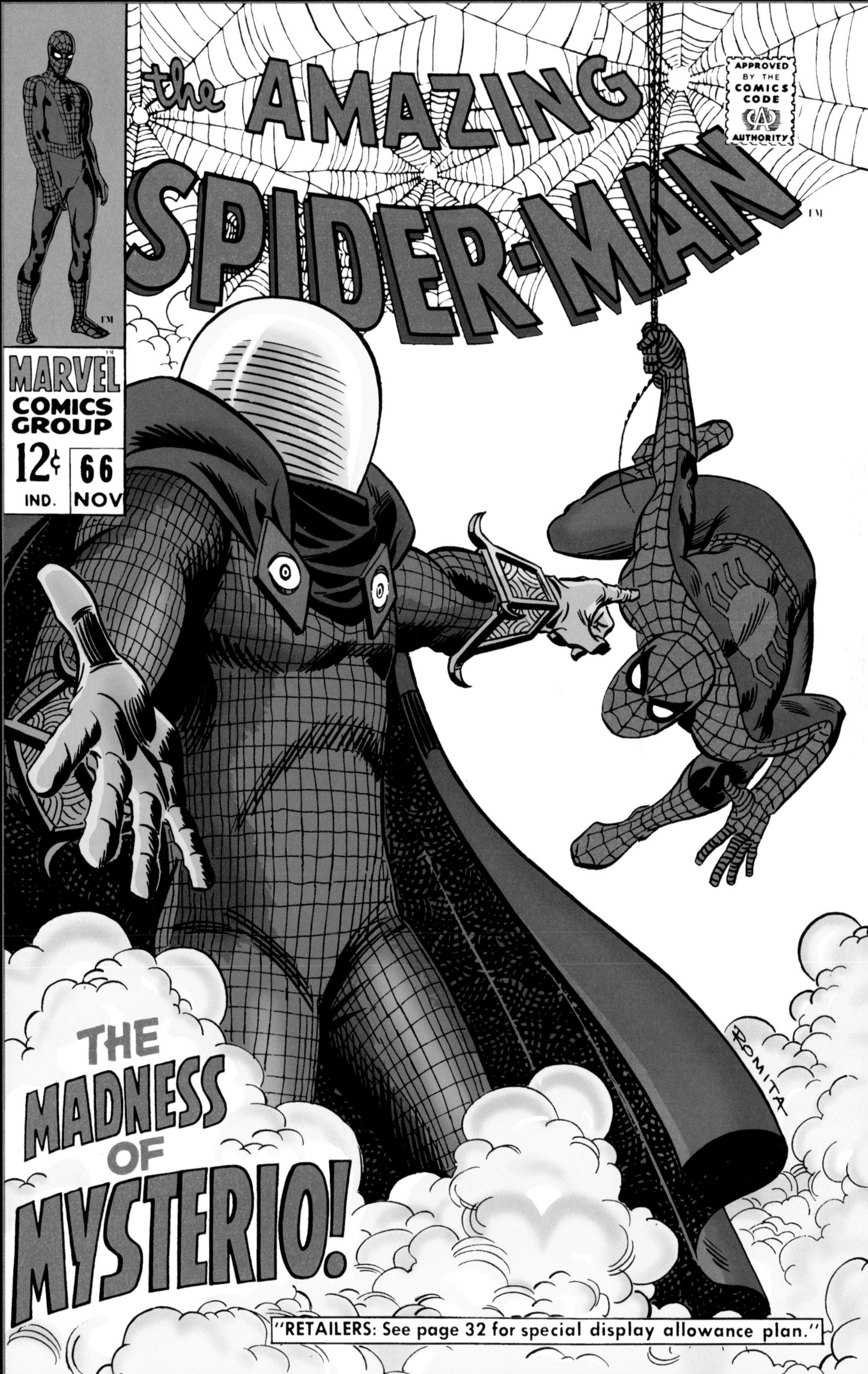
the AMAZING SPIDER-MAN
APPROVED BY THE COMICS CODE AUTHORITY
MARVEL COMICS GROUP
12¢ IND.
66 NOV
THE MADNESS OF MYSTERIO!
ROMITA
"RETAILERS: See page 32 for special display allowance plan."

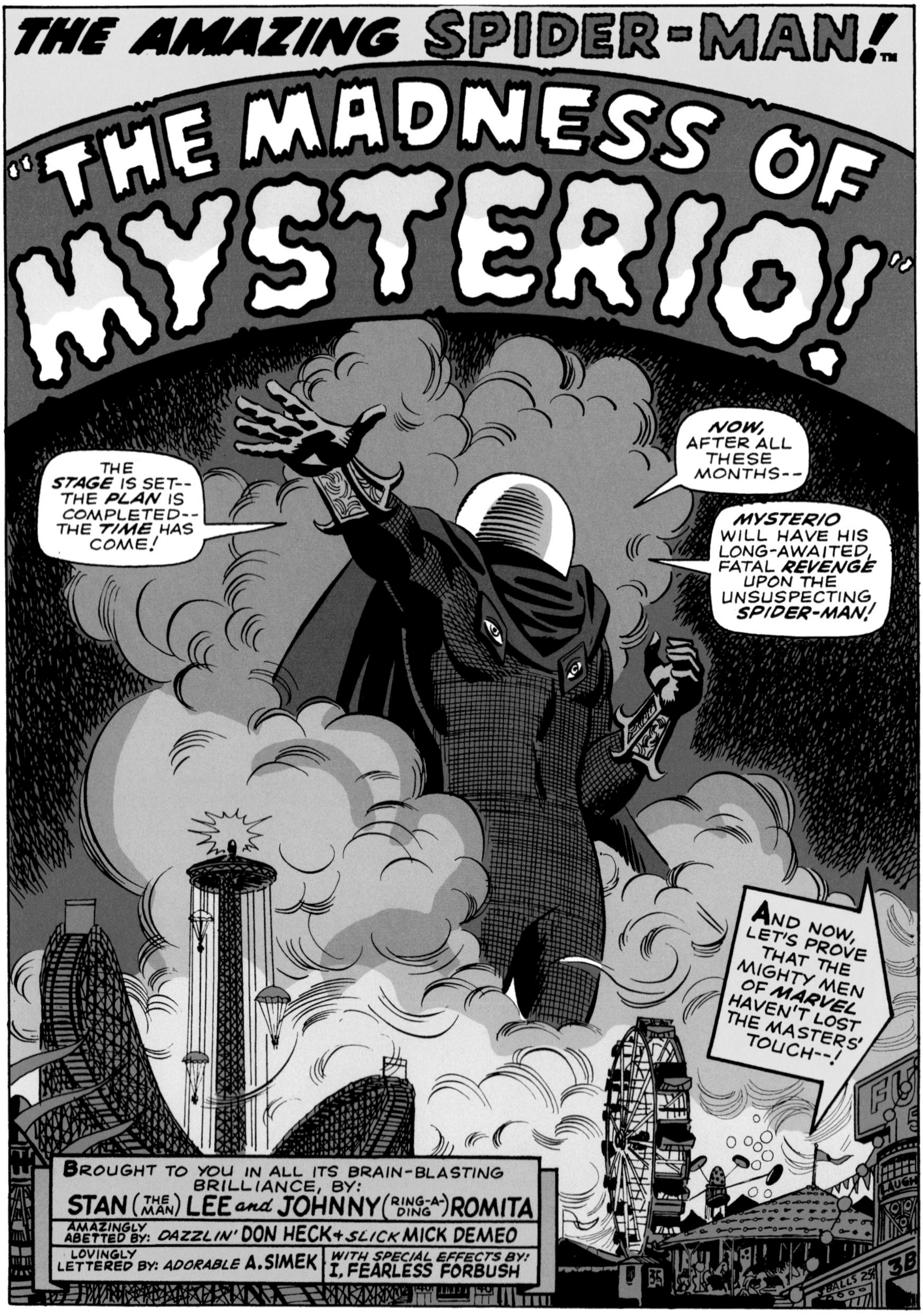
THE AMAZING SPIDER-MAN!™
"THE MADNESS OF MYSTERIO!"
THE STAGE IS SET--THE PLAN IS COMPLETED--THE TIME HAS COME!
NOW, AFTER ALL THESE MONTHS--
MYSTERIO WILL HAVE HIS LONG-AWAITED, FATAL REVENGE UPON THE UNSUSPECTING SPIDER-MAN!
AND NOW, LET'S PROVE THAT THE MIGHTY MEN OF MARVEL HAVEN'T LOST THE MASTERS' TOUCH--!
BROUGHT TO YOU IN ALL ITS BRAIN-BLASTING BRILLIANCE, BY:
STAN (THE MAN) LEE and JOHNNY (RING-A-DING) ROMITA
AMAZINGLY ABETTED BY: DAZZLIN' DON HECK + SLICK MICK DEMEO
LOVINGLY LETTERED BY: ADORABLE A. SIMEK
WITH SPECIAL EFFECTS BY: I, FEARLESS FORBUSH

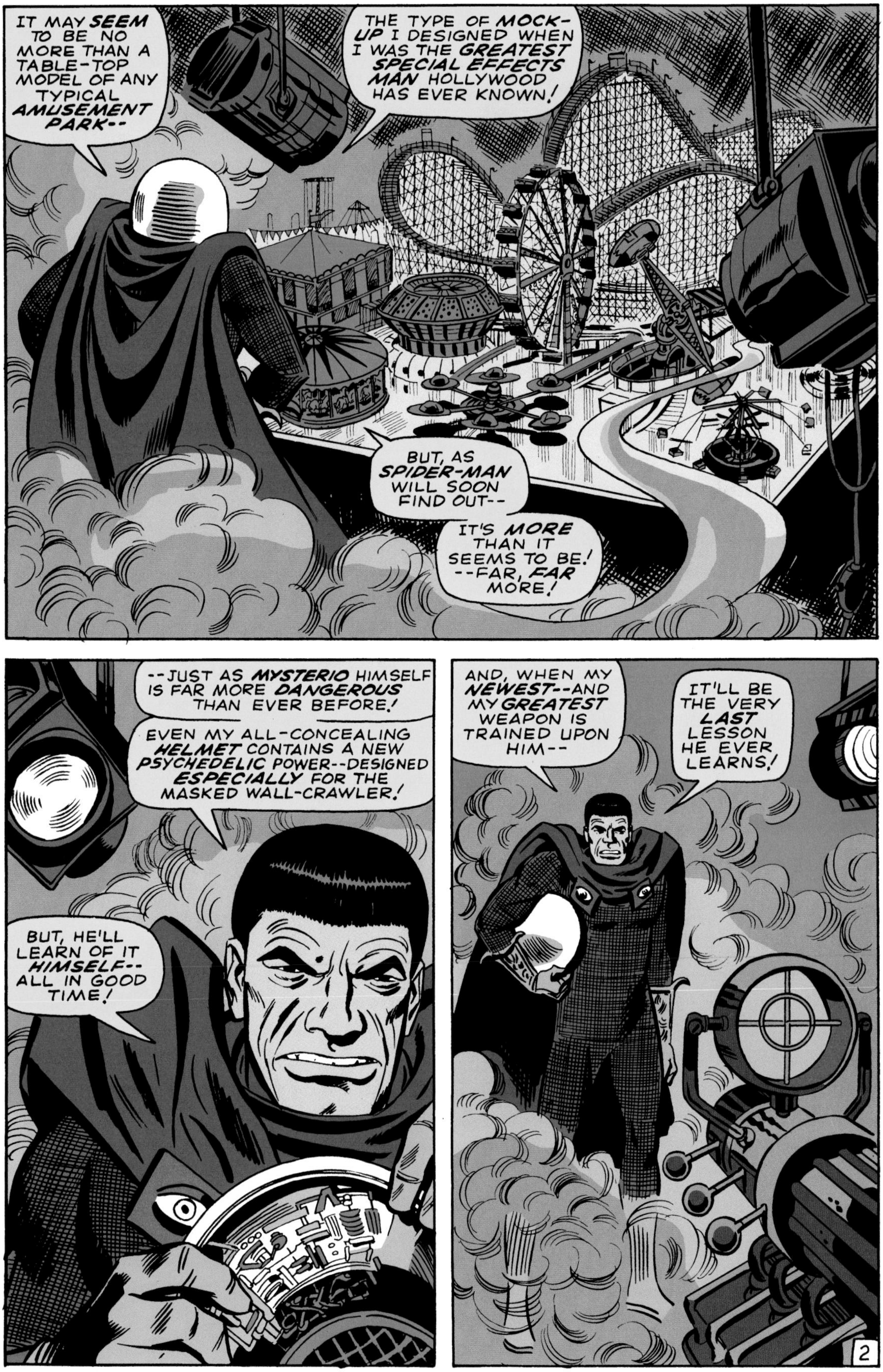
IT MAY SEEM TO BE NO MORE THAN A TABLE-TOP MODEL OF ANY TYPICAL AMUSEMENT PARK--
THE TYPE OF MOCK-UP I DESIGNED WHEN I WAS THE GREATEST SPECIAL EFFECTS MAN HOLLYWOOD HAS EVER KNOWN!
BUT, AS SPIDER-MAN WILL SOON FIND OUT--
IT'S MORE THAN IT SEEMS TO BE! --FAR, FAR MORE!
--JUST AS MYSTERIO HIMSELF IS FAR MORE DANGEROUS THAN EVER BEFORE!
EVEN MY ALL-CONCEALING HELMET CONTAINS A NEW PSYCHEDELIC POWER--DESIGNED ESPECIALLY FOR THE MASKED WALL-CRAWLER!
BUT, HE'LL LEARN OF IT HIMSELF--ALL IN GOOD TIME!
AND, WHEN MY NEWEST--AND MY GREATEST WEAPON IS TRAINED UPON HIM--
IT'LL BE THE VERY LAST LESSON HE EVER LEARNS!
2

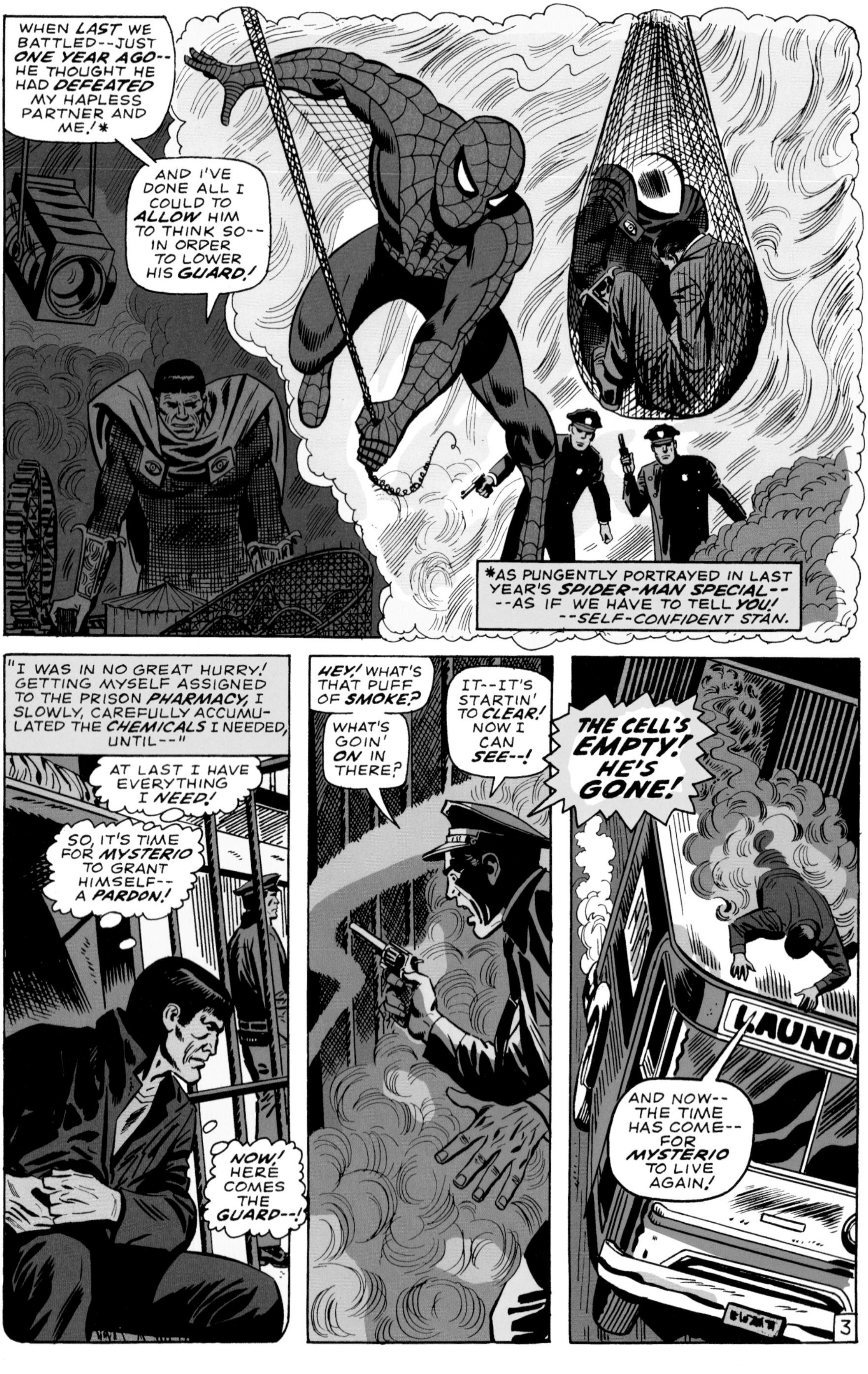
WHEN LAST WE BATTLED--JUST ONE YEAR AGO--HE THOUGHT HE HAD DEFEATED MY HAPLESS PARTNER AND ME!*
AND I'VE DONE ALL I COULD TO ALLOW HIM TO THINK SO--IN ORDER TO LOWER HIS GUARD!
*AS PUNGENTLY PORTRAYED IN LAST YEAR'S SPIDER-MAN SPECIAL----AS IF WE HAVE TO TELL YOU! --SELF-CONFIDENT STAN.
"I WAS IN NO GREAT HURRY! GETTING MYSELF ASSIGNED TO THE PRISON PHARMACY, I SLOWLY, CAREFULLY ACCUMULATED THE CHEMICALS I NEEDED, UNTIL--"
AT LAST I HAVE EVERYTHING I NEED!
SO, IT'S TIME FOR MYSTERIO TO GRANT HIMSELF--A PARDON!
NOW! HERE COMES THE GUARD--!
HEY! WHAT'S THAT PUFF OF SMOKE?
WHAT'S GOIN' ON IN THERE?
IT--IT'S STARTIN' TO CLEAR! NOW I CAN SEE--!
THE CELL'S EMPTY! HE'S GONE!
LAUND
AND NOW--THE TIME HAS COME--FOR MYSTERIO TO LIVE AGAIN!
3

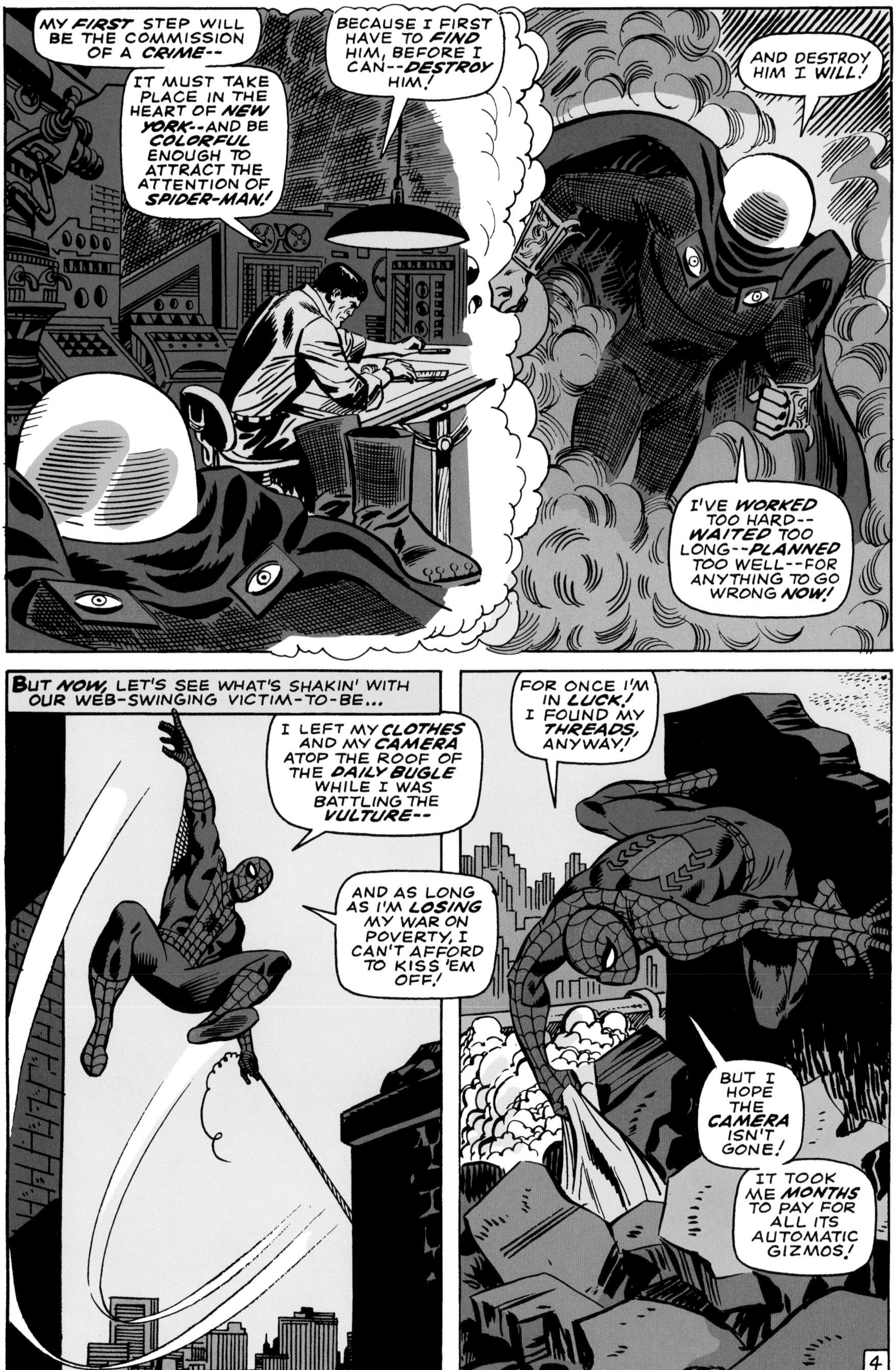
MY FIRST STEP WILL BE THE COMMISSION OF A CRIME--
IT MUST TAKE PLACE IN THE HEART OF NEW YORK--AND BE COLORFUL ENOUGH TO ATTRACT THE ATTENTION OF SPIDER-MAN!
BECAUSE I FIRST HAVE TO FIND HIM, BEFORE I CAN--DESTROY HIM!
AND DESTROY HIM I WILL!
I'VE WORKED TOO HARD-- WAITED TOO LONG--PLANNED TOO WELL--FOR ANYTHING TO GO WRONG NOW!
BUT NOW, LET'S SEE WHAT'S SHAKIN' WITH OUR WEB-SWINGING VICTIM-TO-BE...
I LEFT MY CLOTHES AND MY CAMERA ATOP THE ROOF OF THE DAILY BUGLE WHILE I WAS BATTLING THE VULTURE--
AND AS LONG AS I'M LOSING MY WAR ON POVERTY, I CAN'T AFFORD TO KISS 'EM OFF!
FOR ONCE I'M IN LUCK! I FOUND MY THREADS, ANYWAY!
BUT I HOPE THE CAMERA ISN'T GONE!
IT TOOK ME MONTHS TO PAY FOR ALL ITS AUTOMATIC GIZMOS!
4

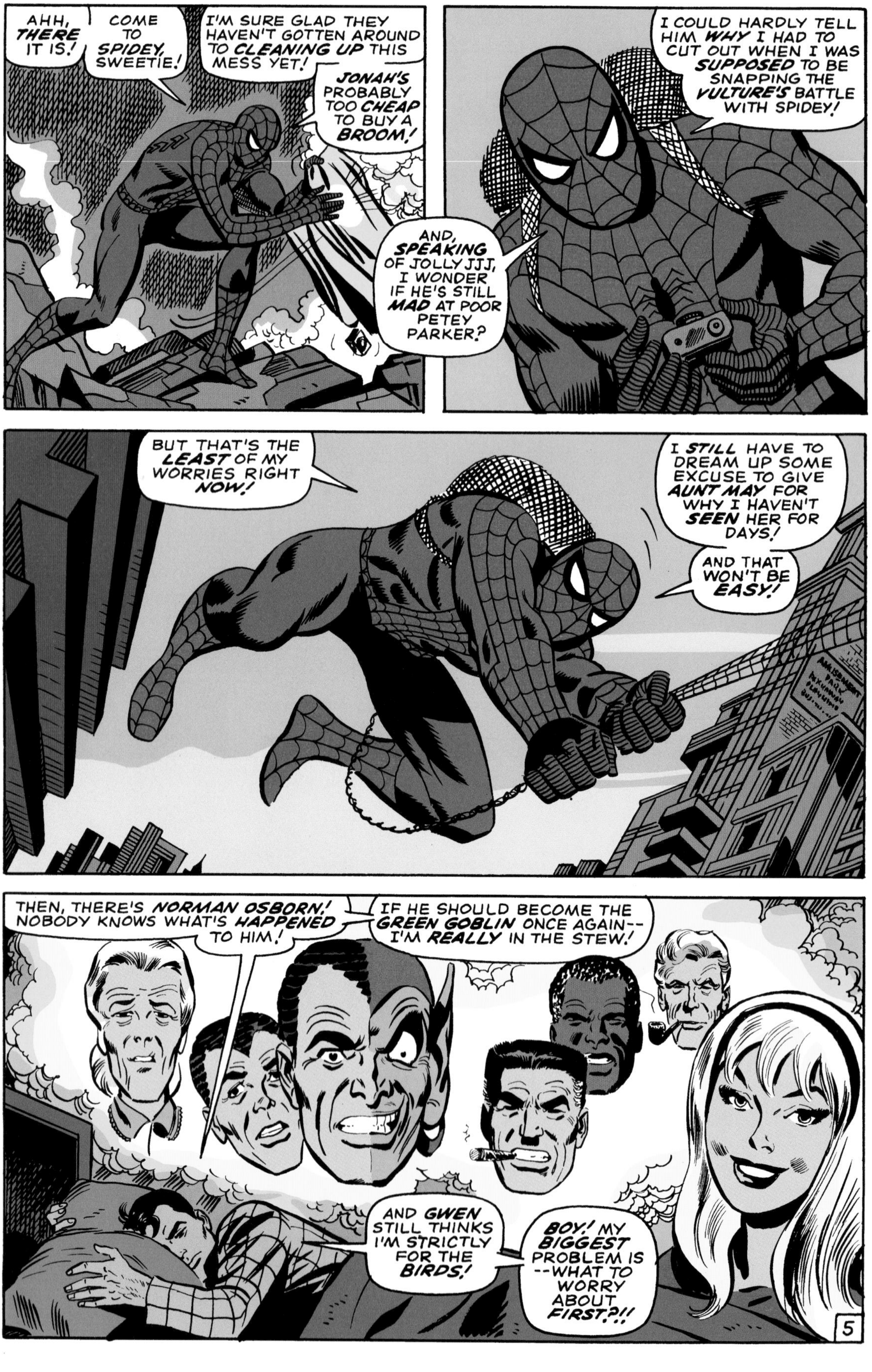
AHH, THERE IT IS.!
COME TO SPIDEY, SWEETIE.!
I'M SURE GLAD THEY HAVEN'T GOTTEN AROUND TO CLEANING UP THIS MESS YET.!
JONAH'S PROBABLY TOO CHEAP TO BUY A BROOM.!
I COULD HARDLY TELL HIM WHY I HAD TO CUT OUT WHEN I WAS SUPPOSED TO BE SNAPPING THE VULTURE'S BATTLE WITH SPIDEY.!
AND, SPEAKING OF JOLLY JJJ, I WONDER IF HE'S STILL MAD AT POOR PETEY PARKER?
BUT THAT'S THE LEAST OF MY WORRIES RIGHT NOW.!
I STILL HAVE TO DREAM UP SOME EXCUSE TO GIVE AUNT MAY FOR WHY I HAVEN'T SEEN HER FOR DAYS.!
AND THAT WON'T BE EASY.!
THEN, THERE'S NORMAN OSBORN.! NOBODY KNOWS WHAT'S HAPPENED TO HIM.!
IF HE SHOULD BECOME THE GREEN GOBLIN ONCE AGAIN-- I'M REALLY IN THE STEW.!
AND GWEN STILL THINKS I'M STRICTLY FOR THE BIRDS.!
BOY.! MY BIGGEST PROBLEM IS --WHAT TO WORRY ABOUT FIRST?!!
5

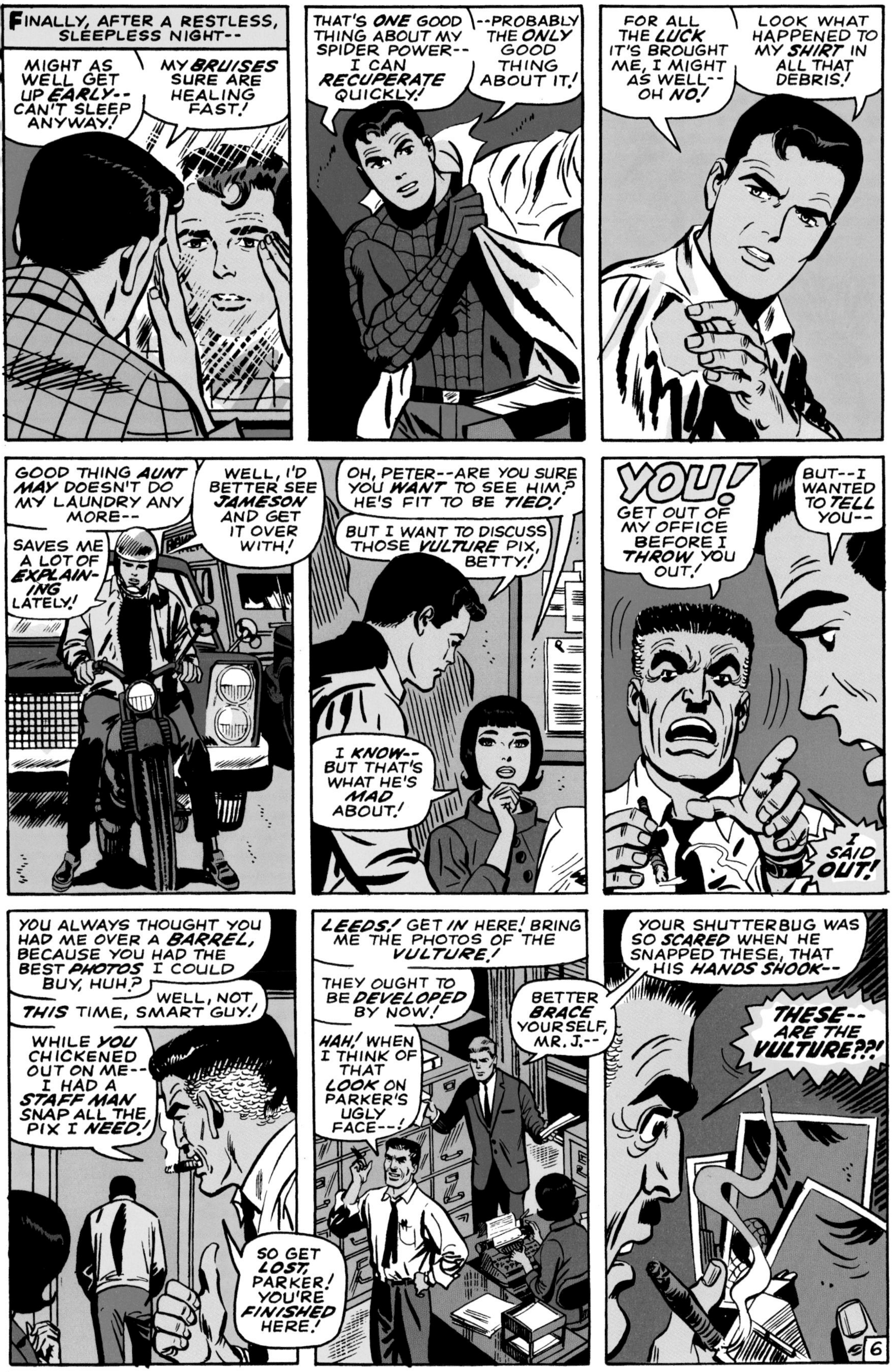
FINALLY, AFTER A RESTLESS, SLEEPLESS NIGHT--
MIGHT AS WELL GET UP EARLY--CAN'T SLEEP ANYWAY!
MY BRUISES SURE ARE HEALING FAST!
THAT'S ONE GOOD THING ABOUT MY SPIDER POWER--I CAN RECUPERATE QUICKLY!
--PROBABLY THE ONLY GOOD THING ABOUT IT!
FOR ALL THE LUCK IT'S BROUGHT ME, I MIGHT AS WELL--OH NO!
LOOK WHAT HAPPENED TO MY SHIRT IN ALL THAT DEBRIS!
GOOD THING AUNT MAY DOESN'T DO MY LAUNDRY ANY MORE--
SAVES ME A LOT OF EXPLAIN-ING LATELY!
WELL, I'D BETTER SEE JAMESON AND GET IT OVER WITH!
OH, PETER--ARE YOU SURE YOU WANT TO SEE HIM? HE'S FIT TO BE TIED!
BUT I WANT TO DISCUSS THOSE VULTURE PIX, BETTY!
I KNOW--BUT THAT'S WHAT HE'S MAD ABOUT!
YOU! GET OUT OF MY OFFICE BEFORE I THROW YOU OUT!
BUT--I WANTED TO TELL YOU--
I SAID OUT!
YOU ALWAYS THOUGHT YOU HAD ME OVER A BARREL, BECAUSE YOU HAD THE BEST PHOTOS I COULD BUY, HUH?
WELL, NOT THIS TIME, SMART GUY!
WHILE YOU CHICKENED OUT ON ME--I HAD A STAFF MAN SNAP ALL THE PIX I NEED!
SO GET LOST, PARKER! YOU'RE FINISHED HERE!
LEEDS! GET IN HERE! BRING ME THE PHOTOS OF THE VULTURE!
THEY OUGHT TO BE DEVELOPED BY NOW!
HAH! WHEN I THINK OF THAT LOOK ON PARKER'S UGLY FACE--!
BETTER BRACE YOURSELF, MR. J.--
YOUR SHUTTERBUG WAS SO SCARED WHEN HE SNAPPED THESE, THAT HIS HANDS SHOOK--
THESE--ARE THE VULTURE??!
6

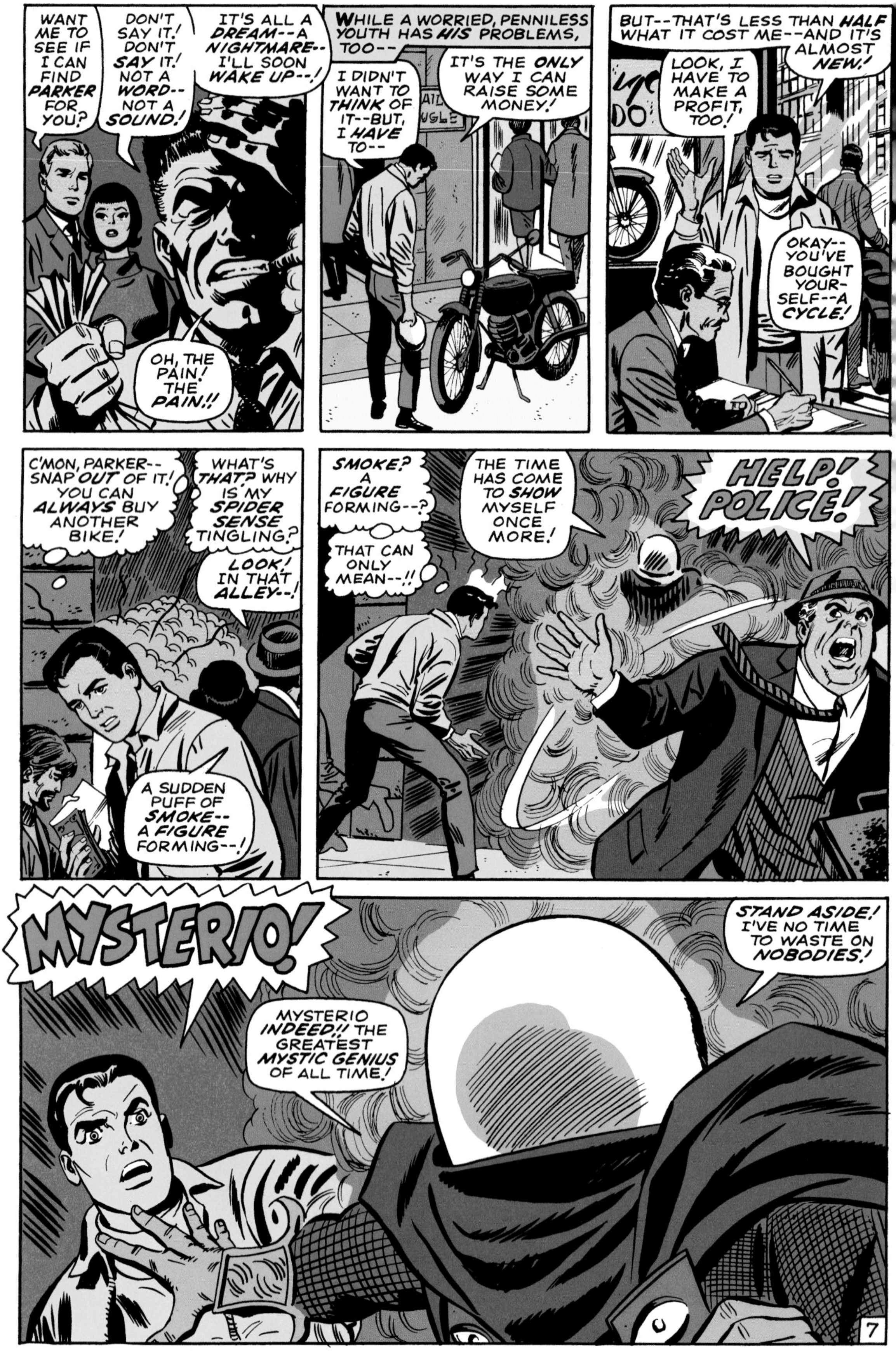

WANT ME TO SEE IF I CAN FIND PARKER FOR YOU?
DON'T SAY IT! DON'T SAY IT! NOT A WORD-- NOT A SOUND!
IT'S ALL A DREAM--A NIGHTMARE-- I'LL SOON WAKE UP--!
OH, THE PAIN! THE PAIN!!
WHILE A WORRIED, PENNILESS YOUTH HAS HIS PROBLEMS, TOO--
I DIDN'T WANT TO THINK OF IT--BUT, I HAVE TO--
IT'S THE ONLY WAY I CAN RAISE SOME MONEY!
BUT--THAT'S LESS THAN HALF WHAT IT COST ME--AND IT'S ALMOST NEW!
LOOK, I HAVE TO MAKE A PROFIT, TOO!
OKAY-- YOU'VE BOUGHT YOUR-SELF--A CYCLE!
C'MON, PARKER-- SNAP OUT OF IT! YOU CAN ALWAYS BUY ANOTHER BIKE!
WHAT'S THAT? WHY IS MY SPIDER SENSE TINGLING?
LOOK! IN THAT ALLEY--!
A SUDDEN PUFF OF SMOKE-- A FIGURE FORMING--!
SMOKE? A FIGURE FORMING--?
THAT CAN ONLY MEAN--!!
THE TIME HAS COME TO SHOW MYSELF ONCE MORE!
HELP! POLICE!
MYSTERIO!
MYSTERIO INDEED!! THE GREATEST MYSTIC GENIUS OF ALL TIME!
STAND ASIDE! I'VE NO TIME TO WASTE ON NOBODIES!
7

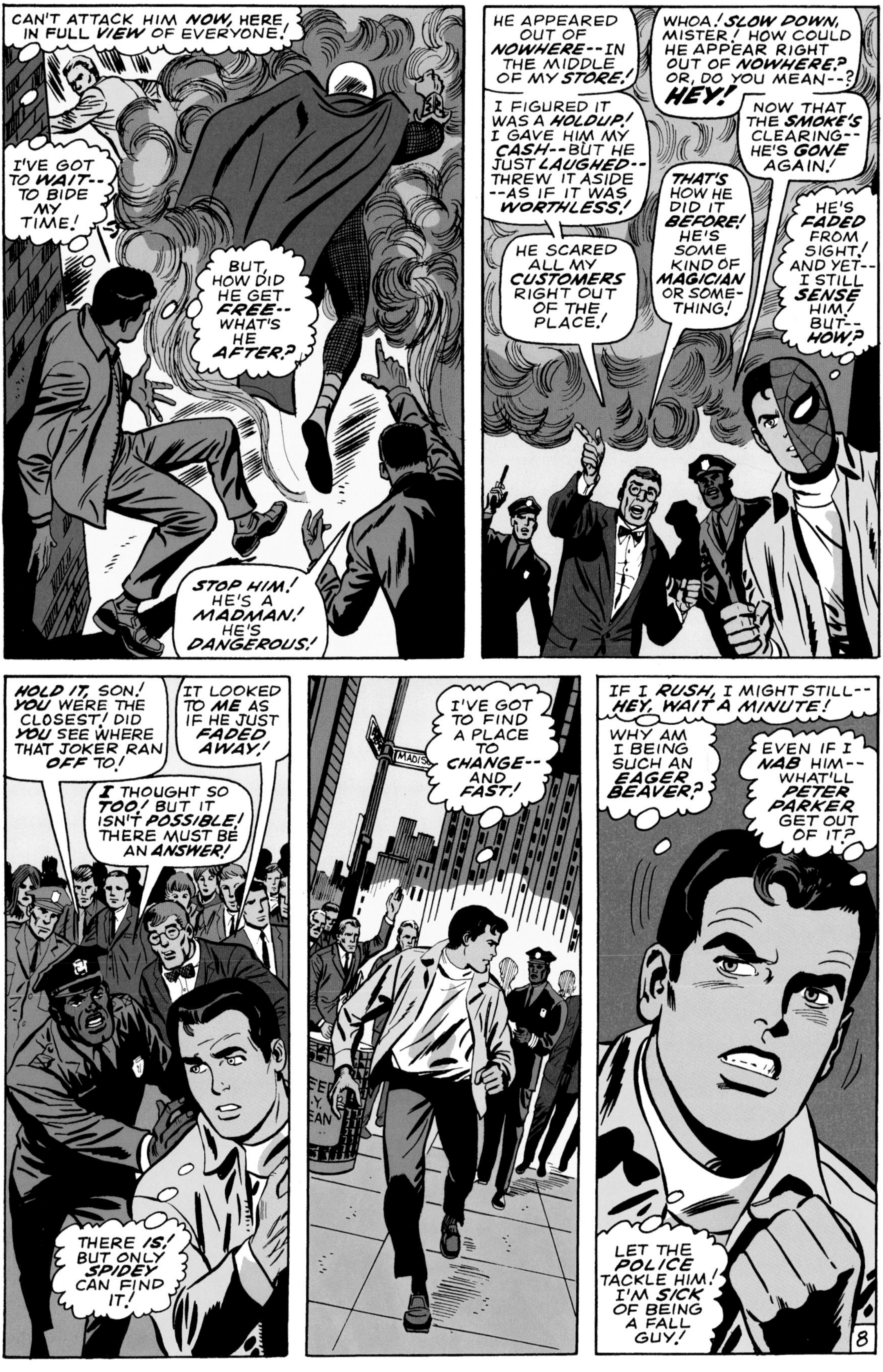
CAN'T ATTACK HIM NOW, HERE, IN FULL VIEW OF EVERYONE!
I'VE GOT TO WAIT-- TO BIDE MY TIME!
BUT, HOW DID HE GET FREE-- WHAT'S HE AFTER?
STOP HIM! HE'S A MADMAN! HE'S DANGEROUS!
HE APPEARED OUT OF NOWHERE-- IN THE MIDDLE OF MY STORE!
WHOA! SLOW DOWN, MISTER! HOW COULD HE APPEAR RIGHT OUT OF NOWHERE? OR, DO YOU MEAN--? HEY!
I FIGURED IT WAS A HOLDUP! I GAVE HIM MY CASH-- BUT HE JUST LAUGHED-- THREW IT ASIDE --AS IF IT WAS WORTHLESS!
NOW THAT THE SMOKE'S CLEARING-- HE'S GONE AGAIN!
HE SCARED ALL MY CUSTOMERS RIGHT OUT OF THE PLACE!
THAT'S HOW HE DID IT BEFORE! HE'S SOME KIND OF MAGICIAN OR SOME-THING!
HE'S FADED FROM SIGHT! AND YET-- I STILL SENSE HIM! BUT-- HOW?
HOLD IT, SON! YOU WERE THE CLOSEST! DID YOU SEE WHERE THAT JOKER RAN OFF TO!
IT LOOKED TO ME AS IF HE JUST FADED AWAY!
I THOUGHT SO TOO! BUT IT ISN'T POSSIBLE! THERE MUST BE AN ANSWER!
THERE IS! BUT ONLY SPIDEY CAN FIND IT!
MADIS
I'VE GOT TO FIND A PLACE TO CHANGE-- AND FAST!
IF I RUSH, I MIGHT STILL-- HEY, WAIT A MINUTE!
WHY AM I BEING SUCH AN EAGER BEAVER?
EVEN IF I NAB HIM-- WHAT'LL PETER PARKER GET OUT OF IT?
LET THE POLICE TACKLE HIM! I'M SICK OF BEING A FALL GUY!
8

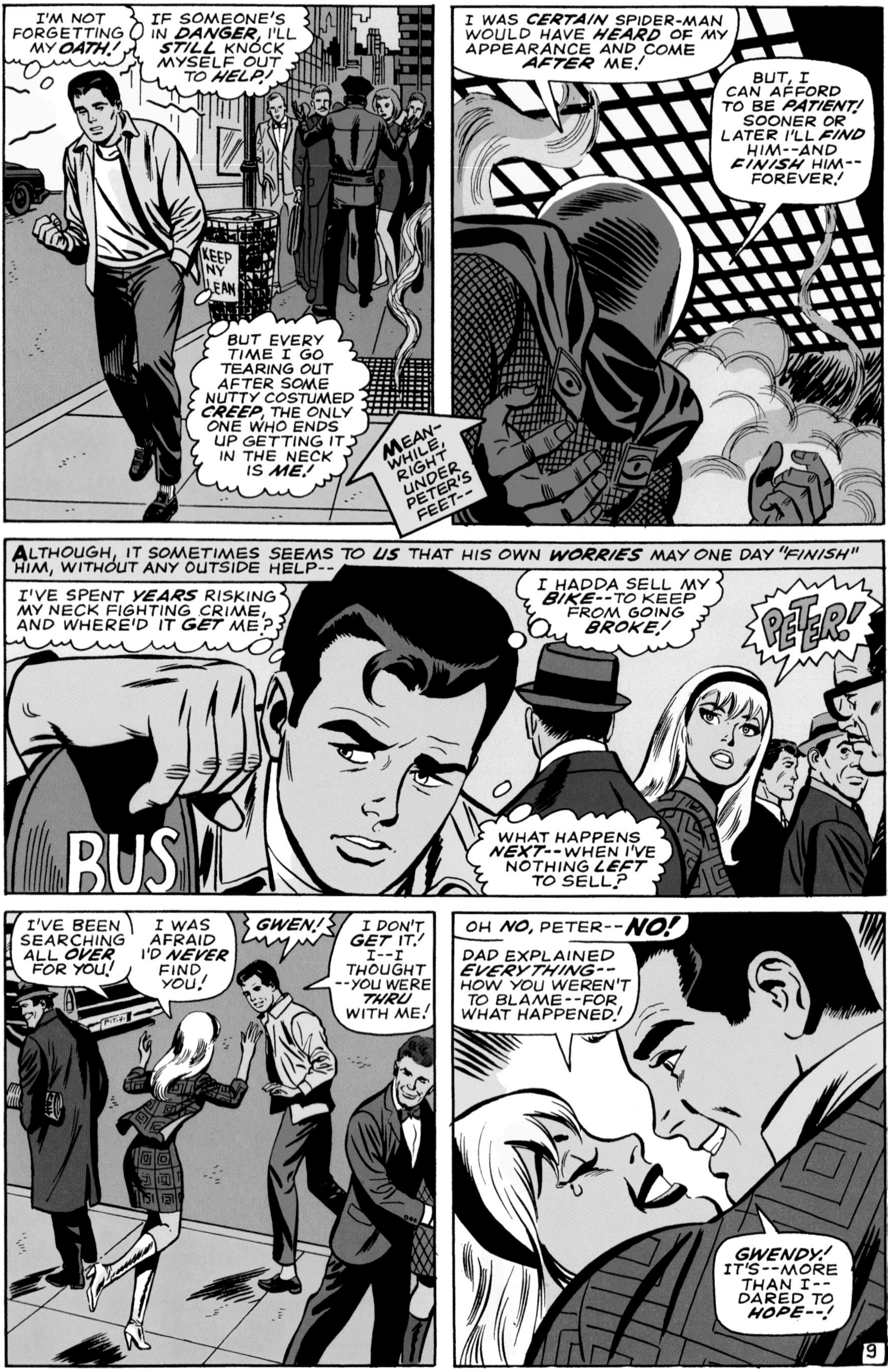
I'M NOT FORGETTING MY OATH!
IF SOMEONE'S IN DANGER, I'LL STILL KNOCK MYSELF OUT TO HELP!
KEEP NY LEAN
BUT EVERY TIME I GO TEARING OUT AFTER SOME NUTTY COSTUMED CREEP, THE ONLY ONE WHO ENDS UP GETTING IT IN THE NECK IS ME!
MEAN-WHILE, RIGHT UNDER PETER'S FEET--
I WAS CERTAIN SPIDER-MAN WOULD HAVE HEARD OF MY APPEARANCE AND COME AFTER ME!
BUT, I CAN AFFORD TO BE PATIENT! SOONER OR LATER I'LL FIND HIM--AND FINISH HIM--FOREVER!
ALTHOUGH, IT SOMETIMES SEEMS TO US THAT HIS OWN WORRIES MAY ONE DAY "FINISH" HIM, WITHOUT ANY OUTSIDE HELP--
I'VE SPENT YEARS RISKING MY NECK FIGHTING CRIME, AND WHERE'D IT GET ME?
I HADDA SELL MY BIKE--TO KEEP FROM GOING BROKE!
PETER!
BUS
WHAT HAPPENS NEXT--WHEN I'VE NOTHING LEFT TO SELL?
I'VE BEEN SEARCHING ALL OVER FOR YOU!
I WAS AFRAID I'D NEVER FIND YOU!
GWEN!
I DON'T GET IT! I--I THOUGHT --YOU WERE THRU WITH ME!
OH NO, PETER--NO!
DAD EXPLAINED EVERYTHING-- HOW YOU WEREN'T TO BLAME--FOR WHAT HAPPENED!
GWENDY! IT'S--MORE THAN I-- DARED TO HOPE--!
9

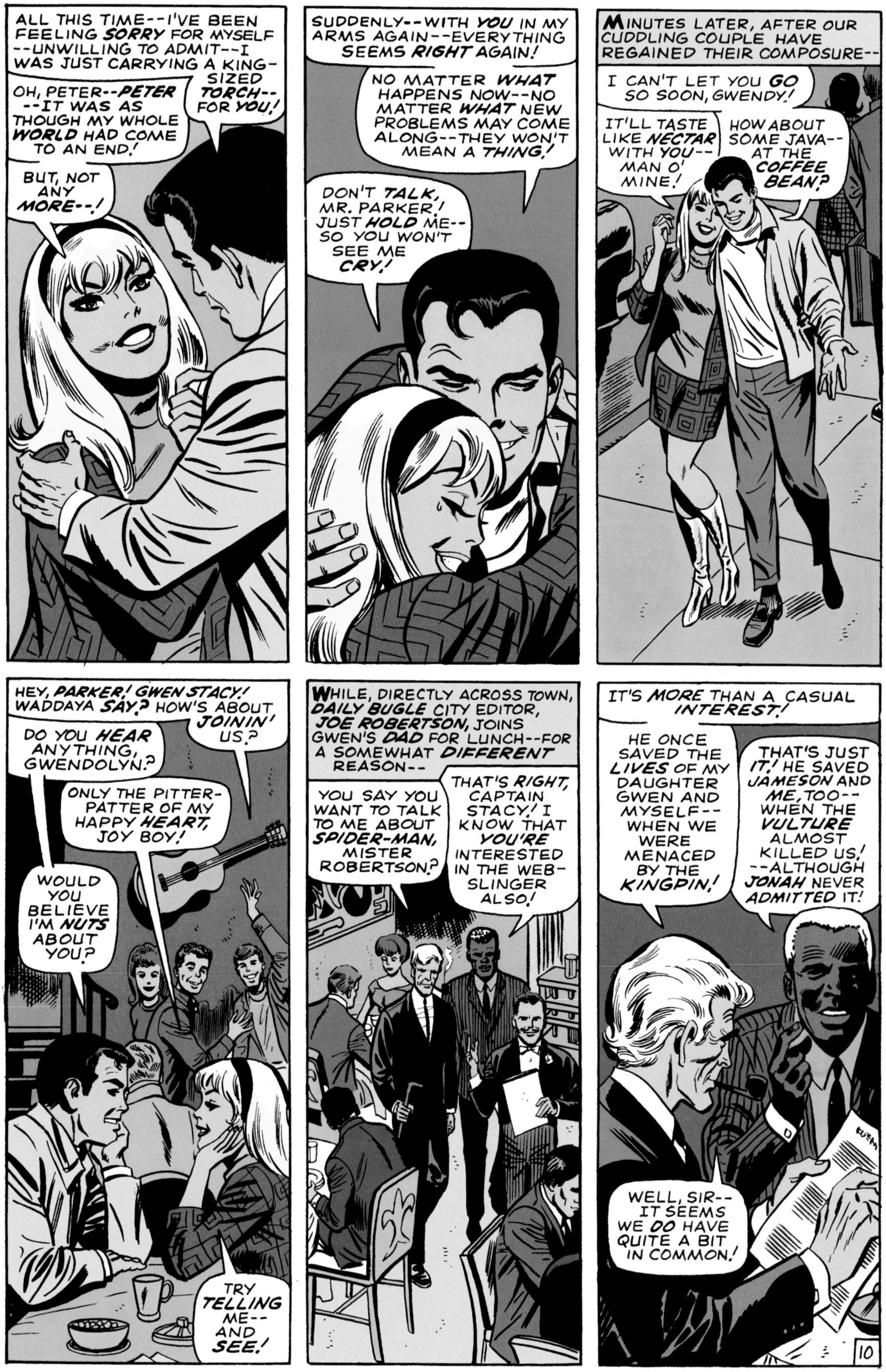
ALL THIS TIME--I'VE BEEN FEELING SORRY FOR MYSELF --UNWILLING TO ADMIT--I WAS JUST CARRYING A KING-SIZED TORCH--FOR YOU!
OH, PETER--PETER --IT WAS AS THOUGH MY WHOLE WORLD HAD COME TO AN END!
BUT, NOT ANY MORE--!
SUDDENLY--WITH YOU IN MY ARMS AGAIN--EVERYTHING SEEMS RIGHT AGAIN!
NO MATTER WHAT HAPPENS NOW--NO MATTER WHAT NEW PROBLEMS MAY COME ALONG--THEY WON'T MEAN A THING!
DON'T TALK, MR. PARKER! JUST HOLD ME--SO YOU WON'T SEE ME CRY!
MINUTES LATER, AFTER OUR CUDDLING COUPLE HAVE REGAINED THEIR COMPOSURE--
I CAN'T LET YOU GO SO SOON, GWENDY!
HOW ABOUT SOME JAVA--AT THE COFFEE BEAN?
IT'LL TASTE LIKE NECTAR WITH YOU--MAN O' MINE!
HEY, PARKER! GWEN STACY! WADDAYA SAY? HOW'S ABOUT JOININ' US?
DO YOU HEAR ANYTHING, GWENDOLYN?
ONLY THE PITTER-PATTER OF MY HAPPY HEART, JOY BOY!
WOULD YOU BELIEVE I'M NUTS ABOUT YOU?
TRY TELLING ME--AND SEE!
WHILE, DIRECTLY ACROSS TOWN, DAILY BUGLE CITY EDITOR, JOE ROBERTSON, JOINS GWEN'S DAD FOR LUNCH--FOR A SOMEWHAT DIFFERENT REASON--
YOU SAY YOU WANT TO TALK TO ME ABOUT SPIDER-MAN, MISTER ROBERTSON?
THAT'S RIGHT, CAPTAIN STACY! I KNOW THAT YOU'RE INTERESTED IN THE WEB-SLINGER ALSO!
IT'S MORE THAN A CASUAL INTEREST!
HE ONCE SAVED THE LIVES OF MY DAUGHTER GWEN AND MYSELF--WHEN WE WERE MENACED BY THE KINGPIN!
THAT'S JUST IT! HE SAVED JAMESON AND ME, TOO--WHEN THE VULTURE ALMOST KILLED US! --ALTHOUGH JONAH NEVER ADMITTED IT!
WELL, SIR--IT SEEMS WE DO HAVE QUITE A BIT IN COMMON!
10

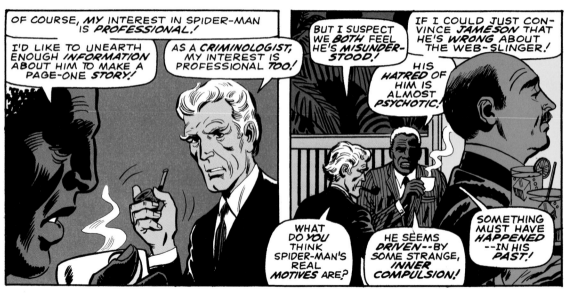

OF COURSE, *MY* INTEREST IN SPIDER-MAN IS *PROFESSIONAL!*

I'D LIKE TO UNEARTH ENOUGH *INFORMATION* ABOUT HIM TO MAKE A PAGE-ONE *STORY!*

AS A *CRIMINOLOGIST,* MY INTEREST IS PROFESSIONAL *TOO!*

BUT I SUSPECT WE *BOTH* FEEL HE'S *MISUNDERSTOOD!*

IF I COULD JUST CONVINCE *JAMESON* THAT HE'S *WRONG* ABOUT THE WEB-SLINGER!

HIS *HATRED* OF HIM IS ALMOST *PSYCHOTIC!*

WHAT DO *YOU* THINK SPIDER-MAN'S REAL *MOTIVES* ARE?

HE SEEMS *DRIVEN*--BY SOME STRANGE, *INNER COMPULSION!*

SOMETHING MUST HAVE *HAPPENED* --IN HIS *PAST!*

FINALLY--

SOMEHOW, I CAN'T ESCAPE THE NAGGING FEELING THAT I *KNOW* HIM!

WE *BOTH* HAVE REASON TO FEEL THAT *HE* KNOWS *US,* AT ANY RATE!

WELL LET'S KEEP IN TOUCH, CAPTAIN STACY!

BY ALL MEANS!

I THINK WE SHOULD COMPARE NOTES MORE *OFTEN!*

*A*ND, WHETHER THAT LITTLE MEETING BODES *GOOD*--OR *BAD* FOR SPIDEY, ONLY TIME WILL TELL! MEANWHILE--

NO MATTER *HOW* MANY THINGS ARE GOING WRONG IN MY LIFE--

NOW THAT I HAVE *GWEN* AGAIN-- *NOTHING'LL* EVER MAKE ME TOSS IN THE TOWEL!

I HOPE *HARRY'S* HOME! I'D LIKE TO--

WELL! SPEAK OF THE *DEVIL!*

PETE! I WAS *WONDERING* WHERE YOU WERE!

ANY WORD FROM YOUR *DAD* YET?

NO--DON'T BOTHER ANSWERING! I CAN TELL BY YOUR *FACE!*

BUT, YOU'VE GOTTA GET *HOLD* OF YOURSELF, MAN! IT CAN'T BE ALL *THAT* BAD!

IT *IS,* PETE! I *KNOW* IT!

I HAVE A FEELING--THAT I'LL *NEVER* SEE MY FATHER-- AGAIN!

THAT'S NOT LIKE *YOU,* BUDDY! WHAT ABOUT HIS *FACTORY?* MAYBE HE'S *RETURNED!* LET'S *TRY* IT!

SURE--SURE! ANYTHING YOU SAY!

11

BUT, UPON REACHING THE SPRAWLING PLANT--

NO, YOUR FATHER HASN'T BEEN HERE FOR DAYS!

WE FIGURED HE'S ON VACATION!

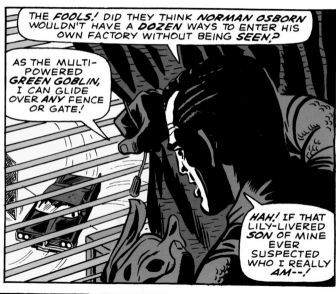

THE FOOLS! DID THEY THINK NORMAN OSBORN WOULDN'T HAVE A DOZEN WAYS TO ENTER HIS OWN FACTORY WITHOUT BEING SEEN?

AS THE MULTI-POWERED GREEN GOBLIN, I CAN GLIDE OVER ANY FENCE OR GATE!

HAH! IF THAT LILY-LIVERED SON OF MINE EVER SUSPECTED WHO I REALLY AM--!

BUT, LET HIM SEARCH FOR ME--

HIM--AND THAT HOLIER-THAN-THOU ROOMMATE OF HIS!

HIS ROOMMATE!

WHY DOES THE MERE THOUGHT OF HIM MAKE MY BLOOD BOIL?

I WON'T BE IN THE DARK MUCH LONGER!

MY MEMORY GETS CLEARER WITH EACH PASSING SECOND!

I CAN'T EVEN TELL HARRY THE TRUTH ABOUT HIS FATHER!

BUT IF OSBORN BECOMES THE GOBLIN AGAIN--AND REMEMBERS WHO I AM--THAT'LL SINK EVERYTHING!

WOULD YOU DROP ME AT MY AUNT MAY'S HARRY?

MIGHT AS WELL... THERE'S NO PLACE LEFT TO LOOK!

SURE YOU WON'T COME IN?

NO THANKS, PETE! I WANNA KEEP DRIVING!

IT'S THE ONLY THING THAT RELAXES ME!

AND THERE'S ALWAYS THE CHANCE--I'LL CATCH A GLIMPSE OF HIM!

OKAY, HARRY! I UNDERSTAND!

I'LL SEE YOU LATER ON!

AND TAKE IT EASY, HEAR?

IT'S JUST AS WELL HE DIDN'T JOIN ME!

AUNT MAY IS SURE TO HAVE A MILLION QUESTIONS TO ASK!

OH NO!

THAT'S HER VOICE!

WHAT'S WRONG? WHAT'S HAPPENING IN THERE??

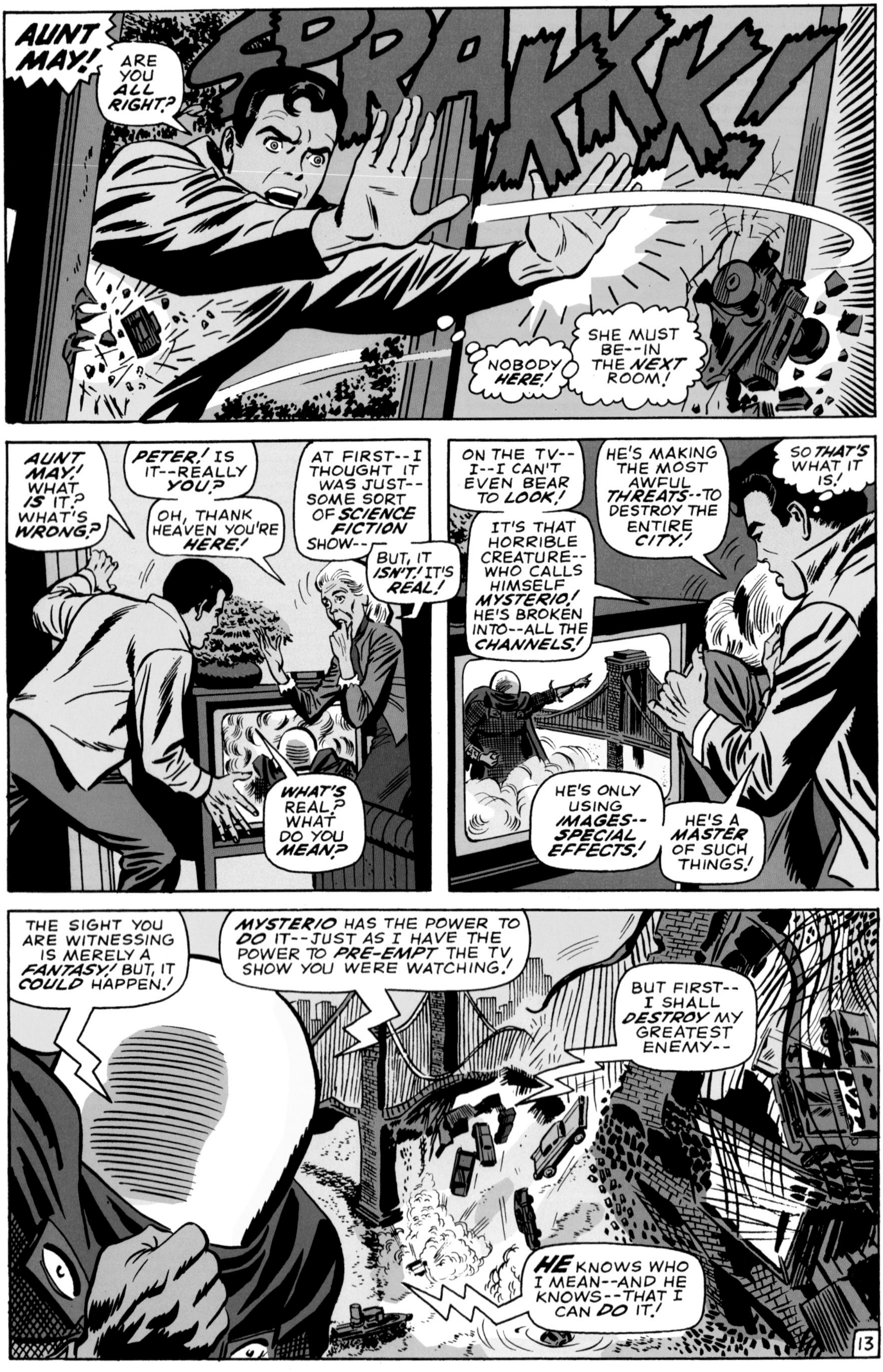
AUNT MAY!
ARE YOU ALL RIGHT?
SPRAKKK!
NOBODY HERE!
SHE MUST BE--IN THE NEXT ROOM!
AUNT MAY! WHAT IS IT? WHAT'S WRONG?
PETER! IS IT--REALLY YOU?
OH, THANK HEAVEN YOU'RE HERE!
AT FIRST--I THOUGHT IT WAS JUST--SOME SORT OF SCIENCE FICTION SHOW--
BUT, IT ISN'T! IT'S REAL!
WHAT'S REAL? WHAT DO YOU MEAN?
ON THE TV--I--I CAN'T EVEN BEAR TO LOOK!
IT'S THAT HORRIBLE CREATURE--WHO CALLS HIMSELF MYSTERIO! HE'S BROKEN INTO--ALL THE CHANNELS!
HE'S MAKING THE MOST AWFUL THREATS--TO DESTROY THE ENTIRE CITY!
SO THAT'S WHAT IT IS!
HE'S ONLY USING IMAGES--SPECIAL EFFECTS!
HE'S A MASTER OF SUCH THINGS!
THE SIGHT YOU ARE WITNESSING IS MERELY A FANTASY! BUT, IT COULD HAPPEN.!
MYSTERIO HAS THE POWER TO DO IT--JUST AS I HAVE THE POWER TO PRE-EMPT THE TV SHOW YOU WERE WATCHING!
BUT FIRST--I SHALL DESTROY MY GREATEST ENEMY--
HE KNOWS WHO I MEAN--AND HE KNOWS--THAT I CAN DO IT!
13

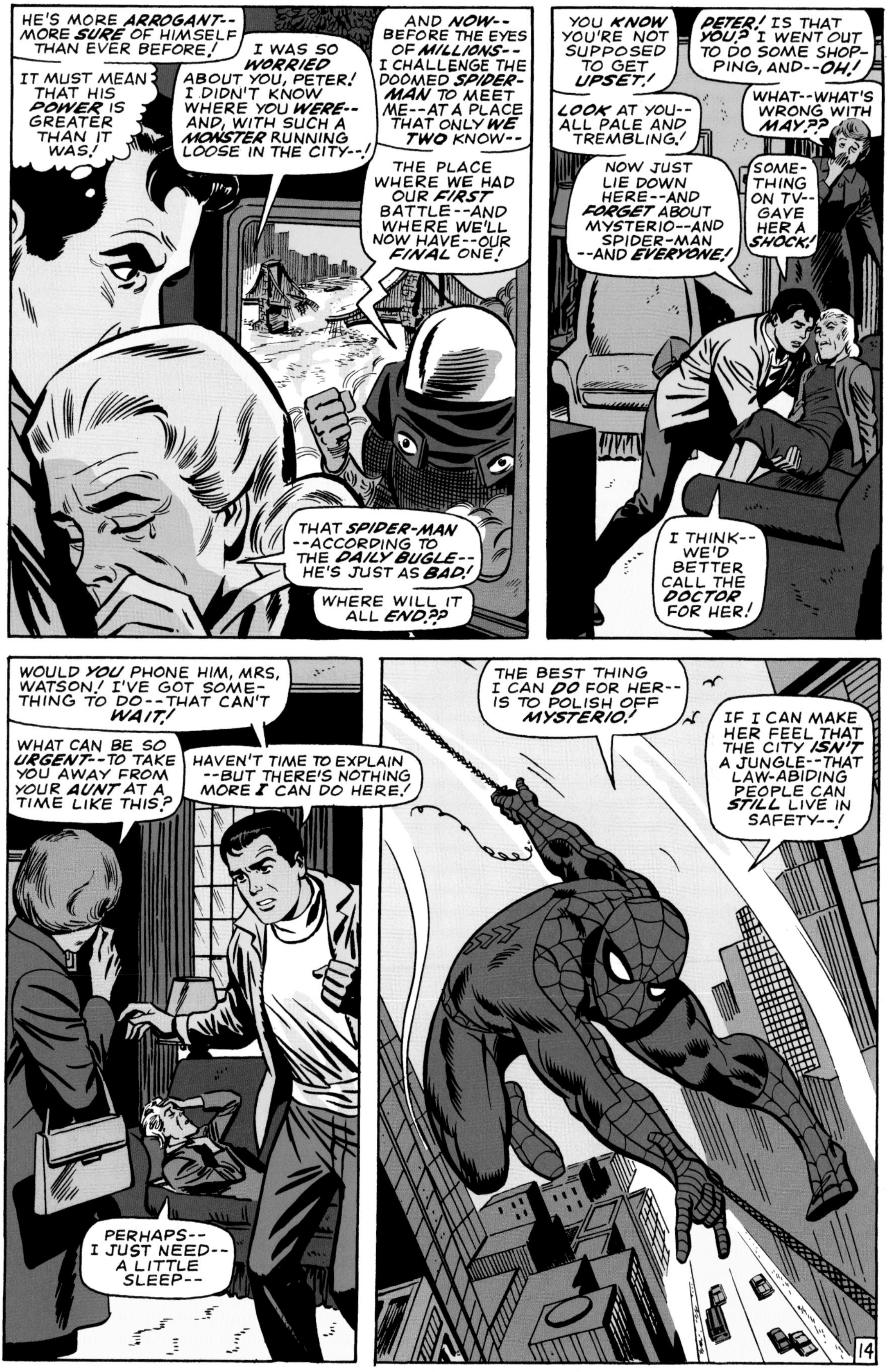
HE'S MORE ARROGANT--MORE SURE OF HIMSELF THAN EVER BEFORE!
IT MUST MEAN THAT HIS POWER IS GREATER THAN IT WAS!
I WAS SO WORRIED ABOUT YOU, PETER! I DIDN'T KNOW WHERE YOU WERE--AND, WITH SUCH A MONSTER RUNNING LOOSE IN THE CITY--!
AND NOW--BEFORE THE EYES OF MILLIONS--I CHALLENGE THE DOOMED SPIDER-MAN TO MEET ME--AT A PLACE THAT ONLY WE TWO KNOW--
THE PLACE WHERE WE HAD OUR FIRST BATTLE--AND WHERE WE'LL NOW HAVE--OUR FINAL ONE!
THAT SPIDER-MAN--ACCORDING TO THE DAILY BUGLE--HE'S JUST AS BAD!
WHERE WILL IT ALL END??
YOU KNOW YOU'RE NOT SUPPOSED TO GET UPSET!
PETER! IS THAT YOU? I WENT OUT TO DO SOME SHOPPING, AND--OH!
LOOK AT YOU--ALL PALE AND TREMBLING!
WHAT--WHAT'S WRONG WITH MAY??
NOW JUST LIE DOWN HERE--AND FORGET ABOUT MYSTERIO--AND SPIDER-MAN--AND EVERYONE!
SOMETHING ON TV--GAVE HER A SHOCK!
I THINK--WE'D BETTER CALL THE DOCTOR FOR HER!
WOULD YOU PHONE HIM, MRS. WATSON! I'VE GOT SOMETHING TO DO--THAT CAN'T WAIT!
WHAT CAN BE SO URGENT--TO TAKE YOU AWAY FROM YOUR AUNT AT A TIME LIKE THIS?
HAVEN'T TIME TO EXPLAIN--BUT THERE'S NOTHING MORE I CAN DO HERE!
PERHAPS--I JUST NEED--A LITTLE SLEEP--
THE BEST THING I CAN DO FOR HER--IS TO POLISH OFF MYSTERIO!
IF I CAN MAKE HER FEEL THAT THE CITY ISN'T A JUNGLE--THAT LAW-ABIDING PEOPLE CAN STILL LIVE IN SAFETY--!
14

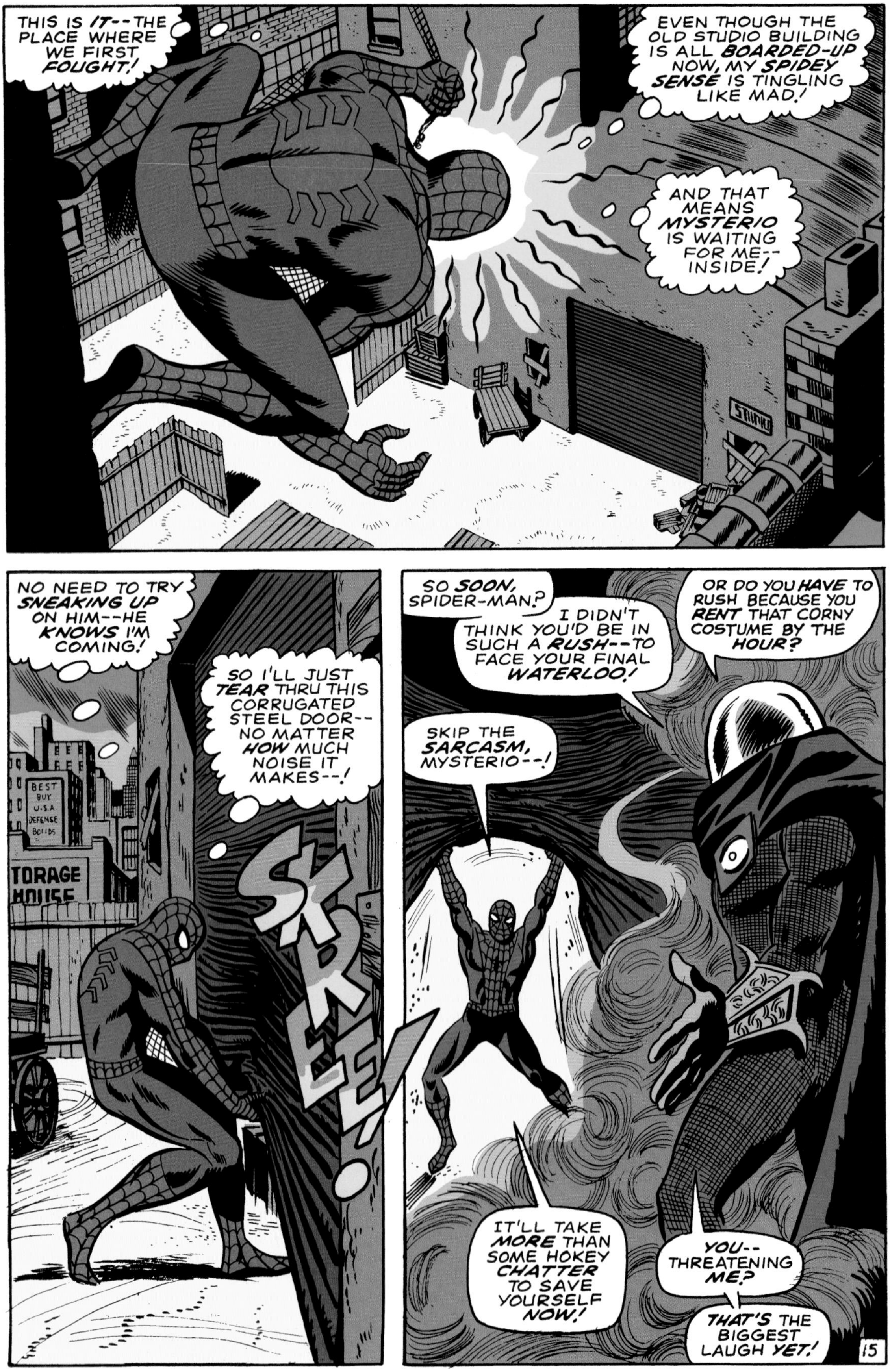
THIS IS IT--THE PLACE WHERE WE FIRST FOUGHT!
EVEN THOUGH THE OLD STUDIO BUILDING IS ALL BOARDED-UP NOW, MY SPIDEY SENSE IS TINGLING LIKE MAD!
AND THAT MEANS MYSTERIO IS WAITING FOR ME--INSIDE!
STUDIO
NO NEED TO TRY SNEAKING UP ON HIM--HE KNOWS I'M COMING!
SO I'LL JUST TEAR THRU THIS CORRUGATED STEEL DOOR--NO MATTER HOW MUCH NOISE IT MAKES--!
BEST BUY U.S.A. DEFENSE BONDS
TORAGE HOUSE
SKREEE!
SO SOON, SPIDER-MAN?
I DIDN'T THINK YOU'D BE IN SUCH A RUSH--TO FACE YOUR FINAL WATERLOO!
OR DO YOU HAVE TO RUSH BECAUSE YOU RENT THAT CORNY COSTUME BY THE HOUR?
SKIP THE SARCASM, MYSTERIO--!
IT'LL TAKE MORE THAN SOME HOKEY CHATTER TO SAVE YOURSELF NOW!
YOU--THREATENING ME?
THAT'S THE BIGGEST LAUGH YET!
15

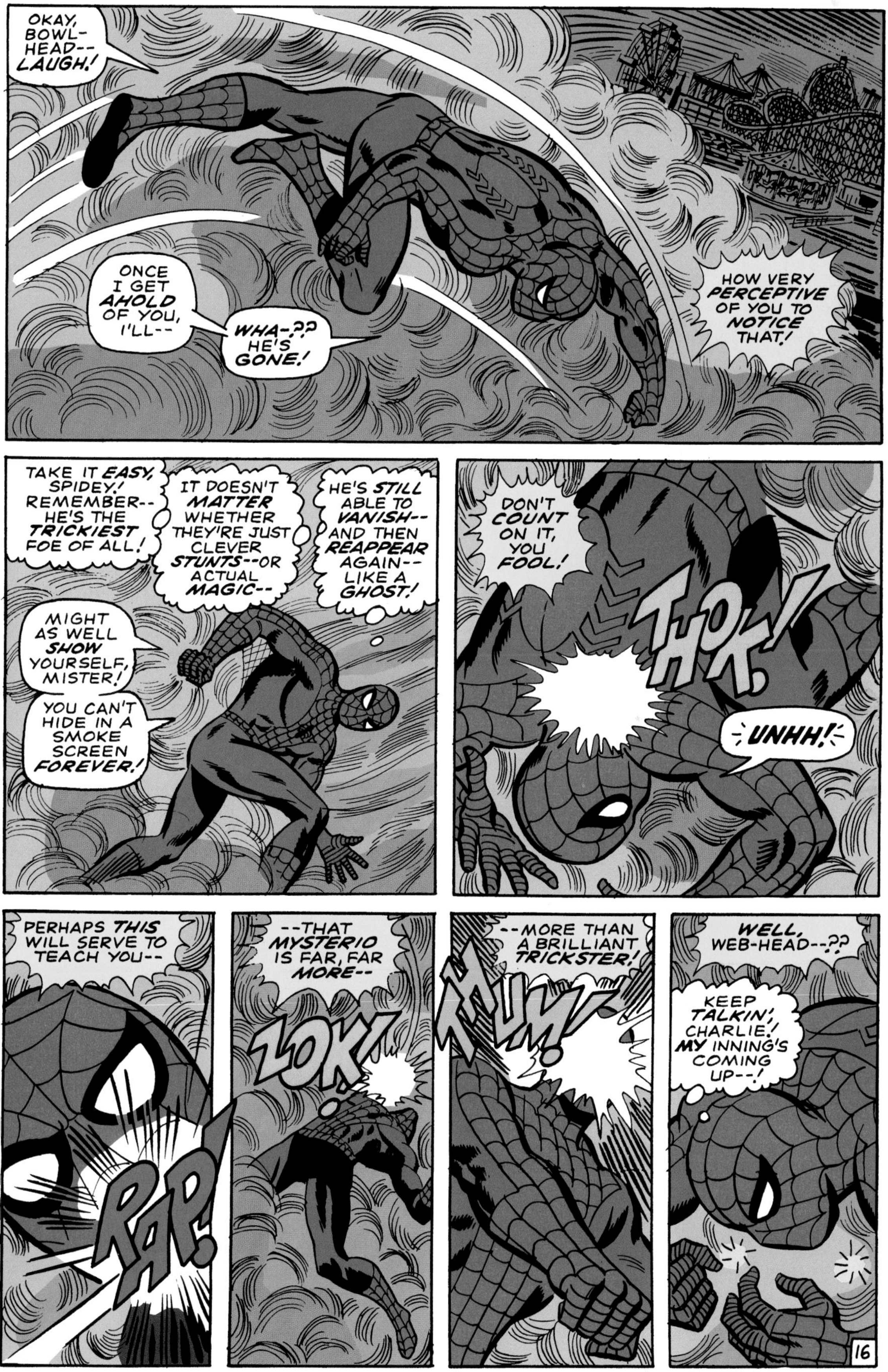
OKAY, BOWL-HEAD-- LAUGH!
ONCE I GET AHOLD OF YOU, I'LL--
WHA-?? HE'S GONE!
HOW VERY PERCEPTIVE OF YOU TO NOTICE THAT!
TAKE IT EASY, SPIDEY! REMEMBER-- HE'S THE TRICKIEST FOE OF ALL!
IT DOESN'T MATTER WHETHER THEY'RE JUST CLEVER STUNTS--OR ACTUAL MAGIC--
HE'S STILL ABLE TO VANISH-- AND THEN REAPPEAR AGAIN-- LIKE A GHOST!
MIGHT AS WELL SHOW YOURSELF, MISTER!
YOU CAN'T HIDE IN A SMOKE SCREEN FOREVER!
DON'T COUNT ON IT, YOU FOOL!
THOK!
UNHH!
PERHAPS THIS WILL SERVE TO TEACH YOU--
RAP!
--THAT MYSTERIO IS FAR, FAR MORE--
ZOK!
--MORE THAN A BRILLIANT TRICKSTER!
THUM!
WELL, WEB-HEAD--??
KEEP TALKIN', CHARLIE! MY INNING'S COMING UP--!
16

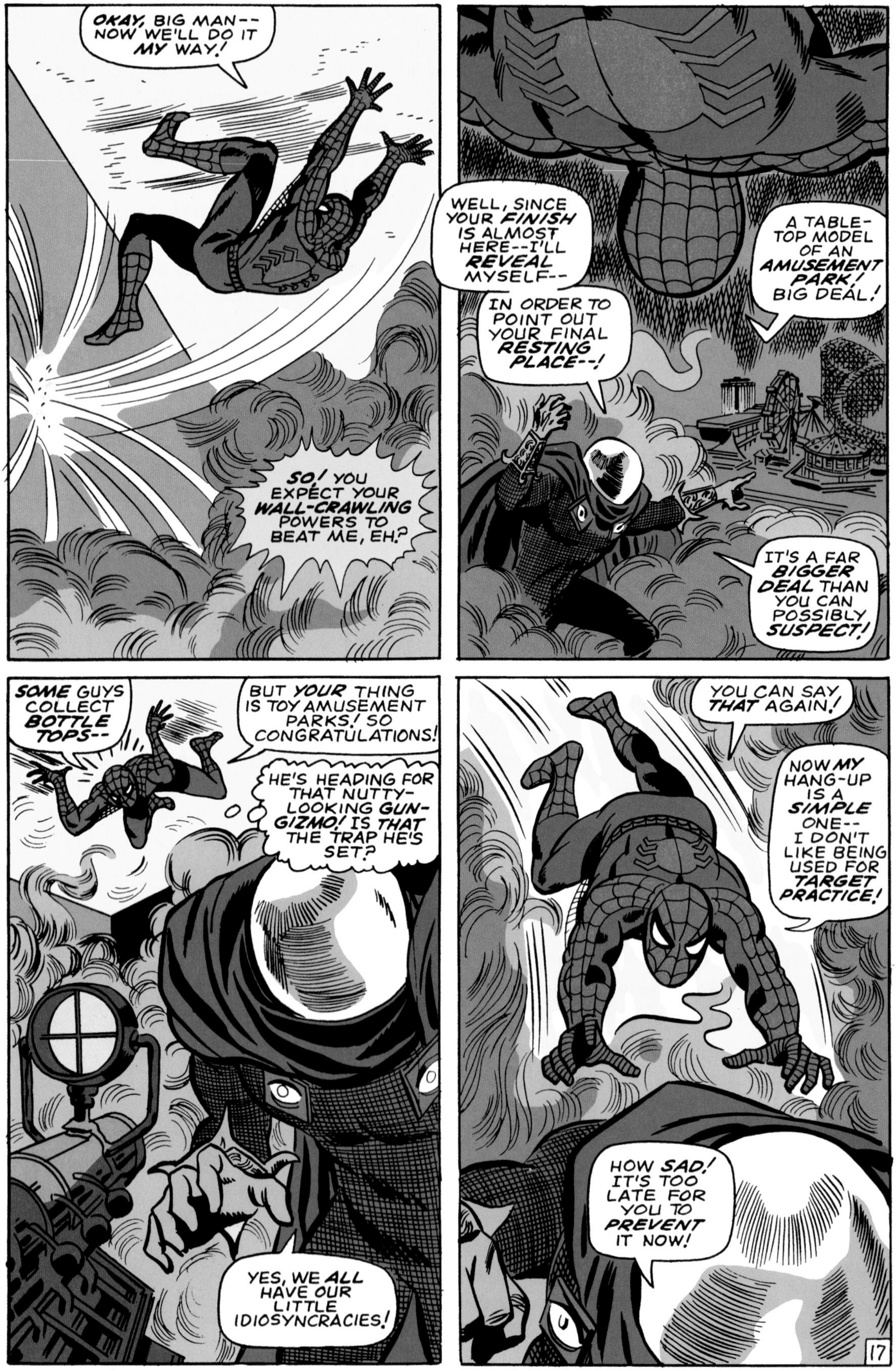
OKAY, BIG MAN-- NOW WE'LL DO IT MY WAY!
SO! YOU EXPECT YOUR WALL-CRAWLING POWERS TO BEAT ME, EH?
WELL, SINCE YOUR FINISH IS ALMOST HERE--I'LL REVEAL MYSELF--
IN ORDER TO POINT OUT YOUR FINAL RESTING PLACE--!
A TABLE-TOP MODEL OF AN AMUSEMENT PARK! BIG DEAL!
IT'S A FAR BIGGER DEAL THAN YOU CAN POSSIBLY SUSPECT!
SOME GUYS COLLECT BOTTLE TOPS--
BUT YOUR THING IS TOY AMUSEMENT PARKS! SO CONGRATULATIONS!
HE'S HEADING FOR THAT NUTTY-LOOKING GUN-GIZMO! IS THAT THE TRAP HE'S SET?
YES, WE ALL HAVE OUR LITTLE IDIOSYNCRACIES!
YOU CAN SAY THAT AGAIN!
NOW MY HANG-UP IS A SIMPLE ONE-- I DON'T LIKE BEING USED FOR TARGET PRACTICE!
HOW SAD! IT'S TOO LATE FOR YOU TO PREVENT IT NOW!
17

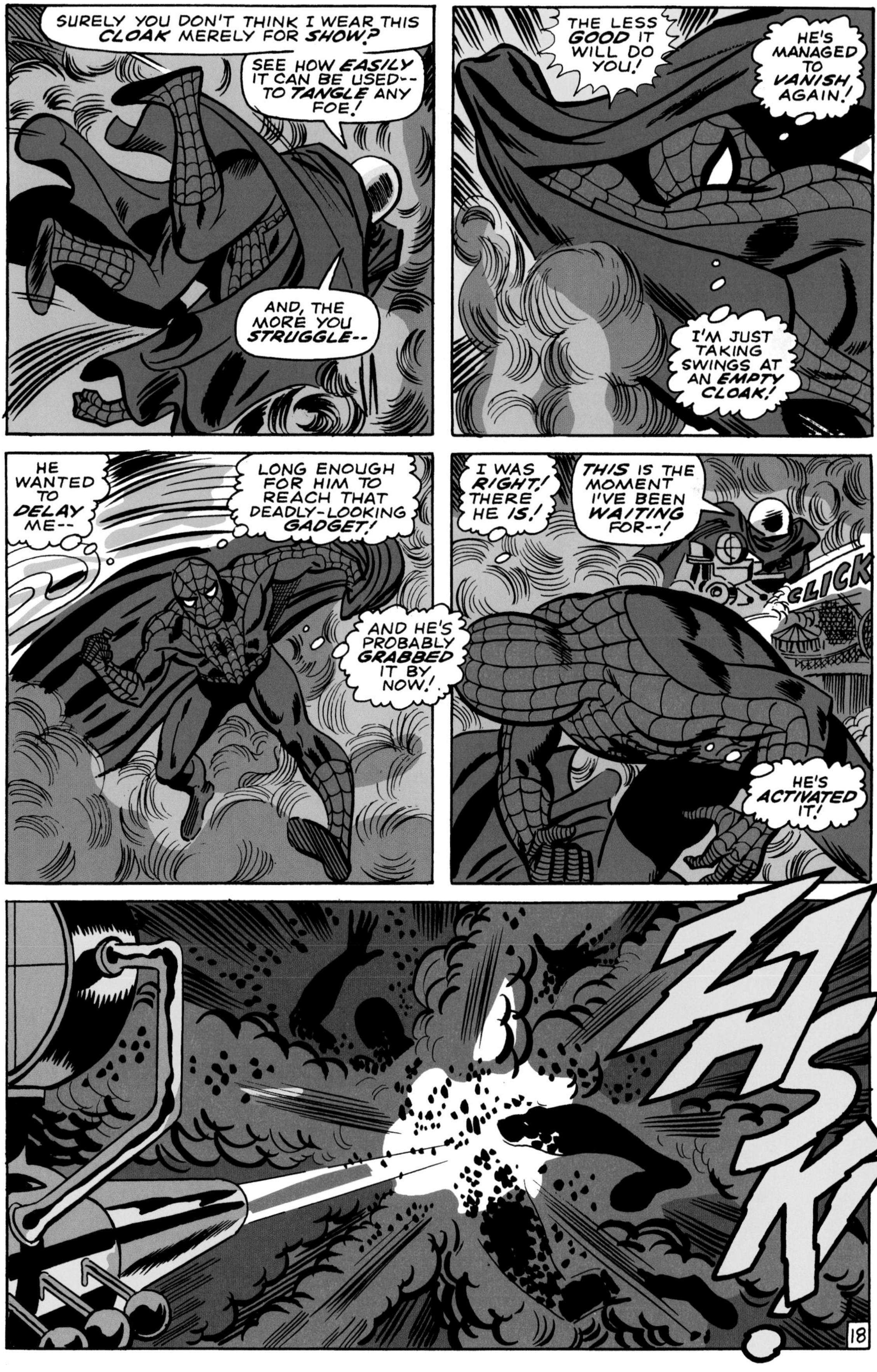
SURELY YOU DON'T THINK I WEAR THIS CLOAK MERELY FOR SHOW?
SEE HOW EASILY IT CAN BE USED-- TO TANGLE ANY FOE!
AND, THE MORE YOU STRUGGLE--
THE LESS GOOD IT WILL DO YOU!
HE'S MANAGED TO VANISH AGAIN!
I'M JUST TAKING SWINGS AT AN EMPTY CLOAK!
HE WANTED TO DELAY ME--
LONG ENOUGH FOR HIM TO REACH THAT DEADLY-LOOKING GADGET!
AND HE'S PROBABLY GRABBED IT BY NOW!
I WAS RIGHT! THERE HE IS!
THIS IS THE MOMENT I'VE BEEN WAITING FOR--!
CLICK
HE'S ACTIVATED IT!
ZZZSK!
18

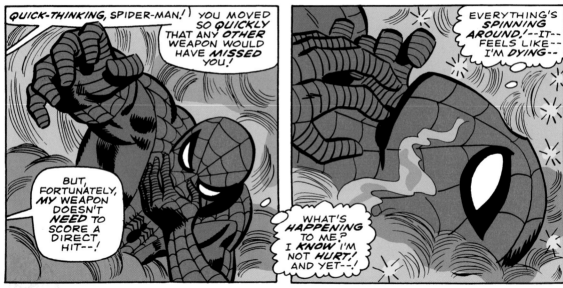

QUICK-THINKING, SPIDER-MAN! YOU MOVED SO QUICKLY THAT ANY *OTHER* WEAPON WOULD HAVE *MISSED* YOU!

BUT, *FORTUNATELY,* MY WEAPON DOESN'T *NEED* TO SCORE A DIRECT HIT--!

EVERYTHING'S *SPINNING AROUND!*--IT-- FEELS LIKE-- I'M *DYING*--

WHAT'S *HAPPENING* TO ME? I *KNOW* I'M NOT *HURT!* AND YET--!

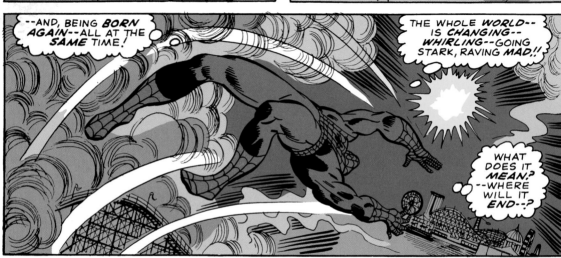

--AND, BEING *BORN AGAIN*--ALL AT THE *SAME* TIME!

THE WHOLE *WORLD*-- IS *CHANGING*-- *WHIRLING*--GOING STARK, RAVING *MAD!!*

WHAT DOES IT *MEAN?* --WHERE WILL IT *END*--?

EVERYTHING *STOPPED!* THE SMOKE IS *CLEARING!*

THERE'S NO *SOUND!* I--NEVER HEARD-- SUCH *SILENCE* BEFORE!

WHY--DO I FEEL--SO STRANGELY *DIFFERENT??*

NO! IT *CAN'T* BE!! IT *CAN'T*--!!

19

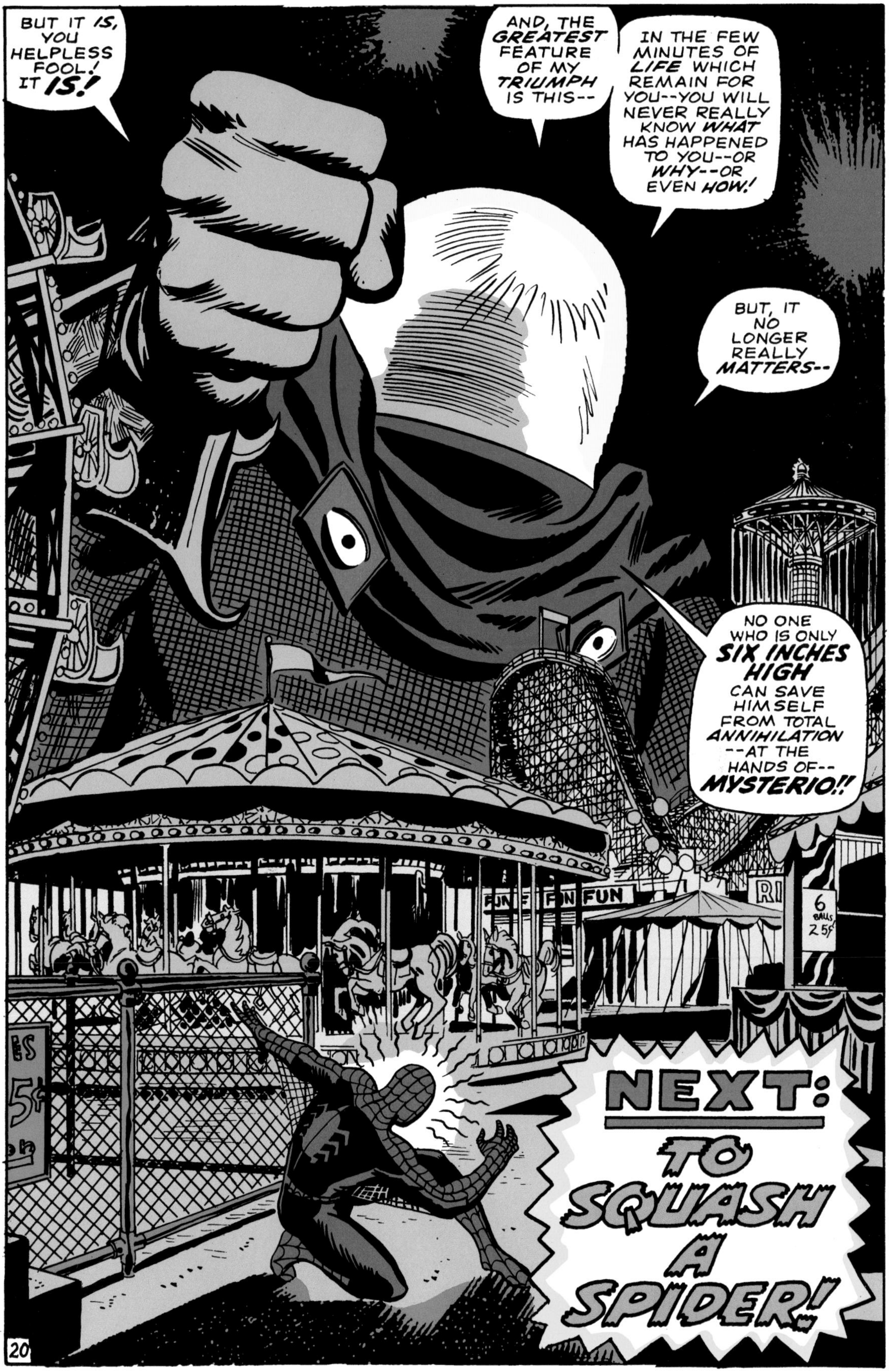
BUT IT IS, YOU HELPLESS FOOL! IT IS!
AND, THE GREATEST FEATURE OF MY TRIUMPH IS THIS--
IN THE FEW MINUTES OF LIFE WHICH REMAIN FOR YOU--YOU WILL NEVER REALLY KNOW WHAT HAS HAPPENED TO YOU--OR WHY--OR EVEN HOW!
BUT, IT NO LONGER REALLY MATTERS--
NO ONE WHO IS ONLY SIX INCHES HIGH CAN SAVE HIMSELF FROM TOTAL ANNIHILATION --AT THE HANDS OF-- MYSTERIO!!
FUN FUN FUN
6 BALLS 25¢
NEXT:
TO SQUASH A SPIDER!
20

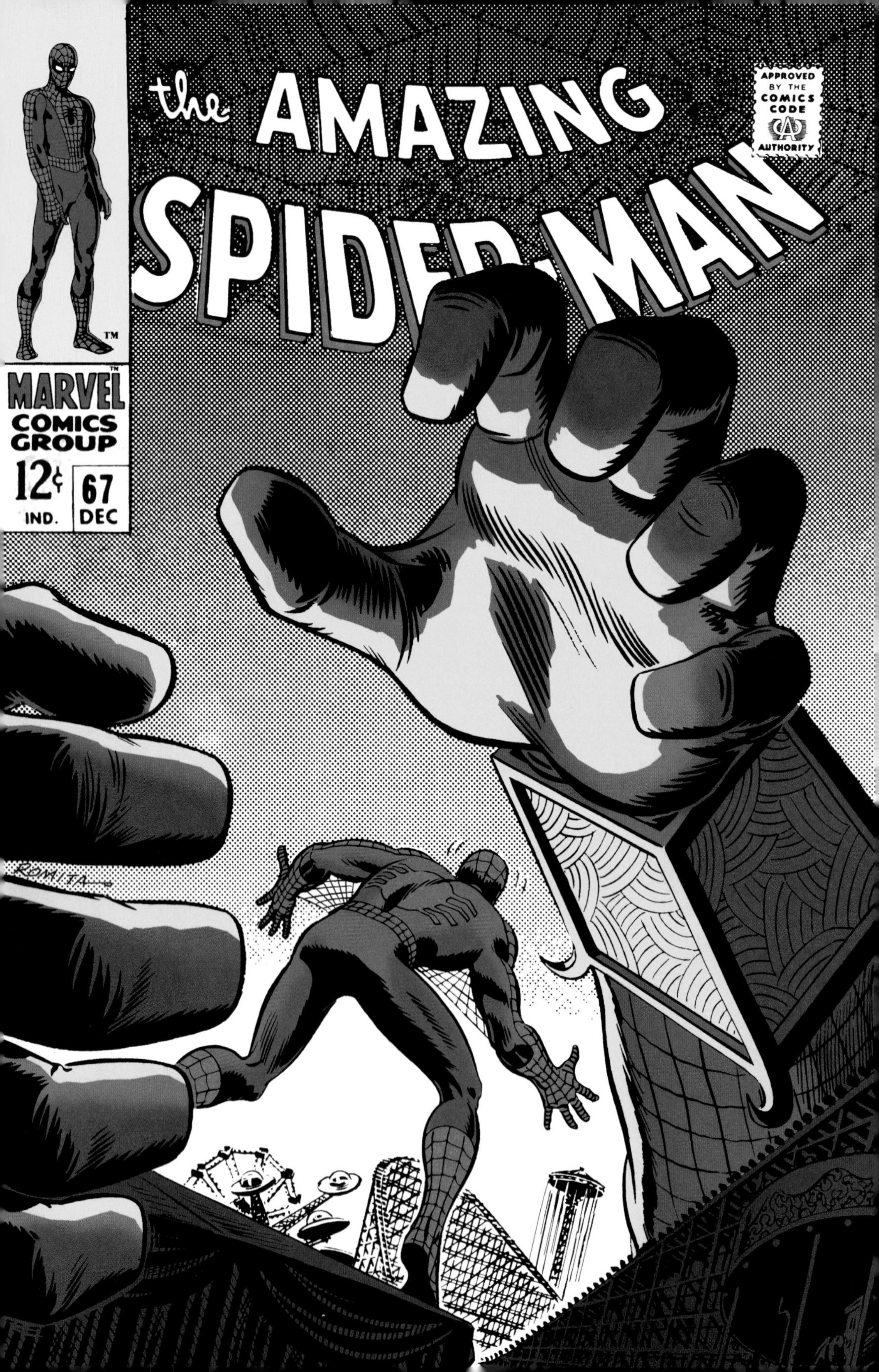
the AMAZING
SPIDER-MAN
APPROVED BY THE COMICS CODE AUTHORITY
MARVEL COMICS GROUP
12¢ IND.
67 DEC
ROMITA

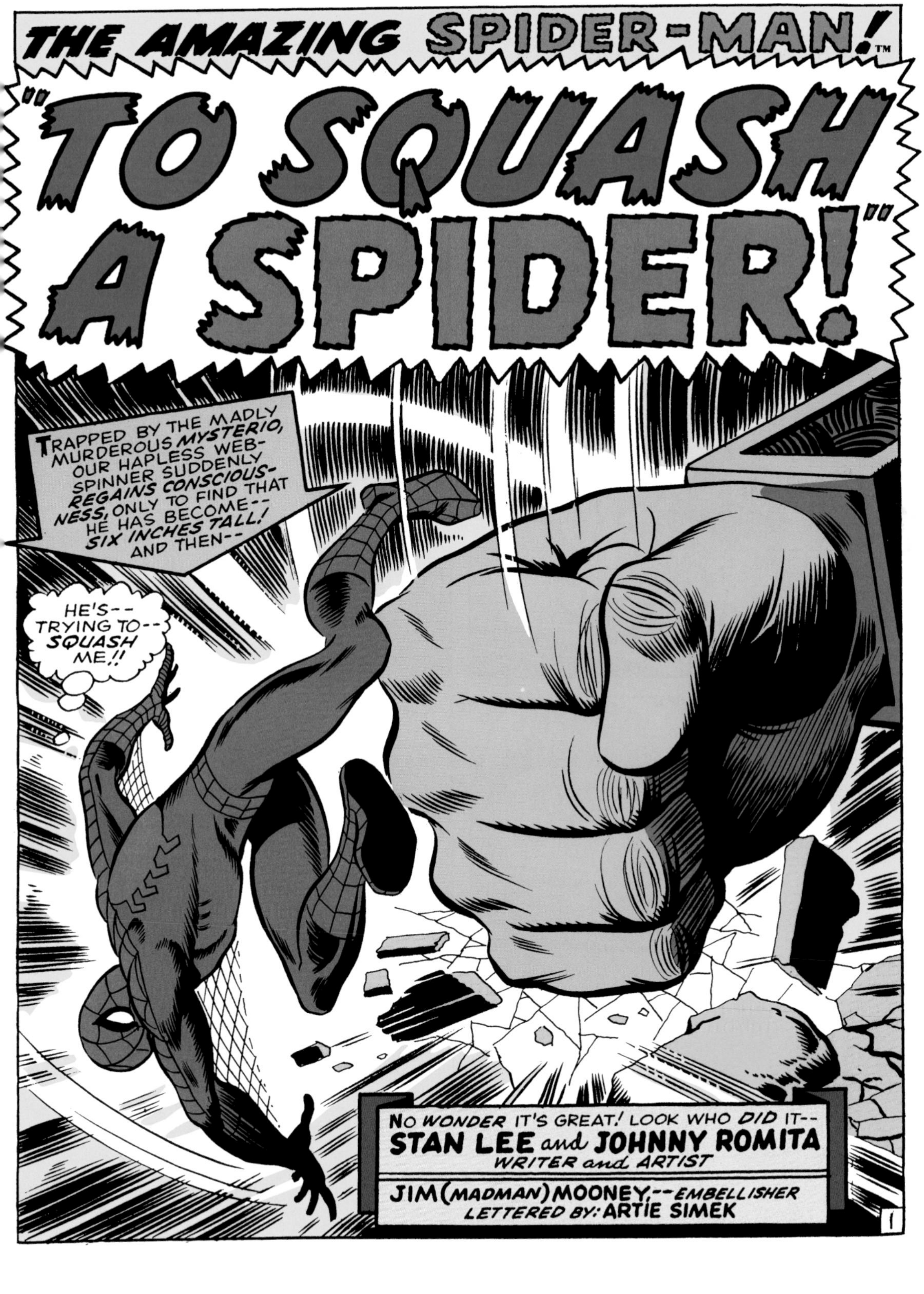
THE AMAZING SPIDER-MAN!™
"TO SQUASH A SPIDER!"
TRAPPED BY THE MADLY MURDEROUS MYSTERIO, OUR HAPLESS WEB-SPINNER SUDDENLY REGAINS CONSCIOUSNESS, ONLY TO FIND THAT HE HAS BECOME-- SIX INCHES TALL! AND THEN--
HE'S-- TRYING TO-- SQUASH ME!!
NO WONDER IT'S GREAT! LOOK WHO DID IT-- STAN LEE and JOHNNY ROMITA WRITER and ARTIST
JIM (MADMAN) MOONEY,--EMBELLISHER
LETTERED BY: ARTIE SIMEK
1

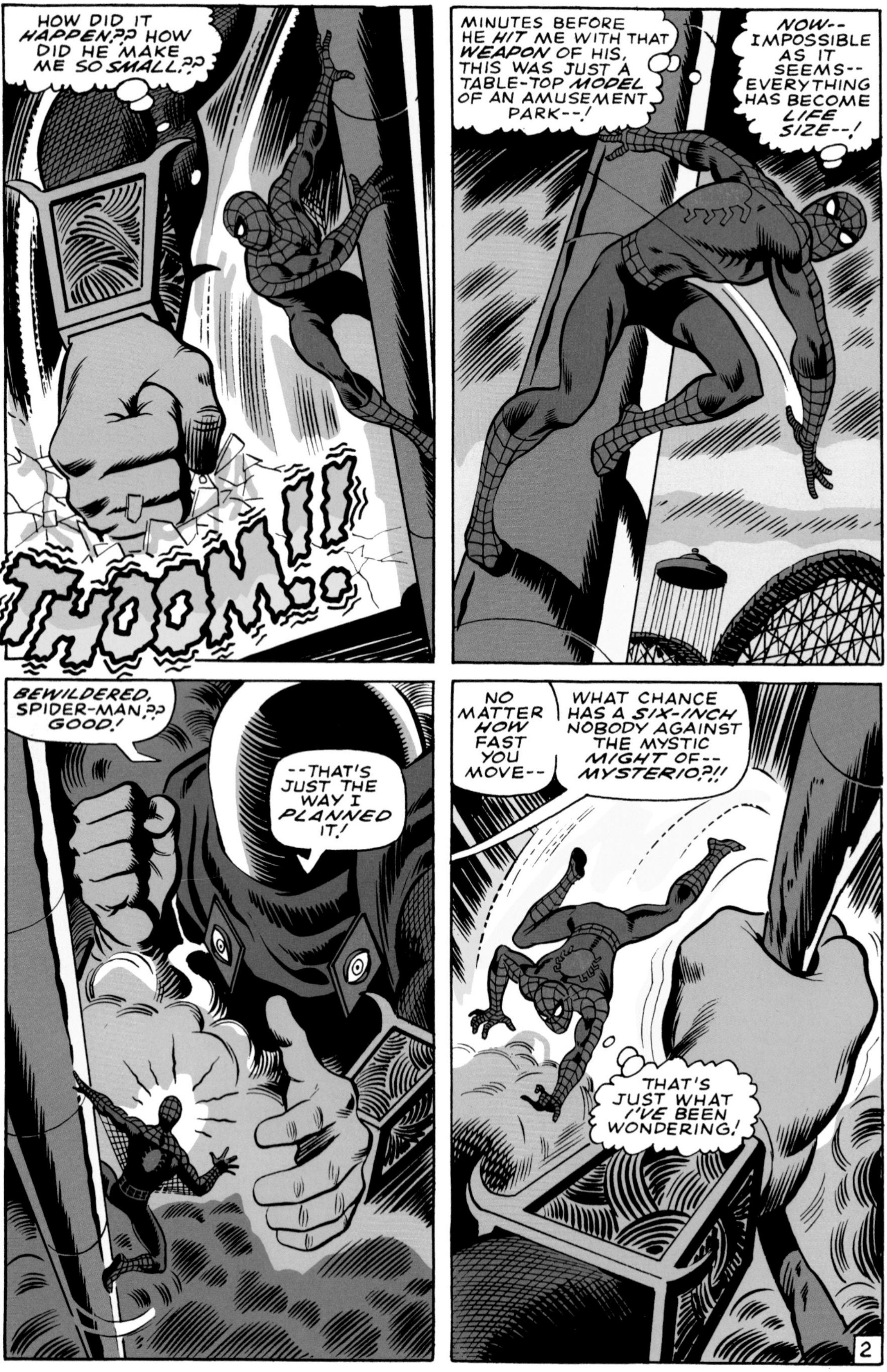
HOW DID IT HAPPEN?? HOW DID HE MAKE ME SO SMALL??
THOOM!!
MINUTES BEFORE HE HIT ME WITH THAT WEAPON OF HIS, THIS WAS JUST A TABLE-TOP MODEL OF AN AMUSEMENT PARK--!
NOW--IMPOSSIBLE AS IT SEEMS--EVERYTHING HAS BECOME LIFE SIZE--!
BEWILDERED, SPIDER-MAN?? GOOD!
--THAT'S JUST THE WAY I PLANNED IT!
NO MATTER HOW FAST YOU MOVE--
WHAT CHANCE HAS A SIX-INCH NOBODY AGAINST THE MYSTIC MIGHT OF--MYSTERIO?!!
THAT'S JUST WHAT I'VE BEEN WONDERING!
2

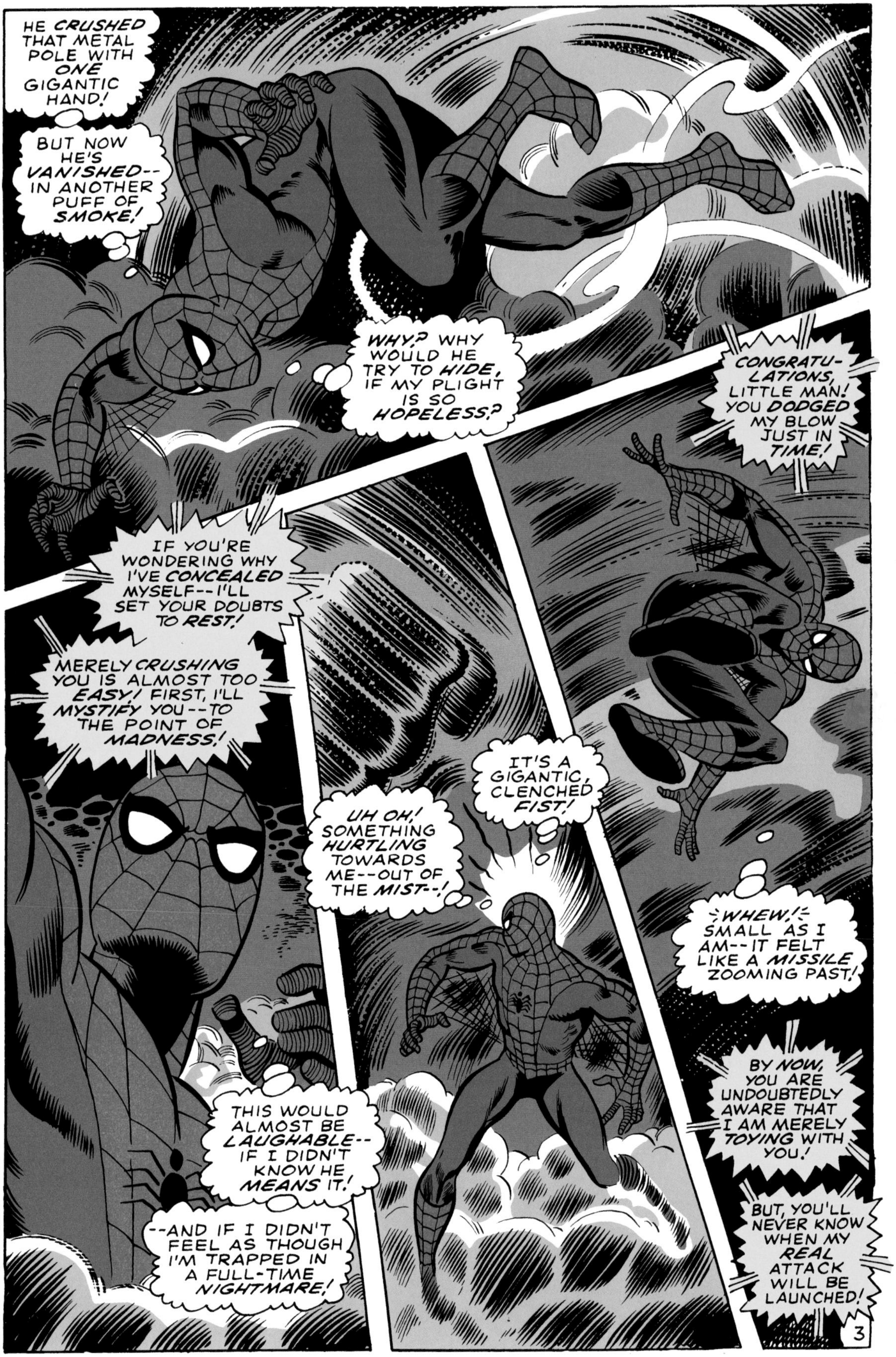
HE CRUSHED THAT METAL POLE WITH ONE GIGANTIC HAND!
BUT NOW HE'S VANISHED-- IN ANOTHER PUFF OF SMOKE!
WHY? WHY WOULD HE TRY TO HIDE, IF MY PLIGHT IS SO HOPELESS?
CONGRATU-LATIONS, LITTLE MAN! YOU DODGED MY BLOW JUST IN TIME!
IF YOU'RE WONDERING WHY I'VE CONCEALED MYSELF--I'LL SET YOUR DOUBTS TO REST!
MERELY CRUSHING YOU IS ALMOST TOO EASY! FIRST, I'LL MYSTIFY YOU--TO THE POINT OF MADNESS!
UH OH! SOMETHING HURTLING TOWARDS ME--OUT OF THE MIST--!
IT'S A GIGANTIC, CLENCHED FIST!
WHEW! SMALL AS I AM--IT FELT LIKE A MISSILE ZOOMING PAST!
THIS WOULD ALMOST BE LAUGHABLE--IF I DIDN'T KNOW HE MEANS IT!
--AND IF I DIDN'T FEEL AS THOUGH I'M TRAPPED IN A FULL-TIME NIGHTMARE!
BY NOW, YOU ARE UNDOUBTEDLY AWARE THAT I AM MERELY TOYING WITH YOU!
BUT, YOU'LL NEVER KNOW WHEN MY REAL ATTACK WILL BE LAUNCHED!
3

PERHAPS-- YOUR TIME IS-- NOW?!!
NOT IF I CAN HELP IT!
AND IT LOOKS LIKE I CAN!
SPTAP!
CAN'T STAY LUCKY FOREVER!
I'VE GOT TO FIND A HIDING PLACE --TO GAIN SOME TIME-- TO THINK THIS OUT!
THWIPP!
THWIPP!
4

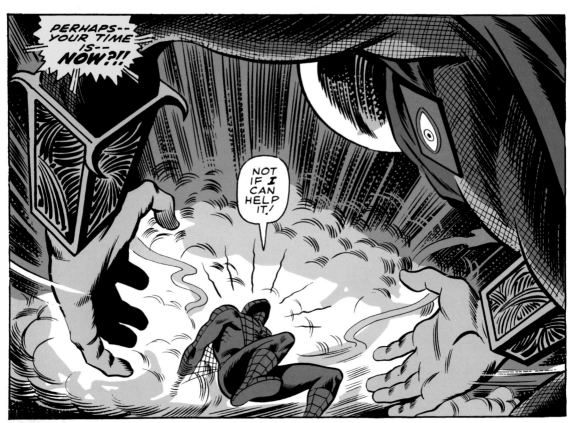

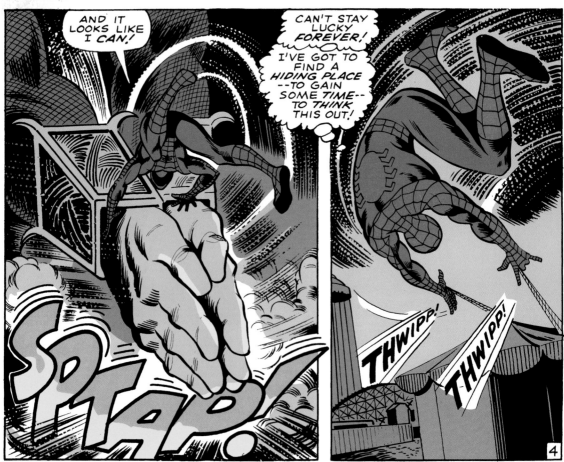

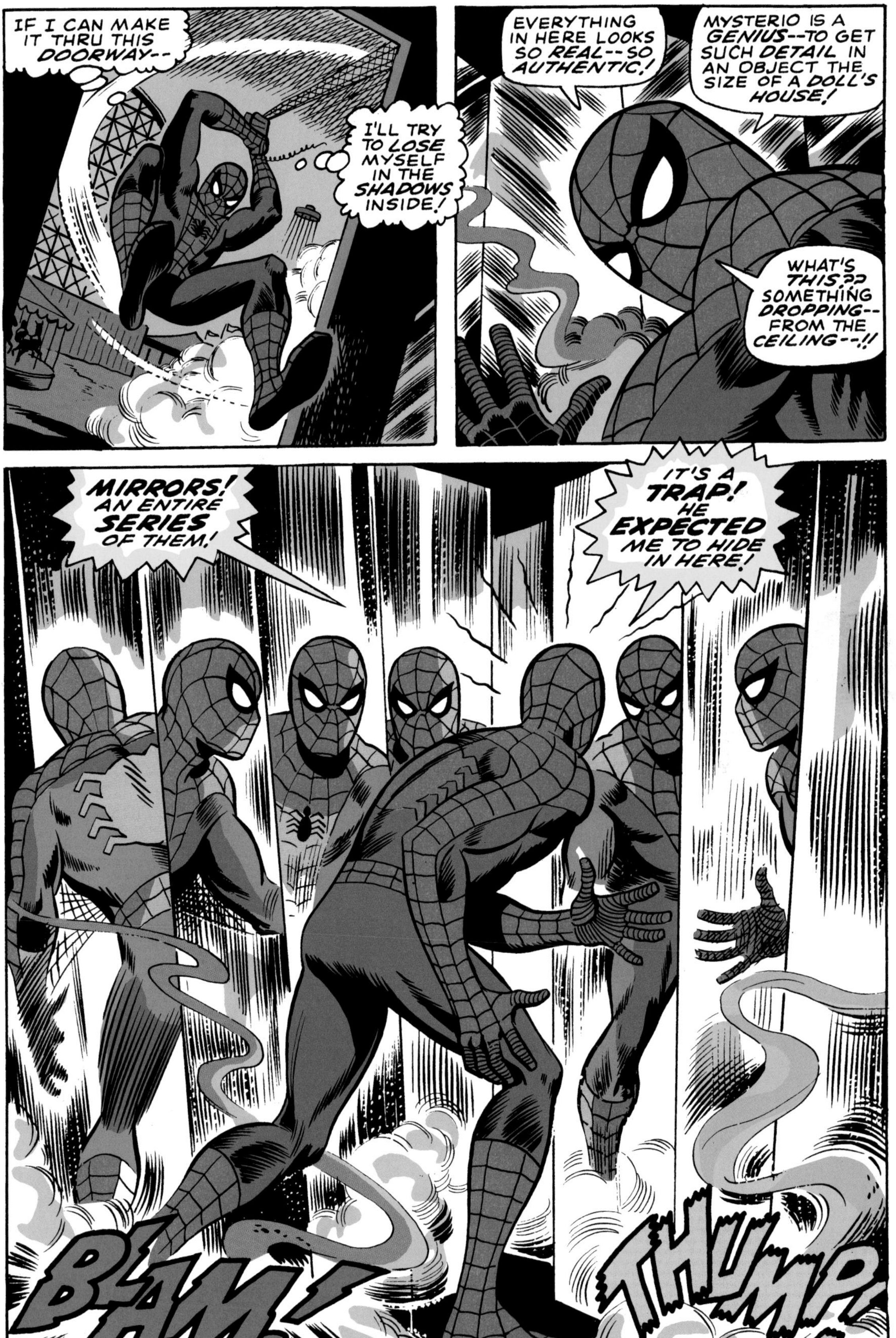

IF I CAN MAKE IT THRU THIS DOORWAY--
I'LL TRY TO LOSE MYSELF IN THE SHADOWS INSIDE!
EVERYTHING IN HERE LOOKS SO REAL--SO AUTHENTIC!
MYSTERIO IS A GENIUS--TO GET SUCH DETAIL IN AN OBJECT THE SIZE OF A DOLL'S HOUSE!
WHAT'S THIS?? SOMETHING DROPPING--FROM THE CEILING--!!
MIRRORS! AN ENTIRE SERIES OF THEM!
IT'S A TRAP! HE EXPECTED ME TO HIDE IN HERE!
BLAM!
THUMP!
5

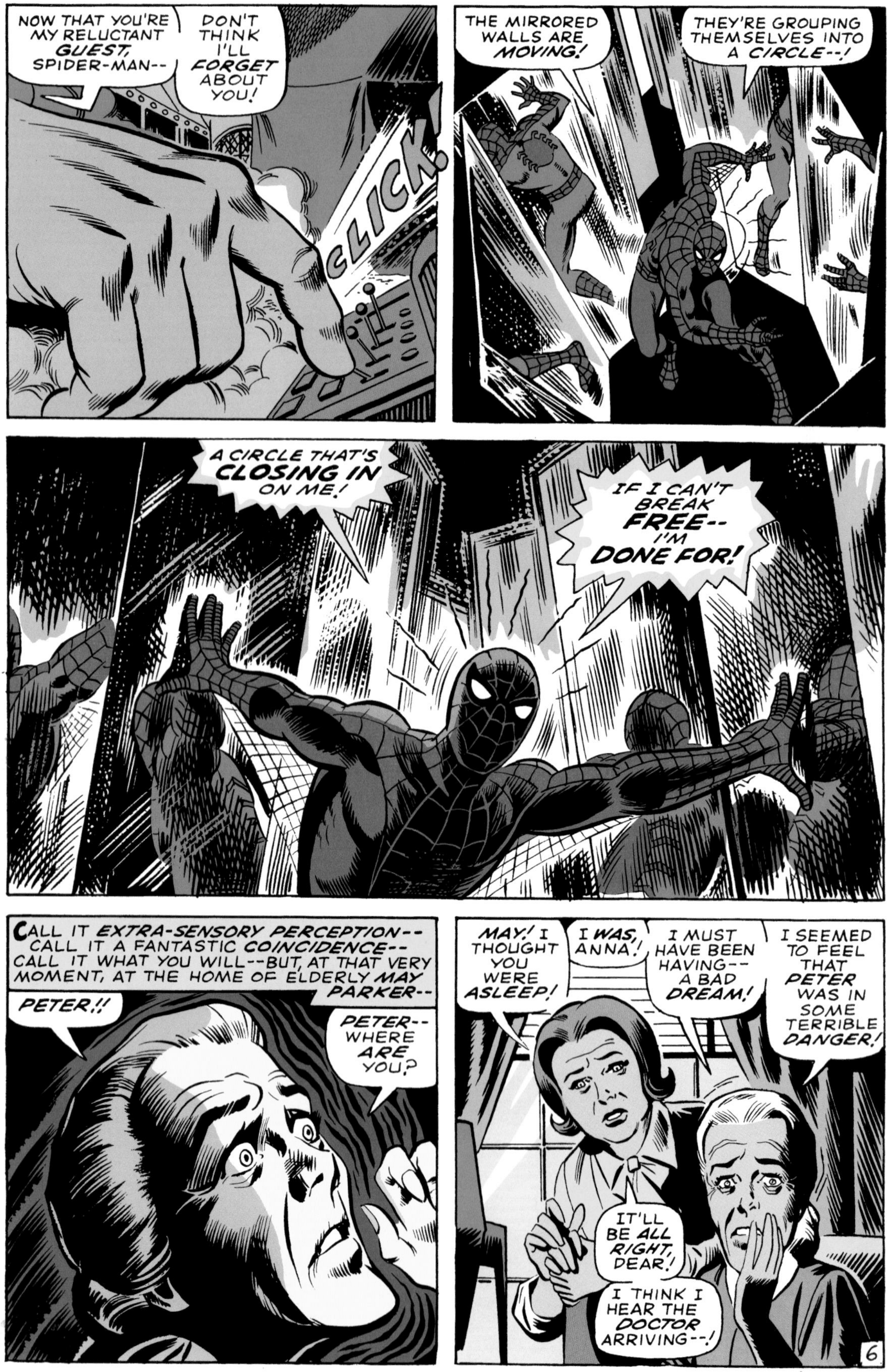
NOW THAT YOU'RE MY RELUCTANT GUEST, SPIDER-MAN--
DON'T THINK I'LL FORGET ABOUT YOU!
CLICK!
THE MIRRORED WALLS ARE MOVING!
THEY'RE GROUPING THEMSELVES INTO A CIRCLE--!
A CIRCLE THAT'S CLOSING IN ON ME!
IF I CAN'T BREAK FREE-- I'M DONE FOR!
CALL IT EXTRA-SENSORY PERCEPTION-- CALL IT A FANTASTIC COINCIDENCE-- CALL IT WHAT YOU WILL--BUT, AT THAT VERY MOMENT, AT THE HOME OF ELDERLY MAY PARKER--
PETER!!
PETER-- WHERE ARE YOU?
MAY! I THOUGHT YOU WERE ASLEEP!
I WAS, ANNA!
I MUST HAVE BEEN HAVING-- A BAD DREAM!
I SEEMED TO FEEL THAT PETER WAS IN SOME TERRIBLE DANGER!
IT'LL BE ALL RIGHT, DEAR!
I THINK I HEAR THE DOCTOR ARRIVING--!
6

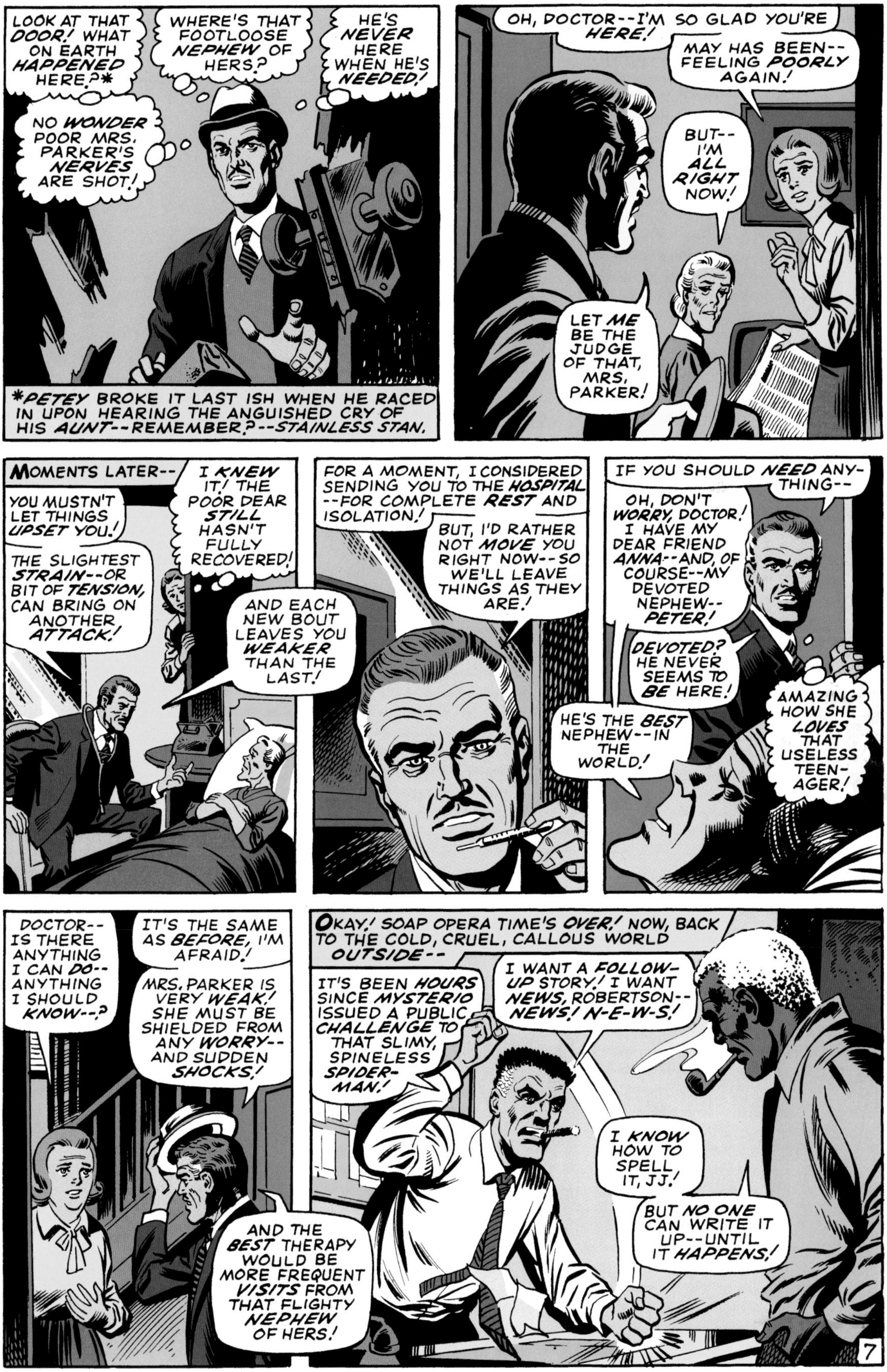
LOOK AT THAT DOOR! WHAT ON EARTH HAPPENED HERE?*
WHERE'S THAT FOOTLOOSE NEPHEW OF HERS?
HE'S NEVER HERE WHEN HE'S NEEDED!
NO WONDER POOR MRS. PARKER'S NERVES ARE SHOT!
*PETEY BROKE IT LAST ISH WHEN HE RACED IN UPON HEARING THE ANGUISHED CRY OF HIS AUNT--REMEMBER?--STAINLESS STAN.
OH, DOCTOR--I'M SO GLAD YOU'RE HERE!
MAY HAS BEEN--FEELING POORLY AGAIN!
BUT--I'M ALL RIGHT NOW!
LET ME BE THE JUDGE OF THAT, MRS. PARKER!
MOMENTS LATER--
YOU MUSTN'T LET THINGS UPSET YOU!
THE SLIGHTEST STRAIN--OR BIT OF TENSION, CAN BRING ON ANOTHER ATTACK!
I KNEW IT! THE POOR DEAR STILL HASN'T FULLY RECOVERED!
AND EACH NEW BOUT LEAVES YOU WEAKER THAN THE LAST!
FOR A MOMENT, I CONSIDERED SENDING YOU TO THE HOSPITAL--FOR COMPLETE REST AND ISOLATION!
BUT, I'D RATHER NOT MOVE YOU RIGHT NOW--SO WE'LL LEAVE THINGS AS THEY ARE!
IF YOU SHOULD NEED ANYTHING--
OH, DON'T WORRY, DOCTOR! I HAVE MY DEAR FRIEND ANNA--AND, OF COURSE--MY DEVOTED NEPHEW--PETER!
DEVOTED? HE NEVER SEEMS TO BE HERE!
HE'S THE BEST NEPHEW--IN THE WORLD!
AMAZING HOW SHE LOVES THAT USELESS TEEN-AGER!
DOCTOR--IS THERE ANYTHING I CAN DO--ANYTHING I SHOULD KNOW--?
IT'S THE SAME AS BEFORE, I'M AFRAID!
MRS. PARKER IS VERY WEAK! SHE MUST BE SHIELDED FROM ANY WORRY--AND SUDDEN SHOCKS!
AND THE BEST THERAPY WOULD BE MORE FREQUENT VISITS FROM THAT FLIGHTY NEPHEW OF HERS!
OKAY! SOAP OPERA TIME'S OVER! NOW, BACK TO THE COLD, CRUEL, CALLOUS WORLD OUTSIDE--
IT'S BEEN HOURS SINCE MYSTERIO ISSUED A PUBLIC CHALLENGE TO THAT SLIMY, SPINELESS SPIDER-MAN!
I WANT A FOLLOW-UP STORY! I WANT NEWS, ROBERTSON--NEWS! N-E-W-S!
I KNOW HOW TO SPELL IT, JJ!
BUT NO ONE CAN WRITE IT UP--UNTIL IT HAPPENS!
7

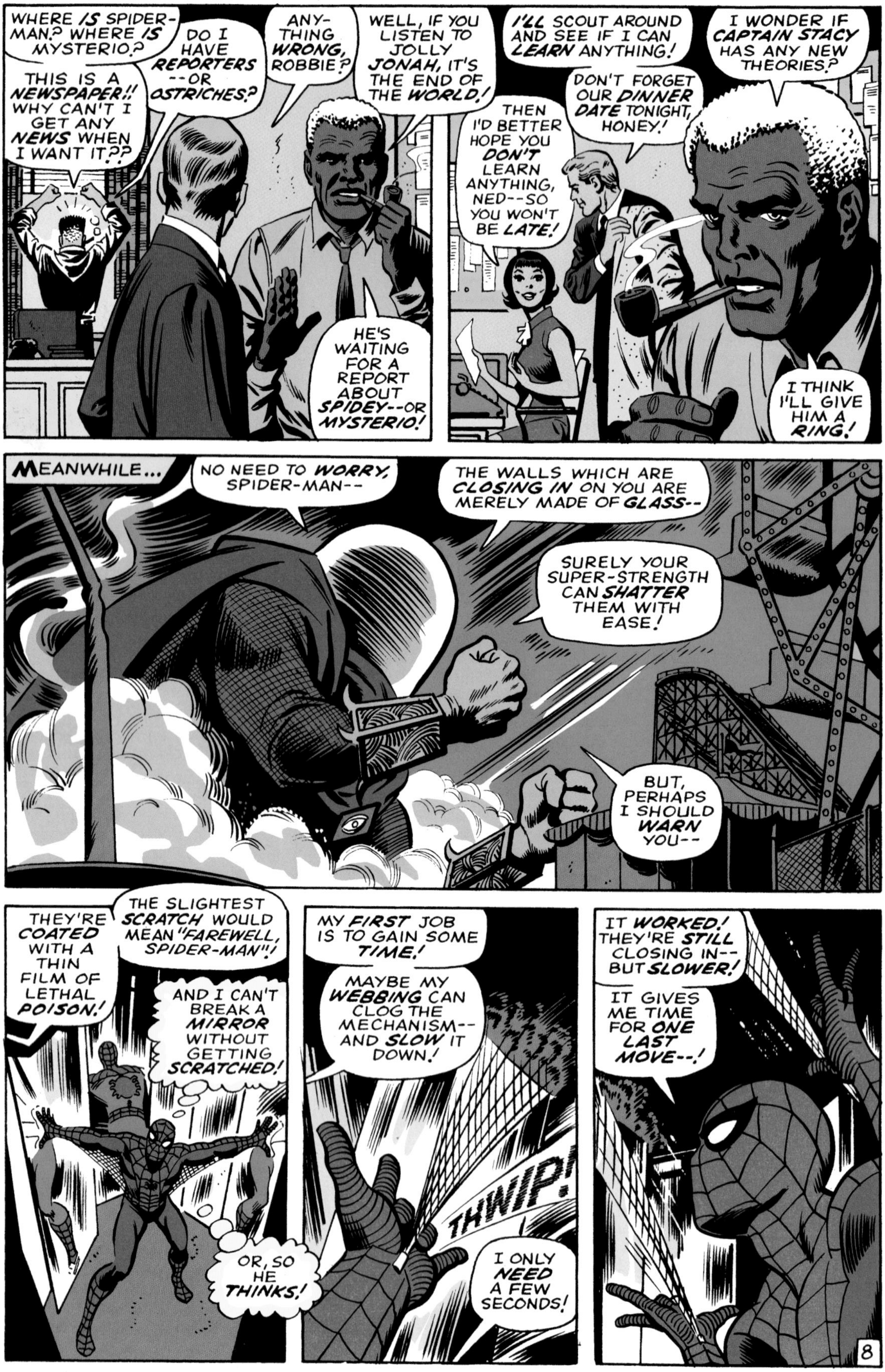
WHERE IS SPIDER-MAN? WHERE IS MYSTERIO?
THIS IS A NEWSPAPER!! WHY CAN'T I GET ANY NEWS WHEN I WANT IT??
DO I HAVE REPORTERS --OR OSTRICHES?
ANYTHING WRONG, ROBBIE?
WELL, IF YOU LISTEN TO JOLLY JONAH, IT'S THE END OF THE WORLD!
HE'S WAITING FOR A REPORT ABOUT SPIDEY--OR MYSTERIO!
I'LL SCOUT AROUND AND SEE IF I CAN LEARN ANYTHING!
THEN I'D BETTER HOPE YOU DON'T LEARN ANYTHING, NED--SO YOU WON'T BE LATE!
DON'T FORGET OUR DINNER DATE TONIGHT, HONEY!
I WONDER IF CAPTAIN STACY HAS ANY NEW THEORIES?
I THINK I'LL GIVE HIM A RING!
MEANWHILE...
NO NEED TO WORRY, SPIDER-MAN--
THE WALLS WHICH ARE CLOSING IN ON YOU ARE MERELY MADE OF GLASS--
SURELY YOUR SUPER-STRENGTH CAN SHATTER THEM WITH EASE!
BUT, PERHAPS I SHOULD WARN YOU--
THEY'RE COATED WITH A THIN FILM OF LETHAL POISON!
THE SLIGHTEST SCRATCH WOULD MEAN "FAREWELL, SPIDER-MAN"!
AND I CAN'T BREAK A MIRROR WITHOUT GETTING SCRATCHED!
OR, SO HE THINKS!
MY FIRST JOB IS TO GAIN SOME TIME!
MAYBE MY WEBBING CAN CLOG THE MECHANISM--AND SLOW IT DOWN!
THWIP!
I ONLY NEED A FEW SECONDS!
IT WORKED! THEY'RE STILL CLOSING IN--BUT SLOWER!
IT GIVES ME TIME FOR ONE LAST MOVE--!
8

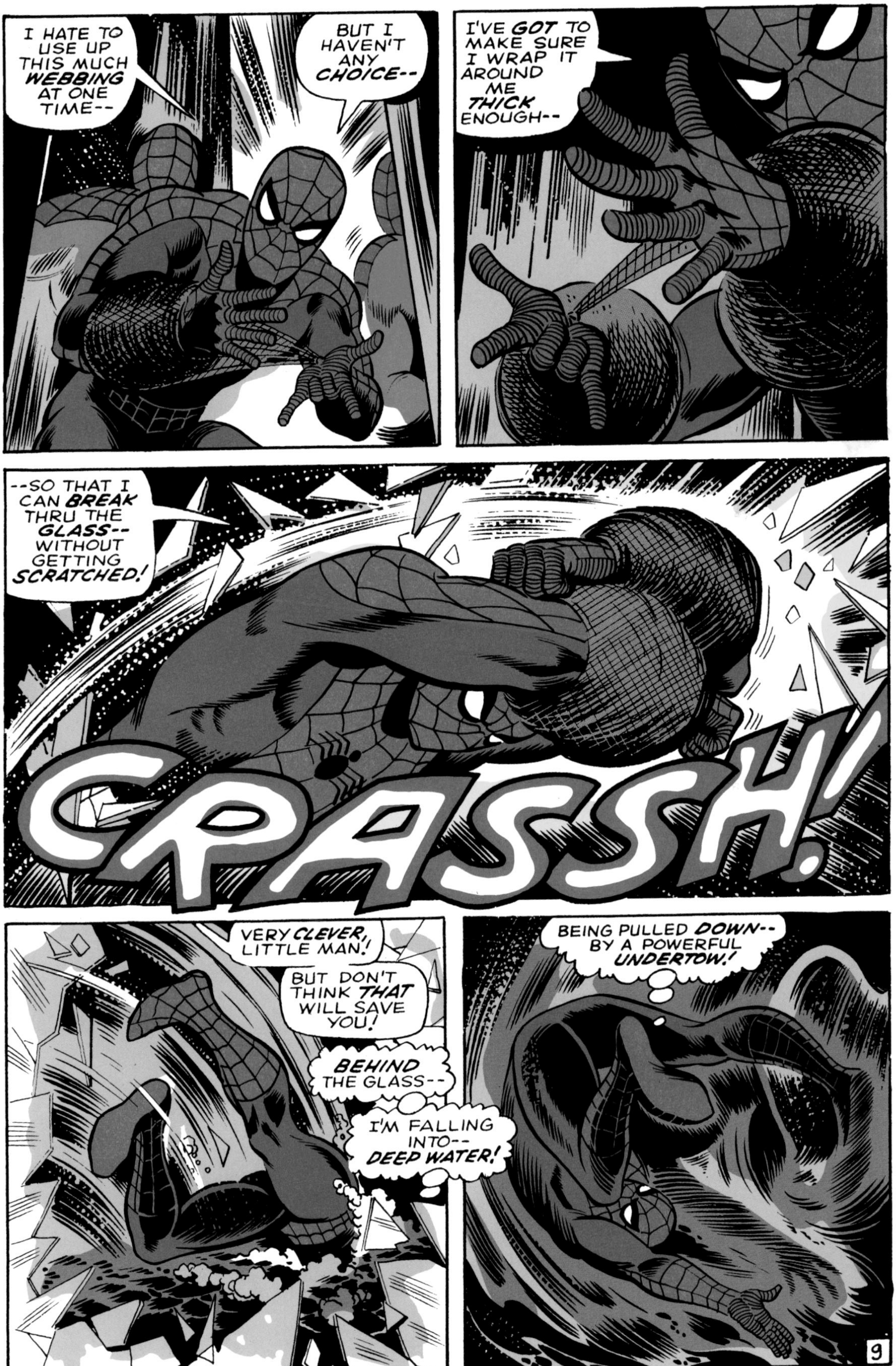
I HATE TO USE UP THIS MUCH WEBBING AT ONE TIME--
BUT I HAVEN'T ANY CHOICE--
I'VE GOT TO MAKE SURE I WRAP IT AROUND ME THICK ENOUGH--
--SO THAT I CAN BREAK THRU THE GLASS-- WITHOUT GETTING SCRATCHED!
CRASSH!
VERY CLEVER, LITTLE MAN!
BUT DON'T THINK THAT WILL SAVE YOU!
BEHIND THE GLASS--
I'M FALLING INTO-- DEEP WATER!
BEING PULLED DOWN-- BY A POWERFUL UNDERTOW!
9

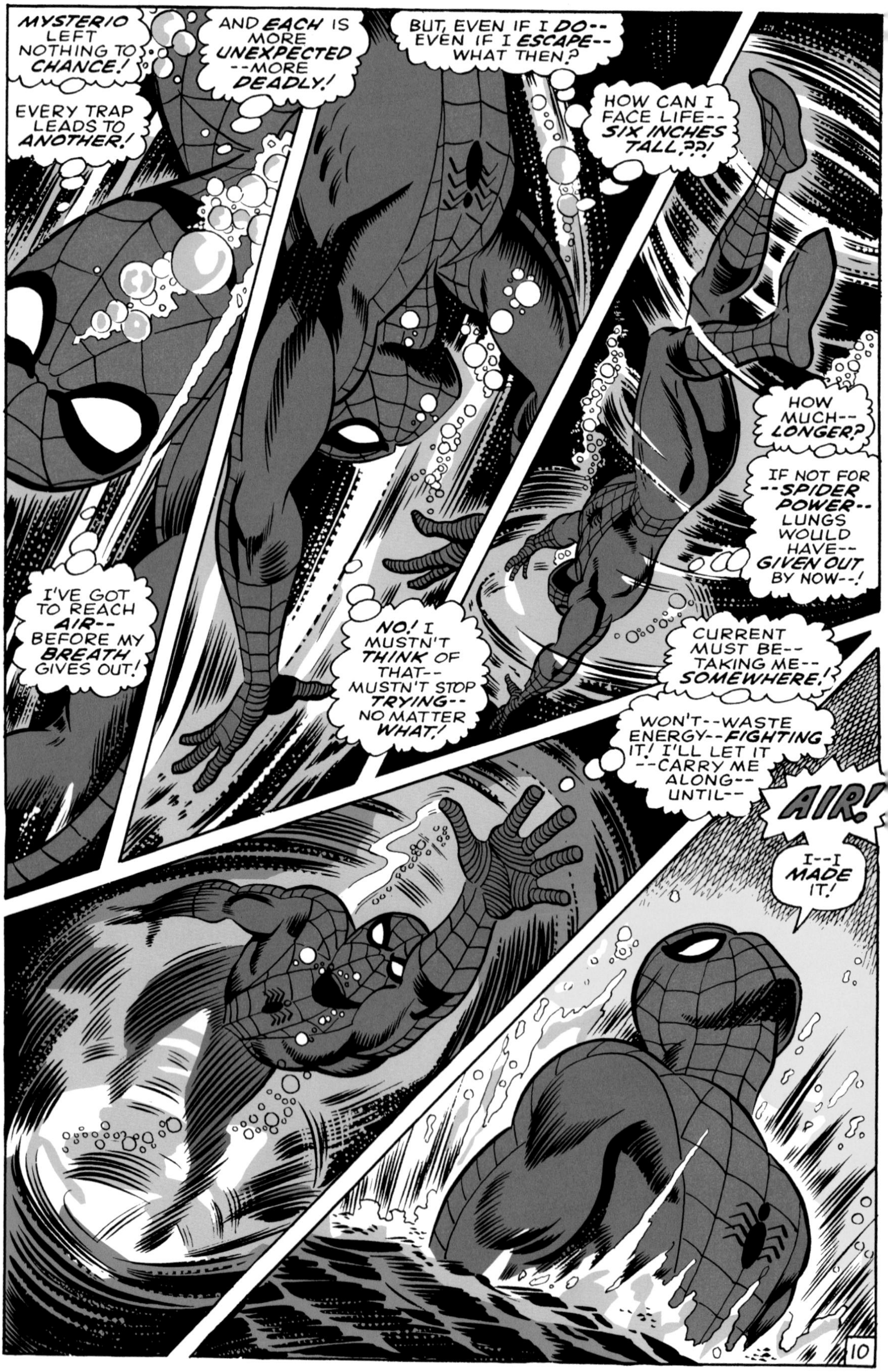
MYSTERIO LEFT NOTHING TO CHANCE!
EVERY TRAP LEADS TO ANOTHER!
AND EACH IS MORE UNEXPECTED --MORE DEADLY!
I'VE GOT TO REACH AIR-- BEFORE MY BREATH GIVES OUT!
BUT, EVEN IF I DO-- EVEN IF I ESCAPE-- WHAT THEN?
NO! I MUSTN'T THINK OF THAT-- MUSTN'T STOP TRYING-- NO MATTER WHAT!
HOW CAN I FACE LIFE-- SIX INCHES TALL??!
HOW MUCH-- LONGER?
IF NOT FOR --SPIDER POWER-- LUNGS WOULD HAVE-- GIVEN OUT BY NOW--!
CURRENT MUST BE-- TAKING ME-- SOMEWHERE!
WON'T--WASTE ENERGY--FIGHTING IT! I'LL LET IT --CARRY ME ALONG-- UNTIL--
AIR!
I--I MADE IT!
10

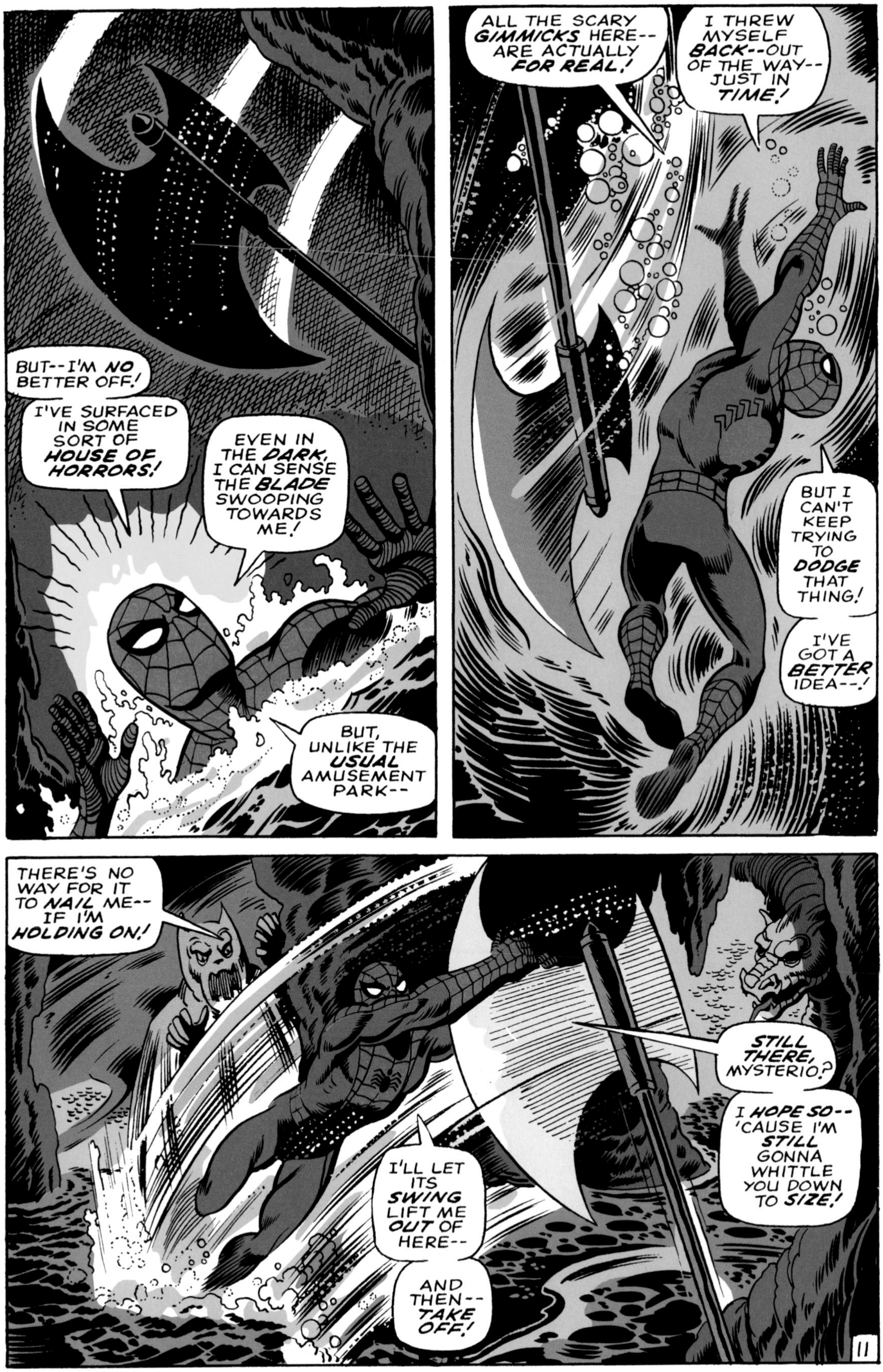
BUT--I'M NO BETTER OFF!
I'VE SURFACED IN SOME SORT OF HOUSE OF HORRORS!
EVEN IN THE DARK, I CAN SENSE THE BLADE SWOOPING TOWARDS ME!
BUT, UNLIKE THE USUAL AMUSEMENT PARK--
ALL THE SCARY GIMMICKS HERE--ARE ACTUALLY FOR REAL!
I THREW MYSELF BACK--OUT OF THE WAY--JUST IN TIME!
BUT I CAN'T KEEP TRYING TO DODGE THAT THING!
I'VE GOT A BETTER IDEA--!
THERE'S NO WAY FOR IT TO NAIL ME--IF I'M HOLDING ON!
I'LL LET ITS SWING LIFT ME OUT OF HERE--
AND THEN--TAKE OFF!
STILL THERE, MYSTERIO?
I HOPE SO--'CAUSE I'M STILL GONNA WHITTLE YOU DOWN TO SIZE!
11

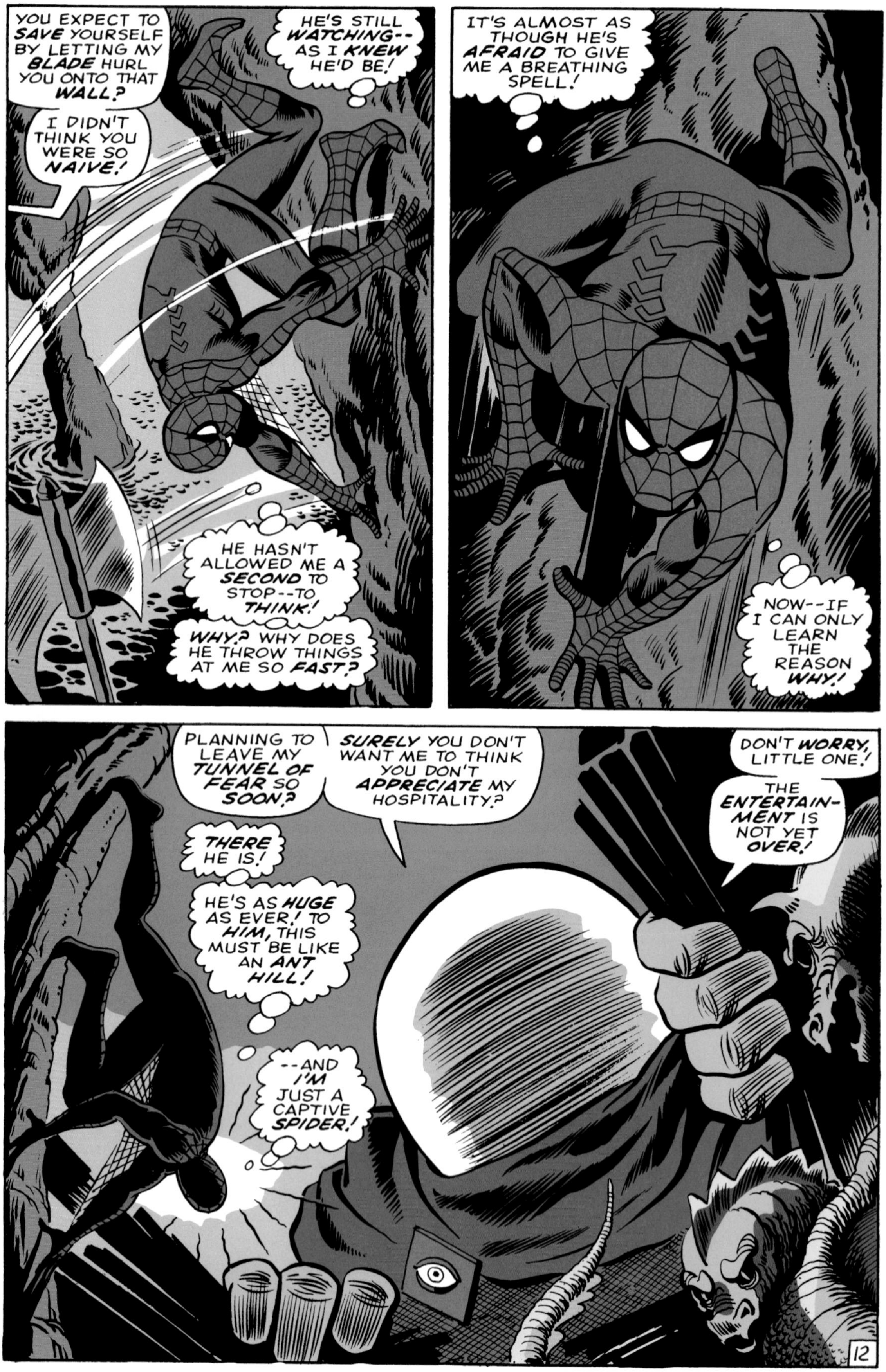
YOU EXPECT TO SAVE YOURSELF BY LETTING MY BLADE HURL YOU ONTO THAT WALL?
I DIDN'T THINK YOU WERE SO NAIVE!
HE'S STILL WATCHING-- AS I KNEW HE'D BE!
HE HASN'T ALLOWED ME A SECOND TO STOP--TO THINK!
WHY? WHY DOES HE THROW THINGS AT ME SO FAST?
IT'S ALMOST AS THOUGH HE'S AFRAID TO GIVE ME A BREATHING SPELL!
NOW--IF I CAN ONLY LEARN THE REASON WHY!
PLANNING TO LEAVE MY TUNNEL OF FEAR SO SOON?
SURELY YOU DON'T WANT ME TO THINK YOU DON'T APPRECIATE MY HOSPITALITY?
DON'T WORRY, LITTLE ONE!
THE ENTERTAIN-MENT IS NOT YET OVER!
THERE HE IS!
HE'S AS HUGE AS EVER! TO HIM, THIS MUST BE LIKE AN ANT HILL!
--AND I'M JUST A CAPTIVE SPIDER!
12

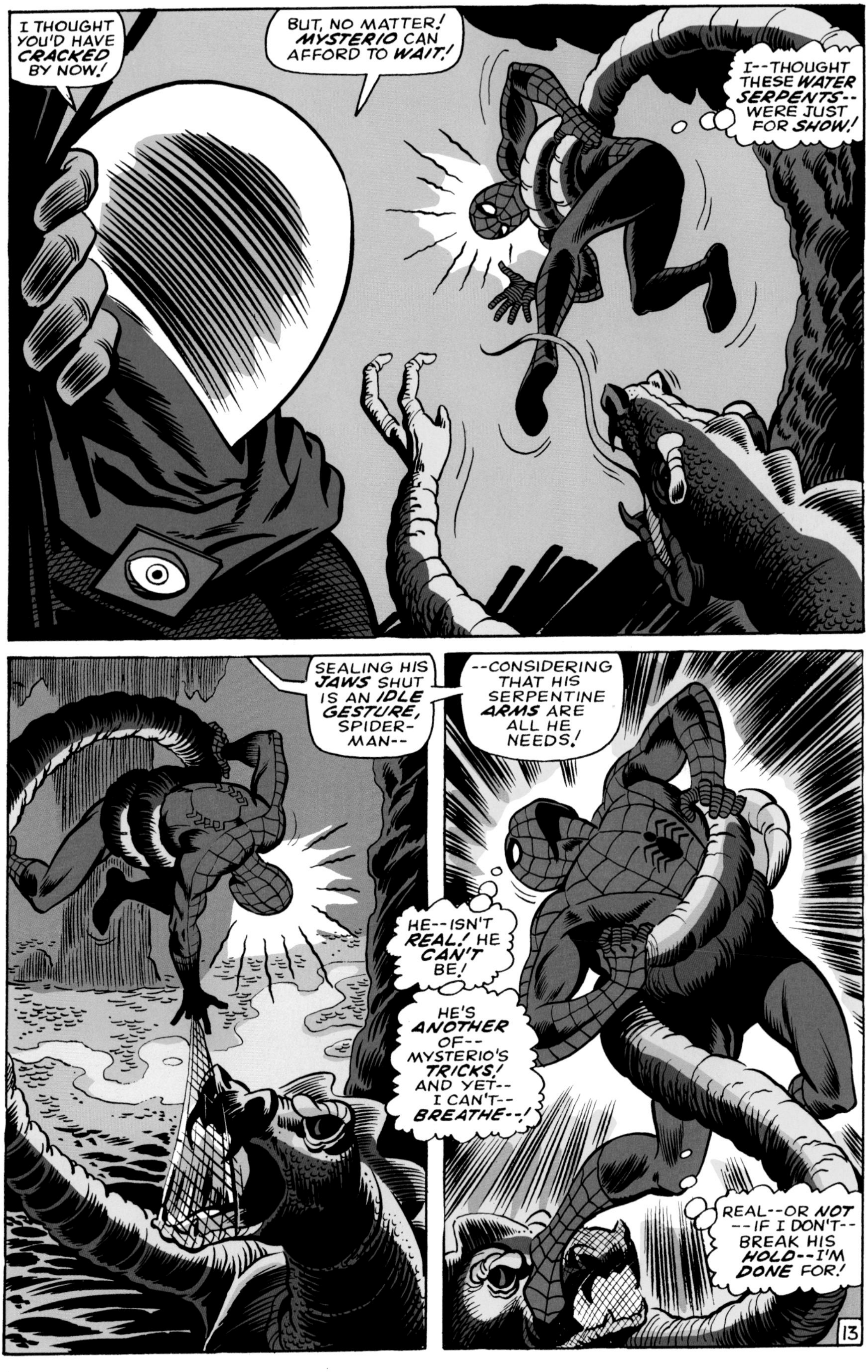
I THOUGHT YOU'D HAVE CRACKED BY NOW!
BUT, NO MATTER! MYSTERIO CAN AFFORD TO WAIT!
I--THOUGHT THESE WATER SERPENTS--WERE JUST FOR SHOW!
SEALING HIS JAWS SHUT IS AN IDLE GESTURE, SPIDER-MAN--
--CONSIDERING THAT HIS SERPENTINE ARMS ARE ALL HE NEEDS!
HE--ISN'T REAL! HE CAN'T BE!
HE'S ANOTHER OF--MYSTERIO'S TRICKS! AND YET--I CAN'T--BREATHE--!
REAL--OR NOT--IF I DON'T--BREAK HIS HOLD--I'M DONE FOR!
13

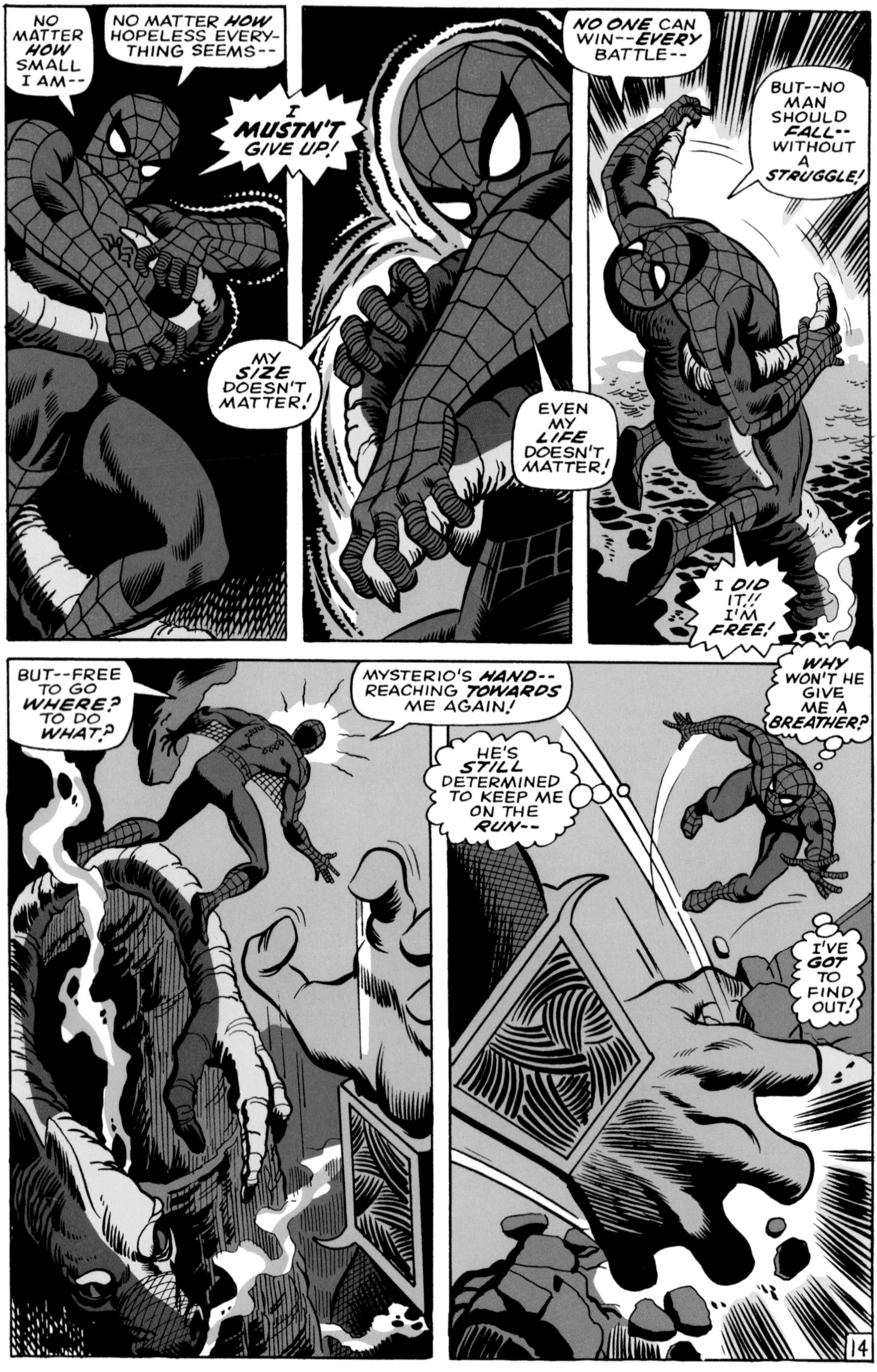
NO MATTER HOW SMALL I AM--
NO MATTER HOW HOPELESS EVERY-THING SEEMS--
I MUSTN'T GIVE UP!
MY SIZE DOESN'T MATTER!
EVEN MY LIFE DOESN'T MATTER!
NO ONE CAN WIN--EVERY BATTLE--
BUT--NO MAN SHOULD FALL--WITHOUT A STRUGGLE!
I DID IT!! I'M FREE!
BUT--FREE TO GO WHERE? TO DO WHAT?
MYSTERIO'S HAND--REACHING TOWARDS ME AGAIN!
HE'S STILL DETERMINED TO KEEP ME ON THE RUN--
WHY WON'T HE GIVE ME A BREATHER?
I'VE GOT TO FIND OUT!
14

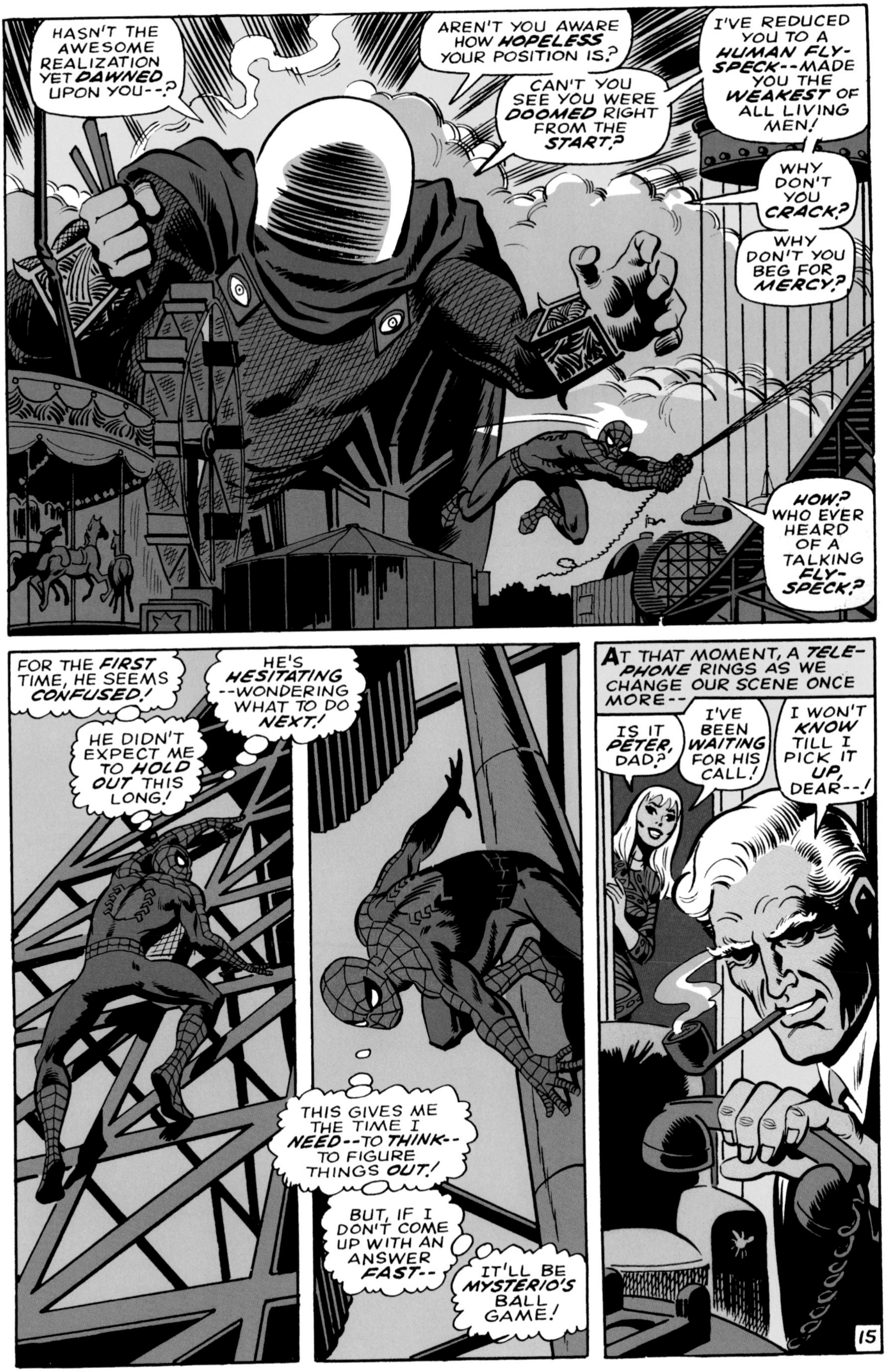
HASN'T THE AWESOME REALIZATION YET DAWNED UPON YOU--?
AREN'T YOU AWARE HOW HOPELESS YOUR POSITION IS?
CAN'T YOU SEE YOU WERE DOOMED RIGHT FROM THE START?
I'VE REDUCED YOU TO A HUMAN FLY-SPECK--MADE YOU THE WEAKEST OF ALL LIVING MEN!
WHY DON'T YOU CRACK?
WHY DON'T YOU BEG FOR MERCY?
HOW? WHO EVER HEARD OF A TALKING FLY-SPECK?
FOR THE FIRST TIME, HE SEEMS CONFUSED!
HE'S HESITATING--WONDERING WHAT TO DO NEXT!
HE DIDN'T EXPECT ME TO HOLD OUT THIS LONG!
THIS GIVES ME THE TIME I NEED--TO THINK--TO FIGURE THINGS OUT!
BUT, IF I DON'T COME UP WITH AN ANSWER FAST--
IT'LL BE MYSTERIO'S BALL GAME!
AT THAT MOMENT, A TELEPHONE RINGS AS WE CHANGE OUR SCENE ONCE MORE--
IS IT PETER, DAD?
I'VE BEEN WAITING FOR HIS CALL!
I WON'T KNOW TILL I PICK IT UP, DEAR--!
15

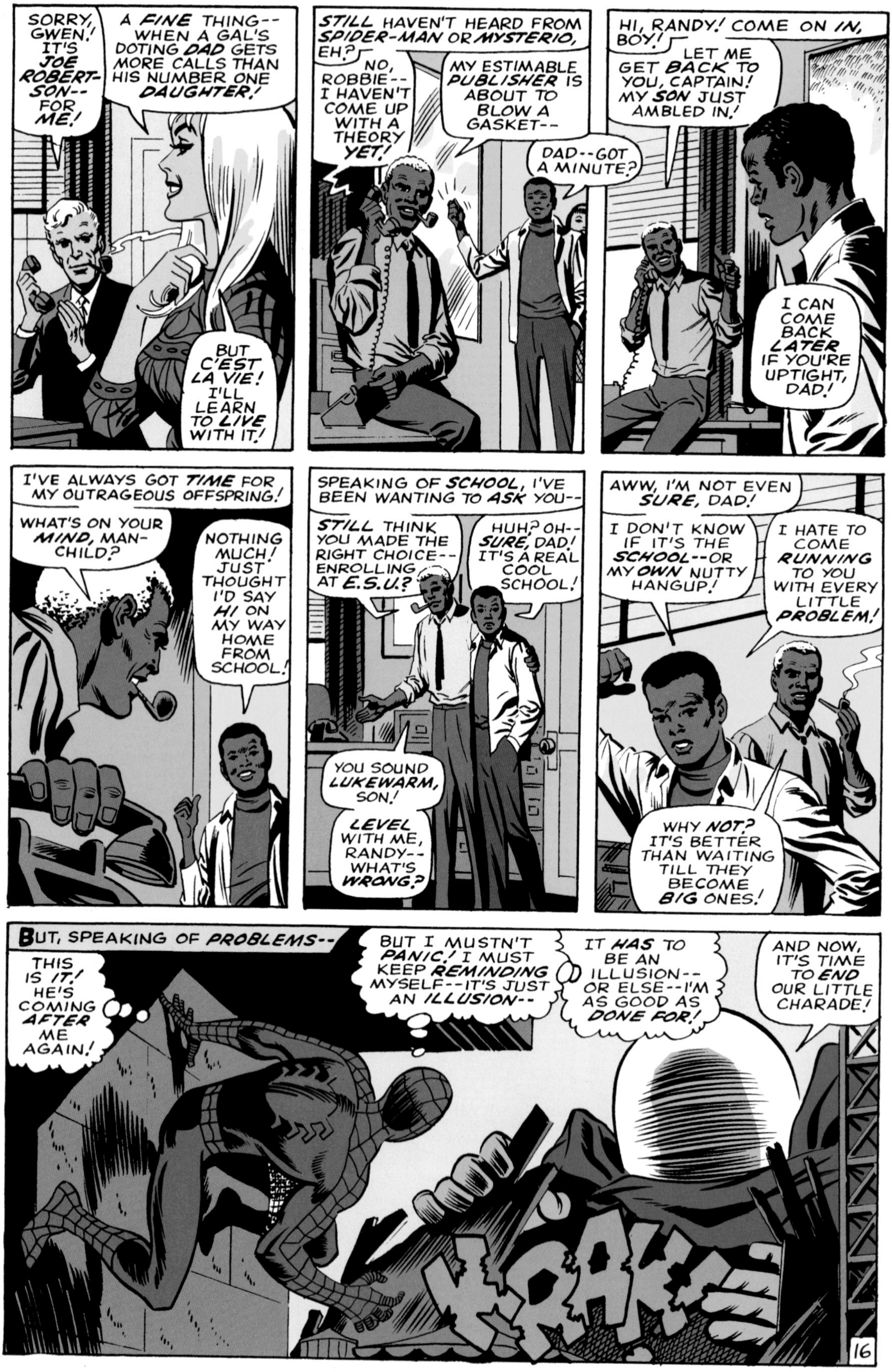
SORRY, GWEN! IT'S JOE ROBERTSON--FOR ME!
A FINE THING--WHEN A GAL'S DOTING DAD GETS MORE CALLS THAN HIS NUMBER ONE DAUGHTER!
BUT C'EST LA VIE! I'LL LEARN TO LIVE WITH IT!
STILL HAVEN'T HEARD FROM SPIDER-MAN OR MYSTERIO, EH?
NO, ROBBIE--I HAVEN'T COME UP WITH A THEORY YET!
MY ESTIMABLE PUBLISHER IS ABOUT TO BLOW A GASKET--
DAD--GOT A MINUTE?
HI, RANDY! COME ON IN, BOY!
LET ME GET BACK TO YOU, CAPTAIN! MY SON JUST AMBLED IN!
I CAN COME BACK LATER IF YOU'RE UPTIGHT, DAD!
I'VE ALWAYS GOT TIME FOR MY OUTRAGEOUS OFFSPRING!
WHAT'S ON YOUR MIND, MAN-CHILD?
NOTHING MUCH! JUST THOUGHT I'D SAY HI ON MY WAY HOME FROM SCHOOL!
SPEAKING OF SCHOOL, I'VE BEEN WANTING TO ASK YOU--
STILL THINK YOU MADE THE RIGHT CHOICE--ENROLLING AT E.S.U.?
HUH? OH--SURE, DAD! IT'S A REAL COOL SCHOOL!
YOU SOUND LUKEWARM, SON!
LEVEL WITH ME, RANDY--WHAT'S WRONG?
AWW, I'M NOT EVEN SURE, DAD!
I DON'T KNOW IF IT'S THE SCHOOL--OR MY OWN NUTTY HANGUP!
I HATE TO COME RUNNING TO YOU WITH EVERY LITTLE PROBLEM!
WHY NOT? IT'S BETTER THAN WAITING TILL THEY BECOME BIG ONES!
BUT, SPEAKING OF PROBLEMS--
THIS IS IT! HE'S COMING AFTER ME AGAIN!
BUT I MUSTN'T PANIC! I MUST KEEP REMINDING MYSELF--IT'S JUST AN ILLUSION--
IT HAS TO BE AN ILLUSION--OR ELSE--I'M AS GOOD AS DONE FOR!
AND NOW, IT'S TIME TO END OUR LITTLE CHARADE!
16

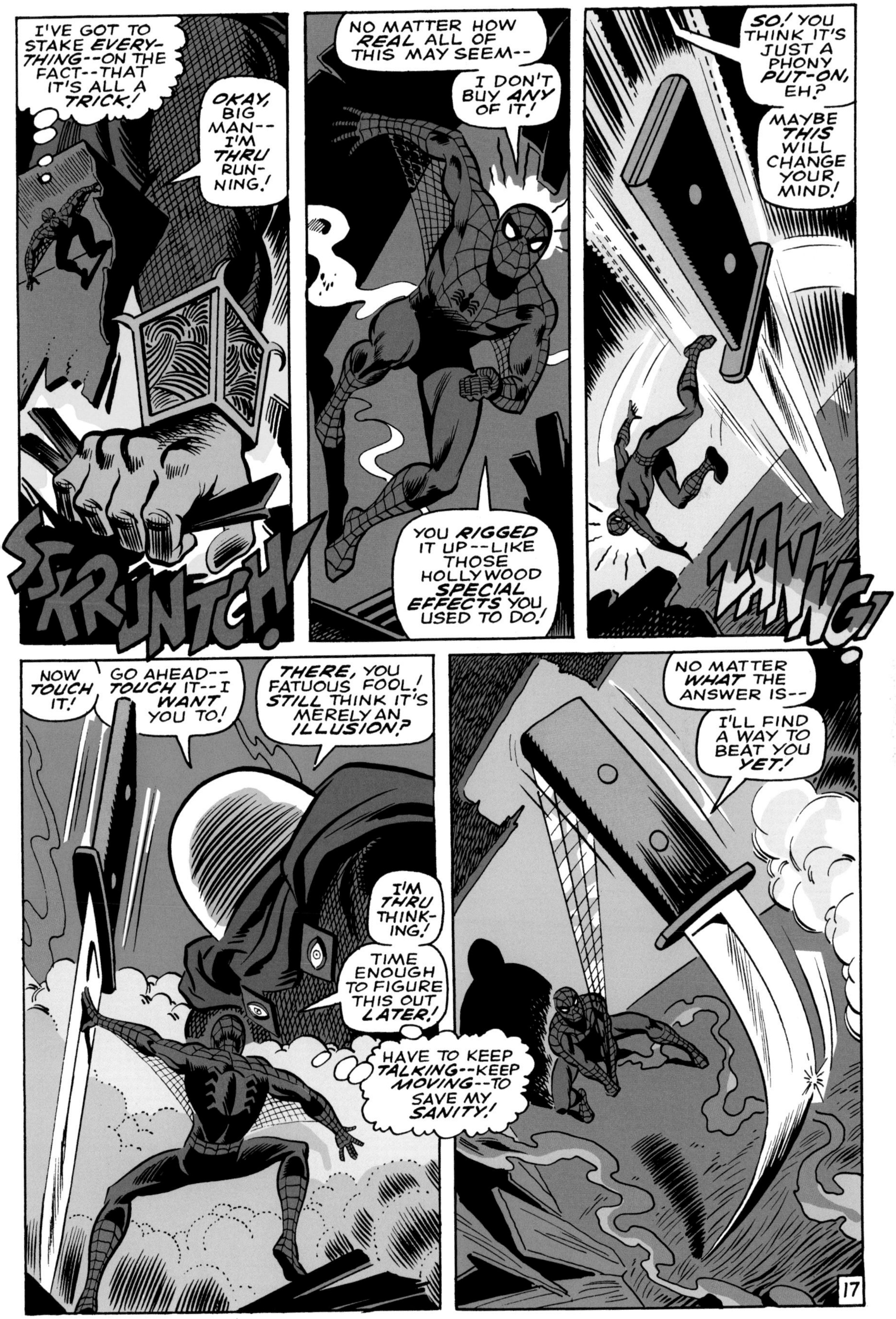
I'VE GOT TO STAKE EVERYTHING--ON THE FACT--THAT IT'S ALL A TRICK!
OKAY, BIG MAN--I'M THRU RUNNING!
SKRUNTCH!
NO MATTER HOW REAL ALL OF THIS MAY SEEM--
I DON'T BUY ANY OF IT!
YOU RIGGED IT UP--LIKE THOSE HOLLYWOOD SPECIAL EFFECTS YOU USED TO DO!
SO! YOU THINK IT'S JUST A PHONY PUT-ON, EH?
MAYBE THIS WILL CHANGE YOUR MIND!
ZANNG!
NOW TOUCH IT!
GO AHEAD--TOUCH IT--I WANT YOU TO!
THERE, YOU FATUOUS FOOL! STILL THINK IT'S MERELY AN ILLUSION?
I'M THRU THINKING!
TIME ENOUGH TO FIGURE THIS OUT LATER!
HAVE TO KEEP TALKING--KEEP MOVING--TO SAVE MY SANITY!
NO MATTER WHAT THE ANSWER IS--
I'LL FIND A WAY TO BEAT YOU YET!
17

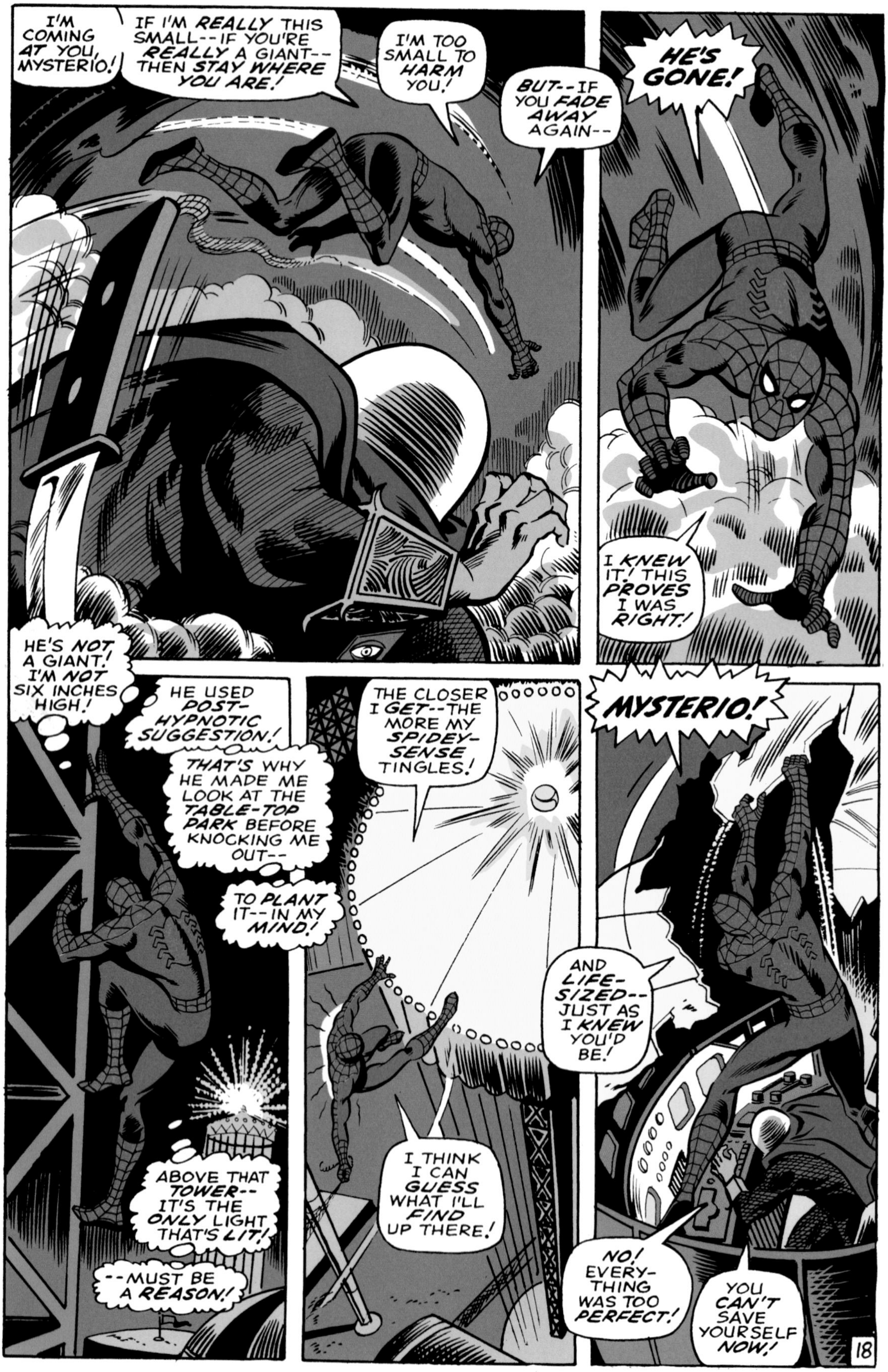
I'M COMING AT YOU, MYSTERIO!
IF I'M REALLY THIS SMALL--IF YOU'RE REALLY A GIANT--THEN STAY WHERE YOU ARE!
I'M TOO SMALL TO HARM YOU!
BUT--IF YOU FADE AWAY AGAIN--
HE'S GONE!
I KNEW IT! THIS PROVES I WAS RIGHT!
HE'S NOT A GIANT! I'M NOT SIX INCHES HIGH!
HE USED POST-HYPNOTIC SUGGESTION!
THAT'S WHY HE MADE ME LOOK AT THE TABLE-TOP PARK BEFORE KNOCKING ME OUT--
TO PLANT IT--IN MY MIND!
ABOVE THAT TOWER--IT'S THE ONLY LIGHT THAT'S LIT!
--MUST BE A REASON!
THE CLOSER I GET--THE MORE MY SPIDEY-SENSE TINGLES!
I THINK I CAN GUESS WHAT I'LL FIND UP THERE!
MYSTERIO!
AND LIFE-SIZED--JUST AS I KNEW YOU'D BE!
NO! EVERYTHING WAS TOO PERFECT!
YOU CAN'T SAVE YOURSELF NOW!
18

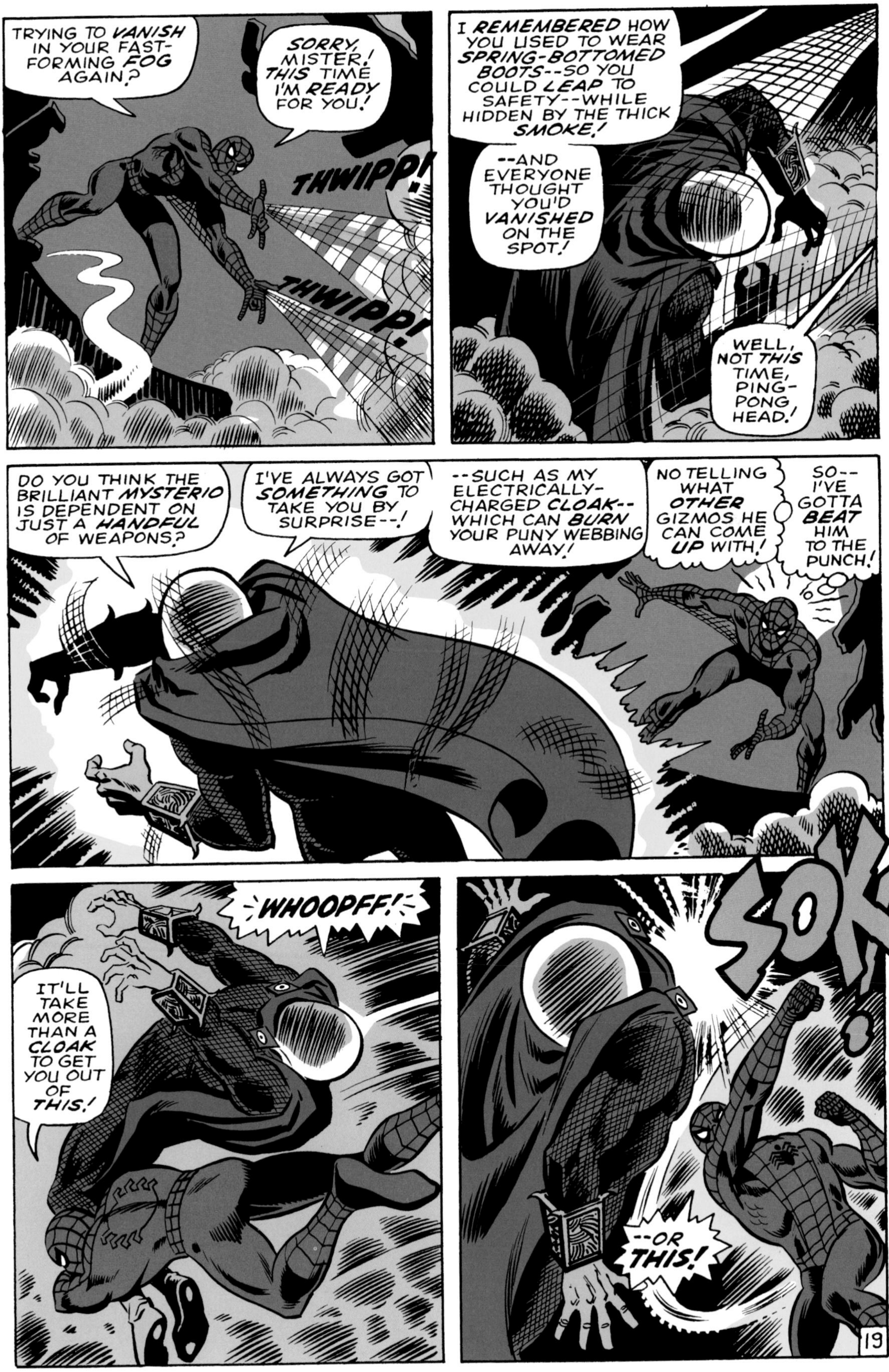
TRYING TO VANISH IN YOUR FAST-FORMING FOG AGAIN?
SORRY, MISTER! THIS TIME I'M READY FOR YOU!
THWIPP!
THWIPP!
I REMEMBERED HOW YOU USED TO WEAR SPRING-BOTTOMED BOOTS--SO YOU COULD LEAP TO SAFETY--WHILE HIDDEN BY THE THICK SMOKE!
--AND EVERYONE THOUGHT YOU'D VANISHED ON THE SPOT!
WELL, NOT THIS TIME, PING-PONG HEAD!
DO YOU THINK THE BRILLIANT MYSTERIO IS DEPENDENT ON JUST A HANDFUL OF WEAPONS?
I'VE ALWAYS GOT SOMETHING TO TAKE YOU BY SURPRISE--!
--SUCH AS MY ELECTRICALLY-CHARGED CLOAK--WHICH CAN BURN YOUR PUNY WEBBING AWAY!
NO TELLING WHAT OTHER GIZMOS HE CAN COME UP WITH!
SO--I'VE GOTTA BEAT HIM TO THE PUNCH!
WHOOPFF!
IT'LL TAKE MORE THAN A CLOAK TO GET YOU OUT OF THIS!
SOK!
--OR THIS!
19

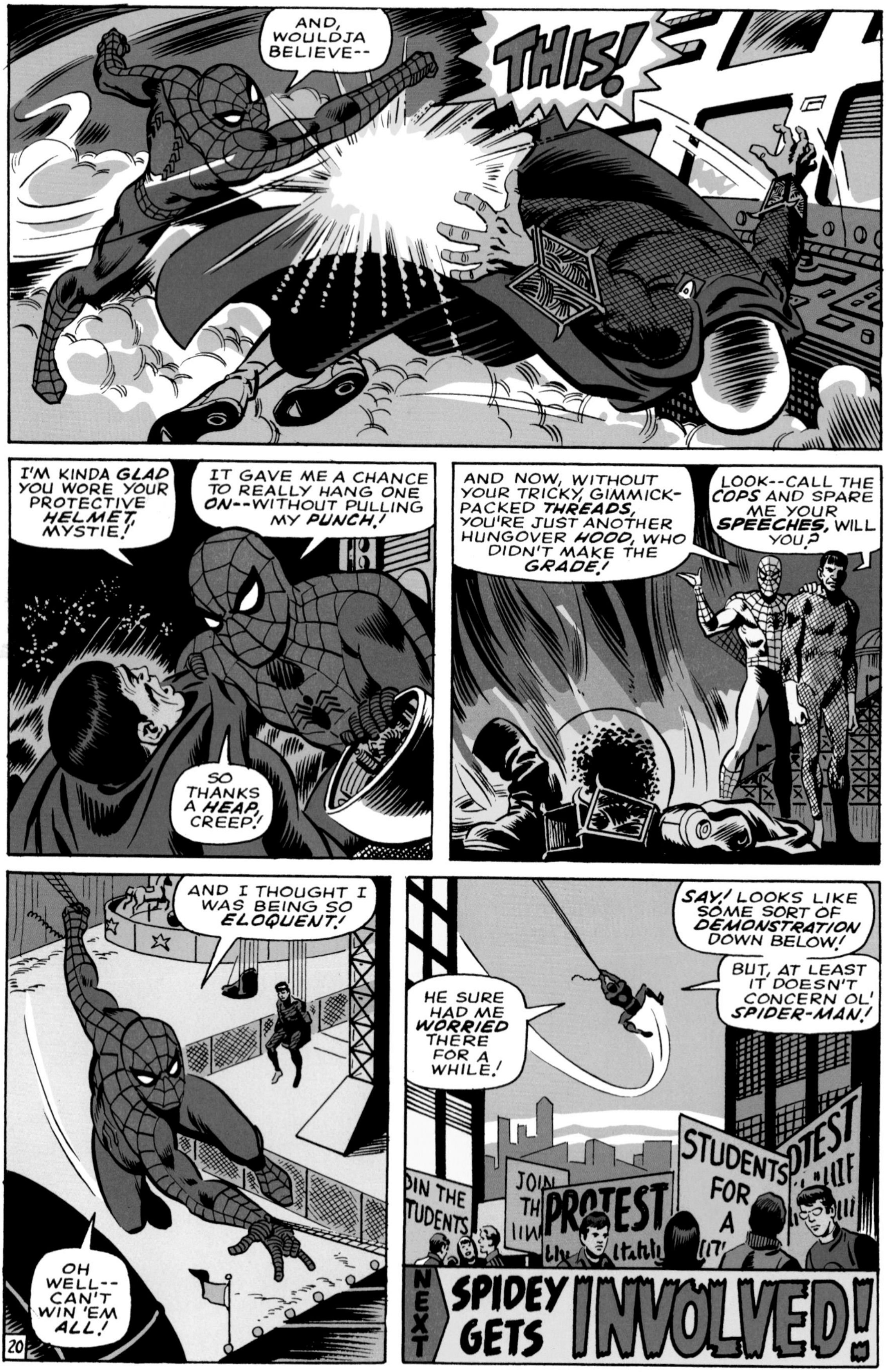
AND, WOULDJA BELIEVE--
THIS!
I'M KINDA GLAD YOU WORE YOUR PROTECTIVE HELMET, MYSTIE!
IT GAVE ME A CHANCE TO REALLY HANG ONE ON--WITHOUT PULLING MY PUNCH!
SO THANKS A HEAP, CREEP!
AND NOW, WITHOUT YOUR TRICKY, GIMMICK-PACKED THREADS, YOU'RE JUST ANOTHER HUNGOVER HOOD, WHO DIDN'T MAKE THE GRADE!
LOOK--CALL THE COPS AND SPARE ME YOUR SPEECHES, WILL YOU?
AND I THOUGHT I WAS BEING SO ELOQUENT!
OH WELL--CAN'T WIN 'EM ALL!
20
SAY! LOOKS LIKE SOME SORT OF DEMONSTRATION DOWN BELOW!
BUT, AT LEAST IT DOESN'T CONCERN OL' SPIDER-MAN!
HE SURE HAD ME WORRIED THERE FOR A WHILE!
STUDENTS FOR A
PROTEST
JOIN TH
PROTEST
OIN THE TUDENTS
NEXT
SPIDEY GETS INVOLVED!

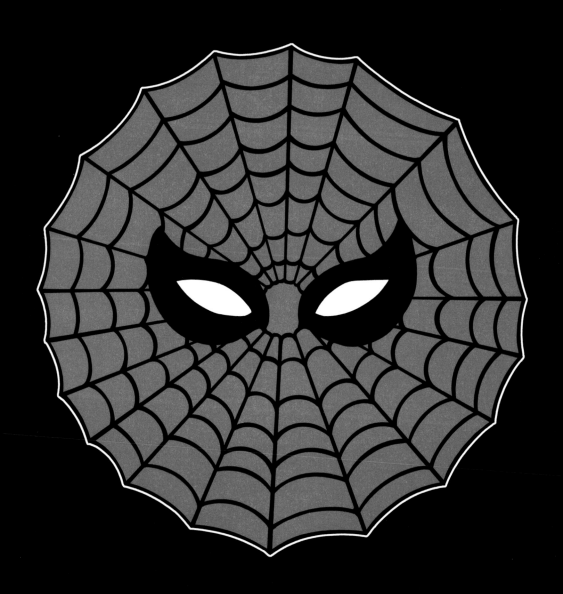

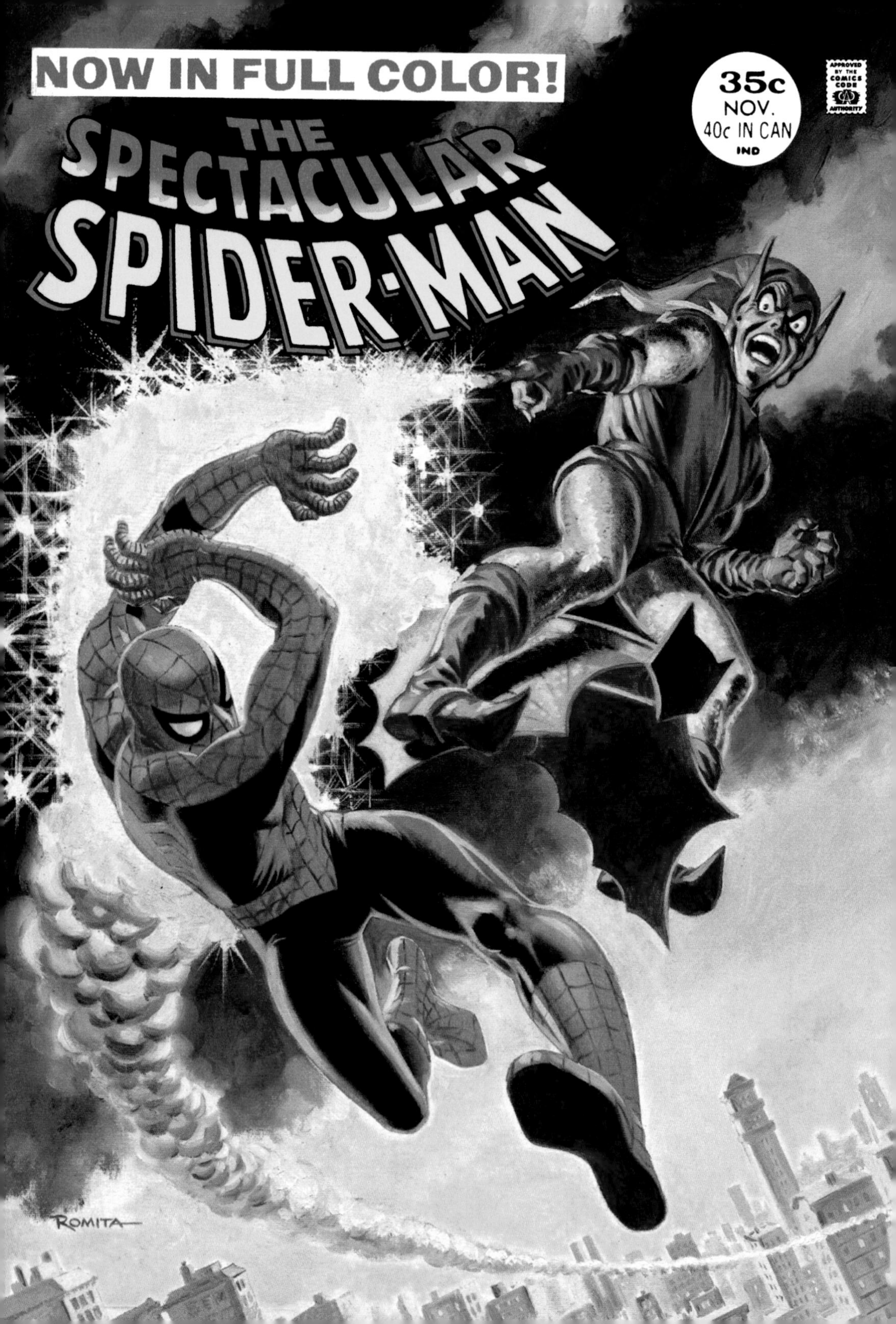
NOW IN FULL COLOR!
THE SPECTACULAR SPIDER-MAN
35c
NOV.
40c IN CAN
IND
APPROVED BY THE COMICS CODE AUTHORITY
ROMITA

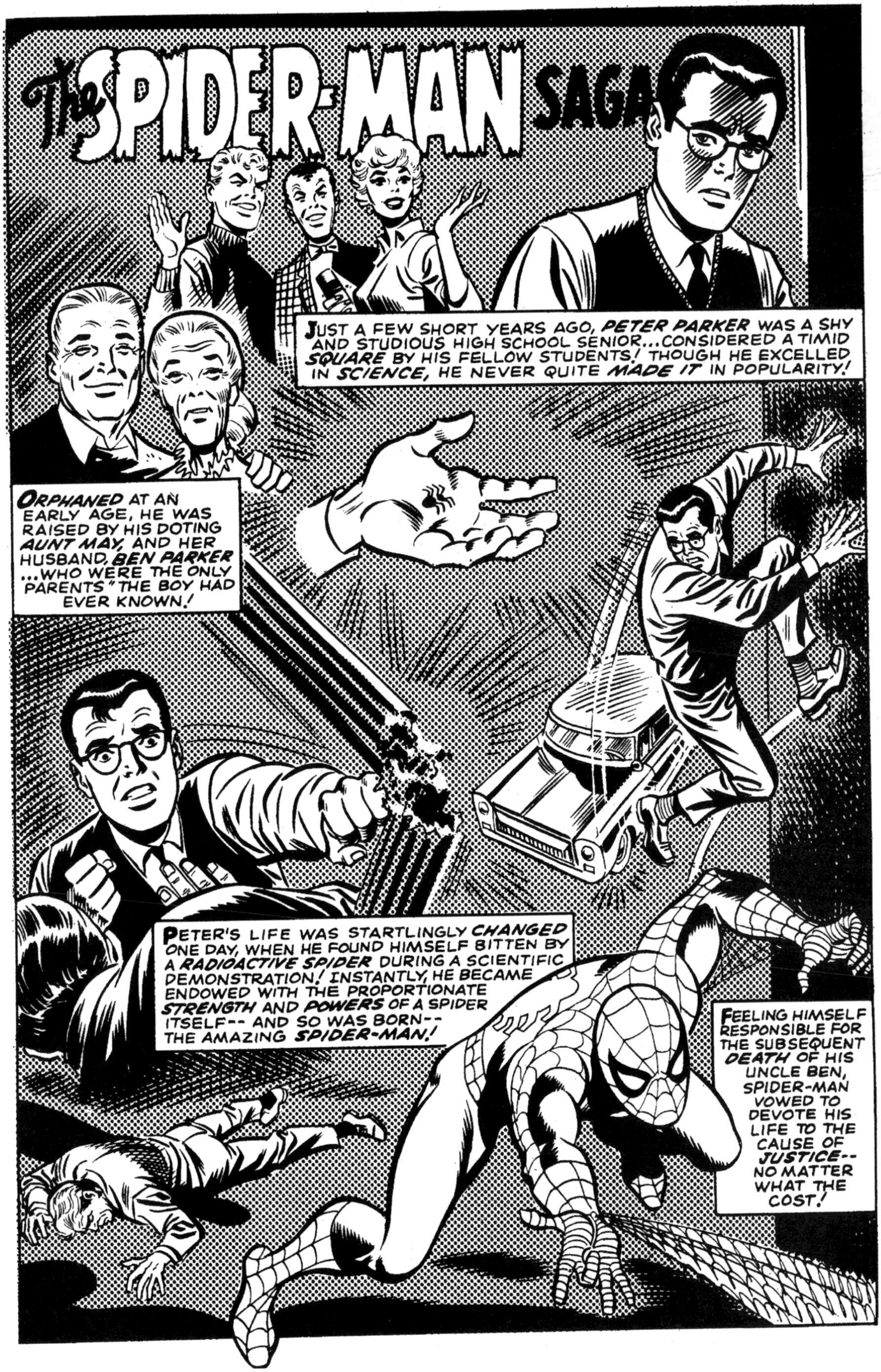
The SPIDER-MAN SAGA
JUST A FEW SHORT YEARS AGO, PETER PARKER WAS A SHY AND STUDIOUS HIGH SCHOOL SENIOR...CONSIDERED A TIMID SQUARE BY HIS FELLOW STUDENTS! THOUGH HE EXCELLED IN SCIENCE, HE NEVER QUITE MADE IT IN POPULARITY!
ORPHANED AT AN EARLY AGE, HE WAS RAISED BY HIS DOTING AUNT MAY, AND HER HUSBAND, BEN PARKER ...WHO WERE THE ONLY "PARENTS" THE BOY HAD EVER KNOWN!
PETER'S LIFE WAS STARTLINGLY CHANGED ONE DAY, WHEN HE FOUND HIMSELF BITTEN BY A RADIOACTIVE SPIDER DURING A SCIENTIFIC DEMONSTRATION! INSTANTLY, HE BECAME ENDOWED WITH THE PROPORTIONATE STRENGTH AND POWERS OF A SPIDER ITSELF-- AND SO WAS BORN-- THE AMAZING SPIDER-MAN!
FEELING HIMSELF RESPONSIBLE FOR THE SUBSEQUENT DEATH OF HIS UNCLE BEN, SPIDER-MAN VOWED TO DEVOTE HIS LIFE TO THE CAUSE OF JUSTICE-- NO MATTER WHAT THE COST!

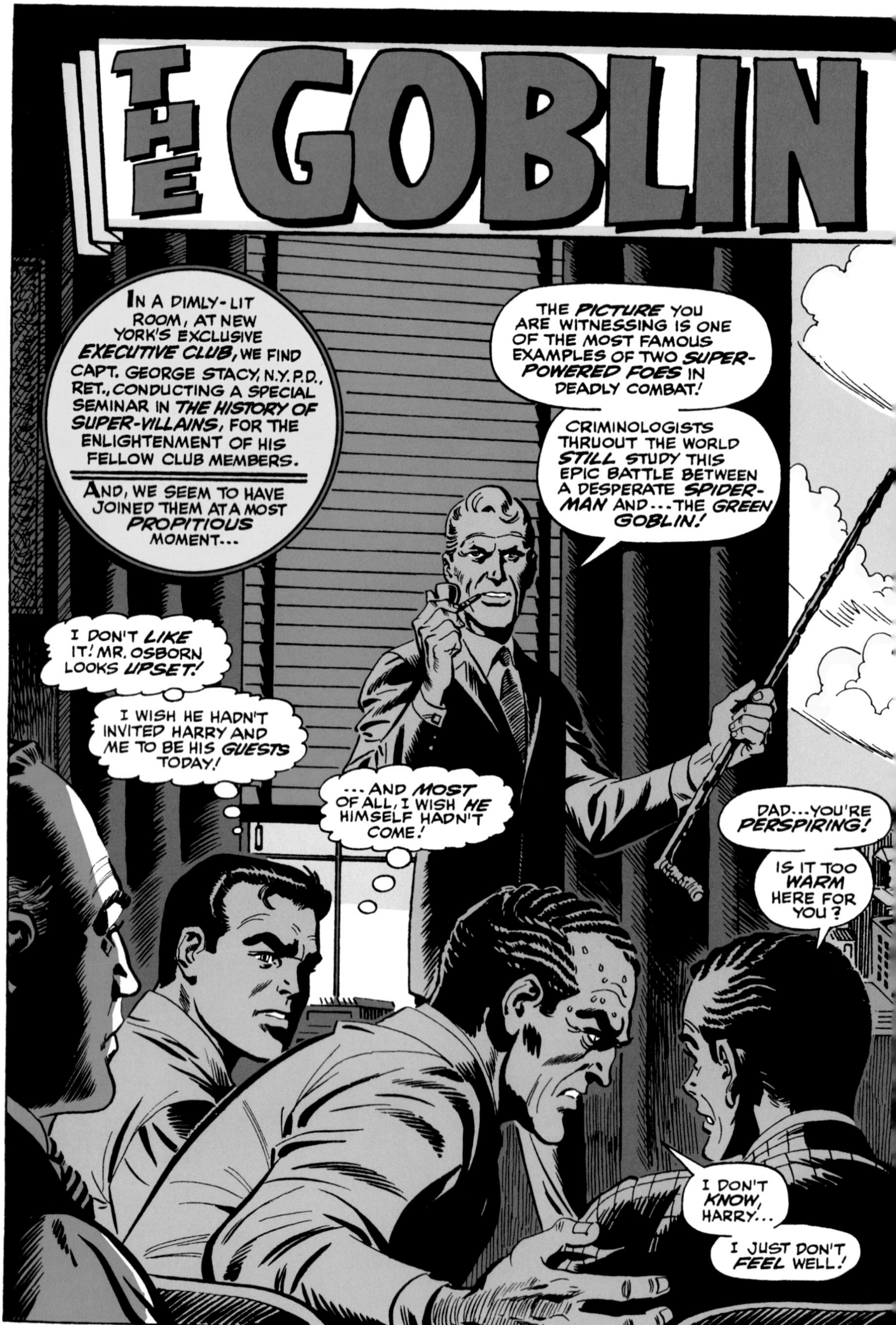

THE GOBLIN
IN A DIMLY-LIT ROOM, AT NEW YORK'S EXCLUSIVE EXECUTIVE CLUB, WE FIND CAPT. GEORGE STACY, N.Y.P.D., RET., CONDUCTING A SPECIAL SEMINAR IN THE HISTORY OF SUPER-VILLAINS, FOR THE ENLIGHTENMENT OF HIS FELLOW CLUB MEMBERS.
AND, WE SEEM TO HAVE JOINED THEM AT A MOST PROPITIOUS MOMENT...
THE PICTURE YOU ARE WITNESSING IS ONE OF THE MOST FAMOUS EXAMPLES OF TWO SUPER-POWERED FOES IN DEADLY COMBAT!
CRIMINOLOGISTS THRUOUT THE WORLD STILL STUDY THIS EPIC BATTLE BETWEEN A DESPERATE SPIDER-MAN AND...THE GREEN GOBLIN!
I DON'T LIKE IT! MR. OSBORN LOOKS UPSET!
I WISH HE HADN'T INVITED HARRY AND ME TO BE HIS GUESTS TODAY!
...AND MOST OF ALL, I WISH HE HIMSELF HADN'T COME!
DAD...YOU'RE PERSPIRING!
IS IT TOO WARM HERE FOR YOU?
I DON'T KNOW, HARRY...
I JUST DON'T FEEL WELL!

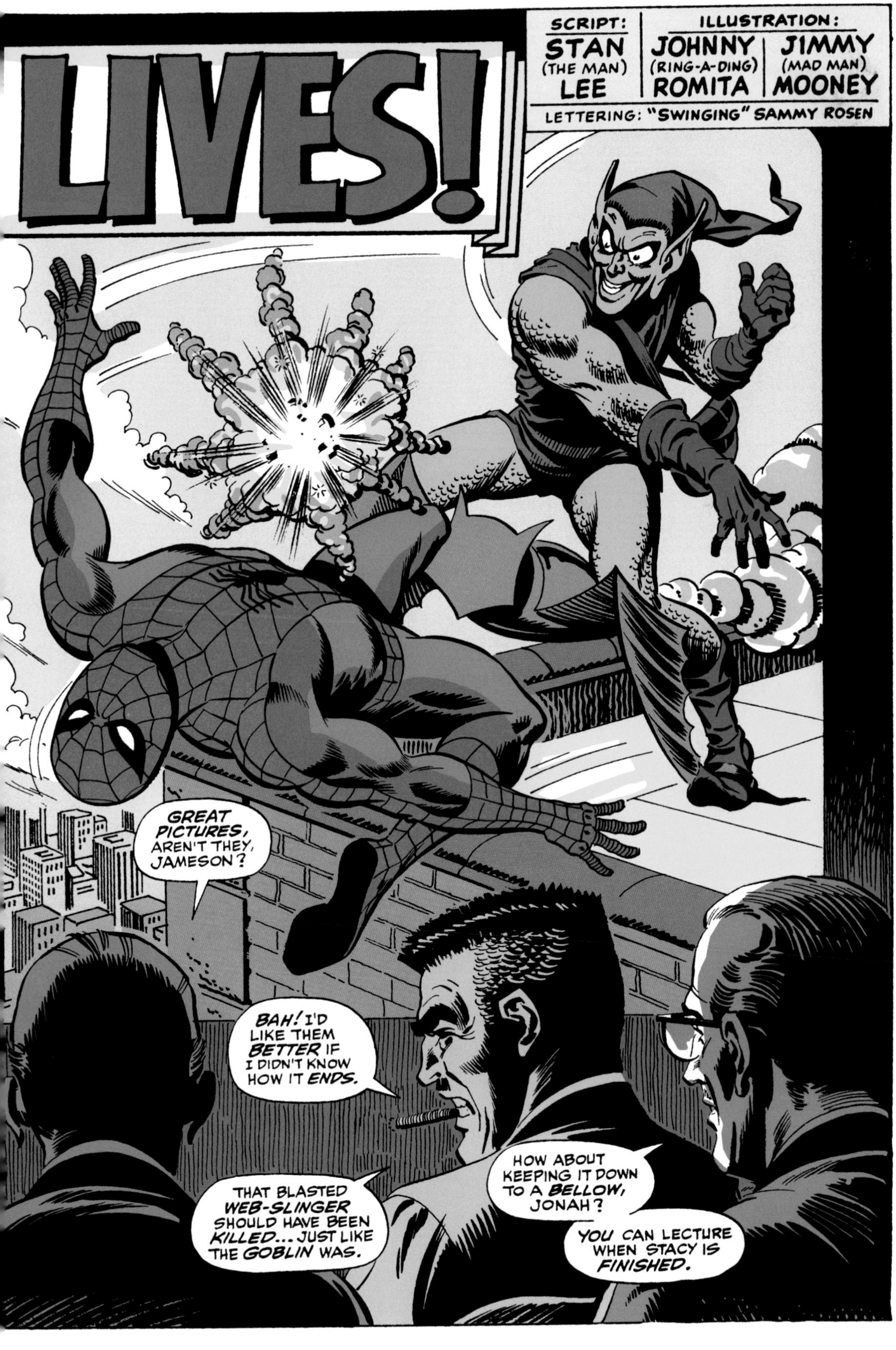
LIVES!
SCRIPT: STAN (THE MAN) LEE
ILLUSTRATION: JOHNNY (RING-A-DING) ROMITA | JIMMY (MAD MAN) MOONEY
LETTERING: "SWINGING" SAMMY ROSEN
GREAT PICTURES, AREN'T THEY, JAMESON?
BAH! I'D LIKE THEM BETTER IF I DIDN'T KNOW HOW IT ENDS.
THAT BLASTED WEB-SLINGER SHOULD HAVE BEEN KILLED... JUST LIKE THE GOBLIN WAS.
HOW ABOUT KEEPING IT DOWN TO A BELLOW, JONAH?
YOU CAN LECTURE WHEN STACY IS FINISHED.

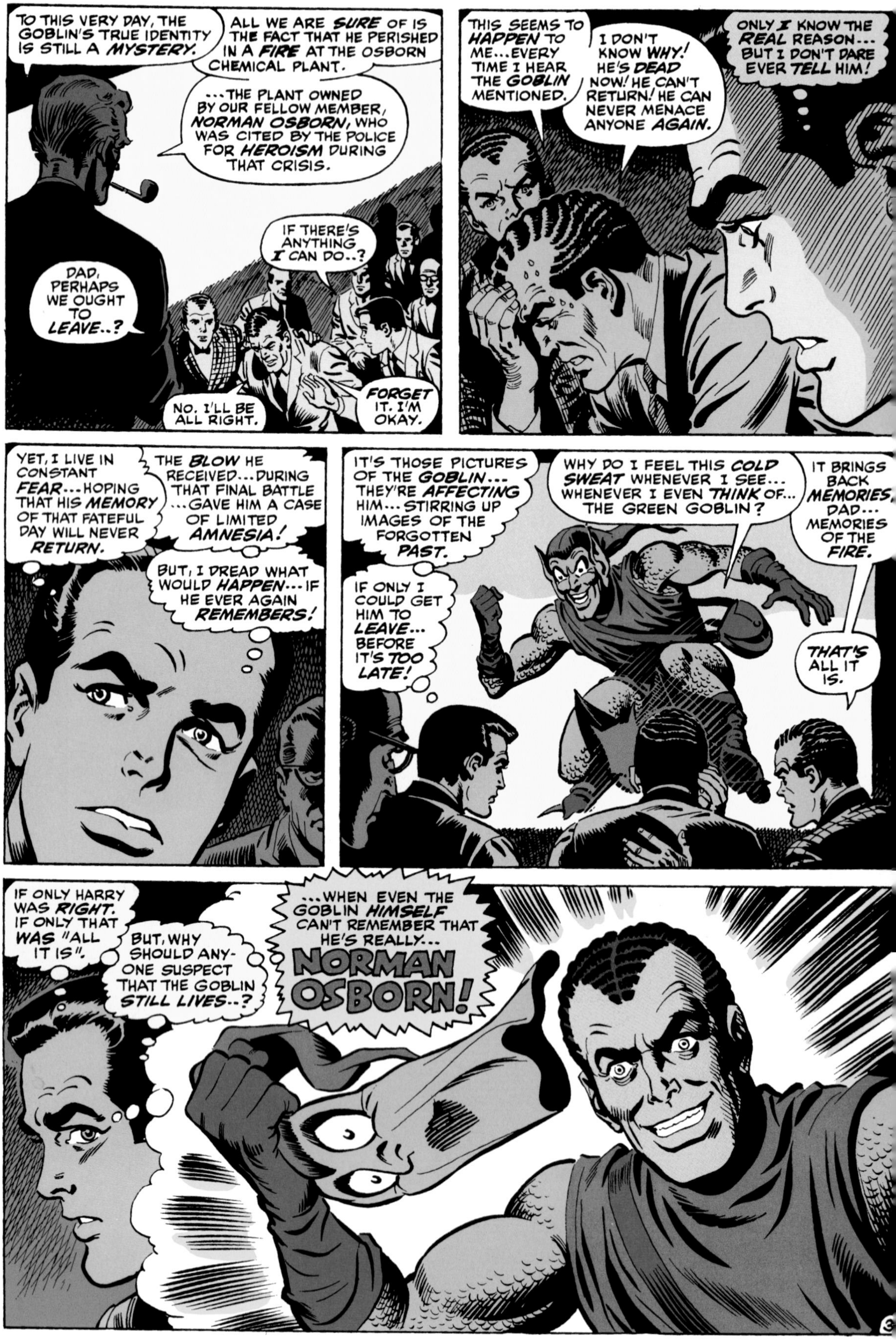

TO THIS VERY DAY, THE GOBLIN'S TRUE IDENTITY IS STILL A MYSTERY.
ALL WE ARE SURE OF IS THE FACT THAT HE PERISHED IN A FIRE AT THE OSBORN CHEMICAL PLANT.
...THE PLANT OWNED BY OUR FELLOW MEMBER, NORMAN OSBORN, WHO WAS CITED BY THE POLICE FOR HEROISM DURING THAT CRISIS.
IF THERE'S ANYTHING I CAN DO..?
DAD, PERHAPS WE OUGHT TO LEAVE..?
NO. I'LL BE ALL RIGHT.
FORGET IT. I'M OKAY.
THIS SEEMS TO HAPPEN TO ME...EVERY TIME I HEAR THE GOBLIN MENTIONED.
I DON'T KNOW WHY! HE'S DEAD NOW! HE CAN'T RETURN! HE CAN NEVER MENACE ANYONE AGAIN.
ONLY I KNOW THE REAL REASON... BUT I DON'T DARE EVER TELL HIM!
YET, I LIVE IN CONSTANT FEAR...HOPING THAT HIS MEMORY OF THAT FATEFUL DAY WILL NEVER RETURN.
THE BLOW HE RECEIVED...DURING THAT FINAL BATTLE ...GAVE HIM A CASE OF LIMITED AMNESIA!
BUT, I DREAD WHAT WOULD HAPPEN...IF HE EVER AGAIN REMEMBERS!
IT'S THOSE PICTURES OF THE GOBLIN... THEY'RE AFFECTING HIM... STIRRING UP IMAGES OF THE FORGOTTEN PAST.
IF ONLY I COULD GET HIM TO LEAVE... BEFORE IT'S TOO LATE!
WHY DO I FEEL THIS COLD SWEAT WHENEVER I SEE... WHENEVER I EVEN THINK OF... THE GREEN GOBLIN?
IT BRINGS BACK MEMORIES, DAD... MEMORIES OF THE FIRE.
THAT'S ALL IT IS.
IF ONLY HARRY WAS RIGHT. IF ONLY THAT WAS "ALL IT IS".
BUT, WHY SHOULD ANY-ONE SUSPECT THAT THE GOBLIN STILL LIVES..?
...WHEN EVEN THE GOBLIN HIMSELF CAN'T REMEMBER THAT HE'S REALLY... NORMAN OSBORN!

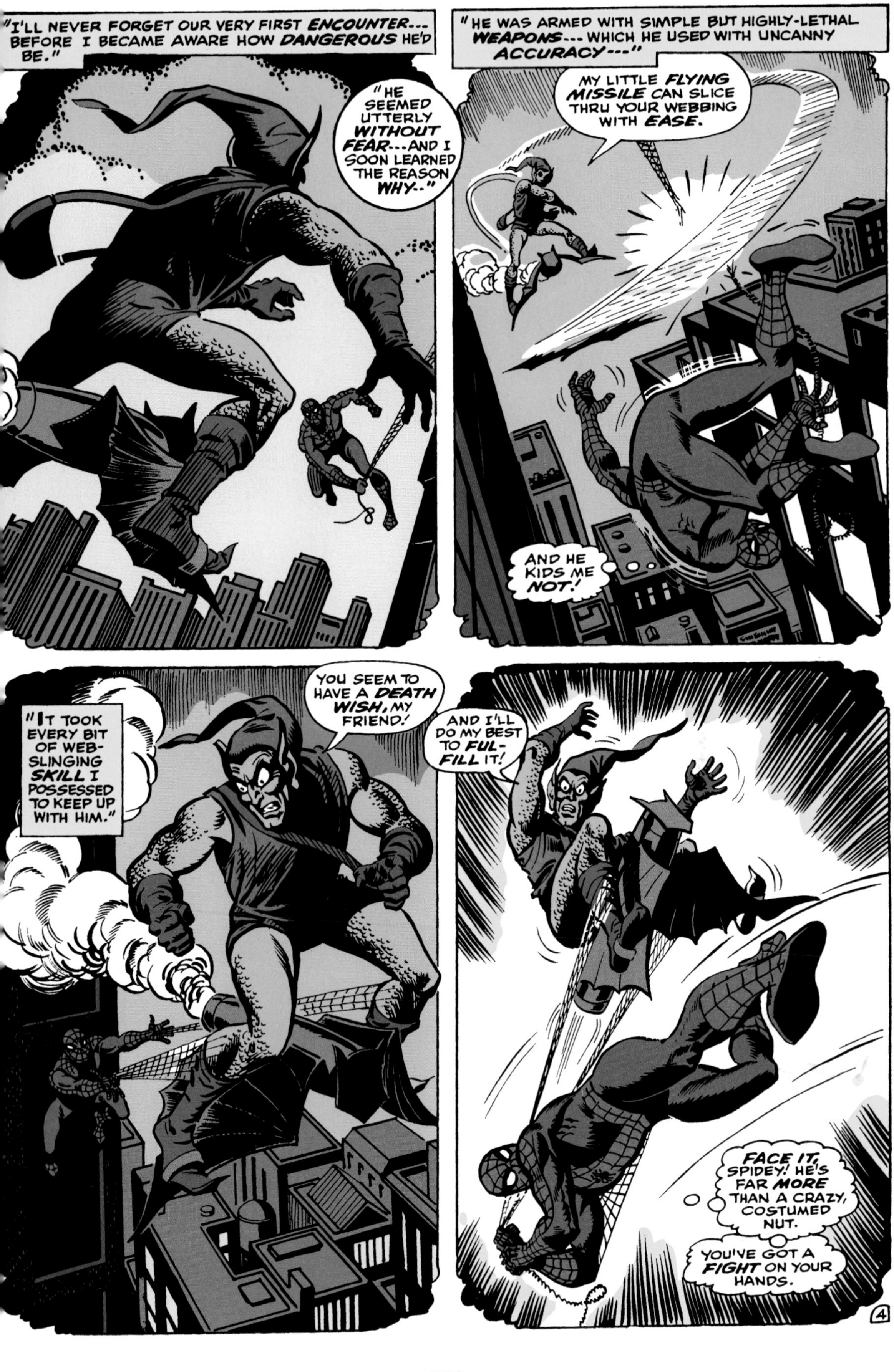
"I'LL NEVER FORGET OUR VERY FIRST ENCOUNTER... BEFORE I BECAME AWARE HOW DANGEROUS HE'D BE."
"HE SEEMED UTTERLY WITHOUT FEAR...AND I SOON LEARNED THE REASON WHY.."
"HE WAS ARMED WITH SIMPLE BUT HIGHLY-LETHAL WEAPONS... WHICH HE USED WITH UNCANNY ACCURACY..."
MY LITTLE FLYING MISSILE CAN SLICE THRU YOUR WEBBING WITH EASE.
AND HE KIDS ME NOT!
"IT TOOK EVERY BIT OF WEB-SLINGING SKILL I POSSESSED TO KEEP UP WITH HIM."
YOU SEEM TO HAVE A DEATH WISH, MY FRIEND!
AND I'LL DO MY BEST TO FUL-FILL IT!
FACE IT, SPIDEY! HE'S FAR MORE THAN A CRAZY, COSTUMED NUT.
YOU'VE GOT A FIGHT ON YOUR HANDS.
4

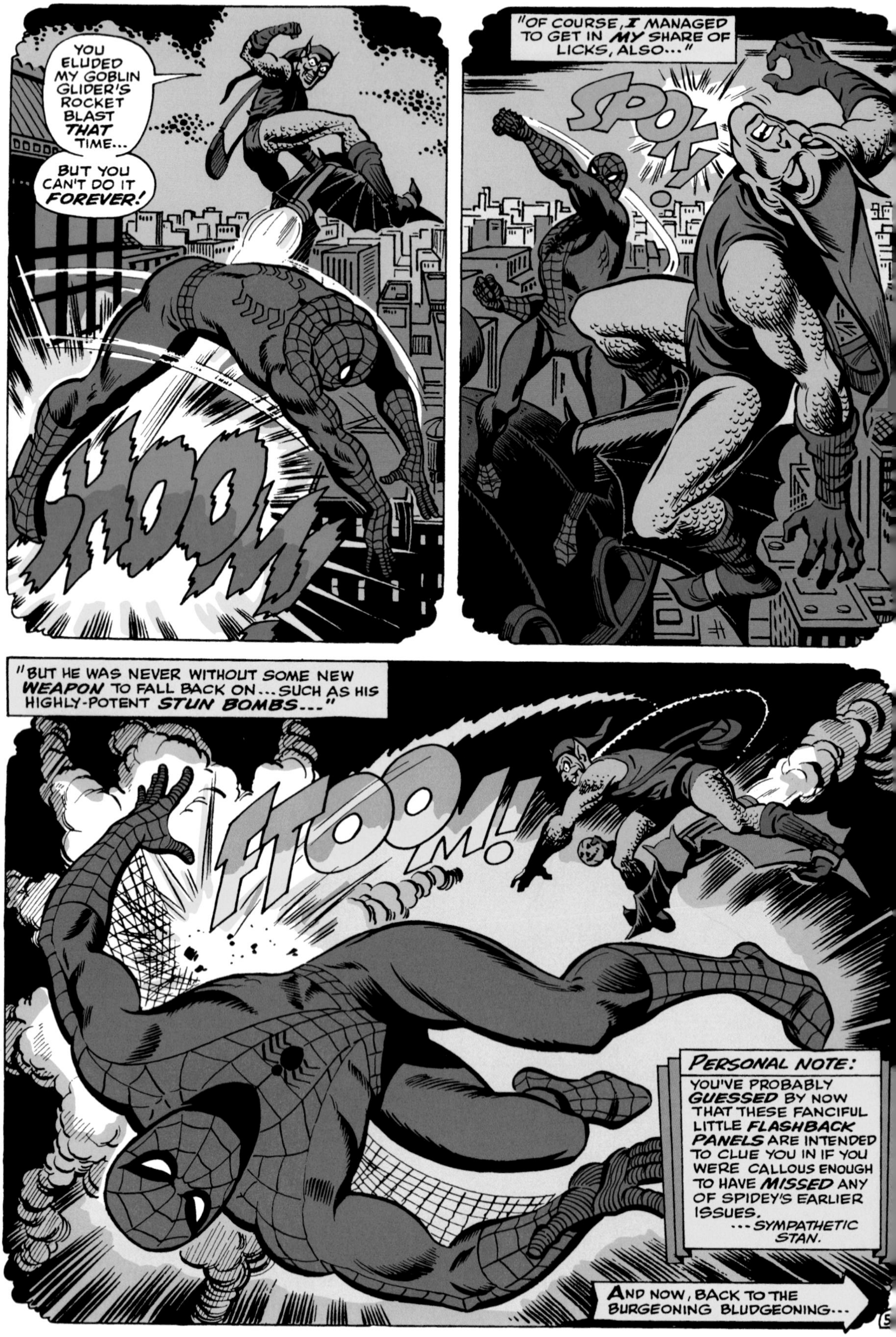
YOU ELUDED MY GOBLIN GLIDER'S ROCKET BLAST THAT TIME...
BUT YOU CAN'T DO IT FOREVER!
"OF COURSE, I MANAGED TO GET IN MY SHARE OF LICKS, ALSO..."
SPOK!
"BUT HE WAS NEVER WITHOUT SOME NEW WEAPON TO FALL BACK ON... SUCH AS HIS HIGHLY-POTENT STUN BOMBS..."
FTOOM!
PERSONAL NOTE:
YOU'VE PROBABLY GUESSED BY NOW THAT THESE FANCIFUL LITTLE FLASHBACK PANELS ARE INTENDED TO CLUE YOU IN IF YOU WERE CALLOUS ENOUGH TO HAVE MISSED ANY OF SPIDEY'S EARLIER ISSUES.
...SYMPATHETIC STAN.
AND NOW, BACK TO THE BURGEONING BLUDGEONING...

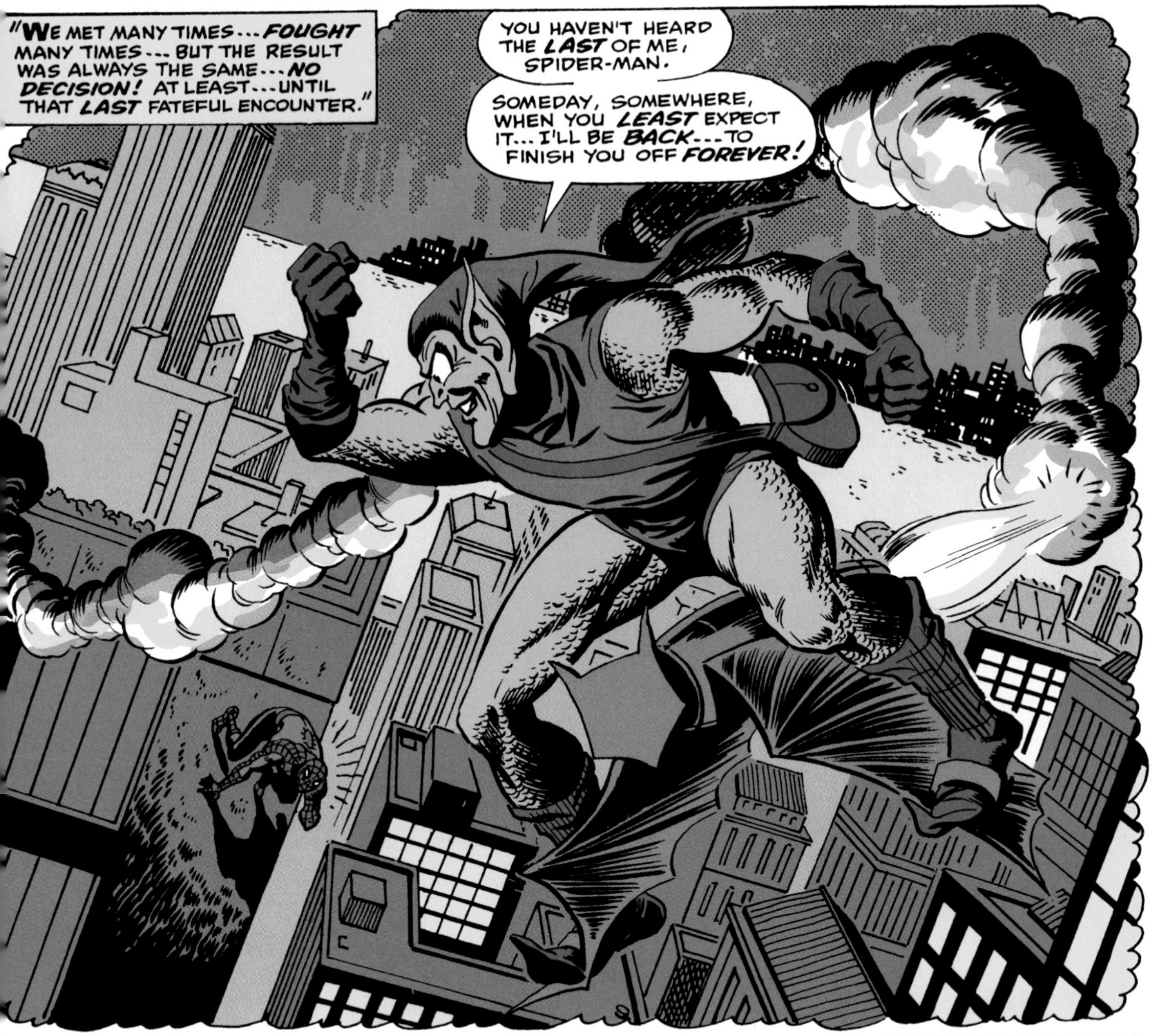
"WE MET MANY TIMES... FOUGHT MANY TIMES... BUT THE RESULT WAS ALWAYS THE SAME... NO DECISION! AT LEAST... UNTIL THAT LAST FATEFUL ENCOUNTER."
YOU HAVEN'T HEARD THE LAST OF ME, SPIDER-MAN.
SOMEDAY, SOMEWHERE, WHEN YOU LEAST EXPECT IT... I'LL BE BACK--- TO FINISH YOU OFF FOREVER!

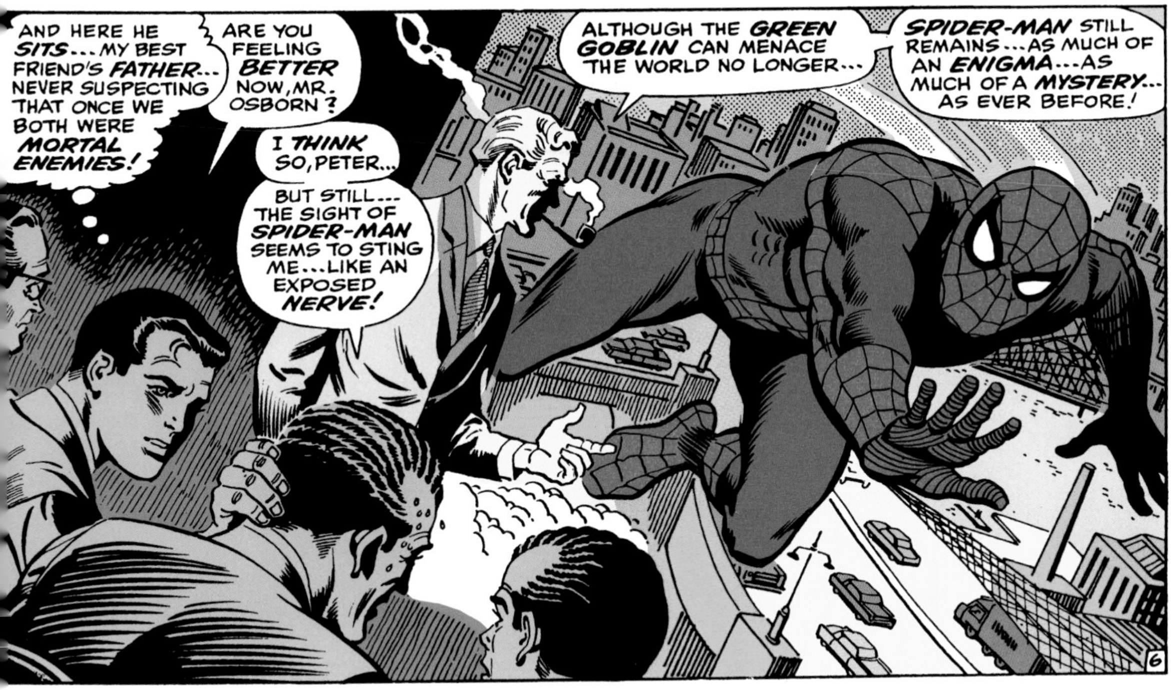
AND HERE HE SITS... MY BEST FRIEND'S FATHER... NEVER SUSPECTING THAT ONCE WE BOTH WERE MORTAL ENEMIES!
ARE YOU FEELING BETTER NOW, MR. OSBORN?
I THINK SO, PETER...
BUT STILL... THE SIGHT OF SPIDER-MAN SEEMS TO STING ME... LIKE AN EXPOSED NERVE!
ALTHOUGH THE GREEN GOBLIN CAN MENACE THE WORLD NO LONGER...
SPIDER-MAN STILL REMAINS... AS MUCH OF AN ENIGMA... AS MUCH OF A MYSTERY... AS EVER BEFORE!
6

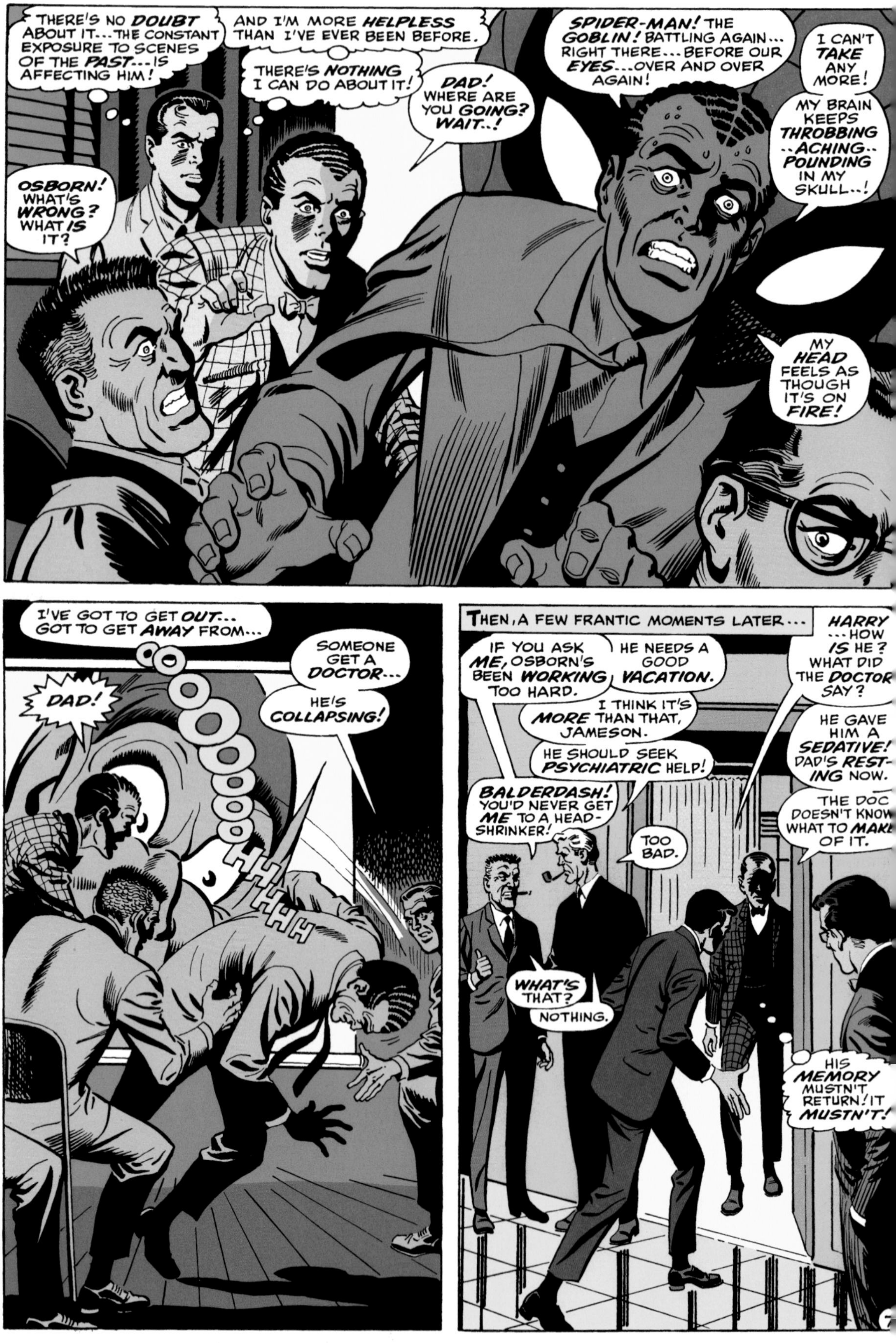
THERE'S NO DOUBT ABOUT IT... THE CONSTANT EXPOSURE TO SCENES OF THE PAST...IS AFFECTING HIM!
AND I'M MORE HELPLESS THAN I'VE EVER BEEN BEFORE.
THERE'S NOTHING I CAN DO ABOUT IT!
DAD! WHERE ARE YOU GOING? WAIT..!
SPIDER-MAN! THE GOBLIN! BATTLING AGAIN... RIGHT THERE... BEFORE OUR EYES...OVER AND OVER AGAIN!
I CAN'T TAKE ANY MORE!
MY BRAIN KEEPS THROBBING ..ACHING.. POUNDING IN MY SKULL..!
OSBORN! WHAT'S WRONG? WHAT IS IT?
MY HEAD FEELS AS THOUGH IT'S ON FIRE!
I'VE GOT TO GET OUT... GOT TO GET AWAY FROM...
DAD!
SOMEONE GET A DOCTOR...
HE'S COLLAPSING!
HHHH
THEN, A FEW FRANTIC MOMENTS LATER...
IF YOU ASK ME, OSBORN'S BEEN WORKING TOO HARD.
HE NEEDS A GOOD VACATION.
I THINK IT'S MORE THAN THAT, JAMESON.
HE SHOULD SEEK PSYCHIATRIC HELP!
BALDERDASH! YOU'D NEVER GET ME TO A HEAD-SHRINKER!
TOO BAD.
WHAT'S THAT?
NOTHING.
HARRY ...HOW IS HE? WHAT DID THE DOCTOR SAY?
HE GAVE HIM A SEDATIVE! DAD'S RESTING NOW.
THE DOC DOESN'T KNOW WHAT TO MAKE OF IT.
HIS MEMORY MUSTN'T RETURN! IT MUSTN'T!
7

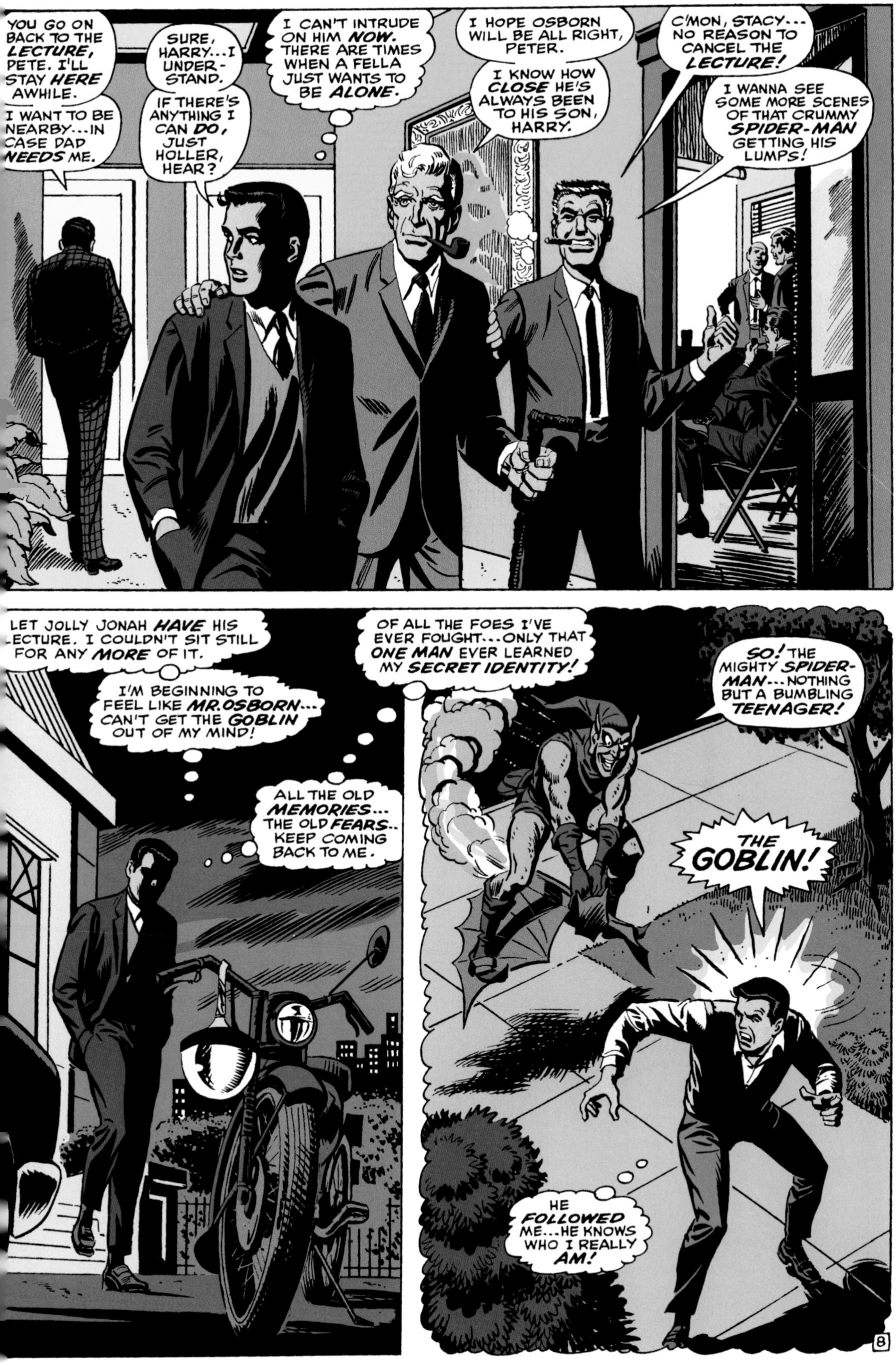
YOU GO ON BACK TO THE LECTURE, PETE. I'LL STAY HERE AWHILE.
I WANT TO BE NEARBY...IN CASE DAD NEEDS ME.
SURE, HARRY...I UNDER-STAND.
IF THERE'S ANYTHING I CAN DO, JUST HOLLER, HEAR?
I CAN'T INTRUDE ON HIM NOW. THERE ARE TIMES WHEN A FELLA JUST WANTS TO BE ALONE.
I HOPE OSBORN WILL BE ALL RIGHT, PETER.
I KNOW HOW CLOSE HE'S ALWAYS BEEN TO HIS SON, HARRY.
C'MON, STACY... NO REASON TO CANCEL THE LECTURE!
I WANNA SEE SOME MORE SCENES OF THAT CRUMMY SPIDER-MAN GETTING HIS LUMPS!
LET JOLLY JONAH HAVE HIS LECTURE. I COULDN'T SIT STILL FOR ANY MORE OF IT.
I'M BEGINNING TO FEEL LIKE MR. OSBORN... CAN'T GET THE GOBLIN OUT OF MY MIND!
ALL THE OLD MEMORIES... THE OLD FEARS.. KEEP COMING BACK TO ME.
OF ALL THE FOES I'VE EVER FOUGHT...ONLY THAT ONE MAN EVER LEARNED MY SECRET IDENTITY!
SO! THE MIGHTY SPIDER-MAN...NOTHING BUT A BUMBLING TEENAGER!
THE GOBLIN!
HE FOLLOWED ME...HE KNOWS WHO I REALLY AM!
8

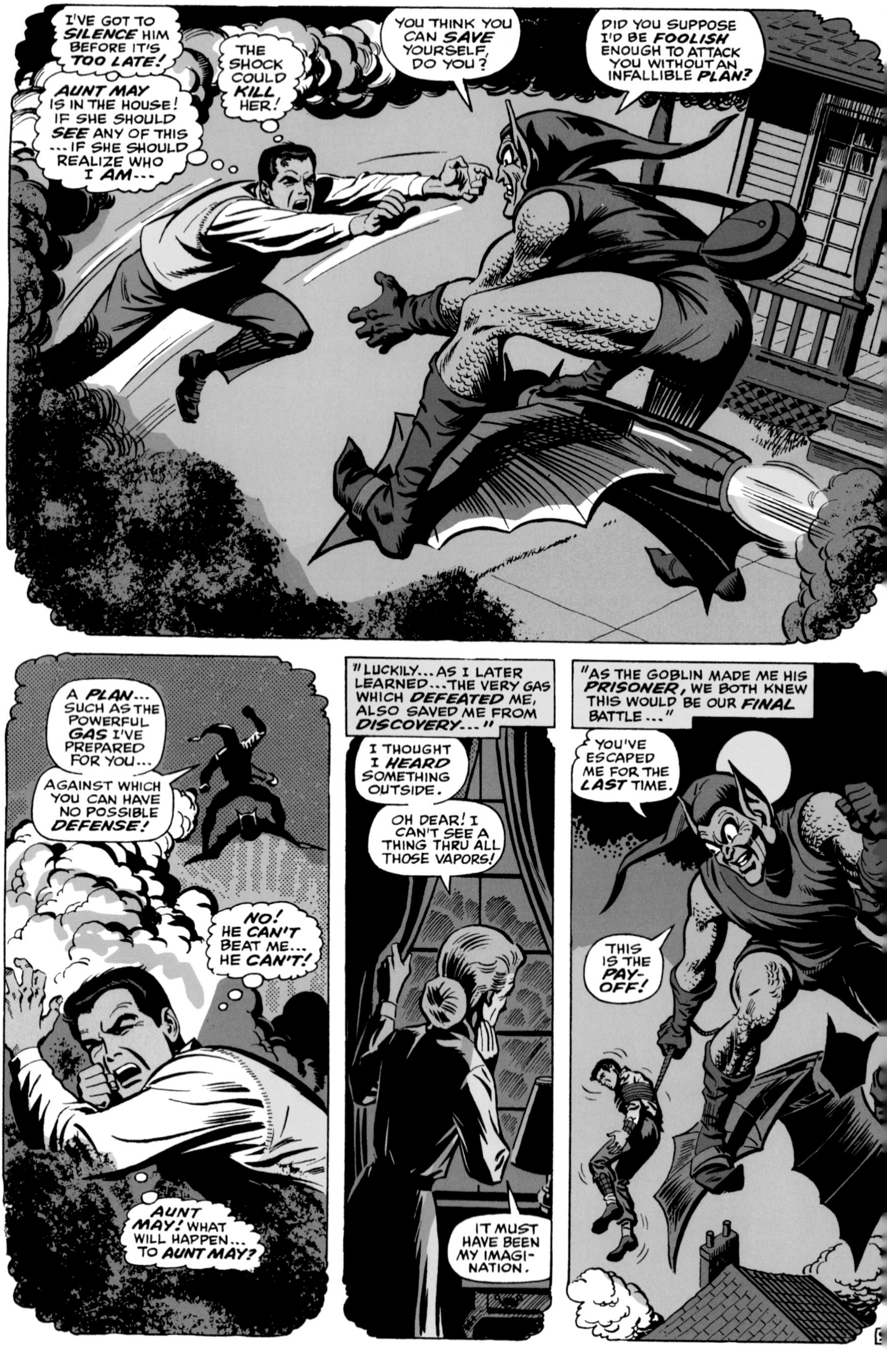
I'VE GOT TO SILENCE HIM BEFORE IT'S TOO LATE!
AUNT MAY IS IN THE HOUSE! IF SHE SHOULD SEE ANY OF THIS ...IF SHE SHOULD REALIZE WHO I AM---
THE SHOCK COULD KILL HER!
YOU THINK YOU CAN SAVE YOURSELF, DO YOU?
DID YOU SUPPOSE I'D BE FOOLISH ENOUGH TO ATTACK YOU WITHOUT AN INFALLIBLE PLAN?
A PLAN... SUCH AS THE POWERFUL GAS I'VE PREPARED FOR YOU...
AGAINST WHICH YOU CAN HAVE NO POSSIBLE DEFENSE!
NO! HE CAN'T BEAT ME... HE CAN'T!
AUNT MAY! WHAT WILL HAPPEN... TO AUNT MAY?
"LUCKILY... AS I LATER LEARNED... THE VERY GAS WHICH DEFEATED ME, ALSO SAVED ME FROM DISCOVERY..."
I THOUGHT I HEARD SOMETHING OUTSIDE.
OH DEAR! I CAN'T SEE A THING THRU ALL THOSE VAPORS!
IT MUST HAVE BEEN MY IMAGINATION.
"AS THE GOBLIN MADE ME HIS PRISONER, WE BOTH KNEW THIS WOULD BE OUR FINAL BATTLE..."
YOU'VE ESCAPED ME FOR THE LAST TIME.
THIS IS THE PAY-OFF!

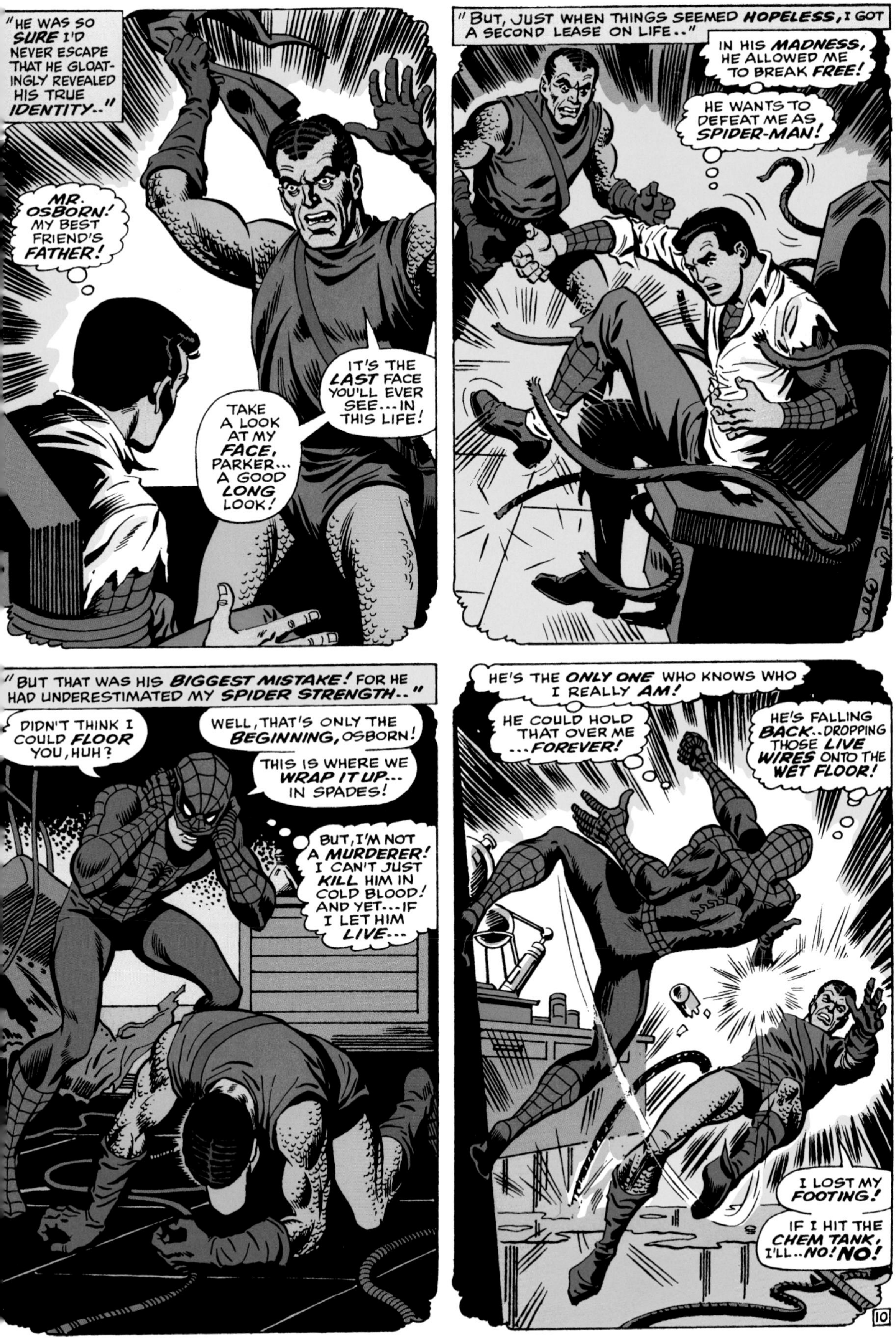
"HE WAS SO SURE I'D NEVER ESCAPE THAT HE GLOATINGLY REVEALED HIS TRUE IDENTITY.."
MR. OSBORN! MY BEST FRIEND'S FATHER!
TAKE A LOOK AT MY FACE, PARKER... A GOOD LONG LOOK!
IT'S THE LAST FACE YOU'LL EVER SEE... IN THIS LIFE!
"BUT, JUST WHEN THINGS SEEMED HOPELESS, I GOT A SECOND LEASE ON LIFE.."
IN HIS MADNESS, HE ALLOWED ME TO BREAK FREE!
HE WANTS TO DEFEAT ME AS SPIDER-MAN!
"BUT THAT WAS HIS BIGGEST MISTAKE! FOR HE HAD UNDERESTIMATED MY SPIDER STRENGTH.."
DIDN'T THINK I COULD FLOOR YOU, HUH?
WELL, THAT'S ONLY THE BEGINNING, OSBORN!
THIS IS WHERE WE WRAP IT UP... IN SPADES!
BUT, I'M NOT A MURDERER! I CAN'T JUST KILL HIM IN COLD BLOOD! AND YET... IF I LET HIM LIVE...
HE'S THE ONLY ONE WHO KNOWS WHO I REALLY AM!
HE COULD HOLD THAT OVER ME ...FOREVER!
HE'S FALLING BACK.. DROPPING THOSE LIVE WIRES ONTO THE WET FLOOR!
I LOST MY FOOTING!
IF I HIT THE CHEM TANK, I'LL.. NO! NO!
10

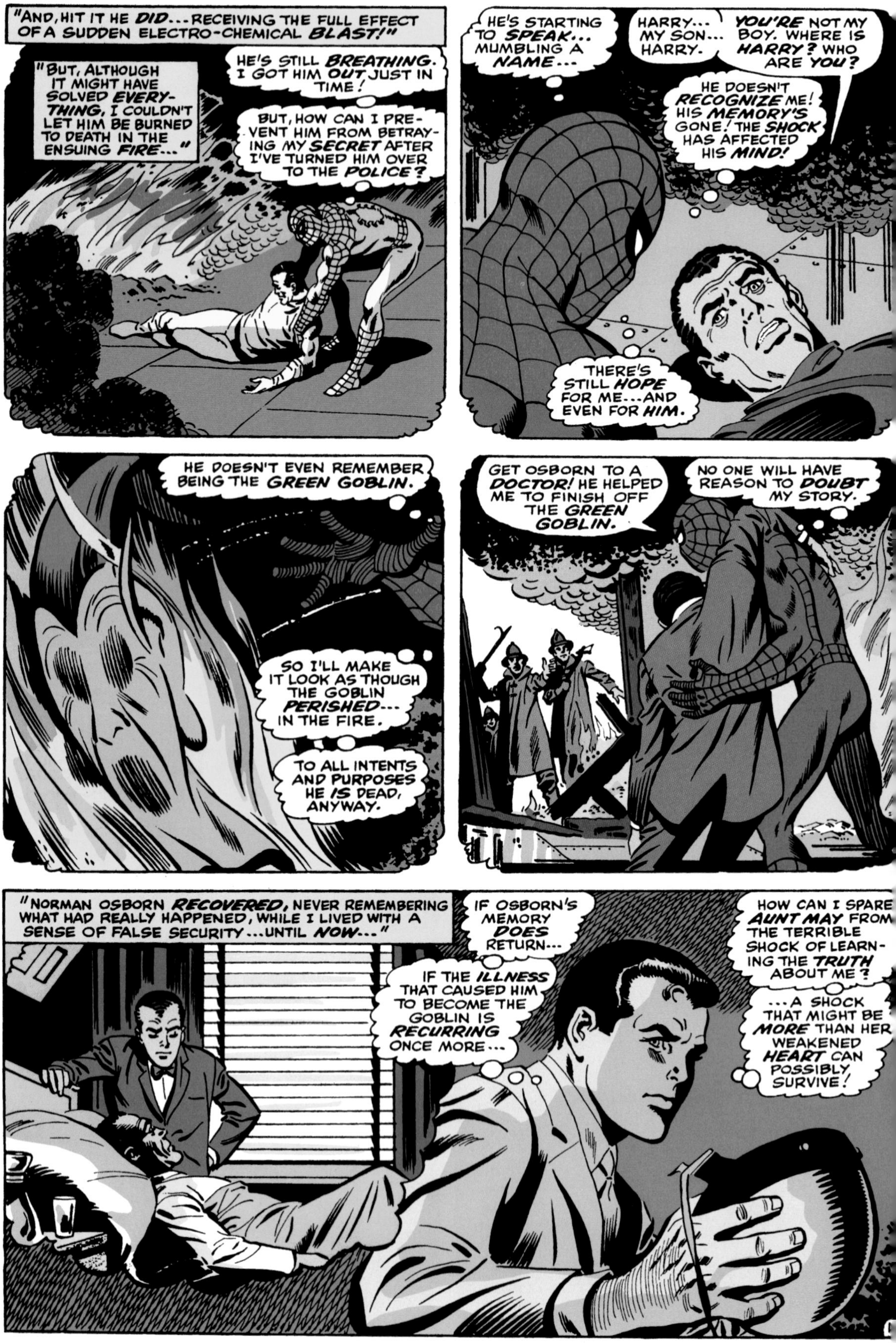

"AND, HIT IT HE DID... RECEIVING THE FULL EFFECT OF A SUDDEN ELECTRO-CHEMICAL BLAST!"
"BUT, ALTHOUGH IT MIGHT HAVE SOLVED EVERYTHING, I COULDN'T LET HIM BE BURNED TO DEATH IN THE ENSUING FIRE..."
HE'S STILL BREATHING. I GOT HIM OUT JUST IN TIME!
BUT, HOW CAN I PREVENT HIM FROM BETRAYING MY SECRET AFTER I'VE TURNED HIM OVER TO THE POLICE?
HE'S STARTING TO SPEAK... MUMBLING A NAME...
HARRY... MY SON... HARRY.
YOU'RE NOT MY BOY. WHERE IS HARRY? WHO ARE YOU?
HE DOESN'T RECOGNIZE ME! HIS MEMORY'S GONE! THE SHOCK HAS AFFECTED HIS MIND!
THERE'S STILL HOPE FOR ME...AND EVEN FOR HIM.
HE DOESN'T EVEN REMEMBER BEING THE GREEN GOBLIN.
SO I'LL MAKE IT LOOK AS THOUGH THE GOBLIN PERISHED... IN THE FIRE.
TO ALL INTENTS AND PURPOSES HE IS DEAD, ANYWAY.
GET OSBORN TO A DOCTOR! HE HELPED ME TO FINISH OFF THE GREEN GOBLIN.
NO ONE WILL HAVE REASON TO DOUBT MY STORY.
"NORMAN OSBORN RECOVERED, NEVER REMEMBERING WHAT HAD REALLY HAPPENED, WHILE I LIVED WITH A SENSE OF FALSE SECURITY...UNTIL NOW..."
IF OSBORN'S MEMORY DOES RETURN...
IF THE ILLNESS THAT CAUSED HIM TO BECOME THE GOBLIN IS RECURRING ONCE MORE...
HOW CAN I SPARE AUNT MAY FROM THE TERRIBLE SHOCK OF LEARNING THE TRUTH ABOUT ME?
...A SHOCK THAT MIGHT BE MORE THAN HER WEAKENED HEART CAN POSSIBLY SURVIVE!

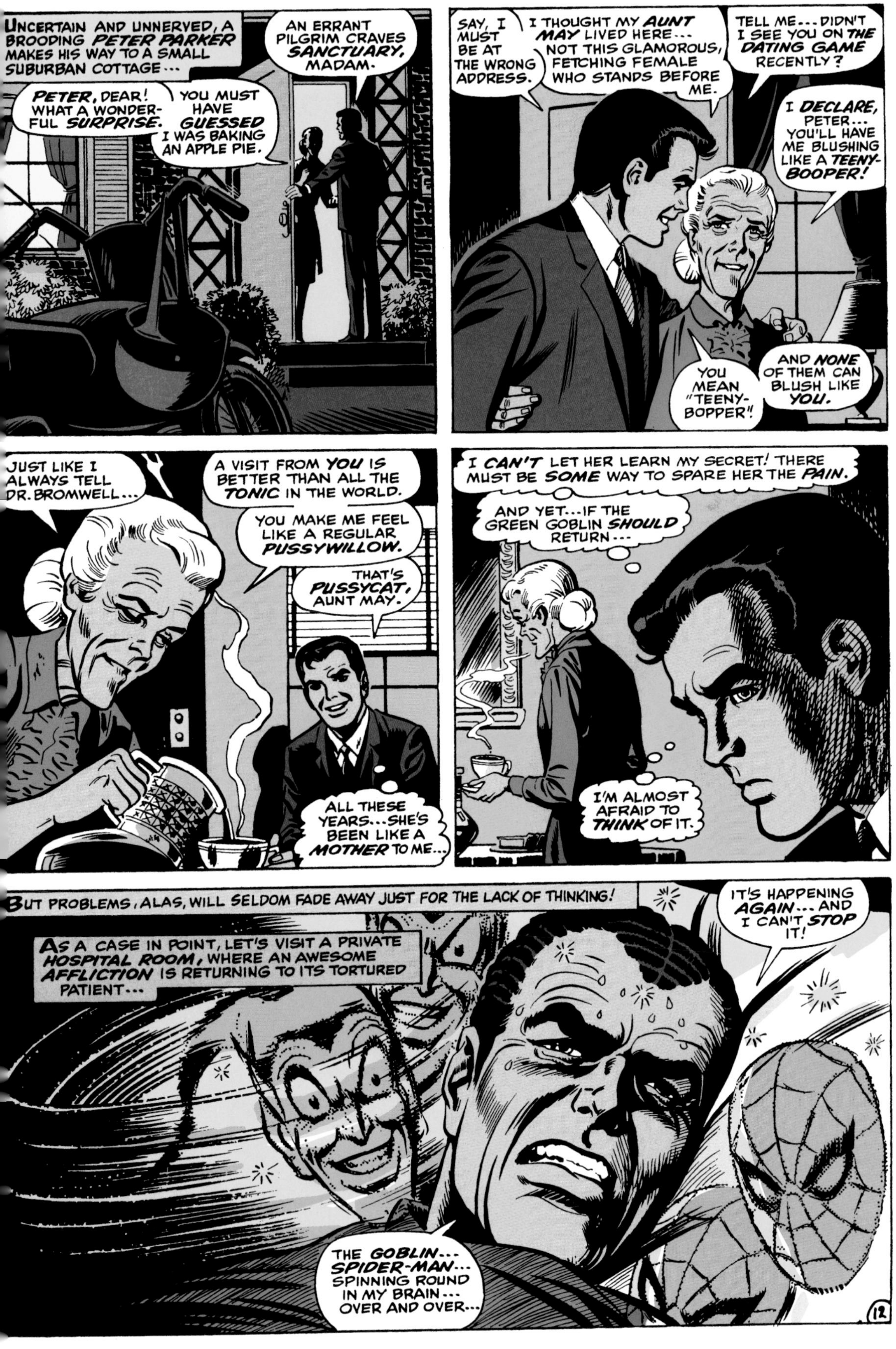
UNCERTAIN AND UNNERVED, A BROODING PETER PARKER MAKES HIS WAY TO A SMALL SUBURBAN COTTAGE...
AN ERRANT PILGRIM CRAVES SANCTUARY, MADAM.
PETER, DEAR! WHAT A WONDERFUL SURPRISE.
YOU MUST HAVE GUESSED I WAS BAKING AN APPLE PIE.
SAY, I MUST BE AT THE WRONG ADDRESS.
I THOUGHT MY AUNT MAY LIVED HERE... NOT THIS GLAMOROUS, FETCHING FEMALE WHO STANDS BEFORE ME.
TELL ME... DIDN'T I SEE YOU ON THE DATING GAME RECENTLY?
I DECLARE, PETER... YOU'LL HAVE ME BLUSHING LIKE A TEENY-BOOPER!
YOU MEAN "TEENY-BOPPER"!
AND NONE OF THEM CAN BLUSH LIKE YOU.
JUST LIKE I ALWAYS TELL DR. BROMWELL...
A VISIT FROM YOU IS BETTER THAN ALL THE TONIC IN THE WORLD.
YOU MAKE ME FEEL LIKE A REGULAR PUSSYWILLOW.
THAT'S PUSSYCAT, AUNT MAY.
ALL THESE YEARS... SHE'S BEEN LIKE A MOTHER TO ME...
I CAN'T LET HER LEARN MY SECRET! THERE MUST BE SOME WAY TO SPARE HER THE PAIN.
AND YET... IF THE GREEN GOBLIN SHOULD RETURN...
I'M ALMOST AFRAID TO THINK OF IT.
BUT PROBLEMS, ALAS, WILL SELDOM FADE AWAY JUST FOR THE LACK OF THINKING!
AS A CASE IN POINT, LET'S VISIT A PRIVATE HOSPITAL ROOM, WHERE AN AWESOME AFFLICTION IS RETURNING TO ITS TORTURED PATIENT...
IT'S HAPPENING AGAIN... AND I CAN'T STOP IT!
THE GOBLIN... SPIDER-MAN... SPINNING ROUND IN MY BRAIN... OVER AND OVER...
12

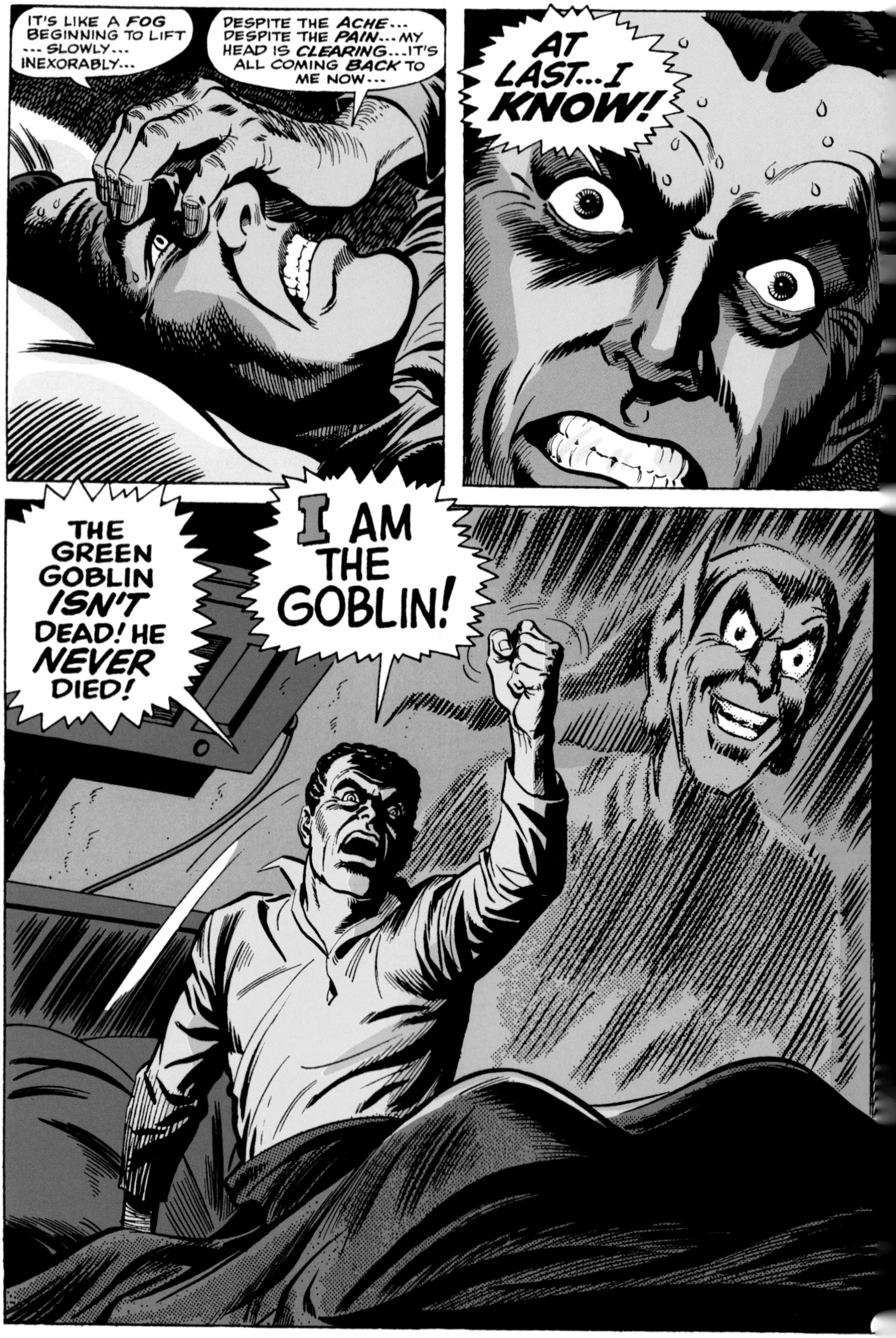
IT'S LIKE A FOG BEGINNING TO LIFT --- SLOWLY--- INEXORABLY---
DESPITE THE ACHE--- DESPITE THE PAIN--- MY HEAD IS CLEARING--- IT'S ALL COMING BACK TO ME NOW---
AT LAST...I KNOW!
THE GREEN GOBLIN ISN'T DEAD! HE NEVER DIED!
I AM THE GOBLIN!

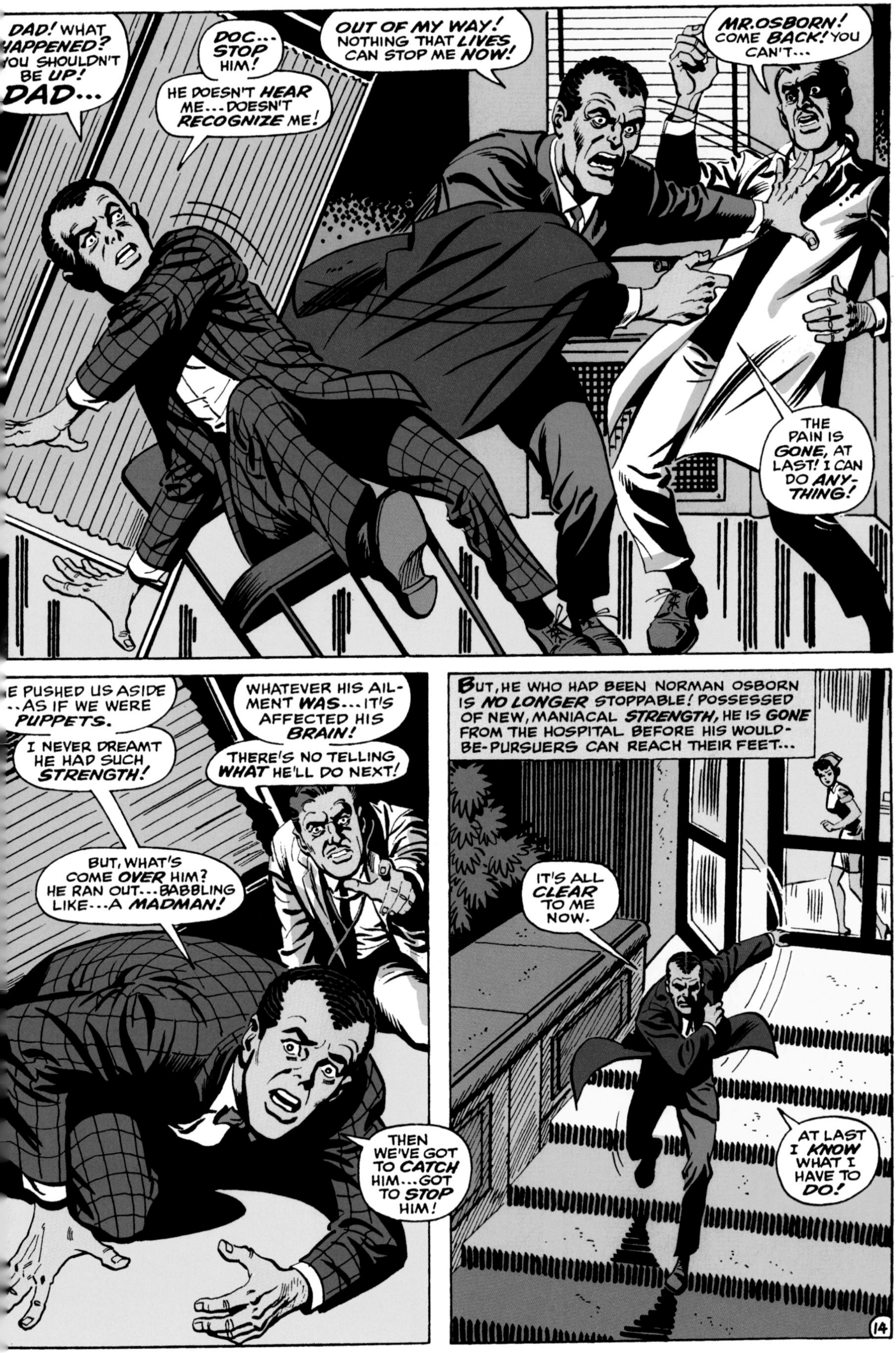
DAD! WHAT HAPPENED? YOU SHOULDN'T BE UP! DAD...
DOC... STOP HIM!
HE DOESN'T HEAR ME... DOESN'T RECOGNIZE ME!
OUT OF MY WAY! NOTHING THAT LIVES CAN STOP ME NOW!
MR. OSBORN! COME BACK! YOU CAN'T...
THE PAIN IS GONE, AT LAST! I CAN DO ANYTHING!
HE PUSHED US ASIDE ...AS IF WE WERE PUPPETS.
I NEVER DREAMT HE HAD SUCH STRENGTH!
WHATEVER HIS AILMENT WAS... IT'S AFFECTED HIS BRAIN!
THERE'S NO TELLING WHAT HE'LL DO NEXT!
BUT, WHAT'S COME OVER HIM? HE RAN OUT... BABBLING LIKE... A MADMAN!
THEN WE'VE GOT TO CATCH HIM... GOT TO STOP HIM!
BUT, HE WHO HAD BEEN NORMAN OSBORN IS NO LONGER STOPPABLE! POSSESSED OF NEW, MANIACAL STRENGTH, HE IS GONE FROM THE HOSPITAL BEFORE HIS WOULD-BE-PURSUERS CAN REACH THEIR FEET...
IT'S ALL CLEAR TO ME NOW.
AT LAST I KNOW WHAT I HAVE TO DO!
14

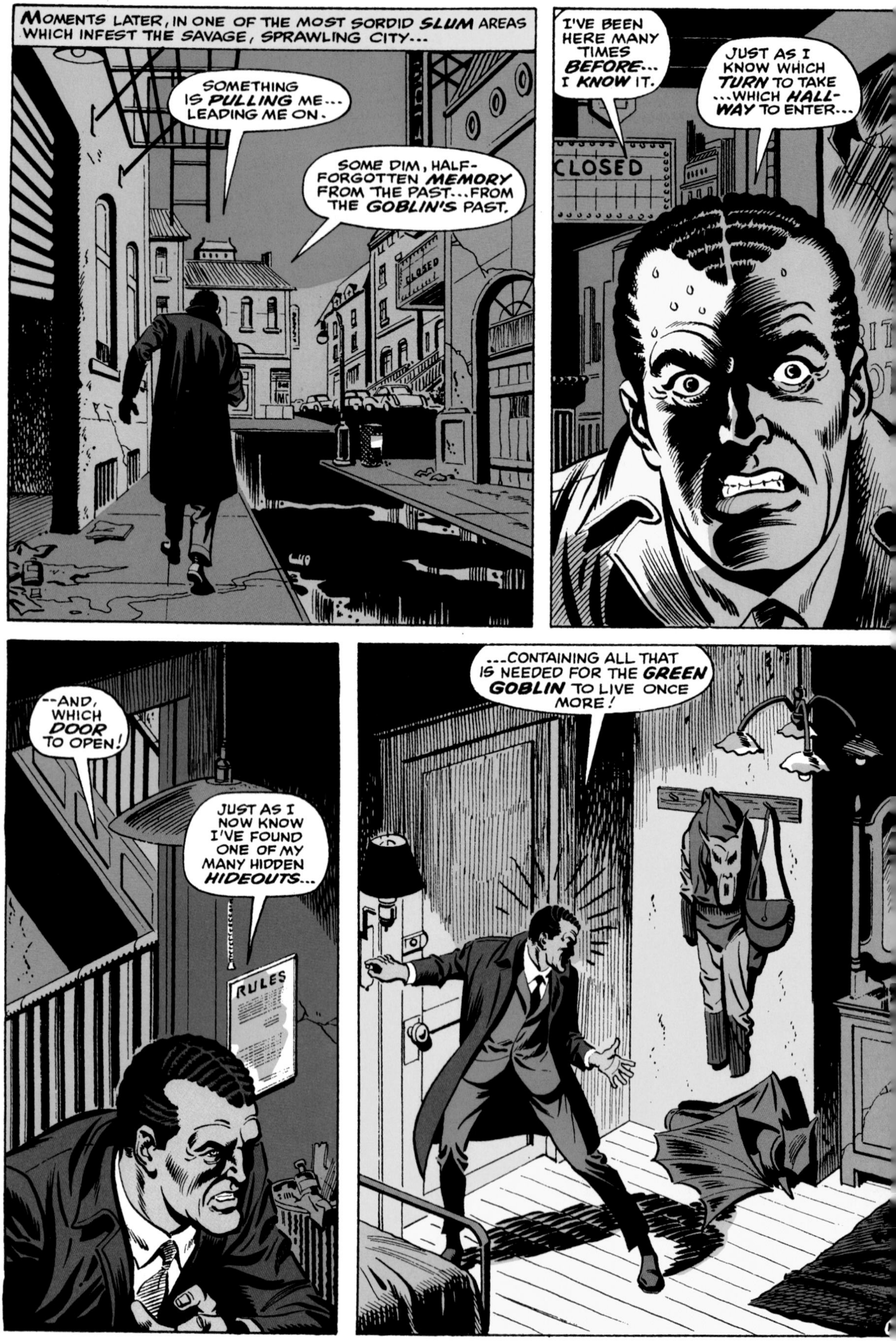
MOMENTS LATER, IN ONE OF THE MOST SORDID SLUM AREAS WHICH INFEST THE SAVAGE, SPRAWLING CITY...
SOMETHING IS PULLING ME... LEADING ME ON.
SOME DIM, HALF-FORGOTTEN MEMORY FROM THE PAST... FROM THE GOBLIN'S PAST.
CLOSED
I'VE BEEN HERE MANY TIMES BEFORE... I KNOW IT.
JUST AS I KNOW WHICH TURN TO TAKE ...WHICH HALL-WAY TO ENTER...
CLOSED
--AND, WHICH DOOR TO OPEN!
JUST AS I NOW KNOW I'VE FOUND ONE OF MY MANY HIDDEN HIDEOUTS...
RULES
...CONTAINING ALL THAT IS NEEDED FOR THE GREEN GOBLIN TO LIVE ONCE MORE!

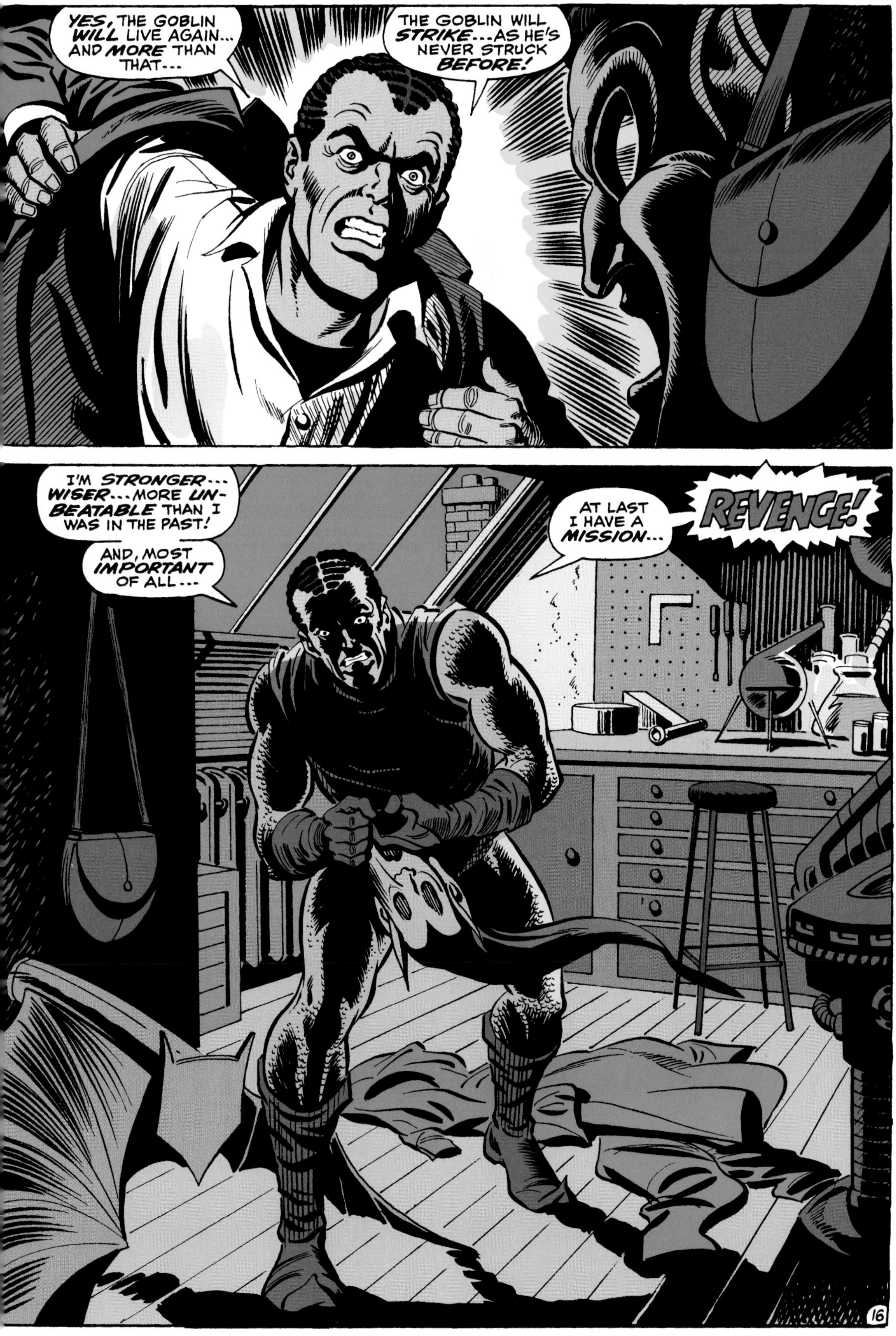
YES, THE GOBLIN WILL LIVE AGAIN... AND MORE THAN THAT...
THE GOBLIN WILL STRIKE...AS HE'S NEVER STRUCK BEFORE!
I'M STRONGER... WISER... MORE UN-BEATABLE THAN I WAS IN THE PAST!
AND, MOST IMPORTANT OF ALL...
AT LAST I HAVE A MISSION...
REVENGE!
16

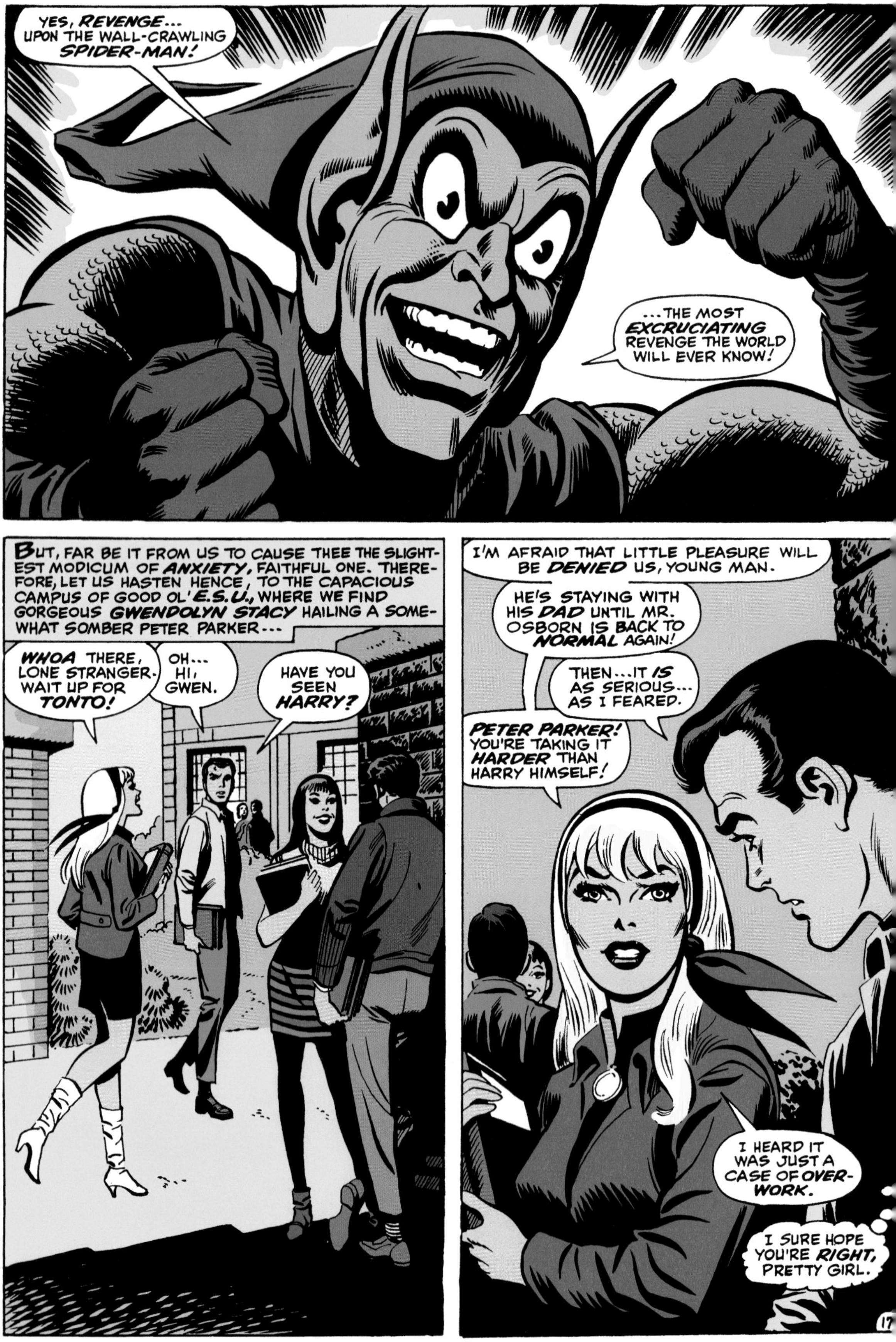
YES, REVENGE... UPON THE WALL-CRAWLING SPIDER-MAN!
...THE MOST EXCRUCIATING REVENGE THE WORLD WILL EVER KNOW!
BUT, FAR BE IT FROM US TO CAUSE THEE THE SLIGHTEST MODICUM OF ANXIETY, FAITHFUL ONE. THEREFORE, LET US HASTEN HENCE, TO THE CAPACIOUS CAMPUS OF GOOD OL' E.S.U., WHERE WE FIND GORGEOUS GWENDOLYN STACY HAILING A SOMEWHAT SOMBER PETER PARKER---
WHOA THERE, LONE STRANGER. WAIT UP FOR TONTO!
OH... HI, GWEN.
HAVE YOU SEEN HARRY?
I'M AFRAID THAT LITTLE PLEASURE WILL BE DENIED US, YOUNG MAN.
HE'S STAYING WITH HIS DAD UNTIL MR. OSBORN IS BACK TO NORMAL AGAIN!
THEN...IT IS AS SERIOUS... AS I FEARED.
PETER PARKER! YOU'RE TAKING IT HARDER THAN HARRY HIMSELF!
I HEARD IT WAS JUST A CASE OF OVER-WORK.
I SURE HOPE YOU'RE RIGHT, PRETTY GIRL.
17

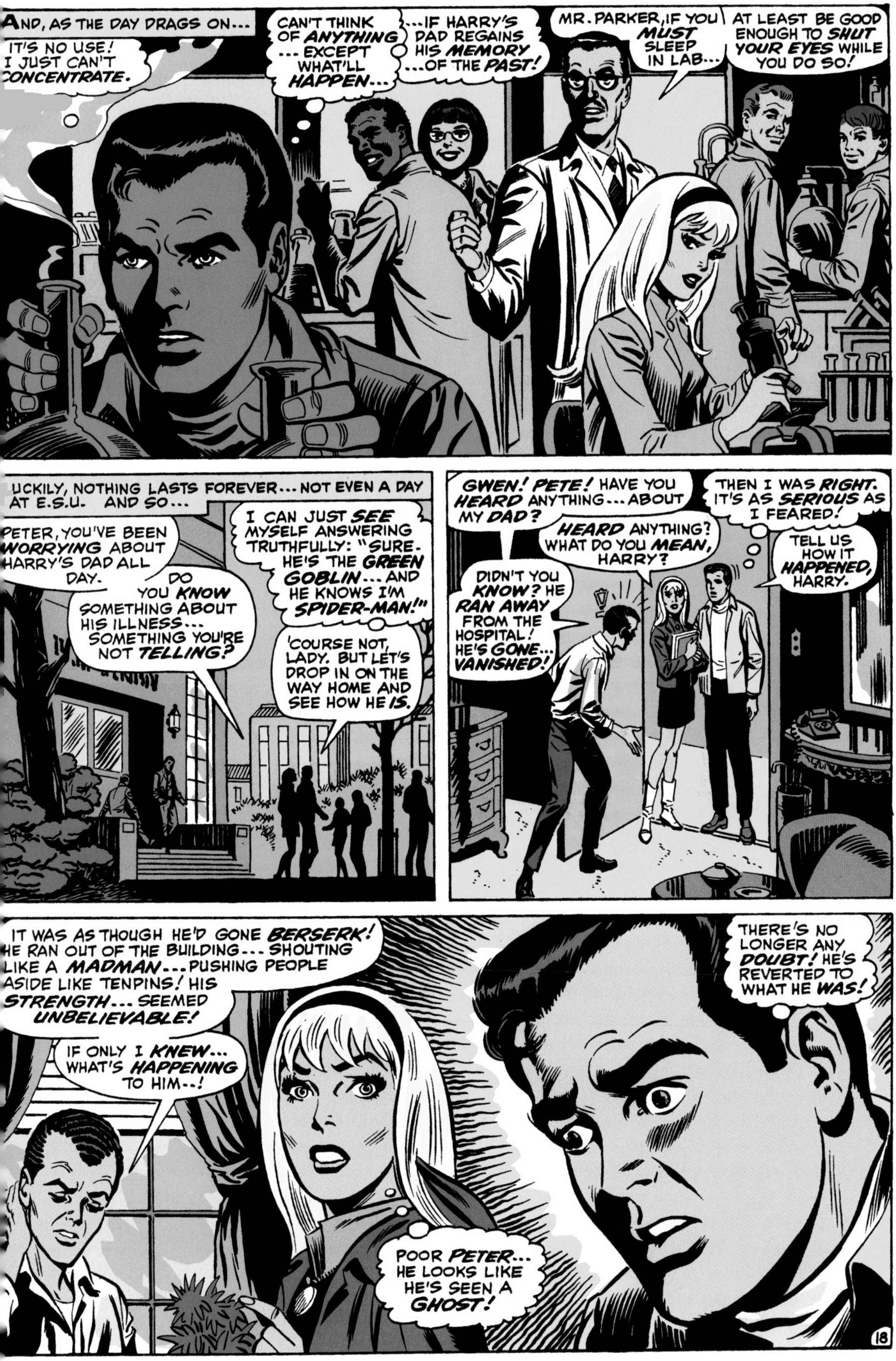
AND, AS THE DAY DRAGS ON...
IT'S NO USE! I JUST CAN'T CONCENTRATE.
CAN'T THINK OF ANYTHING ... EXCEPT WHAT'LL HAPPEN...
...IF HARRY'S DAD REGAINS HIS MEMORY ...OF THE PAST!
MR. PARKER, IF YOU MUST SLEEP IN LAB...
AT LEAST BE GOOD ENOUGH TO SHUT YOUR EYES WHILE YOU DO SO!
LUCKILY, NOTHING LASTS FOREVER... NOT EVEN A DAY AT E.S.U. AND SO...
PETER, YOU'VE BEEN WORRYING ABOUT HARRY'S DAD ALL DAY.
DO YOU KNOW SOMETHING ABOUT HIS ILLNESS... SOMETHING YOU'RE NOT TELLING?
I CAN JUST SEE MYSELF ANSWERING TRUTHFULLY: "SURE. HE'S THE GREEN GOBLIN... AND HE KNOWS I'M SPIDER-MAN!"
'COURSE NOT, LADY. BUT LET'S DROP IN ON THE WAY HOME AND SEE HOW HE IS.
GWEN! PETE! HAVE YOU HEARD ANYTHING... ABOUT MY DAD?
HEARD ANYTHING? WHAT DO YOU MEAN, HARRY?
THEN I WAS RIGHT. IT'S AS SERIOUS AS I FEARED!
TELL US HOW IT HAPPENED, HARRY.
DIDN'T YOU KNOW? HE RAN AWAY FROM THE HOSPITAL! HE'S GONE... VANISHED!
IT WAS AS THOUGH HE'D GONE BERSERK! HE RAN OUT OF THE BUILDING... SHOUTING LIKE A MADMAN... PUSHING PEOPLE ASIDE LIKE TENPINS! HIS STRENGTH... SEEMED UNBELIEVABLE!
IF ONLY I KNEW... WHAT'S HAPPENING TO HIM--!
THERE'S NO LONGER ANY DOUBT! HE'S REVERTED TO WHAT HE WAS!
POOR PETER... HE LOOKS LIKE HE'S SEEN A GHOST!
18

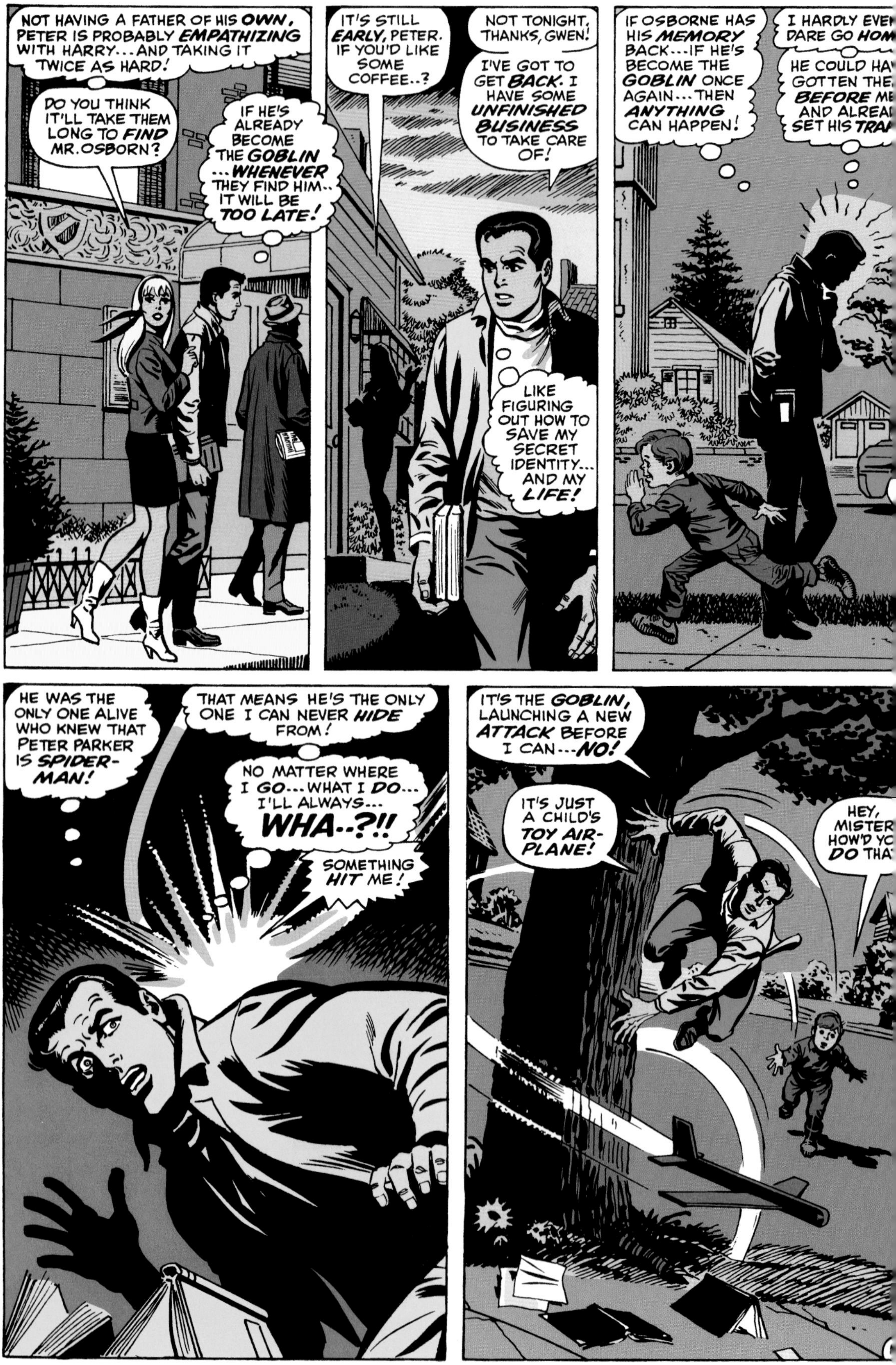

NOT HAVING A FATHER OF HIS OWN, PETER IS PROBABLY EMPATHIZING WITH HARRY... AND TAKING IT TWICE AS HARD!
DO YOU THINK IT'LL TAKE THEM LONG TO FIND MR. OSBORN?
IF HE'S ALREADY BECOME THE GOBLIN ...WHENEVER THEY FIND HIM.. IT WILL BE TOO LATE!
IT'S STILL EARLY, PETER. IF YOU'D LIKE SOME COFFEE..?
NOT TONIGHT, THANKS, GWEN!
I'VE GOT TO GET BACK. I HAVE SOME UNFINISHED BUSINESS TO TAKE CARE OF!
LIKE FIGURING OUT HOW TO SAVE MY SECRET IDENTITY... AND MY LIFE!
IF OSBORNE HAS HIS MEMORY BACK...IF HE'S BECOME THE GOBLIN ONCE AGAIN... THEN ANYTHING CAN HAPPEN!
I HARDLY EVE
DARE GO HOM
HE COULD HA
GOTTEN THE
BEFORE M
AND ALREA
SET HIS TRA
HE WAS THE ONLY ONE ALIVE WHO KNEW THAT PETER PARKER IS SPIDER-MAN!
THAT MEANS HE'S THE ONLY ONE I CAN NEVER HIDE FROM!
NO MATTER WHERE I GO... WHAT I DO... I'LL ALWAYS...
WHA..?!!
SOMETHING HIT ME!
IT'S THE GOBLIN, LAUNCHING A NEW ATTACK BEFORE I CAN...NO!
IT'S JUST A CHILD'S TOY AIR-PLANE!
HEY, MISTER
HOW'D YO
DO THA

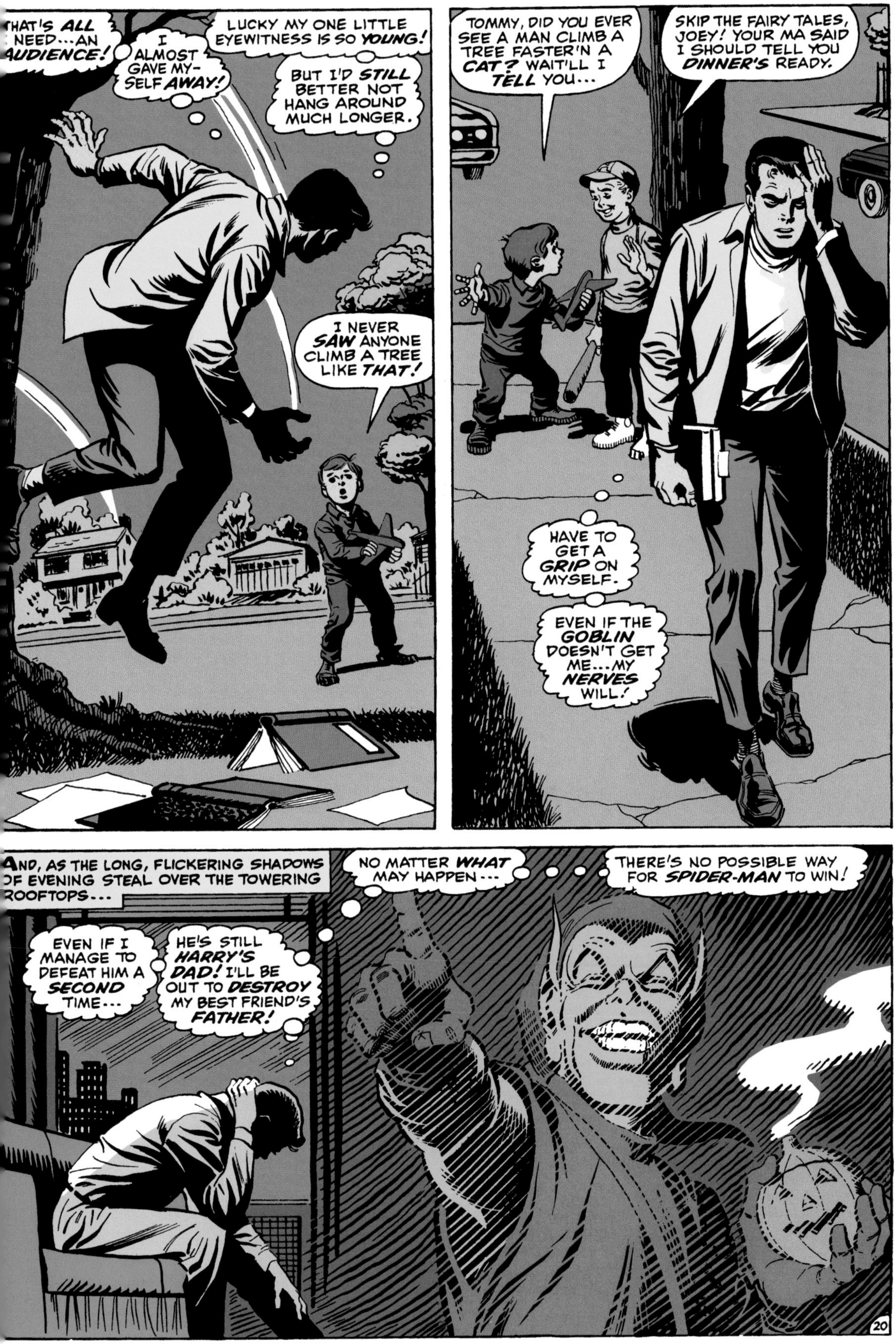
THAT'S ALL I NEED...AN AUDIENCE!
I ALMOST GAVE MYSELF AWAY!
LUCKY MY ONE LITTLE EYEWITNESS IS SO YOUNG!
BUT I'D STILL BETTER NOT HANG AROUND MUCH LONGER.
I NEVER SAW ANYONE CLIMB A TREE LIKE THAT!
TOMMY, DID YOU EVER SEE A MAN CLIMB A TREE FASTER'N A CAT? WAIT'LL I TELL YOU...
SKIP THE FAIRY TALES, JOEY! YOUR MA SAID I SHOULD TELL YOU DINNER'S READY.
HAVE TO GET A GRIP ON MYSELF.
EVEN IF THE GOBLIN DOESN'T GET ME...MY NERVES WILL!
AND, AS THE LONG, FLICKERING SHADOWS OF EVENING STEAL OVER THE TOWERING ROOFTOPS...
EVEN IF I MANAGE TO DEFEAT HIM A SECOND TIME...
HE'S STILL HARRY'S DAD! I'LL BE OUT TO DESTROY MY BEST FRIEND'S FATHER!
NO MATTER WHAT MAY HAPPEN...
THERE'S NO POSSIBLE WAY FOR SPIDER-MAN TO WIN!
20

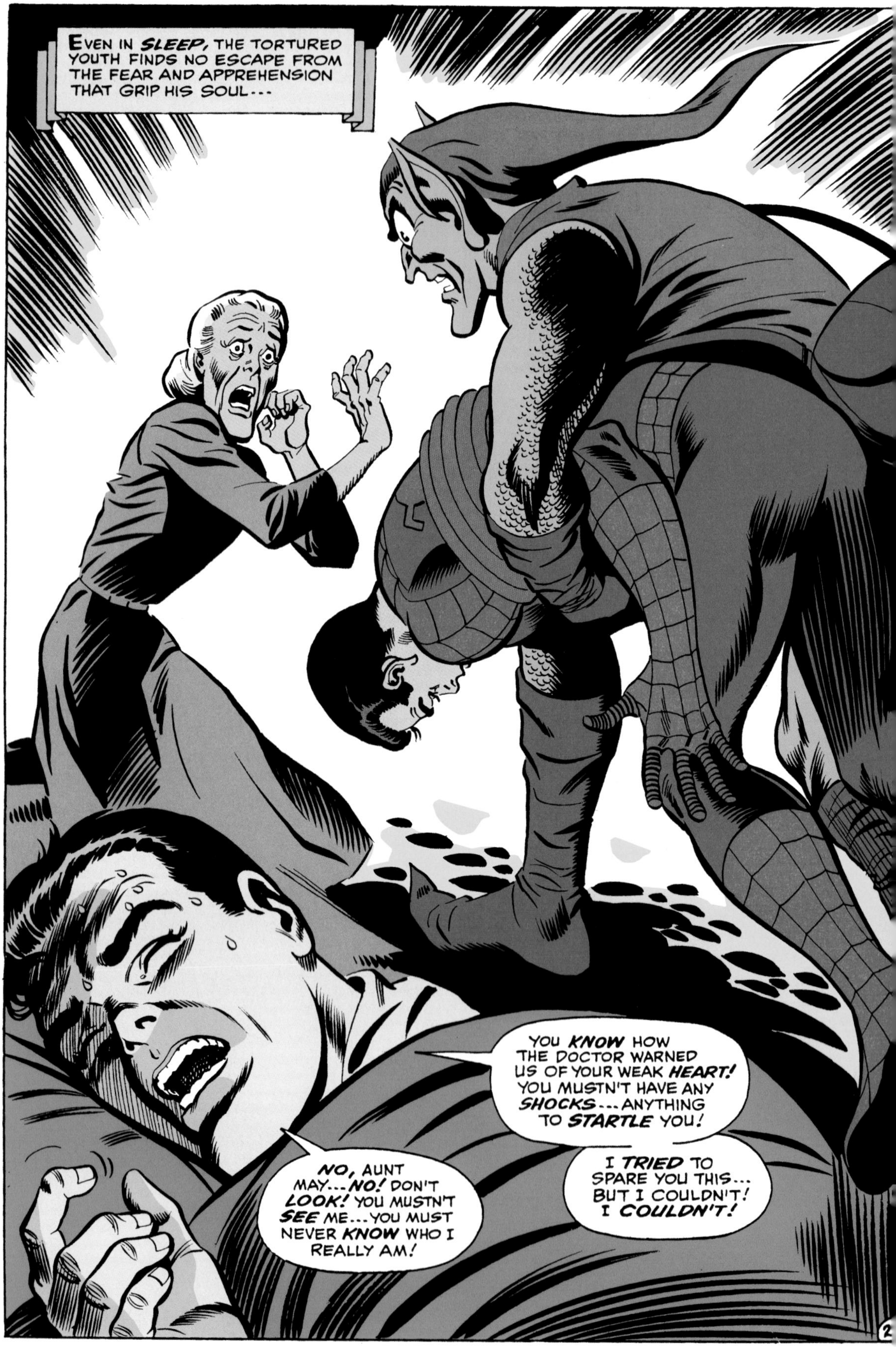
EVEN IN SLEEP, THE TORTURED YOUTH FINDS NO ESCAPE FROM THE FEAR AND APPREHENSION THAT GRIP HIS SOUL...
YOU KNOW HOW THE DOCTOR WARNED US OF YOUR WEAK HEART! YOU MUSTN'T HAVE ANY SHOCKS... ANYTHING TO STARTLE YOU!
I TRIED TO SPARE YOU THIS... BUT I COULDN'T! I COULDN'T!
NO, AUNT MAY...NO! DON'T LOOK! YOU MUSTN'T SEE ME...YOU MUST NEVER KNOW WHO I REALLY AM!
2

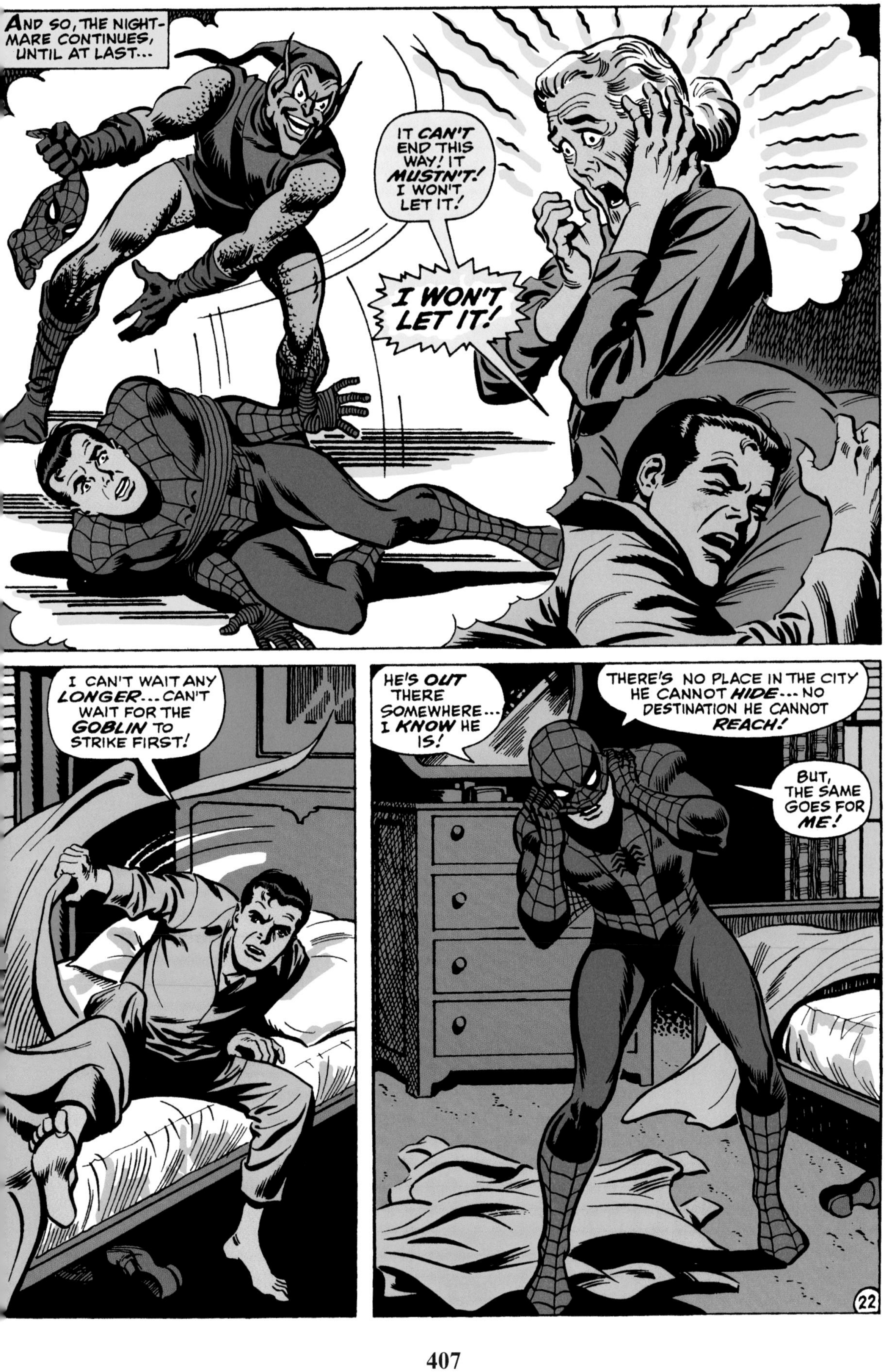
AND SO, THE NIGHT-MARE CONTINUES, UNTIL AT LAST...
IT CAN'T END THIS WAY! IT MUSTN'T! I WON'T LET IT!
I WON'T LET IT!
I CAN'T WAIT ANY LONGER... CAN'T WAIT FOR THE GOBLIN TO STRIKE FIRST!
HE'S OUT THERE SOMEWHERE... I KNOW HE IS!
THERE'S NO PLACE IN THE CITY HE CANNOT HIDE... NO DESTINATION HE CANNOT REACH!
BUT, THE SAME GOES FOR ME!
22

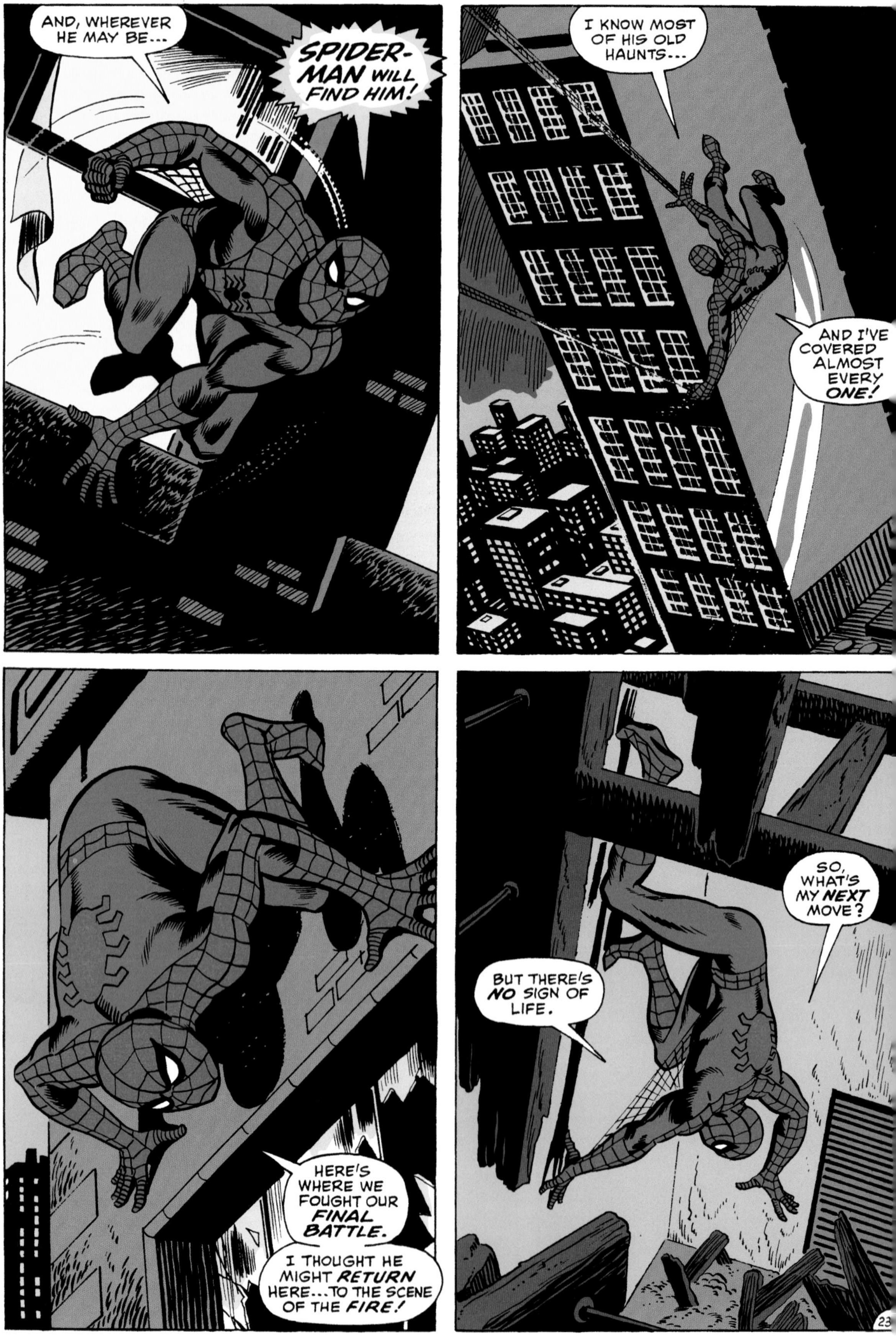
AND, WHEREVER HE MAY BE...
SPIDER-MAN WILL FIND HIM!
I KNOW MOST OF HIS OLD HAUNTS...
AND I'VE COVERED ALMOST EVERY ONE!
HERE'S WHERE WE FOUGHT OUR FINAL BATTLE.
I THOUGHT HE MIGHT RETURN HERE...TO THE SCENE OF THE FIRE!
BUT THERE'S NO SIGN OF LIFE.
SO, WHAT'S MY NEXT MOVE?
23

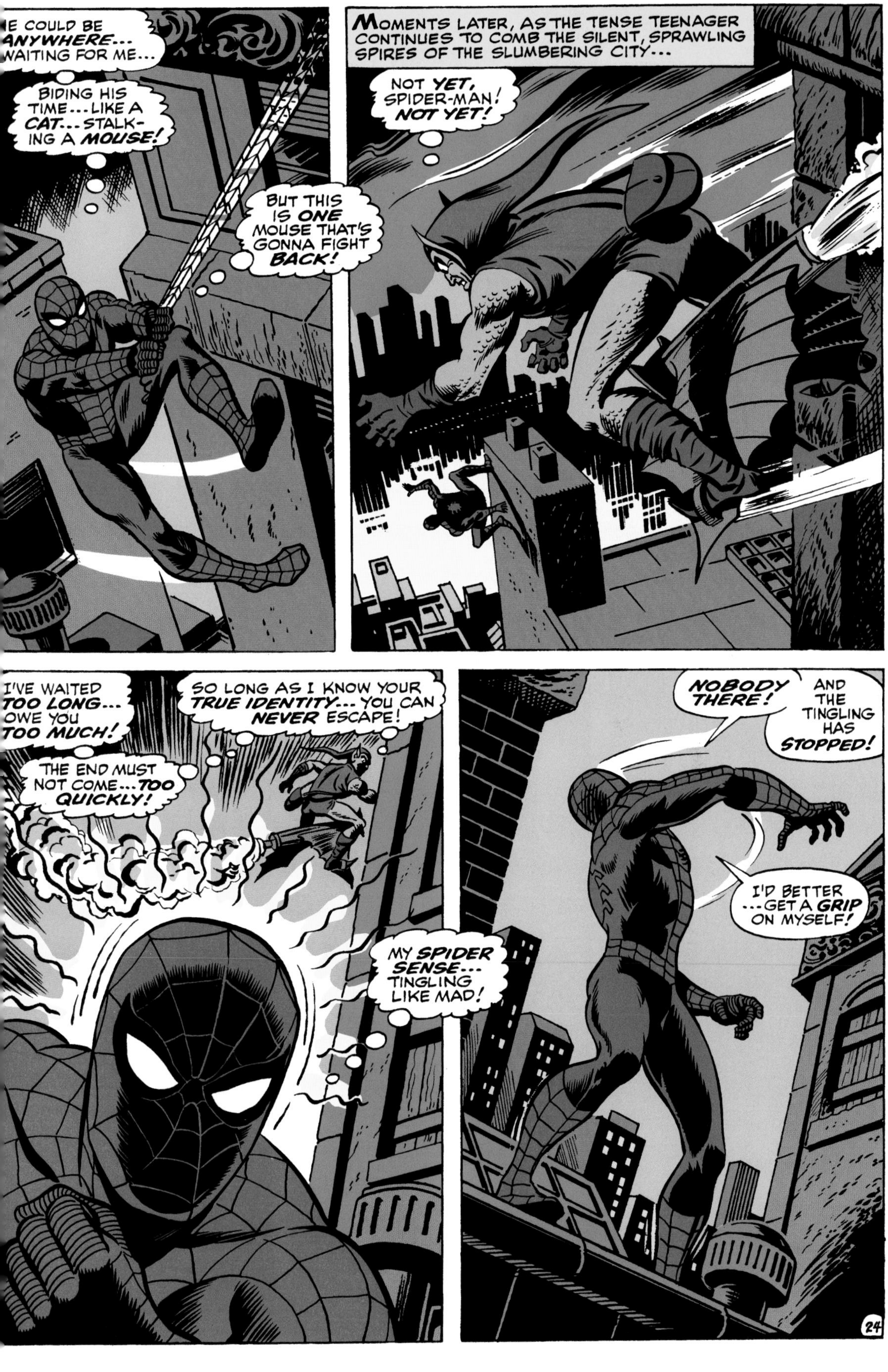

E COULD BE ANYWHERE... WAITING FOR ME...
BIDING HIS TIME... LIKE A CAT... STALKING A MOUSE!
BUT THIS IS ONE MOUSE THAT'S GONNA FIGHT BACK!
MOMENTS LATER, AS THE TENSE TEENAGER CONTINUES TO COMB THE SILENT, SPRAWLING SPIRES OF THE SLUMBERING CITY...
NOT YET, SPIDER-MAN! NOT YET!
I'VE WAITED TOO LONG... OWE YOU TOO MUCH!
SO LONG AS I KNOW YOUR TRUE IDENTITY... YOU CAN NEVER ESCAPE!
THE END MUST NOT COME... TOO QUICKLY!
MY SPIDER SENSE... TINGLING LIKE MAD!
NOBODY THERE!
AND THE TINGLING HAS STOPPED!
I'D BETTER ...GET A GRIP ON MYSELF!
24

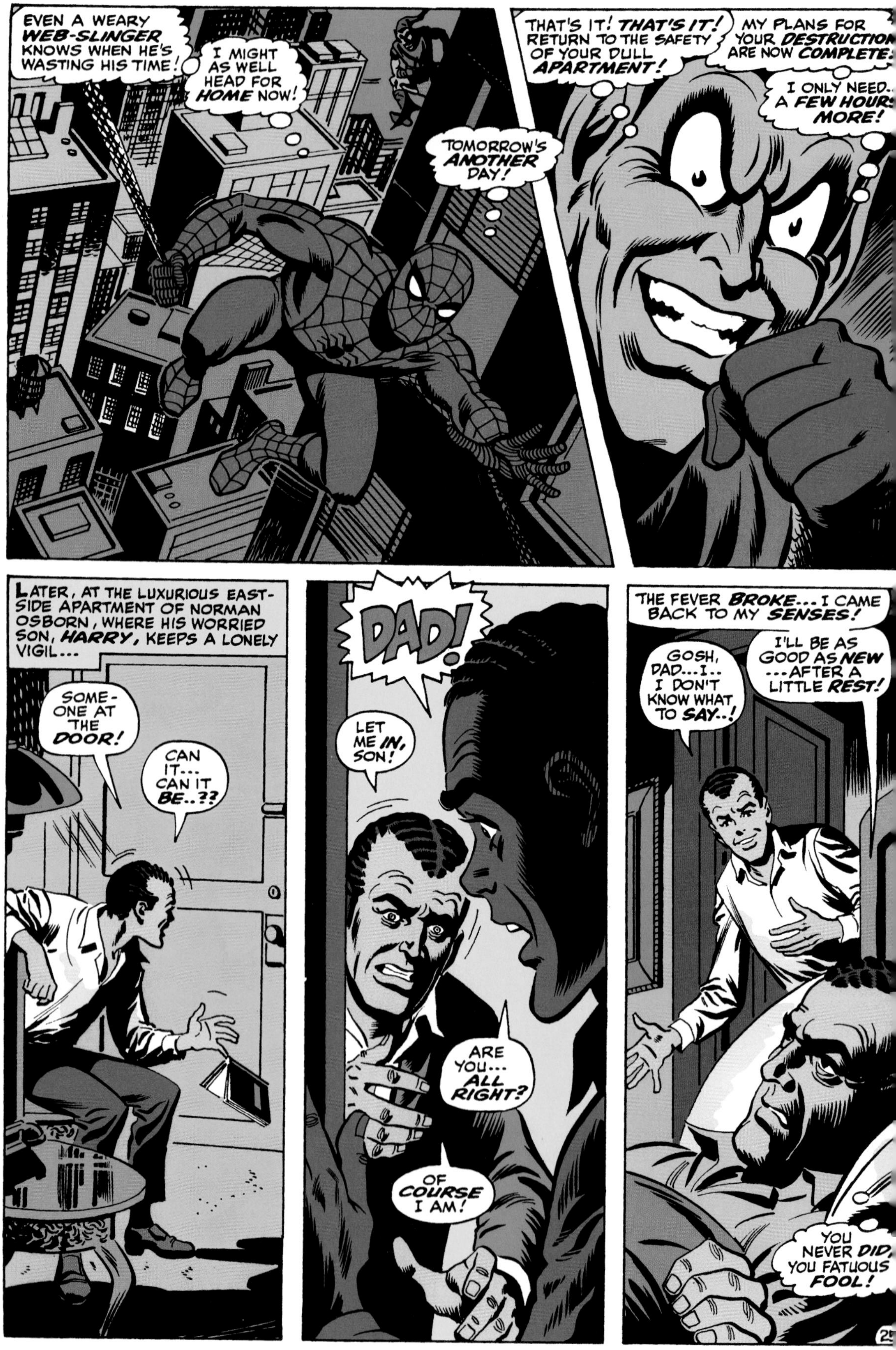

EVEN A WEARY WEB-SLINGER KNOWS WHEN HE'S WASTING HIS TIME!
I MIGHT AS WELL HEAD FOR HOME NOW!
TOMORROW'S ANOTHER DAY!
THAT'S IT! THAT'S IT! RETURN TO THE SAFETY OF YOUR DULL APARTMENT!
MY PLANS FOR YOUR DESTRUCTION ARE NOW COMPLETE!
I ONLY NEED... A FEW HOURS MORE!
LATER, AT THE LUXURIOUS EAST-SIDE APARTMENT OF NORMAN OSBORN, WHERE HIS WORRIED SON, HARRY, KEEPS A LONELY VIGIL...
SOME-ONE AT THE DOOR!
CAN IT... CAN IT BE..??
DAD!
LET ME IN, SON!
ARE YOU... ALL RIGHT?
OF COURSE I AM!
THE FEVER BROKE... I CAME BACK TO MY SENSES!
GOSH, DAD... I.. I DON'T KNOW WHAT TO SAY..!
I'LL BE AS GOOD AS NEW ...AFTER A LITTLE REST!
YOU NEVER DID, YOU FATUOUS FOOL!

NOW, THRU THE MAGIC OF OUR *IMAGINATIONS*... AND THE PRINTED AGE...LET'S SKIP TO THE *VERY NEXT EVENING*, WHERE WE FIND...

THE *PHONE!*

RRRRINNGG

THE WAY THINGS ARE GOING...IT CAN ONLY MEAN ...MORE *TROUBLE!*

YOUR DAD CAME *HOME*, HARRY, AND HE SEEMS HIS OLD *SELF* AGAIN?

SAY--- THAT'S *GREAT!*

OR *IS* IT? IF HE'S *BACK* AGAIN...IT MEANS HE'S *UP* TO SOMETHING!

BUT... *WHAT??*

TO CELEBRATE HIS BEING *WELL* AGAIN, DAD'S THROWING A LITTLE *DINNER PARTY* TONIGHT!

HE WANTED ME TO ASK *YOU*... AND *GWEN*... WHILE I BRING *MARY JANE!*

A *PARTY!* THAT'S NOT *LIKE* NORMAN OSBORN!

HE WANTS *ME* THERE...THE OTHERS ARE JUST A *COVER-UP!*

BUT...I'VE GOT TO GO *THRU* WITH IT!

SURE, HARRY! I... I'LL SEE YOU LATER!

IS HE SO FAR *GONE* THAT HE'D ATTACK ME IN FRONT OF HIS OWN *SON*... AND THE TWO *GIRLS?*

WHAT'S THE *MATTER* WITH ME? I SHOULD KNOW *BETTER*..!

WHEN HE'S THE *GOBLIN*, HE FORGETS *EVERYTHING*...CARES ABOUT *NOTHING*.. EXCEPT HIS OWN DEADLY *PURPOSE!*

26

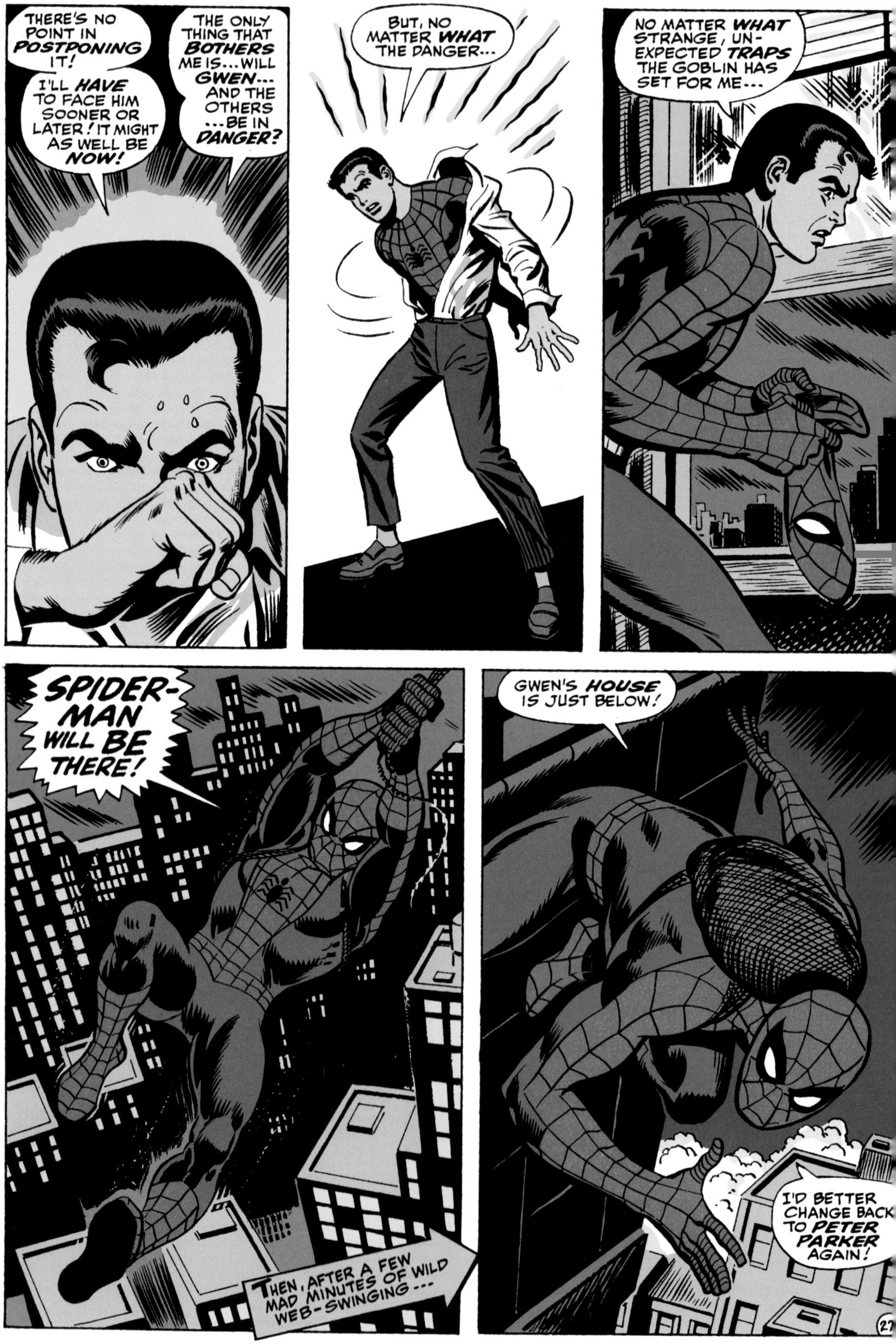
THERE'S NO POINT IN POSTPONING IT!
I'LL HAVE TO FACE HIM SOONER OR LATER! IT MIGHT AS WELL BE NOW!
THE ONLY THING THAT BOTHERS ME IS...WILL GWEN... AND THE OTHERS ...BE IN DANGER?
BUT, NO MATTER WHAT THE DANGER...
NO MATTER WHAT STRANGE, UN-EXPECTED TRAPS THE GOBLIN HAS SET FOR ME...
SPIDER-MAN WILL BE THERE!
THEN, AFTER A FEW MAD MINUTES OF WILD WEB-SWINGING---
GWEN'S HOUSE IS JUST BELOW!
I'D BETTER CHANGE BACK TO PETER PARKER AGAIN!
27

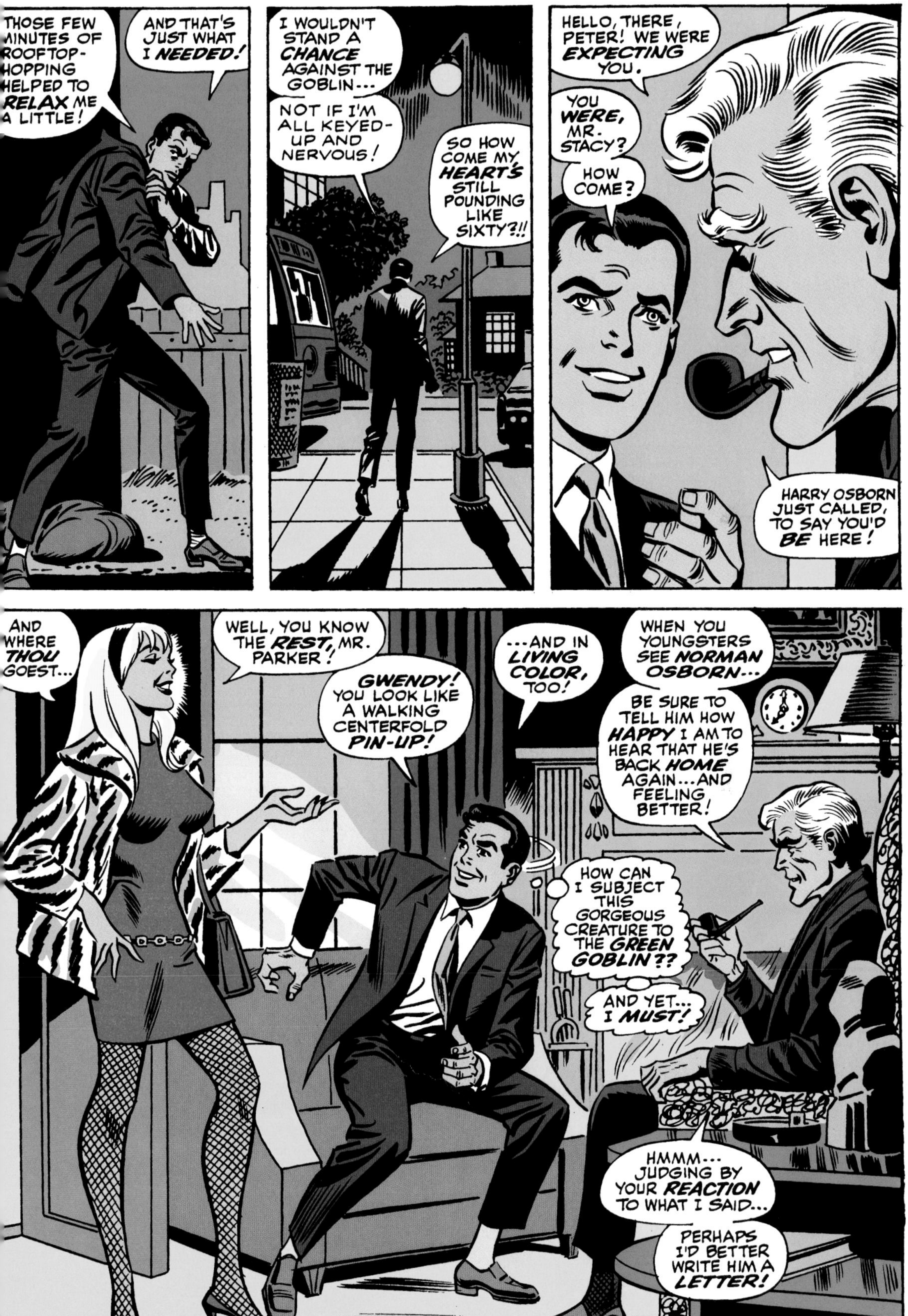

THOSE FEW MINUTES OF ROOFTOP-HOPPING HELPED TO RELAX ME A LITTLE!
AND THAT'S JUST WHAT I NEEDED!
I WOULDN'T STAND A CHANCE AGAINST THE GOBLIN...
NOT IF I'M ALL KEYED-UP AND NERVOUS!
SO HOW COME MY HEART'S STILL POUNDING LIKE SIXTY?!!
HELLO, THERE, PETER! WE WERE EXPECTING YOU.
YOU WERE, MR. STACY?
HOW COME?
HARRY OSBORN JUST CALLED, TO SAY YOU'D BE HERE!
AND WHERE THOU GOEST...
WELL, YOU KNOW THE REST, MR. PARKER!
GWENDY! YOU LOOK LIKE A WALKING CENTERFOLD PIN-UP!
...AND IN LIVING COLOR, TOO!
WHEN YOU YOUNGSTERS SEE NORMAN OSBORN...
BE SURE TO TELL HIM HOW HAPPY I AM TO HEAR THAT HE'S BACK HOME AGAIN... AND FEELING BETTER!
HOW CAN I SUBJECT THIS GORGEOUS CREATURE TO THE GREEN GOBLIN??
AND YET... I MUST!
HMMM... JUDGING BY YOUR REACTION TO WHAT I SAID...
PERHAPS I'D BETTER WRITE HIM A LETTER!
28

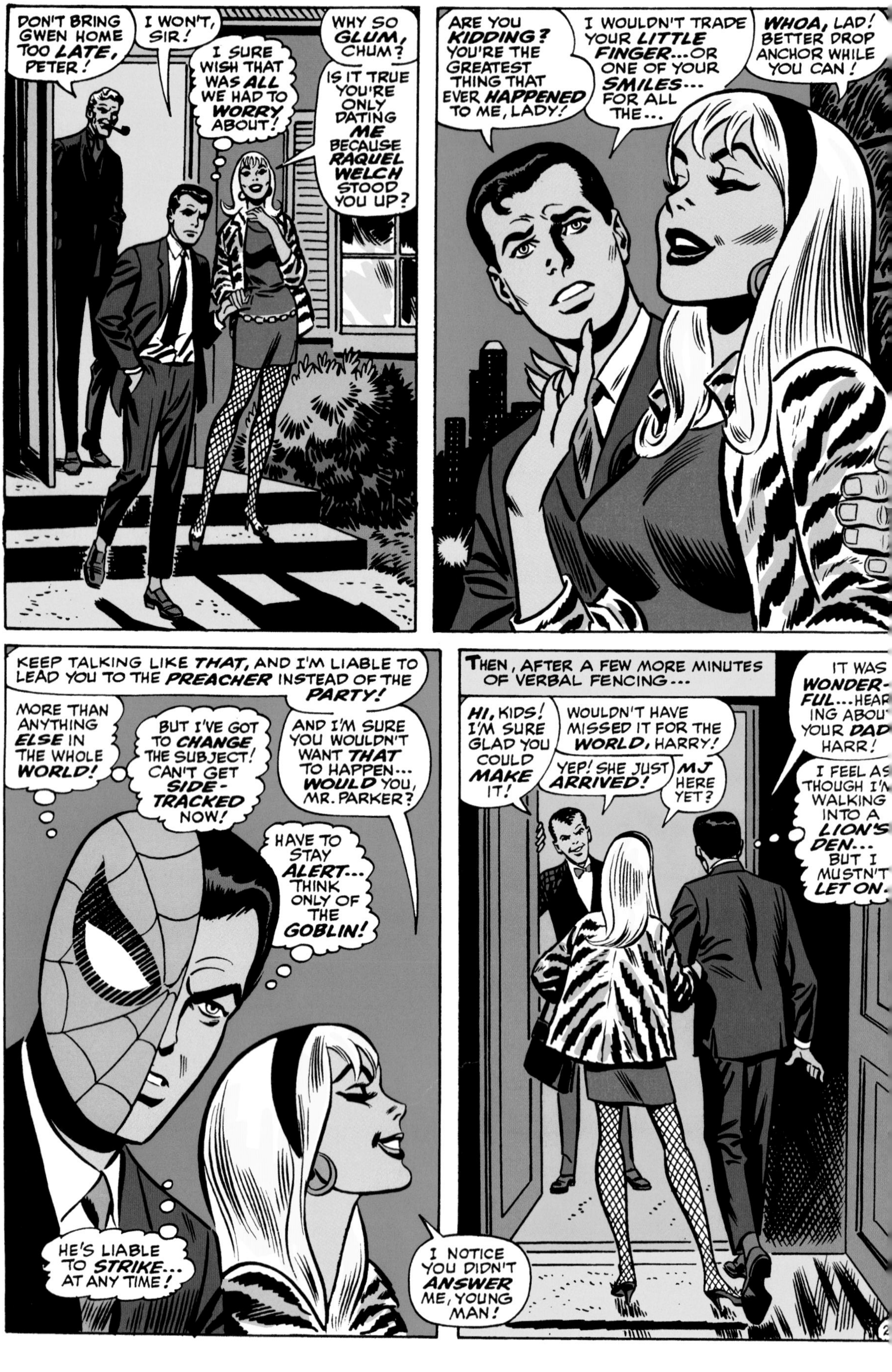
DON'T BRING GWEN HOME TOO LATE, PETER!
I WON'T, SIR!
I SURE WISH THAT WAS ALL WE HAD TO WORRY ABOUT!
WHY SO GLUM, CHUM?
IS IT TRUE YOU'RE ONLY DATING ME BECAUSE RAQUEL WELCH STOOD YOU UP?
ARE YOU KIDDING? YOU'RE THE GREATEST THING THAT EVER HAPPENED TO ME, LADY!
I WOULDN'T TRADE YOUR LITTLE FINGER...OR ONE OF YOUR SMILES... FOR ALL THE...
WHOA, LAD! BETTER DROP ANCHOR WHILE YOU CAN!
KEEP TALKING LIKE THAT, AND I'M LIABLE TO LEAD YOU TO THE PREACHER INSTEAD OF THE PARTY!
MORE THAN ANYTHING ELSE IN THE WHOLE WORLD!
BUT I'VE GOT TO CHANGE THE SUBJECT! CAN'T GET SIDE-TRACKED NOW!
AND I'M SURE YOU WOULDN'T WANT THAT TO HAPPEN... WOULD YOU, MR. PARKER?
HAVE TO STAY ALERT... THINK ONLY OF THE GOBLIN!
HE'S LIABLE TO STRIKE... AT ANY TIME!
I NOTICE YOU DIDN'T ANSWER ME, YOUNG MAN!
THEN, AFTER A FEW MORE MINUTES OF VERBAL FENCING...
HI, KIDS! I'M SURE GLAD YOU COULD MAKE IT!
WOULDN'T HAVE MISSED IT FOR THE WORLD, HARRY!
YEP! SHE JUST ARRIVED!
MJ HERE YET?
IT WAS WONDER-FUL...HEAR ING ABOU YOUR DAD HARR!
I FEEL AS THOUGH I'M WALKING INTO A LION'S DEN... BUT I MUSTN'T LET ON.

OF COURSE, IT WOULDN'T HAVE SHOOK ME UP IF YOU'D ARRIVED A FEW MINUTES LATER!

MARY JANE ISN'T EXACTLY THE *DULLEST* CHICK IN TOWN!

I HEAR SHE'S A *GREAT* CONVERSATIONALIST!

WITH LOOKS LIKE *MINE*, SWEETIE, WHO *TALKS*?

WHY ISN'T HARRY'S *FATHER* HERE?

THERE HE IS *NOW*... ENTERING THE ROOM FROM *BEHIND* ME!

HELLO THERE, PARKER....AND YOUNG LADIES! I WAS *HOPING* YOU COULD MAKE IT!

YEAH! I'LL *BET* YOU WERE!

HARRY TOLD ME HOW *HELPFUL* YOU WERE... DURING MY *ABSENCE*!

I WANT YOU TO KNOW HOW MUCH I *APPRECIATE* THAT, SON!

WE WERE *ALL* CONCERNED ABOUT YOU, MR. OSBORN! AND WE'RE...GLAD YOU'RE *BACK*!

HE'S *TOYING* WITH ME...SQUEEZING MY *HAND*... HARD ENOUGH TO *BREAK MY FINGERS*---IF NOT FOR MY *SPIDER STRENGTH*!

I'VE GOT TO PLAY IT *HIS* WAY...TILL HE MAKES HIS *MOVE*!

THE EARLY PART OF THE EVENING PROGRESSES *SMOOTHLY*, AT LEAST ON THE *SURFACE*! NORMAN OSBORN REGALES THE GATHERING WITH HUMOROUS ANECDOTES AND LIGHT-HEARTED SMALL TALK...WHILE ONLY *PETER PARKER*, AND HIS CUNNING, CONNIVING *HOST*, CAN SENSE THE DEADLY UNDERCURRENT OF *TENSION* WHICH PERVADES EVERY WORD...EVERY MOVEMENT... ...AND THEN, AS *DINNER* IS SERVED...

TELL US ABOUT YOURSELF, PARKER!

EVEN THOUGH YOU'RE MY SON'S *BEST FRIEND*, I FEEL THERE'S SO MUCH ABOUT YOU I DON'T *KNOW*!

OL' PETE'S A REAL *MYSTERY MAN*, DAD!

I UNDERSTAND YOU SOMETIMES *LEAVE* THE APARTMENT FOR A FEW *DAYS* AT A TIME!

NOTHING *MYSTERIOUS* ABOUT IT, SIR! I OCCASIONALLY STAY WITH MY *AUNT*!

HE'S TRYING TO *GOAD* ME... BUT I HAVE TO STAY *COOL*... NO MATTER *WHAT*!

30

415

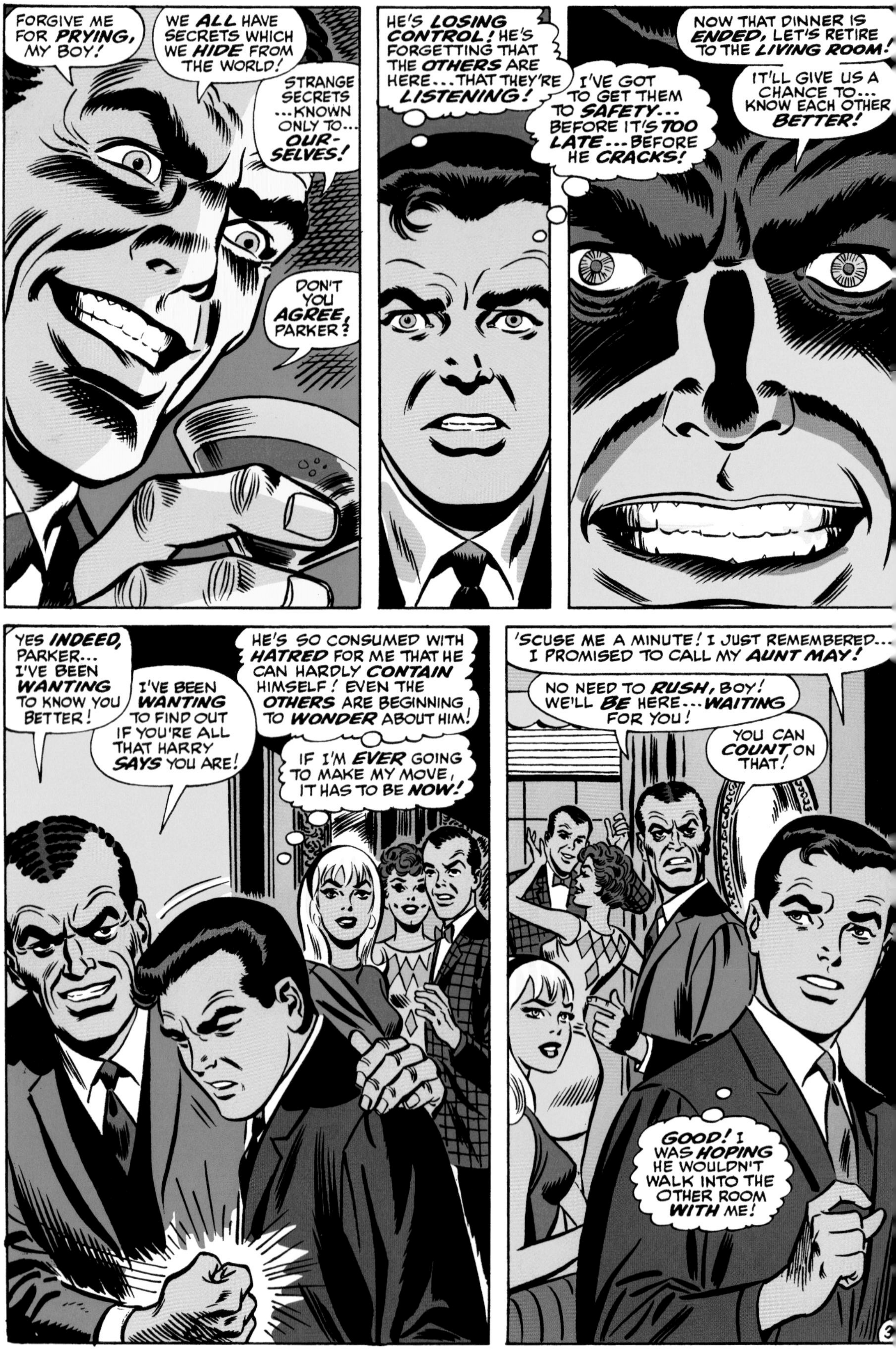
FORGIVE ME FOR PRYING, MY BOY!
WE ALL HAVE SECRETS WHICH WE HIDE FROM THE WORLD!
STRANGE SECRETS ...KNOWN ONLY TO... OUR-SELVES!
DON'T YOU AGREE, PARKER?
HE'S LOSING CONTROL! HE'S FORGETTING THAT THE OTHERS ARE HERE...THAT THEY'RE LISTENING!
I'VE GOT TO GET THEM TO SAFETY... BEFORE IT'S TOO LATE...BEFORE HE CRACKS!
NOW THAT DINNER IS ENDED, LET'S RETIRE TO THE LIVING ROOM!
IT'LL GIVE US A CHANCE TO... KNOW EACH OTHER BETTER!
YES INDEED, PARKER... I'VE BEEN WANTING TO KNOW YOU BETTER!
I'VE BEEN WANTING TO FIND OUT IF YOU'RE ALL THAT HARRY SAYS YOU ARE!
HE'S SO CONSUMED WITH HATRED FOR ME THAT HE CAN HARDLY CONTAIN HIMSELF! EVEN THE OTHERS ARE BEGINNING TO WONDER ABOUT HIM!
IF I'M EVER GOING TO MAKE MY MOVE, IT HAS TO BE NOW!
'SCUSE ME A MINUTE! I JUST REMEMBERED... I PROMISED TO CALL MY AUNT MAY!
NO NEED TO RUSH, BOY! WE'LL BE HERE...WAITING FOR YOU!
YOU CAN COUNT ON THAT!
GOOD! I WAS HOPING HE WOULDN'T WALK INTO THE OTHER ROOM WITH ME!
3

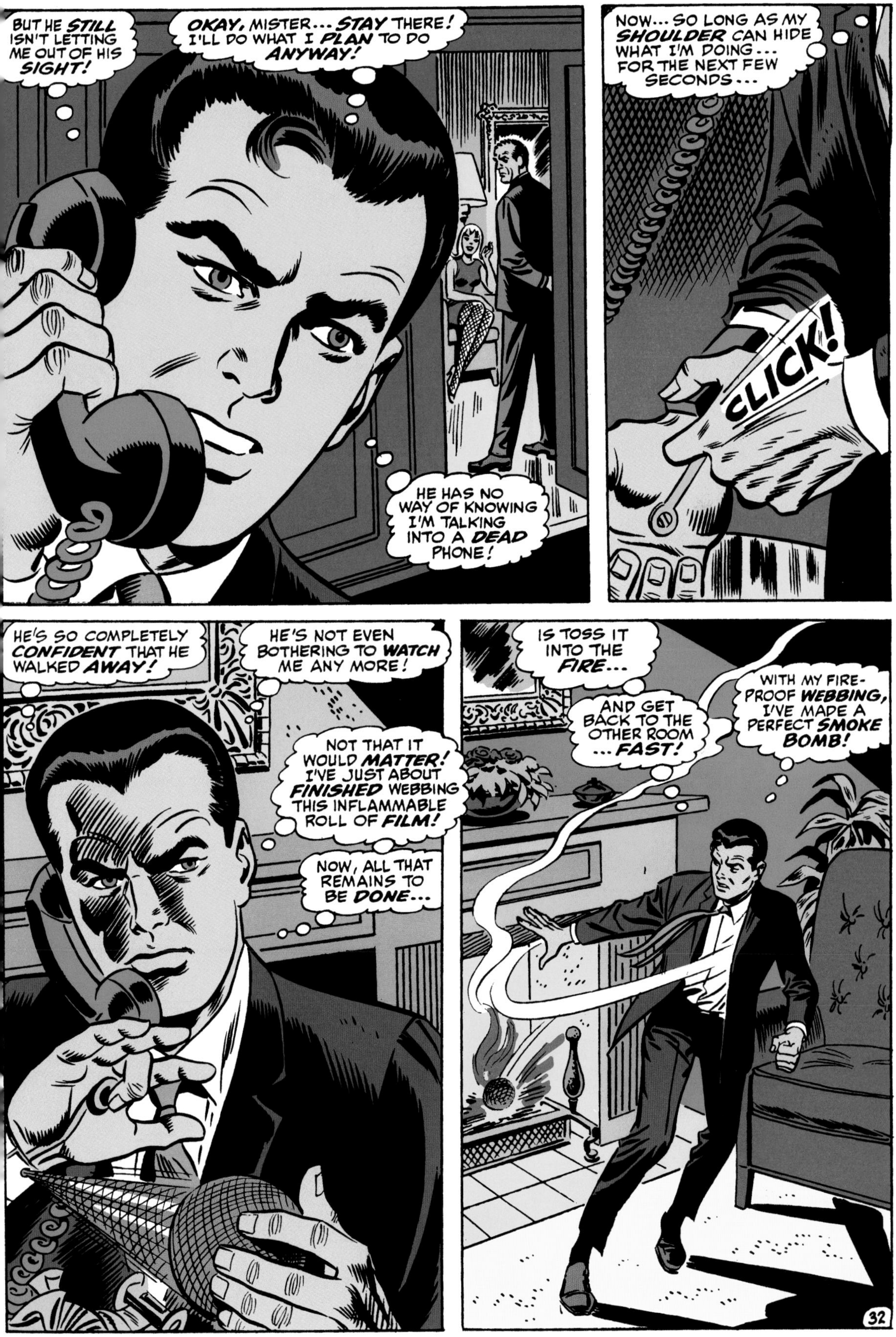
BUT HE STILL ISN'T LETTING ME OUT OF HIS SIGHT!
OKAY, MISTER... STAY THERE! I'LL DO WHAT I PLAN TO DO ANYWAY!
HE HAS NO WAY OF KNOWING I'M TALKING INTO A DEAD PHONE!
NOW... SO LONG AS MY SHOULDER CAN HIDE WHAT I'M DOING... FOR THE NEXT FEW SECONDS...
CLICK!
HE'S SO COMPLETELY CONFIDENT THAT HE WALKED AWAY!
HE'S NOT EVEN BOTHERING TO WATCH ME ANY MORE!
NOT THAT IT WOULD MATTER! I'VE JUST ABOUT FINISHED WEBBING THIS INFLAMMABLE ROLL OF FILM!
NOW, ALL THAT REMAINS TO BE DONE...
IS TOSS IT INTO THE FIRE...
AND GET BACK TO THE OTHER ROOM ... FAST!
WITH MY FIRE-PROOF WEBBING, I'VE MADE A PERFECT SMOKE BOMB!
32

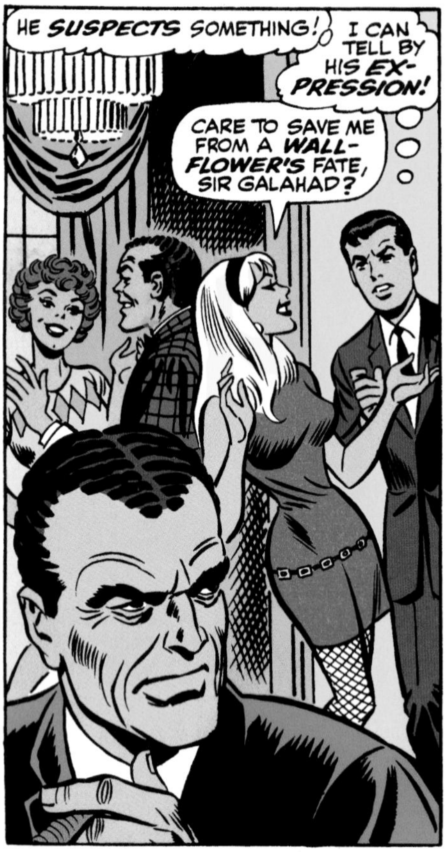
HE SUSPECTS SOMETHING!
I CAN TELL BY HIS EX-PRESSION!
CARE TO SAVE ME FROM A WALL-FLOWER'S FATE, SIR GALAHAD?

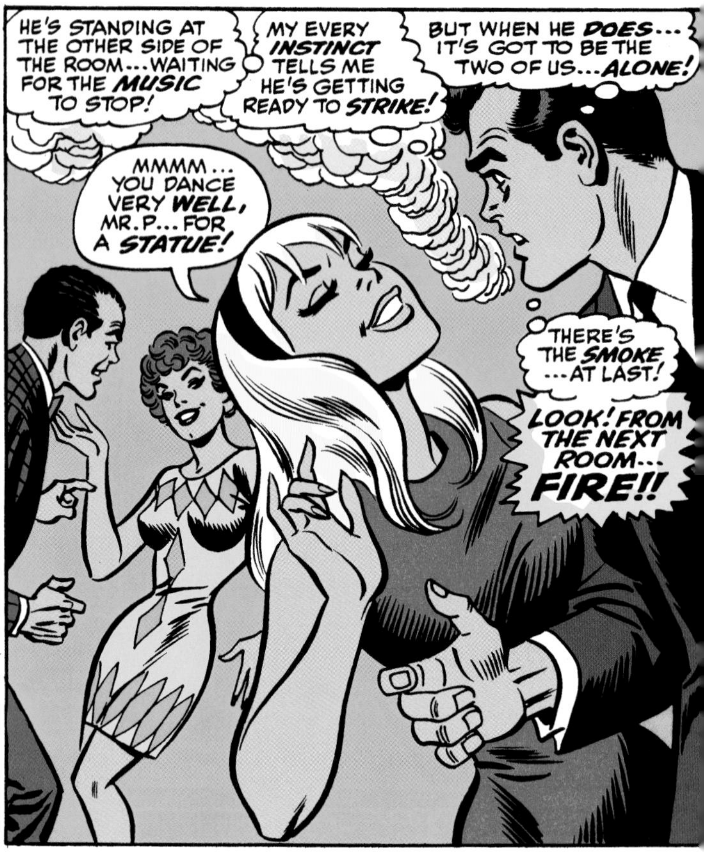
HE'S STANDING AT THE OTHER SIDE OF THE ROOM...WAITING FOR THE MUSIC TO STOP!
MY EVERY INSTINCT TELLS ME HE'S GETTING READY TO STRIKE!
BUT WHEN HE DOES... IT'S GOT TO BE THE TWO OF US...ALONE!
MMMM... YOU DANCE VERY WELL, MR. P...FOR A STATUE!
THERE'S THE SMOKE ---AT LAST!
LOOK! FROM THE NEXT ROOM... FIRE!!

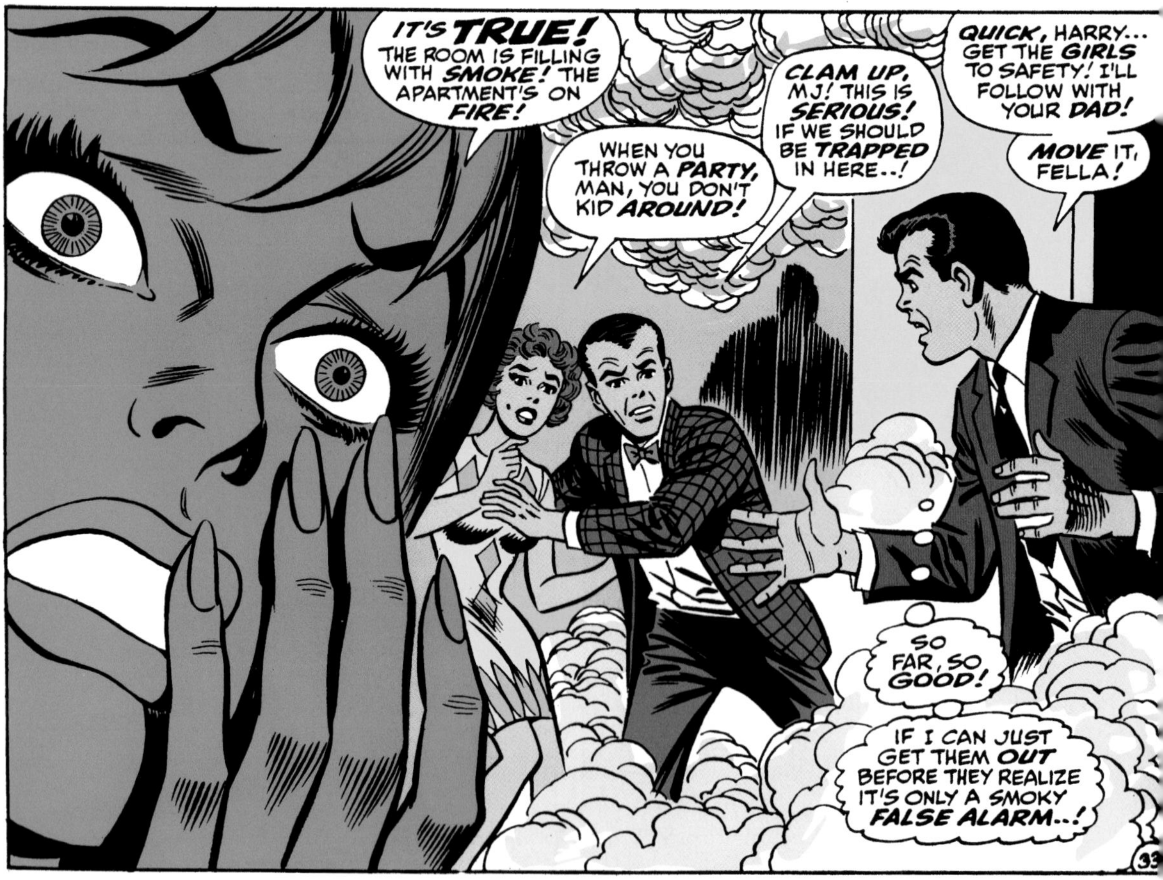
IT'S TRUE! THE ROOM IS FILLING WITH SMOKE! THE APARTMENT'S ON FIRE!
WHEN YOU THROW A PARTY, MAN, YOU DON'T KID AROUND!
CLAM UP, MJ! THIS IS SERIOUS! IF WE SHOULD BE TRAPPED IN HERE..!
QUICK, HARRY... GET THE GIRLS TO SAFETY! I'LL FOLLOW WITH YOUR DAD!
MOVE IT, FELLA!
SO FAR, SO GOOD!
IF I CAN JUST GET THEM OUT BEFORE THEY REALIZE IT'S ONLY A SMOKY FALSE ALARM..!
33

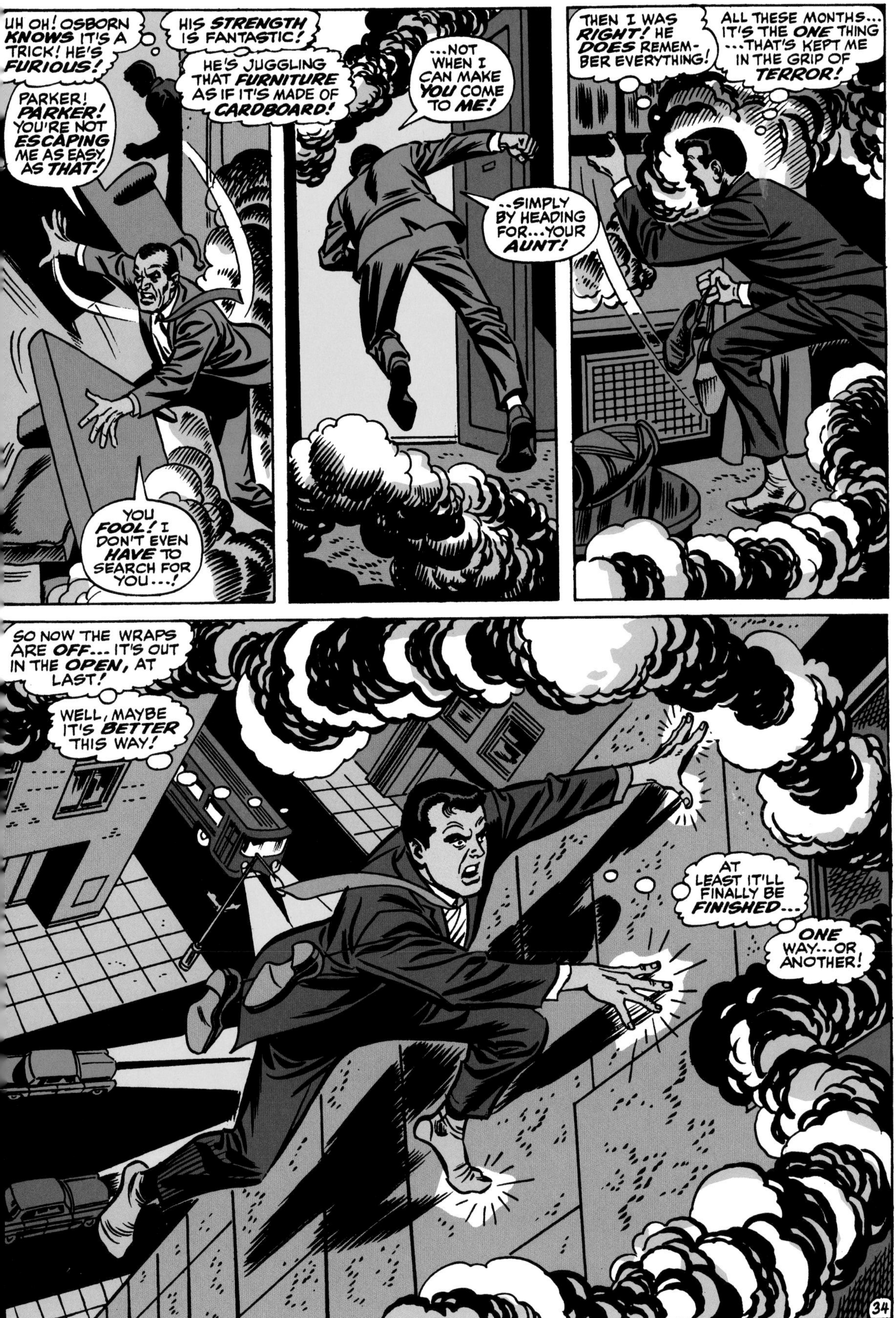
UH OH! OSBORN KNOWS IT'S A TRICK! HE'S FURIOUS!
HIS STRENGTH IS FANTASTIC!
HE'S JUGGLING THAT FURNITURE AS IF IT'S MADE OF CARDBOARD!
PARKER! PARKER! YOU'RE NOT ESCAPING ME AS EASY AS THAT!
YOU FOOL! I DON'T EVEN HAVE TO SEARCH FOR YOU...!
...NOT WHEN I CAN MAKE YOU COME TO ME!
..SIMPLY BY HEADING FOR...YOUR AUNT!
THEN I WAS RIGHT! HE DOES REMEMBER EVERYTHING!
ALL THESE MONTHS... IT'S THE ONE THING ...THAT'S KEPT ME IN THE GRIP OF TERROR!
SO NOW THE WRAPS ARE OFF... IT'S OUT IN THE OPEN, AT LAST!
WELL, MAYBE IT'S BETTER THIS WAY!
AT LEAST IT'LL FINALLY BE FINISHED...
ONE WAY...OR ANOTHER!
34

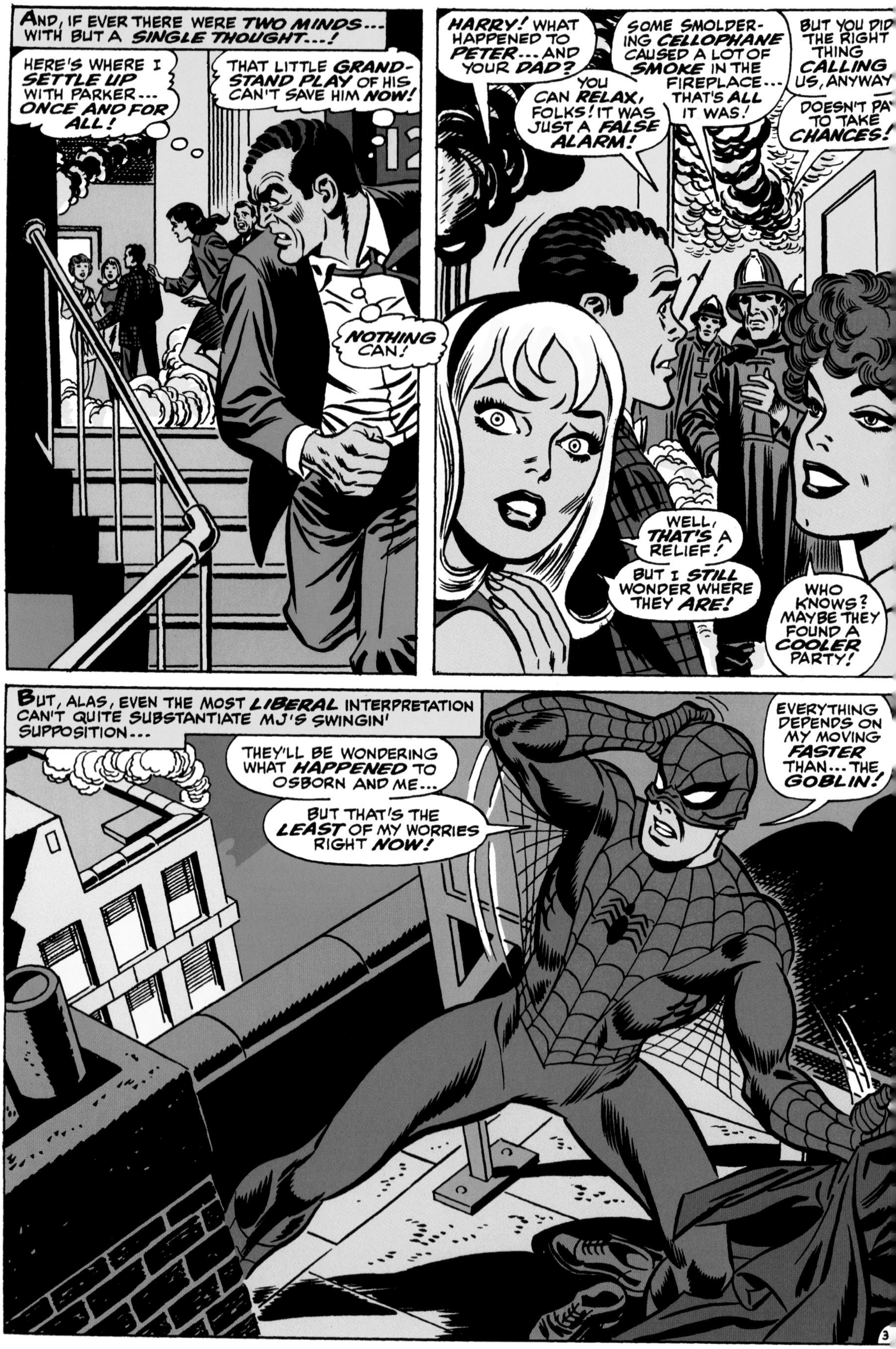
AND, IF EVER THERE WERE TWO MINDS... WITH BUT A SINGLE THOUGHT...!
HERE'S WHERE I SETTLE UP WITH PARKER... ONCE AND FOR ALL!
THAT LITTLE GRAND-STAND PLAY OF HIS CAN'T SAVE HIM NOW!
NOTHING CAN!
HARRY! WHAT HAPPENED TO PETER... AND YOUR DAD?
YOU CAN RELAX, FOLKS! IT WAS JUST A FALSE ALARM!
SOME SMOLDERING CELLOPHANE CAUSED A LOT OF SMOKE IN THE FIREPLACE... THAT'S ALL IT WAS!
BUT YOU DID THE RIGHT THING CALLING US, ANYWAY
DOESN'T PA TO TAKE CHANCES!
WELL, THAT'S A RELIEF!
BUT I STILL WONDER WHERE THEY ARE!
WHO KNOWS? MAYBE THEY FOUND A COOLER PARTY!
BUT, ALAS, EVEN THE MOST LIBERAL INTERPRETATION CAN'T QUITE SUBSTANTIATE MJ'S SWINGIN' SUPPOSITION...
THEY'LL BE WONDERING WHAT HAPPENED TO OSBORN AND ME...
BUT THAT'S THE LEAST OF MY WORRIES RIGHT NOW!
EVERYTHING DEPENDS ON MY MOVING FASTER THAN... THE GOBLIN!
3

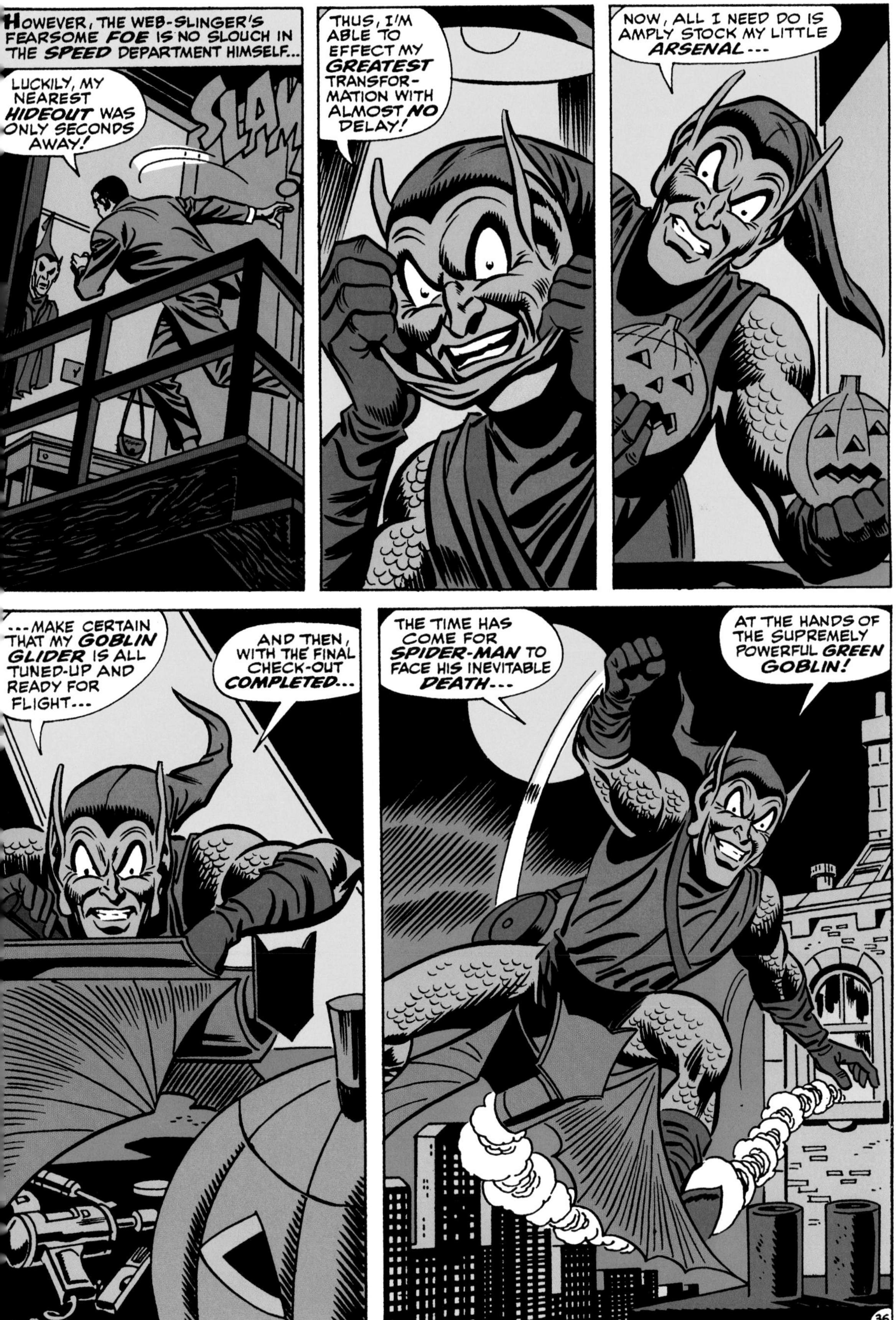
HOWEVER, THE WEB-SLINGER'S FEARSOME FOE IS NO SLOUCH IN THE SPEED DEPARTMENT HIMSELF...
LUCKILY, MY NEAREST HIDEOUT WAS ONLY SECONDS AWAY!
SLAM
THUS, I'M ABLE TO EFFECT MY GREATEST TRANSFORMATION WITH ALMOST NO DELAY!
NOW, ALL I NEED DO IS AMPLY STOCK MY LITTLE ARSENAL---
---MAKE CERTAIN THAT MY GOBLIN GLIDER IS ALL TUNED-UP AND READY FOR FLIGHT---
AND THEN, WITH THE FINAL CHECK-OUT COMPLETED...
THE TIME HAS COME FOR SPIDER-MAN TO FACE HIS INEVITABLE DEATH---
AT THE HANDS OF THE SUPREMELY POWERFUL GREEN GOBLIN!
36

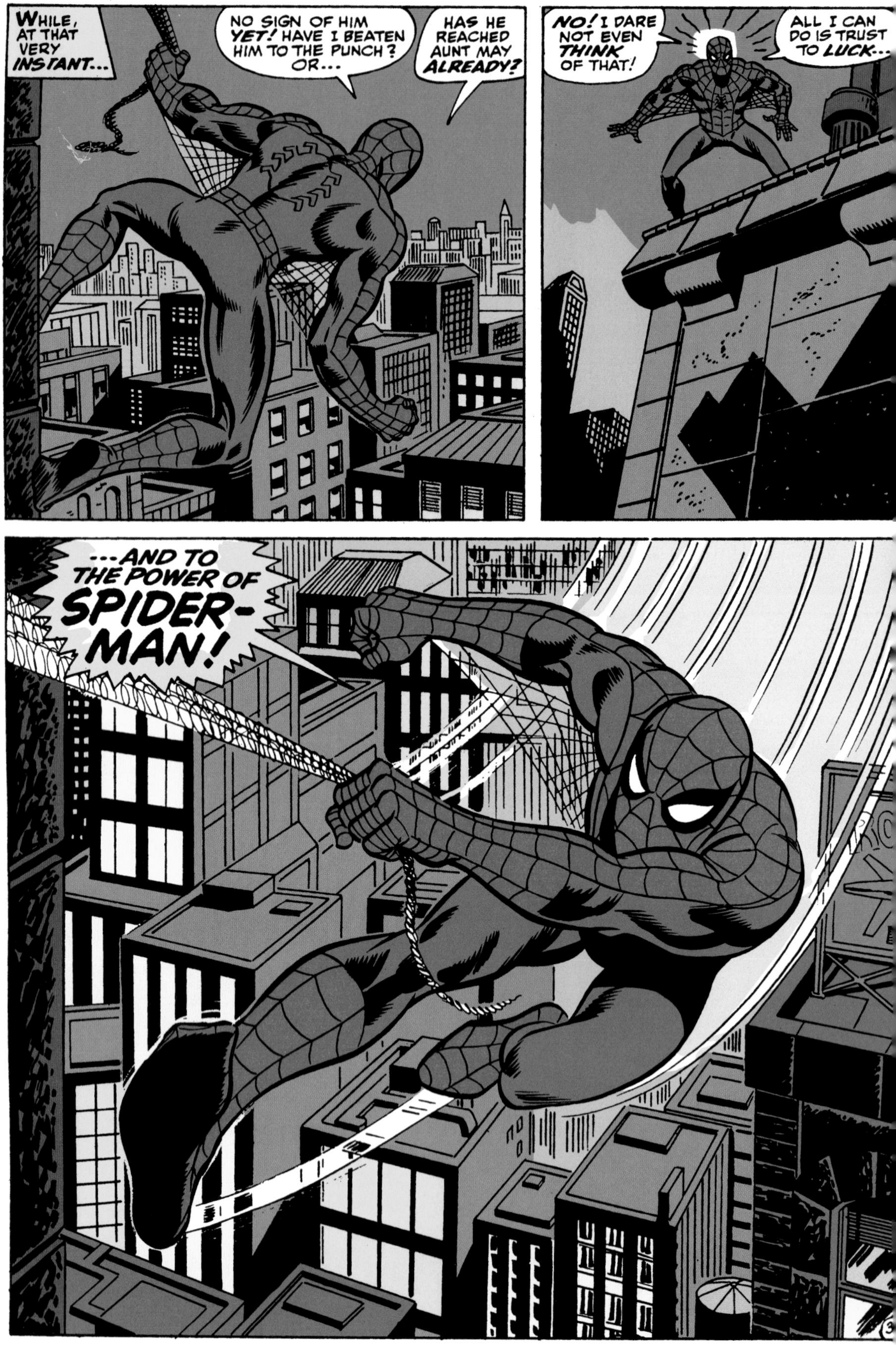
WHILE, AT THAT VERY INSTANT...
NO SIGN OF HIM YET! HAVE I BEATEN HIM TO THE PUNCH? OR...
HAS HE REACHED AUNT MAY ALREADY?
NO! I DARE NOT EVEN THINK OF THAT!
ALL I CAN DO IS TRUST TO LUCK...
...AND TO THE POWER OF SPIDER-MAN!

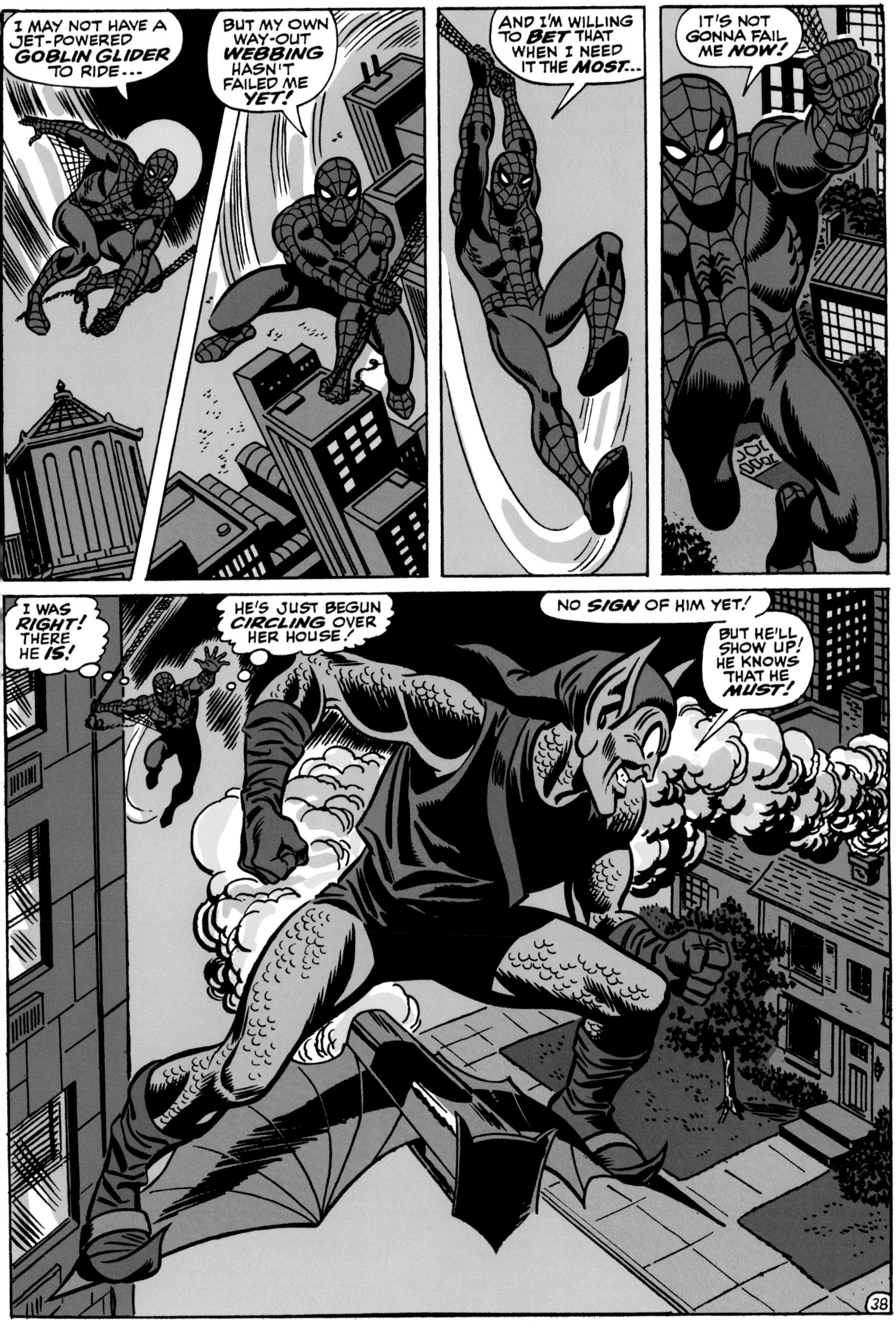
I MAY NOT HAVE A JET-POWERED GOBLIN GLIDER TO RIDE...
BUT MY OWN WAY-OUT WEBBING HASN'T FAILED ME YET!
AND I'M WILLING TO BET THAT WHEN I NEED IT THE MOST...
IT'S NOT GONNA FAIL ME NOW!
I WAS RIGHT! THERE HE IS!
HE'S JUST BEGUN CIRCLING OVER HER HOUSE!
NO SIGN OF HIM YET!
BUT HE'LL SHOW UP! HE KNOWS THAT HE MUST!
38

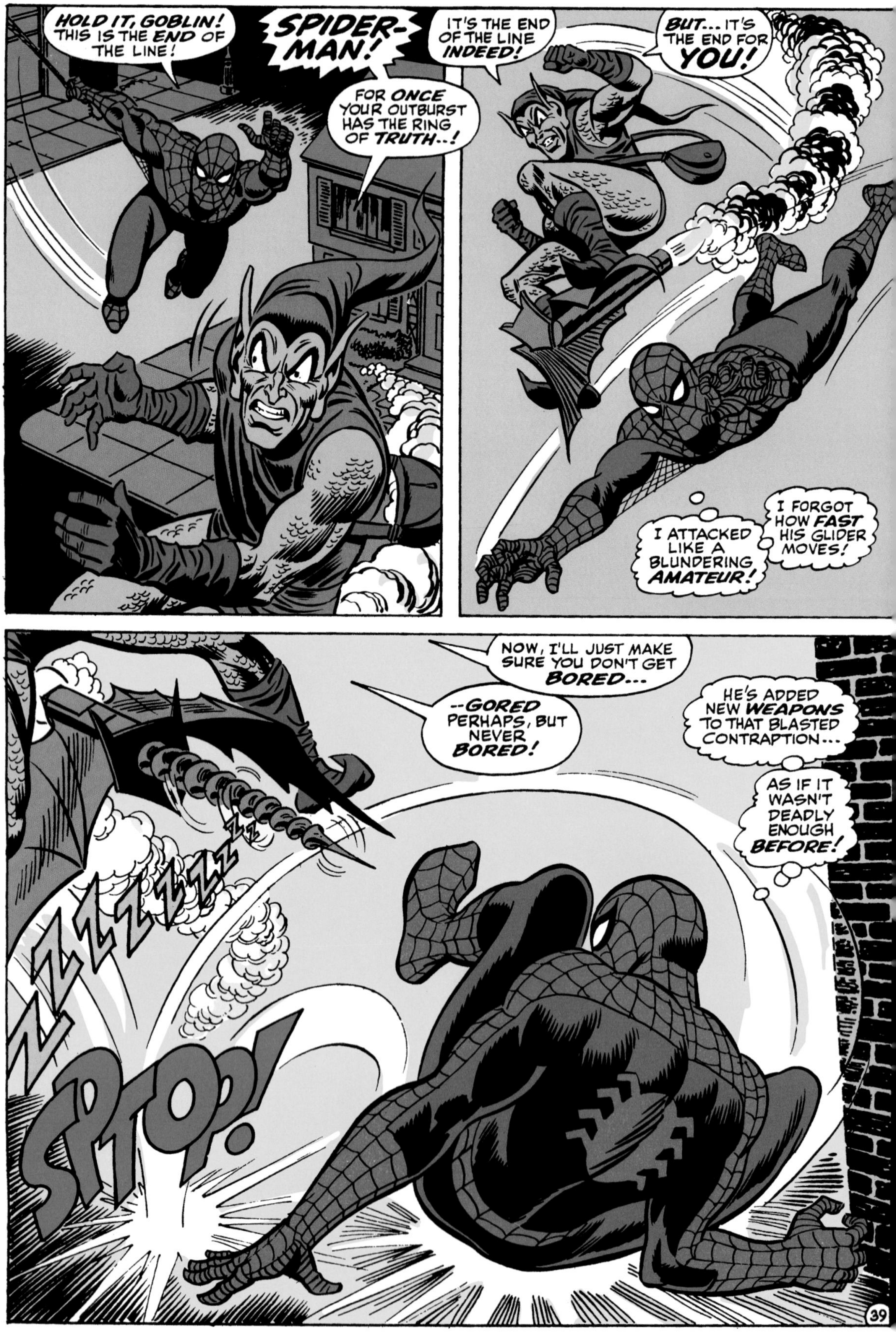

HOLD IT, GOBLIN! THIS IS THE END OF THE LINE!
SPIDER-MAN!
FOR ONCE YOUR OUTBURST HAS THE RING OF TRUTH..!
IT'S THE END OF THE LINE INDEED!
BUT... IT'S THE END FOR YOU!
I ATTACKED LIKE A BLUNDERING AMATEUR!
I FORGOT HOW FAST HIS GLIDER MOVES!
NOW, I'LL JUST MAKE SURE YOU DON'T GET BORED...
--GORED PERHAPS, BUT NEVER BORED!
HE'S ADDED NEW WEAPONS TO THAT BLASTED CONTRAPTION...
AS IF IT WASN'T DEADLY ENOUGH BEFORE!
ZZZZZZZZZZ
SPTOP!
39

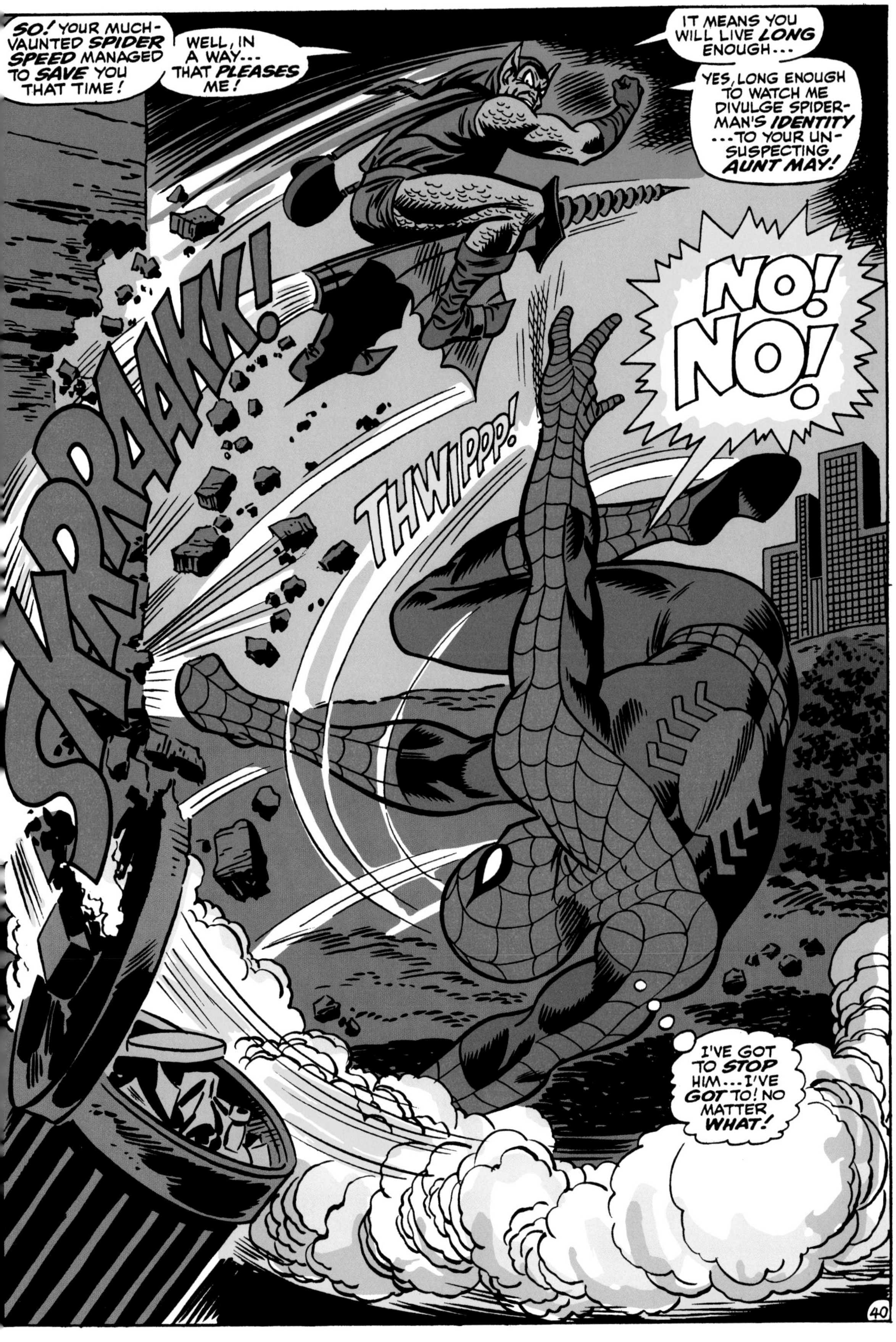
SO! YOUR MUCH-VAUNTED SPIDER SPEED MANAGED TO SAVE YOU THAT TIME!
WELL, IN A WAY... THAT PLEASES ME!
IT MEANS YOU WILL LIVE LONG ENOUGH...
YES, LONG ENOUGH TO WATCH ME DIVULGE SPIDER-MAN'S IDENTITY ...TO YOUR UN-SUSPECTING AUNT MAY!
SKRRAAKK!
THWIPPP!
NO! NO!
I'VE GOT TO STOP HIM...I'VE GOT TO! NO MATTER WHAT!
40

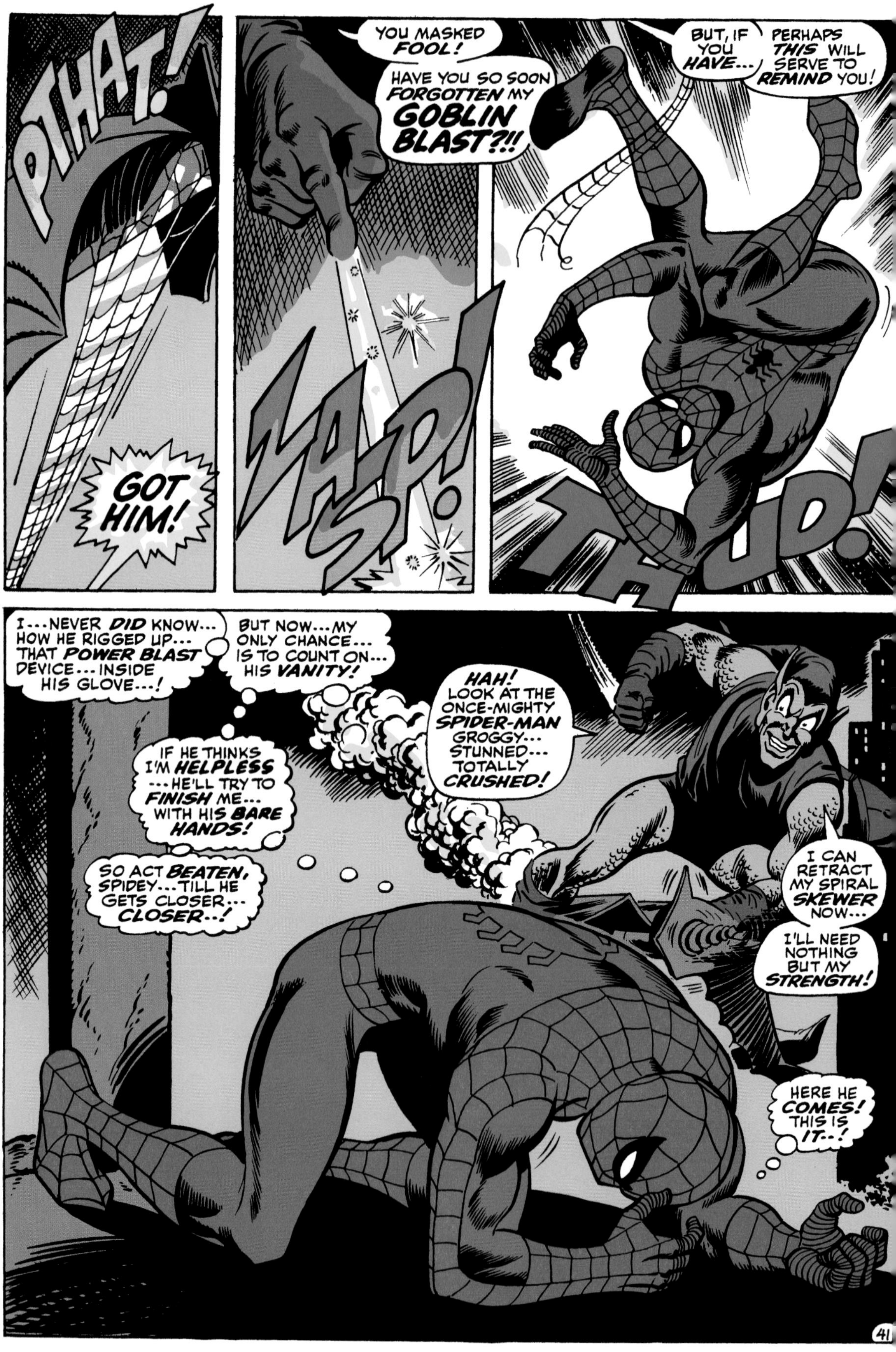
PTHAT!
GOT HIM!
YOU MASKED FOOL!
HAVE YOU SO SOON FORGOTTEN MY GOBLIN BLAST?!!
ZZAAPP!
BUT, IF YOU HAVE...
PERHAPS THIS WILL SERVE TO REMIND YOU!
THUD!
I...NEVER DID KNOW... HOW HE RIGGED UP... THAT POWER BLAST DEVICE...INSIDE HIS GLOVE...!
BUT NOW...MY ONLY CHANCE... IS TO COUNT ON... HIS VANITY!
IF HE THINKS I'M HELPLESS ...HE'LL TRY TO FINISH ME... WITH HIS BARE HANDS!
SO ACT BEATEN, SPIDEY...TILL HE GETS CLOSER... CLOSER..!
HAH! LOOK AT THE ONCE-MIGHTY SPIDER-MAN GROGGY... STUNNED... TOTALLY CRUSHED!
I CAN RETRACT MY SPIRAL SKEWER NOW...
I'LL NEED NOTHING BUT MY STRENGTH!
HERE HE COMES! THIS IS IT..!
41

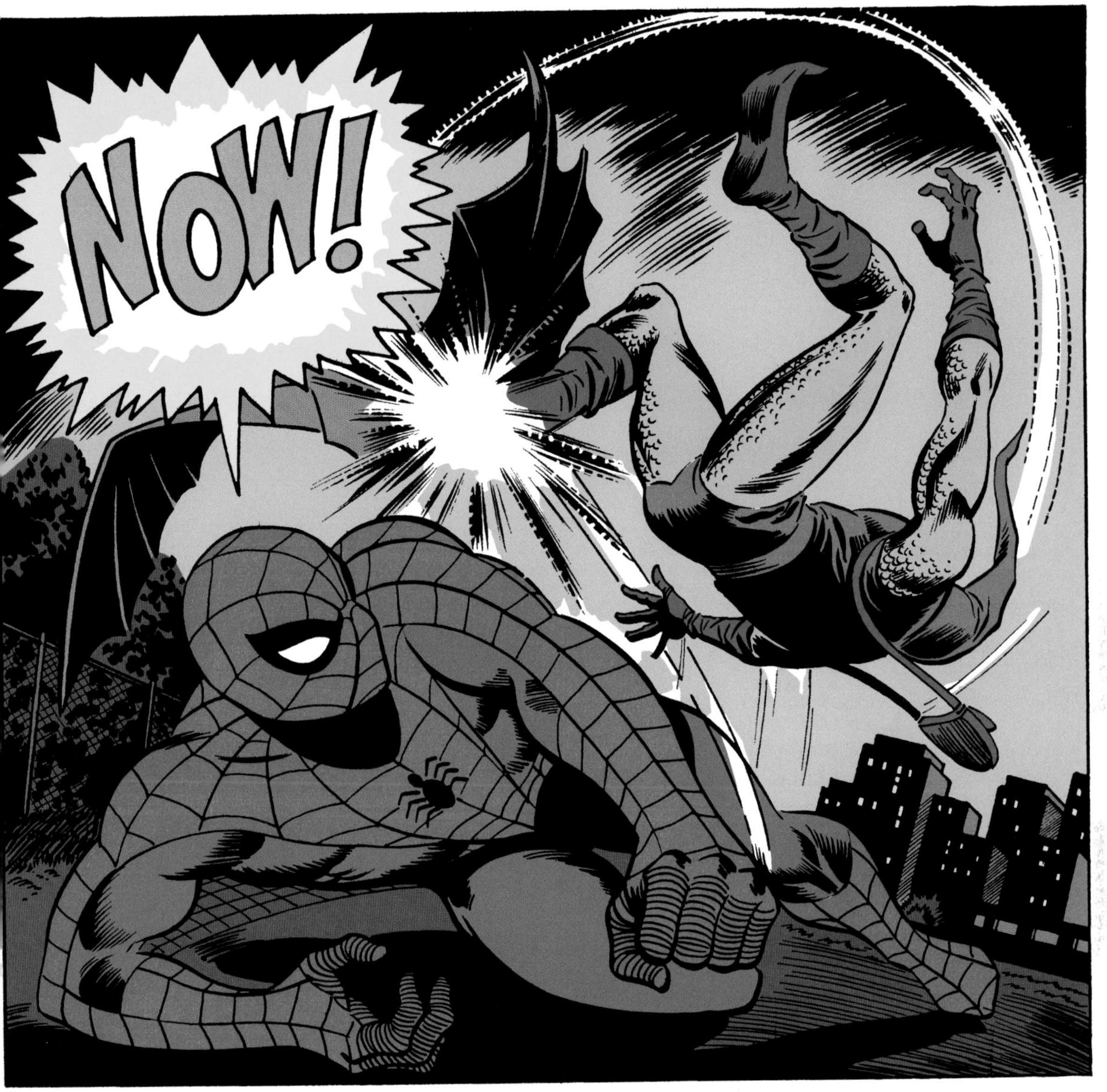
NOW!

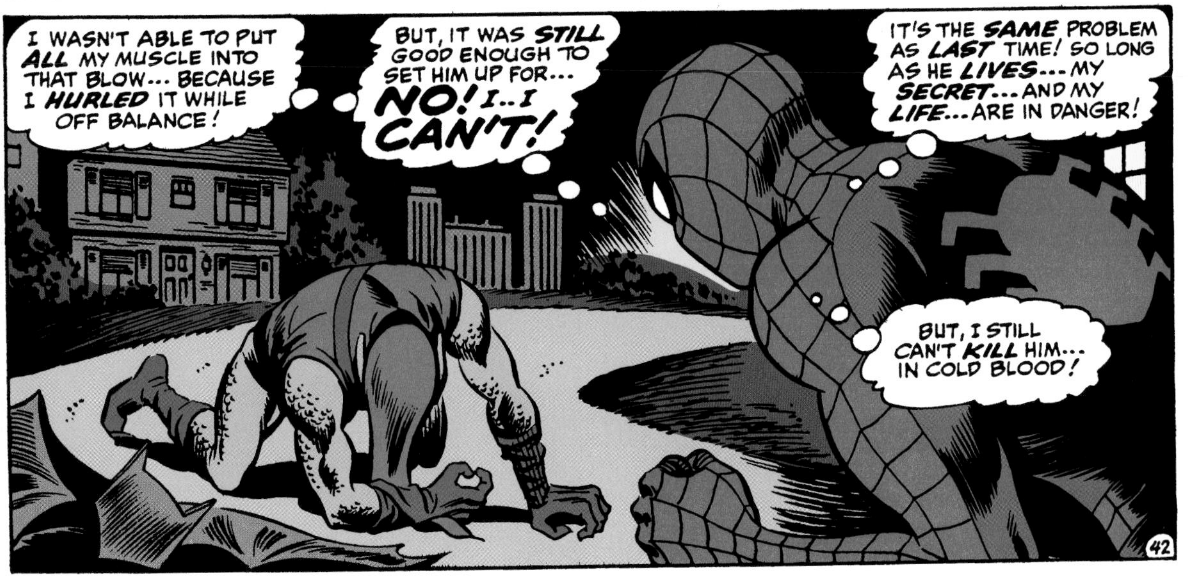
I WASN'T ABLE TO PUT ALL MY MUSCLE INTO THAT BLOW... BECAUSE I HURLED IT WHILE OFF BALANCE!
BUT, IT WAS STILL GOOD ENOUGH TO SET HIM UP FOR... NO! I..I CAN'T!
IT'S THE SAME PROBLEM AS LAST TIME! SO LONG AS HE LIVES... MY SECRET... AND MY LIFE... ARE IN DANGER!
BUT, I STILL CAN'T KILL HIM... IN COLD BLOOD!
42

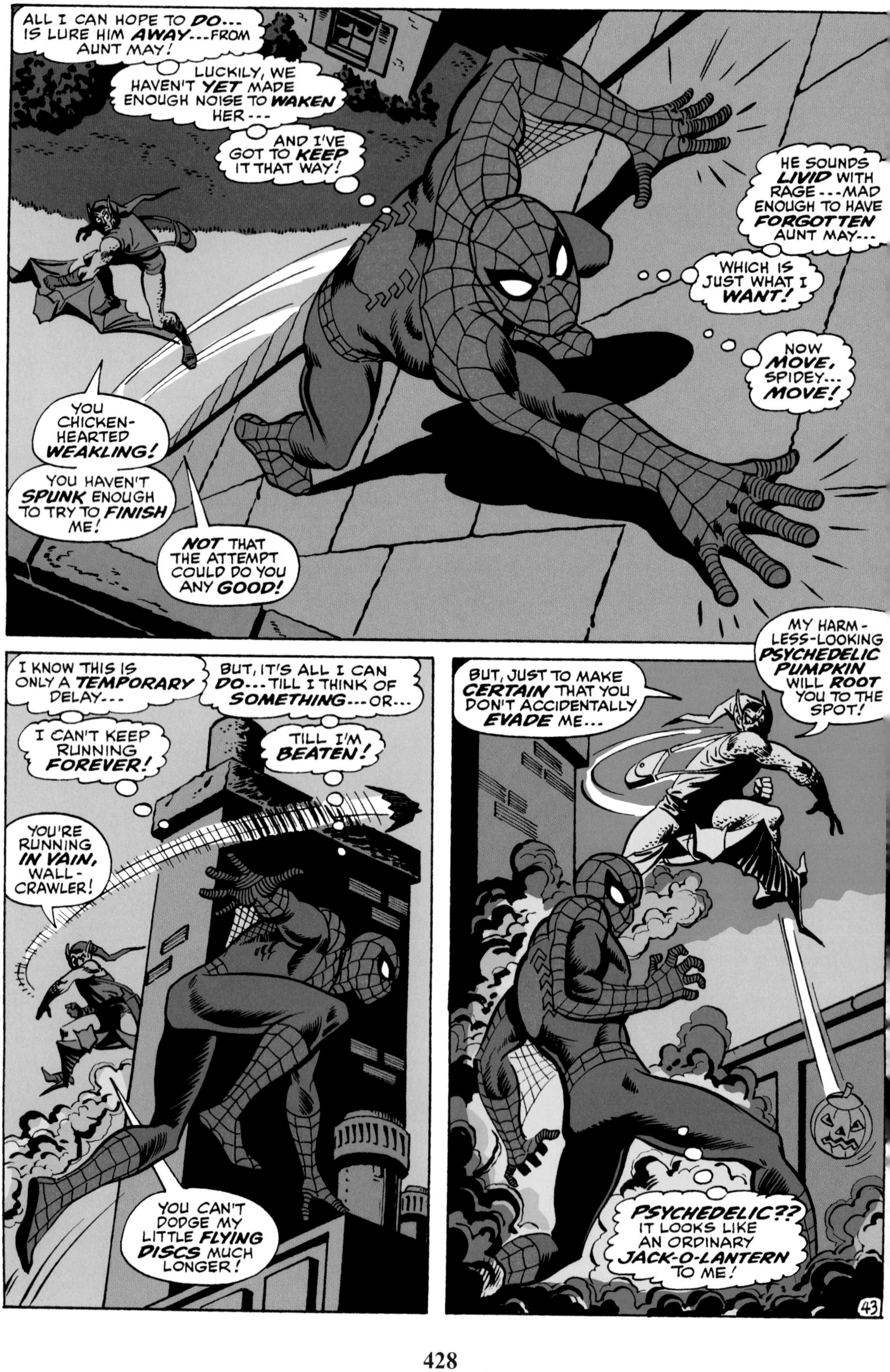
ALL I CAN HOPE TO DO... IS LURE HIM AWAY---FROM AUNT MAY!
LUCKILY, WE HAVEN'T YET MADE ENOUGH NOISE TO WAKEN HER---
AND I'VE GOT TO KEEP IT THAT WAY!
HE SOUNDS LIVID WITH RAGE---MAD ENOUGH TO HAVE FORGOTTEN AUNT MAY---
WHICH IS JUST WHAT I WANT!
NOW MOVE, SPIDEY... MOVE!
YOU CHICKEN-HEARTED WEAKLING!
YOU HAVEN'T SPUNK ENOUGH TO TRY TO FINISH ME!
NOT THAT THE ATTEMPT COULD DO YOU ANY GOOD!
I KNOW THIS IS ONLY A TEMPORARY DELAY---
BUT, IT'S ALL I CAN DO---TILL I THINK OF SOMETHING---OR...
I CAN'T KEEP RUNNING FOREVER!
TILL I'M BEATEN!
YOU'RE RUNNING IN VAIN, WALL-CRAWLER!
YOU CAN'T DODGE MY LITTLE FLYING DISCS MUCH LONGER!
BUT, JUST TO MAKE CERTAIN THAT YOU DON'T ACCIDENTALLY EVADE ME...
MY HARM-LESS-LOOKING PSYCHEDELIC PUMPKIN WILL ROOT YOU TO THE SPOT!
PSYCHEDELIC?? IT LOOKS LIKE AN ORDINARY JACK-O-LANTERN TO ME!
43

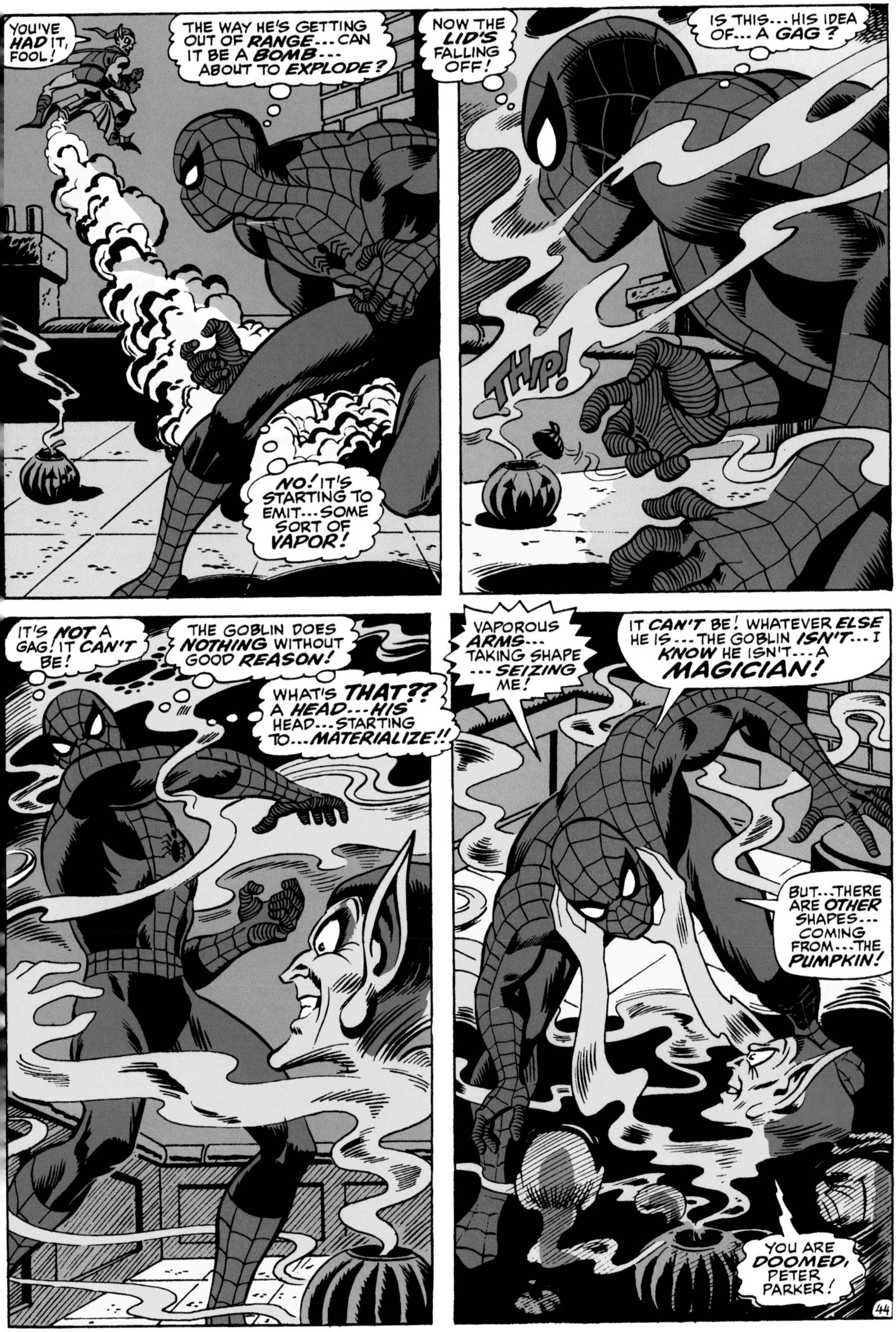
YOU'VE HAD IT, FOOL!
THE WAY HE'S GETTING OUT OF RANGE... CAN IT BE A BOMB... ABOUT TO EXPLODE?
NO! IT'S STARTING TO EMIT... SOME SORT OF VAPOR!
NOW THE LID'S FALLING OFF!
IS THIS... HIS IDEA OF... A GAG?
THIP!
IT'S NOT A GAG! IT CAN'T BE!
THE GOBLIN DOES NOTHING WITHOUT GOOD REASON!
WHAT'S THAT?? A HEAD... HIS HEAD... STARTING TO... MATERIALIZE!!
VAPOROUS ARMS... TAKING SHAPE ... SEIZING ME!
IT CAN'T BE! WHATEVER ELSE HE IS... THE GOBLIN ISN'T... I KNOW HE ISN'T... A MAGICIAN!
BUT... THERE ARE OTHER SHAPES... COMING FROM... THE PUMPKIN!
YOU ARE DOOMED, PETER PARKER!
44

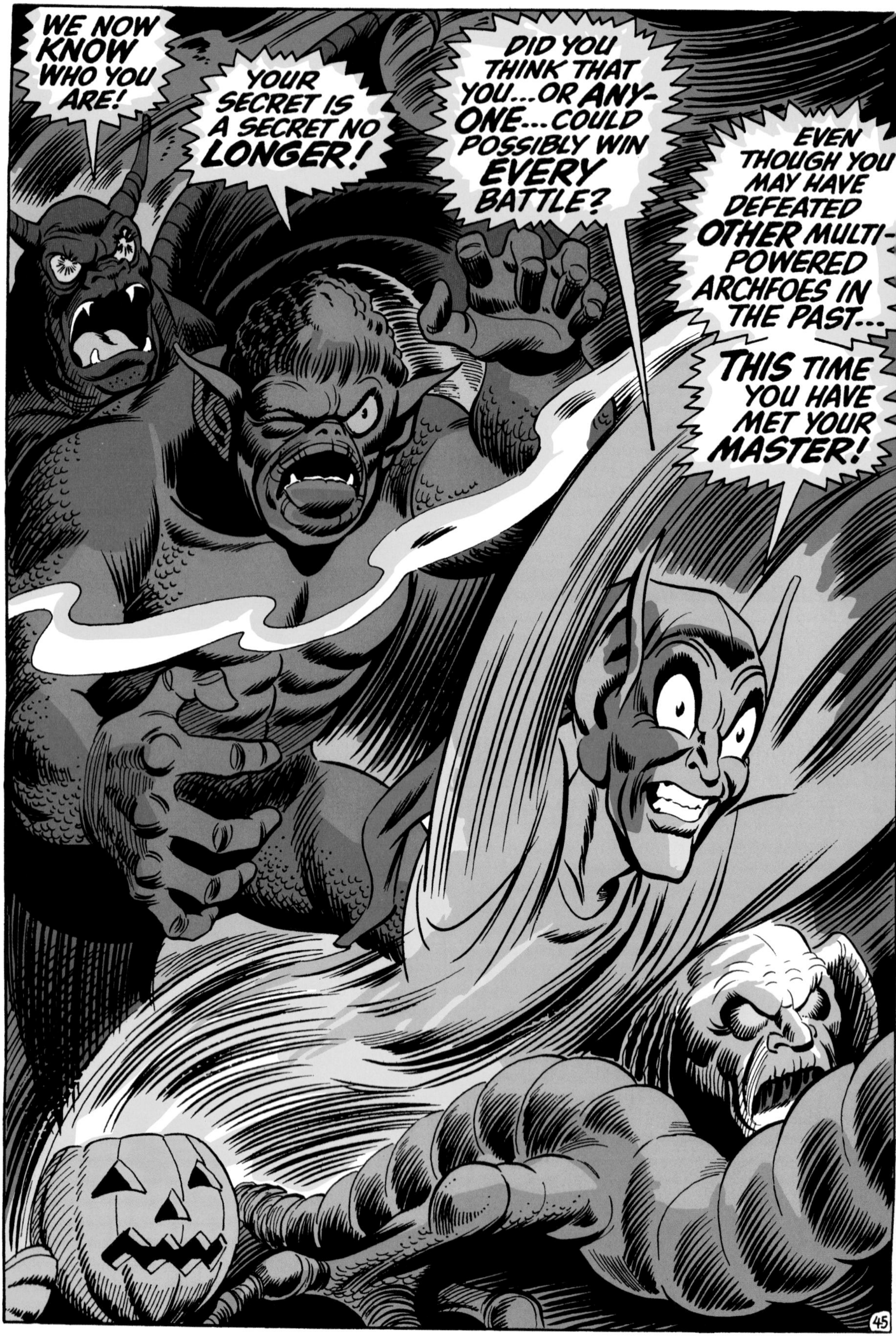
WE NOW KNOW WHO YOU ARE!
YOUR SECRET IS A SECRET NO LONGER!
DID YOU THINK THAT YOU...OR ANY-ONE...COULD POSSIBLY WIN EVERY BATTLE?
EVEN THOUGH YOU MAY HAVE DEFEATED OTHER MULTI-POWERED ARCHFOES IN THE PAST...
THIS TIME YOU HAVE MET YOUR MASTER!
45

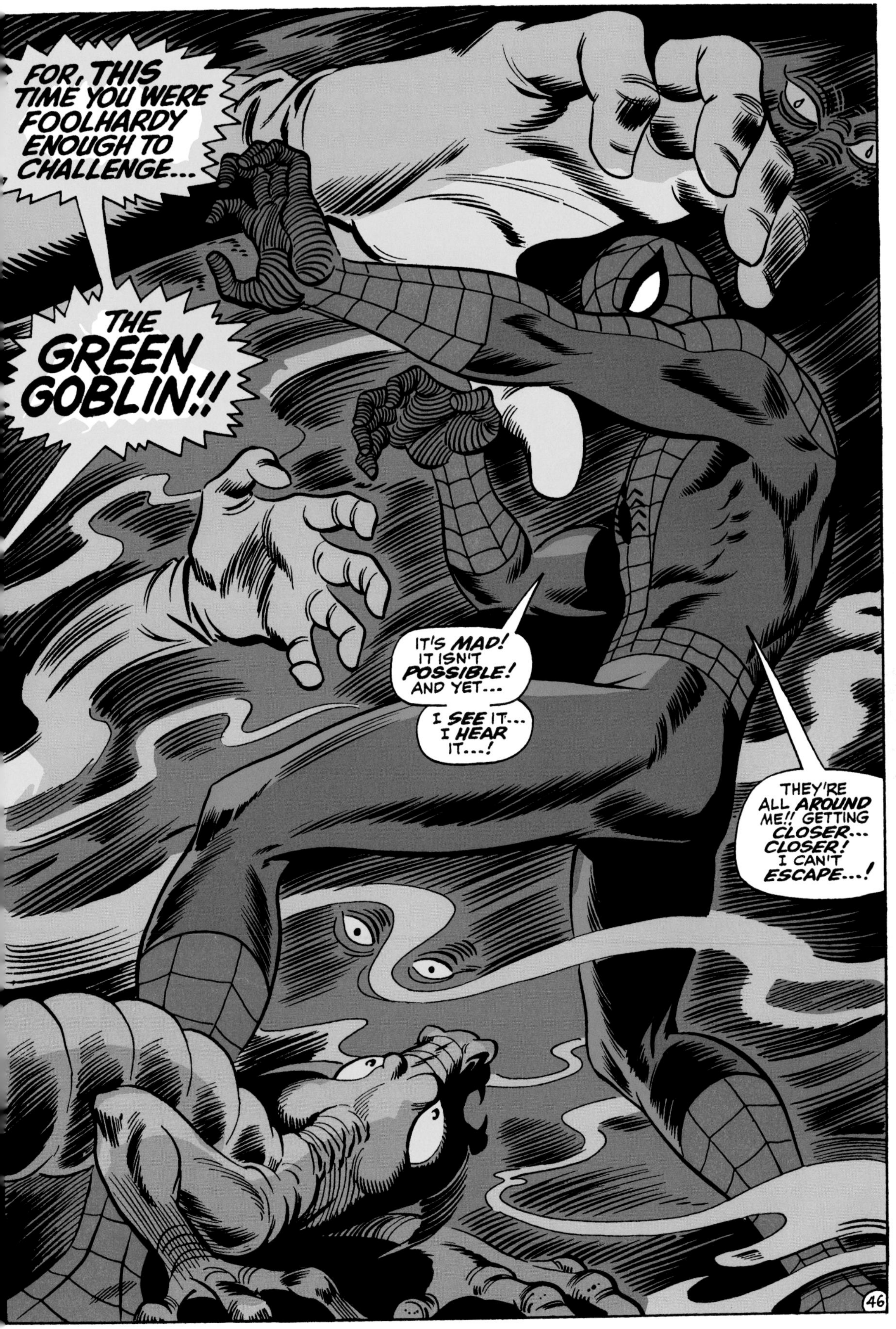
FOR, THIS TIME YOU WERE FOOLHARDY ENOUGH TO CHALLENGE...
THE GREEN GOBLIN!!
IT'S MAD! IT ISN'T POSSIBLE! AND YET...
I SEE IT... I HEAR IT...!
THEY'RE ALL AROUND ME!! GETTING CLOSER... CLOSER! I CAN'T ESCAPE...!
46

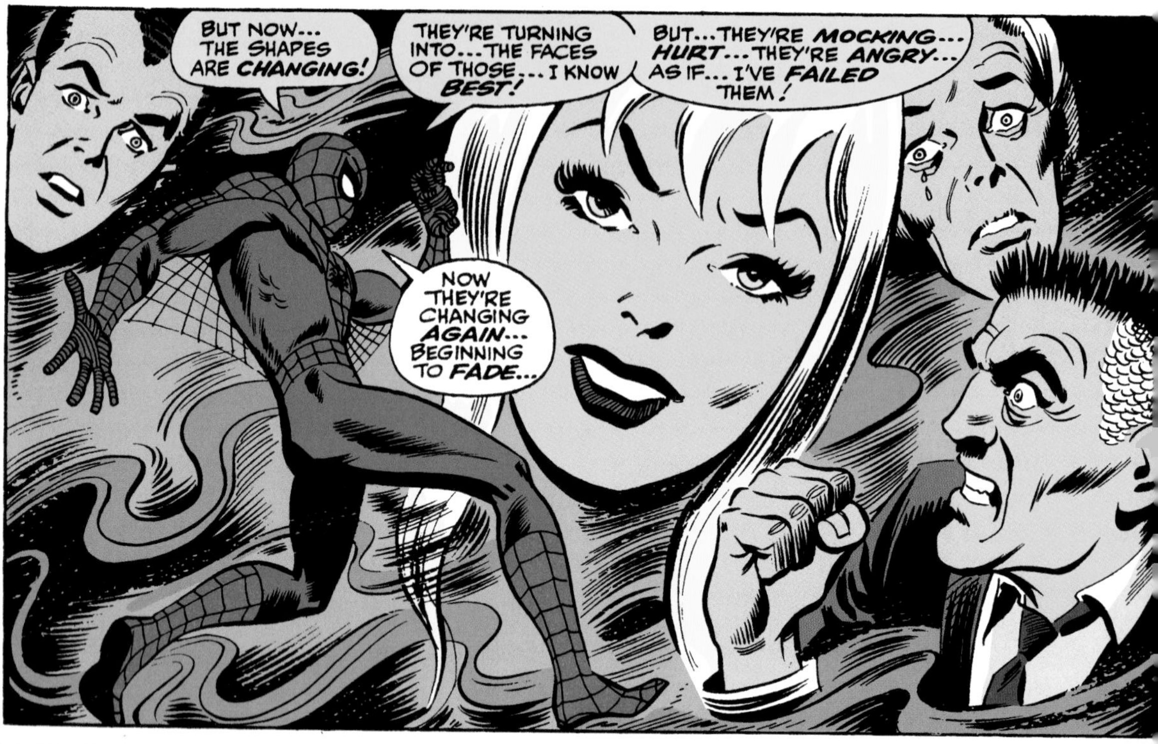

BUT NOW... THE SHAPES ARE CHANGING!
THEY'RE TURNING INTO... THE FACES OF THOSE... I KNOW BEST!
BUT... THEY'RE MOCKING... HURT... THEY'RE ANGRY... AS IF... I'VE FAILED THEM!
NOW THEY'RE CHANGING AGAIN... BEGINNING TO FADE...

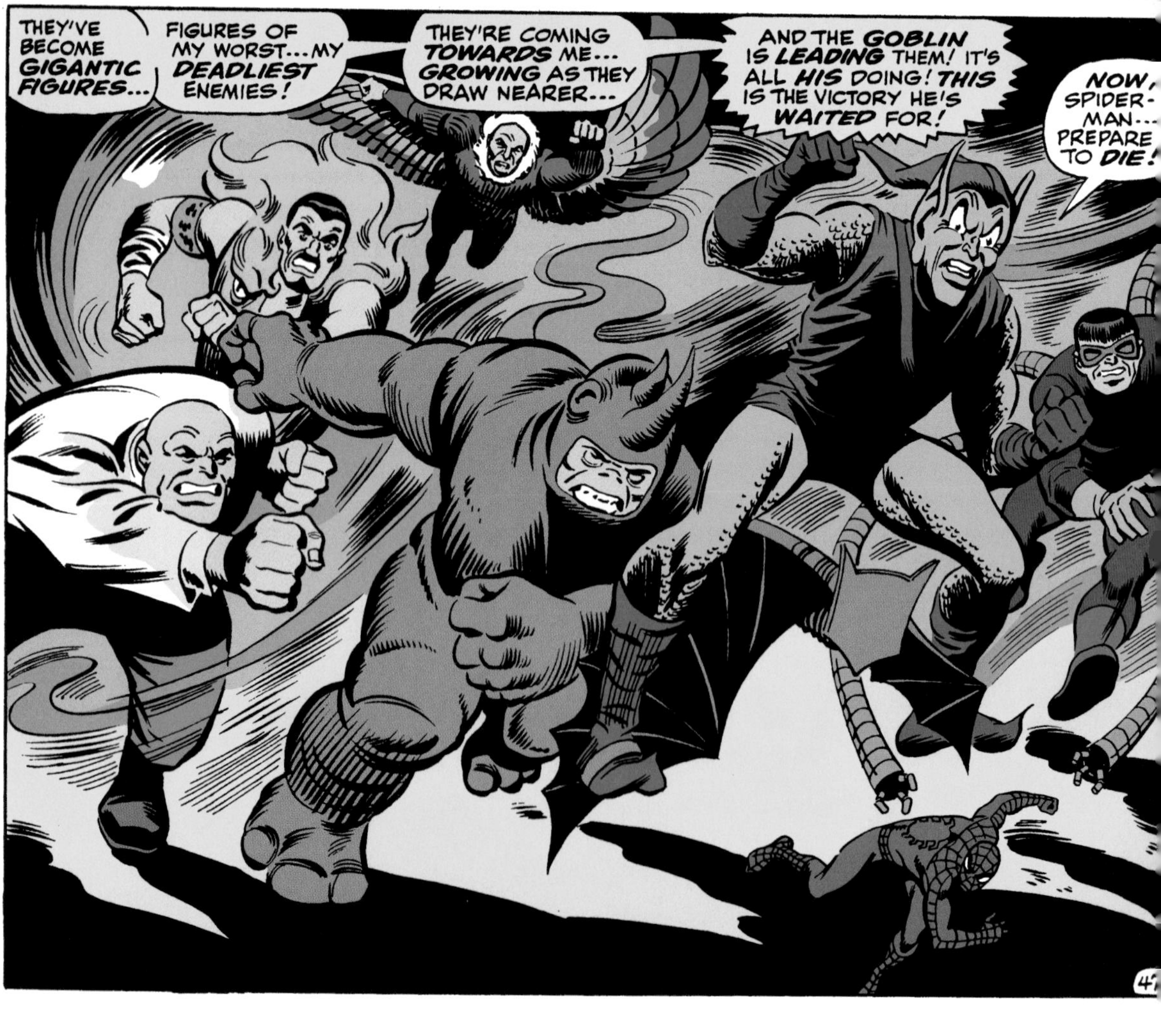

THEY'VE BECOME GIGANTIC FIGURES...
FIGURES OF MY WORST... MY DEADLIEST ENEMIES!
THEY'RE COMING TOWARDS ME... GROWING AS THEY DRAW NEARER...
AND THE GOBLIN IS LEADING THEM! IT'S ALL HIS DOING! THIS IS THE VICTORY HE'S WAITED FOR!
NOW, SPIDER-MAN... PREPARE TO DIE!

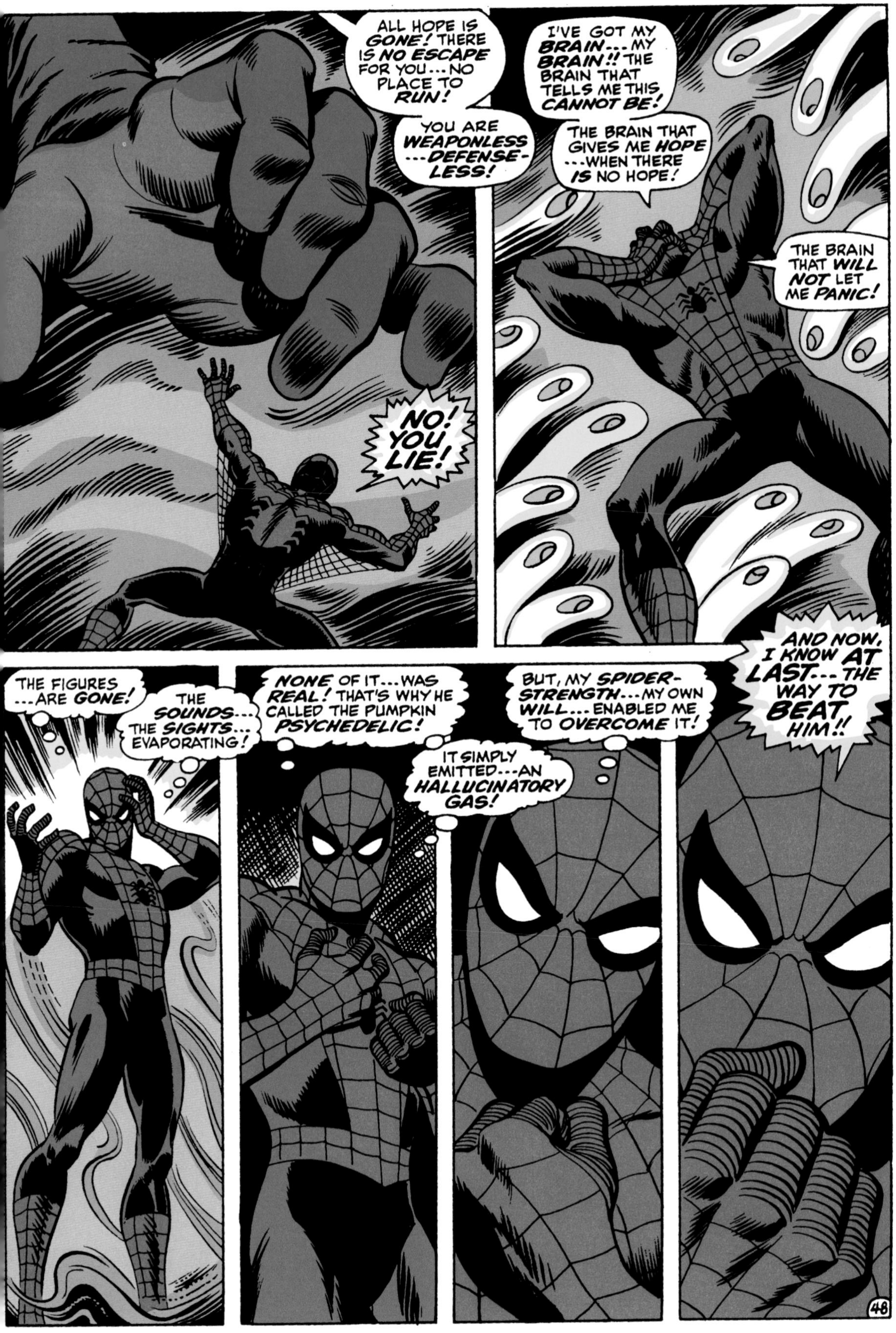

ALL HOPE IS GONE! THERE IS NO ESCAPE FOR YOU... NO PLACE TO RUN!
YOU ARE WEAPONLESS ...DEFENSE-LESS!
NO! YOU LIE!
I'VE GOT MY BRAIN... MY BRAIN!! THE BRAIN THAT TELLS ME THIS CANNOT BE!
THE BRAIN THAT GIVES ME HOPE ...WHEN THERE IS NO HOPE!
THE BRAIN THAT WILL NOT LET ME PANIC!
THE FIGURES ...ARE GONE!
THE SOUNDS... THE SIGHTS... EVAPORATING!
NONE OF IT...WAS REAL! THAT'S WHY HE CALLED THE PUMPKIN PSYCHEDELIC!
IT SIMPLY EMITTED...AN HALLUCINATORY GAS!
BUT, MY SPIDER-STRENGTH...MY OWN WILL...ENABLED ME TO OVERCOME IT!
AND NOW, I KNOW AT LAST... THE WAY TO BEAT HIM!!
48

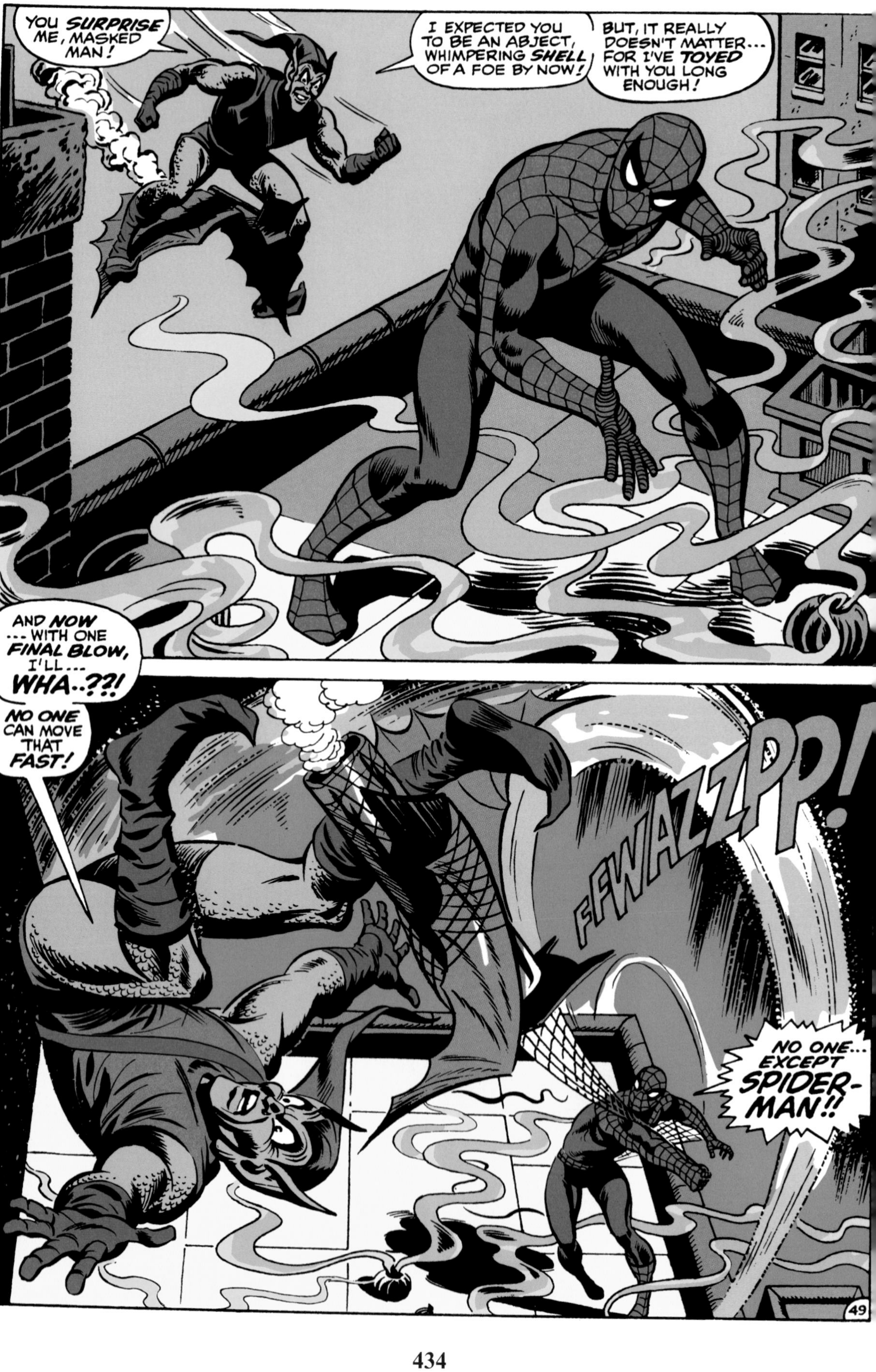
YOU SURPRISE ME, MASKED MAN!
I EXPECTED YOU TO BE AN ABJECT, WHIMPERING SHELL OF A FOE BY NOW!
BUT, IT REALLY DOESN'T MATTER... FOR I'VE TOYED WITH YOU LONG ENOUGH!
AND NOW ... WITH ONE FINAL BLOW, I'LL... WHA..??!
NO ONE CAN MOVE THAT FAST!
FFWAZZPP!
NO ONE... EXCEPT SPIDER-MAN!!
49

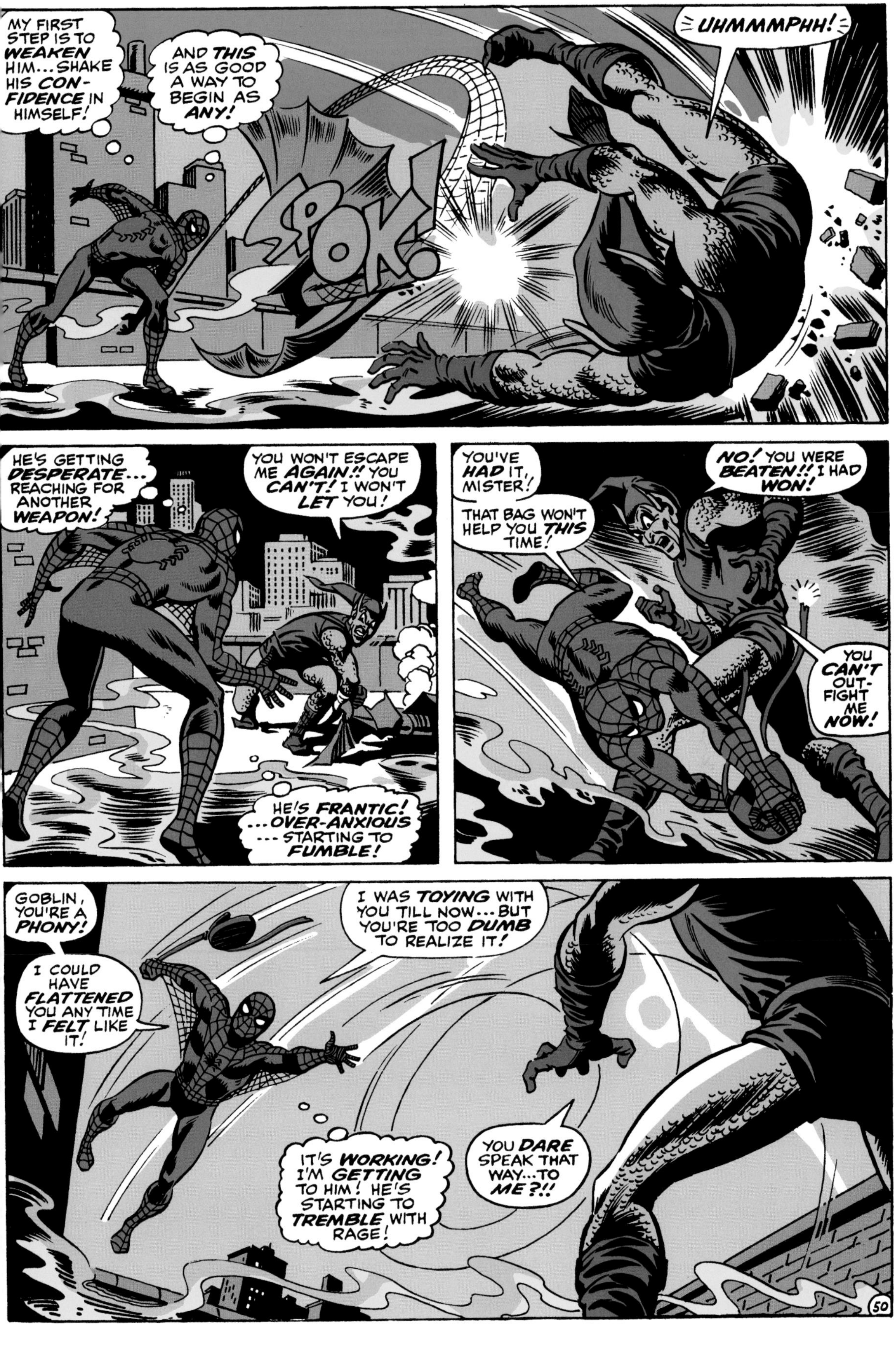
MY FIRST STEP IS TO WEAKEN HIM... SHAKE HIS CONFIDENCE IN HIMSELF!
AND THIS IS AS GOOD A WAY TO BEGIN AS ANY!
SPOK!
UHMMMPHH!
HE'S GETTING DESPERATE... REACHING FOR ANOTHER WEAPON!
YOU WON'T ESCAPE ME AGAIN!! YOU CAN'T! I WON'T LET YOU!
HE'S FRANTIC! ...OVER-ANXIOUS --- STARTING TO FUMBLE!
YOU'VE HAD IT, MISTER!
THAT BAG WON'T HELP YOU THIS TIME!
NO! YOU WERE BEATEN!! I HAD WON!
YOU CAN'T OUT-FIGHT ME NOW!
GOBLIN, YOU'RE A PHONY!
I COULD HAVE FLATTENED YOU ANY TIME I FELT LIKE IT!
I WAS TOYING WITH YOU TILL NOW... BUT YOU'RE TOO DUMB TO REALIZE IT!
IT'S WORKING! I'M GETTING TO HIM! HE'S STARTING TO TREMBLE WITH RAGE!
YOU DARE SPEAK THAT WAY...TO ME?!!
50

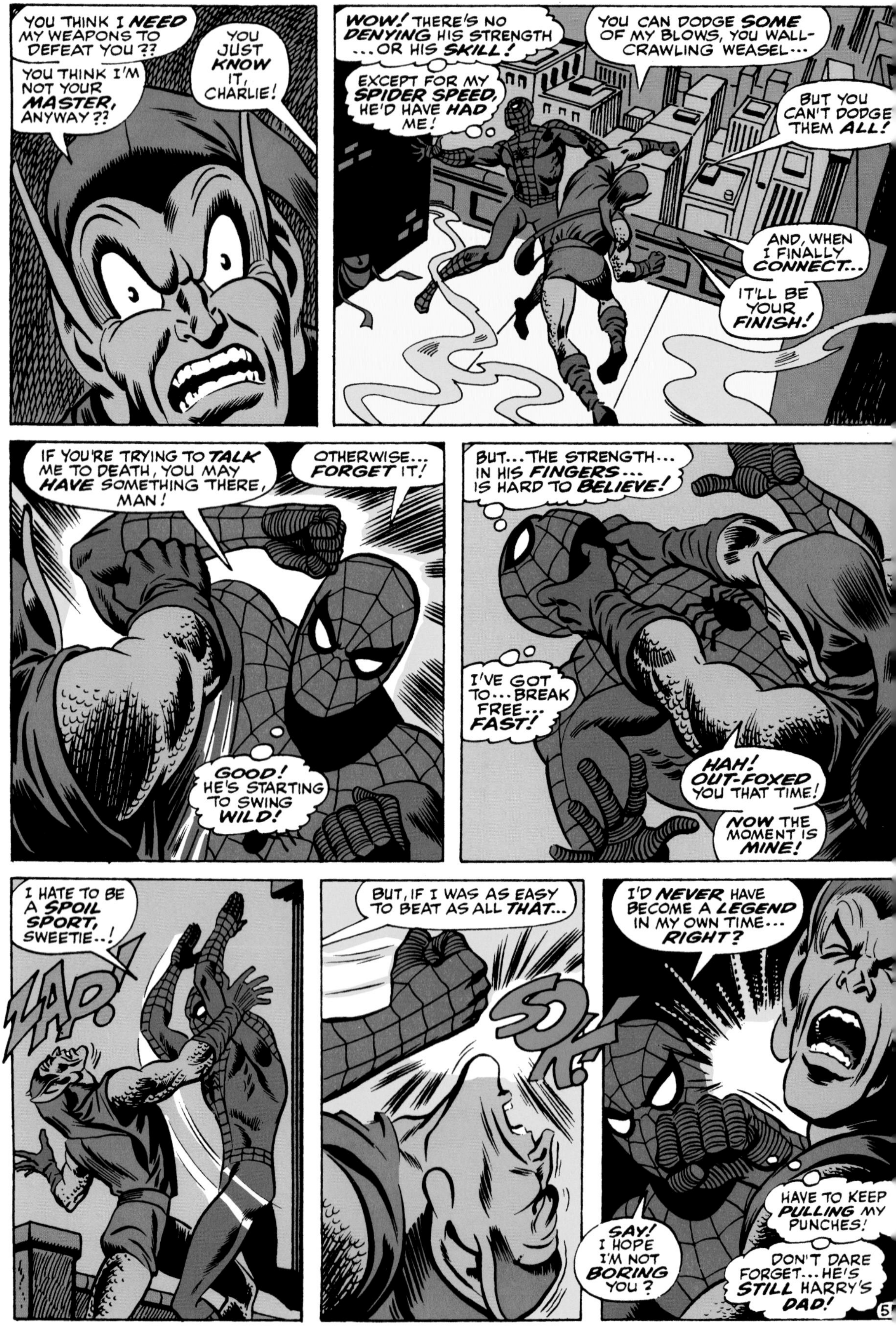
YOU THINK I NEED MY WEAPONS TO DEFEAT YOU??
YOU THINK I'M NOT YOUR MASTER, ANYWAY??
YOU JUST KNOW IT, CHARLIE!
WOW! THERE'S NO DENYING HIS STRENGTH ...OR HIS SKILL!
EXCEPT FOR MY SPIDER SPEED, HE'D HAVE HAD ME!
YOU CAN DODGE SOME OF MY BLOWS, YOU WALL-CRAWLING WEASEL...
BUT YOU CAN'T DODGE THEM ALL!
AND, WHEN I FINALLY CONNECT...
IT'LL BE YOUR FINISH!
IF YOU'RE TRYING TO TALK ME TO DEATH, YOU MAY HAVE SOMETHING THERE, MAN!
OTHERWISE... FORGET IT!
GOOD! HE'S STARTING TO SWING WILD!
BUT... THE STRENGTH... IN HIS FINGERS... IS HARD TO BELIEVE!
I'VE GOT TO... BREAK FREE... FAST!
HAH! OUT-FOXED YOU THAT TIME!
NOW THE MOMENT IS MINE!
I HATE TO BE A SPOIL SPORT, SWEETIE..!
ZAP!
BUT, IF I WAS AS EASY TO BEAT AS ALL THAT...
SOK!
I'D NEVER HAVE BECOME A LEGEND IN MY OWN TIME... RIGHT?
SAY! I HOPE I'M NOT BORING YOU?
HAVE TO KEEP PULLING MY PUNCHES!
DON'T DARE FORGET... HE'S STILL HARRY'S DAD!
5

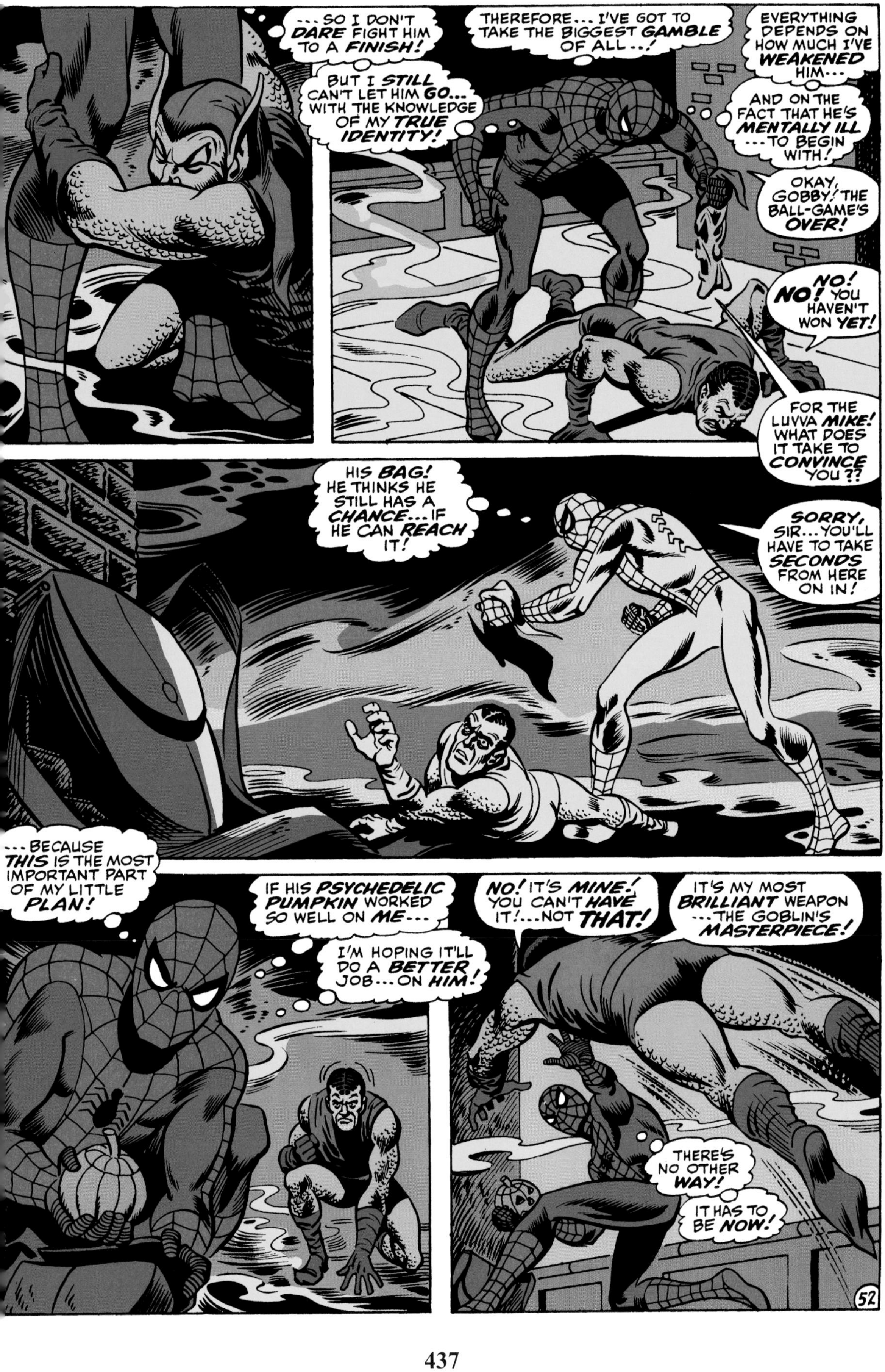
...SO I DON'T DARE FIGHT HIM TO A FINISH!
BUT I STILL CAN'T LET HIM GO... WITH THE KNOWLEDGE OF MY TRUE IDENTITY!
THEREFORE... I'VE GOT TO TAKE THE BIGGEST GAMBLE OF ALL...!
EVERYTHING DEPENDS ON HOW MUCH I'VE WEAKENED HIM...
AND ON THE FACT THAT HE'S MENTALLY ILL ...TO BEGIN WITH!
OKAY, GOBBY! THE BALL-GAME'S OVER!
NO! NO! YOU HAVEN'T WON YET!
FOR THE LUVVA MIKE! WHAT DOES IT TAKE TO CONVINCE YOU??
HIS BAG! HE THINKS HE STILL HAS A CHANCE...IF HE CAN REACH IT!
SORRY, SIR...YOU'LL HAVE TO TAKE SECONDS FROM HERE ON IN!
...BECAUSE THIS IS THE MOST IMPORTANT PART OF MY LITTLE PLAN!
IF HIS PSYCHEDELIC PUMPKIN WORKED SO WELL ON ME...
I'M HOPING IT'LL DO A BETTER JOB...ON HIM!
NO! IT'S MINE! YOU CAN'T HAVE IT!...NOT THAT!
IT'S MY MOST BRILLIANT WEAPON ...THE GOBLIN'S MASTERPIECE!
THERE'S NO OTHER WAY!
IT HAS TO BE NOW!
52

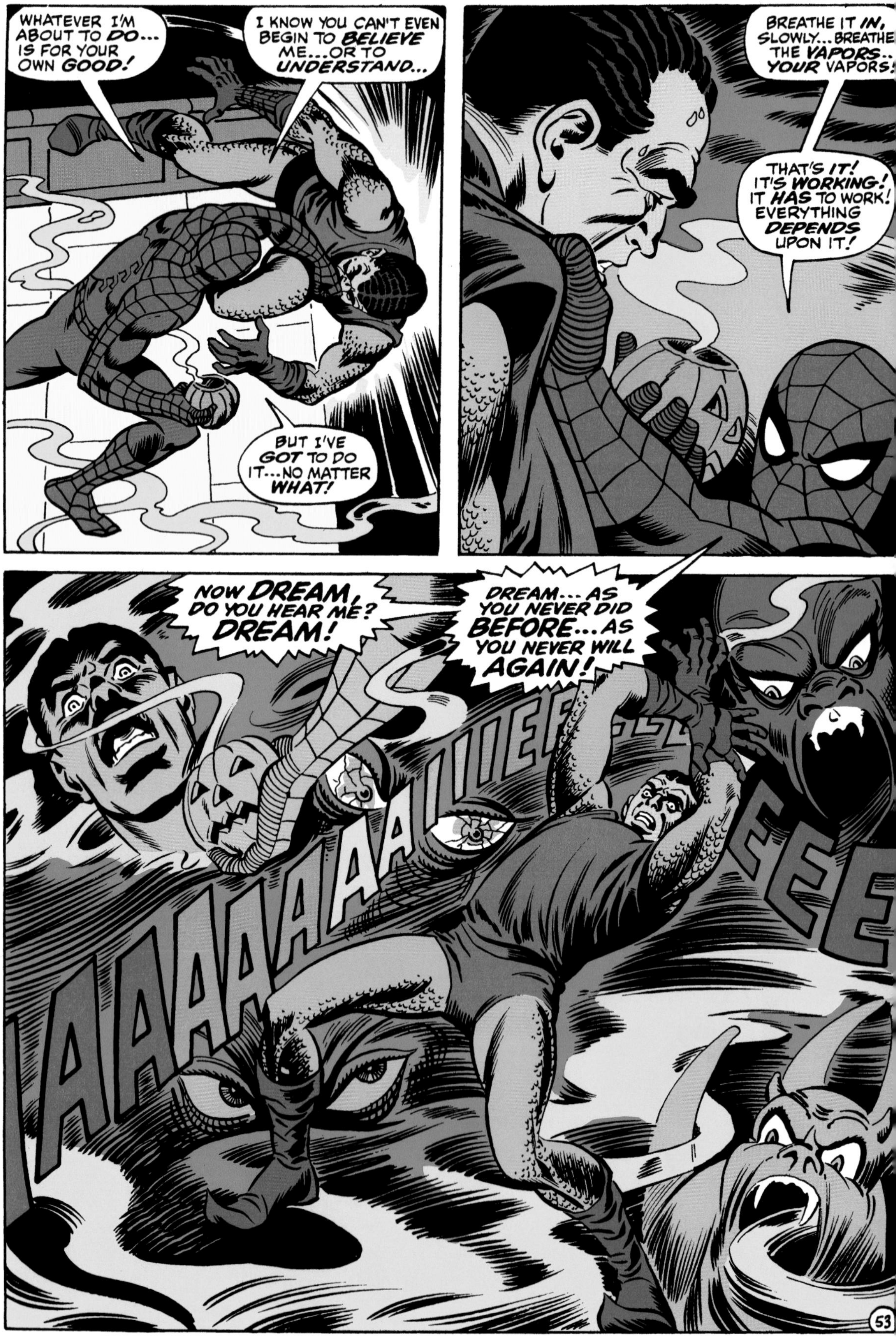
WHATEVER I'M ABOUT TO DO... IS FOR YOUR OWN GOOD!
I KNOW YOU CAN'T EVEN BEGIN TO BELIEVE ME...OR TO UNDERSTAND...
BUT I'VE GOT TO DO IT...NO MATTER WHAT!
BREATHE IT IN, SLOWLY...BREATHE THE VAPORS.. YOUR VAPORS!
THAT'S IT! IT'S WORKING! IT HAS TO WORK! EVERYTHING DEPENDS UPON IT!
NOW DREAM, DO YOU HEAR ME? DREAM!
DREAM...AS YOU NEVER DID BEFORE...AS YOU NEVER WILL AGAIN!
53

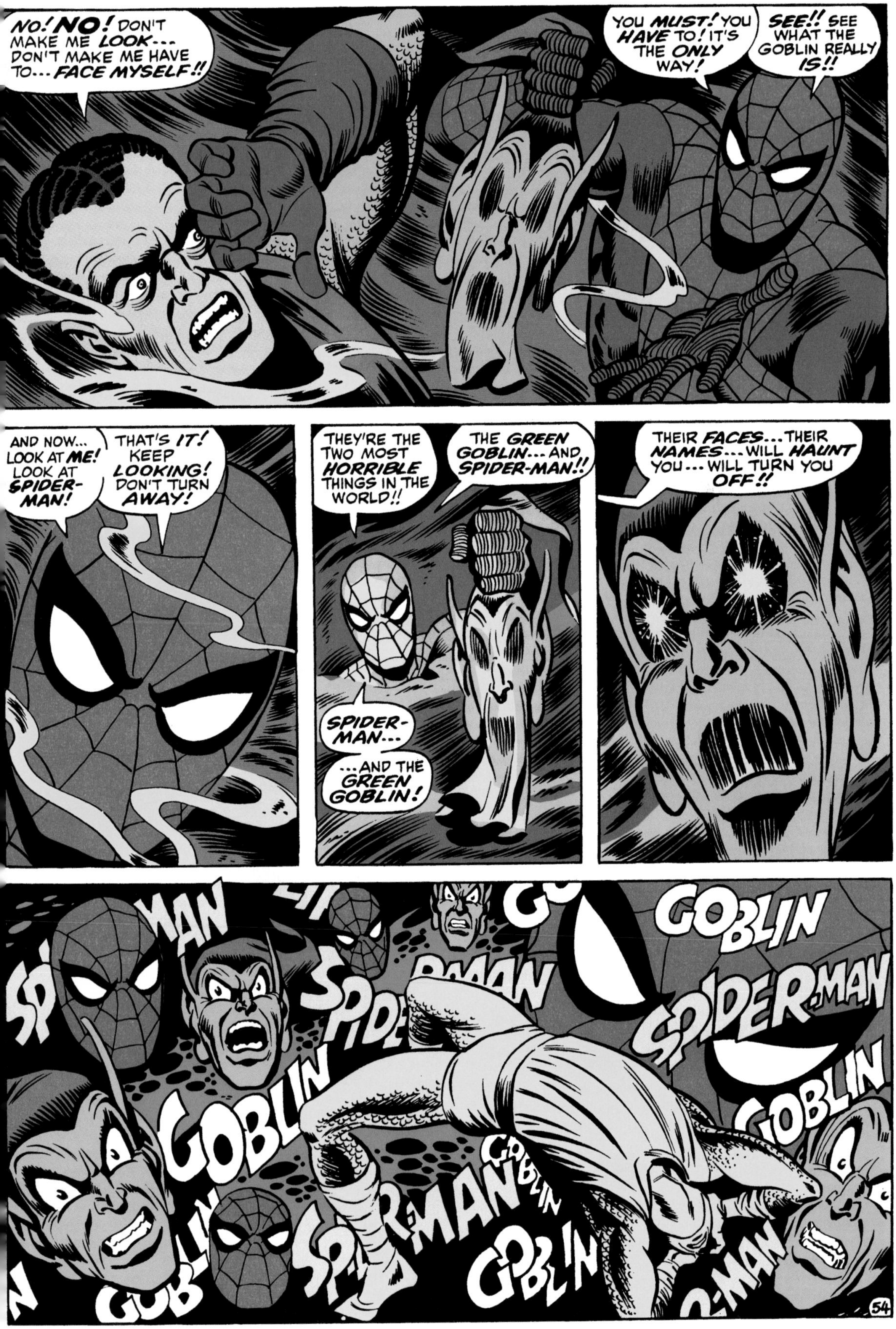
NO! NO! DON'T MAKE ME LOOK... DON'T MAKE ME HAVE TO... FACE MYSELF!!
YOU MUST! YOU HAVE TO! IT'S THE ONLY WAY!
SEE!! SEE WHAT THE GOBLIN REALLY IS!!
AND NOW... LOOK AT ME! LOOK AT SPIDER-MAN!
THAT'S IT! KEEP LOOKING! DON'T TURN AWAY!
THEY'RE THE TWO MOST HORRIBLE THINGS IN THE WORLD!!
THE GREEN GOBLIN... AND SPIDER-MAN!!
SPIDER-MAN...
...AND THE GREEN GOBLIN!
THEIR FACES... THEIR NAMES... WILL HAUNT YOU... WILL TURN YOU OFF!!
GOBLIN
SPIDER-MAN
GOBLIN
GOBLIN
GOBLIN
54

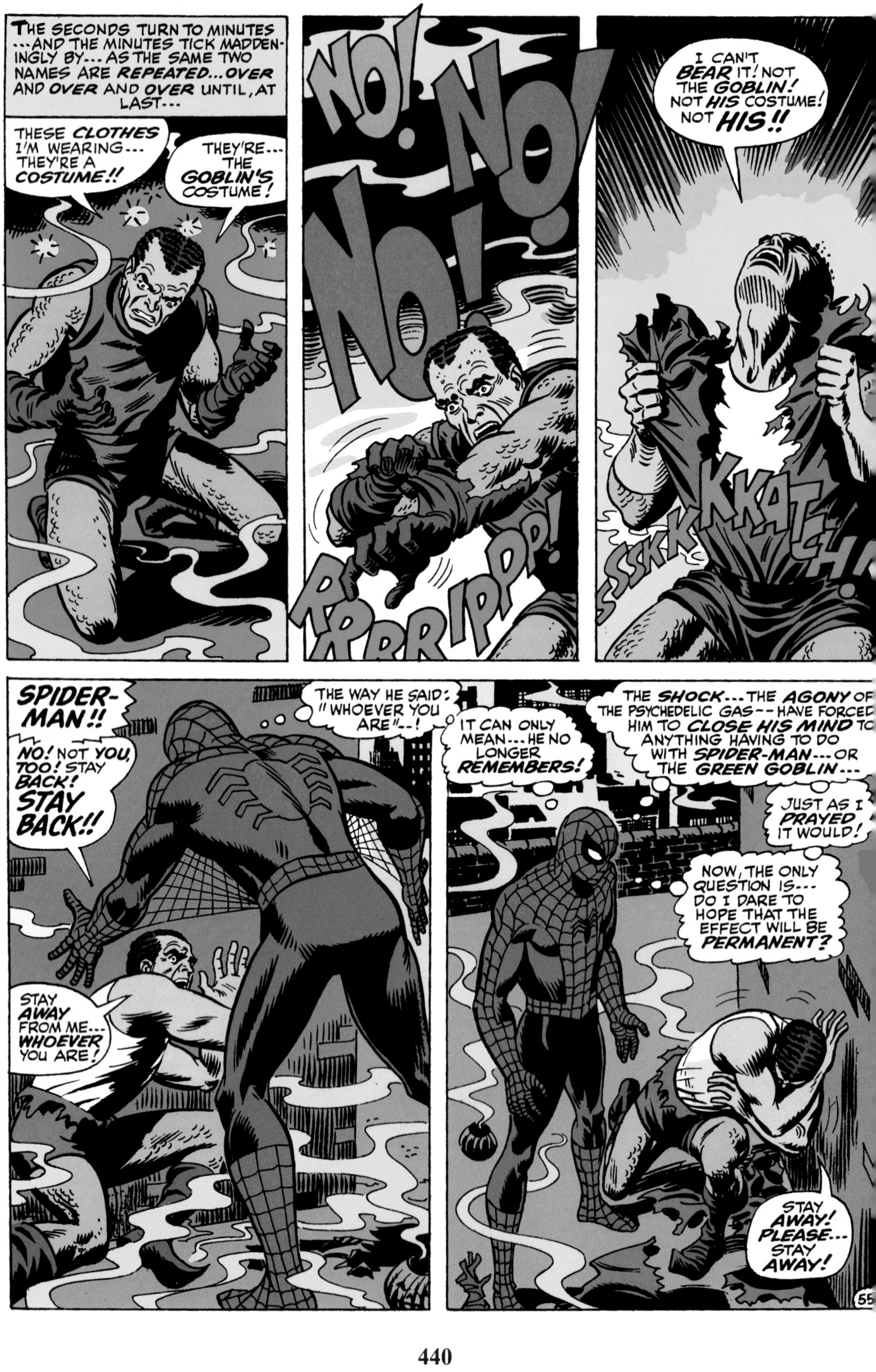
THE SECONDS TURN TO MINUTES ...AND THE MINUTES TICK MADDENINGLY BY... AS THE SAME TWO NAMES ARE REPEATED...OVER AND OVER AND OVER UNTIL, AT LAST...
THESE CLOTHES I'M WEARING... THEY'RE A COSTUME!!
THEY'RE... THE GOBLIN'S COSTUME!
NO! NO! NO! NO!
RRRRIPPP!
I CAN'T BEAR IT! NOT THE GOBLIN! NOT HIS COSTUME! NOT HIS!!
SSSKKKKATCH!
SPIDER-MAN!!
NO! NOT YOU, TOO! STAY BACK! STAY BACK!!
THE WAY HE SAID: "WHOEVER YOU ARE"--!
IT CAN ONLY MEAN... HE NO LONGER REMEMBERS!
THE SHOCK... THE AGONY OF THE PSYCHEDELIC GAS-- HAVE FORCED HIM TO CLOSE HIS MIND TO ANYTHING HAVING TO DO WITH SPIDER-MAN... OR THE GREEN GOBLIN...
JUST AS I PRAYED IT WOULD!
NOW, THE ONLY QUESTION IS... DO I DARE TO HOPE THAT THE EFFECT WILL BE PERMANENT?
STAY AWAY FROM ME... WHOEVER YOU ARE!
STAY AWAY! PLEASE... STAY AWAY!
55

NOW... THE FINAL TEST!

I'LL REMOVE MY MASK... AND SEE IF HE STILL ASSOCIATES PETER PARKER WITH SPIDER-MAN!

NO REACTION!

WHERE HE COULDN'T BEAR THE SIGHT OF SPIDEY... THE FACE OF PETER PARKER HAS SIMPLY RELAXED HIM... HE'S STARTING TO DOZE!

IF MY GUESS IS RIGHT, HE'LL WAKE UP UNABLE TO TALK ABOUT... OR EVEN THINK ABOUT... ANYTHING TO DO WITH THE GREEN GOBLIN... OR SPIDER-MAN!

AND, AT THE SAME TIME, HIS OWN SUBCONSCIOUS WILL SHUT OUT ANY MEMORY OF MY DUAL IDENTITY!

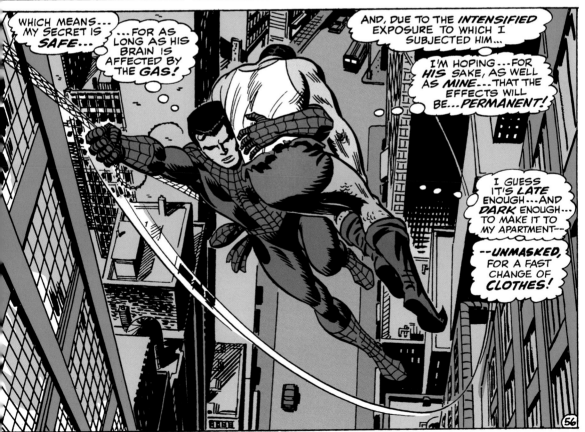

WHICH MEANS... MY SECRET IS SAFE...

...FOR AS LONG AS HIS BRAIN IS AFFECTED BY THE GAS!

AND, DUE TO THE INTENSIFIED EXPOSURE TO WHICH I SUBJECTED HIM...

I'M HOPING---FOR HIS SAKE, AS WELL AS MINE---THAT THE EFFECTS WILL BE...PERMANENT!

I GUESS IT'S LATE ENOUGH...AND DARK ENOUGH... TO MAKE IT TO MY APARTMENT---

--UNMASKED, FOR A FAST CHANGE OF CLOTHES!

56

MINUTES LATER...

NURSE...DO YOU STILL HAVE MR. OSBORN'S OLD *ROOM* AVAILABLE?

OH DEAR! WHAT *HAPPENED* TO HIM?

NOTHING *SERIOUS*, I HOPE! I THINK HE'S JUST *OVER-TIRED!*

PERHAPS HE WAS RELEASED FROM THE HOSPITAL A LITTLE TOO *SOON!*

HIS SON THREW A *PARTY* FOR HIM...AND THE *EXCITEMENT* MUST HAVE BEEN TOO MUCH!

WELL, THE *IMPORTANT* THING IS TO SEE THAT HE GETS PLENTY OF *REST!*

I'LL LOOK AFTER HIM, AND NOTIFY THE *DOCTOR* IMMEDIATELY!

AND *I* BETTER LET *AUNT MAY* KNOW THAT I'M *OKAY!*

BETTER CALL HIS *SON* NOW, NURSE!

IF I KNOW *HARRY*, HE'LL BE *WORRIED* ABOUT HIS DAD!

PETER DEAR! WHY ON EARTH ARE YOU PHONING SO *LATE?*

WHAT? YOU WANTED TO LET ME KNOW...EVERYTHING IS *ALL RIGHT?* THERE'S NO MORE *DANGER?*

WHAT *SORT* OF DANGER?

I'M AFRAID I DON'T *UNDER-STAND!*

OH, *BROTHER!* I REALLY *DID* IT THIS TIME!

WHY DID I HAVE TO CALL HER WHEN I WAS SO *TIRED*---AND NOT *THINKING* CLEARLY?

WHAT AM I GONNA SAY *NOW?*

PETER! IS THERE SOME-THING *WRONG?* WHY ARE YOU ACTING SO *STRANGELY?*

PETER??

NO, AUNT MAY... YOU *MISUNDER-STOOD!* I, EH, REALLY WANTED TO SAY THAT *MR. OSBORN* IS IN NO DANGER! THEY *FOUND* HIM! HE'S *ALL RIGHT!*

OH, YOU *DEAR DEAR* BOY... CALLING ME SO I WOULDN'T *WORRY* ABOUT YOUR *FRIEND'S* FATHER!

HOW VERY *THOUGHT-FUL* OF YOU!

YEAH--- THOUGHTFUL*!!*

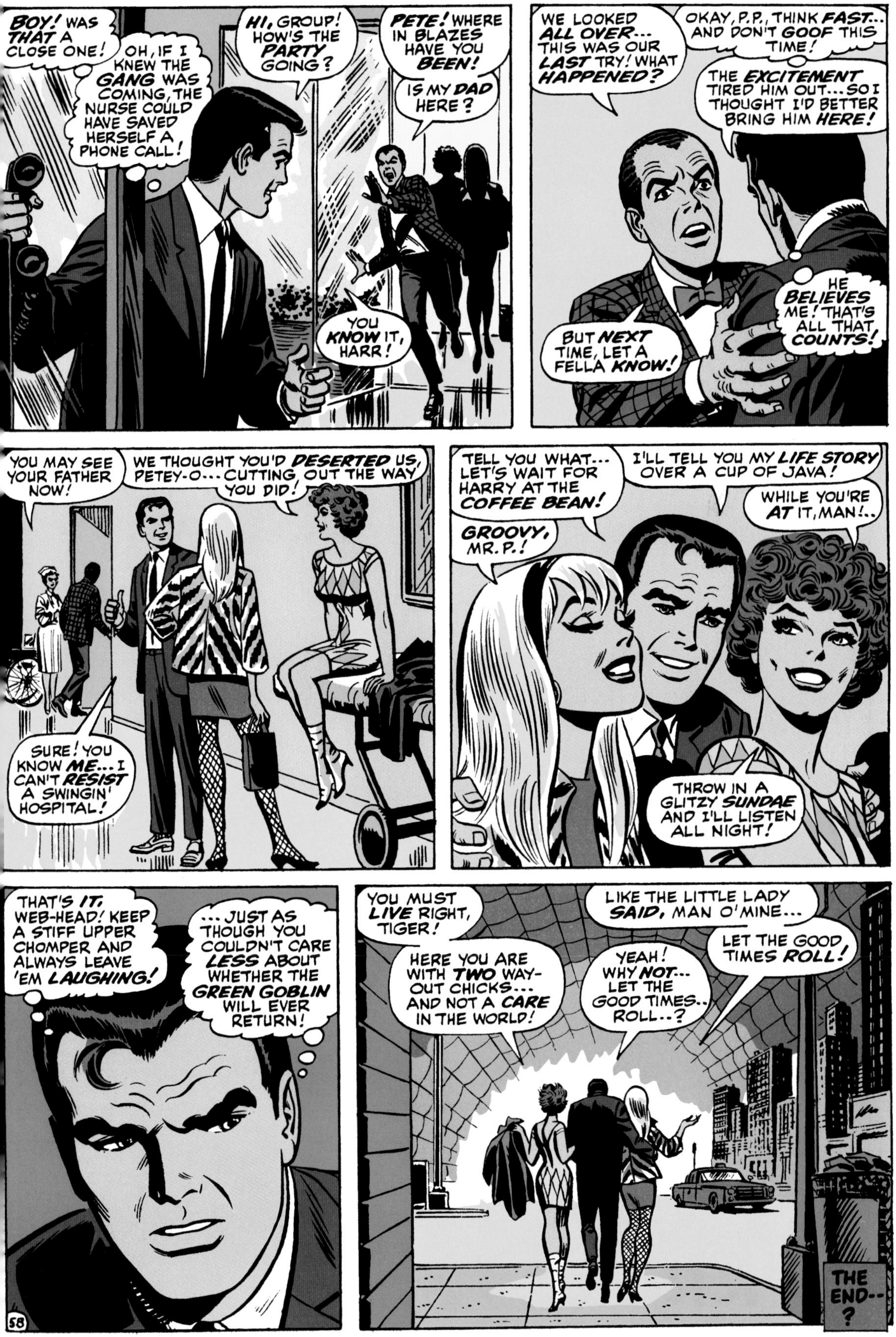

BOY! WAS THAT A CLOSE ONE!
OH, IF I KNEW THE GANG WAS COMING, THE NURSE COULD HAVE SAVED HERSELF A PHONE CALL!
HI, GROUP! HOW'S THE PARTY GOING?
PETE! WHERE IN BLAZES HAVE YOU BEEN!
IS MY DAD HERE?
YOU KNOW IT, HARR!
WE LOOKED ALL OVER... THIS WAS OUR LAST TRY! WHAT HAPPENED?
OKAY, P.P., THINK FAST... AND DON'T GOOF THIS TIME!
THE EXCITEMENT TIRED HIM OUT... SO I THOUGHT I'D BETTER BRING HIM HERE!
HE BELIEVES ME! THAT'S ALL THAT COUNTS!
BUT NEXT TIME, LET A FELLA KNOW!
YOU MAY SEE YOUR FATHER NOW!
WE THOUGHT YOU'D DESERTED US, PETEY-O... CUTTING OUT THE WAY YOU DID!
SURE! YOU KNOW ME... I CAN'T RESIST A SWINGIN' HOSPITAL!
TELL YOU WHAT... LET'S WAIT FOR HARRY AT THE COFFEE BEAN!
I'LL TELL YOU MY LIFE STORY OVER A CUP OF JAVA!
WHILE YOU'RE AT IT, MAN!..
GROOVY, MR. P.!
THROW IN A GLITZY SUNDAE AND I'LL LISTEN ALL NIGHT!
THAT'S IT, WEB-HEAD! KEEP A STIFF UPPER CHOMPER AND ALWAYS LEAVE 'EM LAUGHING!
... JUST AS THOUGH YOU COULDN'T CARE LESS ABOUT WHETHER THE GREEN GOBLIN WILL EVER RETURN!
58
YOU MUST LIVE RIGHT, TIGER!
HERE YOU ARE WITH TWO WAY-OUT CHICKS... AND NOT A CARE IN THE WORLD!
LIKE THE LITTLE LADY SAID, MAN O' MINE...
LET THE GOOD TIMES ROLL!
YEAH! WHY NOT... LET THE GOOD TIMES.. ROLL..?
THE END--?

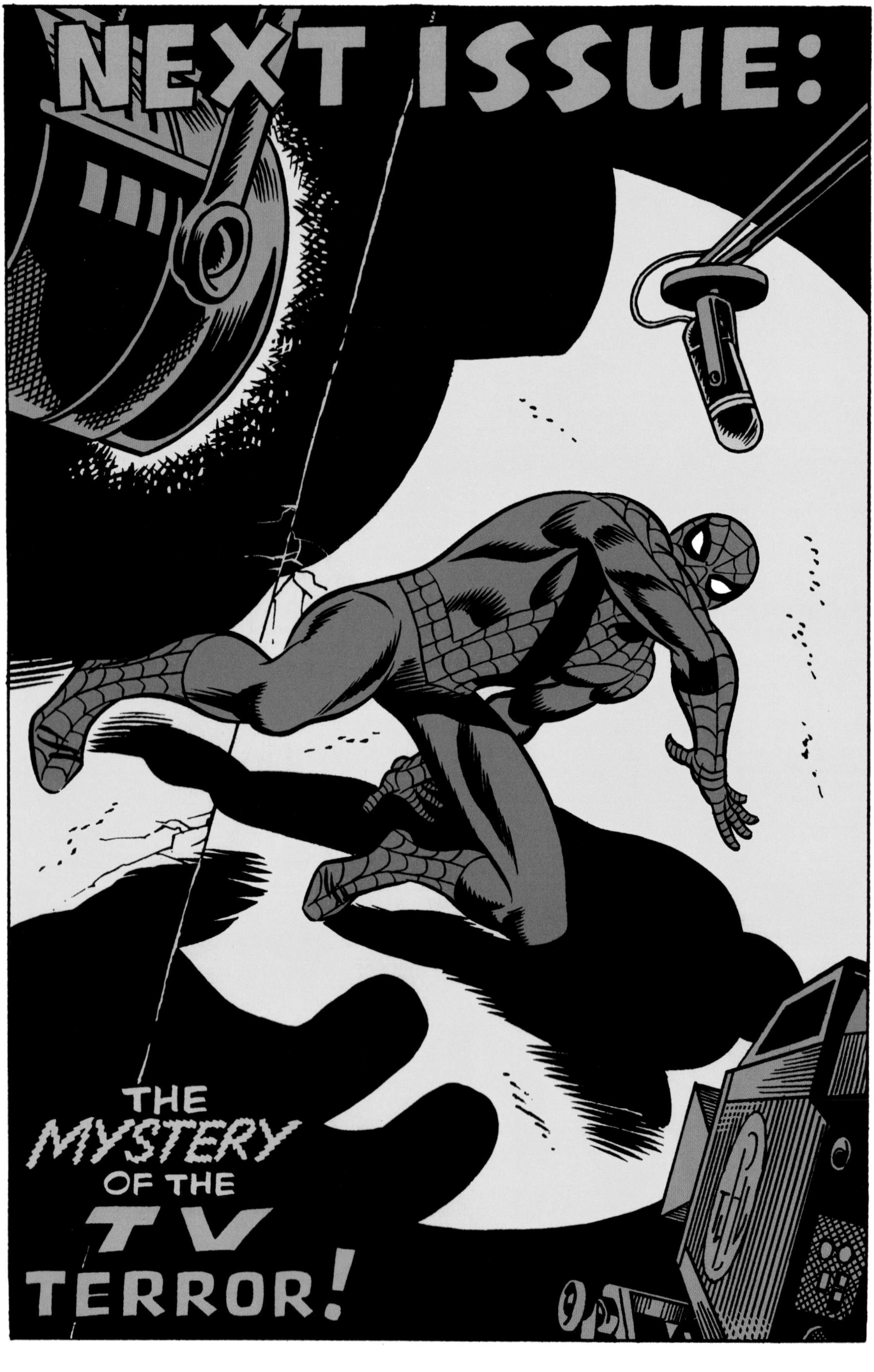
NEXT ISSUE:
THE MYSTERY OF THE TV TERROR!

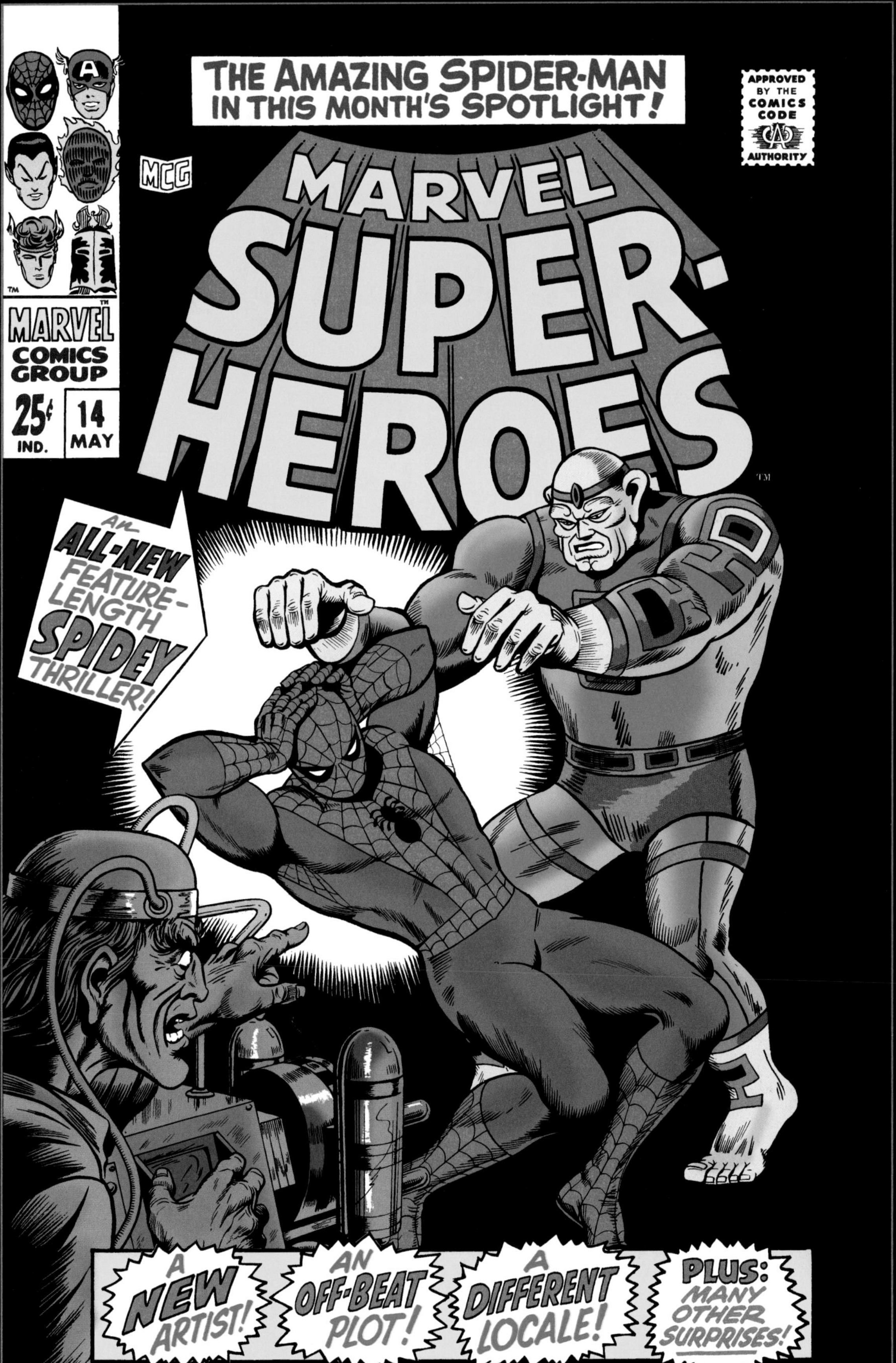

THE AMAZING SPIDER-MAN IN THIS MONTH'S SPOTLIGHT!
APPROVED BY THE COMICS CODE AUTHORITY
MCG
MARVEL SUPER-HEROES
MARVEL COMICS GROUP
25¢ IND.
14 MAY
AN ALL-NEW FEATURE-LENGTH SPIDEY THRILLER!
A NEW ARTIST!
AN OFF-BEAT PLOT!
A DIFFERENT LOCALE!
PLUS: MANY OTHER SURPRISES!

THIS RARE 1968 STORY SHOWCASES FUTURE *AMAZING SPIDER-MAN* ARTIST ROSS ANDRU'S FIRST WORK ON SPIDEY.

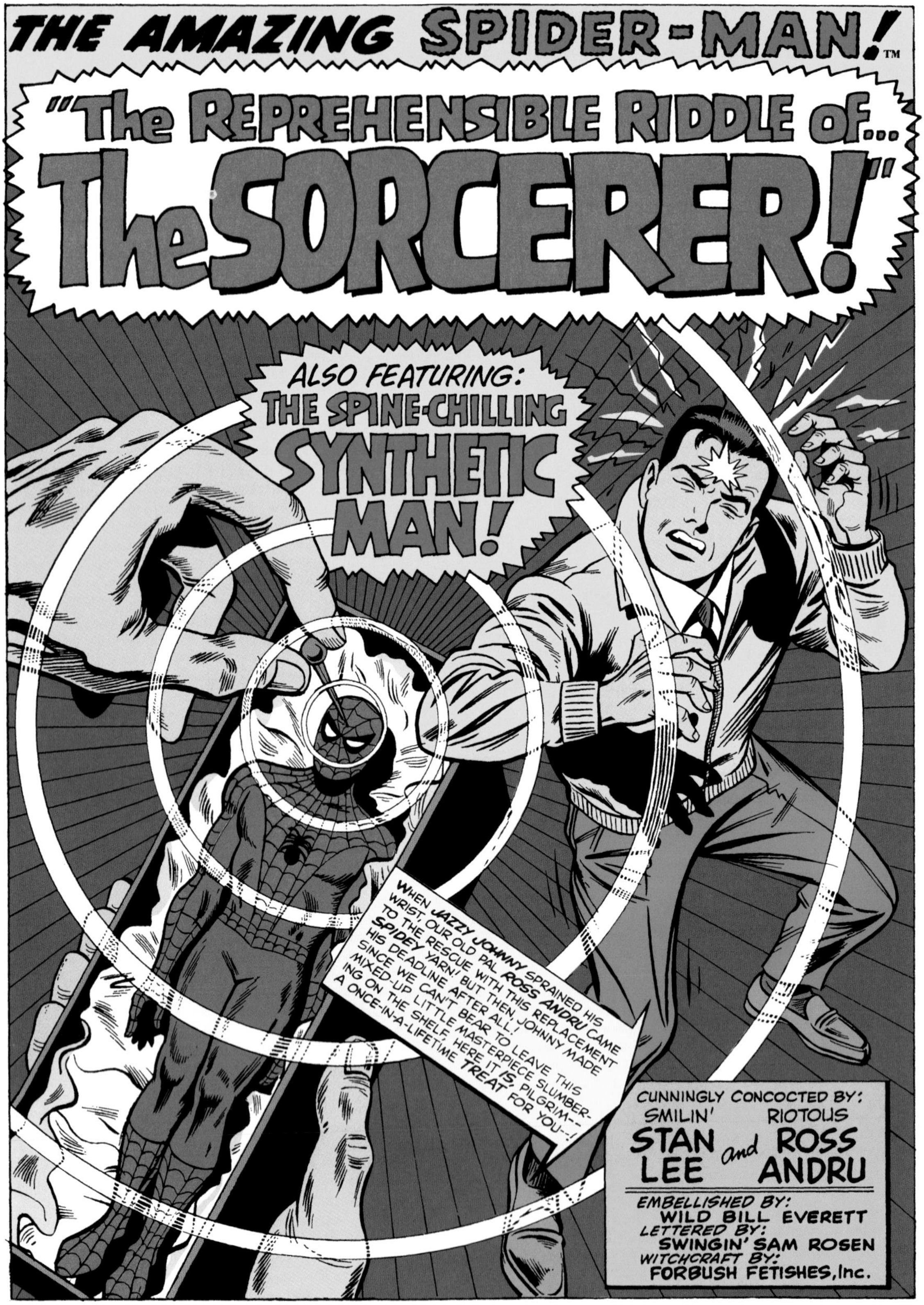

THE AMAZING SPIDER-MAN!™
"The REPREHENSIBLE RIDDLE of... The SORCERER!"
ALSO FEATURING: THE SPINE-CHILLING SYNTHETIC MAN!
WHEN JAZZY JOHNNY SPRAINED HIS WRIST, OUR OLD PAL ROSS ANDRU CAME TO THE RESCUE WITH THIS REPLACEMENT SPIDEY YARN! BUT THEN, JOHNNY MADE HIS DEADLINE AFTER ALL! SINCE WE CAN'T BEAR TO LEAVE THIS MIXED-UP LITTLE MASTERPIECE SLUMBERING ON THE SHELF HERE IT IS, PILGRIM--A ONCE-IN-A-LIFETIME TREAT FOR YOU--!
CUNNINGLY CONCOCTED BY: SMILIN' STAN LEE and RIOTOUS ROSS ANDRU
EMBELLISHED BY: WILD BILL EVERETT
LETTERED BY: SWINGIN' SAM ROSEN
WITCHCRAFT BY: FORBUSH FETISHES, Inc.

MANY ARE THE UNSOLVED MYSTERIES WHICH ABOUND IN THE GREATEST CITY ON EARTH! THE TUMULTUOUS TALE YOU ARE ABOUT TO READ IS THE STARTLING ACCOUNT OF JUST SUCH A MYSTERY---

FROM THE OUTSIDE, IT LOOKS LIKE ANY *OTHER* MIDDLE-CLASS HOME ON A MIDDLE-CLASS STREET, IN THE MIDDLE-CLASS SECTION OF TOWN---

BUT, BEHIND THE GRIM, GREY, SILENT WALLS, WE FIND...

AT LAST! AFTER ALL THESE TORTUROUS MONTHS OF PREPARATION...

I AM *READY!*

...READY TO EXECUTE THE *STRANGEST CRIME* EVER ATTEMPTED!

READY TO *DESTROY* THE VICTIM WHOM I DO NOT EVEN *KNOW*--!

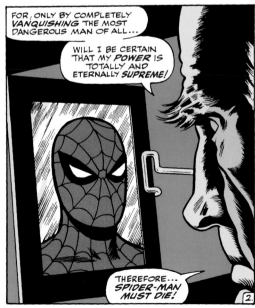

FOR, ONLY BY COMPLETELY *VANQUISHING* THE MOST DANGEROUS MAN OF ALL...

WILL I BE CERTAIN THAT MY *POWER* IS TOTALLY AND ETERNALLY *SUPREME!*

THEREFORE... SPIDER-MAN MUST DIE!

2.

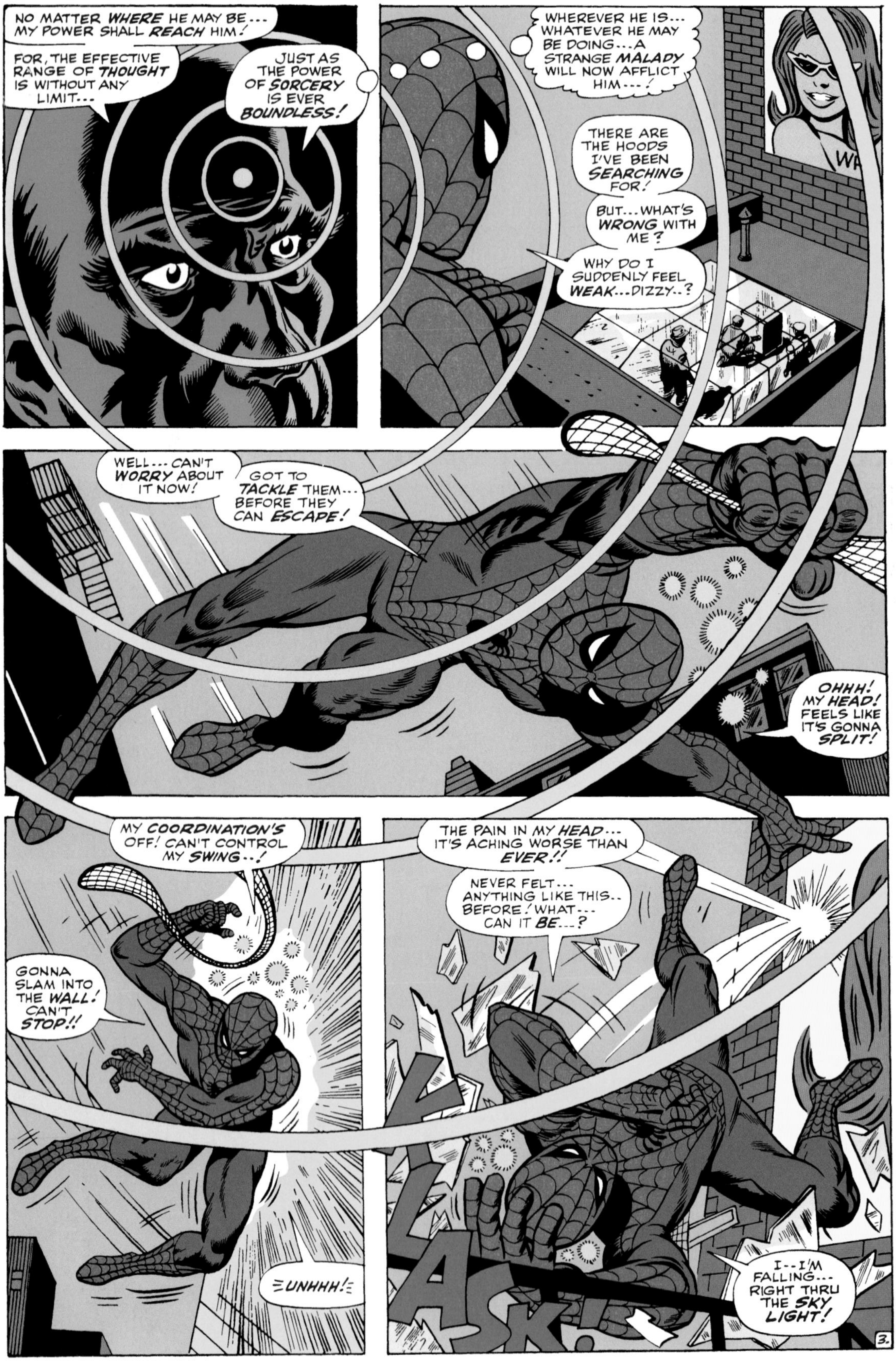
NO MATTER WHERE HE MAY BE... MY POWER SHALL REACH HIM!
FOR, THE EFFECTIVE RANGE OF THOUGHT IS WITHOUT ANY LIMIT...
JUST AS THE POWER OF SORCERY IS EVER BOUNDLESS!
WHEREVER HE IS... WHATEVER HE MAY BE DOING... A STRANGE MALADY WILL NOW AFFLICT HIM---!
THERE ARE THE HOODS I'VE BEEN SEARCHING FOR!
BUT... WHAT'S WRONG WITH ME?
WHY DO I SUDDENLY FEEL WEAK... DIZZY..?
WELL... CAN'T WORRY ABOUT IT NOW!
GOT TO TACKLE THEM... BEFORE THEY CAN ESCAPE!
OHHH! MY HEAD! FEELS LIKE IT'S GONNA SPLIT!
MY COORDINATION'S OFF! CAN'T CONTROL MY SWING--!
GONNA SLAM INTO THE WALL! CAN'T STOP!!
UNHHH!
THE PAIN IN MY HEAD... IT'S ACHING WORSE THAN EVER!!
NEVER FELT... ANYTHING LIKE THIS.. BEFORE! WHAT--- CAN IT BE---?
I--I'M FALLING... RIGHT THRU THE SKY LIGHT!
3.

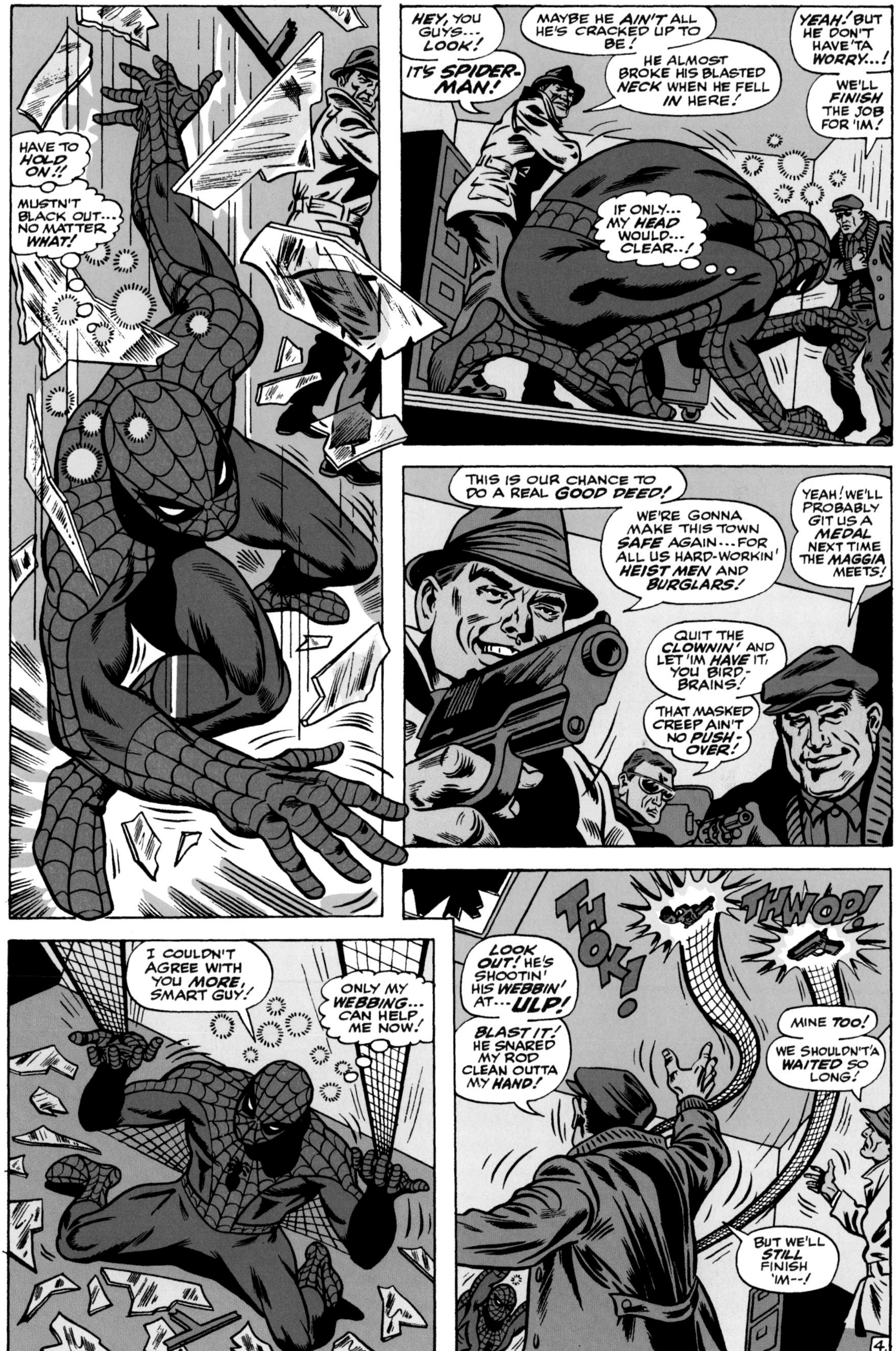
HAVE TO HOLD ON!!
MUSTN'T BLACK OUT... NO MATTER WHAT!
HEY, YOU GUYS... LOOK!
IT'S SPIDER-MAN!
MAYBE HE AIN'T ALL HE'S CRACKED UP TO BE!
HE ALMOST BROKE HIS BLASTED NECK WHEN HE FELL IN HERE!
YEAH! BUT HE DON'T HAVE'TA WORRY...!
WE'LL FINISH THE JOB FOR 'IM!
IF ONLY... MY HEAD WOULD... CLEAR..!
THIS IS OUR CHANCE TO DO A REAL GOOD DEED!
WE'RE GONNA MAKE THIS TOWN SAFE AGAIN...FOR ALL US HARD-WORKIN' HEIST MEN AND BURGLARS!
YEAH! WE'LL PROBABLY GIT US A MEDAL NEXT TIME THE MAGGIA MEETS!
QUIT THE CLOWNIN' AND LET 'IM HAVE IT, YOU BIRD-BRAINS!
THAT MASKED CREEP AIN'T NO PUSH-OVER!
I COULDN'T AGREE WITH YOU MORE, SMART GUY!
ONLY MY WEBBING... CAN HELP ME NOW!
THOK!
THWOP!
LOOK OUT! HE'S SHOOTIN' HIS WEBBIN' AT... ULP!
BLAST IT! HE SNARED MY ROD CLEAN OUTTA MY HAND!
MINE TOO!
WE SHOULDN'T'A WAITED SO LONG!
BUT WE'LL STILL FINISH 'IM--!
4.

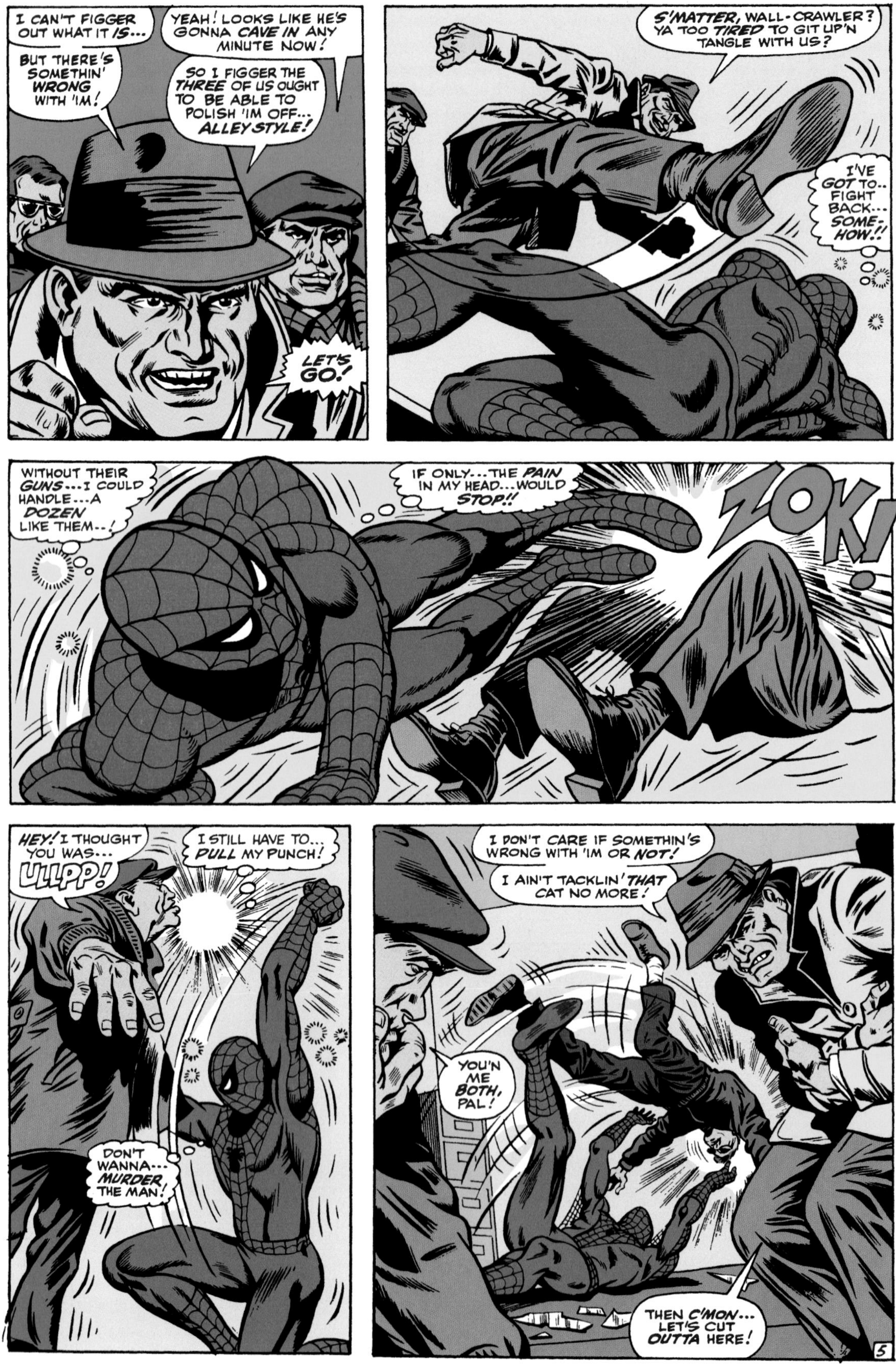
I CAN'T FIGGER OUT WHAT IT IS...
BUT THERE'S SOMETHIN' WRONG WITH 'IM!
YEAH! LOOKS LIKE HE'S GONNA CAVE IN ANY MINUTE NOW!
SO I FIGGER THE THREE OF US OUGHT TO BE ABLE TO POLISH 'IM OFF... ALLEY STYLE!
LET'S GO!
S'MATTER, WALL-CRAWLER? YA TOO TIRED TO GIT UP'N TANGLE WITH US?
I'VE GOT TO.. FIGHT BACK... SOME-HOW!!
WITHOUT THEIR GUNS...I COULD HANDLE...A DOZEN LIKE THEM--!
IF ONLY...THE PAIN IN MY HEAD...WOULD STOP!!
ZOK!
HEY! I THOUGHT YOU WAS...
ULLPP!
I STILL HAVE TO... PULL MY PUNCH!
DON'T WANNA... MURDER THE MAN!
I DON'T CARE IF SOMETHIN'S WRONG WITH 'IM OR NOT!
I AIN'T TACKLIN' THAT CAT NO MORE!
YOU'N ME BOTH, PAL!
THEN C'MON... LET'S CUT OUTTA HERE!
5

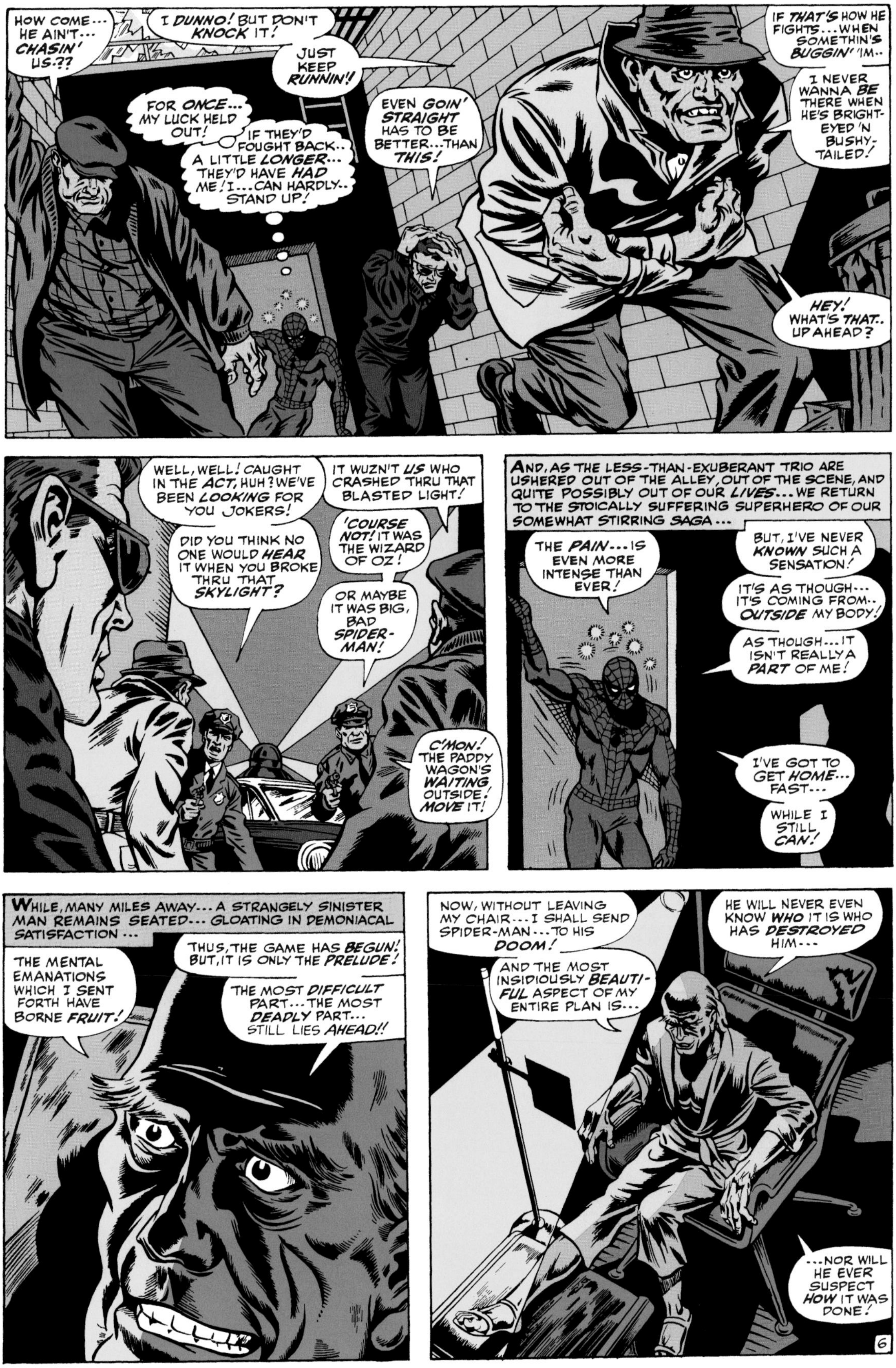
HOW COME... HE AIN'T... CHASIN' US.??
I DUNNO! BUT DON'T KNOCK IT!
JUST KEEP RUNNIN'!
FOR ONCE... MY LUCK HELD OUT!
IF THEY'D FOUGHT BACK.. A LITTLE LONGER... THEY'D HAVE HAD ME! I...CAN HARDLY.. STAND UP!
EVEN GOIN' STRAIGHT HAS TO BE BETTER...THAN THIS!
IF THAT'S HOW HE FIGHTS...WHEN SOMETHIN'S BUGGIN' 'IM..
I NEVER WANNA BE THERE WHEN HE'S BRIGHT-EYED 'N BUSHY-TAILED!
HEY! WHAT'S THAT.. UP AHEAD?
WELL, WELL! CAUGHT IN THE ACT, HUH? WE'VE BEEN LOOKING FOR YOU JOKERS!
IT WUZN'T US WHO CRASHED THRU THAT BLASTED LIGHT!
DID YOU THINK NO ONE WOULD HEAR IT WHEN YOU BROKE THRU THAT SKYLIGHT?
'COURSE NOT! IT WAS THE WIZARD OF OZ!
OR MAYBE IT WAS BIG, BAD SPIDER-MAN!
C'MON! THE PADDY WAGON'S WAITING OUTSIDE! MOVE IT!
AND, AS THE LESS-THAN-EXUBERANT TRIO ARE USHERED OUT OF THE ALLEY, OUT OF THE SCENE, AND QUITE POSSIBLY OUT OF OUR LIVES... WE RETURN TO THE STOICALLY SUFFERING SUPERHERO OF OUR SOMEWHAT STIRRING SAGA...
THE PAIN... IS EVEN MORE INTENSE THAN EVER!
BUT, I'VE NEVER KNOWN SUCH A SENSATION!
IT'S AS THOUGH... IT'S COMING FROM.. OUTSIDE MY BODY!
AS THOUGH... IT ISN'T REALLY A PART OF ME!
I'VE GOT TO GET HOME... FAST...
WHILE I STILL CAN!
WHILE, MANY MILES AWAY... A STRANGELY SINISTER MAN REMAINS SEATED... GLOATING IN DEMONIACAL SATISFACTION...
THE MENTAL EMANATIONS WHICH I SENT FORTH HAVE BORNE FRUIT!
THUS, THE GAME HAS BEGUN! BUT, IT IS ONLY THE PRELUDE!
THE MOST DIFFICULT PART... THE MOST DEADLY PART... STILL LIES AHEAD!!
NOW, WITHOUT LEAVING MY CHAIR... I SHALL SEND SPIDER-MAN... TO HIS DOOM!
AND THE MOST INSIDIOUSLY BEAUTI-FUL ASPECT OF MY ENTIRE PLAN IS...
HE WILL NEVER EVEN KNOW WHO IT IS WHO HAS DESTROYED HIM...
...NOR WILL HE EVER SUSPECT HOW IT WAS DONE!
6

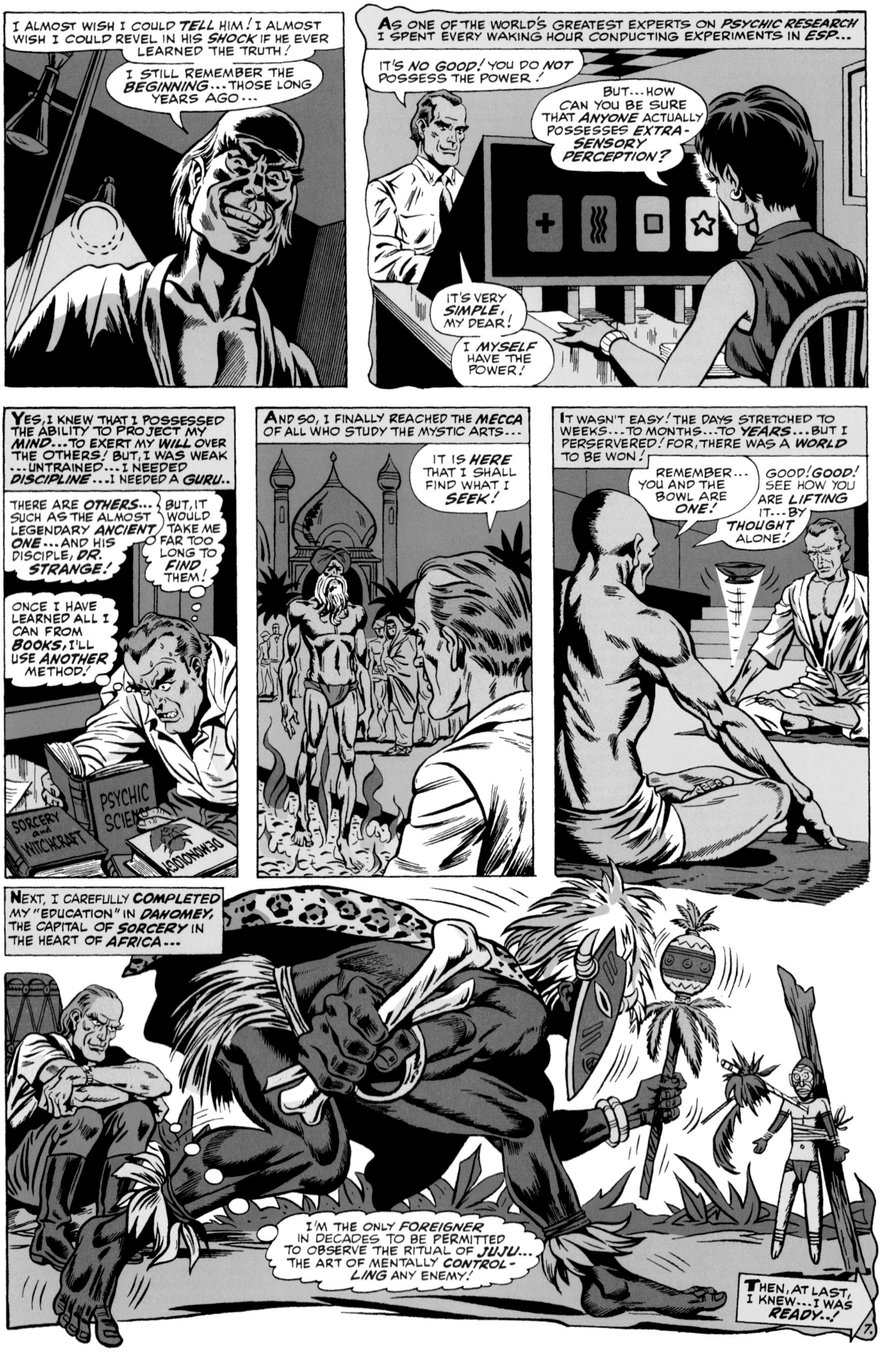
I ALMOST WISH I COULD TELL HIM! I ALMOST WISH I COULD REVEL IN HIS SHOCK IF HE EVER LEARNED THE TRUTH!
I STILL REMEMBER THE BEGINNING... THOSE LONG YEARS AGO...
AS ONE OF THE WORLD'S GREATEST EXPERTS ON PSYCHIC RESEARCH I SPENT EVERY WAKING HOUR CONDUCTING EXPERIMENTS IN ESP...
IT'S NO GOOD! YOU DO NOT POSSESS THE POWER!
BUT...HOW CAN YOU BE SURE THAT ANYONE ACTUALLY POSSESSES EXTRA-SENSORY PERCEPTION?
IT'S VERY SIMPLE, MY DEAR!
I MYSELF HAVE THE POWER!
YES, I KNEW THAT I POSSESSED THE ABILITY TO PROJECT MY MIND...TO EXERT MY WILL OVER THE OTHERS! BUT, I WAS WEAK ...UNTRAINED...I NEEDED DISCIPLINE...I NEEDED A GURU..
THERE ARE OTHERS... SUCH AS THE ALMOST LEGENDARY ANCIENT ONE...AND HIS DISCIPLE, DR. STRANGE!
BUT, IT WOULD TAKE ME FAR TOO LONG TO FIND THEM!
ONCE I HAVE LEARNED ALL I CAN FROM BOOKS, I'LL USE ANOTHER METHOD!
SORCERY and WITCHCRAFT
PSYCHIC SCIEN
DEMONOLOGY
AND SO, I FINALLY REACHED THE MECCA OF ALL WHO STUDY THE MYSTIC ARTS...
IT IS HERE THAT I SHALL FIND WHAT I SEEK!
IT WASN'T EASY! THE DAYS STRETCHED TO WEEKS...TO MONTHS...TO YEARS...BUT I PERSERVERED! FOR, THERE WAS A WORLD TO BE WON!
REMEMBER... YOU AND THE BOWL ARE ONE!
GOOD! GOOD! SEE HOW YOU ARE LIFTING IT...BY THOUGHT ALONE!
NEXT, I CAREFULLY COMPLETED MY "EDUCATION" IN DAHOMEY, THE CAPITAL OF SORCERY IN THE HEART OF AFRICA...
I'M THE ONLY FOREIGNER IN DECADES TO BE PERMITTED TO OBSERVE THE RITUAL OF JUJU... THE ART OF MENTALLY CONTROL-LING ANY ENEMY!
THEN, AT LAST, I KNEW...I WAS READY..!
7.

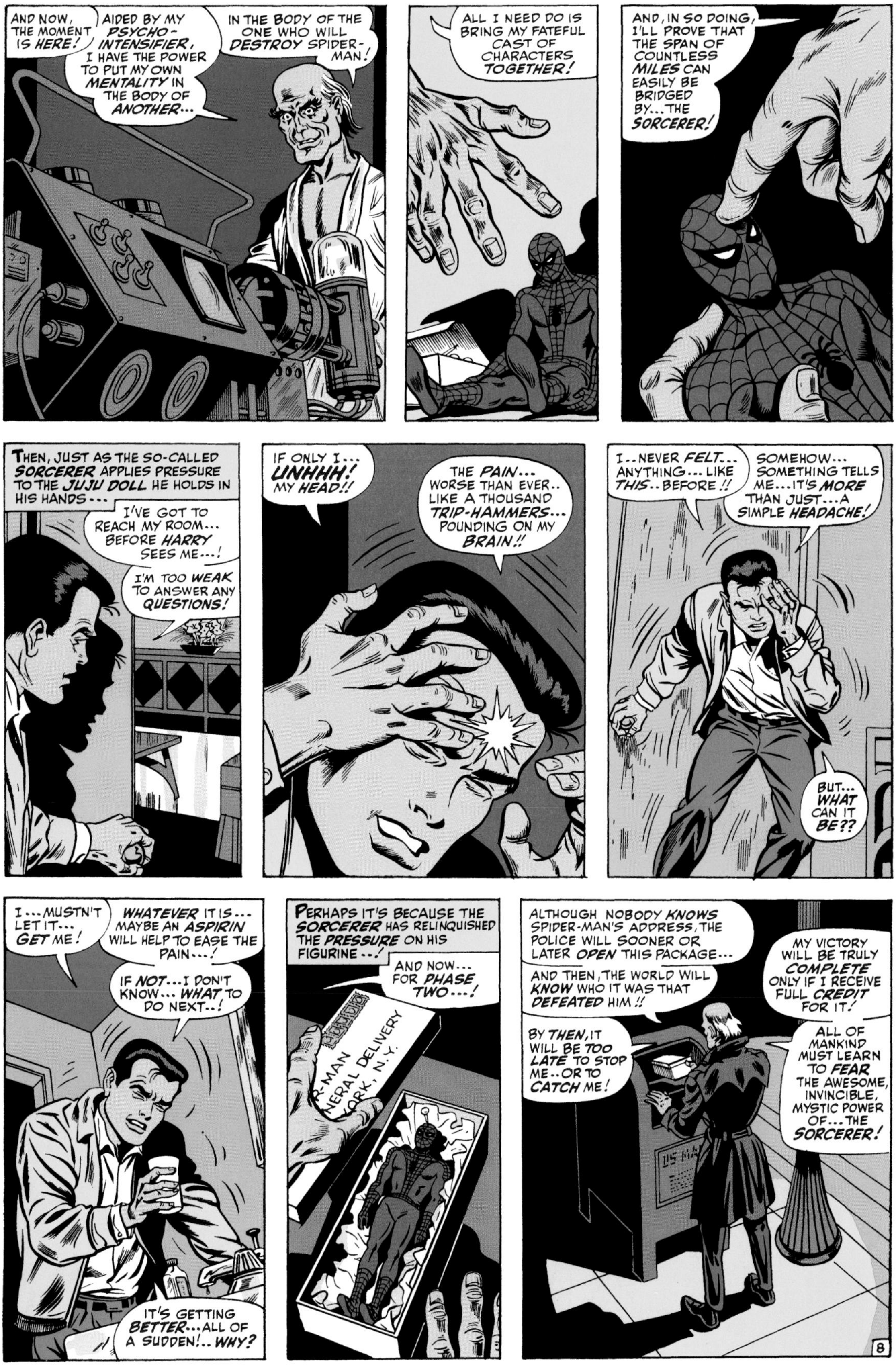
AND NOW, THE MOMENT IS HERE!
AIDED BY MY PSYCHO-INTENSIFIER, I HAVE THE POWER TO PUT MY OWN MENTALITY IN THE BODY OF ANOTHER...
IN THE BODY OF THE ONE WHO WILL DESTROY SPIDER-MAN!
ALL I NEED DO IS BRING MY FATEFUL CAST OF CHARACTERS TOGETHER!
AND, IN SO DOING, I'LL PROVE THAT THE SPAN OF COUNTLESS MILES CAN EASILY BE BRIDGED BY... THE SORCERER!
THEN, JUST AS THE SO-CALLED SORCERER APPLIES PRESSURE TO THE JUJU DOLL HE HOLDS IN HIS HANDS...
I'VE GOT TO REACH MY ROOM... BEFORE HARRY SEES ME...!
I'M TOO WEAK TO ANSWER ANY QUESTIONS!
IF ONLY I... UNHHH! MY HEAD!!
THE PAIN... WORSE THAN EVER.. LIKE A THOUSAND TRIP-HAMMERS... POUNDING ON MY BRAIN!!
I..NEVER FELT... ANYTHING... LIKE THIS.. BEFORE!!
SOMEHOW... SOMETHING TELLS ME... IT'S MORE THAN JUST... A SIMPLE HEADACHE!
BUT... WHAT CAN IT BE??
I... MUSTN'T LET IT... GET ME!
WHATEVER IT IS... MAYBE AN ASPIRIN WILL HELP TO EASE THE PAIN...!
IF NOT... I DON'T KNOW... WHAT TO DO NEXT..!
IT'S GETTING BETTER... ALL OF A SUDDEN!.. WHY?
PERHAPS IT'S BECAUSE THE SORCERER HAS RELINQUISHED THE PRESSURE ON HIS FIGURINE...!
AND NOW... FOR PHASE TWO...!
R-MAN
NERAL DELIVERY
YORK, N.Y.
ALTHOUGH NOBODY KNOWS SPIDER-MAN'S ADDRESS, THE POLICE WILL SOONER OR LATER OPEN THIS PACKAGE...
AND THEN, THE WORLD WILL KNOW WHO IT WAS THAT DEFEATED HIM!!
BY THEN, IT WILL BE TOO LATE TO STOP ME.. OR TO CATCH ME!
MY VICTORY WILL BE TRULY COMPLETE ONLY IF I RECEIVE FULL CREDIT FOR IT!
ALL OF MANKIND MUST LEARN TO FEAR THE AWESOME, INVINCIBLE, MYSTIC POWER OF... THE SORCERER!
8

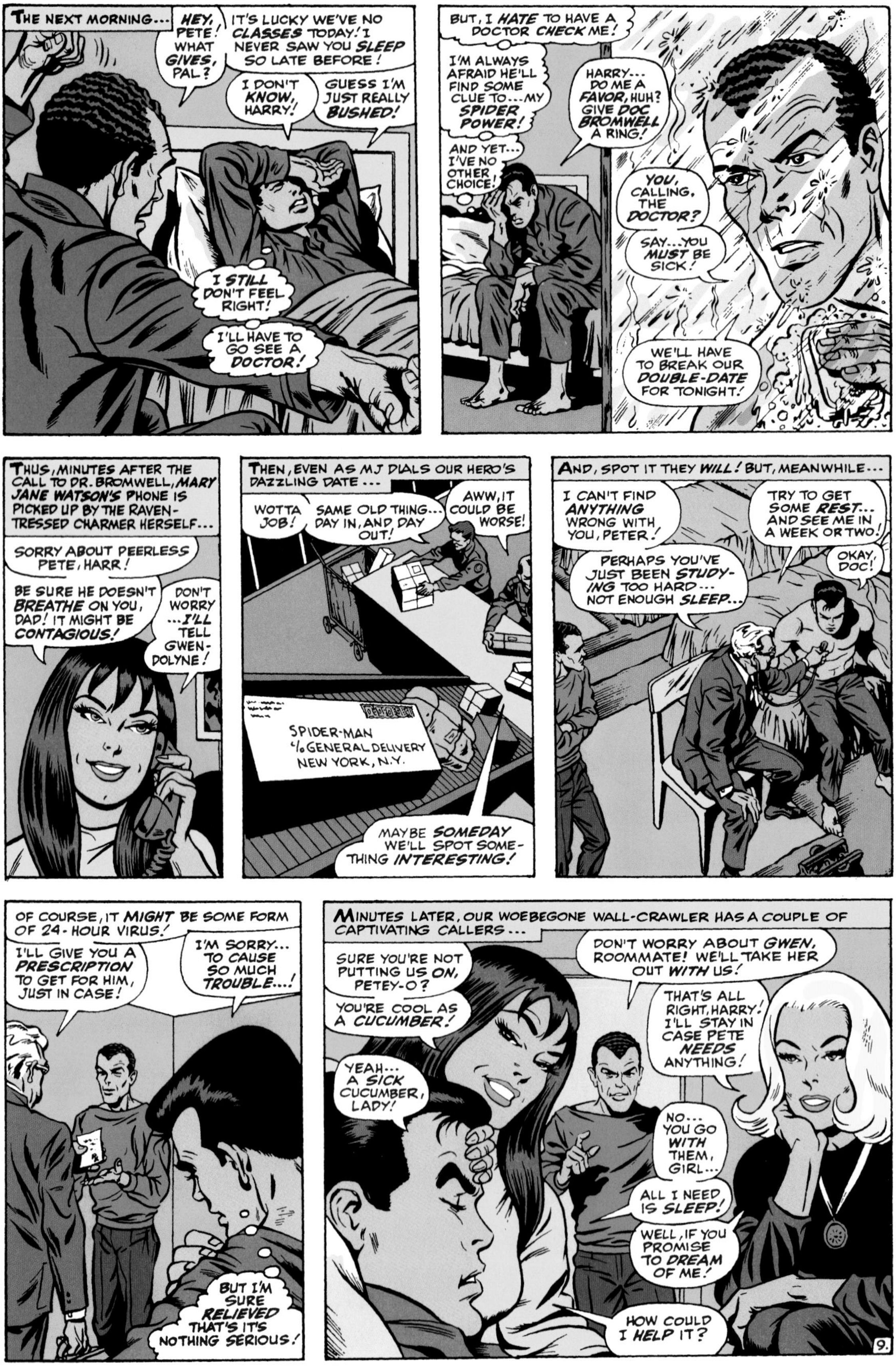
THE NEXT MORNING...
HEY, PETE! WHAT GIVES, PAL?
IT'S LUCKY WE'VE NO CLASSES TODAY! I NEVER SAW YOU SLEEP SO LATE BEFORE!
I DON'T KNOW, HARRY!
GUESS I'M JUST REALLY BUSHED!
I STILL DON'T FEEL RIGHT!
I'LL HAVE TO GO SEE A DOCTOR!
BUT, I HATE TO HAVE A DOCTOR CHECK ME!
I'M ALWAYS AFRAID HE'LL FIND SOME CLUE TO---MY SPIDER POWER!
AND YET... I'VE NO OTHER CHOICE!
HARRY--- DO ME A FAVOR, HUH? GIVE DOC BROMWELL A RING!
YOU, CALLING, THE DOCTOR?
SAY...YOU MUST BE SICK!
WE'LL HAVE TO BREAK OUR DOUBLE-DATE FOR TONIGHT!
THUS, MINUTES AFTER THE CALL TO DR. BROMWELL, MARY JANE WATSON'S PHONE IS PICKED UP BY THE RAVEN-TRESSED CHARMER HERSELF...
SORRY ABOUT PEERLESS PETE, HARR!
BE SURE HE DOESN'T BREATHE ON YOU, DAD! IT MIGHT BE CONTAGIOUS!
DON'T WORRY ...I'LL TELL GWEN-DOLYNE!
THEN, EVEN AS MJ DIALS OUR HERO'S DAZZLING DATE ...
WOTTA JOB!
SAME OLD THING... DAY IN, AND DAY OUT!
AWW, IT COULD BE WORSE!
SPIDER-MAN
c/o GENERAL DELIVERY
NEW YORK, N.Y.
MAYBE SOMEDAY WE'LL SPOT SOME-THING INTERESTING!
AND, SPOT IT THEY WILL! BUT, MEANWHILE...
I CAN'T FIND ANYTHING WRONG WITH YOU, PETER!
PERHAPS YOU'VE JUST BEEN STUDY-ING TOO HARD--- NOT ENOUGH SLEEP...
TRY TO GET SOME REST... AND SEE ME IN A WEEK OR TWO!
OKAY, DOC!
OF COURSE, IT MIGHT BE SOME FORM OF 24-HOUR VIRUS!
I'LL GIVE YOU A PRESCRIPTION TO GET FOR HIM, JUST IN CASE!
I'M SORRY... TO CAUSE SO MUCH TROUBLE...!
BUT I'M SURE RELIEVED THAT'S IT'S NOTHING SERIOUS!
MINUTES LATER, OUR WOEBEGONE WALL-CRAWLER HAS A COUPLE OF CAPTIVATING CALLERS...
SURE YOU'RE NOT PUTTING US ON, PETEY-O?
YOU'RE COOL AS A CUCUMBER!
YEAH... A SICK CUCUMBER, LADY!
DON'T WORRY ABOUT GWEN, ROOMMATE! WE'LL TAKE HER OUT WITH US!
THAT'S ALL RIGHT, HARRY! I'LL STAY IN CASE PETE NEEDS ANYTHING!
NO... YOU GO WITH THEM, GIRL...
ALL I NEED IS SLEEP!
WELL, IF YOU PROMISE TO DREAM OF ME!
HOW COULD I HELP IT?
9.

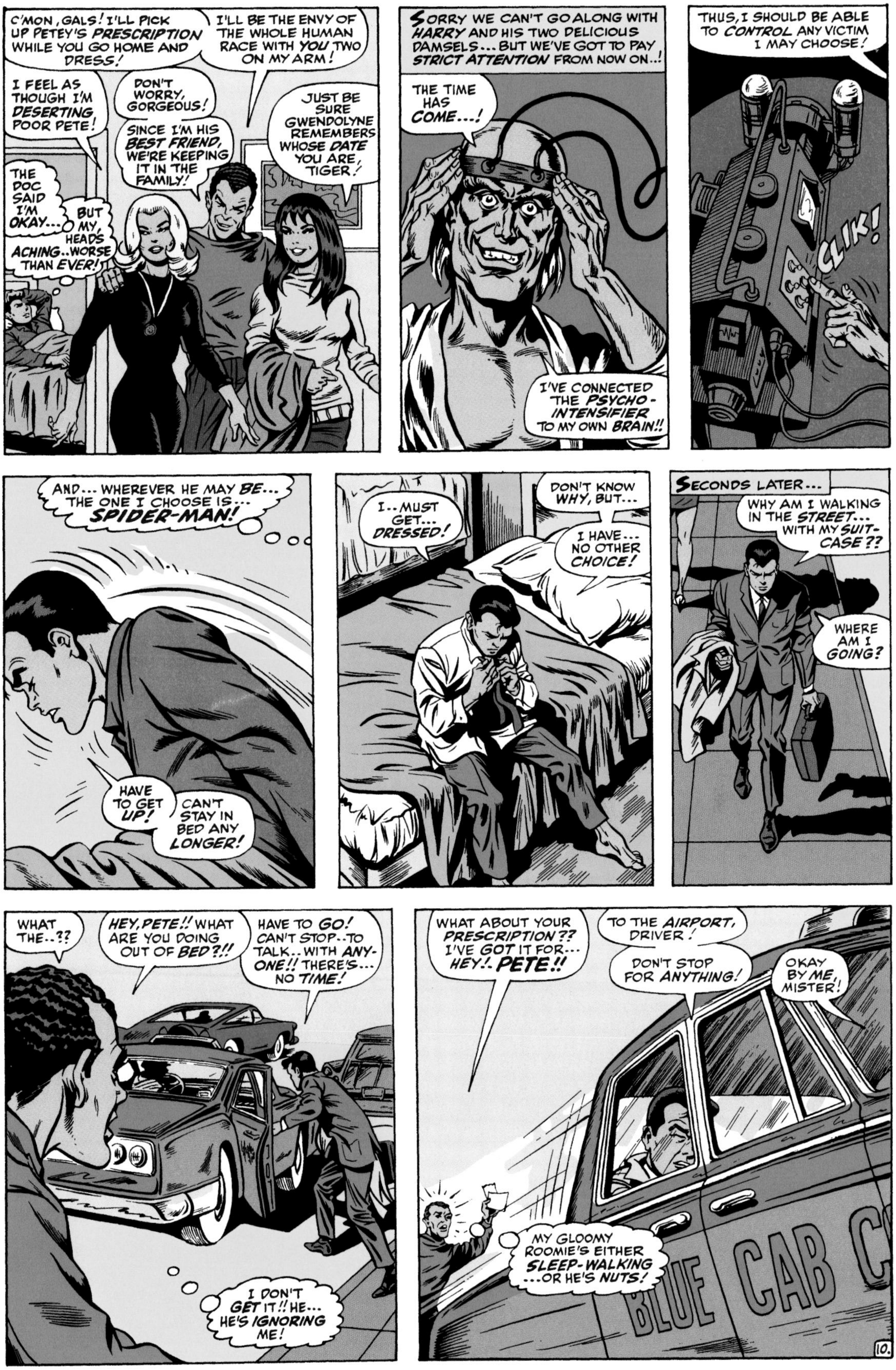
C'MON, GALS! I'LL PICK UP PETEY'S PRESCRIPTION WHILE YOU GO HOME AND DRESS!
I'LL BE THE ENVY OF THE WHOLE HUMAN RACE WITH YOU TWO ON MY ARM!
I FEEL AS THOUGH I'M DESERTING POOR PETE!
DON'T WORRY, GORGEOUS!
SINCE I'M HIS BEST FRIEND, WE'RE KEEPING IT IN THE FAMILY!
JUST BE SURE GWENDOLYNE REMEMBERS WHOSE DATE YOU ARE, TIGER!
THE DOC SAID I'M OKAY...
BUT MY HEAD'S ACHING..WORSE THAN EVER!
SORRY WE CAN'T GO ALONG WITH HARRY AND HIS TWO DELICIOUS DAMSELS...BUT WE'VE GOT TO PAY STRICT ATTENTION FROM NOW ON..!
THE TIME HAS COME...!
I'VE CONNECTED THE PSYCHO-INTENSIFIER TO MY OWN BRAIN!!
THUS, I SHOULD BE ABLE TO CONTROL ANY VICTIM I MAY CHOOSE!
CLIK!
AND... WHEREVER HE MAY BE... THE ONE I CHOOSE IS... SPIDER-MAN!
HAVE TO GET UP!
CAN'T STAY IN BED ANY LONGER!
I..MUST GET... DRESSED!
DON'T KNOW WHY, BUT...
I HAVE... NO OTHER CHOICE!
SECONDS LATER...
WHY AM I WALKING IN THE STREET... WITH MY SUIT-CASE??
WHERE AM I GOING?
WHAT THE..??
HEY, PETE!! WHAT ARE YOU DOING OUT OF BED?!!
HAVE TO GO! CAN'T STOP..TO TALK...WITH ANY-ONE!! THERE'S... NO TIME!
I DON'T GET IT!! HE... HE'S IGNORING ME!
WHAT ABOUT YOUR PRESCRIPTION?? I'VE GOT IT FOR... HEY!. PETE!!
TO THE AIRPORT, DRIVER!
DON'T STOP FOR ANYTHING!
OKAY BY ME, MISTER!
MY GLOOMY ROOMIE'S EITHER SLEEP-WALKING ...OR HE'S NUTS!
BLUE CAB C
10.

BUT ALAS, PETER PARKER IS *NEITHER* SLEEP-WALKING, NOR IS HE *NUTS!* (AT LEAST, SO FAR AS WE KNOW!)

INSTEAD, HE IS FOLLOWING AN *IRRESISTIBLE MENTAL COMMAND,* MADE BY A *SINISTER STRANGER* WHOM HE'S NEVER EVEN SEEN---!

WHAT MADE ME *DO* IT?

WHY DID I BUY AN AIRLINE TICKET TO *NEW ORLEANS??* I DON'T EVEN *KNOW* ANYONE THERE!

CAN I BE... GOING *MAD??*

THEN, A FEW SHORT HOURS LATER...

I FEEL LIKE SOME SORT OF MINDLESS *PUPPET...*

OBEYING THE COMMANDS OF SOME UNKNOWN, UNSEEN *MASTER!*

STILL, I HAVE TO SEE IT *THRU!*

I HAVE TO FOLLOW THIS MYSTIC *PRODDING*...AND SEE WHERE IT *LEADS* ME!

LUCKY I HAD SOME *MONEY* SAVED UP...FROM THAT LAST BATCH OF *NEWS PIX* I SOLD TO JOLLY JONAH!

MIGHT AS WELL ARRIVE IN *STYLE!*

TAXI!, MISTER?

SURE!

ARRIVE *WHERE?!!* WHERE AM I GOING?

I'LL RELIEVE THE *PRESSURE* FOR A FEW MINUTES!

I MUST BE SURE I DO NOT *OVER-TAX* MYSELF... FOR THE *MOMENT OF TRUTH* IS STILL AHEAD!

THAT IS WHEN HE WILL *MEET*... THE *SYNTHETIC MAN!*

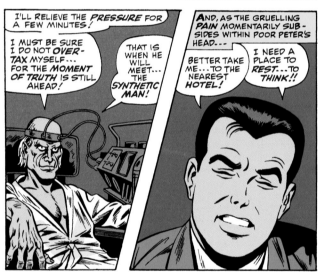

AND, AS THE GRUELLING *PAIN* MOMENTARILY SUB-SIDES WITHIN POOR PETER'S HEAD---

BETTER TAKE ME...TO THE NEAREST *HOTEL!*

I NEED A PLACE TO *REST*...TO *THINK!!*

WELL, IF THERE'S *ONE* THING THEY HAVE PLENTY OF IN NEW ORLEANS... IT'S *HOTELS*...!

NEVER *FELT* THIS WAY BEFORE!

I MADE A *MISTAKE* CALLING DOC BROMWELL!

IT ISN'T A *DOCTOR* I NEED...NOT A DOCTOR LIKE *HIM*, ANYWAY!

I'M RIPE FOR A GOOD *HEAD-SHRINKER!*

GLAD TO HAVE YOU WITH US, SIR!

DO YOU PLAN TO STAY FOR THE ENTIRE *MARDI GRAS?*

I DIDN'T EVEN KNOW THERE *WAS* A MARDI GRAS --!

AS FOR HOW *LONG* I'LL STAY...*YOUR* GUESS IS AS GOOD AS MINE!

YES INDEED! YOU *NEW YORKERS* ARE GREAT LITTLE *KIDDERS!*

11.

SECONDS LATER, WE FIND OUR "GREAT LITTLE KIDDER" DESPERATELY TRYING TO MAKE SOME *SENSE* OF WHAT HAS OCCURRED...

WHY WOULD I SUDDENLY TAKE A PLANE TO *NEW ORLEANS*... FOR NO *REASON* AT ALL?

IT'S AS THOUGH ---I'VE *LOST CONTROL*... OVER MY OWN ACTIONS!

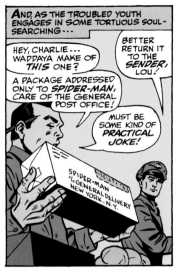

AND, AS THE TROUBLED YOUTH ENGAGES IN SOME *TORTUOUS* SOUL-SEARCHING ---

HEY, CHARLIE... WADDAYA MAKE OF *THIS* ONE?

BETTER RETURN IT TO THE *SENDER*, LOU!

A PACKAGE ADDRESSED ONLY TO *SPIDER-MAN*, CARE OF THE GENERAL POST OFFICE!

MUST BE SOME KIND OF *PRACTICAL JOKE!*

SPIDER-MAN c/o GENERAL DELIVERY NEW YORK, N.Y.

SO, WHILE THE TIGHTLY-WRAPPED *JUJU DOLL* BAFFLES THE POST OFFICE HANDLERS...

SO MUCH *NOISE* OUT THERE... I CAN HARDLY *THINK!*

WHAT'S CAUSING ALL THE COMMOTION?

I SHOULD HAVE *GUESSED!*

THE MARDI GRAS HAS ALREADY *STARTED!*

WELL, I WON'T BE ABLE TO *SLEEP* WITH ALL THAT RACKET...*THAT'S* FOR SURE!

SO I MIGHT AS WELL GO DOWN AND JOIN THE FUN!

GOOD THING I BROUGHT MY *SPIDEY* SUIT ALONG!

WITH EVERYONE *ELSE* IN COSTUME, NOBODY'LL SUSPECT THAT THIS IS THE *REAL* THING!

STRANGE... MY HEAD ISN'T *HURTING* AS MUCH NOW!

WELL... HERE GOES!

UH-OH! I SPOKE TOO *SOON!*

THE PAIN'S *WITH ME AGAIN*... WORSE THAN *EVER!*

AND...SOMETHING SEEMS TO BE... GUIDING MY *FOOTSTEPS*...!

IT'S LIKE I *HAVE* TO WALK... IN *THIS* DIRECTION!

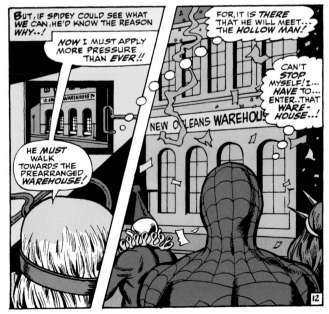

BUT, IF SPIDEY COULD SEE WHAT *WE* CAN, HE'D KNOW THE REASON WHY..-

NOW I MUST APPLY MORE PRESSURE THAN *EVER!!*

HE *MUST* WALK TOWARDS THE PREARRANGED *WAREHOUSE!*

FOR, IT IS *THERE* THAT HE WILL MEET... THE *HOLLOW MAN!*

CAN'T *STOP* MYSELF! I... HAVE TO... ENTER..THAT *WARE-HOUSE*...!

NEW ORLEANS WAREHOUSE

12

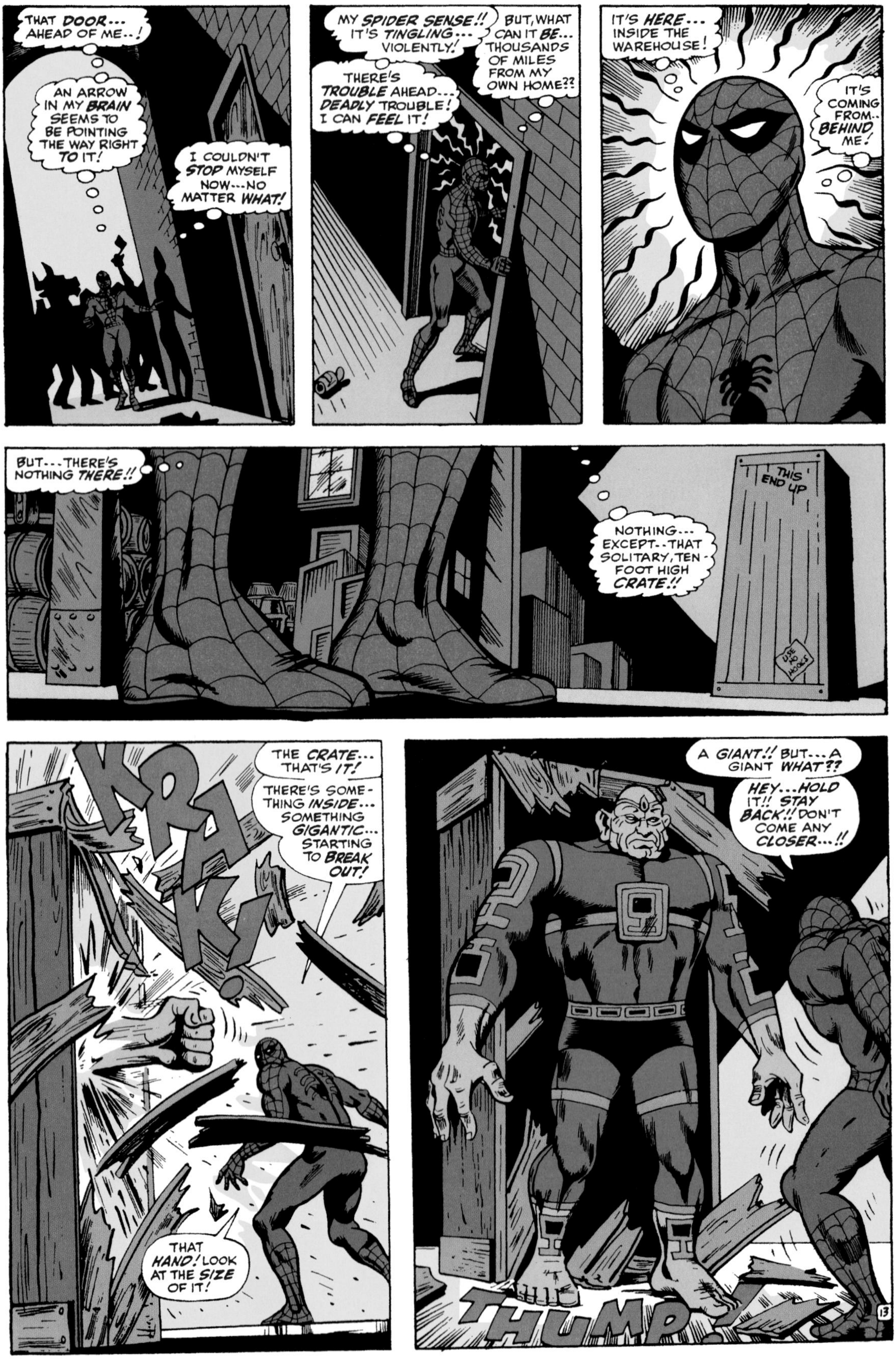
THAT DOOR... AHEAD OF ME..!
AN ARROW IN MY BRAIN SEEMS TO BE POINTING THE WAY RIGHT TO IT!
I COULDN'T STOP MYSELF NOW...NO MATTER WHAT!
MY SPIDER SENSE!! IT'S TINGLING... VIOLENTLY!
THERE'S TROUBLE AHEAD... DEADLY TROUBLE! I CAN FEEL IT!
BUT, WHAT CAN IT BE... THOUSANDS OF MILES FROM MY OWN HOME??
IT'S HERE... INSIDE THE WAREHOUSE!
IT'S COMING FROM... BEHIND ME!
BUT... THERE'S NOTHING THERE!!
THIS END UP
NOTHING... EXCEPT.. THAT SOLITARY, TEN-FOOT HIGH CRATE!!
KRAK!
THE CRATE... THAT'S IT!
THERE'S SOMETHING INSIDE... SOMETHING GIGANTIC... STARTING TO BREAK OUT!
THAT HAND! LOOK AT THE SIZE OF IT!
A GIANT!! BUT... A GIANT WHAT??
HEY...HOLD IT!! STAY BACK!! DON'T COME ANY CLOSER...!!
THUMP!
13

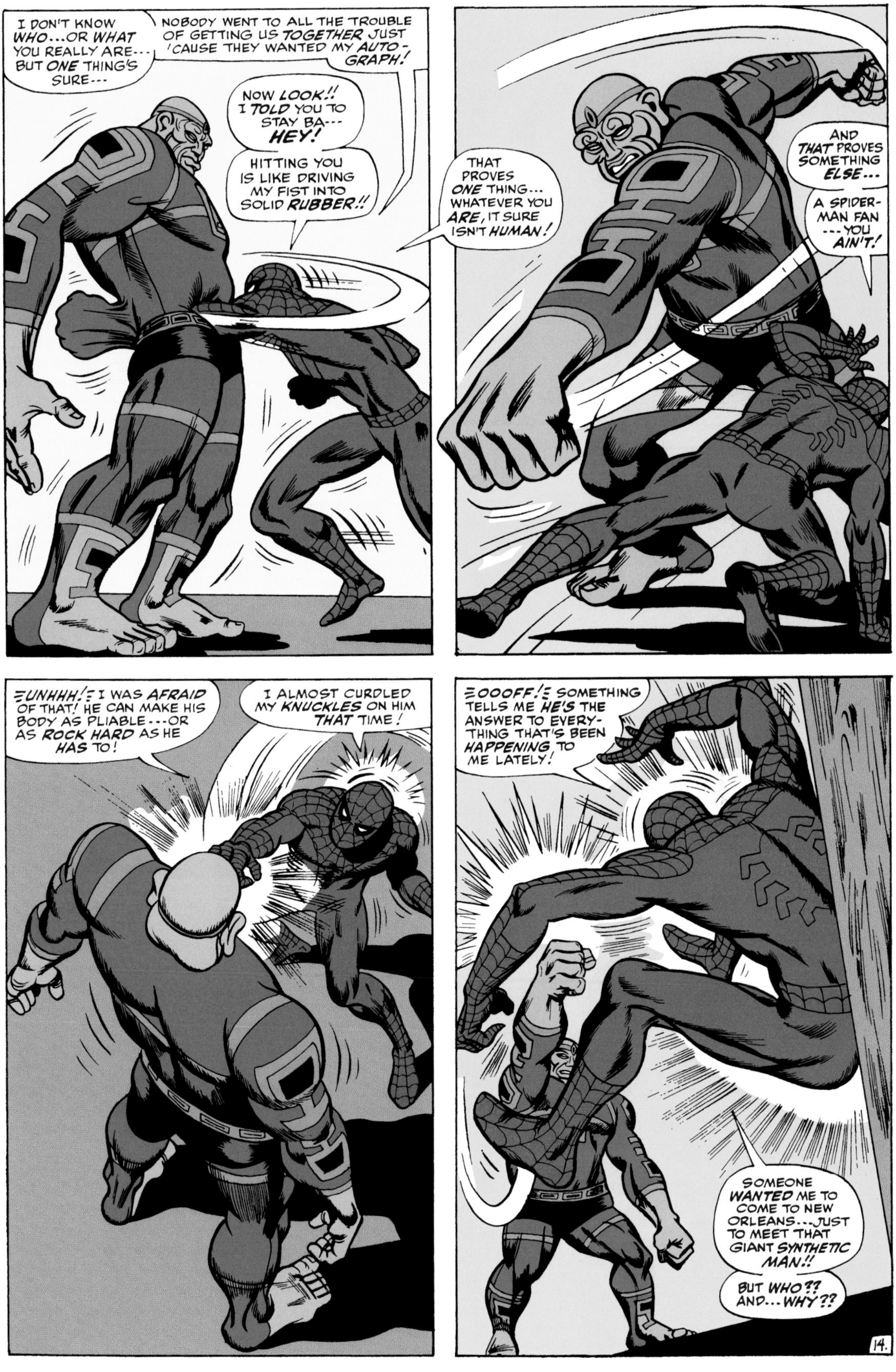
I DON'T KNOW WHO...OR WHAT YOU REALLY ARE--- BUT ONE THING'S SURE---
NOBODY WENT TO ALL THE TROUBLE OF GETTING US TOGETHER JUST 'CAUSE THEY WANTED MY AUTO-GRAPH!
NOW LOOK!! I TOLD YOU TO STAY BA--- HEY!
HITTING YOU IS LIKE DRIVING MY FIST INTO SOLID RUBBER!!
THAT PROVES ONE THING... WHATEVER YOU ARE, IT SURE ISN'T HUMAN!
AND THAT PROVES SOMETHING ELSE...
A SPIDER-MAN FAN ---YOU AIN'T!
UNHHH! I WAS AFRAID OF THAT! HE CAN MAKE HIS BODY AS PLIABLE---OR AS ROCK HARD AS HE HAS TO!
I ALMOST CURDLED MY KNUCKLES ON HIM THAT TIME!
OOOFF! SOMETHING TELLS ME HE'S THE ANSWER TO EVERY-THING THAT'S BEEN HAPPENING TO ME LATELY!
SOMEONE WANTED ME TO COME TO NEW ORLEANS...JUST TO MEET THAT GIANT SYNTHETIC MAN!!
BUT WHO?? AND...WHY??
14.

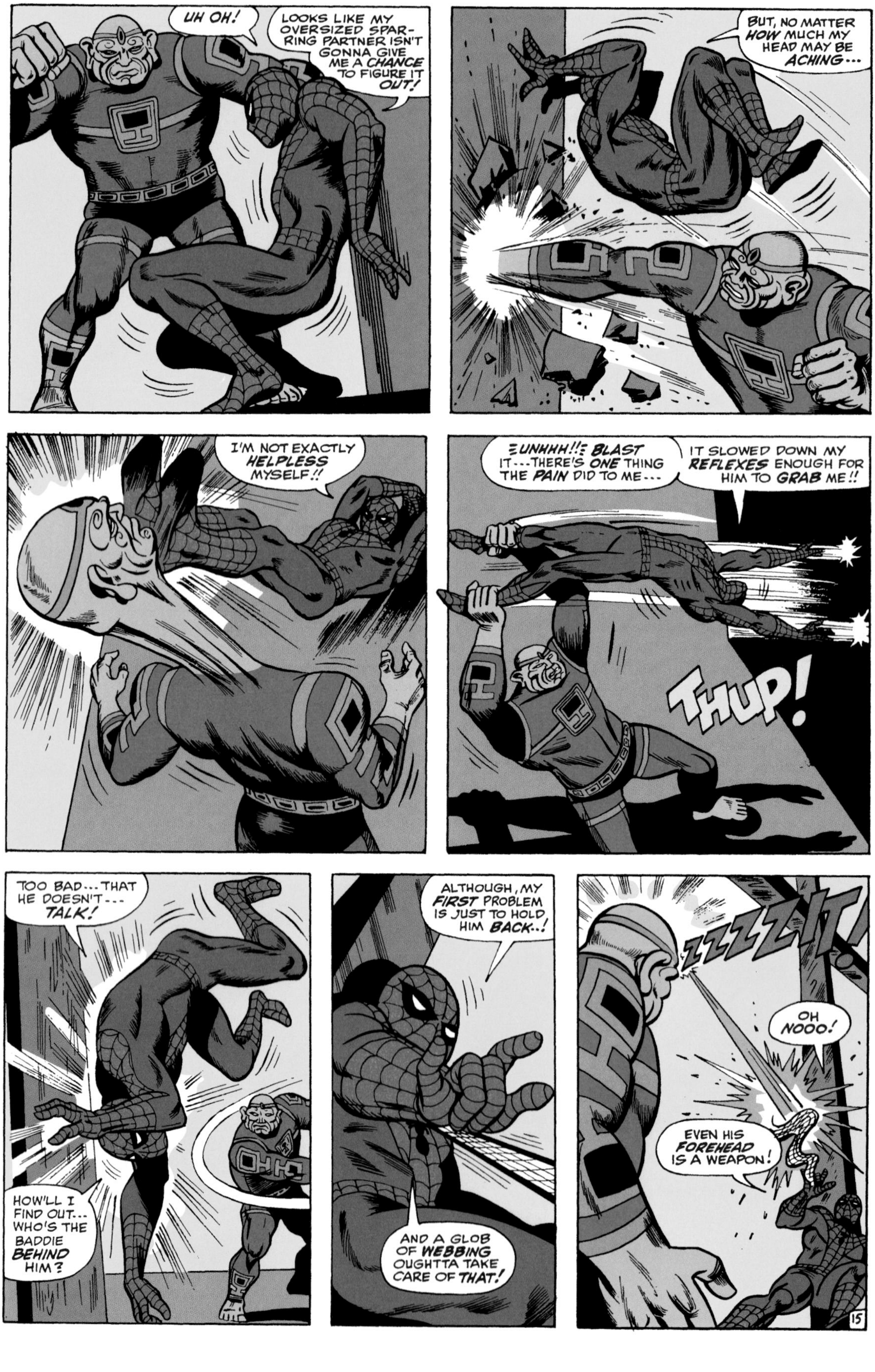
UH OH!
LOOKS LIKE MY OVERSIZED SPAR-RING PARTNER ISN'T GONNA GIVE ME A CHANCE TO FIGURE IT OUT!
BUT, NO MATTER HOW MUCH MY HEAD MAY BE ACHING...
I'M NOT EXACTLY HELPLESS MYSELF!!
UNHHH!! BLAST IT---THERE'S ONE THING THE PAIN DID TO ME---
IT SLOWED DOWN MY REFLEXES ENOUGH FOR HIM TO GRAB ME!!
THUP!
TOO BAD---THAT HE DOESN'T---TALK!
HOW'LL I FIND OUT... WHO'S THE BADDIE BEHIND HIM?
ALTHOUGH, MY FIRST PROBLEM IS JUST TO HOLD HIM BACK..!
AND A GLOB OF WEBBING OUGHTTA TAKE CARE OF THAT!
ZZZZIT!
OH NOOO!
EVEN HIS FOREHEAD IS A WEAPON!
15

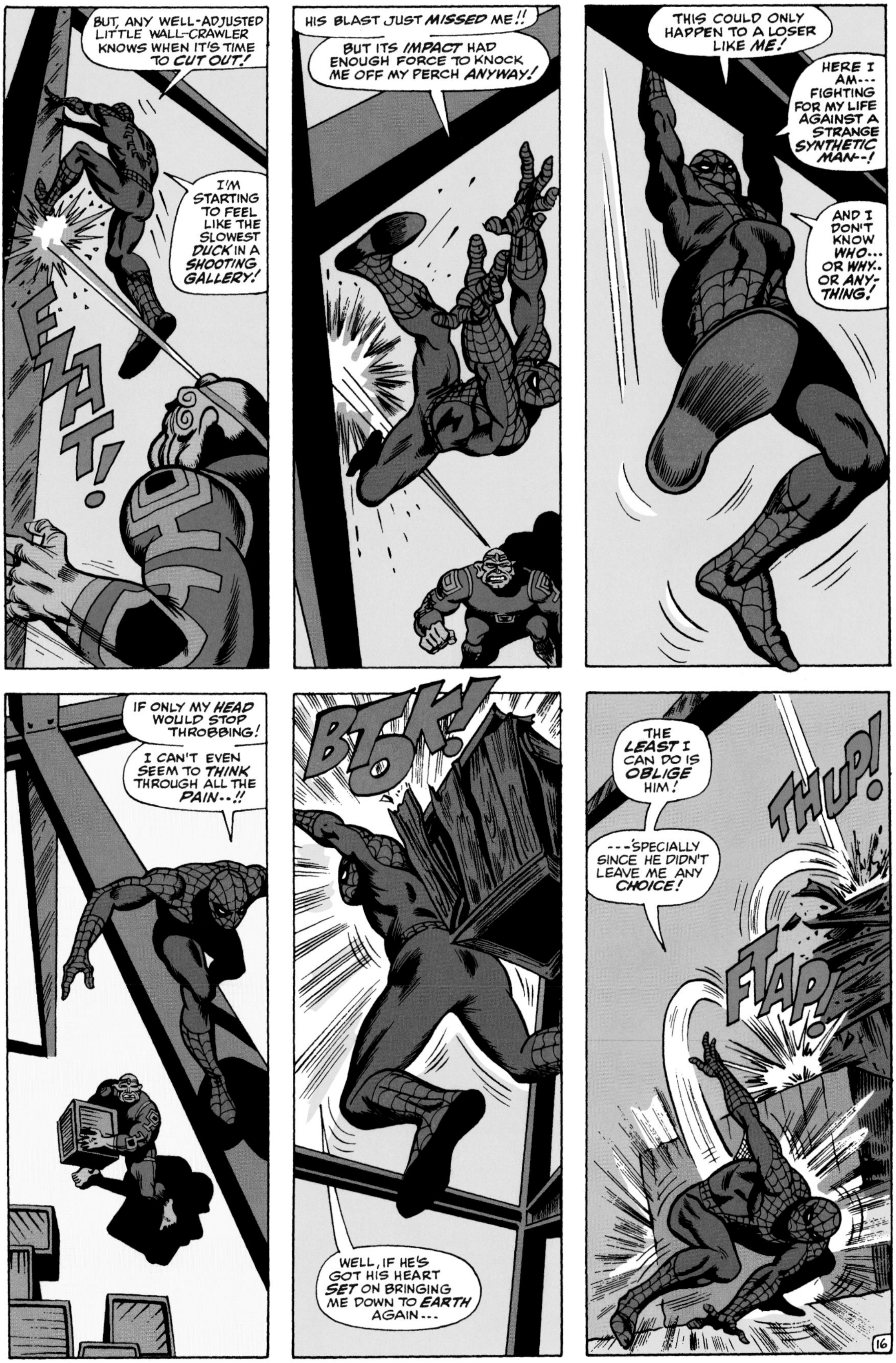
BUT, ANY WELL-ADJUSTED LITTLE WALL-CRAWLER KNOWS WHEN IT'S TIME TO CUT OUT!
I'M STARTING TO FEEL LIKE THE SLOWEST DUCK IN A SHOOTING GALLERY!
FZZAT!
HIS BLAST JUST MISSED ME!!
BUT ITS IMPACT HAD ENOUGH FORCE TO KNOCK ME OFF MY PERCH ANYWAY!
THIS COULD ONLY HAPPEN TO A LOSER LIKE ME!
HERE I AM--- FIGHTING FOR MY LIFE AGAINST A STRANGE SYNTHETIC MAN--!
AND I DON'T KNOW WHO... OR WHY.. OR ANY-THING!
IF ONLY MY HEAD WOULD STOP THROBBING!
I CAN'T EVEN SEEM TO THINK THROUGH ALL THE PAIN--!!
BTOK!
WELL, IF HE'S GOT HIS HEART SET ON BRINGING ME DOWN TO EARTH AGAIN---
THE LEAST I CAN DO IS OBLIGE HIM!
---'SPECIALLY SINCE HE DIDN'T LEAVE ME ANY CHOICE!
THUP!
FTAP!
16

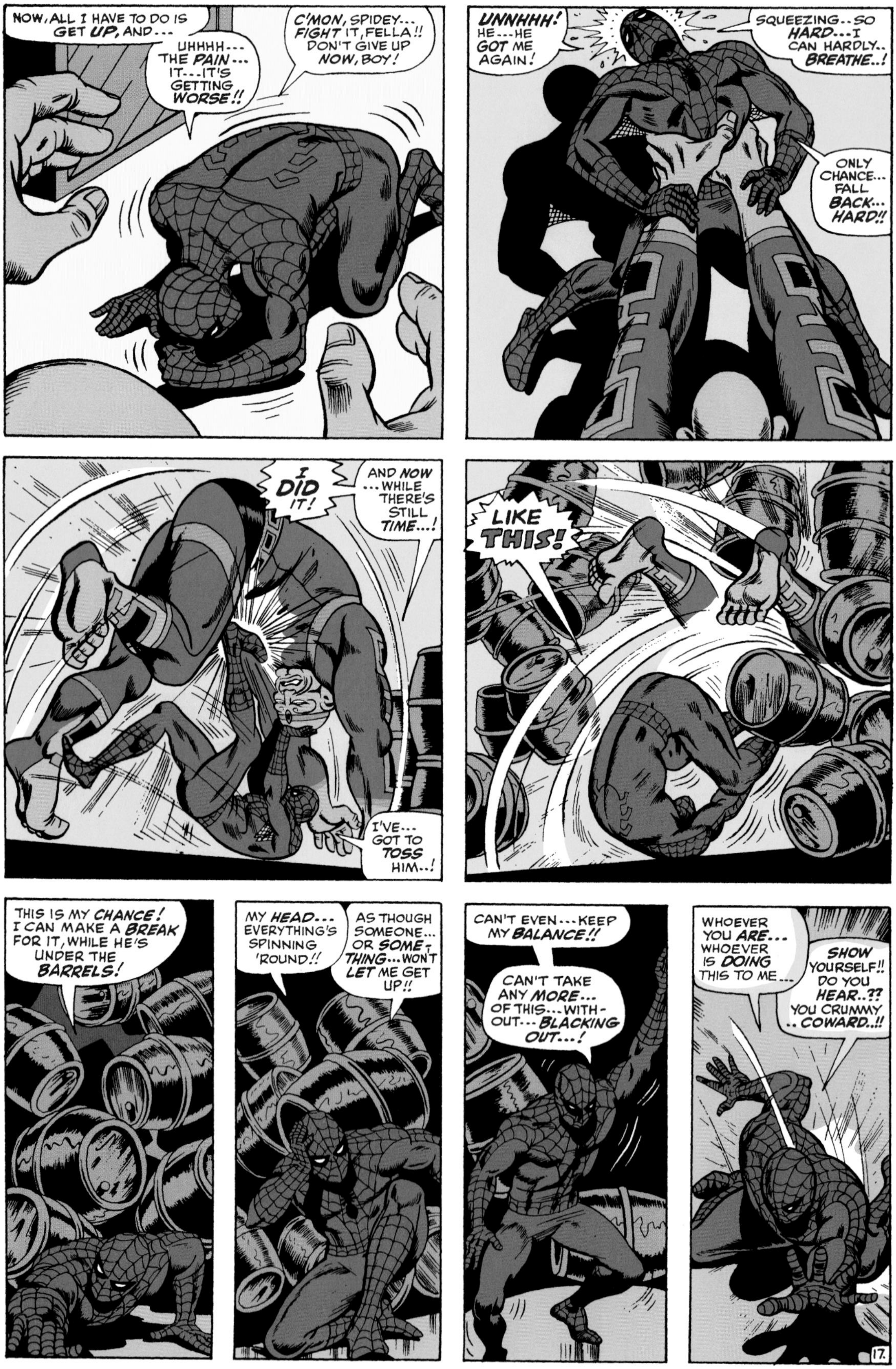
NOW, ALL I HAVE TO DO IS GET UP, AND...
UHHHH... THE PAIN... IT...IT'S GETTING WORSE!!
C'MON, SPIDEY... FIGHT IT, FELLA!! DON'T GIVE UP NOW, BOY!
UNNHHH! HE...HE GOT ME AGAIN!
SQUEEZING..SO HARD...I CAN HARDLY.. BREATHE..!
ONLY CHANCE... FALL BACK... HARD!!
I DID IT!
AND NOW ...WHILE THERE'S STILL TIME...!
I'VE... GOT TO TOSS HIM..!
LIKE THIS!
THIS IS MY CHANCE! I CAN MAKE A BREAK FOR IT, WHILE HE'S UNDER THE BARRELS!
MY HEAD... EVERYTHING'S SPINNING 'ROUND!!
AS THOUGH SOMEONE... OR SOME-THING...WON'T LET ME GET UP!!
CAN'T EVEN...KEEP MY BALANCE!!
CAN'T TAKE ANY MORE... OF THIS...WITH-OUT...BLACKING OUT...!
WHOEVER YOU ARE... WHOEVER IS DOING THIS TO ME...
SHOW YOURSELF!! DO YOU HEAR..?? YOU CRUMMY ..COWARD..!!
17.

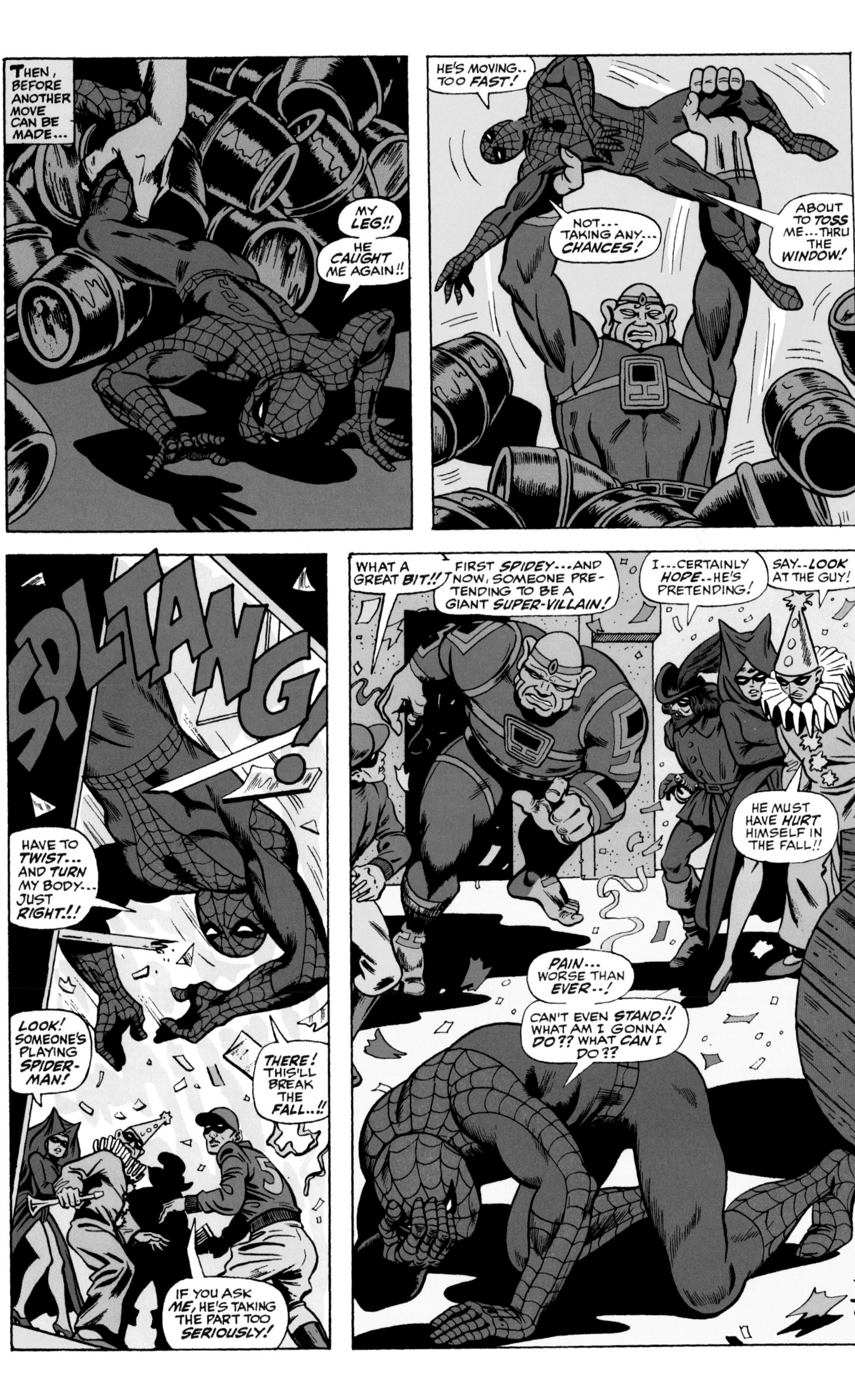
THEN, BEFORE ANOTHER MOVE CAN BE MADE...
MY LEG!! HE CAUGHT ME AGAIN!!
HE'S MOVING.. TOO FAST!
NOT... TAKING ANY... CHANCES!
ABOUT TO TOSS ME... THRU THE WINDOW!
SPLTANG!
HAVE TO TWIST... AND TURN MY BODY... JUST RIGHT!!
LOOK! SOMEONE'S PLAYING SPIDER-MAN!
THERE! THIS'LL BREAK THE FALL..!!
IF YOU ASK ME, HE'S TAKING THE PART TOO SERIOUSLY!
WHAT A GREAT BIT!!
FIRST SPIDEY...AND NOW, SOMEONE PRE-TENDING TO BE A GIANT SUPER-VILLAIN!
I...CERTAINLY HOPE..HE'S PRETENDING!
SAY--LOOK AT THE GUY!
HE MUST HAVE HURT HIMSELF IN THE FALL!!
PAIN... WORSE THAN EVER--!
CAN'T EVEN STAND!! WHAT AM I GONNA DO?? WHAT CAN I DO??
18.

AND, HALF-WAY ACROSS THE CONTI-NENT, A STRANGELY-SMIRKING SORCERER WHISPERS A TRIUMPHANT REPLY...

YOU CAN PREPARE... TO DIE!

NOTHING CAN SAVE YOU NOW!

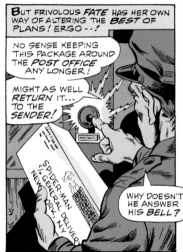

BUT FRIVOLOUS FATE HAS HER OWN WAY OF ALTERING THE BEST OF PLANS! ERGO--!

NO SENSE KEEPING THIS PACKAGE AROUND THE POST OFFICE ANY LONGER!

MIGHT AS WELL RETURN IT... TO THE SENDER!

SPIDER-MAN C/O GENERAL DELIVERY NEW YORK, N.Y.

WHY DOESN'T HE ANSWER HIS BELL?

ALAS, THE PUZZLED POSTMAN HAS NO WAY OF KNOWING THAT THE SHRILL RING OF THE DOORBELL HAS CHANGED THE MYSTIC PITCH OF THE SORCERER'S PSYCHO-INTENSIFIER...

EEEEEEEE EEEE

...CHANGED IT JUST ENOUGH TO CAUSE A DEADLY MENTAL FEEDBACK...

...ONE WHICH NO HUMAN BRAIN ON EARTH CAN HAVE THE POWER TO WITH-STAND!!

NOT EVEN THE DEMONIAC BRAIN OF... THE SORCERER.!!

THEN, AS THE GAUNT, GHOULISH FIGURE SLOWLY GROWS LIMP...AND SILENT...

IT'S JUST A MUSCLE SPASM!

I'LL BE OKAY IN A MINUTE!

BUT...IT DOESN'T LOOK AS THOUGH... I'VE GOT THAT LONG!

HE'S COMING CLOSER...TO FINISH ME OFF..!

CAN'T JUST LIE HERE AND TAKE IT!

C'MON, SPIDEY! YOU CAN DO IT!

YOU'VE... GOT TO... DO IT!

I'VE GOT TO GET UP... GOT TO FIGHT BACK...SOME-HOW!

BUT, JUST AS THE YOUTHFUL ADVENTURER GIRDS HIMSELF FOR ONE FINAL, SUPREME EFFORT...

SOMETHING'S HAPPENED!!...HE'S GONE RIGID!!

HE'S LETTING THE CART FALL TO THE GROUND!

CAN IT BE... SOME SORT OF TRICK...??

19.

464

MAYBE HE WANTED TO THROW ME OFF-GUARD!

HE'S STILL *HEADING* THIS WAY---!

WELL, LET HIM *COME!* MY SPASM'S GONE...!

I DON'T *GET* IT!

HE WALKED RIGHT *PAST* ME...LIKE I WASN'T *HERE!*

HE'S MOVING WITHOUT *SENSE*... WITHOUT *PURPOSE*... LIKE A *SLEEP-WALKER!*

HE'S LIKE SOME GREAT, LIVING *MACHINE*...SUDDENLY GONE OUT OF CONTROL!

IT'S AS THOUGH HE HAD NEVER *FOUGHT* ME... NEVER EVEN *SEEN* ME!

AND...MY *HEAD!* IT'S *CLEAR* AGAIN! THE *ACHE* IS GONE!

IT HAPPENED AT THE *SAME* INSTANT AS *HIS* ABOUT-FACE!

BUT *WHY??*

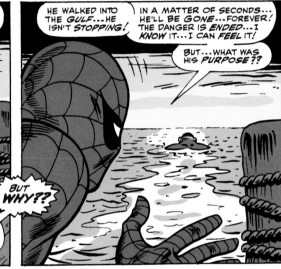

HE WALKED INTO THE *GULF*...HE ISN'T *STOPPING!*

IN A MATTER OF SECONDS... HE'LL BE *GONE*...FOREVER! THE DANGER IS *ENDED*...I *KNOW* IT...I CAN *FEEL* IT!

BUT...WHAT WAS HIS *PURPOSE??*

WEARY AND MYSTIFIED, THE COSTUMED TEENAGER TURNS, HEADING FOR HIS HOTEL ROOM, AND THE LONG JOURNEY HOME!

I'VE FOUGHT ONE OF THE MOST DESPERATE BATTLES OF MY *LIFE*...AGAINST A HIDDEN, NAMELESS FOE!

AND, IN SOME WAY THAT I DON'T UNDERSTAND... THAT I MAY *NEVER* UNDER-STAND---I SEEM TO *KNOW* THAT THE VICTORY IS... *MINE!*

THE END

20

465

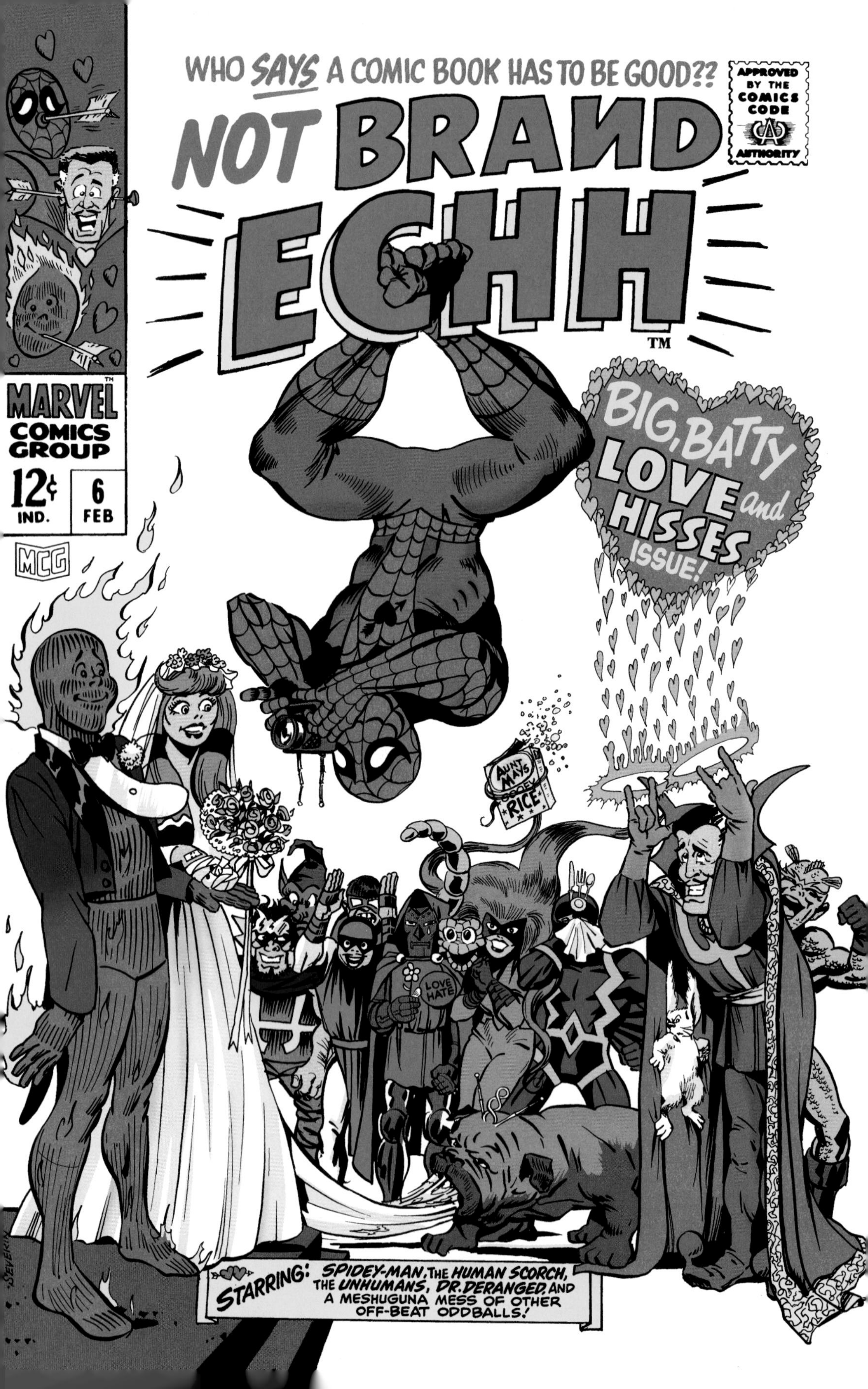
WHO SAYS A COMIC BOOK HAS TO BE GOOD??
NOT BRAND ECHH
TM
APPROVED BY THE COMICS CODE AUTHORITY
MARVEL COMICS GROUP
12¢ IND.
6 FEB
MCG
BIG, BATTY LOVE and HISSES ISSUE!
AUNT MAY'S
RICE
LOVE HATE
STARRING: SPIDEY-MAN, THE HUMAN SCORCH, THE UNHUMANS, DR. DERANGED, AND A MESHUGUNA MESS OF OTHER OFF-BEAT ODDBALLS!

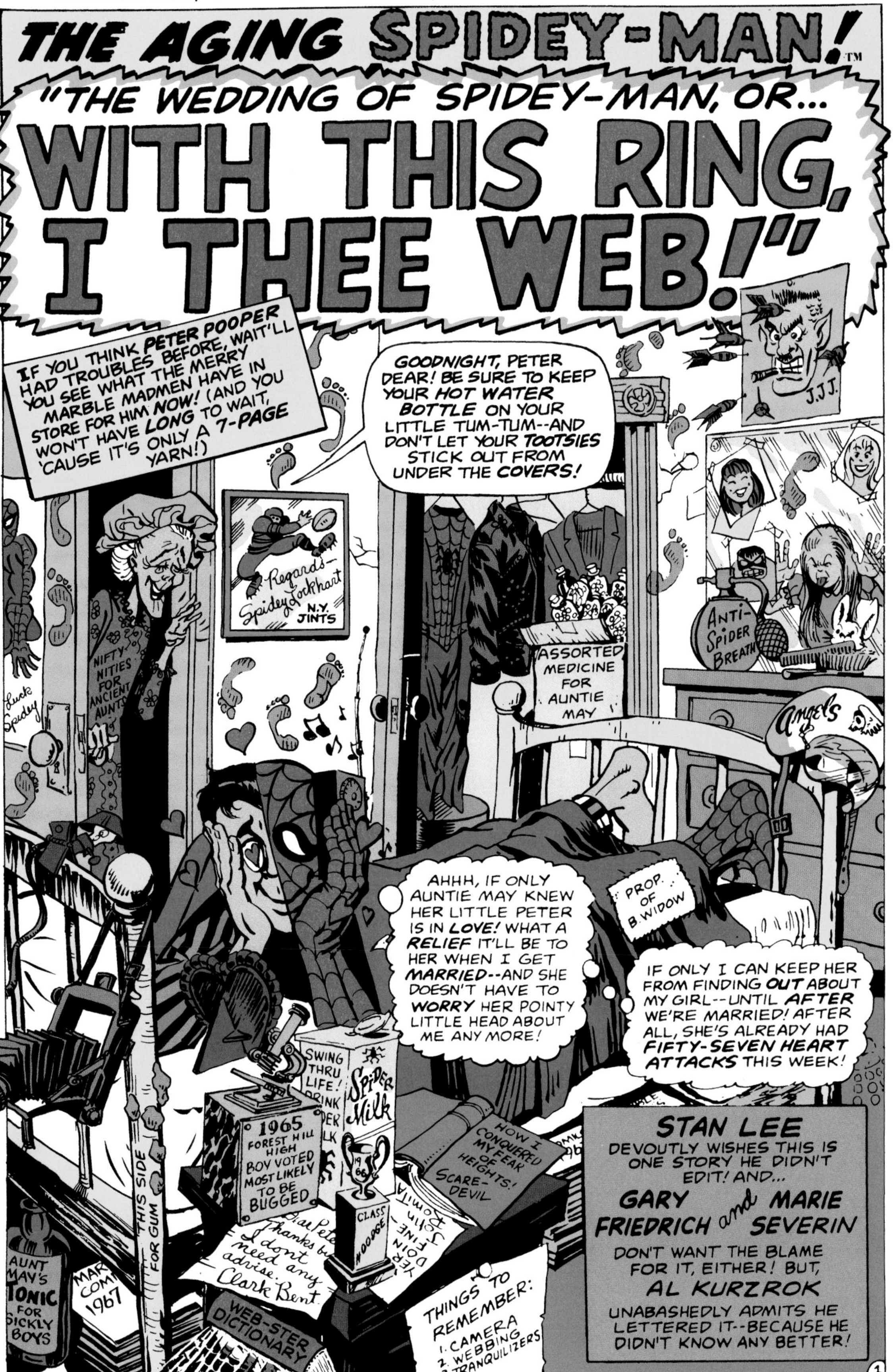
THE AGING SPIDEY-MAN!™
"THE WEDDING OF SPIDEY-MAN, OR...
WITH THIS RING, I THEE WEB!"
IF YOU THINK PETER POOPER HAD TROUBLES BEFORE, WAIT'LL YOU SEE WHAT THE MERRY MARBLE MADMEN HAVE IN STORE FOR HIM NOW! (AND YOU WON'T HAVE LONG TO WAIT, 'CAUSE IT'S ONLY A 7-PAGE YARN!)
GOODNIGHT, PETER DEAR! BE SURE TO KEEP YOUR HOT WATER BOTTLE ON YOUR LITTLE TUM-TUM--AND DON'T LET YOUR TOOTSIES STICK OUT FROM UNDER THE COVERS!
J.J.J.
Regards - Spidey Lockhart N.Y. JINTS
NIFTY-NITIES FOR ANCIENT AUNTS
Luck Spidey
ASSORTED MEDICINE FOR AUNTIE MAY
Anti-Spider Breath
Angels
AHHH, IF ONLY AUNTIE MAY KNEW HER LITTLE PETER IS IN LOVE! WHAT A RELIEF IT'LL BE TO HER WHEN I GET MARRIED--AND SHE DOESN'T HAVE TO WORRY HER POINTY LITTLE HEAD ABOUT ME ANY MORE!
PROP. OF B. WIDOW
IF ONLY I CAN KEEP HER FROM FINDING OUT ABOUT MY GIRL--UNTIL AFTER WE'RE MARRIED! AFTER ALL, SHE'S ALREADY HAD FIFTY-SEVEN HEART ATTACKS THIS WEEK!
Spider Milk
1965 FOREST HILL HIGH BOY VOTED MOST LIKELY TO BE BUGGED
HOW I CONQUERED MY FEAR OF HEIGHTS! SCARE-DEVIL
THIS SIDE FOR GUM
Dear Pete Thanks but I dont need any advise. Clark Bent
WEB-STER DICTIONARY
THINGS TO REMEMBER: 1. CAMERA 2. WEBBING 3. TRANQUILIZERS
STAN LEE DEVOUTLY WISHES THIS IS ONE STORY HE DIDN'T EDIT! AND... GARY FRIEDRICH and MARIE SEVERIN DON'T WANT THE BLAME FOR IT, EITHER! BUT, AL KURZROK UNABASHEDLY ADMITS HE LETTERED IT--BECAUSE HE DIDN'T KNOW ANY BETTER!
1

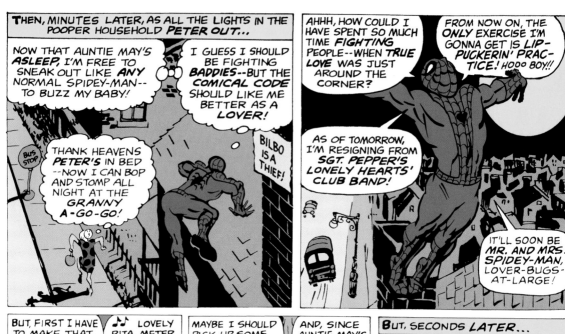

THEN, MINUTES LATER, AS ALL THE LIGHTS IN THE POOPER HOUSEHOLD *PETER OUT*...

NOW THAT AUNTIE MAY'S *ASLEEP*, I'M FREE TO SNEAK OUT LIKE *ANY NORMAL SPIDEY-MAN*-- TO BUZZ MY BABY!

I GUESS I SHOULD BE FIGHTING *BADDIES*--BUT THE *COMICAL CODE* SHOULD LIKE ME BETTER AS A *LOVER!*

THANK HEAVENS *PETER'S* IN BED --NOW I CAN BOP AND STOMP ALL NIGHT AT THE *GRANNY A-GO-GO!*

BUS STOP

BILBO IS A THIEF!

AHHH, HOW COULD I HAVE SPENT SO MUCH TIME *FIGHTING* PEOPLE--WHEN *TRUE LOVE* WAS JUST AROUND THE CORNER?

FROM NOW ON, THE *ONLY* EXERCISE I'M GONNA GET IS *LIP-PUCKERIN'* PRACTICE! HOOO BOY!!

AS OF TOMORROW, I'M RESIGNING FROM *SGT. PEPPER'S LONELY HEARTS' CLUB BAND!*

IT'LL SOON BE *MR. AND MRS. SPIDEY-MAN,* LOVER-BUGS-AT-LARGE!

BUT, FIRST I HAVE TO MAKE THAT *CALL*--SO I'LL JUST SWING ALONG TO THE NEAREST *PHONE BOOTH!*

♪ LOVELY RITA, METER MAID--YOU AIN'T GOT NOTHING ON *SPIDEY!* ♪

MAYBE I SHOULD PICK UP SOME *FLOWERS* FOR HER, THOUGH-- IN CASE I GET TO *SEE* HER TONIGHT!

AND, SINCE AUNTIE MAY'S MEDICINE HAS ME *BROKE* AS USUAL--I'LL JUST BORROW SOME FROM *HERE!*

ETHEL, DO YOU SEE WHAT I SEE?

SURE DO, HARRY! MUST BE ONE OF THOSE FURSHLUGGINER *FLOWER PEOPLE!*

BUT, SECONDS *LATER*...

I'LL JUST PICK *ONE MORE*-- THEN MAYBE I CAN TIE THEM UP IN *HEART-SHAPED* WEBBING, AND...

HEH, HEH! IT MAY NOT BE *HALLOWEEN,* BUT US *GREEN GLOBULES* GOTTA SWING WHENEVER WE *CAN!*

UUURRRKKK!

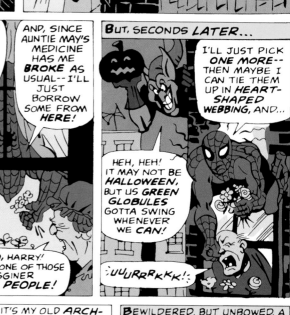

TAKE *THAT*-- YOU NASTY MASKED FELLOW!

SPLAK!

HUH?

HEE, HEE, HEE!

IT'S MY OLD *ARCH-ENEMY--THE GREEN GLOBULE!* WAIT A MINUTE, GLOBBY! I FORGIVE YOU!

I'VE GOT TO *NOW!* I JUST REMEMBERED -- I WAS *KILLED LASH ISH!*

BEWILDERED, BUT UNBOWED, A LOVESICK SPIDEY-MAN REACHES HIS *DESTINATION*...

HI, BABY! WHAT... YOU CAN'T *SEE* ME TONIGHT? BUT WE'RE SUPPOSED TO BE GETTING *HITCHED* TOMORROW!

YOUR TIME IS *UP!* DEPOSIT ONE DIME FOR THE NEXT *THREE* SECONDS, PUHLEEZE!

HUH? OH-- THAT'S *TOMORROW!* BUT, TONIGHT YOU GOT A *DATE?* WELL, AT LEAST I WON'T HAVE TO WORRY ABOUT YOU GETTING *BORED!*

2

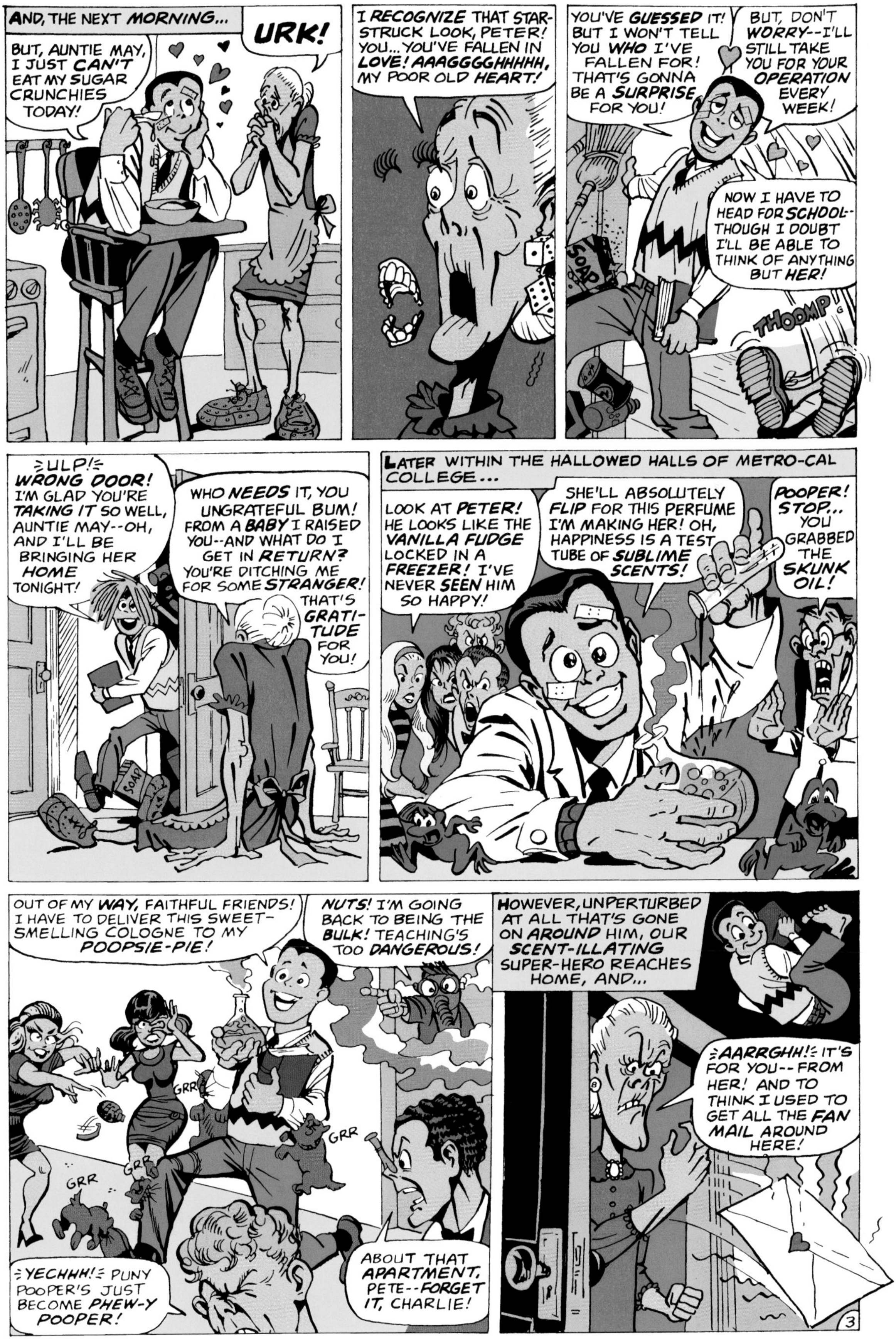
AND, THE NEXT MORNING...
BUT, AUNTIE MAY, I JUST CAN'T EAT MY SUGAR CRUNCHIES TODAY!
URK!
I RECOGNIZE THAT STAR-STRUCK LOOK, PETER! YOU... YOU'VE FALLEN IN LOVE! AAAGGGGHHHHH, MY POOR OLD HEART!
YOU'VE GUESSED IT! BUT I WON'T TELL YOU WHO I'VE FALLEN FOR! THAT'S GONNA BE A SURPRISE FOR YOU!
BUT, DON'T WORRY--I'LL STILL TAKE YOU FOR YOUR OPERATION EVERY WEEK!
NOW I HAVE TO HEAD FOR SCHOOL--THOUGH I DOUBT I'LL BE ABLE TO THINK OF ANYTHING BUT HER!
THOOMP
SOAP
ULP! WRONG DOOR! I'M GLAD YOU'RE TAKING IT SO WELL, AUNTIE MAY--OH, AND I'LL BE BRINGING HER HOME TONIGHT!
WHO NEEDS IT, YOU UNGRATEFUL BUM! FROM A BABY I RAISED YOU--AND WHAT DO I GET IN RETURN? YOU'RE DITCHING ME FOR SOME STRANGER! THAT'S GRATITUDE FOR YOU!
SOAP
LATER WITHIN THE HALLOWED HALLS OF METRO-CAL COLLEGE...
LOOK AT PETER! HE LOOKS LIKE THE VANILLA FUDGE LOCKED IN A FREEZER! I'VE NEVER SEEN HIM SO HAPPY!
SHE'LL ABSOLUTELY FLIP FOR THIS PERFUME I'M MAKING HER! OH, HAPPINESS IS A TEST TUBE OF SUBLIME SCENTS!
POOPER! STOP... YOU GRABBED THE SKUNK OIL!
OUT OF MY WAY, FAITHFUL FRIENDS! I HAVE TO DELIVER THIS SWEET-SMELLING COLOGNE TO MY POOPSIE-PIE!
NUTS! I'M GOING BACK TO BEING THE BULK! TEACHING'S TOO DANGEROUS!
GRR
GRR
GRR
GRR
YECHHH! PUNY POOPER'S JUST BECOME PHEW-Y POOPER!
ABOUT THAT APARTMENT, PETE--FORGET IT, CHARLIE!
HOWEVER, UNPERTURBED AT ALL THAT'S GONE ON AROUND HIM, OUR SCENT-ILLATING SUPER-HERO REACHES HOME, AND...
AARRGHH! IT'S FOR YOU--FROM HER! AND TO THINK I USED TO GET ALL THE FAN MAIL AROUND HERE!
3

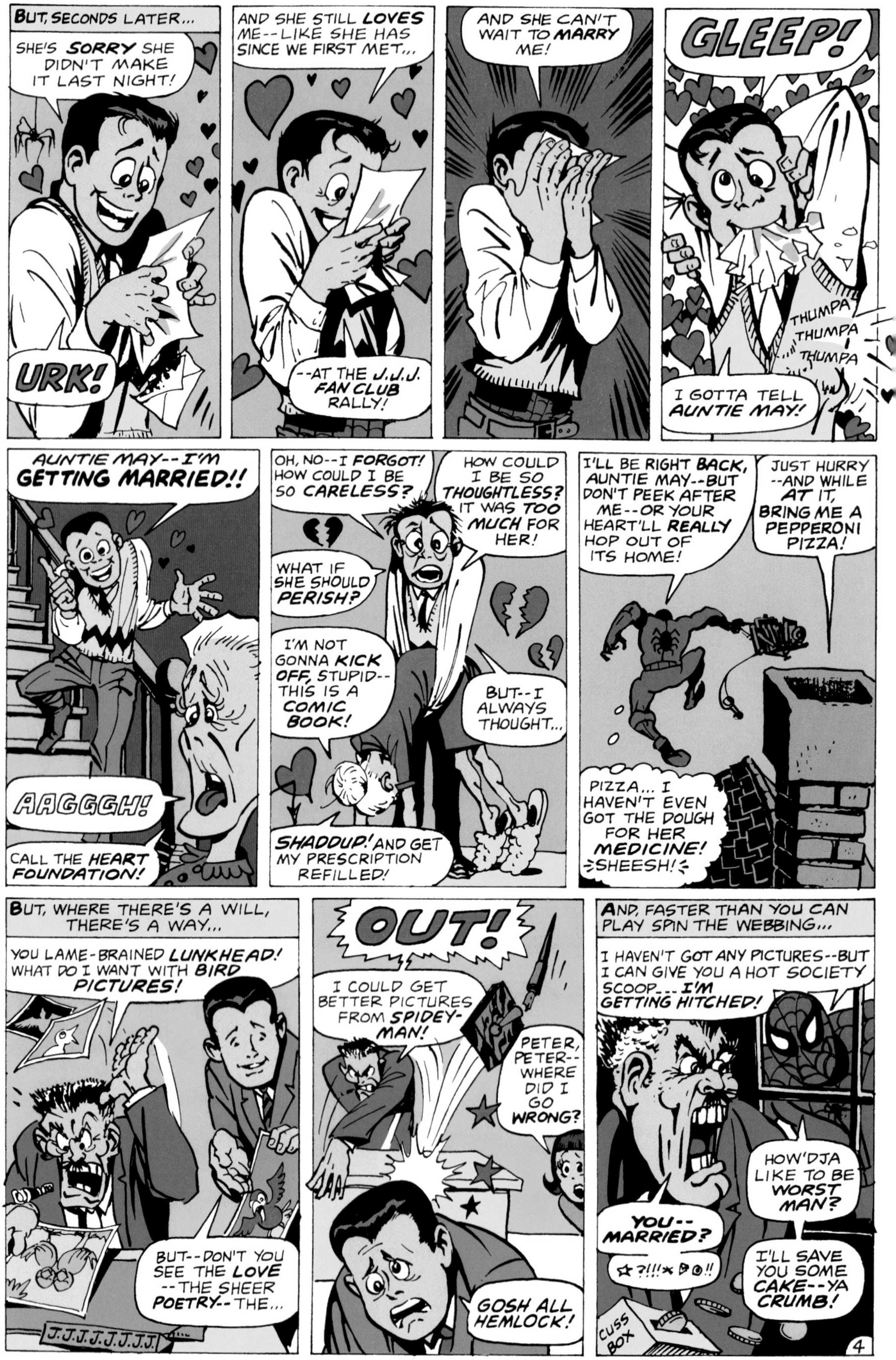
BUT, SECONDS LATER...
SHE'S SORRY SHE DIDN'T MAKE IT LAST NIGHT!
URK!
AND SHE STILL LOVES ME--LIKE SHE HAS SINCE WE FIRST MET...
--AT THE J.J.J. FAN CLUB RALLY!
AND SHE CAN'T WAIT TO MARRY ME!
GLEEP!
THUMPA THUMPA THUMPA
I GOTTA TELL AUNTIE MAY!
AUNTIE MAY--I'M GETTING MARRIED!!
AAGGGH!
CALL THE HEART FOUNDATION!
OH, NO--I FORGOT! HOW COULD I BE SO CARELESS?
HOW COULD I BE SO THOUGHTLESS? IT WAS TOO MUCH FOR HER!
WHAT IF SHE SHOULD PERISH?
I'M NOT GONNA KICK OFF, STUPID--THIS IS A COMIC BOOK!
BUT--I ALWAYS THOUGHT...
SHADDUP! AND GET MY PRESCRIPTION REFILLED!
I'LL BE RIGHT BACK, AUNTIE MAY--BUT DON'T PEEK AFTER ME--OR YOUR HEART'LL REALLY HOP OUT OF ITS HOME!
JUST HURRY--AND WHILE AT IT, BRING ME A PEPPERONI PIZZA!
PIZZA... I HAVEN'T EVEN GOT THE DOUGH FOR HER MEDICINE! SHEESH!
BUT, WHERE THERE'S A WILL, THERE'S A WAY...
YOU LAME-BRAINED LUNKHEAD! WHAT DO I WANT WITH BIRD PICTURES!
BUT--DON'T YOU SEE THE LOVE--THE SHEER POETRY--THE...
J.J.J.J.J.J.J.
OUT!
I COULD GET BETTER PICTURES FROM SPIDEY-MAN!
PETER, PETER--WHERE DID I GO WRONG?
GOSH ALL HEMLOCK!
AND, FASTER THAN YOU CAN PLAY SPIN THE WEBBING...
I HAVEN'T GOT ANY PICTURES--BUT I CAN GIVE YOU A HOT SOCIETY SCOOP... I'M GETTING HITCHED!
YOU--MARRIED?
HOW'DJA LIKE TO BE WORST MAN?
I'LL SAVE YOU SOME CAKE--YA CRUMB!
CUSS BOX
4

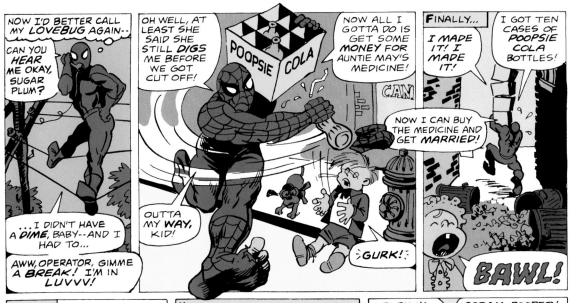

Panel 1:
NOW I'D BETTER CALL MY *LOVEBUG* AGAIN--

CAN YOU *HEAR* ME OKAY, SUGAR PLUM?

...I DIDN'T HAVE A *DIME*, BABY--AND I HAD TO...

AWW, OPERATOR, GIMME A *BREAK!* I'M IN *LUVVV!*

Panel 2:
POOPSIE COLA

OH WELL, AT LEAST SHE SAID SHE STILL *DIGS* ME BEFORE WE GOT CUT OFF!

NOW ALL I GOTTA DO IS GET SOME *MONEY* FOR AUNTIE MAY'S MEDICINE!

OUTTA MY *WAY,* KID!

≷GURK!≷

Panel 3:
FINALLY...

I MADE IT! I MADE IT!

I GOT TEN CASES OF *POOPSIE COLA* BOTTLES!

NOW I CAN BUY THE MEDICINE AND GET *MARRIED!*

BAWL!

Panel 4:
UNTIL...
HERE YOU *ARE,* AUNTIE! ONE BOTTLE OF MEDICATED *JELLY BEANS!* I COULDN'T AFFORD THE *TIME CAPSULES!*

THAT'S *ALL RIGHT,* DEAR! JUST BECAUSE I'VE GIVEN MY *LIFE* FOR YOU DOESN'T MEAN YOU HAVE TO GET THE *BEST* FOR ME!

Panel 5:
HOWEVER, JUST TO SAVE YOUR *SOBS...*
HI, GANG! HERE I AM AT THE OLD *CAFFEIN BEAN!*

AND WAIT'LL YOU HEAR THE *NEWS* ABOUT SPIDEY-MAN GETTING MARR...

Panel 6:
≷BLEHH!≷ IT'S *MR. UNPOPULAR* IN PERSON!

SCRAM, POOPER! BEFORE YOU MAKE MY *MALTED* SOUR!

HOW ARE THINGS IN *SQUARES-VILLE,* PEST?

AND DON'T EXPECT ANY KIND WORDS FROM *ME* UNTIL YOU PAY LAST YEAR'S RENT!

Panel 7:
BUT I HAVE *BIG NEWS!* SPIDEY'S GETTING MARRIED...

AND HE WANTS ALL OF YOU TO COME TO THE *WEDDING!*

EVERYBODY'LL BE THERE! EVEN ARTIE SIMEK!

Panel 8:
BUT...
CAFFEIN BEAN

THAT *TEARS* IT! GET OUTTA HERE-- BEFORE WE SIC THE *GNAT PATROL* ON YOU!

SIGH! THAT'S THAT OLD *GANG* OF MINE!

Panel 9:
WHO *CARES* WHETHER THEY COME OR NOT?

THE MAIN THING IS... *SHE'LL* BE THERE!

AND... LIKE, THE MAN *SAID,* IT ONLY TAKES TWO TO TIE THE *WEB!*

5

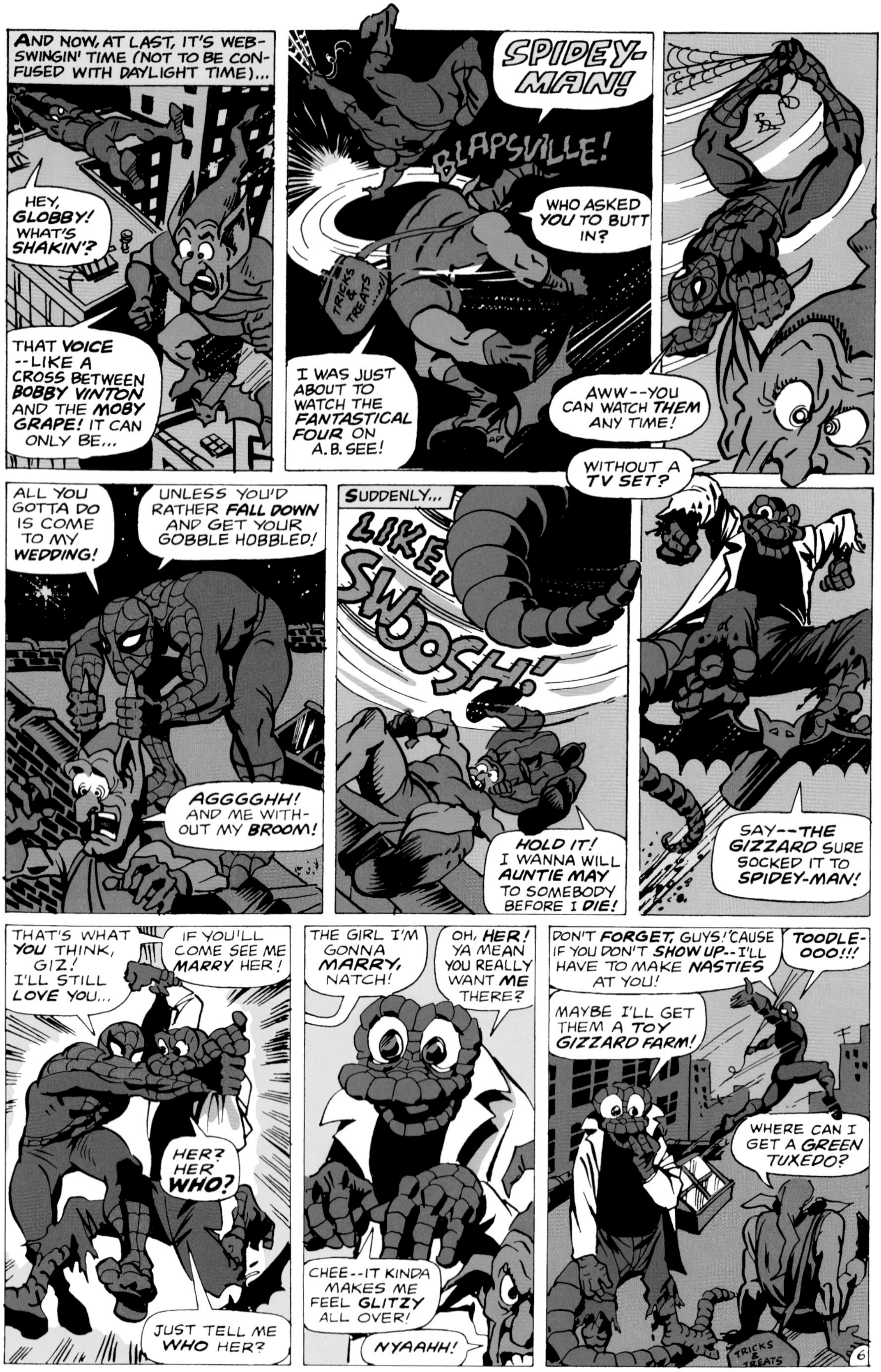
AND NOW, AT LAST, IT'S WEB-SWINGIN' TIME (NOT TO BE CONFUSED WITH DAYLIGHT TIME)...
HEY, GLOBBY! WHAT'S SHAKIN'?
THAT VOICE --LIKE A CROSS BETWEEN BOBBY VINTON AND THE MOBY GRAPE! IT CAN ONLY BE...
SPIDEY-MAN!
BLAPSVILLE!
WHO ASKED YOU TO BUTT IN?
TRICKS & TREATS
I WAS JUST ABOUT TO WATCH THE FANTASTICAL FOUR ON A.B. SEE!
AWW--YOU CAN WATCH THEM ANY TIME!
WITHOUT A TV SET?
ALL YOU GOTTA DO IS COME TO MY WEDDING!
UNLESS YOU'D RATHER FALL DOWN AND GET YOUR GOBBLE HOBBLED!
AGGGGHH! AND ME WITHOUT MY BROOM!
SUDDENLY...
LIKE, SWOOSH!
HOLD IT! I WANNA WILL AUNTIE MAY TO SOMEBODY BEFORE I DIE!
SAY--THE GIZZARD SURE SOCKED IT TO SPIDEY-MAN!
THAT'S WHAT YOU THINK, GIZ! I'LL STILL LOVE YOU...
IF YOU'LL COME SEE ME MARRY HER!
HER? HER WHO?
JUST TELL ME WHO HER?
THE GIRL I'M GONNA MARRY, NATCH!
OH, HER! YA MEAN YOU REALLY WANT ME THERE?
CHEE--IT KINDA MAKES ME FEEL GLITZY ALL OVER!
NYAAHH!
DON'T FORGET, GUYS! 'CAUSE IF YOU DON'T SHOW UP--I'LL HAVE TO MAKE NASTIES AT YOU!
TOODLE-OOO!!!
MAYBE I'LL GET THEM A TOY GIZZARD FARM!
WHERE CAN I GET A GREEN TUXEDO?
TRICKS & TREATS
6

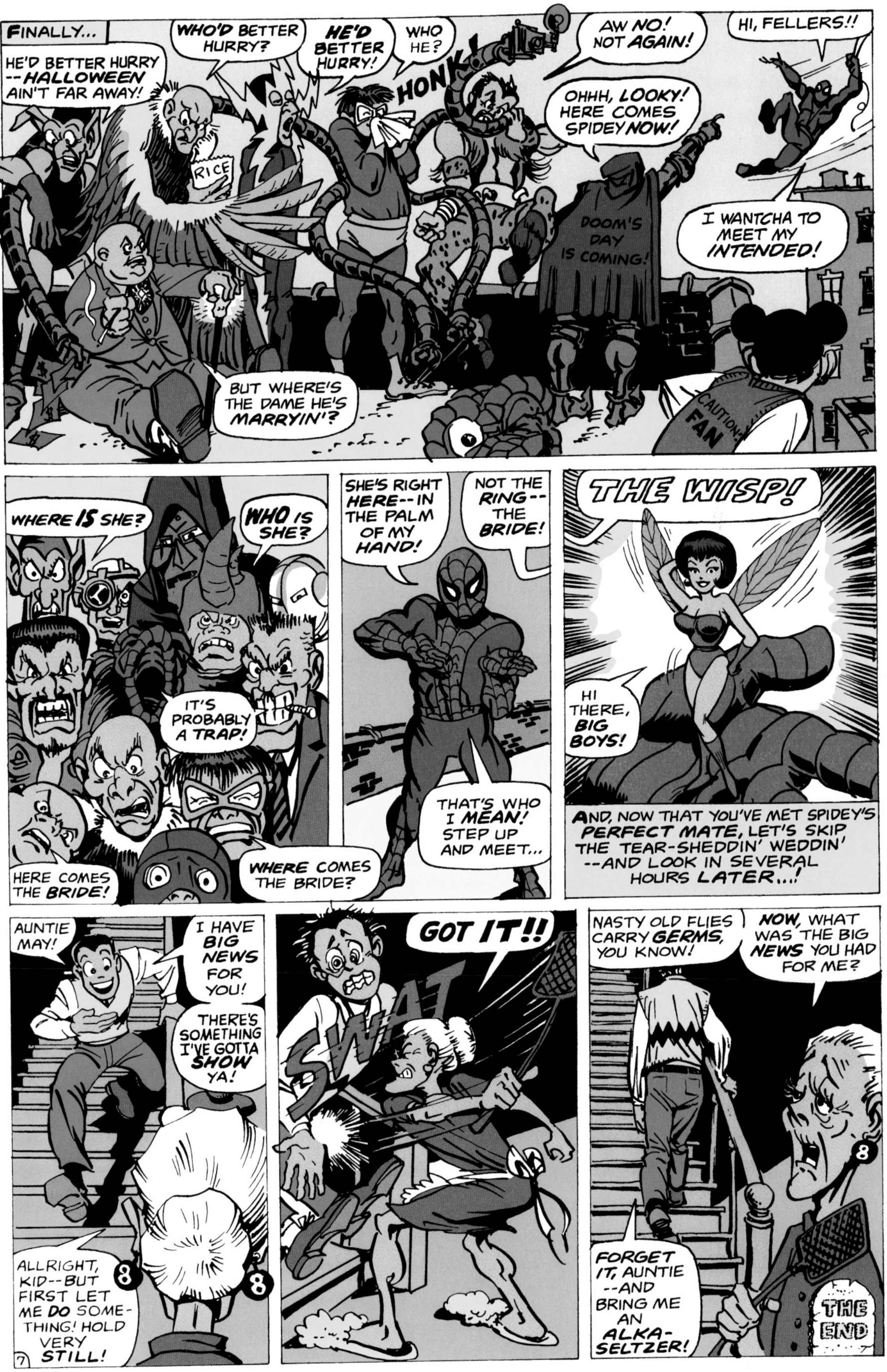
FINALLY...
HE'D BETTER HURRY --HALLOWEEN AIN'T FAR AWAY!
WHO'D BETTER HURRY?
HE'D BETTER HURRY!
WHO HE?
HONK!
AW NO! NOT AGAIN!
HI, FELLERS!!
OHHH, LOOKY! HERE COMES SPIDEY NOW!
RICE
DOOM'S DAY IS COMING!
I WANTCHA TO MEET MY INTENDED!
BUT WHERE'S THE DAME HE'S MARRYIN'?
CAUTION: FAN
WHERE IS SHE?
WHO IS SHE?
IT'S PROBABLY A TRAP!
HERE COMES THE BRIDE!
WHERE COMES THE BRIDE?
SHE'S RIGHT HERE--IN THE PALM OF MY HAND!
NOT THE RING-- THE BRIDE!
THAT'S WHO I MEAN! STEP UP AND MEET...
THE WISP!
HI THERE, BIG BOYS!
AND, NOW THAT YOU'VE MET SPIDEY'S PERFECT MATE, LET'S SKIP THE TEAR-SHEDDIN' WEDDIN' --AND LOOK IN SEVERAL HOURS LATER...!
AUNTIE MAY!
I HAVE BIG NEWS FOR YOU!
THERE'S SOMETHING I'VE GOTTA SHOW YA!
ALLRIGHT, KID--BUT FIRST LET ME DO SOME-THING! HOLD VERY STILL!
GOT IT!!
SWAT
NASTY OLD FLIES CARRY GERMS, YOU KNOW!
NOW, WHAT WAS THE BIG NEWS YOU HAD FOR ME?
FORGET IT, AUNTIE --AND BRING ME AN ALKA-SELTZER!
THE END

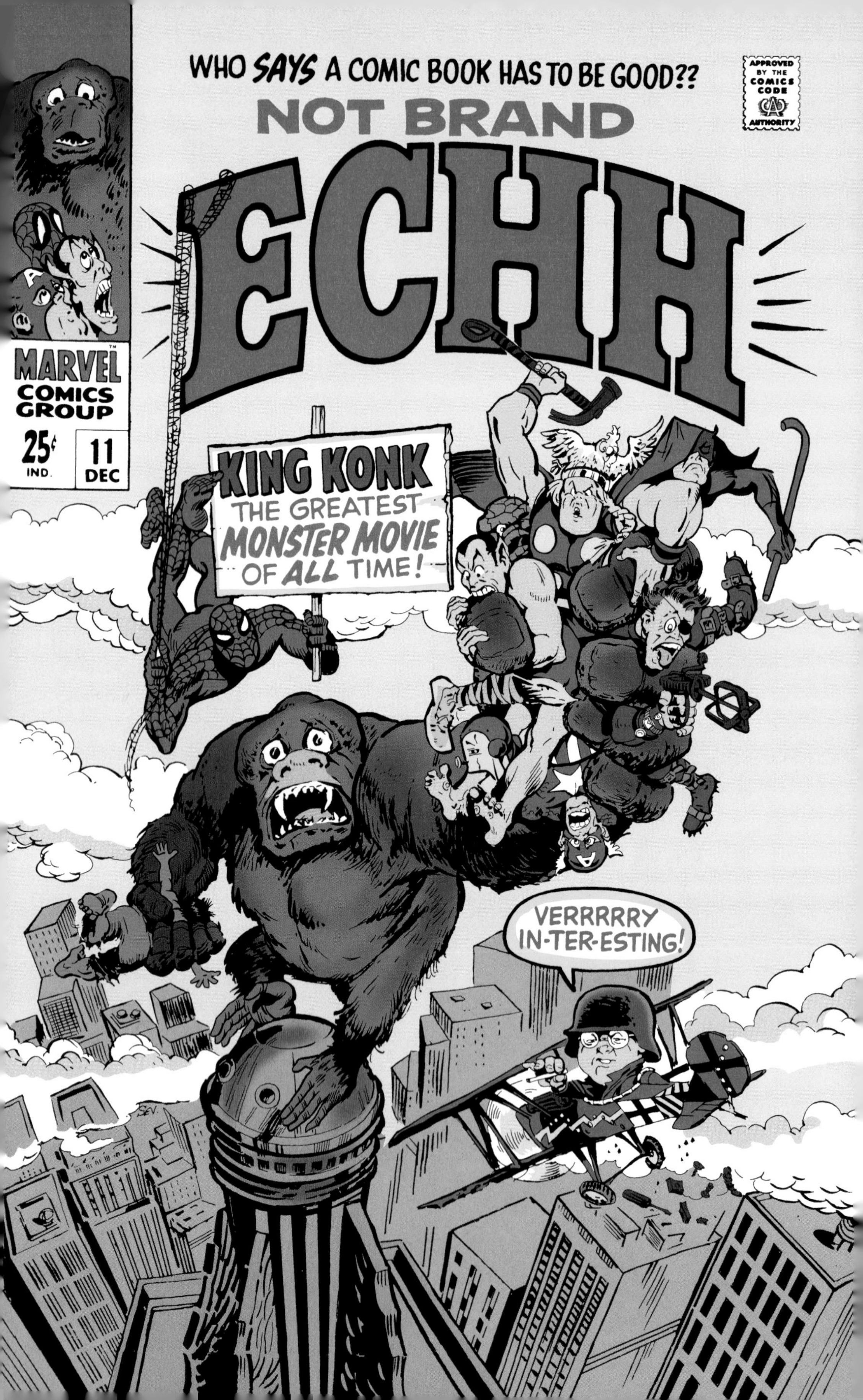
WHO SAYS A COMIC BOOK HAS TO BE GOOD??
NOT BRAND
ECHH
APPROVED BY THE COMICS CODE AUTHORITY
MARVEL COMICS GROUP
25¢ IND.
11 DEC
KING KONK
THE GREATEST
MONSTER MOVIE
OF ALL TIME!
VERRRRRY
IN-TER-ESTING!

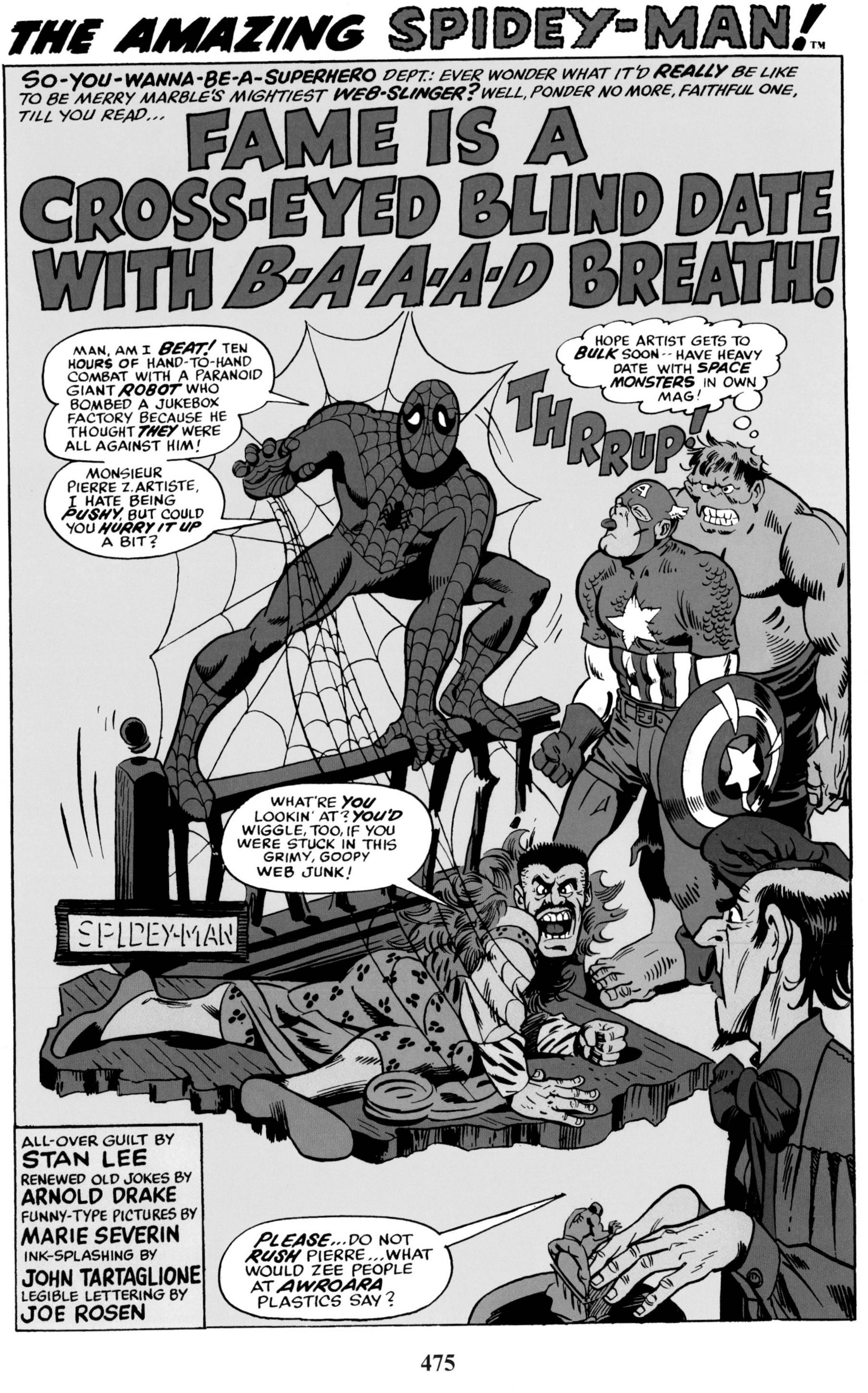
THE AMAZING SPIDEY-MAN!™
SO-YOU-WANNA-BE-A-SUPERHERO DEPT.: EVER WONDER WHAT IT'D REALLY BE LIKE TO BE MERRY MARBLE'S MIGHTIEST WEB-SLINGER? WELL, PONDER NO MORE, FAITHFUL ONE, TILL YOU READ...
FAME IS A CROSS-EYED BLIND DATE WITH B-A-A-A-D BREATH!
MAN, AM I BEAT! TEN HOURS OF HAND-TO-HAND COMBAT WITH A PARANOID GIANT ROBOT WHO BOMBED A JUKEBOX FACTORY BECAUSE HE THOUGHT THEY WERE ALL AGAINST HIM!
MONSIEUR PIERRE Z. ARTISTE, I HATE BEING PUSHY, BUT COULD YOU HURRY IT UP A BIT?
HOPE ARTIST GETS TO BULK SOON-- HAVE HEAVY DATE WITH SPACE MONSTERS IN OWN MAG!
THRRUP!
WHAT'RE YOU LOOKIN' AT? YOU'D WIGGLE, TOO, IF YOU WERE STUCK IN THIS GRIMY, GOOPY WEB JUNK!
SPIDEY-MAN
ALL-OVER GUILT BY STAN LEE
RENEWED OLD JOKES BY ARNOLD DRAKE
FUNNY-TYPE PICTURES BY MARIE SEVERIN
INK-SPLASHING BY JOHN TARTAGLIONE
LEGIBLE LETTERING BY JOE ROSEN
PLEASE... DO NOT RUSH PIERRE... WHAT WOULD ZEE PEOPLE AT AWROARA PLASTICS SAY?

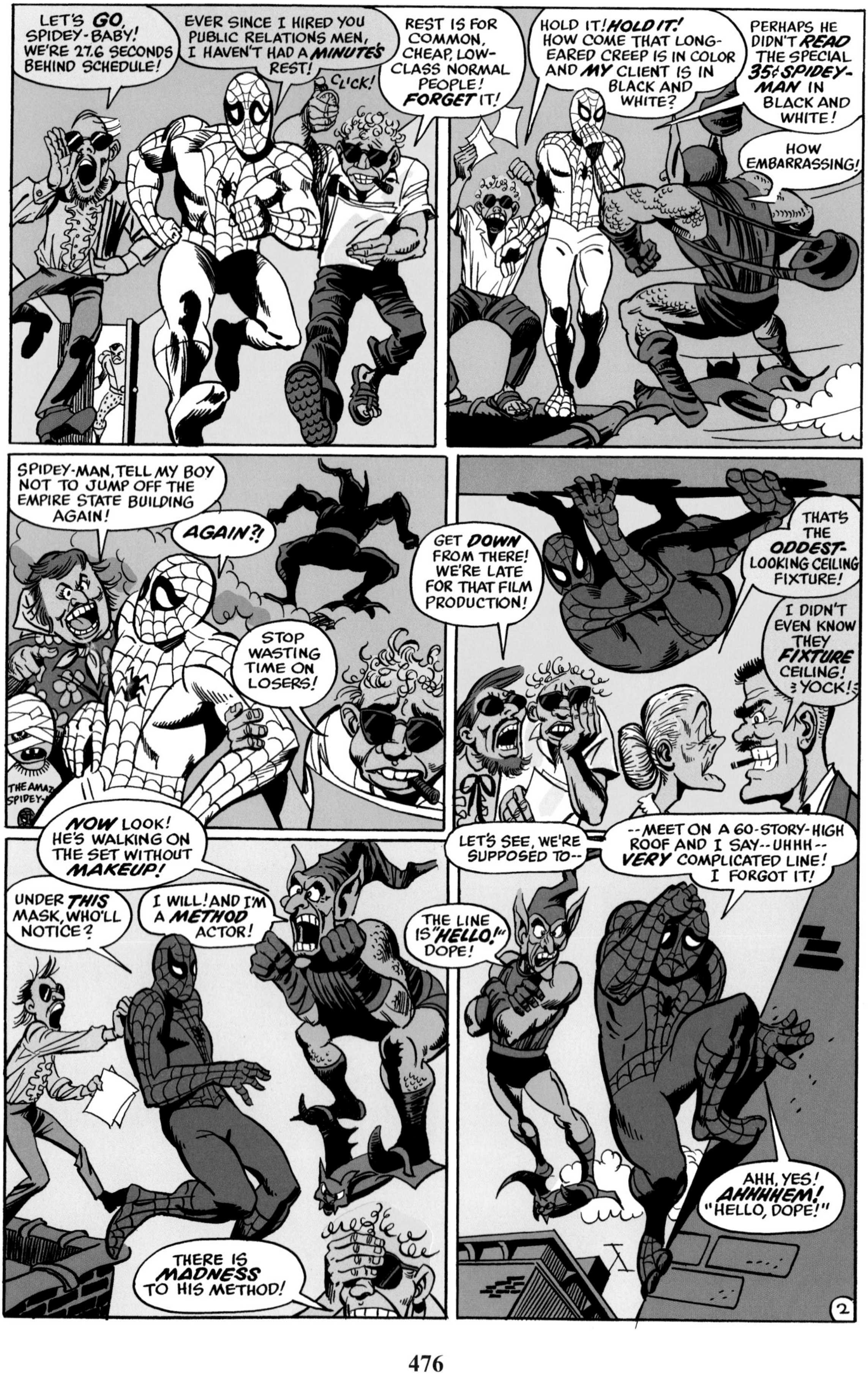
LET'S GO, SPIDEY-BABY! WE'RE 27.6 SECONDS BEHIND SCHEDULE!
EVER SINCE I HIRED YOU PUBLIC RELATIONS MEN, I HAVEN'T HAD A MINUTE'S REST!
CLICK!
REST IS FOR COMMON, CHEAP, LOW-CLASS NORMAL PEOPLE! FORGET IT!
HOLD IT! HOLD IT! HOW COME THAT LONG-EARED CREEP IS IN COLOR AND MY CLIENT IS IN BLACK AND WHITE?
PERHAPS HE DIDN'T READ THE SPECIAL 35¢ SPIDEY-MAN IN BLACK AND WHITE!
HOW EMBARRASSING!
SPIDEY-MAN, TELL MY BOY NOT TO JUMP OFF THE EMPIRE STATE BUILDING AGAIN!
AGAIN?!
STOP WASTING TIME ON LOSERS!
GET DOWN FROM THERE! WE'RE LATE FOR THAT FILM PRODUCTION!
THAT'S THE ODDEST-LOOKING CEILING FIXTURE!
I DIDN'T EVEN KNOW THEY FIXTURE CEILING! YOCK!
NOW LOOK! HE'S WALKING ON THE SET WITHOUT MAKEUP!
UNDER THIS MASK, WHO'LL NOTICE?
I WILL! AND I'M A METHOD ACTOR!
THERE IS MADNESS TO HIS METHOD!
LET'S SEE, WE'RE SUPPOSED TO--
--MEET ON A 60-STORY-HIGH ROOF AND I SAY--UHHH--VERY COMPLICATED LINE! I FORGOT IT!
THE LINE IS "HELLO!" DOPE!
AHH, YES! AHHHHEM! "HELLO, DOPE!"
2

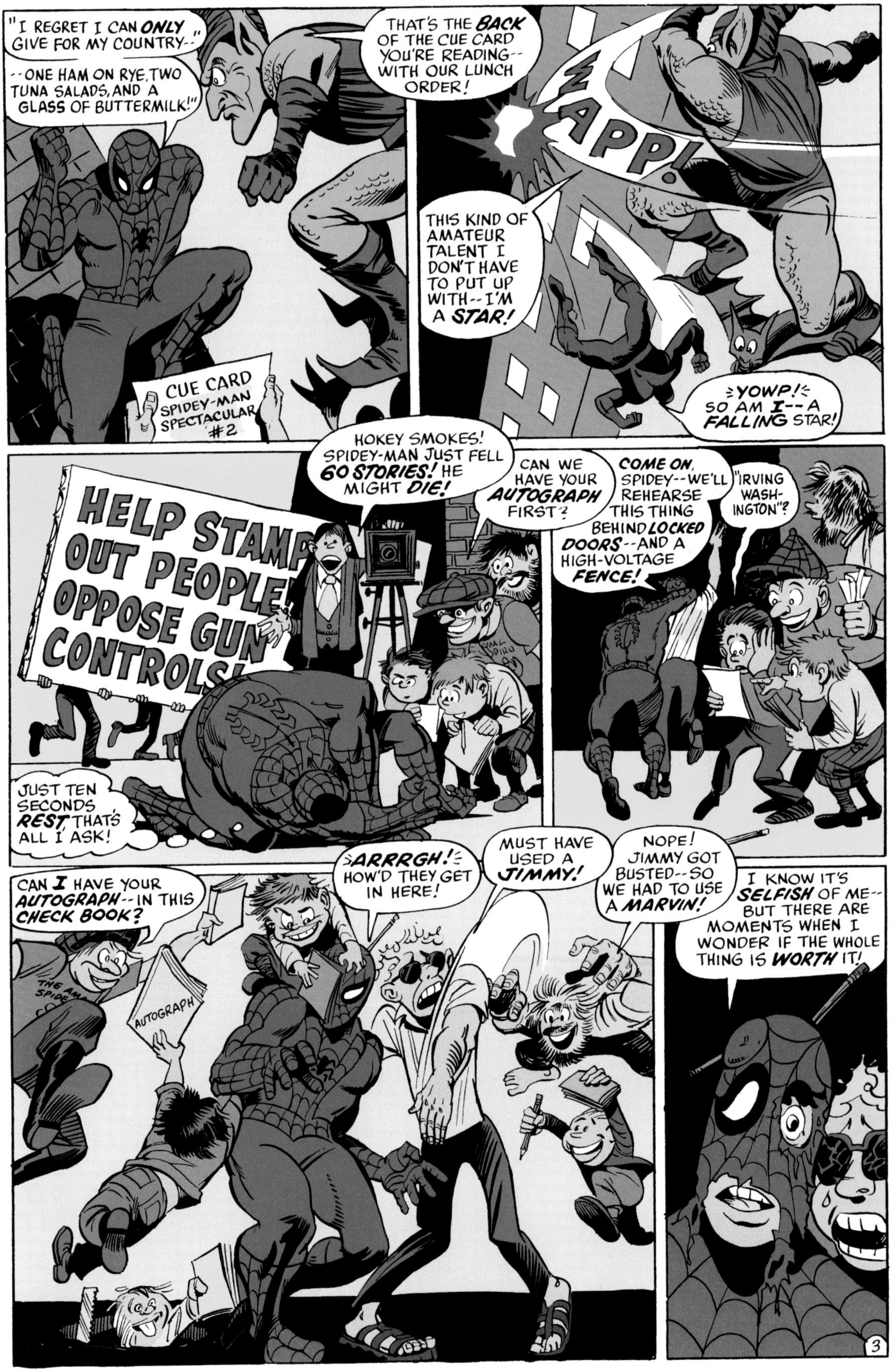
"I REGRET I CAN ONLY GIVE FOR MY COUNTRY--"
--ONE HAM ON RYE, TWO TUNA SALADS, AND A GLASS OF BUTTERMILK!"
CUE CARD SPIDEY-MAN SPECTACULAR #2
THAT'S THE BACK OF THE CUE CARD YOU'RE READING-- WITH OUR LUNCH ORDER!
ZAPP!
THIS KIND OF AMATEUR TALENT I DON'T HAVE TO PUT UP WITH--I'M A STAR!
YOWP! SO AM I--A FALLING STAR!
HELP STAMP OUT PEOPLE! OPPOSE GUN CONTROLS!
HOKEY SMOKES! SPIDEY-MAN JUST FELL 60 STORIES! HE MIGHT DIE!
CAN WE HAVE YOUR AUTOGRAPH FIRST?
JUST TEN SECONDS REST, THAT'S ALL I ASK!
COME ON, SPIDEY--WE'LL REHEARSE THIS THING BEHIND LOCKED DOORS--AND A HIGH-VOLTAGE FENCE!
"IRVING WASH-INGTON"?
CAN I HAVE YOUR AUTOGRAPH--IN THIS CHECK BOOK?
ARRRGH! HOW'D THEY GET IN HERE!
MUST HAVE USED A JIMMY!
NOPE! JIMMY GOT BUSTED--SO WE HAD TO USE A MARVIN!
AUTOGRAPH
I KNOW IT'S SELFISH OF ME--BUT THERE ARE MOMENTS WHEN I WONDER IF THE WHOLE THING IS WORTH IT!
3

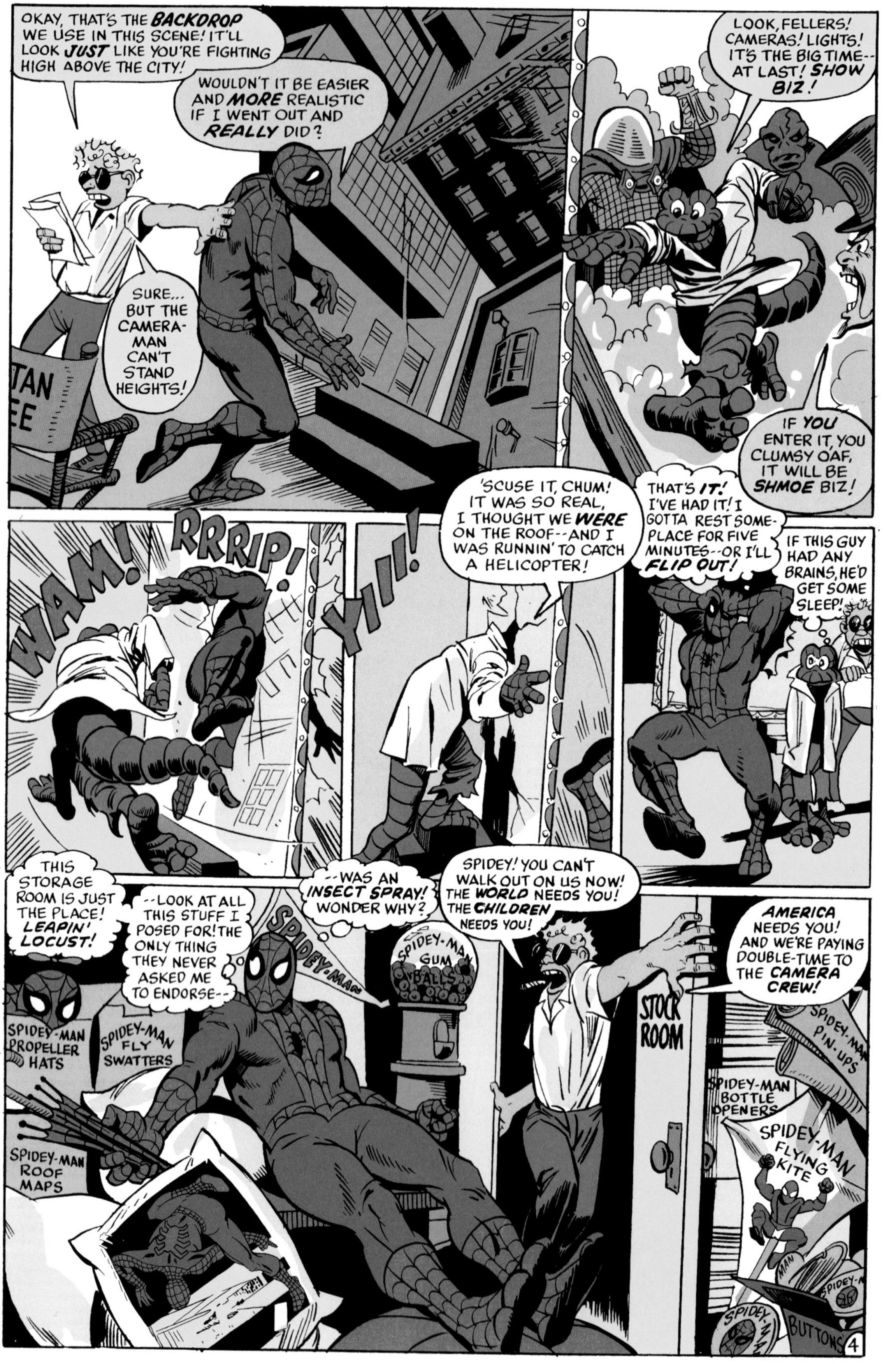
OKAY, THAT'S THE BACKDROP WE USE IN THIS SCENE! IT'LL LOOK JUST LIKE YOU'RE FIGHTING HIGH ABOVE THE CITY!
WOULDN'T IT BE EASIER AND MORE REALISTIC IF I WENT OUT AND REALLY DID?
SURE... BUT THE CAMERA-MAN CAN'T STAND HEIGHTS!
LOOK, FELLERS! CAMERAS! LIGHTS! IT'S THE BIG TIME-- AT LAST! SHOW BIZ!
IF YOU ENTER IT, YOU CLUMSY OAF, IT WILL BE SHMOE BIZ!
WAM!
RRRIP!
YIII!
'SCUSE IT, CHUM! IT WAS SO REAL, I THOUGHT WE WERE ON THE ROOF--AND I WAS RUNNIN' TO CATCH A HELICOPTER!
THAT'S IT! I'VE HAD IT! I GOTTA REST SOME-PLACE FOR FIVE MINUTES--OR I'LL FLIP OUT!
IF THIS GUY HAD ANY BRAINS, HE'D GET SOME SLEEP!
THIS STORAGE ROOM IS JUST THE PLACE! LEAPIN' LOCUST!
--LOOK AT ALL THIS STUFF I POSED FOR! THE ONLY THING THEY NEVER ASKED ME TO ENDORSE--
--WAS AN INSECT SPRAY! WONDER WHY?
SPIDEY-MAN
SPIDEY-MAN GUM BALLS
SPIDEY-MAN PROPELLER HATS
SPIDEY-MAN FLY SWATTERS
SPIDEY-MAN ROOF MAPS
SPIDEY! YOU CAN'T WALK OUT ON US NOW! THE WORLD NEEDS YOU! THE CHILDREN NEEDS YOU!
AMERICA NEEDS YOU! AND WE'RE PAYING DOUBLE-TIME TO THE CAMERA CREW!
STOCK ROOM
SPIDEY-MAN PIN-UPS
SPIDEY-MAN BOTTLE OPENERS
SPIDEY-MAN FLYING KITE
BUTTONS
4

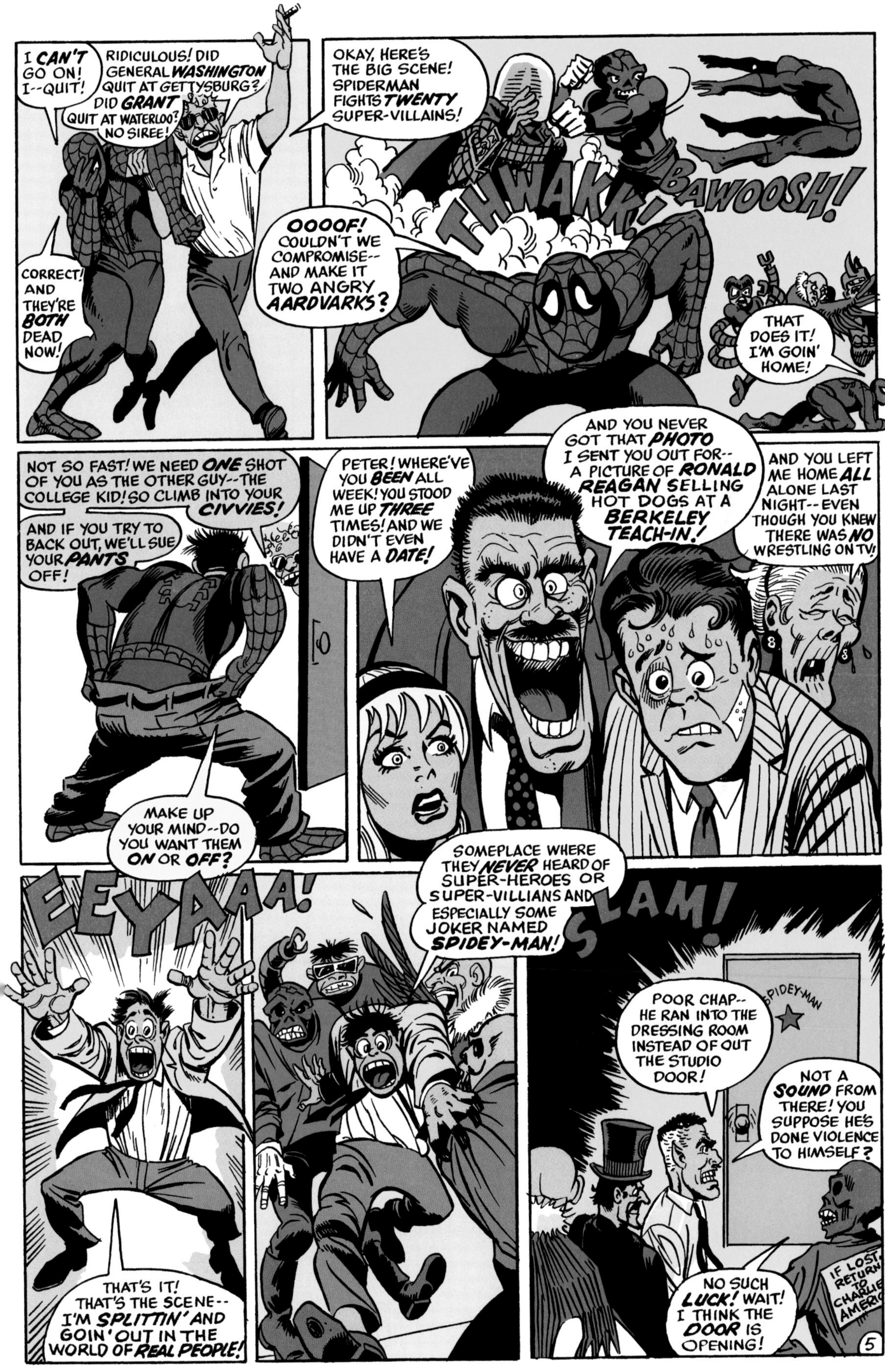

I CAN'T GO ON! I--QUIT!
RIDICULOUS! DID GENERAL WASHINGTON QUIT AT GETTYSBURG? DID GRANT QUIT AT WATERLOO? NO SIREE!
CORRECT! AND THEY'RE BOTH DEAD NOW!
OKAY, HERE'S THE BIG SCENE! SPIDERMAN FIGHTS TWENTY SUPER-VILLAINS!
THWAKK!
BAWOOSH!
OOOOF! COULDN'T WE COMPROMISE-- AND MAKE IT TWO ANGRY AARDVARKS?
THAT DOES IT! I'M GOIN' HOME!
NOT SO FAST! WE NEED ONE SHOT OF YOU AS THE OTHER GUY--THE COLLEGE KID! SO CLIMB INTO YOUR CIVVIES!
AND IF YOU TRY TO BACK OUT, WE'LL SUE YOUR PANTS OFF!
MAKE UP YOUR MIND--DO YOU WANT THEM ON OR OFF?
PETER! WHERE'VE YOU BEEN ALL WEEK! YOU STOOD ME UP THREE TIMES! AND WE DIDN'T EVEN HAVE A DATE!
AND YOU NEVER GOT THAT PHOTO I SENT YOU OUT FOR-- A PICTURE OF RONALD REAGAN SELLING HOT DOGS AT A BERKELEY TEACH-IN!
AND YOU LEFT ME HOME ALL ALONE LAST NIGHT--EVEN THOUGH YOU KNEW THERE WAS NO WRESTLING ON TV!
EEYAAA!
THAT'S IT! THAT'S THE SCENE-- I'M SPLITTIN' AND GOIN' OUT IN THE WORLD OF REAL PEOPLE!
SOMEPLACE WHERE THEY NEVER HEARD OF SUPER-HEROES OR SUPER-VILLIANS AND ESPECIALLY SOME JOKER NAMED SPIDEY-MAN!
SLAM!
SPIDEY-MAN
POOR CHAP-- HE RAN INTO THE DRESSING ROOM INSTEAD OF OUT THE STUDIO DOOR!
NOT A SOUND FROM THERE! YOU SUPPOSE HE'S DONE VIOLENCE TO HIMSELF?
NO SUCH LUCK! WAIT! I THINK THE DOOR IS OPENING!
5

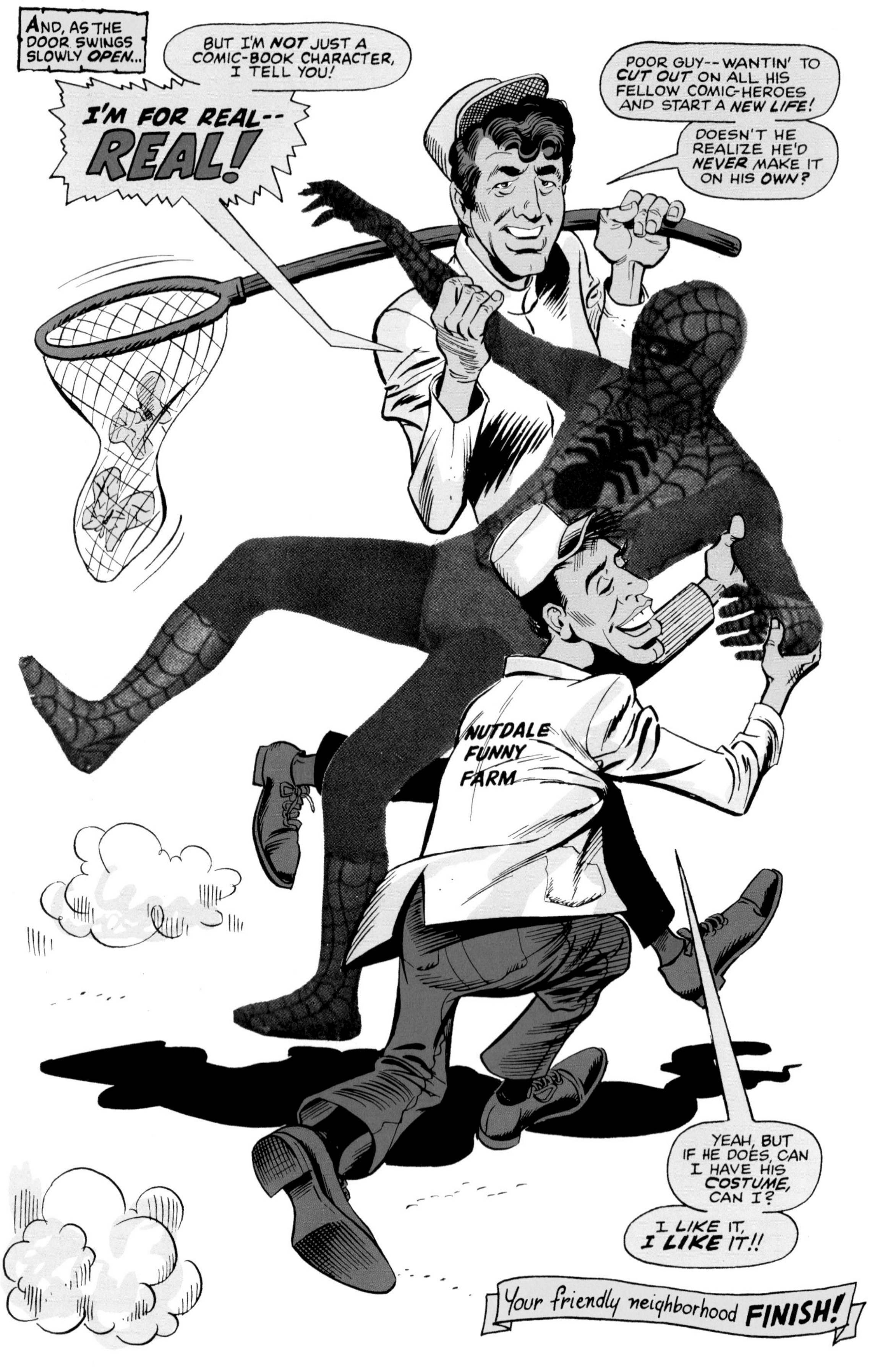
AND, AS THE DOOR SWINGS SLOWLY OPEN...
BUT I'M NOT JUST A COMIC-BOOK CHARACTER, I TELL YOU!
I'M FOR REAL-- REAL!
POOR GUY--WANTIN' TO CUT OUT ON ALL HIS FELLOW COMIC-HEROES AND START A NEW LIFE!
DOESN'T HE REALIZE HE'D NEVER MAKE IT ON HIS OWN?
NUTDALE FUNNY FARM
YEAH, BUT IF HE DOES, CAN I HAVE HIS COSTUME, CAN I?
I LIKE IT, I LIKE IT!!
Your friendly neighborhood FINISH!

SPIDER-MAN #57

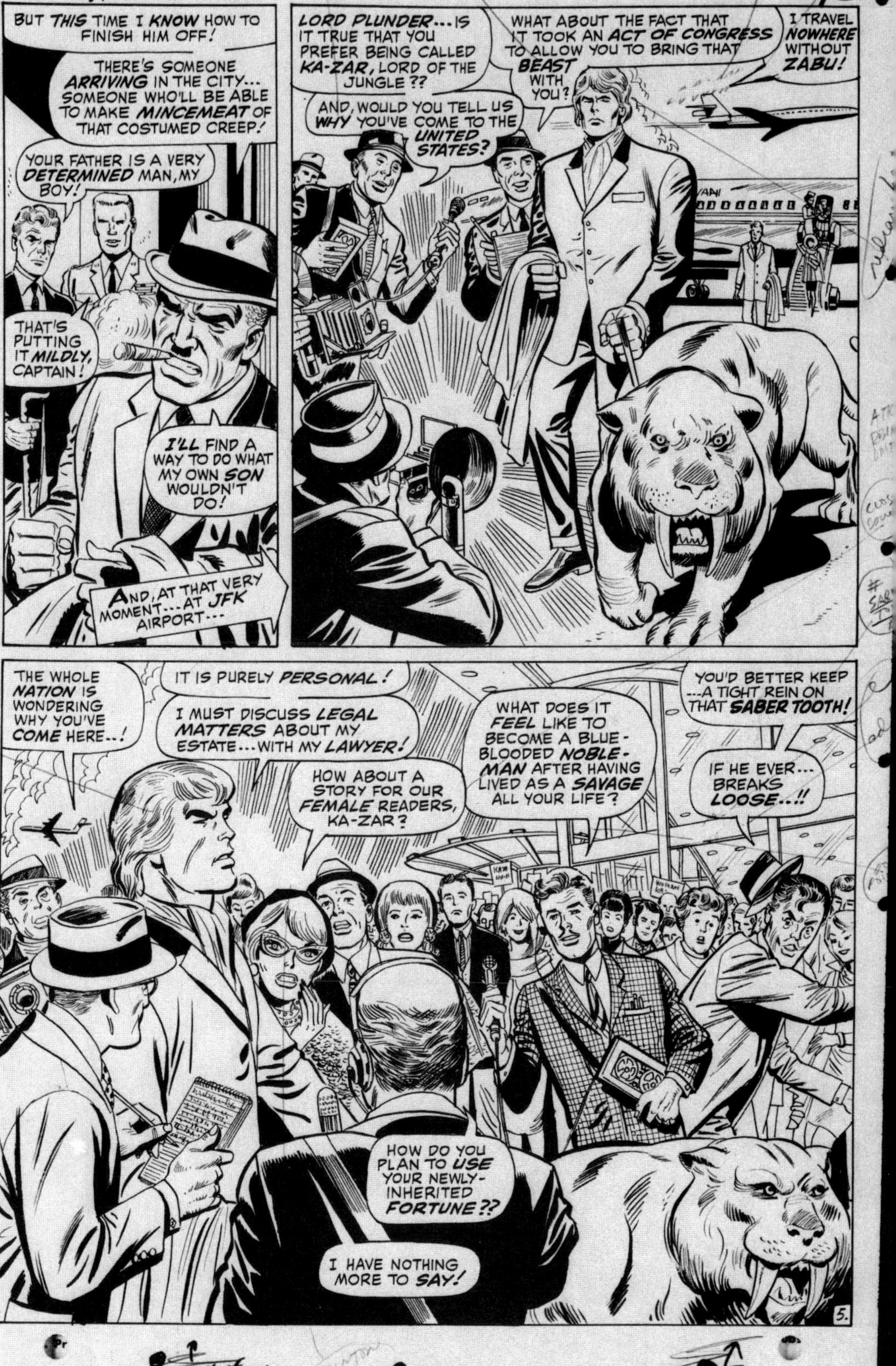

BUT THIS TIME I KNOW HOW TO FINISH HIM OFF!
THERE'S SOMEONE ARRIVING IN THE CITY... SOMEONE WHO'LL BE ABLE TO MAKE MINCEMEAT OF THAT COSTUMED CREEP!
YOUR FATHER IS A VERY DETERMINED MAN, MY BOY!
THAT'S PUTTING IT MILDLY, CAPTAIN!
I'LL FIND A WAY TO DO WHAT MY OWN SON WOULDN'T DO!
AND, AT THAT VERY MOMENT... AT JFK AIRPORT...
LORD PLUNDER... IS IT TRUE THAT YOU PREFER BEING CALLED KA-ZAR, LORD OF THE JUNGLE??
AND, WOULD YOU TELL US WHY YOU'VE COME TO THE UNITED STATES?
WHAT ABOUT THE FACT THAT IT TOOK AN ACT OF CONGRESS TO ALLOW YOU TO BRING THAT BEAST WITH YOU?
I TRAVEL NOWHERE WITHOUT ZABU!
THE WHOLE NATION IS WONDERING WHY YOU'VE COME HERE..!
IT IS PURELY PERSONAL!
I MUST DISCUSS LEGAL MATTERS ABOUT MY ESTATE... WITH MY LAWYER!
HOW ABOUT A STORY FOR OUR FEMALE READERS, KA-ZAR?
WHAT DOES IT FEEL LIKE TO BECOME A BLUE-BLOODED NOBLEMAN AFTER HAVING LIVED AS A SAVAGE ALL YOUR LIFE?
YOU'D BETTER KEEP ...A TIGHT REIN ON THAT SABER TOOTH!
IF HE EVER... BREAKS LOOSE...!!
HOW DO YOU PLAN TO USE YOUR NEWLY-INHERITED FORTUNE??
I HAVE NOTHING MORE TO SAY!
5.

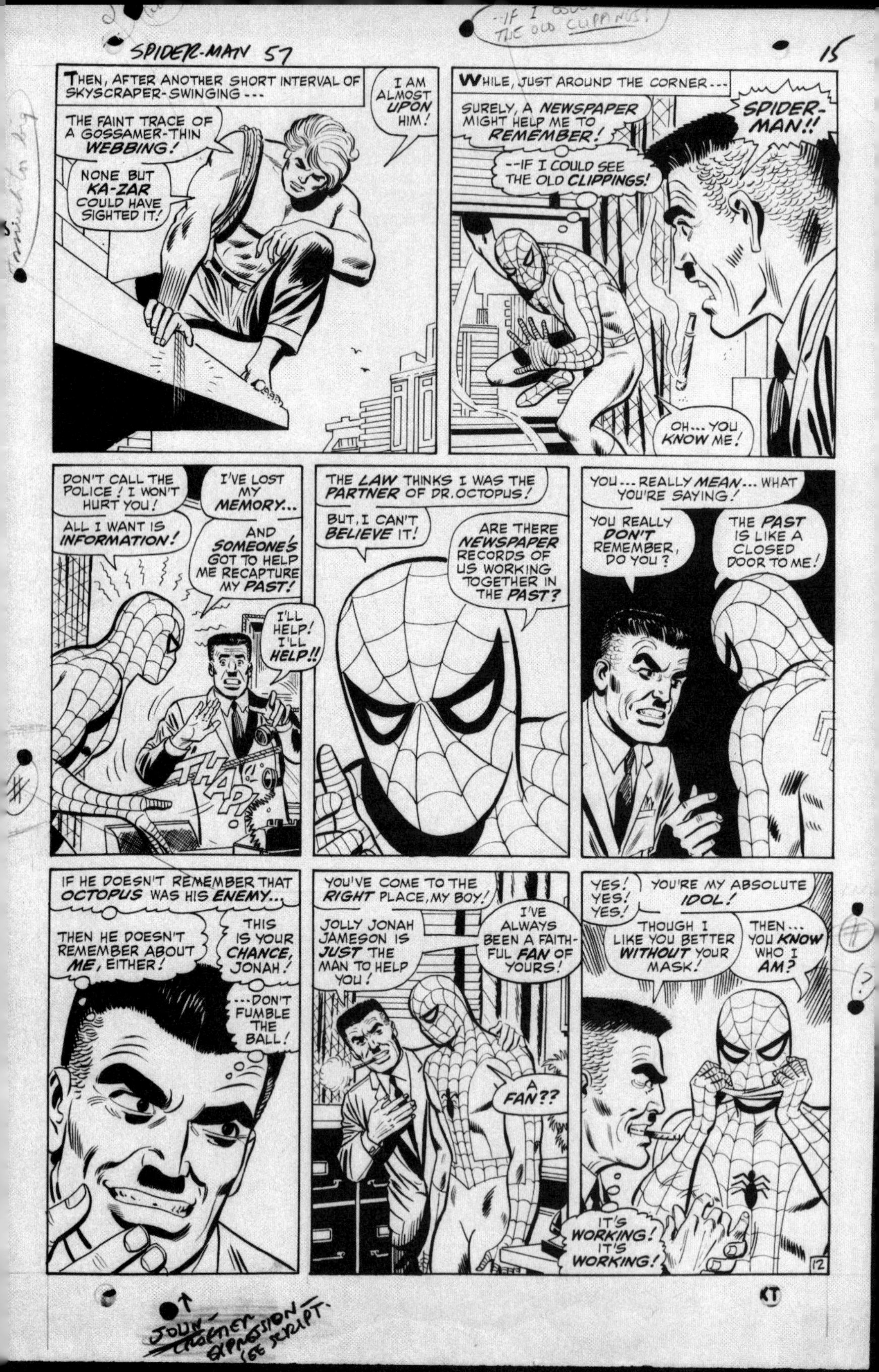
SPIDER-MAN 57
15
THEN, AFTER ANOTHER SHORT INTERVAL OF SKYSCRAPER-SWINGING---
THE FAINT TRACE OF A GOSSAMER-THIN WEBBING!
NONE BUT KA-ZAR COULD HAVE SIGHTED IT!
I AM ALMOST UPON HIM!
WHILE, JUST AROUND THE CORNER---
SURELY, A NEWSPAPER MIGHT HELP ME TO REMEMBER!
--IF I COULD SEE THE OLD CLIPPINGS!
SPIDER-MAN!!
OH... YOU KNOW ME!
DON'T CALL THE POLICE! I WON'T HURT YOU!
ALL I WANT IS INFORMATION!
I'VE LOST MY MEMORY...
AND SOMEONE'S GOT TO HELP ME RECAPTURE MY PAST!
I'LL HELP! I'LL HELP!!
THAP
THE LAW THINKS I WAS THE PARTNER OF DR. OCTOPUS!
BUT, I CAN'T BELIEVE IT!
ARE THERE NEWSPAPER RECORDS OF US WORKING TOGETHER IN THE PAST?
YOU... REALLY MEAN... WHAT YOU'RE SAYING!
YOU REALLY DON'T REMEMBER, DO YOU?
THE PAST IS LIKE A CLOSED DOOR TO ME!
IF HE DOESN'T REMEMBER THAT OCTOPUS WAS HIS ENEMY...
THEN HE DOESN'T REMEMBER ABOUT ME, EITHER!
THIS IS YOUR CHANCE, JONAH!
...DON'T FUMBLE THE BALL!
YOU'VE COME TO THE RIGHT PLACE, MY BOY!
JOLLY JONAH JAMESON IS JUST THE MAN TO HELP YOU!
I'VE ALWAYS BEEN A FAITHFUL FAN OF YOURS!
A FAN??
YES! YES! YES!
YOU'RE MY ABSOLUTE IDOL!
THOUGH I LIKE YOU BETTER WITHOUT YOUR MASK!
THEN... YOU KNOW WHO I AM?
IT'S WORKING! IT'S WORKING!
12
JOHN – CHARACTER EXPRESSION – SEE SCRIPT.

AMAZING SPIDER-MAN #57, PAGE 12 PRODUCTION PHOTOSTAT, FEATURING STORY AND EDITORIAL MARGIN NOTES

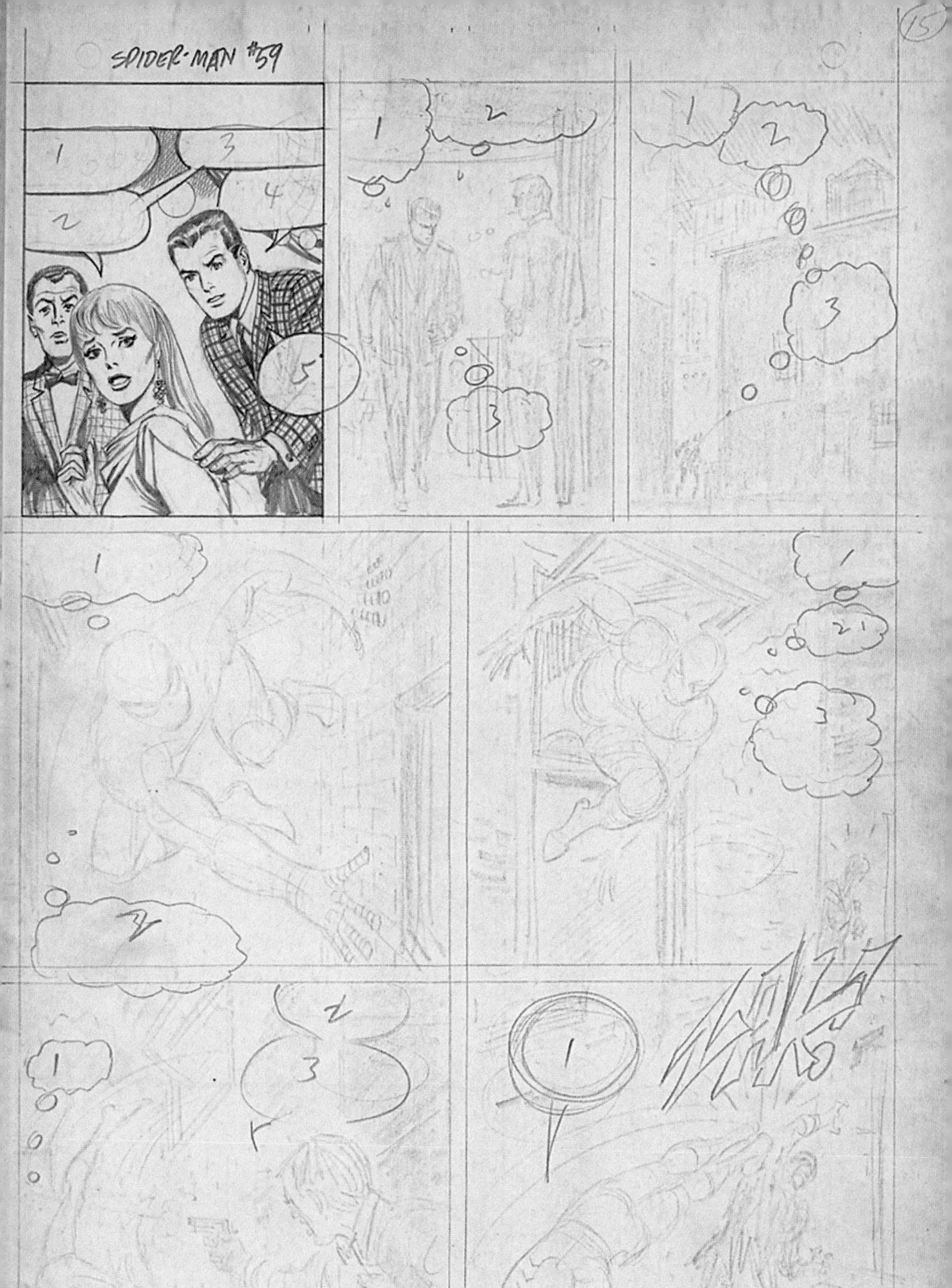
SPIDER-MAN #59
15

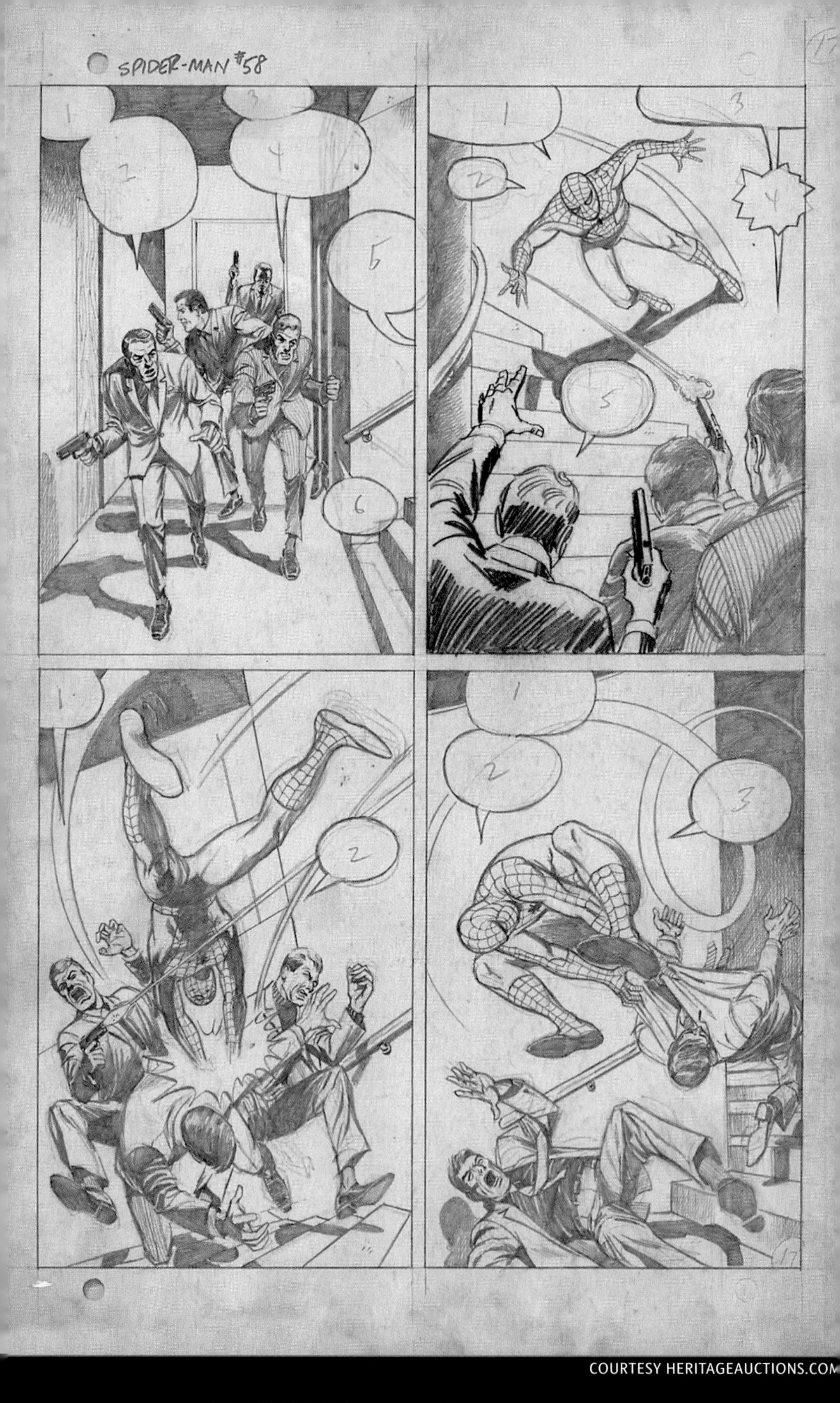
SPIDER-MAN #58
17

AMAZING SPIDER-MAN #59, PAGE 17 UNUSED PENCIL ART,
BREAKDOWNS BY JOHN ROMITA WITH FINISHED PENCILS BY LARRY LIEBER

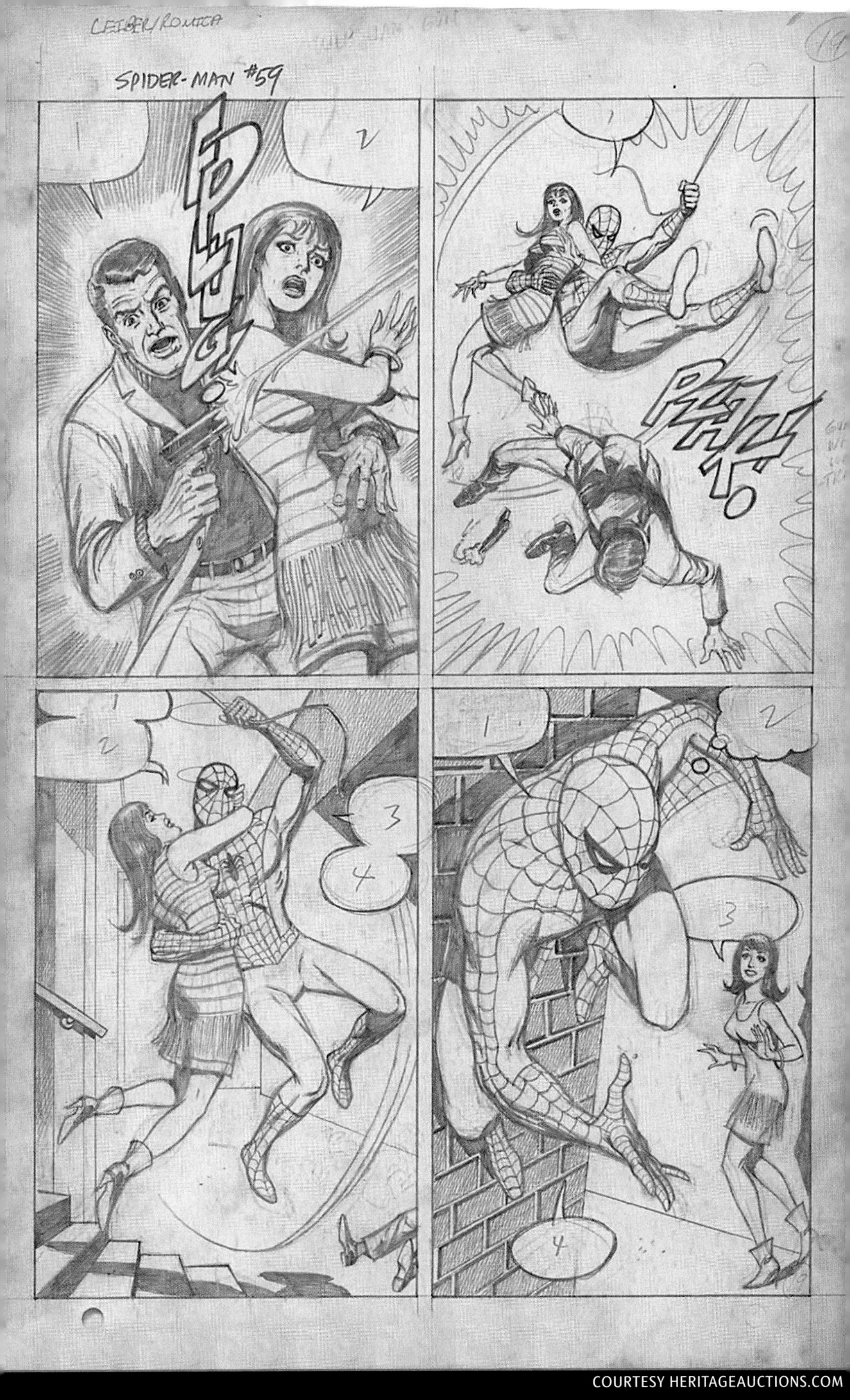
SPIDER-MAN #59

COURTESY HERITAGEAUCTIONS.COM

AMAZING SPIDER-MAN #59, PAGE 19 UNUSED PENCIL ART,
BREAKDOWNS BY JOHN ROMITA WITH FINISHED PENCILS BY LARRY LIEBER

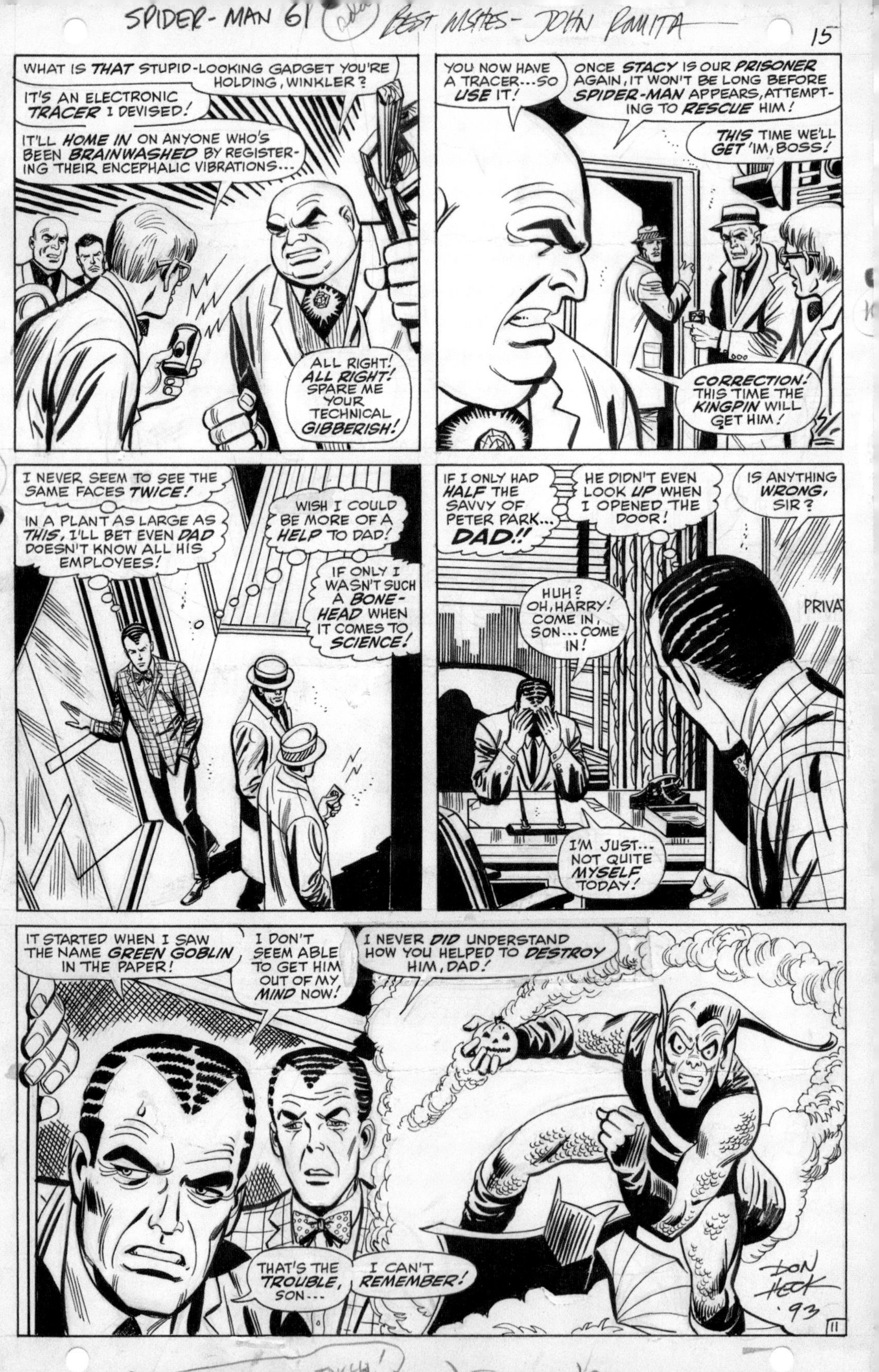
SPIDER-MAN 61
BEST WISHES - JOHN ROMITA
15
WHAT IS THAT STUPID-LOOKING GADGET YOU'RE HOLDING, WINKLER?
IT'S AN ELECTRONIC TRACER I DEVISED!
IT'LL HOME IN ON ANYONE WHO'S BEEN BRAINWASHED BY REGISTERING THEIR ENCEPHALIC VIBRATIONS...
ALL RIGHT! ALL RIGHT! SPARE ME YOUR TECHNICAL GIBBERISH!
YOU NOW HAVE A TRACER...SO USE IT!
ONCE STACY IS OUR PRISONER AGAIN, IT WON'T BE LONG BEFORE SPIDER-MAN APPEARS, ATTEMPTING TO RESCUE HIM!
THIS TIME WE'LL GET 'IM, BOSS!
CORRECTION! THIS TIME THE KINGPIN WILL GET HIM!
I NEVER SEEM TO SEE THE SAME FACES TWICE!
IN A PLANT AS LARGE AS THIS, I'LL BET EVEN DAD DOESN'T KNOW ALL HIS EMPLOYEES!
WISH I COULD BE MORE OF A HELP TO DAD!
IF ONLY I WASN'T SUCH A BONE-HEAD WHEN IT COMES TO SCIENCE!
IF I ONLY HAD HALF THE SAVVY OF PETER PARK... DAD!!
HE DIDN'T EVEN LOOK UP WHEN I OPENED THE DOOR!
IS ANYTHING WRONG, SIR?
HUH? OH, HARRY! COME IN, SON...COME IN!
PRIVAT
I'M JUST... NOT QUITE MYSELF TODAY!
IT STARTED WHEN I SAW THE NAME GREEN GOBLIN IN THE PAPER!
I DON'T SEEM ABLE TO GET HIM OUT OF MY MIND NOW!
I NEVER DID UNDERSTAND HOW YOU HELPED TO DESTROY HIM, DAD!
THAT'S THE TROUBLE, SON...
I CAN'T REMEMBER!
DON HECK '93
11

COURTESY SCOTT DUNBIER

AMAZING SPIDER-MAN #61, PAGE 11 ORIGINAL ART BY JOHN ROMITA, DON HECK & MIKE ESPOSITO

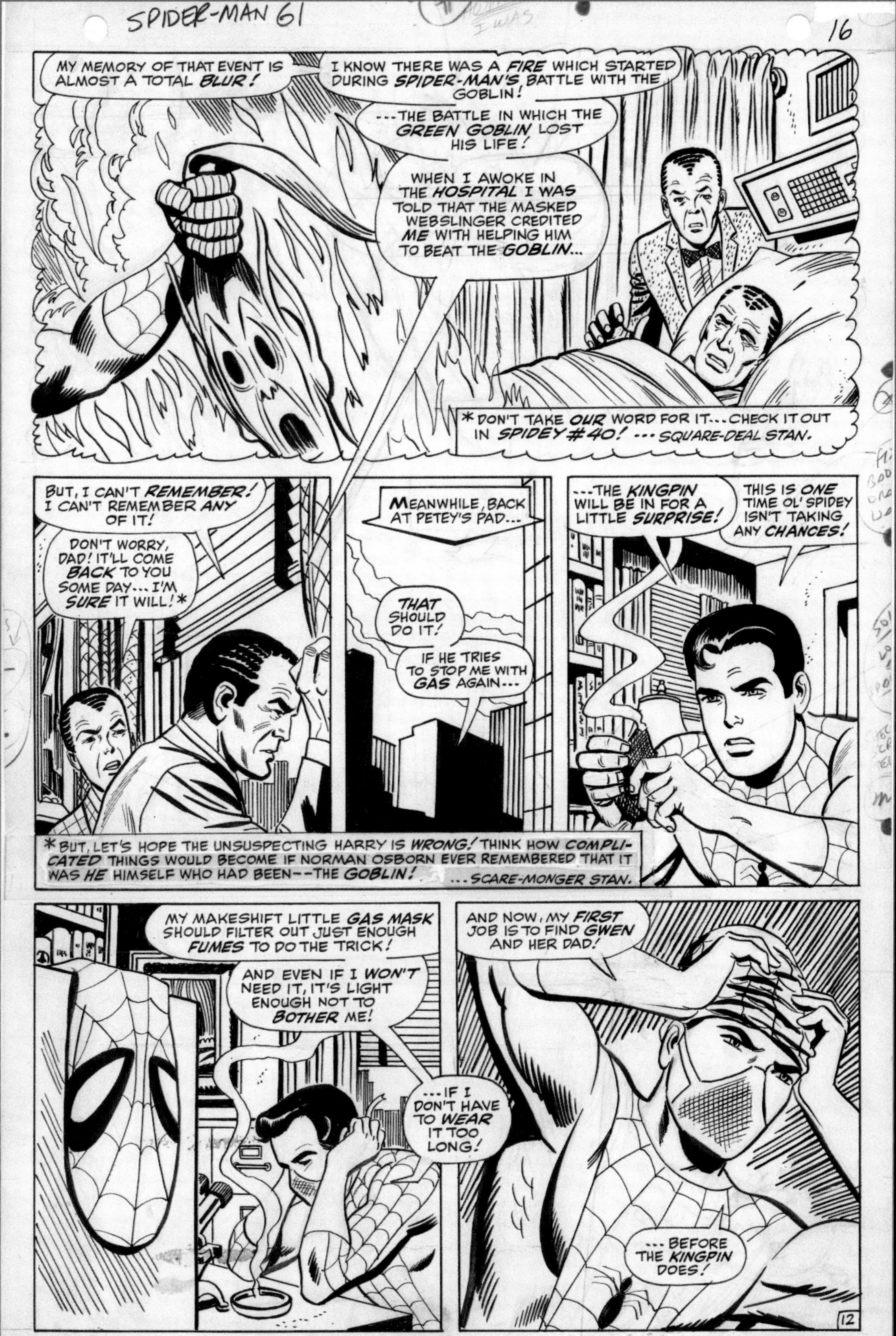
SPIDER-MAN 61
16
MY MEMORY OF THAT EVENT IS ALMOST A TOTAL BLUR!
I KNOW THERE WAS A FIRE WHICH STARTED DURING SPIDER-MAN'S BATTLE WITH THE GOBLIN!
---THE BATTLE IN WHICH THE GREEN GOBLIN LOST HIS LIFE!
WHEN I AWOKE IN THE HOSPITAL I WAS TOLD THAT THE MASKED WEBSLINGER CREDITED ME WITH HELPING HIM TO BEAT THE GOBLIN...
*DON'T TAKE OUR WORD FOR IT...CHECK IT OUT IN SPIDEY #40! ---SQUARE-DEAL STAN.
BUT, I CAN'T REMEMBER! I CAN'T REMEMBER ANY OF IT!
DON'T WORRY, DAD! IT'LL COME BACK TO YOU SOME DAY... I'M SURE IT WILL!*
MEANWHILE, BACK AT PETEY'S PAD...
THAT SHOULD DO IT!
IF HE TRIES TO STOP ME WITH GAS AGAIN...
---THE KINGPIN WILL BE IN FOR A LITTLE SURPRISE!
THIS IS ONE TIME OL' SPIDEY ISN'T TAKING ANY CHANCES!
*BUT, LET'S HOPE THE UNSUSPECTING HARRY IS WRONG! THINK HOW COMPLICATED THINGS WOULD BECOME IF NORMAN OSBORN EVER REMEMBERED THAT IT WAS HE HIMSELF WHO HAD BEEN--THE GOBLIN! ...SCARE-MONGER STAN.
MY MAKESHIFT LITTLE GAS MASK SHOULD FILTER OUT JUST ENOUGH FUMES TO DO THE TRICK!
AND EVEN IF I WON'T NEED IT, IT'S LIGHT ENOUGH NOT TO BOTHER ME!
---IF I DON'T HAVE TO WEAR IT TOO LONG!
AND NOW, MY FIRST JOB IS TO FIND GWEN AND HER DAD!
...BEFORE THE KINGPIN DOES!
12

COURTESY SCOTT DUNBIER

***AMAZING SPIDER-MAN* #61, PAGE 12 ORIGINAL ART, BY JOHN ROMITA, DON HECK & MIKE ESPOSITO**

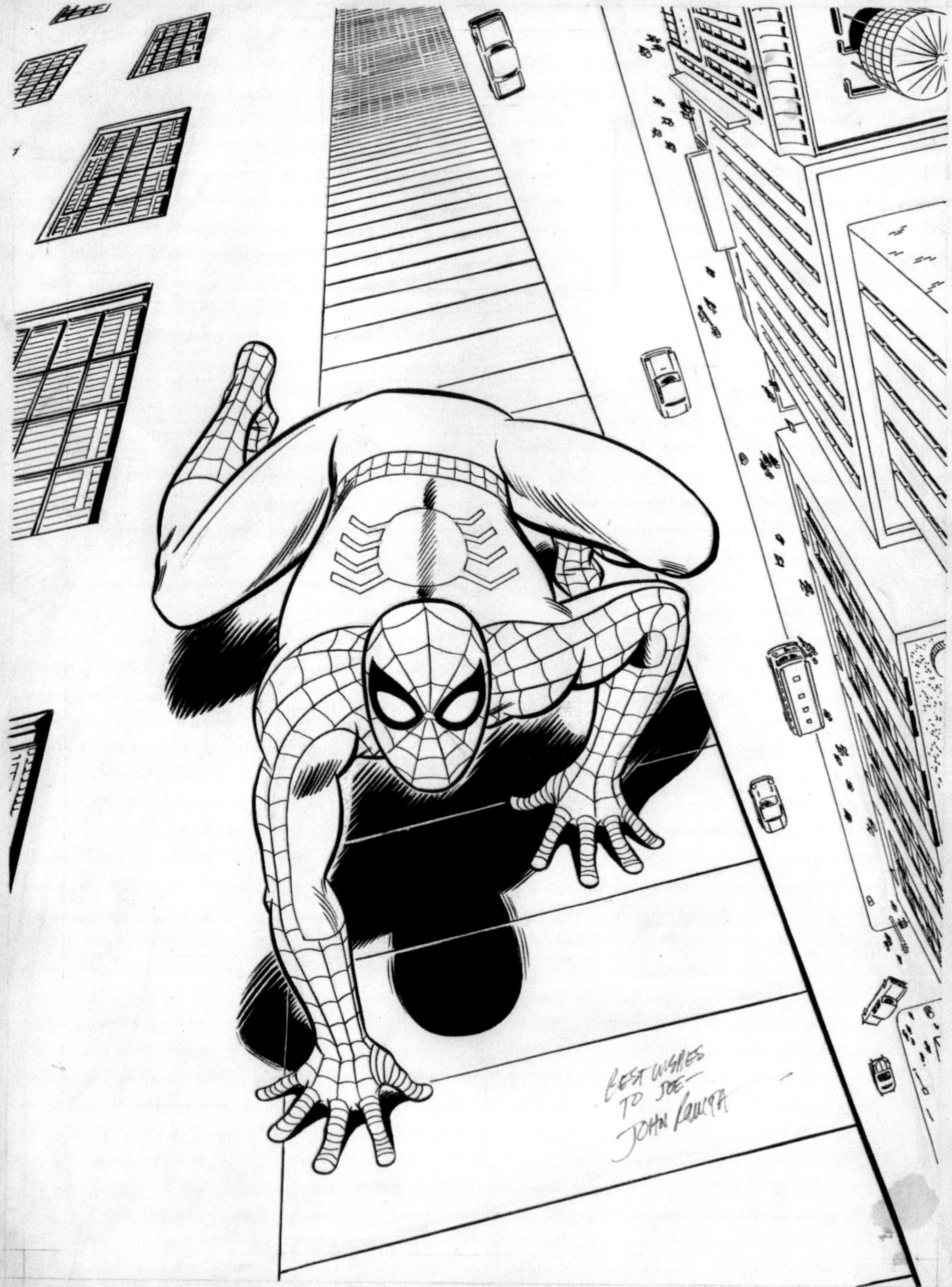
BEST WISHES
TO JOE—
JOHN ROMITA

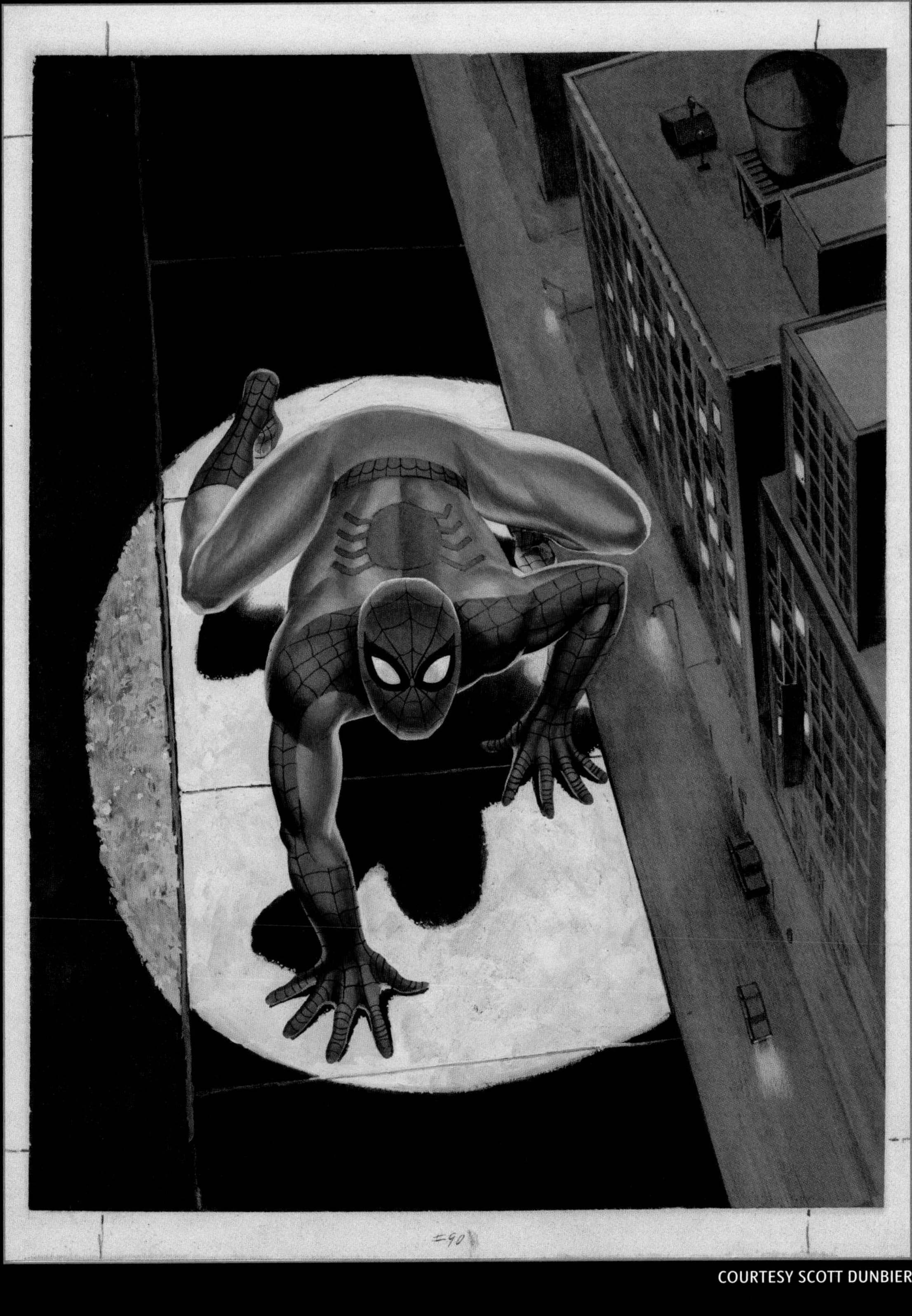

COURTESY SCOTT DUNBIER

***SPECTACULAR SPIDER-MAN* #1, COVER PAINTING ORIGINAL ART, BY HARRY ROSENBAUM**

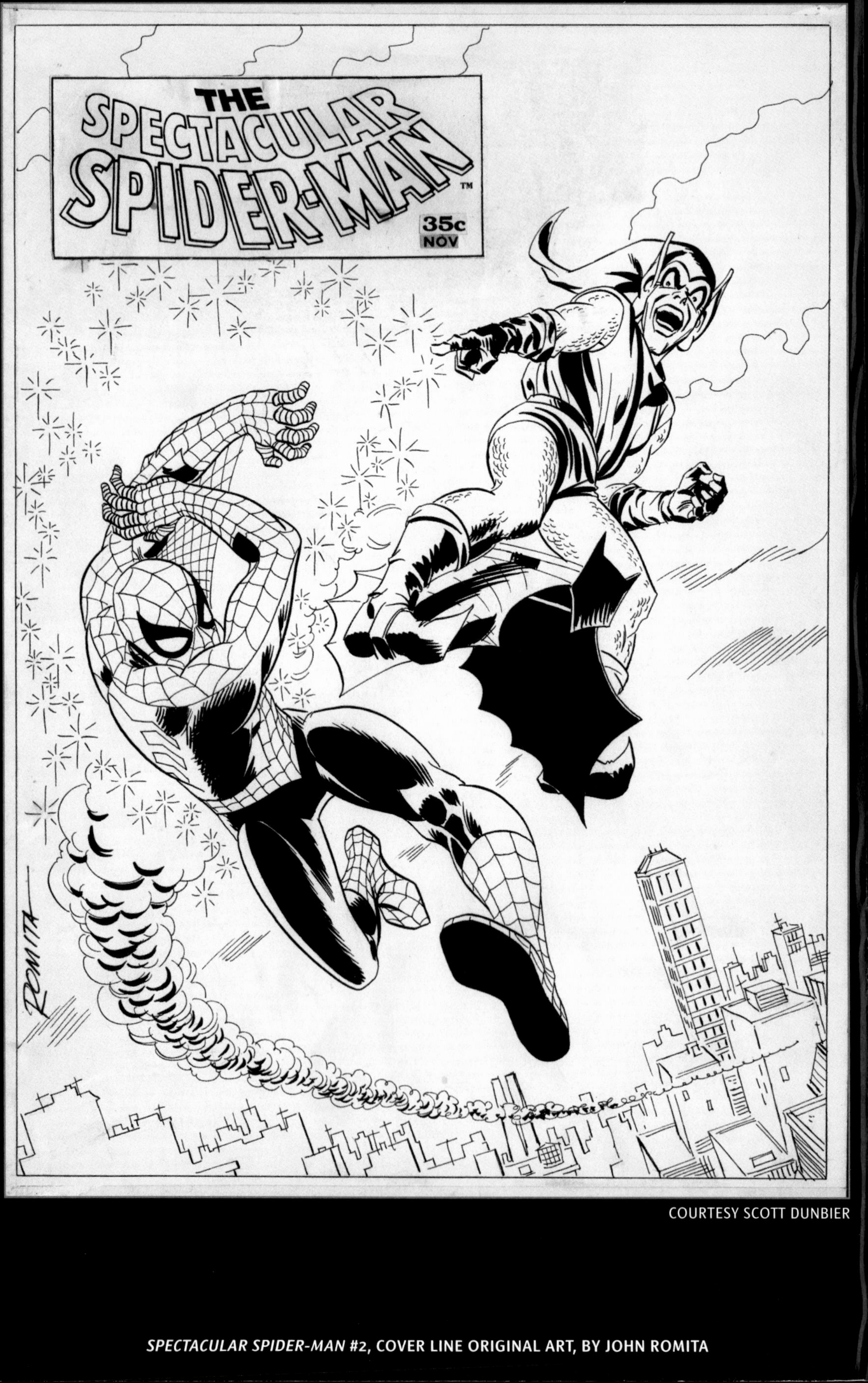
THE SPECTACULAR SPIDER-MAN
TM
35c
NOV
ROMITA

COURTESY SCOTT DUNBIER

SPECTACULAR SPIDER-MAN #2, COVER LINE ORIGINAL ART, BY JOHN ROMITA

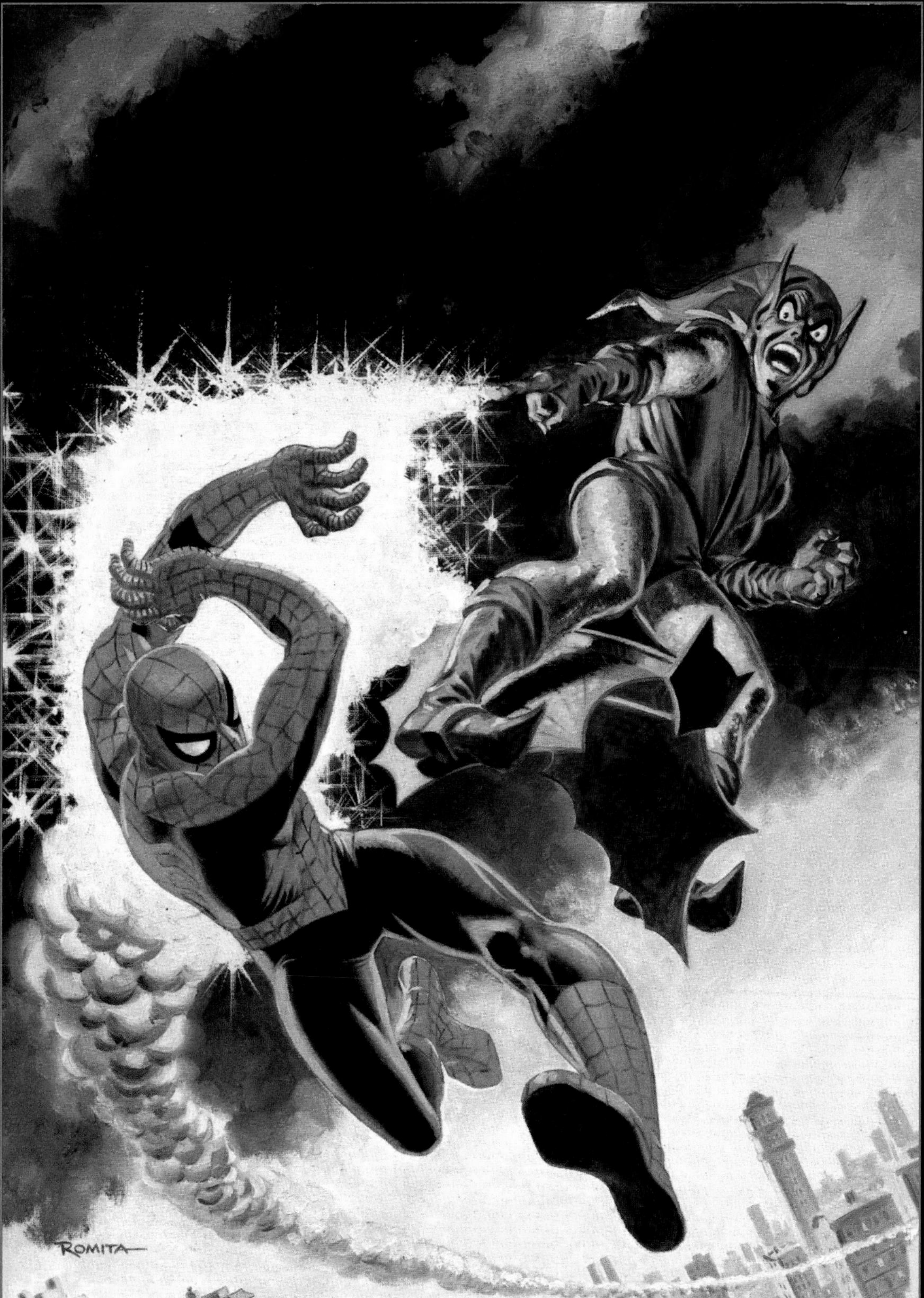
ROMITA

COURTESY HERITAGEAUCTIONS.COM

SPECTACULAR SPIDER-MAN #2, COVER PAINTING ORIGINAL ART, BY JOHN ROMITA

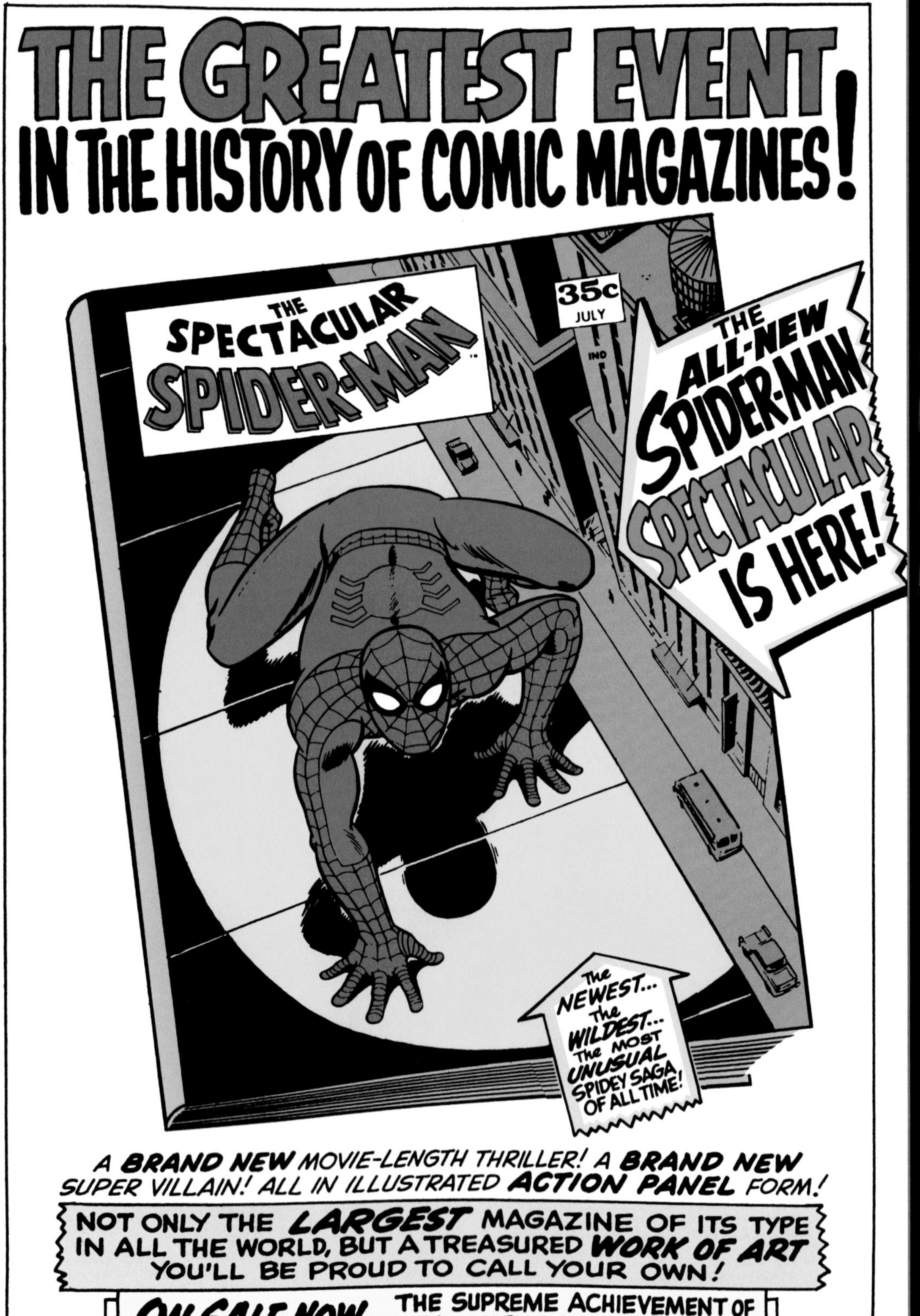

THE GREATEST EVENT IN THE HISTORY OF COMIC MAGAZINES!
THE SPECTACULAR SPIDER-MAN
35c JULY
THE ALL-NEW SPIDER-MAN SPECTACULAR IS HERE!
The NEWEST... the WILDEST... The MOST UNUSUAL SPIDEY SAGA OF ALL TIME!
A BRAND NEW MOVIE-LENGTH THRILLER! A BRAND NEW SUPER VILLAIN! ALL IN ILLUSTRATED ACTION PANEL FORM!
NOT ONLY THE LARGEST MAGAZINE OF ITS TYPE IN ALL THE WORLD, BUT A TREASURED WORK OF ART YOU'LL BE PROUD TO CALL YOUR OWN!
ON SALE NOW... THE SUPREME ACHIEVEMENT OF THE MIGHTY MARVEL AGE!

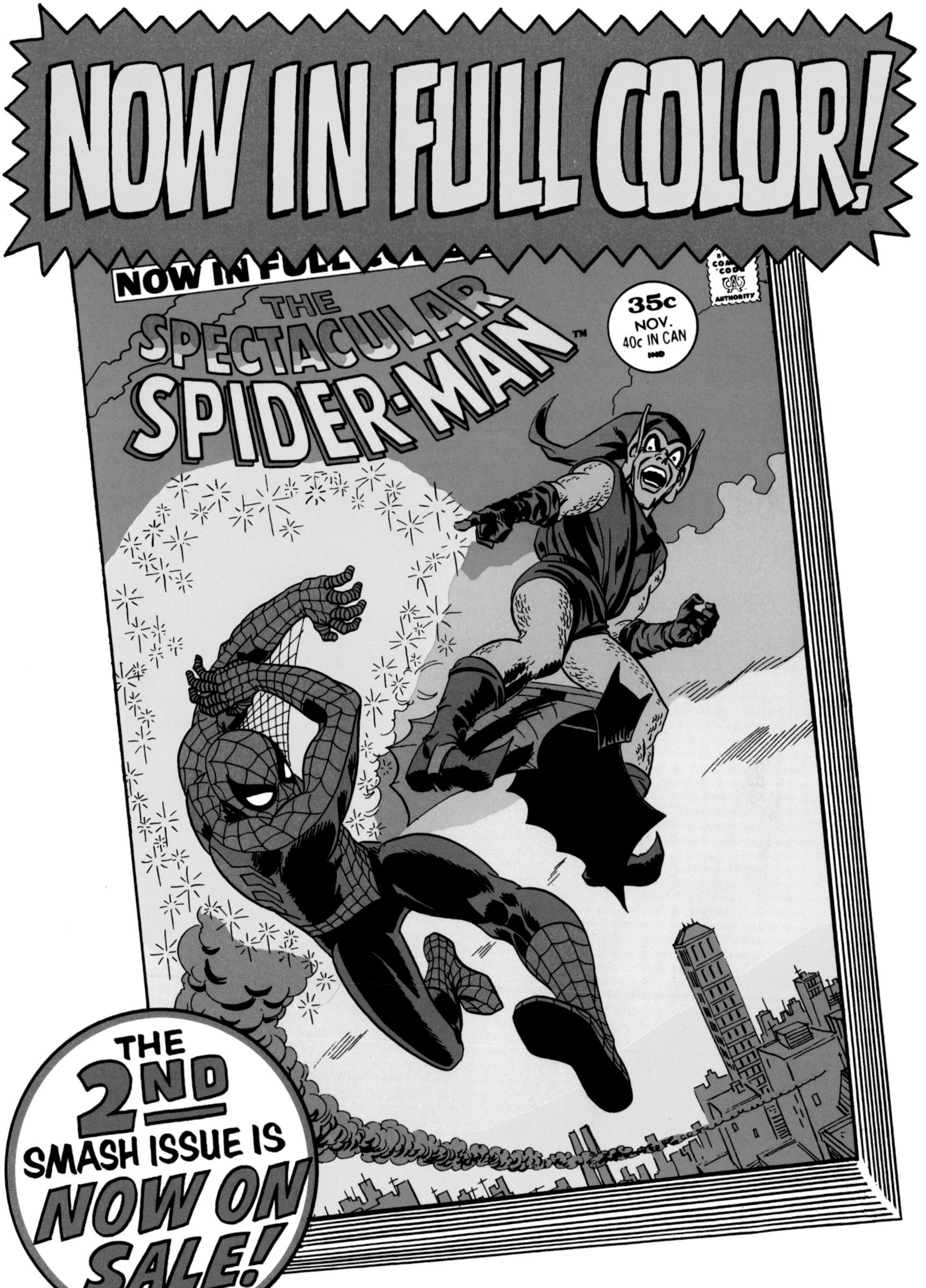
NOW IN FULL COLOR!
NOW IN FULL
THE SPECTACULAR SPIDER-MAN
35c NOV. 40c IN CAN
THE 2ND SMASH ISSUE IS NOW ON SALE!

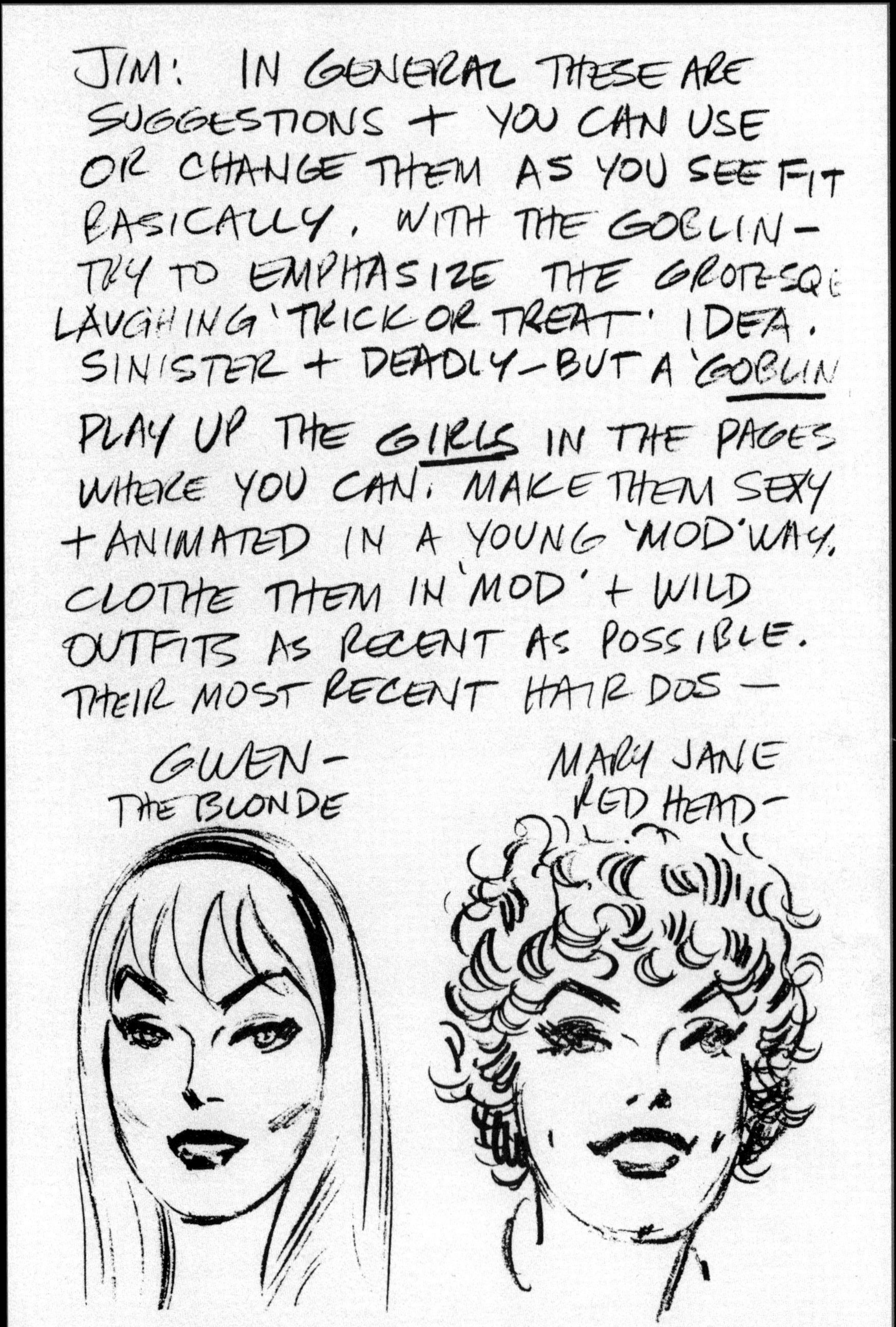
JIM: IN GENERAL THESE ARE SUGGESTIONS + YOU CAN USE OR CHANGE THEM AS YOU SEE FIT BASICALLY. WITH THE GOBLIN — TRY TO EMPHASIZE THE GROTESQ LAUGHING 'TRICK OR TREAT' IDEA. SINISTER + DEADLY — BUT A 'GOBLIN

PLAY UP THE GIRLS IN THE PAGES WHERE YOU CAN. MAKE THEM SEXY + ANIMATED IN A YOUNG 'MOD' WAY. CLOTHE THEM IN 'MOD' + WILD OUTFITS AS RECENT AS POSSIBLE. THEIR MOST RECENT HAIR DOS —

GWEN — THE BLONDE

MARY JANE RED HEAD —

JOHN ROMITA'S CHARACTER AND ART FINISHING NOTES TO JIM MOONEY, CIRCA *AMAZING SPIDER-MAN* #65

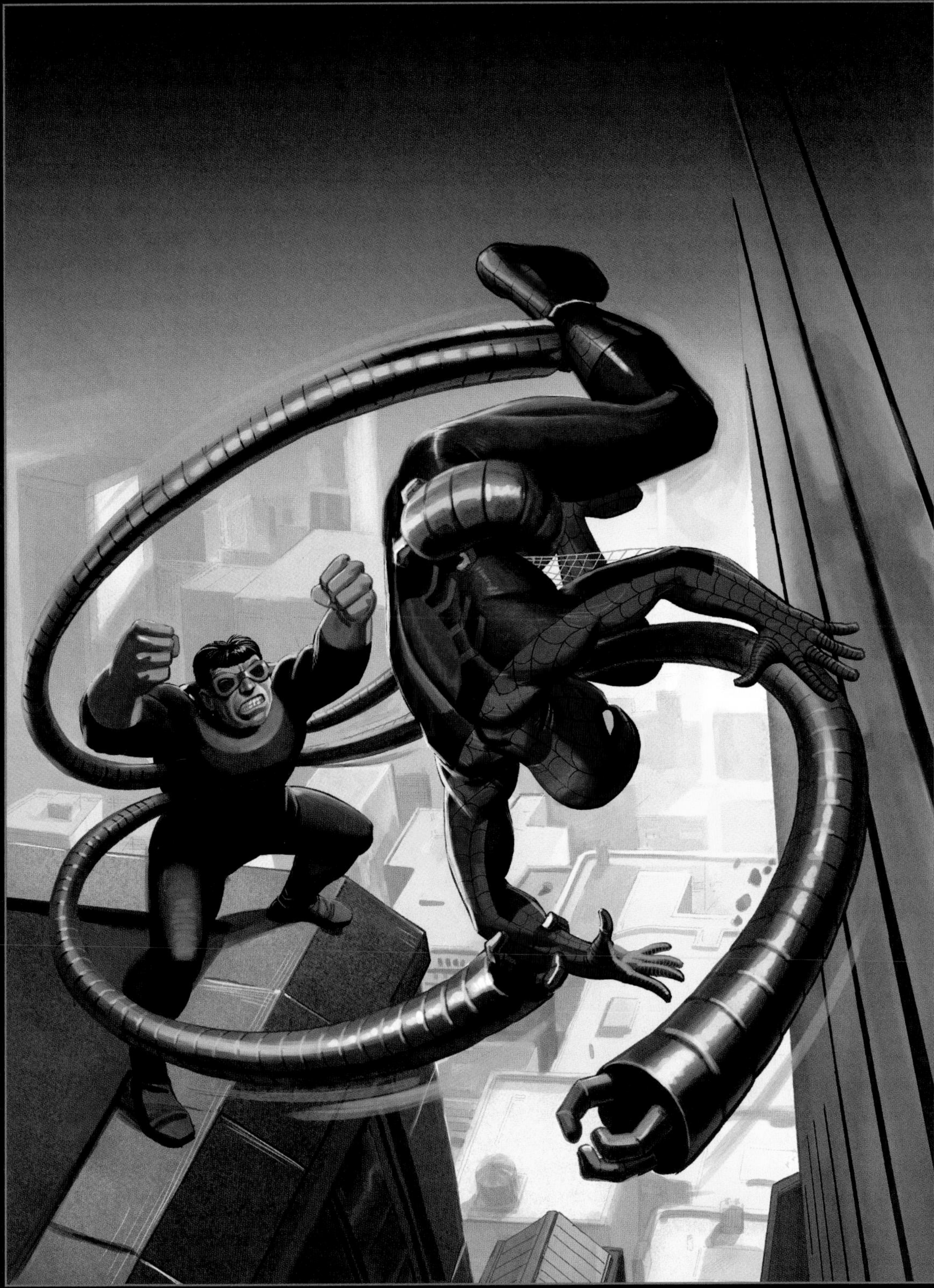

MARVEL MASTERWORKS: THE AMAZING SPIDER-MAN VOL. 6 TPB (2011), COVER, BY JOHN ROMITA & DEAN WHITE

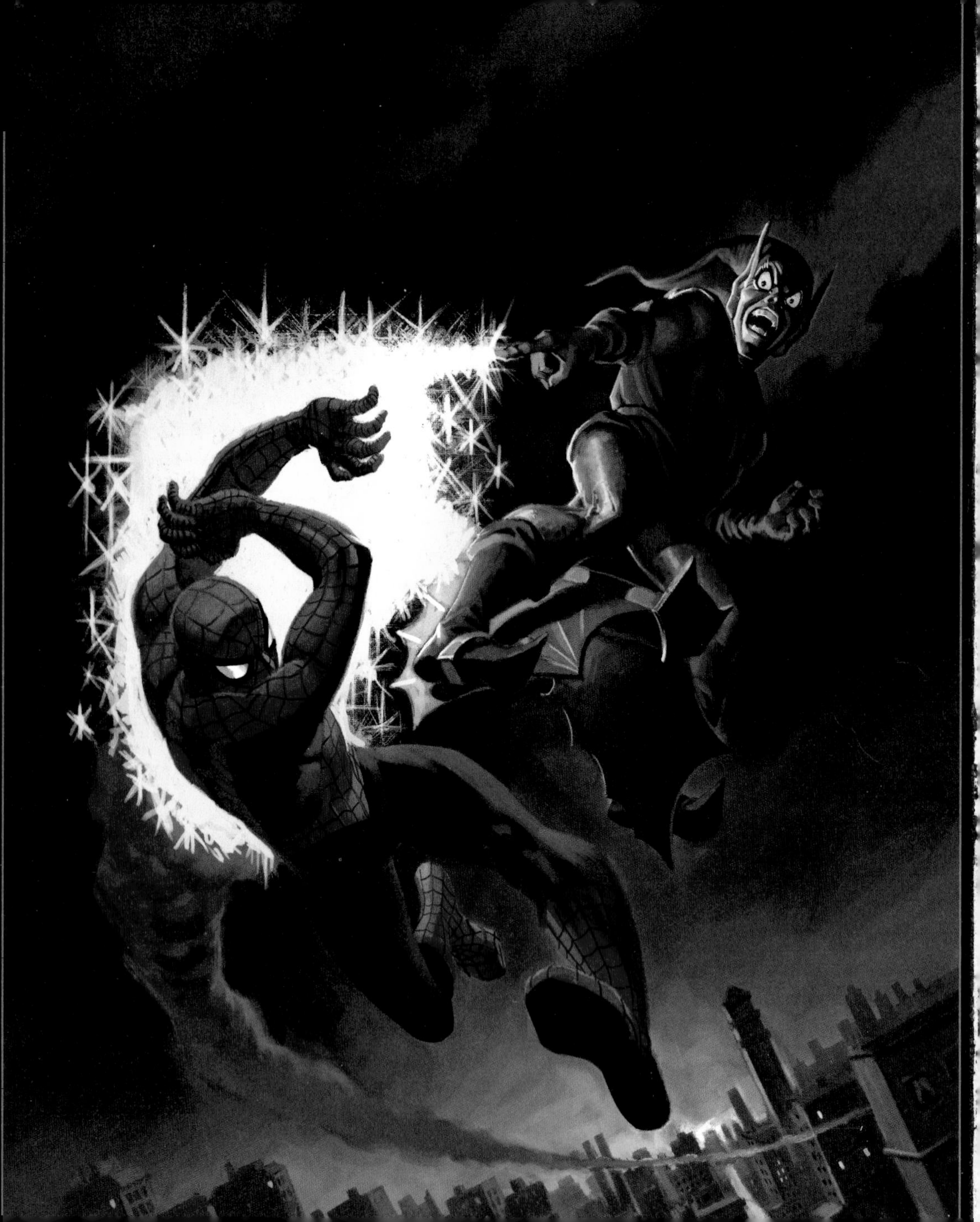